BUYING AIRCRAFT FOR THE ARMY AIR FORCES IN WORLD WAR II

Irving Brinton Holley Jr.

GOVERNMENT REPRINTS PRESS
Washington, D.C.

© Ross & Perry, Inc. 2001 All rights reserved.

No claim to U.S. government work contained throughout this book.

Protected under the Berne Convention. Published 2001

Printed in The United States of America
Ross & Perry, Inc. Publishers
717 Second St., N.E., Suite 200
Washington, D.C. 20002
Telephone (202) 675-8300
Facsimile (202) 675-8400
info@RossPerry.com

SAN 253-8555

Government Reprints Press Edition 2001

Government Reprints Press is an Imprint of Ross & Perry, Inc.

Library of Congress Control Number: 2001093152

http://www.GPOreprints.com

ISBN 1-931641-44-7

♾ The paper used in this publication meets the requirements for permanence established by the American National Standard for Information Sciences "Permanence of Paper for Printed Library Materials" (ANSI Z39.48-1984).

All rights reserved. No copyrighted part of this publication may be reproduced, stored in a retrieval system, or transmitted, in any form or by any means, electronic, photocopying, recording, or otherwise, without the prior written permission of the publisher.

BUYING AIRCRAFT FOR THE ARMY AIR FORCES IN WORLD WAR II

UNITED STATES ARMY IN WORLD WAR II

Stetson Conn, General Editor

Advisory Committee
(As of 1 October 1962)

Oron J. Hale University of Virginia	Maj. Gen. George T. Duncan U.S. Continental Army Command
William R. Emerson Yale University	Maj. General Tom R. Stoughton Industrial College of the Armed Forces
Earl Pomeroy University of Oregon	Brig. Gen. Ward S. Ryan U.S. Army War College
Theodore Ropp Duke University	Brig. Gen. Harry J. Lemley, Jr. U.S. Army Command and General Staff College
Bell I. Wiley Emory University	Col. Vincent J. Esposito United States Military Academy

C. Vann Woodward
Yale University

Office of the Chief of Military History

Brig. Gen. Hal C. Pattison, Chief of Military History

Chief Historian	Stetson Conn
Chief, Histories Division	Col. Louis G. Mendez, Jr.
Chief, Editorial and Graphics Division	Lt. Col. James R. Hillard
Editor in Chief	Joseph R. Friedman

. . . to Those Who Served

Foreword

Buying Aircraft: Matériel Procurement for the Army Air Forces offers the reader a liberal education in military procurement. It examines in depth, and with judicious understanding, the following: procurement of aircraft; budgeting and budgetary changes; contracting; design changes; the nature and development of the aircraft industry; manufacturing techniques, especially in the introduction of mass production into the aircraft industry, and problems in the use of automobile assembly plants for making aircraft; and the War Department's relations with Congress and the Comptroller. Professor Holley recognizes the broad sweep and interrelationship of political, economic, legal, and military problems, and stresses the importance of organization within both government and industry. The volume focuses upon problems inherent in procurement, but does not concern itself with air or ground force doctrine. Its subject matter is the procurement, not the employment, of air power. Because Professor Holley's volume offers concrete examples of problems involved in the design and purchase of complicated and expensive items of military equipment over a period of years, the experiences described should profit the officer engaged in procurement of missiles and aircraft today as well as the student of logistics, and will add immeasurably to the thoughtful citizen's understanding of national defense.

Washington, D.C.
5 November 1962

HAL C. PATTISON
Brigadier General, USA
Chief of Military History

The Author

Irving Brinton Holley, jr., received his B.A. from Amherst College and his M.A. and Ph.D. from Yale University. Enlisting in the Army, he rose to the grade of staff sergeant as an instructor in aerial gunnery, attended the Army Air Forces Officer Candidate School at Miami Beach, Florida, and graduated in April 1944. After serving as a gunnery officer in the First Air Force, he was assigned to technical intelligence at Headquarters, Air Materiel Command, Wright Field, Dayton, Ohio. From 1945 to 1947 he was a member of the faculty of the Industrial College of the Armed Forces.

In 1947 Mr. Holley accepted an appointment in the History Department of Duke University, where he is now a full professor. He holds a commission as a lieutenant colonel, USAF Reserve, and has continued to take an active part in reserve affairs.

Professor Holley is the author of *Ideas and Weapons,* published by the Yale University Press in 1953, as well as numerous articles and reviews in scholarly publications.

Preface

Readers have a right to expect something in the way of answers to two basic questions before they read further in this volume: What is it about and for whom is it written? Although these questions seem simple enough, neither of them can be adequately answered without considerable elaboration.

This book is about procurement in the broadest sense of the word. To be sure, the mechanics of purchasing and contracting are considered at some length, but the term *procurement* is here used to embrace far more than is generally implied by the word itself. The chapters that follow attempt to present the problem of air matériel procurement as a whole: the computation of requirements, the evolution of internal organization, the relationship and accommodation of conflicts between executive and legislative agencies, the character and capabilities of the aircraft industry, and many other similar facets are presented as the vital context without which such topics as contract negotiation and facility expansion can scarcely be understood.

Above all, the author wishes to make clear that he did not undertake this book as an exercise in fulsome praise. He may have leaned in the opposite direction, emphasizing unduly the failures while neglecting the successes. But if this kind of history is to be useful and meaningful, it cannot afford to devote its limited number of pages in adding to the paeans of praise already in print. If the nation is to escape or even minimize the blunders of the past, it cannot neglect to study its mistakes.

If the author has been frugal with praise, he has been no less cautious in apportioning personal responsibility when discussing some of the more egregious failures that marked the procurement program. The search for scapegoats makes exciting journalism and can provide many a political football, but it misses the point. The really meaningful question to be asked of disaster is not "Who was to blame?" but "What were the problems?" Personal censure and recrimination are fruitless; to illuminate even a few of the problems encountered is to help the future avoid the pitfalls of the past.

In the main, then, individuals are accorded their privacy—in success as well as in failure. The major exceptions to this rule are the leaders, both political and military, in the highest echelons. Of necessity, as they themselves must recognize only too well, they forfeited their private lives when they climbed into the realm of folk heroes—or villains—and became a part of the public domain.

This book was not written for the procurement specialist. Nor was it written exclusively for the participants who helped shape many of the events described; for the most part these individuals have left the scene and a rising generation has taken their places. It is this new generation in particular to which this book is addressed. The author has kept his sights consciously trained upon the ambitious young staff officer of tomorrow as well as the general reader. His aim is to provide the broadest possible synthesis of the problems of air arm procurement, giving a comprehensive or general view of the sort required by those who aspire to exercise command as general officers. But the issues discussed here should have meaning for many more readers than those in the limited circle of air arm staff officers, regular and reservist, seeking advancement; the themes developed in this book should provide insights for officers in all the services. Moreover, since military expenditures constitute a major portion of the national budget, no student of public policy who would understand the implications of this spending in the national economy can ignore the intricacies of air arm procurement.

Because this book has been written primarily for a generation that did not experience the mobilization effort of the World War II years, the author has spelled out in considerable detail the peacetime background of both the air arm and the aircraft industry. Participants in the wartime procurement program may feel this belabors the obvious, but the author is convinced that the procurement story of the war era cannot be comprehended unless one is well aware of the assumptions and premises generally held at the time. And precisely because the attitudes were widely if not universally shared, they were often unstated. What everyone takes for granted no one bothers to record. Unless this milieu can be recaptured, a subsequent generation will misunderstand the events of the war years and be led to false conclusions regarding the lessons to be learned from them.

For example, the attitude of the aircraft manufacturers toward plant expansions in 1940 is comprehensible only when seen against the events of the depression just preceding. Readers in the postwar world, who know the aircraft manufacturers only as industrial giants at the top of the national economy, can appreciate the procurement problems of World War II only when they are placed in the context of an industry ranking in fourteenth or fifteenth place among the nation's economic groups. Or again, the decisions and plans of responsible air arm officials, particularly in the crucial prewar months from September 1939 to December 1941, can best be appreciated when seen in the context of their long relationship with Congress and the Comptroller General.

One final caveat remains to be stated. This volume makes no claim of being a definitive account of the subject treated. While it is planned as an integral work, one to be read as an inclusive account of the procurement story as a whole, the writer has sought to avoid needless duplication of the studies done by others in this field, notably R. Elberton Smith, *The Army and Economic Mobilization,* a volume in the official history series, UNITED STATES ARMY IN WORLD WAR II, and Alfred Goldberg's chapters in W. F. Craven and J. L. Cate, THE ARMY AIR FORCES IN WORLD WAR II, Volume VI, *Men and Planes.* With the needs of officers preparing staff papers particularly in mind, the author has been at pains to insert numerous cross references to those and many other published sources bearing on the subjects discussed. The reader will also find, in addition to the usual documentation, a large number of citations leading to archival materials useful to those who wish further illustrative matter for staff studies.

The author will be more than gratified if interested readers are sufficiently provoked to prove that his judgments and interpretations require revision at some points. If this volume stimulates further study and a continuing analysis of the problems of procurement, it will have served its purpose well.

Whatever mistakes *Buying Aircraft: Matériel Procurement for the Army Air Forces* may contain, whether of fact or interpretation, responsibility rests firmly upon the author and not upon the literally hundreds of individuals who shared in one way or another in the preparation of this volume. For their help, however, the author wishes to express his sincere appreciation.

While the author is heavily indebted to the many writers of monographs and special studies cited repeatedly in the footnotes, he wishes to single out as particularly noteworthy the work done by R. R. Russel at Wright Field and J. P. Walsh in the Eastern Procurement District headquarters.

The following individuals, all at one time or another associated with OCMH, read and criticized the entire manuscript: Dr. Kent Roberts Greenfield, Dr. Stetson Conn, Dr. John Miller, jr., Col. Seneca W. Foote, and Mr. R. Elberton Smith. If their strictures on early drafts were occasionally painful, the author is conscious that the net effect of their efforts has been highly constructive. Equally welcome were the evaluations of two outsiders, Mr. T. P. Wright, vice president of Cornell University, and General O. R. Cook, USAF, Retired, both of whom read drafts of the book and prepared elaborate critiques from no other motive than a lifelong dedication to the problems of national defense.

Among those who went far beyond the requirements of their official positions to facilitate the author's research, the following merit particular attention: at Wright Field, Dr. Paul M. Davis and his staff in the Historical Office; at the Industrial College of the Armed Forces, Dr. Marlin S. Reichley and Miss Clara J. Widger with her library staff; at the National War College, George Stansfield; in the Office of the Chief of Military History, Mr. Israel Wice and his staff, Dr. Robert W. Coakley, and Dr. Richard M. Leighton; at the Air Force Historical Division Liaison Office,

Dr. Alfred Goldberg; at the World War II Records Division, National Archives and Records Service, General Services Administration, all those anonymous people who repeatedly performed prodigies in locating obscure and elusive documents from the mounting millions stored there. And for assistance at virtually every turn over the several years during which this book was in preparation, the author wishes to extend his particular thanks to Mrs. Constance McL. Green, Miss Carol S. Piper, and Miss K. E. Brand.

The heavy task of editing the manuscript fell upon Miss Mary Ann Bacon. If the author has bitterly complained that her blue pencil cut off all the colorful peaks in his prose, he cheerfully concedes that she has also managed to fill in most of his otherwise incomprehensible prose valleys. For this he is truly appreciative, as he is to Mrs. Marion P. Grimes, the assistant editor. Mrs. Norma Heacock Sherris arranged the photographs.

Finally, the author wishes to acknowledge the patience, understanding, and help rendered by his wife, Janet Carlson Holley, throughout the years this volume was in preparation.

Washington, D.C. IRVING BRINTON HOLLEY, JR.
5 November 1962

Contents

Chapter		Page
I.	INTRODUCTION	3
II.	THE AIRCRAFT INDUSTRY ON THE EVE OF WORLD WAR II	6
	A Survey of the Industry	6
	The Market for Aircraft	10
	Research and Development	22
	Production	26
	Financing the Aircraft Industry: 1934–38	33
III.	CONGRESS AND THE AIR ARM	43
	Authorized Strength: How Many Aircraft?	44
	Authorizations, Appropriations, and Aircraft	63
IV.	PROCUREMENT LEGISLATION, ORGANIZATION, AND ADMINISTRATION	80
	Organic Legislation for the Procurement of Aircraft	80
	The Organization of the Air Arm for Procurement	93
	The Administration of Procurement	106
V.	PROCUREMENT UNDER THE AIR CORPS ACT	113
	Procurement: 1926–34	113
	Congressional Cloudburst	119
	New Procurement Policy	128
VI.	AIRCRAFT PROCUREMENT ON THE EVE OF WORLD WAR II	132
	The New Policy Reconsidered	132
	The War Department Seeks a Solution	143
	Peacetime Procurement: A Retrospect	146
VII.	PLANNING FOR INDUSTRIAL MOBILIZATION	150
	The Problem	150
	The War Department and Industrial Mobilization	151
	The Air Corps Organization for Mobilization Planning	153
	Air Corps Mobilization Planning	155
	Air Corps Planning in Perspective	166

Chapter		Page
VIII.	THE TIDE TURNS	169
	The President Proposes; Congress Disposes	169
	The First Expansion Program	175
	The Search for a Yardstick	186
IX.	FOREIGN POLICY, POLITICS, AND DEFENSE	194
	Politics and Armament	194
	Aircraft Exports and National Defense	196
	Aircraft Exports and Mobilization Planning	205
X.	REQUIREMENTS	209
	An Essay on Requirements	209
	Origin of the 50,000 Figure	221
XI.	50,000 AIRCRAFT	229
	From Slogan to Program	229
	There's Danger in Numbers: The President's "Must Program"	237
	Return to Reality	243
XII.	ORGANIZING FOR PRODUCTION	247
	Posing the Problem	247
	Evolution of an Organization	249
XIII.	LEGISLATION FOR PROCUREMENT	274
	Wartime Buying With Peacetime Laws	274
	Improvising Legislation in a Crisis	283
XIV.	THE PROBLEM OF INDUSTRIAL CAPACITY	290
	The Beginning of Facility Expansions	290
	Enter Detroit: Air Arm Use of the Automobile Industry	304
	Expansion or Conversion?	316
	The Facilities Program: An Appraisal	324
XV.	THE NEGOTIATION OF CONTRACTS	330
	The Transition to Wartime Buying	330
	The Negotiation of Contracts	337
	The Administration of Contracts	364
XVI.	THE COST-PLUS-FIXED-FEE CONTRACT: NEGOTIATION AND ADMINISTRATION	372
	Some Revolutionary Implications	372
	The Fixed-Fee Problem	374
	The Determination of Allowable Costs	379
	Auditing and Accounting	390
	The Problem of Property Accountability	397
	The Relation of Primes to Subs	401
	The Conversion of Fixed-Fee Contracts	410

Chapter		Page
XVII.	PRICE ADJUSTMENT	421
	Escalator Clauses	422
	Excess Profits and Voluntary Refunds	428
	Statutory Renegotiation	428
XVIII.	CONTRACT TERMINATION	446
	The Background of Termination	446
	The Character of the Termination Problem	447
	The Organization for Termination	451
	Some Illustrative Aspects of Administration	454
	An Afterword	460
XIX.	ORGANIZATION FOR PROCUREMENT	462
	Co-ordination, Control, and Command	462
	Cross Procurement	480
	Centralization and Decentralization	487
XX.	PRODUCTION	511
	The Problem Defined	511
	The Dilemma of Mass Production	512
	Resolving the Dilemma	529
XXI.	THE PROCUREMENT RECORD	548
	A Statistical Summation	548
	The Measure of Success	552
	Counting the Cost	556
	The Contribution of Industry	560
XXII.	SOME CONCLUDING OBSERVATIONS ON MILITARY PROCUREMENT	569
	What Is Air Arm Procurement?	569
	Procurement and Politics	570
	Procurement Leadership in Wartime	571
	Air Power and Organization	572

Appendix

A.	MEMBERSHIP IN THE AERONAUTICAL CHAMBER OF COMMERCE; 1938	575
B.	WARTIME PRODUCERS OF AIRCRAFT	576
C.	MAJOR PRODUCERS OF AIRCRAFT ENGINES: JULY 1940–AUGUST 1945	580

BIBLIOGRAPHICAL NOTE	583
GLOSSARY	588
INDEX	595

Tables

No.		Page
1.	Production of Aircraft Engines	7
2.	Comparative Importance of Military and Civilian Markets	21
3.	A Comparison of the Aircraft Industry With the Automobile Industry	27
4.	Percent of Earnings as Dividends and Surplus, Eighteen Top Aircraft Manufacturers: 1934–38	34
5.	Yearly Increment to Surplus or Deficit Compared With Yearly Increment to Deferred Development Charges, Eighteen Top Aircraft Manufacturers: 1934–38	35
6.	Comparative Cost of Two-Engine and Four-Engine Bombers	142
7.	B–24 Modifications at Willow Run	537
8.	Engine Production by Type: 1940–45	549
9.	Engine Production by Horsepower: 1940–45	549
10.	Propeller Production: 1940–45	549
11.	Number of Airplanes Procured by Army Air Forces, by Type and by Year of Acceptance: January 1940–December 1945	550
12.	Aircraft Deliveries to the AAF: July 1940–December 1945	554
13.	Heavy Bombers Accepted by the AAF	555
14.	Total Military Aircraft Production of Four Major Powers: 1939–44	555
15.	AAF Cash Appropriations and Expenditures: 1935–45	557
16.	AAF Expenditures by Major Categories: 1942–45	558
17.	Expenditures for Modifications and Research and Development: 1942–45	558
18.	Comparison of Civilian Payroll to New Aircraft and Research and Development: 1938–41	559
19.	Average Unit Costs of Selected Aircraft: 1939–45	560
20.	Production of Turbojet Engines: July 1940–August 1945	562
21.	Production of Automatic Controllable Pitch Propellers: July 1940–August 1945	563
22.	Distribution of Employment in Airframe Industry: April 1945	565
23.	Direct Man-hours per Airframe Pound Accepted	565

Charts

1.	Organization Chart Showing Channels of Communication Between the Secretary of War and the Air Corps	95
2.	Organization of OCAC, Washington Headquarters of Air Corps	96
3.	Materiel Division, Wright Field, Dayton, Ohio	98
4.	Composite Organization Chart Showing the Agencies Primarily Concerned With Air Matériel Procurement in the Two Decades After the Air Corps Act of 1926	103

No.	Page
5. Army Air Forces Organization: 9 March 1942	487
6. Organization of the Materiel Command: 19 October 1942	488
7. Organization of the Resources Control Section of the Production Division, Materiel Command: July 1943	489
8. Army Air Forces Organization: 29 March 1943	490
9. Hypothetical Learner Curve	536

Illustrations

U.S. Mail Plane Loading From Mail Truck	13
National Advisory Committee for Aeronautics	24
NACA Full-scale Wind Tunnel at Langley Field	25
Hand Assembly of Stearman Primary Trainers	30
The Morrow Board	47
House of Representatives Committee on Military Affairs	60
Maj. Gen. Oscar Westover	69
Boeing B-17	76
Douglas B-18	77
Maj. Gen. M. M. Patrick	89
Wright Field, 1935	100
Wright Field, 1942	101
Martin B-10	118
Maj. Gen. Benjamin D. Foulois	121
DC-2 Transports in Production	135
B-17 and XB-15	149
War Department Subcommittee of the House Appropriations Committee	176
Secretary Louis A. Johnson	177
Theodore P. Wright	192
President Asks Congress for 50,000 Aircraft	226
Curtiss XP-40	227
British Spitfire	227
Douglas A-26	244
Martin B-26	245
Lt. Gen. William S. Knudsen	256
The B-24	306
The B-25	307
Brig. Gen. Charles E. Branshaw	466
Maj. Gen. Kenneth B. Wolfe	469
General Brehon B. Somervell	478
Brig. Gen. A. J. Browning	479
Secretary Robert P. Patterson	479
Maj. Gen. Oliver P. Echols	479

	Page
Assembly Jig, B-24 Center Wing Section	525
B-24 Assembly Line, Willow Run	526
Boeing B-17 Assembly Line	541

All photographs are from the Department of Defense except for the following: page 227, *Air Force and Space Digest;* pages 24, 25, 177, 192, and 479, National Archives; pages 306, 525, and 526, Ford Motor Company; and page 226, Harris and Ewing, Washington, D.C.

BUYING AIRCRAFT:
MATÉRIEL PROCUREMENT
FOR THE ARMY AIR FORCES

CHAPTER I

Introduction

The strength and structure of the Military Establishment of the United States are responsibilities of the American public expressing its will through Congress. Since the Army is an operating agency with but limited voice in the formation of national policy, it is incumbent upon departmental officials to submit accurate and meaningful reports to the public and its representatives if they are to provide an effective legislative basis for the maximum in national security at the least cost.[1] Unfortunately the information necessary for sound legislation has not always been readily available.

If the American public, congressmen, editors, and the man in the street held a number of serious misconceptions about the Army's air arm and its state of readiness on the eve of World War II, it may very well be that their erroneous impressions were derived from authoritative sources. General Malin Craig, the Chief of Staff, himself assured the people of the United States in his annual report of 1938 that Army planes were "equal, if not superior," to any in the world.[2] Perhaps the aircraft were superior, but a curious congressman might have been forgiven had he asked on what foundation this assurance rested. The Chief of Staff claimed that the outstanding performance of Army aircraft was "convincingly demonstrated" by the flight of six Army bombers on a record-breaking journey to Argentina.[3] The long-distance flight, spectacular and significant as it may have been at the time, was not proof of tactically superior aircraft. Even though the Chief of Staff's logic might be imperfect, the inquiring congressman might still conclude that all was well in the air arm—unless he read further in the official reports of the War Department for the year 1938.

In commenting on the air arm during the fiscal year just past, the Assistant Secretary of War Louis A. Johnson differed with his military colleague and sounded a warning. While the Army's aircraft in 1937 had been, "in general, the best and most efficient in the world," it now appeared that "our former technical superiority" was "no longer clearly apparent." The tone of assurance in the Chief of Staff's boast of aircraft "unexcelled" by the military planes of any

---

[1] Those familiar with the preparation of annual reports within the Army might argue that no one should attach too much importance to such documents, often prepared in haste and sometimes inaccurate. Nonetheless, that some officers recognized their potential importance is attested by the 1934 annual report of Chief of Staff, General Douglas MacArthur, which is paraphrased above.

[2] *Annual Report of the Secretary of War, 1938*, p. 34.
[3] *Ibid.*

nation was not to be found in Johnson's report:

"Recent advances in other countries have equalled if not exceeded our efforts. We have known for some time that foreign nations far surpassed us in the number of military aircraft at their disposal but we also knew that we led the field technically. It now appears that our research and development programs must be accelerated if we are to regain our position of technical leadership." [4] Further, current production programs as well as those contemplated for wartime, he flatly declared, fell far short of providing even a minimum number of aircraft that "any realistic view of the problem would show to be necessary." [5]

If the Chief of Staff and the Assistant Secretary of War appeared to contradict each other, Secretary of War H. H. Woodring did little to clarify the picture. Looking back five years, he recalled that the rest of the world was "setting a fast pace" in the development of air power, while the United States was "floundering along in the ruck." [6] By 1938 the Secretary of War felt free to report a "far more encouraging situation." [7] This was a cryptically vague and entirely relative characterization that might have lent support either to the optimistic view held by the Chief of Staff or to the pessimistic one held by the Assistant Secretary of War.

What, then, was the uninitiated citizen to believe? One official reassured him, another warned him of imminent danger, yet another left him undecided. An inquirer might indeed conclude that freedom of expression prevailed in the War Department. Useful and thought provoking as this diversity of ideas may have been within the Department, the contradictory reports published for public distribution indicated that Congress, the President, and the man in the street would have to seek further for the information so indispensable to an informed and intelligent national policy on air power. This volume may make a contribution toward that quest.

Did the United States have a superior air force on the eve of World War II? The question is now largely academic, but it may well be asked because it poses another, more useful question: exactly what constitutes a superior air force? Air power is something more than a collection of aircraft, the ground installations necessary to keep them flying, and the trained men needed to maintain them in action. In addition, an air arm requires a body of doctrine, for doctrines regarding the strategic and tactical application of air power are as fundamental as the bombers and fighters that execute a wartime mission. Yet even to stop here would be to confine the definition of an air force, by implication at least, to the limits so frequently encountered in newspapers and newscasts. Almost equally important, and less frequently mentioned in public debate, are

---

[4] *Ibid.*, p. 26.
[5] *Ibid.*, pp. 26–27.
[6] *Ibid.*, pp. 2–3. Compare this statement by Secretary of War Woodring with that on page 10 of *Final Report of War Department Special Committee on Army Air Corps* (Baker Board Report), 18 July 1934 (see below, Chapter III), which found U.S. combat aircraft in 1934 "superior to those of any other country." Jane's *All the World's Aircraft* (London: Sampson Low, Marston and Co., Ltd., 1935) whose caustic editor, C. G. Grey, was certainly never one to give an unduly favorable view of U.S. aviation, placed this country at least two years in advance of Europe in 1934.
[7] *Ibid.*, pp. 2–3.

INTRODUCTION

a host of other ingredients that contribute to the sum total called air power. Among these are the productive capacity of the nation's aircraft industry and its potential for expansion, the procedures and practices by which the necessary funds are secured from Congress, as well as the forms and methods governing the procurement of matériel.

In short, although the continuing national debate on air power policy generally takes place in terms of the quest for quantitative and qualitative superiority, other factors essential to a superior air force cannot be slighted with impunity. And in one way or another, the general subject of procurement is related to all of them. It is no exaggeration to suggest that one cannot truly understand the problem of air power without first coming to appreciate something of the enormous complexity of procurement.

The pages that follow seek to illustrate the almost infinite ramifications of the procurement process and its intimate relationship with virtually every other activity of an air force. In addition, the exposition should make it clear that the elements of air power are never static. Science probes further horizons, technology advances, and novel weapons are perfected that require revised conceptions for efficient use. To survive in the ultimate competition of war, an air force must continue to perfect its techniques of procurement no less than its doctrine and its weapons.

CHAPTER II

The Aircraft Industry on the Eve of World War II

A Survey of the Industry

A cross-section view of the nation's aircraft enterprises on the eve of World War II reveals that the industry was in fact a complex of manufacturing enterprises, not all of which were primarily concerned with airplanes. While airplane manufacturers as such constituted the aircraft industry in the popular sense, in reality the term was far more inclusive, covering not only manufacturers of airframes but all those concerns producing engines, accessories, and component parts or subassemblies.

The designation *aircraft industry* thus actually embraced four rather distinct groups. First and best known were the airframe manufacturers. These firms designed new aircraft and produced them, sometimes fabricating nearly all of the items within their own manufacturing organizations and sometimes merely assembling components and subassemblies made elsewhere.

Engine manufacturers constituted a second group. During World War I, aircraft engine production was virtually enfeoffed to the automotive industry. On the eve of World War II this was no longer true. By then seven or eight manufacturers specialized in the production of engines.[1] Two of these firms—the Wright Aeronautical Corporation at Patterson, New Jersey, and the Pratt and Whitney Aircraft Division of the United Aircraft Corporation at East Hartford, Connecticut—dominated the field in terms of numbers produced, dollar volume of business, and units of horsepower delivered. *(Table 1)* A third concern, the Lycoming Division of the Aviation Manufacturing Corporation at Williamsport, Pennsylvania, shared significantly in producing engines for trainers.

---

[1] House Subcommittee of Committee on Appropriations, Hearings on *Supplemental Military Establishment Bill for 1940*, May–June 1939, pages 319-20, mentions the following engine manufacturers: Allison Engineering Co., Indianapolis, Ind.; Continental Motors Corp., Detroit, Mich.; Jacobs Aircraft Engine Co., Pottstown, Pa.; Lycoming Division, Aviation Manufacturing Corp., Williamsport, Pa.; Ranger Engineering Corp., Farmingdale, Long Island, N. Y.; Pratt and Whitney Aircraft Division, United Aircraft Corp., East Hartford, Conn.; and Wright Aeronautical Corp., Patterson, N. J. To this group should be added: Aircooled Motors (Franklin), Kinner Airplane and Motor Co., and Menasco Manufacturing Co., all producing engines in a class below 260 horsepower. Of the firms listed above, Allison, Pratt and Whitney, and Wright Aeronautical produced engines with horsepower ratings above 1000. For a contemporary survey of the engine industry, see *Aviation*, February 1939, pages 55ff.

TABLE 1—PRODUCTION OF AIRCRAFT ENGINES

Manufacturer	1929		1934		1936	
	Number	Percent of Total	Number	Percent of Total	Number	Percent of Total
Curtiss-Wright	2,148	29	1,125	41	1,404	33
Pratt and Whitney	2,010	27	859	31	1,300	31
Other firms	3,220	44	752	28	1,533	36

Source: W. B. Harding, *The Aviation Industry*, pp. 25–26.

Subcontractors constituted a third group within the aircraft industry. Of vital significance in wartime, subcontractors in peacetime were not only fewer but not so well recognized as a definite group with distinctive characteristics.[2] There were very few entirely vertical corporations in the aircraft industry producing airframes, engines, and all major components, but most airplane manufacturers did not rely heavily upon subcontractors for components and subassemblies. Factors such as the absence of manufacturers willing to accept subcontracts, the limited number of units in production runs, the need for close tolerances in precision work, and the necessity for a high order of production co-ordination in an area of frequent and rapid design change, as well as the desire of the airframe manufacturers to find employment for idle sections of their own production forces, all contributed to the peacetime practice of minimizing subcontract work. Even such a relatively large-scale manufacturer as the Boeing Aircraft Corporation fabricated all dies for presses, hammers, and drawbenches in Boeing shops.[3] When the emergency arrived and it proved advantageous to depend upon an increasing number of subcontractors, the lack of widespread peacetime use of subcontractors made wartime expansion in the field difficult. However, even though subcontractors were few in number during the prewar years, they did constitute a distinct part of the aircraft industry.

Vendors or suppliers were the fourth and last group of the aircraft industry. While subcontractors fabricated parts and assemblies to order by special contract with an airframe or engine manufacturer, vendors supplied ready-made items off the shelf. Such standard and semistandard miscellaneous items as wheels, pulleys, rivets, instruments, control cables, turn buckles, and the like made up the vendor's stock in trade. Some vendors, such as the Sperry Corporation, specialized in the field of instruments and controls; others concentrated on difficult-to-manufacture items such as exhaust stacks and collector rings or oleo strut shock absorbers.[4] Among the vendors,

---

[2] For the role of subcontractors in wartime, see below, pp. 401–10.

[3] *Aerodigest* (January 1936), pp. 26–29.

[4] William Barclay Harding, *The Aviation Industry* (New York: C. D. Barney and Co., 1937), pages 30–31, lists the vendors doing a major portion of their business in aviation during 1937 as follows: Air Associates, Aero Supply, Breeze Manufacturing Co., Brewster Aeronautical Corp., Cleveland Pneumatic Tool Co., Irving Airchute, and Sperry Corp. Propeller manufacturers might be listed with this group except that the most important happen also to be aircraft

one will serve as a representative example. Air Associates, Incorporated, combined manufacturing with a mail order house and general store business in aircraft parts. With one store in New York, one in Chicago, and a third on the west coast, Air Associates could supply such standardized items of aircraft hardware as fuel strainers, high pressure hydraulic pumps, relief valves, safety belts, landing wheels, and nuts, bolts, and screws for immediate delivery. Catalogues distributed to 20,000 buyers in a world market attested the scale of the firm's operations.[5] Vendors, whether supplying one complex specialty item such as autopilots or ten thousand minor hardware items from rivets to landing wheels, composed a separate and important segment of the aircraft industrial world.

While the four separate groups—airframe manufacturers, engine manufacturers, subcontractors, and vendors—did exist as identifiable entities, not every concern can be neatly tagged as belonging to one or another. Vertical organizations such as the Curtiss-Wright Corporation cut sharply across the groups, producing engines, airframes, and many component parts within a single managerial domain. Some vendors did subcontract work in addition to selling items from stock by catalogue. Moreover, as if to foreshadow a practice that was to become a problem during World War II, there were occasions when two airframe manufacturers did subcontract work for each other, thus becoming prime contrators and subcontractors at the same time.

That the business of aircraft production was never an integrated enterprise and never became a single, harmonious, smoothly functioning group working entirely within the team rules of a trade organization is perhaps best reflected in the experience of the industry with the National Recovery Administration (NRA) in the early thirties. The various component portions of the industry had such difficulty in finding common ground for agreement that promulgation of an acceptable code proved impossible. When the Supreme Court toppled the whole NRA structure in 1935, the aircraft industry was still without a code.[6]

Although the aircraft industry was thus in reality a complex of several industries, the airframe manufacturers definitely held the center of the stage. As design initiators and as synthesizers of the contributions from all the other groups in the industry, the airframe manufacturers necessarily require more attention and closer study of who they were, where they were located, and what their peculiar problems were on the eve of the war.

Membership in the Aeronautical Chamber of Commerce during 1938 amounted to some 86 manufacturers. This included 8 engine firms, 34 airframe firms, and 44 accessory firms. Of the airframe firms, more than half built only small, low-powered civilian airplanes; 14 handled both civilian and military types;

---

or engine manufacturers. Three important propeller manufacturers were Hamilton-Standard (a United Aircraft Corp. subsidiary), Curtiss, and Lycoming. Bendix Aviation Corp. was a leading vendor in the years immediately before the war, but only about a quarter of its total business lay in the aviation field; therefore, along with RCA, which supplied radio components, it cannot be clearly designated as an integral component of the aircraft industry.

[5] *Aerodigest* (January 1932), pp. 36ff.

[6] L. W. Rogers, "Functions of the Aeronautical Chamber of Commerce," *Journal of Air Law* (October 1935).

and 4 worked almost exclusively on military contracts.[7] *(See Appendix A.)* This listing does not include firms that for one reason or another did not join the Aeronautical Chamber of Commerce. The nonmembers were by no means all unimportant and small-scale producers, including among their numbers such widely different manufacturers as Rearwin Aircraft and Engines, Inc., in the light airplane field and Glenn L. Martin in the large transport and heavy bomber field.

When war came, the nation had about eighteen to twenty manufacturers with considerable experience in building military aircraft and about the same number whose production, though largely in the light airplane field, would qualify them as experienced in component and subassembly fabrication. Taken together, these manufacturers comprised the airframe industry; their skills and techniques would provide the essential basis for the nation's wartime achievements in aircraft production.[8]

A glance at a map of the United States will show how the prewar industry was located about the country. There were four loosely defined areas of concentration: those on the west coast from Los Angeles and San Diego to Seattle; those on the east coast in an area of three or four hundred miles about New York (the Hartford-Buffalo-Baltimore axis); the Detroit-Akron-Cincinnati triangle; and the Wichita-Kansas City-St. Louis triangle. Beyond the fact that the east coast area produced most of the engines and the west coast strip turned out a majority of the airframes, no very clear pattern of production by functional types according to geographic location is discernible. Such widely dispersed plants as Boeing in Seattle, Douglas in Santa Monica, and Martin in Baltimore all produced bombers.

In the light of subsequent wartime pressures for "strategic dispersal," it should be profitable to digress here momentarily to consider why the nation's aircraft industry grew up as it did. As in the case of many another new business, irrational factors such as the sheer accident of the founder's residence probably decided the location of many plants. Few, it appears, made their decisions after a careful weighing of all considerations as did Martin before moving to a site near Baltimore.[9] Some selected a site because local capital was available. Douglas is reported to have been moved by such an inducement. In other cases the presence of other aircraft plants and a pool of trained labor helped determine site selection. Occasionally, as in the case of Wright Aeronautical, a site was chosen because local businessmen made offers of excellent facilities such as a new factory or free use of a municipal flying field. Boeing is said to have gone to Seattle to be near the spruce supply so essential in early aircraft.[10] Year-round flying weather and the presence of the big Navy air arm installation at San Diego helped attract Consolidated to California.[11] There is no evidence to show that stra-

---

[7] House Subcom of Com on Appropriations, Hearings, *Supplemental Military Establishment Bill for 1940*, pp. 319–20.

[8] *Air Commerce Bulletin* (15 May 1938), p. 280.

[9] Glenn L. Martin, "Development of Aircraft Manufacturing," *Royal Aeronautical Society Journal* (October 1931), p. 894.

[10] Denis Mulligan, *Aircraft Manufacture in Chicago* (Chicago, 1939), pp. 30–32.

[11] *Business Week* (February 22, 1936), p. 44.

tegic considerations played any part in plant location before 1939.

When the war broke out in Europe in 1939 the nation's airplane builders were represented in some forty firms whose products ranged from puddle jumpers to four-engine bombers and whose factories were located anywhere from Hartford to Seattle. Large or small, east coast or west, all these manufacturers faced problems of marketing, research and development, production, and financing that, differing in degree, were nonetheless common to the aircraft industry as a whole. A detailed discussion of these four fundamental problem areas is needed to help lay the basis for an appreciative understanding of the aircraft industry with which the nation entered World War II.

The Market for Aircraft

In the aircraft industry in the United States the curve of aircraft production has reflected the curve of demand rather accurately—at least for the period following the market crash of 1929 and during depression when manufacturers learned that frequent design change and high unit costs made the accumulation of unsold items in stock an almost certain prelude to disaster:[12]

Year	Number of Units	Year	Number of Units
1922	263	1931	2,800
1923	743	1932	1,396
1924	377	1933	1,324
1925	789	1934	1,615
1926	1,186	1935	1,710
1927	1,995	1936	3,010
1928	4,346	1937	3,773
1929	6,193	1938	3,623
1930	3,437		

[12] Civil Aeronautics Administration (CAA), *Statistical Handbook 1948*, p. 43.

Observed superficially, these figures would seem to tell little more than the rise and fall of sales in phase with the business cycle of the nation, booming in 1929, hitting bottom in 1933, then staging a comeback, but still far below 1929 levels at the end of the period. Like most statistics, however, these figures representing totals of annual production are deceptive.

Mere numbers, lumping four-engine bombers with two-place puddle jumpers, fail to provide the essential truth. To reduce the annual production totals into meaningful segments, one must ask for whom the aircraft were produced. In broadest terms there are three markets for the industry: the domestic market for civilian aircraft, the domestic market for military aircraft, and the export market for both of these types. Each constitutes a rather distinct problem.

Military aircraft sales, although smaller in number of units than civilian sales, accounted for the larger portion of the industry's dollar volume. For example, in 1928 the 1,219 military planes sold were valued at $19,000,000; in 1933, 466 at $9,000,000; and in 1937, 949 at $37,000,000. In the field of civilian aircraft, the figures for the same years were: 3,542, $17,000,000; 591, $6,000,000; and 2,281, $19,000,000.[13]

[13] Figures are from E. W. Axe and Co., Inc., *The Aviation Industry in the United States*, Axe-Houghton Economic Studies, Series B, No. 6 (New York, 1938) (hereafter cited as *Aviation Industry in the U.S.*), page 70, and *Automotive Industries*, February 23, 1935, page 295, and February 26, 1938, page 262. Values shown do not include parts. It will be noted that the figures given here do not add up to the production totals given in the earlier table. The difference is accounted for by variant systems of enumeration used by the two compilers, one listing

Virtually the same pattern prevailed in the field of aircraft engines.[14] Clearly, military sales, whether for domestic or export destinations, constituted the most important element of the aircraft market even during the years of peace from 1928 to 1938. Without denying the importance of civilian aircraft to the health of the aircraft industry, any appraisal that fails to take full cognizance of the predominating role of the military market will be entirely misleading. Bearing in mind this relatively greater importance of production for military users, it will be easier to retain an adequate perspective when discussing, each in its turn, the three major divisions—civilian, export, and military—of the aircraft market.

The Domestic Civilian Market

Just as it is essential to separate civilian from military sales to perceive the economic realities of the whole aircraft market, so too the civilian market must be subdivided. On the eve of the war there were in the United States more than 20,000 licensed pilots and 10,000 licensed aircraft.[15] However, these figures may give a false impression. In a total of 1,823 civilian aircraft produced in 1938, only 53 were multiengine units. Expressed in other terms, the aircraft industry turned out 1,745 units in the one- to five-place category, but only 42 units with capacities ranging from five passengers up.[16] If this appears to suggest that small aircraft dominated the picture, one should note that the larger aircraft represented an average unit value of nearly $63,000, whereas the average unit value of all the others amounted to only a little more than $3,500.[17] Therefore, the most important single element of the civilian market lay in the sale of multiengine aircraft to commercial carriers or airlines. To understand the character of this key civilian market, so important to the general health of the aircraft industry, one must look for the factors contributing to the sale of transport aircraft in the between-wars period.

By 1938 regularly scheduled commercial airline operations in the United States were "big business," even if far below the railroads in capitalization, tonnage carried, and almost every other basis of comparison. In that year some twenty-odd domestic airlines operated along 30,000 route miles crisscrossing the entire nation. Something of the scale of operations attained by these carriers is indicated in the fact that they employed almost 10,000 people, including 1,135 pilots and copilots, to handle well over a million passengers a year. Revenue from these operations totaled 40-odd million dollars. And this, it should be noted, included domestic carriers only. Two

---

units produced, the other listing units sold, including items from inventory. Moreover, some items listed as export sales represented aircraft sold to buyers in the United States; the same items were listed again in the compilation of export sales.

[14] During the twelve-year period from 1926 through 1937, civilian aircraft sales exceeded military sales (dollar volume) during two years only: 1929 and 1934. In 1930 sales were about equal. See n. 13, above. See also *Barron's* (February 3, 1936), pp. 7–10, table.

[15] Bureau of the Census, *Statistical Abstract of the United States 1939*, p. 433.

[16] CAA, *Statistical Handbook 1948*, p. 51.
[17] *Aviation Industry in the U.S.*, p. 80.

United States international or overseas carriers employed 4,000 more people to carry 100,000 passengers over a world network of 35,000 route miles.[18] By virtually any measuring stick—route miles, passengers carried, or mail ton-miles—the airlines of the United States stood far above those of the other powers.[19] These achievements stand out more vividly when one recalls that only a decade earlier the nation's entire air carrier business involved 34 operators of short lines employing 1,500 people, including 300 pilots, to handle an annual total of 48,000 passengers.[20]

In the decade of rapid growth between 1928 and 1938, the airlines became an important customer of the nation's aircraft manufacturers. For the student of military aircraft procurement problems, the question of airline sales is significant. Not only did airline sales contribute to maintaining a high gross for the aircraft manufacturers and hence foster a healthy industry, airline purchases of big multi-engine transports also stimulated production of a character involving technical problems closely akin to, if not precisely the same as, those encountered in the production of military aircraft.

Certain critical factors fostering the growth of the air carrier industry stand out. They can be readily identified, and even if one cannot assess their relative value in promoting airline growth, mere recognition provides a useful impression concerning some of the types of variables determining the sale of aircraft to airline operators and thus contingently affecting the production of military aircraft.

The Air Mail Act of 1925, often called the Kelly Act after its congressional sponsor, opened the door to private contract mail carriers that replaced the government-operated carrier system in use since 1918. Designed as a virtual subsidy to stimulate the development of airlines, the Kelly Act along with its subsequent amendments achieved its objective, and by 1927 contract carriers handled all airmail. It was, however, in the administration of the act that the aircraft industry felt its full impact. Since the Post Office Department established rigid requirements of financial responsibility in letting airmail contracts, only contract operators with the greater capital resources continued to bid.[21] Thus, while the Kelly Act may be said to have marked the inception of a substantial system of scheduled carriers, from its very passage the administration of the act tended to encourage the few, well-financed operators rather than the many, struggling, small-scale operators lacking financial support. To the aircraft manufacturers both the act and its administration spelled good news. Private contract carriers, seeking lower operating costs in order to underbid, would demand from the industry aircraft of increasingly higher perform-

---

[18] CAA, *Statistical Handbook 1948*, pp. 61–83.
[19] Great Britain Air Ministry, Department of Director-General of Civil Aviation, *The Civil Aviation Statistical and Technical Review, 1938* (London, His Majesty's Stationery Office, 1939), Table IV, compares British, French, Russian, German, and U.S. airlines.
[20] CAA, *Statistical Handbook 1948*, pp. 61–83.

[21] Henry Ladd Smith, *Airways: The History of Commercial Aviation in the United States* (New York: A. A. Knopf, 1942), pp. 94ff. This readable volume contains a running account of the growth of airlines. The author's generalizations and interpretations, although often unsupported by the evidence, are both interesting and provocative.

U.S. MAIL PLANE LOADING FROM MAIL TRUCK, *September 1922.*

ance, whereas earlier the Post Office had operated its own depot for rebuilding and repair, keeping the few available aircraft in operation as long as possible, having little incentive to replace equipment frequently.[22] Moreover, the stipulation of financial reliability imposed by the Post Office increased the probability of airline credit arrangements satisfactory enough for aircraft manufacturers to risk extensive production outlays on transport airplanes for airline operators.

A second landmark appeared in 1926 with the passage of the Air Commerce Act. Encouraged by the precedent of federal aid to seaboard navigation, airline operators and aviation enthusiasts persuaded Congress to assume a similar burden for aerial navigation in the form of radio stations, emergency landing fields, and beacons under Department of Commerce sponsorship. Freed from the obligation of facing the heavy capital charges involved in these necessities, the air carriers could devote more capital to aircraft development.

The regulatory agency established by the Air Commerce Act of 1926 was the Bureau of Air Commerce, a unit within the Department of Commerce. Legislation in June 1938 transferred the functions of this bureau to an independent executive agency, the Civil Aeronautics Board (CAB) although its administrative organization, the Civil Aeronautics Authority (CAA), remained in the Department of Commerce. At the same time,

[22] F. A. Spencer, *Air Mail Payment and the Government* (Washington, Brookings Institution, 1941), p. 25.

Congress substantially enlarged the scope of the agency's powers. Whatever its form or title, the appearance of a federal agency to regulate air traffic had a profound impact on commercial aviation.

Broadly speaking, the Air Commerce Act of 1926 was a piece of organic legislation, collecting the fundamental laws of air carrier operations into a single comprehensive system.[23] While its provisions for aids to navigation gave the air carriers immediate and substantial financial relief, the act's other sections involving uniform traffic and air safety regulations as well as licensing, registration, and inspection requirements, also contributed toward the establishment of a stable, healthy, and vigorous airline industry in the United States.

The tendency toward consolidation received substantial encouragement in 1930 when the McNary-Watres Act amended the Kelly Act in such a way as to give even greater discretionary powers to the Postmaster General in awarding mail contracts. Since the incumbent Postmaster General favored a system of integrated airlines, many small lines combined into networks until a handful of powerful operators dominated the field.[24] By 1934 three airlines flew 65 percent of the nation's route miles, carried 90 percent of the mail, and received 88 percent of the federal mail subsidy.[25]

A third landmark in the history of the nation's airlines was the precipitous rise in passenger traffic that coincided with the era of consolidations. Between 1928 and 1934 airline operations moved off on a new tangent as passenger traffic began to replace mail as a major source of revenue.[26] Passenger volume increased from less than 50,000 in 1928 to almost 500,000 in 1934, climbing steadily thereafter.[27] A number of factors probably contributed to this new trend. A steadily improving safety record may have helped to win the public to air travel.[28] A somewhat more measurable contributory factor was the sharp decline in fares. From 12 cents a mile in 1929, the average passenger fare tumbled to 5.7 cents a mile in 1935. Just how far the air travel fare had to fall in order to challenge the railroads competitively is indicated in the 1929 air rate, which was three and one-half times higher than the average rail fare per mile in that year.[29] Yet another element apparently contributing toward the rise of passenger traffic on the airlines was a provision of the McNary-Watres Act of 1930 changing the method of computing mail payments. The pound-per-mile formula gave place to a new computation based on the amount of space available. This made it advantageous for

---

[23] Air Commerce Act (44 Stat 568), May 20, 1926. For evidence of federal aids to navigation, see *Air Commerce Bulletin* (April 15, 1935), statistical tabulations on airways.

[24] For a general discussion of airline mergers, see Smith, *Airways*, ch. 11, especially p. 243.

[25] Ernest Gugelman, *The American Aviation Industry* (New York: D. D. Magruder, Inc. [1934]), p. 15. Between 1928 and 1934 the number of domestic airline operators dropped from 34 to 24. By 1938 the number had been reduced to 16. CAA, *Statistical Handbook 1948*, p. 61.

[26] J. A. Frederick, *Commercial Air Transportation* (Chicago, 1945), p. 375, Figure 42. Passenger revenue exceeded mail revenue for the first time in 1935.

[27] CAA, *Statistical Handbook 1948*, p. 70.

[28] *Ibid.*, p. 93. Passenger fatalities dropped from 28.2 per 100 million passenger-miles to 4.7 between 1930 and 1935. See also, M. J. Meehan, "Progress in the Aeronautical Industry," *Survey of Current Business* (March 1936), pp. 16–18.

[29] *Aviation Industry in the U.S.*, p. 41.

operators to acquire new and larger aircraft, which, when not filled with mail, invited passenger traffic.[30] Such types as the Ford Trimotor, the Curtiss Condor, and the Douglas DC-2, appearing in succession, did much to popularize air travel.

The appearance of passenger revenue as a major element in the air carrier business marked a definite turning point in the history of air transport. It came just in time to cushion the airlines when the federal government abruptly canceled all private airmail contracts in February 1934.

The airmail scandals of 1934 with their involved interplay of political and economic competition cannot be recounted here at length, but it will be useful to take note of the episode since it shed light upon the peculiar antagonisms behind the record of military aircraft procurement discussed in a subsequent chapter. In February 1934 the President issued an Executive order canceling all airmail contracts and transferring operations to the Army.

When Army airmen attempted to fly the mails on short notice, lacking adequate equipment and training for the task, they were beset with disaster. After a week of midwinter flying and almost daily crashes, the score of catastrophes stood at five pilots dead and six seriously injured. Soon afterward the President rescinded his ban and began negotiations to return the mails to the private air carriers. It was against this setting that Congress passed the Air Mail Act of 1934, which abandoned the subsidy character of previous airmail legislation and reverted to rigid emphasis on low bids regardless of responsibility, reliability, or pioneering investments, all considerations favored in previous awards. As one writer subsequently declared, the 1934 airmail legislation as finally passed had a "punitive aroma." [31]

The airmail carriers must have felt that the 1934 legislation really was "punitive" since their airmail subsidy fell from 23 million dollars in 1933 to 12.5 milions in 1935. Nevertheless, the airlines did not collapse. The volume of mail carried by air mounted rapidly throughout the thirties and by 1939, even under the less favorable legislation of 1934, mail revenues to the air carriers exceeded the sums received before the subsidy legislation had been annulled.[32] More important, however, was the rising volume of passenger traffic, which had turned upward before the 1934 legislation was enacted and which was further stimulated thereby. Had the subsidy cut come earlier, for example in 1928, it might well have been fatal, but in 1934 mail revenues no longer constituted the predominant percentage of air carrier income. By 1938, passenger revenue constituted 57.6 percent of the carriers' income, and the potential market had scarcely been tapped since airline passenger-miles amounted to but 6.8 percent of Pullman passenger-miles.[33]

---

[30] McNary-Watres Act, April 29, 1930, sec. IV.

[31] Hugh Knowlton, *Air Transportation in the United States* (Chicago, University of Chicago Press, 1941), p. 10.

[32] CAA, *Statistical Handbook 1948*, p. 80.

[33] CAA, *Statistical Handbook 1945*, p. 33, and CAA, *Statistical Handbook 1948*, p. 79. The character of the potential passenger volume for air carriers in 1938 is suggested by the fact that ten years later the airlines were carrying 48.5 percent as much traffic as Pullmans. In 1938 it was estimated that less than one-half of one percent of the population flew each year. *Air Commerce Bulletin* (October 15, 1938), p. 98.

The transition of the airlines to a primary interest in passenger traffic had a clearly discernible effect upon aircraft manufacturing in the United States. Many carriers bid on mail contracts at a loss rather than lose their routes, hoping to combine mail and passenger volume for a profit. Faced with almost certain loss unless costs could be pared, operators were more than ever anxious to procure aircraft with improved performance. Engines that could be operated 200 hours rather than 100 hours between overhauls meant increased services at lowered costs and a possible profit. In the same fashion, the transition to passenger traffic fostered a still greater interest in high performance aircraft since airlines studies revealed that improved equipment had a marked influence on passenger volume.[34] Speed in particular had sales appeal. Between 1934 and 1938, the average air speed of the airliners advanced from 127 to 163 miles per hour as one carrier after another secured new equipment with which to hold or capture passenger traffic.[35]

From two directions, then, cost cutting and passenger transport, the carriers were induced to procure new equipment, and four out of five of the biggest operators sold stock in the mid-thirties to raise the necessary funds.[36] That this meant life-giving business for the aircraft manufacturers is clear from the fact that the five largest carriers at that time maintained fleets ranging from fifteen to nearly sixty units.[37] Replacement of any substantial portion of these fleets opened the possibility of true production line output of multiengine aircraft for the first time.

The shift to passenger traffic and the declining mail subsidy might in themselves have effected something of a boom in aircraft manufacture, but by a peculiar coincidence a technical revolution appeared on the very eve of the airmail fiasco. The last transcontinental airmail run before the private contracts were canceled was flown in a Douglas DC–2 on her maiden record-breaking trip across the nation in thirteen hours and four minutes. With successful completion of the record transcontinental flight, the 14-passenger 200-miles-per-hour Douglas airliner rendered obsolete virtually every other airliner in the country. The technical revolution, as embodied in the DC–2, like most revolutions, did not come from any single drastic step forward in design but rather from the cumulative effect of several significant innovations. By coincidence, the development of *monocoque*, all-metal structures replacing the wood, wire, and fabric structures of the previous decade appeared just when a series of major innovations in design provided power plants with vastly more output per pound of engine. The appearance of the DC–2 incorporating all these advances in a brilliant new synthesis forced one carrier after another to discard existing equipment, often long before its actual usefulness had gone, in favor of the new and markedly superior Douglas airplane. There followed a profitless prosperity for the carriers, who were forced to pour the earnings of their growing passenger traffic back into new equipment. The cost of replacement mounted

---

[34] *Aviation Industry in the U.S.*, p. 55.
[35] CAA, *Statistical Handbook 1945*, p. 31.
[36] *Barron's* (February 22, 1937), p. 9.
[37] *Aviation* (April 1937), p. 77.

sharply, rising from approximately $30,000 per unit before the technical revolution to something in the neighborhood of $60,000 after the appearance of the DC-2.[38] The process of replacing equipment was so expensive the airlines continued to show deficits until 1939 despite substantial increases in revenue.[39]

Perhaps the clearest index to the impact of the technical revolution on the airlines is to be found in the size of the total air fleet maintained by the carriers. From a peak of 497 units in 1930, the number fell to 260 in 1938; there were actually fewer units licensed in 1938 than in 1928 despite the enormous increases in passengers, mail, and express carried by the airlines. Not only did the precipitous renewal of almost the entire carrier fleet result in a growing emphasis on production but it also brought to a head all the contingent problems of the technical revolution in aircraft manufacturing. Larger, more expensive, and technically novel aircraft required enlarged facilities, new financing, and extensive tool replacement, all within a very short period of time.

In sum, then, down to fiscal year 1938 there were three outstanding factors conditioning the airline market for aircraft: the Air Mail Act of 1925, the Air Commerce Act of 1926, and the shift from mail to passenger traffic as a primary source of revenue. Each in some measure encouraged the growth of air carriers as customers for aircraft and in varying degree strengthened the aircraft industry as an element of national defense. The carrier market was, however, only one aspect of the three major market areas, domestic, export, and military, that occupied the industry in the late thirties.

The Export Market

In terms of sheer numbers of units, sales of aircraft abroad were by no means inconsiderable. From a mere 37 exported in 1922, the year of doldrums following World War I, exports mounted, erratically and with annual fluctuations, to a total of 631 units in 1937. Aircraft engine exports climbed from 147 in the rock-bottom year 1922 to 1,048 in 1937. Foreign sales in spare parts, replacements, and accessories tell a similar story, growing from $250,000 in 1922 to something over $12,000,000 in 1937. Taken together, aircraft, engines, parts, and accessories in the export trade represented a sizable volume of business for the nation's aircraft industry, in all, over $39,000,000 in 1937.[40]

As an important attribute to national defense, aviation was subsidized in one form or another by all the major powers. For this reason, none of the great nations offered much in the way of markets for aircraft exported from the United States, at least not in normal times of peace. The bulk of the peacetime export market went to lesser states. Almost any year chosen at random demonstrates this distribution. In 1929, for example,

---

[38] *Aviation Industry in the U.S.*, p. 80. *Barron's* (February 22, 1937) gives a somewhat higher figure, running from a pre-1934 cost of approximately $85,000 to a post-1934 figure around $120,000.

[39] *Barron's* (January 15, 1940), p. 25.

[40] *Aviation Industry in the U.S.*, p. 90, based on data compiled from The Aeronautical Chamber of Commerce of America, Inc., and the Bureau of Air Commerce sources. After World War II the name of the chamber was changed to Aircraft Industries Association. See also, CAA, *Statistical Handbook 1945*, p. 123.

only 12 aircraft were exported to Europe, but Latin America took 196. In 1936, when 61 units went to Europe, 192 went to Latin America.[41] Moreover, since the majority of aircraft were exported to the lesser states and smaller powers, the total number of units in any one contract was almost necessarily small and credit arrangements were frequently involved, if not actually precarious.[42]

Regulations conceived to protect the national interest by restricting the export of military secrets constituted a second determinant in the aircraft export trade. These regulations, applying to military aircraft only, required a two-year time lag in the release of current aircraft designs to foreign states. After the passage of the neutrality legislation of the mid-thirties, the export license requirements provided an even greater measure of control than had existed theretofore. In favor of these security restrictions, it was argued that the nation's technical secrets and margin of design superiority were safeguarded. Critics, especially aircraft manufacturers who suffered from the curb, raised a number of points in opposition to the security measure.[43] Restrictions on exports, especially those on export of military aircraft already on contract, reduced the number of units of any one design that could be produced in a single production run.

Perhaps the most important of all the arguments against export curbs on military aircraft was the contention that mere export curbs would not prevent foreign states from securing the most recent military aircraft design details and incorporating them in their own aircraft designs at will. Since the development of facilities and productive capacity was, in the long run, probably as vital to the nation's security as any particular design detail, the export curb to all intents and purposes encouraged or reinforced the creation of productive capacity in foreign states. Finally, there can be little doubt but that restrictions on the export of most recent military designs placed manufacturers in an unfavorable competitive position when pitted against other exporting nations.[44]

Military officials, confronted with frequent proddings from manufacturers, attempted to liberalize the export restrictions as far as possible in order to encourage a healthy aircraft industry. Nonetheless, they continued to insist on the principle of a time lag before releasing current production models for the export market.[45]

A less tangible but no less influential determinant of aircraft exports is to be found in the political and diplomatic sphere. This type of influence on exports may be illustrated best by the case of the

---

[41] *Aviation*, March 1930, p. 596, and April 1937, pp. 84-85.

[42] For some revealing insights on the subject of aircraft export sales, see Special Com Investigating the Munitions Industry, U.S. Senate, Hearings (popularly called Nye Hearings), pt. III, 73d Cong, February 24, 1936, and pt. IV, 73d Cong, Exhibit 304, p. 894.

[43] For an instance of a manufacturer's protest against curbs on exports, see D. L. Brown, "Export Volume and Its Relation to Aviation Progress and Security," *Aerodigest* (December 1934), pp. 15ff.

[44] Competition in the export market between the two wars was sharp. British exports topped those of the United States down to the early thirties, and pressed close behind thereafter. See Air Ministry, Dept of Civil Aviation, *Civil Aviation Statistical and Technical Review 1938; Aviation* (October 1938), p. 35; *Automotive Industries* (March 1939), pp. 574-75.

[45] See ch. IX, below, for a fuller discussion of the export ban.

neutrality legislation of the middle thirties. From the aircraft manufacturer's point of view, considerations such as those raised by the discretionary powers given the President in the neutrality legislation for invoking the ban presented imponderables against which it was virtually impossible to plan. The character of this difficulty becomes evident when it is observed that China was the most important single buyer of aircraft exports from the United States. In the period from 1925 through 1934 the Chinese purchased 6,986 aircraft, while between 1935 and 1938 the number reached 12,406. In both periods the Chinese accounted for something over 13 percent of the nation's total export volume.[46] Had the President found it politically and diplomatically expedient to elevate the China Incident to the rank of a war, by the terms of the neutrality legislation much of this important export trade would have dried up. Thus, the aircraft manufacturer's export trade no less than his sales to domestic air carriers was ultimately and most vitally subject to political decisions often far beyond the scope of any individual manufacturer's ability to influence or even to predict.

In the face of all the imponderables and complexities confronting aircraft manufacturers who pursued the export market, one might well be inclined to ask why they continued to show such aggressive interest in the field. A cursory analysis of aircraft exports in almost any year may reveal the answer. With the crash of 1929 and 1930, the total value of aircraft production fell from $91,000,000 to approximately $61,000,000. In this same period, however, exports fell off only about $250,000, providing between eight and nine million dollars' worth of business to the industry.[47] Expressed in terms of payrolls and employment, the importance of this volume of business in the depression is easily recognized. In 1937 exports amounted to approximately one-third of the nation's total aircraft production, but this third accounted for an estimated 50 percent of the industry's net profits.[48] Unhampered by statutory profit limitations in pricing, export items returned a larger profit than could be extracted in the domestic trade.

While the above illustrations refer to aircraft exports, virtually the same conclusions could be drawn with regard to engines, spare parts, and accessories. In fact, engine exports outstripped aircraft sales annually by almost two to one. During the two worst years of the depression, 1932 and 1933, when aircraft sales ranged between 300 and 400 units, engine sales totaled 2,356 and 2,901.[49]

In short, despite serious obstacles, the export business was extremely worthwhile to aircraft manufacturers in the United States. It might even be argued that the export business was essential to the health of the nation's aircraft industry. By raising the volume of output it

---

[46] Elsbeth Estelle Freudenthal, *The Aviation Business: From Kitty Hawk to Wall Street* (New York: Vanguard Press [1940]), Table IX, p. 141, and Table XIX, p. 271; Harding, *Aviation Industry*, p. 3; Bureau of the Census, *Statistical Abstract of the U.S. 1938*, p. 458.

[47] L. W. Rogers, "Analysis of Aviation Exports," *Aerodigest* (April 1931), p. 45; CAA, *Statistical Handbook 1948*, pp. 43, 58.

[48] *Aerodigest* (July 1938), p. 34; *Aviation* (April 1938), p. 31; Denis Mulligan, *Aircraft Manufacture in Chicago* (Chicago, 1939), p. 8.

[49] *Air Commerce Bulletin* (15 May 1938), p. 280.

increased the probability of mass production and strengthened the nation's position of readiness for war. But even at their best, the domestic carrier and export markets were less important to the cause of national defense than the market for military aircraft in the United States.

The Domestic Military Market

A simple statistical presentation of the total military and commercial aircraft market, both as to numbers and value, should provide a useful point of departure in an analysis of military sales. (*Table 2*) These figures reveal a good deal about the market for military aircraft in the United States. The dollar value of military sales exceeded that of civil sales by a considerable margin despite the lower total number of military units sold. On the basis of continuity and high dollar volume, the military market would appear to have offered an attractive field for aircraft manufacturers. Further detailed study, however, confutes the impression.

Aircraft average unit costs were rising sharply throughout the period of the technical revolution:[50]

Year	Military Aircraft	Civil Aircraft	Military Engines	Civil Engines
1928	$15,641	$4,854	$4,736	$1,551
1932	17,519	4,259	5,872	3,565
1937	39,063	8,413	7,456	3,734

The average unit cost of military aircraft was far in excess of the civil aircraft average unit cost. Several factors contributed. The air arm was building an increasingly larger percentage of bombers, which tended to drive up the average. Where there had been but one bomber to every four pursuit planes in 1926, by 1937 there were eleven bombers to nine pursuits, and the bombers were in many cases four-engine rather than two-engine craft. The complexity introduced with the technical revolution sent engineering costs alone up some 48 percent in the transition from wood to tubular metal structures; with the coming of *monocoque* structures, engineering costs mounted another 50 percent. Many of the heavy charges encountered in military aircraft were not found in most of the civilian types. The early B-17, for example, contained more than $10,000 worth of instruments, not to mention armament and other special military accessories.[51]

The higher average unit cost of military aircraft stemmed not alone from sheer size or complexity; rather it was more directly the result of military emphasis on high performance. Inasmuch as engine horsepower is an important factor in high performance, a comparison will explain the relationship between the higher costs of military aircraft and performance requirements. In 1937 civil aircraft engine production amounted to 2,289 units, but 1,393 of these fell in the under 50 horsepower category and all the rest save 88 were below 600 horsepower.[52] Military aircraft, on the other hand, used no engines in the 50 horsepower category and from a total of nearly 1,800 engines produced for military use, 1,276 were in

---

[50] *Aviation Industry in the U.S.*, p. 71.

[51] Testimony from Hearings before the Subcom of the Com on Appropriations, House, 75th Cong, 1st sess, *1938 Military Establishment Appropriations Bill*, March 1937, pp. 520–22.

[52] CAA, *Statistical Handbook 1948*, p. 51.

TABLE 2—COMPARATIVE IMPORTANCE OF MILITARY AND CIVILIAN MARKETS

Year	Military Units Sold	Value in Thousands	Civilian Units Sold	Value in Thousands
1926	552	$6,154	604	$2,716
1928	1,219	19,066	3,582	17,194
1930	747	10,723	1,937	10,746
1932	593	10,389	549	2,338
1934	437	8,837	772	9,958
1936	1,141	27,836	1,559	12,380

Source: Figures for first three years are from *Automotive Industries* (February 23, 1935), page 295. Figures for last three years are from *Aviation Industry in the United States*, page 70, based on Aeronautical Chamber of Commerce sources.

categories above 700 horsepower.[53] Thus, aircraft manufacturers who wished to compete for the military market were forced to operate with an ever larger capital structure to carry the charges involved in the exceedingly high average unit cost for military aircraft and engines. In addition, the necessity of turning out aircraft of progressively superior performance to meet the tactically competitive requirements of the military market involved the annual investment of large sums for research and development in contrast to the civil aircraft market, where a single basic design occasionally continued to amortize initial development costs over a period of several years.

As a result of the characteristics described above, the market for military aircraft tended to remain in the hands of a comparatively few manufacturers. In 1937, for example, all Army aircraft procurement was with 10 manufacturers, all Navy with 8. And this was from a field of 98 aircraft manufacturers of whom 48 were in active production. In the case of engines, the concentration of business in the hands of a few was even greater. From a total of 23 aircraft engine manufacturers in 1937, the Army's entire procurement came from 3 concerns and the Navy's came from 2.[54] Expressed in somewhat different terms, the concentration of the military market can be seen in the fact that less than a dozen firms manufactured all but 200-odd of the 4,977 aircraft produced for the Army and the Navy between 1931 and 1937.[55] From 1931 through 1937 seven of the largest manufacturers could account for the following percentages of their business through government contracts:[56]

---

[53] *Automotive Industries* (February 26, 1938), pp. 262ff.

[54] *Air Commerce Bulletin* (15 May 1938), p. 280; *Aviation in the U.S.*, pp. 100-101.

[55] *Aviation Industry in the U.S.*, app. VI. Based on Aeronautical Chamber of Commerce figures. Four firms produced three-quarters of this total for the period: Douglas produced 1,194 aircraft for the Army and the Navy between 1931 and 1937, Boeing 684, Curtiss-Wright 681, and North American 551.

[56] Freudenthal, *Aviation Business*, Table VI, p. 128, based on Com on Naval Affairs, House, Hearings on *Investigation Into Certain Phases of the Manufacture of Aircraft and Aeronautical Accessories . . .*, February 2–March 8, 1934 (hereafter cited as Delaney Hearings), and Subcom on Aeronautics of the Com on Naval Affairs, House, *Rpt on Investigation Into Certain Phases . . .*, April 10, 1934 (hereafter cited as Delaney Report), items 18 and 37, respectively, in *Sundry Legislation Affecting the Naval Establishment: 1933-1934*, 1st and 2d sess, 73d Cong (hereafter cited as *Sundry Naval Legislation, 1933-34*).

Manufacturer	Percent of Total Sales
Boeing	59
Chance Vought	75
Consolidated	79
Curtiss	76
Douglas	91
Martin	100
Grumman	75

From these observations a few general conclusions may be drawn regarding the military aircraft market. In dollars, it was the predominant aircraft market, though profits in the field were subject to statutory limits in some cases. In addition, the insistent requirement for ever better performance in military aircraft made the military market probably the most difficult to enter in the technological sense. The need for continuing research and development along with the growing complexity and size of military aircraft made of the military market a costly business, a veritable bottomless pit for funds. And all this, of course, was expense incurred in addition to the investments that all aircraft manufacturers, whether seeking the military market or not, had to face in securing the new facilities and the new tools required by the technical revolution in aircraft structures. As a consequence, the seemingly attractive military market was confined more or less to a dozen manufacturers specializing in military types, and even within this group, four firms received the bulk of the business, largely because they were capable of pursuing a thoroughly aggressive policy of research and development.

Research and Development

In the aircraft industry, the injunction "design or die" has always been virtually axiomatic. Superior performance expressed in higher speeds, greater ceilings, heavier loads, and longer ranges wins contracts. To stay in business, manufacturers soon learned that they must maintain engineering staffs capable of exploiting the latest findings of aeronautical science, translating theory into practical designs. Where there had been but 30 aircraft design groups in the industry of 1918, by 1939 there were 125 different research and development staffs specializing in aircraft, engine, and accessory design work.[57]

The competitive pressure for improved performance made flux in design well-nigh continuous, research and development an unending process. The phrase *research and development* is glibly repeated in discussions of military appeals for higher appropriations, but one seldom finds it concisely defined. In the aeronautical field, as elsewhere, research is of two kinds, fundamental and applied; the former is the peculiar province of the scientist, the latter the task of engineers. Where one deals in abstract theory, the other must make practical application. Thus *research and development* has come to be a shorthand expression for the whole spectrum from the most theoretical exploration of fundamental theory down to the most practical attempts to solve design problems in particular instances.

In aviation, as with other scientific fields, the quest for underlying scientific principles has been carried on extensively in the universities. During the first two decades of flying, few universities offered courses specializing in the aeronautical sciences, but after 1926 the Guggenheim

---

[57] AAF Hist Study 50, Materiel Research and Development in the Army Air Arm: 1914–1945, p. 78.

Fund greatly strengthened fundamental research in the aeronautical sciences with large endowments to nine universities strategically dispersed over the nation.[58] Yet, despite the presence of excellent facilities in several universities, in 1939 only one-seventh of one percent of the Air Corps' research budget, or approximately $15,000, went directly to university research contracts. While indirect contracts and industrial utilization of university facilities increased this figure somewhat, the universities did not match the volume of activities in fundamental research carried on by the federal government.[59]

Among the federal agencies concerned with aeronautical matters, one, the National Advisory Committee for Aeronautics (NACA), stood pre-eminent in the field of fundamental research. This executive agency, established by Congress in 1915 to supervise and direct the scientific study of flight, had grown by 1938 into the nation's leading center of fundamental research. The initial appropriation of $5,000 in 1915 increased during the between-war years until it annually totaled nearly $2,000,000. Following the curve of appropriations, NACA grew from a small group of scientists to a technical staff of more than 500 people administering and operating an elaborate installation of research facilities located at Langley Field, Virginia. This research plant included laboratories for engine and instrument tests, machine shops, a flying field, and wind tunnels. All together, the NACA boasted 11 wind tunnels, among which were a 60 by 30 foot full-scale tunnel, an eight-foot, 500-miles-per-hour tunnel, and other equipment such as vertical and refrigerated tunnels for specialized types of aerodynamic research.[60]

Although in many respects inferior to the research facilities available to European powers, the equipment for fundamental research in the United States, both federally and university sponsored, represented a marked increase over the inadequate equipment of 1918. Over the twenty-year period between the wars, the nation acquired perhaps a dozen centers of advanced aeronautical research, of which the NACA facilities were the best. These research centers were significant assets, not only for scientific achievement but also as training schools for the vitally necessary aeronautical engineers of industry. Science may calculate the ultimate level of aircraft performance, but it is applied research and development carried on by the industry's engineering and design staffs that regulate the actual pace of technical progress.

Army policy on aeronautical research went through several phases in the between-war years. From the armistice until 1926 there was a certain amount of wavering between a policy of support for both fundamental and applied research and a policy of concentrating expenditures in applied research. From 1926 until 1938 it was Army policy to follow the latter course almost exclusively.[61] The

---
[58] *Final Report of the Daniel Guggenheim Fund for the Promotion of Aeronautics, 1930.*
[59] AAF Hist Study 50, pp. 62, 83–85.
[60] *Ibid.,* p. 65.
[61] For a lengthy discussion of the vicissitudes of air arm research and development policies, see Rotary-Wing Aircraft in the Army Air Forces: A Study in Research and Development Policies, 1946, by Irving B. Holley, jr., filed in Wright Field Historical Office (WFHO); and AAF Historical Study 50, page 75.

NATIONAL ADVISORY COMMITTEE FOR AERONAUTICS ANNUAL MEETING, *October 1939.*

preoccupation with applied research was particularly evident on the eve of the war when some 60 percent of the available research funds actually went to industry in contracts for experimental and service test items.[62] Thus, although the sums specifically earmarked by the air arm for research were relatively small, the matériel development contracts awarded to industry represented a hidden subsidy of significant proportions.[63] But this form of research subsidy was not without drawbacks.

During the years from 1926 to 1938 the practice among virtually all manufacturers seeking Army contracts for experimental air matériel was to bid as low as possible, even accepting a loss, on experi-

[62] AAF Hist Study 50, p. 75.

[63] *Ibid.,* p. 49. The following tabulation shows the breakdown for R&D funds for 1937-39:

	1937	1938	1939
Total R&D funds..	$4,518,460	$4,349,890	$3,574,290
R&D.............	2,468,900	2,928,135	2,043,409
Civilian pay......	1,657,060	1,104,950	1,201,550
Service test items..	392,500	316,805	329,331

NACA Full-Scale Wind Tunnel at Langley Field, 1930's

mental work in the hope of recouping later with high-volume production contracts. As long as this practice prevailed, manufacturers had little incentive to execute any form of experimental work other than that promising some more or less immediate return in a subsequent production contract to amortize costs. Under the pressure of this economic restraint, manufacturers were unwilling to indulge in extensive fundamental research. Then, early in 1939, the Air Corps promulgated a new policy that can best be called pay-as-you-go research. Designed to unshackle the pace of design flux from the manufacturers' fears that subsequent production contracts might not be forthcoming, the pay-as-you-go policy developed an unexpected by-product. Not only did the policy tend to speed the pace of design change but it also encouraged individual manufacturers to move into the field of fundamental research, since it was no longer necessary to look for immediate results with which to amortize costs. This trend toward industrial participation in fundamental research created a host of new and difficult administrative relationships between industry and the Army that were still unresolved when the coming of war greatly aggravated the matter.

The acceleration of design change after 1938 presented a problem of critical significance to the aircraft industry. Mass production required standardization. Rapid flux in design is the very antithesis of this. If a manufacturer introduces major design changes in each successive aircraft turned out, efficient production in the sense of large-quantity fabrication by repetitive machine process is patently impossible. Fluid design changes and a high rate of production are mutually exclusive.[64]

To explore this problem further, it is necessary to make a brief survey of the evolution of aircraft production patterns during the twenties and thirties.

Production

The term *production,* unless narrowly defined, can lead to endless trouble in any discussion of the aircraft industry. In aviation circles it means not mere fabrication of items, but mass production, or the approach to mass production in numbers sufficiently great to justify abandoning the handmade, custom-tailoring method of individual unit fabrication in favor of techniques commonly associated with mass production in almost any industry: straight-line assembly, conveyor belts, large runs in unit fabrication, and the like.

The aircraft industry conception of the term *production* was quite different from that of the automobile and other mass production industries. Table 3 reveals much about the nature of the aircraft industry. The automobile makers in 1937 turned out some 1,500 times more units than did the aircraft builders and did the job with a labor force only eight times larger. To be sure, the automobile is less complex than the airplane, but the explanation for the difference in production efficiency is indicated in the different wage patterns of the two industries. For example, in 1937 aircraft workers averaged a 42.3-hour week at an hourly rate of $0.666, while automobile workers worked an average of 35.9 hours each week but drew pay at an average hourly rate of $0.891.[65] This spread may reflect labor's more effective organization in the automobile industry, but clearly the differential was made possible by high volume, which justified a high degree of production tooling to cut unit costs.

As late as 1939, when foreign orders were already mounting, one typical aircraft manufacturer, and a highly efficient one too, turned out only two or three units a day in comparison with Detroit's production of two or three automobiles per minute. Behind this contrast stands the machine. Where Chevrolet's investment per worker in plant and equipment amounted to $2,600, Martin, a leader in the aircraft field in 1939, had an investment of about $800 per worker.[66]

---

[64] CofAC to Chief, Mat Div, 1 Mar 39, and reply, 10 Mar 39; Memo, CofAC to ASW, undated, WFCF 1943, 121.6 Costs, R&D Policy. See also, Air Board Rpt, 23 Mar 39, and TAG to Chiefs of Arms and Services, 15 Sep 39, WFCF 1940, 320.2 Army Aviation. See Chapter VIII in Holley's MS monograph, Rotary-Wing Aircraft in the Army Air Forces: A Study in Research and Development Policies.

[65] Bureau of the Census, *Statistical Abstract of the U.S., 1939,* p. 329.

[66] *Fortune* (December 1939), pp. 74–75; and George Bryant Woods, *The Aircraft Manufacturing Industry* (New York, Boston: White, Weld and Co., 1946), p. 4.

AIRCRAFT INDUSTRY ON THE EVE OF WORLD WAR II

TABLE 3—A COMPARISON OF THE AIRCRAFT INDUSTRY WITH THE AUTOMOBILE INDUSTRY

Year	Number of Establishments		Average Number of Wage Earners		Dollar Value of Products[a]		Number of Units Produced	
	Aircraft	Automobile	Aircraft	Automobile	Aircraft	Automobile	Aircraft	Automobile
1929	132	210	14,710	224,688	71,153,000	2,391,090,000	6,522	5,294,087
1933	64	121	7,816	97,869	26,460,000	1,096,946,000	1,179	1,848,013
1937	92	131	24,003	194,527	106,586,000	3,096,219,000	3,100	4,732,553

[a] For aircraft, value of product includes value of aircraft *and* parts. For automobiles, value of product denotes value of automobiles only.

Comparisons of average dollar output per employee afford another index to the aircraft industry's lack of tooling. In 1937 aircraft workers at something over $4,400 in product value per worker lagged far behind automobile workers, averaging more than $15,000 in product value added per worker.[67]

Thus, although the aircraft industry turned out an increasing number of units in the years following the slump, aircraft *production* was not to be confused with *production* in the automobile industry, where the term meant something quite different. The following figures indicate the relatively inferior rank of aviation in the nation's business as a whole in 1936:[68]

Product	Total Value of Product
Automobiles and trucks	$2,448,000,000
Farm implements	420,000,000
Cans	375,000,000
Refrigerators (retail)	328,000,000
Typewriters and office equipment	153,000,000
Aircraft parts and engines	86,000,000

Combining all these factors—low unit volume, low gross dollar volume, and lack of production tooling—the plight of the aircraft industry in the late nineteen thirties can be summarized as follows: low-priced airplanes waited upon the introduction of production techniques in the industry, but high-volume production could be justified only by a mass market, which waited upon low-priced airplanes. Until some escape from this circle could be found, true mass production in the aircraft industry would remain out of reach. This was the situation prevailing when the crisis appeared in Europe.

Genuine mass production did exist in one branch of the industry. While aircraft manufacturers turned out dozens of units, engine manufacturers turned out hundreds. Where the major aircraft builders often produced several models in a year, every one a distinct production problem requiring independent tooling, two or three engine manufacturers dominated the field with a restricted number of models that they sold for use with numerous different airframes. By way of illustration, as early as 1930, when four leading airframe concerns delivered a total of only 428 military aircraft, a single engine firm produced 666 engines for military use.[69]

---

[67] Computed from Bureau of the Census, *Statistical Abstract of the U.S., 1939*, p. 803.

[68] Figures for 1936. Harding, *Aviation Industry*, p. 69.

[69] Paul A. Dodd, Financial Policies in the Aviation Industry, Ph.D. Thesis, University of Pennsylvania, 1932 (Philadelphia, 1933), apps. F, G, H.

Several factors operated to the advantage of the engine builders. To begin with, the total market for aircraft engines was somewhat greater than that for airframes since airframes normally outlasted engines and most aircraft users procured spare engines in quantities ranging up to 100 percent of the number of aircraft on hand. In addition, aircraft engines, while still under development and subject to continual changes in design during the nineteen thirties, were not in the midst of a violent technological revolution as was the case with airframes. For a comparable revolution in the engine field one might consider the problems subsequently encountered in shifting from reciprocating to jet engines.[70]

The implications of high-volume output in the aircraft engine field were nowhere more apparent than in the new Pratt and Whitney engine facility constructed during 1930 in East Hartford, Connecticut. Here was mass production a whole decade ahead of the airframe builders. The major unit of the Pratt and Whitney plant consisted of a single floor area 1,000 feet long and 400 feet wide. Down the center of this area ran an aisle 15 feet wide. Railroad sidings and truck platforms brought in raw materials at one end of this structure where electric trucks hauled color-coded tote boxes from department to department as fabrication progressed with aluminum machining on one side of the main center aisle and steel machining on the other. Cross aisles facilitated the flow of parts that moved from machining departments to the assembly line where engines grew with the accretion of parts as they moved toward the final inspection point. Beyond the inspection point were located another set of railroad sidings and truck platforms to haul away the finished product.[71] This was a mass production facility. East Hartford had followed the lead of Detroit and pointed the way for the aircraft industry to pursue. Though few of the other engine establishments were so spectacular as the Pratt and Whitney plant, as a group the engine builders were acutely conscious of the need for efficient assembly line operation.[72]

The rising volume of aircraft sales in the nineteen thirties, while small in number and less concentrated than in the case of engines, did have a very real influence on airframe production techniques. Larger orders meant longer runs, justifying the use of more production tooling. But "larger" is a relative term, and increases from three to thirteen airplanes on a single contract did not spell Detroit-style production. More significant in the middle thirties was the impact of the technical revolution.

With the arrival of 40- to 60-place commercial aircraft and four-engine monoplane bombers of *monocoque* construc-

[70] For a discussion suggesting some of the considerations that led the aircraft engine industry into successful production ahead of the airframe industry, see A. H. Leak, "Coordinating Aircraft Engine Design and Production," *SAE Journal* (February 1939), pp. 85–92.

[71] J. W. Marshall, "Line Production the Keynote of New Pratt and Whitney Aircraft Plant," *Iron Age* (July 17, 1930), pp. 152–55. See also Moritz Kahn, "Aircraft and Engine Factory Layout," *Aerodigest* (January 1936), p. 29. Mr. Kahn was at the time of writing a vice president of Albert Kahn, Inc., industrial architects and engineers, a firm that played a significant part in subsequent wartime expansion of the aircraft industry.

[72] The Ranger Engineering Co. facility, built in 1928 at Farmingdale, Long Island, is a case in point. See *Aerodigest* (January 1937), pp. 21–23.

tion sporting wing spans of 60 to 100 feet, one manufacturer after another found his existing facilities utterly inadequate. As fast as available funds and new contracts would permit, the major airframe builders abandoned or enlarged their old facilities—some of them World War I remainders, some of them makeshift conversions from other uses—in favor of new plants constructed specifically for airframe production.[73] In 1935 Consolidated left Buffalo and a twenty-year-old plant with a patchwork of additions sprawling from it, to occupy an entirely new San Diego facility of modern design with a floor area of only slightly less than 450,000 square feet.[74] During the following year Boeing increased floor space to something over 400,000 square feet with a new 60,000-foot addition. This new facility had a single unobstructed assembly area measuring 200 by 300 feet, complete with overhead monorail for the installation of heavy subassemblies such as engines, as well as numerous floor channels with outlets for electricity and compressed air to run power-operated assembly tools.[75]

In explaining Curtiss' decision to expand, President G. W. Vaughan probably spoke for the airframe industry at large when he pointed out that the facility expansion that accompanied the 1929 boom had provided floor space fully adequate until about 1937. Then "it became apparent that aviation was embarking upon an era when quantity production was at a greater premium than at any time in the industry except during the hectic days of the World War." As a consequence, along with most of the other major aircraft manufacturers, Curtiss-Wright planned heavy capital expenditures for increased floor space. Significantly, here as elsewhere in the airframe industry, the expansion of facilities was based upon probable future space requirements rather than current ones.[76] In like fashion, between 1935 and 1939 many of the major airframe producers moved into modern facilities in excess of those required or justified by the prevailing backlog of orders.

Unfortunately for the cause of national defense, the appearance of facilities fully adequate for continuous, straight-line operations did not actually herald the day of mass production. After the mid-1930's the airframe manufacturers did equip themselves with an impressive array of facilities, but, hampered as they were by the lack of orders for large numbers of units justifying long production runs, they continued to fabricate airplanes in piecemeal fashion with handwork the rule rather than the exception. Photographs of the major manufacturer's assembly floors in this era reveal forests of stepladders and but few of the line techniques so characteristic of the auto industry.

During the decade of the thirties important strides were taken toward the eventual achievement of the mass production goal. New tools are a case in point. As the thirties progressed, more and more high-speed, labor-saving devices were to be found in the industry. Almost any well-equipped facility in 1938 could be expected to include high-

---

[73] For a discussion of this question, see W. J. Austin, "Modern Construction Needs of the Industry," *Aerodigest* (October 1937), p. 40.
[74] *Aerodigest* (June 1938), pp. 34-39.
[75] *Aerodigest* (February 1937), pp. 32-34.

[76] *Aerodigest* (June 1938), p. 40.

HAND ASSEMBLY OF STEARMAN PRIMARY TRAINERS AT DOUGLAS PLANT, 1939

speed presses for forming, brakes for shearing, nibblers and bandsaws for sheet cutting, as well as a variety of special precision finishing machines for honing, lapping, and polishing. Pneumatic riveting devices and electric spot-welding equipment were in use to speed assembly, while some of the more recent developments of the industrial world such as optical comparators and Magnaflux units provided accurate, efficient inspection at a production tempo.[77]

Of more interest are those special tools that made possible exceptional savings in production. When Lockheed installed a big 2,000-ton Farrel-Birmingham forming press standing over 25 feet high, it was reported to be the largest in the aircraft industry, but soon afterward North Amer-

---

[77] Extensive surveys of the status of the aircraft industry with regard to tools are hard to find. Most of the articles in the aviation magazines and technical journals are cursory at best, usually dealing in experiences encountered with a single tool or type of equipment. As an example of this type of literature, see J. B. Johnson, "Magnaflux—What Does It Show," *SAE Journal* (February 1939), pp. 59–67. For the most authoritative general survey, see T. P. Wright, "American Methods of Aircraft Production," *Journal* of the Royal Aeronautical Society (March 1939).

ican installed a 3,000-ton model and Baldwin-Southwork produced a 5,500-ton version for use in forming dural parts.[78] With these presses, aircraft manufacturers could turn out sheet metal parts of far greater size and complexity than ever before. Less awe-inspiring than the big presses, but no less significant to the prospect of speeding production, were other special aircraft innovations such as wood and rubber dies, hydraulic stretching devices, and wheeling machines to form intricate shapes at low cost.

One of the heaviest elements of cost for production tooling in most modern industries is encountered in the fabrication of dies for use in forming presses. Where automobile manufacturers retooled once a year, spending millions in the process, aircraft manufacturers introduced major design changes in the midst of production runs many times within the course of a year. To invest large sums of capital in production tools that might shortly be scrapped was neither desirable nor possible under the high-cost low-volume condition of the industry. Fortunately, aircraft manufacturers were able to devise an escape through technology. Unlike the automobile builder, who worked almost entirely with steel, the aircraft manufacturer frequently dealt in lighter metals. As a result, designers discovered that it was possible to construct inexpensive dies for forming presses by replacing tool steel with zinc, which could be readily altered when design changes so dictated. In time, wood and hard rubber dies replaced even the inexpensive zinc dies with further savings in costs and increase in output.

In the quest for lower production costs some manufacturers went even further than the low-cost die and developed the stretching machine, a hydraulic ram device in which jaws gripped sheet stock at the edges and drew it over a wooden frame die. In this fashion such curved surfaces as engine cowling plates and wing tip bows could be formed at little expense. To achieve the same ends by entirely different means, other manufacturers resorted to the wheeling machine, a novel device in which an operator fed sheet stock between two power-operated crowned wheels, tangent to one another, and formed curved sections of sheet by skillful manipulation.[79]

Cheap dies, stretching devices, and wheeling machines were, of course, only a few of the many production innovations that aircraft manufacturers were using on the eve of the war, but they typified the trend toward increased production without the necessity for heavy investment in more or less permanent tooling. Significantly, aircraft manufacturers in the United States were primarily concerned with production tools that cut costs. Those that emphasized labor reduction or high-speed output but involved higher costs remained little exploited until the arrival of a war market.

Although airframe manufacturers frequently used the word *production* in the

---

[78] *Aerodigest* (April 1937), p. 72, and (January 1939), p. 95.

[79] For some interesting comments on production equipment by the president of an aircraft tool firm, Engineering Research Co., see H. A. Berliner, "Special Machines Designed for Flexibility in Aircraft Production," *Aerodigest* (January 1939), pages 65–66, and "European Aircraft Production," *Iron Age* (November 4, 1937), page 45.

late thirties, the industry as a whole was production conscious only to a very limited degree. Perhaps the best evidence of this is to be found in the administrative organizations evolved to produce airplanes. In one typical large-scale manufacturing establishment there were several groups of functional specialists: an aerodynamics group, a landing gear group, an electrical group, a fuselage group, a' weight control group, and, finally, a general group handling details for all groups including such matters as specifications, preparation of handbooks, operating manuals, spares lists, bills of materials, production releases, and contract requirements.[80] Clearly, the engineers dominated the field. Emphasis was on design engineering rather than production engineering, which was lumped in with half a dozen other unrelated administrative chores. Until high volume demanded a change, emphasis would continue upon design rather than upon production.

More evidence of the absence of production-mindedness in the aircraft industry is to be found in a closer analysis. After twenty years of operations, most manufacturers continued to use locally designed, nonstandard business forms, which prevented the speedy accumulation and tabulation of data for production control purposes. The automobile industry had already pointed the way to what could be done with standard forms and punch-card business machines in securing production efficiency through stock control, unit cost control, and planned machine loading. However,

while some aircraft builders recognized the usefulness of these innovations, there were still many who lacked even an adequate stock control system, without which any significant level of production was patently impossible.[81]

Still another index to the lack of production-mindedness amongst aircraft manufacturers before 1939 was the scarcity of articles in the aircraft technical journals and periodicals discussing production problems and production tooling. For every infrequent article on tooling and production engineering in the thirties, one can find literally hundreds of articles on experimental engineering and design.[82]

One manufacturer, who felt that his facility was approaching mass production when it turned out twenty-five units per week, summed up the essential dilemma of the industry concisely. Radiator caps, he reported, cost 20 cents each in small quantities. Produced in lots of 500 or more, the price dropped to 10 cents, but, with an annual output of only 550 airplanes, to produce 500 caps at one time would mean to accumulate an inventory with a once-a-year turnover. When applied to a full line of parts, this process not only involved a high risk of obsoletion in a field of rapid design change but also tied up large sums of working capital.[83]

---

[80] For discussion of an illustrative administrative organization, see *Aerodigest* (June 1938), p. 39.

[81] A revealing view of the industry's lack of production-mindedness is contained in L. Cruikshank, "Standardized Records and Record Keeping," *Aerodigest* (February 1936), page 24.

[82] R. H. Holmes, "Some Principles for the Design of Aircraft Tooling," *Aerodigest* (November 1937), page 24, offers an example of the infrequent production engineering discussion.

[83] W. T. Piper, "Pioneering in Mass Production," *Aerodigest* (September 1937), pp. 56ff. Piper was, at

Without working capital, the introduction of production tooling would be difficult if not impossible. Without improved tooling, low-cost aircraft were not to be expected. Unless the industry could turn out low-cost aircraft, the mass market—barring war—could never be tapped. For this reason, the problem of how the aircraft industry was financed in the years just before World War II takes on particular significance.

Financing the Aircraft Industry: 1934–38

The financial position of the aircraft industry, and particularly the means by which it obtained money, was in the midthirties an element in the nation's defense no less vital than the available strength in aircraft reported each year to Congress. In theory at least, aircraft manufacturers could obtain working capital in three ways: by reinvesting profits, by borrowing, or by selling stock.

For a generation familiar with the millions of man-hours and billions in dollar values that have characterized the aircraft industry since World War II, it may be difficult to recall just how small the prewar business actually was.[84] As late as 1938, Moody's *Industrials,* a widely used barometer of corporate activity, did not consider aircraft manufacturers signifi- cant enough to include them in the firm's annual statistical survey of operating ratios for the nation's major industrial groups.[85] It is against this backdrop that the problems of the aircraft industry's search for funds must be examined.

As a source of capital, profits in the prewar industry appeared favorable—at least on the surface. A composite financial statement for the eighteen top aircraft manufacturers shows a rising curve of net profits:[86]

Year	Net Profit
1935	$1,749,000
1936	5,225,000
1937	8,191,000
1938	17,139,000

This curve seems to spell increasing prosperity, but the round numbers in themselves are deceptive. In the first place, the eighteen top aircraft manufacturers necessarily involve both Curtiss-Wright and United Aircraft, whose corporate earnings include the profits of their engine manufacturing operations along with airframe production, weighting the composite picture abnormally. Moreover, the dollar return of the industry is meaningless unless measured against sales or capital invested.

Profits as a percentage of sales advanced from a deficit in 1934 (again using the eighteen manufacturers' composite state-

---

the time of writing, general manager of the Taylor Aircraft Corporation, one of the more important manufacturers of small, low-powered airplanes.

[84] G. M. Williams, "Growth of the Aircraft Industry," *Prospects and Problems in Aviation,* a series of papers presented at the Chicago forum on aviation (Chicago: The Chicago Association of Commerce, 1945), p. 3.

[85] *Moody's Manual of Investments: American and Foreign: Industrial Securities* edited by J. S. Porter et al. (New York: Moody's Investors Service, 1938, 1940, 1941) (hereafter cited Moody's *Industrials*), p. 145.

[86] Aircraft Industry Financial Summary, 19 Sep 47, National Archives, Rcds of Presidential Comms, etc., Rcd Group 220, Rcds of President's Air Policy Comm, MG2–3.

ment) to 10.9 percent in 1938.[87] Profits as a percentage of capital invested, or net worth, looked even better, rising from 2.9 percent in 1935 to 15.4 percent in 1938. Aircraft manufacturers' profits were certainly improving substantially during the middle thirties, and, in comparison with some of the nation's key manufacturing enterprises outside the aircraft field, they were generally superior in the second half of the thirties in terms of percentages.[88]

A composite financial statement can be misleading, however, for the generally prosperous upcurve of profits obscures the fact that individual firms, even the biggest and strongest in the field, might be encountering disastrous deficits. Boeing, for example, turned in a profit of 7.3 percent of sales in 1936 but suffered a deficit of 27.7 percent of sales in 1938, even though the composite figures for these years reflect a general increase.[89]

Granting the existence of rising profits, it is important to determine where the profits went in order to appraise the industry's capital position. The figures in Table 4 show that the shareholders were not carrying away an abnormal portion of the net. As a matter of fact, aircraft dividends were less than was typical among the nation's manufacturing industries. A substantial share of the industries earnings, an average of 57.4 percent in the period shown, was available to plow back into the business.

TABLE 4—PERCENT OF EARNINGS AS DIVIDENDS AND SURPLUS, EIGHTEEN TOP AIRCRAFT MANUFACTURERS: 1934–38

Year	Dividends	Surplus
1934	0.0	0.0
1935	23.9	76.1
1936	36.8	63.2
1937	52.5	47.5
1938	50.0	50.0

Source: Aircraft Industry Financial Summary, 19 Sep 47; Modley, *Aviation Facts and Figures: 1945*, p. 38.

The amount available as surplus may appear impressive. But compared with deferred development charges (which give some clue to the industry's heavy capital requirements), it is evident that the sums available as surplus for plowing back into the industry may not have been adequate for the abnormal capital requirements of aircraft manufacturers in the thirties, when both plant replacement and design change had to be pursued aggressively to ensure competitive survival. *(Table 5)* The relationship of surplus (undistributed earnings) to deferred development charges (current costs earmarked for future payment) does not necessarily provide an infallible criterion for measuring the degree to which profits were available for use in plant expansion, tool replacement, and design change or development work, since different manufacturers followed different bookkeeping practices in arriving at deferred development charges as published.

---

[87] *Ibid.* Profits as a percentage of sales for the period 1934–38 were as follows: 1934, –.42 percent; 1935, 4.01 percent; 1936, 7.95 percent; 1937, 6.85 percent; 1938, 10.9 percent. Compare these figures with those of Aircraft Industries of America, *Aviation Facts and Figures: 1945*, R. Modley, ed. (New York: McGraw-Hill Book Co., 1946), page 48, based on 12 rather than 18 firms.

[88] See tabulations of percent net income to net worth and percent net income to sales presented in Moody's *Industrials*, 1940, pp. a175ff.

[89] Moody's *Industrials*, 1940, p. a40ff, and Aircraft Industry Financial Summary, 19 Sep 47.

TABLE 5—YEARLY INCREMENT TO SURPLUS OR DEFICIT COMPARED WITH YEARLY INCREMENT TO DEFERRED DEVELOPMENT CHARGES, EIGHTEEN TOP AIRCRAFT MANUFACTURERS: 1934-38

Year	(Thousands of Dollars)	
	Increment to Surplus (or Deficit)	Increment to Deferred Development Charges
1934	$(137)	$883
1935	1,332	1,846
1936	3,301	1,635
1937	3,904	3,154
1938	8,547	5,929

Source: Aircraft Industry Financial Summary, 19 Sep 47.

A common practice in the thirties was to prorate experimental costs over the production life of a given aircraft model, which normally continued to sell for several years. More customary was the practice of selecting a fixed number of aircraft sales against which to prorate development costs. If sales failed to reach the predetermined figure, the firm would show a loss for that particular model. Some manufacturers restricted development costs to the sales of a given model in its initial year of production, showing a profit or loss depending upon the model's sale in that year. It is evident that profits and ultimately the capital available for plowing back into the industry could, within certain limits, be juggled at will by a careful selection of bookkeeping methods and thus make it possible to show a profit or loss in any given year almost according to desire.[90]

Wide deviations in deferment policies suggest grave dangers in seeking an index to the industry's ability to finance itself from earnings by comparing surplus with deferred charges. In addition, the existence of these differing policies suggests a revealing insight into the sometimes surprising spread between extremely high and low bids in price competition on comparable items. Comparisons of one manufacturer with another, in the light of widely different accounting practices, are dangerous to make and difficult if not downright impossible to use with accuracy.

One more factor affects the role of profits as a source of operating capital. In 1934 Congress passed the Vinson-Trammell Act setting a legal profit limit of 10 percent on Navy contracts, including aircraft. Not until later were the provisions of the act extended to cover Air Corps contracts. However, insofar as Navy contracts contributed to the industry's gross during the middle thirties, a ceiling was imposed on the amount of capital aircraft manufacturers could derive from profits.[91] While this ceiling did impound profits of the engine and accessory manufacturers, in practice airframe producers seldom computed profits on military contracts in excess of the ceiling imposed.[92] The Vinson-Trammell Act

---

[90] For a brief discussion of deferred development charges, see *Aviation Industry in the United States*, page 97, and Appendix Table IX, Analysis of Deferred Development Expenses, showing deferred charges as a percent of sales and as a percent of total assets; and amortization of development as a percent of sales and as a percent of deferred development.

[91] Vinson-Trammell Act, 73d Cong, 2d sess, March 27, 1934 (48 Stat 503).

[92] The two major engine producers showed profits over a ten-year period ending in 1937 averaging 17 percent (Harding, *Aviation Industry*, pp. 25-27). Air Corps audits and cost studies covering thirty contracts in 1937 and 1938 showed that accessory manu-

prohibited profits over 10 percent but did not guarantee profits up to that figure. Losses, especially those incurred on research and development or experimental contracts, could and sometimes did absorb the entire margin allowed on more successful production contracts. Although subsequent amendment mitigated this type of loss somewhat, the outlook for creative profits from military contracts was far from bright in the late thirties, a time when manufacturers were looking for capital with which to refurbish the industry.

Even more than legal limits and bookkeeping procedures, the dynamic character of aircraft design itself contributed significantly to the limits on profits during the prewar years of rising sales. The inadequacy of earnings to meet these research charges is suggested by the fact that twelve leading manufacturers poured $5,200,000 into development costs during 1937–38 and deferred sums during the same period amounting to $2,300,000, or nearly half of the total allocated to development.[93] While deferred charges are perhaps unreliable as a measure of capital requirements, other figures contain the same implications. Over the period 1934–38, the aircraft industry as a whole is reputed to have put 9.4 percent of its gross into research, whereas profits amounted to but 5.8 percent of gross.[94] In a period of rapid technical flux, investment in a particular design involved a continuing gamble, for new and more extensive capital outlays on still more advanced designs might be and frequently were required long before the previous model had amortized itself, thus impelling further investment of earnings or deferment of charges or both.

So long as the aircraft industry continued to experience a high rate of design change and a low level of production, even a rising general level of profits proved inadequate as a source of capital. Leaving in abeyance for the moment the relative adequacy of profits as a source of capital, it may be useful to consider borrowing, the second source of capital available to the aircraft builders.

The aircraft industry, like most of the nation's industries, regularly resorted to the banks for cash to meet short-term requirements such as initial inventories or labor costs before payments on delivery of finished products. Bank loans, however, represented only a small portion of the industry's total current assets, about 2 or 3 percent in 1937 and 1938.[95] Moreover, these commercial loans did not represent new capital in the strict sense of the word. They were limited in volume by the liquid assets of the borrower rather than by the prospect of future earnings, as would be the case with funded debt or long-term interest-bearing bonds.

---

facturers averaged profits of 20 percent. Airframe and accessory manufacturers, excluding one serious airframe contract debacle, showed an average profit of 18 percent (Chief, Finance Div. to Maj Gen H. H. Arnold, 1939, AAG 120 Misc, Funds and Disbursements). For evidence of profits in earlier years, see Freudenthal, *Aviation Business*, Table V, p. 123, derived from Delaney Hearings, p. 496, and *Aviation*, October 1938, pp. 35–36.

[93] Aircraft Industries Assn., Industry Planning Memorandum, Financial, Series 13-2, October 1, 1947, Table IV, Composite Balance Sheet for Twelve Leading Airframe Manufacturers, AIA office files.

[94] J. Lloyd, "Stockholders' Panorama of the Aircraft Industry," *Magazine of Wall Street* (November 18, 1939), pp. 146–65.

[95] AIA, Industry Planning Memorandum, cited n. 93.

For a number of reasons the aircraft industry was unwilling or unable to secure capital in the bond market. Long-term debt, whether in the form of mortgages, notes, or bonds, would require fixed interest charges that must be met annually or cumulatively as a part of fixed overhead. So long as the aircraft industry remained dynamic, both as to design and as to production levels, earnings would continue to be problematical and always something of a gamble. Because of these circumstances, the aircraft manufacturers in the thirties continued the practice of the twenties and acquired almost no funded debt.[96] One important exception to this pattern involved a near disaster.

In 1929, near the peak of the boom, the Glenn L. Martin Company moved into an efficient new plant at Middle River not far from Baltimore, Maryland. The collapse of the market curtailed the company's plans to finance the new undertaking with equity capital and, instead, Martin turned to funded debt with 6 percent 5-year notes for some $3,000,000. The continuing depression and a series of misfortunes reduced Martin earnings to deficits despite the fact that the company was a leader in the design field. Unable to meet its obligations maturing in 1934, Martin went through Section 77B of the Federal Bankruptcy Act. The company recovered when the arrival of war sales helped liquidate the notes that had been renegotiated to 1939, but the painful experience stood as an object lesson for all aircraft manufacturers to see.[97] Since such a leader in the aircraft field as Martin skirted disaster with funded debt, it is not difficult to appreciate the reluctance of the industry at large to consider such borrowing to raise capital. Obviously, then, only one source of capital, the stock market, remained to be tapped.

There were serious disadvantages in any extensive use of equity capital. Every share sold in the market diluted managerial control. Moreover, if a given manufacturer intended to rely upon the market for capital to any great extent over a prolonged period of time, he must show occasional profits and pay encouraging dividends or his source of capital might dry up.

There were numerous factors in the middle thirties militating against the sale of aircraft manufacturers' securities. First, some of the major producers, burdened with the unfortunate heritage of the speculative boom, were heavily overcapitalized. Overcapitalization implied a dilution of earnings. Prudent investors normally eschewed the offerings of all such corporations. Second, the high rate of design flux obviously ate heavily into profits, promising the investor a low yield, if any, so long as the pace of development continued to be rapid. Frequent federal investigations of one character or another constituted a third factor weighting the balance against equity capital. Ever since the Hughes investigation of 1918, special hearings on the aircraft industry, congressional or otherwise, followed one another almost annually, and

---

[96] Dodd, *Financial Policies in the Aviation Industry*, pp. 86–90; Harding, *Aviation Industry*, Title XI, p. 64.

[97] *Fortune* (December 1939), pp. 73–77; *Aviation Industry in the U.S.*, pp. 185–89. Curtiss-Wright also labored under a heavy burden of funded debt in the 1930's.

each raised as many problems as it solved, creating a state of permanent uproar, unrest, and uncertainty throughout the industry generally by raising fears of intervention, nationalization, or at the very least, profit limitation. Still another consideration affecting the investor's judgment against aircraft shares is to be found in the very complexity of the industry itself. Dynamic problems of design and production, uncertainties resulting from the political influences affecting the sale of aircraft, and, not least in this enumeration, the diversity of accounting procedures, warned against investment in the aircraft industry.

Among the many pressures against investment in aircraft manufacturing were the warnings of the nation's brokers and market analysts. The aircraft business, warned a writer in *Barron's*, was "swift, turbulent and erratic," clearly "a field for speculation and not for investment."[98] A few months earlier, the *Magazine of Wall Street* declared that there were only twenty-two interesting investment opportunities among the sixty-odd corporate aircraft offerings of the nation and at least half of the twenty-two were regarded as shaky and liable to go under entirely or submit to merger.[99] More significantly, even investment research organizations warned that there were no "gilt edged securities" in the aircraft industry, where shares tended to fluctuate more violently than securities in most other manufacturing industries. The best that could be said of investment in aircraft manufacturing shares seemed to be that it was speculative and therefore "potentially profitable."[100] In short, the experts warned that the aircraft industry presented far too complex a picture for safe investment.

In view of the apparently overwhelming number of considerations advising against investment in aircraft securities, it is certainly surprising to find that the industry was able to raise significant sums in the stock market. From 1936 right on down through the war years of peak production, every aircraft manufacturer who placed offerings in the market was able to sell stock in quantities sufficient to cover current losses and meet working capital requirements.[101] Perhaps the clearest indication of this willingness to absorb aircraft securities is to be seen in the case of Lockheed. Reorganized in 1933 after a period in the hands of a receiver, the corporation had three times sold shares to bring in working capital by 1938. That such a firm could enter the market that frequently and still acquire capital readily is indicative of the availability of equity capital to the industry despite the forebodings of the brokers.[102] Between 1933 and 1939, Bell,

---

[98] H. Lawrence, "New Wings for Aviation," *Barron's* (January 25, 1937), p. 15.

[99] C. M. Turner, "Aviation Begins to Earn Money," *Magazine of Wall Street* (October 10, 1936), pp. 760–62.

[100] Harding, *Aviation Industry*, chs. V–VIII.

[101] Aircraft Industry Financial Summary, September 19, 1947, summary and conclusions based on composite of annual statements of eighteen leading airframe manufacturers.

[102] *Aviation Industry in the U.S.*, pp. 182–84. From 1938 to 1941, the Big Six—Boeing, Consolidated, Douglas, Lockheed, Martin, and North American—all airframe manufacturers, raised their capital and plant by $67,000,000, $23,000,000 or approximately one-third of which came from the sale of securities. See F. A. Callery, "Review of American Aircraft Finance," *Air Affairs* (Summer 1947), p. 485.

Boeing, Curtiss-Wright, Douglas, Fairchild, Lockheed, Martin, Northrop, Republic, and United, to name a few of the larger firms, raised a total of more than $30,000,000 in new capital with anywhere from one to three offerings.[103]

This curious ability to secure equity capital in spite of the numerous drawbacks calls for an explanation. In the first place, there is some evidence to indicate that aircraft shares were heavily if not largely held by speculators rather than investors and therefore somewhat less subject to the normal demands of prudent investment.[104] Thus, while it is true that even shares bought at the market low in 1937 or 1938 would yield only a return ranging from 1.5 to 4.5 percent at best, speculators, anticipating substantial market advances with the probable coming of war, might well be willing to buy aircraft shares.[105] Secondly, whether those who bought aircraft shares were speculators or investors, they appear to have been swayed more by anticipation of future prospects than by the current technical adequacy, managerial competence, or financial position of the industry.[106]

While the stock market proved to be a comparatively ready source of capital for the aircraft industry, each new stock issue imposed its obligation of dividend payments to keep the market interest and each new share diluted earnings and magnified the problems of corporate control. At best the stock market was a last resort, and the extent to which the industry relied upon equity capital is a rough measure of the inadequacy of earnings to meet the demands of the industry. However, this rough measure provides only a relative comparison of these sources of capital; the central problem still remains: to determine the financial condition of the aircraft industry as a factor in its ability to meet the war crisis when it arrived.

The record of rising profits in the 1935–38 period gives a superficial picture of prosperity and fiscal soundness. The volume of business was certainly rising, yet this in itself was no positive indication that the industry was attaining a sounder financial structure. To secure such an indication some yardstick other than profits is essential.

The current ratio of the aircraft industry offers one useful index of the industry's financial position. In effect, the current ratio of an industry, the ratio of its current assets to its current liabilities, is a statement of its working capital position. The current ratio indicates the margin by which available assets, such as cash, inventory, and other easily convertible resources, cover claims such as notes and accounts payable. The lower the current ratio falls, the closer the industry moves to the bare break-even point. A decreasing ratio spells a relatively weak financial position, for an industry with assets barely able to meet its obligations is obviously ill prepared to meet abnormal capital demands or adverse business conditions. The utility of the current

---

[103] Aircraft Industry Financial Summary, 19 Sep 47, summary and conclusions based on composite of annual statement of eighteen leading airframe manufacturers.
[104] Woods, *Aircraft Manufacturing Industry*, p. 35.
[105] Modley, *Aviation Facts and Figures: 1945*, Table 4–10, p. 48.
[106] See, for example, page 492, comments of F. A. Callery, cited n. 102, and analysis of the Brewster firm's fund-raising experience in relation to production record, in Aircraft Industry Financial Summary, 19 Sep 47.

ratio as a yardstick is further enhanced by the circumstance that it provides a basis for comparison between industries without regard for differences in scale of operations.

A comparison of current ratios between the nation's manufacturing industries in general and the airframe industry in particular reveals that during the prewar years airframe manufacturers came to occupy a less favorable financial position than other manufacturers. The following figures indicate the extent to which this was true for an important portion of the industry:[107]

	1935	1936	1937	1938
300 manufacturers (nonaircraft)	4.8	4.2	4.0	4.9
6 major airframe firms	4.9	5.4	2.8	3.5

Enlarging the size of the sample to embrace twelve leading airframe manufacturers does not improve the general picture. The average current ratio for the larger group was 2.0 in 1937 and 2.7 in 1938. This was in contrast to the relatively superior current ratio of 4.0 or higher for the nation's manufacturing industries as a whole.[108] These considerations suggest that the rising curve of aircraft profits was deceptive as a guide to the financial position of the aircraft industry. As the volume of sales mounted, the industry incurred obligations that pressed the industry closer to the bare level of solvency. The financial position of the aircraft industry on the eve of the war became increasingly stringent as current commitments expanded toward the danger point.[109]

The importance of a declining current ratio as a yardstick to the financial position of the aircraft industry is suggested in a comparison of working capital to sales. Where twelve leading aircraft manufacturers increased their working capital 2.6 times between 1934 and 1938, sales in these years increased almost exactly fivefold.[110] All this came at a time when design change and factory refurbishment imposed an abnormally heavy capital requirement upon the industry.

It is possible to identify still other operating ratios that tend to substantiate the current ratio observations. The relationship of inventory to current assets is just such a ratio. A large inventory is a distinct disadvantage because it ties up working capital and increases the probability of losses resulting from design changes that leave obsolete stock in storage. Since the nation's typical prewar manufacturing industry maintained an inventory valued between 40 and 50 percent of current assets while the airframe manufacturers carried inventories valued at 50 to 60 percent of current assets, the inventory capital requirements of the aircraft industry

---

[107] Figures computed from Moody's *Industrials*. Current ratio for U.S. industries 1935-37 based on 316 firms in 1938 edition, p. 41a; 1938 figures based on 307 firms in 1941 edition, p. 46a. Current ratios for six leading airframe manufacturers (Boeing, Consolidated, Douglas, Lockheed, Martin, and North American) from financial statements of these firms in 1940 edition of Moody's *Industrials*.

[108] Aircraft Industries Assn., Industry Planning Memorandum, Financial, Series 13-2, 1 Oct 47, Table 4, Composite Balance Sheet for Twelve Leading Airframe Manufacturers.

[109] Computed from financial statements of six leading airframe manufacturers in Moody's *Industrials*, 1940. For a discussion of the need for adequate capitalization, see L. L. Putnam, "Too Much Money or Too Little—Both Bad," *Airway Age*, vol. 12 (May 2, 1931), 481-84.

[110] Aircraft Industry Financial Summary, 19 Sep 47.

were surely equal to and probably greater than those of most of the nation's manufacturing industries.[111] Under these circumstances, a diminishing current ratio, narrowing the gap between current assets and current liabilities, constituted a serious difficulty adversely affecting the aircraft industry's financial position in the crucial years just before the war.

In assessing the industry's financial condition as an element of the nation's air power on the eve of World War II, the question of the tangible curbs imposed on plant expansion or research and development by capital inadequacies is an insufficient standard of measurement. The attitudes of the directors, corporation officers, and managers who determined policy throughout the industry were likewise important. Most of these men had occupied responsible positions of one sort or another during the preceding decade. The memory of the boom era and its extravagant overexpansion of production facilities and subsequent contraction, collapse, and disaster must have been a painful reality to many of them. The financial position of the aircraft industry in the late thirties, when set against the backdrop of disasters experienced in the early thirties, could scarcely avoid filling industry leaders with a zeal for caution, a reluctance to undertake commitments beyond their ability to consummate, and an almost obsessive desire not to expand capacity beyond the point of anticipated market requirements. These attitudes, seldom directly expressed and therefore hard to document but not necessarily less real for that reason, may offer an important clue to the fuller understanding of the era following 1938. As the crisis mounted and the nation moved slowly toward a war footing, a substantial explanation of manufacturers' reluctance to expand to meet anticipated war orders might be found in the industry's financial position, where a shrinking current ratio heralded a decline to the bare level of solvency and, on occasion, even a dip into deficits.

Yet, despite all its pressing problems, the aircraft industry on the eve of the war was not in a fundamentally unhealthy condition. The rising ratio of earnings to net worth clearly reflected a sound earning power. To be sure, within the general pattern of this healthy condition, the industry was confronted with a knotty problem, an abnormally acute demand for capital resulting from the peculiar coincidence of requirements for funds to push development endlessly while at the same time effecting major plant refurbishments. So voracious was the cry for capital that even this admittedly healthy industry with rising profits was unable to meet its needs. Clearly, the only practical solution was to be found in a high volume of production, which might pile up earnings faster than research and development or facility expansion costs could consume them. Sales, then, held the key to the industry's fiscal difficulties. And

---

[111] Ratio of inventory to current assets for industry in general based on 307 firms, 1934–38, Moody's *Industrials*, 1941, p. 46a. See also 1938 edition, p. 41a. The ratio for aircraft industry is based on an unfortunately small sample covering the years 1934–38, Moody's *Industrials*, 1940, pp. 177–179a. Comparable data for 1939 in L. O. Ballinger and T. Lilley, Financial Position of the Aircraft Industry, Business Research Study, No. 28, Harvard Business School, October 1943, confirm this sample. The author is indebted to this excellent study, covering a somewhat later span of years than those discussed here, for a number of valuable insights into the problems of aircraft industry finance.

so long as a major portion of the market comprised military aircraft, the volume of aircraft production in the United States would in a large measure depend upon the size of the appropriations voted for that purpose by Congress.

CHAPTER III

Congress and the Air Arm

Soon after the outbreak of World War II in September 1939, it became evident that the United States was woefully underarmed. The dramatic assaults of the Luftwaffe drew particular attention to the small size of the air arm and touched off a round of charges and countercharges seeking to pin down responsibility. Some blamed Congress; congressmen were inclined to blame the War Department or the Bureau of the Budget.[1] Seen in the perspective of time, these allegations and recriminations have little significance save insofar as they demonstrate the complexities of the processes by which air strength is decided.

The Constitution empowers Congress to raise and equip armies for the common defense. From its earliest sessions, Congress appropriated funds and passed enabling legislation for military purposes, but the distinction between policy legislation on the one hand and appropriations on the other was never clearly drawn. "Legislation by appropriation" occurred frequently as overlapping committees considered un-co-ordinated departmental bills piecemeal. With the passage of the epoch-making Budget and Accounting Act of 1921, however, Congress introduced revolutionary changes in organization and procedure. In place of piecemeal consideration of estimates by the standing committees of the House and Senate, henceforth all money bills were to be considered by a Committee on Appropriations in each house. These committees held full jurisdiction over all estimates but were specifically enjoined against the inclusion of legislative matter in appropriation acts. Military policies of statutory character thus fell within the purview of a Military Affairs Committee, while consideration of estimates to provide funds to carry out these policies fell to an Appropriations Committee.[2]

The upper limit of strength for the air arm was determined by legislative authorization while the lower limit was determined by the funds actually appropriated. Since the processes of authorization and appropriation involved utterly different sets of factors and were considered by two entirely distinct committees in both the Senate and the House, each must be analyzed in turn.

---

[1] See, for example, remarks on the War Department by Representative J. Buell Snyder, Chairman, House Appropriations Subcom, quoted in Elias Huzar, "Military Appropriations, 1933-42," *Military Affairs*, VII (Fall 1943), 141; remarks by Representative R. A. Collins, of Mississippi, *Cong Rcd*, March 3, 1939, p. 2223. For a prewar instance of War Department efforts to pass responsibility to Congress, see Baker Board Report, pages 48, 54.

[2] For a discussion of the effect of the Budget and Accounting Act of 1921 upon congressional organization and procedures, see William Franklin Willoughby, *The National Budget System, With Suggestions for Improvement* (Baltimore: The Johns Hopkins Press, 1927), chs. II, IV.

Authorized Strength: How Many Aircraft?

The National Defense Act of 1920 constituted a major revision in the legislative basis of the War Department.[3] Supposedly, it represented the best accumulated experience of the World War I years codified into statutory form. Building on the precedents set by the various arms and services in years gone by, the act made no attempt to determine the strength of the Military Establishment other than to impose a ceiling on officers and men and to apportion manpower to the arms and services according to their relative importance. Under this provision the Air Service was allotted a ceiling of 16,000 men and 1,514 officers; no mention of strength in aircraft appeared in the act.

That the troop basis may have been a faulty premise upon which to regulate air arm strength is suggested by the precedent and practice of the Navy. Congress decided upon the number and type of major vessels required for the national defense and then provided the manpower necessary to operate them. In arranging for a manpower allotment in the Air Service without any reference to aircraft strength, the officers who helped to draft the Defense Act and the congressmen who voted for it apparently did not anticipate the strategic potentialities of the air weapon. As a consequence, during the early twenties, the number of aircraft available depended upon the accidents and contingencies that determined the funds given to the Air Service and not upon policy based on strategic considerations.

Funds specifically earmarked for the procurement of new aircraft fell from $6,000,000 in 1921 to something over $2,500,000 in 1925.[4] Lacking well-defined objectives, Air Service officers resorted to expedient makeshifts determined by each year's appropriation. Long-term program planning proved to be impossible, and without comprehensive aircraft procurement programs projected over several years, the Air Service soon acquired a heterogeneous collection of equipment of questionable military utility. Responsible officers began to doubt whether the Air Service could perform the limited tactical role then envisioned for it. To remedy this situation, the Secretary of War appointed a special board under the chairmanship of Maj. Gen. William Lassiter to consider a thorough reorganization suggested by the Chief of the Air Service.

The Lassiter Board

The War Department's special board appointed in March 1923 to study the Air Service could scarcely be said to have been weighted in favor of the air weapon. Five of its seven members were high-ranking officers on the General Staff; another came from the Quartermaster Corps. Only one, the lowest ranking member, was an Air Service officer, and much of his service had been with balloons. Nevertheless, after deliberations lasting more than a month, the Lassiter Board submitted a report that surveyed the air

---

[3] National Defense Act, June 4, 1920 (41 Stat 759), amending the earlier organic statute of the Army, National Defense Act, June 3, 1916.

[4] See War Department Appropriation Act (41 Stat 953) for fiscal year 1921 and successive years.

power problem with unusual perception. Even today the report retains a cogency that commends it to all who seek an understanding of the air weapon. Borrowing freely from the Italian air power theorist, Giulio Douhet, the board divided air power into two categories: air service and air force. The former consisted of those units whose primary function it was to provide service as auxiliaries to the ground arms. Artillery-spotting and observation aircraft fell in this group. The latter embraced pursuit, bombardment, and attack or close support units capable of offensive roles. Both air service and air force were conceived as organic parts of the ground organization, with the number of aircraft required depending upon the number of divisions, corps, and armies contemplated for the ground force in the event of war. On this premise the Lassiter Board visualized a war strength of 8,756 aircraft. The peacetime establishment was set at the minimum necessary to provide an adequate cadre from which to expand to the planned war footing. The board set this cadre requirement at 2,500 aircraft, of which fewer than 25 percent were to be used for flying training. Approved by the Secretary of War, the Lassiter Board report became the fundamental air arm policy of the War Department after April 1923.[5]

The Lassiter report followed the concept implicit in the Defense Act of 1920 in premising air strength upon the Army ground force or a troop basis. In the absence of a well-defined and experience-proven doctrine on air power, the troop basis concept provided a convenient formula for deciding how many aircraft the Army needed. As early as March 1917 the formula had been employed in planning the air component for the million-man army then being organized.[6] General Staff officers continued to use the formula in planning studies during and after World War I, although some Air Service officers, notably Brig. Gen. William (Billy) Mitchell, protested that the number of aircraft required should bear no relation whatsoever to the number of men in the Army as a whole.[7] These voices of protest were ignored for the time being, and air strength continued to be determined by the number of troops available to the Army.

Each time budgetary retrenchment cut back the size of the Army in the early twenties, the Air Service suffered its share of the necessary reduction in manpower. Manpower deficiencies led the General Staff to cut Air Service strength more than 500 aircraft below the approved minimum.[8] Congress, legislating through appropriations, went further, until by June 1925 the air arm had on hand only 1,436 aircraft, of which 1,040 were obso-

---

[5] The full text of the Lassiter report is nowhere available in published form; the Library of the Industrial College of the Armed Forces contains a mimeographed copy of the original. Details concerning the board and the fate of the report, as well as a précis of its text, can be found in Hearings before the Select Committee on *Inquiry Into Operations of the United States Air Service*, House, 68th Congress, 1924–25 (hereafter cited as Lampert Hearings), I–VI, *passim*, especially 1727–28. See also, WPD staff paper prepared for the Howell Comm

Aug 34, mimeographed, Historical Background, WPD–OPD files 888–92.

[6] Lampert Hearings, p. 1257.

[7] *Ibid.*, p. 1894. See also, Irving Brinton Holley, jr., *Ideas and Weapons*, (New Haven, Conn.: Yale University Press, 1953), ch. X, *passim*.

[8] Lampert Hearings, p. 1739.

lete or obsolescent and only 396 were classified as standard.⁹

Air Service officers who protested the condition of the air arm were joined by interested manufacturers in search of contracts. Their combined cries, in conjunction with a series of allegations as to war profiteering and patent abuse and the Mitchell air power controversy, produced an investigation by a congressional committee under the chairmanship of Representative Florian Lampert of Wisconsin.

The Lampert Committee

After taking several thousand pages of evidence during 1924 and 1925, the Lampert Committee reported a number of specific recommendations to Congress. In substance the committee confirmed the findings of the Lassiter Board: the lack of an effective Air Service procurement program had helped to reduce the nation's aircraft industry as well as the air arm itself below an effective minimum level.[10] Since War Department representatives reiterated their intention to fulfill the Lassiter 2,500 aircraft program, pointing out that the Department had actually favored the Air Service with funds originally allocated for other uses, the committee members were led to believe that budget cuts rather than War Department antagonism accounted for the prevailing state of the air arm.[11] To rectify this situation the committee recommended, among many other things, that a definite five-year program of procurement be prepared and that Congress appropriate $10,000,000 each year for new aircraft, leaving the exact number to be procured to the military authorities.[12]

Air Service officers and aircraft manufacturers must have been pleased with the Lampert report, but the committee's recommendations were little more than pious hopes in no way binding upon the War Department or Congress since the recommendations were not immediately enacted into statutes. The Lampert Committee hearings were by no means wasted effort, however. Shortly before the committee published its final report, and perhaps as a counteroffensive in anticipation of that report, the Secretaries of War and Navy asked the President to set up a board to study air power and the national defense. The President complied, appointing a board under the chairmanship of the distinguished banker and Morgan partner, Dwight W. Morrow.

The Morrow Board

After hearing nearly a hundred witnesses and adding four volumes of testimony to the five volumes already published by the Lampert Committee, the Morrow Board submitted its report to the President.[13] While not absolutely binding upon the War Department, the Morrow recommendations, as the considered findings of the chief executive's appointees, carried a weight with War Department officers not generally accorded the earlier congressional report. The

---

[9] Hearings before the President's Aircraft Board, 1925 (hereafter cited as Morrow Hearings), p. 1680.
[10] House Rpt 1653, 68th Cong, 2d sess, December 14, 1925 (hereafter cited Lampert Rpt), pp. 4–5.
[11] Lampert Hearings, p. 1827.

[12] Lampert Rpt, p. 9.
[13] S Doc 18, 69th Cong, 1st sess, *Aircraft in National Defense* (hereafter cited as Morrow Rpt), November 30, 1925.

THE MORROW BOARD AND DOUGLAS TRANSPORT *at International Air Races, Mitchel Field, N.Y., October 1925.*

Morrow Board recommendations differed markedly from those of the Lampert Committee in a number of points not pertinent here but, with respect to the question of air arm strength, the two reports agreed on the need for a comprehensive program of aircraft procurement projected over a number of years. Although the Morrow Board favored a five-year procurement program, in general it was far less emphatic than the Lampert report had been, especially when dealing with technical details. For example, by referring the whole question of aircraft strength to the War Department as a subject for "further study under competent authority," the board evaded one of the major problems that had led to its appointment. The board was equally vague about funds, suggesting only that special appropriations from Congress were "worthy of consideration" over the next few years.[14]

When at last the protracted investigations were over and Congress began to formulate new legislation to cure the ills of the Air Service, there seemed to be general agreement among the investigators on three points concerning air arm strength: a continuing procurement program should be adopted; Congress should appropriate more money for new aircraft; and decisions on the exact numbers and composition of the air weapon should be left to the War Department. In this setting Congress passed the Air Corps Act of 1926, a landmark in air arm history.

[14] *Ibid.*, p. 21.

The Air Corps Act

Following a lengthy study, which made extensive use of the evidence published by the Lampert and Morrow groups as well as by a number of others, the House Military Affairs Committee finally reported out a bill setting up an Air Corps as a combat arm of the line. The bill proposed increased personnel authorizations to be made by additions to the Army total rather than by transfers from the allocations of other arms and services, a provision shrewdly drawn to avoid antagonizing the ground forces. The bill further proposed to authorize a minimum of 2,200 aircraft for the Air Corps. Only standard units not yet declared obsolete were to be included in this number, although the 2,200 total did cover allocations for National Guard and Organized Reserves use as well as provision for an annual replacement increment of approximately 400 aircraft "on order." [15]

Here was specific congressional authorization for a fixed number of aircraft, a policy formulated by the Military Affairs Committee rather than by the Appropriations Committee. But why the figure 2,200? Just as neither the Lampert nor the Morrow report felt competent to decide upon the necessary minimum number of aircraft, the House Committee turned to the military for advice on this point and selected the 2,200 figure on the word of the Secretary of War.[16]

Throughout the twenties, the most enthusiastic advocates of air power protested against War Department unfriendliness toward the air arm. Had the charge been entirely true, the Department would certainly never have sought to preserve the Lassiter program, since the conveniently vague Morrow report provided an easy way to escape responsibility for a drastic cut in the Lassiter recommendation. The 2,200 figure offered by the Secretary of War was far more vulnerable for a reason virtually ignored by the air power advocates. The 2,200 aircraft authorization was premised upon the troops available within the statutory limits on the Army rather than upon a survey of requirements based on the strategic and tactical potential of the air weapon without reference to the size of the Army. By deciding upon the number of troops and then determining how many aircraft this number of men could maintain, General Staff planners made the tail wag the dog. It was as if the Navy had decided on the number of carriers it should have by building enough to use up the men left over after the destroyers and cruisers were provided with crews.

The House and Senate debated the Air Corps bill at length and with great care,[17] but neither made extensive changes in the committee draft except in the matter of procurement procedures.[18] One change, however, although explained on the floor of the House as a simple technicality, was to have far-reaching effects.

---

[15] House Rpt 700, 69th Cong, 1st sess, on H.R. 10827.

[16] *Ibid.*, SW to Chairman, House Military Affairs Com, March 2, 1926.

[17] For the principal debates see *Cong Rcd*, 69th Cong, 1st sess, pp. 8750–67, 10401–03, 10486, 11982, 12254, 12268–73, as well as Senate Rpt 830 and House Rpt 1527. For a full record of the debate, see history of bill under H.R. 10827 in index volume for 69th Congress, 1st session.

[18] For the changes in procurement procedures, see below, ch. V.

Since the clause authorizing 2,200 aircraft included 400 aircraft "on order," the House accepted without debate a request to amend the total to 1,800 aircraft, removing all reference to those "on order" to avoid ambiguity in construction. From the record it seems clear that the legislators believed this adjustment introduced no vital change in the bill.[19] The next ten years were to demonstrate how mistaken they were.

In its final form, the Air Corps Act of 2 July 1926 established a five-year program authorizing the Secretary of War to "equip and maintain a number not to exceed 1,800 serviceable airplanes." To maintain this level of strength the act further authorized the Secretary of War to replace obsolete or unserviceable aircraft from time to time, provided such replacements did not exceed approximately 400 aircraft annually. The language of the act appeared mandatory in specifying that the increases above the prevailing level of strength were to be distributed over five years with an increment of approximately one-fifth of the total number of aircraft procured in each year.[20]

Inasmuch as the first-line or standard aircraft on hand in the Air Service just before the passage of the act numbered only 184 (even including all aircraft procured after the Armistice the figure rose to but 396), the restrictive language of the legislation appears to be anomalous.[21] By insisting upon a gradual increase to minimum strength over a five-year period, the legislators seemed to leave the nation with its defenses below the minimum they considered necessary for years to come. Neither economy nor a failure to appreciate the needs of defense dictated the restrictive provisions, however. They were deliberately inserted with the best of intentions. Were the Air Corps to procure the increase to full strength all at once (the difference between the 1,800 authorized and those on hand, or some 1,400 to 1,600 aircraft), it would create a hump. Five years later, when all these aircraft became obsolete at the same time, the Air Corps would have to replace virtually the whole force, imposing an enormous load upon an industry vitally weakened by the lack of military contracts in the intervening years.

The 1,800 Program in Operation

The limitation on annual replacements to approximately 400 aircraft turned out to be unfortunate. Given a total of 1,800 aircraft with a useful tactical life of approximately five years before becoming obsolete or obsolescent, there should have been 360 replacements each year just to keep the force from obsolescence.[22] This

---

[19] *Cong Rcd*, May 3, 1926, p. 8757. For evidence that the aircraft "on order" should be in excess of the 1,800 ceiling, see testimony of the Chief of the Air Corps, in House Hearings on War Department appropriation for 1928, December 29, 1926, page 501.
[20] Air Corps Act of July 2, 1926 (44 Stat 780). See especially sec. 8.

[21] *Cong Rcd*, May 5, 1926, p. 8758. The figures given are for March 1926. All aircraft in excess of the 396 postwar items were obsolete and eight or more years old, at best little more than junk.
[22] The 360 annual replacements are derived by dividing 1,800 by 5, the arbitrary life figure determined by the Air Corps with the approval of the War Department. Actually, of course, the tactical utility of an aircraft is determined by the character of enemy equipment; thus, an aircraft could be obsolete the day it came off the production line. The

left approximately 40 aircraft, or 2.2 percent of the total strength, to replace those aircraft dropped from the records each year by crashes resulting in a total loss. Since the average annual number of total wrecks over a five-year period amounted to 8.27 percent of the available force, the annual loss of aircraft through crashes exceeded the number of replacements authorized over and above those procured to replace obsolete equipment.[23] On this account alone the Air Corps could never expect to reach the authorized strength of 1,800 aircraft unless it reduced the accident rate to the vanishing point. Since the ratio of accidents to flying time was already exceptionally low, there was little likelihood of escape in this direction from the effects of the ceiling of 400 on replacements despite continual improvement in the accident ratio.[24]

There was yet another factor intrinsically a part of the Air Corps Act that prevented attainment of the full number of aircraft authorized. Experience revealed that upward of 25 percent of the available aircraft strength was normally out of commission during years of peace. Some 15 percent of the force was constantly undergoing overhaul at major repair depots while another 10 percent was often grounded temporarily at air stations for minor repairs or as a result of parts shortages.[25] The number of aircraft actually available for tactical missions in an emergency was thus only approximately 75 percent of the strength annually reported to Congress. Since emergency conditions might reasonably be expected to increase the repair burden, not to mention operational losses, the M-day strength of the Air Corps was considerably lower than it appeared to be on paper.

The number of aircraft out of action for repairs could have been reduced sharply by substantial increases in maintenance, labor, and expansion of depot facilities, but this would have involved large appropriations of a sort Congress was reluctant to make. This situation was accentuated by the fact that the large number of aircraft immobilized for repairs placed an extra strain on those remaining in the field. The aircraft still operational would then require extra repairs, which increased the maintenance burden in the already overworked depots.[26]

One possible way out of the dilemma imposed by the restrictive legislation was to extend the life of all aircraft through administrative action. By keeping aircraft in an active status for more than five years before declaring them officially obsolete, it would be possible to increase the number of first-line aircraft on hand without exceeding the limitation on annual replacements. Although the dangerous implications in such a step were readily apparent, when faced with the budgetary limits of the early thirties the Air Corps decided to adopt this course in order to secure a larger force.

---

five-year-life figure was an administrative convenience based more on past experience with regard to safe operation than on tactical utility, vis-à-vis a potential enemy.

[23] ACofAC to Exec OASW, 25 Feb 32, AHO Plans Div, 145.91-28.

[24] See, for example, Hearings on WD appropriation for fiscal year 1933, p. 995.

[25] Testimony of CofAC, in Hearings on WD appropriation for fiscal year 1938, March 1937, p. 517. Air Corps testimony at appropriation hearings for other years gives figures varying only slightly from these.

[26] *Ibid.*, pp. 517-18.

By arbitrarily declaring the life of all tactical aircraft to be seven years and of all training aircraft to be nine years before classification as obsolete, the Air Corps was following a frugal but hazardous policy.[27] Commercial practice, as indicated by insurance write-down procedure, called for obsoletion after three years.[28] To be sure, the technical revolution in the early thirties, with the transition from wood, wire, and fabric construction to all-metal *monocoque* units, did actually lengthen the safe life span of aircraft. Nonetheless, it is highly significant that the reported practice of the Royal Air Force in 1937 was to write off all tactical aircraft as obsolete after two years.[29]

Experience over the years following 1926 thus clearly demonstrated that the aircraft program set forth in the Air Corps Act was unworkable. Even if Congress had followed the act to the letter, providing approximately 400 replacement aircraft each year, it would never have been possible to reach a total of 1,800 without arbitrarily extending the life of each aircraft beyond five years. Even then, had the 1,800 goal been reached, only about three-quarters of that number would actually have been tactically available. When the five-year program officially expired in 1931, the air arm, with a strength of 1,476 serviceable aircraft, was not up to the minimum contemplated in the Air Corps Act.[30] Understandably enough, Air Corps officials began to urge a reopening of the aircraft program question.

Agitation for Reconsideration

The Chief of the Air Corps cast about for a means of relief. He first tried to secure an interpretation of the act that would remove the offending restrictions. The phraseology of the act provided for not more than 1,800 "serviceable" aircraft. By arbitrarily defining "serviceable" as exclusive of those awaiting overhaul in depots, conservatively estimated to be 12.5 percent at all times, it was possible to maintain that the true ceiling should be 2,058. The Judge Advocate General accepted this interpretation and the Attorney General subsequently handed down an opinion reaffirming it.[31] But the House Appropriations Committee felt otherwise.

In preparing budget estimates for 1933 the Air Corps went ahead on the assumption that 1,800 rather than 2,058 represented the allowable ceiling. During the hearings that followed, an air arm spokesman did mention the fresh interpretation, but the moment was inopportune, and the Appropriations Committee refused to accept the higher figure. This was

---

[27] Memo, CofAC for ASW, 10 Sep 37, AHO Plans Div, 145.93–269. See also, Budget Officer to CofAC, 17 Dec 38, WFCF 1940, 112.05, and Memo, ACofAC for Chief, Mat Div, 10 Apr 35, quoted in E. H. Spengler, Estimating Requirements for AAF Equipment, Supplies, and Spare Parts, WFHO, 1945, p. 3, AHO 2802–2A.

[28] See L. L. Putnam, "Too Much Money or Too Little . . .," *Airway Age*, XII (May 2, 1931), 484.

[29] *The Economist*, CXXVI (February 20, 1937), 401. It seems clear that RAF obsoletion policy was based on the high rate of performance change, which is to say tactical utility, rather than upon the "safe life" of the aircraft.

[30] *Aircraft Year Book 1932*, p. 76.

[31] 36 Op Atty Gen 418, which mentions Army Judge Advocate General opinion of 11 January 1930. Abstract of former in 10 USCA sec. 292b, but *Digest of Judge Advocate General of the Army Opinions, 1914–40*, inexplicably omits the latter opinion.

quite understandable, for a desperate and economy-minded Congress was under great pressure to put immediate retrenchment ahead of potential defense regardless of the fine-spun legalisms of the Judge Advocate General and the Attorney General.[32]

Failing to escape via interpretation, the Chief of the Air Corps looked for another way out.[33] His proposed solution was a frontal assault on the act itself. To this end, he offered an amendment to eliminate the offending clauses. But the General Staff rejected the plan to remove what it termed a "very wise limitation" with the comment, of dubious logic and relevancy, that the "advancement of commercial aviation" would render less necessary each year "the expenditure of increasing funds for replacement of Army airplanes."[34] Blocked in this attempt, the Air Corps chief waited a year before turning to another line of assault. The Morrow Board five-year program was set up only as an immediate goal in an era of rapid development. The time had now arrived, the air arm leader asserted, for a complete reassessment of existing aircraft strength authorizations in the light of the most recent developments.

After extensive studies made in conjunction with the War Plans Division (WPD) of the General Staff, the Air Corps submitted a program of defense requirements.[35] The planners considered such factors as the nation's geographic situation, coast line, and critical areas, the air power of rival states, and the increasing vulnerability resulting from the extended range of aircraft. Here was a genuine attempt to derive aircraft requirements from the tactical and strategic situation of national defense and not, as hitherto, from some such consideration as the number of ground troops available. Moreover, the planning staff did not ignore the all-important premise on which requirements computation existed: the air arm's strength in peace rests upon the assumption that it will be an M-day force sufficiently strong to provide adequate cover during the augmentation of skeletonized units of the Army to war strength. The Air Corps proposal visualized aircraft needs as centering upon four major areas —the continental United States and its three vital outposts, Panama, Hawaii, and the Philippines. To each of these areas the planners assigned aircraft in terms of the number of groups or squadrons sufficient to provide the minimum force believed necessary.

The staff planners' allocations of aircraft by functional types provide a revealing measure of the evolving air power concept of the period. With bombardment groups receiving a larger share of strength than any other class, it is evident that the Air Corps had thrown off the shackles of close-support dogma that had characterized air arm policy ever since World War I. This apparent change in air power thinking should not, however, overshadow another and perhaps more

---

[32] Testimony of ASW (Air) F. T. Davison, January 15, 1932, in House Hearings on WD appropriation for fiscal year 1933 and comments thereon by Representative Collins, pp. 1095–97, as well as testimony of CofAC, p. 993, giving testimony similar to that in the previous year's hearing, p. 681. See also, House Rpt 1215, 72d Cong, 1st sess, May 5, 1932, p. 15.

[33] ACofAC to Exec OASW, 25 Feb 32, AHO Plans Div, 145.91-28.

[34] Memo, CofS G-4 for DCofS, 5 Feb 32, AHO Plans Div 145.91-28.

[35] ACofAC to AG, 15 Mar 33, WFCF 1940, 381.

surprising aspect of the proposed program. Although the Air Corps planners, working in conjunction with the General Staff, supposedly based the new statement of requirements upon a fresh reconsideration of all the elements of national defense, when the various groups and squadrons were added up in terms of aircraft, the total amounted to approximately the same number provided in the act of 1926. Under the circumstances, it is difficult to escape the suspicion that the planners contrived their strategic requirements to coincide with the aircraft already authorized, a case of cutting the pattern to suit the cloth on hand.[36]

Section nine of the Air Corps Act had established the office of Assistant Secretary of War for Air. So long as this office functioned, the Air Corps enjoyed a highly effective though informal channel of communication to the Secretary of War on matters of policy. When the Roosevelt administration came to power the Office of Assistant Secretary for Air was not filled and many of its functions reverted to the Chief of Staff.[37] This shifting of responsibility, coinciding with the aircraft requirements program, led the War Department to appoint a board of officers under the Deputy Chief of Staff, Maj. Gen. Hugh A. Drum, to undertake a comprehensive survey of the air arm.[38]

The Drum Board

The directive received by the Drum Board in August 1933 instructed the members to prepare plans for air operations in conjunction with the "color plans" of the War Plans Division.[39] The board was instructed to accept the assumption that 1,800 aircraft were available for assignment. This premise the board immediately rejected as unsound since 1,800 aircraft not only were not currently available but never would be so long as a considerable percentage of the force remained out of operation at all times for overhaul and repairs. To rest its study of requirements directly upon fundamentals, the board resolved to survey anew the whole question of defense requirements.

The vital areas of national defense, decided the Drum Board, were the continent itself and Panama and Hawaii, but not the Philippines, although the board recognized that air support for the latter would be considered, "should the national policy ever change." As an M-day force, which would be required to defend these vital areas until the nation mobilized, it was assumed that the peacetime air arm should be at all times capable of a maximum effort. Exactly what this entailed, the board set out to determine.

The Drum Board's formula for deciding upon the air strength necessary for the nation ran somewhat as follows:

---

[36] Since the number of aircraft assigned to different types of groups differed from time to time, it is impossible to compute the exact number of aircraft involved in the Air Corps plan.

[37] Although usually attributed to an economy move, the decision not to fill the ASW (Air) office may have come in response to the vigorous exercise of prerogatives by the Chief of Staff, General MacArthur.

[38] Testimony of Brig Gen Andrew Moses, in Com on Military Affairs, House, 74th Cong, 1st sess, Hearings on H.R. 7041, April 1935.

[39] This paragraph and the several that follow concerning the Drum Board are based on the records of the board itself, including the report, exhibits, and related papers filed in AFCF 334.7 Drum Board. See bulky file, this reference. See also testimony of CofAC, in Hearings on WD appropriation, for fiscal year 1935, February 1934, p. 468.

Naval aviation should be equal to or greater than any anticipated enemy force. Air Corps units in the possessions should be "strong enough to meet a sudden emergency" and maintain themselves until reinforced. Observation or Army cooperation aircraft should exist in numbers sufficient to equip all units to be mobilized on M-day. Finally, there should be a General Headquarters (GHQ) Air Force "of sufficient strength and composition" to "insure superiority in theaters where important air operations are contemplated." The GHQ Air Force was conceived as a self-contained organization capable of strategic missions against the enemy's economy as well as operations in direct support of the ground arms.[40]

The Drum Board's analysis seemed to raise as many questions as it answered. What theaters of operations and what potential enemies did the board have in mind? The maximum coalition visualized by the Drum study consisted of the British Empire in alliance with Japan, a combination selected not on ideological grounds but only to envision the worst possible military situation. Another question raised by the Drum study concerned the curious contrast between the formula for aircraft strength suggested for the Navy's air arm and that proposed for the Air Corps. The Navy formula was simple and clear-cut, growing easily out of the slogan "second to none." It was tangible, capable of reduction to relatively exact numbers. The Air Corps formula, on the other hand, rested upon a vague series of ill-defined variables that made it difficult to derive a number so objective and so matter of fact that it could not be easily challenged by a congressional committee.

The Drum Board report recommended that the Air Corps be brought up to full strength with 1,800 aircraft, and that it not go beyond this figure if additional aircraft could be procured only at the expense of the other arms and services. However, the board did amend its conclusions in two important respects. Recognizing that the number of aircraft out for normal overhaul prevented the Air Corps from ever operating at full strength, the board favored the addition of an overhaul factor to the strength authorized by statute. At 12.5 percent of 1,800, or 225 aircraft, this would bring the actual authorization to 2,025. The figure was still further increased to 2,320 by the board's subsequent recommendation of a 25 percent "war reserve" for certain tactical units that were expected to continue in operation during an emergency until reinforced by newly mobilized units.[41]

When the Drum report was filed in its final form late in 1933, the War Department had a new statement of requirements supposedly based upon the very latest political and diplomatic situation. In precise figures the report called for 2,320 aircraft, only a very few more than the number the Secretary of War had asked for when submitting a program to Con-

---

[40] Wesley Frank Craven and James Lea Cate, eds., "The Army Air Forces in World War II," vol. I, *Plans and Early Operations, January 1939 to August 1942* (Chicago: The University of Chicago Press, 1948), pp. 45ff.

[41] Testimony of CofAC, in Hearings on WD appropriation for fiscal year 1935, February 1934, pp. 472–75.

gress before the passage of the 1926 legislation. Moreover, the 2,320 figure did not really constitute an increase but rather a readjustment of strength to ensure a minimum of 1,800 tactically available aircraft at all times, conforming to the original intent of the Air Corps Act and the five-year program. Once again, the evidence strongly suggests that the strategic requirements were drawn to fit the available force.

The increase in the number of aircraft recommended by the Drum Board thus turned out to be no increase at all, only a proposal to bring the air arm up to the level authorized by Congress nine years earlier. And even this concession, the Chief of the Air Corps argued, was quite inadequate since the 12.5-percent overhaul factor allowed fell short of the 15-percent factor actually experienced in the field, to say nothing of aircraft inoperable while grounded for station repair and because of local parts shortages.[42] Nonetheless, even while grumbling at the report's shortcomings, Air Corps officers went ahead and planned procurement for the next fiscal year on the basis of the augmented program.[43] Whether War Department officials believed this augmentation was merely a clarification of the 1926 act requiring no new legislation or expected Congress to pass a new act to authorize the greater strength is not clear. The latter alternative seems unlikely since the Drum Board report was classified as secret and filed away, its existence unknown to Congress.

The 2,320 aircraft program was not destined to remain buried in General Staff files for long, however. Once again the air arm became the subject of political controversy involving investigations that dragged out the War Department's linen for public washing. In the course of the investigations during 1934, War Department officials revealed the existence of the Drum report in response to a congressional request for information, but the details of the 2,320 program were not readily available to members of Congress until nearly a year later when published, and then only in part, in the report of a board headed by Newton D. Baker, a former Secretary of War. This long delay in bringing the new program before Congress antagonized the chairman of the House Military Affairs Committee and led him to suspect the General Staff of seeking to stifle air arm growth.[44] It was just such suspicions that placed congressmen in the mood to launch an investigation of the air arm. The airmail scandal provided Congress with a reason, and soon not one but several investigations were to probe the air arm.[45]

The Baker Board and the Howell Commission

When it became evident that the Air Corps would be investigated by a number of congressional groups, each submitting different and perhaps conflicting

---

[42] *Ibid.*, p. 475.
[43] Acting Exec OCAC to Chief, Mat Div, 14 Jun 34, and 1st Ind, Chief, Mat Div, to CofAC, 27 Jun 34, WFCF 334.7 (1937).

[44] Comments of Representative J. J. McSwain, Chairman, Military Affairs Com, House, 74th Cong, 1st sess, Hearings on H.R. 7041, April 1935, pp. 127, 129–30.
[45] During the early thirties the Black, Nye, and Rogers investigations, to name but the more outstanding, all probed Air Corps policies at length.

recommendations, the Secretary of War decided to act. Following the traditional pattern of parrying congressional investigators with Executive appointees, the Secretary beat Congress to the draw in April 1934 by establishing a board under chairmanship of former Secretary of War Baker to consider the Air Corps and national defense in the broadest context. The board followed these instructions and submitted a report of great importance to the Air Corps in many phases of its operations. Here only the recommendations concerning aircraft strength are pertinent.[46]

Inasmuch as General Drum served as a member of the Baker Board, it is no surprise to find that the new board accepted the recommendations of the earlier Drum Board without challenge. "As a first objective," the Baker report asked for 2,320 aircraft, "the minimum considered necessary to meet . . . peace-time Army requirements." While recognizing that further studies might reveal the need for increases beyond the 2,320 figure, the Baker Board followed the Drum Board in declaring that such increases were not to be accomplished at the expense of the rest of the Military Establishment.[47] Since a majority of the Baker Board were men who, on the record, were not enthusiastic advocates of air power, this relatively modest recommendation for increase in strength could scarcely have been unexpected by the Air Corps, but the air power enthusiasts had another string to their bow.[48]

Under the terms of the Air Mail Act passed in June 1934, the President was authorized to appoint a committee to study the whole question of aviation in the United States. He did so early in July. Officially designated the Federal Aviation Commission, the group was popularly known as the Howell Commission after its chairman, Clark Howell, distinguished editor of the *Atlanta Constitution* and a longtime Democratic National Committeeman.[49] Those who advocated radical increases in air strength may have pinned their hopes upon this body, for the Howell Commission began its five months of deliberation just two weeks before the Baker Board made its final report. They were doomed to disappointment. Significant as many of the Howell recommendations may have been, insofar as they touched on air strength, the commission accepted without question the findings presented by the Drum Board and reiterated by the Baker Board. The proposed 2,320 program was accepted as a "working basis," qualified only by the proviso that changing world conditions might again reopen the question.[50]

Had it wished to do so, the Howell Commission may not have been able to differ with the Drum and Baker conclusions. Covering the whole field of aviation and restricted as to funds and time,

---

[46] See below, for example, p. 159, n. 18.
[47] Baker Board Rpt, pp. 31, 67.
[48] Of the five officers on the Baker Board, only one was an air officer. Of the six civilians, all supposedly chosen for their professional association with air matters, two, Edgar H. Gorrell and Baker, were clearly on the record as seeing the air power problem through General Staff eyes. This would appear to leave the board six to five in favor of a conservative solution for the air arm question.
[49] S Doc 15, 74th Cong, 1st sess, *Rpt of the Federal Aviation Comm*, January 22, 1935.
[50] Ibid., p. 121.

the commission almost necessarily had to decide not to duplicate the work of the earlier board. Moreover, the General Staff made it quite clear that the commission would do well not to meddle with the Baker findings. A request for military witnesses to appear before the commission was brushed off with the comment that the officers were too busy and would remain so for one or two months. And, unless the commission was willing to accept the Baker Board report as it stood, the Secretary of War declared that it would be necessary to present in closed session "considerations that must govern those responsible for the national defense but which cannot be made public." [51] Confronted with broad hints of War Department hostility toward reconsideration of the air power question, the Howell Commission skirted the issue by accepting the Baker report strength figures.

Even if the Howell group had been aggressively determined to explore the question of air arm strength from fresh evidence, there is good reason to doubt that much would have been accomplished in gathering advice from officers in the branch involved. While the commission hearings were taking place, the War Plans Division circularized instructions to the entire Army for the guidance of all called to testify. Officers were directed to familiarize themselves with "approved War Department policy on each of the subjects discussed" and to "conform to these principles" when giving testimony. If called upon for individual, unofficial opinions, officers were authorized to express their private views provided they were clearly identified as such.[52] Experience in numerous earlier public hearings had effectively demonstrated that most officers would be extremely reluctant to express privately held views that were markedly at variance with the positions officially held by their superiors, even when specifically authorized to do so.[53]

The frontal approach to the ear of Congress was closed or at least made dangerous, and individual officers would not attempt flanking tactics by carrying their views and proposals to congressmen privately. War Department directives had also covered the flanks:

"No officer will officially, or otherwise, transmit to any person or agency outside of the War Department, other than through the prescribed channels, any recommendations relative to the introduction, amendment or enactment of military legislation general in scope, or any information intended to be used in the formulation or consideration of such legislation . . . unless specifically authorized by the Secretary of War." [54] Nor was this regulation a dead letter. When the Chief of Staff, General Craig, suspected Air Corps officers of political activity, he urged the Chief of the Air Corps to locate the offenders. The latter admonished his officers, saying, "Expressions of per-

---

[51] SW to Federal Aviation Comm, 31 Aug 34, mimeograph copy, WFCF 1935, 334.8.

[52] Memo, WPD for All General Staff Divs, Arms, Services, etc., 11 Sep 34, WFCF 1935, 334.8.

[53] Support for this contention is abundantly clear throughout the Lampert and Morrow Hearings. Lampert, pp. 1682–83, 1574–76, Morrow, pp. 569–70, 593–633, especially pp. 617–18.

[54] TAG to Chiefs of Arms, Services, et al., 20 Feb 31, quoted in full in Appendix XII of MS, The Army and Congress, 1949, a study of Legislative and Liaison Div SSUSA by Lt Col R. E. Jackson, Jr. See also, G–1 to CofS, 13 Jul 38.

sonal opinion which are at variance with War Department plans and policies, when stated to persons outside the military service, may result in building up opposition within Congress to constructive measures or appropriations recommended by the responsible authorities." [55] Only the official view must reach Congress.

While on the one hand War Department regulations and directives of one sort or another sought to ensure that no opinions of contradictory character reached Congress from individual officers, the Department was elsewhere engaged in setting up machinery to facilitate the flow of official views toward the Hill. Although it was common practice for the War Department to maintain liaison officers with the Senate and House committees, in the early thirties none served with the House because of a temporary dispute over jurisdiction. Possibly as a way round this dispute, the Chief of Staff's office had designated several officers to "cultivate" congressmen in order to have contacts well placed to advise on the merits or faults of pending legislation. A number of officers were so employed "with excellent results." [56]

A free flow of ideas from the War Department to Congress held high promise of mutual advantage. But in facilitating the flow of official views while inhibiting if not preventing the expression of ideas and opinions from individual officers, the War Department may have deprived Congress of free access to the fullest range of data available. [57]

The Baker and Howell groups accepted the Drum report plan for 2,320 aircraft program as it stood. Both rubber-stamped the Drum program without any pretense of going behind the staff studies upon which the program rested. For this reason, criticisms of the proposed program might equally well be directed at the investigators' lack of initiative as at War Department efforts to control the evidence presented to them. However, the Baker and Howell groups were of significance in the question of air arm strength. Their reports were most useful. They brought the Drum study out of its secret classification in War Department files and set up the 2,320 aircraft program as a target figure for public discussion, an action without which authorizing legislation was scarcely expected from Congress.

A New Target: 2,320

A few months after the Baker Board submitted its report in July 1934, the chairman of the House Subcommittee on War Department Appropriations wrote the Secretary of War asking what had

---

[55] Actg CofAC to All Concerned [throughout Air Corps], 6 Nov 35, AFCF 321.9A Organization. See also buck slip, O.W. [CofAC, Maj Gen Oscar Westover] to Gen Craig, 26 May 36, same file.

[56] See MS, Evolution of the Legislative Branch (Legislative and Liaison Br, OCofS, photostat copy covering period 1902–37).

[57] That many congressmen were willing and even anxious to hear individual officers express views at variance with the official War Department position is indicated by remarks sprinkled throughout the budget hearings and verbatim transcripts of the investigations mentioned above. For a formal statement see W. F. James, Chairman, House Military Affairs Com, lecture before Army War College, 16 Jun 27, WF, CADO, Aco 3/75. Particularly revealing are the concluding remarks of the commandant of the college who begged the congressman to ask questions at hearings: "Information often never gets to Congress unless Congress pulls it out of us."

been done by administrative action to fulfill the board's recommendations and what legislative action would be required.[58] In addition to demonstrating the initiative and interest of Congress, this request reflected the importance and prestige attached by members of Congress to such civilian or civilian-influenced bodies as the Baker and Howell groups. This respect for special civilian boards was by no means an isolated case.[59] When considering the question of aircraft strength, some congressmen not only showed a willingness to accept the recommendations of the boards but to favor even more generous increases in strength.

Unfortunately for the Air Corps, the first bills introduced in Congress to implement the increase proposed by the Baker and Howell groups died in committee. Two factors may have contributed to this fate. The first session of the Seventy-fourth Congress—January to August 1935—was considerably exercised over alleged profiteering in aircraft contracts, and on this score alone the time was scarcely propitious for special legislation to augment the air arm. Moreover, one of the more extensively considered bills, calling for 4,834 Army aircraft, coupled the increase with a controversial plan to establish a Department of Air.[60] The proposed increase dropped from sight when the more elaborate departmental proposition did not emerge from committee.

Balked in his first attempt to implement the proposed increase in air strength, the chairman of the House Military Affairs Committee, Representative J. J. McSwain of South Carolina, dropped another bill into the congressional hopper soon after the next session began in 1936. This time he tried a new line of attack. The Air Corps Act of 1926, he said, authorized 1,800 aircraft for the Army and 1,000 for the Navy, a ratio of 9 to 5. Since that time Congress had increased the Navy's authorization to 2,190. If the original ratio were to be preserved, then the Air Corps should have 4,000 aircraft.[61] Representative McSwain justified this 40-percent increase over the 2,320 figure recommended in the Baker report by pointing out that progress had been rapid in aviation since the Baker Board convened, and some European powers were reputed to have between 5,000 and 10,000 military aircraft.[62] The House passed the McSwain bill calling for 4,000 aircraft in five years and sent it to the Senate, where the measure was referred to the War Department for comment.

In reply, the Secretary of War wrote that the 2,320 aircraft favored by the Drum and Baker Boards constituted the minimum safe peacetime strength. Since

---

[58] Chairman, House Subcom on WD Appropriation, to SW, December 7, 1934, cited in House Hearings on WD appropriation bill for fiscal year 1936, p. 49.

[59] See, for example, remarks of Representative Dockweiler, a member of the War Department appropriation subcommittee, who urged compliance with the Baker Board recommendations, erroneously describing the board as "entirely civilian," hence not "militaristic," *Cong Rcd,* February 11, 1936, p. 1819.

[60] H.R. 7041, introduced by Representative McSwain, Chairman, Com on Military Affairs, House.

Text in full in Hearings on the bill, 74th Cong, 1st sess, April 1935.

[61] *Cong Rcd,* February 13, 1936, p. 1992. The McSwain bill was H.R. 11140.

[62] House Rpt 2230, 74th Cong, 2d sess, March 24, 1936, p. 2230.

CHAIRMAN McSWAIN *presiding at a meeting of House of Representatives Committee on Military Affairs, 1935.*

the world situation was growing worse, the need for increases over this figure was "more imminent than remote." Therefore the War Department felt that the proposed ceiling of 4,000 aircraft would not be excessive; a flexible, open-end, unlimited authorization might even be preferable. Nevertheless, despite this willingness to accept increases in air strength, the Secretary informed the Senate that the War Department could not favor the McSwain bill since it was "not in accord with the financial program of the President." The Bureau of the Budget, speaking for the Chief Executive, had written the War Department that only 2,320 aircraft, without limit as to time, would be approved by the President.[63]

Under a long-standing rule of the Bureau of the Budget, the various department heads were forbidden to foster legislation involving expenditure without first securing Presidential approval.[64] This common sense ruling sought to protect the Executive budget by preventing

---

[63] SW to Senator Morris Sheppard, Chairman, Senate Military Affairs Com, May 26, 1936, quoted in full in Senate Rpt 2131, 74th Cong, 2d sess, May 12, 1936.

[64] Bureau of the Budget Circular No. 49, 19 Dec 21, quoted in full in Willoughby, *National Budget System*, pp. 65–66. Reissued periodically in the years following 1921.

end-run Treasury raids, un-co-ordinated legislation backed by heads of departments to the detriment of the comprehensive, integrated Presidential fiscal program. As a financial measure the system was undoubtedly sound. Here, however, fiscal considerations obtruded upon professional military opinion. Because it was not immediately expedient from a fiscal point of view, the President was rejecting a bill designed to provide long-term authorization of aircraft for national defense. The consequences of this circumstance were in all probability unrecognized at the time, but they were serious.

Two alternatives confronted the Senate Military Affairs Committee. One called for 4,000 aircraft in five years; the other called for 2,320 aircraft without time limit. The committee settled the matter by reporting out a bill authorizing 2,320 "immediately." [65] This bill passed the Senate. When the Senate and House conferees met to resolve their separate bills, they compromised on 2,320 aircraft, making no mention of the time limit. In this form the bill passed both houses and became law. [66]

The 2,320 Act

The bills reported out after detailed consideration by the House and Senate Military Affairs Committees both contained careful provision for a time limit. Without such a time specification the authorization might mean virtually nothing. Experience under the Air Corps Act of 1926 had shown that even where a time clause had been inserted, the funds might not be forthcoming. Where the time factor was omitted there would be still less leverage, less positive assertion of "the will of Congress," with which to persuade the Bureau of the Budget and the appropriations committees of the necessity to provide funds to procure the full number of aircraft authorized. Despite this obvious record of past experience, the bills' conferees dropped the time clauses in their efforts to reach an acceptable compromise. Legislative mechanics, the hasty compromise of the conferees, intruded upon the clear intent of the bills as originally framed.

The 2,320 act, as approved by the President on 24 June 1936, authorized augmentation in the strength of the Air Corps above the 1,800 figure established in 1926. The language of the act, subsequently a matter of dispute, stipulated that the increase authorized should not exceed 2,320 aircraft.[67] This figure remained the official ceiling on the size of the air arm until 1939, when the rush of events once more forced a reopening of the question.

It is difficult to determine whether Congress established a peacetime air strength in the 2,320 ceiling that the War Department considered adequate. The Secretary of War flatly asserted on the public record in 1937 that 2,320 aircraft were "sufficient for our needs." At

---

[65] Senate Rpt 2131, 74th Cong, 2d sess, May 12, 1936.
[66] House Rpt 2994, 74th Cong, 2d sess, June 15, 1936, and floor discussion, Cong Rcd, June 19, 1936, p. 10217.
[67] 49 Stat 755, June 24, 1936. Although an authorization of 2,320 aircraft in lieu of the 1,800 prescribed in the Air Corps Act of 1926 was the clear intent of the 1936 statute, the language used in the act actually allows for an alternative interpretation in which the 2,320 aircraft are considered to be in addition to the 1,800 already authorized.

the same time he admitted that peacetime strength should approximate "rather closely" the requirements for war.[68] A year later the Chief of Staff called the 2,320 program "adequate," although subject to revision as world conditions changed.[69] At the same time, when a congressman asked the Chief of the Air Corps if the 2,320 program would provide "all justifiable advance preparation" for a defensive war, the Chief of the Air Corps replied that the program offered "a proper minimum force."[70] Here were public assurances from highly placed officials on the adequacy of the 2,320 program. These assurances are hard to reconcile with statements made elsewhere.

There is reason to believe that the Chief of the Air Corps described the Baker Board's 2,320 program as "a proper minimum force" only in deference to the budget program and not from conviction. Three years earlier, soon after the Baker report appeared, the Air Corps had officially protested to the General Staff that the 2,320 program was inadequate.[71] Certainly nothing had occurred on the international scene after that date to reduce the requirement. In a similar vein, there appears to be a discrepancy in the public statements coming from the Office of the Secretary of War. In his 1937 report the Secretary declared that the 2,320 aircraft program was not only sufficient but approximately equal to war needs. Yet only about a year earlier, his predecessor had officially informed Congress that the need for increases over 2,320 was "more imminent than remote," saying that he would have urged an authorization of 4,000 or more aircraft were it not for budgetary curbs.[72] If Congress at times seemed confused in handling military legislation during the between-war decades, the military authorities were certainly partly responsible.

An Evaluation

The question of how many aircraft should be authorized for national defense resolves itself into two other questions: Who shall determine how many? How shall that figure be determined? To the first the answer is clear. The Constitution gives Congress the job. But inevitably Congress must rely upon the professionals, the military experts, for detailed advice.[73] The military experts were quite willing to give advice, declaring that it was not a difficult problem for a trained general staff to determine the force needed to ensure success.[74] Since Congress showed itself after 1933 generally anxious to give the air arm adequate and even generous support, any inadequacies

---

[68] *Annual Report of the Secretary of War, 1937*, p. 5.
[69] Testimony at Hearings on WD appropriation for fiscal year 1939, February 1938, pp. 10, 34.
[70] *Ibid.*, p. 428.
[71] CofAC to TAG, 1 Nov 34, AFCF 335.5 Baker.

[72] See Senate Rpt 2131, 74th Cong, 2d sess, May 12, 1936.
[73] Far from seeking to take such decisions from Congress, responsible officers urged Congress to take an emphatic stand on such questions as over-all strength. See, for example, testimony of General MacArthur at Senate Hearings on WD appropriation for fiscal year 1936, 27 Feb 35, pp. 4–6. While willing to give advice, military officials were usually anxious to have Congress make the decisions. In the absence of clear and emphatic policy decisions, legislation by appropriation became unavoidable. See also, Elias Huzar, "Congress and the Army: Appropriations," *American Political Science Review*, XXXVII (August 1943), 673.
[74] Baker Board Rpt, p. 11. See also, SW to Federal Aviation Comm, 3 Aug 34, WFCF 1935, 334.8.

in the strength authorized would appear to be the responsibility of the Air Corps and the War Department rather than of Congress.

The evidence available indicates that the failure of the air arm to present its best case to Congress arose in part from the position of the Air Corps within the War Department. While the General Staff actually did treat the Air Corps as a favored child, it was repeatedly asserted that advances in air strength were desirable but not advisable if such gains could only be made at the expense of the other arms and services, which always lingered perilously near and sometimes below the starvation level. Thus the revision of air arm needs reaching Congress was always tempered by the thoroughly understandable desire of the General Staff to ensure equitable recognition for all its arms and services. Since the Constitution gives Congress the task of deciding on questions of military strength and Congress relies on the military experts, it would appear to be a clear obligation of Congress to ensure for itself the fullest presentation of the pleas of every claimant agency.[75]

In the final analysis it is clear that Congress, the General Staff, and the Air Corps, not to mention the President and the Bureau of the Budget, must share the responsibility for determining the air strength of the nation. In one way or another all must bear some measure of responsibility for the size of the air arm actually on hand when the nation finally entered World War II. The subsequent efforts of the politicians and of the officers each to transfer this responsibility to the other were entirely unjustified as the record clearly shows. But the issue of who should determine air strength was only the first half of the problem. Just how the necessary number of aircraft should be determined posed an equally vexing problem.

Authorizations, Appropriations, and Aircraft

If air power advocates were disappointed with the number of aircraft authorized by Congress during the years between wars, they were even less satisfied with the number they actually received. That the funds appropriated were never sufficient to bring the air arm up to authorized strength is immediately evident from the record. Just why this was the case is somewhat more difficult to perceive. For this reason, an analysis of congressional appropriations for aircraft in the twenties and thirties may be useful.

Air Strength in the Booming Twenties

After the confusion of the early twenties, the Air Corps Act of 1926 promised to usher in a new and orderly era by authorizing a minimum force of 1,800 aircraft to be acquired in five annual increments beginning in 1926. Since the act was passed in July, after the current fiscal year had begun, a supplemental appropriation was required to finance procurement of the first increment. The act itself actually called for a supplemental es-

---

[75] Some congressmen saw the issue clearly and submitted bills for a separate air force as the only remedy. However, the separate air force question is so tangled with other issues and motives that it is impossible to single out any one bill as an effort primarily intended to exploit air power to the utmost.

timate, but Congress adjourned without appropriating the necessary funds. Thus congressional inaction delayed the beginning of the five-year program by a full twelve months. Furthermore when air officers subsequently presented their estimates for fiscal year 1928, they asked for 94 fewer aircraft than the number originally specified for the first increment of the program. Under congressional prodding, the airmen revealed that the Bureau of the Budget had compelled this reduction.

Still other factors tended to subvert the intent of Congress. The sudden expansion imposed by the Air Corps Act of 1926 disrupted the normal operation of the air arm. An increase in the total number of aircraft involved a commensurate increase in trained personnel. To secure trained crews, the Air Corps had to break up tactical units in order to find men to run its expanded training schools. This created a greater demand for training aircraft and a temporarily diminished requirement for tactical types. For this reason, when the Bureau of the Budget imposed limitations on the air arm estimates it was the tactical aircraft that suffered. From the 94 aircraft in the first increment selected for elimination by Air Corps officers, 65 were bombers and 20 were attack aircraft.[76]

When the Air Corps presented estimates for the second increment of the five-year program in the budget for fiscal year 1929, Congress appeared to be in a mood to deal generously. The House Appropriations Committee considered the program one of the primary objectives of the Military Establishment and drafted a bill to provide more than enough aircraft to complete the second increment. This supposedly more-than-adequate treatment was deceptive. The 45 aircraft over and above the second increment quota did not make up the deficiency suffered during the previous year. Moreover, the second increment represented quantity and not quality. To keep the tax bill low and still meet the program target in terms of numbers of aircraft, the appropriations committeemen decided to procure some 27 fewer bombers than the original program called for, substituting in their stead a larger number of less expensive units, including 150 observation aircraft of a design already obsolescent.[77]

Justification for the procurement of obsolescent aircraft rested on a bald appeal to economy and nothing more. The Air Corps had on hand several thousand Liberty engines that could be used in conjunction with the obsolescent observation airplanes. To refurbish each of these ten-year-old power plants required an expenditure of but $700, whereas each new engine purchased would cost approximately $7,000. War Department spokesmen made it abundantly clear that they considered procurement of less expensive and obsolescent aircraft types a dubious expedient at best, but the congressmen persisted in their course.[78] Even so, as a general rule Congress treated the air arm as a favored child

---

[76] House Hearings on WD appropriation for 1928, December 29, 1926, pp. 498, 506.

[77] House Rpt 497, 70th Cong, 1st sess, January 31, 1928, pp. 6–13.

[78] *Ibid.* See also, testimony of ASW (Air) Davison, January 6, 1928, House Hearings on WD appropriation for 1929, pp. 449, 464.

CONGRESS AND THE AIR ARM

among the arms and services.[79] Favored or not, when the boom years ended, the Air Corps had not yet reached the minimum strength in aircraft authorized by Congress in the summer of 1926. If the boom years failed to build up the nation's air defense, the depression years were to prove little more successful.

Air Strength in the Depression Years

Even when the depression led to a clamor for economy in federal expenditures, congressmen continued to speak favorably of strengthening the nation's air defense. But speaking favorably about the aircraft program and appropriating money for it were two entirely different propositions. Thus in January 1930, when reporting out the War Department appropriation bill, the House committee proudly noted that the measure provided funds for the full fourth increment of the five-year program. As had been so frequently the case, the "full increment" was achieved only by resorting to a maldistribution of types. While the total number of aircraft procured was up to schedule, there were serious shortages among the combat types specified in the program.

The Appropriations Committee tried to avoid the onus of providing less than the program called for by undermining the very premise of the program itself:

The Five Year Program is not a hard fast schedule which must be adhered to rigidly. It is nothing more than an authorization . . ., subject, of course, to considerations and eventualities that could not be foreseen when the program was adopted. It would be a mistake to expect or require strict adherence to a procurement program for a product so unstable that obsolescence occurs between order and delivery dates. Procurements are so nearly in accord with the program that there is no room for complaint.[80]

The same committee that declared authorizations were little more than suggestions to be accepted or ignored at will had only a year before asserted precisely the contrary. To justify a heavy appropriation covering aircraft procurement to meet the authorized program, the committee had then argued that the expenditures could not be avoided "without disregarding the law." [81]

Something of the contradiction inherent in reporting out a bill providing for a "full increment" and then admitting that the aircraft to be procured were not the proper types was repeated in 1931. The House Appropriations Committee reported a measure that provided for the last increment of the five-year program, bringing it nearly to the verge of completion with the number of aircraft on hand and on order falling only 66 short of the authorized goal of 1,800 units.[82] But the committee's report did not mention that the final increment finishing the five-year program was a full year after the originally contemplated terminal date. When the five-year program was formulated in 1926, it was the clear

---

[79] For examples of Senate and House efforts to make up program deficiencies, see Senate Rpt 381, 70th Cong, 1st sess, February 24, 1928; House Rpt 850, 70th Cong, 1st sess, March 7, 1928; Senate Rpt 1565, 70th Cong, 2d sess, January 28, 1929.

[80] House Rpt 97, 71st Cong, 2d sess, January 6, 1930, pp. 13–14.

[81] House Rpt 1991, 70th Cong, 2d sess, January 3, 1929, p. 3.

[82] House Rpt 2179, 71st Cong, 3d sess, January 5, 1931, pp. 3, 12–13.

intent of all that the question should be thrown open for reconsideration and revision after the five years had elapsed. The five years slipped by, but Congress did not attempt to determine anew whether the authorized ceiling of 1,800 aircraft was adequate.

There was a second discrepancy in the committee's report on the appropriation measure for fiscal year 1932. By suggesting that the five-year program would be nearly finished in 1932, since aircraft "on order and on hand" would total almost 1,800, the committee denied the whole conception of the program as it was understood in 1926. The original program set a target of 2,200 aircraft of which 400 were to be "on order." In the money bill for fiscal year 1932 this was reduced to 1,800 exclusive of those on order, and was interpreted to mean the program was finished when the 1,800 total included those on order.

By the winter of 1933-34, at the very bottom of the depression, the pressure for economy led Congress to abandon all attempts at immediate completion of the five-year program. The evident condition of the Treasury took precedence over the potential requirements for national defense. Although the congressmen had been continually reasserting their desire to favor the aircraft program, the dictates of economy proved more potent.[83] As a consequence, the rate of attrition exceeded the rate of replacement. Where the Air Corps planned to procure 370 aircraft for fiscal year 1934, economy cuts actually left them only 17 units. In the face of such crippling reductions, the Chief of Staff, General MacArthur, appeared before an Appropriations Subcommittee to protest that the nation's defense had been dangerously impaired. He advocated appropriations to complete the five-year program without delay.[84]

General MacArthur was only reiterating what War Department spokesmen had said all along: the 1,800 program was a minimum necessity. Cuts below authorized strength not only resulted in fewer aircraft on hand but hurt the nation's future air defense as well, for a reduction in training aircraft during the depression resulted in a smaller reserve of trained men from which to expand in an emergency. Even if a miracle of mass production should provide more than enough aircraft in a future crisis, there would be great difficulty in expanding the training program fast enough from the minute resources available as a result of the depression cutback in aircraft.[85] Moreover, a failure to procure the program quota in any one year could not be made up by increased procurement the following year because this would result in too many aircraft becoming obsolete at one time. Although War Department officials were fully aware of this situation from the unhappy experience of the early twenties, they explained the matter to Congress only occasionally and rather casually.[86]

The several years of retrenchment in the aircraft program caused the nation's

---

[83] House Rpt 1215, 72d Cong, 1st sess, May 5, 1932, pp. 2-4, 15n; House Rpt 1855, 72d Cong, 2d sess, January 12, 1933, p. 14.

[84] Testimony in House Hearings on WD appropriation for 1935, January 25, 1934, pp. 12-18.
[85] Annual rpt of ASW Davison, 1932, pp. 40-41.
[86] See, for example, testimony of CofAC Westover, in House Hearings on WD appropriation for 1937, December 30, 1935, p. 307.

air arm to fall far below authorized strength. For the five years ending in June 1932, the Air Corps procured an average of 418 aircraft a year, just about all the aircraft allowed within the letter of the Air Corps Act, which restricted annual procurement to "approximately 400." During the next four-year period ending June 1936, the Air Corps procured an average of only 132 aircraft a year. Thus by the beginning of 1937, at a time when Congress had already raised the number of units authorized from 1,800 to 2,320, the Air Corps was 1,247 aircraft under authorized strength.[87]

Relief Funds for the Air Arm

There was a very substantial appeal to congressmen in the idea of using relief money for military purposes. Relief appropriations were popular with great numbers of voters, whereas large sums earmarked for new aircraft nearly always evoked the charge of militarism, at least from a vociferous minority. And in early 1934 the Air Corps needed assistance desperately. Of more than $8,000,000 appropriated for new aircraft in that fiscal year, all but about $1,500,000 was held back by Executive action for reasons of economy. By the same token, about half the appropriation for maintenance and operations was withheld, reducing the Air Corps to a limping pace. In the face of this situation the War Department applied to the Public Works Administration for $39,000,000 to procure new aircraft, receiving $7,500,000.[88] Although this more than replaced the amount of the 1934 appropriation for new aircraft that the President had impounded as an economy measure, it did not actually operate to restore the full program. Even a generous grant of relief money could not restore the aircraft program to the position it would have enjoyed had the original appropriation not been impounded. There were delays in securing the relief allotment, each of which delayed the signing of aircraft contracts, enlarged the gap between procurements, fostered the tendency of humping, and in general disrupted the efficient execution of the program by breaking the essential cycle of annual procurement and obsoletion, which ideally should be spread evenly across the years.

Relief money, air arm officials concluded, was no substitute for regular annual appropriations. When a congressman protested that the reluctance of the Air Corps to apply for relief funds did not sound logical in the light of the prevailing shortages in the aircraft program, the Chief of the Air Corps explained just why relief funds were so unworkable. Those who doled out relief money attached all sorts of conditions to its use. It must be spent within a stated period, it must be distributed over a certain geographic area, and it must ensure jobs for a large number of people in a relatively short time. Obviously, the requirements of procurement by competitive bidding precluded the possibility of following the

---

[87] House Hearings on WD appropriation for 1938, March 25, 1937, pp. 516–17. The shortage indicated includes 742 aircraft on order but not on hand.

[88] Testimony of General MacArthur in House Hearings on WD appropriation for 1935, January 25, 1934, p. 24; Senate Hearings, March 12, 1934, pp. 33–34. See also, House Rpt 869, 73d Cong, 2d sess, March 5, 1934, p. 3.

relief administrators' stipulations. If contracts were to be handed out on the basis of relief needs rather than upon demonstrable superior performance, the air arm could scarcely avoid procuring inferior aircraft. The Air Corps could easily use a hundred million in relief funds, provided it was not tied up with "a lot of strings." [89]

The Air Corps did not even request relief funds during fiscal year 1936, although large sums were available for military use and continued to be available through fiscal year 1940.[90] The House Appropriations Committee joined with Air Corps officials in condemning the use of relief funds for military purposes—but for very different reasons. Relief funds appropriated in lump sums left to the Executive large areas of discretion over which Congress necessarily released control. The committee realized full well that this procedure left control of the funds to the private negotiations of such relief administrators as Mr. Harold Ickes rather than to the public record of congressional hearings and congressional debates published for all to study and criticize. To this end, the committee urged Congress to resume its constitutional duty to raise and support armies and not to delegate this vital function.[91]

Congress as a whole ignored this suggestion and continued to leave the disposition of large sums to Executive discretion for several more years.

The congressmen might have been somewhat less willing to leave the apportionment of relief funds for military purposes in Executive hands had they been fully aware of the backstairs pressures brought by those attempting to influence the administrators. Although it is impossible to believe that any congressman was entirely blind to the practice, many must have been unaware of the extent to which administrators were plagued. One prominent aircraft manufacturer, for example, proposed a plan to channel $10,000,000 from the relief fund to the Army and another $10,000,000 to the Navy for aircraft procurement. "This recommendation is entirely unselfish . . .," he asserted, stemming from a desire to further the aim of the administration in creating jobs.[92] The same manufacturer wrote Maj. Gen. Oscar Westover, Chief of the Air Corps, elaborating upon the $10,000,000 plan and urging the air arm to take the initiative in seeking the funds.[93] The next day the manufacturer telephoned General Westover to report that James Roosevelt was "arranging with Colonel Watson" to let him on the *Houston* when the President started on a fishing trip. "My friend says he can't guarantee the thing, but he says that Jimmie said he thought he could fix it." The manufacturer urged the Chief of the Air Corps, "Get busy on it, and if you can avoid the Director of the Budget, I would

---

[89] House Hearings on WD appropriation for 1935, February 14, 1934, pp. 487–89, and February 15, 1934, pp. 528–29. See also House Hearings for 1936, January 29, 1935, p. 559.

[90] House Hearings on WD appropriation for 1936, January 29, 1935, p. 557. For emergency funds allocated to WD, see Elias Huzar, *The Purse and the Sword, Control of the Army by Congress Through Military Appropriations, 1933–50* (Ithaca, N.Y.: Cornell University Press, 1950), Table III, p. 141.

[91] House Rpt 869, 73d Cong, 2d sess, March 5, 1934, p. 2.

[92] Telg, Mr. . . . to James Roosevelt, 4 Jul 38, AFCF 112.4 Allotment and Appropriation of Funds (A).

[93] Mr. . . . to "dear Oscar" [Westover], 12 Jul 38, same file.

CONGRESS AND THE AIR ARM

certainly do it. If you can't, then let me know and I will get Jimmie busy on the Director of the Budget." The manufacturer was explicit in his promises to the general: "If you get in any trouble . . . I will have influential men there from New York. . . ." [94]

The air arm reaction to this approach was characteristic of the military response to political dealings in general. While admitting that the funds were alluring, the Chief of the Air Corps replied with conscious rectitude that it would be impossible to proceed in the matter in view of certain previous "definite and positive" agreements made with the President and the Bureau of the Budget.[95] Backstairs proposals such as this were probably unavoidable in the allocation of relief funds.

If the air arm was both unable and unwilling to deal politically and relief funds were inherently unworkable, there was no alternative but to resort once again to the normal process of annual appropriation. This, of course, returned the question from the White House to the Hill. The change of scene was disappointing to those who looked for prompt completion of the aircraft program, for the delays that had long hampered air arm exploitation of relief funds returned again in new guises.

Further Delays in Reaching Full Strength

Although by the mid-thirties the Air Corps was certainly not the runt of the de-

GENERAL WESTOVER

fense litter, all was not well. In 1935, nine years after the five-year program began, the Air Corps was still 25 percent under the aircraft strength officially authorized by Congress in 1926. Despite the desire of many in Congress to eliminate this lag, there were a number of obstacles to an immediate solution of the problem. Even military spokesmen, who might be expected to advocate immediate completion of the program, testified before Congress against any plan to make up the deficiency in one jump.[96] To reach full

---

[94] Phone Transcript, Mr. . . . to Gen Westover, 13 Jul 38, same file.
[95] Westover to Mr. . . ., 20 Jul 38, same file.

[96] See, for example, testimony of ASW Woodring, Senate Hearings on WD appropriation for 1937, March 3, 1936, p. 25.

program strength at one time, they pointed out, would incur a series of evils each almost as detrimental in its effect as the original understrength condition. The tactical effectiveness of the nation's aerial defense would rise and fall in a sawtooth pattern as each group of newly purchased aircraft gradually moved toward obsolescence followed abruptly by replacement. Moreover, to absorb the demand for large numbers of aircraft within a short span of time, the aircraft industry would have to expand its facilities, only to face a long period almost devoid of military orders until another peak load appeared several years later.

Capital diverted to the expansion of production facilities to meet abrupt demands for large numbers of aircraft could not be extracted readily for reinvestment in research and development work during the subsequent slack periods of low demand. Without capital for research and development, the aircraft industry could not hope to produce the superior aircraft so much desired by the air arm. In this situation, Air Corps spokesmen could scarcely be reproached for not pressing Congress for large appropriations to bring the program to completion at once.

If air arm officers were above reproach in not having asked for too many airplanes, were they equally faultless in not asking for enough? After careful calculation, air staff planners had determined that it was essential to procure 800 aircraft each year for several years to keep pace with attrition as well as obsoletion and at the same time build up to the strength authorized in 1936. Having determined the 800 figure, the Air Corps went to Congress with estimates for fiscal year 1937 calling for no more than 457 aircraft. An explanation for this seeming contradiction is readily apparent. No matter how much the Air Corps may have desired funds for 800 aircraft, the Bureau of the Budget set the ceiling at 457 and no higher figure could be advocated before Congress.

In the final analysis Congress and not the Bureau of the Budget determined the size of the appropriation for aircraft. In this instance, a probing congressman was helpful enough to ask about the full increment of 800 aircraft and how much more it would cost than the 457 in the estimate. The Chief of the Air Corps replied to the question briefly and there the matter dropped.[97] The opportunity, once presented, did not arise again. For want of a substitute program worked out in detail, and for want of a willingness to press such a plan when the opportunity offered, the air arm let another fiscal year slip by without bringing the air weapon up to authorized strength. When offered no carefully formulated alternative to the budget program, Congress could do little but accept the Executive estimate substantially as it was presented. Some responsibility for the air arm failure to reach authorized strength must therefore rest on military shoulders.

Among the many factors contributing to the lag between aircraft on hand and strength authorized was the general rise in prices that characterized each succeeding year after 1932 or 1933. The original Air Corps estimate for fiscal year 1935 called for 348 new aircraft. Congress appropriated funds for the aircraft, but

---

[97] House Hearings on WD appropriation for 1937, December 31, 1935, p. 341.

sharp increases in unit costs occurring after the year's program had been set up resulted in procurement of only 222 aircraft.[98]

In the following fiscal year the adverse effect of rising prices was even more pronounced. Because of Bureau of the Budget restrictions, the Air Corps estimate asked Congress for only 547 new aircraft, far below the number required to advance toward full program strength.[99] This was only the beginning of difficulties. Between the printing of the budget and the time the Appropriations Committee sent a bill to the House, aircraft prices increased so sharply that the funds proposed in the budget would buy only 450 aircraft, a number barely sufficient to offset the normal attrition rate for obsolescence and washouts.[100] Congress farsightedly added some $4,500,000 to the budget funds earmarked for new aircraft to offset the price rise, but even this increase proved insufficient. Prices continued to rise, and by the year's end the funds were sufficient to procure only 361 aircraft despite the generous efforts of Congress in appropriating more funds than the President asked for.[101]

At the root of the trouble lay the long time lag between budget planning and the ultimate contract and subsequent delivery of new aircraft. Many months elapsed from the initiation of a budget until final appropriation, but by no means did appropriation mark an end to the delays. There were contracts to be negotiated and still further months to wait before new aircraft actually reached Air Corps stations. Even where contracts were all drawn and required only formal approval of the appropriation to go into immediate effect, deliveries usually were months and even years into the future.[102]

Contracts were not always ready for signature as soon as the appropriation bill became law. In fact, at one time during the depression, aircraft procurement officers were specifically instructed to award contracts as late as possible in the fiscal year to slow the rate of cash withdrawals from the Treasury so as to help balance the budget.[103] This process, so familiar to every bill-paying householder, reflected a thoroughly understandable maneuver on the part of the President. It became politically expedient to protect the Treasury, so the President ordered a delay in obligating funds. Delay, coupled with the rise in prices, resulted in procurement of fewer aircraft. It was the President who issued the orders, but it was the congressmen who received the blame.

At times the congressmen became exasperated with the perversities of an aviation program that refused to reach completion in the face of determined efforts to that end, and they had ample grounds for annoyance. Not only were they disturbed by the effect of the time lag between appropriation and actual delivery of aircraft, but in addition they felt they had been deceived when, on occasion, air officers failed to obligate all

---

[98] House Hearings on WD appropriation for 1936, January 29, 1935, p. 535.
[99] *Ibid.*, pp. 556–57.
[100] T. B. Parks in *Cong Rcd*, February 19, 1935, pp. 2214–15.
[101] House Hearings on WD appropriations for 1937, December 30, 1935, pp. 322–23.

[102] *Ibid.*, pp. 327–28.
[103] CofAC to Chief, Mat Div, 5 Aug 37, quoting Budget Office, WD, to CofAC, 3 Aug 37, AFCF 112.4–A.

the funds of one fiscal year before the next year's appropriation bill became law. Why frighten the voter-taxpayers with appropriations larger than need be, argued the legislators, if the funds will not be spent until a later fiscal year.[104] They were further annoyed to learn that air arm officers were asking funds for production contracts when even the types to be procured had not yet been decided upon.[105] Since months and even years might elapse between the formulation of estimates and the final steps of procurement, this was not really surprising. Moreover, considering the rapid pace of design change in aeronautics, rigid decisions as to specific aircraft types in the early phases of budgetary planning might have led to the procurement of obsolete weapons. For many reasons, then, it was difficult if not impossible to close the gap between original estimate and final aircraft, even though these reasons were often obscure to the bedeviled legislator.

There were a number of circumstances that led to the rapid price rises of the middle thirties. One set of motivating causes can be grouped under the heading of social legislation. A second set of factors arose from the increasing technical complexity of aircraft. Four-engine bombers began to replace twin-engine bombers, and the relative proportion of bombers to pursuits increased fivefold in the decade from 1927 to 1937. Improved communications equipment, variable pitch propellers, and the introduction of many sensitive instruments for flight and navigation combined with hundreds of other technical innovations to make each individual aircraft a more intricate and more expensive piece of equipment than ever before. Probably the most obvious index of this rising curve of complexity is to be found in terms of the upward trend in gross weights. A single-place, single-engine fighter weighed 1,600 pounds empty in 1918 and 2,200 pounds in 1933; by the end of the thirties the same type of aircraft ranged between 5,500 and 6,000 pounds.[106]

The appropriation dollar also purchased fewer aircraft pounds with each passing month. Appropriations that seemed adequate when air officers prepared estimates became hopelessly inadequate when the time arrived to sign contracts with individual aircraft manufacturers. Attack bombers, for example, priced at $60,000 each in original estimates, actually cost about $110,000 apiece in the contracts finally drawn several months later, a characteristic pattern throughout the latter half of the thirties.[107]

Congress Tries Some Short Cuts, 1935–38

If prices continued moving up between the time of estimate and the time of contract, the simplest solution was to ask

---

[104] **House Hearings on WD appropriation for 1937,** December 30, 1935, p. 310; House Hearings on Naval appropriation for 1937, March 2, 1936, pp. 520–21.

[105] *Ibid.* See also, House Hearings on WD appropriation for 1937, December 30, 1935, p. 335.

[106] **Figures taken from specifications in** *The Official Pictorial History of the AAF,* pp. 186ff. See also, for description of increased complexity of aircraft and the rising proportion of bombers, House Hearings on WD appropriation for 1938, March 25, 1937, pp. 520–22.

[107] **House Hearings on WD appropriation for 1938,** March 29, 1937, p. 559.

CONGRESS AND THE AIR ARM

Congress for more than enough funds to absorb the difference. Unfortunately, such an obvious maneuver was difficult to execute. In the middle thirties every extra dollar added to appropriations for the military forces had to be made in the very teeth of a popular clamor for the most stringent economies. There was as well the not inconsiderable protests of the pacifists. Confronted with large bodies of hostile opinion, the congressmen had to resolve conflicting objectives. They had to provide sufficient defense without laying themselves open to the charge of war mongering and find ways and means to improve defenses without presenting the bill to the taxpayers—at least not right away. To serve these mutually exclusive ends, Congress resorted to numerous expedients.

One short cut was to use "contract authorizations" in lieu of outright appropriations in any given fiscal year. By this device Congress authorized the air arm to obligate certain sums in contracts for which payment would not fall due until a period beyond the fiscal year in question. By resorting to contractual authorization, in addition to the funds actually appropriated, congressmen hoped they would leave air arm officers free to negotiate contracts and in general to advance the business of defense without having to present the unwelcome tax bill until at least a year later.[108]

Contract authorization may have been a politically expedient device, but there were certain very real drawbacks in its use. When Congress voted for increased contract authorizations rather than outright appropriations, the air arm was unable to contract for aircraft until late in the fiscal year. The sheer complexity of aircraft production was such that hundreds of thousands of dollars in tooling costs and inventory charges were encountered before a single aircraft started down the assembly line. To help manufacturers over these financial hazards, the War Department had instituted a system of partial payments or progress payments to be made in advance of actual deliveries as the preparation for production reached certain predetermined goals. This procedure required large sums of cash soon after the signing of a contract. Where Congress provided contract authorization and left the actual appropriation of cash for the next fiscal year, the requirement for cash disbursals shortly after formal approval of contract made it necessary to delay contract negotiations until just before the next fiscal period, when cash would be available to honor the obligation.[109] This defeated the intent of Congress.

Another drawback in the use of contract authorizations lay in their administrative complexity. Appropriations ran for one year before reverting to the Treasury. Contract authorizations ran for two years. But funds authorized in one fiscal year had to be paid out during the next. Thus in any given year the air arm appropriation might include funds to cover previous contract authorizations, authorizations projecting into the fiscal period ahead, and funds for current obliga-

---

[108] For a frank expression of this evasion, see Senate Hearings on WD appropriation for 1938, May 26, 1937, p. 61.

[109] *Ibid.*, pp. 65–66.

tion.[110] Occasionally some members of Congress appeared bewildered by this maze of overlapping types of appropriations and confessed themselves to be a bit uncertain about the precise nature of a current appropriation measure.

During the late thirties Congress tried yet another device in an effort to satisfy the demand for a defense air arm at full strength without greatly increasing the tax bill. This time the plan consisted of a reduction in the number of spare engines to be procured, using the funds thus gained to buy more aircraft. In 1937 the Appropriations Committee took the initiative in reducing the number of spare engines from 100 percent to 50 percent of the number of aircraft on contract. From the funds so saved, the committee contemplated procurement of fifty-eight additional aircraft, which promised to help close the gap between available strength and strength authorized.[111] Air Corps officers protested that this policy merely robbed Peter to pay Paul. Without an ample reserve of spare engines, they insisted, the Air Corps could not make full use of its increased strength in aircraft. Marked fluctuations in the average number of engines in overhaul at any one time made it imperative that the reserve of spare engines be ample to cover the local needs of a widely distributed and ever-shifting air force.[112]

In the face of air arm protests, Congress continued the 50 percent spare engine policy again in 1938. It was easier for congressmen to point to the tangible evidence of a rising total of aircraft in replies to the taxpayers' questions than to refer to a change in spare engines policy that was elusive if not entirely meaningless to the average citizen. Justifications based on the Navy's policy of 33 percent spare engines were irrelevant, for the Navy kept 50 percent of its aircraft strength in reserve at all times, creating in effect a 100-percent engine reserve even before procuring a single spare engine.[113] The Chief of the Air Corps publicly declared that the 50 percent spare engine policy of Congress was positively dangerous, but the policy continued.[114] One congressman expressed the problem concisely: the legislators were anxious to get more aircraft but they were reluctant to go over the Bureau of the Budget figure.[115] By remaining within that figure, congressmen could make the President shoulder the taxpayers' protests.

There was no escape from the conflicting and mutually exclusive objectives of more aircraft and lower taxes, but with some ingenuity the extremes could be made less antagonistic. By the middle thirties the Navy had devised a scheme that the Air Corps might have emulated with profit. The Navy's plan was simple. Instead of lumping all aircraft procurement under one budget heading for "new construction," there were two headings: "new construction" and "replacement

---

[110] For an example of the overlapping appropriations and contract authorizations, see House Hearings on WD appropriation for 1939, February 8, 1938.
[111] House Rpt 1979, 74th Cong, 2d sess, February 10, 1936.
[112] House Hearings on WD appropriation for 1935, February 15, 1934, pp. 554–55.

[113] Harding, *Aviation Industry*, p. 28.
[114] House Hearings on WD appropriation for 1939, February 8, 1938, pp. 420–21; Senate Hearings, April 1, 1938, pp. 3–5.
[115] House Hearings on WD appropriation for 1938, March 29, 1927, p. 57.

CONGRESS AND THE AIR ARM

aircraft." [116] By segregating those items intended to maintain the force at its current level from those that would increase the force, the Navy sugar-coated the pill. Instead of confusing the congressman with involved charts and intricate tables of figures, the Navy scheme offered but two quantities, one for augmentation, one for replacement. When so tagged, both groups presented psychological hazards to the congressman. If he voted against "replacement," his constituents could criticize him for weakening national defense. If he voted against "augmentation," they would charge him with failing to strengthen national defense. On the other hand, by lumping both types of procurement into a single figure, the Air Corps' estimates obscured the precise character of aircraft requirements.

Congress was by no means solely responsible, however, for the protracted delays that marked the air arm's attempt to reach the full strength authorized. The Air Corps itself shared heavily in this responsibility.

The Air Arm Imposes Delays

Air arm leaders on occasion followed policies closely akin to those employed by Congress in stressing the appearance of strength rather than the real thing. During fiscal year 1938, for example, the Air Corps tried the experiment of lumping two years' supply of bombers in one year while buying no pursuit aircraft and then reversing the procedure in the following year, buying all pursuits and no bombers. By increasing the number of units on contract, the unit price decreased, making it possible to secure more aircraft with the same amount of money.[117] This was a persuasive argument when presented to the Appropriations Committee; unfortunately it ignored a most important consideration. The "two year's supply" plan brought in more units from the funds available, but it failed to take cognizance of the air arm role as an M-day force to be maintained in a condition of constant readiness against surprise attack. By purchasing an excess of one type and none of another type each year, the Air Corps threatened to remain in a continual state of disequilibrium insofar as tactical aircraft were concerned. If pursued extensively, this policy of quantity rather than quality might give the air arm its authorized strength but at the price of combat effectiveness, although it must be admitted that the increased number of aircraft on any one contract resulted in longer production runs, which strengthened the capacity of the industry for mass production.

While the two-year supply procedure did undoubtedly appear to favor numbers rather than performance, the Air Corps did not pursue the policy consistently. Indeed, Congress criticized the air arm for doing just the opposite—delaying production contracts in order to get some new development lying over the horizon. Air Corps spokesmen denied

---

[116] House Hearings on Navy appropriation for 1936, March 13, 1935, p. 546. Contrast the Navy's breakdown with the statement of General Drum on the Air Corps' needs, House Hearings on WD appropriation for 1936, January 14, 1935, p. 53.

[117] House Hearings on WD appropriation for 1939, February 8, 1938, pp. 438–39, and for 1938, March 29, 1937, pp. 552, 557.

BOEING B-17

the charge of delays, pointing out that funds had to be obligated within the fiscal year or revert to the Treasury, but they were quite willing to admit that the air arm actively favored quality rather than quantity.[118]

The Chief of the Air Corps made no secret of the circumstance that the funds appropriated by Congress sometimes bought fewer aircraft than intended in the original estimates for the simple reason that manufacturers turned up at the last minute with superior aircraft of radically improved performance—at a higher price.[119] To ignore this advanced equipment would be to arm the nation with weapons less than the best.

In theory at least, there was no alternative to buying the latest and the best aircraft available, even though it inevitably meant buying fewer units with the funds available. Such a course was the ideal and sometimes the Air Corps pursued it. In practice, however, Air Corps officials did not wish to risk irritating congressmen, who seemed inclined to judge air defense in terms of numbers of aircraft on hand rather than in terms of quality, performance, or tactical suitability.

An episode in April 1937 will illustrate this tendency. The chairman of the Appropriations Subcommittee that handled War Department estimates admitted to the House that he had no great familiarity with military matters. Nevertheless, he recorded his protest against the "unwise" tendency in the air arm to build larger and more expensive bombers such as the Boeing B-17.[120] Less than two months later the effect of this type of criticism became evident. The estimates for fiscal year 1938 called for 177

---

[118] House Hearings on WD appropriation for 1938, March 29, 1937, p. 557.

[119] House Hearings on WD appropriation for 1937, December 30, 1935, pp. 323-24, 338.

[120] *Cong Rcd*, April 29, 1937, pp. 3984, 3988-89.

Douglas B-18

B-18 twin-engine bombers and 13 B-17 four-engine bombers. After operational tests by tactical units, the GHQ Air Force "strongly recommended" that only the B-17 be procured. To buy the more expensive bomber, however, would be to buy fewer bombers. In the face of congressional criticism, Air Corps officers felt it was "impractical" to do so unless the Secretary of War was personally willing to "accept the responsibility to Congress" for decreasing the total number of aircraft in the 1938 budget. Estimates for the four-engine bombers were thus deferred until fiscal year 1939.[121] As a consequence the B-17 units, considered vital to the nation's defense, were not procured until the crisis had already arrived.

The search for quality rather than quantity was not the only Air Corps policy that retarded completion of the authorized aircraft program. Another factor was the air arm's insistence upon a "balanced program" in which procurement of new aircraft remained in phase with the construction of new facilities and the addition of personnel. Experience in past years had revealed what happened when Congress provided new aircraft without increasing the funds available for trained personnel for them. Even worse was the situation in which manpower increased without a commensurate increase in funds for housing. By the same token new aircraft, unless supported with adequate technical facilities —air bases with depot repair shops and the like—did not really strengthen the

---

[121] 2d Ind, OCAC to TAG, 9 Jun 37 (basic unknown), WFCF 452.1 Four Engine Bomber 1936–39. A comparison of the B-17 and B-18 in terms of performance indicates why the decision to delay the B-17 was so critical:

	Boeing B-17	Douglas B-18
High speed.....	256 m.p.h. at 14,000	214 m.p.h. at 10,000
Full load range..	1,327 miles	690 miles
Bomb load......	10,500 lbs.	6,500 lbs.

nation's aerial might. Technical construction—barracks, airstrips, and expensive machine tools in repair depot shops—did not fare as well as aircraft when it came to appropriations. As a result aircraft, although usually understrength, generally ran ahead of personnel and supporting facilities. Since the appropriation acts carried restrictive clauses specifying not less than a fixed amount to be spent for aircraft, air arm leaders could not correct the imbalance by administrative action.

Repeatedly during the thirties Air Corps officers proposed means for overcoming the lack of balance in manpower, air weapons, and supporting facilities. One such recurring suggestion involved a plan to secure in addition to the regular itemized appropriation a lump sum left entirely free for commitment according to administrative discretion. Such a fund would have provided an escape from the embarrassment of having more aircraft than there were trained pilots to fly them, but Congress was unwilling to grant funds without earmarking them rather closely. Legislative fear of Executive encroachment accounted for at least some of this opposition.[122]

Failing to secure funds with which to rectify impossible situations, air arm officers tried another expedient. This time the plan was to forestall trouble in advance by providing Congress with a comprehensive scheme or "balanced program" in which aircraft, personnel, housing, training, and technical facilities were all carefully dovetailed into a five-year plan by which trained pilots would be ready when aircraft left production lines and adequate barracks would be built and waiting for the arrival of newly recruited troops.[123] Above all, those who planned for the air arm wished to avoid the condition created by Congress in fiscal year 1937 when $41,000,000 of total appropriation of $59,000,000 went to the purchase of new aircraft, leaving only $18,000,000 for personnel, maintenance, operation, training, development, and construction of base facilities—an almost impossible situation.[124]

Unfortunately, by 1938 the popular hue and cry called for big increases in manpower, and air arm officials, who had reluctantly curbed the heavy bomber program they really desired in order to keep it in phase with the limited number of men available, found themselves confronted with an abnormal increase in manpower granted by Congress in response to popular pressure.[125] This was frustrating to air arm officers when the crisis arrived because it left them highly vulnerable to uninformed criticism for not having demanded a larger number of aircraft.

Early in February 1938, the Chief of the Air Corps optimistically reported that the end was in sight. If all went well and Congress appropriated the funds as planned, the Air Corps would be able to complete the 1926 "five-year" program, as modified and revised in 1936, during

---

[122] *Cong Rcd*, March 14, 1934, p. 4506.

[123] Acting CofAC to TAG, 5 Aug 36, 321.9A OCAC Organization, and AFCF 360.01A WD Policy Toward Aviation.

[124] Memo, Brig Gen G. R. Spaulding for CofS, 26 Mar 37, AFCF 112.4A, Allotment of Funds.

[125] TAG to CGGHQAF, 28 Mar 38 and TAG to CofAC, 11 Apr 38, 321.9A OCAC Organization, AFCF.

the fiscal year 1940.[126] Who was responsible for this long delay? No one could point to any single group for censure. All who participated in the budgetary process—military officers, Executive agents, and legislators—shared in the result. At best, the limited funds made available by Congress for aircraft procurement in the between-war years reflected the severe limitations if not the inadequacies of the nation's system of budgeting for defense. But even lavish approriations, had they been voted, would not have ensured an adequate air force if the air arm's methods of procurement were not also suitably perfected.

[126] House Hearings on WD appropriation for 1939, February 8, 1938, p. 437.

CHAPTER IV

Procurement Legislation, Organization, and Administration

Organic Legislation for the Procurement of Aircraft

The Statutory Tradition

The legal basis upon which the great bulk of all military procurement has rested is Section 3709 of the Revised Statutes. This section is a codification of a statute enacted in 1861, which itself rested upon earlier precedents dating back to the eighteenth century.[1] The essentials of Section 3709 are contained in a very few words: "All purchases and contracts for supplies . . . shall be made by advertising. . . ." In short, to prevent favoritism in the award of public contracts, the law required advertisement or a public invitation to bid followed by the award of contracts upon the basis of proposals received. The basic statute authorized exceptions to this requirement when the "public exigency" imposed need for immediate delivery, but the spirit and intent of the law are clear. Subsequent legislation made the intent even more specific. A statute of 1884 provided, "the award in every case shall be made to the lowest responsible bidder for the best and most suitable articles. . . ."[2] Contracting officers who sought exceptions to this ruling ran headlong into an opinion of the Attorney General of the United States, who expressed a continued confidence in the wisdom of competition in public contracts when he held that all such contracts must be made according to Section 3709 of the Revised Statutes, save where specifically exempt by law.[3]

There were significant exceptions provided by the express will of Congress. Where but one manufacturer produced a given item, advertisement for bids could be waived. In an instance such as this, the manufacturer was known in the jargon of the services as a "sole source." Another exception, closely related, involved the circumstance in which the manufacturer held a patent on an item sought by the government. Here, too, public advertisement for bids would be to no purpose since only the patent holder could reply. Still another exception authorized by statute permitted the purchase of items that were parts of items already in use. In an organization such as the air arm, where spare parts played

---

[1] Cited as Rev Stat 3709. Based upon act of March 2, 1861 (12 Stat 220), 41 USCA 5.

[2] Act of July 5, 1884 (23 Stat 109).
[3] 22 Op Atty Gen 1, December 20, 1897.

an unusually important role, this exception could be of considerable importance.[4] These and a few other similar deviations granted by Congress did permit some escape from the compulsions of the basic statutes, but probably the most significant modification, insofar as military contractors were concerned, appeared in a law enacted in 1901.

The 1901 statute drew several of the previous stipulations into a single law, adding a noteworthy innovation: "Except in cases of emergency or where it is impractical to secure competition . . . the purchase of all supplies . . . shall be made only after advertisement and . . . shall be purchased where . . . cheapest, quality and cost of transportation and the interests of the Government considered."[5] While reiterating the earlier provisions for protecting the interest of the public, these provisions would appear to broaden the law and leave a wide margin of discretion to responsible officials in the War Department. Both the words *the interests of the Government considered* and the words *where it is impracticable to secure competition* leave a great deal of latitude to the contracting officer. Nevertheless, even though this statute appeared to grant generous exemptions from the mandate to make all military contracts by competition for low bid, in practice contracting officers seldom awarded on any other basis. A number of considerations conspired to this result.

Statutes usually require interpretation. In the normal course of events the laws governing procurement became encrusted with legal barnacles as court decisions, rulings of the Comptroller General, and opinions of Attorneys General or Judge Advocates General operated to define the scope of executive discretion. Just how far this process of legal accretion could go is suggested in the thirteen separate opinions as to what is and what is not a "public exigency" that annotate Section 3709 of the Revised Statutes.[6] Beset with rulings and opinions on every hand, contracting officers were inclined to use the safe ground of compliance with the stipulations placing purchases for the government on a competitive basis.

There were urgings other than legal opinions that induced contracting officers to award on low bid rather than exercise discretion. Low bids could be determined objectively, whereas "quality" or "the interests of the Government" were largely matters of opinion. Being human, contracting officers naturally tended to the safer course since it was far easier to point out the money saved in awarding to the low bidder than it was to prove an alleged increase in quality, performance, or convenience to the government to be obtained from an award to other than the low bidder.

Even the exceptions specifically authorized by Congress were seldom fully exploited in practice because of the conservative tendencies of contracting officers working in the shadow of the military prison at Leavenworth. Competitive procurement with award to the low bidder was the deeply entrenched tradition of military procurement in the United States when World War I arrived to upset the normal pattern.

---

[4] SW D. F. Davis to Judge A. C. Denison, 1 Dec 25, Morrow Hearings, p. 1820. The exceptions are listed here, but their authorizing statutes are not shown.

[5] Act of March 2, 1901 (31 Stat 905), 10 USCA 1201.

[6] See 41 USCA 5, sec. 40.

Procurement Legislation in World War I

In war the regular peacetime procedures for procurement are inadequate. Speed is more important than price; a dollar saved may mean a battle lost. Congress recognized this when framing the basic statutes governing military procurement. In emergencies the Secretary of War and his agents did not need to resort to price competitions; they could negotiate contracts in whatever appeared to be the best interests of the government.[7] This left the selection of contracting procedures to the discretion of the officials representing the War Department. Broadly speaking, the choice consisted of two forms, the fixed-price contract and the cost-plus contract, each representing a fundamentally different philosophy of contractual relationship.

The fixed-price or lump-sum contract, as it was sometimes called, was the conventional form used in peacetime. Whether it was awarded to the low bidder as a result of public advertisement and competition or by negotiation and agreement as to price at the discretion of departmental officials, the fixed-price contract set in advance the price to be paid by the government. The contractor assumed all risks, and in return he was free to increase his profit by improving his efficiency and lowering his costs. For some undertakings, however, the fixed-price form of contract is impractical. Where the product is novel and costs are hard to estimate in advance, contractors are understandably reluctant to assume the risks involved, especially in a period of rising costs in material and labor. To induce manufacturers to bid, officials in the War Department turned to the cost-plus form of contract.

Cost plus is actually a generic term embracing a number of variations, but all share one element in common: the government and not the contractor is expected to assume most of the risks. The latter merely passes his bills for such items as labor and material to the government for payment. His profit for managerial services is then computed by one of several methods. In World War I, profits on this form of contract were computed as a percentage of cost. Such contracts were known as cost-plus-percentage-of-cost (CPPC) contracts. The weakness of such an arrangement is obvious. The contractor had little or no incentive beyond patriotism to hold costs down and considerable incentive for pushing costs up to enlarge his profit.

The dilemma confronting procurement officials within the War Department is readily apparent. They had to draft a contract by which the government assumed the risks but still left an incentive sufficiently strong to induce contractors to hold down costs. Since airplanes had never been mass produced before World War I and the hazards of such an operation were great, it was, logically enough, the members of the Aircraft Board who devised a modified version of the cost-plus contract to resolve the dilemma.[8] Under the terms of the mod-

---

[7] *Ibid.*, sec. 43.

[8] The Aircraft Board was a subordinate agency of the Council of National Defense established by the Defense Act of 1916. Until October 1917 the board was known as the Aircraft Production Board. See C. L. Lord and A. D. Turnbull, *History of Naval Aviation* (New Haven, Conn.: Yale University Press, 1949), p. 118.

ified cost-plus, or bogey, contract, as it came to be called, the government undertook to pay the contractor for all labor, materials, depreciation, and overhead charges, as well as for all special tools and all additional facilities required, retaining title in the case of the latter two items. In addition, the government would pay the contractor a profit or fee representing a percentage on a cost, to be estimated in advance. Thus if actual costs exceeded estimated costs, the contractor could not increase his profit. On the other hand, the advance estimate of cost was to provide a basis for incentive. To encourage contractors to strive for reduced costs, the modified contract offered them a premium of a substantial percentage of any money saved by cutting actual costs below the initial estimate.

The modified cost-plus, or bogey, contract, when applied to airplanes and engines during World War I, made it possible for manufacturers to make rather surprising profits. The Packard Motor Car Company's contract for Liberty engines is a case in point. Government officials set the bogey price in advance at $6,087 per engine. With a 15-percent fee, the manufacturer received a profit of $913.05 per unit regardless of what the engines eventually cost. After it became apparent that actual costs would run somewhat less than originally estimated, the bogey was renegotiated downward to $5,000 and the fee was reduced to 12.5 percent. Even so, Packard managed to earn a profit of $3,750,000 by bringing actual engine costs down to less than $3,200 per unit. But this was only one element of profit, for the contractor received in addition 25 percent of the savings or spread between the bogey and the actual costs.[9]

All together, in fees and premiums, the Packard Company would have earned just under $6,500,000 profit had the contract run to completion. And this, it should be understood, was a contractor with somewhat less than $6,000,000 invested in the plant turning out the engines. Nor were these profits an isolated exception. The Dayton-Wright Airplane Company, which manufactured the only tactical aircraft to go into mass production in the United States during World War I, was in a position to pile up more than $6,000,000 in profits from fees and premiums on a bogey contract even though the corporation's invested capital only amounted to about $1,000,000 supplemented by an advance of $1,500,000 from the government.[10]

Just before the end of the war, public disclosure of apparently excessive profits on air matériel helped to provoke a revulsion to the whole principle of cost-plus contracts for military procurement.[11] In Congress this attitude was reflected in charges of profiteering leveled at contractors and financial profligacy on the part of responsible public officials. The War Department suffered savage attacks from the floor of the House, which usually charged scandalous waste in the con-

---

[9] C. E. Hughes to Atty Gen, 25 Oct 18, Hughes Rpt, in *Cong Rcd*, December 30, 1918, pp. 906–07.
[10] *Ibid.*
[11] S. M. Brannon, JAGD, Discussion of the Legal and Contract Phases of Procurement Planning, for ASW Conference of Planning Branch Officers, 13 Nov 34, in ICAF doc file, Contracts. Actually the estimated scale of profits shown were not in every case realized because of termination or renegotiation, but the cost-plus principle was discredited in the public mind regardless of subsequent changes.

tracting procedures of the War Department.[12] Without question there was waste in the wartime contracts for aircraft, but a good deal less than half of the money spent for air matériel—airplanes, engines, and accessories—used the cost-plus contract and its variants.[13] Much of the waste was inherent in the compulsions of war regardless of the contract form employed. Nevertheless, the cost-plus contract was a dog with a bad name that Congress would not forget.

Something of the congressional reaction to the procurement experience of 1917–18 is evident in the report of a committee investigating wartime expenditures. This committee recommended abolition of the cost-plus contract even for use in wartime, and urged Congress to revoke the power of the Secretary of War to suspend competitive bidding during emergencies as provided in the Revised Statutes, Section 3709.

Finally, the committee actually asked Congress to amend Article III of the Constitution so as to stretch the definition of treason to cover profiteering on war contracts. After World War I, procurement officers of the War Department had to begin their normal peacetime operations in an atmosphere of distrust. Over their heads hung the threats of irate congressmen urging the Department of Justice to bring to book those responsible for wartime losses.[14]

Procurement Under the General Statutes 1918–26

The alleged war scandals, as one manufacturer called them, colored procurement practices for a number of years afterward. The sins of the parents set the teeth of the children on edge. Procurement officers, fearing investigation, were inclined to insist upon public advertisement and competitive proposals, with awards to the lowest bidders. By following the most stringent provisions of the statutes and avoiding the discretionary exceptions, they apparently hoped to safeguard themselves.[15]

In some cases, of course, there was no escape from the use of discretion. When a manufacturer turned up with a new design that promised revolutionary improvements in performance, War Department officials had no alternative but to negotiate with the manufacturer in an attempt to agree upon a mutually satisfactory price. It would be impossible for the government to call for competitive bids on a design the government did not yet possess.

Contracts for experimental airplanes were thus negotiated, but almost all other contracts, especially those calling for airplanes in production quantities, were let

---

[12] See, for example, the charges of Representative W. J. Graham of Illinois, chairman of the postwar committee investigating wartime expenditures. His claim that the War Department spent a billion dollars on aviation and failed to put a single fighting aircraft on the front before the armistice is simply not true. *Cong Rcd,* June 1, 1920, pp. 8144–51.

[13] Hughes Report, *Cong Rcd,* December 30, 1918, p. 885. Of approximately $100,000,000 spent for air matériel, $57,000,000 went out under fixed-price contracts and some $43,000,000 went out under modified cost-plus contracts.

[14] House Rpt 816, 66th Cong, 2d sess, April 1, 1920. Congress did not accept all the committee's recommendations. The National Defense Act of 1916, as amended through 4 June 1920, continued to authorize the President in time of war or when war was imminent to place contracts without regard to the existing statutes (Section 120).

[15] For manufacturers' protests on this situation, see Lampert Hearings, pp. 1505–06 and 1404.

PROCUREMENT LEGISLATION, ORGANIZATION, ADMINISTRATION 85

upon a competitive basis according to the provisions of the statutes. The Air Service spent about $22,000,000 for aircraft in the five-year period 1920–24. Of this, less than $3,000,000 went for the design and development of new types. The spread between the two figures indicates the large amount expended on a competitive basis for items in quantity in contrast to the relatively small sum involved in negotiated contracts for experimental items.[16]

Strict compliance with the statutes governing procurement wrought a number of harmful effects entirely unintended by those who framed the laws. The case of the Martin bomber in 1919 and 1920 illustrates some of the unexpected evils stemming from an insistence upon price competition. During World War I, Glenn L. Martin worked to perfect a superior bomber. The War Department acquired the design rights by purchase. In 1919 the bomber appeared to be the most promising aircraft of its kind in the field. Air Service officers planned to procure 200 units, but they did not invite Martin to negotiate privately on a satisfactory price. Instead, they put the design out to open competition. When the bids were unsealed it was discovered that the Curtiss Aeroplane and Motor Company rather than Martin quoted the lowest price. Two other firms received increments of the order, but Martin, the designer, received no contract at all because he had increased his bid on the production order to amortize the losses he incurred during the initial trial and error experimental phase. Rival firms, with no such costs to cover, were in a position to bid lower.[17]

The evil consequences of a rigid resistance upon competitive bidding appeared abruptly. Deprived of his airplane, Martin no longer had any incentive to improve that particular design. Worse yet, deprived of a profitable production contract as a means of reimbursing his earlier investment, Martin was soon unable to finance further development work.[18] The statutes intended to protect the public's interest here operated to the reverse effect and retarded the pace of research and development.

A sequel only served to confirm the point that aircraft contracts made under the general procurement statutes discouraged the designer and tended to drive him out of business. Some time after the ill-fated Martin bomber affair, the Navy's Bureau of Aeronautics negotiated an experimental contract with Curtiss to build a torpedo-carrying scout-bomber with performance (in terms of range, ceiling, speed, and load) well in advance of current aircraft. The design proved difficult to execute. Curtiss pioneered in the use of new metal alloys to combine strength for bomb carrying with lightness for range. After two years of engineering endeavor the Curtiss staff turned out a superior aircraft, the CS–2, but the effort absorbed $180,000 over and above the contract price negotiated with the Navy. When the Navy sought to purchase forty such aircraft from Curtiss, the

---

[16] Gross expenditures for the period are from Lampert Report, page 3. Experimental expenditures are from testimony of G. C. Loening, based on data inserted in the *Congressional Record*, January 7, 1925, by Representative F. La Guardia (Lampert Hearings, page 455).

[17] Morrow Hearings, p. 1438.
[18] *Ibid.*, p. 1440.

company quoted a price calculated to recoup the firms' loss during the experimental phase. The Navy's cost analysis experts calculated that the Curtiss bid was several thousand dollars higher a unit than it should be. Unable to agree upon a suitable figure, the Navy put the design out to competition, and Martin won with a low bid at $23,000, a figure free from the burden of amortization that increased the Curtiss bid.[19]

Although it so happened that in underbidding each other for production contracts Curtiss and Martin may have achieved a certain rough justice, there were instances under the existing procurement statutes where the designer who failed to get a production contract to amortize his losses had to go out of business.[20] What is more, the operation of the general procurement statutes had still more unfortunate consequence. When the government procured a design for a new or experimental aircraft in a negotiated contract, the assumption was that the designer had turned over a set of drawings, calculations, and specifications, which could be used as the basis of a competition for the production contract. As a matter of fact, no drawings of experimental aircraft were ever quite so complete. Invariably a good deal of shop practice was implicit in the drawings. Symbols and endorsements upon the drawings that might mean much to the staff of the designer were meaningless when handed over to a rival firm chancing to bid low on a production order.[21] No one realized this more than the Curtiss and Martin engineers who tried to build each other's designs. In fact, Martin appreciated this difficulty so acutely that he ignored the CS–2 drawings entirely and had his engineers make up a completely new set of drawings that Martin shopmen would understand. Using a physical sample of the Curtiss CS–2 rather than Curtiss blueprints, the Martin engineers designed the whole aircraft anew, introducing changes where it seemed advisable and even running an entirely new stress analysis on the design.[22] The finished product was quite literally a new aircraft.

Here was the ultimate futility: a close adherence to the general procurement statutes by the military services led aircraft manufacturers into a dog-eat-dog era of destructive competition that penalized the very firms doing most to advance the art. Manufacturers who redrafted each other's designs for production in quantity were engaging in a costly duplication of effort to be condemned on the score of waste alone, not to mention the absurdity involved. And in addition, as the manufacturers themselves admitted, no contractor pushed vigorously to improve a design in the hands of a rival.[23] Officials in the War Department were well aware of this situation even before the CS–2 case came to prominence. Wherever possible, they took steps to remedy the difficulty.

Protests From the Aircraft Industry

Of all the complaints the aircraft manufacturers leveled against the procure-

---

[19] Lampert Hearings, pp. 1144–45; 1404–05; 1628–29.
[20] Morrow Hearings, p. 1439.
[21] Lampert Hearings, pp. 1401–02.
[22] Ibid., pp. 2278–79, 2282.
[23] Ibid., p. 2281.

ment procedures of the government, none reflected such ire as the charge that federal contracting officers failed to respect design rights as proprietary. This, the manufacturers contended, was an issue of the first importance.[24] From this unhappy practice, the manufacturers believed, stemmed many if not most of the other ills besetting the industry.

While most manufacturers were quick to place the blame for the ills of the industry upon the shoulders of federal contracting officers in general and their procurement procedures in particular, there were some few who recognized that at least a part and perhaps most of the trouble experienced by the industry came as a result of overexpansion during the war years. But whether excess capacity from overexpansion or faulty procurement procedures lay at the root of the trouble, everyone seemed to agree that the aircraft industry was heading for the rocks. The Aeronautical Chamber of Commerce in 1924 found the industry dwindling to the point where it would soon "cease to exist."[25] Howard Coffin, wartime head of the Aircraft Production Board, reiterated his report of 1919 when in 1925 he urged immediate action "to prevent a vitally necessary industry from entirely disappearing."[26] Others sang the same refrain in calling for reforms in the procurement practices of the government where aircraft were concerned.

The wails of protest raised by disgruntled manufacturers undoubtedly helped bring about the appointment of the Lampert and Morrow investigating groups.[27] Both boards considered, among all the other aspects of aviation, the broad question of federal procurement policies relating to aircraft. They gathered extensive evidence from manufacturers and government officials alike and spread upon the record a large number of proposals for reform.

Among the manufacturers there was general agreement as to the ills of the industry. Rightly or wrongly, they attributed the trouble to the failure of the government to regard designs as proprietary, to a lack of continuity of orders, to the destructive pricing policies of contracting officers, and to the competition of government factories. In identifying these evils the industry spoke almost with one voice. But making complaints and proposing specific correctives are two entirely different matters. When faced with the opportunity of suggesting concrete proposals, the members of the Aeronautical Chamber of Commerce merely listed their criticisms and then sidestepped the question of detailed recommendations with the comment that any method of procurement overcoming the ills listed would be acceptable to the industry.[28] Possibly the manufacturers realized that any legislation they as a group proposed for the revision of pro-

---

[24] Rpt of the Special Com of the Aircraft Industry to the Members of the Industry, January 5, 1925, signed by representatives of virtually all leading aircraft manufacturing firms. (Reprinted in Lampert Hearings, pp. 1369-71.) Almost every manufacturer appearing before investigating committees at one time or another voiced the protest.

[25] *Aircraft Yearbook, 1924*, p. 1.

[26] Lampert Hearings, p. 1219. For the full text of the Report of the American Aviation Mission, July 19, 1919, called the Crowell Report, in which the condition of the aircraft industry in the United States is reviewed, see *ibid*, pp. 1221-35.

[27] *Ibid.*, pp. 45-57.

[28] Reply of Aeronautical Chamber of Commerce to questionnaire of Morrow Board, October 9, 1925, in Morrow Hearings, p. 1415.

curement procedures might well be enacted. Then, if the revisions proved unworkable in practice they would be in a poor position to complain. Possibly they came to the realization that the problem was infinitely complex.

Perhaps no one should have appreciated the complexity of the aircraft procurement question more completely than Howard Coffin, whose wartime role had plunged him into the very midst of the question. Congress, he declared, had hitherto placed too much reliance upon "curbstone opinions." Having said this, Coffin proceeded to deliver a curbstone opinion. Even while admitting that he was not prepared to make any very profound analysis of the question, he urged Congress to pass legislation permitting the allocation of production contracts to a small group of manufacturers arbitrarily selected as the best qualified. This, of course, was a revolutionary proposal that would do away with the requirement for competitive bidding, but Coffin offered no suggestion as to how it could be achieved without raising the cry of favoritism.[29] In a similar vein Grover C. Loening, an aircraft manufacturer and pioneer designer, favored legislation to permit a "parceling out" of contracts to the established firms maintaining research staffs, provided it could be done without "too much wet-nursing." He too had no suggestions as to just how this could be accomplished.[30]

Glenn L. Martin favored limiting competition to those firms with adequate facilities. The decision as to just which firms were so qualified Martin would leave to the discretion of the contracting officers. No legislation would be required, he felt, provided Congress as well as the Secretaries of War and Navy could be made to understand why such discretionary powers were necessary.[31] There was much to be said for Martin's reluctance to draft fresh legislation. As one witness told investigating congressmen, "new laws search folk's corns out like new boots." [32] Nonetheless, whether one followed Coffin and Loening in a legislative solution or Martin in an administrative one, the objective was the same. Each favored enhanced discretionary powers that would allow contracting officers to limit the competition for government contracts to a select group of manufacturers and, where desirable, permit the allocation of contracts to particular firms.

The manufacturers' spokesmen were not alone in advocating increased powers for contracting officers. One government official after another testified in favor of giving a broader range of discretion to the Secretaries of War and Navy in the procurement of aircraft. Even while admitting the danger of favoritism, Assistant Secretary of War D. F. Davis urged that the proprietary rights of manufacturers be respected and some means found to give production orders to designers—to help them amortize their experimental costs—without resort to competitive bids.[33] The Assistant Secretary of the Navy, Theodore Roosevelt, Jr., echoed the idea, pointing out that the statutes governing procurement were de-

---

[29] Lampert Hearings, pp. 1236, 1250, 1264.
[30] Ibid., pp. 912–13, 922.
[31] Ibid., p. 2279.
[32] Ibid., p. 833.
[33] Ibid., pp. 659, 680.

signed to preserve the public funds, but that it would be a poor economy indeed to preserve the public purse at the expense of adequate aerial defenses for the nation.[34] The Secretary of the Navy was most emphatic: "The principle of competitive bidding is not adapted to aircraft in the present state of the art." [35]

In light of the unanimity of opinion among industrialists and federal officials regarding procedures for aircraft procurement, it is perhaps not surprising that both the Lampert Committee in Congress and the President's appointees on the Morrow Board advocated a drastic and even revolutionary change in the laws governing the procurement of aircraft. Both groups recommended legislation that would amend the existing statutes so as to recognize the manufacturer's proprietary interest in his designs and permit the purchase of air matériel without competitive bidding. These were radical proposals in complete defiance of the historic statutory safeguards on public purchasing, but there was good reason to believe they would be enacted when the Sixty-ninth Congress met and began to consider legislation on aviation matters early in 1926 since nearly everyone concerned with aircraft procurement officially or unofficially seemed to favor the suggested changes.[36]

General Patrick

The Air Corps Act of 1926

Section 10 of the Air Corps Act of 1926 prescribed an elaborate procedure for the procurement of aircraft.[37] Its first subsections—10a to 10i—provided for design competitions to encourage the development of aircraft. They required the Secretary of War and the Secretary of the Navy to advertise in at least three aviation periodicals inviting sealed bids containing not only a graduated table of

---

[34] *Ibid.*, p. 2345. For an excellent exposition of why the Air Service wished to place contracts without competition, see testimony of Maj. Gen. M. M. Patrick, Chief of Air Service, January 27, 1926, in Hearings before the House Military Affairs Com, 69th Congress, 1st session, January 19 to March 9, 1926, pp. 287–89.

[35] SN to Judge Denison, 17 Nov 25, in Morrow Hearings, p. 1734.

[36] The Comptroller General was an important exception. Although the War and Navy Departments had signed an agreement with the Aeronautical Chamber of Commerce promising to "sustain the principle of proprietary design rights," he abstained from ruling on the matter until a specific case came up. Until he did rule on the question, the agreement of the departments and the representatives of industry was relatively meaningless. See testimony of C. L. Lawrence, president of Aeronautical Chamber of Commerce, in Morrow Hearings, p. 1416.

[37] See ch. III, above, for the influence of the act on air strength.

prices on varying quantities of aircraft but, in addition, an aircraft design formulated to meet the rather general specifications laid out in the invitation to bid —or the circular proposal, as it was commonly called. Moreover, Section 10 of the act specified a technique of evaluation by which a board, acting for the Secretaries, assigned a figure of merit expressed in percentiles on each feature of the design.

The design competition feature of the Air Corps Act was an outgrowth of a procedure favored by Representative McSwain, a most active member of the House Military Affairs Committee. By this device the congressman hoped not only to stimulate the inventive genius of the country but also to protect the public from abuse. Every phase of the competition was to receive the fullest publicity. To assure the board's objectivity, its conclusions, expressed as numerical ratings, were to become a matter of public record and subject to challenge by losing competitors, who were provided with formal machinery of appeal. The design competition, McSwain hoped, would provide the government with a means of garnering the best in aeronautical advances without limiting the field to a few big aircraft firms.

The act was not, however, intended to impair the established industry for the benefit of the struggling inventor. Section 10j amounted to a "Buy American" provision. It stipulated that only native-owned and native-operated plants would be eligible for contracts to supply military aircraft. This did not prevent the departments from taking advantage of unique advances made abroad. Section 10k, one of the most important of the act, authorized the Secretaries to purchase aircraft, parts, and accessories for experimental purposes in the United States or abroad, with or without competition. The provision gave the Secretaries a power they had long exercised under a number of legal makeshifts.

Section 10k flatly authorized negotiated contracts in the purchase of items for experimental purposes, a provision no one would dispute. In the years to follow, however, there was a good deal of discussion about the meaning of the rest of the subsection, which read: "if as a result of [experimental procurement] new and suitable designs considered to be the best kind for the Army or the Navy are developed, [the Secretary] may enter into contract, subject to the requirements of paragraph (j) ["Buy American"] . . . for the procurement in quantity of such aircraft, aircraft parts or aeronautical accessories without regard to the provisions of paragraphs (a) to (e) [relating to design competitions]." The phraseology would appear to authorize the Secretaries to give a contract for an experimental aircraft without competition and then follow it up by signing a negotiated or noncompetitive contract with the same manufacturer if it appeared that the experimental contract had resulted in a superior item desirable in quantity. This view is reinforced by the circumstance that although several provisions of the section are specifically excluded—Sections 10a to 10e and 10j—there is no mandatory reference to a subsequent clause requiring competitive bidding under certain circumstances. Had this interpretation continued to prevail and had the Secretaries continued to feel free to negotiate contracts for production quantities following an initial experimental contract, many of the difficulties of the decade before World War II might have been avoided.

Sections 10l and 10m reflect the deep-seated distrust Representative McSwain felt for negotiated contracts consummated behind closed doors. Section 10l provided for extensive government audits of contractors' books, so that even experimental contracts negotiated at the discretion of the Secretaries would be subject to public scrutiny as a check against abuse. Section 10m required the Secretaries to make annual reports to Congress revealing the names of all competitors, prices paid, and the like. A provision, McSwain felt, that would provide "a printed record to be published to the world," and would stigmatize favoritism with publicity.[38] What McSwain did not then realize was that Section 10l burdened Congress with an executive function it was ill-equipped to perform.

Section 10q is one of the most difficult features of the Air Corps Act to understand. On the surface it appeared clear: in procuring aircraft according to designs presented "prior to the passage of this act," designs that had been "reduced to practice" and found suitable, the Secretaries were authorized to negotiate contracts. The subsection, it would seem, merely permitted the departments to exclude from the mandates of the act those aircraft developed before the passage of the act. And so it was interpreted by all in authority after 1926. There is a good deal of evidence indicating that Congress may have had no such limited intent.

During the discussions preceding the passage of the act, Representative Fred M. Vinson of Kentucky, who was then a member of the Committee on Military Affairs, undertook a detailed, item-by-item analysis of Section 10. In dealing with 10q, he said: "This section would authorize the Secretary, when in his opinion the best interests of the Government would be served, to contract for quantity production of aircraft upon designs . . . reduced to practice and found suitable for the purpose intended." He made no mention of any qualifying clause "prior to the passage of this act." Moreover, to show that he visualized 10q as having general application, he went on to describe a hypothetical situation in which a manufacturer builds an aircraft with a markedly superior performance the air arm simply must have. To advertise for competitive bids on such a design by the traditional statutes would be absurd since there would be no guarantee that the low bidder could produce an airplane matching the performance of the original sample. Section 10q, Vinson noted, would obviate this difficulty.[39]

There is further evidence suggesting that 10q was intended to confer upon the Secretaries a continuing power to negotiate contracts for aircraft previously reduced to practice by manufacturers. Representative McSwain had discussed the provision when it appeared in his earlier bills. Far from regarding it as a stopgap applying only to aircraft designed before the passage of the act, he described its operation at length, even to the point of stating that it might seem

---

[38] House Rpt, 1395, June 7, 1926, to accompany H.R. 12471, 65th Cong, 1st sess, p. 5.

[39] *Cong Rcd*, June 29, 1926, p. 12271.

out of harmony with the many safeguards imposed in the other sections of the act. He declared that he expected the departments to use design competition as the normal approach to procurement, although he admitted they might resort to 10k and 10q legally. But, he added, if the authorities abused the privilege, he would be "the first man to rise" seeking to repeal or amend the act.[40] Pledges such as this would be quite unnecessary had 10q applied only to those few aircraft designed before passage of the act, since its applicability would, under that interpretation, have expired almost immediately.

All the evidence leads to the conclusion that the framers of Section 10 probably intended to permit the Secretaries to procure aircraft without competition when the airplanes represented new designs that had been reduced to practice by manufacturers and had been proved superior in actual flight tests. Whatever may have been the intent of Congress, the bare wording of the act itself clearly limited the application of 10q to designs presented before July 1926, and the Secretaries were prohibited from availing themselves of the powers they were intended to have. The wording was unfortunate because it impeded procurement for years to come and inhibited the development of aircraft for military use. Congressmen might be to blame for this legislative mischance, but the full text of the act was referred to the War Department for study, and there was ample opportunity to discover the disparity between what the congressmen said in debate and the way the act actually read. For want of an organization in the air arm adequately equipped to deal with legislation, the text of the act returned from the War Department with the approval of the appropriate officials.[41]

There remains to be considered only one provision of the act. Section 10t stipulated that whenever the Secretaries entered into contracts for aircraft, they were authorized to make the award to the bidder they determined to be "the lowest responsible bidder" that could satisfactorily perform the work required "to the best advantage of the Government." Only the President and the federal courts could review the decisions of the Secretaries as to the awards, their interpretations of the provisions of the contracts, and the subsequent administration of the contracts. Section 10t was revolutionary in that it granted the Secretaries a very large measure of discretion. Not the lowest cash bid but the lowest responsible bidder won the award, and the Secretaries were to make the determination free from the hampering threat of subsequent reversal by reviewing authorities. This was clearly to the advantage of the air arm and promised a solution for many of the troubles besetting aircraft procurement in the years before 1926, provided always, of course, the incumbent Secretaries were willing to exercise their discretionary powers. But in 10t, as in the previous subsections, the officials of the War Department who gave their approval so readily

---

[40] *Cong Rcd*, June 10, 1926, p. 11113. See especially, McSwain to Woodhouse, printed in full there.

[41] See, for example, SW Davis to Representative James, and Chief of the Air Service, Gen Patrick, to James, June 22, 1926, approving sec. 10; both in *Cong Rcd*, June 29, 1926, p. 12278.

PROCUREMENT LEGISLATION, ORGANIZATION, ADMINISTRATION

failed to see the significance of one particular word. The act read: "Hereafter *whenever* the Secretary of War . . . shall enter into a contract. . . ."[42] Did this mean in every case? If so, iot would appear to conflict with the provisions of 10k and 10q by requiring competitive bidding. Uncertainty on this point was to give a handle to subsequent interpretations that inconvenienced the air arm considerably.

For good or for ill, the Air Corps Act of 1926 became the basic law of the air arm and Section 10 determined the forms of procurement for nearly two decades. In retrospect, what precisely were the objectives of Section 10? Perhaps the best statement of the aims behind the section were expressed by Representative J. J. McSwain, the measure's most active sponsor, as he looked back years later. His intention, he wrote, was to stimulate inventive ingenuity in America, protect the government from the evils of favoritism, protect the government against unreasonable charges, and ensure the development of an adequate aircraft industry as a national resource in time of war.[43] Surely all these objectives were present in the Air Corps Act, but they were not equally weighted. Price and performance received more consideration than did the health of the industry, not so much in the act itself but in the interpretations that soon grew up around the act.

Whatever may have been the intention of those who framed the act, its significance stems from the circumstance that it was, after all, the fundamental procurement law of the air arm. Regardless of intent or subsequent interpretation, somehow the Air Corps had to procure airplanes within the terms of the law as it stood on the books, for until World War II there was no legislation enacted to alter Section 10 significantly. The success of the act hung largely upon its execution.

The Organization of the Air Arm for Procurement

A knowledge of the organizations controlling procurement in the air arm is essential to an understanding of the procurement process. The form or structure of an organization tends to influence the conduct of the operations it undertakes, and where tours of duty are short and shifts in personnel are frequent it is the organization rather than the people in it that provides continuity.

Several agencies were involved in procurement. Under the terms of the National Defense Act of 1920, the Chief of Staff and the Assistant Secretary of War occupied parallel positions. Where the former supervised military matters, the latter supervised procurement and procurement planning. While the two were expected to co-ordinate their actions, each was responsible in his own sphere and each had equal access to the Secretary of War. The chiefs of arms and services thus conducted their procurement operations under two heads: they looked to the Chief of Staff and his general staff sections for supervision in the

---

[42] Italics supplied by author.
[43] Representative McSwain to President of Aeronautical Chamber of Commerce, 5 Oct 33, app. C in Recommendations on National Aviation Policy, prepared for Howell Comm by ACC, 12 Sep 34, in AIA file 19. See also, *Cong Rcd*, June 29, 1926, p. 12270, as well as House Rpt 1395 on H.R. 12471, 69th Cong, 1st sess, June 7, 1926.

matter of requirements, both quantitative and qualitative, but they looked to the Assistant Secretary of War and his staff for supervision in the forms and methods of procurement to be employed.[44]

Supervision by the Assistant Secretary of War involved a number of steps. It was his office that drafted and revised the Army Regulations pertaining to procurement, a contribution of considerable importance in overcoming the lack of uniform procedures that had vexed Army purchasing during World War I. In addition, his staff worked constantly to minimize dissatisfaction with the Army's procurement methods by hearing complaints from bidders and contractors. By reviewing contracts before approval to ensure compliance with existing statutes and the various regulations of such executive arms as the Treasury and Labor Departments, the Assistant Secretary sought to prevent troubles before they developed. In general, the function of the Assistant Secretary was to ride herd on all those arms and services performing procurement functions.[45] Insofar as the air arm was concerned, the Air Corps Act of 1926 altered this arrangement slightly by creating an Assistant Secretary of War for Air.[46] The statute left the duties of this office undefined, but in practice the incumbent advanced the interests of the air arm by providing an additional avenue to the Secretary of War.

Thus, from 1926 on, the Chief of the Air Corps, as the head of one of the procuring arms and services, was the responsible officer who made decisions on matters of air matériel procurement within the supervisory purview of the Assistant Secretary and subject, of course, to the final approval of the Secretary of War. To assist him, the Chief of the Air Corps maintained a staff known collectively as the Office, Chief of Air Corps (OCAC). Chart 1 suggests the several routes by which problems confronting the air arm might be brought to the attention of the Secretary and illustrates the relative position of the Air Corps in the hierarchy of the War Department.

The Structure of OCAC

Chart 2 reveals that the staff of the Office of the Chief of the Air Corps was organized into functional units more or less corresponding with those of the General Staff, although the units had different names. In addition, the Air Corps Board, the Air Corps Technical Committee, and the Procurement Planning Board, serving as advisors to the Chief of the Air Corps, were in effect adjuncts of OCAC even though they did not sit in continuous session.

In a sense, all the staff divisions of OCAC worked on planning, but primary responsibility for over-all planning for the Air Corps rested with the Plans Division. Among the many projects undertaken by this division, those of particular relevance to procurement concerned the preparation of war plans—the air arm aspects of the War Department's

---

[44] 41 Stat 764, sec. 5a, and 5 USCA 182.

[45] The duties of the Assistant Secretary of War and the Office of the Assistant Secretary are defined in Army Regulation 5–5. See also the annual reports of the Assistant Secretary for 1937 and 1938 for the OASW role in current procurement.

[46] Act of July 2, 1926, sec. 9 (44 Stat 748), 5 USCA 182a.

PROCUREMENT LEGISLATION, ORGANIZATION, ADMINISTRATION

CHART 1—ORGANIZATION CHART SHOWING CHANNELS OF COMMUNICATION BETWEEN THE SECRETARY OF WAR AND THE AIR CORPS

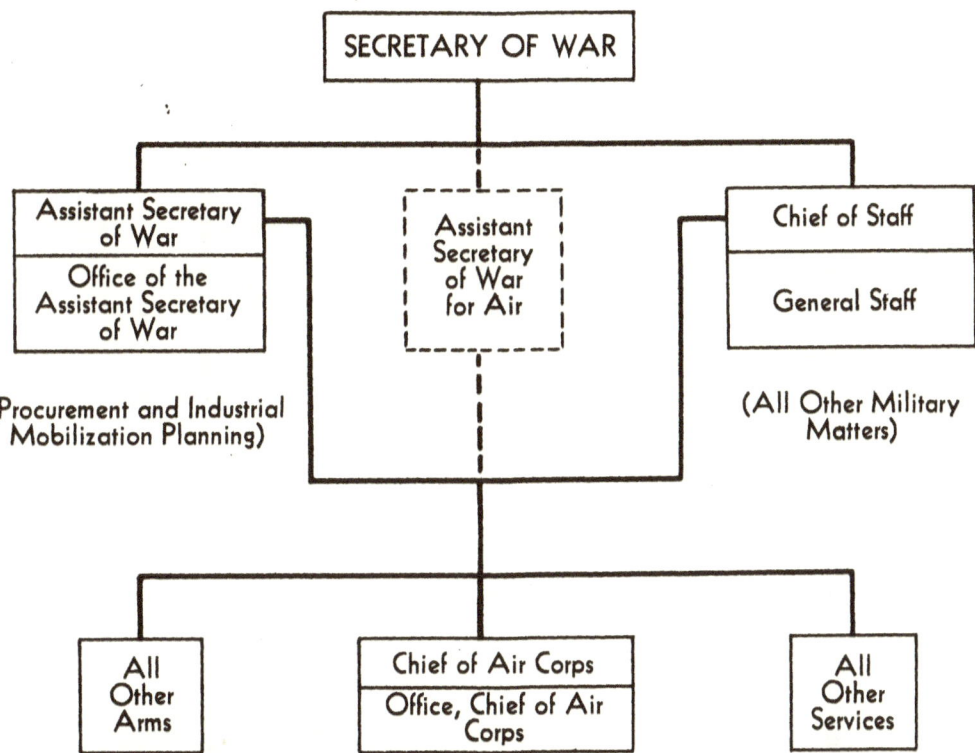

"color plans"—the formulation of requirements to meet these plans, and the drafting of legislation as a basis for congressional action in authorizing programs.[47] Although the organization chart suggests that the Air Corps Board functioned in an advisory capacity to the Chief of the Air Corps, in practice it functioned as a service group to the Plans Division, turning out studies on doctrine, technical equipment, and policies in general, including many bearing in one way or another upon the question of procurement.

In matters directly concerning procurement, the Supply Division of OCAC was the agency of primary concern. In one form or another and under different names from time to time, the organization for handling matériel questions in OCAC always posed a peculiar problem since the headquarters and all the other staff divisions of OCAC were in Washington, while after 1926 the staff for matériel was actually located at Wright Field at Dayton, Ohio, with only a small liaison section in Washington.[48]

---

[47] For a view of Plans Division functions in practice, as differentiated from the role assigned by directive, see R&R, Actg Chief, Plans, to Exec, 23 Aug 38, AHO Plans Div 145.91-244.

[48] See AAF Hist Study 10, p. 27.

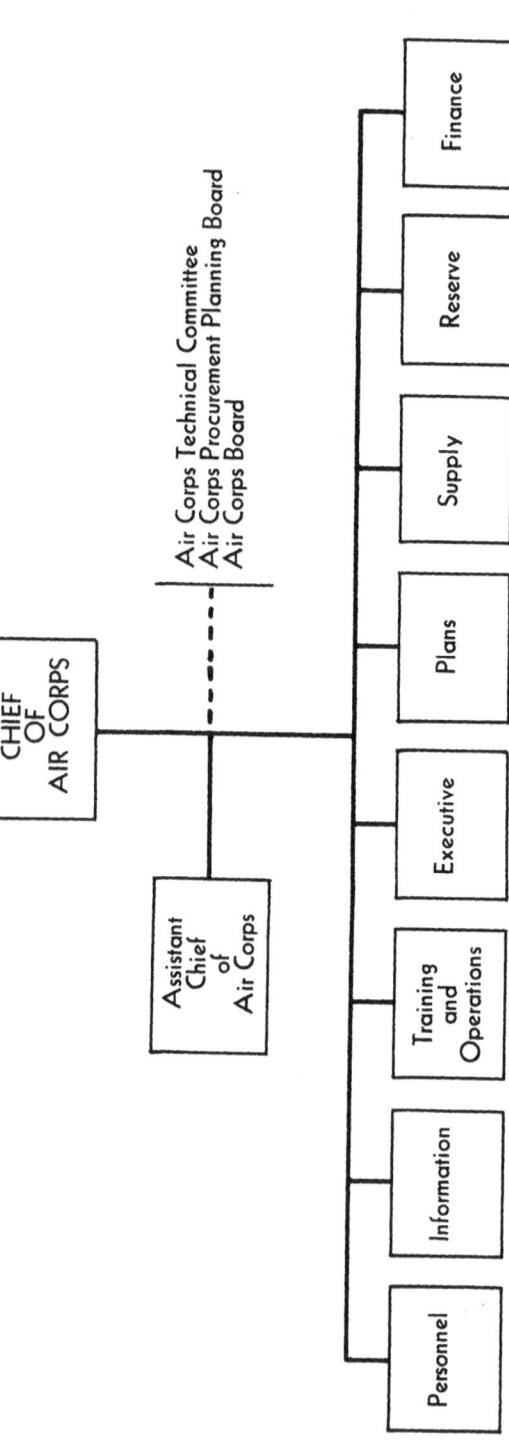

CHART 2—ORGANIZATION OF OCAC, WASHINGTON HEADQUARTERS OF AIR CORPS

Source: Memo, Exec, OCAC, to all Divisions, 15 Jan 36, AHO, Plans Div 145.93–171, and AAF Historical Study 10, revised Apr 47.

Just as the Air Corps Board served in practice as a special adjunct for the Plans Division regardless of what its directives might say, so too the Air Corps Technical Committee and the Procurement Planning Board were closely related to the functions of the Materiel Division. Each of these special groups performed a co-ordinating function of particular importance. The Technical Committee, with representatives from the Materiel Division reflecting the engineering and manufacturing point of view and representatives from the Operations Division defending the user's point of view, sought to resolve the conflicting objectives of these groups. The committee's task was to make an acceptable or workable recommendation for the Chief of the Air Corps to use as a basis for his decision on matériel problems.[49]

The role and composition of the Procurement Planning Board were similar to those of the Technical Committee, but there the decisions to be reached were fiscal rather than technical. The board's central function was to try to match the funds available to the aircraft. In short, the board had to compromise the desired with the possible.[50] While the Technical Committee and the Procurement Planning Board did make recommendations that led to decisions issued in the name of the Chief of the Air Corps, the great bulk of the work relating to procurement came to Washington from the Materiel Division at Wright Field.

The Materiel Division

The functions of the Materiel Division insofar as procurement was concerned may be explained by considering its five major sections. *(Chart 3)*

The operations of the Engineering Section were fundamental to the activities of all the other branches, for it was from the various experimental aircraft and accessories sponsored by this section that the items subsequently procured in quantity were ultimately selected. The staff of the Engineering Section endeavored to keep itself informed about advances in science and technology on every horizon in order to formulate programs of experimental development resulting in superior air weapons. The Engineering Section initiated contracts with industry for the manufacture of experimental items, prepared specifications to secure uniformity and acceptable quality where standardization was possible, and tested the prototype models turned out by the contractors. Finally, when users of finished equipment returned reports of unsatisfactory performance, the Engineering Section sought to rectify the shortcomings. The entire Materiel Division was shorthanded in the decade before the outbreak of war, but nowhere was the lack of skilled officers more acute than in the Engineering Section. For example, as late as 1937, there were only four proj-

---

[49] AR 850-25, as issued in the years before World War II, outlined the functions of technical committees for the arms and services generally but left the mechanics of administration undefined. No analytical history has been written to evaluate the role of the Air Corps Technical Committee before the war.

[50] For a discussion of the Procurement Planning Board, see Memo, Chief, Proc Sec, for Chief, Mat Liaison Sec, with Incl, 1 Jun 34, WFCF 334.8 Hearing 1935; and testimony of Brig Gen H. C. Pratt, February 14, 1934, House Hearings on WD appropriations for 1935.

CHART 3—MATERIEL DIVISION, WRIGHT FIELD, DAYTON, OHIO

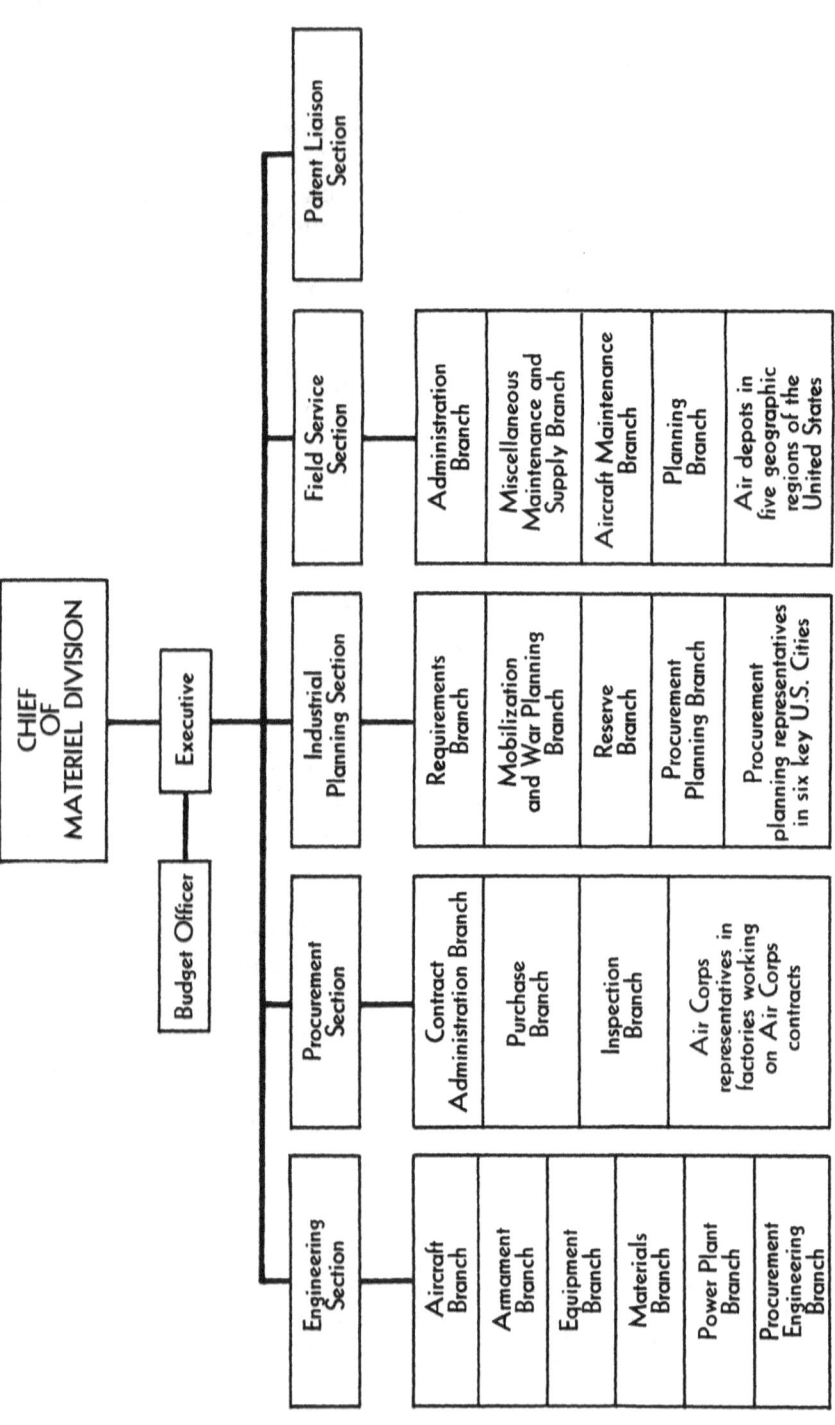

ect officers in the Aircraft Branch to monitor all the various aircraft projects under way at that time.

To the Procurement Section fell the actual business of conducting the purchasing operations of the Materiel Division. Procurement Section officers drafted the circular proposals that were distributed to the aircraft industry. It was they who drew up the contracts, checked them for legal sufficiency, and negotiated with manufacturers over the terms to be included. If changes were required in the terms once the contract had been signed, it was the officers of the Procurement Section who helped process the necessary legal papers, and it was they who arranged for the inspection of the final product before acceptance. In the Procurement Section the shortage of officers was also chronic. Despite the expenditure of more than $30,000,000 for air matériel in 1937, to consider but a single year, there was only one officer available at Wright Field to supervise the important function of inspection. Although there were more than a dozen officers carried on the Procurement Section roster, most served as resident representatives in the factories of manufacturers holding Air Corps contracts and only a few remained at Wright Field to conduct the involved operations centering there.

Of the three remaining sections of the Materiel Division, the Industrial Planning Section, which also played a vital role in the Materiel Division, will be treated in a subsequent chapter.[51] The Field Service Section performed the supply and maintenance services of the air arm and thus is of marginal interest save insofar as the section initiated the purchase of spare parts, supplied information on requirements, and compiled the unsatisfactory reports that influenced the procurement process. The last section of the division to be accorded the status of a major unit was the Patent Liaison Section, a designation that is misleading since the staff of the section generally consisted of only one officer from the Judge Advocate General's Department.[52]

All five sections of the Materiel Division were located at Wright Field, an elaborate air base consisting of landing fields, hangars, workshops for handling maintenance and housing tests, laboratories for conducting research and development work, and offices containing not only the files of contracts and related correspondence but complete sets of specifications as well. A summary of the paper work turned out at Wright Field during 1938 indicates the scope of the administrative functions carried on by the division: over 63,000 copies of specifications were printed during the year for distribution to manufacturers; 53,000 engineering change notices were mailed to contractors; nearly half a million pages were prepared to keep the *Status of Equipment Book* ever current, and the division's big machines turned out three miles of blueprints, for the most part consigned to manufacturers at work on contracts covering aircraft or accessories for the War Department.[53]

---

[51] See ch. VII, below.

[52] The three preceding paragraphs are based on the following: Mat Div GO 6, 9 Dec 36, and Chief, Mat Div, to CofAC, 5 Nov 37, AHO Plans Div 145.91–391.

[53] Annual Rpt of Mat Div, draft copy, 27 Aug 38, WFCF 321.9 Annual Rpt 1938.

WRIGHT FIELD, 1935, BEFORE EXPANSION

Procurement of air matériel involved three echelons between the Secretary of War on the one hand and the manufacturer who actually fulfilled a contract on the other. Each of the three—the Assistant Secretary and his staff, the Chief of the Air Corps and his staff, and the Chief of the Materiel Division and his staff—constituted a clearly defined administrative entity, different in location and personnel. Concerning the organization of these three echelons there need be no confusion, but the definition of their functions is by no means so simple. The exact line of demarcation between the three was not always clear. Where duties were assigned by statute— as for example in the Air Corps Act of 1926, which required the Secretary of War to approve contracts purchased under its terms—there was no confusion, but where no statutory provisions were present there was a good deal of uncertainty and overlapping. Acute problems of co-ordination and command appeared on every hand to complicate procure-

Wright Field, 1942, Showing Expansion of Facilities

ment operations as officers in each of the several echelons tried to perform their duties.

Problems of Co-ordination and Command

One of the most important misunderstandings that troubled procurement operations grew out of the failure of air arm officers and general staff officers to reach a meeting of minds on doctrine regarding the tactical and strategic employment of air power. So long as there was an Assistant Secretary of War for Air, the air arm could count on ready access to the department head, regardless of the attitude of the General Staff. While this had certain advantages, it suffered the disadvantages of channeling problems past the Chief of Staff rather than through him—and problems he did not handle he could scarcely be expected to appreciate, let alone solve.[54] The

---

[54] For a discussion of the problems in command raised by the existence of an Assistant Secretary of

decision of President Roosevelt in 1933 not to appoint an Assistant Secretary of War for Air terminated the uncertainty in the chain of command induced by the existence of this official, but almost immediately a new dilemma appeared.

During 1935 the War Department established the General Headquarters Air Force, which, in the minds of the airmen if not to all others in the Army, was to constitute a great concentrated striking force of strategic air power at the disposal of the high command. Even if this force turned out to be something less than great, and even if there were no complete accord in the matter of doctrine, there could be no denying the importance attached to the quality of the aircraft procured to perform the special functions of this striking force. In such a situation there was need for the most proficient co-ordination possible between the users (the GHQ Air Force) and the suppliers (the Air Corps). Despite this obvious need for co-operation, the War Department created the GHQ Air Force not as a subordinate section of the Chief of the Air Corps but rather as a virtually independent command reporting directly to the Chief of Staff. There were many reasons for making this arrangement, but none of them obviated the difficulties in the procurement process that resulted from the separation of users and suppliers.[55] Since the only authoritative channel between the two air arms lay through the Chief of Staff, and since the airmen often believed this official to be unappreciative if not actually hostile to their concepts of air power, they regarded the arrangement as highly unsatisfactory. The experience of World War I, when the users, represented by the Division of Military Aeronautics, and the suppliers, represented by the Bureau of Aircraft Production, were similarly separated, gave ample evidence of the need for closer co-ordination than the existing organization could provide.[56]

The problems of co-ordination and command that disturbed the functioning of the air arm were by no means all external to the Air Corps itself. One of the most difficult questions, one that appeared again and again, was the matter of the relationship of the Washington headquarters to Wright Field—the relationship of OCAC to the Materiel Division. For the first ten years after the passage of the Air Corps Act in 1926, the Materiel Division functioned on a bureau basis as an organic part of the Washington headquarters, though physically located in Ohio. A small liaison staff remained in Washington to handle papers for the remote division, but this staff was a service agency only.

During 1935 and 1936 criticism of the prevailing arrangement led to the creation of a Supply Division in OCAC as the primary advisory agency on matériel for the Chief of the Air Corps. This removed the Materiel Division from its

---

War for Air, see testimony of Chief of Finance *et al.*, in House Hearings on WD appropriation for 1935, January 26, 1934, pp. 59–60, 465–66, and Senate Hearings on same, March 12, 1934, pp. 27–28, as well as Baker Board Report, p. 66.

[55] For a discussion of the various factors influencing policy regarding the chain of command for GHQ Air Force, see AAF Hist Study 10, *passim*.

[56] The precedent from World War I is treated at length in Holley, *Ideas and Weapons*, Chapter IV.

PROCUREMENT LEGISLATION, ORGANIZATION, ADMINISTRATION

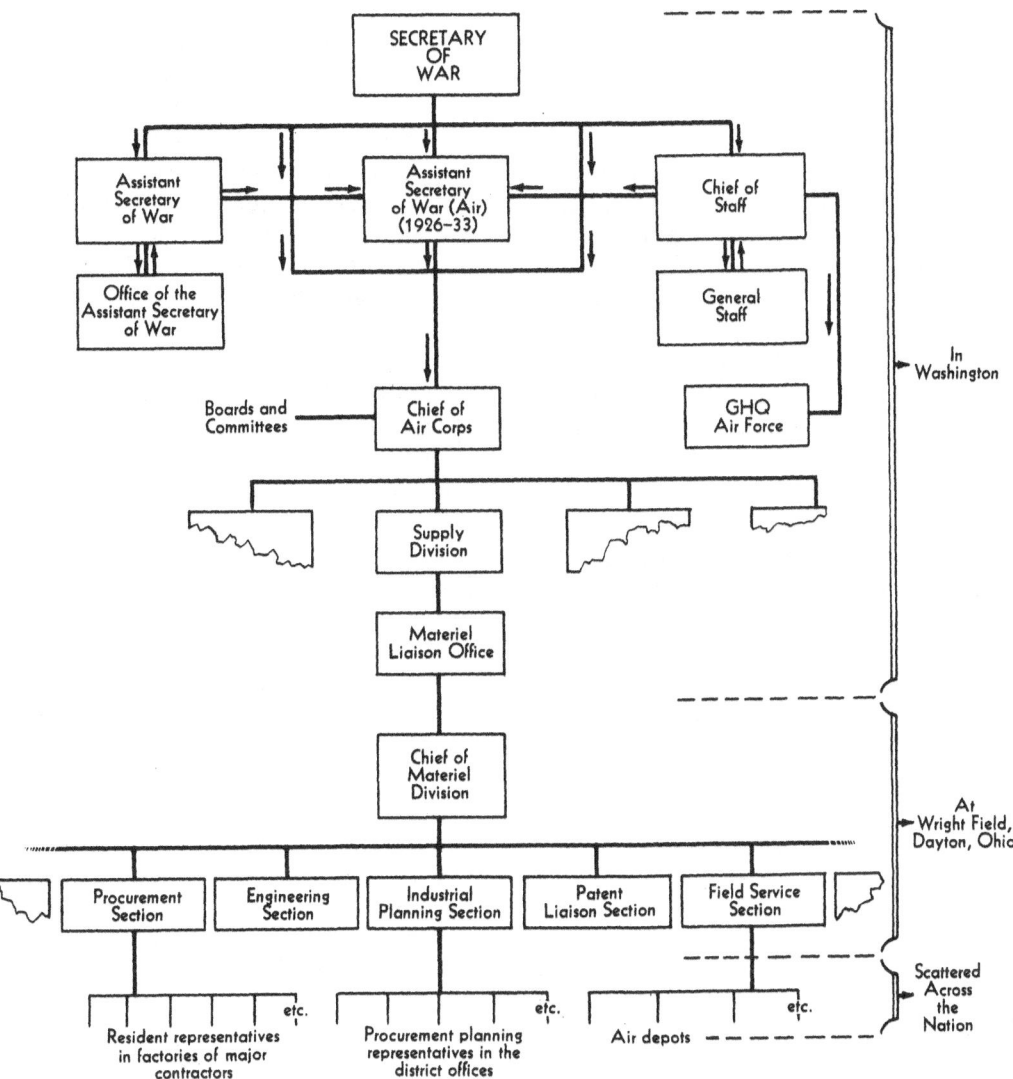

CHART 4—COMPOSITE ORGANIZATION CHART SHOWING THE AGENCIES PRIMARILY CONCERNED WITH AIR MATÉRIEL PROCUREMENT IN THE TWO DECADES AFTER THE AIR CORPS ACT OF 1926

position as the advisory staff for the air arm on matériel matters and led to the anomalous situation in which the Chief of the Supply Division in Washington, a major, exercised more power and made more decisions than did the Chief of the Matériel Division, a brigadier general, at Wright Field. *(Chart 4)* After a year of this system, the Chief of the Matériel Division moved to Washington to assume his rightful role as primary adviser on air matériel matters, retaining both the Supply Division in Washington and the Materiel Division in Ohio with somewhat duplicating functions and a good deal of uncertainty regarding the exact responsibilities of each.[57]

As though the relationship of the Materiel Division to OCAC were not a sufficiently complex problem in itself, in the mid-thirties a General Staff directive complicated the matter still further by ordering the Chief of the Air Corps to reactivate the Air Corps Technical Committee, which had been allowed to fall into disuse. The prevailing Army Regulation on technical committees for the arms and services in general left the precise powers of the committees vague and ignored the special circumstances raised by the widely differing organizations upon which such committees were imposed. The new Air Corps Technical Committee was to begin operations by confronting the Chief of the Air Corps with an interesting problem in command: he had to determine between the relative merits of the recommendations of the Technical Committee on one hand and the Materiel Division on the other.[58]

As a result of organizational uncertainty and instability, the system for procurement was forever in flux. Officers were so occupied accustoming themselves to new administrative arrangements that they found little opportunity to perfect the operation of the minor mechanics in the procurement system. The whole procedure for procurement never really became a well-oiled routine. This situation was further complicated by the high rate of turnover in personnel. To acquire only the barest rudiments in the extremely technical area of administration involved in monitoring an experimental engineering program, conducting aircraft design competitions, and negotiating contracts requires long years of training and experience. Rapid turnover in personnel militated against the training of a highly proficient staff of procurement specialists save where civil service employees supplemented the military staff.

Even if the philosophy implicit in the Army practice of assuming that assignment confers competence is correct, it must be recognized that the individual officer assigned to procurement duties, competent though he may have been, found the frequent shifts in organization confusing. And, as a result, few officers could be expected to understand the full implications of the operations they conducted. Thus, despite the well-nigh continual search for improved organization and administration that marked the growth of the Air Corps in the decade before the war, there remained a number of inadequacies in the staff.

Some Staff Difficulties

Perhaps no single shortcoming of the air arm was more crucial than its apparent inability to handle legislation advantageously. And the formulation of legislation, whether seeking enlarged appropriations or a revision in the statutes

---

[57] AAF Hist Study 10, pp. 55–58.
[58] TAG to CofAC, 24 Oct 36, AFCF. See also AC Project Rcds, folder 18, Policies, Procedures and Organizations Governing Supply Functions of the Mat Div (Lyon Papers).

PROCUREMENT LEGISLATION, ORGANIZATION, ADMINISTRATION 105

governing purchasing, was of central significance to procurement.

Among the several staff divisions of OCAC, the Information Division might be expected to have played an active part in handling legislation for the Air Corps. It did not do so. The Information Division, as its name suggests, was an office for handling information, not for evaluating it. The use of the word *information* in place of *intelligence* in the division title is highly significant. The Military Intelligence Division of the General Staff, G-2, fought vigorously in the between-war years to prevent any encroachment upon its functions by the arms and services. For this reason OCAC never developed an agency to perform the intelligence function in the fullest sense of the word. As a consequence, the Information Division did little concerning legislation but maintained a reference file of current bills and reports. There was no effort to provide the air arm with strategic and tactical intelligence concerning the highly important battles on Capitol Hill. At best, the Information Division before the war was scarcely more than a public relations office and a convenient reference library for OCAC.[59] In general, all questions of legislation were referred to the Plans Division for consideration.

No single unit of OCAC was more important than the Plans Division. Upon the division's officers hung responsibility for much of the creative planning for the air arm. Unfortunately, the division also suffered from the usual shortage of personnel—as late as 1938 there were only four officers assigned to this vital activity.[60]

There were able officers in the Plans Division, but ability alone was no substitute for effective procedures in handling problems. Especially was this true in the involved business of legislation. Plans officers themselves were aware of the deficiencies in their office routine for dealing with legislation.[61] They realized that some sort of system was essential since the number of bills churned out by a single Congress was often staggering. In one session, for example, Plans officers found themselves confronted with more than 140 bills to study, and, where the bills moved forward, they had committee reports and amendments in the House and Senate to watch with care and report upon.[62]

Plans Division officers tried to formulate standing operating procedures for use in processing legislation, but there were no real specialists in the subject.[63] In general, work on legislative matters was just an additional duty. When confronted with highly technical problems such as the legal aspects of procurement, Plans officers tended to look about for experts on whom to rely. In the matter of legal questions, with which procurement legislation abounded, perhaps not unnaturally the Plans officers turned to the lawyers most readily available, officers with commissions in the Judge Advocate General's Department assigned to

---

[59] AAF Hist Study 10, p. 26.

[60] *Ibid.*, pp. 36-38.
[61] Memo, Actg Chief, Plans Div, for CofAC, 28 Dec 35, AHO Plans Div 145.91-31.
[62] Memo, Chief, Plans Div, for CofAC, 26 Nov 35, AHO Plans Div 145.91-31.
[63] OCAC Office Memo, 10-27, 18 Feb 36, AHO Plans Div 145.91-30.

the Patent Section of the Supply Division or the Materiel Division. The opinions rendered by these patent lawyers on the legal points raised in pending legislation on procurement, as one might suspect, frequently tended to be highly technical, narrowly defined, and legalistic. Without in any way disparaging the talents of the lawyers, their outlook was extremely cautious and, as the subsequent discussion of procurement legislation shows, the interests of the air arm were at times adversely affected as a result. Opinions legally sound might satisfy a judge but they leave a congressman unmoved. For want of legislative specialists, air arm legislation suffered.

There were civilian specialists on procurement at Wright Field, men widely familiar with the intricacies of procurement legislation, but Wright Field was far from Washington. When the Plans Division found it necessary to report on a measure before action by Congress, often there was no time to refer the matter to the trained staff at Wright Field, and Plans officers had to act as best they could with commensurately inadequate results.[64]

The net result of these several circumstances was to leave the Plans Division a faulty instrument for dealing with legislation, especially procurement legislation originating outside the Air Corps. Throughout the prewar years there was an elaborate administrative hierarchy extending on down from the Secretary of War to guide procurement, but for all the achievements of these tiers of agencies, they were weak in at least one vital respect: they failed to establish adequate devices to deal with the essentially political problems underlying the procurement of air matériel. This circumstance made the tasks of procurement officials immeasurably more difficult.

The Administration of Procurement

An Air Corps study prepared in the mid-thirties, in an elaborate chart purporting to trace the exact formalities that resulted in the procurement of aircraft in quantity, described the chain of events that led from the idea for an aircraft to the finished product.

First, a tactical unit initiated a request for a new item of equipment. The request was then studied by the Air Corps Board, where the idea was considered in terms of its relationship to doctrine. On the basis of this analysis, the Air Corps Technical Committee propounded a statement of military characteristics—desired attributes such as speed, load, range, armament—which the committee sent to the General Staff for approval. If the General Staff found the proposed statement of military characteristics acceptable and within the scope of official Army doctrine, the approved paper was returned to the Technical Committee, where a development project was officially set up and the Engineering Section of the Materiel Division was authorized to procure a design either by direct purchase or by holding a design competition as prescribed in Sections 10a–10i of the Air Corps Act. If the resulting design was approved by the Technical Committee, the Engineer-

---

[64] See, for example, the action of OCAC on S. 215 (the Logan Bill), 74th Cong, 1st sess, WFCF 334.8 and 032, 1935, *passim*.

ing Section proceeded to purchase an experimental item with the assistance of the Procurement Section. If tests by the Engineering Section showed the experimental item to be acceptable, it was approved for trial. Then, if the General Staff and the Assistant Secretary of War gave their assent, the Procurement Section prepared a contract for a service test quantity, that is, the number of aircraft deemed necessary to secure an adequate test of tactical suitability in the field. This number ranged from three or four to a full squadron of thirteen or more depending upon the type of aircraft and the novelty of its design. When the tactical unit in the field completed its service test, its recommendations went to the Technical Committee where, if the evidence warranted, a decision was made to recommend the aircraft for standardization, another way of saying that the committee recommended the aircraft for purchase in quantity. If the General Staff and the Assistant Secretary of War approved, the Engineering Section recorded the design in its book of standards and, when funds became available, the Procurement Section proceeded to procure in quantity.

The elaborate ritual described may look very official and impressive, but it is doubtful if any airplane ever followed the route there prescribed. The specified procedure, like most complicated prescriptions, does not reflect reality. It is at once too simple and too complex. It does not begin to show the many concurrences and authoritative approvals required at stages along the way. The purchase of an experimental item was never a simple matter between the Engineering and Procurement folk at Wright Field. With a formal development directive in hand from the Technical Committee, it was still essential to secure the approval of a number of other officials such as the budget officer.[65] And even after a contract had been negotiated, it did not become valid until forwarded to the Chief of the Air Corps who, by law, had to secure the approval of the Secretary of War.

On the other hand the route set forth in the Air Corps study is idealized and unrealistic in that it prescribes a procedure far too regular and stereotyped. In practice many of the steps were omitted. The functions assigned to the Technical Committee, for example, were often taken over by the Chief of the Air Corps relying upon advice from the Materiel Division, and more often than not ideas for new aircraft originated elsewhere than with the tactical units.[66] Yet, for all of these discrepancies, the study illustrates clearly, if perhaps imperfectly, how much emphasis air arm officials placed upon authorization and co-ordination.

Procurement officials, living always in the shadow of congressional investigation, were particularly insistent upon getting formal authorizations and approval of their decisions by higher authority. They were equally zealous in co-ordinating with all appropriate agen-

---

[65] See, for example, Actg Chief, Mat Div, to CofAC, 16 Mar 35, WF Proc and Contract files, 360.01. See also, Materiel Division study concerning development, standardization, and procurement planning... [1936], AF Documentary Reference and Research Br, document file, Doc 13/US/14.

[66] For a rather different version of the route from idea to aircraft, see Mat Div Bull No. 30, 30 Aug 35, AF Doc Reference and Research Branch doc file, Doc 13/US/11.

cies. Co-ordination, as any staff officer knows, all too often means getting a signature scratched upon a document even though the signer has little idea of its contents. Officials concerned with procurement repeatedly issued directives perpetuating and even enlarging the practice since officers in each echelon hoped to spread responsibility as broadly as they could and if possible shed it entirely either up or down the line in the event of a kickback.

Some of the required co-ordinations and approvals were entirely necessary, but whether they resulted from necessity or from a desire to provide self-defense, the number of steps in the processing of paper work for procurement seemed always to grow greater. As a result, the already inherently complex pattern of procurement tended to consume increasingly longer periods of time between the inception of a design and the day when it reached mass production.

By the end of 1937 the average time lapse between idea and aircraft was five years. At least six months went into the formulation of specifications for an aircraft desired to meet a particular tactical need. One or two years more passed during the development of an experimental item for evaluation, which was itself a time-consuming process. Service tests by tactical units often required another six months to two years, and at every step in between these operations there were delays of greater or lesser duration as papers shuttled through the in and out baskets at each staff echelon.[67]

Five years was only an average figure. Actually, the elapsed time varied widely depending upon the particular form of procurement involved, for the time required to conduct a formal design competition was obviously far greater than that required to buy an aircraft already perfected by a manufacturer and available for purchase on a sole source basis.[68]

One prolific source of delays lay in the change orders frequently encountered in contracts for experimental aircraft. When in the course of such a contract the manufacturer devised changes in design or construction that improved the product, the government's interest was clearly served if the improvement could be incorporated, regardless of the specifications. But who was to pay for such modifications? While the contractor was always anxious to improve his product, there was a limit on the number of changes he could undertake without running his costs above the price set in his contract. Where air arm officials felt the proposed modification was not only desirable but essential, they would consent to a change order that virtually amounted to an amendment of the contract, providing for agreed upon increases in the manufacturer's compensation to cover the cost of the variation over the original specification.

Air arm officers believed that contractors abused the change order privilege on occasion. A contractor could bid low in his initial response to a circular proposal, then, having won the contract, he could proceed to recoup the losses inevitable on his low bid by persuading

---

[67] CofAC, Lecture, Current Procurement and Allied Problems, Army Industrial College, 11 Dec 37, ICAF files.

[68] ESMR 50–101, 31 Oct 34, WFCF, 008 Policy: Procurement.

procurement officers to allow him a number of change orders each with its allowance of increased compensation. To offset the temptation presented by this possibility, the officials who negotiated change orders surrounded them with nearly all of the elaborate procedures of a contract itself. Since a change order involved an expenditure of funds, approval of the highest echelons of authority was required. The net result of all these formalities was an increase in the time between the signing of an initial contract and the delivery of the first item. But paper work, the necessity of securing formal approval and the desired co-ordination, was not the only cause of delay growing out of change orders. There was an element of delay inherent in the negotiation itself. Procurement officers were particularly on guard against the efforts of manufacturers to increase prices unduly by this backdoor route, and in pursuit of this end they ran headlong into manufacturers with precisely the opposite intention.[69] Since anticipated costs in any proposed modification were hard to estimate, the negotiators for the two different interests were sometimes completely unable to agree upon a figure. Meanwhile, precious time sped past and the gap between idea and completed aircraft grew larger and larger.

The gap between drawing board and flying field may not have been of critical importance in peacetime, but in war victory might hinge upon an ability to reduce the span appreciably. The nation that can create new aircraft rapidly and then inject modifications on the assembly line with a minimum of delay and confusion obviously has the advantage. Insofar as procurement officials delayed the process of modification by encumbering it with legalistic requirements and formalities, they set up stumbling blocks that would one day have to be removed when the nation went to war. The rigid time-consuming contractual formalities that grew up in peacetime were utterly unsuited for the demands of war.

At best, the progression from idea to aircraft was a difficult journey. It would have been difficult in a long-established organization where each office was manned by highly skilled specialists with years of experience. How much more involved the task must have been in an organization where the very form of the structure as well as the rules of the game seemed to be in an almost continual flux and the officers in charge were subjected to rotating tours of duty. In spite of this serious handicap, the procurement staff at Wright Field did manage to hammer out a number of highly effective operating procedures, most notably those that made possible an objective evaluation of aircraft and aircraft designs submitted by rival manufacturing concerns.

In perfecting administrative tools to assist in the selection of superior equipment, Air Corps officers had a number of historic precedents on which to draw. As far back as 1907, when the Signal Corps called for bids on its first airplane,

---

[69] For an interesting example of a manufacturer's attitude on change orders, see testimony of J. L. Callan, January 28, 1925, in Lampert Hearings, p. 1499ff. For restrictions placed on the free use of change orders, see AC Policy 133 in Digest of Policy, 9 Apr 37, AFCF 161. See also, CofAC to Chief, Mat Div, 13 Dec 35 and 23 Mar 36, AFCF 161.

there was a substantial problem of evaluation.[70] Air officers acquired a great deal of experience over the next thirty years, and by the end of the 1930's they could boast of a system that went far toward fulfilling the ideal of objective evaluation.

The first step in the formal process of evaluation was the appointment of two or three separate boards of officers. The first, composed of pilots, put each airplane entered in competition through a series of tests to determine its maximum performance: speed, rate of climb, service ceiling, endurance, and so forth. The second board was composed of engineering officers who studied each aircraft in competition from the standpoint of engineering and design. They reported on the features that favored ease of maintenance or simplified engine change, on the relative ease with which each airplane in competition might be put into mass production, and so on. The third board, made up of officers from tactical units, evaluated the entrants in terms of their suitability for the specific tactical function expected of them. A transport, for example, would be expected to excel in load-carrying capacity, whereas a fighter might be judged more heavily on high speed and maneuverability. Sometimes both performance and engineering features were evaluated by the same board, but the characteristics evaluated remained as described above.

In a contest amongst a number of airplanes, absolute objectivity in the selection of the best is no doubt unobtainable. The use of three separate boards, each with different personnel, made possible, however, the virtual elimination of errors stemming from an improper relationship between an officer and a manufacturer. Not only did the number of members on each board dilute the importance of any individual member's contribution, the very existence of three separate boards, each representing a different point of view, served to subordinate further the ultimate importance of any single member. Moreover, the boards were not generally appointed until a short time before the actual evaluation, thus reducing the period during which any very purposeful influencing might be attempted by the manufacturers.

Once satisfied that the system of multiple boards provided sufficient safeguards against collusion, procurement officials took further steps to perfect the operation of the boards themselves. With the best of intentions, sincere but inexperienced officers might unwittingly blunder in their evaluation and selection unless guided by a standing operating procedure especially contrived to ensure the highest possible degree of objectivity. Such a procedure actually had been fashioned by the middle thirties. To begin with, each board was required to submit a formal memorandum report on its findings. These staff papers, following a prescribed format, were in themselves a strong incentive to objectivity since they required that all con-

---

[70] The Army's first airplane specification issued 23 December 1907, is found in Charles deForest Chandler and Frank P. Lahm, *How Our Army Grew Wings* (New York: The Ronald Press, [1943]), pages 145–61 and Appendix 6. For an interesting comparison with British techniques of evaluation, see *Army Military Airplane Competition*, 1912, Report of Judges Committee. (A command report available in the Library of Congress.)

PROCUREMENT LEGISLATION, ORGANIZATION, ADMINISTRATION

clusions be deduced from facts presented as evidence in the body of the report. In addition, each board had to use a prescribed formula by which each item in competition could be graded by a system of points ranging down from a maximum of 1,000. For all those characteristics subject to exact measurement, the formula provided a precise conversion into points. For features not susceptible to exact measurement, the board had to assign points arbitrarily. This was not entirely objective, but, since each assignment so made had to be fully justified in the final report in relation to the other competitors, the opportunity for gross injustices in the award of points was substantially minimized.[71]

In practice, understandably enough, the evaluation of aircraft in competition often fell somewhat short of the ideal pattern prescribed. Records of the Materiel Division reveal that many of the boards appointed to appraise aircraft fulfilled the provisions of their directive imperfectly and incompletely. Many of their omissions were undoubtedly attributable to inexperience. Some were the fault of the system itself. For example, the board conducting the engineering phase of the evaluation procedure was required to assess the aircraft at hand in terms of its adaptability to quantity production. With one eye cocked on the ever-present possibility of war, this provision made sense. But what did the board regard as mass production? Was it a dozen units or 50 or 500? Moreover, the board evaluated the aircraft itself, not the manufacturer. Was he equipped with tools and talent, with capital and all the other essentials of mass production? These the boards ignored in making their evaluation even though the Air Corps Act explicitly authorized the Secretary of War to reject any bid if it served the public interest to do so, and an award to a manufacturer unable to produce his winning aircraft in quantity clearly fell within this discretion.

The operation of evaluation boards in the prewar years was indeed imperfect; nevertheless, to minimize the importance of the system for objective evaluation would be a grave error. The real significance in the formulation of a technique for the impartial determination of winners in a competition did not lie in the promotion of honesty and the defeat of favoritism, though these achievements were certainly significant in themselves. Rather, the greater accomplishment lay in the circumstance that the operation of boards tended to free the selection of aircraft from the caprice of command. Subjective selection is no more valid when ordered by men with the full powers of high command than it is when ordered by ill-trained underlings. The procedure for objective evaluation evolved within the air arm made it difficult for responsible officers in the highest echelons to act otherwise than objectively. To be sure, they could overrule a board's decision, but to do so without ample reasons in support was to invite criticism and even congressional investigation—an outcome many officers regarded as the ultimate in disaster.

---

[71] For an account of evaluation procedures, see Mat Div Bull No. 31, 29 Aug 36, AF Doc Reference and Research Br doc file, Doc 13/US/13.

To appreciate fully the significance of a system that went far toward freeing the air arm from decisions made on the whim of individual commanders, one has only to turn to the record of those who have operated without such a system. In this connection the records of McCook Field, the old engineering center of the Air Service before 1926, are both amusing and meaningful.[72] Selection of airplanes seems to have been colored if not dominated by what might be called the joy stick approach of General Mitchell. Still flying in the romantic tradition of World War I or, as old-timers would proudly say, by the seat of his pants, the ever-enthusiastic General Mitchell would leap out of an experimental aircraft, pronounce it a "hot ship" and urge its immediate procurement.

Perhaps an even more telling example of the catastrophe that might follow when the selection of weapons depends upon the will of individuals in high command is the notorious example of the Nazi state during World War II. When Hitler relied upon bare intuition, in reaching vitally important engineering decisions, as he did, for example, in the production of jet fighter planes, disaster followed. Interference of this sort became, as General Henry H. Arnold later declared, a secret weapon highly advantageous to the enemies of Germany.[73]

Without question, the procedures evolved by the air arm to ensure an impartial selection of aircraft played a most important part in assuring the all-around superiority of the weapons chosen.[74] But these and the many other techniques worked out by Air Corps officers were not achieved without heartbreaks and trial and error extending over many years.

---

[72] The old McCook Field records of the engineering center are now filed in a body along with the retired section of the Wright Field Central Files cited herein as WFCF.

[73] Henry H. Arnold, *Global Mission* (New York: Harper & Brothers, 1949), pp. 496, 516. See also, F. D. Graham and J. J. Scanlon, Economic Preparation and Conduct of War under the Nazi Regime, Div WDSS, 10 Apr 46, as well as Military Intelligence Division (MID) reports of 8 and 14 Jun 45 by Captured Personnel and Materiel Branch, OCMH.

[74] For a rather full account of the steps in negotiating a contract, see testimony of General Pratt, House Hearings on War Department appropriation for 1935, February 4, 1934, pages 482–89.

CHAPTER V

Procurement Under the Air Corps Act

Procurement: 1926–34

The Air Corps Act of 1926 contemplated three normal methods of procurement. First, there was the design competition leading to the purchase of one or more aircraft constructed according to the winning design as prescribed in Sections 10a to 10g of the act. Second, there was the provision for experimental contracts in Section 10k, which permitted the Secretary of War to buy any experimental aircraft at his discretion without competition. Finally, Section 10t required competition where aircraft were to be procured on grounds other than those mentioned above, but allowed the Secretary to exercise discretion in determining "the lowest responsible bidder." Still another section, 10q, authorized procurement without competition, but the stipulations of this section were assumed to be of a temporary character applying only to aircraft already reduced to practice from designs presented before the Air Corps Act was passed in 1926.

The normal procedure for procurement contemplated by Representative McSwain and others who helped formulate Section 10 of the Air Corps Act called for the use of the design competition. When the Army needed aircraft it would send out circular proposals asking for the submission of designs. When the designs had been evaluated and a winner selected, a contract could be awarded for the production of a single unit to test its adequacy in practice. If subsequent service tests of a small number of units proved the aircraft satisfactory in the field, a large production order might follow. Occasionally, a manufacturer might present an idea that air arm officials considered to be of sufficient interest to justify immediate procurement, without holding a design competition. For such situations, Section 10k, authorizing purchases to be made at a negotiated price without competition, provided a legal basis for action. Whenever air arm officers found that neither the design competition nor the experimental contract clauses suited the problem at hand, they could resort to Section 10t.

Unfortunately for the air arm, procurement operations conducted "by the numbers," following the apparent intent of the law as expressed by its framers, did not attain the results desired. In practice the idea of design competition proved unworkable, for it yielded nothing more tangible than a paper promise to perform. When circular proposals went out inviting bids on a certain type of aircraft, a whole flood of replies returned to Wright Field. Inexperienced designers were more than willing to dream up aircraft alleged to possess the most superlative flying qualities and performance capabilities—as yet unattained. Until a physical sample or experimental airplane could be built around the winning design there was no telling whether the evaluating board had picked a leader or a lemon. If they chanced to choose a lemon, a great deal of money and time had to be spent before the error could be confirmed.[1]

There were other flaws in the concept of a design competition. The time allowed for replies to a circular proposal, a few months at best, prevented manufacturers from working up realistic plans to accompany their bids. The winning design generally had to be worked out in detail after the original bids had been returned. Actual costs usually outstripped the estimates initially submitted, since the bidders had little or no detailed data on which to base exact price figures. As a consequence, manufacturers usually lost money on airplanes evolved from design competitions.

Since the design competition was unworkable, there was only one thing to do: abandon the use of Section 10a to 10g in favor of the authorizations contained in 10k or 10t, even though this had not been the intent of those who framed the Air Corps Act. Procurement officers began to purchase experimental airplanes under the authority of Section 10k, which is to say, the Air Corps simply contracted for a finished experimental airplane at a negotiated price.[2] But here lay a new source of trouble.

While the negotiated contract resulted in the purchase of a successful airplane more often than did the design competition, manufacturers still lost money. In their zeal to get the air arm to contract for an experimental item they deliberately bid below cost in the hopes of putting such a desirable product in the hands of Air Corps officers that a quantity order would soon be forthcoming. But unlike the provisions of the law that authorized the award of contracts for airplanes in quantity to the winner of a design competition without further advertisement, Section 10k only authorized the purchase of experimental airplanes. The section made no mention of quantity procurement. Whenever the Air Corps wished to procure airplanes in quantity, the language of Section 10t clearly called for competition by means of a new circular proposal and a new evaluation. In following this procedure there would be a strong possibility that a manufacturer other than the designer would submit the low bid and win the contract.

The use of Section 10k to authorize procurement of experimental airplanes followed by the use of Section 10t to authorize procurement in quantity would thus threaten to return the whole question of air matériel procurement to the chaotic and undesirable situation of the period before 1926. If designers were to lose money on experimental aircraft and then be denied an assured oppor-

---

[1] Maj Leslie MacDill to Chief, Mat Div, 13 Dec 29, WFCF 008 Proc.

[2] ESMR 50-12, 17 Feb 32, Present Air Corps Policy Concerning Procurement of Experimental Articles, WFCF 008 Proc.

tunity of recouping their losses with a production order because of the possibility that a rival firm might underbid them, would they be any better off after the passage of the Air Corps Act than they had been before? Manufacturers foresaw the threat and protested.[3]

Judge Advocate General officers in both the Army and Navy agreed that 10k did not sanction the award of contracts for airplanes in quantity without competition.[4] On the other hand, they were inclined to believe that the prohibition on the use of 10k to authorize quantity procurement need not result in such disasters as the manufacturers predicted. After all, they contended, Section 10t granted discretion to the Secretaries of War and Navy. One advisor felt that the very intent of 10t was to dwarf price as a factor in making the award.[5] Another was equally explicit in pointing out that the Secretaries were empowered to consider such factors as quality and the need for an adequate industrial preparedness in addition to low bids.[6] By taking advantage of factors other than price, the military lawyers felt, awards under 10t could be made to the designer even when his bid was not the lowest submitted. No doubt this was sound law, but it turned out to be faulty practice; as one manufacturer put the matter, a Secretary would have to display "an extraordinary amount of courage" if he were to exercise his discretion and award a contract to other than the low bidder.[7]

Manufacturers were not the only ones to protest the possible use of the narrow interpretation of 10t, which emphasized price.[8] Administrative officers within the departments also deplored the tendency. One naval officer bluntly charged that the Secretaries studiously avoided the use of 10t for quantity procurement of aircraft because the "political consequences" made the exercise of discretion required by 10t "intensely distasteful on personal grounds."[9]

In short, regardless of what the law said, administrators did not award quantity contracts on grounds other than low bid because they feared political criticism. With good reason, manufacturers protested that they were heading back toward evil days such as those before 1926. Fearing that they might not win production contracts to amortize their losses from experimental work, prudent firms began to doubt the wisdom of accepting any military contracts for experimental projects.[10] Without willing

---

[3] See, for example, C. M. Keys to Representative Carl Vinson, 31 Jan 27, cited in Pickens Neagle to Vinson, 5 Feb 27, photostat copy in JAG (Army) Gen Rcds Sec, 400.12, 11 Nov 35.
[4] See Memo, Col J. I. McMullen, JAGD, 8 Nov 26, and Memo, Lt M. E. Gross for Maj Gen J. A. Hull, JAG, 10 Nov 26, both in JAG (Army) Gen Rcds Sec 400.12 Proc, 17 Nov 26; JAG (Navy) to SN, 12 Feb 27, JAG (Army) Gen Rcds Sec 400.12 Proc file, 11 Nov 35.
[5] Neagle to Vinson, 5 Feb 27, cited n. 3.
[6] Memo, JAG for ASW, 20 Oct 30, JAG (Army) Gen Rcds Sec 400.12 Proc.

[7] Keys to Vinson, 31 Jan 27, cited n. 3.
[8] Memo, JAG (Maj Gen E. A. Kreger) for Lt Col J. I. McMullen, 15 Sep 30, JAG (Army) Gen Rcds Sec 400.12 Proc.
[9] Memo, Comdr S. M. Kraus, 1 May 31, cited in W. O. Shanahan, Procurement of Naval Aircraft: 1907–1937, Naval Aviation History Unit, vol. XVII, p. 355.
[10] Chief, Mat Div, to CofAC, 3 Sep 30, WF Proc 032 Gen Legislation. For evidence on losses sustained by manufacturers doing experimental work, see President, ACC, to McSwain, 22 Nov 33, app. C in Recommendations on National Aviation Policy prepared for Howell Comm by ACC, 12 Sep 34, AIA file 19.

manufacturers, progress in the quest for superior aerial weapons would be doomed. From this fate there appeared to be no escape unless some loophole could be found to circumvent the difficulty.

Since the procurement provisions of the Air Corps Act seemed to offer no practicable means of securing aircraft in quantity without resorting to competition after an initial experimental order under Section 10k had produced a superior model, there was an obvious solution: amend the law. The chief of the Procurement Section at Wright Field urged that "all possible pressure" be brought to secure an amendment from Congress. The desired result could be obtained very simply by inserting the phrase "with or without competition" in the language of Section 10k where it alluded to quantity procurement.[11] A pair of bills to this effect were drafted,[12] but the chief of the Air Corps refused to support them, confessing quite candidly his fear that any extended discussion of the Air Corps Act in Congress might lead to new legislation restricting the exercise of discretion by the Secretaries even further than was already the case under the statute as it stood.[13] The official Air Corps policy was thus to leave well enough alone—to preserve the existing advantages of the Air Corps Act rather than risk losing all in an attempt to rectify its obvious deficiencies.

An Artful Evasion

The reluctance of the War Department to sponsor amendment of the Air Corps Act meant that some other means had to be found. Actually, there was an out, hitherto unrecognized as such within the provisions of the act, one subsequently labeled an "artful evasion" by critics of the policy. If the Air Corps Act of 1926 failed to contain adequate authority, then procurement officers could turn elsewhere, in particular to the voluminous Army Regulations governing procurement.[14]

Among other provisions, Army Regulation 5-240 prescribed that competition might be avoided in certain special circumstances in which competition was impractical—for example, when the item sought was patented or when the manufacturer of the article was the sole source and no similar or suitable item could be procured elsewhere. By construing Army Regulation 5-240 to define the

---

[11] Chief, Procurement Sec to Exec, Mat Div, 11 Sep 30, and to Chief, Mat Div, 8 Dec 30, WF Proc 032 Gen Legislation.

[12] H.R. 11569 and S. 4531, 72d Cong, 1st sess, April 1932. Both bills died in committee. H.R. 9359, 70th Cong, 1st sess, was an earlier effort to amend 10k, apparently sponsored by the Navy. This bill also died in committee. For a brief note on the content of these bills, see Notes on the Chronology of Section 10 . . . (Air Corps Act). **AF Documentary Reference and Research Br, Doc 13/US/9.**

[13] 2d Ind, OCAC to TAG, 9 May 32, basic, McSwain to SW 29 Apr 32, WF Proc 032 Gen Legislation. For an example of air arm fears that new legislation would "open the door" detrimentally, see 1st Ind, Exec OCAC to Chief, Mat Div, 11 Jan 30, basic Chief, Mat Div, to CofAC, 3 Jan 30, WFCF 032 Legislation 1939. Interestingly enough, about the same time Rear Adm. W. A. Moffett, Chief of the Bureau of Aeronautics, was urging the Secretary of Navy to "leave well enough alone" in the Air Corps Act of 1926. Shanahan, Procurement of Naval Aircraft: 1907–1939, p. 359.

[14] 10th Ind, OASW to CofAC, 24 Aug 27, basic unknown, quoted in "Notes on the Chronology of Section 10 . . ." (Air Corps Act). See also, 6th Ind, OASW to TAG, 29 Jul 27, JAG (Army) Gen Rcds Sec 452 Aircraft, 12 Jul 27 file.

PROCUREMENT UNDER THE AIR CORPS ACT 117

manufacturer of an experimental aircraft purchased under Section 10k with a negotiated contract as a sole source, procurement officers found a means of authorizing the award of production contracts without resorting to competition.

The history of a single well-known aircraft design in the early thirties illustrates this policy.[15] Glenn L. Martin designed and built the Martin XB–10, a twin-engine bomber, for the Air Corps. The Martin experimental contract came under the authorization of Section 10k of the Air Corps Act. The price was negotiated. Since the first or experimental item showed promise, air arm officials purchased 10 more items, designated YB–10, to conduct service tests. These, too, were procured at a negotiated price under the authorization of Section 10k, since the quantity was limited and the item was still experimental in many respects. Each successive item coming off the assembly line in this service test order was modified in one way or another as Martin engineers and designers corrected minor deficiencies and introduced novel features improving on the original design. By the end of the service test phase, the B–10 represented an advanced design reflecting the accumulated experience of the manufacturer with that particular type of aircraft.

Clearly, Martin had become a sole source. No other manufacturer could take the original design purchased under Section 10k and reproduce the same airplane exactly. Much of the art wrapped up in the B–10 lay in the experience of Martin engineers and could not be committed to drawings. Procurement officers might then readily certify that there was no counterpart in the commercial world and that no other suitable similar article was obtainable. Whereupon they would be free to authorize a production contract under the provisions of Army Regulations 5–240 referring to procurement without competition.[16]

In terms of dollars expended, the record of purchases made during the years from 1926 to 1934 clearly reflects the extent to which the air arm procurement officers managed to conduct their operations without resorting to the destructive competition so detrimental before 1926. After spending well over $16,000,000 in experimental contracts under 10k, procurement officers negotiated contracts involving more than $22,000,000 under the terms of Army Regulation 5–240, which permitted noncompetitive purchases from a sole source. But what of the alternative, Section 10t, which imposed the necessity of competition? Between 1926 and 1934 the air arm procured scarcely more than $750,000 worth of matériel under the terms of this clause.[17]

A year-by-year analysis of the types of legal authorization employed in air arm contracts after 1926 points up even more vividly the extent to which procurement officers used negotiated contracts rather than competitive contracts. During 1927 virtually all contracts used the authorization contained in 10q. Of the 389 aircraft on contract in 1928, all but one used the "sole source" authorization for negotiated contracts. Virtually the same pat-

---

[15] *Aircraft Yearbook, 1934*, pp. 125–26.

[16] Memo, Chief, Proc Sec for Chief, Mat Liaison Sec, with Incls, 1 Jun 34, WFCF 334.8 Hearing, 1935.
[17] "Notes on the Chronology of Section 10 . . ." (Air Corps Act).

Martin B-10

tern recurred from 1929 through 1931. Of 413 aircraft put on contract in 1932, not one was advertised competitively.[18]

Procurement officers obviously had perfected means of circumventing the insufficiencies or the inadequacies of the Air Corps Act. But in finding legal justification to avoid competition in placing contracts, the officers were in no way guilty of any clandestine evasion of the law. Each year the annual report issued by the Assistant Secretary of War received wide public distribution. Contained in every such report was a tabular listing of all contracts awarded for air matériel. Each contract showed the legal basis for the award. Moreover, every contract signed by procurement officers was duly reported to Congress. Less they could not do, for Section 10m of the Air Corps Act specifically required full and itemized reports to Congress on every contract signed. From 1926 to 1934, year after year, the air arm made each contract for air matériel a matter of public record in the annual report on procurement sent to Congress.

An impartial observer could scarcely help but conclude that the forms of law had been duly observed. Nonetheless, in January 1934 the Washington *Post* published a report that grave charges of irregularities in air arm procurement were about to be laid before the House. The *Post* report was a signed feature article, but it gave no source for its accusations, which can be summarized in a single quotation from the whole text: "Over the protests of Comptroller General McCarl with Congress ignorant of what was going on, the War Department for seven years has been procuring aircraft for the Army Air Corps in contravention of the intent of the sponsors of the act of 2 July 1926. . . ."[19]

The accusation of wrongdoing in the Air Corps implied that the law had been evaded and procurement officers had indulged in the "crime" of negotiated contracts. The charge that air arm officers had hoodwinked Congress was patently

---

[18] Unsigned Memo on JAG letterhead, sub: Procurement Under the Air Corps Act, 11 Apr 34, JAG (Army) Gen Rcds Sec 452.1 Aircraft.

[19] Washington *Post*, January 27, 1934.

PROCUREMENT UNDER THE AIR CORPS ACT

false; each of the contracts negotiated was legal, but, accurate or not, the damning allegations were sufficiently serious to suggest the need for careful investigation. When Congress did turn attention to the indictment of wrongdoing, charges and countercharges, investigations and recriminations rained down with the fury of a cloudburst.

Congressional Cloudburst

The wave of congressional criticism that seemed about to inundate the air arm began in January 1934 when the House Military Affairs Committee started routine hearings to weigh the respective merits of the various bills placed in the legislative hopper at the opening of the session.[20] It became evident to War Department observers that Congress was in an unusually aggressive mood. Hearings that had been scheduled to consider strengthening the Air Corps along the lines proposed by the Drum Board soon began to expand into problems far beyond the scope initially contemplated.[21]

The Merchants of Death

To reconstruct the atmosphere in which Congress conducted the air arm hearings of 1934 one need not go far afield. Since the preceding fall Senator H. D. Black of Alabama had been conducting an investigation of the federal subsidies received by private airmail contractors. The senator pushed his attack with the zeal of an ambitious district attorney, and soon the headlines were reporting accusations of scandalous profiteering by airline firms abusing government subsidies.[22] The public was left with the impression that most if not all of the big airlines were guilty of gross plundering. Since many of the leading aircraft manufacturers were linked by corporate ties to the airlines, the brush that tarred the airlines tarred the manufacturers as well. Rightly or wrongly, the Black investigations brought the aircraft manufacturers into generally low repute.

In similar fashion the so-called Pecora hearings impaired the prestige of the aircraft industry. Justice Ferdinand Pecora of New York, investigating stock exchange practices for a Senate committee, struck a glancing blow at the industry by uncovering what many felt to be grave abuses practiced by financiers rigging the market in aviation stocks for the advantage of insiders.[23] The evidence uncovered was sparse and concerned only a few people, but the disclosures appeared at a crucial moment, for this was precisely the time when the press and the public were in hot pursuit of war profiteers. Only a few months earlier a War Policies Commission, at the request of Congress, had studied the

---

[20] For example, H.R. 7413, H.R. 7601, and H.R. 7657, all introduced by Representative McSwain. See also New York *Times,* January 7, 1934, p. 10, and February 21, 1934, p. 10.

[21] SW to McSwain, 21 Feb 34, mimeo copy in National Archives, Rcd Group 94, AGO central files, box 249, file 031-032.

[22] Hearings before Special Com on Investigation of Air Mail and Ocean Mail Contracts, Senate, 73d Cong, 2d sess, pts. 1-9.

[23] Banking and Currency Com, Senate, 72d Cong, Hearings on *Stock Exchange Practices.* See especially, pts. 6 and 16, *passim,* March 1933 and March 1934.

record of profit making in World War I.[24] While the Pecora hearings were still under way a sensational book entitled *Merchants of Death* came off the press.[25] It was but the best known of many works charging the munitions makers with evil intent. The munitions makers, according to the critics, would supply everything for a war "from cannons to a *casus belli*" in their selfish pursuit of profits.[26]

Against the background of fear, mistrust, accusation of wrongdoing, outright peculation and plundering of the public treasury, alleged or proven, Congress considered budgets for the military services. A more inopportune time could scarcely have been found.

From the military view, the first real misfortune arising from the suspicious mood of Congress fell upon the Navy. Testimony presented at the hearings on the Navy's appropriation bill in January 1934 brought out evidence to show that at least one manufacturer holding a Navy contract for air matériel during the boom years had reaped profits in excess of 43 percent on the sum of the contract.[27] The reaction was immediate. Already aroused to the menace of profiteering, House members were quick to take up the scent, and soon a committee was busily investigating the Navy's procurement procedures. Subsequent findings by the committee revealed that the enormous earnings were confined to an isolated instance where one engine manufacturer had indeed made excessive profits but only for a short period.[28] It took time to bring out such clarifications, and meanwhile the damaging charges of profiteering continued to rankle in the minds of congressmen as headlines played the allegations for all they were worth.

When the Chief of the Air Corps followed his Navy opposite number to the Hill to present his budget for the ensuing year, he found the congressmen armed with questions suggested by the recent disclosures and allegations. Maj. Gen. Benjamin D. Foulois, the incumbent chief of the air arm was a vigorous advocate of air power. He enjoyed a record of many years of honorable service, but he was not noted for his tact.[29] When the committee fired questions at him, he responded to them bluntly and without guile. In reply to a query he asserted, "We generally negotiate contracts." This was literally true, but the truth might have been explained in its proper context if the general had wished to continue the practice. He apparently did not realize the extent to which the "negotiated contract" had become anathema on the Hill in recent months. This

---

[24] See app. I in report of SW for fiscal year 1932, and Proceedings of War Policies Comm, H Doc 163 and Misc H Doc 271, 72d Cong, 1st sess.

[25] H. C. Engelbrecht and F. C. Hanighen, *Merchants of Death* (New York: Dodd, Mead and Co., 1934).

[26] The quip is from "Arms and the Men," *Fortune*, March 1934.

[27] House Hearings on Navy Dept appropriation for 1935, January 2, 1934, pp. 421–22.

[28] Naval Affairs Com, House, Hearings, item 6, *Information as to the Method of Awarding Contracts for Ships and Aircraft for the U.S. Navy*, January 24–February 2, 1934, in *Sundry Naval Legislation 1933–34*.

[29] For an example of the vigorous expression of the Chief of the Air Corps, see Washington *Post*, April 1, 1933, report of his testimony before the House Military Affairs Committee, and the reaction to this report in Memo, Chief, Budget and Legislative Planning Branch, for General Drum, 1 Apr 33, in National Archives, Record Group 94, AGO central files, box 211, file 011.

PROCUREMENT UNDER THE AIR CORPS ACT

in itself might not have stirred up much trouble, but the general took the bait a second time. In response to a leading question he asserted that it was air arm policy to procure from already established concerns.[30] The congressmen were left to infer from this that the Air Corps favored big business rather than small business and dealt by preference with the insiders. Such a remark dropped in the context of recurrent charges of fraudulent stock market deals and illicit procurement practices was scarcely calculated to calm congressional fears.

Still later, when discussion revealed that procurement officers allowed a 15-percent profit margin in negotiated contracts, the fat was fairly in the fire.[31] For critics of air arm policies, here was "evidence" to justify investigation.

If congressmen began to feel that surely something must be wrong with the system of procurement or the men who ran it, their attitudes were perhaps understandable within the context of the times. General Foulois testified on 14 and 15 February 1934. Only three or four days earlier the President had, as a consequence of the disclosures of the Black Committee, canceled the airmail contracts held by the privately owned airlines. Until some permanent solution appeared, he ordered the Air Corps to carry the mails. Scarcely a week later one of the Army pilots assigned to the mails died in a crash. Shortly thereafter there was another crash, and then another. Each successive death seemed to reinforce the suspicions of the congress-

GENERAL FOULOIS

men and to confirm the allegations of the scandalmongers by linking the profiteering of the airlines to the inferior airplanes operated by the Army. For this reason alone, the Air Corps could expect a thoroughgoing investigation, but worse was yet to come.

The Delaney Committee

When the cry of profiteering on Navy contracts first appeared, Representative Carl Vinson, the experienced chairman of the House Naval Affairs Committee, launched an immediate investigation with a subcommittee headed by Representative J. J. Delaney of New York. After two months of listening to a

---

[30] House Hearings on WD appropriation for 1935, February 14, 1934, pp. 478-79.
[31] *Ibid.*, p. 551, February 15, 1934.

parade of witnesses and accumulating some 800 pages of recorded testimony, the committee published a final report.[32] Its findings were in sharp contrast to the charges of profiteering and corruption that had led to the investigation in the first place. The profits made by contractors doing business with the Navy on air matériel, the committee found, were "moderate and reasonable." Aircraft manufacturers had garnered an average of only 11.5 percent on their costs before state and federal income taxes. Navy procurement policies were not only free from taint of collusion, the committee reported, but were also "prudent and practicable," inducing keen competition even in a limited field. In fine, the investigators learned, as had the Lampert and Morrow groups before them, aircraft "cannot be handled in exactly the same way as . . . commodities in an open market." Sometimes negotiated contracts were essential.[33]

Had the public at large and the members of Congress all read the report of the Delaney Committee with its temperate findings, the furor over the procurement of air matériel might have abated rapidly. This was not to be the case. The headlines charging the Navy with laxity and accusing manufacturers of profiteering made more lurid reading than did a sober recital of facts in statistical array. The charges made exciting copy for nearly a month; the denials issued by the committee exonerating the Navy and the manufacturers made copy for but a single day. While the New York *Times* made a front page story of Congressman Vinson's decision to investigate huge profits in Navy contracts, the report of the committee over two months later was buried far back on the fifteenth page.[34]

The unfavorable cast of public opinion was still further distorted when a single member of the Delaney Committee accused the majority of whitewashing the Navy and filed a minority report contradicting the findings of the group. The author of the minority report spread his case in the *Congressional Record*, while the report of the majority remained virtually buried in a hard-to-find publication of miscellaneous hearings. As so often before, the newspapers picked up the sensational minority report and gave it a play. The New York *Times* quoted the author in declaring that "new evidence" of illegal procurement had been turned up, but refrained from analyzing the "new evidence."[35] Had they wished to do so, the members of the committee majority might easily have demonstrated that the minority report was misleading because it rested upon dubious premises and made flatly contradictory recommendations.[36] Nonetheless, they remained silent. The sensational minority report stood uncontroverted, and the public at large was left to believe what it wished. As a consequence, the issues at hand became thoroughly confused.

---

[32] Delaney Hearings and Delaney Report, items 18 and 37, respectively, in *Sundry Legislation Affecting the Naval Establishment 1933–34*, cited n. 56, ch. II, above.

[33] Delaney Rpt, pp. 1470–71. Delaney Hearings, pages 1113–36, contains discussion of the committee in framing the report.

[34] New York *Times,* January 30 and March 9, 1934.
[35] *Ibid.*, March 19, 1934.
[36] Delaney Rpt. See also, *Cong Rcd*, May 30, 1934, pp. 10034ff.

A Confusion of Issues

As soon as the Delaney Committee began to probe Navy procurement practices, there were demands for a similar investigation of the Army. One congressman demanded to know if the Air Corps allowed its contractors to reap immense profits such as those mentioned in the Navy investigation.[37] Another complained that unbeknownst to Congress, air arm procurement officers were violating the Air Corps Act of 1926. "We had not the slightest idea that practically every bid is let without real competition."[38] Yet another asserted positively (and quite erroneously) that the United States ranked eighth among the nations of the world in the number of aircraft engine factories. This "very backward position" he attributed to the "bankers' control of the American aviation industry." All this, the speaker felt, demonstrated the existence of a giant "air trust," a combination that set the high prices government procurement officers were obliged to pay.[39]

Some of the charges aired in and out of Congress were too vague to be denied. Yet, taken all together, the various claims of wrongdoing added up to a formidable if somewhat confused accusation. There were, of course, a few voices raised in protest over the inaccurate and misleading character of statements repeatedly made, but these attempts at rebuttal were lost in the clamor.[40] As usual, the blackest headlines went to those who shouted scandal and promised spectacular revelations—to be produced in full somewhat later.

Although proposals for reform were numerous, everyone seemed to agree upon at least one point. A thoroughgoing investigation of air arm procurement methods should be held. Representative McSwain, in his strategic position as chairman of the Military Affairs Committee, took advantage of this unanimity of feeling to secure passage of a resolution directing his committee to undertake an investigation of the air arm. The committee, McSwain declared, would endeavor to find how abuses in the procurement of air matériel came about and to frame legislation to prevent their recurrence.[41] The actual work of conducting hearings and gathering evidence fell to an eight-man subcommittee headed by Representative W. N. Rogers of New Hampshire, from whom the group took its popular name.

The Rogers Committee

The committee began its investigation of the air arm in a mood far less hostile than might have been expected from the prevailing temper of Congress. Representative McSwain promised that the investigation would undertake no junketing, nor would it "besmirch any reputation upon hearsay evidence." More significantly, while begging the House to drop all partisan charges, he urged the Congress not to prejudge the case.[42] Amidst the numerous misrepresentations

---

[37] New York *Times*, February 8, 1934.
[38] *Cong Rcd*, March 2, 1934, p. 3617.
[39] *Ibid.*, March 6, 1934, pp. 3863–67.
[40] See especially, remarks of Representative Collins of Mississippi, in *Cong Rcd*, March 8, 1934, p. 4018.

[41] *Cong Rcd*, March 2, 1934, pp. 3613–14.
[42] *Ibid.*

of the allegations of the day, this was welcome objectivity. Moreover, the members of the committee seemed generally to favor the concept of air power, holding that the Air Corps would soon become the first line in the nation's defense if it had not already reached that stature.[43] And, finally, at least two of the committee members had served previously with congressional groups investigating the procurement problem in the air arm.[44] All the auguries indicated a fair investigation would be forthcoming.

When the Rogers Committee opened its hearings, the Chief of the Air Corps requested that the testimony be heard in executive session. The committee obligingly complied. No doubt considerations of military security carried some weight with the members—or the chairman may have recalled the unhappy experience of the Lampert Committee, which suffered from an unscrupulous use of its published hearings as a sounding board for disgruntled claimants against the government. Whatever the motives, the hearings were closed. This decision could not have been easy, since to close the hearings to the press meant to forego a great deal of publicity.

In haste and under pressure conjured up by the temper of the times the Rogers Committee's findings and recommendations were just what one might have expected under the circumstances: a demand for competition on all contracts for procurement in quantity and a return to aggressive design competitions for experimental contracts as contemplated in the original McSwain measure of 1926.[45]

The revisions in procurement policies demanded by the Rogers Committee were one response to the outcry against profiteering, but they were by no means the only response. The several hearings in Congress—investigations by committees and subcommittees in both the House and Senate—produced a number of plans for rejuvenating air arm procurement. Every congressman seemed to have his pet scheme for saving aviation.

Congressional Panaceas

Taken collectively, the numerous proposals suggested for reforming air matériel procurement fell into three or four broad groups. Some felt that greater economy and efficiency would result from a system of joint Army and Navy procurement, but proposals leading to such a scheme soon became involved in the highly controversial question of a department of defense that blurred the focus and tended to drop the procurement question from sight.[46] Some felt that a solution to the problem of air matériel procurement lay in turning the

---

[43] See, for example, the committee's final report in House Rpt 2060, 73d Cong, 2d sess, June 18, 1934, reprinted in Cong Rcd, 74th Cong, 1st sess, June 15, 1935, p. 9384.

[44] Representative Rogers served on the Lampert Committee in 1925, and Representative James was a member of the committee that considered Section 10 of the Air Corps Act in 1926.

[45] Cong Rcd, June 18, 1934, p. 12479, and House Rpt 2060.

[46] This discussion of joint Army-Navy procurement may have induced the President to create by Executive order a co-ordinating agency, the Aviation Procurement Committee, under the Procurement Division of the Treasury. The venture was short lived. WFCF 334.8 Minutes of Aviation Proc Com, 1935.

manufacture of all aircraft and aircraft accessories over to the government. Some merely favored curbs of excessive profits. Still others were sure that only a revision in the laws governing procurement would save the nation from abuses. Each group of proposals deserves consideration in some detail.

Government manufacture of aircraft as a way out of the difficulties over procurement attracted a good deal of attention. Considering the current talk about munitions makers as merchants of death and in view of the diminished prestige of private enterprise near the bottom of a depression, this faith in government-owned factories was scarcely surprising. Something of the bitterness toward "big business" that motivated advocates of government factories was expressed by the congressman who felt that the aircraft manufacturers had made "something like a racket" of Air Corps contracts. Government manufacture, he believed, "would have a good deal to do in preventing war." [47] Since the Navy already had such a facility—an aircraft factory at Philadelphia, which built planes during World War I—attention turned to the utilization of this plant.

There were only a few congressmen who actually advocated production or even the manufacture of any large percentage of military aircraft at the government plant; nevertheless, there were many who seemed to feel that a vigorous use of the Naval Aircraft Factory would serve as an ideal weapon to drive down excessive prices charged by privately owned concerns. In addition, some also saw in the government plant a useful measuring stick by which procurement officers could acquire firsthand information on the actual costs involved in aircraft fabrication.[48] The President himself seems to have toyed with this idea at one time.[49]

For many reasons, however, costs determined in a government plant could not readily be employed to measure private costs. For example, the use of civil service employees imposed a number of special conditions upon federal projects that did not apply in private industry. This consideration alone seriously obscured the cost figures of government plants. In addition, government accounting and budgeting practices did not require federal facilities to carry all the burdens of depreciation, capital costs, maintenance, and overhead costs that are inescapable in a private venture. One Navy spokesman expressed the matter bluntly: costs computed at the Naval Aircraft Factory would be "quite useless" as a check on private industry.[50] Nevertheless, Congress went right ahead and, to the distress of many military officials, tacked a rider on an important naval authorization bill stipulating that at least 10 percent of the aircraft procured should come from government-owned, government-operated plants.[51]

Those who favored profit curbs as a means of preventing abuse in military procurement found a ready audience.

---

[47] Testimony quoted in House Rpt 1506, 73d Cong, 2d sess, May 7, 1934, p. 15.

[48] Delaney Hearings, pp. 952–53.

[49] Actg SW Woodring to President, 29 Nov 35, SW and OASW files, AC Gen Questions.

[50] Note on table prepared by Navy Dept showing record of operations at Naval Aircraft Factory, printed in Minority Rpt by a member of the Delaney Subcom, Delaney Rpt, p. 1473.

[51] 48 Stat 503; 34 USC 494, March 27, 1934.

Had not the papers been filled with reports of fantastic profits in the aircraft industry? Was not the government the major market for aircraft in the United States? Then surely it must follow that the government's laxity in negotiating contracts had served to line the pockets of the manufacturers. Such was the line of reasoning pursued by those who urged a limitation on profits. Obviously, these abuses must end, so, in addition to the 10-percent rider pertaining to the Naval Aircraft Factory that encumbered the naval expansion bill of 1934, Congress put a limit of 10 percent on the profits of all manufacturers with contracts for naval matériel, including aircraft.

Congress accepted the limit on profits in the belief that such a ceiling was necessary to prevent profiteering. But the voices shouting profiteer were more shrill than accurate. The facts revealed a very different story. Over the years from 1926 to 1933, the aircraft manufacturers had not made the fantastic profits claimed for them. The major airframe manufacturers took a profit of 0.2 percent (on cost) of their combined Army, Navy, and commercial sales. Even adding in the far more profitable business of the engine manufacturers, the average profit (on cost) came to but 10 percent on the combined total business.[52] Considering only Air Corps contracts for the years 1926 through 1933, the profits earned by airframe and engine manufacturers were even less, ranging around 9 percent on cost. Moreover, these firms suffered an average loss of 50 percent on cost in experimental contracts.[53] Combining the experimental losses with the production gains produces an average profit of around 8 percent, hardly fantastic. Audits of Navy contracts revealed only slightly higher profits, returning 11.5 percent on costs of combined experimental and production orders.[54] Such figures clearly showed that neither the Army nor the Navy had permitted any wholesale profiteering. Net earnings ranging between 7 and 11.5 percent of costs before taxes were by no stretch of the imagination excessive for such a high risk venture as aircraft manufacturing.[55]

While the 1934 law limiting profits provided for the recapture of all earnings in excess of 10 percent, there was no corresponding floor under losses. If the limit were to be applied in good years, preventing the accumulation of surpluses, how would the manufacturers carry their overhead charges in lean years?[56] Questions such as this the advocates of profit ceilings left unanswered. As a consequence, there were repeatedly voiced proposals in Congress calling for a radical revamping of the existing statutes governing procurement.[57]

The demand for revision of the law was at least in part from responsible sources and could not be ignored. If the law were to be revised, it became relevant to ask, what had been the ob-

---

[52] From tables prepared by Bureau of Supplies and Accounts, Navy Dept, Delaney Hearings, p. 503.

[53] *Ibid.*, pp. 502–03.
[54] *Ibid.*, pp. 1040–41.
[55] Testimony of C. E. Orton, Chief Auditor for AC, House Hearings on WD appropriation for 1935, February 15, 1934, p. 533.
[56] The case against rigid profit curbs is presented in Delaney Hearings, pp. 807, 815–16, 829–30, 1039, 1088.
[57] *Ibid.*, pp. 556, 584–85.

jective of the Air Corps Act? Those who had framed the act asserted a threefold aim: they wished to procure aircraft of maximum performance at a minimum price while at the same time ensuring a healthy aircraft industry as a national resource of advantage in time of danger.

Those who advocated a return to strict competition had a decided advantage—the idea of competition in the award of public contracts was a tradition of long standing. "Competition" was a good word implying equality of treatment and opportunity for struggling small business in the best American tradition. The converse of competition was "monopoly" or "trust." As for "negotiated contracts," it was easy to conjure up pictures of insidious practices, secret meetings, and generally devious doings of a pernicious nature whenever negotiation took place.

Actually, "competition" and "negotiation" tended to become rather careless generalizations and catch phrases. An undue emphasis upon competition could defeat the main objectives that the proponents of the Air Corps Act sought to achieve.[58] Moreover, negotiated contracts were by no means entirely noncompetitive. Engines might be purchased by a negotiated contract on a sole source basis, but they entered into competition indirectly. Aircraft designers specified the engine to be used in any given airframe, and where the aircraft was bought competitively, the engine shared in that competition.[59] Furthermore, even where the Air Corps awarded a contract for an aircraft in quantity at a negotiated price following an earlier experimental order there was competition, albeit indirect. Air arm procurement officers required manufacturers to submit options for production quantities when accepting an experimental order. Thus, even if the subsequent production order was not thrown open for bids there was competition, for the manufacturer recognized that the prices quoted in his production option could have a determining effect upon the purchase of his original experimental aircraft.[60]

After a hasty study touching briefly on most of the proposals discussed above, the Rogers Committee reported out recommendations urging a drastic return to competition. In addition, the committee found the Air Corps "inefficient" and "expensive," while using "various subterfuges" that added up to a "pernicious, unlawful" system of procurement. On top of all this the committee charged the Chief of the Air Corps with gross misconduct, and held him guilty of "deliberate, willful and intentional violations of the law."[61]

Despite the intemperate language of the Rogers Committee report and in the face of the committee's vigorous recommendation for a return to competition in procurement, Congress adjourned

---

[58] The case for negotiating production contracts with the manufacturer of a successful aircraft developed on an experimental contract appears in virtually every important hearing. For the arguments presented in 1934, see Delaney Hearings, pp. 473–75, 693, 724–26, 750–51, 911–12.

[59] Ibid., pp. 464–65; Memo, OASW for CofS, 17 Aug 36, SW and OASW files, AC Gen Questions, item 363.

[60] Delaney Hearings, p. 849.

[61] House Rpt 2060, 73d Cong, 2d sess, June 18, 1934, reprinted in Cong Rcd, p. 9384, June 15, 1935, 74th Cong, 1st sess.

without amending the Air Corps Act of 1926. It may be that mere legislative accident played some part in the decision not to amend the Air Corps Act in 1934. On the other hand, at least a partial explanation of why the congressmen were unwilling to amend the law may be found in the new procurement policy promulgated by the Assistant Secretary of War within the terms of the 1926 act.

New Procurement Policy

The new procurement policy contrived by Assistant Secretary of War H. H. Woodring was, in essence, a return to competition. In his testimony before Congress as well as in his reports to the President and to the public, the Assistant Secretary went out of his way to publicize his decision to insist upon competition. He assured Congress repeatedly that he personally favored competitive contracts with all their safeguards of sealed bids and attendant publicity in preference to the prevailing procedure of negotiated contracts. Indeed, the Assistant Secretary fairly cut the ground from under all those congressmen who advocated radical changes in the Air Corps Act of 1926. In achieving by administrative action what the congressmen hoped to accomplish by statutory mandate, Secretary Woodring spiked their guns and probably forestalled amendment of the Air Corps Act.

The circumstances that induced Mr. Woodring to take a firm stand in favor of competitive procurement reflect one of the dilemmas of air matériel procurement. Interestingly enough, Mr. Woodring's decision to insist upon competition in aircraft procurement antedated the agitation in Congress.

To begin with, as a man of wide legislative experience the Assistant Secretary must have recognized the importance of leaving a complicated piece of legislation undisturbed upon the statute books. After eight years, Section 10 of the Air Corps Act had become an integral part of the air arm. Much of the administrative routine at Wright Field stemmed from its provisions. And these procedures or administrative routines represented a wealth of experience painfully accumulated through mistakes made in applying the Air Corps Act in practice. Perhaps of even greater importance were the many rulings of the Comptroller General, and the legal opinions of the Attorney General and the Army's Judge Advocate General interpreting the Air Corps Act. Since neither the General Accounting Office nor the legal advisors would give rulings or opinions on hypothetical cases in advance, to draft a new law would mean that opinions and rulings would have to wait until specific cases came up for interpretation. In short, since every new statute passed by Congress carries with it the threat of undoing years of work, Mr. Woodring had good reason to seek a solution to his problem by means other than amendment.

To purchase aircraft in production quantities during fiscal 1933, Congress, it will be recalled, appropriated somewhat more than $10,000,000,[62] but the President then impounded $7,000,000 of this sum as an emergency economy measure. Toward the end of the year the admin-

---

[62] See above, ch. III.

PROCUREMENT UNDER THE AIR CORPS ACT

istration's policy shifted, and the Public Works Administration (PWA) agreed to make available to the Air Corps $7,500,000 in relief funds. This sum was slightly larger than that impounded by the President several months earlier, but because of rising costs during the interval it would now buy fewer aircraft.[63]

When the PWA money became available late in 1933, the Air Corps found itself with a shortage of more than 700 aircraft; the planes on hand were not even enough to equip the units already activated.[64] In addition, aircraft were needed to replace equipment rapidly approaching obsoletion. The situation called for prompt action if the air arm was to avoid virtual disarmament, but the need for haste did not cancel the necessity for procuring aircraft of superior performance. For this reason air arm officials decided to follow the same procurement method used during the previous several years. They negotiated production contracts with manufacturers who built aircraft of the highest known performance, justifying their action by affirming that the manufacturer of a superior aircraft was a sole source as defined in Army Regulation 5–240. On this basis the Chief of the Air Corps forwarded a number of contracts to the Assistant Secretary of War for routine approval before obligating the available PWA funds.

To understand the Assistant Secretary's reaction to the Air Corps request one must be aware of the particular circumstances of the period. From the moment the new administration took office in 1933, officials of the War Department were under an increasing pressure from various groups seeking a share in the contracts at the disposal of the government. Federal contracts, once shunned, were now sought. Labor unions and business leaders in dozens of communities urged the Secretary of War to pursue a spread-the-work policy.[65] Aircraft manufacturers were no exception to the rule.[66] As the depression's bite cut deeper, the pressure upon the War Department reached the point where it could no longer be ignored. Just at this juncture the Air Corps sent up the contracts that had been negotiated to obligate the PWA funds. On the heels of the unsigned contracts came two disgruntled manufacturers to complain at being left out when the War Department had $7,500,000 to spend on production model airplanes.[67] The Assistant Secretary, fully aware of the potential danger of their complaints uttered in the prevailing "merchants of death" milieu, refused to approve the negotiated contracts. Instead, he decided to reconsider the whole question of air matériel procurement and its underlying principles.

The dilemma confronting the Assistant Secretary was very real. On the one hand he must be sure to obtain aircraft

---

[63] House Rpt 1506, 73d Cong, 2d sess, May 7, 34, pp. 2–3, and House Hearings on WD appropriation for 1935, February 15, 1934, p. 564.

[64] See above, p. 66.

[65] For examples of the pleas reaching the War Dept, see Members of the Bristol, Pa., Exchange and Rotary Club to Senator J. J. Davis, 15 Jul 32, and Davis to SW, 17 Jun 32, as well as G. B. Cole, Secretary Local 18886 Aeronautical Workers National Union, to SW, 21 Dec 34, WFCF 004.4 Manufacturing, 1939 file.

[66] Annual Rpt of SW, 1934, p. 27, and House Rpt 1506, 73d Cong, 2d sess, May 7, 1934, p. 9.

[67] House Hearings on WD appropriation for 1935, February 15, 1934, pp. 487, 514–15, 519.

capable of the maximum known performance, while on the other he must somehow contrive to retain effective competition as to price. Here was the selfsame difficulty that had confronted the Lampert and Morrow investigators. How could the Assistant Secretary reconcile the mutually exclusive ends of price and performance?

Furthermore, the Assistant Secretary must maintain a large number of aircraft manufacturers in a financially healthy condition as an essential national resource for future periods of emergency. If he attempted to spread the available funds more or less evenly over the industry in an effort to ensure economic health, how could he contract for aircraft of maximum performance at the minimum price? Airplanes purchased on the basis of price competition might lower the cost to the government but would afford no guarantee as to performance. Conversely, airplanes purchased solely on the basis of performance might well and often did cost more than airplanes purchased with competition as to price. In either case the objective of a healthy industry would be ignored, for whether there was competition as to price or performance, the greatest volume of business tended to cluster as a few efficient firms attracted more business than they could handle with dispatch while many other idle firms rolled to the edge of bankruptcy. What procurement procedure could the Assistant Secretary devise to resolve all the conflicting requirements that had troubled air arm officers and congressmen for nearly a generation?

At first, Assistant Secretary Woodring believed that the rules governing federal procurement in general should be applied to air matériel. Further study persuaded him, as it had so many other ardent advocates of competition before, that air matériel constituted a special case. Which is not to say, however, that he conceded his position on competition entirely.

In reply to Mr. Woodring's queries, Air Corps officials claimed that negotiated contracts were absolutely necessary. If they were forced to buy superior airplanes competitively, to be sure of buying the best, they would have to write up a specification that more or less defined the best known aircraft of any given type. This, they protested, would play directly into the hands of the manufacturer who had perfected a particular airplane. He and he alone could bid effectively. Clearly, such a procedure would defeat the desire of the Assitant Secretary to ensure competition. Fortunately for the future of the service, under the Assistant Secretary's prodding, several Air Corps officers managed to work out a procedure for getting around this difficulty. And they did so before 3 January 1934, when the second session of the 73d Congress opened. The Assistant Secretary's new policy was thus formed before the agitations in Congress led to so much investigation of the Air Corps.

The solution contrived by the air arm officers was a relatively simple one. They proposed to let each manufacturer bid on his own specification, and to inject the necessary element of competition they included a speed requirement. But instead of specifying the maximum known high speed or the high speed desired, they stipulated a minimum high speed. Manufacturers submitting entries offering top speeds lower than the minimum established in the invitation would be rejected. The advantage of this arrangement is evident: it permitted competition as to performance while at the same time excluding all but those within a narrow margin of the desired performance.

Furthermore, by limiting competition to those manufacturers who had previously submitted an aircraft (similar to the one they placed in competition) for test and approval by the staff at Wright Field, the air arm could eliminate any bidder whose aircraft was structurally unsafe or failed to comply with the requirements of the *Aircraft Designer's Handbook* regarding the incorporation of standardized accessories and the like. Finally, by requiring bidders to submit a physical sample for test, those who evaluated bids would no longer be troubled with paper promises that failed to materialize. Henceforth, evaluation of bids for production contracts was to be based on actual performance of the sample airplane as tested in flight.

The Assistant Secretary of War thus came to the Hill early in 1934 prepared to report that he had a new policy already in effect. He would approve negotiated contracts under Section 10k of the Air Corps Act only for the procurement of experimental aircraft. For production contracts he would insist upon competition, using the provisions of Section 10t as legal authorization. Hereafter, he assured the congressmen, competition was to be the watchword. Where there was a conflict between price and quality, if the aircraft of highest performance was not the low bidder, the Secretary could avail himself of that provision in 10t authorizing him to make an award on his own discretion "to the best advantage of the Government." By insisting upon the submission of physical samples of aircraft the Secretary could rest his decision upon reports of performance actually demonstrated rather than solely upon a manufacturer's paper claims. Taken all together, the various elements of the new procurement policy appeared to have resolved the basic difficulties of air matériel procurement.

Perhaps the most important attribute to the new policy had nothing to do with its intrinsic characteristics but rather with its timeliness. When the Assistant Secretary appeared before a committee of Congress, which was irate over the alleged profiteering of the aircraft industry, he held an excellent tactical position. He could say that the War Department was already complying with the committee's wishes. Congress need not legislate because the administration's policy provided virtually every safeguard the critics in Congress demanded. In short, Assistant Secretary Woodring managed to forestall amendment of the Air Corps Act because he took the wind out of the congressional sails.

CHAPTER VI

Aircraft Procurement on the Eve of World War II

The New Policy Reconsidered

Broadly considered, the new procurement policy contrived in 1934 by War Department officials under the goad of congressional criticism had one main characteristic: insistence upon competition. Competition was to apply in the procurement of individual experimental aircraft no less than in the procurement of production quantities. In contracts for aircraft in production quantities the real novelty introduced by the new policy was the requirement that all bids be accompanied by a physical sample of the aircraft to be evaluated. Rigorous competition among sample airplanes was to be the watchword of the day. With this in mind, Air Corps officers during 1934 sent out circular proposals to the industry, inviting the submission of bids and samples.[1]

While eager to secure the broadest kind of competition, procurement officers had to make every effort to ensure a high degree of standardization. Since the bids were invited on the basis of a performance specification only, each manufacturer was entirely free in the matter of design. Without some guidance by the Air Corps such a policy could, over a period of years, result in a heterogeneous collection of equipment. To impose a degree of uniformity and standardization, procurement officers provided each bidder with substantial instructions in the form of the *Handbook for Aircraft Designers,* the Air Corps standards book, as well as an index of all pertinent Army, Navy, and federal specifications for materials and subassemblies. Moreover, bidders were required to use government-furnished equipment (GFE) for many accessory installations. Thus instruments, armament, oxygen, communications, and other items could be standardized. The GFE, along with engines and propeller installations often amounted to half the cost of the complete aircraft.[2] By concentrating procurement of GFE in Air Corps hands, it was possible to ensure a high degree of uniformity and interchangeability and to improve the quality of competition as well. By reducing the number of variables in the various sample aircraft offered, the area of competition was narrowed and became commensurately fairer.

---

[1] Service Sec, Proc Div, ATSC, Prewar Procurement by the Air Corps, undated [c. 1946], ICAF Doc file, pp. 12–13. See also, Mat Div Bull No. 30, 30 Aug 35, AF Doc R&R Br, Doc 13/US/11.

[2] House Hearings on WD appropriation for 1935, p. 566.

AIRCRAFT PROCUREMENT ON THE EVE OF WORLD WAR II

Premature Boasts

The Secretary of War was enthusiastic over the new policy for aircraft procurement. Although by his own admission more than two years and a full cycle of procurement would have to pass before any judgment on the new policy would be possible, scarcely twelve months after issuing the first circular proposal for a sample aircraft competition, the Secretary was ready to praise the new procedure. He reported to Congress that the new policy brought out more rather than fewer bidders as some critics had feared. In addition, the samples submitted showed remarkable advances in performance over the types currently standardized in the Air Corps. About ten months later, in June 1936, he reiterated his contention that the policy was a success. In the following year the Assistant Secretary of War spoke out just as emphatically. He stressed the "salutary effect" of the sample aircraft competition and declared the policy "fully justified."[3]

There were, no doubt, some appreciable gains attributable to the wave of congressional criticism and the new policy formulated as a consequence. Probably the most obvious gain appeared in the improved procedures hammered out by procurement officers at Wright Field. Evaluation methods were standardized and made more objective.[4] Office routines were formalized and procurement officers circularized the industry to inform all bidders of the new procedures.[5]

Another gain directly attributable to the trials and tribulations of 1934, although somewhat less immediately a part of the new policy, concerned legislation. After 1934 Air Corps officers displayed a keener appreciation of the need for facing proposed legislation squarely. Rather than depend upon off-the-cuff arguments mustered in the Washington headquarters against bills threatening to upset air arm procurement methods, Air Corps officials learned to send such measures to Wright Field. There, specialists familiar with the complexities of procurement could draft staff papers so well informed as to be overwhelmingly persuasive. When Representative McSwain offered a bill early in 1935 that seemed apt to alter the air arm's procurement policy adversely, the success of the new procedure was evident. A logical, informative staff paper in the form of a memorandum report drafted at Wright Field provided the basis for a convincing reply by the Secretary of War that helped forestall passage of the measure.[6]

Though the new procurement policy of 1934 and 1935 did improve procedures and raise standards of objectivity in evaluation, avoiding some of the worst aspects of the aircraft procurement used

---

[3] SW G. H. Dern to McSwain, Chairman, Com on Military Affairs, House, August 15, 1935, and January 13, 1936, *Cong Rcd*, January 15, 1936, pp. 452–54; *Annual Report of the Secretary of War, 1935*, p. 8, and "Annual Rpt of the Assistant Secretary of War," in the Secretary's annual rpt for 1937, pp. 26–27.

[4] Mat Div Office Memo [draft] 233, 19 Sep 34, WFCF 008 Proc; ESMR 50–74, 23 Apr 34, CADO WF, Doc 13/107. For a glimpse of the confusion characterizing procurement earlier, see ESMR 50–12, 17 Feb 32, CADO WF, Doc 13/87.

[5] AC Policy 168, 17 Sep 35, Digest of AC Policies, OCAC, AF Doc R&R Br, and 2d Ind JAG to ASW, 13 Nov 34, JAG (Army) Gen Rcds Sec 400.12.

[6] See ESMR 50–12, Addendum 3, 1 Apr 35, CADO WF, Doc 13/87, for comments on McSwain's H.R. 6810, 74th Cong, 1st sess, and ASW to McSwain, 25 Apr 35, JAG (Army) Gen Rcds Sec 452.1 Aircraft.

before 1934, a number of problems still remained to be solved. One such centered around the relationship of performance and price. While the new procedures for evaluation improved the degree of objectivity possible in determining the merits of two or more samples as to performance, how could price be equated with performance? To which bidder should an award go when one brought in a markedly superior aircraft at a price considerably higher than the price quoted by his rival with an admittedly inferior aircraft? If performance alone was to determine the selection, the manufacturer who knew his sample to be superior could inflate his price and profit unreasonably. When the Air Corps set out to procure transport aircraft during 1934 just such a problem as this came up, and in answering the questions raised, air arm officers brought the procurement process a long stride forward.

The Transport Case

During August 1935 the Air Corps issued a circular proposal on a transport aircraft, calling for bids returnable in the following year. Three manufacturers, Douglas, Curtiss-Wright, and Fairchild submitted fully acceptable bids and samples, which were evaluated under the new procedures. Douglas, with 786 points, won first place in the competition. Curtiss-Wright, with 692.5 points, and Fairchild, with 599.7 points, lagged far behind, so an order for a production quantity of transports went to Douglas. The new procurement policy seemed to be working smoothly until the time arrived to pay the contractor. When Douglas' contract was submitted for approval, the Comptroller General held up payment on a complaint from Fairchild. Upon investigation the Comptroller found that while the Douglas sample had indeed won the competition in terms of performance, the Douglas bid of $49,500 was nearly twice as high as those of Curtiss-Wright's $29,500 and Fairchild's $29,150. In a competition for production quantities of aircraft, the Comptroller felt that there could be "no proper evaluation" where price was disregarded. Unless the practice of ignoring price were curbed, the Comptroller held, it would be possible for a manufacturer whose sample exceeded those of his competitors by a very few points or a narrow margin of superior performance, to win a contract even though his bid was way out of line on price.[7]

Here once again the Comptroller General was raising the question that had so vexed the framers of the Air Corps Act of 1926. Which was more important, performance or price? If one bought on price alone, then one could not command superior weapons. If one bought on performance alone, then one could not be certain of securing a low price. In raising this question anew, the Comptroller appeared almost to be unaware of the years of discussion already spent on this very point. More significantly, in raising the question in the precise terms he did, the Comptroller appeared to display a lack of understanding of the importance of superior performance in the aircraft purchased for military use. In commenting on the competition between Douglas,

---

[7] Text of Compt Gen decision of February 19, 1936, given in 1936 U.S. Aviation Report 268. See also, Compt Gen to SN, December 16, 1935, quoted in *Cong Rcd*, March 23, 1936, p. 4201.

DC–2 Transports in Production *at Douglas Santa Monica plant, June 1934.*

the high bidder, and Fairchild, the low bidder, the Comptroller found fault because the contract went to Douglas even though the performance of the Fairchild sample was "far in excess of the minimum" performance required by the terms of the circular proposal. That an aircraft merely "in excess of the minimum" required was poor economy indeed when matched against an enemy aircraft designed at the utmost limit of the art seems to have escaped the Comptroller's notice.

A further review of the facts raises additional doubts as to the Comptroller General's appreciation of the problem at hand. To begin with the initial circular proposal had announced that the "figure of merit," or performance rather than price, would be the "primary consideration" in making the award. Thus the bidders knew before they entered that the competition would center around performance and not price. Moreover, much of the disparity in price between the Douglas entry and those of the other two companies was rendered irrelevant by the fact that the Douglas entry was a twin-engine transport whereas both the other competitors offered single-engine designs. Further, the Douglas sample at the time of the competition was already in production as the DC-2 (Air Corps C-32), the immediate lineal predecessor of the famous DC-3, or C-47, the work horse of World War II fame. In fact, the sample evaluated was actually borrowed by Douglas for that purpose from a commercial airline customer.

Even so, the Comptroller's protests could not be ignored. To secure the matériel essential to the air arm, officials in each echelon of the procurement organization had to meet the challenge represented by the Comptroller's opinion. The differing reactions of officers in the several organizations concerned with procurement not only provide a cross-section appraisal of the many points of view regarding the nature of aircraft procurement but also spell out the complexities of that process.

At Wright Field the officers who helped evaluate the sample aircraft in the transport competition were men in close contact with tactical operations. They were in many instances the men who would themselves use the equipment purchased. They had no doubt about what they wanted. The Douglas aircraft was superior, so they selected it as the winner even though it was more expensive. In short, the pilots in the field wanted the best available.

In Washington, the Chief of the Air Corps viewed matters in a somewhat different perspective. As the individual responsible for the success or failure of air arm operations, the Chief of the Air Corps was understandably reluctant to buy the more expensive Douglas aircraft when to do so meant getting eighteen units rather than the thirty-six originally contemplated when the budget was set up nearly two years earlier. This in turn would mean falling further than ever behind the authorized strength established for the air arm. While the Chief of the Air Corps undoubtedly wanted the best equipment he could get, he could not ignore the annual hearing on appropriations where he must face congressional critics who would demand to know why the arm failed to reach aircraft strength authorized after Congress had so generously appropriated funds in the preceding year. Beside the general influences that would work upon any Chief of the Air Corps, there was a particular consideration operating upon the incumbent officer during 1935. After the excoriation of General Foulois by the Rogers Committee, the Chief of Air Corps, anxious to avoid the charge of "deliberate, willful and intentional violations of the law," was under great pressure to award on the basis of price rather than performance. Understandably he did so recommend, but when the Secretary of War overruled him in favor of the superior Douglas aircraft [8] he was free from attack and so approved the award to Douglas that the Comptroller subsequently challenged.

The issue, then, was clearly drawn. On the one hand the Comptroller General held that the air arm's competition was illegal because it failed to provide any means of establishing the exact relationship between performance and price, thus leaving the award entirely to a competition on performance. The Secretary of War, on the other hand, held that any arbitrary formula that evaluated price

---

[8] For general résumé of this affair, see G. Brown, Development of Transport Airplanes and Air Transport Equipment, WFHO, 1946, pp. 70-73.

along with performance would deprive the Secretary of the discretion legally vested in him by Section 10t of the Air Corps Act of 1926. While the Secretary might, if he so desired, give price a greater or lesser weight in evaluating bids, he maintained that the discretion entrusted to him by Congress in 10t was specifically intended to permit flexibility in making awards in order to serve the best interests of the air arm.[9]

The conflict of views between the Secretary and the Comptroller posed an interesting constitutional problem. The Comptroller General was the agent of Congress; the Secretary of War was the agent of the President. If either had chosen to take his case to his superior, a difficult question of legislative and executive relationship might have arisen. Fortunately, Congress has provided a somewhat simpler solution for more routine questions by authorizing appeals from such conflicts to the Attorney General. The Secretary of War therefore presented his case to the Attorney General for a ruling. In addition to the relevant facts, he described the chaos that would result from a reversal and concluded, "Should you be forced to decide the question presented adversely to the views of the War Department, I hesitate to predict the effect upon National Defense. . . ."[10] Four months later the Attorney General ruled substantially in favor of the Secretary of War.[11] Douglas, which had long since completed deliveries of the transports, at last received its money.[12] Thus a procurement project begun in August 1934 finally reached completion sometime after April 1937. Much of this delay seems attributable to the failure of the Comptroller General to appreciate the latitude given to the Secretary of War under the terms of the Air Corps Act of 1926.

In another case of interest to the Air Corps, the Comptroller also apparently ruled without fully grasping the problem in hand. Toward the end of 1934 the Comptroller held up payment on an aircraft contract on the grounds that it had been improperly awarded. He ruled that there had been ample time since the passage of the Air Corps Act in 1926 for the air arm to determine specifications for the airplanes it required. In eight years, the Comptroller implied, the Air Corps should have had more than enough time to prepare specifications and blueprints "down to the last wire . . . or the last bolt. . . ." Such specifications would permit all qualified manufacturers to compete on price, declared the Comptroller, and there would be no need for evaluations permitting charges of "favoritism and fraud" in the award.[13] This opinion clearly assumed that aircraft designs were static rather than dynamic, that once one achieved an acceptable design it could be frozen for procurement purposes. But in aircraft design the preparation of detailed specifications and drawings down to the last bolt is impossible. Procurement officers knew that no War Department personnel could prepare

---

[9] The Secretary's position was ably formulated in 5th Ind, JAGO to SW, 27 Oct 36, JAG (Army) Gen Rcds Sec 400.12.
[10] SW to Atty Gen, 28 Dec 36, JAG (Army) Gen Rcds Sec 400.12.
[11] 39 Op Atty Gen 23, April 9, 1937.

[12] Memo, Capt Park Holland, OASW, for Maj F. P. Shaw, JAGO, 9 Feb 37, JAG (Army) Gen Rcds Sec 400.12.
[13] Compt Gen to SW, 12 Dec 34, JAG (Army) Gen Rcds Sec 163 Bids.

such drawings. If such drawings were possible, the Secretary of War noted, they would actually restrict rather than encourage competition since it would be necessary to specify a particular airplane previously proven to meet the needs of the air arm. A particular airplane would, of course, be the design of one manufacturer who would thus gain an enormous advantage in any competition.[14]

Since all disbursements are ultimately subject to the approval of the Comptroller General, it is obviously imperative for those who wish their procurement projects to move along without delay to learn to live with the Comptroller General and the General Accounting Office. Awareness of this may have motivated Air Corps officials to reach an agreement while the Douglas case was still pending. The Comptroller had insisted that price should be formally evaluated in the competition; the Secretary of War had contended that he had an express grant of discretion to weigh price as he saw fit. Although the Attorney General ultimately ruled on the Douglas case in favor of the War Department, procurement officers recognized that the problem of price would continue to be a point of criticism in the Accounting Office. They arranged with the Comptroller, therefore, to include price as a factor for evaluation in all future competitions.

The formula contrived to satisfy the Comptroller was simple but ingenious. After determining a figure of merit on the basis of performance, the figure was to be divided by the dollar cost bid by the manufacturer. The resulting price factor would favor the bidder with the lowest price and the highest performance.[15] In conceding this point, however, War Department officials insisted that discretion still rested with the Secretary—there would be no determination of the winner "by a purely mathematical formula." The figure of merit and the price factor together would serve as a guide to the Secretary, who nevertheless remained free to make an award to other than the winning bid combination of price and performance provided there were substantial reasons for so doing.

If the new arrangement helped allay congressional criticism and if it led aircraft manufacturers to feel they were getting fair play, it was probably a success. But the relationship of price and performance was an aspect of Assistant Secretary Woodring's new procurement policy that raised other significant difficulties when put into practice.

Drawbacks of the New Policy

Although the top political officials of the War Department boasted of the success of the new procurement policy that substituted competition for negotiation in the award of aircraft contracts, the

---

[14] SW to Compt Gen, undated draft by OCAC, revised by JAGO, JAG (Army) Gen Rcds Sec 163 Bids.

[15] Memo, Exec, OASW, for CofS, 17 Aug 36, SW and OASW files, AC Gen Questions, item 363. For description of price-performance formula, see CofAC to OSW, 4 Feb 37, JAG (Army) Gen Rcds Sec 400.12, 11 Nov 35 file. See also, Mat Div Bull No. 31, 29 Aug 36, AF Doc R&R Br, Doc 13/US/13, and Bull No. 30A, 1 Jul 39, entitled Proc Policy and Procedure . . . , AFCF in AC Project Rcds (Lyon Papers), Book 56. The Navy had concocted a price-performance formula at least four years earlier, but there is no evidence that Navy experience was studied by Air Corps officials. See Mat Div BuAer, to Asst Chief, BuAer, 7 Mar 32, in Delaney Hearings.

Chief of the Air Corps was more cautious. He preferred to withhold judgment until extended experience decided the issue.[16] As events were to prove, his caution was fully justified.

Under the new policy, with its emphasis on competition, experimental contracts involved a return to the use of design competitions as authorized by Section 10a *et seq.* of the Air Corps Act in preference to negotiated contracts under 10k. Procurement officers, from their unhappy experience immediately following the passage of the Air Corps Act in 1926, knew that the design competition was a virtually unworkable system for purchasing experimental aircraft. Nonetheless, they were driven to return to the design competition at the insistence of the Military Affairs Committee and its chairman, Representative McSwain.[17]

Early in 1935 the Air Corps sent out circular proposals on a design competition for a pursuit aircraft. In May sixteen bids were opened. During the next five months the several evaluating boards did their work, and in September the Secretary of War announced the awarding of a contract to the Wedell-Williams Air Service Corporation, which had presented the winning design. In the meantime another manufacturer had presented not only a design but a sample aircraft at Wright Field with actual flight performance superior even to the paper promises of the Wedell-Williams design. The superiority of the airplane was in large measure attributable to a new and more powerful engine that appeared on the market after the Wedell-Williams bid had been received.

To proceed with a contract for constructing an experimental aircraft according to the winning design was obviously futile. When Wedell-Williams began to redesign its aircraft to utilize the newly developed engine, the Judge Advocate General raised objections. An award could not legally be made for such a modified design without obvious detriment to the other competitors. Whereupon, procurement officers determined to cancel the design competition award entirely and negotiate for the modified Wedell-Williams design, using the powers conferred by Section 10k. However, Wedell-Williams, convinced that the airplane had no future, subcontracted the job, thus defeating a major purpose of the Air Corps Act—to encourage firms with design staffs rather than "production only" shops.

Here was the ultimate absurdity. If the design competition, Section 10a *et seq.*, was to be used to avoid the favoritism alleged to color the use of negotiated experimental contracts (Section 10k), but 10k had to be used to bail out the shortcomings of the design competition, then surely the design competition was unworkable. After three failures in 1926 and 1927, procurement officers had avoided the use of design competitions until driven to try four more during 1935. Two others in a modified form were tried

---

[16] Testimony of Gen Foulois at House Hearings on WD appropriation for FY 1936, January 29, 1935, pp. 558–60.

[17] For influence of Military Affairs Com on WD policy, see Gen Pratt to E. P. Warner, 10 May 34, WFCF 008 Proc. See H.R. 6810, 74th Cong, 1st sess, March 18, 1935, and McSwain to SW, 19 Mar 35, JAG (Army) Gen Rcds Sec 452.1 Aircraft. See there also, ASW to McSwain, 25 Apr 35, and SW to President, undated draft by JAGO, indicating the measure proposed by McSwain was sufficiently dangerous to justify seeking Presidential aid in defeating it.

during 1938. Significantly, none of the aircraft used in World War II had its inception in a design competition.[18] In 1935 Air Corps procurement officers once again reached the conclusion of 1927: paper promises to perform were meaningless. The design competition was unworkable.

The clear failure of the design competition in the matter of experimental contracts served only to emphasize the importance of the sample aircraft competition in determining the success or failure of the new procurement policy of the War Department with regard to production contracts. Yet here, too, departmental officials found complications and obstacles. The sample aircraft competition proved difficult to administer. The procedure, it will be recalled, involved the mailing of a circular proposal containing type specifications in terms of the minimum performance acceptable. This left the maximum performance to the skill of the designer, who was required to demonstrate the attainments of his design by actual flight performance with a sample aircraft.

To ensure absolute fairness to all competitors, procurement officers ruled that after a manufacturer entered a competition he was to receive no help whatsoever from officers at Wright Field. On the surface this appeared to be a sensible safeguard, but in practice it led to a whole train of adverse consequences. The ruling prevented Wright Field engineers from making suggestions that would improve designs. Worse yet, by requiring Air Corps officers to ignore the manufacturer entirely until the sample was actually flown to Wright Field for evaluation, the air arm was denied an opportunity of studying the aircraft in the mock-up stage, where numerous flaws in design might have been remedied easily.[19] Modifications introduced after the plane reached Wright Field for evaluation could be effected only through change orders—tedious and expensive amendments of the contract.

A further drawback inherent in the sample competition was the necessity of drafting the invitation or circular proposal comprehensively enough to allow the widest possible freedom to the designer yet explicit enough to bring in bids suited to the requirements of the air arm. If the invitation was insufficiently explicit the bidders would have no way of knowing just what was desired; if the invitation was too explicit, it would stultify innovations in design.

Yet another difficulty cropped up in the sample competition. Samples were to be used only for production or quantity contracts. Since the needs of the service required that the winner be put into production as soon as possible, it was assumed that the samples submitted would be fully developed airplanes ready for production. But to win the competition, manufacturers were under pressure to submit aircraft embodying new design features that by their very novelty were not proven by long use in service. Thus competitions intended to attract production models brought in what

---

[18] This whole account of the design competition story is taken from Prewar Procurement by the Air Corps, by Service Section, Procurement Division, Air Technical Service Command, pages 8–11.

[19] A mock-up is a dummy aircraft of full scale erected before fabrication of the first flying model. It is used to assist in planning the location of parts and accessories.

amounted to experimental models instead, which is to say that using the sample competition for production contracts virtually converted production contracts into experimental ones.[20]

A major criticism leveled against the new procurement policy by air arm officers was the high cost involved in its administration. The Chief of the Air Corps, preferring the negotiated contract, was undoubtedly more than ready to muster arguments showing the excessive cost of managing competitions. Yet even if these defensive arguments are discounted, it was indeed expensive to hold competitions. At times the mere list of bidders circularized ran to eighty mimeographed pages. It mattered little that 95 percent of these firms never responded with bids. To satisfy Congress that competition prevailed, all must be circularized. Sending out proposals and evaluating bids necessitated an annual payroll of more than sixty thousand dollars, not to mention the diversion of engineers from research and development projects to work at evaluating competitions.[21]

The high costs of the new procurement policy were not confined to administrative charges. Manufacturers found the sample aircraft a costly proposition to build, especially when a contract failed to materialize and the entire investment had to be absorbed from company funds. During the decade of the thirties airframe costs increased between threefold and fourfold.[22] In addition to the impact of social legislation and rising labor costs, the advancing complexity of aircraft structures drove costs upward. As the average number of items on contract increased, unit costs fell, but tooling costs rose rapidly, thus requiring a heavier initial outlay by manufacturers. As airframes grew heavier and more complicated, the time for fabrication stretched out from a few months to more than two years in some cases. The step from twin-engine bombers to four-engine bombers marked the most spectacular rise in costs. (*Table 6*) As the decade of the thirties advanced, manufacturers who undertook to build sample aircraft on the chance of recouping their losses with the award of a government contract risked larger and larger sums of money.

Almost everyone concerned with the building of military aircraft began to issue dire predictions about the future of the aircraft industry if the War Department persisted in its sample aircraft policy. Brokers interested in raising capital for the industry warned their clients that manufacturers were becoming "increasingly reluctant" to risk entrance into competitions. If unsuccessful, a manufacturer might lose his entire investment since the possibility of finding a purchaser other than the government for a highly specialized military aircraft was limited at best. On the other hand, manufacturers were virtually driven to

---

[20] The difficulties mentioned here as well as many others are discussed in memo for files by Maj J. P. Dinsmore, JAGD, 2 Nov 34, JAG (Army) Gen Rcds Sec 400.12. See also, JAG (Army) Gen Rcds Sec 156 Claims, 23 Jun 36, *passim*. Some Wright Field views are contained in ESMR 50–74, Addendum 3, 14 Jun 34, and ESMR AG–51–20, 18 Jun 34, both in WFCF 008 Proc.

[21] Engr Sec Office Memo 182, 12 May 34; Maj A. J. Lyon to Maj C. W. Howard, 7 Sep 34; Chief, Mat Div, to CofAC, 1 Nov 34. All thru in WFCF 008 Proc Policy.

[22] Mat Div Budget Officer to CofAC, 12 Jun 34, AHO Plans Div 145.93–260.

Table 6—Comparative Cost of Two-Engine and Four-Engine Bombers

	Martin B-10B	Douglas B-18	Boeing YB-17
Quantity	103	82	13
Total cost aircraft	$72,000	$105,000	$302,100
Airframe cost with changes	45,450	72,243	246,030
G F E cost	13,650	16,957	23,261
Engine cost each	6,500	8,200	8,200
Engine cost per craft	13,000	16,400	32,800

Source: Exhibit A, 2d Ind, Chief, Info Div, OCAC, to Chief, Mat Div, 29 Apr 36, WFCF 121.6 Cost of Airplanes. The price jump between the twin-engine B-18 and the four-engine B-17 would be reduced somewhat if like quantities were considered, but the spread between the two would still remain great.

enter competitions, for failure to do so might leave a firm far behind its competitors in technical development.[23]

The complaints leveled by brokers, manufacturers, and others against the use of sample aircraft competitions were, of course, special pleading by partisans. On the other hand, air arm officers who were partisans only for superior equipment raised similar objections to the system. In the Navy, where the Bureau of Aeronautics procured aircraft under a sample competition not unlike that of the Air Corps, there were like complaints. The bureau chief was apprehensive over the declining number of bidders who cared to risk capital on a sample aircraft. With good reason, manufacturers shied from such risks. In one competition for a relatively light aircraft, a dive bomber, two firms bid with prices around $80,000 whereas one actually spent $125,000 and the other actually spent $200,000 developing the samples.[24] Such heavy outlays could and did on occasion drive firms toward bankruptcy when they failed to win production contracts.[25]

The sample competition had hardly been fairly tried before the Chief of the Air Corps suggested the danger lurking in the policy. Of ninety-odd circular proposals sent out inviting the submission of a sample bomber for competition, only one firm replied.[26] By the end of fiscal year 1936 the Chief of the Air Corps was anxious to try possible expedients for shoring up the faltering policy. He questioned whether manufacturers could afford to lose more than two competitions in a row, if that many, and recommended changes in the procurement system to alleviate the difficulty.[27] A year later manufacturers were displaying a decided lack of interest in government busi-

---

[23] Harding, *Aviation Industry*, pp. 6-8; Callery, "Review of American Aircraft Finance," *Air Affairs* (Summer 1947), p. 484; *Aviation Industry in the U.S.*, pp. 98-162; *Manual of Magazine of Wall Street* (March 6, 1937), p. 43.

[24] Testimony of Rear Adm E. J. King in House Hearings on Navy Dept appropriation for 1936, March 13, 1935, pp. 543, 547.

[25] Remarks of Senator R. S. Copeland, *Cong Rcd*, March 18, 1936, p. 3934.

[26] Testimony of Gen Foulois, House Hearings on WD appropriation for 1936, January 1935, p. 560.

[27] Annual Rpt of CofAC, 1936, AFCF 319.1.

AIRCRAFT PROCUREMENT ON THE EVE OF WORLD WAR II 143

ness. Improved conditions in the business world and growing sales to commercial airlines no doubt contributed to this situation but, the Chief of the Air Corps felt, so did the procurement methods of the air arm.[28] During 1938 and 1939 procurement officers continued to urge changes in the sample competition. Now, however, their requests had become demands. Changes in procurement procedures "must" be adopted, they claimed, for it was becoming impossible to get competition. The sample aircraft represented "an insuperable barrier" to manufacturers, whose capital resources were too slender to permit "an undertaking frought with such risk of financial loss."[29]

The War Department Seeks a Solution

Since air arm officers and industry spokesmen continued their barrage of objections to the costly sample competition, War Department officials were compelled to give the question some attention. If the policy was really unworkable and changes proved necessary, the War Department would be thrust into an embarrassing position. The civilian Secretaries, it will be recalled, had gone way out on a limb in declaring the new policy a success. Perhaps their declarations were politically necessary at the time, but having praised the policy loudly, they were in a poor position to ask for its revision.[30] Whether for political or other reasons, the faults in the administration of sample aircraft competitions continued to be a cause of agitation well into the crisis period before the outbreak of World War II in 1939, and repeated attempts were made to meet the difficulties.

The Air Corps made the first attempt. Procurement officers proposed to conduct the sample competition as usual and award a contract to the winner under Section 10t. Then, if the second and third ranking samples in the competition proved to be designs of exceptional value only slightly less desirable than the winning aircraft, these could be purchased as experimental aircraft under the authority of Section 10k at negotiated prices.[31] The prices paid for the second and third ranking aircraft would necessarily be less than the sum paid the winner and might not even cover the full cost of constructing the samples, but the mere possibility that there would be some reward to others beside the winner was expected to lure in more bidders on each competition. Thus, purchasing the best of the losers would serve not only to sharpen rivalry and create superior weapons for the air arm but at the same time would strengthen the industry financially and provide the nation with a greater productive capacity in time of war.

Though the Air Corps plan had advantages insofar as the competitors were concerned, the advantages were offset by defects from a budgetary standpoint. Funds for production contracts (10t)

---

[28] Lecture at Army War College by Brig Gen O. Westover, Materiel Division Developments of Fiscal Year 1937, WFCF 350.001 Lectures.

[29] Chief, Legal Br, to Chief, Proc Sec, 10 Feb 38, AFCF 032, 1926, and R&R, Comment 2, Chief, Supply Div, OCAC, to Exec, 17 Mar 39 same file. See also, Memo, Budget Officer (Mat Div) for ASW, Feb 39, WFCF 111.3 Expansion Program.

[30] 6th Ind, JAG to SW, 1 Jun 37, JAG (Army) Gen Rcds Sec 400.12.

[31] CofAC to G-4, 19 Mar 37, AFCF 112.4A.

came from one budget while funds for development contracts (10k) came from another. Thus the purchase of the sample competition winner in quantity would be on the production budget while any money paid out for the second and third place samples in the same contest would have to come from the research and development budget.[32]

With Congress anxious to build up the air arm to authorized strength, appropriations for production contracts were easier to secure than those for research. Air arm officers would have preferred to buy the second and third ranking items from the easier-to-get funds, but legal considerations blocked the way. Appropriations for production contracts carried a mandatory clause ordering that "not less than" a given figure be spent. If the second or third ranking samples failed to materialize or contained no features worth buying, the War Department could find itself with earmarked funds unspent at the end of the fiscal year. This would be damaging if the Air Corps sought larger appropriations the following year since many congressmen tended to regard unspent funds as a presumption of padded estimates rather than as evidence of economical spending.

If, on the other hand, procurement officers used research and development funds to buy the runners-up in a sample competition, they encountered other vexations. To divert research funds to the sample aircraft contest was to rob research in order to provide what amounted to a subsidy for the industry. Since the second and third ranking samples were avowedly production models, their value for experimental use was highly specialized at best and often not at all in the area of research most needing money.

Thus, the Air Corps plan for making sample competitions workable turned out to be of dubious merit. While the remedy could be applied to advantage, the administrative drawbacks accompanying it suggested that some other expedient must be devised.

Several aircraft manufacturers, feeling themselves to be relentlessly driven to the wall by the excessive costs of sample aircraft, came forward during 1938 with suggestions of their own. Probably the most elaborate plan was that of Reuben H. Fleet, president of the Consolidated Aircraft Corporation. Once a procurement officer in the Air Service, Fleet had for many years taken an active interest in procurement problems and the general question of legislation dealing with the air arm.

Although Fleet presented several proposals, they all boiled down to one central idea: legislation should be enacted to authorize the War Department to procure aircraft in production quantities by negotiated contracts rather than by sample competitions. Since to have favored Fleet's proposals would have put the Air Corps in the position of favoring the practice of negotiation so stigmatized by Congress, the War Department recommended against the proposal.[33] The language of the War Department rejection was obviously calculated to allay any sus-

---

[32] TAG to CofAC, 11 Apr 38, and 1st Ind, OCAC to TAG, 22 Apr 38, AFCF 321.9A.

[33] Memo, Capt Holland, OASW, for Gen Arnold, 12 Feb 38; Chief, Legal Br, Proc Sec, to Chief, Proc Sec, Mat Div, 10 Feb 38; SW to A. J. May, 21 Feb 38, draft by Plans Div, OCAC. All in AFCF 032 1926.

picion in Congress that the department might still harbor a desire for negotiated contracts in preference to competition. This solicitude for congressional opinion may well have been necessary, nevertheless it may be significant that Congressman McSwain had died, and a new incumbent with a somewhat different attitude toward public contracts presided over the House Military Affairs Committee.

Though the officials of the various echelons concerned with aircraft purchases believed it expedient to reject Fleet's proposed amendment, they could not drop the matter there. Other proposals to amend would surely follow, and Congress might take unfavorable action. There had to be some solution and soon, for the sample competition policy seemed on the verge of breakdown. In at least one instance, a medium bomber project, plans for a competition were canceled when procurement officers found that not one manufacturer was willing to bid.[34]

Confronted with a knotty problem of policy, leaders in the War Department resorted to a traditional Army expedient, appointing a formal board of officers to study the question and report a solution.[35] The board met and gathered evidence. Air Corps officials and numerous individual aircraft manufacturers presented testimony on their respective points of view. For the industry as a whole the Aeronautical Chamber of Commerce offered a series of recommendations—an example of the useful collaboration between an industry lobby and the War Department, which was to prove most fruitful in the war crisis soon to arrive. The revised procurement procedure ultimately recommended by the board was an amalgam of the various suggestions and proposals made on every hand.

Essentially, the board recommended what amounted to a compromise between the advantages of the sample aircraft competition and those of the design contest. It recommended that before issuing circular proposals for aircraft in quantity, the Air Corps should invite manufacturers to submit designs for evaluation. One or more designs would then be awarded experimental contracts (10k) for the construction of one or more aircraft. Similarly, the authority of 10k could be used to purchase the design data of the losers where warranted by the nature of the design. While all bidders could not be assured compensation for the engineering data submitted with their bids, the mere idea that some return was possible to firms other than the winner of first place was expected to encourage manufacturers to enter competitions that they might otherwise have avoided.

Increasing the number of bidders in military aircraft competition was, of course, one of the major objectives sought by the board, but there were other advantages anticipated from the proposed scheme. Detailed type specifications would not be prepared for quantity procurement until after the design winner or winners passed the final mock-up stage. This would permit air arm officers to exchange ideas freely with the manufacturers and to suggest changes during the period of construction without risk of showing favoritism to any one

---

[34] Memo, Exec, OASW, for ASW, 6 Jul 38, OASW files, AC Proc Board, 1938.

[35] Proceedings of the board, 8 Jul 38, *et seq.*, OASW files, AC Proc Board, 1938.

competitor. Finally, after garnering all the best design ideas of the design competition, the Air Corps could issue a circular proposal for a sample aircraft to be offered in competition by manufacturers seeking to supply aircraft in production quantities. The manufacturer offering a sample aircraft with superior performance could normally expect to win a production contract. Competitors were not confined to winners of the design competition. Any manufacturer who could afford to build a sample aircraft meeting the required specifications could submit a bid.

The board expected other advantages to accrue from the revised procedure. By subsidizing at least one and sometimes several experimental airplanes in the first phase of the new routine, the War Department would provide an assured supply of bidders for production proposals. At the same time, by leaving the sample aircraft contest open to all bidders, no one could protest that full free competition had been denied. In retaining the requirement of a sample aircraft in production competitions, the board preserved the best feature of this system of procurement: objective evaluation based on actual performance.

Although the purchase of design data and subsidizing of the construction of winning designs would involve a considerable increase in initial costs, the plan was expected to make great savings by reducing the number of change orders authorized after the contract had been signed. This was one of the persuasive arguments offered in support of the board's proposed scheme. Air arm officers would get more nearly the design they wished, and get it cheaper, while manufacturers would get into production with fewer delays.[36]

During October 1938 the Chief of Staff approved the board's proposal for a revised procurement procedure and urged a like course upon the Assistant Secretary.[37] If given time, the War Department might have gone ahead to perfect a highly workable system of procurement that was both fair to the industry and acceptable to those critics in Congress who insisted upon the fullest competition. But the War Department was not to be given time. The revised procedure had scarcely been drafted when the crisis that was to end in war shattered all hope of an orderly evolution in aircraft procurement methods.

Peacetime Procurement: A Retrospect

What general observations appear to stand out from a twenty-odd year survey of procurement methods? What conclusions appear to be so obvious as to lie virtually beyond dispute? To begin with, it is highly significant that the Air Corps was still seeking to improve its procurement procedures when the crisis came. Even the briefest of surveys over twenty years of aircraft procurement shows that the process was essentially a matter of resolving conflicting objectives and mutually exclusive ends. To such a fundamental question as whether or not contracts should have been let by negotiation or by competition, experience over the years showed that there could be no

---

[36] See G-4 Memo for CofS with G-3 and WPD concurring, 10 Oct 38, AFCF 452.1.
[37] Ibid.

clear-cut answer. Each method had its advantages, each had its shortcomings. While low price was of importance, so too was superior quality. Equally impossible to decide was the conflict between strategic necessity on the one hand and the economic health of the aircraft industry on the other. Clearly, there were no black and white formulas or right and wrong means to employ. Resolving mutually exclusive ends involved compromises.

Yet, conceding the existence of diverging ends or goals, there still remained the question of means, the matter of administering the search for those ends. Experience demonstrated again and again the importance of well-informed administrators. Time after time breakdowns in the procurement process might have been avoided had those who administered the law been familiar with the precise text of the statutes. The War Department and its subordinate echelons were of necessity in constant flux. Officers seldom remained for long at any one post. Therefore, the formulation of standing operating procedures was even more essential in the Military Establishment than would be the case in many civilian organizations. But organization by itself is never enough. The best of procedures will not operate efficiently without well-informed, assertive officials willing to accept political responsibility. They must select legal advisors who are resourceful and imaginative, advisors who will find legal ways in which desirable ends may be secured rather than proliferate arguments to show why a given course may not be followed.

The need for well-informed and able administrators was not confined to the higher echelons of the War Department. The need for assertive, imaginative officials extended clear down through all those echelons at Wright Field, where procurement took place. Effective procurement called for imaginative officers who could devise procedures above criticism by the Comptroller General, the General Accounting Office, and a host of disgruntled competitors. In sum, the ideal in procurement administration called for officials who could get what the necessities of defense required and still stay within the law.

All of which leads to yet another question. What was the law concerning procurement? Early in 1939 an attorney-at-law wrote to the War Department asking for information on the rules and regulations governing aircraft procurement. An Air Corps officer detailed to prepare a reply simply referred the attorney to the Superintendent of Documents for a copy of the Air Corps Act of 1926. The officer who sent this amazing answer may have been naive, ignorant, or merely lazy—clearly "the law" of procurement was only the beginning. Every statute upon the books was encrusted with an intricate overlay of judicial decisions, Judge Advocate General and Attorney General opinions, and Comptroller General rulings as vital to the procurement process as the statute itself.

In short, statutes were only the visible portion of a most intricate process whose very complexity made tampering essentially dangerous. To change a statute is to upset an elaborate and delicate mechanism. After a statute has remained upon the books for any considerable period it accumulates not only rulings, opinions, and decisions, but in addition it becomes the core for a number of administrative procedures that only extended experience can perfect. A congressman may be entirely sincere in proffering a bill to end some abuse, real or alleged, in the procurement system, but, if passed, his bill may actually do more harm than good. If the record of aircraft procurement between the wars shows anything at all, it reveals the immense difficulties attending every effort to change the laws. If air arm officials had been able to make this circumstance clear to all legislators, the cause of national defense might have been greatly enhanced.

Clearly "the law" is a most subtle concept. The same statute may remain on the books over a period of many years and yet be a very different matter one year from another. The organic statute of the air arm, the Air Corps Act of 1926, was just such a law. A great deal depends upon who is to administer it. A change in administration, even without conscious decision by the President, may mean a drastic alteration in the spirit in which an act is interpreted. Changes other than political also work subtle differences in the law. The Air Corps Act was drafted before the technical revolution of the late twenties had altered the whole structure and scale of the aircraft industry. After this revolution wrought profound changes in the industry, the Act of 1926 no longer meant the same thing that it had when first written. An act conceived for a large number of relatively small firms now operated upon a very different type of industry led by a handful of major producers.

Perhaps the most important conclusion to be drawn from the history of twenty years of aircraft procurement is that no conclusions can be drawn; there are no formulas, no cut and dried rules to follow in every case. Procurement methods that work in one era may be utterly unworkable in another. The corporate character of the industry changes, the mood of the Congress changes, and a new President enters the White House. Conclusions drawn on the situation of 1938 might well be no longer valid in 1968. The same congressmen who insisted upon stringent economy and competitive procurement in 1934 may well have voted billions for defense while joining the clamor for negotiated contracts to speed the placement of contracts in 1941.

The record further suggests the critical importance of studying the whole procurement process rather than isolated segments. As late as March in 1940, when the threat of war was hovering over the nation, the Secretary of War boasted that his system of procurement had resulted in aircraft "superior to any in the world."[38] Japanese Zeroes and German Messerschmitts were soon to raise some doubt regarding the Secretary's view. In defense, the rejoinder might be offered that the triumphant B–17 was a product of the Secretary's "sample" competition and should on its record vindicate his methods. The war record of the B–17, the Boeing Flying Fortress, cannot be denied, but the success of the B–17 does not prove the utility of the "sample" procurement policy. The B–17 was indeed a

---

[38] Hearings of Senate Military Affairs Com on S Res 244, 76th Cong, 3d sess, March 28, 1940, p. 3.

COMPARATIVE SIZE OF B-17 *(upper)* AND XB-15 *(lower).*

private venture submitted by the manufacturer as a bid in a sample competition, but a further probing after facts reveals that before the B-17 came the XB-15, also a four-engine bomber, an experimental project sponsored and paid for by the Air Corps. The design experience derived from the XB-15 made the B-17 possible.[39] To weigh the sample competition apart from its context is to distort the record and draw conclusions from half truths. In short, there is no ideal formula for aircraft procurement.

---

[39] Draft of annual report for Mat Div, p. 9, 27 Aug 38, AFCF 321.9 Annual Rpt.

CHAPTER VII

Planning for Industrial Mobilization

The Problem

Probably no aspect of the nation's experience in World War I seems less successful than the record of War Department procurement. The Army, trained for little more than garrison duty, suddenly found itself expanded to a force of several million men. To equip this force for the exigencies of modern warfare called for the purchase of nearly three-quarters of a million different types of items. The War Department was unprepared for such a program.

Within the Army alone, half a dozen agencies began to compete with each other for the services of manufacturers who could provide the items needed. Taking all the government procurement agencies together, by the war's end there were literally hundreds of different contract forms in use. Each had its peculiarities involving special interpretations. As a consequence, war contracts filled the federal courts with costly litigation for decades after the armistice. And the price of unpreparedness cannot be reckoned in dollars alone. Delays in production cost lives.

Because the War Department had to formulate its requirements after the outbreak of World War I, many leading contractors were barely able to reach production before the war ended. The sudden rush of orders that belatedly hit the nation's manufacturers led to a wild scramble for the limited available supply of raw materials. Acute shortages developed in several key materials and prices rose alarmingly. Marked fluctuation of price levels reflected the impact of war on the national economy. Manufacturers fortunate enough to receive munitions contracts absorbed all available materials or labor and profited. Others, less fortunate, were driven out of business. Even the firms with war contracts found it difficult to attain capacity production. As soon as one shortage seemed solved, others appeared to upset hoped-for schedules. Bottlenecks in transport, in power, and in machine tools all rose to delay the total mobilization effort. In the scramble, the Army bid against the Navy for the nation's productive capacity, war contractors competed with one another for the nation's resources, and the nation as a whole paid heavily for its unpreparedness.

Out of the chaotic experience of utilizing the nation's potential in World War I came the realization that the preparations for war must be carefully thought out in advance. There had to be a mobilization plan if the mistakes of the past were to be avoided. And beyond the plan, all agreed, administrative machinery had to be created to regulate the flow of the

The War Department and Industrial Mobilization

The National Defense Act of 1920 gave legal recognition to the need for industrial mobilization planning. Section 5a placed the task squarely on the shoulders of the Assistant Secretary of War.[1] Although the job of procurement planning for wartime posed enormous difficulties, by the middle thirties the Office of the Assistant Secretary of War had carried the task a long step forward.[2] The objectives to be achieved were recognized; the problems to be solved were defined. All that remained was the actual business of filling in the details that would give substance to a mobilization plan.

The work of filling in the details fell to organizations for the most part within the Office of the Assistant Secretary of War. The Assistant Secretary delegated his statutory obligation for industrial mobilization planning to a Planning Branch in his office staffed by civilian employees and Army officers. To ensure a supply of trained officers for this assignment, the Assistant Secretary sponsored a special training school, the Army Industrial College. But Army activity in economic planning, no matter how intelligently executed, could not alone solve the problems raised. Soon after the Planning Branch began to function, it became evident that, to be realistic, all planning must include the Navy despite the silence of the 1920 Defense Act on this point. To offset this statutory deficiency, the Secretaries of War and Navy by administrative action created the joint Army and Navy Munitions Board (ANMB), which became the authoritative source of joint mobilization plans. The bulk of the detailed spadework continued to be performed by the Planning Branch of OASW and its naval counterpart.

By 1931, with the publication of the Industrial Mobilization Plan prepared the year before, the phase of trial and error was over, and detailed planning began in earnest. As more information accumulated, new problems and complications emerged. Modifications in concept and procedure were necessary. Subsequent revisions of the plan, appearing in 1933, 1936, and 1939, sought to obviate the shortcomings of earlier versions.

The planners learned much from their study of World War I, but as they began to fill in the details of their initial plans they gradually came to realize that they had set up impossible goals. Subsequent revisions—for example, the so-called Protective Mobilization Plan—scaled down the size of the force to be put into uniform immediately following the outbreak of war, after staff studies revealed that the nation's facilities simply could not get the desired items of equipment in the

---

[1] 41 Stat 764, June 4, 1920. For an extended discussion of the various plans contrived by the War Department to erect a civilian superagency on the skeletal planning staff of OASW, see Harold W. Thatcher, *Planning for Industrial Mobilization: 1920–1940*, QMC Historical Studies, 4 (Washington, 1943, reprinted 1948). See also R. Elberton Smith, *The Army and Economic Mobilization*, UNITED STATES ARMY IN WORLD WAR II (Washington, 1959), ch. II.

[2] The following résumé of OASW planning is based on the several mobilization plans and on Harry B. Yoshpe, Study of Experience in Industrial Mobilization in World War II, Army Industrial College, 1945.

desired quantities within the time initially believed possible. Perforce, the planners revised their conception of mobilization to fit the facts.[3] This alone may have justified the entire planning effort, but its usefulness certainly extended beyond the matter of changing perspectives. Probably of equal importance was the opportunity to perfect operating procedures.

Over the years of the "Long Armistice," the mobilization planners worked out a number of fundamental procedures to provide for an orderly economic mobilization in time of war. Among other things, this involved taking steps to prevent the scramble of purchasers that occurred in World War I, overloading some districts or regions of the country and ignoring others. The planners sought to apportion the load as evenly as possible across the various regions of the nation so all could share the benefits and the burdens.

"Apportioning the load" involved having some means of measuring the productive capacity of any given facility. This led the planners to perfect their administrative tools and define their terms still further. After some experimenting they hit upon the scheme of assuming the output of a plant in a normal eight-hour day to be 100 percent. Then, assuming a war situation, the plant would work three shifts around the clock. Allowing a margin for tool changing, cleaning time, and so forth, the planners reasoned that any given facility had a total capacity in wartime of 250 percent of its normal output. By arbitrarily reserving 50 percent of any facility's normal production for civilian use, this left some 200 percent of normal productive capacity to be assigned to military production.

Equipped with this measuring stick, procurement planning officers of the various arms and services surveyed individual facilities by the thousands and returned their findings to the Planning Branch in OASW. Where their reports showed that more than one service was bidding for the productive capacity of any facility, the Planning Branch formally "allocated" that plant, earmarking its production for one or another of the services. Where conflicts with the Navy appeared, the joint Army and Navy Munitions Board reconciled the rival claims by assigning the disputed facility to a "reserved" status in which the board doled out capacity on an *ad hoc* basis. By the eve of World War II the *Directory of Allocated and Reserved Facilities* published by OASW contained over 10,000 separate facility listings. Each listing represented a means of safeguarding against the concentration of orders that so impeded production in World War I.

Concentration of contracts was only one of many evils. Another was the manufacturers' all too frequent lack of familiarity with the military items they were expected to produce. Ideally, an educational order was the best way to familiarize manufacturers with unusual military items; however, in the absence of funds to finance more than a very few such orders, the mobilization planners did the next best thing. They co-operated with manufacturers in drawing up

---

[3] Compare the conception of mobilization presented by Woodring, in "Report of the Assistant Secretary of War," *Annual Report of the Secretary of War, 1936*, page 20, with that of Louis B. Johnson, "Report of Assistant Secretary of War, 1938," *ibid.*, page 20.

an "accepted schedule." This was not a contract but a statement of the quantities and rates at which a specific item would be required. To explore the possibilities of actually meeting this schedule, the planners further co-operated with the manufacturers in drawing up "factory plans" that attempted to outline the steps necessary to convert to military production and to formulate a statement of the labor, materials, and so forth required in the event of war.

Although the Defense Act of 1920 charged the Assistant Secretary of War with responsibility for mobilization planning, much of the work was actually delegated and redelegated in the twenty-odd years between the wars. However, one major division of labor is evident. The Assistant Secretary and his immediate staff assumed responsibility for providing the conceptual framework of mobilization and undertook to establish rules and procedures to co-ordinate procurement and control the national economy in time of need. On the other hand, most of the detail of surveying, planning, and scheduling was left to the individual arms and services. Only in this context is it possible to appraise the role of the Air Corps in the field of mobilization planning.

The Air Corps Organization for Mobilization Planning

Just as the Assistant Secretary of War delegated his statutory obligation for mobilization planning, so too did the Chief of the Air Corps. Since air arm mobilization was largely concerned with matériel, the problem inevitably fell into the sphere of the Materiel Division, which unlike the other units of the Office, Chief of Air Corps, was physically located at Wright Field near Dayton, Ohio. Thus, an Industrial Planning Section (IPS) at Wright Field shouldered the special tasks of industrial mobilization planning imposed by the Assistant Secretary's directives.[4]

Standing instructions charged the officers of IPS with "continuous study" to familiarize themselves with the nation's industrial resources, new processes, and developments that might affect the pattern of mobilization.[5] In actual practice, the officers assigned to the Industrial Planning Section found themselves swamped by the sheer volume of routine administration without taking on added burdens of "continuous study." In the main, their work involved the task of keeping the details of the mobilization plan current, utilizing the reports sent in by the Procurement Planning District representatives who operated in six geographical regions centered around New York, Buffalo, Cleveland, Detroit, Chicago, and Los Angeles.

The fundamental work of procurement planning was really done by the district officers. It was they who met the individual manufacturers face to face. It was they who surveyed a facility and filled out Form 100, the standard information sheet that went forward through IPS at Wright Field to the Planning Branch in OASW, where the over-all mobilization plan was constructed. Aside from such obvious information as the location of the facil-

---

[4] For a representative view of the Materiel Division agency for mobilization planning, which evolved slowly over the years after 1920, see Mat Div Industrial Planning Cir No. 203–1, 25 May 37.

[5] *Ibid.*, p. 4.

ity being surveyed, a roster of its key officials, its organization, its financial status, its production record, and the like, the reports returned from the districts went into considerable detail where manufacturers agreed to accept a schedule of production in an emergency. Such reports gave descriptions of the manufacturing methods to be used, compiled a bill of materials, and listed subcontractors whose services would be required.[6]

Although the district representatives surveyed literally thousands of facilities, not every survey resulted in a factory plan or an accepted schedule. There were so many items to be handled that only the most critical, those most intricate or those most difficult to manufacture, were carried all the way through the detailed planning and scheduling stage. For many items only an informal plan and schedule seemed necessary. This was especially true of commercial items that offered no manufacturing difficulties. Even items for which a detailed plan might have been useful or helpful did not always get formal schedules. The Industrial Planning Section was more than fully occupied in keeping plans up to date upon only the most critical items.[7]

Though the staff officers in IPS failed to complete a number of their plans and schedules, it is easy to find mitigating circumstances in their favor. They were perpetually understaffed. Air Corps authorities felt no urgency about mobilization plans, which they considered rather theoretical. Confronted with a chronic shortage of officers, the Air Corps gave first priority on manpower to tasks regarded as more pressing and more important. Even had more officers been available, they could not have been assigned to mobilization planning work because the appropriation acts passed during the decade before the war generally employed restrictive language that limited the planning staff to its strength in previous years.[8]

Another consideration militating against effective mobilization planning was the difficulty encountered in establishing a working harmony with the representatives of industry. Officers engaged in survey work found themselves at a disadvantage when dealing with industrialists because of the wide differences in their salaries. Since most of the officers conducting the surveys were in the lower pay brackets, it was not always easy for them to negotiate on equal terms with high-ranking officials of the nation's largest industrial firms. In addition, the planners were initially handicapped by standing instructions warning them against antagonizing manufacturers with too frequent requests for information, questionnaires, and so forth. All their relations with the manufacturers rested upon good will or the patriotic desire of individual businessmen to be co-opera-

---

[6] The operations of the district representatives are briefly described in Review of Methods Employed by the AAF in Estimating Productive Capacity and in Placing Production Schedules: 1922–1945, 15 May 46, prepared by ATSC's Logistics Planning Div, Plans (T–5), ICAF.

[7] Keeping the plans current seems to have swamped others besides the planners in the Air Corps. In 1936 the Assistant Secretary reported the task "Herculean" and noted that three years after the appearance of the 1933 Mobilization Plan, the job of working out the details on requirements had at last been completed. "Report of the Assistant Secretary of War," 1936, p. 21.

[8] See, for example, Lt Col F. J. Riley to ASW, 29 Mar 37, WFCF 381 Mobilization, 1939.

tive. Businessmen were under no legal obligation to provide information, nor were they under any compulsion to permit surveys or to agree to "accepted schedules." Some manufacturers refused to sign schedules, although they might otherwise be co-operative, because they feared a recurrence of their mistakes in World War I. They recalled having accepted production goals they could not meet because they had failed to appreciate the rigid standards imposed by government specifications. Others may have refused to sign accepted schedules for fear of being branded warmongers or merchants of death. Some manufacturers flatly refused to supply information on the ground that to do so would weaken their position vis-à-vis their competitors. At the other extreme there were manufacturers who were quite willing to sign schedules that were hopelessly unrealistic. Since accepted schedules were not contracts and not legally binding, they could be signed with breezy irresponsibility. As a consequence, accepted schedules, duly signed and placed on file, often meant little or nothing.[9]

Under such circumstances, one can readily appreciate how difficult was the task confronting the officers working on the problem of industrial mobilization for the Air Corps. Nonetheless, in spite of many handicaps, the accomplishments of the Air Corps planners seemed substantial. Over the years between the wars, the Industrial Planning Section at Wright Field accumulated vast files of information concerning the aircraft industry in the United States. Hundreds of factory plans were on tap ready for use in converting the industry from a peace to a war footing.

Thus, at least on the surface, the Air Corps appeared ready for M-day. There existed an organization, a staff, plans, and carefully recorded procedures for mobilization of the nation's aircraft industry. Yet when war finally did come, virtually the entire planning effort evaporated: most of the planning and much of the accumulated data were either scrapped or ignored. If the past has any meaning at all for the present, surely one might inquire as to what mistakes were made that thought, foresight, and vision might have avoided.

Air Corps Mobilization Planning

Was the mobilization planning effort of the Air Corps a success or a failure? In the final analysis, the air arm was not prepared when the war came; the plans for mobilization were faulty and inadequate. But before appraising the Air Corps' effort in procurement planning, it might be well to restate the problem. Leaving aside for the moment the matter of creating economic controls for the nation's economy as a task to be performed by the Army and Navy Munitions Board and some civilian superagency to be set up for the purpose, the essentials of mobilization planning fall into two separate phases: first, the determination of requirements, both qualitative and quantitative, and, second, the location of adequate productive capacity to meet these requirements. While the Air Corps did contribute information leading to the

---

[9] For an excellent summary of the problems besetting the planners, see AAF Hist Study 40, The Expansion of Industrial Facilities Under Army Air Force Auspices: 1940–1945, ATSC Hist Office, 1945, p. 16.

promulgation of requirements, final determination lay in the hands of the General Staff and thus beyond air arm decision. This in itself complicated the task of planning, but even more detrimental was the highly volatile nature of the variables that entered into the computation of requirements.

Take, for example, the matter of design as a qualitative factor of requirements. In the field of aviation the speed of technical change was, as the Secretary of War once remarked, "downright astonishing."[10] Each change in design involved some sort of recomputation of requirements. Since design change was continual, the computation of requirements was forever unsettled; approved programs were always "about to be revised." Propeller blades offer a case in point. The mobilization plan of 1933 listed blades as a critical contributory item, but the blades in discussion were made of wood. Shortly thereafter steel blades replaced wooden ones. Then hollow steel forgings came into use. Finally variable-pitch designs began to elbow out fixed-pitch models. During this evolutionary sequence, imaginative and resourceful manufacturers with aggressive research staffs pushed ahead of less progressive firms.[11] Each change in design, each new technique of production, and each newly formed company upset the calculations on requirements.

Sometimes design change involved the introduction of an entirely new item rather than development of an existing item. Fractional horsepower electric motors are an example. They were virtually unheard of as aircraft appliances during the 1930's, yet during World War II each B-29 used over a hundred such units. Planners would have had to have been blessed with great prescience to have scheduled in advance such yet unknown requirements.

The variables introduced by design changes alone, it would appear, were enough to make of requirements computation a well-nigh impossible task. Added to this difficulty were the further complications introduced by changes in doctrine. The between-war years were characterized by sharp disagreements as to the proper strategy and tactics of air power. Even amongst those most avid in their faith in aircraft there was disagreement as to the most effective form of weapon. The fighter school of thought vied with the bomber school, and advocates of heavily armed bombers argued with the advocates of fast, lightly armed bombers. As one or another of these groups gained dominance, requirements changed colorations. On the eve of World War II, for example, strategic plans called for 37 percent of the available productive capacity to be reserved for observation aircraft.[12] When the war finally arrived, this whole class of aircraft proved unusable and was abandoned as a separate type.[13]

Design and doctrine were not the only fluid variables that troubled the calcula-

---

[10] *Report of Secretary of War, 1935*, p. 7. See also, comments of Maj Gen. O. Westover, CofAC, before industry representatives, 6 Sep 38, WFCF 381 Emergency Proc.

[11] See, for example, the rivalry described in ESMR, M-51-394, 13 Sep 37, WFCF 004.4 Manufacturing, 1939.

[12] Lt Col Farthing to Lt Col H. V. Hopkins, 7 Mar 38, AHO Plans Div 145.93-183.

[13] Evolution of the Liaison-Type Airplane, 1917-1944, ATSC, 1945.

PLANNING FOR INDUSTRIAL MOBILIZATION 157

tion of requirements. There were differences of opinion within the Army as to the proper method by which such calculations should be made. General Staff directives for the earliest mobilization plan laid down a standardized rate of manpower induction, to which munitions production was to be geared. Air Corps efforts to work out the details soon revealed the flaw in this approach. The proposed rate of induction far exceeded the most optimistic rate of aircraft deliveries to be expected from the existing industry. Since the dynamic state of aircraft design made it unfeasible to maintain a large, ready reserve of aircraft to make up the difference between the rate of induction of manpower and the rate of production of equipment, some change in plan was essential.

General Staff officers recognized the validity of the Air Corps criticism but protested that the proposed solution of delaying inductions until equipment was ready was "in conflict with the fundamental concept of the War Department General Mobilization Plan," which was "based on personnel and not upon supply and equipment." The Air Corps was ordered to comply with the War Department plan, "not through making the availability of equipment the determining factor before new units are directed to commence their mobilization, but by reducing the requirements of Air Corps units in any period to a reasonable number based on expectation of production." [14]

Here was a major dispute over a fundamental premise. General Staff officers used the traditional troop basis for calculating requirements. Yet the troop basis was an entirely inadequate formula upon which to determine aircraft requirements, with the possible exception of certain types of close-support equipment. Strategic and tactical necessity for air power, not the number of men mobilized, constituted the only effective basis for determining the major aircraft requirements of the Air Corps. If the General Staff officers who established requirements for the first mobilization plans based their calculations on strategic and tactical considerations at all, they emphasized tactical or close-support aspects to the detriment of strategic functions. They insisted, for example, that the Air Corps should give "absolute" priority to observation aircraft for assignment to armies and corps.[15]

To be sure, the example cited above represents only a single episode in the early thirties. General Staff officers were not always so intransigent in their directives on air power. Nonetheless, the illustration has a point—it shows the absence of agreement upon the techniques to be employed in computing requirements. And in the absence of such agreement another variable was introduced that worked to upset and confuse the orderly process of Air Corps mobilization planning.

Thus, from the very outset, the Industrial Planning Section of the Air Corps was beset with virtually insurmountable difficulties. So many variables entered into the calculation of requirements that

---

[14] TAG to CofAC, 12 Jun 30, quoted in 1st Ind, OCAC to ACTS, 10 Feb 33, basic ACTS to OCAC, 24 Jan 33, AHO Plans Div 145.93-165.

[15] *Ibid.*

any planning rested upon foundations of sand. Planners were repeatedly forced to rely upon "educated guesses."

The story of Air Corps planning for aluminum well illustrates the difficulties of working from uncertain assumptions. In 1932 after more than a decade of preparation for mobilization, the Air Corps still had no plan for this vital commodity. A civilian employed at Wright Field finally offered to work up a plan during his two weeks of active duty as a reserve officer.[16] In 1936 Air Corps officers were still computing the aluminum requirements for the 1933 mobilization plan, but an entirely new plan, the revision of 1936, was soon to appear, invalidating much if not all of the calculations already made. In 1937 the requirement was still unsettled, and air arm officers continued to make "educated guesses" rather than exact computations of the need for aluminum. The dubious nature of this sort of data for planning purposes is even more obvious when one notes that even the "educated guess" disregarded such conditioning factors as the availability of skilled labor, raw materials, and machine tools, not to mention possible shortages in accessory equipment and delays arising from the introduction of design changes during production.[17]

Despite the unknowns and the variables with which they had to work, Air Corps planners had to go ahead and plan anyhow. They knew they were working with imponderables in search of solutions to a hypothetical question. Moreover, they knew full well that if war should break out they would be criticized for failing to come up with a smoothly operating plan. Staff officers in the Industrial Planning Section at Wright Field were like the one-eyed hunter who is standing in a fog and is asked to shoot with a broken gun at ducks he cannot see.

Air Corps officers put into their planning for wartime procurement much effort but not enough thought. They worked conscientiously and hard but tended to busy themselves largely with the routines of filling in details upon an existing conceptual framework. Rarely did they define their assumptions and even more rarely did they question those assumptions. On occasions when they did recognize the premises underlying their plans, they not infrequently failed to think them through to their ultimate implications. A review and appraisal of the major assumptions that underlay the Air Corps planning effort may help reveal some of the planning officers' difficulties.

A Healthy Industry: Key to Defense

With air power, as with other forms of military might, preparedness may take one of two forms. A nation may choose to maintain an aerial fleet-in-being or, as an alternative, it may choose to rely upon its capacity to build an air fleet in time of emergency. The fleet-in-being or "Big Stick" form of preparedness has certain advantages. It can be used as a diplomatic weapon to terrorize an opponent into surrender without a fight, as Hitler found. But at the same time, the fleet-in-being has serious limitations. Obso-

---

[16] Chief, Materials Br, Mat Div, to S. N. Colby (Alcoa), 13 Jul 32, WFCF 381 Mobilization, 1939.
[17] Dir, Planning Br, OASW, to CofAC, 1 Nov 37, and 1st Wrapper Ind, OCAC to Chief, Mat Div, with Incls, 9 Nov 37, as well as 2d Wrapper Ind, Mat Div to CofAC, 3 Dec 37, AHO Plans Div 145.93–182.

lescence in aviation is so great that large numbers of old aircraft rapidly become relatively vulnerable to fewer aircraft of newer design and superior performance, as France found to her sorrow after the outbreak of World War II. In the United States, officers of the War Department in general and the Air Corps in particular were firmly committed to a policy that emphasized the importance of capacity to build, the importance of industrial potential, the power to create and replenish an air force, rather than a fleet-in-being. This idea was repeatedly promulgated formally as official doctrine on many occasions.[18] Nevertheless, the implications of the policy were not thought out to their further limits.

Educational orders constituted but one of the several means by which the Air Corps could have helped assure the existence of a strong and healthy industry ready to climb to peak output soon after receiving orders for items in mass-production quantities. An educational order is an order designed to familiarize a manufacturer with the item he will be expected to produce in an emergency. In its simplest form, an educational order might involve little more than acquainting the contractor with the item he is to make. In its most complex form it might even include the construction of jigs and fixtures as well as tools and dies to be held on a stand-by basis.

The Defense Act of 1920 authorized the use of educational orders, but the actual execution of contracts depended upon the willingness of Congress to appropriate funds.[19] Beginning in 1927 the War Department asked for funds to launch an educational order program. Similar measures were introduced repeatedly thereafter, but Congress showed little enthusiasm to provide funds for "if and when" purposes.[20] Not until the mounting threat of the dictatorships in Europe and Asia was dangerously far advanced did the legislators relent. In June of 1938 Congress authorized funds for educational orders, but the sum allowed was only $2,000,000, to be spread amongst all the arms and services. As the international crisis became more acute the War Department returned to Congress to present plans for a larger educational order program. In 1939, with the menace of war too obvious to ignore, Congress responded generously, but by then it was too late.[21] The carefulful preparations that might have been secured at slight expense in the years of peace were at that late date to be had, if at all, only at tremendous cost.

Thus, in the matter of educational orders as in so many other instances, military leaders could retire behind congressional skirts. Since Congress provided no funds, let Congress shoulder the blame. War Department officers could rightly

---

[18] Baker Board Rpt, p. 64. Since the Baker findings were declared official policy by the President, the Baker report takes on more importance than a mere recommendation. See also annual report of the Assistant Secretary of War, 1936, p. 25, in the Secretary's Report, and testimony of ASW Woodring at Senate Hearings on WD appropriation, March 3, 1936, p. 30.

[19] 41 Stat 764, sec. 123.

[20] For an example of congressional attitude on educational orders in the mid-thirties, see remarks of Representative C. C. Bolton of Ohio, Cong Rcd, February 19, 1935, p. 2224.

[21] See summary of WD interest in educational orders in the report of the Assistant Secretary of War, 1939, pp. 16–17.

claim to have recognized the need for educational orders to broaden the base of the aircraft industry for an emergency. But was this enough? There is a good deal of evidence in the record to suggest that the officers of the Industrial Planning Section at Wright Field did not think through the whole problem and see its many ramifications.

Perhaps the decided limitations in the imagination of planning officers in the Air Corps were spelled out most clearly when the Office of the Assistant Secretary asked for recommendations on educational orders from the Air Corps. When Congress seemed about to authorize funds, the War Department asked for a report as to what jigs, dies, and gauges the Air Corps would wish to procure with its share of the money. The Air Corps replied at length explaining that aircraft design was in continual flux, and as a consequence, prewar investment in production tools was "neither practical nor economical." [22] This was certainly true—but it begged the question.

In refusing to spend money on production tools for airframes as such, the air arm was probably pursuing sound policy. But this view of the problem utterly failed to consider the matter of standardized components and accessories. Oleo struts afford an example. The oleo strut is a piston and cylinder assembly used to cushion the shock of landing by forcing hydraulic fluid through a restricted orifice. The machining of oleo struts calls for skilled craftsmanship, work done to close tolerances, and a considerable amount of production experience. In the rush to rearm for World War II an acute bottleneck developed in the production of these struts. While not an entirely standard item, the oleo strut did lend itself to the educational order program. A little money spent during 1937 and 1938 on training if not on tooling up for production might have gone far to eliminate the bottleneck that endangered the air rearmament program after the crisis arrived.

The objection of Air Corps planners to the use of educational funds was not limited to the idea of prewar production tooling alone. They rejected the whole concept of educational orders for air arm items. One of the officers most actively engaged in the work of preparedness planning on the eve of World War II flatly asserted that the use of educational orders was not "practicable" for air arm matériel. He argued that the "proprietory nature" of so many individual items of Air Corps equipment that might lend themselves to the application of educational orders would preclude the use of such orders. Manufacturers, he claimed, would be unwilling in time of peace to turn over drawings, specifications, and tools to "outside interests" or potential competitors.[23] This may have been true, but there is no indication that the Air Corps ever undertook an extensive program to persuade the manufacturers of critical items to consider the substantial advantage they would enjoy if they selected and "educated" their own secondary sources in peacetime rather than waiting for war when arbitrary assign-

---

[22] R&R, Plans Div to Exec, OCAC, 1 Nov 37, with inclosed draft Memo for OASW, AHO Plans Div 145.91–182.

[23] Exec, Mat Div, to Chief, Mat Div, and CofAC in turn, 18 May 37, WFCF 032 Legislation, 1939.

ments of proprietory rights to alternative sources might prove necessary.

Clearly then, while Air Corps officers admitted the assumption that a healthy aircraft industry was vital to national defense, they failed to explore even the immediate environs of their premise, let alone its outer orbits. Unfortunately, this myopia was not confined to the single premise concerning the need for maintaining a healthy industry. A similar shortsightedness seems to have been prevalent elsewhere too, notably in connection with the fundamentally important policy of whether or not wartime production expansion should be achieved by expanding the small extant aircraft industry or by converting existing facilities of others, such as the automotive industry.

Conversion Versus Expansion

On one point, at least, there was substantial agreement by all concerned with mobilization planning. If war should come, the existing aircraft industry would prove entirely inadequate to provide the many thousands of aircraft required. Additional sources would be necessary, whether they were found by expanding the existing industry after the arrival of an emergency or by converting the productive capacity of manufacturers normally outside the aircraft industry. The selection of one or the other of these alternatives necessarily depended in some measure upon the definition or conception of the problem framed by the staff officers responsible for a solution to it.

There seems to have been a good deal of confusion as to the exact nature of the job to be done. The plans of the War Department for an emergency were for the most part conceived in terms of an M-day. In his report for 1938 the Secretary of War specifically warned the nation against the danger of assuming that there would be a cushion of time for eleventh-hour preparedness as there had been in the years 1914–17.[24] Yet, at the same time, air arm officers went on assuming that the Navy was still the first line of defense and the Air Corps would not be called upon to provide a substantial force for immediate action. Officers of the Industrial Planning Section at Wright Field, on whom the Assistant Secretary placed the burden of decision, saw their task primarily as one of speeding the production of aircraft *after* M-day.[25]

As a consequence of this confusion and uncertainty in defining the exact nature of the job to be done, the planners had a rather hazy base upon which to decide whether to convert or to expand. The record of experience in World War I, which might have been helpful, was not readily available. An elaborate history of the aircraft production effort in World War I never reached publication. One copy of the manuscript was destroyed in a fire and another was, to all practical purposes, lost in the files where it was "discovered" during World War II, too late to be of real use. For want of specific evidence, even the most fundamental questions remained unanswered. As a result, decisions had to be made on the basis of opinions, not facts.

[24] *Report of the Secretary of War, 1938*, p. 2.
[25] AAF Hist Study 40, p. 5. For delegation of responsibility for decision on conversion or expansion, see OASW, Planning Br Cir No. 2, 20 Jul 33, AHO Plans Div 145.93–187.

Between 1920 and the beginning of World War II, opinion in the Air Corps moved to and fro on the question of conversion versus expansion. In the twenties most officers favored conversion. Later there was a tendency to favor production by the aircraft industry, leaving to outsiders the roles of parts suppliers and subcontractors. Finally, in the middle thirties responsible officers in the Air Corps again swung back to the idea of conversion.[26] However, having made this decision, the planners promptly ignored the alternative of expansion.[27] They made no exploratory studies of the problems that might be encountered in an expansion of the aircraft industry, apparently assuming that the decision to rely upon conversion would never be reversed.

Once they had decided upon conversion instead of expansion, the officers of the Industrial Planning Section selected the automobile industry as the logical source of industrial capacity for aircraft production in wartime. But their choice was valid only insofar as staff officers could sell the idea of conversion to the aircraft manufacturers as well as the automobile firms. Unfortunately, the parties concerned were not always enthusiastic. One of the major automobile manufacturers on whom the wartime burden would of necessity be thrust was reported to be opposed to making even so much as a study of the subject until war came.[28] On the other hand, aircraft builders were understandably reluctant to encourage any genuine interest in aircraft construction in automotive circles, where such interest might ripen into competition. A wide gap separated the thinking of the car builders and the aircraft manufacturers.[29]

If conversion of the automotive industry in wartime was to become a reality, Air Corps officers somehow had to bring together the men who produced aircraft and those who turned out automobiles. There was much ground to be covered in getting the two industries to the point where they could exchange ideas, talk the same language, and in general appreciate each other's problems so as to be ready for a high order of co-operation when war came.[30] Nonetheless, Air Corps officers responsible for procurement planning appear to have taken relatively few steps in this direction in the between-war years.

In April 1938, when war in Europe seemed more than ever imminent, they finally took the initiative. The Chief of the Air Corps himself asked the Secretary of War to approve a plan to use Air Corps transportation to fly a number of engineers from Detroit to the west coast to study production problems in the aircraft industry. Apart from the cost of the flights themselves, the expedition would be at the manufacturers' expense.

---

[26] AAF Hist Study 40, pp. 10–11.
[27] *Ibid.*, p. 13.
[28] Glenn L. Martin to Capt C. H. Welsh, Proc Planning Representative, New York City, 12 May 36, AHO Plans Div 145.93–182.

[29] For evidence on this gap, see, for example, Eugene Edward Wilson, *Slipstream: The Autobiography of an Aircraftsman* (New York: Whittlesey House [1950]), page 265, mentioning the "feud" between the mass production industry and "the carriage trade."
[30] Apart from getting aircraft and automobile makers to understand each other, the Air Corps faced the problem of training its own officers to understand each of them. See, for example, Lecture, CofAC, Current Proc and Allied Problems, AIC.

In the weeks immediately ahead during the spring of 1938 the automobile engineers faced a slack period and could afford to be away from their regular jobs. Unfortunately, for reasons unstated, the Secretary rejected the request and suggested that the matter be raised again "in the fall."[31] "In the fall" was too late. By then the slack season had passed and before another fall rolled around, the aircraft manufacturers were far too busy with foreign orders to entertain visitors from Detroit. The lost opportunity could not be recaptured. Once the war actually broke in Europe, trained aircraft engineers became an even scarcer commodity, and the War Department had to pay dearly for their services.

Much of the record of Air Corps' planning to convert the automobile industry tells of lost opportunities, though the account is not entirely one of frustration. There were some substantial efforts made by industrial planning officers in the Air Corps to work out the detailed steps for converting the car industry to aircraft production. In some instances the planners actually drew up formal "factory plans" that helped to bring the problems of conversion into clearer focus. A representative factory plan completed in June 1938 illustrates the limits that circumscribed the thinking of officers engaged in the work of the Industrial Planning Section at Wright Field.

District officers, using the procedures and instructions drafted by IPS, prepared a factory plan for the Packard, Graham-Paige, and Hudson facilities in Detroit.[32] The three firms were to be converted to production of a twin-engine bomber. Although the bomber actually used for planning purposes was the Glenn L. Martin production model B–10, which was already approaching obsoletion in 1938, the planners were less concerned with the B–10 as such than with the general problem: Can a twin-engine bomber of 12,000 to 14,000 pounds gross weight be successfully manufactured in the facilities available for conversion?

The Air Corps planners had to break the aircraft into its components to determine whether or not the available labor skills, engineering talent, machine tools, floor space, and the like were available in the facilities selected for conversion. At this point the planning officers were plunged into difficulties. They found the Detroit manufacturers utterly inexperienced in appraising the problems to be encountered in aircraft production through a study of drawings and samples. This was scarcely surprising, in view of the differences in the items produced by the two industries, but instead of training the manufacturers by thrusting upon them the task of making a production analysis, thus helping them to learn by experience, Air Corps officers used a study prepared by Glenn L. Martin. The Air Corps lacked funds and the automobile manufacturers were unwilling to spend their own for a fresh approach, so the planners did the next best thing and borrowed a production study. This was ex-

---

[31] CofAC to SW, 26 Apr 38, copy with marginal notes on reply by Gen Westover, AHO Plans Div 145.93–182.

[32] The following paragraphs are based upon the factory plan of 25 June 1938, copy in AMC Historical Office files.

pedient, but it missed the whole point of the exercise.

By imposing upon the automobile manufacturers a production analysis based on Martin's shop practices, the planners tended to force the patterns and techniques of the job-shop aircraft industry upon the mass-production automotive industry. And at the same time, the Detroit manufacturers did not get the value of the experience they would have acquired had they actually come to grips with the problem of making a production analysis of a twin-engine bomber. The stock response industrial planning officers subsequently gave to this criticism was that there were no funds available and planners had to rely entirely upon the willing co-operation of the manufacturers. This was certainly true, but since it was and the results were unsatisfactory, the officers of the Industrial Planning Section were under a clear obligation to push aggressively for educational funds. Instead, they rejected invitations from the Assistant Secretary of War to lay plans for spending educational order money when it became available.[33]

If one accepts the limits imposed upon procurement planning and advance training by lack of funds as unavoidable, there still remain grounds for criticizing the vision of those who drew up the factory plans. The B–10 bomber plan, for example, reflects a touching faith in the ability of the automobile manufacturers because of their "enormous capacity."[34]

While it was true that the facilities being surveyed did have "enormous capacity," the phrase was meaningless. The factory plan itself failed to provide a detailed list of the machine tools available, nor did it indicate whether the available tools could work to the tolerances required in aircraft construction. In short, the plan retired into vague generalities at exactly the point where precise information would be most useful in an emergency.

In at least one respect the B–10 factory plan probably justified itself. Procurement planning officers discovered that despite the "enormous capacity" of Packard, Graham-Paige, and Hudson with a combined total of over 7,750,000 square feet of floor space, an additional 500,000 square feet of new construction would be necessary. Assembly areas would have to be provided near the fly-away point with bay areas of sufficient dimension to accommodate the wings of a bomber. Even in the case of the B–10 with its modest wing span of 70 feet 6 inches, the available bay areas were inadequate. The B–18, a production model twin-engine bomber in 1938, had a wing span of 89 feet, 6 inches, and the trend in bombers was toward even greater spans.

Thus, in practice, the Air Corps' policy of conversion could not be taken at face value. Conversion might of necessity also involve a certain amount of expansion, as the B–10 factory plan clearly revealed. But the IPS officers failed to act upon this consideration. What is more, the record suggests that they were not very resourceful in making use of the experience on expansion already available from British precedents.

In the mid-thirties the British Government launched an extensive preparedness

---

[33] R&R, Plans Div to Exec, OCAC, 1 Nov 37, with enclosed draft Memo for OASW, AHO Plans Div 145.91–182. See also, Interview with Detroit Dist Hist Office, 1945, same file.

[34] Factory Plan of 25 Jun 38, copy in AMC Hist Office files.

program of which one feature was the so-called shadow factory plan. Among these shadow factories were airframe and engine assembly plants erected at government expense to be operated by managerial and labor skills outside the regular aircraft industry. One such was the airframe assembly plant erected near the famous Austin factory near Birmingham. The aircraft to be produced was designed by the Fairey aircraft firm, but the labor and management in an emergency were to be recruited from the Austin force while the nearby Austin plant itself would manufacture parts to supply the shadow assembly plant.[35]

The military attachés of the United States stationed in London reported on the shadow factory program of the Air Ministry at great length.[36] The program as a whole embraced six major and twelve minor facilities. By the end of 1937 it involved an investment of some £7,500,000 ($37,500,000).[37] Out of this expenditure came a wealth of experience concerning facility expansion, contract forms, techniques of compensation, techniques for perfecting liaison between designers and producers, as well as much other information.

Officers of the Planning Branch in the Office of the Assistant Secretary of War were aware of the opportunities offered by British activity in the field of procurement planning. They sought and received permission for representatives of the War Department to visit some of the British shadow establishments. Moreover, they invited the Industrial Planning Section at Wright Field, amongst others, to submit a list of questions to guide the representatives in their dealings with the British Air Ministry.[38] This was in December 1936. The officer who was then Chief of the Industrial Planning Section responded with unusual enthusiasm.[39] Not content merely to compile questions for others, he asked for authority to send some representatives from his organization at Wright Field.[40] Unfortunately, the request was still shunting to and fro in the Air Corps paper mill in the summer of 1938.[41] Once again a potentially fruitful idea lost its point by being delayed and deferred until too late.

Officers of the Industrial Planning Section could have profited from British experience with shadow factories, even without sending observers abroad. Military attachés recorded much of value about the shadow factory program. Some of their reports gave references to published articles on the program. Both the attaché reports and the published matter were available in the Technical Data Library at Wright Field. Once again, however, the officers of the Industrial Planning Section appear to have discovered them

---

[35] Military Attaché, London, Rpt 39281, 4 Mar 38, AMC CADO F35/332.

[36] See, for example, Military Attaché, London, Rpt 38310, 19 Oct 36, a 55-page survey of the whole British rearmament program, and subsequent reports, *passim*, in CADO C21/4/6 et al.

[37] Military Attaché Rpt 39047, 5 Nov 37, AHO Plans Div 145.93–182.

[38] Memo, Dir Planning Br, OASW, for CofAC, 11 Dec 36, AFCF 360.02A Foreign Aviation.

[39] See reply to questionnaire by Mat Div, 24 Dec 36, AFCF 360.02A Foreign Aviation.

[40] Chief, Industrial Planning Sec, to CofAC, 4 Jan 38, AHO Plans Div 145.93–182. Note the time lag between the questionnaire and the request.

[41] 1st Ind, Mat Div to CofAC, 28 Jun 38, basic unknown, WFCF 381.4 Shadow Factories 1940; Chief, Plans Div, to CofAC, 10 Jun 38, AHO Plans Div 145.93–182.

too late. When inspected after the war, the library charge-out cards indicate that they had been used only once. The only name on virtually all of the cards was that of the officer in charge of mobilization planning. The date on each was November 1938, a date after the President had touched off the program to expand the air arm. In sum, then, although Air Corps officers expected to rely upon conversion of automotive facilities to produce aircraft in adequate quantity during an emergency, their exploratory studies of conversion were limited both in scope and in imagination.

The Chief of the Air Corps was by no means unaware of the many weaknesses in air arm mobilization planning. In 1938, on the eve of the expansion program that ultimately was to transform the Air Corps into a mighty force, he called a conference of representative aircraft manufacturers. He hoped to secure their co-operation in the mobilization that loomed ahead. In his introductory remarks he suggested some of the questions that would have to be asked and answered if the coming mobilization was to be rapid, orderly, and economical. Would aircraft builders allow manufacturers outside the industry to reproduce their designs? On what basis? Should converted automobile manufacturers draw parts and components from their own regular suppliers or should the air arm undertake a vast program to provide government-furnished equipment? Should the government provide assembly facilities? If so, should the government operate the plants? Should the automobile manufacturers or the old-line aircraft builders assume responsibility? Should the government immediately erect shadow plants or should industry take the initiative?[42] These were all intelligent questions. They were the right questions to pose because they reflected problems yet unanswered. They had to be answered before the Air Corps could expect production to the limit. But the formulation of such questions in September 1938 was decidedly late in the game. If mobilization planning is to be truly helpful it has to be done in the years of peace to prevent the chaos of last-minute improvisation.

Air Corps Planning in Perspective

A Signal Corps officer once remarked that prewar mobilization plans were "in-the-safe-mirages," an apt description when applied to Air Corps planning efforts. The annual report of the Materiel Division at Wright Field stated in August 1938 that air arm mobilization planning had become more "practical" in recent months, yet at that very time much of the effort expended by IPS officers still went into the task of converting the 1933 mobilization plan into the Protective Mobilization Plan.[43]

To say the very least, many features of the air arm mobilization plan were unrealistic. The officers who worked out the details often seemed to have lost touch with the realities of war during the long years of peace. Some, for example, believed that the way to achieve increased production was to freeze design.[44] Such

---

[42] Comments by Gen Westover, cited n. 10, above.
[43] Draft of annual rpt, Mat Div, 27 Aug 38, WFCF 321.9 Annual Rpt.
[44] Ltr, Plans Sec to IPS, 7 Mar 38, AHO Plans Div 145.93–182. This entire letter reflects the lack of realism that colored much procurement planning work.

PLANNING FOR INDUSTRIAL MOBILIZATION 167

views ignored the bitter experience of World War I: to gear mobilization plans to a concept of rigidly frozen designs was to invite disaster and to ignore the alternative. The alternative, of course, was to establish a system that would introduce modifications into the production line without retarding output. Such in-line modifications are at best difficult to administer, but planning officers certainly did nothing to improve the situation by ignoring the matter entirely during the prewar years.

What the planners needed most, it would appear, was the stimulus to self-criticism. They needed some means by which they could subject their plans, their work, even their thinking, to objective, disinterested criticism or evaluation. Most military organizations are probably deficient in this respect in peacetime, but the theoretical character of their work probably made the mobilization planners exceptionally vulnerable. Some officers had recognized this deficiency, for from time to time those in charge conducted command post exercises and war games to test the efficacy of the planning being done.[45] This was a move in the right direction, no doubt, but the war games were largely routine. They gave an opportunity to check the adequacy of procedures and practices already established but did little to question the soundness of underlying assumptions.

Only a few war games were conducted. At best they seem to have been of limited use. Perhaps the best indication of their unimportance and occasional character is to be seen from the manner in which many of the records of these exercises were filed: Material on "War games" was placed under "Games," along with "Athletics" and "Physical training" in the central files.

In general, few attempts were made at self-criticism although on occasion, of course, there were individual officers who did question the premises underlying mobilization planning. After one meeting of procurement planners at Air Corps headquarters, an officer representing one of the procurement districts wrote a scathing criticism of the whole conference and the ideas presented there. With more courage than tact he contrasted the subject of the conference as advertised in the agenda with the subjects actually discussed. Then with unusual prescience he launched into a number of specific criticisms of Air Corps planning that events in the following months were to prove only too valid. He scored particularly the absence of adequate planning data and the failure to use current procurement as a point of departure.[46] Unfortunately, the criticism was not welcomed and was not weighed for what it might be worth. Somewhat later a complaint to headquarters from Wright Field described this particular critic as "overzealous" in "trying to make a worthwhile showing" and as one "impatient" with

---

[45] See Memo, Chief, Allocations Div, OASW, for Plans Div, OCAC, 21 Jul 38, AHO Plans Div 145.93-182. See also, AFCF 353.6 *passim*.

[46] Mimeograph MS, Comments on New York District on Resume of Procurement Planning Conference Held in OCAC, 6 Sep 38; and Proc Planning Representative, New York City, to CofAC, 25 Oct 38. Both in AHO 145.92-182. For an interesting postwar opinion tending to confirm these criticisms, see transcript of testimony by Maj Gen O. P. Echols, 29 Sep 47, before President's Air Policy Comm, National Archives, Rcds Group 220, box 6, file 37-1d.

the overworked IPS staff.[47] Officers engaged in the work of industrial planning evinced little desire to submit their presuppositions and their work to criticism, even to the criticism of officers within the organization.

From the perspective of the postwar era, it is possible to see the problem of Air Corps industrial mobilization planning with some clarity. By and large the central difficulty seems to have been the tendency of the planners to emphasize organization rather than operations, form rather than function. The planners concocted highly complex mobilization plans but failed to come to grips with the heart of the matter, the assumptions underlying their plans. They put more emphasis upon the office than upon the idea. Yet, for all the stress upon the details of planning to the neglect of principle, in actual point of fact the Industrial Planning Section at Wright Field did not even do a very good job of housekeeping.[48]

---

[47] Exec, Mat Div, to Col A. H. Hobley, 28 Jan 39, AFCF 004.4 Firms and Factories.

[48] Perhaps the most dramatic evidence of the air arm's ineffective planning for war is to be seen in the memo drafted by the Planning Branch, OASW, for the Assistant Secretary to send to the President in reply to his rearmament proposals, 10 November 1938. The productive capacity of the nation's aircraft industry was, he confessed, "unknown." (AHO Plans Div 145.93–182) If the judgments rendered in this critique seem harsh on the planners, they are no harsher than the criticisms rendered after World War II by the industrial planning officers who sought to profit from their earlier mistakes. See, for example, Pre-World War II Industrial Preparedness, Air Coordinating Com Project 5, prepared by Industrial Mobilization Planning Div, AMC, 10 Mar 48, especially secs. E, F, and G, WFHO.

CHAPTER VIII

The Tide Turns

*The President Proposes;
Congress Disposes*

During the summer of 1938 President Roosevelt reached the conclusion that drastic steps would have to be taken to rearm the nation in the face of menacing dictatorships in Europe and Asia. A number of people contributed to the formulation of this crucial decision. No doubt Hitler's speech at Nuremberg, which the President heard on the radio a scant fortnight before the betrayal of Czechoslovakia in 1938, helped to precipitate the decision to rearm.[1] But there were others, too, who helped to condition the President's mind and to prepare him for a new tack his administration was about to follow. Ambassador Hugh R. Wilson sent frightening reports to the President from Berlin. Businessmen returning from visits to German factories communicated their alarm indirectly through officials in the War Department.[2]

When at last Ambassador William C. Bullitt returned from France with evidence confirming these reports, the President made up his mind.[3] There was no alternative: the United States must rearm, whatever the cost, and air power must play a leading role in national defense.

White House Meeting

On 14 November 1938 the President summoned a number of his political and military advisors to the White House. He did not ask for advice, he laid his policies on the line. The Army air arm, he declared, must be built into a heavy striking force. After noting the sorry position to which the United States had fallen in contrast to recent advances in German air power, the President asserted that the Air Corps alone required a strength of 20,000 aircraft backed by an annual productive capacity of 24,000 units. Unfor-

---

[1] Robert E. Sherwood, *Roosevelt and Hopkins: An Intimate History* (New York: Harper and Brothers, 1950) pp. 99–100.
[2] Memo, Exec, OASW, for ASW, 23 Jun 38, SW files, item 568. See also, Wilson to President, 11 Jul '38, SW files, item 608. The Ambassador was influenced not alone by the reports of attachés and other such officials but also by conversations with at least two aircraft manufacturers from the United States who, as trained observers, grasped the implications of what they saw in the German factories they visited. In addition to reports of Glenn L. Martin

and James H. Kindelberger mentioned by Wilson, see Memo, E. E. Aldrin for CofAC, 17 Oct 38, item 710. An earlier report, by Mr. T. P. Wright of Curtiss-Wright, indicated that by 1936 German aircraft production was already three times that of the United States and Britain combined. See Wright to Brig Gen William H. Harris, Chief of Military History, 13 Oct 61, OCMH.
[3] Mark Skinner Watson, *Chief of Staff: Prewar Plans and Preparations*, UNITED STATES ARMY IN WORLD WAR II (Washington, 1950), pp. 131–32.

tunately, the President went on to point out, if he were to ask for any such number, Congress would vote him half as much. Far better, he felt, to ask for 10,000 to begin with and have some assurance of congressional support. The 10,000 aircraft, the President explained, could be procured over a two-year period. One-fourth of the total could be training craft; the remainder, all tactical or combat types, would be divided equally; half in active use, half in reserve.[4]

The White House meeting marked a turning point in the history of national defense. Military advisors who had been urging increases in strength upon the President for months, if not for years, now found themselves directed to plan an expansion of air power considerably larger than any for which they had ever dreamed of asking. Where, then, did the President get his figures?

Why 20,000? Did the President suggest this number initially to the generals or had the generals previously suggested the figure to the President? War Department officials had made numerous proposals during the summer of 1938 to increase Air Corps strength above the 2,320-unit limit then prevailing. Many programs were discussed, but none of those seriously considered seems to have exceeded a ceiling of 7,000 aircraft before the President set 10,000 as a goal.[5] The Chief of the Air Corps, Maj. Gen. Henry H. Arnold, undoubtedly did give the President some figures through Harry Hopkins, as he states in his memoirs, but his own subsequent testimony before a congressional committee indicates that it was the President rather than the generals who exerted the initiative.[6] Moreover, none of the programs mentioned in the War Department even remotely touched the figures initially considered by the President. As it now appears, the President privately decided that 30,000 not 20,000 aircraft were needed to face the German menace, but the cost of 30,000 aircraft induced him to set his "requirement" in the White House conference at 20,000. And even this figure he felt compelled to halve on grounds of political necessity.[7]

The President's Message to Congress

When the President sent a special message on national defense to Congress on 12 January 1939, he was fulfilling a political role as well as observing a constitutional and ceremonial rite. The President felt that a larger air force was necessary, but he also knew what such a force would cost. Rumors that the President intended to ask for 10,000 airplanes when Congress assembled were not denied at the White House. For six weeks before the opening of Congress newspaper writers speculated on the number of aircraft the President would seek. Instead of 10,000 or 8,000, or any of the other

---

[4] *Ibid.*, ch. V.

[5] General Arnold mentioned the 7,000 figure; Secretary Woodring said he had never heard of any figure above 10,000 mentioned in the War Department before the President's conference. See House Hearings on WD supplementary appropriation for 1940, May 19, 1939, p. 54, and June 5, 1939, pp. 275–79.

[6] Arnold, *Global Mission*, pp. 177–79; Arnold's testimony, House Hearings on WD appropriation for 1940, January 30, 1939, p. 296.

[7] The President's original aim of 30,000 aircraft is mentioned in Watson notes on interview with Maj Gen J. H. Burns (Ret), 7 Feb 47, OCMH.

figures guessed in the press, the Chief Executive suggested that funds should be provided for an increase of not less than 3,000 aircraft.[8] Congress gave an almost audible sigh as most congressmen admitted a "feeling of relief" that the President had been so "moderate" in his demands.[9] It was the essence of the Chief Executive's political skill to agree that half a loaf was better than none. Clearly, the President had trimmed his request to make it politically acceptable. Were his generals doing any differently when they in their turn went to Congress for funds?

The Air Corps Budget:
Fiscal Year 1940

By time-honored custom, appropriation committeemen opened hearings on the executive budget in the first month of the new year. Representatives of the War Department, including the Chief of Staff and the Chief of the Air Corps, were summoned to the Hill to defend the estimates they had prepared long since for approval by the Bureau of the Budget. Toward the end of January 1939, when General Arnold took his turn before the committee, his requests were something of an anticlimax. If the President had surprised Congress by asking for approximately 3,000 rather than the rumored 10,000 aircraft, General Arnold produced yet another surprise. He asked less money for new equipment than had been sought in the previous year, a figure sufficient to procure not more than 219 new aircraft. This minute request, he implied, was necessitated by the approach toward the authorized ceiling of 2,320.[10]

Thus the Air Corps was placed in the absurd position of curbing its request to stay within the legal limit even though the President had already informed the War Department of his desire for 20,000 aircraft and Congress had received his message asking for funds to provide at least 3,000. The congressmen might have been willing to accept this absurdity, knowing as they did that the budget was formulated nearly a year before, but there was an obvious discrepancy in the testimony given before them. While the Chief of the Air Corps solemnly declared that the Air Corps could not ask for more aircraft because of the 2,320 ceiling on authorized strength, a few days earlier the Chief of Staff, General Malin Craig, had informed the committee that the authorized ceiling was not 2,320 but 4,120.[11]

When the Chief of Staff had approved the War Department's estimates several months earlier, he had certainly seemed to believe 2,320 was the authorized ceiling on air strength. Moreover, his annual report, which by coincidence reached the newspapers on 14 November, the day of the White House meeting, had warned against the dangers of favoring one arm, such as the Air Corps, at the expense of the others.[12] Yet barely a month later he was claiming that 4,120 rather than 2,320

---

[8] *Cong Rcd,* January 12, 1939, p. 218ff.
[9] *Aviation* (February, 1939), p. 80. See also, comments in New York *Times* quoted in CWO Merton England and Dr. Chauncey Sanders, Legislation Relating to the Army Air Forces Training Program, 1939–1945, AAF Hist Studies, 7, revised 1946, copy in OCMH, p. 4.

[10] House Hearings on WD appropriation for 1940, January 30, 1939, pp. 11, 283. The 219 aircraft included 178 for the Regular Army and 41 for the Organized Reserves and National Guard.
[11] *Ibid.,* pp. 11, 294.
[12] New York *Times,* November 14, 1938.

was the legal ceiling on air power. His explanation was simple. The Air Corps Act of 1926 authorized 1,800 aircraft. The Act of 24 June 1936 authorized 2,320. If one construed the measures as supplementary, then the number of aircraft authorized amounted to the sum of the two, or 4,120.

The discrepancy between the testimony of the Chief of Staff and that of the Chief of the Air Corps led to an obvious question in Congress.[13] If 4,120 was the authorized ceiling, why then did the Air Corps come to the Hill asking for only enough new aircraft to reach 2,320, even though the President had urged Congress to provide for far more? Air Corps officers had not mistaken the meaning of statutes all along. On the contrary, there is ample evidence to show that they had tried to construe 4,120 as the ceiling but had met with resistance from within the War Department.[14] There it had been held that such an increase in air strength was "in excess of requirements" and would require a "huge annual increase" in the estimates presented to Congress in future years merely to maintain the enlarged air arm.[15]

Thus, when the Chief of the Air Corps testified in behalf of estimates based on a 2,320 ceiling, he was defending a figure that he had been constrained to accept by higher authority. When the Chief of Staff, who had long been unwilling to give the air arm an abnormal share of the War Department budget, testified in January 1939 that the legal ceiling on aircraft was 4,120, he spoke as a very recent convert. In fact, his conversion to a belief in air power seems to have dated from the White House meeting in November.[16]

In sum, the Air Corps estimate for fiscal year 1940 suggests that budgetary considerations determined the official statement of requirements presented to Congress by General Arnold far more than did tactical or strategic considerations. Which is to say, the generals seemed to be doing the very thing the President was condemned for doing: defining defense requirements not in terms of strategic necessity but upon a basis of what was politically feasible.

Executive Leadership

Bewildered congressmen might well have wondered what to believe when asked to vote on vital questions of national defense. The Air Corps asked for funds to reach a ceiling of 2,320 airplanes, and then in the very midst of the congressional hearings on this estimate the Chief of Staff declared that the legal ceiling was really 4,120, or nearly twice as many aircraft. On the other hand, the President let his intimate associates talk for nearly a month about 8,000 or 10,000 airplanes then, when Congress opened, asked for only 3,000.

Seen in retrospect, the President's tend-

---

[13] See exchange in Senate between Senator Sheppard and Senator Alben W. Barkley, *Cong Rcd*, February 27, 1939, pp. 1915–16.

[14] Copy, Memo, G–4 for CofS, 17 Jun 38, JAG (Army) Gen Rcds Sec 452.1 Aircraft; Memo, OASW for G–4, 29 Jul 38, SW files, AC, item 963; Memo, OCAC Fiscal Officer to Gen Arnold, 29 Nov 38, AFCF 360.01A.

[15] Unsigned Memo, undated but sometime following 16 October 1938, staff study offering arguments against 4,120 as a ceiling figure, WPD–OPD 3807–28A.

[16] Watson, notes on interv with Gen Burns.

ency to blow first hot and then cold, now 10,000, now 3,000, was perhaps deliberate and not haphazard planning. The President's 10,000-airplane goal may have served as a most useful trial balloon. Carefully "leaked" to the press, it gave the President an opportunity to provoke discussion on the point, an opportunity to accustom the public in general and congressmen in particular to the immense increases in air power that he sought.[17] Once the critics had fired all their ammunition at this trial balloon, the President could then ask for somewhat less and appear moderate in so doing. But there appears to have been a second purpose in the President's strategy. Besides convincing the public of the need for more air power, the President may have been working to convert individuals within the War Department as well. The long feud between the air and ground components had conditioned air arm officers to minimize their requests for funds and aircraft.[18] Rather than stir up the old fight annually, they seemed inclined to ask for less, to accept 2,320 as a ceiling rather than fight for 4,120. Thus the President's bold suggestion of 10,000 served as a dramatic catalyst that jarred Air Corps officers into thinking and planning in large numbers.

In the light of these developments, the requests of the Chief Executive appear to have been purposeful elements of political tactics. On the other hand, the Air Corps' request for funds to reach a ceiling of 2,320 rather than the 4,120 permitted by law was equally understandable. Neither folly nor blindness, this request merely reflected the obvious consequences of inflexibility in the legally prescribed system for budgetary planning. As any experienced congressman would know, the estimates presented by the Air Corps stemmed from plans initiated anywhere from eighteen months to two years earlier. If the Air Corps was to be held responsible for a blunder in asking for 2,320 when the real ceiling was 4,120, the responsible officers might with justice point out that the estimates presented were those approved by the Bureau of the Budget and the President himself. Moreover, the terms of the 1921 Budget and Accounting Act required the officers who presented an estimate to defend it loyally and take no initiative in asking for more.[19]

Between the time when the Bureau of the Budget originally approved the War Department estimates for fiscal year 1940 and the time when General Arnold went to the Hill to defend the air arm estimate, the diplomatic and strategic setting had changed most drastically. The President had changed his mind regarding expenditures for defense. So had the Chief of Staff. But the Budget and Accounting Act of 1921 made no provision for such changes. Designed to provide for or-

---

[17] The strategy of the President's leaks to the press may be followed clearly in the New York *Times,* viz., October 14, 1938, p. 13; October 15, p. 1; November 6, p. 1; November 13, sec. X, p. 8; November 19, p. 4; November 24, p. 22; December 5, p. 16; December 27, p. 3.

[18] Long after the President indicated his intention, in October 1938, of encouraging big increases in national defense, the War Department continued to inspire stories calling for increases in air strength up to 3,000 or 4,000. Even the Chief of the Air Corps hinted to reporters that an increase of 2,000 more aircraft would be the limit; see New York *Times,* October 16, p. 31; October 23, p. 8; October 23, sec. X, p. 5.

[19] 42 Stat 20, sec. 206. See above, pp. 60–61.

derly treatment in fiscal matters, the act proved too rigid in a dynamic political situation. The Chief of the Air Corps was thrust into the uncomfortable position of defending an estimate based upon a 2,320-aircraft ceiling in January 1939 even though the President, in November 1938, had already told him to work for 10,000.

The Congress Disposes

Early in February 1939 the chairman of the House Military Affairs Committee introduced a bill calling for an increase in air power to an authorized ceiling of 6,000 aircraft. The 6,000 figure was neither the 10,000 suggested by the President in November, the 3,000 he asked for in January, nor a plausible compromise suggested in Congress to adjust the two extremes. As a matter of fact, the proposed measure was a departmental bill. It was more or less drafted by officials in the War Department and presented to Congress as a desired objective.[20]

The transitions from 10,000 to 3,000 to 6,000 airplanes were the essence of the President's political art. His original intention in November had been to secure 10,000 aircraft for the Air Corps in two years, with three-quarters of the force to be combat types. During the latter half of November and throughout December the President read the omens as they appeared. He encountered considerable opposition from within the Army in favor of a balanced force rather than abnormal expenditures on air power alone. At the same time, when the President learned the probable cost of 10,000 airplanes as estimated by air arm officers, he began to doubt whether it would be possible to secure the necessary funds from a reluctant Congress. Once again he trimmed sail to meet the prevailing winds and agreed to accept a program of 5,500 aircraft with provision for a ceiling at 6,000, which allowed a margin for units on order.[21] Since there were on hand at the end of 1938 some 1,797 aircraft, of which 351 would soon be obsolete, the net available strength was 1,446. By adding to this the aircraft on order or about to be ordered from current appropriations there was a total of 2,464, which subtracted from 5,500 left 3,032.[22] So the President had asked Congress for about 3,000 airplanes.

The President's maneuver was exceedingly adroit, as events proved. His request for 3,000 won him support from the very people who had been most alarmed by the rumors of 10,000 or more aircraft emanating from "usually reliable sources" and undenied at the White House.[23] Yet even as his request for 3,000 was made, Air Corps officers were readying a bill asking for a ceiling of 6,000. This, of course, would not bear the White House label and in any event by the time it appeared the President would already have garnered the dividend of his apparent moderation.

---

[20] *Cong Rcd*, February 14, 1939, p. 1389.

[21] Watson, *Chief of Staff: Prewar Plans and Preparations*, pp. 139–43.

[22] Figures presented by ACofAC in committee Hearings quoted in *Cong Rcd*, February 14, 1939, p. 1377.

[23] See, for example, editorial in *Aviation* that praised the President's message as "very reasonable" and promised to back the administration to the hilt even though previously dubious about the big programs mentioned in the press. *Aviation* (February, 1939), p. 81.

THE TIDE TURNS

From Bill to Statute

Seen in contrast to the rising might of the Luftwaffe, the President's request for 3,000 aircraft came as a surprise. It tended to disarm the opposition. To ask for less would clearly be criminal negligence. As soon as the debate on the new aircraft ceiling began on the floor, the Republicans announced that an opposition caucus had agreed to support the administration measure in the interests of national defense.[24] But even with victory for the measure assured in principle, it was not carried without a fight. Isolationists and members of the economy bloc made a determined effort to scuttle the bill with amendments that would have spread the procurement program over a greater number of years.[25] Despite the determination of the bill's opponents, both Houses passed the measure. Adjustments in conference consumed the inevitable number of weeks, so it was not until April 1939 that the 6,000 ceiling became law and the Air Corps could actually proceed with the 5,500 program.[26]

The First Expansion Program

The White House meeting of 14 November 1938 touched off a furor of planning activity unlike anything seen in the War Department since the days of World War I. And in the midst of this furious bustle was the Assistant Secretary of War, Louis A. Johnson.

The Role of Louis Johnson

On the day following the White House meeting, Louis Johnson, as Acting Secretary of War, sent a directive to the Chief of Staff mapping out the steps to be followed in carrying out the President's orders. Taking his cue from the President, he asked for detailed plans to provide for an Air Corps of 10,000 aircraft in two years, half of which were to be in a reserve status without operating personnel and base facilities. To provide the productive capacity asked by the President, the Assistant Secretary directed the Chief of Staff to draw up budgetary plans for the construction of seven government-owned aircraft factories, each with an average capacity of 1,200 units per year. This capacity, in conjunction with the anticipated expansion of the existing industry would, he hoped, be capable of meeting the total production potential desired at the White House.[27]

Louis Johnson, with restless drive and tireless energy, built fires on every hand to break through the administrative routines with which the War Department had become encumbered during the long years of peace. Though Congress was slow in appropriating the funds necessary to start the aircraft program on its way, Johnson would not permit this to become an excuse for delay. He ordered all the necessary aircraft contracts to be prepared and ready for formal approval the moment the President signed the appropriation bill.[28] Again and again when opportunity offered, the Assistant Secre-

---
[24] *Cong Rcd*, February 14, 1939, pp. 1375–76, debate on H.R. 3791.
[25] *Ibid.*, pp. 1378–87. See also, House Rpt 32, February 8, 1939; Senate Rpt, February 22, 1939; and Doc 38, March 16, 1939.
[26] 53 Stat 555, April 3, 1939.

[27] Memo, Actg SW for CofS, 15 Nov 38, SW files, AC.
[28] CofAC to Chief, Mat Div, 1 Mar 39, AFCF 452.1 Proc of Aircraft.

WAR DEPARTMENT SUBCOMMITTEE OF THE HOUSE APPROPRIATIONS COMMITTEE *at the White House, February 1939. Left to right: Edward T. Taylor, Chairman J. Buell Snyder, Joe Starnes, David T. Terry, John H. Kerr, and John C. Pugh.*

tary seized the initiative to drive the air rearmament program ahead with vigor.[29]

The aggressive leadership of Johnson brought results. A scant ten days after the White House meeting, the Chief of Staff approved the formal staff plan for the two-year, 10,000-aircraft program. Some staff officers were ordered to draft the special legislation required by the program, while others were directed to study possible means of speeding procurement under existing statutes. For a start, plans were laid to build at least 2,000 of the 10,000 aircraft in government-owned

---

[29] Examples of Johnson's vigorous leadership are many, e.g., ASW to CofS, 28 Nov 38, WPD–OPD 3807–28A; Actg SW to Atty Gen, 10 Nov 38, JAG (Army) Gen Ref Br 700.12, 29 Oct 38; ASW to Lockheed *et al.*, 30 Jul 38, SW files; *Aerodigest* (June 1939), p. 26. For a considered appraisal by an officer who worked closely with Johnson during his term as Assistant Secretary of War, see Gen Burns to TAG, 7 Feb 47, filed in OCMH with Gen Burns Interv.

stand-by facilities, air arsenals, as they were called, to be built at Ogden, Utah; Denver, Colorado; Dayton, Ohio; Harrisburg, Pennsylvania; and at three other sites to be selected upon the basis of available land, strategic vulnerability, labor market, postwar utility to the Air Corps, and the like. Production was to be by private management using privately developed designs. Only the facility would be government-owned.[30] Louis Johnson's energy soon made itself felt in every echelon.

The 10,000 aircraft program had scarcely been defined before the Chief of the Air Corps directed his Plans Staff to do some "deep thinking" on the long-range problems involved. The expansion program posed many problems but none more vexing than the one the Chief of the Air Corps himself posed for his plans staff. How, he wished to know, would it be possible to develop enough productive capacity to meet the requirements of the mobilization program on time and still maintain a volume of business large enough to keep the industry healthy after the program strength had been reached at the end of two years. If the Air Corps used up every bit of available capacity and urged the construction of additional facilities to meet the desired objectives of the expansion program on time, then would not the industry find itself at the close of the two-year program with virtually no orders on hand? "Somehow," said General Arnold,

LOUIS JOHNSON

"we must find a way to lick that problem."[31]

General Arnold was right. If the Air Corps expected the full co-operation of the industry, somehow a plan had to be worked out to provide assurances that the aircraft manufacturers would not be left high and dry—and out of business—once the Air Corps reached full strength. Without the enthusiastic co-operation of the industry the whole program was obviously doomed. With or without government-owned air arsenals, the aircraft designers and the managerial skills of the industry would be indispensable.

The Industry's Reaction

As General Arnold clearly saw, the long-term interests of national defense

---

[30] AAF Hist Study, 22, Legislation Relating to the AAF Materiel Program, 1939–1945, USAF Hist Div Aug 49, p. 5; Memo, ASW for President, 19 Nov 38, AFCF 319.1A Rpts; AC Project Rcds (Lyon Papers) 2-C, Data for Defense of 5500 Program; Memo CofAC for CofS, 28 Nov 38, WPD–OPD 3807–28A.

[31] Memo, CofAC to Col Carl Spaatz, 18 Nov 38, AFCF 360.01A.

were best served by adding productive capacity in the aircraft industry. If the nation did not become embroiled in war there would be no rush of orders, and the expanded industry would atrophy. An enlarged capacity and an economically sound industry were both sound assets for national defense. From the military point of view both had to be considered. On the other hand, it is hardly surprising that the aircraft industry as a whole tended to be more concerned with the immediate problem of orders than with the ultimate possibility of a wartime demand too great for the existing industry to handle. After the long, lean years of depression the industry preferred, quite understandably, to work around the clock and even expand if necessary rather than see the government set up a series of air arsenals that might absorb enough government orders, after the program was completed, to drive some of the privately owned aircraft manufacturers out of business.

The president of the Aeronautical Chamber of Commerce, who could speak for the industry if anyone could, was certain that the existing industry could meet the Army's requirements "without straining." Other industry spokesmen joined the chorus to this effect, especially after the rumored target of 10,000 had been cut down to the realities of the 5,500 units in the expansion program.[32] No doubt the industry actually could have met the demands of the program in hand. But this was no guarantee that adequate capacity existed to meet the vastly greater requirements of mobilization should war come. Responsible officers in the Air Corps were well aware of this. Their staff studies indicated that productive capacity was "far below" mobilization requirements.[33] Nevertheless, more and more they came to accept the manufacturers' point of view.

Between the time of the White House meeting in November 1938 and the passage of the expansion program bill the following April, Air Corps' policy changed markedly. The original plan, which emphasized building up productive capacity, gave way to a plan that stressed the need for keeping existing capacity loaded with a sufficient volume to save manufacturers from bankruptcy. Unfriendly critics of the industry were inclined to suggest that "profits" won out over "preparedness." It would be fairer, perhaps, to put the contention another way: of the twin objectives sought by the air arm in the name of defense, that concerned with fostering a healthy industry won out over that concerned with building up productive capacity for war. Both objectives were valid. Neither could safely be ignored.

When Air Corps leaders took the short-term rather than the long-term view their action was entirely understandable. The possibility of being swamped with war orders too numerous for the industry to supply was a contingency of the remote future, but the complaints of the manufacturers were decidedly immediate. It was all very well to talk in grandiose terms about preparedness and air arse-

---

[32] *Aviation* (February 1939), p. 81; *Aerodigest* (February 1939), p. 42; E. N. Gott to W. W. Barbour, 1 Mar 38, quoted in *Cong Rcd*, March 1, 1939, p. 2073.

[33] CofAC to Chief, Mat Div, 25 Mar 39, WFCF 452.1 Adaptability of Aircraft to Production.

nals and stand-by capacity, but while Congress debated there were no funds and without funds there could be no contracts.

Between the reluctance of Congress to appropriate vast sums for preparedness and the frequently voiced demands of manufacturers seeking more business, Air Corps policy makers began to stress the immediate rather than the remote. As late as April 1939, the Chief of the Materiel Division seriously proposed stretching out current Air Corps contracts over a longer period of time to save manufacturers from having to discharge their trained employees at the end of the current program.[34] Similarly, the Chief of the Air Corps suggested a plan to stretch the available appropriations by purchasing airframes without armament, signal equipment, and other accessories.[35] Both these proposals were rejected, but the mere fact that they were made suggests the extent to which Air Corps officials were preoccupied during the first half of 1939 with the task of assuring the industry enough business to keep it alive.

Until special or emergency appropriations were forthcoming there could be no contracts placed for aircraft in quantity over and above the few provided for in the regular annual appropriation. Without such contracts, manufacturers continued to worry about filling up the acres of idle capacity in their plants. The more they worried, the more they were inclined to report that they had plenty of capacity available to meet military requirements. The more often these assurances were voiced, the more remote became the air arsenal program.

Even before Congress assembled, officials in the War Department had begun to cast about for alternatives. A hasty survey by air arm officers indicated that a comparatively small investment of private capital could increase aircraft output by as much as 50 percent.[36] On the other hand, the air arsenal program would require millions in appropriations from Congress. Since private financing was more expedient than public, the President's plan for preparedness in the form of stand-by capacity simply faded away. By April the aviation press was reporting that the administration's proposal for "nationalized" facilities had been shelved.[37]

The month of April 1939 marked a conscious turning point in the attitude of the industry toward the rearmament program. Down to the passage of the bill authorizing a 6,000 aircraft ceiling, most manufacturers were worried about filling their plants. Thereafter, more and more manufacturers began to worry about finding enough floor space to meet their production requirements. Money, of course, made the difference. Toward the end of April Congress appropriated nearly $27,000,000 for immediate expenditure on new equipment, more than $31,000,000 more for expenditure during the fiscal year, and over $18,000,000 to cover previous authorizations. In all, Congress provided some $57,000,000 for new equipment. The golden rain had

---

[34] Chief, Mat Div, to CofAC, 15 Apr 39, AFCF 004.4.
[35] G-4 to DCofS, 3 Feb 39, WPD-OPD 3807-32-40.
[36] Memo, ASW for CofAC, 22 Dec 38; and Memo, CofAC for ASW, 5 Jan 39. Both in AFCF 452.1 Proc of Aircraft.
[37] Sayre and Stubblefield, "Measures for Defense," *Aviation* (April 1939), p. 21.

begun. Passage of a supplementary military appropriation in July in response to an appeal from the President brought the Air Corps another $89,000,000 for immediate expenditure plus contract authorization of $44,000,000 more.[38] The day after the regular fiscal year 1940 appropriation bill passed, Air Corps officials announced the signing of contracts for 571 airplanes worth some $19,000,000. When the supplementary funds became available in July, an even greater torrent of orders went out to the industry. On 10 August the Air Corps contracted for nearly $86,000,000 worth of aircraft, the largest single day of business in the history of the industry up to that time. In fact, this one day's orders amounted to more business than the industry had known in any full year in peacetime down to 1937.[39]

Inevitably, however, all this good fortune was to be compounded with difficulties. Even before the torrent of funds could be transmuted into contracts, there were warning cries of shortages from the industry. While most preparedness discussion had been centered around airframe capacity, the equally menacing question of capacity in accessory plants and material suppliers had been virtually ignored.

Aluminum offers a case in point. The average airframe was almost 70 percent by weight aluminum and 29 percent steel. Aluminum producers were sure they could meet the demand. At an average of 7,000 pounds of aluminum per airframe, the total weight required for the expansion program fell well within the aluminum industry's annual capacity. Unfortunately, airframe manufacturers' orders and indeed their needs could not be spread evenly over the entire year. They required most of the necessary weight in aluminum toward the beginning of their production runs and virtually all began producing at about the same time, since the Air Corps placed the bulk of its contracts all within a few hours of one another. This concentration of orders, which threatened to swamp the aluminum industry, was bad enough in itself, but there was a further complication. The aluminum industry was fully capable of meeting the total demand of aircraft manufacturers in aluminum sheet of standard gauges, but forgings, castings, and extrusions raised an entirely different problem. Throughout the decade of the thirties these items had been coming into greater use. With the arrival of big orders, longer production runs—real mass production—their use, especially extrusions, might be expected to increase.[40]

Aluminum was only one item for concern. Elsewhere other shortages threatened. Production delays on the part of a wheel manufacturer brought shortages in the Curtiss plant that held up production of the P-36 for five days. A shortage of gun-synchronizers delayed production for twenty days. Hard-to-manufacture hydraulic pumps for use in retraction

---

[38] 53 Stat 606, Military Appropriations Act, 1940, April 26, 1939, and 53 Stat 995, Supplementary Appropriation, July 1, 1939.

[39] *Aerodigest* (May 1939), p. 28 and *Aviation* (September 1939), p. 52.

[40] Intercompany Memo, J. E. Schaefer, Stearman Division of Boeing, to J. P. Murray, 13 Apr 39, AHO Plans Div 145.93–182. Breakdown of average airframe by weight in aluminum and steel is based on Brig Gen G. H. Brett, "Procurement for Defense," *Aviation* (August 1940), p. 42.

THE TIDE TURNS

gear and other similar applications soon became critical as the two or three firms skilled in making this item found themselves flooded with orders.[41] When manufacturers, hard pressed for highly skilled labor, began to raid each other's shops to lure away men, it became evident that some sort of action on the part of the government would be necessary to ensure a smooth and efficient flow of resources to the industry.[42] The War Department had mobilization plans setting up agencies to control the flow of resources in case of war, but the United States was not yet at war. The problems had arrived before the war; the mobilization plans were inadequate.[43] Improvisation would be necessary. At the end of June 1939 the Chief of the Air Corps sent invitations to a large number of leaders throughout the aircraft industry, inviting them to a conference to be held in his office during July to consider their common problems.

OCAC Conference, July 1939

The call that went out to industry leaders offers something of an index of the progress in air arm planning since the inception of the expansion program during the previous November. Then a peacetime atmosphere prevailed. Economy was the watchword. Manufacturers attending a conference in Washington in the summer of 1938 were merely instructed to come with data on the productive capacity of their plants.[44] But by July 1939 a new vitality was evident. Invitations to the industry specified the agenda in detail. Moreover, individual manufacturers were instructed to bring not opinions on the capacity of their plants but facts, explicit information concerning floor space, employees, facility costs, and the like.[45]

Just as the invitations to the July conference reflected something of the growing awareness of the real problems that beset the expansion program, so too the welcoming remarks of the presiding officials gave a revealing insight on War Department leadership. Assistant Secretary of War Johnson spoke of preparedness. With singleness of purpose he saw the ultimate objective: adequate productive capacity to provide the nation's air power requirements in time of war. For Johnson there seemed to be no doubt that war was inevitable, and he bent every effort to meet that war prepared. In contrast to the views of the Assistant Secretary were those of General Arnold. He saw two problems before the conference. First there was the immediate problem, the Air Corps' expansion program, which was actually in hand. Second, there was

---

[41] Shortage complaints are scattered throughout the files for this period. See, for example, Curtiss-Wright to Chief, Mat Div, 18 Jan 39, SW files, Aircraft, item 1110a; and Memo, CofAC for SW, 25 Jul 39, AHO Plans Div 145.93–182.

[42] Memo, CofAC to ASW, 21 Feb 39, AHO Plans Div 145.93–182.

[43] R&R, Plans Sec to CofAC, 17 Apr 39, AHO Plans Div 145.93–182.

[44] Actg CofAC to Glenn L. Martin et al., 16 Aug 38, SW files, AC Gen Questions, item 550a, 16 Aug 38. The request for estimates of productive capacity in terms of dollar values suggests the crudity of the measurements involved. For an example of the acute emphasis on economy that dominated at the time, see, Dir, Planning Br, OASW, 145.93–182. West coast procurement planning officers were not invited to the Washington conference in order to save travel expenses.

[45] ASW to leading aircraft industry manufacturers, 30 Jun 39, AFCF 004.4.

a possible future problem, an emergency program, if war should come.[46]

Once again General Arnold saw clearly the essential dilemma of the Air Corps. A solution to one problem did not of necessity mean a solution to the other. Rather than impose orders from above, he moved hesitantly and cautiously. He made no effort to force the manufacturers into any pattern or plan predetermined by the Air Corps. "You are going to write your own ticket," General Arnold told his audience. In short, the manufacturers learned that leadership by cooperation would substitute, for mandates from above, the "Government regulation," which so many of them resented. This method could be called an abdication of leadership to the business interests. Before judging, however, one should see the whole problem. The Chief of the Air Corps was responsible for the aerial defense of the nation. When General Arnold assumed command in September 1938 he found the nation virtually without air defense against the growing might of the dictatorships. He knew he must depend upon the manufacturers to provide the requisite airplanes. No hastily contrived government-owned facilities could supply the need without the fullest co-operation of the existing industry in providing the necessary designs and engineering talent. General Arnold's most significant contribution to the cause of national defense may have been his early recognition that the Air Corps could no more order production from the aircraft industry than it could order appropriations from Congress. As the subsequent war years were to reveal, a skillful and timely use of the carrot with only an occasional use of the club won the best results in both cases.

The problem before the conference, regardless of who formulated the answer, was one of increasing productive capacity to meet first the requirements of the expansion program and then the needs of a possible future emergency. After raising the first obvious solution of using multiple-shift operations, General Arnold opened the conference for discussion.

One means suggested for increasing production was the extensive use of subcontracting. Some of the manufacturers present opposed the idea. For the most part the objections came from the larger firms with heavy investments in floor space and tools. They wanted to keep their plants working at capacity even when the expansion program came to an end. They were obviously anxious not to encourage a whole host of small parts manufacturers, each with a low overhead, to become competitors. On the other hand, some of the smaller firms were quite enthusiastic about subcontracting. Some of them had already discovered they could make more money in supplying specialty items to the larger firms than they could hope to make in the high-risk business of entering competitions to build complete military aircraft. Some manufacturers with but limited capacity and inadequate capital favored subcontracting because it permitted them to accept production contracts beyond their immediate capacity in the hope of earning profits to plow back into expansion. To

---

[46] Proceedings of Air Corps Procurement Conference (hereafter cited July Conference Proceedings), 10 Jul 39, AFCF 337.1 Conference. Unless otherwise stated, the following discussion of the conference is based on this source.

this a representative of OASW, long concerned with the problems of wartime mobilization, added a warning note: it would be well to learn to make use of subcontractors in peacetime because various shortages in wartime might make plant expansion impossible.

The conference reached no simple solution to the matter of subcontracting. All agreed that some subcontracting would be necessary, but a wide difference of opinion persisted as to the degree desirable. In any event, whether extensive or limited, subcontractors would have to be trained. This in turn gave rise to a discussion of educational orders.

In 1939 Congress provided first $2,000,000 and then later an additional $14,500,000 to support an educational order program for Army items.[47] At last substantial sums were available to educate new sources. But instead of educating a large number of inexperienced producers, the Air Corps devoted its share of the first grant to the purchase of a training aircraft from two aircraft manufacturers. The industrial planners of the air arm felt that airframes rather than accessories would constitute the most serious chokepoint in production. Airframes, engines, and propellers, they argued, were the basic items upon which available educational funds should be spent.[48] Since the ground rules of OASW stipulated that only items that would long remain standard should be considered for educational orders, this led air arm officials to select cargo and training airplanes as most suitable for educational orders.[49]

As the expansion program gathered headway it became increasingly clear that accessories and components were to be the really serious bottlenecks. Early in the summer of 1939 it was apparent that collector rings (exhaust manifolds for air-cooled engines) and oleo struts were going to be critical items for which it would be well to educate new sources.[50] By the following summer the fundamental mistakes in Air Corps policy regarding educational orders became evident. Not airframes but dozens of components were the real candidates for education. Magnetos, carburetors, starters, prop hubs, camera lenses, gyro-pilots, and a flock of other items were critically short. Any or all of these accessories would have responded favorably to educational orders.[51] Unfortunately, by the time this was recognized the Air Corps had lost its opportunity; the Assistant Secretary had long since precluded the use of any further educational order funds on air arm projects inasmuch as the aviation expansion program was itself a gigantic educational order.[52]

Industry and Army representatives at

---

[47] 52 Stat 707, June 16, 1938, authorized educational orders, and 52 Stat 1153, June 25, 1938, appropriated $2,000,000 for the purposes. 53 Stat 560, April 3, 1938, authorized $34,500,000 for educational orders, but the regular appropriation act for 1940, 53 Stat 595, April 26, 1939, actually appropriated only $2,000,000. A supplementary act, however, 53 Stat 995, July 1, 1939, subsequently appropriated $14,500,000 for educational orders in fiscal 1940.
[48] Chief, Industrial Planning Sec, to Chief, Mat Div, 1 Mar 39, AFCF 032k; Exec, OCAC, to ASW, 2 Mar 39, AFCF 030 President and Congress.

[49] Memo, Lt Col R. L. Walsh for Gen Arnold, 23 Aug 39, AHO Plans Div 145.93-182.
[50] Ibid.
[51] Unsigned Memo for Chief, Mat Div, 10 Jul 40, AC Project Rcds (Lyon Papers), folder 11, Educational Orders and Industrial Planning, AFCF.
[52] Notes prepared for Gen Arnold on Education Orders, 1 Nov 39, AC Project Rcds (Lyon Papers), folder 11, Educational Orders and Industrial Planning, AFCF.

the July 1939 conference realized that even extensive subcontracting would not provide all the necessary additional production capacity for an emergency or wartime program. Even if educational order funds were plentiful and wisely expended, it would be impossible to push up the level of airframe production indefinitely by this method. There were, as everyone present realized, only two alternatives left. The government could erect shadow factories, stand-by facilities, or the individual manufacturers could expand their own plants.

Where possible, subcontracting was to be preferred to building new facilities. This was the official War Department policy. As to the choice between government-built plants and privately financed expansions, the industry in July 1939 wanted neither but preferred the latter alternative. Col. H. K. Rutherford, representing the mobilization planners of OASW, probably reflected industry opinion fairly when he labeled shadow factories "unsatisfactory, expensive" and a "last resort." [53] Privately financed expansion, then, was to be favored. But the aircraft manufacturers were still not anxious to expand.

Ever since the President had suggested a 10,000-aircraft program, aircraft builders had been warning one another not to get caught with productive capacity too great to be profitably employed when the current program concluded. The memory of the long depression was too vivid

to forget. "Having faced the cold shadows of a vacant factory," said an official of United Aircraft, "we had no appetite for more of the same." [54] "Don't let's get stampeded" into building needless capacity, editorialized *Aviation* magazine with a worried look at the long-term future and its bleak prospects.[55] When Glenn L. Martin told all those present at the conference that the industry had sufficient capacity to do the job on hand, he was only voicing an opinion widely accepted by the trade. Why expand when existing facilities would be more than ample? [56]

The industry was unanimous in its opposition to expansion—or so it would seem. When speaking for the group or to the public at large each individual manufacturer opposed expansion. But in practice, the manufacturers behaved quite differently. When confronted with tempting offers for long production runs beyond their existing capabilities, individual firms seemed to have no qualms about expanding when necessary. Airframe manufacturers had already built a million square feet of floor space in the first six months of 1939, an increase of 17 percent. Moreover, productive capacity of the engine manufacturers had been increased 20 percent in the same period.[57]

In short, the aircraft manufacturers were like large-scale commodity farmers. They agreed in conclave that increased production would threaten a market glut, then hurried home to consider means for

---

[53] July Conference Proceedings, p. 18. For a long detailed opinion from the industry on this point, see C. A. VanDusen, Consolidated Aircraft Corp., to Procurement Planning Representative in Los Angeles, 12 Jun 39, AFCF 004.4.

[54] Wilson, *Slipstream*, p. 220.
[55] *Aviation* (December 1938), p. 19.
[56] July Conference Proceedings, pp. 12–13.
[57] ACC news release, November 13, 1939.

expanding their plants. Glenn L. Martin offers a case in point. He was sure the existing industry could do the job, yet even as he spoke, workmen were putting the final touches upon a magnificent new plant with nearly a half-million feet of floor space that he had just constructed to handle a big order from the French Government.[58]

The phenomenon was quite simple. Those who received orders and needed to expand went right ahead and did so. But the industry as a whole protested in unison that plenty of capacity was available. Even after war broke out in Europe, the aviation press still carried warnings against foolish plant expansions, and those with orders went right ahead and ignored the warnings.[59] Behind these contradictions lay an obvious explanation. Throughout the industry there was an underlying fear of the administration's air arsenal plan. Individually and collectively, manufacturers felt impelled to insist that plenty of idle capacity was available, partly in the hope of attracting new orders to themselves and partly to forestall the threat of government-financed stand-by plants that might be but a first step toward nationalization of the industry.[60]

Not surprisingly, then, the manufacturers who attended the Air Corps procurement conference in July 1939 displayed no enthusiasm for further expansion and were quite willing to assert that plenty of capacity existed to meet the requirements of the expansion program. Their contentions were, however, merely opinions and not facts. Moreover, those who attended the conference could give no assurances, not even opinions, on whether or not the extant industry could meet the requirements of mobilization if war should come. The truth was that nobody knew what sort of production the industry might achieve under wartime conditions. Never having enjoyed really large orders, most manufacturers had little idea of the maximum level of output they might achieve if fully tooled for mass production.

Would the industry have to expand to meet the demands of war? Without some means of determining productive capacity no one could tell. Manufacturers' opinions were far too subject to coloration by the hope of further business and the fear of competition from government-owned plants. Objective criteria were needed to measure productive capacity impartially. General Arnold asked for constructive proposals. He wanted a yardstick that would measure productive capacity accurately and fairly. Although a number of the industry representatives present made helpful suggestions for such a yardstick, they preferred to leave the details to a military board. In a highly competitive industry, each manufacturer was willing to co-operate with air arm officials but reluctant to divulge production data to a rival.[61] The close co-opera-

---

[58] *Fortune* (December 1939), pp. 12, 73.
[59] Marcus Nadler, "Economic Study of Fighting Nations Indicates No War-Order Windfall," *Printers Ink* (October 6, 1939), p. 11; *Aviation* (October 1939), p. 53.
[60] See, for example, ACC Info Bull No. 16, 28 Nov 39, with facsimile article, S. B. Altick, "Across the Skyways," New York *Sun*, November 18, 1939, article captioned, "Nationalization of Entire Aviation Industry Threatened by Left Wingers in Washington."

[61] July Conference Proceedings, pp. 4-9.

tion among manufacturers that marked the war years was still a long way off.

So the conference ended. Army officers and manufacturers alike realized that no long-term planning was possible until the necessary facts could be obtained. It must have been evident to all that what the Assistant Secretary of War said in November 1938 was still true: the productive capacity of the aircraft industry was unknown. But now only two months remained before World War II would break out in Europe.

The Search for a Yardstick

When the industry and air arm leaders finished their deliberations at the Office of the Chief of Air Corps in July 1939, at least one conclusion was evident: no further mobilization planning was possible without "facts." Yet even upon this seemingly obvious word there was no real agreement.

Long before the OCAC conference in July, Air Corps officers had recognized the acute need for accurate information on the capacity of the nation's industry to turn out aircraft. The matter had been discussed at a similar meeting with industry representatives almost a year earlier.[62] Everyone present seemed to agree that the existing factory plans drawn up by officers of the Industrial Planning Section at Wright Field were unreliable. Even the manufacturers whose plants were surveyed and scheduled admitted this. On the other hand, these were the very men who protested that the preparation of really accurate surveys to measure potential productive capacity would require a great deal of time and money.[63] Such surveys demanded the services of highly paid and highly skilled production engineers whom few aircraft manufacturers would or could afford to divert from their normal duties. The Air Corps response to this reluctance was the so-called data contract.

Data Contracts

After some preliminary delays between October 1938 and April 1939 while funds were secured and specifications drawn up, procurement officers negotiated a number of data contracts with aircraft and engine firms. Subsequently, the effort to purchase "information" was broadened considerably by including a data clause in all regular contracts for supplies. By this means manufacturers were led to deliver reports on future productive capabilities along with the items they turned off their assembly lines.

The effort of air arm officers to secure facts on which to base decisions concerning mobilization was undoubtedly sound. Unfortunately, the plan was a partial failure in execution. Insofar as the data contract program induced manufacturers to think and plan in terms of large-scale mass production even before they received large orders, the program was a

---

[62] This and the following several paragraphs are largely based upon Critical Analysis and Evaluation of AAF Pre-World War II Purchased Procurement Planning Data Program, 1 Jul 47, prepared by Industrial Planning Sec, Proc Div, AMC, pp. 8ff.

[63] *Ibid.*, pp. 10–11. See also Wilson, *Slipstream*, pp. 213–16, attributing to one leading aircraft builder the opinion that the work of the air arm mobilization planners amounted to "twenty years of hogwash."

success.[64] But the data actually purchased (at a cost of something over $100,000 for the initial phase of the program alone) was never effectively utilized.[65]

A fundamental flaw in conception virtually wrecked the whole program. Instead of purchasing surveys of each manufacturer's facilities as a whole, the studies bought were posited upon an assumed production of a single aircraft, engine, or accessory. When that item became obsolete or when the manufacturer in question took on additional orders—from the French, the British, or the Navy for example—the purchased data lost much if not all of its meaning. Similarly, the data lost much of its value since it failed to consider the possibility of redesigning items to facilitate mass production.[66]

In the last analysis, of course, estimated production schedules prepared by individual contractors themselves were not to be relied upon. The manufacturers tended to reason from assumptions that were too optimistic. In promising a given level of bomber production for some future date such as M-day plus twelve months, for example, a manufacturer assumed rather too readily that design would be frozen, labor would be available in sufficient quantities, all items of government-furnished equipment would be on hand when required, additional machine tools could be procured when needed, and so on.[67] Such idealized assumptions made for unrealistic scheduling. At best, the average manufacturer was caught in a crossfire of conflicting interests. He was anxious to sell air arm officers on the idea that he had plenty of available capacity in the hope of landing a big production order. Yet at the very same time he may well have been anxious to secure government assistance in financing a plant expansion. In short, the manufacturer with a data contract was a special pleader rather than an objective reporter. A contract that asked him to estimate his productive capacity for some future date asked for an opinion, an opinion based as much upon aspiration as upon fact. Thus, manufacturers were asked to provide the very information they were least able to give objectively. And, ironically, they were not asked—until almost too late—to provide the data they were entirely capable of delivering: full, factual data concerning their facilities and operations—the available floor area in their plants, employees in each shift, and so on.

Data contracts were not the only source of information available on the nation's aircraft productive capacity. The Aeronautical Chamber of Commerce, representing 90 percent of the industry, offered a possible alternative means of determin-

---

[64] Wilson, *Slipstream*, page 234, indicates that United Aircraft was inspired by the discussions alone, without waiting for a data contract, to undertake rather elaborate advance war planning. Other leading firms followed suit.

[65] Critical Analysis and Evaluation of AAF Pre-World War II Purchased Procurement Planning Data Program, which concludes bluntly: "The purchased studies were of little use...."

[66] *Ibid.*, p. 3. See list of "major deficiencies of the Purchased Planning Data Program."

[67] Chief, Mat Div, to CofAC, 25 Jul 39, AHO Plans Div 145.93–182. Some manufacturers were fully aware of the falseness of these assumptions and as a consequence were reluctant to take data contracts. See Chief, Mat Div, to CofAC, 4 May 39, AHO Plans Div 145.93–182.

ing capacity. British experience with a counterpart organization, The Society of British Aircraft Constructors, suggested that this industry trade association and clearinghouse could provide a very useful liaison between individual aircraft manufacturers and the air arm procurement organizations.[68] Self-interest would ensure the enthusiastic co-operation of the Aeronautical Chamber of Commerce. Moreover, in the role of confidential agent, the ACC might be able to secure information from the various manufacturers that each would be reluctant to report to government officials for fear of impairing his bargaining position in subsequent contract negotiations. Finally, and perhaps of most importance, the ACC could command from the ranks of its members the very best in technical skills.

A committee sponsored by the ACC to measure the nation's productive capacity could be depended upon to have the services of some of the best aircraft production engineers in the country. Such a survey actually compiled by the ACC during the summer of 1939 reflected this competence the more pointedly by the contrast it presented to similar surveys made by the officers of the Industrial Planning Section at Wright Field.[69]

On the other hand, if there were advantages in relying upon the Aeronautical Chamber of Commerce, there were also decided disadvantages. If Air Corps officers depended upon this trade association for the basic data upon which to make vital decisions concerning national defense, they would lay themselves open to the politically dangerous charge of having surrendered to the business interests. General Arnold probably selected the wisest course when he ordered Materiel Division officers to make their own estimates of available productive capacity. But at the same time, he held the door open for the ACC by authorizing it access to the classified military contracts of its members. By this means the ACC was retained as an important supplementary source of information and a medium for bringing suggestions and criticisms from the industry to Air Corps headquarters.[70]

While General Arnold's decision no doubt retained full responsibility for the mobilization effort where it properly should have rested, there was, nevertheless, some loss of effectiveness. Officers who were admittedly not production specialists had to grope and fumble for solutions to highly technical questions. Inevitably they made mistakes while learning anew what the production engineers already understood. This was essentially the position of those officers who were ordered to serve on a special board directed to contrive some sort of yardstick for measuring the aircraft productive capacity of the United States.

---

[68] Military Attaché, London, Annual Rpt, 13 Sep 38, AMC CADO, C 21/38 Great Britain.

[69] For an example of the kind of detailed survey made by ACC, see Curtiss-Wright, St. Louis Div to ACC, 17 Jul 39, AFCF, 004.4 Mfrs.

[70] Memo, CofAC for Col Echols, 21 Aug 39, WFCF 381. For a discussion of the problems encountered when a government agency hands over some of its functions to private hands, see the account of Frederic C. Lane (*Ships for Victory: A History of Shipbuilding Under the U.S. Maritime Commission in World War II* (Baltimore: The Johns Hopkins Press, 1951, pp. 97ff.) on the relations of the Maritime Commission with the firm of Gibbs and Cox.

THE TIDE TURNS

The Yardstick Board

Less than a week after the July 1939 conference in OCAC, the chief of the Materiel Division appointed a special board of officers to study aircraft production.[71] This group, known informally at Wright Field as the Yardstick Board, was to devise a method or formula with which it would be possible to measure the capacity of any given facility in the industry. Despite the years of study devoted to the general problem by the Industrial Planning Section, the facts and figures necessary for the board's deliberations were not at hand. A new questionnaire had to be sent out to the industry. Not until the end of July 1939 could the board begin its work; its final report appeared during the middle of September, after the outbreak of war in Europe.[72]

The board had at its disposal a number of tools or techniques for estimating productive capacity if its members would but seek far enough. For a very crude index, there was the industry's production record in two previous periods of mass production. During World War I, aircraft yearly output rose from 400 units in 1916 to 2,000 units in 1917, and finally to 14,000-odd units in 1918. Had the officers of the yardstick board actually used these figures they would have obtained a false impression of the acceleration in production to be expected in World War II. Over a comparable period of years, from 1938 to 1941, aircraft output was never much more than double that of the previous year. Interestingly enough, the more recent experience of the boom years 1926–29 provided a far more accurate picture of what to expect. The rate of increase in the boom was almost exactly that achieved during the years 1938–41. At best, to be sure, the record of accelerating output in previous periods of mass production was suggestive only. The validity of this earlier experience as a basis for comparison was, to say the least, made questionable by the intervening technical revolution in aircraft structures.

Dollar value of output offered another crude yardstick to measure capacity in the aircraft industry. Since statistics on total dollar output, average unit costs, total unit production, and the like were readily available, it was a relatively simple matter to make some rough correlations between expenditures and output. Dollar volume as a yardstick had the advantage of providing a convenient basis of comparison between manufacturers of widely different types and models. Moreover, this yardstick had been used before by the Air Corps and was a familiar one in the industry.[73] On the other hand, dollar volume as a measurement of production suffered from several intrinsic weaknesses. To begin with, factors such as the different levels of wages in various parts of the country and the generally rising level of wages and material costs injected variables that upset the formula. More significantly, just as in the case of World War I or the boom years, rapid changes in technology threatened to nul-

---

[71] Memo, ACofAC for ESW, 26 Jul 39, AFCF 004.4 Mfrs.
[72] TWX, Contract Sec, WF, to Plans Sec, OCAC, 1 Aug 39, and extract, Proceedings (of Yardstick Board) 15 Sep 39, AFCF, AC Project Rcds (Lyon Papers), bk. 22, Capacity of the Aircraft Industry.

[73] Actg CofAC to Glenn L. Martin, 16 Aug 38, SW files, AC Gen Questions, item 550a.

lify the validity of much past experience. As manufacturers received larger orders, they installed more and more production tooling. As mass-production techniques replaced job-shop methods, output increased surprisingly. Estimates of potential production based on assumptions framed in terms of job-shop conditions had to be scrapped to make way for the new situation. Clearly, the commonly used dollar volume yardstick was no longer accurate.[74]

When General Arnold asked the manufacturers attending the OCAC conference for help in contriving a yardstick, he roused a lively discussion and turned up some useful ideas. Everyone present seemed to agree that the old dollar volume yardstick was inadequate. The real problem was to devise a common denominator, a measurement valid whether applied to giant bombers or puddle jumpers, the Army's tiny liaison airplanes. James H. Kindelberger of North American suggested airframe pounds as such a common denominator. General Arnold preferred airframe pounds per square foot. Then Mr. Kindelberger suggested that man-hours of productive labor per square foot of plant in relation to airframe pounds produced was a formula already employed by the Germans. Mr. L. L. Bell, of Bell Aircraft felt this formula might be improved if some consideration could be given to whether or not the aircraft in question had ever been in production before.[75]

These and a number of other ideas put forth by the representatives of the aircraft industry at the conference provided a useful starting point for the Yardstick Board. Fortunately at least one engineer, Mr. T. P. Wright, who at the time was director of engineering for the Curtiss-Wright Corporation, had gone beyond this starting point and had published a thoughtful paper on this very question of estimating capacity.[76] The problem Mr. Wright posed was virtually identical to that facing air arm planners: can the existing industry handle the expansion program proposed by the President? To answer this question he worked out in detail a series of formulas using airframe pounds, productive floor space, man-hours, and the like. Then, having derived his formulas as tools, he proceeded to apply them to the specific situation in hand. As an interested party, an aircraft builder, looking for military orders, Wright's conclusions might be subject to challenge. But this in no way minimized his brilliant contribution in suggesting methods for analyzing capacity.

The available evidence does not make clear the extent to which the Yardstick Board relied upon Wright's study.[77] The degree of the board's obligation is probably unimportant since the real significance of Wright's work was that it for-

---

[74] For a rather harsh judgment on the failure of Air Corps officers to foresee the importance of production tooling, see Review of Methods Employed by the AAF . . ., cited ch. VII, n. 6.

[75] July Conference Proceedings, pp. 4–9.

[76] T. P. Wright, "America's Answer: Gearing Our Aviation Industry to the National Defense," *Aviation* (June 1939), pp. 26ff.

[77] Although the board's report does not mention Wright's study, it must have been available to the members of the board. The Chief of the Materiel Division actually went out of his way to urge that the Chief of the Air Corps read the study. See TWX, Brett to Arnold, 6 Sept 39, WFCF 008 Policy file, Pay-as-you-go. Plans officers, OCAC, were familiar with Wright's article also. See Maj M. R. Wood to Col Spaatz, 14 Aug 39, AHO Plans Div 145.93–182.

malized some of the ideas used by various leading production engineers and helped make the techniques commonplace.

After extended deliberations the Yardstick Board concluded that the simplest and most expressive measure of productive capacity was airframe pounds per square foot per month. A carefully drawn questionnaire brought in the necessary data from virtually every producing unit in the industry. By combining the arithmetic average and a modified median of these returns, the board found that the average figure of production was 1.20 pounds per square foot per month. By similar means the board found that the area per productive laborer at maximum concentration was 145 square feet, that only 81 percent of total area was actually productive, that the number of pounds per month per man averaged 80, that the maximum amount of subcontracting was 20 percent, and, finally, that second-shift operations were only 74 percent and third shift only 57 percent as efficient as first-shift operations.[78]

To work the formula of the Yardstick Board, air arm planners had only to apply the facts of a given case to these known industrial indicators. Thus, for example, a manufacturer with 100,000 square feet of floor and 250 productive workers would give the following projection or estimate:

a. 250 employees × 80 lbs./man/mo. = 20,000 lbs./ mo. current output.

b. 100,000 sq. ft. × .81 (% of area productive) = 81,000 sq. ft. productive.

c. 81,000 sq. ft. productive × 1.20 lbs./sq. ft./mo. = 97,200 lbs./mo. maximum production.

d. 97,200 lbs./mo. production × .20 (% subcontracted) = 19,400 lbs. farmed out to subcontractor.

e. 81,000 sq. ft. productive ÷ 145 sq. ft./man = 558 first-shift employees at maximum.

f. 558 first shift × .74 (second-shift efficiency) = 413 employees on second shift at maximum.

g. 558 first shift × .57 (third-shift efficiency) = 318 employees on third shift at maximum.[79]

Though subsequent experience and the passage of time demonstrated that the board's coefficients were not infallible,[80] the yardstick evolved by the board, with the help of the industry, gave air arm officers a reasonable basis on which to premise plans for subsequent steps in the expansion program. In short, the Yardstick Board accomplished in a matter of weeks what the Industrial Planning Section failed to do over a period of years.

Tools for Planning

The formula derived by the Yardstick Board marked an important milestone along the route if not the beginning of the use of effective statistical techniques as a basis for reaching authoritative policy decisions on mobilization planning in the aircraft field. After this rather

---

[78] Extract, Proceedings of Yardstick Board, 15 Sep 39, AFCF AC Project Rcds (Lyon Papers), bk. 22, Capacity of the Aircraft Industry.

[79] *Ibid.*

[80] Where, for example, the board found productive area at 81 percent of total area, subsequent studies changed this figure to 85 percent. See K. Perkins and M. A. Tracy, Airplane Manufacturing Capacity Based on Factory Areas, OPA Aircraft Rpt 13–A, 31 Oct 41, AFCF, Outsize, 452.1 Aircraft Manufacturing Capacity.

THEODORE P. WRIGHT

hesitant start, a whole series of statistical tools were developed for measuring productive capacity, costs, labor requirements, and the like. These were almost entirely the work of Mr. Wright and his associates serving as aircraft specialists with the Advisory Commission to the Council of National Defense (NDAC) and its successor agencies, Office of Production Management (OPM) and War Production Board (WPB). There is no need to expound these formulas in full. The detailed reports are readily available for those interested in them. Here it should be sufficient to suggest something of the complex range of subjects for which statistical tools were developed. In addition to those devised for production planning, similar formulas made it possible to estimate probable costs for budgetary planning. Others, which estimated unit costs in advance, gave contract negotiators tools for use in close pricing.[81]

Unfortunately, there is evidence to show that at least some highly placed air arm officers were inclined to ignore the formulas. Although the various formulas were made available to officers of the Materiel Division, then urged upon them, it seems safe to conclude that it was the staff of consultants within NDAC and its successors who made best use of these tools.[82] If Air Corps officers failed to utilize all the statistical tools available to them, in some instances it may be attributable to sheer blindness on the part of individuals. But far more significant was the breach that separated the regular air arm procurement organization from the temporary civilian agencies such as NDAC. Hastily built, of necessity, the civilian production and planning agencies paid a heavy price in terms of inadequate liaison with corresponding elements of the military organization.

The Realities of September 1939

There were unavoidable delays in getting together the information from which the Yardstick Board reached its conclu-

---

[81] Aircraft Br, WPB, Aircraft Manufacturing Capacity Based on Factory Area, Aircraft Rpt 13-X, 15 Mar 42, AFCF 004.4 Bulky. See, for example, T. P. Wright and A. E. Lombard, Report on Prices of Military Airplanes, Airplane Div NDAC, Rpt 5, 10 Jul 40, AFCF 452.1–191.
[82] T. P. Wright to Chief, Mat Div, 10 Jul 40, AFCF 452.1 Aircraft Gen; R&R, CofAC to Chief, Mat Div, 25 Jul 40, "Does this mean anything or is it just another report?" Comment 2, Chief, Mat Div, to CofAC, "A good rule of thumb ... if one wants to take the trouble to figure it out," "My people use it in connection with estimates." Comment 3, CofAC to E. H. Beebe, and No. 4, Beebe to CofAC, 27 Jul 40, "It should be useful for planning future purchases ...," AFCF 452.1–91.

THE TIDE TURNS

sions. Until the board reported, no detailed planning could be undertaken; almost every major decision regarding the expansion of capacity remained suspended.[83] No one could be sure just how much it would be necessary to enlarge the existing industry. Assistant Secretary Johnson felt that it must be expanded "several times" above current capacity. The Chief of the Materiel Division directed his staff officers at Wright Field to commence plans for a possible fivefold expansion [84]—and this only a matter of weeks after many of the industry's most distinguished leaders had assured the President that no expansion would be needed.[85]

Since the Yardstick Board did not report formally until mid-September 1939, the vital decisions regarding expansion were delayed until after war broke out in Europe. Precious months were lost to the mobilization effort largely because of a failure to contrive adequate administrative tools for realistic planning during the years of peace.

If the hour was late and the war very real indeed —in Poland if not in France —air arm officers in September 1939 could at least take some comfort from the progress of the past nine months of gestation. The Air Corps had a program, Congress had provided the funds, the aircraft industry was growing rapidly on its own initiative, and at last there were administrative tools to assist in making the vital decisions necessary to plan for an efficient mobilization of the nation's productive capacity. When the President took note of the war in Europe and declared a state of limited national emergency, some air arm officers felt that the last necessary ingredient for success had been added; the impetus of war and a national emergency, they hoped, would banish most of the obstacles that impeded the effort to mobilize the air arm while it was still at a peace.

---

[83] For evidence of delays imposed by failure to have information in hand from the industry, see Actg Chief, IPS, to Asst Tech Exec, Mat Div, 9 Sep 39, WFCF 400.12.
[84] AAF Hist Study 40, pp. 19–20.
[85] Down to the actual outbreak of war in Europe, the Aeronautical Chamber of Commerce continued to issue assurances that the industry had capacity "sufficient for quick deliveries on all future orders both at home and abroad." See news release from the ACC, August 28, 1939.

CHAPTER IX

Foreign Policy, Politics, and Defense

When the President declared a state of limited emergency soon after the outbreak of war in Europe in September 1939, he apparently hoped to secure the legal advantages and psychological impetus of a crisis to speed rearmament in the United States. The realities of the blitzkrieg in Poland, terrifyingly heralded in lurid headlines and newsreels, seemed to justify his declaration. Each new Wehrmacht thrust was an argument of the need for stronger national defense.

Military intelligence reports indicated that the German Air Force had something over 8,000 combat aircraft on hand; in the United States the Air Corps could muster only some 2,400, at best.[1] Congress had authorized the expansion program of 5,500 aircraft, yet more than half this number remained on paper. There were 1,178 aircraft on order but undelivered, 1,291 on contracts currently under consideration, 1,143 in competitions still being evaluated, and 186 on options that could be exercised.[2] Even if every one of these aircraft were to be made immediately available to the Air Corps, the total strength on hand would fall far below that of the German air arm. The 5,500 program, which held such promise in the spring of 1939 seemed inadequate during the fall. In contrast to the Luftwaffe, the Air Corps seemed woefully underarmed.

Only if Congress authorized a larger force and granted still larger appropriations did it appear possible for the air arm and the nation's industry to close the gap. Unfortunately for the cause of national security, the political moon was in an awkward phase during most of the period of limited emergency—1940 would be an election year.

Politics and Armament

The first session of the Seventy-sixth Congress ended 5 August 1939. Thus it turned out that Congress was not in session when war broke out in Europe on 1 September. The President hastily called a second session to convene on 21 September. Meanwhile, the German forces had overrun Poland, and its downfall was only ten days away. Had the blitzkrieg continued, Congress might well have authorized impressive increases in the Air Corps without further delay, but the blitz did not continue. Even before

---

[1] Aircraft Strength and Production Capacity of European Air Powers, Chart as of Jul 39, 15 Jan 40, AHO Plans Div 145.91–135 QQ. Postwar data showed this estimate actually understated German strength. See United States Strategic Bombing Survey, Aircraft Division Industry Report, 2d ed., Jan 47, copy in OCMH, exhibit III A and figure IV–1.

[2] Draft Memo, Plans, OCAC, for ASW, 30 Aug 39, AHO Plans Div 145.93–183. Cf. notes on staff meetings of division chiefs 1939–40, entry for 23 Oct 39, AFCF 337 Special.

Congress adjourned on 3 November, Poland had capitulated and the powers were settling down to an apparent stalemate behind the West Wall and the Maginot Line.

When the third session of the Seventy-sixth Congress opened in January 1940, insofar as the major powers were concerned blitzkrieg had turned into "sitzkrieg." The menace of Axis might to the democracies was as great as before, but the sense of urgency had passed. The headlines no longer provided daily reminders of the destructive potential of air power.

Shortly after the beginning of the new session, the President presented his budget. He asked something over $1,750,000,000 for defense.[3] This extraordinary request raised the level of planned expenditures far beyond expected income. Next, the President asked an election year Congress to pass a tax bill to make up the anticipated deficit. "To Congressional realists," *Time* magazine remarked, this proposal was "sheer romance."[4] Congress was clearly in a mood for economy—perhaps not so defiantly as during the previous winter when one representative had declared that a force of 15,000 or 20,000 aircraft would "bankrupt" the nation,[5] but certainly the legislators as a group had little enthusiasm for passing tax bills in an election year.

Four months later, in April 1940, when the Appropriations Committee reported out a measure to provide funds for the War Department during the following fiscal year, the committee chairman boasted of having cut, with the approval of the Bureau of the Budget and the President, more than a hundred million dollars from the estimates requested by the Department.

Subsequent events were to prove these economies ill-advised, to say the least. Yet they were not made without reason. The Appropriations Committee contended that foreign orders placed in the United States were stepping up the nation's capacity to produce aircraft at no expense to the government. Increased productive capacity seemed to obviate the need for a stand-by reserve to cover the lag between production and mobilization requirements in an emergency, so why burden the taxpayers?[6] Without foreign orders, the committee recognized, the proposed cuts would be fatal,[7] but the bill as presented assumed that the French and British were mobilizing the aircraft industry in the United States. If export orders could take the place of educational orders, so much the better.[8]

The proposal to make French and British aircraft orders vital cogs in the nation's mobilization effort was not the first occasion when foreign orders played such a central role in the defense of the United States. In the months leading up to this nation's entry into World War I, the situation was remarkably similar in many ways. In 1917, as in 1940, procurement officers found the marketplace swarming with French and British purchasing missions. They learned in 1917 the important lesson that mobilization is not an isolated activity of the War De-

---

[3] H Doc 529, 76th Cong, 3d sess, January 4, 1940.
[4] *Time*, January 15, 1940, p. 14.
[5] *Cong Rcd*, March 3, 1939, p. 2223.

[6] House Rpt 1912, 75th Cong, 3d sess, April 2, 1940, pp. 19–20.
[7] *Ibid.*, pp. 2–3.
[8] *Ibid.*, pp. 10–11.

partment alone but part of a complex whole, a pattern in which export orders as well as Navy orders must be taken into consideration.

Aircraft Exports and National Defense

When Italy had threatened Ethiopia in 1935, the furor over arms manufacturers as warmongers and merchants of death once again claimed the attention of Congress. The congressmen passed a neutrality measure that held out to the public the promise that neutrality in a warring world could be had by legislation. The terms of the measure made it unlawful for citizens of the United States to sell or transport arms to belligerents who had been labeled as such by the President. Sales of arms to nonbelligerents could be consummated only under license from a Munitions Control Board in the State Department, with an accompaniment of full publicity. In 1936 Congress widened the neutrality law to prohibit loans to belligerents. In 1937 these measures were replaced with an entirely new act. While reaffirming the previous curbs on the sale of arms to belligerents, the new law permitted the sale of arms to nonbelligerents only if they agreed to pay cash and to take delivery in the United States.[9]

The official policy of President Roosevelt's administration was, therefore, to discourage traffic in arms. Diplomatic and consular officials received instructions to deny their good offices and the use of official channels of communication to armament dealers.[10] Similarly, the Export-Import Bank adopted a policy of refusing loans to foreign nations wishing to purchase arms in the United States.[11]

Occasionally the President found a way around the law. This was the case, for example, in 1937 when the Japanese invaded China. A strict application of the neutrality statutes would have required him to cut off the flow of arms from the United States to both nations, since the law made no distinction between aggressors and their victims. By refusing to declare the "China Incident" a war, admittedly a technicality, the President was able to avoid the automatic imposition of an embargo on the flow of arms so essential to the victim of Japanese aggression.

The various neutrality laws passed by Congress were by no means dead letters, forgotten statutes moldering on the books. Each of the successive acts had teeth and could be enforced. At least one group of leading aircraft manufacturers was tried early in 1939 under the provisions of a neutrality statute and subsequently fined more than a quarter of a million dollars for selling airplanes and machine guns to warring states in Latin America.[12]

The effect of the national neutrality policy was to inhibit sales in the very area where they would do the most good in

---

[9] Jt Res 51, which became Public Res 27, May 1, 1937 (50 Stat 121).

[10] R. W. Moore, Dept of State, to U.S. diplomatic and consular offices, 21 Nov 35, AFCF 360.01 B.

[11] Memo, Maj W. R. Carter for Gen Arnold, 19 Apr 39, AFCF 452.1–3295.

[12] *Fifth Report of the National Munitions Control Board*, H Doc 876, 76th Cong, 3d sess, July 3, 1940, ch. VII. The case mentioned here, involving several affiliates of Curtiss-Wright, concerned violations of Public Resolution 28, May 28, 1934 (48 Statutes 811) applying exclusively to the Chaco war.

building up facilities for national defense. Faith in the use of neutrality legislation to keep the nation clear of war seemed to obscure the need for maintaining a healthy armament industry as an essential to national defense. But curbs on the export of arms were not all chargeable to Congress and to the prevailing spirit of isolationism in the nation at large. Some restrictions on exports were imposed by the military leaders.

To protect military secrets during World War I, Congress had passed the Espionage Act of June 15, 1917, which provided heavy penalties for those guilty of revealing such secrets to an enemy. Inevitably, these grew up an elaborate body of administrative practices and policies as military men sought to apply the law. Amongst these rules and regulations were those providing a means for releasing items of equipment from their classification as military secrets when their increasing obsolescence no longer required such a status.

Common sense clearly urged the release of items from a classified status as soon as possible. If items of equipment classified as secret during peacetime were not released until they were so utterly obsolete as to be virtually worthless, manufacturers could not hope to find secondary markets. As the sole purchaser, the government would have to amortize the full cost of the item in question. On the other hand, if the government released an item from its secret status promptly and permitted export sales, the manufacturer might be able to enlarge his volume of production substantially. With lower unit costs and larger margins of profit, he would be in a position to bid lower on subsequent government contracts. This was especially true with regard to aeronautical equipment, where the rate of change in design was particularly rapid.

The procedures governing the release of aircraft and aircraft equipment were minutely specified, but the principles involved can be stated simply: military aircraft purchased by the United States or designed according to specifications of the military services were not to be released for export until after the lapse of time, running up to as much as one year following the start of production.[13] In practice, this meant that no aircraft was released until several years after it left the design stage and had already long since been compromised by public disclosure. Although the details of the policy changed from time to time in the between-war years, the principles involved remained constant into 1939.

Curbs on the release of military aircraft until they were "approaching obsolescence" [14] virtually destroyed all hope of large-scale export sales. The best potential customers are nations at war, and no warring nation willingly buys inferior arms. Thus, since the military services in the United States were anxious to build up the nation's capacity to produce aircraft in an emergency, they were under pressure to liberalize their release policy by authorizing the earliest possible sale and export of aircraft initially designed for the United States.

---

[13] See, for example, *Release Policy for Aircraft and Aircraft Equipment*, prepared by the Aeronautical Board (Washington, 1938).

[14] General Arnold used the phrase in describing the existing release policy on the eve of the war. July Conference Proceedings, p. 26.

Since the release of military equipment from security classification had a definite influence on the volume of export sales and hence on the development of productive capacity in the United States, the prevailing definition of "military secrets" assumes no little significance. Some items of equipment are clearly identifiable as military secrets. So long as the mechanism of the Norden bombsight was kept from the enemy, it gave the United States a decided advantage. With other items, airframes for example, the concept of military secrecy is less obvious. New principles are infrequent and advances are more in the nature of variant applications, differences in engineering rather than in fundamentals. While "gadgets" may often constitute military secrets, most airframes lose this status almost as soon as they come out the factory door.[15] On the other hand, by encouraging the export of military aircraft (lacking obviously secret appliances) it was possible to strengthen the nation's productive capacity without added expense to the taxpayers. Moreover, by controlling the supply of spare parts the producing nation could even minimize the tactical importance of aircraft already sold. As one aircraft manufacturer suggested, the ability to supply means more than the available supply.[16] Thus, insistence upon a policy that tended to delay the date for releasing military aircraft for export well beyond their first public appearance may have been highly detrimental to the national interest since it undeniably cut export sales at a time when aircraft manufacturers desperately needed them.[17]

For years air arm officers had followed the easy course of classifying all recent and current aircraft as military secrets. Then, in 1939, they found themselves caught in a most awkward position when they began urging the utility of exporting current models. Congressmen quite understandably asked, "Won't we be giving away military secrets?" In the lexicon of politics "military secrets" are sacrosanct no matter how expedient the justification for disclosure.

On two counts, then—faith in the efficacy of neutrality legislation and the safeguarding of military secrets, real or alleged—national policy frowned upon the export of arms. Yet, despite these considerations and even while the official administration line remained one of adherence to strict neutrality, the President was whittling away at the letter of the law wherever executive discretion allowed. When, for example, French military representatives asked during 1938 for permission to fly the Air Corps' P-36 with an eye to possible purchase, the President readily gave his consent.[18] Later in the same year he saw to it that the Export-Import Bank arranged a $25,000,000 military loan to China. The standing policy against credits for military purchases was easily evaded on the pretext that the loan would be spent on "essential" supplies other than arms and ammunition—a distinction that harked

---

[15] See comments of Gen Arnold before Senate, Hearings on WD appropriation for 1941, May 2, 1940, p. 96.

[16] See comments of Brig Gen George H. Brett and Glenn L. Martin, July Conference Proceedings, p. 26.

[17] See comments of Martin, pp. 19-26, and J. T. Hartson, p. 21, as well as Jouett, p. 27, in July Conference Proceedings.

[18] Memo, Exec, OASW, for SGS, 21 Jun 38, SW files.

back to the classic struggles of international jurists to define contraband.[19]

Although the President boldly seized the initiative in undermining the spirit of the neutrality statutes and in liberalizing the War Department's release policies whenever he felt he could safely do so, Air Corps officers did not at once follow his lead. General Westover, Chief of the Air Corps in July 1938, obeyed the regulations to the letter even though doing so meant forbidding the undeniably friendly Canadians so much as a peep at the XFM–1 Bell fighter, which they had asked to see, presumably with the President's encouragement.[20] Then abruptly there occurred one of those turns of fate, at once tragic and comic, that thrust the whole question before the public.

In January 1939 a group of French officers on a purchasing mission visited the Douglas aircraft plant in California. There, with Air Corps permission, one of their number flew in a Douglas experimental bomber with a company pilot. While demonstrating acrobatic maneuvers at low altitude the bomber crashed. The French observer, Capt. Paul Chemidlin, survived the accident. As he was rushed to a hospital, company officials, well aware of the possible ramifications in any disclosure of the mission's intentions, attempted to disguise the observer's real identity by describing him to newsmen as a company mechanic named Smithins.[21] The truth was soon out, and President Roosevelt found himself in the very midst of a political tempest.

Isolationist Senator Bennett Champ Clark of Missouri regarded the President's release to the French of a bomber designed for the United States as downright "shocking." Senator Gerald Prentice Nye of North Dakota went even further. He felt that the permission granted to the French was nothing less than a "military alliance." In short order a Senate Committee was baying down the trail after detailed evidence on the President's role in the whole affair. Although the Chief of Staff, General Craig, testified that military men had granted permission for the French flight only reluctantly and under pressure from the White House, it soon became apparent that no laws had been violated.[22] The release policies guiding the President were, in the final analysis, executive promulgations quite within the power of the President to disregard if he so desired.

L'affaire Chemidlin may have been a blessing after all. It brought the President's policy out into the open and revealed a stronger sentiment in favor of his policies than he himself apparently had expected. Press reaction to the incident, apart from rabidly isolationist journals, was generally favorable.[23] Aid for the British and French against the dictatorships was clearly regarded as a most expedient form of national self-interest.

---

[19] Edward R. Stettinius, Jr., *Lend-Lease: Weapon for Victory* (New York: The Macmillan Company, 1944), p. 16.
[20] Memo, CofAC for CofS, 27 Jul 38, SW files.
[21] K. P. Wolfe to Gen Arnold, 28 Jan 39, AFCF 161 French and Swedish Contracts. This file contains several items dealing with the affair.

[22] New York *Times*, January 29, 1939, 1:8. Craig's testimony was in executive session, thus in fairness it should be stated that his testimony is reported only as leaked by senators present.
[23] For specific comment to this effect, see *Nation*, February 11, 1939, p. 168. See also New York *Times* editorial, January 30, 1939, 12:1, and Arthur Krock's column, January 31, 1939, 20:5.

The net effect of the Chemidlin episode was to establish a precedent permitting a more liberal release of equipment designed to Army and Navy specifications. Where previous foreign orders had been largely confined to training aircraft, export sales now included bombers and fighters as well. In a matter of weeks after the Douglas crash, the trickle of orders from foreign purchasing missions turned into a torrent. During February 1939 a British purchasing mission increased earlier orders to a total of 650 aircraft, committing something over $25,000,000 for aircraft and facilities with North American and Lockheed. Several days later a French mission placed orders totaling 615 aircraft with Douglas, Curtiss, Martin, and North American, involving more than $60,000,000. Corresponding orders for engines went to Pratt and Whitney and to Wright Aeronautical. In the months that followed French and British orders increased, and other nations followed suit, pressing aircraft builders for early deliveries. Canada, Australia, Belgium, Norway, Sweden, and Iraq, to mention but a few, all placed contracts for varying numbers of military aircraft. Moreover, during the year no less than a million dollars' worth of aircraft went from the United States to the USSR.[24]

The importance of the rising volume of export orders to national defense would be hard to overestimate. In some cases orders began to arrive just in time to save manufacturers from dismissing their trained cadres of production workers for want of business.[25] Coming as they did before Congress provided funds for the 5,500 Air Corps expansion program, the big foreign orders helped make manufacturers in the United States think in terms of large-scale production. When export orders continued to pile up on top of the volume of business created by the 5,500 program, crowding facilities and burdening the existing labor force, the double load encouraged expansion and forced manufacturers to train large numbers of additional employees. The need for meeting delivery deadlines while absorbing unskilled production workers led aircraft builders to undertake production tooling to an extent undreamed of in the past.

Perhaps the greatest contribution of the foreign orders lay in their psychological value to the aircraft industry. The prospects of a sharply rising curve of export sales seem to have put manufacturers in a mood to take bigger risks, to sink more capital in plant expansions and in costly tooling for mass-production assembly operations. Had the export orders contributed nothing more than the psychological preparation of the nation's aircraft builders, they would have been fully justified.

Only one cloud hovered on the export horizon. By the terms of the 1937 neutrality legislation, arms could not be shipped to nations officially declared belligerents on the outbreak of war. What if Hitler turned one of the recurring in-

---

[24] For a good summary of the early French and British orders, see Memo, Exec, OCAC, for SW, 16 Jun 39, AFCF 161. See there also, R&R Proc Sec (Supply Div OCAC) to Gen Arnold, 4 Apr 39 and, Memo, Maj D. G. Lingle for Gen Arnold, 2 Sep 39, as well as New York *Times*, February 5, 37:4; February 15, 1:7; November 11, 3:8; December 2, 1939, 3:1.

[25] Wilson, *Slipstream*, pp. 218–19.

cidents into a *casus belli* and the foreign purchasers became forbidden belligerents? Editorial writers warned that the hundreds of aircraft on order might become undeliverable. Who, then, would pay for them?[26] This ominous threat, while not dissuading manufacturers from accepting orders from abroad, did induce them to drive hard bargains with foreign purchasers.

The two major producers of engines for military aircraft, Pratt and Whitney and Wright Aeronautical, were reluctant in 1939 to undertake vast additions to plants that might become liabilities if the neutrality legislation abruptly terminated foreign purchases. They agreed to accept the staggeringly large engine orders proffered by the French and British on condition that the foreign purchasers agree to underwrite the cost of necessary plant expansion. Only the French agreed to accept these terms. They had little choice in the matter. Production in the nationalized aircraft plants of France had fallen disastrously far behind German output. Virtually the only alternative was to make up the deficit with purchases in the United States. After the fall of France the British took over all such commitments, and by the final accounting the two nations had invested more than $84,000,000 in the United States on engine plants alone.[27] Export orders clearly played an important role in gearing the manufacturers of military aircraft engines for the task of war.

Despite the precautions taken by individual manufacturers to save themselves from sudden loss of markets on the outbreak of war, the neutrality act did affect aircraft production seriously. During September and October 1939, while Congress debated whether or not to revoke the neutrality statutes, aircraft deliveries slumped. After reaching a production peak of 238 military aircraft per month during the summer, in September only 51 units left the assembly lines.[28] Quite apart from the merits of the case on diplomatic or legal grounds, the prosperity stemming from big production contracts offered convincing arguments for amending the neutrality statutes.[29] Early in November 1939, Congress gave way and relaxed its earlier prohibitions sufficiently to permit the sale of arms to belligerents on a cash-and-carry basis.

With the neutrality barriers out of the way, war orders from abroad increased rapidly. Where contracts for aircraft previously had stipulated hundreds, they now called for thousands. The experience of a single manufacturer serves to illustrate the impact on the whole industry. Douglas Aircraft reported just after Congress approved the cash-and-carry measure that there were 2,500 men standing in line outside the company office seeking employment. Already the Douglas labor force totaled 11,000, and

---

[26] See, for example, S. Stubblefield, "Washington Windsock," *Aviation* (October 1939), p. 53.

[27] Wilson, *Slipstream*, pp. 221–22; New York *Times*, November 4, 1939, 1:2; Stettinius, *Lend-Lease*, p. 22.

[28] Senate Hearings on WD appropriation for 1941, May 2, 1940, pp. 90–91. The production figures given here do not square with those in House Hearings on WD appropriation for 1941, March 7, 1940, p. 479.

[29] The threat of U.S. aircraft builders to erect plants in Canada outside the neutrality curbs may have helped persuade Congress to revoke the neutrality measures. See *Aviation* (October 1939), p. 52, and New York *Times*, September 12, 1939, 7:5.

the firm had a backlog of $78,000,000 in unfilled orders — half of which were for export.[30]

In light of the fact that the Air Corps appropriation for new aircraft in fiscal year 1939 was only some $32,000,000, the tremendous significance of foreign orders as a stimulus to rearmament becomes apparent. From a backlog of aircraft industry orders totaling $630,000,000, at the end of 1939, some $400,000,000 was attributable to foreign purchasers.[31] So long as these orders served as a goad to production, who could complain? But such sales posed problems for the Air Corps' own rearmament program.

The rising volume of aircraft exports spelled success if by success one means fulfillment of the policy pursued by Congress—letting foreign orders build up aircraft production capacity in the United States at no expense to the nation's taxpayers. But success in this respect was tinctured with many complications and considerations quite apart from cost.

Early in 1940 War Department spokesmen trooped to the Hill to present their presidentially approved estimates for fiscal year 1941. The formal estimate called for no more than 496 aircraft, just enough to meet the normal attrition rate and to sustain the 5,500 program at its planned strength. Although the number of aircraft asked for in this estimate was no more than Congress had authorized in 1939 and no more than had been anticipated from the beginning of the expansion program, the appropriation hearings gave ample evidence that the congressmen were more than willing to find ways of reducing the cost of rearmament.[32] The officers who defended the estimate for the War Department were fully aware of this situation and recognized the necessity of contriving tactics to meet it.[33]

Shortly before presenting their estimates, the War Department officials had agreed, with some urging from the President, to permit manufacturers with government contracts for military aircraft to defer deliveries to the Air Corps in favor of export sales.[34] A number of factors lay behind this decision. To begin with, the President had favored the release of current models of military aircraft as a matter of foreign policy, insuring survival of the French and British, which in turn would, he hoped, keep the war from the New World. But as soon as aircraft manufacturers were allowed to export current military models a new dilemma appeared. Which customer should take priority in delivery?

Manufacturers were in a position to favor deliveries to foreign countries rather than to the Air Corps. Since the foreign purchasers were desperate, they were will-

---

[30] New York *Times*, November 3, 1:6, and November 9, 1939, 9:1–4.

[31] *Congressional Record*, November 1, 1939, page 1267, gives a table of expenditures for new aircraft for 1920–40. See also Review of Methods Employed by the AAF . . . , Logistics Planning Div, Plans, ATSC, p. 94. The $400,000,000 in export orders involved more than 4,500 aircraft ordered from twelve of the approximately twenty major manufacturers. See Chief, Mat Div, to Aeronautical Board, 18 Jan 40, AFCF 452.1 Sales Abroad.

[32] House Hearings on WD appropriation for 1941, February–March 1940, *passim*.

[33] See, for example, General Marshall's fear of an economy wave, Hearings of Senate Military Affairs Com on S Res 244, 76th Cong, 3d sess, March 28, 1940, p. 15.

[34] House Hearings on WD appropriation for 1941, February–March 1940, *passim*.

ing to pay premium prices. With premium payments from foreign sales, manufacturers could afford to channel all their output to the export market and use a small part of the ample profit margin thus derived to pay the penalty for delayed deliveries to the Air Corps as specified in the government's liquidated damage clauses. Air Corps officers came to the realization that whether they liked it or not they might find themselves in competition with foreign purchasers.[35]

On the other hand, there were some decided advantages to be gained from the situation.[36] With the coming of war the pace of technical development and design changes in the field of aviation accelerated sharply throughout Europe. Each nation sought feverishly to turn out aircraft of superior performance. As a consequence the rate of change became so rapid that in the United States aircraft ordered by the government at the beginning of the expansion program threatened to be obsolete by the time they were delivered months later. To insist upon delivery on schedule of all aircraft due the Air Corps might turn out to be a guarantee of acquiring obsolete equipment. By deferring deliveries and allowing foreign purchasers to buy directly off the end of the production line, the Air Corps could take later delivery of improved models.

By granting belligerent nations the output of current production, the Air Corps could secure realistic tests for its equipment under actual combat conditions without the loss of a single man. And, as experience revealed, the latest Air Corps equipment proved deficient in armor, armament, and a number of other details such as self-sealing fuel tanks. By taking delivery at a later date, the Air Corps would not only secure improved equipment but also lower prices since sales abroad would tend to absorb some of the cost of the modifications found necessary.

Undoubtedly there was a very real danger in buying obsolete equipment for the air arm. And upon this ground War Department spokesmen could present valid arguments justifying the delayed deliveries to the Air Corps.[37] They apparently felt, however, that the argument of obsolescence would be insufficient to persuade the economy-minded congressman with an eye to the on-coming elections. To meet this difficulty the War Department representatives offered further bait.

Foreign sales of military aircraft, the Chief of Staff told Congress, built up the productive capacity of the industry. The original 5,500 program called for 3,300 active and 2,200 reserve aircraft. But the ratio of reserve to active units—2,200 to 3,300—was premised upon the estimated

---

[35] *Ibid.*, 42, pp. 476–78.
[36] For an extended survey of the pros and cons of export sales, see Rpt of Meeting in OCS, 19 Mar 40, AFCF 452.1 Sales Abroad. See also, Gen George C. Marshall and Gen Arnold, Statement of Policy, for President, 21 Mar 40, AC Project Rcds (Lyon Papers), 59–108F, and testimony of SW Woodring before Senate Military Affairs Com, Hearings on S Res 244, March 18, 1940.

[37] General Marshall noted later that the War Department "could not afford to do anything else" but defer deliveries to export channels, so serious was the problem of obsolescence. Senate Hearings on WD appropriation for 1941, May 1, 1940, p. 64. General Arnold, when prodded by Senator Henry Cabot Lodge, Jr., also admitted that obsolescence had become a serious problem since the outbreak of war in Europe. *Ibid.*, pp. 73, 105.

productive capacity of the industry when the expansion program was first formulated. Export sales, by stimulating plant expansion, increased productive capacity and reduced the need for a large reserve. On this basis, both General Marshall and General Arnold offered to cut the original estimate of 496 new aircraft for fiscal year 1941 to a total of 166 items.[38] This reduction, volunteered by the War Department, appealed to the congressmen; it represented a possible saving of some $27,000,000 in the budget.[39] Unfortunately, in suggesting this economy, the military leaders opened Pandora's box.

Why, reasoned the Appropriations Committee, should they stop at 166 aircraft? If the entire 496 aircraft in the estimate were to fill the reserve and if export sales obviated the need for a reserve, why buy any of the 496 aircraft? Following this line of reasoning, the committee reported out a bill providing only 57 new aircraft for fiscal year 1941 and the House promptly passed the measure.[40] While rushing to the Hill to beg the Senate to restore this cut, the Chief of Staff may have reflected somewhat ruefully on the impropriety of letting the camel get his nose under the tent.

Undoubtedly there was a good deal of dismay, if not irritation, in the War Department when responsible officers there saw how the congressmen had seized the initiative, using the Department's own arguments.[41] This rather unexpected reversal must have been disconcerting in itself; worse yet, it did not mark the end of the difficulty. The tactic of tying export sales to a reduced appropriation in an effort to woo Congress with an economy package held other dangers.

No matter how justifiable the export of current models of military aircraft might be as foreign policy, such sales posed serious problems to those responsible for national defense. Insofar as diversions of equipment to foreign countries delayed delivery to the Air Corps, they threatened to delay the expansion program. Ostensibly, the units deferred were destined for a reserve status, but any acceleration in the training program would immediately create a need for some of the reserves.[42] True, by not deferring deliveries the Air Corps would get obsolescent aircraft, but for training purposes even obsolete aircraft would be better than none at all. Furthermore, export orders tended to drive up costs since in their desperation the foreign purchasers were willing to negotiate contracts with wider profit margins to ensure speed in production. Manufacturers receiving

---

[38] *Ibid.*, p. 21. See also, Senate Military Affairs Com Hearings on S Res 244, March 28, 1940, p. 12.
[39] Hearings on S Res 244, March 28, 1940, p. 10.
[40] H.R. 9209, WD appropriation for 1941, 76th Cong, 3d sess. See H Rpt 1912, April 3, 1940. See also, remarks of Representative Snyder in *Cong Rcd*, April 3, 1940, 3932ff.

[41] Both General Marshall and General Arnold described the 496 aircraft in the estimate as "replacements," items falling in the reserve portion of the 5,500 program, thus providing a handle for the committeemen to eliminate most of the aircraft as they did. House Hearings on WD appropriation for 1941, February 23, 1940, p. 21, and March 8, 1940, p. 519.
[42] Actually, as Generals Marshall and Arnold subsequently admitted, the reserve was not a reserve after all. It did not provide any reserve in heavy bombers, and some units were designated reserve "only because at the time the appropriation was made they were not yet out of the experimental stage and air arm officers did not wish to buy 'paper' aircraft." Senate Hearings on WD appropriation for 1941, April 30, 1940, p. 38, and May 2, 1940, pp. 115–22.

these foreign contracts were then in a position to bid lavishly for the output of vendors and suppliers, and this in turn tended to drive prices higher for the Air Corps.[43]

The President did not make the policy of favoring exports easy to take. He continued to exert pressure in favor of foreign purchasers until the Air Corps found itself hard put to carry out the successive phases of the expansion program. By the summer of 1940, about 70 percent of the military engines delivered by the two leading engine manufacturers went to foreign purchasers.[44] Worse yet, export sales actually threatened to wreck the air arms' all-important heavy bomber program.[45]

The discomfiture of Air Corps leaders was acute. They were caught in a crossfire of executive will and military necessity. The Chief of the Air Corps repeatedly protested, within the Department, that an excessive release of aircraft for export could cripple the air arm seriously, although in public he continued to accept the President's leadership without qualification. When rumors of his private protests reached the newspapers he disavowed them—quite properly—as inaccurate.[46] Yet, ironically enough, when some junior officers, reflecting his own irritation, berated the President's policy of favoring aid to the Allies over rearming the Air Corps, General Arnold slapped them down pointedly. Criticism of the President's policy, he declared, was a "flagrant breach of discipline."[47]

To use a phrase more nautical than aeronautical, the Air Corps was caught in a bight. The whole matter of exploiting the export trade in aircraft as an element of national defense clearly had not been thought out to its hither limits before the crisis arrived. In a sense this was a serious shortcoming in the vital field of mobilization planning.

Aircraft Exports and Mobilization Planning

During August 1939, on the eve of World War II, General Arnold began to have serious doubts concerning the value of the existing Air Corps mobilization plans. Only a few days before the German invasion of Poland he ordered a restudy of the whole problem—clearly in anticipation of a sweeping revision.[48]

The organization for mobilization planning that ultimately would have to comply with General Arnold's request was at best a blunt instrument.[49] Moreover, just as the planners entered upon the most difficult tasks of the limited emergency, the already inadequate organization received a crippling blow.

---

[43] Testimony of Admiral J. H. Towers, House Hearings on Navy Dept appropriation for 1941, January 8, 1940, p. 488.

[44] Mat Planning Sec, Mat Div, Chart: Proportion of Accepted Deliveries of Aircraft Engines by Customer..., Jan–Aug 40, 26 Sep 40, AC Project Rcds (Lyon Papers), 59-10 F.

[45] CofAC to ASW thru CofS, 14 Jun 40, and Memo, CofAC for CofS, 17 Sep 40, AFCF 452.1 Sales Abroad.

[46] CofAC to Senator Sheppard, 4 Apr 40, AHO Plans Div 145.93-263.

[47] CofAC to CGGHQAF, 1 Oct 40, AHO Plans Div 145.91-246.

[48] Unsigned Memo for Brig Gen B. K. Yount, 18 Aug 39, AFCF 381A War Plans; Notes, Div Chiefs' Staff Meetings, 1939–40, AFCF 337 Special, as well as Memo, Col Echols for Gen Arnold, 23 Aug 39, AFCF 452.1 Aircraft, Gen. See also, 1st Ind CofAC to ASW, Apr 39, on basic, Planning Br (OASW) to CofAC, 27 Mar 39, WFCF 381 Mobilization.

[49] See above, ch. VII.

Foreign orders and the outbreak of war in Europe forced the Chief of the Air Corps to give more attention to mobilization planning at the headquarters in Washington. Congressional queries and the need for detailed information on the part of all the various agencies of the War Department led to a decision to transfer a part of the Industrial Planning Section at Wright Field to Washington, where it was to serve in a liaison capacity. This transfer of officers in September 1939 reduced the already undermanned planning staff at Wright Field by one-third. What is more, the cut came at the very moment when the workload at Wright Field began to increase enormously. To make matters worse, the officers sent to Washington were soon afterwards lured off into other duties. The planning function lost ground on both fronts.[50]

The whole industrial planning operation began to fall behind the rapidly changing pace of events. One rather glaring example of this should suffice to illustrate the tendency. Among other duties, the mobilization planners were responsible for working out the details for lining up the aircraft industry to meet the requirements of the Protective Mobilization Plan (PMP) of 1939.[51] Since the Air Corps possessed no currently approved Tables of Organization and Basic Allowance, all the detailed work on PMP had either to wait or to be evolved from obsolete data. Even if the necessary tables had been available, however, they would not have solved all problems. The air component of PMP was geared to the authorization of 1936 totaling 2,320 aircraft. By mid-1939 this ceiling had been raised to 6,000 and procurement of 5,500 units was under way. Air arm officers suggested to the General Staff that further work on a PMP premised upon 2,320 aircraft was, to say the very least, "open to question."[52]

The hint had very little effect. During May 1940, a General Staff query blandly asked for further information on PMP, including the desirability of additional observation balloons. General Arnold pointed out that this sort of planning had no real value since, in terms of PMP, the Air Corps was already beyond the 2,320 limit—was in fact already mobilized.[53] But the mobilization planners at Wright Field lagged far behind General Arnold in their conception of the problem; they continued to plod along with the details of PMP and its augmentations. As late as August 1940, after the fall of France had entirely altered the situation, a furious officer was still trying to shut off the "asinine" work of the mobilization planners at Wright Field who lumbered along, several laps behind reality, working out PMP.[54]

In blunt truth, the industrial planners at Wright Field went on shoeing dead horses from September 1939 until well

---

[50] AAF Hist Study 10, p. 58. Unsigned Memo, 24 Apr 40, sub: Major Time Consuming Projects of Industrial Planning Sec, and Memo, Maj A. W. Marriner, Asst Tech Exec for Chief, Mat Div, 4 May 40, WFCF 381.
[51] For air arm aspects of PMP 1939, see AHO Plans Div 145.93-249.
[52] Dir, Planning Br, OASW, to CofAC, 27 Mar 39, and draft by Plans Div, OCAC, to TAG, 9 Jun 39, AHO Plans Div 145.93-182.
[53] TAG to CofAC, 8 May 40, and 1st Ind, CofAC to TAG, 6 Aug 40, AHO Plans 145.93-250.
[54] IOM, Maj B. E. Meyers to Tech Exec, Mat Div, 24 Aug 40, Air AC Project Rcds (Lyon Papers), 59-11.

into the summer of 1940. Their fundamental shortcoming, it appears, was a failure in conception; they did not seem to realize that the air arm's expansion program of 1939 was really phase one of the mobilization for war. Their thinking was far too rigid to fit actualities that did not mesh perfectly with their preconceived notions of how war would come; the M-day for which they were planning had already passed.

Even more serious than the inability of the Wright Field planners to anticipate a creeping M-day was their failure to foresee the contingencies that might arise from foreign orders for aircraft in wartime. Here again they ignored the experience of World War I with unfortunate consequence. When the President and the Congress decided to utilize French and British orders for aircraft as an integral aspect of the nation's defense, the mobilization planners at Wright Field had no clear path to follow. Perforce, they had to grope and blunder in solving the problems raised by the policy.

The contingencies stemming from the precipitous rise in export orders for military aircraft took any number of forms. For example, air arm contracts in force when the crisis arrived contained no provisions preventing foreign purchasers from securing priority on deliveries by paying the liquidated damage penalties imposed by the Air Corps for delays. Had air arm officers anticipated the situation their contracts might have been better drawn.

Similarly, the record of the first few months of war makes it quite clear that Air Corps officers were taken off guard by the extremely high rate of design change in military aircraft. As Generals Arnold and Marshall both admitted, the release of military aircraft from the United States to Europe was not only desirable but essential if this nation was to avoid being left with obsolete equipment. Realistic experience with military equipment (without loss of lives to the Air Corps) was a useful and necessary *quid pro quo* for the release of recent production models to foreign users. Clearly the relationship between the "release policy" or regulations as to military secrets on the one hand and deferred delivery to foreign purchasers on the other had not been thoroughly thought out before the war came.

The whole point and purpose of peacetime planning is to avoid hasty improvisation in time of crisis. The mobilization planning of the air arm was not only faulty in conception but inadequate in execution. The failure was not alone that of the mobilization planners at Wright Field who did the detail work. It was a failure of higher command as well. The congressional decision to accept export orders as a vital aspect of national defense required of the Air Corps a whole series of corollary responses and adjustments that only the upper echelons of leadership could make. Since these decisions were not made in advance, improvisation in the crisis was unavoidable. The cost—in confusion and delay—is a matter of record.

During the dreadful days of May and June 1940 when so many illusions were shattered, air arm officers woke up to the realization that the policy of letting foreign orders mobilize the aircraft industry, the policy they had been led to accept and approve, was now turning out badly. On 10 May the Germans invaded neutral

Holland and Belgium. Twenty days later British troops faced disaster at Dunkerque. On 10 June Mussolini declared war on France. A week later the French were begging an armistice. And in this crisis the Air Corps was inadequately armed. Once again air arm officers were learning from painful experience, as an earlier generation had learned in the months leading up to April 1917, that politics, foreign policy, and mobilization planning cannot be separated.

CHAPTER X

Requirements

When President Roosevelt went before Congress on 16 May 1940 with his dramatic appeal for arms, he asked among other things for 50,000 airplanes. How did he arrive at the number 50,000? One version is that the President was disappointed at the lack of imagination displayed by military leaders when asked to state their maximum needs, so he plucked a number—25,000—from the air, possibly with an eye to World War I experience. But when he asked the British production chief, Lord Beaverbrook, for an opinion, that worthy is alleged to have replied, "Why be a piker; 100,000 makes better headlines." So the President split the difference and asked for 50,000 aircraft.[1]

On the other hand, in his memoirs, Secretary of State Cordell Hull recalls a conversation with the President during May 1940, as the French Republic was about to collapse, when the President spoke of merely doubling the existing military appropriation. Hull urged him to go far beyond that and "aim for a production of 50,000 planes a year." The President, Mr. Hull tells us, was speechless at the size of this figure, an eightfold increase over existing programs.[2]

Conceding the accuracy of Mr. Hull's memory, his account of the origin of the 50,000 figure is no more bizarre than the Beaverbrook anecdote. Here, too, the figure is a round number plucked from the air, casually and quite unscientifically. How then, one may well ask again, was the 50,000 figure actually derived? Before seeking an explicit answer to this question it may be useful to digress and explore the general question of requirements as well as the several factors conditioning the computation of requirements.

An Essay on Requirements

The computation of requirements is a central problem in any study of military procurement. The procurement process cannot begin until at least three essentials are determined: how much of what and when—quantity, quality, and schedule. This applies not only to aircraft, but to all related items as well, for maintenance tools, field servicing equipment, and special facilities for ground crews are just as vital as the aircraft themselves. When there is no aqua system, no high-speed pump, and no tank truck for refueling, ground crews must resort to bucket brigades. Under such circumstances refueling a heavy bomber takes hours rather than minutes, and the aircraft on hand are "tactically available"

---
[1] Wilson, *Slipstream*, p. 233.
[2] Cordell Hull, *The Memoirs of Cordell Hull*, 2 vols. (New York: The Macmillan Company, 1948), p. 766.

fewer hours per day. Bitter experience in the early months of World War II made the truth of this only too evident; accessories proved to be every bit as important as airframes and engines. An aircraft without guns or without an oxygen system was hardly better than no aircraft at all. When landing gear production—wheel, strut, or tire—lagged, so did air power. The discussion that follows is cast largely in terms of airframes or engines in order to simplify the analysis, not to minimize the importance of spares, maintenance equipment, and accessories. Within the framework of this arbitrary limitation, it should be possible to review the parameters—the several variable factors—that enter into the formulation of requirements for the nation's air power; and surely no single factor is more important to the computation of requirements for air power than a clear definition of the meaning of air power itself: the doctrine or agreed-upon mission of the air weapon.

Mission Unknown

Although it is patently impossible to formulate an accurate statement of requirements without first defining the mission of the weapons to be procured, the fact remains that as late as 1939 the doctrine or accepted mission of the Army's air arm remained in uncertain flux. In the early 1930's the Chief of Air Corps flatly asserted that the air arm had no officially defined wartime role.[3] Such neglect of doctrine suited the era when hopeful statesmen sought a formula

---

[3] Testimony of Gen Foulois, House Hearings on WD appropriation for 1933, January 5, 1932, p. 1014.

for world peace at Geneva. All their attempts failed but not from want of cooperation by the War Department. In 1933 the President and the Secretary of War had even been willing to abolish bombardment aviation as a contribution to disarmament.[4] Little wonder that air power enthusiasts in the Air Corps mistrusted the War Department. The long struggle of the air arm to win General Staff approval of its heavy bomber doctrine of strategic air power is well known. There is no need to retrace those steps here save to observe that by 1938 a number of studies were made within Air Corps circles spelling out the strategic role of air power in considerable detail, though the studies by no means represented official doctrine approved by the General Staff.[5] Thus down to the outbreak of war in 1939 there was no real agreement between the Air Corps and the General Staff on the mission of the aerial weapon.[6]

When the Air Corps rearmament program began to take shape after the crucial White House conference in November 1938, the lack of an approved

---

[4] *Secretary of War Annual Report, 1933,* pp. 48–49.
[5] See, for example, AC Board Study 44, Air Corps Mission Under the Monroe Doctrine, 17 Oct 38, AHO files; and student com rpt, ACTS, A Study of the Air Defense of the Western Hemisphere, 12 May 39, AHO Plans Div 145.93–141.
[6] TAG to CofAC, 23 Mar 39, AFCF 381.A War Plans. For examples of conflicting views of General Staff and Air Corps, see Memo, G–4 for Gen Marshall, 5 Apr 39, AGO Rcds, G–4 27277–19; Memo, OASW for Gen Marshall, 2 Mar 39, AGO Rcds, WPD–OPD 3807–32–40. Of particular interest is the Air Corps effort to obtain more freedom in defining military characteristics for aircraft to be procured. See CofAC to TAG, 10 Jun 39, WFCF 452.1 Military Characteristics; AC Policy 181, 10 Jul 39, Digest of AC Policies, AF Doc Br.

statement of mission for the air arm led to trouble. Congress, following the proposals of the administration, launched a program calling for 5,500 aircraft, but was this expansion actually geared to the needs of the Air Corps? Procurement had scarcely begun when the Secretary of the General Staff suggested that the number of aircraft authorized by Congress had been "arrived at hurriedly" and "without a sufficiently thorough estimate of the situation...."[7]

The outbreak of war in Europe served only to emphasize the need for an improved foundation of doctrine in formulating aircraft requirements. The blitzkrieg in Poland must have led to some sobering second thoughts about air power, for by the end of October 1939, a new harmony seemed to mark the relations of air and ground staff officers. "For the first time," one air arm officer reported after a conference with representatives of the War Plans Division, "we are approaching the problem of air requirements in a logical way. We are analyzing the problem first in order to determine the character of the tools needed."[8] In short, on the testimony of participants on both sides of the issue, their inability to reach decisions on doctrine had left the formulation of requirements unsettled until the crisis of war itself. The War Department had been forced to begin buying its weapons before deciding what weapons it wanted.[9]

The failure of officers within the War Department to resolve their differing views on air power was not the only way in which doctrine affected the calculation of requirements. Between the Army and Navy the role of air power was subject to still sharper dispute —and this too was unresolved when war broke out.

The Army and the Navy Agree To Disagree

Early in the nineteen thirties Chief of Staff Douglas MacArthur told some congressmen that the Army-Navy dispute over air power and coastal defense was "completely and absolutely settled."[10] He was, it would seem, a bit optimistic, for not long afterward the Aeronautical Board, the appropriate agency for resolving such joint conflicts between the Army and Navy, reported that its members were unable to reconcile their conflicting views and arrive at a mutually acceptable statement on the proper mission of Army air power.[11]

The dispute of the Army and Navy over air power was by no means academic. It was often expressed in seemingly trivial terms—for example, minor overlaps in functions such as the operation of patrol planes—but behind the façade of details lay a fundamental struggle for power. Navy spokesmen held that "sea operations" were "inherently a function of the

---

[7] Memo, SGS for WPD, 20 Oct 39, AGO Rcds, WPD–OPD 3807–41.

[8] Memo, Capt H. S. Hansell for Col I. C. Eaker, 31 Oct 39, AFCF 337.1 Conference. The co-operative attitude expressed here appears to have been developed while working out the details of the Army's new strategic plan based on the joint RAINBOW 1 plan approved in August 1939.

[9] See complaints of ASW Johnson on this point, *Aerodigest* (January 1939), p. 51.

[10] Testimony on H.R. 9920, May 25, 1932, quoted in Craven and Cate, eds., *Plans and Early Operations*, p. 62.

[11] Aeronautical Board Case 59, 27 Apr 34, AGO Rcds, WPD–OPD 888–90–91.

Navy . . . whether . . . carried out by surface ships, subsurface ships, or aircraft." Army representatives with little confidence in the future of strategic bombers might be willing to concede this much, but how could they accept the Navy contention that "money spent on our Army could, with more profit toward guarding our continental coastline, be spent in augmenting our naval strength. . . ."?[12] With so much in the way of pay, promotion, the hope of command, and the whole question of career tied up in the matter, it was difficult for either Army or Navy officers to take an utterly detached view.

Unable to reach any fundamental agreement on doctrine, Army and Navy officials resorted to an old formula: they would agree to disagree. All controversial discussions of Army-Navy operations, warned a General Staff officer, should be studiously avoided.[13] This was the essence of the "solution": solve the problem by virtually ignoring it. High-ranking officers contrived an accord only by defining the respective missions of the services in very general terms that avoided exploring the areas of overlap too closely,[14] and once this "agreement" was drawn, they fended off every effort to reopen the question.[15] Air power advocates within the Army who urged reconsideration in light of the rapidly increasing potential of long-range bombers were repeatedly silenced with the argument that the precarious Army-Navy accord must not be upset. The admittedly faulty definitions of respective missions, "arrived at after years of acrimonious and injurious controversy" had best be left undisturbed.[16]

The consequences of the Army-Navy failure to work out a solution as to their respective overwater missions were obvious. With one whole potential area of air arm activity left in uncertainty, it was next to impossible to compute quantitative and qualitative requirements. Highly suggestive evidence of the gap separating Army and Navy thinking and hence requirements is to be found in a dispatch of the War Department's Hawaiian commander written soon after the outbreak of war in Europe. He reported, in secret and with evident surprise, that his recent conversations with naval officers in the islands revealed "an apparent acceptance of the idea that the Navy might sometime call upon the Army Air Corps in this area for assistance." If the Air Corps hoped to co-operate effectively, the Army commander pointed out, no time should be lost in establishing flight strips on the islands within bomber range of Hawaii. Thus, when Hitler was rolling through Poland, the Army was just beginning to

---

[12] Rear Adm J. K. Taussig to Clark Howell, 6 Dec 34, AGO Rcds, WPD–OPD 888–92.

[13] Memo, G–1 for WPD, 9 Apr 35, AGO Rcds, WPD–OPD 3774–13.

[14] WPD draft, Employment of Army Aviation in Coast Defense, 16 Aug 34, AGO Rcds, WPD–OPD 3774–13. Something of the precarious character of the accord is suggested by the following buckslip from Kilbourne to Drum covering the draft ". . . we'll never silence the junior officers without some very drastic discipline." See also Memo, WPD for CofS, 13 Jan 40, which mentions the Army-Navy joint action accord, saying this "admittedly does not meet the main issue." WPD 888–103.

[15] See, for example, Memo, DCofS for WPD, 13 Oct 37, and related papers, AGO Rcds WPD–OPD 888–100–102; Memo, WPD for CofS, 22 Dec 38, in WPD 888–03.

[16] Memo, WPD for CofS, 22 Dec 38, AGO Rcds, WPD–OPD 888–103. See also, Memo, Chief, Plans, OCAC, for CofAC, 5 Mar 38, AFCF 321.94 Organization; Arnold, *Global Mission*, pp. 176–77.

REQUIREMENTS

think in terms of such far-flung bases as Christmas Island, Midway, and the like,[17] which had to be considered in any plan of aerial defense for the Hawaiian Islands.

On two counts then—uncertainty as to its role within the Army and uncertainty vis à vis the Navy—the air arm faced imponderables when attempting to tally its needs. Unfortunately, these were not the only variables involved. There were also political factors that had to be taken into account.

The Political Factor in Requirements

On the first of July 1939 President Roosevelt issued a military order. In his capacity as Commander in Chief, he placed the Joint Army and Navy Board, the Aeronautical Board, the Joint Economy Board, and the Munitions Board directly under his leadership in the Executive Office.[18] The shift involved some adroit political maneuvering that need not concern us here, but it is of significance insofar as it clearly indicated the President's intention to rule the military arm as well as reign.

Since the services would naturally follow the President's lead, military officials accepted an obligation to back up his leadership with adequate steps in support. The evolution of the nation's foreign policy offers a case in point. Here the President was a leader; he inched along cautiously, making one change at a time, seeking always to be sure the public substantially supported him. Thus, over the months and years before the war, the nation's foreign policy was modified decidedly, albeit gradually, and as a consequence the nation's military obligations altered too. Each new Presidential promulgation and pronunciamento in the field of foreign relations brought with it a corresponding need for at least a review and in some cases a revision of national military strength.

During 1937 planning officers in the War Department regarded the Army's mission as the defense of the United States and its territories. Then, early in 1938, President Roosevelt warned Congress that increases in armament were necessary to keep "any potential enemy many hundred miles" from the coasts.[19] Clearly the concept of continental defense was expanding. Six months later, speaking at Kingston, Ontario, the President assured his listeners that the United States would not stand idle if Canada were threatened. Here, by implication at least, was a further extension of military obligation. In November 1938, at the time of the White House conference at which the initial target of 10,000 aircraft was suggested, the President directed his military chiefs to prepare plans to meet any attack on the Western Hemisphere, from pole to pole. When Congress convened soon thereafter in January 1939, he announced this pattern of hemisphere defense publicly.[20]

Each step in the evolution of foreign policy implied a response in military terms—a revision of strategic thinking,

---

[17] Maj Gen C. D. Herron to TAG, 5 Oct 39, and 2d Ind, OCAC to TAG, AFCF 381 War Plans.
[18] Military Order 129, by FDR, July 1, 1939, *Federal Register*, vol. IV (July 7, 1939), p. 2786.
[19] *Cong Rcd*, January 28, 1938, p. 1216.
[20] Stetson Conn and Byron Fairchild, *The Framework of Hemisphere Defense*, UNITED STATES ARMY IN WORLD WAR II (Washington, 1960), ch. I. See also *Cong Rcd*, January 4, 1939, p. 74.

new areas to defend, new bases to plan or prepare, a revision in the capabilities and number of the weapons required. A few words from the President and the existing heavy bomber might no longer be adequate. New specifications, new statements of military characteristics, and so on would then have to be devised to suit the new situation.[21]

The influence of Executive discretion on military requirements was by no means limited to the extension or contraction of defense spheres. The President's leadership in extending aid in the form of aircraft to friendly powers was another aspect of his ability to shape military requirements. Each time the President or his agents agreed to deliver military aircraft to British, Soviet, Chinese, or other forces, the sum of military requirements in the United States varied accordingly.[22]

War Department staff officers who tried to compute aircraft requirements thus faced a dismaying number of variables. Their plight was not unlike that confronting the manager of a ball team who discovers, when he sets about his business, that his team cannot decide which players will play what positions. For that matter, the team is not sure of the rules of play, and the dimensions of the playing field are subject to continual change. Finally, there is some question whether the home team will receive the available equipment or whether it will be distributed elsewhere.

Unfortunately for the staff officers concerned, the inherent complexity of their task did not absolve them from responsibility. Difficult, even impossible though the job may have been, they had to try to compute the needs of the service. Moreover, there were still other conditioning factors that had to be taken into account, although happily not all of these were as erratic as those already mentioned. Some factors, such as the matter of spare parts and the problem of attrition, lent themselves, in theory at least, to almost finite calculation.

Computing Requirements for Spare Parts

Perhaps the first requisite to understanding the computation of spares required is an appreciation of the size and importance of the job. Experience during World War II showed, for example, that a single bombardment group flying approximately 31 Boeing B–17's on 15 sorties per month burned up in that period some 19,000 spark plugs—about three tons of them.[23] Surely no one would dispute the magnitude or the importance of the whole problem of spares. German Air Force leaders minimized the significance of spare parts before World War II only to discover, when facing the supposedly inferior Soviet Air Force, that they had committed a critical mistake that helped bring on disaster.[24] Common sense alone would suggest that it is false economy to ground a $100,000 aircraft

---

[21] Memo, Lt Col G. S. Warren, Fiscal Officer, OCAC, for Col Loughry, 27 Jul 39, AFCF 030 President and Cong. See also, *Aide-mémoires* for Use in . . . Army Air Corps Program, 6 May 39, AGO Rcds, WPD–OPD 3807-30-31.

[22] See AFCF 381.3A Lend-Lease Aid, *passim;* WFCF 032 Lend-Lease, *passim.*

[23] Data from WFHO.

[24] Rpt to SN, Unification of the War and Navy Departments and Postwar Organization for National Security (Eberstadt Rpt), October 22, 1945, print of Senate Com on Naval Affairs, p. 231.

for want of an $8,000 engine or a $1.00 spark plug.[25]

The term *spares* involves several different categories. There are spare engines purchased along with new aircraft, since engines wear out faster than airframes and require more frequent overhaul. But engines, both spares and those in use, require stocks of spare parts, individual components, especially items subject to heavy wear and breakage such as piston rings and spark plugs. Although spare airframes are designated as reserves or depot reserves rather than spares, there is a category of airframe spares—parts such as wing tips, wheel assemblies, control surfaces, and so forth, all subject to replacement. *Spares*, then, unless defined, might embrace any one of several different groups of items. But whether taken individually or collectively, spares posed a great many difficult problems for the staff officers responsible for computing the number required.

Throughout the years of peacetime planning, officers accumulated "experience factors" on spares, yet to the very eve of World War II the debate over the question of replacement parts remained unsettled. It was difficult to obtain agreement on exactly what percentage of spares should accompany the procurement of new equipment,[26] and even where there was agreement, funds were not always available to procure the spares desired.[27]

Consider, for example, the case of spare engines. In the fiscal year 1936 Congress provided funds for 100 percent spare engines but authorized only 50 percent in the following fiscal year. In 1938 the Air Corps begged for more than 100 percent spare engines; the Bureau of the Budget favored 75 percent, while Congress allowed 50 percent. Then abruptly in 1939 the vast new air rearmament program brought novel factors into play.[28]

If policy on spare engines fluctuated widely in the three years before the rearmament program began, the introduction of other variables during the period of rapid expansion did little to simplify matters. Under normal peacetime conditions, newly procured aircraft were delivered over a period of many months and sometimes over one or two years, since manufacturers assembled units a few at a time on a job-shop basis. As a result, few engines reached the point where they required overhaul (after two or three hundred hours of operation) at any given time. The introduction of mass production in the hurried rearmament of 1939–41 changed all this. With large numbers of aircraft being delivered at approximately the same time, great numbers of engines reached the overhaul stage almost simultaneously. Because of this, even 100 percent spare engines proved inadequate since the overhaul load arrived at the repair depots all at once. With engine overhaul consuming anywhere from 150 to 200 man-hours per engine—nearly a month of working days—the only alternatives were to pro-

---

[25] Draft Memo, Plans, OCAC, for ASW, 3 Sep 37, AHO Plans Div 145.93–269.
[26] For a classic statement on the problem of spares centering around the feasibility of procuring 9,000-pound B-17 wing butts as spares, see Col F. M. Kennedy to Gen Brett, 13 May 40, AFCF 452.1–H Parts.
[27] See above, ch. IV.

[28] CofAC to TAG, 12 Mar 37, AFCF 112.4-A, and ASW to Senator Copeland, 31 Mar 38, reprinted in Senate Hearings on WD appropriation for 1939, April 1, 1938, pp. 1–5.

cure more spare engines or to improve the facilities of the repair depots to provide for engine overhaul on a large-scale or mass-production basis.[29]

Engine overhaul on a mass-production or assembly-line basis became possible for the first time during the expansion program and promised savings in both time and money. However, only extended experience could show how much these savings would be. Meanwhile, to be absolutely certain that the air arm would be capable of sustained action after M-day, Air Corps staff officers had to compute requirements for engines in terms of the peak load anticipated even if doing so subsequently meant having a number of usable engines left over long after the aircraft for which they were procured had been written off.[30]

There were other complications stemming from the expansion program that tended to vex the computation of the spares required. Many new air bases, located at ever more distant points, forced Air Corps planners to give increasing attention to the question of distribution. As the pipeline grew bigger and longer it swallowed spares in what must have seemed to be a geometric progression. Even in peacetime the nation's fifty-odd air bases had to stock parts for a dismaying array of engines. Just before the war there were about a hundred different engine models in use.[31] The rearmament program multiplied the number many times.

Staff planners in peacetime were fully aware of the "distribution" or "pipeline" factor in computing requirements, but throughout the decade of the thirties they expressed it entirely in terms of time rather than quantity. They visualized the pipeline factor as a delay in delivery rather than as an absolute increase in quantity. In their calculations they thereupon proposed to absorb this delay by moving up the dispatch of spares 15, 30, 60, or 90 days to ensure delivery at the point desired at the time desired.[32] Unfortunately, as the expansion program got under way experience was to prove that there were other factors involved. Newly created air bases in the field, and even old, long-established stations when rapidly expanded, tended to lose control, at least temporarily, over spares. Unmarked boxes of spares without identifying shipping tickets were to all practical purposes unavailable even if physically present, and operating units made duplicate requisitions, thus absorbing more spares than peacetime experience factors might justify statistically.[33]

Clearly, then, the problem of computing requirements in spares was inherently complex though by no means impossible when undertaken by imaginative staff officers capable of using statistical tools or experience factors once they had

---

[29] Maj Meyers to CofAC, 20 Feb 39, AFCF 452.1 Proc of Aircraft; Memo, CofAC for ASW, 10 Sep 37, AHO Plans Div 145.93-269.

[30] For a tragic example of the disasters stemming from the want of a minor part, see account by R. L. Watson in Craven and Cate, eds., *Plans and Early Operations*, p. 227.

[31] Memo, CofAC for ASW, 10 Sep 37, AHO Plans Div 145.93-269.

[32] See Industrial Planning Sec, WF, Computation of AC Requirements Based on Gen Mobilization Plan, 1933, AHO Plans Div 145.93-189, and draft (by Plans Div) CofAC to TAG, 18 Apr 39, AHO Plans Div 145.91-391.

[33] See, for example, R&R, CofAS, to OCAC, 7 Oct 41, AFCF 452.1-H Parts, and Memo, ACofAS, A-4, for Dir, Military Requirements, 20 Jul 42, AFCF 360.01-C.

REQUIREMENTS

been accumulated. While not impossible, however, the task, which proved difficult enough during peacetime, was to become enormously more involved in war.[34] Here the problem has been arbitrarily confined to spares—spare engines, spare parts for engines, and the like. When the problem is projected to embrace such replacement items as fuels, lubricants, and ammunition, the intricate ramifications to requirements calculations become evident. Unfortunately for the planner, estimating requirements, the calculation of spares and distribution factors, brings no end to his labors. Yet to be considered is the attrition or wastage factor of actual operations.

The Attrition Factor in Requirements

Attrition or wastage by definition includes all losses of operating aircraft, those destroyed in accidents as well as those lost to enemy action. Since operational losses bear a direct relationship to the number of missions, strikes or sorties made, it becomes a matter of considerable moment in computing replacement needs to know the number of sorties per month a given type of aircraft is expected to make. This in turn depends upon the concept of the mission or doctrine officially established for the air arm in general and each type of aircraft in particular. Because the official doctrine of air power was, at best, in a state of flux during the years leading up to the war, it was difficult if not impossible to determine probable replacement requirements with any degree of precision.

Staff officers at various echelons in the War Department gave a good deal of thought to the question of wartime attrition in the years before World War II. The Air Corps Board set the loss rate at 1 percent per day, or 30 percent per month, in 1938, but officers in G-4 considered this too low, citing British sources favoring 50 percent per month as probably more realistic.[35]

The derivation of an accurate attrition formula was vital. If set too low, replacements would not be available when needed in combat. If set too high, it would impose a needless strain upon the national economy and upset the delicate balance of resources and facilities involved in the nation's industrial mobilization.

Vital as the attrition formula was, staff officers seeking to derive it were groping largely in the dark. They had very little definite information to confirm or deny the attrition figure suggested by the Air Corps Board. Not until the very eve of the rearmament program did the War Plans Division belatedly ask G-2 for hasty reports on the attrition experience of the forces fighting in China and in Spain.[36] This information, although far from ideal, was better than none at all; however, the Chief of Staff himself warned against accepting any formula based upon it. Shortly after the outbreak of war in Europe in 1939 he suggested that it would be advisable to wait until events there provided a broader basis for computing attrition rates.[37]

---

[34] See below, ch. XX.

[35] Plans Div, OCAC to AC Board, 30 Mar 38, AHO Plans Div 145.91-528.

[36] WPD to G-2, 31 Oct 38, AGO Rcds, WPD-OPD 3807-27.

[37] Memo, CofS for ASW, 17 Nov 39, AFCF AC Project Rcds (Lyon Papers), bk. 22.

This is what the staff had to do. The inevitable penalty was paid in months of delay.

British operational experience, helpful as it was, proved to be no panacea for determining attrition rates. Objective observations at firsthand were hard to secure. The British were co-operative, but different observers sent conflicting information to the United States. Moreover, actual wartime operations uncovered a number of hitherto neglected variables and upset some preconceived notions. For example, while Air Corps planners believed crew exhaustion rather than the availability of equipment would be the limiting factor in deciding the number of missions per month, British experience suggested that matériel rather than physical limitations was the critical factor.[38] Weather, too, played a far more limiting role than prewar studies had anticipated. Experience in the RAF showed that there was a decided difference in the mission rate—and hence in the attrition rate—between winter and summer, a difference that could have profound consequences upon the over-all replacement rate.[39]

The attrition formula officially promulgated early in 1941, after an extended study of British experience, was substantially different from the official estimate of 1938. The revised formula anticipated a wastage of 20 percent per month as a combined average for all types of aircraft in a theater of operations. In the zone of interior and in the possessions not active as theaters, the rate was set at 3 percent per month.[40]

Seen in perspective, it is difficult to believe that this or any other formula for attrition could be much more than very rough yardsticks. Utterly different conditions in many different theaters ranging from the arctic to the tropics against two entirely different enemies produced wastage figures that fluctuated so erratically as to defy most generalizations drawn upon them. Yet elusive as they undoubtedly were, such factors as attrition, distribution, and spares were at least tangible. A far more subtle factor in the computation of requirements was the tendency of staff officers to carry habits of thinking and the long-established administrative practices of peacetime over into the period of crisis. As George Orwell might have put it: staff officers on the eve of war were inhibited by peacethink.

Peacetime Thinking and Wartime Requirements

Peacetime thinking was budgetary thinking; this was not a peculiar form of military narrowness but an acute awareness for the facts of life—the political and statutory realities. The inevitable result of this phenomenon was that peacetime

---

[38] AC Board Study No. 6A, 28 Mar 38, revised to 3 May 41, AHO. See also, Dir, AC Board, to CofAC, 27 Jan 41, and R&R, Chief, Intelligence Div, OCAC, to Plans, 15 Feb 41, AFCF 452.1 Aircraft Gen.

[39] Unsigned Memo for Gen Brett, 12 Feb 41, with Incls (see especially 2, 3, and 4), AFCF 452.1 Aircraft Gen.

[40] TAG to CofAC, 21 Jan 41, AFCF 452.1 Aircraft Gen. This formula was not again revised until long after Pearl Harbor. See Dir, Military Requirements, to CGSOS, 30 Apr 42, AFCF 400.12 Proc. For shrewd estimates of attrition by a civilian observer, see T. P. Wright, "Winged Victory . . . ," *Aviation* (April 1940), and "The Truth About Our National Defense Program," *Aviation* (January 1941).

thinking tended to continue until the actual outbreak of war even though the real crisis developed many months before the shooting began. As a consequence, budgetary thinking continued even when the time was ripe for a shift to a "needs basis" from a "cost basis."[41]

The tendency to think in budgetary terms even as war aproached had its consequent influence upon the computation of requirements. Take, for example, the matter of planning replacements. The normal peacetime practice in providing replacements for aircraft on hand was to write them off as obsolete after a predetermined number of years. This obsoletion policy obviously constituted a bookkeeping device. It provided an orderly and systematic means for estimating fiscal requirements for the years ahead while at the same time ensuring automatic disposition of aircraft after several years of service.

Unfortunately, automatic obsoletion at the end of five or six years, though good bookkeeping, had little or no bearing upon aircraft performance and no relationship whatever to enemy capabilities. Some Air Corps officers were fully aware of this difference between peacetime fiscal obsoletion and wartime performance obsoletion. Wartime obsoletion, they saw, would be determined by the enemy.[42] Superior output by the enemy could, and in the event did, make some of this nation's aircraft obsolete even before they rolled off the production line.[43] Nevertheless, the habit of thinking in peacetime and fiscal terms tended to persist.

Long after the start of the expansion program, the imagination of those computing requirements continued to be colored by the question: "What can we afford?" rather than the question: "What do we need"?[44] And what better evidence of persistence in peacetime thinking could there be than the report from Wright Field that an effort was under way to rid all combat aircraft of such peacetime accretions as built-in drinking water containers and baggage compartments! This, be it noted, did not occur until the summer of 1940, after the fall of France and more than a year beyond the start of the rearmament program.[45] The computation of requirements, it would appear, required far more than mere addition.

*Requirements Computation:
A Summary*

The computation of requirements posed a seemingly insurmountable task. Each variable was only a beginning; each in turn suggested countless ramifications, permutations, and multiple variations. One conclusion is inescapable: the formulation of requirements was a search in which absolute answers were unobtainable. This, however, was no solution. Military necessity compels staff officers to

---

[41] Sherwood, *Roosevelt and Hopkins*, pp. 280–81; Troyer Anderson, MS study of OASW–OUSW in World War II, 1948, OCMH, ch. VI, pp. 124–28.

[42] Chief, Mat Div, to CofAC, 6 Mar 39, AC Project Rcds (Lyon Papers), bk. 2; CofAC to TAG, 14 Apr 39, AFCF 452.1–A Proc of Aircraft.

[43] Memo, CGAAF for Lovett, 23 Feb 43, AFCF 452.01–A Production.

[44] For an excellent illustration of the need for breaking away from budgetary inhibitions in computing requirements, see Sherwood, *Roosevelt and Hopkins*, pp. 162–63.

[45] R&R, Chief, Mat Div, to Arnold, 16 Jul 40, AFCF 452.1–H Parts.

come up with answers of some sort. If the only possible answers had to be approximations, then it would seem beyond argument that the approximations should have been as accurate and as comprehensive as intensive study of available data would permit. Nevertheless, in the opinion of responsible staff officers in the War Plans Division of the General Staff, down almost to the very eve of war in Europe, no really comprehensive study of air power needs had ever been drawn up by the Army. Actually, the turning point came in March 1939 when the lack of a carefully defined statement of mission for Army aviation finally led the Chief of Staff to appoint a special Air Board to make a thorough investigation of the subject. The board's report proved to be an epochal document. On 1 September 1939, the very day war broke out, the Chief of Staff, General George C. Marshall, informed the Secretary of War that the Air Board report established for the first time a specific mission for the Air Corps. Two weeks later the approved report was circulated through the Army as official policy and for months thereafter the War Plans Division computed aircraft requirements on the basis of the board's findings.[46]

The appearance of the Air Board report did indeed mark a turning point, for until its publication no computation of aircraft requirements had been based upon a sound, thoroughgoing analysis of all the factors involved. The available record suggests that the few requirement studies undertaken earlier at various staff levels within the air arm were neither comprehensive nor informed. More often than not they tackled only a portion of the total problem. While ignoring some factors entirely, they accepted others without sufficiently questioning the assumptions and premises upon which they rested.[47]

Though responsible military officials fell short in the matter of calculating requirements until the war was nearly upon them, there were a number of contributing causes behind their failures. Not least among these were the inherent complexity of the problem and the prevailing organizational or administrative structure that let the task of computation fall between two organizations, the General Staff and the Air Corps.[48] But the major

---

[46] Watson, *Chief of Staff: Prewar Plans and Preparations*, pp. 100-101; WPD for CofS, 21 Dec 39, AGO Rcds, WPD-OPD 3807-41.

[47] For an example of the piecemeal approach, see Chief, Plans, OCAC, to CofAC, AFCF 381-B War Plans. See also, Ray S. Cline, *Washington Command Post: The Operations Division*, UNITED STATES ARMY IN WORLD WAR II (Washington, 1951), pp. 34-37. The best evidence in support of this generalization is to be found by comparing the prewar concept of "requirements" with postwar thinking. See, for example, the treatment contained in Special Text No. 97 on mobilization, issued by the Army Industrial College before World War II, in contrast with postwar studies such as Industrial College of the Armed Forces study L 48-29, Problems Inherent in the Determination of Requirements. For background of requirements problems in World War I, see Holley, *Ideas and Weapons*. For WPD condemnation of earlier studies, see Memo, WPD for CofS, 21 Dec 39, AGO Rcds, WPD-OPD 3807-41.

[48] For a revealing example of this conflict in responsibility, see unsigned staff study, OCAC, entitled Discussion of the Memo to Chief of Staff, subject: Air Force Requirements . . . , 30 May 41, in which General Staff officers are alleged to have left out "certain vital considerations." AFCF 321.9-E. The adverse effect of organizational inadequacy upon requirements computation was nowhere more obvious than in the sphere of intelligence. See Arnold, *Global Mission*, pp. 533-35; Memo, CofAC for G-2, 20 Feb 37, AFCF 360.02A Foreign Aviation. See also, AAF Hist Study 10, p. 92.

difficulty lay elsewhere: the whole question of requirements was never adequately studied by air arm officers as it should have been, broadly and philosophically, until after the publication of the Air Board study in the spring of 1939. Before then, all too often when staff officers worried about requirements, it was in connection with some particular and pressing problem for which an answer was required yesterday, if not sooner.[49] There were no wide-ranging studies made of requirements in the abstract. There were no staff manuals to which harried officers could turn and find suggestive discussions of the elements to be considered.[50] Instead, lessons on the art of formulating requirements had to be found amongst the obiter dicta of previous studies, themselves wrought in haste and under pressure. Under such circumstances one should hardly be surprised if even the ablest of staff officers failed to make adequately comprehensive studies of requirements. The first major staff paper on aviation requirements to appear after the outbreak of war in Europe gives evidence of solid accomplishment in the face of obstacles. Without a doubt it marked a decided advance over any previous study of the topic.

Within the context of the foregoing digression, it may prove useful to return to the original topic of this chapter and consider something of the background of the President's call for 50,000 airplanes and the military role in shaping that figure.

Origin of the 50,000 Figure

Looking back after the event, Air Corps officials felt free to report that they had determined the Army's requirements for aircraft "efficiently and effectively," at the outbreak of war in September 1939.[51] Perhaps they had, considering the many imponderables involved, but easy complacency and self-serving compliments hardly seem warranted by the facts. War Department spokesmen believed that the officially promulgated statement of requirements was, when war came in Europe, inadequate. To begin with, as a G-4 officer observed, despite the President's earlier directives both in public and in private, the Army's aircraft requirements as stated in September were still premised upon the funds appropriated by Congress rather than a sound study of the needs of national defense.[52] Moreover, beyond this faulty premise, even the mechanics of computation were in error. The officially approved statement of aircraft requirements that had been drawn up by the General Staff to accompany the Protective Mobilization Plan was not in accord with the existing realities. Although the plan assumed that 9,745 aircraft would be on hand at the beginning of this phase of the mobilization, Congress had authorized only 6,000 and had actually provided appropriations for less than 5,500.[53] Clearly the PMP figures bore no relation to the facts. Far from being content with previous computations, planning officers on

---

[49] For a characteristic instance of the do-it-yesterday type of directive, see Memo, CofAC for WPD, 1 Nov 38, AFCF 381.A War Plans.

[50] Watson, *Chief of Staff: Prewar Plans and Preparations*, pp. 100–101; Memo, WPD for CofS, 21 Dec 39, AGO Rcds, WPD–OPD 3807–41.

[51] Memo, ACofAC for Gen Marshall, 19 Dec 40, AFCF 452.18 Proc of Aircraft.

[52] Memo, G-4 for CofS, 7 Sep 39, AFCF 452.1 Airplanes, Gen.

[53] Memo, G-4 for WPD, 2 Sep 39, AGO Rcds, G-4 27277–19.

the General Staff undertook a new survey of aircraft needs soon after the invasion of Poland in September 1939.

Hemisphere Defense Reconsidered

No one recognized the deficiencies of previous requirements computations more than the officers who studied the question anew. The flaws of all previous staff studies on the subject were only too evident. Not one of the studies, the planners reported in December 1939, had been based upon an adequate appraisal of the need for hemisphere defense. Worse yet, most of the previous studies seemed to have been "aimed at justification of a predetermined number of planes rather than at a reasoned derivation of the number required." Here again was an old and only too familiar practice: earlier planners had cut the pattern to suit the cloth on hand.[54]

The horrors of the German blitzkrieg in Poland seem to have induced a higher caliber of staff work and a more careful weighing of existing assumptions.[55] The result was a staff paper undoubtedly superior to any that had preceded it. In the new paper the General Staff planners conscientiously sought to encompass the many variables involved. They considered a wide range of factors such as probable or possible theaters of action, composition of the forces required, attrition rates, and so on. Each variable they subjected to a searching analysis in terms of the evidence available. If the evidence was inadequate, as it indubitably was in a number of respects, they nonetheless pressed their study as far as they could.

In estimating the number of missions per month, for example, they had few experience factors on which to rely. British bomber operations in World War I offered a precedent rather too remote to be meaningful; alternatively, they could lean on the recent report from the Air Corps Board, which explored the question with imagination and ingenuity. Using the Department of Commerce safe limit of 100 hours per month for airline pilots as a maximum for endurance, the board had applied the maximum cruising radius and known speed of the several aircraft types on hand to arrive at an estimate of the probable mission rate per month.[56]

The results achieved were still only estimates, but they were informed estimates—in contrast to the guesswork that had characterized so many of the previous staff studies on requirements. On the other hand, the survey was by no means exhaustive. The planners still virtually ignored political considerations such as foreign aid and made no mention of the distribution or pipeline factor. Nevertheless, the resulting statement was probably the most logical and comprehensive yet contrived. It laid down a requirement for 2,726 tactical aircraft for active operations, 1,960 for reserve, and 6,831 for training purposes.[57]

In all, the General Staff study called for 11,517 aircraft to provide for hemisphere defense. More than three months

---

[54] Memo, WPD for CofS, 21 Dec 39, sub: Estimate of Number of Aircraft Required in Hemisphere Defense, AGO Rcds, WPD–OPD 3807–41. See above, ch. V.

[55] See memo cited in preceding note.

[56] *Ibid.*, tab G.

[57] *Ibid.* Original date of this portion of report is 21 December 1939. Figures vary in subsequent revisions.

REQUIREMENTS

were consumed in arriving at this conclusion; the problem was inherently difficult, and staff studies on requirements are by their very nature slow in production. Yet even after this statement of needs had been formulated, there remained a whole series of co-ordinations and approvals before the paper could become the official aircraft requirement of the War Department for planning purposes. Begun in October 1939, the study was still in the headquarters paper mill the following spring.[58] In April 1940 G-2 initialed the paper but suggested that it was by then out of date.[59] Events had overtaken the planners. When the Air Corps finally sent a formal directive to Wright Field authorizing procurement planning on the basis of the much revised and amended General Staff statement of aircraft requirements, it was too late;[60] "sitzkrieg" had once again become blitzkrieg with the invasion of the Low Countries, and the Western Allies seemed about to flounder.

Aircraft Requirements in the Crisis of May 1940

Sometime on 10 May 1940, the President's military aide, Brig. Gen. Edwin M. Watson, sent him a sheaf of pages from the War Department. On the attached buck slip General Watson wrote, "Louis Johnson gives this as the most important summary of our needs yet presented by him." Among other items of equipment, the "summary of needs" included aircraft. Congress, the Assistant Secretary noted, had authorized 6,000 aircraft but had appropriated funds for somewhat fewer than 5,500. The legislators should be asked to provide $300,000,000 to close the gap.[61] Only that morning the New York *Times* had carried a column headlined "Mighty Air Forces Demanded by Army" and "Plea for 500 Flying Fortresses Will Be Put Before Congress Now."[62] This inspired story, so obviously leaked from an "informed source" in the War Department, coupled with the Assistant Secretary's memorandum to the President, clearly defined the immediate upper limit of aircraft requirements contemplated by responsible military officials.[63] On 8 May, two days before he became Prime Minister, Win-

---

[58] The sequence of co-ordination and approval is indicated in the following: Memo, CofAC for WPD, 6 Jan 40, urged approval even if inadequate, since data were needed as point of departure for industrial planning. See also, G-3 to WPD, 24 Jan 40; Memo, WPD for CofS, 18 Apr 40; Memo, WPD for CofS, 10 and 27 May 40. All in AGO Rcds, WPD-OPD 3807-41.

[59] G-2 to CofS, 22 Apr 40, AGO Rcds, WPD-OPD 3807-41.

[60] CTI-46, 10 May, AFCF AC Project Rcds (Lyon Papers), bk. 24.

[61] Memo, E. M. W. (Watson) for President, Memo, ASW for President, both 10 May 40. Johnson's memo was based on a detailed study prepared by the Executive, OASW, Col. J. H. Burns, 10 May 1940, which appears to have been sent along to the White House as a supporting document. Franklin Delano Roosevelt Library, Speech File, 16 May 40.

[62] New York *Times*, May 10, 1940, p. 8. See also, Memo, Chief, Mat Div, for ASW, 10 May 40, justifying the need for 400 heavy bombers, and Memo, Louis Johnson for President, 10 May 1940, asking for permission to ask the Congress to provide funds to begin procurement of these additional bombers. Roosevelt Library, Speech File, 16 May 40.

[63] According to the New York *Times*, May 10, 1940, page 8, some military officials estimated that the combined Army, Navy, and foreign or export requirements for aircraft from U.S. manufacturers would amount to 16,000 units over the following 16 months. Since they expected export orders to reach 8,000, the size of the force anticipated for the Army and Navy is evident.

ston S. Churchill had admitted in the House of Commons—in public—that the failure of British troops in Norway was largely attributable to lack of air power.[64] This, from the doughty First Lord of the Admiralty, had not left War Department officials unmoved. Indeed, as the New York *Times* reported, they demanded a "mighty" air force, but their conception of such a force seemed to revolve around 400 or 500 additional airplanes and at the outside lingered within the authorized ceiling of 6,000 units.

The rush of events in Europe soon made such official thinking on requirements obsolete. German troops had invaded Belgium, Luxembourg, and the Netherlands on the 10th. By the 14th the Dutch Government was in flight to Britain and every hour signaled new disasters along the Allied front. To responsible officials in the United States, the menace of German might loomed more terrifying than ever before. The time had come for courageous action and imaginative thinking. If the nation's defenses were to be erected in time, someone had to cut through the existing restrictions, so necessary in peace and so frustrating in a crisis.

There was no lack of boldness among the President's political advisors. The Secretary of the Treasury, Henry Morgenthau, Jr., urged the President to ask Congress for a discretionary fund of $100,000,000 to be used to expand productive capacity for defense.[65] The Secretary of the Navy, Charles Edison, went still further. He wanted the President to ask Congress to provide a five, or even ten, billion dollar blank check for the President to spend on defense at will. Secretary Edison recognized full well that such a blank check was a radical idea, but he was equally certain that the nation faced a real crisis: "The totalitarian mob," he wrote, "must be shown that democracies can act in emergencies—can cut through the delays and ineffectiveness of legislative processes when the need comes."[66]

This kind of thinking, at once bold and dramatic, must have appealed to the President. He directed Assistant Secretary of War Johnson to make a study of the additional productive capacity required to raise the nation's total aircraft output to a level of 50,000 units a year.[67] Johnson responded to this request with an estimate. Meanwhile, however, the sequence of disasters in Europe seems to have led him to reconsider the statement of requirements he had sent to the President on 10 May. To this end he directed his able executive, Col. James H. Burns, to work out a revised statement of aircraft requirements.

Colonel Burns's reply was disturbing. The Army, he reported, had formal plans for expanding manpower beyond existing strength, but no decision on such matters had been made for aircraft.

---

[64] Parliamentary Debates, Commons, vol. 360, pp. 1348–62, May 8, 1940. The New York *Times*, May 9, 1940, page 4, carried the speech in full and spread its message in a page 1 headline.

[65] Memo, Morgenthau for President, 14 May 40, Roosevelt Library, Speech File, 16 May 40. The Secretary's vision did not exclude his own interests: his memo suggested that he himself be appointed chairman of a committee with "ultimate authority," under the President, to use the money.

[66] Memo, Edison for President, 14 May 40, Roosevelt Library, Speech File, 16 May 40.

[67] Memo, ASW for President, 14 May 40, Roosevelt Library, Speech File, 16 May 40.

Rather than continue floundering amongst imponderables any longer, Colonel Burns suggested an entirely arbitrary statement of aircraft requirements for planning purposes. He projected the requirement for tactical aircraft on the existing troop basis, approved by the General Staff:

Mobilization Phase	Army Manpower	Tactical Aircraft	
1. Extant Force	500,000	3,000	appropriated for under 5,500 program
2. PMP	1,200,000	7,500	increased in direct proportion to manpower
3. PMP Augmented	4,000,000	24,000	

Using this table and an assumed attrition rate of 15 percent per month, Colonel Burns estimated that support of the third phase would require some 28,800 replacements a year for tactical aircraft alone—by his estimate a threefold increase over the nation's existing airframe production capacity.[68]

Colonel Burns's computations were admittedly not based upon any logical and systematic analysis of strategic needs; they were nothing more than expedient makeshifts, extrapolations, to establish a target for planning purposes. The approach was imaginative; the figures, if inaccurate, were at least bold.[69] Assistant Secretary Johnson may have felt that Colonel Burns's figures were too bold or perhaps politically unfeasible. At any rate, the next day, 15 May 1940, when he sent a revised statement of aircraft requirements to the White House for the President to use in an emergency message before Congress, he pared Colonel Burns's 28,800 down to 19,000. This cut he justified by saying that pilot training was limited to 19,000 per year and the production of pilots governed the production of airplanes [70]—an assumption that time was to prove grossly mistaken.[71] Insofar as the written record goes, the 19,000 figure was the War Department's last word on aircraft requirements before the President's special appeal to Congress in behalf of national defense.[72]

On the question of military preparedness the President kept an open mind. Fully aware of the speed with which the surge of military operations in Europe was altering so many assumptions and plans, he was reluctant to set any targets for defense production. On 12 May he resolved to ask Congress for more money, but as late as the 13th he had not decided upon the precise number of aircraft he

---

[68] Memo, Exec, OASW, for ASW, 14 May 40, Roosevelt Library, Speech File, 16 May 40. In his computation, Colonel Burns assumed that the attrition rate would apply only to the aircraft in active status, or approximately two-thirds of the totals shown. The remaining one-third was carried as an operating reserve.

[69] The Air Corps mobilization plan extant at the outbreak of war in September 1939 visualized the requirement for tactical aircraft in PMP augmented to H plus 1½ years at just over 20,000 units. See Photostat of Chart by Proc Plans Div of Planning Br, OASW, 3 Aug 39, AFCF 452.1 Aircraft Requirements Program.

[70] Memo, Louis Johnson for President, 15 May 40, AGO Rcds, SW file. The communication is a masterpiece of political composition. It flatters the President, paints a horror picture of current need, absolves the War Department from blame for the situation, and ends with a statement of needs neatly tied up with a budget-oriented price tag.

[71] By 1944, pilot training reached an annual total of 57,590, airframe production, 95,272 units. AAF Statistical Digest (Washington, 1945), pp. 64, 112.

[72] Supporting the apparent lack of evidence to the contrary is an item in the New York Times, May 14, 1940, p. 13. In the midst of lively speculation on the number of aircraft the President would ask Congress to provide, the Army and the Navy each proposed increases of about 2,000 units.

THE PRESIDENT ASKS CONGRESS FOR AT LEAST 50,000 AIRCRAFT, *May 1940.*

would demand.⁷³ His military advisors were providing him with staff papers on aircraft requirements, but the President's vision ranged far beyond the Army, or even beyond the Army and the Navy together. He looked past the mere addition of figures from Army and Navy staff studies and calculated the requirements of all the enemies of fascism everywhere. On 15 May he received cables from Ambassador Bullitt in France and Ambassador Kennedy in England. Both relayed requests for shipments of aircraft.⁷⁴ With the French and British requests before him, the President could see the aircraft requirements of the Army and Navy in fuller perspective, and from this vantage point he went to Congress with his famous call for a program of no less than 50,000 "military and naval" aircraft a year for the nation's defense.⁷⁵

The President's request for 50,000 aircraft showed him capable of breaking

---

⁷³ New York *Times,* May 14, 1940. See remarks of Press Secretary Stephen Early.

⁷⁴ Cordell Hull, *Memoirs,* pp. 765–66.
⁷⁵ *Cong Rcd,* May 16, 1940, p. 6244, and H Doc 751.

CURTISS XP-40

BRITISH SPITFIRE

loose from the restraints and inhibitions that of necessity conditioned the calculations of so many military officials. Easily forgotten in the wake of subsequent events is the hesitant pace that characterized so much military activity before the President's sweeping request. For example, sometime earlier, Canadian officials had generously lent the Air Corps a Spitfire for tests; in return they requested a P–40 Warhawk. But no, such a step seemed undesirable—at least in some staff circles. On the very day that the President went to Congress for 50,000 airplanes, an Air Corps legal officer advised against the P–40 loan; this would be a technical violation of the obligations of a neutral. Rather than "risk adverse criticism," any such decision should be referred to "high Government officials" willing to take the initiative.[76] The President was willing to do just this, and accepted the responsibility.

In the crisis of May 1940 the War Department did indeed supply the President with a statement of aircraft requirements. But the 50,000 figure finally used was neither an Army nor a Navy figure—it was a Presidential figure concocted by the President and his political associates.[77] The President's big round number was a psychological target to lift sights and accustom planners in military and industrial circles alike to thinking big. The 50,000 figure was not a logical summation of strategic and tactical requirements; in view of this circumstance, Secretary Hull's claim that he thought up the 50,000 figure and even the Beaverbrook anecdote on its origin may contain more than a grain of truth. In any event, the implication is clear: in the crisis it was the politicians acting more or less intuitively rather than the generals with their staff studies who set the 50,000-aircraft goal; when the War Department was unready to state its air power needs adequately, the job fell to the President.

---

[76] Chief, Patents Sec, to ACofAC, 16 May 40, AHO Plans Div 145.93-23.

[77] Judge Samuel I. Rosenman is somewhat ambiguous on this point. He says *(Working With Roosevelt* (New York: Harper and Brothers, 1952), page 94), the Army and Navy "furnished us with the materials and statistics on military requirements." While it is true that some figures were supplied, as the Roosevelt papers cited above clearly show, the final 50,000 figure does not appear in the papers sent to the White House from the War Department. On the "glacial pace" of those bound by peacetime conventions, see Sherwood, *Roosevelt and Hopkins,* page 159. He also quotes Donald M. Nelson on the President's vision, "his foresight was superior . . . and this foresight saved us all," (page 160). See also, MS study of OASW-OUSW by Troyer Anderson, Ch. V, p. 4: and Bruce Catton, *The War Lords of Washington* (1st ed.; New York: Harcourt, Brace and Co. [1948]), page 21, who claims some Air Corps officers felt the 50,000 figure was "pretty wild," and William L. Langer and S. Everett Gleason, *The Challenge to Isolation, 1937–1940,* (New York; Harper and Brothers, 1952), pages 473–75, especially 474, suggesting that the President's figures should not always be taken too literally.

CHAPTER XI

50,000 Aircraft

From Slogan to Program

No doubt the President's appeal for more aircraft expressed in round numbers served as a stimulating psychological target to raise the sights and fire the imagination of the nation—taxpayers, voters, and aircraft builders—as well as congressmen. The big round number could serve equally well as a political symbol. It gave newsmen a convenient handle with which to persuade the people that the administration stood for all-out defense. But to staff officers fell the task of converting this political slogan into meaningful programs.

Matching Ends With Means

There is a great difference indeed between a target such as 50,000 aircraft—either as an air force in being, or as an annual productive capacity for that number such as the President demanded—on the one hand, and a procurement program for 50,000 aircraft worked out in detail and down to the last penny on the other.[1] A procurement program involves prior agreement on how many of what and when—quantity, quality, and schedule — but these fundamentals are not enough. In addition, plans for any given number of items conforming to any given specification, to be delivered at any given date, must be based upon funds against which contracts can be written. On this last point the Constitution is explicit. Clearly then, the process of translating the President's 50,000 slogan into a detailed program involved first of all matching ends with means—getting the necessary appropriations and authorizations.

On the surface the task of wresting adequate appropriations from Congress would appear to have been a simple one since the disasters in Europe had won so many converts to the cause of adequate defense. The mood of Congress had shifted, and congressmen were asking "How soon can we get it?" rather than "How much will it cost?"[2] Under such circumstances why not simply ask for the money and order the airplanes—all of them—without further ado? Unfortunately, the mechanics of government by consent are never quite so direct. The Air Corps was not operating in a legislative vacuum; it was not free to start from scratch with a clean slate and draw up a logical, orderly, comprehensive, procurement program that would cover its share of the 50,000 airplanes and distribute the load evenly across the available

---

[1] President's Message to Congress, *Cong Rcd*, May 16, 1940, p. 6244.

[2] Watson, *Chief of Staff: Prewar Plans and Preparations*, p. 166.

productive facilities of the industry. Instead, air arm planners had to carry on from where they stood, in the midst of the game so to speak, changing course to the new bearings indicated by the President as Commander in Chief. The plans they drew up had to be fitted into the living present, the contracts in process of execution, appropriations under consideration, and so on, whether this proved orderly and logical or not.

When air arm officers sat down to consider the President's new target figure in May 1940, the "living present" in which they found themselves took something of the following shape: the 50,000 target figure was a goal for the Army and Navy combined. Thus, after conferences with the Navy and an entirely arbitrary slicing of the pie, the Air Corps' share was some 36,500 aircraft, a figure derived by deducting the Navy's existing program of 13,500 from the Presidential 50,000 and assigning the remainder to the Air Corps.[3] Clearly, it was the President and not the military who dictated the character of the subsequent program.

Dividing the President's 50,000 target between the Army and the Navy simplified the task in some ways so far as the Air Corps was concerned, but complicated it in others. Where the President spoke in sweeping terms, in actual practice the detailed fulfillment of his goal would have to be divided between two separate agencies with consequent confusion arising from different methods of doing business (often with the same manufacturer) and the increased need for coordination.

Even within the Air Corps, the target of 36,500 airplanes was by no means devoid of complications. Aircraft already on hand had to be taken into account. Allowing for obsoletion and attrition from accidents, available strength by the end of fiscal 1940 was estimated at 2,760 aircraft. Moreover, there were yet undelivered on current contracts some 2,936 aircraft ordered on the 5,500 program of fiscal years 1939 and 1940.[4] Finally, when the President made his dramatic appeal in May 1940, Congress was considering the appropriation for the regular military budget of fiscal 1941. The aircraft asked for by the War Department in this budget numbered only 166, and the House had moved to cut the figure to 57.[5] But the crisis broke as the debate proceeded, and Congress hurriedly approved the full 166 sought and added a supplemental measure providing 1,900 more or a total of 2,066 aircraft in the Army appropriation. Thus, even before Air Corps planners began to consider the 36,500 program in detail, there were 7,700-odd aircraft on programs of one sort or another.[6]

Subtracting the 7,700-odd aircraft already on program from the 36,500 that constituted the Air Corps' share of the 50,000 total left some 28,000 airplanes yet to be ordered if the President's objec-

---

[3] Unsigned, undated note in AC Project Rcds (A. J. Lyon Papers), bk. 29, 36,000 Program, AFCF; Watson, *Chief of Staff: Prewar Plans and Preparations*, p. 175. See also, photostat Memo, CofAC for CofS, 5 Jun 40, marked "Tentatively O K, GCM," AFCF 321.9-C.

[4] Copy, Memo, CofAC for ASW, 9 Jul 40, AC Project Rcds (Lyon Papers), bk. 24, AFCF.

[5] See ch. IX, above.

[6] Mat Planning Sec, Mat Div, OCAC, Summary of Air Corps Programs, 28 Jun 40, AC Project Rcds (Lyon Papers), bk. 30, AFCF; and Mat Div, OCAC, CTI-80, 19 Jul 40, WFCF 111.3 Munitions Program 1-31 Jul 40. See also H.R. 9209, 76th Cong, 3d sess.

tive was to be seriously pursued. Air Corps officers set about drafting plans to place orders that would secure not only the 28,000 aircraft (17,000 tactical types and 11,000 trainers) but would also look to the provision of a proportionate share of the productive capacity amounting to 50,000 units a year as demanded by the President before Congress.[7]

Air Corps plans, however, were not evolving in complete isolation. In the office of the Assistant Secretary of War, staff officers were also trying to convert the President's remarks into military programs. In the absence of an official schedule, Colonel Burns, an imaginative officer, proposed the following timetable:[8]

> By 1 October 1941, an Army of 1 million men
> By 1 January 1942, an Army of 2 million men
> By 1 April 1942, an Army of 4 million men

This, of course, was entirely arbitrary timing, but for want of anything else, it provided a troop basis and a series of target dates against which to project a comprehensive munitions program.

Understandably enough, the planners in the Office of the Assistant Secretary wanted to include aircraft in this general munitions program. In doing so, however, they applied an old Army formula uncritically, tying the aircraft program to the troop basis even though observant officers had pointed out on a number of occasions from 1918 onward that the two could not be meaningfully correlated.[9]

There may indeed have been ample justification behind the use of a troop basis in planning a munitions program for the ground forces, but harnessing the aircraft program to the timetable thus derived resulted in a schedule bearing little or no relation to the needs of the air arm or the President's target. The proposed ground and air arm mobilization schedule appeared as follows:

> By 1 October 1941, 1 million men and 9,000 aircraft
> By 1 January 1942, 2 million men and 18,000 aircraft
> By 1 April 1942, 4 million men and 36,000 aircraft

Having established the doubling and redoubling of the troop basis, the planners simply equated the air with the ground figures by taking the Air Corps' share of the President's target and then spreading it back over the schedule in the same doubled and redoubled pattern.[10]

When the combined air and ground program received approval from the Chief of Staff and the President, the fate of the air arm production schedule was sealed. Soon afterwards, when hasty surveys revealed that the capacity expansions necessary to meet the ultimate program

---

[7] Notes for General Brett on 50,000 aircraft by JFP:JAL (Lt Col J. F. Powell?), 18 May 40, bk. 22; Conference in OCAC, Army Requirements, 36,500 Aircraft, 19 Jun 40, bk. 29; TWX E733, Lyon to Brett, 31 May 40, bk. 24A. All in AC Project Rcds (Lyon Papers), AFCF.

[8] Watson, *Chief of Staff: Prewar Plans and Preparations*, pp. 174–75. Obviously Colonel Burns was applying the same line of reasoning followed in his memo to Louis Johnson of 14 May 1940. See above, pp. 224–25.

[9] See above, pp. 44–45, 48, and Holley, *Ideas and Weapons*, ch. III.

[10] Watson, *Chief of Staff: Prewar Plans and Preparations*, p. 175. That this is what actually happened is further supported by evidence that Colonel Burns used the same formula only a few days before. See Memo, Burns for ASW, 14 May 40, Roosevelt Library, Speech File, 16 May 40.

threatened to delay attainment of the more immediate objectives, the Chief of Staff and the President agreed to concentrate on the intermediate goal, two million men and 18,000 aircraft, leaving the ultimate goals to some remoter date. The recent catastrophe in Europe made 18,000 aircraft in hand seem definitely preferable to some 36,000 in the industrial bush.[11] The consequences of this decision were crucial. Where air arm planners had been aiming at the fulfillment of the dual Air Corps goal of 36,500 aircraft on hand plus an annual productive capacity for that number, they were now told to lower their sights. They were to work toward a goal of 18,000 not only in the matter of strength but even with respect to the expansion of productive capacity. For the ground arms, however, while the immediate objective for strength on hand was cut back, the goals for the expansion of productive capacity were left at the original "ultimate" figure.[12]

There is no evidence to suggest that it was ground arm opposition to air arm aspirations that motivated the disproportionate cutbacks. Economic feasibility rather than doctrinal differences virtually compelled a reduction in the program.[13] The President's fears that the cost of the aircraft program would prove embarrassing may have been misplaced, for the Luftwaffe's furious assault on Britain seems to have shattered most lingering doubts in Congress as to the wisdom of pouring astronomic sums into defense. But the fact that national defense policy was inseparable from political considerations should not be overlooked. Thus, even after the air arm target had been cut back to 18,000 aircraft, Air Corps planners were unable to present a request to Congress for appropriations to procure this number because the price tag threatened to be too high.

The Bureau of the Budget took one look at the $1,500,000,000 required to procure 18,000 aircraft and immediately began cutting. Using methods acquired over the peacetime years the bureau staff trimmed some 1,400 aircraft from the 18,000 total. More important than these few aircraft, however, was the continuing pressure exerted to cut down all along the line on the current budget. As a consequence, the Air Corps came to Congress for funds not to finance 18,000 airplanes, or 18,000 minus the 1,400-odd trimmed off by the Bureau of the Budget for the President, but for a mere 3,000, the "first increment" of the 18,000 program. The original 50,000 target, or the Air Corps share of 36,500, was virtually lost to sight as air arm planners shelved it until the "military situation" in the future seemed to justify reconsideration.[14] Even the 3,000 aircraft of the

---

[11] Watson, *Chief of Staff: Prewar Plans and Preparations*, pp. 176–79.

[12] Memo, CofS for Actg SW, 1 Jul 40, cited in *ibid.*, p. 179. For an informed opinion favoring a reduced goal for the immediate future, see T. P. Wright, "50,000 Planes a Year: How Much? How Long?" in *Aviation* (July 1940), and Wright, "The Truth About Our National Defense Program," *Aviation* (June 1941).

[13] Watson, *Chief of Staff: Prewar Plans and Preparations*, p. 179, especially the remarks attributed to the President.

[14] Draft Memo, OCAC for G–4, 20 Jul 40, AFCF 452.1–13F Proc of Aircraft; Mat Planning Sec, Mat Div, OCAC, Summary of Air Corps Programs, 28 Jun 40, AC Project Rcds (Lyon Papers), bk. 30, AFCF; Mat Div, OCAC, CTI–80, 19 Jul 40, WFCF 111.3 Munitions Program 1–31 Jul 40. Though the

"first increment" became 2,181 aircraft when rapidly rising costs subsequently made it impossible to procure the full number with the appropriation secured.[15]

Gearing procurement programs to appropriations was clearly an intricate task. Delicate political decisions joined with the procedures of congressional government to make the end product something far removed from the initial Presidential proposal. But the drafting of procurement programs was not confined to matching ends with means, complex as this task was. Also involved was the necessity of deciding exactly which from a number of possible models and types of aircraft should be procured and put into production.

How Many of What Kind?

In the years leading up to World War II, air arm officers had emphasized the role of strategic air power. If many of them tended to attach undue importance to the doctrine of heavy bomber employment, it must be recalled that they did so as crusaders selling an idea in the face of considerable opposition. In consequence, when the Battle of Britain in the summer of 1940 abruptly demonstrated the critical importance of a defensive fighter force, there were some at least among the air power advocates who found their mental breastworks facing the wrong way. While not intending to neglect fighters, their preoccupation with bombers and strategic doctrine may have resulted in a neglect of defense. The result appeared in a decided doubt as to the proper composition of the air arm to be procured under the President's appeal in the crisis.

The few to whom, as Churchill said, so many owed so much in Britain left a deep impression in Air Corps circles as to the use to which the immediately available funds should be put. Although unwilling to abandon ultimate faith in the bomber, Air Corps officers began in haste to reconsider the role of the fighter. Their uncertainty is reflected in the wide disparities in plans and rapid fluctuations in strength proposed by Air Corps officers planning the budget to be set before Congress.[16]

As long as doctrine remained unsettled, requirements could never be clearly defined. And so long as requirements remained in doubt, those who drafted procurement programs worked in the dark. Those who sought to translate the President's 50,000 aircraft objective into orderly procurement programs had perforce to resort to guesses, makeshifts, and temporary expedients, always subject to change.

President and the Bureau of the Budget continued to use peacetime habits of thought even after the crisis justified a change, they were following a well-defined pattern. For example, Louis Johnson, an official of wide political experience, usually sent statements of military requirements to the White House expressed in terms of dollar costs. For one example among several in this period, see Memo, Johnson for President, 10 May 40, Roosevelt Library, Speech File, 16 May 40. William S. Knudsen in an interview with H. F. Pringle, 15 December 1945, asserted that the President's reluctance to ask Congress for money because of the political campaign definitely was a difficulty in the effort to rearm during the summer of 1940. See Pringle Papers, Knudsen, OCMH.

[15] AAF Hist Study 22, n. 120.

[16] Compare the differences in composition of force in the following, both of 31 May 1940: TWX, E733, Lyon to Brett, and TWX, E739, Lyon to Brett, AC Project Rcds (Lyon Papers), bk. 24A, AFCF.

The need for matching ends with means and the necessity of planning with imponderables in the form of uncertain requirements as to both the number and the composition of the force to be procured, serious as they were, did not exhaust the roster of obstacles to effective planning and programming. The relationship between productive capacity and the size of the air arm desired had to be taken into consideration as well.

*Productive Capacity Versus
Aircraft on Hand*

The President's call for 50,000 aircraft provided the stimulus that set in motion the wave of orders already mentioned. Though budgetary exigencies delayed procurement by spreading appropriations over a period of time rather than providing for the full number all at once, the cumulative effect was still great. As the summer of 1940 wore away and as the backlog of orders began to swamp one manufacturer after another, the planners paused to reflect upon the consequence of the mounting productivity.

By the middle of August 1940, there were somewhere between 26,000 and 30,000 military aircraft on order in the United States on Army, Navy, and British contracts.[17] Sometime between June 1941 and June 1942 these orders would reach a peak of deliveries and then taper off rapidly. But the menace of foreign dictators might not taper off so conveniently. What then? To base the nation's continued defense upon the aircraft already produced would be to rest upon a progressively more obsolescent force. And to do this would involve demobilizing the productive capacity of the aircraft industry, for without adequate orders manufacturers would be forced to cut back on their production shifts.

To impair the newly developed productive capacity of the aircraft industry would be to invite disaster akin to the fate of France, where aircraft output had never reached an adequate level. But to go on producing at full speed would mean piling up aircraft in undreamed of quantities. The dilemma was real indeed and not unlike that vexing Alice: How can one run at top speed and still remain in the same place? General Arnold never doubted for a moment which policy the air arm should pursue: "It makes no difference what disposition is made of these surplus planes," he said, "so long as industry is kept working at full speed. . . ."[18] He even went so far as to consider a plan attributed to the Germans whereby obsolescent aircraft were melted down for scrap in order to keep industry at full blast on more recent models.[19]

The problem, in fine, was this: Might not the President's goal become a grave? Was the real weapon of national defense any fixed number of aircraft or was it rather productive capacity maintained at full blast? In retrospect the problem appears academic. War came before aircraft production reached its peak, so the decision never had to be made. Looking back upon the event it is easy to ignore the very real debate on the question that

---

[17] Memo, CofAC for ASW, 12 Aug 40, AFCF 452.1-13F Proc of Aircraft.

[18] *Ibid.*

[19] Memo, CofAC for ASW, 15 Aug 40, SW file, Aircraft.

persisted for weeks in staff circles.[20] Even though Pearl Harbor made a choice unnecessary, to a generation engaged in the prolonged agony of a cold war, the road not taken here is well worth study by those who would understand the complexities of translating political slogans into procurement programs.

Planner's Lament

Reduced to practice, the simple clarity of the President's 50,000 goal became a hodgepodge of piecemeal appropriations, overlapping procurements, compromises in timing, and uncertainties in composition. And to top it off, the achievement or fulfillment of the goal by a triumph of mass production would, paradoxically, bring the danger of defeat by obsolescence—unless war arrived soon enough to absorb the full output of the clattering assembly lines.

Ideally, staff officers would pursue an orderly, logical, all-embracing, and comprehensive program in which orders to the aircraft industry could be assigned all at once and facilities as well as production tools, material orders, and subcontracts for the ultimate program could be planned from the start. But the world of reality is never like this. In practice, air arm staff officers found themselves driven to makeshifts—they had to contrive not a program but a patchwork of programs, each an expedient compromise, each an *ad hoc* solution of a current difficulty.[21] Each such momentary solution, each such temporary adjustment, was destined to give place to some new version as new circumstances appeared. The ink was scarcely dry on each "ultimate" program before revisions had to be considered.[22]

As a consequence of this piecemeal approach, the whole intricate manipulation of national resources, called industrial mobilization, was of necessity disordered, makeshift, and jerry-built. But, as these pages have suggested, this was not so much for want of planning or want of vision as it was the result of having to do the job within the framework of the forms of law and a government of discussion and consent.

Just how confusing the many variables could make the procurement process must be evident to any reader who has tried to follow the mutations and permutations of the 50,000 program already described. The proliferation of programs and their various alterations were confusing even to the planners who lived in the midst of them during the rush to rearm in the summer of 1940. One can readily sympathize with the harassed officer who explained one phase of the program to a colleague in words to this effect:

The 1,900 program is really the 2,066 program and the 3,000 program is really the

---

[20] See, for example, Chief, Mat Div, to CofAC, ESMR, SM, Ex-18, 25 Oct 40, AFCF 452.1-13F Proc of Aircraft; Memo, Exec, OASW, for DCofS, 1 Oct 40, SW files, Aircraft, item 1783; Exec, OASW, to CofS, 15 Oct 40, same file, item 1839, cross reference from SW classified file, item 1096.

[21] For evidence on the piecemeal character of the program and the long delay between conception and approval, which contributed to the chaos of production, see CofAC to TAG, 5 Jul 40, and CofAC to ASW, 12 Sep 40, with ASW approval 19 Sep 40, AFCF 452.1 Aircraft Gen.

[22] T. P. Wright *et al.*, Report on Army and Navy Program for Procurement of Airplanes on Engines, Fiscal Years 1941-2, Airplane Division Report 3-A, NDAC, 1 Jul 40, rev 8 Jul 40. See also, CTI-80, 19 Jul 40, WFCF 111.3 Munitions Program 1-30 Jul 40.

2,181 program which is the first increment of the 36,500 program, but these two together are actually called program A. The 2,181 were not formerly included in the so-called 18,000 program but are now, and the 18,000 has been reduced to 16,575 [by the budget cut of 1,425]. Thus, the 15,819 obtained by subtracting 2,181 from 18,000 is now 14,394. Therefore the grand total of 20,066 has become 18,641. Cheerio! [23]

If the programs for procurement were, of necessity, confusing, overlapping, and piecemeal, it is not surprising to find that the arming and equipping of tactical units followed suit. The First Aviation Objective established during June 1940 as the initial allocation of tactical aircraft anticipated a total of 54 combat groups.[24] Since delays in production made it impossible to procure the aircraft for the full strength of 54 groups all at once, even the First Objective had to be broken into phases known as the First Aviation Strength and Second Aviation Strength. The former called for the activation of all 54 groups on a cadre basis as aircraft became available. The latter activated no additional groups but simply provided for full strength in all the units under the 54-group objective.[25]

The first and second strengths of the First Aviation Objective should not be confused with the Second Aviation Objective, which called for 84 groups. The Second Objective was derived by computing the size of force necessary to provide a demand for replacements sufficient to sustain on one-shift operation an aircraft industry capable of producing 36,500 aircraft a year on full-shift operations.[26] Capacity to produce rather than immediate tactical requirements thus dictated the Second Aviation Objective.

In short, what had started off so grandly as the President's 50,000 goal became in practice something far more complicated and something considerably smaller. The 50,000 had become some 33,000 and this was not just an Army-Navy figure but a total reflecting Army, Navy, and British orders combined. Moreover, the Air Corps "ultimate" goal of 36,500 was no longer scheduled for 1 April 1942. Instead, it was put off to a remote and indefinite future with the more obtainable goal of 18,641 aircraft by 1 July 1942 placed in its stead.[27]

The President's target, 50,000 aircraft, was undoubtedly useful. But there is no profit in being deceived by one's own propaganda: a psychological incentive is not a procurement program. The journey from slogan to program not only watered down the target, but may also have transformed it significantly. The objective sought turned out to be not just numbers but a whole host of considerations of time and composition, of model and type, of financing and productive capacity all wrought as variables in not one but a series of interrelated programs.

---

[23] Summary of Air Corps Programs, undated, initialed "K," AC Project Rcds (Lyon Papers), bk. 29.
[24] Memo, Asst CofAC for CofS, 6 Aug 40, AFCF 321.9 C; CTI-80, 19 Jul 40, WFCF 111.3 Munitions Program 1–31 Jul 40. The number of aircraft in each group varied, of course, depending upon the tactical function performed by the group.
[25] Gen Arnold to Brig Gen H. W. Harms, 9 Aug 41, AFCF 321.9F.
[26] Memo, G–3 for CofAC thru SGS, 26 Apr 41, AFCF 321.9E. It will be observed that the military planners apparently did not include capacity for exports in their calculations.
[27] Draft of lecture, Gen Arnold, AIC, 5 Oct 40, WFCF 350.001 Lectures, 1941.

50,000 AIRCRAFT

In short, by the time the President's big round number had been converted into detailed programs it became something altogether different from the catch phrase or slogan it had been originally.

There is no need to spell out here all the numerous variations that subsequently stemmed from the President's 50,000 figure. It should be sufficient to shed some light upon the implications of planning within the context of the Presidential target, which remained the official aircraft production goal until after June 1941.[28] Clearly, this kind of target had its utility, even if modified and compromised in use. It is possible, however, to be seduced by such target figures.

There's Danger in Numbers: The President's "Must Program"

Programs in Evolution

To show how even the admittedly useful psychological target may prove dangerous or even disastrous at times will require a digression. By abandoning the chronological thread of narrative for the moment to look ahead and consider events over the three or four years following the fall of France some of the dangers inherent in big round number political slogans may become evident.

For more than a year after the President's request to Congress in May 1940, 50,000 remained the pole star of the aircraft program. Variations and modifications were introduced and British orders raised the over-all total greatly, but 50,000, with 36,500 as the air arm's share, for months remained as the outside target figure. To be sure, the content or composition of this figure changed considerably. Air Corps officers won increasing political support for the production of heavy bombers for long-range strategic missions.[29] During May 1941, for example, the President formally directed the Secretary of War to increase the production of heavy bombers to 500 per month.[30] After years of dispute the heavy bomber had at last acquired a partisan in the White House. Bomber production was to be increased "even at the expense of closing down . . . pursuit factories if necessary to obtain material, labor and tools."[31]

By the fall of 1941 it had become evident that the air arm had moved well beyond the point where the momentum of the President's 50,000 target of May 1940 had any further significance. Bolstered by successive instances of White House support, the newly established Air War Plans Division (AWPD) in September 1941 drew up an "ultimate" production target for the Army air arm. This plan called for an interim goal of 59,727 and an ultimate total goal of 63,467 air-

---

[28] NDAC Official Bull, Defense, 20 Dec 40, p. 3. See also, WPD 3807-83, *passim*.

[29] ASW R. A. Lovett to President, 23 Apr 41, and Memo, Lovett for Arnold, 7 May 41, both in AFCF 452.1, 1856 Bomber Program. See also William Frye, *Marshall: Citizen Soldier* (Indianapolis: Bobbs-Merrill, 1947), p. 285.

[30] FDR to SW, 4 May 41, SW files, Aircraft, item 2004. Three months later air arm officers were proposing from 750 to over 1,000 heavy bombers per month as suitable objectives. See Memo, CofAC for CofAAF, 28 Aug 41, AFCF 452.1, 1856 Bomber Program; Memo, Secy Air Staff for CofAC, 30 Aug 41, AFCF 452.1 Aircraft, Gen.

[31] Memo, Exec, OCAC, for Gen Brett, 8 May 41, AFCF 452.1 1856 Bomber Program. See also, TAG to CofAC, 9 Jun 41, AFCF 321.9E.

craft, including tactical and training types.[32] These figures were still under consideration when the disaster at Pearl Harbor swept the nation into the war and precipitated anew the question of production targets.

Confronted with an urgent request to prepare a statement of requirements for an all-out war or a Victory Program, Air Corps officers simply turned to the extant AWPD study and lifted out the figures calling for an ultimate production in the neighborhood of 60,000 aircraft for the Army's air arm by 1 January 1944. Yet even in providing General Arnold with this target figure for an all-out effort, the Acting Chief of the Air Corps noted that it was really not an ultimate figure since AWPD studies were even then considering a 35-percent increase.[33] One can only conclude that "final" and "ultimate" in the military vocabulary are something akin to the term "supercolossal" in Hollywood. Ultimate or not, these figures represented the scale of military planning for air power at the time of the Roosevelt-Churchill ARCADIA Conference in Washington at the end of 1941.

The President's New Targets

The traditional state of the union address to both Houses, falling as it did so soon after Pearl Harbor, gave the President an excellent opportunity to present Congress with a new set of production targets suited to the new situation of actual war. The President laid down a whole string of production objectives to guide the nation's armament program. And at the head of the list came aircraft. For 1942, the President asked a total of 60,000 aircraft, of which some 45,000 were to be tactical types and the remainder trainers. For 1943, the goals were higher: a total of 125,000 aircraft, of which 100,000 were to be tactical types.[34]

The President's target figures were precise—so precise, in fact, as to raise questions as to their origin. The figures could have been just another set of psychological targets, sufficiently higher than the last, of course, to goad on both aircraft producers and military planners. On the other hand, they could have been supplied to the President from military or industry sources. The record does indeed show that the staff planners within the War Department supplied the President with figures before he returned his procurement directive asking in substance for fulfillment of the goals enumerated before Congress. It was common practice for officers within the Department to write their own tickets, which is to say, frame directives to themselves for the President's signature.[35] This may well have occurred in this particular case. Significantly, however, the goals ordered by the President, 60,000 and 125,000 aircraft in 1942 and 1943, were not the figures sent to the White House from the military planners.

The President, it seems, took the figures supplied as a maximum by military officials and arbitrarily raised them. When Harry Hopkins protested at this cavalier disregard for the facts of produc-

---

[32] Craven and Cate, eds., *Plans and Early Operations*, pp. 131–32.
[33] Memo, Actg CofAC for Gen Arnold, 21 Dec 41, AFCF 452.1 Aircraft, Gen.
[34] *Cong Rcd*, January 6, 1942, p. 34.
[35] FDR to SW, 4 May 41, and Lovett, ASW (Air), to President, 23 Apr 41, AFCF 452.1, 1856 Bomber Program.

tion, Mr. Roosevelt is said to have replied "Oh, the production people can do it if they really try."[36] This certainly suggests that the President regarded the figures both as rational goals and as psychological targets. Other evidence helps confirm this view. In sending the targets to the military men for compliance, the President suggested that the Secretaries of War and Navy might wish to confer in working out the precise distribution of the totals.[37] Had they compiled the figures in the first place from a study of their joint requirements presumably no such after-the-fact conference would be necessary. And finally, the President himself hinted that the new production targets were propaganda for internal as well as external consumption when in his address before Congress he pointedly called the attention of the nation's enemies to the big new production goals they had inspired by the attack on Pearl Harbor.[38]

For better or for worse, 60,000 and 125,000 became the aircraft production targets for 1942 and 1943. Almost immediately critics denounced the President's figures as impossible.[39] It might well prove entirely possible to manufacture 125,000 aircraft by 1943, but what kind of aircraft: the types needed, models suitable for combat, or mere numbers? To reach the prescribed targets in the allotted time might signal a triumph of production, but would it ensure victory in the air; would the aircraft turned out be superior to those of the enemy? Some air arm officers in grim jest branded this emphasis on quantity "the numbers racket."

"The Numbers Racket"

Evidence of the adverse effect of the President's apparent preoccupation with numbers without corresponding concern for performance began to accrue almost immediately. Before the President's appeal to Congress, the air arm budget for the coming fiscal year called for procurement of some 33,000 aircraft. After the President's address calling for 60,000 and 125,000 aircraft over the next two years, the Chief of the Materiel Division, who was responsible for procurement, sent up a hurriedly revised program asking for 39,000 rather than 33,000 aircraft without increase in the covering appropriation. This remarkable stretching of funds, it seems, was to be accomplished by removing some 700 expensive heavy bombers from the procurement program and substituting a greater number of fighters, dive bombers, and trainers. The heavy bombers were to be deferred to a

---

[36] Rosenman, *Working With Roosevelt*, p. 325. Robert Sherwood vouches for the story as one who was actually present at the time. Roosevelt, adds Sherwood, "was never afraid of big round numbers." *Roosevelt and Hopkins*, pp. 473–74. Donald Nelson credits Roosevelt with saying that he reached the program figures by "my usual rule of thumb method." Donald M. Nelson, *Arsenal of Democracy* (New York: Harcourt, Brace and Company, 1946), pp. 185–86.

[37] FDR to SW, 3 Jan 42, AFCF 452.1 Aircraft, Gen. Craven and Cate, eds, *Plans and Early Operations*, page 247, citing a secondary source, indicates that the President's directive to the Secretary of War, 3 January 1942, called for 131,000 aircraft in 1943 rather than 125,000. The different figures suggest that the President was juggling the target figures considerably between 3 and 6 January 1942.

[38] Rosenman, *Working With Roosevelt*, p. 325; *Cong Rcd*, January 6, 1942, p. 34.

[39] Rosenman, *Working With Roosevelt*, p. 325.

subsequent program.⁴⁰ Such evidence is, of course, inconclusive when standing alone, but it certainly suggests a tendency on the part of some air arm officers to take their cue from the President and stress numbers at the expense of tactical need. In trying to provide the number of aircraft set up in the target without due consideration for all the other factors involved, some of the planners may have been pursuing the form while losing the substance.

By the fall of 1942 there were increasingly serious doubts expressed in the upper echelons of production planners as to whether or not it would be possible to attain the goals established by the President. Even after cutting down on the number of spare parts to be procured along with the aircraft on program in order to turn out a greater number of flyable units, production still lagged behind the target figures. The goals might be reached, a planning committee reported, if the air arm program were given priority over all other consumers and if no design changes (which would slow down production) were introduced.⁴¹ The implication of this report was clear: the President's goals could be reached only by sacrificing all else. To attain the desired level of production it would be necessary to rule out the very design changes that were essential to the production of aircraft superior to those of the enemy. And by the same token it would be impossible to attain the goals set and still procure those spare parts without which even the best of flyable units would soon be depleted by cannibalization under combat conditions in the field.⁴²

When asked to revise his production goals in October 1942, the President remained adamant. He was "seriously disturbed," he said, by the existing production failures but insisted that he expected full compliance with the 125,000 goal set in January 1942. This meant, he reiterated, an output of 100,000 tactical aircraft during 1943 and not merely the attainment of that rate of production by the end of 1943. "I am convinced," the President wrote, "that this is not an impossible production requirement and can and should be carried out."⁴³

Even after the President had formally insisted upon fulfillment of the established production goals, agitation for a cutback continued in air arm circles. Some officers felt that the goals were unrealistic. One officer intimately concerned with production planning suggested that the President's target figures might actually lie beyond the resources of the nation. The production record gave some support to this view. During September 1942, the last reported month then available, actual deliveries were only 51 percent of scheduled deliveries.⁴⁴

The record of actual output in con-

---

⁴⁰ R&R, Chief, Mat Div (draft by Maj Meyers), to Fiscal Div, 2 Feb 42, AFCF 452.1–13F Proc of Aircraft.

⁴¹ Jt Aircraft Planning Com, WPB, to D. M. Nelson, 26 Sep 42, USW files, ASF Planning Br, 452 Aircraft.

⁴² Interestingly enough, the officer who signed the WPB report, Major Meyers, was the same man who had drafted a directive for the Chief of the Air Corps in October 1940 to reduce spare parts procurement so as to increase the number of completed aircraft procurable from limited funds. Memo, CofAC for Chief, Mat Div, 11 Oct 40, AFCF 452.1–13F Proc of Aircraft.

⁴³ Memo, FDR for JCS, AFCF 334.7 Bulky, President's Aircraft Program.

⁴⁴ R&R, AFADS to AFDAS, 6 Oct 42, AFCF 334.7 Bulky, President's Aircraft Program.

trast to scheduled output must have influenced the President, for soon afterward he relented somewhat from his earlier stand. At his request the Air Staff surveyed the whole field of requirements once again, and he formally approved a revised statement of operational needs. Instead of a production target of 125,000 aircraft for 1943, the new goal was to be 107,000 aircraft—82,000 tactical types and 25,000 trainers.[45] Even this lower target proved difficult to hit.

As the first quarter of 1943 slipped by, more and more air arm officials began to doubt that the new goal could be reached even though they were not anxious to have it reduced. The Deputy Chief of the Air Staff declared flatly that without "prompt relief"—concessions of labor and materials being absorbed by ground force and naval programs—fulfillment of the objective would be a "remote possibility."[46] The Assistant Secretary of War for Air, Robert A. Lovett, believed the same thing. He fed this information into the White House via the backstairs route, Mr. Harry Hopkins.

Lovett felt that a total of 88,000 rather than 107,000 aircraft in 1943 would be a realistic estimate.[47] He urged Hopkins to sell this to the President. Experience had shown that the changing needs of combat required a shift from inferior models already in production to superior models just emerging from an experimental status. Such a shift would unavoidably reduce aircraft output. Why should not the President explain this candidly to the public, Lovett urged, so there would be no misunderstanding? The production goals could thus be lowered to an obtainable figure, and the public would know why.[48]

A single episode early in 1943 will serve to illustrate the unintended absurdities stemming from an emphasis on sheer numbers without corresponding attention to performance or quality. The Douglas A-26, just emerging from experimental status, was reported to be "the sweetest flying aircraft" ever built for the air arm. Staff officers representing the users or tactical arms pointed out that the A-26 would go 100 miles per hour faster and carry more bombs than either the North American B-25 or the Martin B-26. They urged that production of the two medium bombers be tapered off (rather than increased as currently planned) and the A-26 substituted instead. "Fifty 100 percent aircraft," said the Director of Military Requirements, "are of more value than a hundred 50 percent aircraft in actual combat." If it proved necessary to pay for this increased performance with decreased production, he argued, it might still increase over-all combat effectiveness.[49] Superior performance or quality was clearly a more desirable objective than mere numbers, mass production, or quantity; at least this was the view of those who had to fly against the enemy.

---

[45] FDR to SW, 29 Oct 42, SW files, Aircraft, item 2180. See also, Adm W. D. Leahy to D. M. Nelson, 26 Nov 42, AFCF 400.17A.

[46] R&R, DCofAAF, to CGMC, 17 Mar 43, AFCF 452.01-B Production.

[47] Lovett to Hopkins, 25 Mar 43, AFCF 452.01-B Production. Lovett was not far off. Actual production in 1943 was just under 86,000 units.

[48] *Ibid.*

[49] R&R, Military Requirements to MC, 23 Jan 43, comment 3; see also, comments 1 and 2, AFCF 452.01-A Production.

On the other hand, the suppliers were in a position quite different from the users. They too wanted to procure superior aircraft. But they were judged as succeeding or failing not in terms of quality but of quantity. The Chief of the Materiel Command agreed "in principle" with the request of the users, but then went on to explain why it would be impossible to comply. General Arnold had stated as a "must" a total of 133,000 aircraft in 1943 in place of the Roosevelt goal of 125,000. Practical considerations such as ground force and naval requirements coupled with the limited resources of the nation led him to accept, however reluctantly, 107,000 aircraft as the maximum production feasible. The Materiel Command, then, felt committed to reach this target. "We cannot get even approximately the number of aircraft which we are directed to produce unless we adhere to existing types and models with the absolute minimum of changes."[50] In short, those responsible for supplying aircraft took their quantitative goals more seriously than their qualitative goals. This reply evoked an immediate outcry.

As spokesman for the users, the Director of Military Requirements denounced the tendency to place greater emphasis on numbers than upon tactical usefulness. He saw the issue as one of utmost importance and trotted out some horrible examples to support his case. Experience in operations showed the need for winterizing airplanes, modifying production models to make them suitable for all-weather operation in northern climates. Production authorities argued against winterization since the introduction of such modifications would cut down on the total output. If they had won their point, the consequences would have been appalling. Airplanes not winterized could not be flown to the Soviet Union over the northwestern or Alaskan route; by delaying winterization greater numbers could be produced, but any attempt to fly such unmodified aircraft through Alaska would surely have encountered heavy losses.

Worse than the delays in winterization resulting from an emphasis on quantity rather than quality was the continued production of obsolete types. The Director of Military Requirements regarded the Vultee A–31 as a "splendid example" of what happened when the demand for quantity was allowed to dominate. Long after the airplane was recognized as obsolete and unsuited for combat, it was continued in production, using up labor, materials, and productive capacity.[51] Obviously there was no profit in producing airplanes nobody wanted.

Observations on the Numbers Game

If the suppliers became so engrossed in the numbers game that they lost sight of tactical usefulness, then the value of the President's psychological targets might well be questioned. On the other hand, as British experience had shown, "the best is the enemy of the good." Too much stress on performance would leave

---

[50] R&R, CGMC to Dir, Military Requirements, 30 Jan 43, comment 4, AFCF 452.01–A Production.

[51] R&R, Dir, Military Requirements, to CAS, 5 Feb 43, comment 5, AFCF 452.01–A Production. Much the same thing could be said of the A–35 and A–36. See Memo, Arnold for Lovett, 22 Feb 43, AFCF 452.01–A Production.

airplanes forever on the drawing board and never in the hands of troops in the field.

To balance quantity and quality called for genuine daring from those in command. To stop production of an aircraft model, no matter how obsolete, was to draw public criticism. Unavoidably, labor would have to be laid off until a newer and superior model could be tooled up for production. And the layoffs would take place even as everyone in the community, from schoolboys to housewives, was urged to join the war effort. On the other hand, it also took courage not to discontinue a model already in production when a markedly superior model appeared on the horizon. The A-26 was indeed superior to the B-26 in several respects, but performance was not the only factor to be considered. Elaborate training schools were established to provide the B-26 with crew members and maintenance mechanics. Spare parts were piling up in appropriate depots all over the map. Until these elements could be adjusted, the superior A-26 might well prove unable to carry as much punch to the enemy as the inferior B-26 simply for want of spare parts and mechanics trained to cope with its particular eccentricities.

One final consideration should be brought to bear when appraising the President's production targets. Big round numbers, such as 125,000 aircraft in 1943, utterly failed to take account of the rising gross weight of military aircraft. In January 1942 when the President announced his target for 1943, the average airframe weight was 4,520 pounds. A year or so later the average airframe being produced weighed some 8,900 pounds, or nearly twice as much.[52] With some justice the Materiel Command could claim that the President's target had been more than fulfilled if one used a 1942 rather than a 1943 yardstick. But if this was so, responsible officers of the command should have been doubly careful not to be coerced by the numbers game into stressing quantity out of proportion to quality.[53]

Return to Reality

Following the President's call for 50,000 aircraft in May 1940, air arm officers worked day and night to complete the necessary contracts. At one time during the summer and fall of 1940 procurement officers were signing as many as 1,000 contracts a day at Wright Field purchasing everything from flying boots to four-engine bombers. Most of these, of course, were for accoutrements and maintenance supplies, but aircraft constituted the largest dollar volume. Two weeks after Congress made funds available for the Air Corps share of the 50,000 program, the Secretary of War closed contracts for 11,000 airplanes. For the first time since World War I, the War Department purchased more than a thousand aircraft on a single order. The billions of dollars available were quite enough, as General Arnold said, "to stagger any

---

[52] Memo, Gen Echols for Bureau of the Budget, 10 May 43, AFCF 452.01-B Production.

[53] There is evidence that "coercion" was employed to ensure a high level of acceptances regardless of quality. See, for example, Deputy Air Inspector to Chief, Technical Inspection Div (Air Inspector), 14 Jun 43, with inclosures, citing instances of ferry pilots forced to take delivery of aircraft that still had ten days of work yet undone. AFCF 333.5 Contract Investigation.

Douglas A-26

"mere officer" and "seemingly sufficient to buy anything for anybody at any time." [54]

Schedules Versus Deliveries

Billions of dollars to spend and staggering production targets, 50,000, 60,000, and even 125,000 aircraft, made a brave show—for the future. The current realities were sobering in contrast. Against the grand programs involving tens of thousands of aircraft scheduled for delivery, the production actually achieved— the aircraft actually "accepted" officially for the air arm—amounted to little more than a trickle. During one week in November 1940, more than six months after the President announced his 50,000 target, the air arm received only two tactical aircraft from the entire industry. There were, it is true, nearly 40 small trainers turned out in that same week, but even this was utterly inadequate compared with the scheduled requirement for trainers. Nor was this halting pace an isolated instance.[55] Production throughout the remainder of 1940 and well into 1941 remained painfully low. The result: a virtually unarmed air force.

An Unarmed Air Force

During the summer of 1941 General Arnold grimly took stock of the consequences of the disastrous gap between orders and deliveries. The GHQ Air Force, supposedly the air arm's great offensive or striking arm, could muster only two groups of heavy bombers (70 aircraft), two groups of medium bombers (approximately 114 aircraft), two groups of light bombers (approximately 114 aircraft), and three groups of pursuit (225 aircraft), nine groups or a paper total of 523 airplanes in all. But even this force was, the General felt, something of an

---

[54] Arnold, lecture, AIC, 5 Oct 40, WFCF 350.001, 1941; *Aviation* (October 1940), p. 71.

[55] Chief, Mat Planning Sec, to Tech Exec, 20 Nov 40, and Memo, Asst CofAC for ASW, 12 Dec 40, both in AFCF 319.1 Production Rpts.

Martin B-26

absurdity since it lacked the mobile air depots essential for sustained operations in the field and, worse still, to operate even those nine groups involved the use of obsolete equipment—B-18's and P-36's without leakproof tanks, gun turrets, armor and all the other modifications shown necessary by the war in Europe.

The Army's aerial striking force, said General Arnold, was at "zero strength." He concluded bluntly: the air arm was not ready for war. Not until sometime after March 1942 would aircraft production be expected to begin outstripping training and pile up a backlog of aircraft.[56]

The small number of aircraft available to tactical units in the field was in itself alarming, but this was not the only danger present. Even those aircraft reported as "tactically available" by the pitifully few groups and squadrons in the field were not always really available. At one point during the summer of 1941, for example, the Chief of the Air Corps reported that two whole squadrons of heavy bombers, B-17's, and an entire group of medium bombers were grounded for want of parts or because of structural defects appearing after delivery.[57]

In some cases even aircraft officially "accepted" by the War Department were not in fact complete. Production of Bell P-39 fighters, for example, ran well ahead of propeller production. To avoid a pile-up, air arm officers arranged to accept the units as assembled, fly them to an air base, remove the propeller, ship it back to Bell, fly away another, and so on.[58] Whatever the paper records may have indicated to the contrary, the air arm had a number of lame ducks on hand. Even after Pearl Harbor, tactical units continued to list aircraft on strength

---

[56] Memo, CofAAF for WPD, 7 Jul 41, AFCF 321.9E.

[57] Memo, CofAC for Lovett, 14 Jun 41, AFCF 452.1 Airplanes, Gen.

[58] Chief, Production Engr Br to Statistics Sec, 2 Sep 41, AFCF 319.1 Production Rpts.

reports even though they lacked guns, turrets, radios, and bombsights—without which they would be of little use in a shooting war.[59]

If every aircraft assigned to tactical units were fully equipped and ready for operations in the field, the available strength at the time of Pearl Harbor would still have been dangerously inadequate. As subsequent experience during World War II was to show, there is many a slip between the end of the production line and airplanes actually brought to bear on the enemy target. By the middle of the war, the record revealed, out of every 1,000 aircraft accepted, 38 percent, or 380, remained in the United States with training units or in local defense organizations. Of the remaining 62 percent, or 620 aircraft, reaching theaters of operations, on any average mission day, some 45 percent, or 279 aircraft, were undergoing repairs. This left 55 percent, or 341 aircraft, available for strikes against the enemy. But on an average mission 20 percent of this force, or 68 aircraft, failed to reach the target. This left 80 percent, or 273 aircraft—27.3 percent of the 1,000 originally accepted—as the effective force available.[60] At any given moment, therefore, perhaps one-quarter of the net output of the production lines could be brought to bear against a distant enemy.

A number of factors lay behind the delays that hindered the growth of the air arm. Diversions of production abroad, notably to the Russians and the British contributed substantially. So too did the decision, when the crisis arrived, to buy aircraft still on the drawing board or in the experimental stage rather than go ahead with current production models. In buying "paper aircraft" and unproved experimental models the Air Corps undoubtedly slowed down production, since there were inevitable bugs to be eliminated before production could begin. But at the same time, the decision resulted in the ultimate production of markedly superior aircraft, the B–17's for example, rather than the B–18 or B–23 bomber.[61]

Fundamentally, of course, the delays in equipping the air arm stemmed from the nature of the problem itself. The aircraft industry was asked to effect a revolution almost overnight. During the 1930's War Department orders for aircraft ranged anywhere from 100 to 600 items a year. Then rather abruptly they soared, first to several thousand in early 1940 and then to tens of thousands twelve months later.[62] This flood of orders led to a scramble—for labor, materials, factory capacity, machine tools, and the services of subcontractors. Only by careful co-ordination and control could the wild scramble be synchronized into an orderly mobilization of resources and only by understanding the administrative organizations contrived to achieve this synchronization can one fully appreciate the difficulties besetting procurement for the air arm in this period of stress.

---

[59] Memo, Maj Luther Harris for Gen Arnold, 20 Jan 42, AFCF 452.1 Airplanes, Gen.

[60] Memo, Gen Arnold for SW, 20 Jan 44, AFCF 452.01–D Production.

[61] For a good general review of factors delaying aircraft production, see Mat Div, OCAC, Memo Rpt for Rcd, 8 Apr 41, AFCF 452.1 Airplanes, Gen.

[62] R&R, Chief, Mat Div, to Exec, 31 May 41, AFCF 452.1–13–F Proc of Aircraft, Actg Chief Stat Control Div to ASW (Air) 12 May 43, AFCF 452.01–B Production.

CHAPTER XII

Organizing for Production

Posing the Problem

Military Foresight

Of the many lessons available to the War Department from the experience of mobilization in World War I, perhaps none stood out more vividly than this: If the nation were to avoid the scramble that marred the rush to arm in 1917, any future attempt at mobilizing the nation's resources for war must be co-ordinated and controlled by a single, central agency under civilian control. This conclusion was embedded in the policies of the War Department and in the thinking of its officials. The Army Industrial College, the special military school on economic mobilization for war, laid down the dictum in its teachings and its textbooks.[1] With more than 800 graduates scattered throughout the arms and services of the Army, not to mention the Navy, the influence of the school was certainly appreciable. Moreover, the official mobilization plans actually drawn up on the eve of the war spelled out in unmistakable terms the principle of civilian dominance over a single, central agency.[2]

The official mobilization plan of 1939 visualized the agency specifically as a War Resources Administration (WRA) staffed by "patriotic business leaders of the nation" and topped by an administrator, or economic czar, appointed by and responsible to the President. Pending the selection and formation of such an organization in time of crisis, the planners provided for an interim or caretaker arrangement by which the Army and Navy Munitions Board would undertake to co-ordinate the mobilization effort until the WRA was ready to take over. Thus the planners, the officers who had drawn up the official mobilization plan and had spent the between-war years studying the special problems involved, would for the time being become operators.

The ANMB officially consisted of the Assistant Secretaries of War and Navy, with their appointees. In practice, the actual operation of the board fell to a working staff recruited largely from the office of the Assistant Secretary of War. The interim function anticipated for the board in preventing a scramble for resources followed several broad paths. A facilities division would try to allocate or apportion available industrial capacity for production among the various claimant agencies; a commodities division would seek to assure a fair division of available material resources amongst the various claimants by resorting to a

---

[1] See, for example, AIC, Special Text No. 97, published just before World War II. See also, ASW, "Annual Report," p. 7, in the Secretary's annual report for 1940.
[2] S Doc 134, 76th Cong, 2d sess, *Industrial Mobilization Plan*, Revision of 1939, pp. 6–7.

system of priorities; and other similar divisions would do the same for power, transportation, and so on, in each case co-ordinating all phases of the mobilization in one grand synthesis, balancing ends with means.[3]

After twenty-odd years of study, military officials had contrived a logical, flexible organization as well as a number of more or less elaborate administrative procedures to meet the emergency when it arrived. But the very excellence of this forehandedness may have been deceptive. At least some officials placed an exaggerated trust in the utility of the advance arrangements.[4] When war did break out in Europe in the fall of 1939, for example, the Assistant Secretary of War promptly asked the supply services if any bottlenecks were anticipated. To this question an air arm officer replied in the negative, blandly announcing that the Air Corps would crack down on defaulting manufacturers by purchasing "in the open market," making the defaulters pay the difference in cost.[5] Here was faith indeed in the efficacy of advance planning. But would there be any "open market" to which one could turn in a crisis when the productive capacity of every manufacturer was strained to the utmost?[6] It was all very well in theory to take a cavalier attitude and talk of coercing compliance or to rely confidently upon procedures worked up in advance to facilitate mobilization, but in the event theory did not always coincide with practice.

Theory and Practice

Events did not obediently follow in the footsteps of the planners. Of immediate and unavoidable concern was the troublesome reality of politics. When the crisis arrived, the President considered establishing a War Resources Board which, at least according to plan, would in an emergency be converted into a single central civilian agency (WRA) to control and co-ordinate the mobilization. But, desirable as such an agency might be from the standpoint of efficient operations, the President found that the board appointed simply was not politically expedient at the moment.[7] New Dealers—

---

[3] *Ibid.*, pp. 8–12. For a brief description of ANMB, WRB, and the plan, see H. J. Tobin, "Preparing Civilian America for War," *Foreign Affairs* (July 1939), p. 686.

[4] For a good example of this faith in the efficacy of the planners' work see Assistant Secretary of War (Louis Johnson), "Annual Report," 1940, which claims that ANMB had led Army and Navy to a "complete understanding of each other's problems in industrial mobilization" (page 7), as well as the claim: "So far these plans have proved workable and of material value." "No need for revision of these plans in any important particular is apparent" (page 8).

[5] Memo, Maj R. H. Magee for CofAC, 2 Nov 39, AFCF 319.1–A. See also, ASW to Douglas, 27 Nov 39, AFCF 452.1 Airplanes, Gen, and Memo, CofAC for Chief, Mat Div, 30 Jan 40, AFCF 321.9 B, for examples of the tendency on the part of military officials to "order" production according to plan, while refusing to "tolerate" delays.

[6] Interestingly enough, Louis Johnson had himself made a special point of the circumstance that there would be no "open market" in which to buy munitions in wartime. See ASW "Annual Report," 1940, p. 10.

[7] See above, ch. VIII. See also, Civilian Production Administration, *Industrial Mobilization for War: History of the War Production Board and Predecessor Agencies, 1940–1945* (Washington, 1947), and R. Elberton Smith, *The Army and Economic Mobilization*, UNITED STATES ARMY IN WORLD WAR II (Washington, 1959), pp. 99–102. For a partisan account, see B. Rauch, *Roosevelt: From Munich to Pearl Harbor* (1st ed.; New York: Creative Age Press, 1950), pp. 158–59, 207. For a brief but more objective account, see Langer and Gleason, *Challenge*

even within the Cabinet—protested that the businessmen selected for the board might undermine the social gains of the administration. Union leaders were outspoken in deploring the lack of labor representation on the board, and at least one senator professed to find the board dominated by "Morgan interests." The very title of the board proved an embarrassment. The President was currently engaged in trying to persuade Congress to amend the neutrality laws. While assuring the legislators that such a move would not carry the nation nearer to war, he could scarcely afford to grant a *War Resources Board* large powers over the national economy. As a consequence the War Resources Board was disbanded, and the President tried to co-ordinate the nation's mobilization efforts by a series of expedient makeshifts.

Not until January 1942, more than two years after the beginning of hostilities in Europe, did the President finally create a really substantial superagency for centralized co-ordination and control. Moreover, even this agency, the War Production Board (WPB), received powers that were neither all-inclusive nor overriding. In brief, it took more than two years of

---

to Isolation, pp. 269–72. For a fuller treatment, see Troyer Anderson MS in OCMH, History of the Office of the Under Secretary of War: 1914–1941, ch. 4, passim, and Harry B. Yoshpe, Plans for Industrial Mobilization: 1920–1939 (AIC Study 28), pp. 67–68, as well as Thatcher, Planning for Industrial Mobilization: 1920–40. For WRB report and other documents as well as testimony regarding WRB and the failure to use the mobilization plan, see Hearings of Special Com Investigating the National Defense Program (Truman Com), pt. 42, *Industrial Mobilization Plan*, 1948. For what purports to be a White House view of WRB, see J. Alsop and R. Kintner, *American White Paper; The Story of American Diplomacy and the Second World War* (New York: Simon and Schuster, 1940), pp. 49–51, 64.

acute crisis and confusion on the production front to bring theory and practice into line—to establish the agency that, long before the war arrived, the military planners had considered to be necessary.

During the two years of delay between the time the President dropped the War Resources Board and the day he established the War Production Board, responsible officials, both military and civilian, had to hammer out organizations to guide industrial production in the United States. The organizations they contrived did indeed work. Alternate solutions might have worked better—or worse. But this, at least, must be stated: their task was vastly complicated by the President's delay in creating a centralized agency that every mobilization study between the wars had shown to be so necessary.

Evolution of an Organization

The President's call for 50,000 aircraft marked the real beginning of "wartime" mobilization for the Air Corps. While it is true that the *de jure* M-day did not arrive until after Pearl Harbor, the air arm's *de facto* M-day fell on 16 May 1940. Thus it came about that the situation anticipated by the planners simply did not materialize. Because the actual mobilization of the air arm took place before the nation legally engaged in war, and because the President never felt that it was politically feasible during that period to set up a powerful co-ordinating superagency such as the proposed War Resources Administration, virtually the whole prewar rearmament effort had to be conducted without effective, centralized leadership.

For eighteen months the law lagged

behind the facts. Nonetheless, the law of supply and demand was in full operation. Just as the planners had anticipated, there ensued a scramble for labor, materials, and productive capacity or facilities. The abrupt increase in demand signaled by the President's message, even if it did eventually simmer down to substantially less than 50,000 aircraft, sent manufacturers scurrying to their vendors and suppliers with ever larger orders. Their requests soon exceeded the supply, and one manufacturer after another, confronted with rapidly approaching delivery dates, brought stories of shortages to the attention of the War Department contracting officers.

The President had scarcely returned from the Hill to the White House before the impact of his call for 50,000 aircraft was felt in War Department circles. The air arm hastily sent a list of "anticipated chokepoints" to the Assistant Secretary. Gone was the cavalier assurance of the previous fall. No responsible official now talked of buying in the open market.

For some items there was no source at all; for many others only premium prices would command deliveries. Aluminum castings, for example, precision castings for engine crankcases, threatened to be unobtainable. Limited supplies of forgings, die steel, electric furnace steel, machine tools, nylon and linen for parachute harnesses, and many other items all seemed about to wreck the rearmament program.[8] Sometimes the critical item was minute indeed. Iridium, for instance, used in electrical contacts or breaker points in spark plugs and various control mechanisms, posed a trivial problem in terms of tonnage but an acute problem technically for want of a feasible substitute. Sometimes the shortages came in entirely unexpected fields. Steer hides offer a case in point. While substitutes for leather flying suits might be readily found, at the time leather seemed to be an essential component in self-sealing fuel tanks. Since the very idea of such tanks was a novel one first found in captured German airplanes, no advance provision to obtain steer hides for the purpose had been made. The supply of aircraft engines was especially critical. So desperate did the mounting shortage of power plants become during the six months following the President's request, Air Corps officials were driven to the expedient of borrowing engines from one of the leading commercial airlines in order to fly off otherwise completed B–17 bombers.[9]

Probably no single material shortage caused more alarm and confusion than did aluminum. Before the beginning of 1940, Army-Navy estimates on aluminum forgings contemplated a maximum requirement of 600,000 pounds per month. By August 1940, Alcoa was actually producing 1,500,000 pounds of forgings a month—but even this was not enough to meet the mounting demand.[10] Aircraft manufacturers were unimpressed by the claim that Alcoa had far exceeded anticipated production. They responded to the facts as they saw them. Alcoa deliv-

---

[8] Memo, Acting CofAC for ASW, 5 Jun 40, SW files, Airplanes, item 1558a. See also, TWX, PES to Tech Exec, OCAC, 29 Nov 40, WFCF 111.3 Munitions Program Requirements. This whole file is filled with details on shortages.

[9] R&R, Maj Gen G. H. Brett to Gen Arnold, 21 Dec 40, AFCF 400.114.

[10] Memo, Maj Wood for Col Spaulding, 27 Aug 40, AGO Rcds, ASF Planning Br file, 452.11 P&A.

ORGANIZING FOR PRODUCTION

eries on forgings were far behind schedule. To keep assembly lines from stalling, aircraft builders resorted to the expensive expedient of substituting components machined out of solid billets of aluminum. This was slow, costly, and put a heavy strain on already overworked tool rooms with the further effect of aggravating the machine tool shortage.[11]

There were indeed numerous delays in the production of aluminum forgings. Dies were difficult to fabricate, die sinkers were hard to train, and heavy forging hammers were scarce. But not all these delays were attributable to the suppliers. Alcoa representatives pointed out that aircraft manufacturers were guilty of long delays in providing drawings for the parts ordered. Merely placing an order was not enough. Detailed drawings and specifications had to accompany an order. Without these it was impossible to begin work on the construction of forging dies. If, as was often the case in 1940, aircraft manufacturers were trying to put models into production directly from the drawing board, it is not surprising that all too frequently the necessary detailed drawings were not available when orders for parts went out to the suppliers. Even when drawings were sent with the initial order, it sometimes happened that subsequent design changes were introduced and the partially finished dies had to be reworked.[12]

While suppliers and aircraft manufacturers were busy blaming one another, General Marshall asked, with some irritation, how the aluminum producers could protest that there was no shortage at the very moment the aircraft builders were explaining away their failure to produce by pointing to unfilled orders for aluminum products.[13] Government officials exploring the question began to uncover some of the answers. Apart from the intrinsic difficulties already mentioned, they found that aircraft builders wanted to receive an entire order of forgings in one delivery. This not only simplified inventory control but permitted the aircraft builders to work or machine the forgings with a single tool setting. But to provide such bulk deliveries for each and every aircraft builder would require hammer capacity on the part of the material supplier far in excess of that available. Moreover, any such arrangement would involve the supplier in a feast and famine cycle—coping with peak loads just after the aircraft manufacturers placed their orders, then trying to survive periods of idleness.[14]

Clearly the solution to this problem was to schedule deliveries to aircraft manufacturers in monthly installments, rationalizing the flow by balancing the supplier's capacity with the actual needs of the manufacturer's assembly line. In short, if the suppliers, such as Alcoa, on the one hand and the aircraft manufacturers on the other, were to be kept from bootless recrimination and unrealistic delivery schedules, some sort of impartial arbiter would have to ride herd on all parties concerned.

---

[11] See, for example, comments from North American Aviation, initialed "L.A.," 6 Aug 40, AFCF 004.4.

[12] Notes on Conference on Export Aluminum Alloy Aircraft Production, 8 Jan 40; R&R, Chief, Mat Div, to Exec, OCAC, 7 Aug 40. Both in AFCF 004.4.

[13] Memo, CofS for ASW, 9 Dec 40, SW files, Airplanes, item 1906.

[14] E. R. Stettinius, Jr., to ASW, 10 Dec 40; SW files, Airplanes, item 1906. See also, Telg, Douglas to NDAC, 6 Dec 40, same file.

In the absence of a central co-ordinating agency, the attempt to bring order out of confusion fell to the existing agencies of the Executive and to hastily improvised expedients. Moreover, for want of centralized co-ordination and control from 1939 on, the nation's mobilization was confused, disordered, and at cross purposes. The process of mobilization thus entailed a great deal of overlapping effort and lost motion as the parties concerned sought some means of relating their efforts.

In Search of Co-ordination

By the terms of the mobilization plan of 1939, the Army-Navy Munitions Board was to serve as an interim agency for co-ordination until some superior civilian agency such as WRA could be established. The problems of aircraft production commanded the board's attention immediately. Since the demand for military aircraft far exceeded available capacity, it was readily apparent that joint planning would be necessary. There were no air arm representatives regularly assigned to ANMB, so the board set up a special *ad hoc* "aircraft planning committee" as a working staff. The committee proposed to ensure that all material and industrial capacity requirements for the Army and Navy air arms were presented on a common basis.[15] This was a useful beginning, but, unfortunately, the need for co-ordination was not limited to conflicts of interest between the Army and Navy.

As early as July 1939, even before the outbreak of war in Europe, President Roosevelt directed ANMB to set up a clearance committee to help place foreign orders for military aircraft and other munitions.[16] The work of the clearance committee was useful insofar as it kept the military services informed as to the nature and extent of the load being imposed upon domestic capacity by export orders, but knowledge after the fact was not the same as positive control. Even if it had been granted full powers over export orders, the ANMB would obviously have been in no position to exercise them disinterestedly since the two military services were themselves claimant agencies seeking an ever larger share of the aircraft production pie.

In December 1939 the President removed the clearance committee function from ANMB and assigned it to an informal committee of Army, Navy, and Treasury representatives with instructions to report through the Secretary of the Treasury to the White House. This group, with its membership revised, the President subsequently gave official status as the Interdepartmental Committee for Co-ordinating Foreign and Domestic Military Purchases—the President's Liaison Committee, as it was commonly termed for convenience.[17]

Although the President's Liaison Committee was officially assigned the task of co-ordinating procurement of foreign and domestic arms to prevent conflicts over materials and facilities, the President appears to have been less interested in co-

---

[15] R&R, Maj Lingle to CofAC, 20 Jul 39; Col Rutherford to CofAC, 13 Dec 39; Rutherford (as chairman of Aircraft Planning Com, ANMB) rpt of 5 Mar 40. All in AFCF 334.7 ANMB.

[16] ASW, "Annual Report," 1940, p. 6.

[17] Watson, *Chief of Staff: Prewar Plans and Preparations*, pp. 300, 367; *U.S. Government Manual*, July 1940, pp. 59, 62–63.

ordination than he was to ensure a flow of supplies to France and Britain. As the Secretary of the Treasury blandly put it when looking back on the event several years later, the Treasury had "a less parochial view" than either the Army or the Navy. While this may have been true, there were still more compelling reasons why the President turned to the Secretary of the Treasury. So long as isolationist Secretary Woodring remained at the War Department, the President had good reason to prefer dealing with Secretary Morgenthau, whose views more nearly coincided with his own on aid to the fighting allies.[18] Thus it came about that the interim co-ordinating role contemplated by the planners for the ANMB did not work out as anticipated. The prewar mobilization planners had not only ignored politics and personalities but diplomacy as well. They had given no real consideration to the possibility of foreign orders as a factor in the market. As a consequence, instead of serving as a stopgap agency building up effective co-ordinating procedures until a civilian superagency could be formed to take them over, the ANMB remained merely a joint board of the two military services without authority to exercise practical control over export orders, which comprised a major share of armament production. This was the administrative situation that prevailed in the spring of 1940 when the President asked Congress for 50,000 airplanes.

Production of 50,000 airplanes threatened to swamp the aircraft industry. The President knew full well that co-ordination was more than ever necessary; makeshift arrangements such as the Liaison Committee would no longer do. Therefore, in May 1940, he directed that all aircraft contracts be cleared through Henry Morgenthau at the Treasury until final machinery could be set up. Thus, contrary to the expectations of the prewar planners and in apparent violation of all logic, the Secretary of the Treasury actually served as chief of the nation's military aircraft production—at least for a brief period.[19]

From its very inception, the President definitely regarded Morgenthau's aircraft production role as temporary. Even before assigning it he had begun to toy with the possibility of erecting some sort of civilian mobilization agency as a substitute for the discarded WRB, but he moved with the utmost caution, for here as elsewhere Mr. Roosevelt was reluctant to let major policy decisions slip out of his own hands. Moreover, the time could scarcely have been less propitious politically. The major party conventions in the summer of 1940 were only weeks away, and virtually any steps taken could cause difficulty; the President would be damned for whatever he did do as well as for whatever he failed to do.

On 28 May the President called in White House newsmen to explain his

---

[18] Henry Morgenthau, "The Morgenthau Diaries," *Colliers* (October 18, 1947), p. 17ff. Morgenthau implies that the President was reluctant to force Woodring out because of Woodring's many friends on the Hill.

[19] Memo, FDR to SW and CofS, 24 May 40, and Memo, FDR for Secy Treas, 6 Jun 40, SW files, Airplanes, item 1522a. See also, cross reference, Exec, OCAC, to Chief, Mat Div, 14 Jun 40, AFCF 452.1–13–F Proc of Aircraft, and CPA, *Industrial Mobilization for War*, p. 24. For suggestions of the irritations caused in the Air Corps by Treasury interference, see Arnold, *Global Mission* pp. 184–87, 193, 197.

next move. Having released several trial balloons during the preceding week, he apparently felt sure of his ground.[20] To ask Congress for new legislation, the President explained, might cost weeks of delay. He had decided simply to make use of an all-but-forgotten statute on the books since 1916. Under this statute the President could have formed a Council of National Defense composed of selected Cabinet members. But this portion of the law he chose to ignore in favor of a more promising provision that authorized the appointment of seven civilian experts as advisors to the Council. Using this authorization the President established a substitute for the ill-fated WRB, a substitute that came to be known as the National Defense Advisory Commission (NDAC), but was formally named the Advisory Commission to the Council of National Defense.[21]

In forming the new agency the President was certain of one thing: he would not repeat the mistake that had virtually forced him to shelve the WRB. Instead of manning the new NDAC entirely with businessmen, he pointedly added a prominent labor leader to the list. His choice, Sidney Hillman, was carefully selected to avoid alienating labor votes. Hillman, the President confided to reporters off the record, was "just half way between John Lewis and Bill Green."[22]

The question of leadership for the commission as a whole was not so readily solved. When a perspicacious reporter raised this question, the President was evasive. "Why bring up the subject?", he parried.[23] To co-ordinate its several members, the commission was to have no chairman other than the President himself, who would preside over a full-dress meeting once a week. Republican critics charged that the President was playing politics with national defense.[24] Even within Executive circles there was concern lest the President's expedients impair the functioning of the civilian agencies long planned for the day of mobilization.[25]

For better or for worse, this was the situation with the coming of summer in 1940: an immense mobilization had begun to gather headway. More than a billion dollars of abnormal expenditures sent disturbing shock waves through the national economy. In failing to establish the civilian agency sought by the planners, the President left the task of co-ordinating the mobilization effort to

---

[20] See, for example, the advance build-up reflected in the New York *Times*, May 19, 1940, 6:1; May 21, 22:5; May 22, 10:4; May 26, 1:1; and May 28, 12:4. The most important preparatory step taken within the administration came on 25 May 1940 when the President used the authority given him in the 1939 reorganization of the Executive to establish the Office for Emergency Management (OEM), as an administrative catchall for defense agencies. See Bureau of the Budget, *The United States at War* (Washington, 1946), pp. 21–23. See also, Sherwood, *Roosevelt and Hopkins*, pp. 157–60.

[21] Transcript of Press Conference, 28 May 1940, Samuel I. Rosenman, compiler, *The Public Papers and Addresses of Franklin D. Roosevelt*, vol. 9 (New York: The Macmillan Company, 1941), 241ff. See also, Act of August 29, 1916 (39 Stat 649), and Smith, *The Army and Economic Mobilization*, pp. 102–03.

[22] Press Conference, 28 May 40, in Rosenman, *Public Papers and Addresses of Franklin D. Roosevelt*, 246.

[23] *Ibid.*, p. 249.

[24] See criticisms of Herbert Hoover and Governor Thomas E. Dewey reported in New York *Times*, May 30, 1940, 9:4 and 15:4.

[25] F. L. Kluckhohn in a signed article, New York *Times*, May 28, 1940, 13:1, reported objections by officials responsible for national defense.

a whole series of more or less parallel and conflicting agencies that had to grope their way toward some sort of *modus vivendi*.

As any brand new second lieutenant soon learns, there is a great difference between issuing an order and getting it obeyed. This the President clearly understood.[26] Merely appointing a commission to co-ordinate the mobilization effort would not immediately achieve that goal. In fact, the results were to be quite the reverse at first since the creation of a new agency such as the NDAC injected a further complication into an already confused pattern of administration.

To begin with, there was the matter of recruiting a staff. Mr. William S. Knudsen of General Motors agreed to serve as commissioner of production and Mr. Edward R. Stettinius, Jr., of U.S. Steel accepted a post as commissioner of raw materials. In addition to Mr. Hillman, who was, as previously mentioned, to be responsible for the labor supply, there were four other commissioners concerned with prices, farm products, transportation, and consumer interests—all elements of the economy liable to abnormal stress under the impact of millions on millions of dollars to be poured out in war orders. Naming the seven commissioners was only the beginning. Beyond these seven a whole series of staff members had to be located and then persuaded to accept the pleasures and tribulations of public service. The big banner headlines at the end of June may have made it appear that the commission was indeed a fact, but for the people involved the process took longer. It required time to shift gears mentally as well as to adjust physically to the job in Washington. Since the NDAC continued to recruit staff during the rest of the year, it continued to suffer from the unavoidable annoyances of a shakedown cruise throughout the period.[27]

The three busiest commissioners, Knudsen, Stettinius, and Hillman, were all men of wide experience and acknowledged capabilities in their respective spheres. Nonetheless, like old dogs in new beds even the most experienced of men needed time to trample out routines for doing business. The commissioners as well as lesser men had to discover exactly what their jobs would be. The President had defined the function of NDAC in general terms but left to time, circumstance, and the commissioners themselves the more detailed refinement of the agency's role.

Demarking the precise limits of NDAC power was not easy. If the new commissioners and their staff members had only vague and general notions of their functions and procedures, the various arms and agencies with whom they were to deal were no better informed.[28] Two

---

[26] Press Conference, 28 May 40, in Rosenman, *Public Papers and Addresses of Franklin D. Roosevelt*, p. 245.

[27] Mr. Knudsen and Mr. Stettinius seem to have cleaned out their corporate desks rather briskly. See New York *Times* reports of June 2, 1940, IV, 7:1; and June 5, 1:3. For continuing recruitment of staff see, for example, June 14, 13:1; June 30, 8:1; and October 23, 13:6.

[28] For evidence of initial efforts to define the role of NDAC, see *U.S. Government Manual*, July 1940, pp. 50–53. Compare with comments in NDAC Official Bull 3, Defense, 30 Aug 40, and WPB Doc Publication 1, *Minutes of the Advisory Commission to the Council of National Defense, passim.*

GENERAL KNUDSEN

weeks after the formation of NDAC, the executive at OCAC noted that the President had set up "two commissions" that would "undoubtedly have dealings with the Air Corps." He sent a staff officer scurrying to dig up the facts about this new development, a job that took five days.[29] In short, even old-line, established organizations such as the Air Corps had to hammer out a working relationship with the NDAC, while the newly appointed commissioners and their staffs decided what their own jobs actually should be.[30] Instead of the well-drilled and smoothly functioning team envisioned by the mobilization planners in peacetime, the President's alternative turned out to be something more akin to a pick-up team of strangers who had never played together before and lacked general agreement on the rules of the game.

Insofar as the air arm was concerned, the NDAC meant for the most part the Aeronautical Section of Commissioner Knudsen's Production Division. As head of the Aeronautical Section, Knudsen chose George J. Mead, a former vice-president and engineer at United Aircraft where he had helped develop the famous Wasp engine. Mead had come to Washington earlier at the call of the Secretary of the Treasury to study the problems of engine production, so he was already at least partially acclimated. Capt. S. M. Kraus of the Navy's Bureau of Aeronautics and S. Paul Johnston, former co-ordinator of research for the National Advisory Committee for Aeronautics (NACA), came in to serve as administrators in the new organization, while Mr. T. P. Wright (Vice President and Director of Engineering at Curtiss-Wright) and A. E. Lombard, Jr. (of California Institute of Technology) brought to the staff professional skills of the utmost importance in dealing with the immediate problem of production scheduling.[31]

Broadly speaking, the NDAC was "to coordinate" the nation's defense effort.

---

[29] R&R, Exec, OCAC, to Chief, Info Div, 14 Jun 40, and notes in reply, 19 Jun 40, AFCF 334.8 OPM.
[30] For details, see WPB, MS, Relations Between the Armed Services and NDAC, Special Study No. 3, 5 Nov 43. For an unfortunate example of NDAC–AC relations, see Wright to Arnold, 23 Aug 40, and related correspondence, AFCF 452.1-191.

[31] WPB, Aircraft Production Policies Under the National Defense Advisory Commission and Office of Production Management: May 1940–December 1941, Special Study No. 21, 30 May 46, p. 4.

ORGANIZING FOR PRODUCTION

But what did that mean? According to the old capitol saw, a co-ordinator is simply a fellow with a desk between two expediters. As a matter of fact, the NDAC undertook both functions. Sometimes the expediting was imaginative and beneficial. This was certainly true, for example, when NDAC took the lead in urging the armed services to use "letters of intent" authorizing manufacturers to proceed with construction even before completing the details in formal contracts.[32] On the other hand, there were times when NDAC officials seemed to go beyond co-ordinating and expediting to intrude in what were essentially military decisions. The borderline was not always clearly defined, of course, but the military men were understandably disturbed when, for example, NDAC officials in search of greater output questioned the advisability of putting the four-engine B–17 bomber into mass production.[33]

Probably the most important contribution of the NDAC to aircraft production is to be found in the comprehensive series of reports undertaken by the Aeronautical Section staff to survey the task at hand and define the nature and scope of the job to be done. The titles of the several staff studies are sufficient to suggest their value. Report No. 1, 11 June 1940, Military Air Force of the United States; Present and Anticipated set up production targets. Report No. 2, 14 June 1940, Aluminum Alloy Requirements for Airframes, Engines, and Propellers; 50,000 Plane Program tackled one of the most pressing bottlenecks. Subsequent reports went on to measure available productive capacity for airframes, engines, and other major components.[34] These studies were of value (even if not always fully exploited) insofar as they helped familiarize the civilian staffs with the question as a whole and to survey and define the tasks in hand.[35] But to survey the problems was not to solve them. While it is undoubtedly true, as "Boss" Kettering has said, that "a problem defined is half solved," a very large half was yet to be mastered. There were shortages growing daily more pressing, and somehow or other the makeshift administrative organizations charged with orienting the national drive to rearm would have to prevent the uncontrolled scramble that had marred the pace of mobilization in previous wars.

The NDAC and the Air Corps

When the NDAC first began to function as an agency for co-ordinating the rearmament effort, the whole vexing problem of shortages had already become

---

[32] Memo, Mr. Eaton (NDAC legal consultant) for Col Schulz, OASW, 29 Jul 40, SW files, Airplanes, item 1652.

[33] Memo, ASW for Knudsen, 18 Oct 40, SW files, Airplanes, item 1824. See also, TWX, Echols to Brett, 23 Jul 40, WFCF 111.3 Munitions Program. The tendency of NDAC officials to slight military considerations (range, etc.) in emphasizing production offers an interesting counterfoil to the contentions of Eliot Janeway in *The Struggle for Survival* (New Haven, Conn.: Yale University Press, 1951), pages 212–18, regarding the role of NDAC–OPM in weapon design, etc.

[34] See above, ch. VIII.

[35] By no means insignificant was the NDAC role in educating the public, manufacturers, etc., in the nature of the task at hand and in the problems to be expected. See, for example, Wright, "50,000 Planes a Year: How Much? How Long?" *Aviation* (July 1940). Although written before Wright joined NDAC, the article suggests the kind of familiarization that was undertaken.

acute for the aircraft industry as well as other elements of the economy. The plight of the industry can be explained most readily by coming down to cases. For example, when an important air arm subcontractor complained of a pressing need for a certain machine tool necessary to continue his flow of production uninterruptedly, he asked if there were not some standard, routine procedure whereby he might qualify for a priority to obtain the desired tool without delay. This was a legitimate request and a most logical one too, since the mobilization planners were generally understood to have spent the long peacetime years preparing for just such an eventuality. Unfortunately, the air arm had little positive response to make other than to cite a recent enactment of Congress authorizing such priorities.[36] Obviously the new law would remain entirely meaningless until it was translated into administrative procedures and put into force.

The plain truth of the matter was that after more than six months of effort, no detailed procedures had been worked out to cope with the intricate question of priorities; all seemed to wait upon the action of Congress, which finally came at the end of June 1940.[37] Thus, as the newly appointed civilian staff of NDAC assembled, the officers in ANMB were only beginning to contrive ways to execute the system of priorities. The peacetime planners had visualized the civilian agency as taking over a going concern set in motion at the onset of the crisis. In the event, the civilian NDAC began to consider the question of priorities at almost the same time as did the military ANMB.[38]

The ANMB, of course, was only a headquarters agency for resolving Army-Navy conflicts, in this instance the relative importance of the claims of their respective contractors. The actual point of contact between business and the armed services remained, for the Army at least, the Ordnance Department, the Quartermaster Corps, the Air Corps, etc. It was these services conducting day-to-day business with the contractors that received the complaints and passed them on to the ANMB. For the Air Corps, this point of contact with manufacturers was not the office of the Chief, OCAC, in Washington, but the remotely located arm of that office, the Materiel Division at Wright Field. The typical Air Corps contractor, of course, had only the vaguest notion of the ANMB, whereas he was actually dealing with the engineering and contracting officers at Wright Field. It was, therefore, both logical and sensible to direct contractors with priority requests to file them through already familiar channels. The arrangement involved a minimum of confusion and delay, but at the same time it created a new problem in itself. With Wright Field in Ohio and the ANMB sitting in Washington, who would plead the case of air arm

---

[36] Adel Precision Products Corp., Burbank, Calif., to Arnold, 28 Jun 40, and reply, 11 Jul 40, AFCF 004.4.

[37] Act of 28 June 1940, Public Law 671, 76th Cong. For evidence of earlier War Department concern with the priority question, see, for example, ASW to Pump Engineering Service Corp, 1 Dec 39, SW files, Air Corps Gen Questions, item 734.

[38] See Memo, Secy, ANMB, for CofAC, 17 Jun 40, for details of the board's priority committee and its formation. A priority procedure was worked out about a month later. See Proposed Procedure, 10 Jul 40, AFCF 334.7 ANMB.

ORGANIZING FOR PRODUCTION

priorities before the ANMB? To resolve this difficulty the Chief of the Air Corps established a Priorities and Allocations Section in OCAC to serve as a special mediator and advocate for all air arm requests.[39]

The advantages of maintaining a special advocate in Washington were obvious. The Priorities Section was ever ready to present arguments in favor of giving priority treatment to aircraft manufacturers for tools, materials, and component items. Air arm officials believed, not without reason as it turned out in practice, that it would pay dividends to "retain counsel." On the other hand, there were also some disadvantages in this arrangement. The more layers or echelons placed between contractors in the field and the top of the ladder in Washington, the more numerous the opportunities for misunderstanding, delay, and multiplication of papers—not to mention the difficulties involved in educating the staff members concerned in each additional echelon.

The general procedure worked out by ANMB and the services for handling priorities was to deal with individual cases as they arose.[40] When, for example, Bell Aircraft asked for a priority on the delivery of a much needed Warner-Swasey turret lathe, the request went to Wright Field where most of Bell's earlier contractual contacts had been made. After surveying the situation, officials there found that a lathe of the desired type could be secured by diversion from an order previously placed by another Air Corps contractor, the Lycoming Manufacturing Company. This information was sent as a claim or request to the Priorities and Allocations Section of OCAC, where it was presented for adjudication to the ANMB priorities committee.

The officers of ANMB did not take long to discover that decisions such as the one raised by the Bell request were exceedingly difficult to make. Was the end product at Bell more important than the end product at Lycoming? Is an airframe more important than an engine? And even where the relative importance of the end products was clear, as in extreme cases, it proved difficult if not impossible to make intelligent decisions on priorities since seldom were all the facts in hand. Before assigning priorities on vertical boring mills, for example, it was necessary to determine the number and specifications of all those required by contractors holding current orders and the number available or on order with the tool builders. This involved a series of telegrams and phone calls to muster the desired data—not only for boring mills and machine tools in general but for other critical items as well such as raw materials and component parts.

The competition for tools and supplies was not, of course, confined to contractors supplying the Air Corps. Airline operators, anxious to expand with the war boom, began to place orders in increasing numbers with the aircraft manufacturers. Since no statutory profit limit curbed the aircraft builders' net on sale to commercial carriers, such orders held a considerable allure even against the large volume promised in military con-

---

[39] Chief, Allocations and Priorities Sec, to Admin, Exec, 2 Dec 40, and 21 Dec 40, and Col W. F. Volandt, OCAC, to Secy, ANMB, 13 Nov 40. All in AFCF 321.9D.

[40] For a description of this procedure, see ANMB Priorities Com Cir No. 1, 9 Dec 40, AFCF 334.7 ANMB.

tracts. The obvious result was a conflict of interests: civilian versus military production. This was equally true in the matter of export customers for military aircraft. The second half of 1940 was the peak period of foreign armament purchases in the United States, and aircraft represented a major element of these transactions. Thus not only did manufacturers find foreign orders more profitable, but in a number of instances they accounted for a larger volume of business than sales to the Army and Navy.[41] As a consequence, the contests for materials and other scarce items were not always confined to Army versus Navy or even military versus civilian orders but also included domestic versus foreign orders. And in some instances, where a manufacturer held orders from all of the rival consumers, the contest did not even involve different firms but the relative priority of orders on the bench within a single concern.

The whole summer and most of the fall of 1940 were devoted to the search for a workable procedure for dealing with priorities to rationalize the scramble for resources.[42] The task moved slowly. In mid-November the officer in charge of priorities in OCAC could still complain: "An effective system of prior-ity control does not exist."[43] There were a number of explanations behind this confession. To begin with, the officers tackling the problem were but recently assigned and the job was novel. There were no established routines to pursue. This alone might readily account for much of the delay, but there were even more significant factors involved. Mustering information from so many diverse sources proved hard work. Aircraft and component manufacturers were slow to submit reports on the tools and materials they required, even when they were urged to do so. And when they did reply to such requests they sometimes submitted their data in such a useless or incomplete form, requiring follow-up requests for more information before the priorities committee could act with something approximating full information in hand. Air Corps contractors, while calling desperately for machine tools, failed to include in their requests sufficient information as to the specifications of the tools desired or the end products for which the tools were to be used.[44] Air arm staff officers had to educate manufacturers to appreciate the importance of, and the real need for, backing up their priority claims with full supporting data if they hoped to receive favorable action from ANMB.

One explanation for the halting evolution of an effective priorities system may be found in the "business as usual" atmosphere that seemed to persist in Washington. At least one journalist repeatedly jibed at the "national defenders" who "stacked their arms" at lunch until three, quit at four-thirty each day, and

---

[41] Bureau of the Budget, *United States at War*, p. 19. For evidence on significance of airline and export orders, see SW to Donald Nelson, 25 Nov 40, SW files, Airplanes, and related correspondence filed there, especially Memo, CofAC for ASW, 30 Sep 40, item 1794; Memo, ASW for Knudsen, 10 Aug 40; and Lockheed to ASW, 27 Sep 40, item 1860.

[42] A good insight on the problem is contained in Chief, Allocation and Priorities Sec, to Tech Exec, 27 Nov and 4 Dec 40, AFCF 319.1-D. For representative illustrations of the kinds of priority problems encountered, see Chief, Facilities Sec, to Stat Sec, 7 and 28 Jul 41, same file.

[43] Chief, Allocations and Priority Sec, to Tech Exec, 20 Nov 40, AFCF 319.1 Production Rpt.
[44] *Ibid.*

ORGANIZING FOR PRODUCTION

then took Saturday afternoon off.[45] These strictures may have been unduly harsh, but it was undeniably true that the Air Corps was not yet on a war footing administratively, and OCAC had not entirely shaken off its peacetime routines.[46]

There was yet another consideration that tended to retard the air arm in its rearmament effort. The headquarters organization of the Air Corps, OCAC, simply was not geared to the task of mobilization. Apart from individuals of considerable capacity, the organization suffered from a want of administrative talent.[47] One deficiency in particular stands out: the air arm headquarters lacked some of the most necessary tools of command. Procedures adequate for a small peacetime force had become obsolete as the scale of operations mounted. As the number of units and items under discussion rose from tens and hundreds to thousands and tens of thousands, crude manual techniques of office routine broke down. And at the very moment that officials of the newly created NDAC were seeking statistical data on which to premise major plans, air arm officials were just beginning to use machine record tabulations at OCAC.[48]

If the NDAC was a hastily contrived and makeshift organization quite unready to shoulder the tasks confronting it for a long period after its formation, almost the same thing could be said of such permanent military organizations as OCAC and ANMB. For the reasons advanced, the processing of priority requests proceeded at a most painfully slow pace. As late as December 1940, not a single case of interest to OCAC had even reached NDAC; not one had even cleared ANMB.[49]

The officer in charge of priorities at OCAC put his finger on the heart of the matter when he declared that the officials of ANMB had "neither the knowledge, ability or authority" to cope with the priority problem. He was not insulting the individuals concerned but appraising the situation as it existed. The delays in ANMB stemmed from the circumstance that the board was attacking problems quite beyond its terms of reference. The contentions requiring resolution were not, as we have seen, limited to

---

[45] *Aviation,* October 1940, p. 71, and December 1940, p. 99.

[46] While individual officers did indeed work beyond duty hours, the fact remains that during the fall of 1940, the OCAC working day ran from 8:45 to 4:15 with a half day on Saturday, and the record reveals no civilian employees earning overtime pay. See Memo, OCAC for all divisions, 19 Sep 40, and Memo, Plans for Exec, 2 Oct 40. Both in AHO Plans Div 145.91-246. For evidence on petty peacetime restrictions that continued to inhibit operations, see, for example, TWX, PES to Admin Exec, OCAC, 13 Dec 40, WFCF 111.3 Munitions Program Requirements.

[47] For general criticisms of administrative efficiency, see Memo, CofAC for Plans, 8 Apr 40, AFCF 321.9-B; R&R, Exec, OCAC, to Chiefs, Mat, Plans, and T&O Divs, 17 Oct 40, AHO Plans Div 145.91-246; as well as Secretary Patterson's postwar reflections on lack of "management" in the Air Corps, 6 Dec 45, Pringle Papers, 18h.

[48] Machine record tabulations had long been used in supply operations at Wright Field, but despite frequent discussions on the subject from 1938 on, little was done in OCAC to provide effective administrative tools of this character until well into the war period. See Rpt of special com of Mat Div (SO 217), 14 Sep 40, AHO Plans Div 145.91-246, and Col Farthing to Col Spaatz, 22 Dec 39, AHO 145.91-391. Machine records were first initiated at OCAC in November 1940, almost six months after the real mobilization began. See, Memo, J. M. Farrar for CofAS, 28 Oct 41, AFCF 321.9 AAF Stat Control.

[49] Allocations and Priorities Sec, OCAC, Weekly Activities Rpt, 11 Dec 40, AFCF 319.1-D.

those arising between the Army and Navy but were conflicts involving domestic airlines and orders placed by the British Purchasing Commission (BPC) as well as other foreign orders. What was needed, the OCAC officer insisted, was a "procurement priority" to superimpose upon the existing system of "military priorities." While the ANMB could iron out conflicts between the military services, it was clearly beyond the powers of the board to cope with the current difficulty since the real rivalry of the moment was between the orders of the armed forces on the one hand and of the airlines and foreign nations on the other. In such a situation only a national civilian agency such as NDAC could hope to reconcile priority contests effectively.

Far from trying to enlarge the powers of ANMB or the military services at the expense of the civilian agency, the air arm priorities officer urged that all final decisions on priorities should rest with NDAC, "the only agency with the necessary perspective and jurisdiction to consider the aircraft industry as a unit and . . . successfully administer priorities." In this proposal he was supported by his superiors, who urged that just such a course be followed.[50] Indeed, so pressing was the need for a single, strong, centralized means of co-ordination and control, air arm officials urged the appointment of a single head to "adjudicate conflicts" currently being encountered in the several agencies dealing with aircraft production—the Treasury, OCAC, OASW, the Navy's Bureau of Aeronautics, the ANMB, and the British Purchasing Commission, all in addition to the Production Division of NDAC.[51]

In the light of subsequent strictures by civilian officials in the great mobilization effort, it is of interest to note that air arm officers sought to enhance the powers of NDAC rather than curtail them. The officers did this when they discovered anew from experience what they had known in theory all along: effective mobilization of the national economy for war is impossible without some form of central co-ordination. Co-ordination, they came to realize, involves more than the mere recording of facts in some central agency. Co-ordination implies a synthesis or rationalization of strategic plans with production schedules, an apportionment of resources—men, materials, facilities, and output—among the various claimant groups so as to match in the most efficacious way the complex ends desired with the limited means available. As matters stood, no single agency existed that could provide such a synthesis. The semiautonomous commissioners of NDAC were certainly not organized to do the job. They lacked not only co-ordination among themselves but were uncertain where their powers began and the powers of others left off.[52] Until this particular difficulty could be resolved and until a truly effective agency for co-ordination emerged, the mobilization effort

---

[50] *Ibid.* See also, Memo, Asst CofAC for ASW, 12 Dec 40, Weekly Activities Rpt, 19 Dec 40, AFCF 319.1-D.

[51] Memo, Asst to CofAC (Gen Brett) for ASW, 19 Dec 40; Memo, Asst to CofAC for Gen Marshall, 19 Dec 40. Both in AFCF 452.1 Airplanes, Gen. See also, AC Project Rcds (Lyon Papers), bk. 56.
[52] WPB Special Study 3, pp. 1–2.

ORGANIZING FOR PRODUCTION

seemed doomed to suffer an endless series of inefficient and wasteful conflicts.[53]

The Achievement of Co-ordination

Although the culmination of the mounting demands for an effective system of centralized co-ordination and control over the national mobilization did not come until December 1940, insofar as aircraft were concerned, responsible officials had taken a long step in that direction months before with the formation of a special co-ordinating committee for aircraft production. From amidst the welter of wartime agencies, this committee in particular offers insights of significance into the general problem of organizing production in time of national crisis.

Until the President established the NDAC, responsibility for co-ordinating aircraft export sales with Army and Navy procurement rested, in theory at least, with the President's Liaison Committee. This committee, it will be recalled, reported through the Secretary of the Treasury for reasons of political expediency. However, since the Treasury was in an echelon parallel to the War and Navy Departments, the committee faced an inherently impossible task in its effort to cope with the rivalry of Air Corps and British spokesmen for the lion's share of available aircraft output. Far from serving as a passive recorder of facts or even as an impartial arbiter, Secretary Morgenthau became a litigant in the rivalry.[54]

With the formation of the NDAC, this anamolous situation began to clear up. In July Commissioner Knudsen of the Production Division arranged a meeting of representatives from the Army, the Navy, and the British Supply Council to decide upon a slicing of the aircraft production pie.[55] All present agreed that it would vastly facilitate aircraft production if a single authoritative committee could be set up embracing Army, Navy, and British members to make binding decisions on all three parties concerning the apportionment of productive facilities in the United States, rationalizing the flow of materials, and so on.

While the formal establishment of an Army-Navy-British (ANB) committee on aircraft was still under discussion, the enormous value of such a group was demonstrated by two steps taken on the basis of the informal collaboration already accomplished. The first step took the form of a production schedule projected by NDAC staff members from the division of output agreed upon in July at the meeting conducted by Knudsen. This schedule spread the aircraft in the current procurement program month by month over the next two calendar years. For the first time since the beginning of the rearmament effort, it was possible to plan comprehensively, and individual manufacturers could find out what total

---

[53] For an insight on the misunderstandings that marred the teamwork of the period, see Memo, Exec, OASW, for CofS, 9 Dec 40, SW files, Airplanes, item 1901, as well as the retrospective comments of Maj Gen J. H. Burns in Memo for M. S. Watson, 20 Feb 48, OCMH.

[54] Details of this difficult situation are suggested in Watson, *Chief of Staff: Prewar Plans and Preparations*, pp. 305–09.

[55] For an excellent brief account of this meeting and the agencies formed as a consequence, see R. D. Masters, *Handbook of International Organizations*, Carnegie Endowment for International Peace (New York: Columbia University Press, 1945), pp. 249–53.

burden they might be expected to shoulder. For the first time individual manufacturers were able to get a comprehensive view of their tasks and decide whether or not facility expansions would be necessary. In addition, the month-to-month schedule made it possible to order materials and component parts on a rational basis of scheduled need rather than all at once in panic lots that swamped vendors and suppliers alike.[56]

Meanwhile, at Wright Field the second by-product of the ANB meeting in July was coming to fruition. Manufacturers had repeatedly pointed out that standardization among Army, Navy, and British purchases would pay large dividends in production by permitting the use of single assembly lines, longer production runs, and lower unit costs. The absurdities to which the absence of standardization could lead were perhaps never better demonstrated than in the situation at Douglas Aircraft where seven different models of the same aircraft, each embodying minor variations to satisfy different customers, were all proceeding toward completion simultaneously.[57]

While it was readily apparent to everyone concerned that month-by-month schedules and standardized designs would be a great stride forward in rationalizing and thus increasing production, it was equally apparent that neither the schedules nor the standardized designs decided upon were decisions that would stay put. Each week, even each day, would raise new difficulties and introduce new and unexpected variables jeopardizing or voiding the steps already taken. The obvious answer lay in the formation of an agency or administrative mechanism to continue to make such decisions, revising the monthly schedules as circumstances dictated and reaching decisions on standardization in the case of each new item of equipment developed. After many conferences and informal meetings during the summer of 1940, the organizational solution finally contrived was officially designated in mid-September as the Army-Navy-British (ANB) Purchasing Commission Joint Aircraft Committee.[58]

Formation of the Army-Navy-British Purchasing Commission Joint Aircraft Committee marked the beginning of a genuinely effective system for co-ordinating aircraft production in the United States. Although the committee represented the bulk of the aircraft orders currently placed, its membership did not

---

[56] WPB Special Study 21, p. 35; ARCO Admin Office, History of the Aircraft Resources Control Office of the Aircraft Production Board and Predecessor Agencies: May 1940–September 1945 (hereafter cited ARCO Hist), 29 Sep 45, p. 4.

[57] Lt Col C. E. Branshaw, resident representative at Douglas Aircraft, to Asst Chief, Mat Div, 27 Jun 40, WFCF 452.1 Standardization of Aircraft. For a survey of this topic in general, see USAF Hist Study 67, Standardization of Air Materiel 1939–1944: Controls, Policies, and Procedures, Nov 51. See also, ARCO Hist, pp. 62–68.

[58] In addition to *Handbook of International Organizations,* and WPB Special Study 21, see Joint Aircraft Committee Organization and Function, pamphlet issued 1 Jan 42 by JAC, AFCF 334.8 JAC. The long delay in establishing the joint committee, 23 July to 13 September 1940, may have been but one of the unfortunate results of the dispute at this time between the Air Corps and the Navy over their respective aerial functions. See AGO Rcds Sec, WPD–OPD 3807–41 and 888–103, as well as Memo, CofAC for CofS, 3 Jul 40, with related correspondence, AFCF 360.01B, and Memo, CofAC for CofS, 5 Jun 40, AFCF 321.9–C. For further information on the origin of JAC, see AAF Hist Study 6, Distribution of Air Materiel to the Allies: 1939–1944, AHO, Jul 44, *passim.*

ORGANIZING FOR PRODUCTION

at the start embrace the whole of the nation's output. In addition to the export orders placed by the British and those taken over by them when the French government fell, there were dozens of foreign states placing aircraft orders in this country, orders that were still handled by the Secretary of the Treasury through the Liaison Committee. Likewise, orders from the domestic airlines fell outside the competence of the committee. For all its advantages, the committee was not all embracing and could not hope to co-ordinate the aircraft program in one grand synthesis. This piecemeal assault on the problem could be—and subsequently, was—rectified by executive action redefining the committee's authority to include control over all aircraft produced in the United States.[59] Nevertheless, so long as it continued to operate parallel to but apart from the NDAC staff, the ANB Committee was certain to be of limited value. This became increasingly evident after a month or two of operations and led to agitation for recasting the committee with broader powers over the aircraft program.

In every echelon of activity in the national mobilization as the fall of 1940 wore on, responsible officials came to recognize the crying need for centralized, high-level, decision-making bodies to co-ordinate and control the intricate game of production currently under way. They were beginning to learn from experience what they already knew from departmental doctrine. Thus it came about that during December 1940 the various agitations in military circles for a strong central co-ordinating agency coincided with favorable circumstances elsewhere. By this time the Presidential elections were safely over, and the NDAC had more or less completed its shakedown.

Just before Christmas the President took a major step forward when he decided to establish the Office of Production Management (OPM).[60] By this move he superimposed a co-ordinating agency on top of the existing NDAC, absorbing virtually all of its functions. This was undeniably an awkward arrangement. However, the involved considerations inducing the President to create a form of dual leadership with Knudsen and Hillman as director general and associate director general have already been suggested in the discussion of the NDAC, and need not be recounted here.[61] It is sufficient to note that the formation of OPM carried the administration of the national mobilization one step nearer to a single centralized agency such as the War Resources Administration conceived by the prewar planners.

Though not an ideal co-ordinating agency, OPM at least offered greater possibilities than the loosely contrived NDAC. Once the initial confusion accompanying the formation of OPM had

---

[59] Memo, ANBPC Jt Com for SW, 5 Nov 40; Memo, CofAC for CofS, 22 Nov 40. Both in AFCF 400.174. See also, Actg SW to Chairman, President's Liaison Com, 20 Nov 40, SW files, Airplanes, item 1885a.

[60] See Executive Order 8629, January 7, 1941, creating OPM, in Rosenman, *Public Papers and Addresses of Franklin D. Roosevelt*, IX, 689, item 154. See there also, Administrative order and attached note, 7 Jan 41, and item 147, p. 622, and item 153, p. 679, press conferences explaining OPM.

[61] For suggestions on the political problems behind the formation of OPM, see Bureau of the Budget, *United States at War*, pp. 50–55, and *Barron's*, September 16, 1940, p. 4, and November 25, 1940, p. 4.

subsided, the Aircraft Section of OPM (taken over from the NDAC) was combined with the existing Army-Navy-British Purchasing Commission Joint Aircraft Committee. The officials of the OPM Aircraft Section had the legal responsibility for co-ordinating the mobilization effort in general and the aircraft program in particular. Moreover, they alone could co-ordinate the aircraft program with the mobilization as a whole through the machinery of OPM. On the other hand, the ANB Joint Committee in its turn was capable of a unique contribution too. Its members represented three different going concerns. Each of these had its long established relationships with industry, and each had its years of accumulated experience. In addition, the members of the committee either occupied positions high in the military hierarchy and near the point of effective decision making or enjoyed ready access to those who did. Clearly the combination of organizations offered decided advantages, and on 22 April 1941 by mutual agreement the interested parties decided upon just such a move.[62]

The expanded committee, which added OPM representatives as voting members to the Army-Navy-British Purchasing Commission group, styled itself the Joint Aircraft Committee (JAC).[63] The two War Department members were Maj. Gens. Henry H. Arnold and George H. Brett. The Navy members were Rear Adm. J. H. Towers and Capt. D. C. Ramsey; thus both the Air Corps and the Bureau of Aeronautics were represented by officers in the top echelon of command. The two members from the British Supply Council were Sir Henry Self and Mr. C. R. Fairey, both from the British Purchasing Commission, the former an Under Secretary in the British Air Ministry, the latter a well-known British aircraft manufacturer. The two members from OPM were Mr. Merrill C. Meigs, head of the OPM Aircraft Section, and Mr. T. P. Wright, whose work in the NDAC and OPM had already won him considerable recognition quite apart from his reputation in engineering circles.

By the terms of its organic directive, the JAC was put in a position to give the aircraft program the kind of co-ordination and control it required. The directive vested the committee with power to schedule all deliveries: Army, Navy, British, other foreign orders, and domestic commercial orders. This included the power to schedule the production of component parts as well as end products, and the power to make decisions prescribing standardization to be binding on all the parties concerned.[64]

In practice the mandate of the JAC brought several far-reaching results. Disputes among the several users or agencies sharing in the end products could be settled speedily by frank discussion among the principals, who had authority to make their decisions binding.[65] This was par-

---

[62] WPB Special Study, 21, pp. 14-15.
[63] SW to Gen Arnold, 22 Apr 41, AGO Rcds, SW files, Airplanes. The term *Joint* was, in the light of subsequent developments, rather unfortunate, for *joint* came to be used for Army-Navy agencies whereas the term *combined* was used for U.S.-British agencies.

[64] *Ibid.*
[65] For illustrative instances of the type of disputes confronting JAC, see SW to SN, 8 Mar 41, and JAC to CNO and CofS (April 1941), in AGO Rcds, WPD-OPD 888-103, as well as Chief, Bureau of Aeronautics, to CGAAF, 14 Feb 42, and Memo, Exec, Mat Div, to CofS, 16 Feb 42, AFCF 452.1 Production.

ORGANIZING FOR PRODUCTION

ticularly significant in the matter of standardization. Having pursued their courses independently and freely for many years, the Army, the Navy, and the British had each evolved numerous items of equipment along entirely different lines. This was especially true with regard to armament, communications, oxygen equipment, and other such accessories. Standardization in these areas would require great concessions by all if substantial gains in the direction of simplification were to be attained, and, especially after the passage of the Defense Aid Supplemental Appropriation Act in March 1941, standardization was more than ever essential if the production authorities were to increase output by reducing the number of different types of the same item being turned out.[66]

Probably no single function of JAC was more important than its role in issuing continual revisions of the aircraft production schedule. This the committee accomplished by simply revising repeatedly the initial effort NDAC made in scheduling. Report 8 on airframes was projected through a series of revisions designated 8A, 8B, through 8L in March 1943, when a major recasting took place to convert the schedules from a "target" basis to a more realistic basis of deliveries believed to be possible. Similar schedules were extended from the original NDAC Report 9 on engines and Report 10 on propellers.[67]

The three reports and their revisions constituted a most useful tool for mobilization planning and control. All depended upon these basic schedules. Not only were they vital in planning to keep each of the three major items—airframes, engines, and propellers—in proper relation to one another, each schedule also provided the directive for an enormously complex series of activities following in its wake. If, for example, the official airframe schedule called for a monthly rate of production that a given aircraft builder could not meet, then expansion of facilities might be required. This would set up a demand including such critical items as structural steel and machine tools with which to equip the new facilities—in addition to the raw materials and components required to construct the prescribed number of airframes on the basic schedule. Each such collateral demand—for steel, tools, components, etc.—of itself set in motion a similar chain of events that involved an equally complex set of responses. The schedule was the heart of an intricate network of impulses. The task of the planners and co-ordinators was to keep the whole delicate network in balance. If combat operations showed an aircraft type to be obsolete, it might have to be removed from the schedule. Or a manufacturer might fail, despite all urging and assistance, to meet the output prescribed in the schedule. In either event the schedule was revised accordingly. This in turn involved a careful reapportionment of all the various types

---

[66] JAC, Organization and Function, 1 Jan 42, especially exhibit entitled "Organization and Function of Working Subcommittee on Standardization of the JAC." Typical items standardized, in addition to aircraft as such, included: safety belts, seats, pyrotechnique equipment, spare parts for engines, and self-sealing fuel tanks. Mr. T. P. Wright served as chairman of this committee throughout the war.

[67] ARCO Hist, pp. 31–39, and WPB Special Study 21, pp. 15–22.

of contributory items that were being fed toward the end product. Unless these items too were diverted and directed into useful channels, much of the national mobilization effort would be lost. The great contribution of JAC stemmed from its capacity to make and enforce the decisions so vital in keeping the production schedule sensitively balanced, attuned to the facts of the ever-evolving mobilization scene.

That JAC was a successful agency is perhaps best attested by its survival to the end of the war. Since it was a successful administrative device, it may well justify careful analysis. This seems especially true inasmuch as the prewar mobilization planners never mentioned any organization similar to the JAC. What were the peculiar characteristics or features making this unique and entirely unplanned agency so useful and so successful in surviving the periodic reorganizations that beset all other wartime agencies?

The JAC in Retrospect

One explanation of the survival and effective operation of JAC during the war years can be found in its stature. The agency was established high enough in the chain of command to speak with authority. Its decisions were binding. But this very advantage carried with it an inherent disadvantage, for the higher one goes in the echelons of command, the further one gets from the facts of the case. As one mounts further and further from the level of day-to-day operations, the more difficult it becomes to secure the information so necessary in making sound decisions. While it is all very well to create an agency at the highest echelon to speak with authority, the decisions of such an agency are no better than the facts and figures fed to it. This problem —the fundamental need for a close relationship between the decision-making and the operating echelons—was recognized by a number of experienced air arm officials. Some, indeed, were only too well aware of the frustrating isolation that beset "desk" officers in Washington remote from the engineers at Wright Field.[68] Although the special circumstances that separated the Washington headquarters from the matériel functions at Wright Field made this a particularly difficult matter for the air arm, the problem applied to any hierarchical organization.[69]

The Joint Aircraft Committee was no exception to this general rule. It had to face the fundamental problem of how an agency can keep its head in the upper stratosphere of command and still retain its feet upon the solid ground of fact derived from a working familiarity with operations at the grass-roots level. Broadly speaking, the solutions JAC contrived involved two separate administrative devices.

The first administrative mechanism to be tried was the "working subcommittee." For this device there was ample precedent in the experience of the Joint Board, which for years had freed its high-ranking members from well-nigh impossible burdens by assigning most if not all of the staff papers to working parties of

---

[68] For pointed illustrations, see IOM, Chief, Mat Div, for CofAC, 13 Sep 39, AFCF 321.9 Mat Div Organization; and Memo, ACofAS, MM&D, for CGMC, 4 Jun 43, AFCF 452.01B Production.

[69] ANMB, for example, encountered much the same sort of difficulty. See Secy, ANMB, to CofAC, 10 Sep 40, AFCF 334.7 ANMB.

younger officers. Thus, JAC appointed subcommittees on allocations, standardization, and so on, with appropriate subgroups specializing in everything from armor plate to windshields. The subcommittees, of course, could be no better than the talent serving them, so in the composition of these working parties lay the success or failure of the device. But here lay the rub. To transplant a well-informed engineer from Wright Field to Washington was to cut him off from the roots that continuously nourished him with new information—precisely the information that made him valuable to the committee. This difficulty was resolved by the use of visiting witnesses, experts, project engineers, and the like, men thoroughly familiar with their own specialties, who could be called in to give evidence before the committee when needed but not kept so long as to remove them from intimate contact with their work.[70]

Insofar as the problem of standardization was concerned, JAC successfully blended the authority of high rank with the technical ability of specialists by the use of visiting experts, but in the matter of scheduling and allocation somewhat different techniques were required. The compilation of accurate production schedules projecting many months into the future depended more upon the realism of the estimates supplied by the manufacturers than upon the technical skill of individual witnesses before JAC or its subcommittees. In July 1943, for example, JAC received information to the effect that the Fisher long-range fighter, P–75, anticipated the following production in 1944: 1 unit in May, 10 in June, 50 in July, 100 in August, 175 in September, and 250 in October.[71] If this projection was accepted by the JAC scheduling subcommittee, a whole sequence of correlated factors would be set in train: an appropriate number of Allison V–3420 engines would have to be earmarked to meet this schedule as well as propellers, landing gears, and hundreds of other components, accessories, and materials. As it turned out, the P–75 never emerged from the test stage, let alone reached full production.[72] To have scheduled the flow of vast quantities of materials for the P–75 would have impaired the war effort by diverting scarce resources into what turned out to be a dead-end road. Clearly the schedule makers could be no more accurate than the data received by them. And it was realization of this circumstance that led JAC to its second solution for keeping its feet on a firm foundation of accurate information.

Besides authorizing the use of expert witnesses, the directive establishing JAC also provided for the formation of a working echelon, the Air Scheduling Unit (ASU), at Wright Field. The ASU was to serve as a central clearinghouse for information from the industry to JAC and from JAC to the industry.[73] The directive did not devise the scheme of

---

[70] For insights on some of the problems involved in the use of expert witnesses before the working subcommittees of JAC, see IOM, Asst Exec, Mat Div, OCAC, for Tech Exec, WF, 21 May 41; Chief, Engr Sec, Mat Div, OCAC, to Chief, PES, WF, 28 Aug 41; and IOM, Chief, PES, for CGMC, 28 Mar 42. All in AFCF 334.8 JAC.

[71] Memo, ACofAS, MM&D, for JAC, 21 Jul 43, AFCF 452.01B Production.

[72] *Army Aircraft Model Designation*, June 1946, pp. 76–79. Total number procured (of 2,500 on production contract) was six.

[73] SW to Gen Arnold, 22 Apr 41, SW files, Airplanes.

the working echelon for JAC but merely took official cognizance of an arrangement that had been in operation for some time. Like JAC itself, the Air Scheduling Unit was not planned; it grew out of the accidents of circumstances.

When the President replaced the NDAC with OPM during January 1941, the civilian officials charged with co-ordinating aircraft production realized the futility of trying to perform the mass of detailed work on production co-ordination with a yet-to-be-recruited staff in Washington when the Air Corps already had a trained staff doing this very type of work at Wright Field. Discussion was still under way on a plan to establish a working echelon for OPM at Wright Field when in February 1941 a directive from Knudsen, the new director general of OPM, ordered the Aircraft Section (OPM) to utilize the existing Production Engineering Section of the Air Corps' Materiel Division at Wright Field as a working staff and point of contact with the industry. By April it had become apparent that even with the best will in the world, an air arm monopoly in the flow of information to the Aircraft Section of OPM as well as to JAC was hardly conducive to the ideal of impartiality. By mutual agreement, therefore, the existing unit, the Air Scheduling Unit of the Production Engineering Section at Wright Field, was modified to serve the several contending interests of the Washington echelon—the Army, the Navy, the British, and OPM—by adding representatives from the parties involved.[74]

In practice the modified ASU was a board of three officers, Army, Navy, and British, along with an OPM representative. These men together served as a field staff (for JAC as well as OPM) reconciling conflicts whenever possible without reference to Washington. Of course, three or four officials in Ohio were no more capable of handling the vast array of details—surveys, allocations, etc.—involved in scheduling the aircraft program than were three or four officers sitting in Washington, even if those in Ohio were nearer to the vital source of information. The ASU had to rely upon the existing staff services of the Air Corps Materiel Division at Wright Field. By the end of 1941 more than 100 officers and 800 civilians at the Materiel Command headquarters were employed in executing the mechanical details of scheduling: assembling bills of materials, compiling flow charts and delivery schedules, reconciling conflicts, and adjusting other difficulties. In 1942 more than 3,000 civilian and military personnel, including both Army and Navy officers, were absorbed in this work.[75]

The task performed for ASU was truly staggering. There were some 6,000 or 7,000 different types of end items to handle. These involved more than 9,000 different bills of materials, any one of which might embrace from one to literally hundreds of different types of components and basic raw materials.[76] All the items and quantities had to be coded

---

[74] WPB Special Study 21, pp. 16–19.

[75] Col W. S. Cave, RAF, British History of the Aircraft Scheduling Unit, May 45, copy in ICAF Library, pp. 5–6. This historical sketch, including illustrative supporting documents, gives an excellent cross section of the ASU in operation. Colonel Cave was the British representative on ASU throughout its life.

ORGANIZING FOR PRODUCTION

and carded for machine records tabulation. Then, when total requirements had been compiled—for any given moment and always subject to major change—the gap between need and available supply had to be reconciled in terms of the end item preferences laid down in JAC directives, by whatever expedients seemed best. Sometimes ASU would divert a shipment of materials or components from one user to another to meet a temporary crisis, arranging meanwhile to "repay" the loan in the next shipment. Sometimes ASU "borrowed" components already delivered and in stock at one end-product assembly plant and "loaned" them to another similar end-product plant to prevent impending stoppages along the assembly line. On at least one occasion an ASU agent broke up an impending shortage by pleading successfully with an alcoholic diemaker to stay sober just long enough to finish the critical item he had in hand.[77]

In general, the technique of ASU was informal. Staff members worked by phone, telegram, letter, or personal visit to arrange *ad hoc* adjustments, based on the willing co-operation of the parties concerned. Only as a last resort, in about one case in a hundred, was it necessary to employ mandates, formal compulsory directives binding under law.[78] Surely, here was impressive evidence of the patriotic spirit of the nation's often maligned businessmen. Shortages needing relief frequently ran to more than 1,000 a month. Between 1942 and 1945 ASU received formal requests for assistance in reducing 50,000 bottlenecks, and this figure ignores entirely an unknown number of informal requests.[79]

Accident and chance played a large part in the evolution of the Air Scheduling Unit. The name itself tells the story. What started out as a unit within a branch of a section in the Air Corps' Materiel Division ultimately became an international or combined Army-Navy-British and OPM agency for adjusting the flow of materials for an aircraft program involving literally dozens of claimant nations on a worldwide basis. In a sense, the story of ASU is the story of JAC. Neither was planned; both evolved. They were the expedient outgrowth of experience—men groping pragmatically until they hit upon workable and successful organizations to cope with situations confronting them.

To call JAC a success is to oversimplify. This device of command did indeed work and on the record worked well. But if administrative history is to have any real meaning, it would seem to be of more importance to know why JAC worked well than to sing in praise of its

---

[76] The Air Scheduling Unit, prepared under direction of Brig Gen E. W. Rawlings, Sep 45, in Pringle Papers, OCMH, p. 6.

[77] For an excellent account of ASU in operation, supplementing Colonel Cave's account mentioned above, see History of Navy Membership in the Aircraft Scheduling Unit, 1941–1945 prepared by the Bureau of Aeronautics representative on ASU, Jun 45.

[78] Cave, British Hist of ASU.

[79] The ASU, p. 5. History of Navy Membership in ASU gives the following breakdown of 47,000 critical shortages mentioned on page 18: 56 percent concerned materials and 44 percent concerned components. Of materials, 21 percent were in steel, 22 percent in aluminum, 9 percent in other nonferrous metals, and 4 percent in nonmetallic items. Of aircraft components, 23 percent were in bearings, pumps, valves, fittings, etc.; 13 percent were in electrical equipment; 3 percent in landing gear; 2 percent in engine accessories; and 3 percent in radio and instruments. This sample was taken after February 1943 and thus does not accurately reflect the whole war period.

accomplishments. The individuals who served on the committee deserve full credit for their contribution to whatever effectiveness it may have had, but, in attributing achievements to the men involved, it is possible to overlook the part played by the conditioning circumstances —the organizational structure and procedures that gave scope to and made possible the work they did. In other times chance will place different men in these or similar roles, and the varying abilities of those who served in the past will be of far less moment than the historical record of the organization in which they served.

The Joint Aircraft Committee bridged the gap between the authority of high command on the one hand and on the other the familiarity with technical details found in the operating echelons. This it did by a series of administrative devices: working subcommittees, visiting experts, field parties with delegated powers, and so on—each evolved in practice. Sometimes the evolutionary process was halting and painful. There were stresses and strains, not to mention repeated malfunctionings. As rival interests jockeyed for power there were personality clashes and instances of acute interservice competition against and amongst the representatives of JAC.[80] On occasion the whole mass of paper in the JAC mill seemed to lag and accumulate in hopeless confusion.[81] Yet out of all this there emerged an effective tool of administration. Moreover, at least some of those in positions of authority actually did garner significant lessons from this experience, as subsequent events were to demonstrate.

After Pearl Harbor the more centralized War Production Board (WPB) replaced the OPM, but through most of 1942 this change had little direct effect upon the organization for aircraft production beyond alterations in terminology. During the fall of 1942, however, the continuing gap between the vast programs of aircraft production planned and the disappointing level of output on the assembly lines led to an agitation for reform.[82]

As chairman of WPB, Donald Nelson was inclined to attribute much of the trouble to the existing administrative system. Whatever his intentions were, in air arm circles they were regarded as an effort to build up a Washington staff —perhaps in the nature of a Ministry of Supply—to replace that already functioning at Wright Field. General Arnold's memory extended back to World War I when a similar concentration in Washington was tried with results that were unimpressive if not disastrous. In the light of this experience, he pointed out

---

[80] For an example of the political hazards encountered by JAC, see Memo, Maj Timberlake for Col Meyers, 10 Oct 41, and Gen Arnold to Senator Lister Hill, 14 Oct 41, AFCF 334.8 JAC. For an example of personality conflicts, etc., see Memo, Rear Adm R. Davison for Brig Gen G. E. Stratmeyer, 19 Mar 43, with related correspondence, AFCF 334 JAC. For examples of the tendency of various claimants to seek membership on JAC, see Brig Gen B. E. Meyers to Dir, Gen Dept of Munitions and Supply (Canada), 19 Sep 42, and CGASC to CGAAF, 30 Jan 43, with Inds, AFCF 334 JAC.

[81] Memo, Deputy Recorder, JAC, for Chairman, Subcom on Production Programs, 26 Apr 43, AFCF 334 JAC. For a typical example of the grist in the JAC mill, see Memo, Actg CofAC for CofAAF, 31 Dec 41, AFCF 334.8 JAC.

[82] ARCO Hist, pp. 21–22.

ORGANIZING FOR PRODUCTION

certain fundamental weaknesses in the Nelson scheme: a board such as the one that seemed to be proposed could speak neither authoritatively for command, as could JAC, nor could it possess the knowledge of technical details available to ASU.[83]

General Arnold must have placed his shots well; in the subsequent reorganization of the aircraft production organization, the features he had identified as essential were retained. The Joint Aircraft Committee remained intact. And, although the Aircraft Branch of WPB was abolished, its functions were absorbed by the newly created Aircraft Resources Control Office (ARCO), which served as a secretariat or working party for the Aircraft Production Board (APB) established within WPB as the top decision-making and co-ordinating agency for air matériel.

Significantly, both of the newly established agencies, APB and ARCO, made use of the principles for which General Arnold had argued. As soon as it was set up, ARCO delegated most of its operations to the ASU at Wright Field, which continued operating as if no change had occurred. Equally revealing was the composition of the new Aircraft Production Board. It mirrored the pattern found successful in JAC and drew its members from the ranks of officials in the highest echelons, both military and civilian, who could speak with informed and decisive authority—men who knew what they were talking about and had the power to act.[84]

Not least among the external factors contributing to the effectiveness of the new machinery for co-ordinating aircraft production was the physical location of the offices involved. Whereas the original Aircraft Branch of WPB had been housed in the Social Security Building, where Mr. Nelson had his headquarters, the reconstituted Aircraft Board and its administrative offshoot, ARCO, were moved into the Pentagon. This greatly facilitated dealing with military procurement officials. At the same time, there was no loss of contact with WPB, for the chairman of the Aircraft Production Board, Mr. C. E. Wilson, was also vice chairman of WPB.

Thus, by the end of 1942, when the penultimate aircraft production reorganization took place, insofar as air matériel output was concerned the agencies for controlling and co-ordinating production had been hammered into a rough approximation of what the mobilization planners had recommended for many years during peacetime. To be sure, the actual forms of the organizations finally contrived were certainly unlike anything visualized by the prewar planners, but the principles underlying them were essentially traditional: centralization of authority for co-ordination and decision and decentralization of operations in order to leave the technical details in the hands of those familiar with them.

---

[83] CGAAF to Donald Nelson, 22 Nov 42, AFCF 452.01A Production.

[84] ARCO Hist, pp. 23–30, as well as British and Navy histories of ASU cited.

CHAPTER XIII

Legislation for Procurement

Wartime Buying With Peacetime Laws

The Problem: Inadequate Laws

At the momentous White House meeting of November 1938 the Administration turned a corner in policy and decided upon aerial rearmament.[1] At that time the President called for 10,000 aircraft in two years' time. This Executive pronouncement stirred up a flurry of planning activity in Air Corps and War Department circles as crash programs were concocted to meet the new target figures. And in short order the major obstacle blocking completion of the President's bold new program became all too evident.

To procure 10,000 aircraft in the United States—or even half that many—within the two years prescribed was patently impossible if the War Department were constrained to use the forms of competition prescribed by law and by administrative ruling.[2] Under the prevailing system of competitive procurement evolved during the thirties, contracts for production quantities of aircraft were awarded to the manufacturer who submitted the best sample aircraft in an open competition involving advertising for bids months in advance, the laborious fabrication of samples to be submitted, a careful evaluation of these samples, and, finally, the drafting of contracts with the winning manufacturer in each competition. This process may have been scrupulously fair and quite above reproach politically, but it was time consuming. Moreover, it led to a well-nigh fatal concentration of business. Who won the competitions? Presumably the most efficient manufacturers. The rearmament program had no sooner got under way than it became clear that the bulk of the production contracts was concentrated in the hands of three or four firms who soon had more work than they could handle. To deliver within the two-year program period these firms would have to expand their facilities. But meanwhile more than a dozen aircraft manufacturers, the losers, were confronted with empty factories and idle assembly lines for want of aircraft orders. Unless some means could be found to circumvent the requirements on competitive bidding, it would be impossible to meet the President's target figure in time.

The laws governing aircraft procurement were peacetime laws hardly suited to an emergency situation with its crash programs seeking overnight results. The

---
[1] See above, ch. VIII.
[2] Memo, CofAC for ASW, 28 Feb 39, AFCF 452.1 Proc of Aircraft. See above, chs. IV and V.

normal, legally prescribed procedure, for example, stipulated that advertisements for competitive bids had to be carried in three leading aviation journals inviting returns in ninety days. When Air Corps staff officers tried to carry out the President's hurry-up program during February and March 1939, they discovered that aeronautical journals as well as aircraft manufacturers had to have lead time. Not until the issues of the following month could they insert their invitations to bid, and this would mean that bids would return no sooner than the following July.[3] The forms of law were geared only to the needs of peace. As a consequence, Air Corps attack bombers, a type in which the air arm was sadly deficient at the time, even if promptly procured with funds from fiscal year 1939, would not be delivered until July 1941, two years hence.[4]

If the President's instructions were to be carried out, Air Corps officials had to find some way to circumvent the obstacles in the law and spread the production load over the entire aircraft production capacity of the nation.[5] Their first effort in this direction was to scan the language of the existing laws themselves in the hope of finding some loophole to cope with the situation. Sure enough, the legislators had anticipated exemptions and deviations under certain circumstances. The Defense Act of 1920, for example, authorized the Secretary of War to procure by direct negotiation, without regard to the usual statutes calling for competition, "in time of war or when war is imminent." This would seem to provide just the authority desired. Unfortunately, this convenient escape route was blocked as a solution to the problem. An old opinion of the Attorney General held that "emergency" procurement for a time when war was "imminent" could only be construed to mean "unanticipated" procurement. Since the President's 10,000 aircraft program was hardly unanticipated, this door was closed.[6] Similar restrictions blocked all practical use of the escape clause in Revised Statute 3709 which stipulated the general use of competition in government procurement. Here too accretions of legal barnacles vitiated the clear intent of the laws when the emergency the lawmakers had anticipated finally did arrive.[7]

Inasmuch as the procurement laws appeared to offer no obvious or convenient loopholes, Air Corps officers had perforce to cast about for alternatives. It might be possible, they believed, to attain the ends sought by administrative action within the existing laws. With this in mind officials at Wright Field turned to the Air Corps Act of 1926 and dusted off the long unused device of the design competition authorized in Sections 10a to 10i. The use of a design competition gave the War Department a good deal of latitude.

---

[3] Memo, Dir, Current Proc, OASW, for CofAC, 4 Mar 39, SW files, Aircraft, item 1107.

[4] Memo, Gen Arnold for SW, 20 Oct 38, AFCF 452.1.

[5] For a detailed argument on the need for spreading the work load across the productive capacity available, see Memo, Exec, OCAC, for ASW, 13 Mar 39, AFCF 452.1–13E, Proc of Aircraft. See also, Memo, CofAC for ASW, 24 Oct 38, same file.

[6] Memo, W. M. Reading for Gen Arnold, 21 Oct 38, and unsigned Memo (not sent) for JAC, 22 Oct 38. Both in AFCF 452.1A Proc of Aircraft. See National Defense Act of June 3, 1916, as amended June 4, 1920, sec. 120.

[7] Service Sec, Proc Div, ATSC, Prewar Procurement by the Air Corps, p. 18.

Not only did it shorten the time for opening bids but it also authorized direct negotiations with more than one manufacturer on production contracts under certain circumstances. However, by no stretch of the imagination was the design competition a panacea. Design competitions in 1939 and 1940 were sure to suffer from the same faults that led to their abandonment before. Instead of buying a known product, a sample aircraft reduced to practice, with the design competition the Air Corps would be buying a paper promise to perform that might or might not turn out satisfactorily.[8] And what is more, even when using a design competition a firm already filled beyond capacity with production orders might well win the contest.

The Solution: New Legislation

When War Department officials and Air Corps officers failed to solve their problem either within the existing statutes or by administrative action, they concluded that there was only one course left open. They would have to seek new legislation from Congress authorizing them to abandon competition in aircraft procurement during the current emergency. With new legislation such as this, they could negotiate directly with manufacturers at will, placing contracts wherever the exigencies of the situation and the availability of capacity dictated.

In short order the headquarters paper mill began to grind out draft bills, officers in OCAC as well as OASW and the Army JAGO contributing. The final version stated in part: [9]

... hereafter, whenever the Secretary of War ... determines such action to be in the public interest, he may in his discretion, in addition to any other method prescribed by law, purchase ..., with or without competition, such aircraft, aircraft parts, aeronautical equipment, or aeronautical accessories from such sources as he may elect. ...

But almost as soon as this proposed bill was polished to a proper finish, War Department officials began to have sober second thoughts about the wisdom of putting it into congressional hands. Any attempt to introduce novel legislation, however desirable, might well open the gate to congressional tampering with some of the most useful aspects of the existing laws, notably section 10k of the Air Corps Act. In fact, some congressmen had already done just what air arm officers most feared: proposed legislation that in curing one complaint would cause a whole new sequence of ills by introducing violent changes in the existing scheme of statutes.[10] Moreover, as air arm representatives discussed their proposal on the Hill, they discovered that congressional sentiment was cool indeed to the whole idea of negotiated contracts. There were a number of factors that seemed to have helped in shaping congressional opinion

---

[8] Memo, CofAC for ASW, 22 Mar 39, AFCF 452.1 Aircraft Requirements Program; and Immediate Action Letter, Chief, Mat Div, to CofAC, 22 Mar 39, AFCF 452.1-13E Proc of Aircraft.

[9] Memo, Dir, Current Proc, OASW, for JAG, 12 Nov 38, and 1st Ind, JAGO to ASW, 18 Nov 38, Army AG Gen Rcds Sec 400.12 (18 Nov 38); Memo, CofAC for CofS with Incls, 14 Dec 38, AFCF 030 President and Congress; Memo, Col Warren for CofAC, 2 Mar 39, AFCF 452.1-13E Proc of Aircraft.

[10] H.R. 3804, introduced February 7, 1939, 76th Congress, 1st session, for example, would have imperiled Section 10k of the Air Corps Act. See draft of SW to Representative May, Chairman, House Military Affairs Com, 16 Mar 39, AFCF 032 Air Corps Act and Amendments.

on the subject of negotiated contracts. In part, faith in competitive bidding was a product of the general congressional climate prevailing ever since the sensational hearings of the middle thirties.

Another circumstance that may have helped to shape opposition on the Hill was the fact that the aircraft manufacturers themselves, speaking through the Aircraft Chamber of Commerce, were opposed to abandonment of the established principle of competition in quantity procurement of aircraft. Several considerations were present to motivate such a seemingly contradictory stand taken by the manufacturers, many and even most of whom did not hold production contracts for military aircraft. To begin with, President Roosevelt's scheme for a series of air arsenals or government-owned facilities to provide standby capacity against any sudden demand for output in war frightened many manufacturers.[11] To some, no doubt, this reeked of socialism; even for less doctrinaire partisans any such plan spelled trouble in the form of increased competition in a business already subject to periods of feast and famine.

Even if the President did not press his air arsenal idea, a very similar threat had appeared in another quarter. This was a Senate bill proposing the establishment of an Aviation Engineering Center, a sort of aircraft TVA to be used as a yardstick on costs in the aircraft industry.[12] This project, a hardy perennial in Congress, was quite sufficient to intimidate the industry at large. There was little need to fear that undue profits would be exposed for few if any manufacturers in the industry were so fortunate as to enjoy them, but all knew, as one journalist expressed it, that any government yardstick would never be 36 inches long.[13] The aircraft manufacturers took the only course that seemed open to them. They climbed on the congressional bandwagon and signed the pledge as faithful believers in the higher virtues of good old-fashioned competition—among themselves, that is, and not between privately owned and government-owned facilities.[14]

Under the circumstances, air arm staff planners realized there was little hope for the legislation they proposed. The War Department bill, which would have authorized the placement of contracts without competition, was filed away in the traditional departmental pigeonhole until Congress in general, and the House Military Affairs Committee in particular, adopted a more receptive mood.[15]

Without the amelioration expected from new legislation authorizing negotiated contracts, the troubles of the Air Corps continued to mount. Moreover, each temporary and expedient improvisation failed, as had makeshift arrangements in the past. Which is to say, because the Air Corps lacked the power to place contracts rationally, where capacity was available, business continued to concentrate in the hands of those few firms that won in open competition. In a total

---

[11] See above, pp. 177–79.
[12] H.R. 5197 and S. 1738, 76th Cong, 1 sess. See also, Senate Military Affairs Com, Hearings on S. 1738 to establish a military aircraft engineering center, April 7, 1939.
[13] Stubblefield, "Washington Windsock," *Aviation* (August 1939), p. 53. See also above, pp. 124–26.
[14] J. H. Jouett for ACC to ASW, 1 Feb 39, with Incls, AFCF 030 President and Congress.
[15] R&R, Supply Div to CofAC, 17 Feb 39, cited in AAF Hist Study 22, p. 65.

of 537 pursuit aircraft for which funds were available, the necessity of awarding contracts competitively brought the apparently inevitable result: a single manufacturer won the competition and received orders for 524 of the 537 to be purchased. Yet on every hand rival manufacturers—the losers—continued to stare at virtually empty factories and silent production lines.[16]

Air Corps attempts to ease the situation by awarding service test contracts helped to distribute the load somewhat. Service test aircraft were classified as experimental items and could be purchased without competition under Section 10k of the Air Corps Act. At best, however, this remedy had only limited utility since, under the prevailing legal interpretation of Section 10k, not more than fifteen aircraft of any one type could be purchased in this manner.[17] Nevertheless, even an order for fifteen items was helpful in encouraging manufacturers to get production under way.

For a brief period during the fall of 1939 air arm officials believed they had stumbled upon an ingenious solution for their difficult problem. They hoped they could avoid the time-consuming delays encountered in awarding contracts only through competition by the simple expedient of exercising options on those contracts, extending the number of items to be purchased as desired. Here again, unfortunately, the law stood in the way. The prevailing ruling held that options could not be extended endlessly, even if the bidders were willing—which was not always the case.[18]

One after another the various administrative expedients failed. At last it became apparent that a trip up to the Hill could no longer be delayed. If Army airmen were to be provided with adequate air power in the current emergency —in quantity and on time—remedial legislation would have to be sought no matter how dangerous such a step might be and no matter how unpropitious the climate around the Capitol.

Return to the Hill

When War Department leaders finally decided to secure a revision of the statutes governing aircraft procurement, they planned their maneuver with considerable care. As a first step, they tried to persuade Congress that the War Department had no intention of proposing a permanent departure from the prevailing practice of competitive procurement. General Arnold let it be known that he was deeply attached to the principle of competition. He professed to oppose the whole idea of negotiated contracts—in principle. But as to the present emergency, that was another matter. Without abandoning one iota of his belief in the benefits of competition as a general rule, he urged the necessity of deviation in time of crisis. The present moment, he declared, was just such a crisis.[19]

---

[16] CofAC to ASW, 8 Jul 39, AFCF 452.1-13F Proc of Aircraft.
[17] *Ibid.*
[18] 1st Ind, Current Proc Br, OASW, to CofAC, 30 Sep 39, basic unknown, AFCF 452.1 Aircraft Requirements Program; P. G. Johnson, of Boeing, to J. P. Murray, 19 Mar 40, SW files, Aircraft, item 1454.
[19] See, for example, testimony of Gen Arnold, Hearings of Subcom of House Appropriations Com on supplementary WD appropriation for 1940, May 19, 1939, p. 62.

LEGISLATION FOR PROCUREMENT 279

As a second step in their campaign to sell the idea of negotiated contracts to Congress, War Department officials had doctored the text of their original bill to make it more palatable—to congressmen if not to the aircraft industry. They tacked on a proviso which ostentatiously applied the profit limitations of the Vinson-Trammell Act of 1936 to all procurement that might be effected under the proposed measure.[20] Taking the profits out of war, forestalling the profiteers, was certain to alienate few votes and it might go far to dispel any notion that the War Department had a sinister purpose in mind when it asked for power to negotiate contracts rather than adhere to the tradition of sealed bids.

As a third step, supplementing the other preliminary approaches to the Hill, the Assistant Secretary urged the President to lend the prestige of his backing to the measure sought by the War Department.[21] But the President no doubt recognized a hot potato when he met one. Although he approved the bill drafted by the Department, he was apparently unwilling to give it his blessing or come out publicly and wholeheartedly for it. Journalistic scuttlebutt at the time hinted that the President's reluctance stemmed from his unwillingness to contradict himself; having used General Foulois and his negotiated contracts as a scapegoat in the airmail and aircraft procurement hearings of the middle thirties, it was suggested, he was now unwilling to ask for the power to negotiate that he had so recently criticized.[22] Whatever his motives, the President gave the bill no special backing.

With all the preliminaries out of the way, War Department officials in July 1939 hopefully sent their bill to the Hill.[23] There it made no headway at all. This was not surprising in view of the long prevailing mood of Congress. Even the doctored version of the bill failed to excite any enthusiasm in the House Military Affairs Committee. The committee members, no less than the President, were well aware of the attitude of Congress on the question of negotiated contracts. Confronted with the chill reception at first base, the staff officers riding the bill lost no time in bemoaning its fate. They knew the measure would never carry, so they returned to the task with a compromise, a bill drafted along entirely different lines.[24]

The new proposal did not ask Congress to grant the War Department what military officials really wanted and needed, that is, blanket authority to negotiate aircraft contracts at the Secretary's discretion and without resort to competitive bidding. Instead, it called for competi-

---

[20] Memo, Col Warren for CofAC, 2 Mar 39, AFCF 452.1–13E Proc of Aircraft.

[21] Memo, Dir, Current Proc, OASW, for ASW, 8 Jul 39, with inclosed drafts of letters for President to sign, AFCF 452.1–13F Proc of Aircraft. See also, AAF Hist Study 22, p. 69.

[22] Stubblefield, "Washington Windsock," *Aviation* (September 1939), p. 53.

[23] The bill was introduced by Representative May, Chairman of the House Military Affairs Com, as H.R. 7111, 76th Cong, 1st sess, July 10, 1939.

[24] The new bill, sponsored by Representative Dow Harter of Ohio, was H.R. 7267, 76th Cong, 1st sess, July 10, 1939. See SW to Representative May, 21 Jul 39, SW files, Aircraft, item 1229, and AAF Hist Study 22, p. 70. Perhaps the most striking evidence of congressional suspicion is to be seen in Public 168, 76th Congress, July 13, 1939 (53 Statutes 1000), which authorized procurement of secret devices "without advertising" but only after first securing three reputable bids.

tion as in the past but with a new twist. Now, instead of awarding an entire production contract to a single winner, the compromise bill proposed to authorize awards, at the Secretary's discretion, to the first, second, and third bidders in order of merit.[25] This was the so-called split-award provision.

The split-award measure, which included the profit-limiting proviso of the earlier War Department bill, retained the advantages of competition and thus, in the eyes of Congress, protected the public purse. Yet, at the same time it did provide the Department with some latitude in permitting negotiations on price with the second and third place winners. On balance, the split-award bill would appear to have been a rather watered down compromise to which no one would take exception. However, even this limited authorization was resisted on the floor of the House, where the fear of negotiated contracts was repeatedly expressed. One member, for example, asked, with characteristic if erroneous distress, if the proposed measure would not permit awards to the "highest bidder."[26] Against such opposition even the compromise split-award bill made slow progress. Introduced in July 1939, it was not finally made into law until March 1940, only two months before the disaster that was soon to befall the democratic cause in Europe.[27]

Procurement Law: An Appraisal

This, then, was the situation at the beginning of the new year 1940. Even as Hitler posed his forces for the dramatic and terrifying assaults that marked the early spring, the Congress continued to see no emergency. As a consequence, Air Corps procurement for the coming year had to be by formal advertisement and bids—by the traditional safeguarded procedure of competition.[28]

If the law lagged dangerously behind the facts in the matter of authorizing emergency power to negotiate contracts, this was equally true with regard to other statutory provisions concerning procurement. Certainly it was so with most of the statutes originally enacted to promote social welfare rather than military efficiency. Many of the welfare statutes, indubitably meritorious in conception and intent, created serious problems for those concerned with national defense as a few illustrative instances will show.

The Buy American Act of 1933, as its name implies, was intended to encourage domestic industry by requiring all purchases for the government to come from within the nation.[29] Just as the Buy American Act was to protect the nation's businessmen, the Walsh-Healey Act of 1936 and the Eight-Hour Law of 1912 were designed to protect labor.[30] The Eight-Hour Law, drafted originally to abolish the notorious stretch-out, forbade all labor in excess of the eight-hour day

---

[25] Merit was determined by the formula that had been worked out to equate performance, utility as to types, price, etc. See above, p. 138.

[26] *Cong Rcd*, July 31, 1939, p. 10538. See also, Appendix, p. 4107, extension of remarks by Representative Harter, as well as testimony in Hearings of Senate Military Affairs Com on S. 2868 (H.R. 7267) 76th Cong, 1st sess.

[27] Public 426, 76th Cong, March 5, 1940 (54 Stat 45).

[28] TWX, Exec, OCAC, to Tech Exec, WF, 24 Jan 40, WF Proc files, 400 Proc Method.

[29] Public 428, 72d Cong, March 3, 1933 (47 Stat 1521).

[30] Walsh-Healey Act, Public 846, 74th Cong, June 30, 1936 (49 Stat 2036); Eight-Hour Act, Public 199, 62d Cong, June 19, 1912 (37 Stat 137).

on public works. Among its many provisions the Walsh-Healey Act required contractors on government work to meet the prevailing minimum wage and pay time and a half for labor in excess of the 40-hour week. Similarly, the various anti-kickback acts imposed heavy fines and prison sentences on contractors extorting rebates from employees engaged on public works.[31]

The statutes mentioned above, a list representative rather than exhaustive, were broadly conceived as social legislation for general application in time of peace. Congress had recognized, specifically in some cases, that amendment or outright suspension would be necessary in time of war. But what about the twilight zone that was neither peace nor war? What about the period of rearmament from the White House decision in November 1938, to the attack on Pearl Harbor? In present-day jargon, this was an era of cold war, but most unfortunately the statutes made no mention of such a circumstance.

As the aircraft expansion program gathered headway in the summer of 1939 and, one after another, contracts were let, the War Department began to receive a wave of complaints. Many manufacturers were dismayed at the inclusion of the Eight-Hour Law stipulations in their contracts. They were more than willing to pay time and a half for overtime, they assured the Department, and had made their bids accordingly. Only belatedly had they discovered that the Comptroller General insisted upon the eight-hour clause in their contracts as an absolute prohibition on work in excess of eight hours in any single day. Even with overtime work allowed, the shortage of skilled labor constituted a serious deterrent to the rearmament program. Responsible procurement officers believed that the Comptroller's intransigent insistence upon the exact letter of the law might bring outright disaster by leaving the nation unarmed in its hour of peril.[32]

There followed a frantic appeal to the Attorney General whose lawyers went burrowing after precedents to authorize an escape. The search was no doubt hastened on when one of the nation's leading engine manufacturers, in fact the sole source for liquid-cooled, in-line engines, flatly refused to bid on an Air Corps contract containing the Eight-Hour Act provisions. This refusal was neither autocratic nor unpatriotic; the manufacturer was quite willing to pay for overtime work but to comply with the eight-hour curb on labor would have disrupted his entire plant, which was already at work on an overtime basis.[33] For months the various legal advisors of the Government passed this question to and fro. At last, during the catastrophic days of May 1940, Congress acted to suspend the Eight-Hour Law during the emergency.[34] Meanwhile, nine precious months had been lost.

---

[31] See especially, Public 798, 71st Cong, March 3, 1931 (46 Stat 1494); Public 324, 73d Cong, June 13, 1934 (48 Stat 948); and Public 403, 74th Cong, August 30, 1935 (49 Stat 1011).

[32] Memo, CofAC for ASW, 15 May 40, AFCF 161 Contract Requirements. See also, Compt Gen to SW, 19 Oct 39, WF Proc files, 016 Compt Gen Decisions; and 17 Compt Gen 937.

[33] TWX, Contract Sec, WF, to Contract Sec, OCAC, 14 May 40, for Allison case; J. K. Northrup to Contracting Officer, Mat Div, 25 Jun 40. Both in WF Proc files, 016, Compt Gen Decisions.

[34] Copy, SW to Compt Gen, 13 Feb 40, and related correspondence, SW files, Aircraft, item 1411.

Another difficulty arose from a strict compliance with the Walsh-Healey Act and its related statutes. For effective enforcement, these laws required the submission of public contracts to the Secretary of Labor for approval. In addition, manufacturers were required to inform the Secretary of the Treasury each week the exact wages paid to each employee engaged on a public contract, including not only the labor force of the prime contractor but the employees of all subcontractors as well. Even in peacetime, compliance with these provisions imposed a heavy burden of administrative overhead. As the nation rearmed during 1939 and 1940, the difficulties of administration became well-nigh insupportable. The number of subcontractors on many contracts multiplied from tens to hundreds. By the spring of 1940, the average airframe manufacturers had between 300 and 400 subcontractors and one airframe builder had more than 700 of them.[35] Employment rose, sometimes almost overnight, from hundreds to tens of thousands. Obviously, under such circumstances, full compliance with legislation drafted when labor desperately needed such safeguards threatened to become utterly unworkable in a period when labor had a seller's market.[36] The national defense effort, including work on the B-17, Boeing's famous Flying Fortress, appeared to be menaced by a bookkeeper's nightmare—all because no legislative provision had been made to take into account the situation presented by a period of rearmament that was neither peace nor war.

Probably no statute better shows up the difficulties than does the Buy American Act. As the flood of defense orders began to absorb a larger and larger portion of the nation's resources and acute scarcities appeared in many raw materials, manufacturers and suppliers began to protest against the restrictions of the law that required military purchases to be made within the United States. Their complaints reached something of a climax over the problem of supplying aviation fuel for Air Corps units stationed in the Panama Canal Zone. Tank storage there was inadequate, and tankers were not always available. As an expedient, the supplier, Standard Oil of New Jersey, wished to transport aviation gasoline from the United States to Aruba, the Dutch isle off the coast of Venezuela where the corporation had ample storage facilities. From Aruba, Standard Oil could readily supply the needs of the Panama defense forces without delay. However, since the tanks at Aruba also stored oil from Venezuelan sources, the corporation could not honestly certify that the product withdrawn from the common tankage was the very same as that shipped originally from the United States. After a delay of weeks, War Department attorneys found a way out of this dilemma in a five-page legal opinion holding fuel to be a fungible commodity comparable to grain in a common elevator and therefore not identifiable.[37]

---

[35] Col M. C. Cramer, JAGD, to Actg Asst Solicitor Gen, 23 May 40, JAG (Army) Rcds Gen Sec, 160 Contracts (4 Dec 39).

[36] A good illustration of the staggering administrative burden involved in compliance with the statutes in question may be found in: Murray, of Boeing, to Chief, Mat Div, 30 Oct 39, and Memo, JAG for ASW, 13 Dec 39, WF JAGO Kickback file.

[37] Memo, Asst to Dir, Purchases and Contracts, OASW, for JAG, 13 Aug 40, and 1st Ind, JAG to ASW, undated. Both in WF JAGO, Buy American file.

LEGISLATION FOR PROCUREMENT

Thus it turned out that some six weeks after the President had declared aviation fuel "essential to defense" by formal proclamation, the Buy American Act still intruded delays in the national mobilization program.[38] It continued to do so until well after Pearl Harbor, for as late as June 1942 contracting officers were still worried over the legality of contracts that omitted, at the direction of the Secretary of War, the Buy American stipulation.[39]

To pursue the roster of statutes that posed difficulties to the nation's rearmament program is unnecessary. The examples cited illustrate that the statute books contained laws for peace and laws for war, but the laws were inadequate for an era of cold war or half-war such as that existing from the time the Air Corps expansion program began in 1938, or at least from the outbreak of war in Europe during 1939, to Pearl Harbor.

Improvising Legislation in a Crisis

The Turning Point

President Roosevelt's message of 16 May 1940 in which he asked for 50,000 aircraft marked the real turning point for procurement legislation in the United States. Where before the Congress was suspicious, it was now openhanded. The President took an entirely unqualified stand in behalf of more arms—such a stand as he had not taken during the previous summer when Assistant Secretary Louis Johnson urged him to support

even so modest a request for discretionary powers as that contained in the split-award bill. But now the rush of events had caught up with him. After the Wehrmacht triumphs in Europe, his dramatic plea for 50,000 aircraft was no longer far out in advance of public opinion, nor, for that matter, was it far ahead of congressional thinking; the mood of Congress had changed. Where only a few short months before congressmen had refused to see the emergency described by military officials, they now asked, "What can we do to strengthen the nation's defense?"[40] "Tell us your needs," senators urged the Army and the Navy, as they hastened to give priority to defense legislation already on the Hill and to consider whatever additional legislation the emergency required.

Emergency Legislation

The first fruits of the new enthusiasm in Congress for military measures took the form of money bills—vastly enlarged appropriations to finance defense spending.[41] Even more significant, however, were the bills drafted to speed up the procurement process. In the week following the President's plea for 50,000

---

[38] Proclamation 2413, July 2, 1940, in *Federal Register*, V, No. 30, July 4, 1940, 2467.

[39] TWX, Contract Sec (Washington) to Contract Sec (WF), 22 Jun 42, WF JAGO, Buy American file.

[40] For congressional reluctance to recognize the emergency as such, see House Hearings on supplementary WD appropriation for FY 1940, May 19, 1939, p. 62. See also *Aviation* (September 1939), p. 53. For the changing mood of Congress, see, for example, *Cong Rcd*, May 14, 1940, p. 60844, and House vote on H.R. 9850, 76th Cong, 3d sess, May 24, 1940.

[41] Appropriation for FY 1941, June 13, 1940, Public 611; 1st Supplement, June 26, 1940, Public 667; 2d Supplement, September 9, 1940, Public 781; 3d Supplement, October 4, 1940, Public 800. All 76th Cong, 3d sess.

aircraft at least half a dozen measures of signal importance to national defense were referred to committees for consideration. In the Senate and House both the military and the naval committees set to work on these proposals and in a matter of days reported out bills that would effect fundamental and even revolutionary changes in military buying.

The first bill of importance to military procurement to be enacted after the President's address was not, strictly speaking, an Air Corps bill, although it was to have a far-reaching effect upon air arm operations. The act authorized the Reconstruction Finance Corporation (RFC) to lend money or to buy stock in corporations organized to promote national defense. The Defense Plant Corporation (DPC) set up under this act was empowered to extend loans to manufacturers needing working capital and to finance facility expansions. The underlying philosophy of the act is evident: the RFC could absorb any postwar losses better than could private bankers who were understandably reluctant to underwrite the high risk of immense wartime expansions, which might become utterly uneconomical at the close of hostilities. The application of this act can best be discussed in the following chapter; for the moment it is sufficient to see it as but a single item on the roster of emergency laws.[42]

The second emergency measure to be enacted was one sponsored by Congressman Vinson of Georgia, chairman of the House Naval Affairs Committee. This was essentially a Navy measure; as passed, however, some of its terms applied to the War Department. The Vinson Act (the National Defense Expediting Act) was an involved piece of legislation with many sections and subsections, but the powers it conferred and the curbs it imposed may be summarized briefly.[43]

The act authorized the Secretary of the Navy to negotiate contracts in his discretion. The inhibitions, the fear of fraud that had marked past congressional thinking, were now swept away in a broad grant of powers safeguarded only by the Navy's promise not to use the privilege save when necessary.[44] The act did not stop with negotiation; the Secretary of the Navy was even empowered to modify existing contracts where the exigencies of defense warranted such action. The act also provided for the payment of advances of as much as 30 percent on the contract price to help contractors get defense production started. Once begun, partial or progress payments were authorized before completion of the contract, to help manufacturers meet their operating costs when undertaking projects far beyond the normal range of their working capital.

The Vinson Act also authorized the use of cost-plus-fixed-fee (CPFF) contracts, provided the fee did not exceed 7 percent of the estimated cost. The cost-plus-a-percentage-of-cost (CPPC) contract made odious during World War I was expressly prohibited. In banning the CPPC contract, Congress hoped to deny manufacturers any incentive to pyramid their costs and thus their profits.

---

[42] Public 664, 76th Cong, 3d sess, June 25, 1940 (54 Stat 573). See also, AAF Hist Study 40, pp. 30–32, and ch. XIV, below.

[43] Public 671, 76th Cong, 3d sess, June 28, 1940 (54 Stat 676).

[44] House Rpt 1863, 76th Cong, 3d sess, June 20, 1940, p. 7.

The CPFF contract, on the other hand, gave manufacturers no reason to increase their costs, although it must be admitted that it gave little incentive for reducing them either. But the advantage of the CPFF contract to the government was obvious: using it, manufacturers with little or no experience in operations on the scale proposed in the defense program could be induced to sign contracts they would never touch if compelled to sign the conventional risk-type or fixed-price contract form.

The discretionary powers mentioned above were available only to the Navy, but some provisions of the Vinson measure were intended to govern both Army and Navy procurement. One such was the profit limit on all Army and Navy aircraft contracts. Where previous profit curbs had been set at 10 and 12 percent, the new ceiling stipulated was 8 percent. If actual cost was less than the contract price, the contractor was then allowed to retain 8.7 percent of this cost as his profit. The act also subjected subcontractors to this profit limit whenever the sum involved reached $25,000.

A final feature of the Vinson Act applying to the Army as well as the Navy was the section authorizing the Secretaries to certify to the Commissioner of Internal Revenue as to the necessity for and cost of any additional facilities required by manufacturers to fulfill a defense contract. Certification amounted to a decided tax advantage to manufacturers with munitions contracts since they could write off their capital costs by the amount certified rather than the 5 or 10 percent normally allowed under the prevailing peacetime statutes. All in all, the Vinson measure gave the Navy, and to a lesser extent the Army, broad discretionary powers with which to hasten defense production.[45]

The third major procurement bill enacted after the President's appeal was one sponsored by Representative May, chairman of the House Military Affairs Committee. In its final form this measure was far more sweeping than the Vinson legislation.[46] It authorized the Army to make use of negotiated contracts, CPFF contracts, advance payments, and actually authorized the government to undertake the erection of facilities even when this had to be done on private sites. These provisions conferred powers nearly parallel to those given the Navy. In addition, Representative May's measure included statutory language granting the broadest sort of powers to the President so that he might "provide for emergencies," exercise wide discretion, and buy "with or without competition."

The three acts described above were "emergency legislation" in every sense of the phrase and as such they were noteworthy. The acts gave the Army and Navy what they needed most desperately —sweeping grants of discretionary power to escape the time-consuming restraints of peacetime competitive buying and to place orders with smaller and weaker concerns that could never have won orders competitively, thus broadening the base of defense production.

On the other hand, the character and content of the three acts suggest some-

---

[45] This discretion included the power to suspend certain civil service and social welfare statutes where necessary. For an extended discussion, see Smith, *The Army and Economic Mobilization*, ch. IX.

[46] Public 703, 76th Cong, 3d sess, July 2, 1940 (54 Stat 712).

thing of the inherent difficulty encountered when enacting emergency legislation. Although the problem of industrial mobilization confronting the services was a common one, Congress, operating within the traditional framework of separate committees for the Army and Navy in each house, came up with separate bills for each service. As a consequence, even though there was some overlapping with laws common to both, the Secretary of the Navy enjoyed some powers not given the Secretary of War and vice versa. The two services, then, rushed to rearm under numerous statutes that gave them inequitable and unbalanced powers for dealing with the common tasks of mobilization.[47]

Even more significant than the differing statutory bases of Army and Navy operations was the character of the laws themselves as indicative of the difficulties to be met in emergency legislation. True, the emergency statutes granted broad powers to the responsible civilian Secretaries and even broader powers to the President, but the powers were only a beginning. Discretionary powers—such as the authority to negotiate contracts—were certainly of the utmost utility to the services in speeding procurement. Nevertheless, generous grants of power, when hastily conferred at the penultimate crisis, are no substitute for legislation built out of years of experience, legislation carefully tailored to suit the needs of the services as revealed in practice.[48] In fact, the very passage of the statutes authorizing procurement without competition brewed trouble. The newly authorized power to negotiate contracts opened a whole new field of activity that was soon crying for clarifying legislation—a field hitherto unknown and unexplored, since many of the problems encountered when negotiated contracts were introduced simply did not exist so long as procurement had been restricted to sealed bid competition.

Still another difficulty inherent in emergency legislation was the matter of timeliness. The wide discretionary powers that Congress granted to the military services were adequate only so long as the government enjoyed a buyer's market. Such a situation had existed when the War Department first sought permission from Congress to negotiate contracts. When at last Congress did grant this authority, the whole outlook of the industry had changed. Where before most Air Corps contracts had tended to cluster in the hands of a few successful manufacturers, leaving the rest of the industry idle and begging for work, now, especially after Dunkerque and the fall of France, a flood of orders from abroad had induced a seller's market—the aircraft manufacturers, vendors, and suppliers had more work than they could handle. The military services were authorized to negotiate contracts, but by this time the manufacturers were not particularly interested in negotiating since the industry's order backlog was already mounting by millions of dollars. What is more, export orders were not subject to the profit curbs imposed by Congress. Why, asked the manufacturers, should we dicker with the government and submit

---

[47] By way of illustration, the Secretary of the Navy received authority to seize facilities when necessary by the Act of June 28, 1940, although the Secretary of War did not receive comparable authority until ten weeks later.

[48] See Chapters IV and V for discussion of the importance of operating experience in making new legislation meaningful.

to all the inconveniences and disadvantages of military purchasing when we can sell abroad virtually without strings? Desperate states in Europe with their backs to the wall, ordering in panic, could scarcely afford to bargain as closely with the aircraft manufacturers as procurement officers for the military services at home were certain to do. Some manufacturers, already swamped with domestic as well as foreign orders, even urged procurement officers to give the available orders to their competitors.[49]

In a word, the emergency statutes of June and July 1940 were not only obsolete, already lapped by the course of events when passed, but also created new problems that in turn required legislative solution. Even though conscientiously drafted to permit the widest possible latitude to the departments, the emergency statutes were of necessity only the beginning of a long series of acts, each a piecemeal or patchwork attempt to hasten and foster the nation's defensive mobilization.

Patchwork Laws

Congressional zeal for the cause of defense did not burn itself out with the passage of the laws already mentioned. Symptomatic of the co-operative spirit on the Hill was the resolution, introduced by Senator Tom Connally of Texas, proposing that all defense contracts be required to go on full shift, twenty-four-hour operation. This was enthusiastic co-operation indeed; it was, in fact, a bit too enthusiastic. As War Department spokesmen pointed out, some items in the armament program were less urgently required than many others, and to insist, by compulsory legislation, that all contracts be pursued at full force around the clock might well lead to needless overloading of production capacity to the detriment of the defense effort.[50]

Enthusiastic support from the Hill was most welcome to the War Department, but less compulsion and more elaboration of discretionary powers would seem far more appropriate. During the summer of 1940, experience gathered when operating under the emergency statutes passed just after the President's call for 50,000 aircraft clearly demonstrated the need for further legislation to meet the deficiencies in the measures. New statutes would be needed not only to handle the difficulties growing out of the novel practice of negotiating contracts but also to cope with the exigencies of a seller's market. Congress would have to concoct measures—inducements or coercions—to secure the productive capacity of the nation's manufacturers for the defense effort.

By early fall Congress was ready with a set of legislative patches to cover the flaws the summer's operations had revealed. Within the span of a relatively few days a large number of laws went on the statute books. These, too, were emergency laws, yet in a very real sense the underlying philosophy on which they rested had subtly shifted from what it had been earlier in the season. In the spring the assumption had been that once freed of the requirements of competition,

---

[49] See AAF Hist Study 40, ch. III, n. 23.

[50] S Res 289, 76th Cong, 3d sess, July 1, 1940, text in *Cong Rcd*, July 1, 1940, p. 9098. See also, AF Hist Study 22, pp. 75–76.

contracts could be freely entered with the nation's munitions manufacturers. This second round of emergency laws rested upon a skillful mixture of carrot and stick. Manufacturers were confronted with a series of blandishments and compulsions to participate in the great national defense effort.

The first legislative patch was distinctly carrot. In addition to lavish appropriations to expedite production, the act contained inducements to new and inexperienced firms of uncertain financial standing. Procurement officers were authorized to waive bid bonds, hitherto required of all contractors to guarantee satisfactory performance or money back on the items procured. If some congressmen had had their way, the carrot would have tasted far better; they proposed to raise the profit curb on aircraft manufactured for the United States from 8 to 12 percent of contract price. To the chagrin of the manufacturers, however, this provision was stricken before enactment. On the other hand Congress, ever anxious to take the profits out of war, reduced the allowable fee in CPFF contracts to 6 percent of cost.[51]

The second bit of legislative patchwork insofar as military procurement was concerned took the shape of a club slipped into the epochal Selective Service Act of 16 September 1940. It was, no doubt, shrewd politics to balance the encroachments of the draft upon personal freedom with a commensurate restraint on corporate freedom. At any rate, Congress seized this convenient moment to impose on all government orders an obligatory priority that would ensure delivery on defense contracts ahead of export sales. In conjunction with this, Congress gave the Secretary of War power to seize production facilities from recalcitrant or unco-operative manufacturers who delayed the defense effort. Procurement officials had little desire to wield this club, but its mere presence in the department's legislative arsenal was expected to animate manufacturers with a willingness to negotiate rather than lose their facilities and suffer the heavy fine or imprisonment imposed as penalties.[52]

A month later Congress was still blending incentives and mandates to shore up the system of negotiated procurement with whatever additions and corrections events had shown to be necessary. Of particular interest was a statute designed to help smaller business firms by authorizing the assignment of claims. Under the terms of this act, manufacturers working on defense orders could assign to banks their claims for payments by the government in return for advances in working capital, a practice hitherto precluded by a century-old law.[53]

Without doubt, the most important bait offered by Congress to cajole manufacturers into the defense effort appeared in the Second Revenue Act, 8 October 1940. In this statute, Congress suspended

---

[51] Public 781, 76th Cong, 3d sess, September 9, 1940 (54 Stat 872). See also, House Rpt 2810, July 31, 1940.

[52] Public 783, 76th Cong, 3d sess, September 6, 1940 (54 Stat 885). See also, Cong Rcd, 20 June 1940, p. 8680, and following for evolution of S. 4164, and J. H. Ohly, History of Plant Seizures During World War II, 1947, draft MS, OCMH.

[53] Public 811, 76th Cong, 3d sess, October 9, 1940 (54 Stat 1029). See also, CPA, Policies Governing Private Financing of Emergency Facilities, Hist Rpts on War Administration, WPB, Special Study 12, p. 24.

the profit limit on aircraft entirely.[54] Capitalism rather than compulsion, the congressmen hoped, would induce greater production. And the profits allowed, having served their purpose, would be taken up in the excess profits taxes laid on elsewhere in the same statute. Removal of the profit limitation on aircraft manufacturers was not merely a concession granted under pressure but rather an effort to return the aircraft manufacturers and shipbuilders to the status of all other manufacturers. So long as aircraft and shipbuilding firms, and they alone, labored under profit limitations, they found it difficult if not impossible to get subcontractors (who were subjected to the same profit limitation imposed on the prime contractors) to enter negotiations.[55] And why should subcontractors accept aircraft orders if there were jobs to be had in other segments of industry producing munitions for defense that did not impose profit curbs? Another feature of the Revenue Act, decidedly more persuasive than peremptory, was the section authorizing rapid, five-year depreciation of new facilities certified as necessary for defense by the Secretaries of War and Navy.[56] Under this provision, manufacturers expanding their productive facilities for defense could, on certification, write off 20 percent of their capital outlay each year as depreciation, an unusually advantageous deduction in a period of abnormally high taxes.

In 1941 Congress enacted virtually no legislation of significance to military procurement. The broad powers already conferred left the War Department with a relatively free hand to work out its own problems. Thus, from October 1940 to December 1941, apart from a few relatively minor items such as an extension of the statutory authority already granted, Congress did not alter the procurement laws.[57] Some few bills were proposed calling for important changes, but none passed.[58]

If procurement officers lacked adequate latitude in negotiating contracts before Pearl Harbor, Congress tried to rectify any such omission in the First War Powers Act of 18 December 1941, which authorized the President and his agents to enter contracts without regard to the provisions of existing law when to do so would hasten the war effort. At last all restrictions on the negotiation of contracts were swept away. Insofar as procurement legislation was concerned, this was a capstone.[59] Congress did, of course, continue to add patches and pieces of legislation throughout the war. But with the possible exception of the renegotiation statute which can be considered more conveniently in a subsequent chapter,[60] for all practical purposes, with the passage of the First War Powers Act, procurement officers had just about all the major discretionary powers they needed.[61]

---

[54] Public 801, 76th Cong, 3d sess (54 Stat 974, Title IV).

[55] H. Rpt 2810, 76th Cong, 3d sess, July 31, 1940, p. 8.

[56] 54 Stat 974, Title III. For an extended discussion of the amortization plan in operation, see Smith, *The Army and Economic Mobilization*, ch. XX.

[57] Public 89, 77th Cong, 1st sess, May 31, 1941, (55 Stat 236).

[58] See H.R. 1615, 1775, and 4945, 77th Cong, 1st sess.

[59] Public 354, 77th Cong, 1st sess, December 18, 1941 (55 Stat 838). The Second War Powers Act, March 27, 1942 (56 Stat 176), contained no powers of interest to War Department procurement officers.

[60] See ch. XVII.

[61] For evidence on the adequacy of existing laws for procurement, see IOM, JAG (WF) for Chief, Contract Sec, 30 Sep 41, AFCF 400.12.

CHAPTER XIV

The Problem of Industrial Capacity

The Beginning of Facility Expansions

The Foundations of Policy

The President's call for 50,000 airplanes precipitated a veritable avalanche of correspondence upon the desks of Air Corps staff officers. Not least among their troubles was the question of capacity. Would the productive facilities of the nation's aircraft manufacturers be sufficient to meet this new and vastly enlarged requirement?

The Air Corps had paid a good deal of attention to the problem of productive capacity during the prewar years.[1] Officers concerned with mobilization planning throughout the twenties and early thirties had drawn up rather elaborate factory plans calling for the manufacture of aircraft in the automotive facilities of Detroit during an emergency. All these plans rested upon the assumption that aircraft builders would freely consent to hand over their latest designs for mass production. With the coming of a real emergency, however, this general principle, which had seemed sound enough on paper, now lost much of its appeal.

When War Department officials tried to bring individual airframe and automobile manufacturers together, most of the aircraft builders shied off. They argued that the automobile manufacturers lacked aeronautical engineers and facilities with adequate clearances for the wing span of current aircraft. More significant, perhaps, was the reluctance of the old-line aircraft builders to invite postwar competition among car builders with their well-known reservoirs of tooling skills and working capital. Under the circumstances, Air Corps officers found it necessary in the fall of 1938 to recast entirely their mobilization plans. Thereafter, it was agreed, all final airframe assembly work would be performed by old-line, established aircraft firms as prime contractors. The automotive manufacturers would serve only as subcontractors providing the primes with parts and subassemblies.[2]

As a consequence of this reversal, which redefined the anticipated role of the automotive firms, the detailed factory plans compiled over the past two decades had to be scrapped. Since they were admit-

---

[1] See above, chs. VII, VIII, and IX.

[2] ASW to CofAC, 23 Sep 38, and 1st Ind, CofAC to ASW, 12 Oct 38, WFCF 381 Mobilization (1939); AAF Hist Study 40, pp. 17, 21. The decision not to use automobile manufacturers as prime contractors on aircraft appears also to have rested on lessons derived from the British shadow factory plan. The whole subject of the influence of British experience on U.S. policy is one that could profitably be studied at length. See especially, London Military Attaché Rpt 39854, 4 Jan 39, WF CADO F35/375.

tedly faulty, their demise probably occasioned little real loss.³ Nevertheless, it was this turn of events that led the Air Corps to enter the period of acute national crisis with a policy but no plans.

The Detroit car builders were not the only competitors feared by the aircraft manufacturers. The President's air arsenal scheme was even more disturbing in its implications. To manufacturers who could remember with distaste the acres of empty floor space that burdened them during the depression years, the prospect of competition from federal aircraft plants could scarcely be regarded as other than ominous. Not surprisingly, the industry as a whole broke into a chorus of assurances that the Air Corps rearmament program could readily be accomplished without further plant additions.⁴ In such an environment of fear and misgivings, serious consideration of possible wartime plant expansions was difficult, to say the least, since any suggestion of government-financed facilities, however necessary they might be for war purposes, was bound to bear the taint of nationalization for manufacturers acutely sensitive on this point.

Further complicating the task of determining whether or not the nation's aircraft manufacturers could handle the load was the shifting character of that load itself. What had begun as the President's goal of 10,000 in November 1938, was watered down to some 5,500 in Congress the following winter, only to leap up to 50,000 in May 1940. Each such gyration in quantity, not to mention the matter of quality, models, types, and so on, brought drastic variations in the estimates of capacity required.

All these difficulties were in themselves decidedly upsetting to the mobilization planners, but, as the reader will recall, throughout most of the 1939 build-up period air arm staff officers were actually unable to measure productive capacity with any reasonable degree of accuracy. The program of modified educational orders or production data contracts helped to clarify the problem but did so only belatedly. More useful were the findings of the Yardstick Board, which gave Air Corps staff officers a most necessary tool for planning. But even this measuring stick became available only after war broke out in Europe, and by then the whole problem of aircraft production capacity in the United States had entered a most crucial phase.⁵

By the time the industry had been resurveyed with the Yardstick Board's criteria, several more precious weeks had passed. Therefore, not until the late fall of 1939 did it become generally apparent that vast new facilities would be required in the aircraft industry. In tenor with the prevailing attitude, these were envisioned as additions to existing facilities owned by the aircraft manufacturers rather than as air arsenals or government-owned installations.⁶

---

³ See above, ch. VII.

⁴ ASW to C. W. Larner (Baldwin Locomotive Works), 11 May 39, SW files, Airplanes, item 116Y; Review of Methods Employed by the AAF . . . , ATSC Logistics Planning Div, p. 16. The planners at Wright Field accepted the assumption that the President's air arm build-up could and should be done without further plant expansion. See Chief, Mat Div, to CofAC, 22 Dec 38, AFCF 452.1A Proc of Aircraft. See also above, pp. 175–79.

⁵ See above, pp. 189–93.

⁶ Memo, Dir, Planning Br, OASW, for CofAC, 3 Oct 39, and 1st Ind, reply, 10 Oct 39, AFCF 004.4.

Thus it turned out that in the months immediately before the President's call for 50,000 airplanes, the Air Corps staff officers responsible for mobilization planning were only just emerging from the exploratory stage in which they had endeavored to find out how much aircraft production capacity the nation really did possess. Of necessity, their program for expanding facilities was little more than a sketch, tentative and unfinished. The planners themselves confronted their tasks with a good deal of uncertainty; not only were they inexperienced in the problems of facility expansion, they had to set about their tasks before the necessary enabling legislation had been passed.[7]

The problems of industrial mobilization—including accurate measurement of capacity and the planning of facility expansions—are far too complex and too laden with variables to lend themselves to simple solutions or easy generalizations on policy before the event. Because of this, useful and detailed mobilization planning in advance for facility expansions was difficult if not impossible to achieve. Responsible officers may have been sorely at fault for their prewar failure to explore alternatives of policy with vigor and imagination, but insofar as detailed planning is concerned, it is doubtful whether the most prescient of staffs could have drafted plans to encompass the many parameters of the national scene during the early months of 1940. Whether the military staffs were remiss or not in failing to provide suitable plans in advance for the crisis of May 1940 is now beside the point. The fact remains no plans were available. Even the very nature of the task at hand was unclear.

In his call for 50,000 airplanes the President had boldly set a production target; now the problems involved in reaching this goal required definition.

Commissioner Knudsen of the NDAC suited the needs of the occasion. He was an industrial titan with great prestige. Moreover, he was trained by his industrial experience to look at the "big picture" and reduce it to simplest terms. Having looked, in those agonizing days of May 1940 when all Europe seemed to collapse, Mr. Knudsen drew the whole problem into focus with two blunt questions: "How much capacity do you need?" and "When do you need it?"[8]

How Much and When?

Knudsen's questions defined the job in hand and set in motion a train of action in the War Department.[9] Hitherto no one had so narrowly defined the character of the problem. The President himself had been vague concerning the implementation of his production goal. Soon after his address before Congress, he received a group of reporters as he worked in shirtsleeves at his desk. Engine production was the real bottleneck, he told them; there was already an ample margin of idle airframe capacity. If plant expansions should be needed, private capital rather than public money would do the job.[10] The Secretary of War echoed these assurances—the War

---

[7] See above, chs. VIII and XIII.

[8] Watson, *Chief of Staff: Prewar Plans and Preparations*, p. 174 and n. 106. The words are attributed to Knudsen by Colonel Burns, Executive Assistant to Mr. Johnson. Memo, Burns for ASW, 13 Jun 40.
[9] *Ibid.* See also Wright, "50,000 Planes a Year: How Much? How Long?" in *Aviation* (July 1940).
[10] New York *Times*, May 22, 1940, 10:5.

Department had no intention of erecting aircraft plants with federal funds.[11]

But the President and the Secretary were expressing opinions and intentions, not facts. Mr. Knudsen's provoking challenge showed up their words for what they were and touched off a furious round of conferences and staff studies to get the facts that would answer the questions Knudsen posed.[12]

On the first of July 1940, a month and a half after the President's address before Congress, the combined efforts of the military and civilian agencies produced the necessary answers. On that date the Airplane Division of the NDAC submitted its crucial report on the nation's aircraft productive capacity.[13] To approximate the President's program, a 200-percent increase in floor space would be required. And along with this there would have to be a 400-percent increase in the labor force, widespread agreement on standardization, and willingness to spread the work load across the available capacity, particularly by greater use of subcontracting. To these prescriptions the authors of the NDAC report added an explicit caveat: any attempt to reduce the expansions indicated in the report by postponing the completion date of the program should be avoided as dangerous to national security. Moreover, they warned, manufacturers should be informed in advance of the whole load expected of them. Any other course of action would result in confusion and lost motion by forcing individual aircraft builders to revise and rework their plant expansions with every subsequent alteration in program.

With the facts in hand, it was a relatively easy matter for Army and Navy officials to reach agreement on a slicing of the productive pie. Having decided upon a 36,500 to 13,500 split, each service assumed responsibility for sponsoring the facility expansions required by the manufacturers with whom it held contracts. Where individual manufacturers served both the Army and Navy, the service with the lion's share of business took cognizance.[14]

Although the division of labor agreed upon by the Army and Navy mentioned only airframe and engine facilities, the problem of facilities for accessory items was not ignored. Accessory items were absolutely vital to completed aircraft, but, so long as the small and inadequate staff at Wright Field was preoccupied with airframes and engines, consideration of

---

[11] SW to Joplin, Mo., Chamber of Commerce, 29 May 40; SW to Senator Morris Sheppard, 31 May 40; SW to Senator Tom Connally, 5 Jun 40. All in SW files, Air Corps, Gen Questions, item 809a.

[12] See, for example, AC Project Rcds (Lyon Papers), bk. 29, OCAC Conference, 19 Jun 40.

[13] T. P. Wright and A. E. Lombard, Report on a Study of Airplane Manufacturing Capacity, 1 Jul 40, Airplane Div, NDAC, Rpt 4, copy in AC Project Rcds (Lyon Papers), bk. 22. Report No. 7, 22 July 1940, treated engine capacity. See also, Study 21, p. 26ff.

[14] For Army-Navy agreement of 3 July 1940, see Memo, ASW for ASN, 16 Jul 40, SW files, Airplanes, item 1612. The division was as follows:

Army: airframes: Beech, Bell, Boeing, Cessna, Curtiss, Douglas, Fairchild, Lockheed, Martin, North American, Republic, Ryan, Stearman, Stinson, Vultee
engines: Allison, Continental, Jacobs, Lycoming, Menasco, Wright
Navy: airframes: Brewster, Grumman, Spartan, Vought, Consolidated
engines: Pratt and Whitney, Ranger

See also, CofAC to ASW, 8 Jul 40, AFCF 451.1 Airplanes, Gen. For an indication that the agreement was not foolproof, see Memo, Asst CofAC for CofAC, 10 Dec 40, AFCF, 004.4 Manufacturers.

accessories would have to wait; first things had to come first.[15] Furthermore, just as airframe capacity was hard to measure, so too was it difficult to get precise figures on accessory output. There was no convenient yardstick to estimate capacity for these items; the only alternative was to start from scratch with a new inquiry. A flash survey, pending more exhaustive study, revealed that a substantial number of accessory manufacturers would require plant additions. Magnetos, carburetors, starters, turbo-superchargers, and almost all panel instruments—to mention but a few items—threatened to become dangerous chokepoints unless facilities were immediately expanded.[16]

The NDAC report on capacity had insisted that manufacturers should be informed in advance of the total load to be assigned them so they could plan accordingly. This was sound advice, but it was an ideal scarcely to be achieved. Staff officers were still apportioning the total load and planning expansions to suit this load when it became evident that the "total" capacity figures rested upon an unsound premise. In computing the load, the NDAC officials had assumed that spares and spare parts could be produced in sequence to regular production runs rather than concurrently with them. Thus in the case of propellers, all units turned out were earmarked for use on aircraft scheduled to be produced. There would be no productive capacity available for manufacturing spares until the end of the program. Such an arrangement was utterly unacceptable to the air arm. Concurrent production of spares had to be provided. This meant that "total load" had to be revised upward and manufacturer's plans for facility expansions altered accordingly.[17]

Thus, finding the answer to Mr. Knudsen's questions proved to be slow work. Not until well into the middle of July 1940, did the expansion program gather headway. Even then the question of facilities for the production of accessories had yet to be decided. Moreover, still remaining was the vexing problem of ways and means: how should the proposed facility expansions be financed?

Financing Facilities

On the day following the President's statement on 50,000 aircraft, the Secretary of War had called in a number of officials from the War and Treasury Departments to discuss the problems that might be anticipated in any effort to reach this target figure. All those who met with the Secretary were well aware of the extent to which the nation's aircraft industry had already expanded to meet the demands of foreign purchases. During 1939 aircraft, engine, and propeller plants had been enlarged by approximately a third, to a total of 13,000,000 square feet. The French and British Governments had contributed some $72,000,000 toward accel-

---

[15] AAF Hist Study 40, p. 73.
[16] R&R, Exec, OCAC, to Chief, Mat Div, 28 Jun 40, WFCF 111.3 Munitions Program, and reply, 9 Jul 40, AFCF 452.1 Airplanes, Gen. See also, TWX, PES (WF) to Engr Sec (Washington), 5 Jul 40, WFCF 111.3 Munitions Program, and draft Memo (ASW) for Knudsen, NDAC, 26 Sep 40, AFCF 452.1. For an interesting insight on the question of expanding the facilities of accessory manufacturers, see Fairchild Aviation Corp. to Col Volandt, 23 Jul 40, and reply, 31 Jul 40, AFCF 004.4.

[17] Memo, Actg CofAC for ASW, 12 Jul 40, AFCF, 004.4; TWX, Engr Sec (Washington) to PES (WF), 20 Jul 40, WFCF 111.3 Munitions Program.

THE PROBLEM OF INDUSTRIAL CAPACITY

erating airframe production alone, and there were, of course, numerous additions in floor space and equipment privately financed by manufacturers receiving foreign orders. The Secretary of War and the officials who met with him had every reason to recognize the nation's enormous debt of gratitude to those foreign states, notably Britain and France, who had done so much to hasten the pace of rearmament.[18] Now, however, if further expansions were to be undertaken, they would have to be financed at home. But how? That was the problem.

The various federal officials who considered the problem of facility financing in the weeks immediately following the President's call thought almost entirely in terms of private investment. The government had no intention of financing facility expansions with public funds. Indeed, insofar as plant financing was concerned, the government had no plans at all.

Not until after the President's message to Congress on 16 May 1940 was any really sustained and serious consideration given to the general question of financing the construction of whatever new capacity might be needed in the nation's emergency. Those who finally did begin to grapple with the problem undoubtedly started out with a predilection for private financing, but this did not prevent them from exploring and finally using a number of alternatives.[19]

One rather obvious procedure suggested but immediately rejected as a solution was to add a small increment to the unit cost of each item purchased on a production contract. The advantage of such a scheme was its simplicity. There would be no new and complicated procedures to evolve, no problems of special financing apart from the basic supply contract signed by a contractor who would simply handle the whole expansion problem in the traditional way, and gladly so, since he would be reasonably protected against loss.

There were, however, decided disadvantages to any plan to pay for new capacity by added charges to unit costs. The nation would be in the position of having presented all those fortunate enough to hold such war contracts with free factories. Moreover, this would be over and above any profits that might have been earned and without regard to whether or not the contractor had performed efficiently or not. Even if a manufacturer's wartime production record had been sufficiently impressive to win him some sort of bonus, an outright gift of a new plant was unthinkable and, to say the least, indefensible, if for no other reason than on the grounds that it would give unfair advantage in the postwar market to the favored manufacturers who were in a position to receive such gifts during the war.[20]

A second alternative means of paying for emergency plant extensions lay in outright government ownership. Whatever additions were required would be built, paid for, and owned by the government but operated by private con-

---

[18] SW to ASW, 17 May 40, SW files, Airplanes, item 1525a. See also, Wesley Frank Craven and James Lea Cate, eds., "The Army Air Forces in World War II," *Men and Planes* (Chicago: The University of Chicago Press, 1955), ch. IX, pp. 299–304.

[19] See especially CPA, Policies Governing Private Financing of Emergency Facilities, WPB Special Study 12, pp. 9–10.

[20] Compt Gen to SW, 16 Aug 40, AFCF 016.

tractors. This was the government-owned, contractor-operated (GOCO) plan. The arrangement offered one decided advantage: expansions could be undertaken at need without thought for postwar competitive considerations that inevitably colored the thinking of contractors building plants on private account. But in this arrangement there were admittedly some disadvantages too. If the scheme were adopted, the War Department would have to foot the entire cost of construction at once, and in the fall of 1940 the heavy demands on available appropriations made it expedient to avoid such immediate outlays where possible. Then too, the many legal and administrattive complications arising from construction under the auspices of the Corps of Engineers constituted another argument against this form of financing. Although the Ordnance Department did eventually use the GOCO arrangement extensively—for the very good reason that virtually no one would be interested in owning a shell-loading plant in peacetime—the air arm used this form of financing only in a few exceptional instances.[21]

In air arm circles, special tax concessions such as the five-year depreciation or tax-amortization scheme, already mentioned, were far more popular than outright government construction and ownership. This is hardly surprising, for ever since the outbreak of war in Europe in 1939 manufacturers in the aircraft industry had been urging the War Department to approve some form of rapid amortization. There was much to commend the idea, since as matters stood under the prevailing tax laws, even when foreign states such as France and Britain built and paid for facility expansions to speed aircraft and engine production of individual manufacturers in the United States, the money so spent was regarded as additions to capital and was taxed as such.

Not surprisingly, manufacturers looking ahead fearfully to the lean times anticipated for the postwar era had no desire to carry the burden of excessive plant charges for 10 or 20 years—or long after the current emergency—which would be the case at the usual depreciation rate ranging from 5 percent to 12 percent for plant and equipment.[22] Individual manufacturers argued that the government's interest as well as that of the manufacturers would best be served by a rapid tax-amortization allowance.[23] Rapid tax amortization was not all give-away. If, for example, a manufacturer had been allowed to take a 20-percent depreciation allowance for 5 years beginning in 1939, he would have written off the plant by 1943, and with no depreciation to take thereafter would have had to meet the full bite of wartime taxes for 2 more years. Thus, when some manufacturers urged immediate and total depreciation of extraordinary or emergency facility costs and others suggested two-year writedowns, they did so with the knowledge that it would lay them open to the full burden of wartime taxation on earned

---

[21] AAF Hist Study 40, pp. 43–44. See also Smith, *The Army and Economic Mobilization*, p. 496ff.

[22] Smith, *The Army and Economic Mobilization*, pp. 456–60.
[23] United Aircraft Corp. to CofAC, 18 Sep 39, SW files, Airplanes, item 1350; Allison Engineering Co. et al., to CofAC, 1 Sep 39, AHO Plans Div, 145.93–183.

income. At first blush these proposals might seem to be in the nature of an outright steal or what would amount to a free gift of plant from the government, but even in France, where the socialists had not been notably friendly to private contractors, three-year tax amortization was the order of the day in emergency facility expansions.[24]

Perhaps the most telling argument in favor of tax amortization was raised by the officials of United Aircraft Corporation. They pointed out that only by heavy expenditures on tooling and equipment—quite apart from mere floor space —could the aircraft industry hope to cut over-all production costs and hence reduce unit prices to the government.[25] If the government failed to grant depreciation concessions, manufacturers would be loath to install the very tools that could be counted upon to lower prices and speed delivery to the government as purchaser.

All the points mentioned above were raised privately in discussions between manufacturers and government officials in the months following the outbreak of war in Europe. And although the idea of tax amortization was not brought out officially in public until the President spoke of it in his fireside chat some ten days after he urged Congress to provide 50,000 airplanes, the proposals of the eight or nine months just past were not entirely in vain if they helped educate War Department officials to the intricacies involved.[26]

Unfortunately, once the proposition to grant rapid depreciation concessions entered the public forum on Capitol Hill, a new difficulty appeared. Manufacturers who were dickering with the government for facility expansions during the summer of 1940 were reluctant to tie themselves into any rigid contract when far more favorable terms might be just around the corner in pending legislation.[27] Thus, ironically, it turned out that the provision for rapid depreciation, which promised to be of major importance in encouraging manufacturers to undertake vast expansions to increase production for the emergency, actually had the short run effect of delaying those expansions—at least until October 1940 when Congress finally enacted a whole basketful of legislation coupling excess profits taxes with the rapid depreciation privilege and repeal of the amended Vinson-Trammell profit curb.[28]

In their zeal to prevent individual manufacturers from getting undue advantage under the depreciation privilege, the congressmen wrote into the law a provision requiring War Department officials to certify that prices in all contracts held by a contractor using rapid depreciation contained no hidden increment of facility cost buried in his showing of production costs. In short, Congress wanted to make absolutely certain that no contractor received double reimbursement for his facilities. On its face a sound pre-

---

[24] J. C. Ward, president, Fairchild Aircraft, The French Aircraft Industry: 1940, Lecture, AIC, 7 Oct 40.

[25] Wilson, *Slipstream*, pp. 225–28.

[26] Smith, *The Army and Economic Mobilization*, p. 459.

[27] See, for example, North American Aviation to ASW, 23 Jul 40, SW files, Airplanes, item 1637; and ASW to Representative Francis Case, 14 Aug 40, SW files, Airplanes, item 1702; as well as lecture draft by Materiel Division, for General Arnold to give at Army Industrial College, 5 Oct 40, WFCF 350.001 (1941).

[28] See above, ch. XIII.

caution, in practice this provision proved virtually impossible to administer. Item costs were extremely difficult to analyze with accuracy in a time of economic flux, and cost analysts found it difficult enough to squeeze out suet from every item of product cost without in addition having to pay special heed to facility costs. After causing untold delays and annoyances, this certification stipulation was removed by Congress.[29]

Although the rapid depreciation provision was eventually widely used, the depreciation privilege alone did not provide a full answer to the question of paying for emergency extensions to plant.[30] Even the most liberal tax concessions offered no assurance to a manufacturer that his earnings would be sufficiently high to meet the costs that vast factory additions would inevitably involve. Moreover, if rapid depreciation did meet the departmental objection to direct government financing by forestalling an immediate drain on the available appropriations, it did not answer the cries of the banking community, which anxiously clamored for an opportunity to participate in the expansions about to be launched across the country.[31] For these reasons, as well as to provide a means of proceeding while waiting for Congress to act, government officials and members of the banking fraternity contrived yet another means for financing facility construction. This was the emergency plant facility (EPF) contract.

The EPF contract was specifically designed to lure private capital into emergency construction work. Under its terms a manufacturer would undertake to build whatever facility the government wished him to, and he would build it big enough to meet the needs of the emergency without regard to postwar economics. For its part, the government would agree to buy back the facility from the contractor with a series of equal payments spread over sixty months.[32]

The advantages of the EPF contract are readily apparent. To begin with, it promised to place no immediate and overwhelming drain on War Department appropriations. Because it was designed to be bankable, the EPF contract was expected to simplify the manufacturer's task of borrowing through normal banking channels the funds required for factory construction contracts. At the same time, by leaving the actual problems of designing and building to the manufacturer, the War Department gave him a great deal of latitude if not a free hand. Along the same line, the manufacturer would enjoy virtually complete freedom in operating his plant since title would not transfer to the government for sixty months, which, it was assumed, would extend beyond the emergency. On the other hand, to keep the contractor from extravagance in conducting the expansion, he was given an option of buying the plant at the end of the emergency. Obviously, the lower the initial cost, the lower the price he might expect to pay eventually.

When put into practice, the EPF contract revealed a number of unexpected shortcomings. Although the EPF con-

---

[29] Smith, *The Army and Economic Mobilization*, pp. 467–71.
[30] *Ibid.*, p. 473, Table 50.
[31] AAF Hist Study 40, p. 37ff.

[32] This account of the EPF contract is based on AAF Historical Study 40, and Smith, *The Army and Economic Mobilization*, pages 476–84.

tract had been devised at least in part to give private banking circles an opportunity to participate in financing the vast expansion program, the conservative banking community insisted upon writing in safeguards to the point where EPF financing became cumbersome if not unworkable. Fearing that Congress might not finally appropriate the full amount committed for five years in the future, the bankers included a clause in the contracts that, in practice, forced the War Department to maintain a cash reserve sufficient to meet the whole obligation. This led to the ridiculous situation in which the government on one hand had to pay up to 4 percent in interest charges to the banks for loaning money to the manufacturers—who passed on this burden as a cost of doing business—while on the other hand the government, which is to say the War Department, carried balances sufficient to liquidate the entire obligation at once.[33] Under such circumstances it was advantageous for the government to take title immediately by prompt payment of the construction costs, thus saving needless interest charges.

There was an additional advantage for the manufacturer in prompt payment of the EPF contract. So long as a manufacturer retained title to a plant under the EPF arrangement, he had to pay state taxes on it. In California, where an important segment of the airframe industry lay, the state government even insisted that manufacturers receiving EPF repayments for facility expenditures had to report them as income and pay state taxes accordingly.[34]

The anticipated advantages of the EPF contract were clearly outweighed by its drawbacks, but there were only revealed by experience. Thus, although the air arm entered 11 EPF contracts beginning with the Boeing B-29 plant in Seattle, by 1945 all of these save two, the Ford Dearborn plant and the Martin Middle River plant, were either canceled, amended, or converted to other types of contracts.

Probably the most attractive form of emergency facility financing was the Defense Plant Corporation (DPC) arrangement, which came to be used in place of the EPF contract. During June 1940, Congress authorized the depression-born Reconstruction Finance Corporation (RFC) to set up the DPC as a wartime holding company, but opposition from the banking community delayed the operation of this agency for some time. Under DPC auspices a manufacturer selected for expansion by the War Department—or any other military agency for that matter—sized up the task at hand and applied for DPC financing. On approval, DPC put up the cash and the manufacturer occupied the plant on a rental basis, full title resting with the government from the very start.[35]

There was much to commend the DPC form of financing although it, too, did not want for difficulties in administer-

---

[33] The charges involved were by no means trivial. For a single project, Ford Dearborn, the interest amounted to approximately $1.25 million. See Smith, *The Army and Economic Mobilization*, p. 481, n. 15.

[34] That the state tax could make the difference between profit and major loss is suggested by the California state tax of $800,000 imposed on the Douglas Long Beach facility constructed under an EPF contract. See Smith, *The Army and Economic Mobilization*, pp. 481-82.

[35] This summary of DPC financing is based on Smith, *The Army and Economic Mobilization*, pp. 484ff. and AAF Hist Study 40, pp. 39-42.

ing.[36] Because it was not tied down by prolonged advance negotiations with the bankers and because it did not require certifications such as those necessary to secure tax amortization, the DPC arrangement was fast and flexible. Moreover, when an expansion project had to be modified or enlarged in midstream—and experience proved this was to be the typical situation—a simple amendment could be worked out on the initial DPC agreement to cover the increased costs.

DPC financing had still other advantages. With clear title to the expanded facility never out of government hands, there could be no difficulty with state governments over taxes. And under the prevailing federal statutes DPC, as a quasi-independent governmental corporation, was not subject to audit by the General Accounting Office, a circumstance that might have raised the fears of some critics but certainly contributed notably toward speeding the rearmament program, not only in freeing DPC officials from cumbersome bureaucratic routines but also in avoiding the need for accumulating literally tons of bookkeeping records.

The DPC scheme was especially acceptable to the War Department during the hurried months of defense build-up in the latter half of 1940 and throughout 1941 when the rush of work fairly swamped departmental staff officers, particularly those charged with supervising the construction projects undertaken for the government. Since DPC provided a supervisory staff of its own on DPC projects, War Department officers were released for work elsewhere. Just as it stretched personnel, so too the DPC arrangement stretched funds. Although Congress appropriated seemingly astronomical sums for defense after May 1940, the War Department was trying to overcome a generation of disarmament all at once; even the most lavish grants seemed never enough for the tasks at hand. Thus, insofar as it was able to transfer the burden, even temporarily, to DPC, the War Department could stretch its defense dollars just so much further.

A less obvious but no less substantial advantage in the DPC scheme of construction was that it removed the question of facilities from the immediate concern of those using them. Thus the Army and Navy, instead of disputing over who should expand a facility and thereby get the inside track, could place the project in the somewhat more objective hands of the DPC. This was a particularly advantageous settlement in the matter of secondary manufacturers who served as vendors and suppliers to the prime contractors producing for the services, since here it was not at all uncommon to encounter individual firms serving prime contractors for all the using arms.

By the same token, the dispassionate or detached quality of DPC administration made it possible for the government to drive harder bargains in arranging for construction of facilities by individual supply contractors. Since DPC officials had nothing to do with end-item procurement, they were not subject to the same pressure that beset War Department contracting officers who might be intimidated by manufacturers who could insist

---

[36] For an insight on at least one of the difficulties met, see the suggestive exchanges contained in IOM, Chief, PES, to Chief, Mat Div, 25 Sep 40, and related correspondence, AFCF 004.4.

THE PROBLEM OF INDUSTRIAL CAPACITY

that the provision of facilities on generous terms was a necessary prerequisite to early delivery of the aircraft and other munitions so eagerly sought by the using arms.

Insofar as air matériel was concerned, the DPC arrangements proved in practice to be a most popular method of financing facility expansions during the emergency period. Beginning as a rather hesitant experiment in August 1940 with a DPC plant for the Packard Motor Car Company to build the British Rolls-Royce aircraft engine, DPC projects attracted more and more favor until the end of the war when the total of DPC projects sponsored by the War Department reached 935 and involved some three billion dollars in capital. Of these, more than 80 percent were air arm projects.[37]

Financing expansions of productive capacity was one of the crucial problems of defense. Until decisions were reached here, construction could not go ahead. Because mobilization planners in the War Department, Treasury, and even Congress itself had not prepared effective financing procedures in advance, all had to be done in haste during the summer and fall of 1940. As a result, the decisions actually reached and the forms of financing finally selected in individual cases were determined less by logic than by accident—the accident of whatever alternative arrangement was readily available at the moment. This was true almost down to Pearl Harbor, by which time legislation had combined with experience to make possible a more informed and rational selection of fiscal instruments.

Perhaps the prewar planners could not possibly have foreseen and prepared for the difficult problem of facility financing, but this much at least is clear: the delays encountered while various officials worked out suitable financial instruments seriously retarded the nation's rearmament effort. Delay was the penalty of improvisation. At the beginning of August 1940, nearly three months after the President had galvanized the country with his call for an air armada of 50,000, the Air Corps had signed contracts for but 33 additional aircraft, although this figure rose to 343 by 20 August.[38] To be sure, Air Corps contracting officers had been ready and waiting, pen in hand, since June, but the manufacturers were inclined to drag their feet. Understandably enough, contractors were reluctant to sign until Congress made up its mind on rapid depreciation, excess profits, and profit limitations, and on the whole subject of emergency facilities.

Some manufacturers were hardy enough—or foolhardy enough—to go ahead with the patriotic business of rearmament without waiting for Congress and the financial experts to conclude their deliberations. But in the main, the first round of Air Corps contracts for facility expansion initiated in July 1940 took several months to reduce to terms.

The First Round of Expansion

The initial series of facility expansions undertaken by the Air Corps involved

---

[37] Smith, *The Army and Economic Mobilization*, pp. 494-96, especially Tables 51 and 52.

[38] Craven and Cate, eds., *Men and Planes*, p. 307.

some twenty projects.³⁹ After a preliminary bout of informal discussions, official letters of intent went out on a single day in the middle of July 1940 to the first thirteen manufacturers selected to receive factories. In line with the policy agreed upon by the prewar mobilization planners, all of these proposals went to old-line, established firms in the aviation industry, both airframe and engine builders—the firms with design skills, production experience, and technical know-how.⁴⁰

The expansion projects evolved during the summer of 1940 varied according to the need in each case. The Boeing Airplane Company, for example, undertook an extension of its Seattle plant to assemble B–17 heavy bombers (Flying Fortresses) and in addition agreed to build a whole new plant for fabricating subassemblies at Wichita, Kansas, the two involving an outlay of over $10,000,000. Glenn L. Martin agreed to double the floor space at its Middle River plant near Baltimore to increase production of the B–26 medium bomber (the Marauder), a project expected to cost nearly $7,000,000. And this was only the beginning, since changes, overruns, and additions almost invariably led to increased expenditures in plant expansion projects. North American Aviation received nearly $2,500,000 for an addition to the firm's plant at Englewood, California, and at the same time agreed to erect an entirely new $6,500,000 plant at Dallas, Texas, for the production of training aircraft.

In addition to the projects mentioned above, Bell, Curtiss-Wright, Republic, Vultee, Ryan, Fairchild, and Beech had, by the end of October, agreed to various types of expansions. These of course were only the first in a list that was to grow longer and longer as time passed. There is no need to describe all of the projects sponsored by the Air Corps.⁴¹ Nevertheless, some of the difficulties encountered in almost every facility expansions are suggested by a typical example.

The plant expansion sponsored by the Air Corps for the Bell Aircraft Corporation in Buffalo, New York, was neither the largest nor the smallest undertaken.⁴² It reflects nonetheless a considerable body of meaningful experience. The initial Bell proposal called for an assembly plant of 240,000 square feet, a floor area 400 by 600 feet, to be used to speed production of the P–39 Airacobra pursuit. Negotiators for the manufacturer and the air arm dickered at considerable length over the amount that would be allowed the contractor under an EPF contract to construct the proposed plant for the government. At last they agreed upon a figure just over a million dollars.

The agreement with Bell had scarcely passed through the long chain of official approvals required—the Secretary of War, the NDAC, and the President himself—before Bell representatives were back asking for the inclusion of $100,000 for "contingencies not previously considered." Even while the negotiators had bar

---

³⁹ LI–65, Chief, Mat Div, to Asst Chief, Mat Div, 21 Aug 40, AFCF 452.1 Aircraft, Gen; Rpt of New Productive Capacity, OCAC, Mat Planning Sec, 5 Sep 40, AFCF 004.4 Manufacturers.
⁴⁰ AAF Hist Study 40, p. 73ff.

⁴¹ An excellent brief survey of the over-all program is published in Craven and Cate, eds., *Men and Planes*, p. 308ff.
⁴² For the Bell story in general, see AFCF 004.41 Bell EPF, *passim*.

THE PROBLEM OF INDUSTRIAL CAPACITY 303

gained, it appears, the cost of materials and equipment had spiraled—a process familiar to those with knowledge of the behavior of the national economy under the stress of a war boom. A week later Bell officials were back again. This time they wanted a change order approving a $60,000 increase to cover the interest charges paid by the manufacturer on the money borrowed to finance construction of the new plant. When these extras were approved the manufacturer returned with a long list of things allegedly forgotten in the initial negotiations. A sewer pump, an incinerator, and fluorescent lighting, among other such items, were presented for approval as justifying an increase over the initial fixed-price contract.

Gradually the irony of the situation began to dawn on responsible officials in the Air Corps. It was the familiar old story of air matériel procurement during the previous twenty years repeated all over again. Before signing a contract, manufacturers were willing to promise the moon itself; after signing a contract they asked for change orders increasing the contract price for every little item not included when the original fixed price was under consideration. In fairness, it must be recognized that many such change order requests were fully justified. In a highly fluid situation it was inevitable that unforeseen contingencies would occur. The Bell requests mentioned above may well have been justified, but the Chief of the Materiel Division, as the officer directly responsible, began to have qualms. "Some day," he said, "there has to be an accounting." The cold shadow of a Leavenworth cell block fell across the future. If air arm negotiators were too liberal, if they failed to drive adequately hard bargains, the Chief of the Materiel Division observed, it would be "terrifically hard to explain" at any postwar day of reckoning.[43] The appropriate subordinate officials at Wright Field were admonished accordingly. But tightening the purse strings, where at all possible, met only one of the many problems of facility expansion.

If the problems of financing vexed operation of the various facility expansions sponsored by the air arm, even more troublesome were the complications arising out of the perpetually changing scope and scale of the projects undertaken. The original Bell expansion involved some 240,000 square feet. By the summer of 1941 air arm officers were perfecting a plan to provide Bell with 500,000 square feet of additional space in an entirely new DPC plant to build B–17 subassemblies. Despite pressure from OPM officials who urged that this new plant be located in some other labor area less saturated with war work, air arm officers argued that Bell management resources were too thin to allow cadres to be split off in order to set up an operation remote from the parent plant. Only a few months later, soon after Pearl Harbor, air arm officials again urged Bell to undertake an expansion. This time, apparently ignoring their earlier assertions regarding Bell's lack of depth in management, they pressed the manufacturer to operate a giant $14,000,000 B–29 Superfortress heavy bomber assembly plant outside Atlanta, Georgia.

---

[43] Chief, Mat Div, to Asst Chief, Mat Div, 16 Oct 40, AFCF 004.4.

The record of Bell's experience in facility expansion shows that the problem of productive capacity kept changing. Events in Europe and Asia continually raised the sights for aircraft output. As a consequence, no grand synthesis, no overview, was ever quite possible. One day's "ultimate" program was utterly lapped by needs rising over the next day's horizon. If mobilization planning and facility expansion were to be logical, orderly, and rational, as T. P. Wright had noted in his earliest production studies for NDAC, it was essential to get a picture of the "whole load." Yet in practice it was precisely this "whole load" that never could be discovered. Not only did the turn of events, both military and diplomatic, keep changing the requirement for aircraft output, but Congress made available larger and larger funds and more flexible means of financing facilities. In a very real sense the rules of play were in continual flux during the entire game. And at the same time the industrial managers were themselves changing. Bell officials who thought they faced a big job when they set to work on their first million-dollar expansion at home in Buffalo were not staggered when asked to tackle a $14,000,000 project in Georgia only a little over a year later.

The Bell story illustrates the fact that it was difficult to plan for procurement when all the factors turned out to be widely fluctuating variables. What had been visualized as the full expansion program in the early summer of 1940 ended up as merely the first round in a long series of expansions. That the first round of expansions was entirely inadequate became increasingly apparent during the fall of 1940.[44] By the time the President described the nation as the Arsenal of Democracy during his fireside chat at the end of December 1940, it was already clear that it would be necessary to look elsewhere for increased aircraft production—to Detroit, for instance, with the as yet virtually untapped resources of the automobile industry and its vast congeries of vendors and suppliers.[45]

Enter Detroit: Air Arm Use of the Automobile Industry

Mr. Knudsen Takes the Initiative

The old-line, established aircraft manufacturers of the country feared the automobile industry as a potential competitor, and this attitude on the part of aircraft manufacturers seems to have colored the thinking of air arm officers who did business with them. The officers spoke in a general way of utilizing the productive capacity of the automobile industry, but when it came down to cases in the frantic summer of 1940, they sponsored large expansions for the old-line aircraft firms long before they turned to Detroit. Commissioner Knudsen of the NDAC broke the pattern. No one knew the productive potential of Detroit better than Knudsen, and it was he, rather than the automobile men themselves or air arm officers immediately concerned,

---

[44] Memo, CofAC to Chief, Mat Div, 21 Oct 40, AFCF 452.1 Production. See also AAF Hist Study 40, pp. 79ff.

[45] For a concise account of the growing realization of the need for more aircraft production capacity, see William L. Langer and S. Everett Gleason, *The Undeclared War: 1940–1941* (New York: Harper and Brothers, 1953), pp. 238–40.

THE PROBLEM OF INDUSTRIAL CAPACITY

who took the initiative in calling in the automobile manufacturers.[46]

To recruit the Detroit manufacturers Mr. Knudsen appeared before them in person in October 1940, first at a meeting of truck and automobile builders in New York City and then before a much larger gathering in Detroit including not only the big automotive leaders but representatives of the body manufacturers and parts suppliers, as well as the tool and die firms serving them, a cross section of the entire industry assembled through the auspices of the powerful Automobile Manufacturers Association (AMA), an organization ideally suited to such a function.[47] By appearing in person, Mr. Knudsen made his proposal immensely appealing. It was not the brainchild of some theorist or politician but a proposition from Big Bill Knudsen, whose rise to power from the shop floor to the top of General Motors won him immense respect, not least of all from his former competitors. Moreover, Mr. Knudsen skillfully cast his proposal in dramatic and daring terms. Specifically, he called for 12,000 bombers over and above those currently on program. The government would erect two large assembly plants to be operated by experienced airframe manufacturers, but it was up to Detroit to utilize its available capacity to produce the parts and subassemblies to feed into these plants. Without the aid of Detroit, Knudsen declared, this vast new program could never be accomplished.

If Knudsen's approach to the automobile manufacturers appealed to their patriotism, equally skillful was the accompanying appeal to the intense pride of the industry in its technical skills. While Knudsen was up in front making his pitch, some imaginative officers were busy setting up displays of typical aircraft parts and subassemblies as well as blueprints to suggest to manufacturers in the Detroit family how their various productive capacities might be utilized.[48]

When confronted with the twofold challenge to their pride and their patriotism, the automobile manufacturers accepted with enthusiasm. They set up a committee to consider ways and means of meeting the challenge. The committee, called the Automotive Committee for Air Defense (ACAD), was no empty formality. Its members, drawn from the top echelons of the industry, included such leaders as Edsel Ford, K. T. Keller of Chrysler, and Charles E. Wilson of General Motors. It was an auspicious beginning. Detroit had enlisted with enthusiasm. Indeed, Mr. Knudsen had succeeded in recruiting his forces before the plans to employ them had actually been completed. The precise details of the government's bomber plant program, which he outlined in Detroit, had yet to be hammered out.

---

[46] Memo, drafted by Maj Lyon for SW, 26 Oct 40; Memo, ASW for Brig Gen Carl Spaatz, 23 Oct 40. Both in AFCF 004.4 Manufacturers. See also *New Republic* (November 11, 1940), p. 659.

[47] Automobile Manufacturers Assn., *Freedom's Arsenal: The Story of the Automotive Council for War Production* (Detroit, 1950), pp. 1–9; AAF Hist Study 40, p. 79ff; and app. VI, text of Knudsen's speech of 25 Oct 40. See also, WF Memo Rpt, Insp–M–40–36–E, 29 Oct 40, AFCF 452.1 Production.

[48] The record is unclear as to just who was responsible for the challenge to the automobile industry's technical skills implied in the parts exhibit in Detroit. Knudsen had it in mind even before he went to Detroit on 25 October 1940, but the idea may have originated elsewhere. See Memo, ASW for Gen Spaatz, 23 Oct 40, SW files, Airplanes, item 1834. By the end of 1940, more than 800 firms had studied the exhibit. AMA, *Freedom's Arsenal*, 37ff.

THE B-24

The Bomber Plant Program

The automobile manufacturers and others on the ACAD lost no time in getting the government bomber plant program under way. As they visualized the task, it fell into four equal parts. Approximately 25 percent of the work would involve the fabrication of parts. Making subassemblies would account for another 25 percent. These two jobs would be the responsibility of the automotive industry. The manufacture of fuselages would take up another 25 percent, which, coupled with the installation of parts and final assembly by the old-line aircraft manufacturers who were to manage each of the two government-furnished plants, would round out the program.[49] As one

automotive manufacturer saw the process in retrospect, it was a wedding of the aircraft and automobile industries without benefit of shotgun. The fear of old-line airframe producers that automobile builders would run away with the postwar airplane market was laid by an explicit promise to the contrary, and soon more than a thousand design and production men from Detroit were swarming through the aircraft plants studying the problems they would have to face.[50]

Air Corps officers in charge of the project knew only too well that getting government bomber plants into production would inevitably turn out to be a long and complex undertaking. To begin with, the necessary funds were not readily available and would have to be found somewhere. Once construction had begun, it would still take an estimated ten to twelve months to complete the plants; thus the first trickle of production could scarcely be expected before another year, and full production was not anticipated in less than eighteen months. To make matters worse, Air Corps officers were unable to decide exactly which bombers should be produced in the government plants. Consolidated's experimental four-engine heavy bomber, the XB-24, might turn out to be superior to the tried and tested Boeing Flying Fortress, which was already several model changes along the way as the B-17E. Similarly, the twin-engine Martin medium bomber, B-26, might prove superior to the North American B-25 in tests yet to be conducted. Thus it was necessary to start the program and bring automobile builders into cooperation with aircraft builders even be-

---

[49] WF Memo Rpt, Insp-M-40-4-A, 6 Dec 40, WF Contract files, 321.91 Organization.

[50] AMA, *Freedom's Arsenal*, p. 24.

fore anyone was certain just which airplanes would be built.[51]

The selection of sites for government-owned assembly plants presented another problem almost certain to delay the program. No one in the War Department had specialized experience along this line, and the instructions drafted for the first Plant Site Board were amateurish indeed, though there was actually no reason for this floundering. Nearly a month before work commenced on the bomber plant projects, the Aeronautical Chamber of Commerce, with a wide range of executive skills at its disposal throughout the industry, had drafted an able and imaginative check list for site board work; the check list was not used. In addition, the industrial development department of the Baltimore and Ohio Railroad had proffered the services of its skilled and experienced staff, but this, too, seems to have been ignored.[52] And even when the Air Corps finally did send survey teams out into the field to study possible sites, it took some time to shake off the cumbersome administrative routines of peacetime. Occasionally compliance with existing regulations led to situations nothing short of absurd. Each long distance call placed by a board in the field, to take but one illustrative example, had to be authorized in writing in advance. Thus it not infrequently happened that a board

THE B–25

had to run up heavy bills in per diem charges for want of permission to make a call costing a few dollars at the most.[53]

The officials who selected facility sites had to reconcile a number of conflicting interests. For many years it had been accepted doctrine that any major expansion of the aircraft industry in an emergency should be in the interior of the country, "behind the mountain chains" for obvious strategic reasons. In practice the doctrine was largely ignored. Manufacturers built new plants and expanded their old plants where it was most economical to do so. Even when the government footed the bill as it did in the first round of expansions during the fall of 1940, responsible air arm officers were unwilling to ignore the contention of many manufac-

---

[51] Memo, CofAC for ASW, 4 Oct 40, AFCF 004.4 Manufacturers; Memo, Actg SW for President, 16 Nov 40, AFCF 030. See also, AAF Hist Study 40, p. 84.
[52] Memo, OASW for CofAC, 22 Jul 40, and ACC release of 10 Jun 40, as well as B&O RR to Brig Gen C. T. Harris, 3 Jul 40. By way of contrast, see the site survey prepared by a manufacturer's engineer, J. T. Hartson, of Glenn L. Martin to Col Volandt, 13 Dec 40. All in AFCF 004.4.

[53] Memo, Chief, Plans, OCAC, for Exec, 8 Jan 41, AFCF 311.3 Phone Calls.

turers that to build secondary plants in the interior, at a distance from parent plants, would seriously slow down production.[54] On the other hand, those responsible for site selections were subjected to a good deal of pressure from various localities in the interior urging their advantages and the need for an equitable distribution of defense orders.[55]

Neither political nor purely strategic considerations called the turn. The matter was decided, rather, by inescapable economic factors. The government assembly plants were ultimately located in communities not already burdened—or blessed—with defense contracts. And each site was selected only after the most careful survey showed that the available housing, power, transportation, labor supply, flying weather, and the like justified the choice.[56]

The Site Board surveys made it apparent that the initial plan for two government bomber plants was not feasible. To erect new plants expecting to hire upward of 20,000 employees in any one industrial area threatened to impose an impossible strain on the local resources in labor, housing, transport, and so on. The obvious solution was to divide the load. Thus, by the end of 1940 there were four rather than two government bomber plants under way in or near Omaha, Nebraska; Kansas City, Kansas; Tulsa, Oklahoma; and Fort Worth, Texas. Each of these localities was to receive a bomber plant big enough for use in assembling the largest designs on the experimental horizon, the XB-29 or the XB-32, for example, even though the immediate plan only called for the production of medium bombers at Omaha and Kansas City.[57]

While the surveys leading to the selection of sites proceeded, Mr. Knudsen's negotiators were busy trying to bring the automotive and aircraft manufacturers together. The task was extremely involved. First, each individual airframe firm had to be persuaded to do business with a particular set of automobile companies. With this basic agreement reached, the interested parties had to decide what parts or subassemblies each would make, what patent licensing would be required, and how the flow of design data would be arranged, since the exigencies of battle would inevitably keep designs in a high state of flux even after mass production had begun.

The government bomber plant program, or Knudsen automotive program as it was sometimes called, finally took the following form: Glenn L. Martin of Baltimore agreed to produce the B-26 medium bomber in the government-built plant at Omaha, using parts supplied by the Chrysler Corporation and the Hudson Motor Car Corporation of Detroit and the Goodyear Aircraft Corporation of Akron. North American agreed to assemble the B-25 medium bomber at the Kansas City plant, using parts and

---

[54] Wichita, Kans., Chamber of Commerce, to SW, 20 Mar 39, with 2d Ind, OCAC to TAG, 8 Apr 39, AHO Plans Div 145.91-244, and SW to Senator Arthur Capper, 15 Dec 37, SW files, Air Corps Gen Questions, item 471, offer some insight on the subject.

[55] See, for example, telegrams of Senator Josh Lee of Oklahoma to Gen Arnold, 10 Dec 40, and Senator Sheppard to Gen Brett, 13 Dec 40. Both in AFCF 004.4.

[56] Gen Brett to J. J. Cochran, 30 Dec 40; Col Volandt to Shreveport, La., Chamber of Commerce, 9 Jan 41. Both in AFCF 004.4.

[57] Memo, CofAC for ASW, 27 Nov 40, AFCF 004.4.

THE PROBLEM OF INDUSTRIAL CAPACITY 309

subassemblies provided by the Fisher Body Division of General Motors and its related subcontractors and suppliers. Although the Boeing B–17 had been the favored heavy bomber when the automotive program was first broached, by the time negotiations were completed early in 1941 it had been decided to concentrate on the B–24 designed by the Consolidated Aircraft Corporation of San Diego. Consolidated agreed to set up a second B–24 assembly line in the government-built plant at Fort Worth, while the Douglas Aircraft Corporation undertook to open still another for the same aircraft in the government plant at Tulsa. To feed the big assembly units at Tulsa and Fort Worth, the Ford Motor Company agreed to supply a total of a hundred sets of knockdown airframe parts per month, each set consisting of virtually all the major components of the bomber—fuselage, wings, tail, landing gear, and so forth.

All but one of the automobile manufacturers contributing airframe parts and assemblies arranged to do so in their existing plants or in privately financed expansions. Ford was the exception. Ford persuaded the government negotiators that it would be necessary to erect an entirely new plant in addition to the $2,000,000 conversion job done at the River Rouge factory. The new facility that grew out of this decision was the multimillion dollar project at Willow Run some thirty-odd miles west of Detroit.[58]

The expansion of aircraft engine production followed close on the heels of airframe expansion. Even before Knudsen's appeal to Detroit, Wright Aeronautical had received government assistance for the erection of a facility at Lockland, Ohio, near Cincinnati. This new plant, with its installations of automatic equipment, not only increased the output of Wright R–2100 radial engines but also constituted what was probably the nearest approach to automation in a World War II engine factory. The foremost manufacturers of in-line aircraft engines, the Allison Division of General Motors, undertook a large expansion of its Indianapolis plant without government assistance, while the Lycoming Division of Aviation Corporation received a $1,500,000 expansion to speed output of the R–680 engine for use in training planes. But even these additions to plant were insufficient to keep up with the rising curve of demand.

With engines as with airframes, government officials soon turned to Detroit. The first automobile manufacturer to enter the field was the Packard Motor Car Company, which agreed to produce the British Rolls-Royce Merlin engine, V–1650, for delivery to the British as well as to the United States. Because the top management of Pratt and Whitney felt that its staff had already been spread thin on the expansions sponsored for the firm by the French and British, it seemed wise to increase the output of the Pratt and Whitney R–2800 engine by utilizing the management resources of Ford. Ford was duly licensed and built a new plant on the River Rouge site at a cost initially estimated at $22,000,000.[59] To increase production on yet another Pratt and Whitney engine, the R–1830, in phase

---

[58] AAF Hist Study 40, pp. 87–89.

[59] *Ibid.*, pp. 77–78.

with the anticipated output of the two government-built B–24 assembly plants at Tulsa and Fort Worth, as well as to meet British requirements, the Buick Motor Division of General Motors agreed to sponsor a $31,000,000 facility financed by the government at Melrose Park near Chicago. Similarly, to step up the output of the Wright B–2600 engine to match the expected demands of the B–25 assembly plant at Kansas City, the Studebaker Corporation agreed to operate three plants, located in Chicago, South Bend, and Fort Wayne, which the government would finance at a cost of just under $50,000,000.[60]

The expansions mentioned here, both airframe and engine facilities, constituted only the beginning of a long sequence. As events in Europe and Asia led to increased requirements, further additions to plant were undertaken. In some cases even before ground was broken for these initial projects, it was decided to double or even triple the floor space involved. A whole new group of manufacturers was brought into the program too. Moreover, extensive facility expansions were granted to the firms producing accessory items—gun turrets, landing gear assemblies, and the like.[61]

By July 1941, the end of the fiscal year, the air arm could report that there were over 24,000,000 square feet of floor space in the aircraft industry, double the area available in January 1940. The labor force directly employed in the industry had tripled to 180,000 workers. Counting suppliers and vendors as well as prime and subcontractors, the air arm had sponsored some 45,000,000 square feet in facility expansions, which, together with outlays for tools, cost a total of $721,000,000.[62]

All these undertakings held promise of enormously increased production—when completed. Unfortunately, since many involved new construction rather than conversion of existing plant, a long delay between inception and fulfillment was inevitable. The public, never fully informed of the difficulties involved, was doubtlessly led to expect too much too soon. It was all too easy to confuse the big bold headlines—promising 12,000 bombers from Detroit—with the reality of fully functioning production lines. Among those disturbed at the gap between promise and fulfillment at Detroit was Walter Reuther of the CIO United Auto Workers, who sought to bridge the distance in what came to be known as the Reuther Plan.

The Reuther Plan

During December 1940, Mr. Reuther offered the government a plan by which he claimed the automotive industry could produce 500 fighter aircraft a day after a mere six months spent in tooling up. Automobile output was to continue unabated at existing levels. This miracle of mass-produced aircraft was to be achieved entirely by utilizing the excess floor space of Detroit. With its capacity equal to 8,000,000 units a year but currently turning out a scant 4,000,000, the automobile industry should be fully ca-

---

[60] *Ibid.*, pp. 90–91.
[61] *Ibid.*, pp. 93–94.

[62] Hearings of Special Com Investigating the National Defense Program (Truman Com), July 15, 1941, pt. 6, p. 1527–28.

pable of building 500 fighter aircraft a day, if the manufacturers involved would but accept three proposals Mr. Reuther proceeded to spell out. First, they would have to agree to forego the usual annual car model change for production year 1942 in order to free the industry's tool and die men to work at tooling up the aircraft project. Second, the participating manufacturers would have to agree to pool their machine tools so that particular tools could be moved about from one plant to another as the occasion might require. Third, Mr. Reuther called for the formation of a nine-man board of supervisors or directors to conduct this great co-operative effort. The board would include three representatives from management, three from the government, and three from organized labor.[63]

The Reuther Plan and the uproar it engendered can be understood only in the context of the running feud of unions and management in the decade of the nineteen thirties. On the part of organized labor, Mr. Reuther was anxious to hold and even expand the social and legal gains already won by the unions. Not least among these objectives, as stated by Reuther, was the hope of forcing Ford into full compliance with the terms of the Wagner Act.[64] On the other hand, some spokesmen for management seemed to feel that the whole Reuther scheme was an effort to prepare for a drive for more pay and shorter hours by discrediting management's record in the defense effort before management could do the same to labor.[65]

As soon as the Reuther Plan was publicized, both sides indulged in a good deal of blatant grandstanding. A number of stories rather obviously inspired in Detroit appeared in the news. They all sang the same refrain: only a very small proportion of the tools and equipment in the automotive industry would be suitable for use in airframe and aircraft engine work. One spokesman flatly declared that not more than 10 percent of the industry's tools could be used.[66] This intramural fencing for advantage tended to make truly objective evaluations and decisions on the Reuther Plan extremely difficult.

Even the most cursory examination of the plan by government officials revealed that it was based on a number of misunderstandings. To begin with, 500 fighter aircraft a day were far more than the Air Corps needed, wanted, or could use. The Air Corps desired bombers—long-range, multiengine, heavy bombers—with immense wing spans that were far too great to permit assembly in the narrow bays of the existing automobile factories.

Perhaps the most serious objection to the Reuther Plan was that it did not come to grips with the most difficult and central problem of design: just how would Mr. Reuther transfer the design of an aircraft, continually in flux as a design, from the drawing boards of an aircraft

---

[63] The Reuther Plan was officially titled, Program for Utilization of the Auto Industry for Mass Production of Defense Planes. A copy is available in the records of the OEM Library in the National Archives, but, for easier access, see the New York Times, December 23, 1940, 1:1, and December 24, 1940, 1:1. For a brief description, see AAF Hist Study 40, p. 82.

[64] See, for example, remarks by Walter Reuther in radio address reported in New York Times, December 29, 1940, 20:6.

[65] See feature story, datelined Detroit, in New York Times, December 29, 1940, sec. X, 4:6.

[66] Ibid. See also, same issue, sec. IV, 5:8.

manufacturer to the production lines of Detroit. This task, by no means impossible, nevertheless imposed acutely difficult problems on management. Yet the management Mr. Reuther sought to establish was not one already perfected as a team with years of experience but a co-operative affair pooling individuals from a number of firms, an arrangement almost certain to lose the advantages that government officials hoped to gain when they turned to Detroit. One of the important reasons for selecting Ford, Chrysler, and General Motors as key producers was that each of these corporations had built up elaborate purchasing organizations whose experience would be invaluable in dealing with the host of subcontractors, vendors, and suppliers necessarily involved in the government's bomber plant program.[67] If these drawbacks were not in themselves sufficient to induce rejection of the plan, Reuther himself offered the *coup de grâce* by suggesting that the whole Detroit aircraft effort be managed by a mixed commission of representatives from labor, management, and government. Such a proposal was almost certain to kill off enthusiasm even among those anxious to co-operate with organized labor.

The objections to the Reuther Plan were immediately apparent to responsible officials in the government, but to reject it out of hand was inexpedient. Since the whole scheme had come into focus as a contest of organized labor versus big business, no matter how cogent the arguments against Mr. Reuther's proposal, the administration could not afford to come out immediately in favor of one side over the other. Instead, it was necessary to play for time. An aircraft was provided to carry Mr. Reuther on a tour of aircraft and engine plants to study the application of his plan. The trip was well worth the trouble. An officer assigned to the expedition observed that as a result of their several conferences, the attitude of the manufacturers toward Reuther changed from hostility to tolerance. And, for his part, Reuther appeared to come away with a far greater appreciation of the technical difficulties that would be encountered when building airframes in automobile plants. After learning at first hand that many aspects of the aircraft job required watchmaker's precision work, the union leader was not quite so self-assured as he had been when he blandly excoriated the "bugaboo of tolerances" in his initial proposal. Then he had said "we'll add more gauges"; now he was not quite so sure.[68]

Although the Reuther Plan did have serious shortcomings, there was indeed considerable merit to the claim that aircraft production could be substantially increased if the automotive manufacturers would subordinate all work in preparation for their 1942 models in favor of defense contracts. Mr. Reuther might have served the cause of defense better had he concentrated on this central theme without the obfuscation of the 500-airplane-a-day promise. Of course, it might well be argued that he would never have found any listeners had he not first presented such an extravagant proposition. Without the headlines captured by the

---

[67] AMA, *Freedom's Arsenal*, p. 37. See Rpt of NDAC decision of 18 Dec 40.

[68] Memo, Maj D. W. Watkins for Gen Arnold, 28 Jan 41, AFCF 333.1 Contract Inspection. See also Wilson, *Slipstream*, pp. 247–48.

plan, it would have been more difficult to urge labor's claim for a seat in the councils directing the nation's economic mobilization. And, as the debate over the plan clearly showed, this was by no means the least important purpose visualized by its author.[69]

The moment was opportune for a bid to further power by labor. A Gallup poll conducted toward the end of 1940 revealed that 58 percent of the nation's voters were inclined to blame the Roosevelt administration for the lag in defense production.[70] Mr. Roosevelt's answer to this criticism was to superimpose a coordinating agency, OPM, on top of the loosely correlated NDAC.[71] As Director General of the new organization, the President appointed Mr. Knudsen, the representative of big business. But, significantly, at the same time he named labor's Mr. Hillman as Associate Director General. Seen from the vantage point of organized labor, Mr. Reuther's Plan would appear to have been highly successful—at least in one respect.[72]

While it may be true that the Reuther Plan had to be broached in extreme form —500 aircraft a day—to stir up excitement and attract attention to make gains for labor, these advances were not made without losses in another direction. Since a program of 500 fighter aircraft a day was manifestly impractical, it drew upon itself the withering fire of the automotive industry. Many of the objections leveled against this aspect of the plan were entirely valid, but that only served to obscure the real issue. After all, Mr. Reuther's main point was not precisely 500 fighters a day but rather a fuller utilization of the available capacity in Detroit. Once the headline writers identified the Reuther Plan with "500-a-day," the damage was done; soon afterward the union proposal was tacitly shelved.[73]

The Reuther Plan, if taken as a whole, was certainly not feasible. With knowledge of all the factors involved, its author himself would doubtlessly have accepted this conclusion. But rejection of the plan as such did not dispose of Mr. Reuther entirely. Even if he conceded that only 10 percent of the automobile manufacturers' tools were suitable to conversion to aircraft work, Mr. Reuther argued effectively that this scant 10 percent represented a pool far in excess of the tools currently in use throughout the entire aircraft industry. And if the car manufacturers would but defer their preparations on their 1942 models, their equipment could be converted promptly to aircraft work. The trouble was not that the automobile makers refused to cooperate in the defense effort but that they insisted on doing so on their own terms. They would build aircraft, some labor spokesmen claimed, only if they received new plants supplied by the government or won big tax concessions, and even then

---

[69] See, for example, the radio address by R. J. Thomas, president of UAW, CIO, urging adoption of Reuther Plan, as reported in New York *Times*, January 4, 1941, 7:8.

[70] New York *Times*, January 4, 1941, 7:3.

[71] See above, ch. XII.

[72] For an interesting perspective on the advantage to Reuther himself growing out of the plan, see Nelson, *Arsenal of Democracy*, p. 318.

[73] The whole newspaper debate on the Reuther Plan offers an excellent case history on political practice. The plan was adroitly done to death by killing off a nonessential feature and then leaving it in suspended animation, neither accepted nor rejected, denying its frustrated author sufficient leverage for further action. See especially, New York *Times*, January 2, 1941, 8:4, and January 3, 1941, 8:6.

only if they were allowed to continue building automobiles too.[74] If they were to enter the defense effort, Mr. Reuther charged, the automobile manufacturers wanted the prestige of producing end products, aircraft and engines, and not just parts appearing under someone else's brand name.[75] In fine, the union view suggested that the automobile manufacturers put profits ahead of preparedness, that they were lagging rather than leading in the nation's defense effort.

Leading or Lagging?

There was a measure of justice in the charge that the automobile manufacturers were dragging their feet rather than leading in the rearmament program. Hardly a day passed but some news account out of Detroit explained just why the industry could not be converted to aircraft production as Mr. Reuther suggested.[76] No doubt many of these stories were inspired by manufacturers frightened by the more extreme features of the Reuther Plan. In their anxiety they apparently allowed themselves to be drawn to the opposite extreme, greatly underestimating the extent to which Detroit's capacity could be used for aircraft work. This was unfortunate, for the industry was just at this time in the midst of a boom in automobile production, the like of which had not been seen since 1929. Thus, by their own words the automobile manufacturers were cast in the role of those who put the profits of production ahead of the patriotism of conversion for defense. Before condemning them, however, it might be useful to consider the question in a somewhat broader context.

There were actually a number of very good reasons why the facilities of Detroit could not readily be diverted immediately to aircraft use. To begin with, no single manufacturer, acting individually and on his own initiative, could decide to omit the usual tooling up for model 1942. For a single automobile builder to do this in the highly competitive automotive field would be market suicide. It was a case of all firms omitting the changes or none. Similarly, no single firm could drop automobile production entirely in favor of aircraft work, as some critics suggested. The whole empire of dealerships and distribution channels as well as carefully nourished customer relations made any unilateral action in this direction simply unthinkable. To ask automobile manufacturers to act individually in accepting aircraft orders would be to ask a higher order of patriotic response from them than from the nation as a whole.

One solution of the difficulty was to have guns and butter, continuing automobile output in existing facilities while building new ones to absorb the aircraft load. It was this duplication of facilities that union spokesmen were inclined to regard as a selfish grab at the taxpayer's expense. However, it should be noted that the manufacturer's preference for

---

[74] See CIO Outlook as quoted in New York *Times*, December 29, 1940, 19:2.

[75] Memo, Maj Watkins for Gen Arnold, 28 Jan 41, AFCF 333.1 Contract Inspection. Reuther's remarks were doubtlessly aimed especially at Ford, whose insistence on an assembly plant at Willow Run made the charge appear valid. See AAF Hist Study 40, p. 88.

[76] See, for example, J. S. Edgerton, Aviation Editor, in Washington *Star*, January 22 and 31, 1941; and New York *Times*, February 9, 1941, 39:3.

THE PROBLEM OF INDUSTRIAL CAPACITY

new construction rather than the conversion of existing plants stemmed, in part at least, from a peculiarity in the regulations on financing production acceleration. Neither the War Department nor the Defense Plant Corporation would generally agree to pay for reconversion or nonrecoverable charges such as the cost of removing and returning machinery, strengthening floors to carry heavier equipment, and other similar expenditures in privately owned buildings. Since making the conversion changes in some instances ran up formidable totals, manufacturers were inclined to favor operations in new government-built plants rather than in portions of their own plants converted to aircraft use.[77]

Although individual Detroit manufacturers did show an understandable reluctance to enter aircraft production if it involved dropping automobile output or unless they received additional facilities in which to do the job, the fact remains that while the debate raged over Detroit's failure to convert rapidly to defense, an increasingly heavy volume of aircraft contracts was placed with them. Even before Mr. Reuther leveled his charges, Douglas had placed a $20,000,000 order for wing assemblies with the Murray Body works, and other aircraft manufacturers soon followed suit.[78] Nor should it be forgotten that other branches of the services were pouring orders into Detroit. By the end of March 1941, for example, the industry was turning out military vehicles at the rate of more than 13,000 a month. By the end of June 1941, more than half of Detroit's $2,000,000,000 defense load was concerned with air matériel, the remainder being motor vehicles, marine equipment, guns, and ammunition.[79]

While it was entirely feasible for the automotive industry to absorb aircraft contracts gradually, there were many obstacles to any effort at sudden or abrupt transition to military production.[80] As the British had learned at great cost in the early phases of their mobilization, any attempt to cut automobile production suddenly leads to mass unemployment and severe economic dislocation. Officials on the planning staff in the Under Secretary's office were well aware of this difficulty as were a number of air arm officers, but it was not always easy to get this point over to critics in and out of government who urged an immediate transition to all-out defense. Those who favored the latter course presupposed that orders for military aircraft were all ready to place in the hands of the automobile builders. Such was not the case.[81] It was easy to criticize Detroit for not cutting off production sooner, but firms could scarcely be blamed for wishing to retain automobile production until they

---

[77] AAF Study 40, p. 85.
[78] *Business Week* (November 2, 1940), p. 17.
[79] AMA, *Freedom's Arsenal*, pp. 46, 58.
[80] Mr. Nelson has pointed out (*Arsenal of Democracy*, page 218) that there is no such thing as partial conversion of a modern production line. It is a case of all or nothing. Although this is undeniably true with regard to the automobile assembly lines, it does not apply to the satellite subcontractors and suppliers who not only could but did gradually move into aircraft work.
[81] Memo, Dir, Planning Br, OUSW, for USW, 21 Apr 41, in app., vol. II, ASF Control Div, Monograph, The Period of Military Preparedness: June 1940–December 1941, OCMH; Memo, Asst CofAC for USW, 22 Jan 41, AC Project Rcds (Lyon Papers), bk. 56, Proc Data.

actually had large-scale defense orders in hand.

Seen in retrospect, it seems clear that automobile production should have been curtailed sooner or at least the 1942 model changes should have been curbed more drastically. But to place responsibility for these steps upon the manufacturers themselves is to charge them with a leadership in the nation's economic mobilization that they did not possess. If responsibility rests anywhere, it rests with those officials—civilians and military alike —who shared the burdens of authority in the period of national crisis. But, although they legally held authority to take the necessary steps and provide for the nation's defense, they could not exercise that authority until it was politically feasible to do so. Since the public—if its opinions had been gauged aright—was believed to feel that the production of both guns and butter was not only entirely possible but desirable, no orders categorically directed Detroit to stop automobile production until after the United States entered the war.[82]

The capacity of Detroit was not adequately used for aircraft production before Pearl Harbor, but this was not so much the result of poor planning by government officials or egregiously selfish conduct on the part of the automobile makers as it was a product of the inherent difficulties involved in any attempt to mobilize a competitive, capitalist economy within the framework of a politically free state. Walter Lippmann may have put his finger on the very heart of the problem when he charged that Knudsen and Hillman had been trying to act as umpires between industry and labor instead of taking command.[83] But command rests ultimately upon the threat of coercion rather than co-operation and, at least until the Japanese struck, it was probably not possible to resort to coercion. The nation's formal declaration of war after 7 December 1941 changed the nature of the facility problem drastically but by no means solved it.

Expansion or Conversion?

Big Business and Small Business

The automobile industry was not the only segment of the national economy to face the dilemma of expansion or conversion even though the question first came into focus there. During each successive month of 1941, as material shortages became increasingly acute, more and more small business firms were driven to seek contracts for military items, contracts that would assure their material requisitions a priority status. Small business, generally defined by the Army as concerns employing 500 or fewer workers, had hitherto avoided government contracts because of the inevitable mass of administrative overhead involved.[84] When

---

[82] Indicative of the guns and butter attitude is the following from *Business Week* (November 23, 1940), page 4, "There is no point in curtailing auto production . . . so that body plants can devote themselves to (aircraft) assemblies. . . ." Even a year later, attempts by OPM to curb production of butter for guns encountered opposition. A *Fortune* poll, November 1941, page 200, showed that 75 percent of the nation's businessmen felt that the New Deal was using the crisis as a pretext to push its social program.

[83] Walter Lippmann, syndicated column "Today and Tomorrow," January 16, 1942.

[84] See chs. IV, V, and VI, above.

THE PROBLEM OF INDUSTRIAL CAPACITY

faced with the alternatives of military contracts and their interminable rules, regulations, and intricacies on the one hand and, on the other hand, the prospect of going out of business for want of certain raw materials available only to those holding priority ratings, however, small businessmen clamored for defense orders.

Somewhat to their surprise, many small firms had their offers of idle capacity rejected. On every side they heard laments that munitions output was far below requirements, yet they returned empty handed from their search for contracts. Procurement officers for the supply services were passing out orders involving millions, but all seemed to go to big business. Appeals to these contract winners for subcontracts often brought no better results. This was confusing and disturbing in itself; what followed was even more so. At the very moment that small businessmen were casting about anxiously and even desperately for defense orders to occupy their idle factories, the newspapers were filled with reports of vast new facilities being erected at government expense to speed munitions output. Was this gross favoritism to big business or the result of flagrantly bad planning? A special Senate group, popularly called the Truman Committee, was soon investigating this alleged discrimination in the award of contracts.[85]

The irritation felt by many disgruntled small businessmen was reflected in an early interim report of the Truman Committee. The special investigators were inclined to place the blame on Army and Navy shoulders. The military services, the committee found, had failed to make adequate peacetime preparations. As a result there had ensued a mad scramble for matériel. True, the services did try to co-ordinate, but their efforts in this direction fell short. For want of preliminary planning, procurement officers were left at the mercy of the contractors. When manufacturers who were anxious to continue the production of civilian goods while taking on military contracts insisted that they would require new plants if they were to meet delivery deadlines, procurement officers were in no position to argue. In their eyes, early delivery was at least as important as cost. Furthermore, the committee reported, lack of experience prevented procurement officials from scrutinizing manufacturers' proposals in sufficient detail to determine whether or not they provided for the maximum amount of subcontracting. Although a great many small business firms might have been converted to war work by forcing prime contractors to subcontract work wherever possible, the committee concluded that procurement officers in the military services had taken the line of least resistance and had authorized generous facility expansions for prime contractors instead of insisting on conversion of existing facilities where it was feasible to do so.[86]

The charge of the Truman Committee that procurement officers had favored big business over small business was hard to contest. By midsummer of 1941 approximately three-quarters of the $10,000,000,000 in defense orders already placed were in the hands of some 50-odd large

---

[85] S Res 71, 77th Cong, 1st sess, March 1, 1941.

[86] Senate Rpt 480, 77th Cong, 1st sess, November 17, 1941, pt. 3, pp. 2-4.

corporations. Worse yet, some of these favored firms had been granted facility expansions that increased their capacity well beyond existing requirements—and this at a time when more and more small firms were slowing down for want of priorities on scarce materials.[87]

The fabrication of oleo struts offers a case in point. During the fall of 1940, Wright Field procurement officers recognized that difficult-to-manufacture hydraulic shock-absorber struts were threatening to become a dangerous bottleneck. Airframe firms on every hand reported shortages in this item. The civilian officials in NDAC lacked sufficient staff to deal with the problem, so it fell to the Air Corps by default. A hurried survey revealed that the leading manufacturers of oleo struts were swamped with business. Under heavy pressure for results, procurement officers moved fast.[88] Less than seventy-two hours after the survey had been completed, they dispatched a letter of intent to one of the most important strut makers, the Cleveland Pneumatic Tool Company, authorizing expenditures up to $4,500,000 for enlarging floor space and buying new tools to triple the firm's output of struts.[89] In the weeks and months that followed, half a dozen other firms received similar assistance in the rush to build up production to meet the needs of the successively larger aircraft programs as they were announced. These expansions continued for nearly a year until finally, in October 1941, one of the newly financed strut manufacturers, the Hughes Tool Company of Houston, found itself fairly teeming with capacity but no orders.[90]

At first glance the plight of a manufacturer with production capacity enlarged at government expense but standing idle would appear to confirm the most damaging charges leveled by the Truman Committee. The actual situation, however, was somewhat different. Production of oleo struts still lagged behind demand, but aircraft builders primarily interested in early deliveries preferred to place their orders with the more experienced strut makers rather than with firms just coming into production. Thus, until procurement officers at Wright Field could persuade airframe manufacturers to place orders filling up the newly erected capacity, the air arm itself had to award contracts for standard sizes of struts to keep the newly expanded firms occupied.[91] This was an awkward arrangement, but the same situation would have occurred even if strut production had been enlarged by conversion rather than by new construction. Moreover, even if the expansions granted to the several strut manufacturers did run production capacity ahead of orders placed by aircraft builders, this was no evidence that expansion was unnecessary or undesirable, for air arm officials were consciously planning not alone for current or on-order needs but also for potential needs should

---

[87] *Business Week* (August 16, 1941, page 7, and August 23, 1941, page 15) reflects the growing irritation of small business with the Army's failure to spread orders across the economy. See also Nelson, *Arsenal of Democracy*, pp. 271–72.

[88] Memo, CofAC for Gen Brett, 28 Nov 40, and reply, 2 Dec 40, AFCF 452.1–H Parts.

[89] Col Volandt to Cleveland Pneumatic Tool Co., 30 Nov 40; TWX, Tech Exec, WF, to Facilities Sec, OCAC, 25 Nov 40, AFCF 004.4.

[90] Memo, Chief, Mat Div, for USW, 17 Oct 41, AFCF 452.1–H Parts.

[91] *Ibid.*

THE PROBLEM OF INDUSTRIAL CAPACITY

war come. As a matter of fact, for certain critical raw materials there had been a conscious policy shift early in 1941 from expansions predicated upon orders in hand to expansions based upon anticipated orders.[92] Seen in this perspective, the enlargement of strut capacity beyond the level of current orders was clearly justified as prudent military planning. But this still does not come to grips with the general question of why procurement officials resorted so frequently to expansion—new construction—in preference to conversion of extant facilities throughout the nation.

There were, in practice, a number of reasons why both Air Corps procurement officers and prime contractors favored the construction of new plants over the conversion of old ones. To begin with, it is entirely understandable that procurement officers preferred to deal with well-known, old-line, established firms rather than with newly converted strangers. To take the example of oleo struts again, it was certainly much simpler administratively to award the Cleveland Pneumatic Tool Company an 800,000-foot expansion in floor space than to go out and round up one or more idle plants under different management to get the same amount of productive area. A newly located firm might or might not turn out to be capably managed or financially sound; its technical skills might very well fail to measure up to the exacting requirements of strut fabrication, and even if its labor force and available machine tools were of the highest quality, it would still be necessary to spend a considerable period in tooling up and training. Even after such obstacles as proprietary rights and patents were cleared away, a newly converted firm would have to co-ordinate its production line with the design changes introduced by the initial manufacturer. Under the circumstances it often seemed patently easier to accomplish this intricate task under one roof and one management.

There were still other reasons why the construction of new floor space and the installation of brand new machine tools sometimes appeared preferable to the conversion of extant facilities. Some small manufacturers represented themselves as eager to convert their idle plants to the production of military end items when in reality what they wanted was to have the government put them in business, providing a plant, tools, working capital, and orders, or just about everything, including a guaranteed profit.[93] Sometimes the facilities offered were little more than junk—several acres of floor space in a Chicago railway carshop, for example, empty throughout the depression, encrusted with rust and still haunted by the memories of 1929.[94]

Not least among the reasons why prime contractors urged expansions for themselves instead of subcontracting to converted manufacturers was their reluctance to build up potential competitors among the subcontractors they trained. This was by no means a purely hypothetical fear. One manufacturer trained as a subcontractor by Glenn L. Martin,

---

[92] Memo, Asst Chief, Mat Div, for USW, 25 Mar 41, AFCF 470.1-B.

[93] See, for a characteristic case, W. S. Knudsen to E. Schram, RFC, 3 Oct 40, SW files, Airplanes, item 1797a.

[94] Maj F. M. Hopkins to Col Volandt, 19 Mar 41, AFCF 004.4.

to take but a single illustration, ended up by luring away eight Martin engineers and then applying to the Air Corps for an independent prime contract.[95]

On balance, then, the charges of the Truman Committee were not without merit, but it should be clear that decisions on whether to build new floor space or convert existing facilities were at best difficult to make. With the perspective of time it now appears that procurement officials did on occasion undertake expansions where they probably should have pressed for conversions. No one would deny the need for new construction in providing vast assembly plants with bays wide enough to accommodate the largest wing spans, but the erection of new factories for accessory and equipment manufacturers posed a different problem. Doubtlessly a watertight case could be made for the erection of an entirely new Curtiss-Wright engine facility planned for efficient mass production just outside Cincinnati, but would it be possible to do the same for the thirty satellite subcontractors and suppliers around this prime contractor, who also received facility expansions? Occasionally a new process, magnesium casting, for example, made new construction unavoidable, but it is difficult to believe that each and every firm among the thirty was a unique or exceptional case for which conversion was entirely impracticable.[96]

Air Corps procurement officers probably gave too little consideration to the potentialities of conversion. Certainly the conversion of existing facilities, especially the capacity of small business, was desirable for both economic and political reasons, but it is imperative to remember that the decisions taken must ultimately be judged in terms of military necessity, which is to say in this instance, speed of delivery and quality of product. To reach any conclusion on this point it will be useful to defer judgment, at least momentarily, so as to first survey the facilities question as a whole. Suffice it to say that by midsummer 1941 more and more small business firms were driven from their normal channels by "priority shortages."[97] Their reiterated complaints brought mounting pressure from Congress.

The Facilities Problem After Pearl Harbor

From midsummer through 7 December 1941 the official position held that expansion was over. Future increases in capacity would be achieved by conversions. Only in unusual circumstances where the need for specialized facilities made new construction unavoidable was it anticipated that deviations from this stand would be granted. Nonetheless, the nation had scarcely awakened to the shocking realities of war in the days immediately following the Japanese assault before this policy was discarded and the air arm set off on yet another round of new construction.

There were a number of reasons for the apparent reversal in policy. When the nation at last plunged into war, it did

---

[95] Memo, Chief, Mat Div, for CofAC, 3 Jan 41, AFCF 452.1 Airplanes, Gen.

[96] Hearings of Special Com Investigating the National Defense Program (Truman Com), April 15, 1941, pt. 1, p. 24.

[97] For a statement of policy, see R&R, Chief, Mat Div, to Personnel Div, 4 Nov 41, AFCF 004.4.

so under the most undesirable circumstances—the blow fell before the rearmament program reached completion, and it came simultaneously on two fronts. The sudden and appalling prospect of a two-ocean war made existing computations of requirements seem utterly inadequate and led to the formulation of new and higher goals. Moreover, since the shooting war arrived before the conversions that were taking place throughout the mass-production industries had begun to pay off with impressive records of output, responsible officials in the air arm and the civilian agencies alike may well have underestimated the potentialities of the as yet unconverted capacity of the nation. Whatever their reasoning may have been, they gave the signal for the construction of a large number of entirely new plants.[98]

Before the nation had been two weeks at war, North American, Bell, Curtiss-Wright, Douglas, Republic, and the Fisher Body Division of General Motors all launched new facility construction projects, at costs ranging from 20 to 50 million dollars each, to increase production of fighters, bombers, and heavy transports. In addition, most of the major airframe manufacturers who had received facility projects during the first round of building in the fall of 1940 were now authorized to enlarge them with further additions. Nor was this all. Small- and medium-sized airframe concerns were now deluged with orders, mostly for training aircraft, and they too received authorizations for new facilities commensurately scaled to their needs. Included in this group were such firms as Aeronca of Middletown, Ohio; Beech of Wichita, Kansas; Bellanca of New Castle, Delaware; Fairchild Aviation of Hagerstown, Maryland; and Northrop of Hawthorne, California, to name but a few of the better known.

Manufacturers of accessory and equipment items—instruments, superchargers, magnetos, and the like—shared in the wave of newly authorized facilities as did the engine manufacturers, not only those previously mentioned but other companies as well. New construction provided for the engine manufacturers was even more lavish than that for the airframe builders. Projects ranged from $50,000,000 up. The largest of these, a 6,750,000-square-foot expansion for the Dodge Division of the Chrysler Corporation at a cost of $173,000,000, turned out to be the largest facility project sponsored by the air arm during the war, larger even than the more widely publicized Willow Run plant. A most graphic indication of the impact all this new construction had on the nation's economy was to be observed in the priority issued by OPM for some 7,000,000 tons of structural steel to begin work on these facilities. In short, despite all the hue and cry about the desirability of conversion rather than expansion, the new construction authorized (for the most part in the first four months after Pearl Harbor) actually exceeded the facilities provided during the previous year.[99]

The unhappy truth was this: most officials were ready to admit that it was highly desirable to convert rather than expand, but no one had any really effective scheme of conversion ready to use or ready to assure results. The air arm

---

[98] AAF Hist Study 40, pp. 109–11.

[99] *Ibid.*, pp. 111–13.

no less than the other military services lacked a comprehensive plan for this purpose. Although Mr. Knudsen had first raised the question of conversion in Detroit during October 1940, as late as January 1942 General Arnold was only just beginning to urge that a study of idle facilities be conducted there, and an officer in the area responded that although the facilities there were inadequate for assembly work, it might be well to collect data to determine whether or not they could be utilized for depot repair work.[100] Twenty years of industrial planning and facility survey work seem to have been largely in vain.

The military services, of course, were not alone at fault when conversion was not pushed as aggressively as it might have been. Employers in some of the larger firms receiving military orders were sometimes fearful of the dislocations that were expected to accompany the change-over from civilian to military production. Skilled workmen and vital foremen might be lured away and then prove unwilling to return later on. Labor, too, feared unemployment and loss of seniority rights during a prolonged period of conversion. Many small firms with less ample capital resources, even those successful in getting war contracts, worried about the costs of financing conversions. Tooling up for production of items for which a firm lacked any experience whatsoever was a venture into the unknown not to be undertaken lightly.[101]

Although various federal statutes on the books authorized the Executive to convert industries to war production by commandeering wherever necessary, such a course was clearly inexpedient, politically as well as technically, in all but the most extreme cases.[102] Since even a commandeered factory must be managed and a coerced management was liable not to be very co-operative, plant seizure by the government was obviously only a last resort.

The most effective method for bringing about a wide-scale conversion of facilities to war production, as the preceding pages have shown, was the obvious expedient of shutting off the flow of raw materials to nonessential industries. In the auto industry, the war itself called the turn; the Japanese advance cut off the supply of raw rubber, making curtailment in the production of civilian automobiles virtually unavoidable. For most other industries, however, the granting or withholding of raw materials required a fine adjustment of conflicting considerations—precisely the role long anticipated for a civilian superagency set up to ride herd on the nation's war economy. Neither NDAC nor OPM had measured up to the task, but the shift in public opinion that accompanied the nation's plunge into war so strengthened the administration's hand that the President finally felt able to take the step long urged upon him. He created the War Production Board (WPB) under Donald Nelson, with powers at last sufficiently broad to dominate the economy at least to the extent of forcing conversions by

---

[100] Asst AAG to CofAC, 15 Jan 42; unsigned Memo for CofASC, 26 Jan 42. Both in AFCF 004.4.

[101] AAF Hist Study 40, p. 114. See especially the sources cited on pp. 111–13.

[102] See, for example, the National Defense Act of June 4, 1920, Section 120, as well as the acts passed during the summer and fall of 1940 as described in Chapter XV.

THE PROBLEM OF INDUSTRIAL CAPACITY

systematic curtailments in the flow of resources.[103]

The WPB did indeed play a major role in enforcing conversions to war work, not only by driving in the small producer, but also by putting pressure on the military services to meet these offers of capacity halfway with prime contracts for end items and by forcing big contractors to utilize the converted capacity of small business by a greater distribution of subcontracts. Yet, in crediting this role to WPB, it is important not to overlook other factors that were at work. After Pearl Harbor, conversion carried with it the sanction of patriotic enthusiasm, and many of the miracles of the shift to military production accomplished by industry were unquestionably the work of determined men driven by zeal for victory. To reinforce this patriotic zeal, a significant innovation appeared in the rules for government financing of facilities. Hitherto, officials responsible for the most attractive financing arrangement, the DPC scheme, had virtually refused to underwrite more than 5 percent of a manufacturer's anticipated postwar rehabilitation costs. A few weeks after the outbreak of war, this allowance was raised to 10 percent. Similar relaxations appeared all along the line. Applications for facility financing were less closely scrutinized; contractors were permitted to include sizable contingency allowances in their estimates; purchases of general-purpose machine tools (which would have postwar value) were authorized with relatively little question. In short, the new rules made conversion far more attractive.[104]

As it turned out in practice, conversion proved less painful than many had anticipated. There were, it is true, as many as 150,000 unemployed workers in Detroit during the spring of 1942, to cite an important example, but as the tooling-up process reached completion, unemployment virtually disappeared. Strenuous efforts were begun to import labor from outlying areas, while local housewives were pressed to take up jobs in the factories. Despite earlier contentions, by the middle of June 1942, nearly 70 percent of the Detroit pool of machine tools was being used on war contracts—a backlog of orders then amounting to some $14,000,000,000 in contrast to the $4,000,000,000 worth of orders on the books in Detroit on 7 December 1941.[105] The pattern laid down in Detroit was substantially repeated throughout the nation in other segments of the economy as the curtailed flow of resources, wartime fervor, and simplified administrative regulations induced more and more manufacturers to convert their facilities to war production.

Although conversion rather than expansion was increasingly enforced after April 1942, there was a certain amount of new construction authorized after that time. Nevertheless, in the final analysis, it turned out that more than 75 percent of the facilities sponsored by the air arm in World War II had been authorized before the end of 1942, and most of this construction was begun before the end of the first quarter.[106] The few projects that came afterward were for the most part those made necessary by the exigencies of

---

[103] AAF Hist Study 40, pp. 114–20.
[104] Ibid., pp. 124–28.
[105] Ibid., pp. 121, 123.
[106] Ibid., p. 130.

the war or the appearance of new technical processes, rather than any general shortage of capacity.[107] Once again, it would appear, the air arm, and for that matter the military services in general, repeated the pattern of 1941, preaching conversion but practicing expansion whenever military exigency seemed to require immediate results. A careful appraisal of the record in retrospect should shed some light on whether or not this policy—if it could be called such—was justified.

*The Facilities Program:
An Appraisal*

The Record of Achievement

During the war years from 1940 through 1945 the air arm sponsored some 190 facility projects. Of these, 57 involved factories for building airframes, gliders, or subassemblies; 8 involved engine plants; and 107 involved plants for fabricating parts, equipment, or accessories. The remaining 18 projects developed modification centers where postproduction alterations could be introduced in finished aircraft.[108] To pay for these projects the air arm authorized some $3,000,000,000 in direct expenditures. In addition, tax amortizations or rapid depreciation privileges accounted for an additional $840,000,000. As the following figures show, more than half of the direct expenditures were authorized in 1942, and by far the greatest proportion of this amount came in the first few months of the year—just after the nation entered the war:[109]

Year	Expenditure Authorized	Percent of 5-Year Total
1940	$151,298,472	4.9
1941	629,999,116	20.3
1942	1,665,972,004	53.8
1943	426,360,787	13.8
1944	222,504,289	7.2

All the new construction connoted by these billions in disbursements, taken in conjunction with the existing aircraft industry already enlarged under the stimulus of foreign orders, plus the conversions effected during the war, represented an enormous increase in productive capacity. Between September 1940, when the government began its facility expansion program, and the end of 1944, the year of peak production, the weight of aircraft actually produced rose 1,900 percent. And even at that, privately financed expansions had already greatly enlarged the industry in 1939. Available capacity rose more rapidly than actual output of airframes. During the year following September 1940, aircraft production in the United States doubled. By the end of another year, in the fall of 1942, capacity had doubled the 1941 figure and during 1943 this multiplication was more than repeated. Thus by the middle of 1944, in time for the invasion of Europe, aircraft productive capacity—not output— was estimated at about 2,000 percent of the level available in September 1940.

The record of the nation's increasing capacity to turn out airplanes is an im-

---

[107] *Ibid.*, ch. 8, *passim.*
[108] Craven and Cate, eds., *Men and Planes*, p. 318. The subject of modification centers is treated at greater length in Chapter XX, below.
[109] AAF Hist Study 40, p. 222. Unless otherwise indicated, the contents of this section are based on Chapter X of the study.

THE PROBLEM OF INDUSTRIAL CAPACITY

pressive one. In a period of five or six years the aircraft industry jumped to first place among the nation's manufacturing enterprises, reflecting at once the imagination and energy of those who participated in the expansion and the lavishness with which facilities were provided.[110] Nevertheless, to be meaningful in shaping policy for the future, this record of achievement must be studied from a number of perspectives.

The Cost in Time

Vastly expanded productive capacity is of little value if it is not ready when needed. The facilities program of the air arm must be measured ruthlessly against this unyielding criterion: How long did it take?

For newly constructed airframe factories, from green grass to the day the first acceptable airplane rolled off the assembly line, the average time lag experienced in World War II amounted to 18 months. From green grass to full production averaged 31 months—in contrast to the 18 or 20 months anticipated by some Air Corps planners in 1940. Averages, of course, are deceptive. Some fighter plants were built, equipped with machinery, and attained full production in 24 months. And at the other extreme, the newly constructed plants for the Boeing Superfortress, the B-29, consumed about 40 months from green grass to full production, although technical difficulties in the aircraft itself as well as delays in plant construction contributed to the extended lag. As a general rule, the time required to get into full production was appreciably less where the aircraft design in question was well out of the experimental stage when the tooling process began.

In contrast to the time involved in construction at entirely new or green grass sites, is the time spent in building additions to existing plants. Here the span from the decision to build to the achievement of full scheduled production averaged 21 months. The time lag from the decision to build to the day the first acceptable aircraft appeared is thus significantly less than was the case with entirely new plants. Nonetheless, the step up from first production item to full production in the expanded plants took just about as long as did the process in entirely new plants, since difficulties such as the recruitment of labor, training of supervisors, and so forth were involved in both cases.

Even when a manufacturer was already in full production on a given type of aircraft, such as a civilian transport, the experience of the war years showed that it required an average of 28 months to switch over to full production of a military aircraft. This did not mean that there had to be a gap of 28 months with no production whatever, of course, since work on one type could be tapered down while the other was building up. In such change-overs only about 5 months actually elapsed between the last month of peak production on the old line and the first month of peak production on the new. The rest of the 28-month period was spent in tooling up and pilot line work on the new model.

Whether one takes the extreme of 40 months or the most favorable minimum

---

[110] Williams, "Growth of the Aircraft Industry," *Prospects and Problems in Aviation*, p. 3.

of 18 months, it took a painfully long time to accelerate production in the emergency. When one recognizes the enormous advantage the nation enjoyed in the facility expansions undertaken during the year or two before Pearl Harbor, the implications of an 18- to 40-month delay in reaching full production is all too obvious.

What was true of airframes was almost equally true of aircraft engines. Where the government undertook to build entirely new factories, from green grass to full production required an average of 23 months. From the beginning of building to the first acceptable item required an average of 14 months.

Taking the experience of airframes and engines together, it is clear that the quickest way to accelerate production by building was to make additions to existing plants rather than begin work on entirely new sites. But any attempt to apply this conclusion in the future would have to assume that adequate pools of labor and other resources would be readily available at the site of each going concern to be expanded.

Conversion or Construction?

The experience of World War II shows that it required just about the same length of time, on the average, to convert automobile factories to aircraft engine production as it did to build an entirely new plant, tool it up, and get into production at full schedule. This seeming paradox is explained largely by the fact that the manufacturing of aircraft engines in mass-production quantities called for the installation of numerous special-purpose tools. Production could not begin until these intricate tools were themselves fabricated and installed. During the long months in which the machine tool builders were at work on them, it was quite possible to erect new floor space. Thus it turned out that the converted automobile plants and the newly erected plants started just about even when their special tools were delivered.

For airframes, a comparison of the relative merits of conversion and new construction is difficult if not impossible to make—at least with any degree of validity. Only one automobile manufacturer, Ford, actually converted to the fabrication of complete fly-away aircraft and, ironically, this was done largely, though not entirely, in a newly constructed plant at Willow Run. The facts of Ford's production record are available but are extremely difficult to interpret. From the decision to locate at Willow Run, it required 18 months to turn out the first acceptable item. This time span is not, however, an entirely meaningful one since the original Ford program called for the production of knockdown sets of parts at Willow Run for assembly by aircraft manufacturers elsewhere; only belatedly was it decided to build complete airplanes at the Ford site. Some 38 months went by before Willow Run had full scheduled production, in contrast to delays running from 25 to 32 months encountered in the three other plants making the same bomber, the Consolidated B-24 Liberator. But here again the measuring stick is not adequate, for much of Ford's trouble stemmed from the difficulty of luring labor out to Willow Run, a location that offered inadequate housing.

In terms of direct man-hours of labor

expended per pound of airframe turned out, the Ford Willow Run plant for a brief period held the best record in the entire industry. And even this favorable ratio could easily have been improved had Ford been allowed to go all out once the obstacles to production had been circumvented, but by that time the end of the war was in sight and the need for an indefinite number of B-24 bombers had passed. The record of low labor outlay per airframe pound turned out was not won without cost, for the special tooling that made it possible was extremely expensive. In short, the Ford triumph in proving that the mass-production methods of the automotive industry could be utilized for aircraft was won at a cost in time lag and tooling dollars that went far to offset the subsequent savings in labor costs and the ultimate achievement of mass production.

By the yardstick of cost per square foot of floor space obtained, the facility program of the air arm in World War II shows that airframe capacity could be obtained by conversion at approximately one-third of the initial outlay by the government needed for new construction. But even here initial costs could be deceptive, since the long-run cost of new construction would have to include sums recovered by plant sales at the war's end, rents paid for the duration, and the potentially lower prices chargeable on end products procured from manufacturers using government-owned facilities in contrast to procurement from manufacturers using their own facilities. The differences in taxes paid between these two classes of contractor would still further complicate any valid comparisons drawn between them.

It is impossible to determine whether it is faster and cheaper in the long run to convert or construct airframe and engine facilities in an emergency. Even after conceding that speed is more important than cost in wartime, it is still not possible to derive a positive conclusion on the relative merits of these two courses. A Scots verdict is seldom popular and never dramatic; it fails to give a clear-cut answer to those who want a simple rule of thumb for use in guiding policy. But frustrating or not, there it must stand insofar as airframes and aircraft engines are concerned.

In the matter of facilities for manufacturing aircraft accessories and equipment, the data available are inadequate to permit any conclusions on the problem of conversion or construction, but the same factors that conditioned aircraft and engine facility policy might be expected to apply. For those items requiring special tooling and special-purpose machine tools consuming months to build, new facilities might easily be erected while the tools were on order, offsetting the most important time saving offered by conversion. Once again, it would appear that tools and tooling lay at the heart of the facility question and should be studied with particular care.

Although the air arm spent some $3,000,000,000 in direct financing of facilities during the war, by no means all of this money went into the construction of new floor space. Actually, only 35 percent went toward new construction. An additional 4 percent went for the purchase of land for building sites, railroad spurs, and the like, but the remaining 61 percent was spent for the purchase of tools.[111] Since in many instances new tools had to be provided whether the floor space utilized was secured by new construction or conversion, the total of direct air arm expenditures charged up to *facilities* can be misleading. Far from indicating a preference on the part of the air arm for new construction in lieu of conversion, these expenditures merely show that machine tools rather than floor space constituted the real problem. For if the major facility cost to the government was in tools rather than floor space, then the crucial question of policy, the vital choice between the alternatives of construction and conversion, comes down at last to a series of decisions on tools.

In sum, conversion offered no real saving in time over construction where special tools had to be built and installed before production could begin. Moreover, many other factors such as dispersion, labor availability, and the like must also enter the equation, for the most part in favor of new construction. On the other hand, where general-purpose tools would serve well enough for the manufacturing tasks in hand and were available, conversion was certainly to be preferred over new construction, other things being equal. Where procurement officers of the air arm urged government financing of new construction and the purchase of new tools when conversion of existing plants and utilization of existing general-purpose tools were entirely feasible, they erred. That they did err in this respect is clear.

There were, of course, good reasons to explain if not to excuse the course pursued by air arm procurement officials. They were under pressure from their superiors for results, early deliveries and a rapid build-up of output, so they were especially vulnerable to contractors who brought in studies showing that new tools and new floor space at government expense were essential if the desired production targets were to be met. What is more, some contractors may have felt an incentive to inflate their estimates as to the additional tools and plant required, since they might reasonably expect to buy up any such facilities from the government at bargain prices at the end of the war. While a big airframe manufacturer might be wary of overloading with millions of square feet of excess assembly area in peacetime, a manufacturer of accessory and equipment items whose business was not exclusively oriented toward aircraft products need have no such fear. For him, the inducement to seek generous financial assistance for facilities was strong indeed.

If one concedes that the air arm did finance some unnecessary facilities for equipment and accessory manufacturers, yet another extenuating circumstance should be considered. The great bulk of these expansions, whether in tools or in floor space, was authorized in the frenzied early months of the war. Procurement staffs were totally inadequate to the task, and it proved impossible to scrutinize each facility application as closely as it should have been—and would have been had the more rigorous criteria of the pre-Pearl Harbor period been continued in use.

The mad rush to provide adequate productive capacity to meet the military requirements of World War II only served

---

[111] Craven and Cate, eds., *Men and Planes*, p. 317.

to prove anew what the public, Congress, and military planners had known all along: haste makes waste. A failure to build up adequate productive capacity by appropriating enough for aircraft procurement in peacetime made the scramble to provide that capacity in wartime both expensive and dangerous. The reluctant taxpayers and their congressmen must share in this responsibility for the wartime rush to secure facilities, but that fact did not relieve military officials from their own responsibilities. Perhaps the greatest weakness of the air arm in World War II insofar as facilities were concerned lay in its failure to perfect or expand an administrative organization capable of obtaining and using the information without which sound decisions on such questions as construction or conversion can scarcely be made. The facilities problem was far too complex to have permitted anything in the way of detailed advanced planning, but broad surveys and studies of general policy were entirely feasible. And here the pre-Pearl Harbor record of the air arm proved to be one of inadequacy.

CHAPTER XV

The Negotiation of Contracts

The Transition to Wartime Buying

The Variable Objectives of Military Purchasing

Buying aircraft for the United States was a far more involved process than mere purchasing. The very objectives of procurement had a subtle way of changing direction and shifting in emphasis while the buying went on.

In time of peace the mechanics of purchasing aircraft and their related equipment revolved primarily around the problem of equating quality (especially that aspect of quality expressed in terms of maximum possible performance) and price.[1] In time of war a number of rather different and infinitely more diverse objectives came into play. At least at first, prices declined in relative importance, and, although maximum performance remained highly desirable, speed of delivery and ability to produce in quantity contended for first-ranking importance. As wartime shortages mounted, the ability to produce while conserving scarce resources—manpower, transport, materials, facilities, and the like—became an ever more insistent objective. Gradually, however, as the supply of munitions grew larger and the nation's strength in weapons in relation to those of the enemy became increasingly favorable, low cost once again rose to pre-eminent importance. Other desirable objectives such as the prevention of excessive profits to war contractors reflected a similar rise and fall in emphasis and importance. The extremes to which the pendulum of emphasis could go are perhaps best illustrated by two examples: in the fall of 1940 the President still listed the reduction of unemployment as one of the aims of the rearmament program; in 1951 a group of industrial spokesmen studying the aims of military procurement failed even to list speed of delivery as a factor of significance.[2]

Those charged with buying military equipment had to contrive means to accomplish their immediate ends—the delivery of weapons—while taking into account the elusive and often transient goals comprehended within the general subject area labeled "military procurement." Somehow, responsible officers had to devise contract forms that would accomplish these varying objectives to the satisfaction of a legion of critics. But

---

[1] See above, chs. IV, V, and VI.

[2] H Doc 950, 76th Cong, 3d sess, September 13, 1940, and Industry Advisory Com on Military Contractor Relàtionships, Rpt to Munitions Board: Review of Major Problems in Military Procurement and Recommendations, 31 Aug 51, p. 37. For a survey of official promulgations reflecting shifts in procurement objectives, see Smith, *The Army and Economic Mobilization,* pt. IV, "Army Purchasing Problems and Policies," *passim.*

the contract itself was only half the battle. Once signed, contracts had to be administered; their clauses had to be interpreted and their discretionary phrases approved. In short, procurement officials were expected to make continual and rather subtle adjustments in the rules of the game while running the bases.

A final judgment—whether the military buyers bought wisely or foolishly—need not concern us here. The mere recital of their efforts should afford meaningful insights into the problem of military procurement as a whole. Within this context, the relatively large share of the total falling to the air arm (approximately half of munitions expenditures in the first few months after the President's call to arms in May 1940 and upward of a third thereafter) makes a close scrutiny of air matériel procurement especially worthwhile. And no phase of the whole procurement story is more crucial than the difficult era of transition from the pace and practice of peacetime to the urgent and expedient methods of war—where possible, by administrative action; where necessary, by legislative enactment.

Speeding Procurement by Administrative Means

At the very beginning of the rearmament program, Air Corps officials had recognized that the protracted procurement sequence of peacetime would have to be drastically streamlined if the air power essential for national defense were to be delivered on time. A number of steps could be taken to this end. Some of them represented major shifts in policy; others involved seemingly trivial changes in practice but brought substantial reductions in the time span of the procurement cycle.

Typical of the major changes in policy taken at executive discretion was the decision to buy untried designs for production model aircraft, off the drawing board as it were, instead of requiring manufacturers to submit samples reduced to practice beforehand. There were serious shortcomings in such a procedure. Of this procurement officers were fully aware, but the new policy promised to shorten the procurement cycle by several months and the need for speed in arming the nation seemed to justify the risks involved.[3]

Of the minor changes in procedure that helped to shorten the procurement cycle appreciably, perhaps none was more significant than the inauguration of a daily air courier service between Wright Field and the Washington headquarters. Even a later generation accustomed to the easy communication made possible by the almost unrestricted use of leased telephone lines to Ohio should be able to appreciate the delays and frustrations that continually beset the business of aircraft procurement before regular courier service was introduced. Another administrative innovation, seemingly trivial but of far-reaching effect, was the directive ordering all contractual papers to be "hand carried" through the headquarters paper mill. In normal peacetime practice a contract could spend days and even weeks wending its way at a leisurely pace from

---

[3] For background on the relative merits of design competitions and the sample aircraft method of procurement, see above, pages 132–43 and 247–49. See also, Service Sec, Proc Div, ATSC, Prewar Proc by the Air Corps, pp. 14–18, and Gen Arnold, Lecture at AIC, 5 Oct 40, WFCF 350.001 Lectures, 1941.

out basket to in basket as it gathered the co-ordinations and approvals required by law or regulation. The stipulations in themselves could not easily be evaded, but by assigning an individual pusher or runner to each contract it was at least possible to cut down on the time papers customarily spent merely waiting for pickup and delivery.[4]

The number of minor peacetime routines that could be modified by alert officials to effect appreciable savings in the time required for procurement was, for the most part, limited only by the ability to break through peacetime habits of thought. Occasionally, however, even the petty mechanics of administration proved difficult to alter because they involved matters beyond departmental discretion. The little matter of corporate seals presented just such a case. As the buying rush mounted, contracting officers at Wright Field repeatedly found manufacturers' negotiators ready to sign a contract but inhibited for want of the official corporate seal, without which the signatures of the company's officers would not be binding. Even though this was clearly a minor technicality, neither contractors nor contracting officers wished to risk evasion however expedient it might appear. Inquiries were hurriedly dispatched to Washington: would the Government Accounting Office invalidate a contract without the corporate seal? Two months later the Comptroller General's favorable reply reached Wright Field.[5]

Meanwhile, one is left to imagine, the representatives of multimillion dollar aircraft firms flew in to Wright Field lugging twelve pounds of corporate seal in their briefcases.

Skillful streamlining of procedures by administrative action could and did cut down on the time lag in the procurement cycle. But in the crisis of May 1940, when all Europe seemed about to collapse, no amount of procedural improvement could overcome the major cause of delay—aircraft manufacturers showed increasing reluctance or, in some cases, downright refusal to sign production contracts.

Manufacturers' Resistance to Government Contracts

The President's call to arms of 16 May 1940 galvanized the air arm procurement organization to furious action. Negotiations were already afoot with the leading aircraft manufacturers before the President spoke, but now the number of units to be produced increased spectacularly. Unfortunately, as the need for airplanes went up, so too did the demands of the manufacturers. As one Air Corps officer euphemistically expressed it: the negotiations ran into "legal difficulties." By this he meant that the airplane builders now insisted upon all sorts of changes in the proposed contracts before they would sign them. They wanted escalator clauses to protect them against unanticipated increase in the cost of labor and materials; they refused to sign liquidated damage clauses that would penalize them for belated deliveries; and they were reluctant to include the usual option clauses granting the government the right to pro-

---

[4] R&R, Asst Exec, OCAC, to Maj Bevans, 25 Jun 40; Memo, Asst to Dir of Purchases and Contracts, OASW, for CofAC, 14 Aug 40. Both in AFCF 161 Contracts.

[5] Chief, Contract Sec, to CGMC, 27 Nov 42; and GAO to CGMC, 29 Jan 43, AFCF 161 Contract Requirements.

THE NEGOTIATION OF CONTRACTS

cure further increments of aircraft in the future at stated prices. In short, as an officer at Wright Field complained with impressive understatement, the manufacturers were making things "very difficult." [6]

Doubtless many public officials became exasperated as days of tedious negotiation dragged on before contracts were signed. It would be grossly unfair, however, to condemn these businessmen without a full awareness of the considerations that operated on both sides of the bargaining table. To begin with, the sums involved and the tasks proposed—even if dwarfed in retrospect—seemed staggeringly large at the time. Individual firms were being invited to undertake projects far beyond the normal range of their capital. This alone would inspire hesitation. But there was another consideration in the calculations of the negotiators. The manufacturers naturally wanted to make a profit but, more particularly, they were anxious to avoid loss. When considering a multi-million dollar contract on a small base of capitalization, even a slight miscalculation or ill-advised concession at the bargaining table could bring not only a failure to profit but destructive, bankrupting corporate loss. Procurement officers with long experience knew that managements on the verge of bankruptcy, or fearful of that threat, did not achieve creative wonders in design, development, and production. While it is easy to look back and condemn the leading aircraft manufacturer who took so long to sign contracts in the desperate spring and summer of 1940, such criticisms may not invariably be warranted.

One can find evidence suggesting that certain manufacturers did take advantage of the nation's exigency, but judgments should not be made without knowledge of the circumstances. One airplane builder, for example, did refuse to guarantee the performance of the airplanes he turned out. The facts show, however, that the manufacturer was being asked to put a novel design directly into large-scale production, and he had already lost over a million dollars on Army and Navy contracts during 1940.[7]

The fear of loss made men reluctant to act. Sometimes corporate officers preferred to accept a contract foregoing profits if only they were guaranteed against loss.[8] Ironically, as events were to demonstrate, "no profit" or limited profit contracts turned out to be something less than desirable from the government's point of view since they offered little or no incentive to efficiency. Yet, for all the valid fears of loss, there were actually manufacturers at the other end of the spectrum who went full steam ahead—and damn the torpedoes—ordering materials, getting production under way, incurring liabilities even while still haggling around the negotiation table at

---

[6] R&R, Brig Gen G. H. Brett to Gen Arnold, 6 Jun 40; TWX, Prod–T–6, Brett to Volandt, 31 May 40. Both in AFCF 161 Contracts. The fear of litigation resulting from entering contracts in haste was not without foundation in fact. Several millions of dollars of contract values from U.S. procurement in World War I were still being contested in the courts when World War II arrived. Office of Fiscal Dir (Army), History of Fiscal Services: 1940–1945 (1946), p. 829.

[7] Hearings of the Special Com Investigating the National Defense Program (Truman Com), August 22, 1941, pt. 6, pp. 1856–57.

[8] Wilson, *Slipstream*, page 253, vividly illustrates the attitude of one representative corporation official.

Wright Field to get as much contractual protection as possible.⁹

Between the rigidity of the laws, which no amount of administrative simplification could entirely offset, and the looming fears of the manufacturers, who refused to sign contracts, the aircraft procurement program seemed destined toward fatal delay. In desperation officials in the War Department, always reluctant to tamper with the procurement statutes, decided to ask for and received legislative relief.¹⁰ The new statutes sought to hasten procurement from two directions: first, by authorizing procurement by negotiation, and, second, by authorizing cost-plus-fixed-fee (CPFF) contracts. Unfortunately, even the most skillfully drawn statutes did not in themselves resolve all the problems of execution or administration.

Special Legislation No Panacea

The emergency statutes of the spring and summer of 1940 did grant sweeping powers to procurement officials. As one of them expressed it, the new laws allowed contracting officers to do just about anything short of selling the Washington Monument. It would seem that such powers should have opened the floodgate to a veritable deluge of buying utterly uninhibited by the traditional restraints. In practice, however, military negotiators found that they enjoyed a good deal less freedom of maneuver than the statutes seemed to grant.

The emergency laws had scarcely been passed before the Secretary of War began to whittle them down with supplementary interpretations and instructions. Negotiated contracts in lieu of the customary competition, he directed, should be used only where "necessary" to accomplish the defense program. Cost-plus-fixed-fee contracts were to be used only where the Assistant Secretary of War gave his personal approval. Initially, the declared policy of the War Department was to oppose the use of CPFF contracts for the purchase of equipment.¹¹ The official line was to use the new powers hesitantly, if at all. Under such circumstances it was only the boldest negotiators who sought to use the powers contained in the emergency statutes. When officers must justify their decisions to their superiors at every turn, they tend to act conservatively.

Quite apart from the matter of departmental policy, there was another very good reason why CPFF contracts were not immediately favored: there simply were no appropriate contract forms or clauses ready to use. Despite all the talk in the between-war years on the probable use of some sort of cost-plus contract in a future emergency, a very rough draft of the contract form was all that had been prepared. Only after the crisis arrived and Congress had hurriedly approved the cost-plus principle did procurement officers begin to work out the detailed mechanics of a form for CPFF contracts. More than a month after Congress acted, no CPFF contract form suitable for aircraft procurement was available.¹²

---

⁹ See, for example, Telg, Kindleberger to Arnold, 27 Jun 40, AFCF 161 Contracts.
¹⁰ See ch. XIII, above.

¹¹ Actg SW to CofAC *et al.*, 2 Jul 40, AFCF 032; Memo, Maj E. C. Langmead for Chief, Mat Div, 8 Jul 40, AFCF 452.1 Airplanes, Gen.
¹² OASW to CofAC *et al.*, 23 Jul 40; Memo, CofAC for ASW, 8 Aug 40. Both in AFCF 161 Contracts.

If much of the evidence suggests that leadership in the field of procurement from the top echelon of the War Department seems to have been something less than sure-footed, it should be recalled that the incumbent officials were still new to the job. Secretary of War Stimson was not appointed to his office until late in June 1940. Assistant Secretary Patterson arrived several weeks later. These men had to learn the ropes; inevitably, in doing so they groped and stumbled until they found their bearings.[13]

The Assistant Secretary, for example, worked hard to safeguard the government's interest in CPFF contracts. This was a laudable purpose; unfortunately it missed the mark. As a lawyer and a judge, Patterson tended to see the ends sought in terms of honesty and equity. But when the new Assistant Secretary tried to impose equity by requiring all CPFF contracts to use a standard form without deviation unless personally authorized by himself, air arm officers had to educate the new civilian chief of procurement. The plain fact of the matter was that the recently revised standard War Departmen CPFF form would not cover all the special considerations involved in aircraft procurement. As if to drive this point home, the very first CPFF contract entered by the air arm was a most unusual one, a three-party deal involving the United States Government, the British Government, and the Packard Motor Car Company. Until the newly appointed Secretaries came to understand the endless complexities of their jobs, the aircraft procurement program continued to encounter delays from that quarter.[14]

The delays marking the initial use of CPFF contracts should not be attributed entirely to the hesitant policy of the civilian Secretaries. Several responsible air arm officers also opposed this type of contract. They argued with considerable point that the use of the CPFF arrangement would lift responsibility from the manufacturer's shoulders, and the government would lose control of its program. With the government footing all the bills, what would stop a manufacturer from paying labor whatever it demanded? How, they asked, could the government ensure delivery by the dates specified in the contract schedule? With no profit incentive a manufacturer was under no great pressure to produce. The CPFF contract was designed to allay the manufacturer's fears regarding costs over which he had no control. Might it not quiet these fears rather too much, making manufacturers too little concerned with results, leaving them content to let the government pay their costs and collect their fees when at long last they finished the work on contract?[15]

Experience was to reveal a host of difficulties yet unmentioned. Nonetheless, General Arnold and Mr. Knudsen decided to use the cost-plus approach. Since most manufacturers in their fear of uncontrolled costs flatly refused to accept traditional fixed-price or lump-sum con-

---

[13] Anderson, Hist of OUSW, ch. IV.

[14] TWX, DHQ-T-1120, Brett to Volandt, 5 Sep 40, AFCF Contracts; Memo, Asst to Dir of Purchases and Contracts, OASW, for CofAC et al., 30 Dec 40; AFCF 161 Contract Requirements; TWX, Cont-T-27, Contract Sec, WF, to Bolandt, 14 Jan 41, AFCF 161 CPFF Contracts.

[15] R&R, Chief, Mat Div, to Arnold, 31 Jul 40, AFCF 161 CPFF Contracts.

tracts in any event, the CPFF contract, for all its obvious drawbacks, seemed to be the only practical escape.[16]

Even the final decision to utilize the CPFF principle in major aircraft contracts did not immediately uncork a flow of signatures on contracts. The necessary forms were not available and would take days or weeks to perfect. And at the same time, manufacturers who were abruptly presented with an opportunity to accept allegedly loss-preventing CPFF contracts as well as some of the other novel features of the emergency statutes discovered that the innovations raised as many problems if not more than they solved. Not surprisingly, the manufacturers began to boggle over a new set of difficulties. How would the new "certificates of necessity" affect their depreciation? Would the Bureau of Internal Revenue agree with the War Department on this? If not, would the hapless contractor find himself in the middle of a bureaucratic brawl?[17]

Questions such as these and a dozen other legal niceties threatened to consume further weeks of precious time in protracted negotiations. Clearly some way had to be found around the legal roadblocks that continued to arise from the very statutes Congress had provided to obviate such difficulties. Here was a situation calling for the utmost in executive leadership.

The newly appointed Assistant Secretary of War was far from settled in his office; nevertheless he saw clearly that the hour called for prompt and imaginative action.[18] To meet the occasion he came forward with a legal stopgap, the so-called letter of intent, which would authorize manufacturers to go ahead on the preliminary steps to production with the full assurance of indemnification while the negotiators and legal experts took their time about working out all the details of a formal contract.

Whether it was the Assistant Secretary or one of his subordinates who initially conceived the letter of intent is now of little moment.[19] The Secretary made the idea his own; he accepted the risks involved in its application and deserves substantial credit for whatever it accomplished—and the letter of intent accomplished a great deal. It proved to be just the device needed to get production rolling. Soon air arm negotiators were doing a land office business.

A Land Office Business

By the middle of August 1940, letters of intent had gone out to just about every major airframe and engine manufacturer in the United States. By the end of the month most of the firms had accepted the letters and had started to work even though formal contracts were yet to be negotiated.[20] This task, involving so

---

[16] R&R, CofAC to Brett, 31 Jul 40, AFCF 161 CPFF.

[17] For a good résumé of some of the important difficulties delaying contracts, see Memo, Actg CofAC for ASW, 11 Jul 40, AFCF 161 Contract Requirements; Memo, CofAC for ASW, 30 Jul 40, SW files, Aircraft, item 1652 b.

[18] For an informed and highly personal view of the Assistant Secretary during his first few weeks in office, see Anderson, Hist of OUSW, ch. IV, pp. 14-19.

[19] The record is unclear on the origin of the letter of intent. For Patterson's views, see report of conversation with him, 6 Dec 45, in Pringle Papers, 18h.

[20] Asst to Chief, Mat Div, to Asst Chief, Mat Div, 9 Aug 40, AFCF 452.1-13-F Proc of Aircraft; ASW to NDAC (Knudsen), 14 Aug 40, SW files, Aircraft, item 1686; Memo, Asst CofAC for ASW, 27 Aug 40, AFCF 161 Contracts.

THE NEGOTIATION OF CONTRACTS 337

many important contracts all at once, threatened to swamp the small staff of negotiators at Wright Field. To avoid any such eventuality as well as to keep the contractors' representatives from falling over one another in the corridors and crowding each other out of hotel space, the procurement staff at Wright Field set up an orderly schedule inviting contractors to come in on fixed dates to negotiate. By this means, before the end of September 1940, more than 9,000 aircraft were actually placed on contract.[21]

In all, approximately 300 contracts with 100 manufacturers of airframes, engines, and accessories were drawn. At the time this looked like an immense volume of business. Two years later, when the Air Force was buying from some 4,000 different concerns, the 1940 roster of contractors no longer looked very impressive,[22] but in those two years air arm procurement officials were to learn from painful experience that it was the negotiating and administering of contracts that caused most of the difficulties, not the mere profusion of contracts.

The Negotiation of Contracts

The Letter of Intent

The utility of the letter of intent lay in the speed with which it could be applied. In essence, it authorized a manufacturer to incur expenses in starting production and obligated the government to reimburse him for expenses whether or not a formal contract could subsequently be agreed upon. By this device, weeks of debate over detailed contract terms did not hold up production. What is more, by using the letter of intent, it was possible to escape, at least temporarily, the normal delays encountered in the headquarters paper mill. Much of this delay revolved around the need for collecting all the required signatures of approval and the initialed co-ordinations that, as the office wags put it, helped spread the responsibility against the day of investigation. In short, the letter of intent was simply "an agreement to try to agree later." Yet even this expedient at times proved too slow, and during the late summer of 1940 some letters of intent actually took the form of telephone calls to manufacturers authorizing them to begin work immediately without even waiting for a confirming letter, which would be mailed later.[23]

Naturally this improvisation could not continue for long. To be sure, the letter of intent was again widely used during the rush to place orders after Pearl Harbor. January 1942 was the biggest procurement month of that year. At Wright Field alone, orders were placed for $6,000,000,000 worth of equipment. Most of the orders were originally placed as letters of intent and ranged all the way from a single aircraft production order of approximately $200,000,000 down to "small" orders for accessory items such as $6,000,000 worth of starters, $3,000,000

---

[21] TWX, DHQ-1137, Echols to Brett, 9 Sep 40, AFCF 161 Contracts; Memo, ASW for SW, 20 Sep 40, SW files, Aircraft, item 1767.

[22] Memo, Actg CofAC for ASW, 17 Jul 40, AFCF 400.12; Budget Office, AFAMC, to CGMC, 23 Dec 40, AFCF 161 Contracts.

[23] Interv with J. W. Schwinn, WF, 25 Jul 55. For an illustration of the utility of the letter of intent in cracking a manufacturer's reluctance to act, see Asst Tech Exec, Mat Div, to Chief, Mat Div, 14 Sep 40, AC Project Rcds (Lyon Papers), 59-32.

worth of sights, and so on.²⁴ Procurement officials also found the letter of intent helpful as a means for hastily obligating unexpended funds that would otherwise revert to the Treasury at the end of a fiscal year. But continued use of the letter led to revisions and improvements until finally it was converted into a short form or letter contract. This new form was undoubtedly a tighter instrument legally; unfortunately, it was also far less flexible than the original letter of intent and for that reason lost a great deal of its utility.²⁵

Here was the classic pattern of administration; the expedient and flexible short cut gradually became encumbered with so many formalities and "improvements" that it lost the very characteristics that made it valuable in the first place. The time had arrived for further innovation, for the discovery of new short cuts and escapes.²⁶

During the desperate summer and fall of 1940 the letter of intent probably justified its use by saving precious weeks of time, but there were drawbacks attending its application. Manufacturers found that once they started work under a letter of intent they had the government at a decided disadvantage in the subsequent negotiation of formal contract terms. Although it was the policy of the War Department to convert outstanding letters into contracts as soon as possible, some manufacturers were able to spin out negotiations for many months. The longer the delay, the more difficult it became for procurement officers to negotiate a contract to the government's advantage. Despite the determined efforts of the procurement staff at Wright Field, as late in the war as December 1944 the Air Forces still had outstanding 177 letters of intent representing over a billion dollars in procurement.²⁷

The Setting for Negotiation

Broadly speaking, the task confronting procurement officers when they sat down to negotiate contracts was to get buyer and seller into agreement on the terms and conditions of a formal contract. The emergency statutes passed during the summer of 1940 authorizing negotiated contracts greatly simplified the procurement process by permitting military buyers to narrow the range of possible

---

²⁴ See Asst to CofAC to Asst Chief, Mat Div, 2 Feb 42, AFCF 004.4 Manufacturers. See also, Lecture 22, Production Statistics, by Maj D. R. Tyson, AAF Contracting Officers School, WF, Winter 1944–45. The lectures before the AAF Contracting Officers School at Wright Field are to be found in the Wright Field Historical Office files and in a file in the possession of Mr. Schwinn, a key wartime employee at Wright Field. Neither set of lectures is complete.

²⁵ The annual report of the Under Secretary of War for 1941, pages 30–31 mentions the revised form.

²⁶ For a brilliant illustration of a suggested innovation, consider the proposal (JAG, WF, to Chief, Contract Sec, WF, 7 Jan 42, JAG files WF, Proc 10K) to use the compulsory powers of Section 9 in the Selective Service Act of 1940, not to coerce unwilling manufacturers but to give legal sanction to reimbursement for work done before the signing of a contract. The record is not clear on just why this idea was not widely used. It may have been because co-operating manufacturers feared that even the amicable use of the compulsory power would carry a stigma.

²⁷ Memo, Col A. J. Browning, Special Representative of USW, for CGMC, 28 Sep 42; CGMC to CG, Mat Center, 30 Sep 42. Both in AFCF 161 Contract Requirements. For an illustration of a letter of intent that misfired, see Memo, Wright for Meyers, 14 Mar 42, AFCF 400.12 Proc. See also, Negotiation and Administration of Contracts, Lecture, by Lt Col J. G. Scarff, AAF Contracting Officers School, WF, 12 Dec 44, WFHO.

THE NEGOTIATION OF CONTRACTS

contractors or suppliers quite arbitrarily to manageable numbers, if necessary to a single source. On the other hand, this freedom to negotiate did not leave the military buyers utterly untrammeled agents at liberty to bargain as they would. Contract negotiators for the War Department had to operate within a rather rigid set of rules, the Procurement Regulations laid down by the Assistant Secretary of War under authority granted in the Defense Act of 1920.

The Procurement Regulations of the War Department, or PR's as they were commonly called, consisted of a numbered series of instructions prescribing the general policies and forms to be used for all departmental buying. The regulations not only spelled out uniform procedures to be followed by procurement personnel but amassed in one convenient place all those provisions, prohibitions, inclusions, and exclusions that had been laid down by Congress in one statute or another over a great period of years but never gathered together and issued in codified form until the summer of 1942. The PR's were the procurement bible, a dismayingly intricate compendium synthesizing scattered statutory mandates, departmental regulations, opinions of the Attorneys General and rulings of the Comptrollers General, not to mention all those administrative procedures and practices that had evolved from experience over the years.[28]

To write a contract required threading one's way through the complex maze of directives, prohibitions, and prescriptions laid out in the Procurement Regulations.[29] A number of stock contract forms simplified the task by providing at least a point of departure for the use of the negotiators. There was, for example, the stock form for cost-plus-fixed-fee contracts, which had been drafted with so much difficulty during the summer of 1940. The intricacies of this form are such that it will be convenient to defer consideration of it until later. A second standard form was available for use in the purchase of standard units such as nuts, bolts, and other similar off-the-shelf items. This form, an informal contract, was called a purchase order. It amounted to little more than an order blank with conditions prescribed. By far the most important instrument in the arsenal of the Procurement Regulations was Form 32, the one that was provided for the normal pattern of procurement—fixed-price or lump-sum contracts. Such contracts were formal documents representing mutual agreements certified by the participating parties with their seals and signatures.[30]

---

[28] To read the Procurement Regulations of the War Department as they are published at any one time is as deceptive as judging the whole reel from the appearance of a single frame of film. To understand the PR's one must study them in evolution. Unfortunately the files are inconveniently organized for this purpose. There is apparently no extant historical file of PR's available anywhere that reflects all the changes introduced. AF Records Section, Record Group 506, A 51–66, contains some suggestive material of this sort but is not complete.

[29] There are almost no accounts of the negotiating process available. Of the few to be found, the following are most useful: Lecture 1, The Procurement Function of the AAF, the ATSC, and the Contracting Officer, by Brig Gen D. C. Swatland; Lecture 10, Negotiation and Administration of Contracts, by Scarff. Both lectures before AAF Contracting Officers School, WF, Winter 1944-45, filed in WFHO.

[30] For a detailed analysis of contract forms, especially the fixed-price contract, see Lecture 11, Provisions of Fixed Price Contracts, by Maj L. A. Mincer, AAF Contracting Officers School, WF, 11 Dec 44, WFHO.

Each stock contract form consisted of a series of articles or numbered paragraphs specifying the terms of the agreement. By and large the articles fell into two fairly distinguishable categories. On the one hand there were those inescapable stipulations that for the most part reflected congressional mandates. Typical of this category were the labor requirements of the Walsh-Healey Act, which were a compulsory feature of every government contract above a given dollar volume. Another required article was that prohibiting interested officials from benefiting under the terms of a contract. In the jargon of the trade, articles such as these were "boiler plate"—not subject to negotiation in the absence of unusual circumstances. On the other hand, the second category of articles comprised all those normally open to bargaining. In this group were to be found clauses covering the nature and specification of the items to be purchased, the character of the inspection required, the components to be supplied by the government to the manufacturers, the additional facilities to be provided where necessary, and, finally, the critically important factor of price.

The use of standard contract forms might be expected to speed up negotiations by narrowing the area of discussion to those articles actually negotiable. One might assume that the boiler plate articles would be taken for granted since they were in any event unavoidable. In practice, the use of boiler plate clauses and articles did not work out this way. To begin with, not all manufacturers were familiar with the stock articles. The rush of war orders brought thousands of businessmen into association with military buyers for the first time. Lack of familiarity bred caution. As a consequence, procurement officers frequently found themselves involved in prolonged sessions struggling to convince would-be contractors that there were no hidden catch-phrases in the boiler plate. As a matter of fact, even those manufacturers long familiar with government business practices were inclined to mistrust the apparently innocuous articles. It must be admitted that their fears had a certain justification, for even the boiler plate articles belied their name. Frequent additions as well as alterations and special deviations to meet unusual circumstances kept the supposedly unchanging "standard" clauses in a state of flux. Since even slight changes in terminology could affect the margin between profit and loss, manufacturers showed a good deal of reluctance to act without first exploring every line of contractual text for pitfalls. Inasmuch as some of the larger contracts embraced several hundred pages of text, this line-by-line search could be exceedingly time consuming. To placate manufacturers' fears and to save time, procurement officers actually went so far as to include a special article in each contract identifying in detail any deviations from the standard or conventional contractual verbiage.

That the procurement staff at Wright Field appreciated the need to forestall manufacturers' fears concerning possible pitfalls in the standard articles of military contracts is evident from the peculiar history of Form 32, the stock instrument for fixed-price contracts. In 1935 the Treasury Department issued the original Form 32 for use by all governmental purchasing agencies. The initial instrument had fifteen articles. Over the years, as experience showed the need for clarifications and additions, more and more articles were added, until by 1942 it had become a bulging document of 42 articles. Inevitably this growth by accretion involved a good deal of overlapping and duplication in the various clauses.

Early in 1943 the procurement staff decided that a redrafting was long past due and set about revising, trimming down, and lopping off the obvious deadwood in Form 32. This was clearly desirable, but it threatened to hold up negotiations simply because it was new. Procurement officers recognized that businessmen, especially those most familiar with the old form, would recoil suspiciously from a novel contractual instrument and insist upon giving it to their legal advisors for close scrutiny—and weeks of delay would follow. To minimize the time lag unavoidably arising from this sort of reaction, an ingenious officer arranged to label the new instrument "Form 32"—Materiel Command Form 32 rather than Treasury Form 32. Under this flag, manufacturers' fears could be soothed with an oblique reference to "the same old form" merely pruned and reshuffled, which, indeed, was the truth.[31]

In short, procurement officers discovered that they had to spend a great deal of time "negotiating the unnegotiable," allaying the fears and suspicions with which manufacturers regarded the fine print and the changes in the fine print that continually occurred.[32]

The British Ministry of Supply when confronted with this same mistrust of the fine print on the part of manufacturers faced the problem somewhat differently. The whole gamut of stock articles the Ministry commonly employed in contracts were numbered serially and published in a bound booklet readily available through His Majesty's Stationery Office to all who applied for it. Businessmen, including those infrequently entering government contracts, were thus free to study the fine print at length even before so much as considering a particular bid on government work. By this simple device the boiler plate portion of many British munitions contracts was reduced to a mere listing by cross references to appropriate articles in the published catalogue of standard provisions.[33]

If the fine print in the boiler plate articles of air arm contracts led to difficulties and delays at the bargaining table, how much more so was this true of those articles and clauses open to give and take—those actually subject to formal negotiation? Whether they concerned specifications defining the nature of the end item itself, patent rights, the provision of additional facilities, or equipment for production at government expense, or the procedures for inspection, packing, and shipping, these negotiable articles opened endless opportunities for dispute and disagreement.[34]

By way of example, consider the possibilities of misunderstanding and delay in the matter of tooling. Who should pay the cost of special tooling, the jigs,

---

[31] *Ibid.*

[32] A candid expression of a typical management attitude can be found in Lecture, Aircraft Production, by J. T. Hartson, vice president of Glenn L. Martin, AIC, 6 Nov 41.

[33] C. F. Robinson, R. C. Kyser, and J. D. Millett, Foreign Logistical Organizations and Methods: A Report for the Secretary of the Army, Oct 47, p. 163, OCMH.

[34] Negotiation and Administration of Contracts, Lecture by Scarff.

fixtures, dies, and the like, that made mass production possible? To begin with, the line of definition between general- and special-purpose tools was often difficult to discern, let alone agree upon. If the government agreed to pay for certain tools and tooling and retained title to them, would the manufacturers then be responsible for wear and tear or loss resulting from breakage? Would contractors be free to lend this tooling to subcontractors where necessary? If special tooling owned by the government could be used to produce for the commercial market—in fabricating a cargo airplane, for example—should the contractor be authorized to do so? If so, how would the government's representatives meet the cry of inequity that might arise from rival firms? Since virtually every negotiable article of a contract offered equally complex grounds for discussion and disagreement, the opportunities for delays in signing air arm contracts were almost without limit.[35]

One of the most vexatious articles in the negotiation of wartime contracts was that covering the provision of spare parts. Aircraft contracts signed in wartime called for the delivery of an initial complement of spare parts concurrently with the aircraft themselves. Unfortunately, no one, not even the airplane's designer, knew in advance precisely which spare parts would be required. Each individual aircraft design presented a novel problem, and only after extended operation in the field could enough experience be accumulated to indicate with any degree of accuracy just which parts would be required in great numbers as replacements and which not at all. In such a situation to ask a manufacturer to sign a contract placing an itemized price tag on each replacement part in advance was to expect him to base his production costs on unknown quantities.

In almost any field of manufacturing the length of the production run bears an appreciable influence on unit cost. Manufacturers were readily tempted to cut costs on spares by running off additional quantities when turning out the parts required for the aircraft on contract. With luck and a good deal of shrewd estimating a manufacturer could save both time and money in this fashion, but heavy risks were involved. In wartime, especially, the flux in design was rapid. Each change in design could involve extensive retooling; thus a manufacturer who tried to be forehanded could, and sometimes did, end up with a warehouse full of spares made obsolete by subsequent alterations in design.

The elaborate contractual arrangements by which the difficulties encountered in procuring spare parts were eventually circumvented, if not entirely resolved, need not be spelled out here. Suffice it to say, the fundamental difficulty of buying and selling unknown quantities of spare parts continued to plague contract negotiations throughout the war.[36]

Framing appropriate articles to cover the complexities of tooling, spare parts, or any of the other problems mentioned

---

[35] Chief, Proc Div, WF, to Chief, Legal Br, Dir of Materiel, ASF, 6 May 44, AFCF 161 Contract Requirements.

[36] Lecture, Spare Parts Procurement, 13 Dec 44, by Lt Col E. R. Wardell; Negotiation and Administration of Contracts, Lecture by Scarff. Both lectures before AAF Contracting Officers School, WF, Winter 1944–45, filed in WFHO. See also, A. F. E. MacInerny, *Production of Airplane Spares* (Lockheed Aircraft Corp., 1944).

THE NEGOTIATION OF CONTRACTS

above created obstacles for the negotiators on both sides of the table, but in the final analysis these were often subordinate to the fundamental and pervasive question of price. It was in negotiating the all-important price of the article that air arm procurement officials faced their most serious challenge. No one would ever dream of disputing the pivotal role of price, yet, oddly enough, it was here that the negotiators found themselves literally groping in the dark.

Negotiating in the Dark

One subtlety that requires precise explanation is the difference between a "negotiated contract" and "contract negotiation." When procurement officers spoke of "negotiating a contract," they referred to the discussion that led up to the signing of any contract. A "negotiated contract," on the other hand, was specifically one in which the crucial question of price was reached by agreement between the parties involved rather than by competition involving the use of invitations, sealed bids, and public opening.

By March 1942 air arm procurement officials operated under Army directives stipulating that all procurement must employ the negotiated contract in preference to competitive bidding unless explicitly exempt by the Under Secretary.[37] From its status as the unusual exception to be used with circumspection, the negotiated contract had come full circle to rank as the general rule. This was not just a simple shift in procedure but a revolution in military procurement. As such, it encountered something less than an enthusiastic reception in some circles.

Use of the negotiated contract made it possible to abandon competition in the open market in favor of direct dealings with arbitrarily selected individual firms. To deal directly with such firms without the cumbersome mechanics of competition, sealed bids, and all the rest was expeditious as well as efficient and therefore highly desirable in wartime, but the advantages could not conceal the inherent drawback in negotiated contracts. If the great arbiter — competition — which policed price albeit imperfectly via the pressures of the market place, were once abandoned, then some alternative had to be substituted to accomplish the same end. If the machinery of normal competition would no longer maintain continuing downward pressure on price, the burden necessarily fell upon the government negotiators. Protecting the public interest required skilled horse traders, negotiators who could achieve by shrewd bargaining over the table what the general economic forces of the market had formerly done. This was the challenge of the negotiated contract.

An impartial observer in 1942 might well have questioned whether the challenge would be met. The outlook at that time was hardly favorable. To begin with, whether they chose to use the fixed-price or the cost-plus-fixed-fee contract, the government's negotiators had to be able to make a rather close estimate of probable costs. In the fixed-price contract, such an estimate was needed to hold a manufacturer to a close price that would still cover his costs adequately. Which is to say, a price had to be set tight enough to give him an incentive to improve his

---

[37] Memo, OUSW for CofAC *et al.*, 4 Mar 42, AFCF 161 Contract Requirements. Based on WPB Directive No. 2, 3 Mar 42.

methods and increase his profits, yet slack enough to ensure him against disastrous losses resulting in delayed delivery or downright failure to produce at all. And similarly, in the CPFF contract, a careful study of probable costs was essential before the government could compute intelligently the allowable fixed fee, not to mention appropriations and budgeting. In the last analysis, without data on which to make such estimates, air arm procurement officials really could not even make an intelligent selection of the appropriate contractual instrument—the fixed-price or fixed-fee form—let alone work out a close price.

Accurate cost analysis hinges upon two factors: first, highly experienced negotiators with a thorough grasp of the manufacturing processes entering into the fabrication of every different type of end item purchased, and, second, information on the current market in all the many ingredients contributing to that heterogeneous class called air matériel. These ingredients included not only semifabricated and self-contained component parts but also raw materials in bulk such as sheet aluminum, strip copper, and the like, each in a bewildering array of grades and varieties, every one of which carried a price tag that fluctuated daily. In addition to the materials costs were costs of labor reflecting not only the varying wage levels in different parts of the country but also the individual pay scales established for the whole gamut of skills encountered in the aircraft industry—from tinsmith to time clerk. Effective negotiation demanded trained men fully armed with vast quantities of up-to-date information on a host of costs.

At Wright Field the air arm did have a handful of highly experienced contract negotiators, but for many months, especially in the early days of the war, these men found themselves working virtually in the dark. The few tools they had at their disposal were rudimentary at best. The procurement staff had acquired some experience in price negotiation during the peacetime years when lining up contracts for experimental aircraft under the provisions of Section 10k of the Air Corps Act of 1926. And there was, in addition, a considerable quantity of cost data available in the audits of aircraft manufacturers' books authorized by the Air Corps Act, but much of the information was hopelessly outdated by the inflationary pressures that had sent prices spiraling upward ever since the outbreak of war in 1939.

The experience in negotiating experimental contracts and the data derived from audits did indeed have some utility, but both suffered from an almost fatal defect. Each applied to a volume of operations utterly dwarfed by the immense rush of war orders. Production costs valid for orders measured in tens or hundreds obviously did not hold true when applied to thousands. The Wright Field negotiators were well aware of the "learner curve" worked out for the aircraft industry in the thirties by T. P. Wright. By using the system of projections conceived by Mr. Wright, they were able to estimate the reductions in labor costs per unit that should be obtained by any given increase in the total number of units in production. Even when skillfully applied, however, these curves or projections gave only crude estimates so long as it remained impossible to verify all the cost factors introduced to construct the curves. At

THE NEGOTIATION OF CONTRACTS

this point the Wright Field negotiators were really handicapped, for they simply did not have the necessary information at their finger tips.[38]

Although virtually disarmed by want of adequate factual data, the air arm negotiators did not succumb to the manufacturers across the table. What they lacked in the way of information they tried to make up in rigorous bargaining, even though there was no substitute for full and up-to-date cost data.[39] The urgency of wartime demand gave high trump cards to the manufacturers' representatives. As the cry for increased production became more frantic, Wright Field negotiators were placed under heavy pressure to sign contracts in the shortest possible time, even if this meant doing so without a thorough cost analysis beforehand.

The nadir of orderly procurement seems to have come in March 1942 when the chief of the Contract Section himself confessed that the process had by then devolved to one of "price asking" by the manufacturers and "price taking" on the part of the government.[40] This, it would seem, was tantamount to conceding an utter breakdown in the air arm's ability to bargain effectively. Even after allowing for a certain hyperbole in the contract chief's remarks, they still imply that the procurement organization at Wright Field suffered from a serious deficiency. Bluntly stated, that organization was still not ready for the rush of war orders some two years after the rearmament program began and months after the fall of France had unleashed torrents of appropriations for air matériel.

Perfecting the Organization

The difficulties confronting the Contract Section at Wright Field in driving effective bargains for the government when the real wartime crisis arrived suggests the existence of a defect in the organization, which, in theory at least, had labored throughout the peacetime years to be ready for the tasks of war. There were, to be sure, a few really able negotiators on the permanent civil service staff who had perfected their skills in the years before the war, but their experience, if wide in scope was limited in scale. In 1939, for example, they purchased only 865 aircraft and wrote only 353 formal contracts. The whole civilian staff of the Contract Section numbered but 70-odd persons. The modest scale of their operations is probably best suggested by the annual tabulation of GFE items—engines, accessories, and the like—purchased by the Air Corps. As late as 1939 the entire list could be itemized on three or four sheets of paper.[41]

When the rush of war orders finally arrived it literally overwhelmed the Contract Section at Wright Field. In 1939 the air arm had spent some $35,000,000

---

[38] Interv with Mr. Schwinn, 25 Jul 55.

[39] See, for example, TWX, Echols to Brett, 26 Aug 40, AFCF 452.1-13-F Proc of Airplanes.

[40] IOM, Chief, Contract Sec, for Chief, Mat Div, 2 Mar 42, quoted in M. L. McMurtrie, History of the AAF Materiel Command (Materiel Center): 1942, WFHO, Aug 46, p. 92. See also, Memo, Brig Gen H. A. Shepard, Chief, Proc Div, for Maj Gen O. R. Cook, 13 Jan 50, WFHO Proc and Production Activities.

[41] Mat Div Annual Rpt, FY 1939; M. L. McMurtrie, and P. M. Davis, History of the AAF Materiel Command: 1926 Through 1941, WFHO, Nov 43, app. vol. II, E, tab 2.

for such categories of matériel as aircraft, engines, and other GFE items; by the end of fiscal 1942 commitments for the same items involved outlays in excess of $11,-500,000,000.[42] And by that date the staff at Wright Field was negotiating an average of 392 formal contracts each month, not to mention handling 2,500 informal contracts or purchase orders at the same time. Clearly the small staff of highly trained civilian negotiators could not be stretched over this immense volume of business. Those in authority responded to this challenge by calling for additions in staff.

Although large numbers of people were recruited for the procurement staff—by the end of fiscal 1942 the Contract Section alone employed over 850—individuals with appropriate talents were virtually impossible to find, let alone hire on existing civil service pay scales. The obvious alternative was to train men almost from scratch, but this could be done only with great effort and by prolonged exposure to experience, a process necessarily time consuming. Thus, when the ultimate crisis arrived after Pearl Harbor, the procurement staff, though already vastly enlarged, was still dangerously undermanned.

Civil service procedures as to personnel and budgetary limitations, at least down to Pearl Harbor, went far to inhibit the opportune development of an organization capable of handling the increased volume of buying.[43] Perhaps the most serious criticism that has been brought against those in command is that they continued trying to solve the procurement problem by additions to staff long after it should have been clear that sheer numbers (even if appropriately skilled individuals were obtainable) could no longer keep pace with the mounting workload. Not until several months after the United States entered the war did those in command undertake a thorough overhaul of the procurement organization at Wright Field in an attempt to deal with the enormous difficulties inherent in wartime purchasing by means other than additions of personnel in ever greater numbers.

To be sure the procurement staff did continue to expand rapidly after Pearl Harbor, and the statistics of that expansion are impressive. In a sense they are too impressive. Their sheer magnitude in contrast to the recent past is so striking, so dramatic, as to divert attention from the underlying lessons and implications behind the facts. During the first half of 1942, for example, each month found several thousand visitors—agents, manufacturers, negotiators, and the like —thronging the corridors at Wright Field in search of contracts. Each visitor required time and attention. Each brought new complications to be faced. By the year's end the Air Force was doing business with some 7,000 prime contractors and over 60,000 subcontractors.[44] Obviously, absolute additions to staff were unavoidable if this upsurge of business was to be handled at all. More negotiators, more expeditors, more file clerks, and more typists were hired until the

---

[42] *Ibid.*

[43] For a general discussion of this question, see McMurtrie and Davis, Hist of AAF MC: 1926-41, ch. V.

[44] *Ibid.*

Contract Section doubled, redoubled, then doubled again. But this kind of expansion only obscures the far more significant refinements of organization that were gradually introduced during 1942 and 1943.

The organizational innovations that restored the air arm's contract negotiations to effectiveness involved a host of lesser details introduced piecemeal over many months, but virtually all of the changes grew out of one central principle: the functional breakdown of the procurement process into subdivisions performing highly specialized activities. Before the war a small group of men in the Purchase Branch at Wright Field did nearly all the negotiating necessary for the entire service. These men were experts broadly qualified by experience to conduct negotiations on whatever contract came their way, be it aircraft engine or parachute, fuel truck, or flying boot. So long as the volume of work remained small and time was not of the essence, such an arrangement was doubtlessly efficient. A few widely qualified generalists who could handle almost any task were less costly to maintain than a whole stable of specialists.

With the coming of war, however, the advantage of the peacetime organization disappeared. What is more, the weakness of peacetime planning for the wartime procurement organization stood clearly revealed as the inevitable happened: the workload rapidly outstripped the available staff while those in command frantically sought to recruit manpower even though it might reasonably have been anticipated that highly trained negotiators would prove difficult to hire in the midst of a war boom. Not until well after Pearl Harbor—which is to say not until after the most hectic months of procurement were past—did the responsible authorities undertake a functional breakdown or subdivision of the procurement organization into a series of narrow specialties for which experts, if they could not always be hired, might be trained fairly rapidly.

Within the context of limitations that beset the peacetime air arm, those in command can scarcely be criticized for resorting to the form of organization they had used in the prewar years. But can the same be said of their planning for war? For that matter, was any really serious consideration given to the problem of staff and organizational planning before the crisis arrived? If there was, little documentary evidence of such activity remains, and the piecemeal manner in which the reorganization of the procurement function actually took place during 1942 and 1943 strongly suggests that it was done pragmatically and under the pressure of events rather than as a consequence of conscious foresight. Planning for the contingencies and imponderables of a remote future is always difficult, but the trouble in this instance seems to have stemmed not so much from faulty planning as from an almost complete absence of planning.[45]

The air arm's failure, until belatedly,

---

[45] Probably the easiest way to trace, at least superficially, the course of organization change at Wright Field is by use of the data supplied in McMurtrie and Davis, Hist of AAF MC: 1926–41, app. vol. II. For further comment on organizational weaknesses at Wright Field, see Lt Col L. S. Friedman, IGD, rpt to IG, Inspection of Procurement Operations at Wright Field, 11 Nov 43, AFCF 331.1 Inspection (Bulky).

to resort to functional subdivision and specialization on a large scale is the more surprising because the principle involved had long since been applied by the very aircraft manufacturers with whom officials at Wright Field were negotiating every day. Before the war, most aircraft firms employed a relatively large percentage of highly skilled workmen, each one almost a master machinist capable of proceeding from sketchy blueprints containing a minimum of detail and fully able to work without close supervision. With the coming of mass production in wartime when such highly skilled men were not to be found, the aircraft concerns solved their problem by a series of progressively smaller breakdowns that brought more and more tasks into the range of semiskilled or narrowly trained workers. But even with this example at hand, the air arm was slow to follow suit.

Not until 1944 did the procurement organization at Wright Field reach what may be called maturity. By then the old catchall Purchase Branch had been moved up to the superior status of a section within which the various purchasing functions were parceled out on functional lines: an Aircraft Procurement Branch, still further subdivided into separate units buying airframes, engines, and propellers, was paralleled by a General Procurement Branch with individual subunits buying GFE items, maintenance equipment, and so on. In each of these several internal organizations were to be found highly specialized negotiators, each an expert in his particular field—fuels and lubricants, instruments, electrical equipment, and the like. Obviously an officer who in civilian life had been a commission throwster in the silk trade would make a more sensitive negotiator in the parachute field than would a man whose entire civilian experience had been confined to selling heavy machinery to highway contractors, although the latter might make a highly competent negotiator buying fuel trucks and other such equipment.

In a word, a major key to the effectiveness of the mature procurement organization was to be found in its reliance upon negotiators—as well as others—who were specialists. Yet this was by no means the only significant organizational change introduced.

While the principle of specialization applied to negotiation was highly important, perhaps even more so was the proliferation of units designed to improve the flow of vital information toward the negotiators who most needed it. In the Purchase Section, to consider but one illustration, was established a Cost Analysis Branch manned by an officer and ten civilians. One group in this branch, the Industrial Cost Unit, analyzed the cost estimates presented by manufacturers negotiating for contracts by working up detailed reports on the adequacies of the estimates presented on tooling, labor time, and materials costs. The data compiled by these people was then sent to the government negotiators at the bargaining table—the procurement firing line—to help them in their efforts to establish a close but fair price. A second group within the branch, the Corporate Profit Unit, supplied negotiators with information on a contractor's over-all profit picture to help them drive harder bargains where in the past a manufacturer's profit had been excessive or to be somewhat more generous where he had suffered loss, especially where the loss stemmed from circumstances beyond his control.[46]

The reorganization of the Contract Section paralleled that of the Procurement Section. In prewar days and during the early rearmament rush, the procurement staff often negotiated contracts and then sent them to the legal staff to be drafted in proper legal form. For several months after the outbreak of war the legal talent for this task continued to be drawn on a part-time arrangement from the base judge advocate's office, which handled all the other customary legal burdens of an air field, including military justice and small claims. After Under Secretary Patterson himself had singled out this glaring organizational weakness for criticism, a full-time Legal Branch was established within the Contract Section and staffed with lawyers concentrating on highly specialized segments of the broad field of procurement law. The mature Legal Branch of late 1943 and early 1944 employed 40-odd officers, almost all of them attorneys, and well over 200 civilians.[47] This was a remarkable increase in numbers, to be sure, but here too it would be well not to let mere increases in staff conceal the more meaningful trend toward functional breakdown or job simplification that lay at the root of the procurement organization's vastly enhanced wartime capabilities.

Substantial as were the improved efficiencies of the mature procurement organization, the forward steps taken were not without some costs and losses. Although an elaboration and subdivision of functions did provide a highly useful flow of information to assist the negotiators in their work and helped pit well-informed government specialists against manufacturers' representatives operating in their own home territory, the sheer bulk of the data fed up to them tended to become unmanageable. By 1944 the various offices at Wright Field were turning out some 115 recurring reports: 17 daily, 15 weekly, 16 monthly, and so on. A dozen of these originated within the purchasing organization itself.[48] Admittedly much of this information was absolutely vital to sound negotiation, but its compilation and use did lead to numerous difficulties.

Many manufacturers complained at the burdens imposed by the preparation of the many recurring reports expected of them. This is hardly surprising considering their number. Boeing, for instance, took tally at one point in the war and discovered that the Air Force required the corporation to submit 425 different reports each month.[49] Some manufacturers wryly suggested that the Air Force expected contractors to turn out more weight in paper than in airframes.

People as well as papers complicated the task of co-ordination. As the procurement organization doubled and redoubled, it was difficult to keep the right hand aware of what the left hand did. The increase in staff at Wright Field repeatedly ran ahead of construction work on new floor space. The various sections and branches had to use office accommo-

---

[46] For a general description of the Procurement Division as it approached maturity, see Office for Organizational Planning, Materiel Command, Report on Decentralization of Procurement Division, 11 Sep 43, WFHO Research file.

[47] McMurtrie, Hist of AAF MC: 1942, p. 63.

[48] R. R. Russel, History of the Air Technical Service Command: 1944, WFHO, May 46, p. 63.

[49] Proc Div Decentralization Progress Rpt, 30 Sep 43, WFHO.

dations where they could be found. Throughout the first two years of the war, branches of a section and units of a branch frequently had to set up shop in offices remote from one another. When the overflow led to the use of rented office space and even to the conversion of an old high school building in downtown Dayton, expansion of staff had long since passed the point of diminishing returns. The loss of effective co-ordination implicit in all this may be inferred from the following statistics: by 1944 the Materiel Command as a whole had expanded to a total of 43,821 people (34,304 civilian and 9,517 military) in contrast to a total of but 1,900 in 1939. The procurement staff over this same period grew from 70 people to 876 (542 civilian and 334 military).[50]

Clearly, the advances toward efficiency wrought by specialization were offset at least in some measure by a decline in close, timely co-ordination of operations and a decided impairment of comprehensiveness in over-all supervision. When the force at Wright Field swelled from hundreds to thousands and then to tens of thousands, general officers in command could not avoid finding it increasingly difficult to maintain a "general" view of operations in their charge.

That the problem of co-ordination would become more pressing as the procurement force grew larger was inevitable. And just as inevitable was the high cost—in time as well as money—of every administrative device installed to keep all interested parties informed of what was going on. Quite apart from the expense in terms of manpower, salaries, office space, and the like, each device added to improve co-ordination increased the administrative time lag by minutes or hours and even days. Despite repeated efforts to cut down on the time it took to process contracts, the lag continued to be, as one official declared, "something appalling." Toward the end of the war, when procedures were well oiled, it still took an average of thirty days to get a contract to the point of agreement around the bargaining table. And this was not the culmination but only the beginning of the paper chase, since formal contracts still had to go up through several echelons of the Air Force for signatures and co-ordination. What is more, such contracts often had to make parallel journeys back through a manufacturer's organization to get appropriate corporate approvals at the home office. At the very end of 1944 it still took an average of seventy-eight days after reaching agreement by negotiation to get a signed and legally binding contractual instrument safely back in the files at Wright Field.[51]

Sometimes it happened that manufacturers' bids would expire while previously agreed upon terms were plodding through the headquarters mill gathering signatures of approval. Prudent manufacturers placed time limits on the acceptance of their quotations for sound business reasons. It would never do to be called upon to perform on a quotation given at a date much earlier in the inflationary spiral, since a geometric progression in labor and material costs could make any bid totally unrealistic in a matter of months or even less. If the air arm negotiators were to avoid returning to

---

[50] Russel, Hist of AAF ATSC: 1944, app. IV.

[51] Negotiation and Administration of Contracts, Lecture by Scarff.

THE NEGOTIATION OF CONTRACTS

the bargaining table all over again, it was imperative to hold the delays in the headquarters mill to the minimum.[52]

Some critics were tempted to condemn the delays of the headquarters paper mill as "typical Army red tape." Part of this criticism is undoubtedly justified; the elaborate and hastily expanded administrative machinery of the procurement organization certainly offered grounds for improvement. But were most of the imposed delays really avoidable? Unless time-consuming follow-ups, co-ordinations, cross-checks, and approvals were provided, the occasions for costly errors to slip by would have been legion. Experienced procurement officers, even those who most deplored the creaking slowness of the paper mill, were convinced that most of the steps along the way to a fully signed and co-ordinated contract were well worth the trouble and entirely justified by the savings effected.[53]

The prevention of fraud or monetary loss was only a part, probably a minor part, of the benefit to be derived from the elaborate administrative routine applied to contracts. A full flow of accurate and timely information was essential to a taut and efficient mobilization of the national economy where resources were in short supply and available quantities had to be apportioned with care among many competing users. Unless each contract was co-ordinated and cleared with those directing the national mobilization, unless these officials were supplied with full and early information on each contract signed, the whole complex task of rationalizing the flow of resources fell into chaotic disarray. Yet it is precisely here that the delays began. Clearing a contract through the mobilizers imposed unavoidable costs mounting through hours to days of delay.[54] And it is these delays that the uninitiated found easy to deplore as the consequence of Army red tape and inefficiency.

Among the many factors contributing to the delay in getting air arm contracts completed, none was more vexing than the stipulation that all must be approved not only by the top officers of the command in the Washington headquarters but by the Under Secretary of War as well. The outlying position of the major procurement staff at Wright Field made this requirement even more cumbersome than might otherwise have been the case. The delays inherent in the circuitous journey to Ohio could have been disastrous had they not been eliminated or reduced.

Shortly after Pearl Harbor Under Secretary Patterson laid down some broad outlines of policy for wartime leadership. "War," he said, "calls for the same boldness and imagination in procurement as it does in the . . . field."[55] To show that his words were not empty symbols, he proceeded to demonstrate a good deal of "boldness and imagination" in the exercise of his high office. His method was

---

[52] For a wartime insight on this problem, see TWX, Asst Chief, Mat Div, WF, to Chief, Mat Div, OCAC, 9 Dec 41, WF, JAG file, Proc 10K.

[53] For an extended statement of the reasons for retaining time-consuming co-ordinations, see Negotiation and Administration of Contracts, Lecture by Scarff.

[54] A rather brief résumé of some of the steps taken by a requirement on the way to becoming a completed contract will be found in Procurement Statistics, Lecture by Tyson.

[55] Quoted in OUSW Purchasing and Contracting Dir No. 8, 14 Jan 42, abstract in WF JAGO file, War Powers Act.

simplicity itself: he delegated vast segments of the power legally vested in him to approve contracts. By passing the power of final approval to a long chain of subordinates, endowing each with authority to make the ultimate decision on sums commensurate with his rank, the Under Secretary hastened the procurement process immeasurably. Successive modifications of the original order from time to time increased the total contract values that subordinate officials could approve until toward the end of the war the following cascade of delegations and redelegations were in force:[56]

All contracts of $5 million or more required signature of Under Secretary.

All contracts of $1 to $5 million required signature of Commanding General, Materiel Command.

All contracts of $100,000 to $1 million required signature of Chief, Procurement Division.

All contracts of less than $100,000 required signature of contracting officer only.

Delegation of authority can be a powerful instrument in the arsenal of leadership. A timid man is afraid to delegate power; a selfish man refuses to do so. Under Secretary Patterson was neither. Nevertheless, even while admitting the impetus given to procurement by his decision to delegate final authority, some detractors have been inclined to scoff that far from being bold, Judge Patterson's decision was belated.[57] Indeed, it might better have come long before Pearl Harbor, perhaps as early as the summer or fall of 1940 when the paper mill bottleneck on contract approvals first became acute. With some justice the Under Secretary's critics could point out that to delegate wide contractual authority after Pearl Harbor may have required imagination but only a minimal boldness, for by then the public, the voting public, was badly frightened and willing to follow the nation's leaders without too much cavil. Genuine boldness, it can be argued, would have risked such a delegation of power—would have risked censure —in the broader interest of national defense months earlier at a time when such a move was almost certain to provoke political fireworks.[58]

Against the charge of timidity a number of relevant circumstances must be considered. To begin with, directives issued by OPM required that all contracts over $500,000 be submitted for review by the OPM staff. So long as this practice prevailed, Judge Patterson understandably insisted upon scrutinizing every Army contract of that size before it was released to OPM. It was at least in part because of his insistence that OPM relaxed this requirement after Pearl Harbor. Furthermore, Judge Patterson did not even come to the War Department until July 1940 when he became Assistant Secretary of War. He assumed the title of Under Secretary in December 1940. Inevitably, some months were to pass before he could grasp the intricacies of his

---

[56] Negotiation and Administration of Contracts, Lecture by Scarff.

[57] Typical of the criticism leveled against the Under Secretary is IOM, Asst Chief, Mat Div, for Chief, Mat Div, 1 Oct 41, AFCF 400.12.

[58] To understand just how scathing such criticism could be, the reader need only to recall the political roasting described above, pages 119–128 and 128–131.

THE NEGOTIATION OF CONTRACTS

office.[59] Delegations of authority were utterly out of the question until the Under Secretary came to know and trust the men with whom he had to work and to whom he would apportion fractions of his power. Probably no aspect of procurement administration illustrates more pointedly the crucial importance of mutual confidence among the top political and military officials of the War Department. Similarly, confident redelegations of power down within the military echelons were possible only when those with political and military responsibility at the top of the system knew they could rely upon the ability and integrity of the men inside the procurement organization, where most of the actual buying took place. For this reason a closer look at some of the types of personalities and positions involved—both as buyers and as sellers—might be appropriate.

A Note on Buyers and Sellers

Peacetime practice and the terminology of the Procurement Regulations enshrined the contracting officer as the military buyer. He was the legally responsible official, the legal link between the government and the manufacturer. But the subdivision of functions made necessary by the vast expansion of procurement during the rearmament period tended to bring an increasing differentiation in function between those who negotiated contracts on the one hand and the lawyers on the other hand who drafted the formal instrument in legally acceptable terms.

As the pressure to turn out weapons became acute after Pearl Harbor, many contract negotiators grew more and more impatient with the lawyers. In the negotiators' view, once the really vital terms had been agreed upon—price, delivery schedules, and so on—the real work of buying was done. The formal contract with all its technical niceties and fine print they were inclined to regard as "lawyer's nonsense." To them the contracting officer was simply the last man up the line who put his signature on the contract. At best, the negotiators saw the lawyers as necessary evils; at worst, they blamed them for injecting staggering delays into the procurement process.[60]

In a sense, the negotiators were right. The legal details in formal contract writing did account for much of the time lag in the procurement paper mill. It is also true that lawyers were reluctant to seek new and radical legislation authorizing sweeping powers to hasten procurement by expedient means. But this conservatism was not simply congenital professional blindness to innovation. Legal officers knew only too well that new powers and expedient means would inevitably upset the hard-wrought body of procurement procedures and practices and make it necessary to obtain new rulings and decisions at the cost of much delay and many mistakes.[61]

As the war progressed the impatient negotiators came increasingly to recognize and appreciate the intrinsic importance of the legal draftsmen and their con-

---

[59] Anderson, History of the Office of the Under Secretary of War, Chapter IV, sheds a good deal of light on the difficulties of the incumbents coming to understand the powers and responsibilities of the office.

[60] Proc Function of AAF, Lecture by Swatland.

[61] See, JAG (WF) to Chief, Contract Sec, 30 Sep 41, WF JAGO file, Proc 10K.

cern for the seeming minutiae of language. This change in attitude came, in part at least, from a rather subtle transformation in the nature of contract negotiations that took place during the years of crisis. In peacetime, contracts were negotiated by principals. For the air arm, the ranking contracting officer headed the list. And on the manufacturer's side, as often as not, the top corporate official of an aircraft concern sat across the table. On both sides the men were personally interested in airplanes. They flew them, they designed them, and they built them; they knew and understood aircraft. With the massive expansion that characterized the rearmament program much of this intimacy and dealing among principals was lost. The principals might still come to Wright Field, but now they came with a retinue of lawyers and accountants, men who were specialists in taxes and amortization procedures, insurance experts, and the like.[62] If the air arm wished to bargain skillfully and protect the government's interest, it too must add specialists. For this reason there was a marked tendency, at least during 1944 and 1945, to add legal experts and the contracting officer to each group of negotiators, making procurement the work of an integrated team rather than a series of separate steps in sequence.[63] Such teams may have turned out better contracts, but unavoidably they took more time doing so.

By the time the air arm procurement organization reached maturity it numbered literally dozens of buyers on its staff if one included all those specialists purchasing bits and pieces. Nevertheless, a relatively small group of men, including both officers and civil servants, negotiated contracts for most of the major components such as airframes, engines, and propellers, which accounted for the overwhelming preponderance of the dollar volume obligated. These men, who spent billions of dollars and dealt with some of the best paid corporate executives in the country, did a large portion of their work on salaries and at ranks that can only be described as modest.[64]

While there was remarkably little change of personnel in the teams negotiating for major items during the war, this was not the case with those charged with procuring the hundreds of small items comprising the broad category of accessories and related equipment. Here there was a continual and substantial turnover in personnel, which raised a number of vexing problems. Specialist negotiators were hard to recruit in competition with industry. When commissioned officers filled these slots the abler men won promotions and generally moved off to other duties. Into their places moved young reservists and OCS graduates who may have been able enough but had considerably less general business experience than was desirable. Inexperience was a far more seri-

---

[62] IOM, Asst Chief, Mat Div, for Chief, Mat Div, 1 Oct 41, AFCF 400.12.
[63] Proc Function of AAF, Lecture by Swatland.
[64] See, for example, IOM, Chief, Contract Sec, for Chief, Mat Div, 27 Sep 41, AFCF 161 CPFF. Among those who served prominently as negotiators were Col K. B. Wolfe, a production man, Col F. P. Shaw, a JAG officer, Col A. E. Jones, wartime chief of the purchasing organization, and two career civil servants, J. W. Schwinn and F. E. Roush, although to single out these may seem to disparage others by neglect.

ous matter than dishonesty among negotiators.[65]

With but a very few exceptions, air arm procurement officials turned in a remarkable record for probity during the war.[66] The exceptions, notably one case concerning a civilian and another, an officer, occurred in cases involving small sums of money.[67] Though small, the amounts concerned did not in any way diminish the degree of error, for these breaches, especially that of the officer, did unquestionably harm the morale of the procurement staff as a whole.[68] Where absolute personal integrity could not be vouchsafed with reasonable assurance, those in positions of top command were unable to allow that freedom of action that saves time and simplifies many administrative complications.

While breaches of the public trust by dishonest procurement officials were few, those attributable to inept or inexperienced buyers were more numerous. Understandably, the permanent records, the files at Wright Field, are scarcely teeming with carefully documented instances of this sort of lapse. Nonetheless, the record of subsequent activity along the line of repricing and renegotiation amply indicates a quality of negotiation that, to say the very least, could often have been improved. Ironically, legislators and public critics spent their energies in hot pursuit of dishonesty—which was all but negligible—while virtually ignoring the far more important problems of recruiting, compensating, and training or retraining buyers, especially in the accessory or small item field, where the greatest opportunity for improvement undoubtedly lay.

The discussion thus far has concerned itself with but one side of the table. What of the spokesmen for industry on the other side? The old-line airframe and engine builders who had been visiting Wright Field for years were all familiar with many of the peculiarities and pitfalls of government procurement, and without doubt this factor of experience was of decided advantage to them in negotiating contracts. Yet even amongst these old-line firms there were substantial differences in effectiveness at the bargaining table, sometimes springing from variations in corporate policy and sometimes from the individual personalities involved.

In a study such as this, a discussion of the respective merits of rival firms or the personal attributes of individual corporate executives is patently out of place. Suffice it to say that air arm negotiators for one reason or another found a relatively uniform pattern in their opposite numbers at the bargaining table. Negotiations with some firms were consistently harmonious and expeditious, conducted in an atmosphere of mutual understand-

---

[65] Lecture, The Procurement Function of the AAF . . . , by Lt Col J. G. Scarff, AAF Contracting Officers School, WF, Winter 1944–45, WFHO; Memo, J. M. L. for Brig Gen A. E. Jones, 2 Nov 43, AFCF 161 Purchasing and Contracting. For an interesting comparison with a similar problem in World War I, see Procurement Correspondence: 1923, Staff Study on World War I experience, WFHO file, Proc.

[66] This generalization is based on a study of the reports of congressional investigations searching for fraud, the confidential reports of inspectors general and intelligence units assigned to fraud cases, as well as interviews with a number of civilian and military officials on duty in the procurement organization throughout the war period. Needless to add, the documentary record is at best imperfect evidence in such matters.

[67] The sordid details are extensively documented in Hearings of the Special Com Investigating the National Defense Program, 80th Cong, S Res 46, November 5–21, 1947, pt. 43.

[68] *Ibid.*, p. 27152.

ing and co-operation. On the other hand, some firms invariably proved recalcitrant, suspicious, and un-co-operative. In the last analysis, however aggressively their representatives may have haggled, the firms of the old-line aircraft industry were willing to give and take across the bargaining table.

Somewhat different were the attitudes and practices of the industrial giants—for example, the major automotive concerns —firms whose business was not exclusively or even predominantly in the field of aviation. With these, the military buyers had a great deal of difficulty. The giants were no less honest or more profit conscious than the aircraft industry, but the fact remains that negotiations with them tended to encounter exasperating delays and disruptive points of disagreement. When the industrial giants first began to consider air arm contracts in substantial volume, they sent highly paid corporate officials to Wright Field accompanied by whole phalanxes of advisors who left the impression that they looked down on the "junior officers" and "minor functionaries" negotiating for the government. They also left the impression that they were doing the government a favor in accepting military contracts. Neither of these attitudes lasted long, but they did little to facilitate negotiations.

Galling as the intangibles of attitudes may have been, they were not the main reason why it proved difficult to come to terms with the larger industrial firms. The heart of this difficulty lay elsewhere: the great industrial combines, like the military buying agencies, were bureaucracies in themselves. They had promulgated corporate policies and procedures based on long experience in the industrial world. They wished to alter their policies and practices no more than the government negotiators wished to break Procurement Regulations.[69] In brief, negotiations between the air arm and the giant industries tended to be difficult precisely because buyer and seller were so much alike.

The question of integrity on the part of the manufacturers dealing with the air arm cannot be dismissed in a single or simple generalization. Insofar as fraud is concerned—leaving the matter of excessive profits to later discussion—the major aircraft and engine manufacturer came through the war with a noteworthy record for integrity. There were, to be sure, charges of improper workmanship, diversions of resources, and so on, but investigation almost invariably revealed the charges to be untrue or attributable to minor employees rather than willful acts of corporate policy. Although the vast majority of smaller firms doing business with the air arm were no less honest than the major airframe and engine companies, among the several thousands involved there were some cases of outright fraud, but these, of course, were exceptions to the general rule.[70]

---

[69] The generalizations of this and the immediately preceding paragraph are of necessity based largely upon the opinions of air arm officers and civilians who served at Wright Field during the war.

[70] Only one old-line airframe firm seems to have fallen into the hands of persons of questionable integrity, and that company sold the air arm only two aircraft in the years 1940–45. See MID rpt 2D–3630, 10 Apr 41; FBI to G–2, 29 Jul 41. Both in AFCF 004.4 Manufacturers. For an example of minor peculation within a major contractor's organization, see Asst to Atty Gen to SW, 23 Feb 42, AFCF 333.5 Investigation of Contracts. For suggestions that some contractors were not unwilling to resort to the use of influence short of fraud, see AAF Hist Study 40, pp. 216–18.

THE NEGOTIATION OF CONTRACTS

If the record of business honesty indicated here seems to suggest flattering generalizations on the national character, it might be well to point out, with no intent to disparage the business community, that there were certain very real deterrents to fraud in military contracts. Heavy penalties on the statute books coupled with the activities of a legislative investigating committee backed by legions of patriotically motivated informants, not to mention the government's sweeping powers of audit in air arm contracts, all combined to minimize peculation. But surely a major deterrent to fraud must have been the relative ease with which ample profit margins could be acquired under war boom conditions.

Negotiating at High Noon

By the end of 1944 the negotiators at Wright Field were more or less consistently writing contracts that contained fair and reasonable price clauses. The Procurement Regulations defined "fair and reasonable" prices as those "close enough to costs so that producers must exercise careful management and ingenuity to increase production and decrease costs in order to earn a reasonable profit."[71] The goal of the government negotiator was to achieve prices sufficiently close to make contractors hold down their costs.

Without a mass of detailed factual information at his finger tips, the most skillful negotiator was relatively helpless. For this reason, one of the most significant tools of the air arm negotiators was the Standard Proposal Form, which all prospective contractors were required to submit signed under oath. This document probed so searchingly into the inner workings of a contractor's business and asked such an array of questions that many manufacturers grumbled over its use, which, they said, made them sit at the bargaining table with all their cards face up. It did. The proposal form required separate price quotations on each major component of any item purchased, then demanded a cost breakdown showing labor, material, and overhead charges with a full explanation of how each was derived. In addition, the form required an itemized statement of cost experience on similar articles, if any, turned out by the bidder. Further questions exacted information on labor requirements, tax burdens, royalties, facility requirements, the bidder's balance sheet, operating statement, and so on.[72]

The data derived from the Standard Proposal Form and its supplements became powerful weapons in the negotiators' arsenal, but the completed forms were not always easily come by. Most large corporations, accustomed to operating under the glare of public scrutiny, supplied the desired information readily enough. Among the smaller firms doing business with the air arm, however, there were many who resented the necessity of divulging the details of their operations.[73] This circumstance, it would appear, was

---

[71] Proc Function of AAF, Lecture by Swatland.

[72] See Materiel Command Form 43.1 and PR 243.1 (1944). The Standard Proposal Form is described at length in Training Section, Readjustment Division, Materiel Command, Readjustment Training Course Manual, WF, 1945, copy in ICAF files.

[73] Negotiation and Administration of Contracts, Lecture by Scarff.

not without some relevance to the alleged favoritism shown by military buyers to "big business." Certainly the reluctance—or inability—of many small firms to reveal the intimate details of their operations must be assessed as a factor in any attempt to weigh the relative distribution of orders between "big business" and "small business."

The government's negotiators did not content themselves with the use of the Standard Proposal Form. They exploited other sources of information as well. Within the organization at Wright Field extensive records were accumulated to assist in the procurement process as a corps of clerks maintained up-to-date alphabetical files, by product and by maker, showing every item purchased for the Air Force. To these were added the reports of contract audits as they became available and, later, the reports of renegotiators.[74] Comments and reports by resident representatives within the manufacturer's plants, procurement district officers, and project officers of the Engineering and Production Divisions at Wright Field added to the growing store of information.[75] Late in 1943 still another flow of data became available when the War Department began to publish weekly indices on prices paid throughout the technical services. These provided not only a comprehensive survey of price trends but a factual basis for spot comparisons as well.[76]

[74] Renegotiation is discussed in Chapter XVII, below.
[75] For comments on the information sources used by negotiators, see Proc Statistics, Lecture by Tyson; Negotiation and Administration of Contracts, Lecture by Scarff.
[76] The refinement of Army pricing techniques is discussed in Smith, *The Army and Economic Mobilization*, pp. 311-25.

Armed with numerous readily available sources of fact, trained and experienced negotiators had several courses of action open to them in undertaking a given purchase. Even after WPB Directive No. 2 made mandatory the use of negotiated contracts, procurement officials could make use of competitive bidding when the circumstances seemed to warrant such action. If the situation justified the use of a negotiated contract, there were two general techniques that could be used to reach agreement on a close price—the price comparison method and the cost analysis method. Air arm buyers in actual practice frequently resorted to a combination of two or more of these tools as the best means for protecting the public interest.

Although the exigencies of war made the procurement of aircraft by the traditional procedure of invitation and bid out of the question, this was not true with a large number of smaller items, especially where more than one manufacturer turned out similar commercial counterparts. In such instances, the military buyers frequently sent out invitations or circular proposals to seven or eight and sometimes to as many as fifteen potential bidders. The number of bids submitted in response was almost always disappointing; only infrequently would more than three or four manufacturers reply. Probably no other evidence better illustrates the fundamental weakness of competitive procurement in wartime. In a seller's market, where so many manufacturers already had more orders than they could handle, there was little incentive to seek additional orders. Those who did respond were under little or no pressure to compute their bids as carefully and as

THE NEGOTIATION OF CONTRACTS

closely as possible. In consequence, the primary benefits of competition were lost.

Nonetheless, competition was by no means useless as a technique of buying. If it only brought in three interested manufacturers, the resort to competition accomplished an important function. Under the authority of the emergency statutes, the military buyers were under no obligation to award a contract to the low bidder at his quoted price. Instead, the price could be used as a point of departure for subsequent negotiations. Many, indeed, were the price reductions effected around the bargaining table after competition had isolated or identified the low bidder in the field.[77]

Another tool in the buyer's hands involved the use of comparative prices. After a year or two of high-volume procurement, the accumulation of historical records on prices in the Wright Field files began to provide a useful basis for comparison on costs of like or similar items. And even where no information was available on a directly comparable procurement, the records on price were useful in showing general price trends. There were, admittedly, certain serious limitations on comparative pricing as a tool for negotiators: the prices paid in earlier purchases of a given item might themselves have been out of line, either too high or too low; if the prices on file represented purchases effected many months earlier, subsequent shifts in wages and material costs might well have invalidated the record for meaningful subsequent comparisons.

Procurement officials at Wright Field during the war years found that a combination of competitive and price comparison techniques oftentimes brought excellent results in the direction of close pricing.[78] If an invitation to bid brought in two or three proposals, the prices set might be far too high, but at least they offered a valid basis for comparison. Here all prices to be compared were current prices and no adjustments for wage or material costs would be necessary as was the case with historical comparisons. Moreover, since each bidder had to submit a cost breakdown in his Standard Proposal Form, discrepancies would loom immediately. For example, when three manufacturers bid on the same item and one showed material costs substantially higher than the other two, explanations were immediately in order. If it turned out that the higher figure was justified by a larger percentage of subcontracting, material costs could be legitimately higher but the indicated labor cost must then in consequence fall proportionally lower since there would be less inside fabrication involved. If they did not, the manufacturer's figures were open to the suspicion of error and invited further scrutiny.

Scrutiny was precisely what was involved in cost analysis, the third tool available to the military buyers. By all odds, cost analysis was the most difficult technique of negotiation to administer, yet it offered the highest rewards in terms

---

[77] Proc Function of AAF, Lecture by Swatland.

[78] The material in this and the several paragraphs following is based largely upon Lecture, Price Analysis in Relation to Procurement, by Lt Col A. P. Smith, Jr., AAF Contracting Officers School, WF, Winter 1944–45, WHFO.

of close pricing. Although the various elements of cost can be divided and subdivided into an almost endless number of categories, the usual breakdown employed at Wright Field during the war was: materials, labor, manufacturing and administrative overhead, tooling, and profit. In essence, to apply the cost analysis method of negotiation was to study every accessible bit of information on one, several, or all of these classes of estimated expense in an effort to locate needless fat.

To the uninitiated, cost analysis may look like a highly technical field open only to certified public accountants. Actually the task was far less esoteric than it looks. To be sure, a few aspects of the job required the services of highly trained experts, but a large part of the most effective kind of cost analysis could be accomplished by an intelligent but relatively inexperienced staff willing to indulge in a great deal of plain hard work. The available evidence on the point is unclear, but looking back after the war it seems that at least one reason for the agonizingly slow development of an effective cost analysis staff at Wright Field during the war was the tendency of those in command to believe that only trained accountants and the like could handle the job.[79] Whether or not they were correct in this belief may be apparent from a study of the steps actually involved in cost analysis work.

Material costs were probably the easiest of all to verify. Raw material prices cited in a manufacturer's estimate could be checked against market quotations. For even greater accuracy reflecting transportation costs, discounts, and so forth, analysts could study a manufacturer's general purchase records to compare his material estimates in the Standard Proposal Form with his payments on materials for customers other than the government. For other types of materials such as purchased parts and subcontracted assemblies, cost analysts could require a manufacturer to reveal the procedures he followed to ensure close pricing in his purchases from suppliers and subcontractors. If his methods seemed unsatisfactory, the analysts sometimes went directly to the suppliers and subcontractors to study their pricing techniques. While there was patently nothing abstruse about all this, it could involve days of gruelling work with meticulous attention to detail.

Testing the accuracy of a manufacturer's estimate on direct labor presented a considerably greater challenge than did the analysis of material costs. Rates could be checked readily enough by comparison with prevailing rates on other jobs in a manufacturer's own plant, with rates in his community, or with rates in the industry at large. Hours, on the other hand —a manufacturer's estimate of the number of direct labor hours required to complete the contract—were extremely hard to pin down.

Meaningful appraisals on this kind of estimate demanded the services of skilled estimators. Such men had to be capable

---

[79] There is much evidence on the delay in perfecting a cost analysis organization in the air arm. See, for example, the remarks of General Swatland, late in 1944, in lecture to AAF Contracting Officers School, The Procurement Function of the AAF: "We are gradually getting in a position where our negotiators and cost analysts personnel can smoke out the unjustified items in the cost breakdowns furnished by contractors." See also, Friedman, rpt to IG, Inspection of Proc Operations at WF, 11 Nov 43.

of reading a blueprint and formulating an independent appraisal of the wage-hours and machine time needed to finish any given part. For such work the buying staff had to find the necessary talent. Sometimes the Engineering and Production Divisions could supply project officers or engineers experienced in one or another of the processes involved in the fabrication of a given item. On occasion, where the dollar volume involved warranted still closer study, the price analyst could request the Air Force resident representative or area representative to run individual time studies on a contractor's shop floor to verify a disputed estimate.

Engineering studies of costs and manufacturing methods were most useful in analyzing estimates, but they were often unobtainable. Highly trained production men and experienced estimators were all working full tilt in the fundamental job of speeding up war production. Few were available for counter-checking cost estimates, even if they felt so inclined. In consequence, it was virtually impossible for the procurement organization at Wright Field to build an elaborate staff for this purpose. The sheer variety of production processes used by the hundreds and thousands of manufacturers who served the air arm as contractors and subcontractors made insoluble the task of assembling a fully competent staff of estimators. To have maintained a huge staff covering every manufacturing process would have left many of the experts relatively idle for long periods while at the same time withdrawing them from the production field where their skills were desperately needed. The alternative—the solution actually used during the war—was to engage a small staff of experienced estimators and manufacturing methods men, using their skills to the utmost while recognizing their limitations.

The difficulties encountered in compiling accurate estimates of direct labor requirements for any given contract may be better understood when one considers the many imponderables usually present. An airframe production contract, for instance, might call for a run of deliveries spread over a period of six months beginning twelve months after the contract was signed. Given the dynamics of a wartime economy, the efforts of negotiators to verify the labor needs indicated in a manufacturer's proposal was something of a voyage into *terra incognita*. Labor productivity hinges upon a host of factors. Included among them are such elusive intangibles as the extent of dilution with unskilled workers, the state of worker morale, and the effectiveness of the control exercised over the flow of materials to the assembly point, for example. Clearly, no watertight verification of direct labor requirements ever was possible. Nevertheless, air arm negotiators did have some rough and ready tools whose use could at least force manufacturers to keep some semblance of reason in their estimates.

First in importance among the techniques for rough verification of direct labor computations was the "learner curve." Experience in aircraft construction had shown that every time the number of units in production was doubled, the direct man-hours of labor required dropped about 20 percent. This formula, or one of its derivatives, when projected for a given contract was called the "learner curve." Thus, for example, while the first B-17 Flying Fortress turned out by Douglas at Long Beach absorbed over 100,000 man-hours of direct labor, by the time the 1,000th item rolled off the line, the figure had been cut to something in the neighborhood of 16,000 man-hours.[80]

When the learner-curve yardstick, be it ever so crude, was applied at the bargaining table, manufacturers were less inclined to submit grossly inflated, padded, or simply careless estimates. With good reason they might haggle over the precise point to be chosen as the beginning of the projected curve, for the high flux of design typical in the early stages of production might well delay the normal projection of the curve even where a manufacturer exercised due diligence to secure maximum labor efficiency. But whatever difficulties attended its application, the use of this negotiator's tool was more than justified by the realism it induced in the figures submitted by most manufacturers.[81]

There were other tools available for cross-checking manufacturers' estimates on direct labor needs. One such device was the simple expedient of applying a manufacturer's computed labor figure against his anticipated rate of production to see if the results obtained would square with the delivery schedule promised. Finally, in the later months of the war after a good deal of experience had accumulated, air arm negotiators found it useful to check a manufacturer's labor estimates on previous contracts with his actual requirements under those contracts as a measure of the adequacy of his methods.

Analyzing overhead charges in manufacturers' cost estimates gave just about as much trouble as direct labor. Manufacturing overhead included such items as the indirect labor of supervisors and inspectors as well as heat, light, and so on, while administrative overhead covered such costs as taxes, administrative salaries, and accounting. The greatest difficulty arose, of course, when one tried to allocate these costs among several different contracts held by a manufacturer at one time. Where a firm held governmental and nongovernmental contracts simultaneously, air arm analysts had to be alert to see that the government contracts were not loaded with an undue portion of the total overhead. When a manufacturer entered a number of government contracts in sequence, the cost analysts had to exercise great care to be sure that each successive contract did not repeat overhead payments already absorbed in earlier jobs. This was particularly true where other governmental buyers, such as the Navy Bureau of Ordnance, were dealing with the same concern. With co-ordination among the buyers at best something less than ideal, if the cost analysts were not everlastingly alert the government could end up paying the same overhead charge two or three times.

---

[80] Lecture, Special Characteristics of Aircraft Procurement, by Lt Col J. G. Scarff, undated but approximately 1944, data in folder, AAF Proc Program, prepared by MC, filed in USAF Hist Div Liaison Office, Hq USAF. See also, Negotiation and Administration of Contracts, Lecture by Scarff.

[81] Beginning in July 1943, the Aircraft Resources Control Office began turning out an index of airplane production efficiency (Report 17 *et seq*.) that measured the relative efficiency of various manufacturers in terms of output per airframe pound or horsepower per man per day. The wide differences in the performance of various manufacturers as revealed by the reports was expected to stimulate a spirit of competition and a consequent improvement in manpower utilization.

THE NEGOTIATION OF CONTRACTS

While some manufacturers may have flagrantly loaded their overhead accounts, by no means all of those who did so were guilty of deliberate padding. In the confusion and rush of wartime business, manufacturers were themselves oftentimes utterly lost in the intricacies of cost analysis. In fact, there is a good deal of evidence scattered through the records to suggest that the cost analysis work done for and by the negotiators at Wright Field taught a number of manufacturers a great deal about the inadequacies of their own business methods. An illustration may be to the point.

At a crucial juncture during the war, the military buyers at Wright Field approached a well-known manufacturer and invited him to come in as an additional source producing a rather complicated gear box assembly. He submitted an estimate showing a unit cost of $2,450. A quick comparison showed that this figure was not too far from the $2,300 charged by the existing source, the manufacturer who had long been producing this gear box and whose experience might be expected to bring his costs down substantially. Thus, superficially, on the basis of price comparison alone, the estimate seemed acceptable. However, to verify this figure before negotiations, the staff at Wright Field began a cost analysis. Almost immediately it appeared that the estimated price simply would not hold water. The analysts could not reconcile the overhead rate indicated in the manufacturer's Standard Proposal Form reply with the rate shown in his annual balance sheet and operating statement. Surprisingly enough, it wasn't that the rate was too high; it was much too low! Which is to say, the manufacturer appeared not to be absorbing enough of his legitimate overhead on the government contract. On the other hand, the direct labor estimate seemed excessive. To get at the bottom of this confusion the manufacturer was summoned to Wright Field for a conference. Confronted with the questions raised by the analysts, the manufacturer admitted that he had set the $2,450 unit price quite arbitrarily (probably with one eye on the price charged by the original maker of the gear box) and had then simply hypothesized all the elements of cost after inserting the profit figure desired. The manufacturer further admitted that he had never actually made a detailed cost analysis or breakdown even for his own use. When he did so, after the conference at Wright Field, he came up with a unit price for the gear box below the price charged by the original and presumably more practiced firm. Subsequent production experience revealed that his revised bid was a fair one allowing an adequate profit. On this one negotiation alone "close pricing" saved the government over two million dollars.[82]

Tooling costs also gave the cost analysts a great deal of trouble. Here, too, it was important to be sure the government was not buying something it already owned, for jigs, fixtures, and special tools used in one contract were often usable in another with slight modification. Another danger against which the negotiators had to guard was the possibility of paying for jigs and fixtures once under the guise of overhead and a second time as tooling. By the end of the war the Air Force contract negotiators had acquired a considerable

---

[82] Price Analysis in Relation to Proc, Lecture by Smith.

knack for ferreting out such duplications as these.

In sum, negotiations at high noon—the work of the mature procurement organization at Wright Field late in the war—were much closer to the ideal of close pricing. There was room for improvement, to be sure, but the horse trading was certainly shrewder than it had been in the months just before and just after Pearl Harbor. For whatever the figures may mean, an Air Force spokesman at Wright Field toward the end of 1944 claimed that on cost-plus-fixed-fee contracts alone the negotiators had squeezed a billion and a quarter dollars from the estimates submitted by manufacturers. And this would result in a saving of some $45,000,000 on the single item of fees, if nothing else.[83] Clearly, cost analysis was a most lucrative device for rending the suet from manufacturers' proposals. Moreover, the savings effected were by no means limited to reductions in fees and profits. Far more significant were the reductions in costs brought about by close pricing with its stimulus to efficiency and economy. The savings wrought by pressure in this quarter were far greater than those accomplished by reductions in fees and profits.[84]

If it does no more than begin to suggest the complexities besetting those who negotiated Air Forces contracts, the foregoing account will have served its purpose.

Unfortunately the contract, when negotiated, signed, sealed, and on file at Wright Field, marked only the beginning of administrative difficulties. Still ahead were the burdens of contract administration, a field of endeavor certainly no less complex than negotiation and replete with trials and tribulations of its own.

The Administration of Contracts

The term *contract administration* embraces the whole range of governmental supervision required to get delivery of the end product desired in the least time and to the best advantage of the public. Included in this phrase are such functions as production expediting, inspection, and auditing, each a vital element in the procurement process. In the following pages the focus is limited entirely to those aspects of administraiton performed personally by the contracting officer.

The Contracting Officer

Although production men and engineers working out practical problems on the shop floor were often inclined to regard contracting officers as mere paper pushers, these much maligned individuals were actually of crucial importance —they represented the focal point in the relationship between military officials and manufacturers. No matter how intimately the technical staff of the buyer and seller may have co-operated in working out the engineering details of a given contract, when it came to the all-important matter of dollars and cents, the contracting officer held the whip hand. His signature and his alone made a government

---

[83] Negotiation and Administration of Contracts, Lecture by Scarff.

[84] See especially the comment by Smith, *The Army and Economic Mobilization*, pages 324–25, that the true industrial patriot was not the entrepreneur who emerged with the lowest profit, but the one who succeeded in producing at the lowest cost. The question of profits and fees is discussed in Chapter XVII, below.

contract legal. Without his consent the manufacturer could collect not a penny of recompense.

Patently, then, the contracting officer was far more than a *pro forma* signer of documents. As a matter of fact, he occupied a rather unique status in the military hierarchy. Although subject to the command of his immediate superior for administrative purposes—pay, promotion, and the like—he did not sign contracts "by order of" that superior. Instead he signed: "The United States of America, by Richard Rowe, Contracting Officer." When acting as such, the contracting officer represented the government. His discretion and his alone validated a contract. He could be removed by his superior, but he could not be coerced either in signing a contract or in making determinations under its terms.[85]

The essence of the contracting officer's role in contract administration, as distinguished from contract negotiation, is to be found in his obligation to make determinations and give approvals as provided in the terms of the instrument. In signing a contract, the contracting officer accepted a large number of working responsibilities. Even in relatively simple procurements, substantial discretionary powers were almost invariably left in his hands. For example, the standard form used during the war for fixed-price procurements mentioned the contracting officer some nineteen different times and each mention afforded him one or more opportunities or obligations to act at one time or another during the life of the contract.

There is no need to enumerate all nineteen instances of the contracting officer's discretionary power to convey an appreciation of his role in contract administration. A few will suffice. For example, Article V in the standard fixed-price form provided certain penalties for delays in deliveries beyond the time specified in the contract. Whether or not these delays were excusable was for the contracting officer to determine. In extreme cases he could go out into the open market and buy the items on contract from other sources, holding the original contractor liable for their cost as a result of his default. Obviously, when armed with such powers a contracting officer, by the character of his decisions, might easily make or break a manufacturer. Needless to add, during the war this latent power was seldom exercised adversely. Even in 1944, the year of peak production when nearly 50 percent of all Air Forces contractors were behind schedule in their deliveries, only twenty-five firms were declared officially in default.[86]

One of the heaviest burdens of administration placed on the contracting officer's shoulders grew out of changes in the design of an end item arising during the life of the contract. Article II of the standard fixed-price instrument author-

---

[85] Manual for Contracting Officers Engaged in the Administration of Contracts, prepared by ATSC Proc Div, 10 Jan 45, ATSC Reg 70-31, ICAF.

[86] MC, Readjustment Div, Readjustment Training Course Manual, Aug 44, pp. 100-01. For an example of an aggravated default, see IOM, Chief, Contract Sec, for CGMC, 4 Sep 42, AFCF 164 Performance and Non-Performance, as well as other correspondence in this file. For a hardship case, see DeLong Hook and Eye Co., to WF, 17 Jun 42, and subsequent correspondence, AFCF 164. By way of contrast, see also, Memo Rpt CM-1187, Contract Sec, 9 Sep 41, AFCF 163 Bids (K).

ized the contracting officer to make whatever changes the exigencies of the service might require in the specifications of the item on order. The necessity for injecting alterations in the design of production model airplanes to ensure superior performance in the face of the enemy inevitably led to a more or less continual flow of change notifications. And for every one of these changes involving an appreciable amount of work, the manufacturer was entitled to an equitable adjustment in the amount of his compensation. Contract administration, then, became a matter of negotiating an endless series of supplementary agreements to cover the changes injected along the way.

During the war, as the number of design modifications in a given aircraft on the production line mounted astronomically, the peacetime practice of writing supplemental contracts for each modification proved utterly unworkable. In the first place it was scarcely feasible to hold up an urgently needed modification on the production line while procurement officials haggled over price with the manufacturer. Secondly, since many modifications were introduced on the strength of oral directives from project engineers, it sometimes proved difficult to recall all the necessary information when tying up the contractual details at a later date. For example, some eighteen months after production had been ended on the Martin B-26C at Omaha, procurement officers were still trying to tidy up the contract for that aircraft to embrace all the changes introduced. The solution finally worked out to meet this problem of supplemental agreements was to compile serial lists of all modifications made from day to day but to leave all discussions as to price until quarterly sessions, when the changes accumulated to date could be lumped and a single appropriate adjustment in contract price negotiated.[87]

Though the procedures worked out by procurement officers in peacetime to handle contract changes proved cumbersome in wartime, there were extenuating considerations that should not be overlooked. Changes in design had always been authorized in fixed-price contracts, but the process of writing supplemental agreements as practiced in peacetime was a long and complicated one. Still more difficult to accomplish were any other kinds of amendment. Mutual mistakes, even when admitted freely by both parties, were all but impossible to correct and then only with the approval of the Comptroller General.[88]

The reason why the amendment of contracts in peacetime was made difficult is not hard to discern. Then, the emphasis of procurement laws and administrative regulations was upon dollar economy rather than speed of delivery. If amendment were too simple, it would be a relatively easy matter for a manufacturer to win a contract with an abnormally low bid and then make up his losses by wan-

---

[87] Contract Change Notification, Lecture by Maj D. Sommers, 14 Dec 44; Proc Function of AAF, Lecture by Swatland; Flexible Pricing in Fixed Price Contracts, Lecture by Maj L. W. Dinkelspiel; Negotiation and Administration of Contracts, Lecture by Scarff. All lectures before AAF Contracting Officers School, WF, Winter 1944-45, WFHO.

[88] For an illustration of the unwillingness of GAO to relax the rules on reformation of contracts, see Compt Gen to SW, 15 May 41, AFCF 161 Contract Requirements. See also, Lecture, Supplemental Agreements, by Maj K. Masters, and Lecture, Contract Adjustments Without Consideration, by Maj J. G. Hodges, AAF Contracting Officers School, WF, Winter 1944-45, WFHO.

gling a succession of high-priced supplemental agreements more than covering the cost of modifications introduced after the contract was too far along to cancel.

The passage of the first War Powers Act in 1941 went far to remove the rigidities prevailing in the peacetime years. As amplified in Executive Order 9001, it not only permitted contract amendments where mutually agreeable but also authorized follow-on orders increasing the number of items on contract without the necessity of redrawing the whole instrument. This marked a radical deviation from peacetime practice, which rigidly prescribed the number of items on order and the unit price to be paid, allowing no increases without further competitive advertising. Just how extensively the flexible wartime powers were actually used may be suggested by the case of the complex three-party Rolls-Royce engine contract drawn by Packard, the British, and the War Department in 1941. Five years later the same contract was still in force—it was far too involved to renegotiate repeatedly—but 199 supplementary agreements had been added to it. In its final form the bare text of the contract required several reams of paper standing in a pile a foot high.

The greater flexibility in contract amendment authorized in wartime proved highly convenient to procurement officers and manufacturers alike. For example, the use of supplemental agreements in lieu of a succession of separate contracts resulted in substantial savings in accounting, and many manufacturers found that it brought about economies in marking and labeling tools and parts as required by shipping instructions. On the other hand, the new flexibility was not without its drawbacks. Contracting officers learned that the preference shown by many manufacturers for supplemental agreements rather than new contracts was not invariably innocuous. It sometimes happened that the original contract contained clauses that were highly advantageous to the manufacturer but were subsequently outlawed by statute or regulation. A good example of this is to be seen in the generous reconversion allowances written into some of the early large-scale contracts negotiated in the disastrous summer of 1940 but excluded from later contracts as a matter of policy. So long as the manufacturer continued to add supplemental agreements to the original contract, he could legally expect the benefits specified therein, even if he would no longer be eligible for them when entering into a new contract for precisely the same items contemplated in the supplements.[89]

In yet another sense the simplified process for wartime contract amendment tended to increase the burdens of contracting officers. Whenever a contract was negotiated containing new and favorable clauses—for example, highly advantageous provisions for covering termination costs not included in earlier instruments—the word would spread by grapevine. Soon dozens of other manufacturers would come flocking in clamoring to have their contracts similarly amended. As a consequence contracting officers found themselves on a veritable treadmill, continually rewriting the terms of previously drafted contracts. By 1944, in addition to their major task of

---

[89] Supplemental Agreements, Lecture by Masters.

negotiating new contracts, Wright Field contracting officers found they were grinding out no less than 2,000 changes on existing contracts every month.[90]

Contract changes, especially those involving price adjustments, while extremely burdensome, constituted only one of many facets of the job contract administration. Among their other duties, contracting officers had to approve the various subcontractors selected by primes, certify as to a contractor's progress in order to permit partial payments, issue tax exemption certificates, and perform many similar functions. Activities such as these obviously presupposed that the contracting officer would maintain an almost continual personal supervision over every individual contract of substantial size. Although in peacetime, when the number of contracts written each year was small and the problems of administration less numerous and certainly less pressing, it may have been feasible for contracting officers to maintain close supervision from their desks in the procurement organization at Wright Field, in time of war such a procedure was patently impossible. Manufacturers could hardly be expected to go all the way to Wright Field for the approvals and determinations required under their contracts, and contracting officers could scarcely be expected to spend time traveling to the manufacturers. Nonetheless, the terms of the instrument were explicit: the contracting officer was the only person who could legally implement those clauses calling for his discretion.

---

[90] Negotiation and Administration of Contracts, Lecture by Scarff.

Changing Concepts of the Contracting Officer

If air arm procurement officials were to avoid a hopeless legal snarl detrimental to the whole supply program, some means had to be contrived to escape the impossible situation in which contracting officers found themselves. The solution was expedient and simple. Originally "the contracting officer" was a designation that meant just what it said: the officer who actually signed the instrument for the government in the first place. But when it became evident that the contracting officer who signed a contract at Wright Field could not possibly administer that contract personally, procurement officials simply enlarged the concept of "the contracting officer" to include three different sets or levels of contracting officers to handle the different categories of functions legally required of the officer who signed a given contract. First, there were the contracting officers at Wright Field who negotiated contracts in the original instance. Next, there were contracting officers located in the procurement district headquarters geographically decentralized around the country. Finally, where the size or complexity of a contract justified such a course, there were individual contracting officers actually stationed in manufacturers' plants. In short, under the pressure of wartime demand, the initial conception of the contracting officer gave place to a new view in which the term *the contracting officer* came not to mean a single or particular individual but rather *a contracting officer*, any accredited contracting officer duly assigned to the task. The change did not result from any deliberate study by those in command; the practice simply evolved as a matter of practical necessity and was then confirmed after the fact as official policy.

By making contracting officers interchangeable—for this was the effect of the new policy—air arm procurement authorities established a functional division of labor among them. No matter how far away a manufacturer's plant might be, there were some tasks of contract administration that could best be handled at Wright Field. Price adjustments, changes in government-furnished equipment, terminations, insurance agreements, and so on were more easily handled at headquarters because only there could the pertinent information and the trained specialists be found. On the other hand, those facets of contract administration that virtually necessitated local supervision were assigned either to a contracting officer operating out of a procurement district headquarters or to one permanently located in a manufacturer's plant as a member of the resident representative's military staff.[91]

Although the new scheme of interchangeable contracting officers did make for simpler administration, the gain was won at a considerable cost. When the concept of the contracting officer was enlarged to encompass more than one person, the risk of conflicting interpretations and contrary rulings was substantially increased. Unless the most rigorous care were exercised in co-ordinating the decisions of contracting officers at every echelon, a manufacturer might find himself getting one decision or ruling from a local contracting officer, another from a district contracting officer, and still another from a contracting officer at the Wright Field headquarters. In fact, some shrewd manufacturers soon learned that they could exploit the split personality of the interchangeable contracting officers by playing one off against another to extract rulings most favorable to themselves.[92]

To prevent manufacturers from shopping up and down the line for advantage, regulations were drafted specifying the contracting officer to whom a manufacturer should turn on any particular question. Needless to say, the mere publication of a parcel of regulations did not curb the practice entirely. Manufacturers continued to go over the heads of local contracting officers seeking more authoritative or more lenient decisions from headquarters. This was hardly surprising. Experienced contracting officers were hard to find, and the best of them were generally retained at Wright Field to carry on the critical work of negotiating new procurements. The men sent out to serve as local contracting officers were thus all too often inexperienced and unsure of themselves. Even some of the abler men, when bereft of the support readily available through consultation when stationed at headquarters, showed a distressing tendency to refer all questions to Wright Field for authoritative

---

[91] Lecture, Administration of Fixed Price Contract, by Maj J. G. Hodges, AAF Contracting Officers School, WF, Winter 1944–45 WFHO; Chief, Proc Div, to Proc Br, MM&D, 17 Jul 43, AFCF 161 Purchasing and Contracting, as well as MC, Contract Sec, Office Memo 42-394 (1942).

[92] Proc Function of the AAF, Lecture by Swatland.

opinions.[93] Manufacturers, sensing this lack of self-confidence, were quick to take advantage of it by making informal appeals to the higher echelons paralleling those of the local contracting officer in an effort to influence the advice subsequently sent down to him.

If in theory the local contracting officer was fully competent to exercise discretion in all matters legally within his jurisdiction without coercion or compulsion from his superiors, he frequently felt that his power was substantially eroded in practice. The local contracting officer was inclined to complain that he became a whipping boy, whose main purpose in life was to take the blame for all decisions unfavorable to the contractor. For example, a resident representative (they were usually production men and therefore anxious to maintain harmonious relations with the manufacturer being supervised) found it convenient to insinuate that he would be more than pleased to permit a certain course of action desired by the manufacturer were it not that the local contracting officer refused to countenance it. Then, making a virtue of a necessity, he could piously point out that while the contracting officer was actually one of his military subordinates as a member of the resident air arm staff at the manufacturer's plant, official regulations forbade any coercion in the exercise of his discretion. One cynical observer of this situation was led to remark that the only real jobs left to local contracting officers were the distasteful ones such as renegotiating prices downward or taking the rap for approving aircraft for payment when they were actually lacking countless parts.[94]

Disputes and Appeals

Although most local contracting officers regarded themselves as the underdogs of contract administration, many contractors seemed to feel that they and not the officers were the actual underdogs. The essence of the manufacturers' complaint was that the deck had been stacked too heavily in favor of the government. They found it difficult to deal with local contracting officers, who operated out at the end of a long chain of command and were guided almost entirely by regulations, orders, and instructions they themselves had little or no part in framing. "You can't talk with the man who put the clause in the contract," protested one prominent aircraft manufacturer; "you can't reason with the principal party." [95] Naturally this breakdown in communication led to all manner of disputes in the normal course of contract administration.

In anticipation of disputes between manufacturers and contracting officers, Article XII of the standard fixed-price instrument provided for appeals to the department head on disputed points. But this procedure proved to be less than satisfactory. Since all questions of fact arising under a contract were, under its terms, decided finally and conclusively

---

[93] See especially, Memo, Chief, Mat Div, for Gen Brett, 24 Feb 41, AFCF 300.6; Lecture, CPFF Administration, Maj R. H. Demuth, AAF Contracting Officers School, WF, Winter 1944–45, WFHO. See also, Memo, C. Lynde for the Air Inspector, 3 Apr 44, AFCF 333.1 Misc.

[94] Maj J. G. Allen, IGD, to IG, 21 Oct 42, AFCF 333.1A Consolidated; CPFF Administration, Lecture by Demuth.

[95] Hartson, Aircraft Production.

THE NEGOTIATION OF CONTRACTS

by the contracting officer, manufacturers were inclined to feel that the trumps lay with the government. During 1942 repeated complaints of this situation led to the creation of a Board of Contract Appeals to provide a more equitable consideration of disputes. The new board devised a set of simple procedures for deciding questions of fact with a judicial detachment scarcely to be expected from a department head relying upon a case prepared by interested parties as had been the practice hitherto.[96]

The vastly enlarged scale and scope of wartime procurement, not to mention the imperatives of speedy delivery, brought about something of a revolution in the field of contract administration. Changes in the fundamental conception of the contracting officer inescapably led to a whole string of collateral changes in the procedures of contract administration. The account above has discussed these changes and the shifting character of the contracting officer more or less in the abstract. For a fuller understanding of the broader implications of contract administration, it will be necessary to pursue the topic along lines of discussion at once more tangible and more specialized. To this end the chapters that follow are devoted to such major facets of contract administration as those raised by the cost-plus-fixed-fee instrument, the question of price adjustment, and the problem of terminations.

---

[96] For a brief published account of the organization and operation of the board, see J. W. Gaskins, "New Method for Handling Appeals Under War Department Contracts," *Engineering News-Record* (July 1, 1943), p. 80.

CHAPTER XVI

The Cost-Plus-Fixed-Fee Contract: Negotiation and Administration

Some Revolutionary Implications

From the day in 1940 when Congress authorized its use, the cost-plus-fixed-fee contract (CPFF) was an unwanted stepchild. Cost-plus transactions had been generally discredited by the abuses perpetrated under this name during World War I, and post-World War I congressmen in the early nineteen twenties legislated explicitly against the use of cost-plus-a-percentage-of-cost (**CPPC**) contracts.[1] However, the cost-plus method of contracting had far too much functional utility to be legislated into oblivion. The notorious CPPC instrument was only one of several versions of the cost-plus contract. To destroy a useful principle for the shortcomings of a single application would be absurd. The CPPC contract, by defining profits as a percentage of costs, offered a positive incentive for a manufacturer to enlarge his costs and thus pyramid his profits. The CPFF contract, on the other hand, reimbursed a manufacturer for his expenses but limited his fee or "profit" to a figure rigidly fixed beforehand. The two forms were alike in that they were intended to repay a contractor for his legitimate costs, but they were intrinsically unlike insofar as the element of profit was concerned.

To say the very least, the War Department officials who secured congressional authorization to employ the CPFF contract displayed a certain lack of semantic sensitivity when they continued to use the phrase *cost plus* in spite of all its obnoxious connotations. Since the CPPC and CPFF contracts were so substantially different, there would have been no loss of candor in calling the latter instrument a *fixed-fee* contract or some other harmless name. While honorable officers certainly did not wish to deceive Congress by a misrepresentation of the facts, little was to be gained and something was almost certainly lost by deliberately courting guilt by association through the careless application of terminology. Thus, as it turned out, the CPFF contract began life in 1940 facing an uphill fight. Congress authorized its use reluctantly and only after repeated departmental assurances that the defense program would break down unless some escape were provided from the limitations of the conventional fixed-price form of contract.[2]

[1] See above, ch. IV.

[2] ASF Purchases Div, Monograph, Purchasing Policies and Practices, Sep 1939–Jun 45, 1945, OCMH, p. 231ff. See also, Smith, *The Army and Economic Mobilization*, ch. XII, *passim*.

The arguments in favor of the CPFF device were exigent: many manufacturers simply would not accept fixed-price contracts to turn out complex items of equipment for which they had no production experience and for which the elements of cost were unknown. The difficulties encountered in the procurement of gliders will amply demonstrate the point. Since the whole aircraft industry was swamped with aircraft orders, glider production was deliberately placed outside the industry—with furniture firms in Grand Rapids and with piano makers across the land. Waco, the old-line firm that had designed the production model glider, estimated unit costs at $14,000. The average unit cost actually encountered on the first 1,000 units produced came closer to $26,000. The inexperienced firms demanding CPFF contracts in such circumstances were evidently entirely justified.[3]

Lack of production experience was not the only consideration urging the use of the CPFF form. Where government orders ran a firm's total output far beyond its normal business volume, even old-line manufacturers with extensive cost data in hand and a good grasp of production methods refused to negotiate the usual fixed-price contract. Lack of working capital, not lack of patriotism, often lay at the root of the matter. The firm turning out struts for the Boeing Flying Fortress, by no means an industrial giant, suddenly found itself with billings running as high as $7,000,000 a month, far beyond the normal scope of its capital resources.[4] Some form of CPFF contract, for all its revolutionary implications, seemed to offer the most obvious line of escape from this difficulty.

The introduction of the CPFF contract did indeed bring a revolutionary change in air arm procurement, a change no less significant than that wrought by the shift from competition with sealed bids to negotiated contracts. On the surface at least, resort to the CPFF form seemed to remove most of the conventional economic pressures from a manufacturer's shoulders. With the government paying all bills for labor, for materials, and so on, a manufacturer would appear to have little incentive to make the most economical use of available resources. In protecting a producer from unforeseen and incalculable costs, the CPFF instrument threatened to protect him too much by removing virtually all the goads to efficiency found in the customary fixed-price contract. To a certain extent this inherent weakness did militate against the use of the CPFF form, but experience in World War II was to demonstrate that the drawbacks, while real, were not insurmountable, provided only that those in command recognized fully the implications of the CPFF contract and took appropriate steps to cope with them.

The key to effective use of the CPFF contract can be found in a single word: responsibility. Just as the switch from competitive to negotiated contracts forced officials at Wright Field to evolve techniques of bargaining to substitute for the pressures of the market place, so too the introduction of the fixed-fee contract required a significant transfer of responsi-

---

[3] Lecture, CPFF Contracts, by Maj D. Sommers, AAF Contracting Officers School, WF, 12 Dec 44. copy in possession of Mr. Schwinn.

[4] *Ibid.*

bility. Procurement administrators had to develop methods of supervision to replace the normal profit and loss incentives bearing upon a contractor. Although no blanket judgment on the relative merits of the fixed-fee contract as opposed to conventional fixed-price or lump-sum contract can be made, the record suggests that each type possessed substantial, even compelling advantages for meeting widely different situations. The many problems arising under the fixed-fee form of contract become vastly more meaningful if they are viewed not merely as *ad hoc* solutions of particular difficulties, but collectively, as attempts to achieve by administrative measures what competition and the incentives of the profit motive system would normally accomplish in peacetime without such close governmental supervision.

Procurement officials in the top echelons of the War Department certainly did not foresee all the many convolutions and ramifications to which the administration of CPFF contracts would eventually lead, but from the very day Congress authorized the use of CPFF they did recognize that the government would have to assume far more responsibility for the detailed supervision of a manufacturer's operations than was habitually the case with fixed-price contracts. All the technical services were enjoined to exercise the closest supervision in the administration of fixed-fee contracts in view of "the many difficulties inherent" in them, and each was urged to supply the Office of the Assistant Secretary with all instructions promulgated for this purpose.[5] Significantly, five months had passed before the air arm complied with a special directive establishing procedures for supervising fixed-fee contracts. Even then the instructions were couched almost entirely in vague generalities.[6] Neither the delay nor the inadequacies of the directive stemmed from want of interest in the problem. It was rather the inevitable result of an attempt at prospective rule making in an area beyond the realm of experience.

Air arm officers had to learn, as their brethren of the bench and bar have found, that case law was far more responsive to the infinite complexities of life than code law ever could hope to be. The attempt to draft instructions for the supervision of fixed-fee contracts was an example of code law, and as such it was virtually foredoomed to insufficiency. For the sake of clarity it will be convenient to divide the following highly interrelated problems into separate discussions: the fixed-fee problem; determination of allowable costs; auditing and accounting; property accountability; the relationship of prime and subcontractors; and, finally, conversion from fixed-fee to fixed-price contracts. While by no means exhaustive, this list of subject areas should prove adequately representative of the problems encountered in the administration of CPFF contracts.

The Fixed-Fee Problem

In a CPFF contract the fee corresponds, in theory at least, to the element of profit in a conventional fixed-price

---

[5] Memo, Dir, Current Proc, OASW, for CofAC et al., 29 Jun 40, AFCF 161 CPFF Contracts.

[6] Chief, Mat Div, OCAC, Tech Instruction–425, 25 Nov 40, AFCF 161 CPFF Contracts.

THE COST-PLUS-FIXED-FEE CONTRACT

contract. Therefore, to understand the practice with regard to fixed fees, one must first appreciate the official stand on profits in general as worked out for traditional purchasing under fixed-price contracts. Air arm policy in negotiating lump-sum agreements was to try to allow manufacturers no more than a 9- to 10-percent profit on estimated costs. Naturally, this profit range was not invariably applied; special considerations from time to time made a much lower return suitable. Where a manufacturer with a lump-sum arrangement proposed to subcontract a large portion of the job to a single outside firm, the negotiators at Wright Field would try to hold the profit allowed the prime contractor to 6 or 7 percent on costs. Similarly, where a manufacturer used government-owned facilities or working capital from public sources in excess of his own, these factors were considered by the negotiators when working out the rate of profit they wished a manufacturer to retain. In practice, of course, no matter what profit margin the negotiators intended to allow, a manufacturer who proved himself more efficient than contemplated in the preliminary estimates could realize profits well beyond those anticipated for him.[7]

With the CPFF arrangement, a somewhat different pattern emerged. No matter how much a manufacturer exerted himself to improve efficiency, the savings attained would not accrue to him as profit. His take depended almost entirely upon the sum initially fixed as his fee, and thus much of the energy and business zeal of a manufacturer's managerial organization tended to be concentrated upon the fee-setting negotiation.

The amount of the fee awarded on any given CPFF contract depended upon two variable factors: the estimated total cost of the work to be done and the percentage of that total authorized by statute and allowed by administrative discretion. The process by which an approved "estimated cost" figure was obtained need not be elaborated here beyond the observation that the manufacturer had every incentive to make it as large as possible while the government's buyers did their best to hold it down. To this end air arm negotiators employed all the special techniques of close pricing.[8] In this respect negotiations on CPFF contracts were little different in principle from the bargaining encountered on conventional fixed-price instruments. On the other hand, the whole question of the percentage allowable on the estimated cost raised problems as novel as they were knotty.

The 1940 statute authorizing use of the CPFF form of procurement set the upper limit on fees at 7 percent of estimated cost. Most manufacturers hoped to secure this maximum figure. The government's negotiators were equally anxious to settle for less than the allowable limit. As it turned out, quite unexpected and accidental circumstances operated to exert a downward pressure on fees from the very first. The emergency statute of June 1940 explicitly permitted the use of the CPFF form and the 7-percent maximum fee in aircraft pro-

---

[7] Negotiation and Administration of Contracts, Lecture by Scarff.

[8] See ch. XV, above.

curement.⁹ A subsequent statute, written for a somewhat different purpose, limited fees payable on "public works" contracts to 6 percent. Procurement officials at Wright Field professed to be in doubt as to whether or not air matériel fell within the definition of "public works." If this was but a subtle form of leverage devised by the negotiators to lower the ceiling on fixed fees, there is no evidence to prove the point. Pending a definitive legal opinion they persuaded manufacturers to accept the lower percentage. Although it was eventually determined that contracts for aircraft and other such items of armament did not constitute "public works," the Comptroller General refused to allow any upward amendment of fees on a conditional basis. Once the pattern of fees at less than the maximum authorized had been started, it proved easier to conclude subsequent negotiations at 6 percent and even lower.¹⁰

Although a fee of 5 percent of estimated costs appears decidedly modest in contrast to the expectations of normal business practice, a number of air arm contractors managed under this meager percentage to pile up profits that could certainly be described as more than generous when equated to the prewar level of returns. For example, by 1944, four of the old-line airframe firms—Bell, Boeing, Lockheed, and Republic—had so increased their output that the value of their unfilled orders had expanded to 100 times their net worth. Under such circumstances, fees set at a mere 5 percent of estimated costs tended to yield a return on capital so spectacularly high as to arouse adverse criticism. Some manufacturers, as the report of one inspector general noted, in a single year earned fees that were in excess of their entire investment.¹¹

As they became aware of the limited capital invested and the large profits some manufacturers were reaping, the buyers at Wright Field undertook to work out a few rules of thumb for scaling down fee percentages. One such was the formula limiting a contractor's fee to 4 percent whenever his volume of business exceeded four times his invested capital. Similarly, it was decided to cut all fees to 4 percent where a firm held government orders of more than half a billion dollars. Throughout the war there was a good deal of agitation for further reductions in fee percentages, but procurement officials joined with the manufacturers in resisting these moves. They argued that a ceiling of less than 4 percent on fees would make the range of allowable compensation too narrow. Negotiators would find it difficult to differentiate between those contractors who contributed engineering skill, facilities, or working capital and those who did not. For the negotiators tried, whenever possible, to make the size of the fee contingent upon the degree of special contribution made by any given manufacturer. This was doubtlessly wise policy,

---

⁹ Public 671, 76th Cong. 3d sess, June 28, 1940 (54 Stat 676–6).

¹⁰ Public 781, 76th Cong. 3d sess, September 9, 1940 (54 Stat 872–3); Interv with Mr. Schwinn, 25 Jul 55, WF.

¹¹ ASF Purchases Div, Purchasing Policies and Practices, p. 259ff. See also, Friedman to IG, 11 Nov 43, AFCF Bulky 333.1 Inspection.

but it led to rather troublesome administrative difficulties.[12]

Probably no single aspect of the whole fee problem gave more concern than the matter of equity. Where differential rates were applied, disgruntled manufacturers time and again would complain to higher headquarters that a rival firm doing substantially similar work had been flagrantly favored with a higher fee. The answer was always the same: beware of easy generalizations; each CPFF contract represented a case unto itself. All the facts must be in hand before meaningful or valid comparisons could be made.[13]

The most obvious differential in fees was that between designers and producers. For a long while it was air arm policy to put an upper limit of 6 percent on the fees granted to firms contributing aircraft designs, while auto manufacturers who put these designs into mass production were generally held to a maximum of 5 percent. Although the distinction was readily apparent in this particular instance, there was still room for jealousy and misunderstanding.[14]

The Ford Motor Company's charges of discriminatory treatment offer a case in point. In November 1942 Ford accepted a 5-percent fee on a large contract. This was the lowest fee percentage awarded up to that time. Presumably the Ford management agreed to accept this fee because it would return an adequate profit. Then, too, the Ford representatives may have been led to believe that as leaders in the industry they would set the pace toward lower fees and other manufacturers would follow suit. It was with considerable vexation that Ford saw Chrysler receive a 6-percent fee and Studebaker a 7-percent fee on seemingly comparable contracts. At first blush it might appear that a manufacturer who was less willing to co-operate and more zealous in driving a hard bargain had been rewarded with a higher fee. A full survey of the facts reveals that it was not all so simple. At least one of Ford's 5-percent contracts had allowed the corporation to enjoy the interest-free use of sizable sums of working capital, a concession not written into most subsequent contracts. Also in at least one of Ford's contracts there was a clause providing for reimbursement by the government for the firm's reconversion costs at the close of hostilities. Contracts with most other manufacturers did not include this feature. Finally, it is relevant that the negotiators allowed a somewhat higher fixed fee whenever a manufacturer was willing to accept over-all price renegotiation or agreed to include repricing clauses on government business.[15]

In retrospect it appears that air arm officials might have found negotiations on CPFF contracts a good deal smoother if, as a matter of policy, they had taken pains to educate and inform the manufacturers concerned of the many and complex variables that entered into the computation of fees. In practice, pro-

---

[12] ASF, Purchases Div, Purchasing Policies and Practices, p. 259ff.

[13] 2d Ind, Hq AAF to IG, 13 Jan 44, reply to IG Ltr cited in n. 11, above.

[14] Memo, CGAAF for CGASF, 2 Jul 42, AFCF 333.1 Contract Inspection.

[15] TWX, 1766, Contract Sec, WF, to Col Volandt, 11 Jul 42; Memo, Col Browning, Special Representative of USW, for Col Volandt, Asst to CGMC, 18 Jul 42. Both in AFCF 161 CPFF.

curement officers, harassed by the rush of war work, were sometimes not only uninformative but downright curt—to the great damage of harmonious relations with industry. A case in point with somewhat amusing overtones can be found in the record of negotiations with Emerson Electric of St. Louis, an important manufacturer of aircraft gun turrets. Between the time air arm and Emerson representatives agreed upon the terms of a CPFF contract and the time of final departmental approval of the document, the War Department changed its policy on maximum allowable fees. Emerson was notified that a lower fee percentage would be used in the contract. Understandably disturbed, the president of the Emerson turret plant, Mr. W. S. Symington, wrote Wright Field asking for a copy of the directive reducing fixed fees. Instead of returning a candid answer, a colonel in the Contract Section summarily dismissed the request with the bald assertion that it was contrary to policy to release such administrative memoranda.[16] Under the circumstances, Mr. Symington might have been forgiven had he charged the negotiators at Wright Field with double dealing. It might be interesting to speculate on the reactions of the colonel when Mr. Symington later became Assistant Secretary of War for Air and then Secretary of the Air Force.

If, on occasion, some procurement officers were insensitive in their dealings, it may also be true that some manufacturers tended to put themselves in a bad light by their intransigent stand against reductions in fees.[17] There were indeed a number of reasons why fixed fees should have been retained at relatively generous levels, but as a matter of good public relations it might have been better tactics for the manufacturers to espouse lower fees with sacrificial and patriotic enthusiasm while assuring themselves the substance of adequate profits when negotiating the fringe benefits. This was precisely what French manufacturers had done in a like situation. Contrary to the common notion that Frenchmen will debate endlessly over principle and lose the substance while their allegedly more expedient Anglo-Saxon neighbors with their genius for compromise eschew theory and principle for the substance, at least insofar as procurement matters were concerned, the very opposite proved to be true. Where many manufacturers in the United States laid themselves open to a good deal of criticism by resisting every move to lower fees, French manufacturers accepted a modest fee at face value but then made sure to protect themselves against loss by insisting on bookkeeping arrangements specifying just what would and what would not be included in the costs allowed by the government accountants.[18]

Here was the very essence of the matter of fees. If manufacturers could be

---

[16] Chief, Contract Sec, to Symington, 21 Nov 41, and 27 Nov 41, WF Contract files 360.01.

[17] Douglas, for example, invited adverse publicity in the fall of 1942 by resisting introduction of the 4-percent fee in CPFF contracts until Air Force officials threatened to employ the coercive mandates provided in the Selective Service Act. See Lecture, Mandatory Orders, by Maj L. S. Robinson, AAF Contracting Officers School, WF, Winter 1944–45, copy in possession of Mr. Schwinn.

[18] French Aircraft Industry, Lecture by Ward, AIC, 7 Oct 40.

assured both fair and generous treatment with regard to their claims for reimbursement of costs under CPFF contracts, they could afford to accept relatively small sums in the form of fees. On the other hand, so long as manufacturers feared that contracting officers and the auditors of the General Accounting Office would disallow numerous items of expense incurred under CPFF contracts, they felt constrained to demand high fees as a protective buffer against loss. Thus, no definitive understanding of the fee question is possible without a contingent study of the whole problem of just which costs were to be allowed and which disallowed.

The Determination of Allowable Costs

In principle, a manufacturer with a CPFF contract was entitled to reimbursement for his costs. But there lay the rub. Precisely what items of expenditure were to be classified as legitimate elements of cost? Were bonus payments to the executives of a corporation to be allowed as part of the cost of a bomber contract? Could a barbecue for the production workers in a parts plant be regarded as reimbursable? By the terms of the contract all such decisions lay with the contracting officer. His word was binding within the War Department unless a contractor wished to file a protest under the disputes clause and carry his case to the Board of Contract Appeals. But even where a contracting officer gave final approval to a particular item presented for reimbursement by a manufacturer, there was another hurdle to cross. The General Accounting Office studied all vouchers submitted for payments, and where disbursements seemed to have been made contrary to the terms of the contract or in defiance of existing law, the Comptroller General could suspend subsequent payments to a manufacturer to cover the contested amounts. What costs were allowable? Whatever charges a manufacturer could get both the contracting officer and the GAO to accept under the terms of the contract.

The crux of the matter lay in the contract itself; every CPFF contract contained an Article III, which attempted to cover the question of allowable costs. One approach—that actually followed by the Navy and the Ordnance Department—was to spell out in great detail in Article III all the points of conflict, clearly labeling the costs allowed and those disallowed. In practice, however, this approach fell short. It proved impossible to foresee all the many and varied types of conflicts over costs that cropped up in the life of most contracts. No matter how elaborately detailed were the stipulations of Article III, disputes over allowable costs seemed almost unavoidable.[19] When they first undertook to use the CPFF form, the contract writers at Wright Field decided that they could never hope to anticipate all the cost problems that would surely be met when aircraft were put into mass production for the first time. Almost of necessity they turned to an alternative course when drafting fixed-fee contracts.

Rather than make any attempt to spell out the scope of allowable costs in detail, air arm contract drafters simply wrote into Article III a cross reference

---

[19] CPFF Contracts, Lecture by Sommers.

to an existing Treasury Department decision, TD-5000. This regulation or directive had been worked out as an accounting guide or procedural manual for use in the determination of excess profits under the Vinson-Trammell Act of 1934. Because it was founded in actual experience and embodied a list of disallowances based on specific cases arising in the past, TD-5000 promised to provide a surer guide for contracting officers' decisions than would any prospective regulation drawn up without benefit of experience. Moreover, TD-5000 laid down several general principles for reimbursements: to be allowed, a cost must be necessary to the performance of the contract as written, must be reasonable, and must not be specifically disallowed by the contract.[20]

Equipped with a list of specific disallowances and a set of principles, air arm contracting officers set out to administer the CPFF contracts that had been written. They soon came to realize that TD-5000, while helpful, did not provide the answers they sought. TD-5000 was designed for use with a profit-limiting statute, and the criteria it established were not always suited to the very different function of determining allowable costs under CPFF contracts. Moreover, the directive raised as many questions as it answered. What costs were necessary? What costs were reasonable? Ultimately such questions called for the exercise of discretion, and in this contracting officers found it difficult to agree among themselves let alone reach decisions acceptable to GAO.

The uncertainties beclouding the question of allowable costs led to a chain of unfortunate consequences. Each day's mail brought in its quota of complaints from manufacturers protesting a disallowed cost. Often the complaint concerned a relatively insignificant sum of money, but at a time when managerial skills in the aircraft industry were spread woefully thin, every diversion of time and attention delayed the main job of production just so much more.

Anxious to meet the problem of allowable costs squarely, the procurement staff at air arm headquarters invited suggestions from the industry. This was a move in the right direction. Unfortunately, its execution was somewhat bungled. The manufacturers were requested to submit their grievances in ten days. Here was a major question of policy growing out of a revolutionary shift in procurement procedure; certain to be involved were numerous and intricate questions of accounting calling for the most concentrated and thoughtful study if effective supplements to TD-5000 were to be promulgated, yet the manufacturers were expected to respond in ten days. Some of them, especially those on the west coast, scarcely had time enough to receive the request before their replies were due.[21]

The pattern reflected in this episode was uncomfortably characteristic of far too much air arm administration in the war years. Pressed to the limits of endurance in their efforts to get production, procurement officers sometimes lost

---

[20] *Ibid.* See also, ASF Purchases Div, Purchasing Policies and Practices, p. 269. For TD-5000, 29 Jul 40, see Code of Federal Regulations, sec. 26.9, ch. 1, title 26.

[21] Asst to Chief, Mat Div, to all major contractors, 14 Jun 41, AFCF 161 CPFF.

sight of the ultimate in their preoccupation with the immediate, handling questions of high policy in the same way that they dealt with the day-to-day details of operations. Surely one of the gravest weaknesses revealed in the air arm at war was the absence of adequate staff arrangements for lifting policy problems above the daily round of effort. For, in the last analysis, sound policies are often little more than meaningful generalizations based on operational experience subjected to reflective study.

Where the line operates, the staff should reflect. But as every experienced officer knows, staffs have a fatal tendency to drift into operations at the expense of reflection. Not all the buyers at Wright Field were blind to the need for "procurement doctrines," carefully formulated statements of policy on allowable costs, but the structure of the organization within which they operated made inadequate distinction between line and staff. Perceptive officers who clearly grasped the need for broad and all-embracing statements of policy found themselves so heavily engaged in current negotiations that they were unable to devote even a fraction of their time and energy to that mature reflection without which doctrine cannot be distilled from practice. That the whole question of allowable costs in fixed-fee contracts demanded the most careful study by highly experienced procurement officials scarcely needs demonstration. Nonetheless, a brief account of a few representative problems should serve to illuminate the complexities besetting those who sought to promulgate general rules for administering CPFF contracts. Most of the claims for reimbursements that came into dispute fell into one of three areas—overhead, salaries, and taxes—and it will be appropriate to consider some representative cases arising under each heading.

Where a manufacturer's plant was entirely devoted to war work on a fixed-fee contract, overhead costs posed few problems, since virtually all costs could be charged to the government. On the other hand, manufacturers operating plants with several different types of contracts—one or more fixed-fee jobs under the same roof with some conventional fixed-price contracts—raised many headaches. In those instances where the manufacturer combined both fixed-price and fixed-fee arrangements with the government in the same plant with his regular commercial business, the task of segregating overhead brought on an accountant's nightmare. Typical in this respect was the situation encountered when dealing with the General Motors Corporation.

Like most other contractors apart from the old-line aircraft firms, General Motors edged into the field of munitions production only gradually. Aircraft parts and engine contracts were initially a side issue in contrast to the immense volume of automobile production. In fact, until 1941, the corporation's policy was to charge none of the main office overhead to the government contracts currently held. As automobile production had to be tapered off, however, and the corporation gradually moved toward almost total preoccupation with war orders, this arrangement broke down. The costs incurred by the central corporate management had to be absorbed somewhere. How, was the question.

In administering the air arm fixed-fee contract held by General Motors' Fisher Body Division, just what element of the home office overhead should be charged as its proportionate share? Since this problem came up after a number of General Motors contracts had been under way for weeks or months, the contracting officer, in whose hands decisions of this sort lay, faced a knotty problem. If he directed the contractor's salaried employees in the home office to keep records of the time they spent on each contract, he knew that no effective audit was possible, either retrospectively or currently. Yet without audit there would be no way of determining to the satisfaction of the GAO whether or not charges properly assignable to the manufacturer on his fixed-price jobs had been slipped off onto the government's shoulders in a fixed-fee contract. On the other hand, if the contracting officer allocated overhead salary costs arbitrarily in proportion to direct labor costs on each different contract, he was just as likely to err in the other direction. Such a course could work a serious injustice to the manufacturer since different kinds of contracts and different phases of the same contract involve widely varying amounts of managerial effort. Moreover, the novelties and technical difficulties usually encountered when getting munitions production started entailed far more exertion in the front office than did the regular run of business. Whatever decision he made to resolve this dilemma, the contractor remained vulnerable to review by GAO.[22]

Among the many annoying questions on allowable overhead costs, few were more frequently raised than those pertaining to advertising. To what extent should advertising be an allowable charge against the government? When a manufacturer devoted 100 percent of his facilities to war work on public contracts was no institutional advertising to be allowed? If not, what would become of the useful and service-rendering trade association journals that made a genuine contribution to the war effort but depended almost entirely upon institutional advertising? Was a manufacturer's house organ such as the *Douglas Airview* promotional advertising or a necessary morale builder for the firm's employees? If it started out as the latter but drifted toward the former, was the contracting officer going to impose a censorship on editorial policy? If he did not, there was always danger that GAO would disallow the claim for reimbursement at some later and inconvenient date after large sums had been spent by the manufacturers in good faith.[23]

In the matter of contributions, TD-5000 authorized those that were encountered in the ordinary run of business. A contracting officer might safely approve vouchers for gifts to the Red Cross and the local Community Chest, but what about a manufacturer's donation to a British war relief fund? It lay within the contracting officer's discretion to pass such a claim if it seemed both "reasonable" and "necessary."

The problem of allowability in regard

---

[22] Orton, Exec Accountant, AAF, to Fiscal Officer, Hq AAF, 14 May 42, AFCF 161 CPFF.

[23] Col Volandt to Quigley Publishing Co., AFCF 161 Contract Requirements; Chief, Proc Div, to Air Inspector, 18 Nov 44, AFCF 333.1–A Douglas.

to contributions illustrates as well as any other aspect of the overhead problem the precarious position into which the discretionary roles of the contracting officer and GAO thrust a manufacturer holding a CPFF contract with the government. After a number of disputes had cropped up over reimbursement for donations, the War Department issued an official "interpretation" in December 1942. The directive, or policy statement, held that contracting officers could approve reasonable charitable contributions under fixed-fee contracts. This they proceeded to do in the normal course of business until August 1944, when the Comptroller General flatly ruled that all such payments were nonreimbursable. Contracting officers accordingly began to reject all vouchers for charitable contributions, leaving the manufacturers, who had acted in good faith under the War Department's earlier interpretation, to foot the bills out of their fixed fees.[24]

So long as the Comptroller General's rulings concerned only such marginal items as donations, there was little cause for alarm; these pinpricks were annoying, but they could be ignored since the sums involved were relatively small. In time, however, GAO suspended so many vouchers for all manner of overhead items that several aircraft manufacturers were seriously affected. Since overhead vouchers, unlike claims for labor and materials, were reimbursed only once a year, after-the-fact disallowances could be financially embarrassing. In all good faith and with the formal assent of the contracting officer in charge, a manufacturer could incur a series of heavy overhead charges only to wake up one morning months later to find his claims disallowed or, if already paid, to find a like amount withheld from some current and uncontested voucher.[25]

Quite understandably, some manufacturers felt that they were helplessly caught between two impersonal bureaucratic grindstones. Air Force officers never receded from the War Department's contention that the decisions of a contracting officer were binding unless shown to be arbitrary, in bad faith, or fraudulent. On the other hand, while GAO would sometimes back down on a specific disallowance after a showing of the facts, the Comptroller General would never concede any impairment to his right of independent review of all federal contracts.[26] If GAO had confined its work to mere auditing—verifying the accuracy of the accounts rendered, there would have been no ground for complaint. But the Comptroller General went far beyond mechanical audits and undertook not only to interpret individual contracts but to develop a philosophy of procurement considerably at variance with that held by air arm contracting officers.

During the prolonged dispute on overhead payments the Comptroller General took the stand that many of the disallowed items were supposed to be financed as a matter of course by the contractor out of his fixed fee. At that very moment the War Department was engaged in a campaign to force manu-

---

[24] ASF Purchases Div, Purchasing Policies and Practices, p. 270.

[25] *Ibid.*, pp. 271–72; CPFF Administration, Lecture by Demuth.

[26] ASF Purchases Div, Purchasing Policies and Practices, p. 272.

facturers to accept lower fixed-fee percentages to prevent the accumulation of abnormal or excessive profits. Here were two diametrically opposed conceptions of the fixed fee. If the Comptroller General and his staff at the Accounting Office regarded the fixed fee as a slush fund to cover miscellaneous operating expenses, how could the Under Secretary of War talk about fees as "profits." [27] With no little justice, manufacturers caught between these two interpretations might argue that it was grossly unfair to belabor them as profiteers or to imply a lack of patriotism in their resistance to lower fees when at the same time burdening these self-same fees with all manner of overhead costs.

Although there were numerous other items of overhead frequently in dispute, further elaboration would serve little purpose. On the other hand, the related problem of salary raises should prove well worth closer study. To what extent should salary increases be allowed under fixed-fee contracts? How were contracting officers to curb the understandable temptation of contractors to hand themselves raises at government expense?

After the air arm's first few CPFF contracts had been in operation for several months, detailed audits began to turn up some rather startling statistics. One leading automobile manufacturer building aircraft engines for the government had given out raises to certain classes of supervisory personnel averaging 41 percent over the level of pay prevailing before the firm took on a war contract. Another manufacturer jumped an official's salary from $12,000 to $19,200 when the corporation signed a CPFF contract. Reports such as these and many others like them indicated the pressing need for a refinement of policy in this area.[28]

To be sure, many salary increases were entirely justified. After the lean depression years the return of full employment inevitably required a good deal of adjustment regardless of whether the fixed-fee or the fixed-price contract was to be used. Moreover, the rapidly expanded aircraft industry desperately needed large numbers of managers and supervisors, more than could readily be found in the old-line firms unless relatively junior men were hastily moved upward. Such promotions certainly justified marked increases in salary. But air arm officials were genuinely concerned when the president of a west coast aircraft firm reported his 1942 salary at $50,000, a figure some $30,000 over that of the year before.[29] Enlarged responsibilities and the incentives necessary to maximum production must be taken into account, but it is pertinent to observe that a considerable number of draftees were then currently being asked by their "friends and neighbors" to risk their lives for a cash incentive of no more than $50 a month.

The rush of war orders precipitated by the Japanese attack on Pearl Harbor made clarification of policy on salary increases more than ever necessary. Although a number of proposals had been

---

[27] *Ibid.*, p. 270.

[28] Memo, Dir, Purchasing and Contracting, OUSW, for CofAC, 16 Jun 41; Lt Col J. M. Rae, IGD, to IG, 30 Mar 42. Both in AFCF 161 CPFF.

[29] MS sheet showing pay of all officials making over $5,000 in the aircraft company. 1941–42 AFCF 333.1B.

THE COST-PLUS-FIXED-FEE CONTRACT 385

broached from time to time in the preceding months, none seemed satisfactory.[30] Finally, taking their cue from some remarks in an address by the President, the buyers at Wright Field set an entirely arbitrary limit of $25,000 as the maximum amount reimbursable on salaries paid to fixed-fee contractors.[31] Not until a number of contracts had been written with this limitation was it discovered that the President had been thinking in terms of a posttax salary of $25,000 rather than a pretax maximum of $25,000 as written into fixed-fee contracts at Wright Field.[32] This difference could place the air arm at a distinct disadvantage vis-à-vis the other services since manufacturers could scarcely be blamed if they preferred to take advantage of the more generous terms offered elsewhere.[33] Nevertheless, to change policies in midstream threatened to be even more disadvantageous.

To revert to the simple formula laid down in TD-5000, as some favored doing, was decidedly inexpedient. To do this would be to reimburse contractors for all "reasonable" salary increases above the $25,000 maximum. Since the contractors had made their original estimates knowing that all salary costs above the maximum would have to be derived from income provided by the fixed fee, any shift in policy that belatedly permitted them to be reimbursed for these sums would in effect amount to granting them a windfall in the form of an enlarged fee.[34] Obviously GAO would hold such a course utterly unwarranted.

Under the circumstances it is no wonder that contracting officers found the entire question of allowable costs an exercise in frustration. Men resort to written contracts in a quest for certainty, yet the broad areas of discretion allowed in fixed-fee contracts marked the very antithesis of finality. Where they enjoyed discretion under the terms of a contract, contracting officers were confronted with a bewildering and oftentimes conflicting array of statutes, Executive orders, and command policies, both advisory and obligatory. The multiplicity of these directives alone would make it difficult to apply them even though their very purpose was to attain uniformity and equity. The margin for error and misunderstanding was in no way reduced by the circumstance that these prescriptions were never fixed and permanent but remained in a continuing flux that left neither manufacturers nor government officials with much sense of certainty when they considered salary increase cases or any other facet of the topic of allowable costs.

Though the matter of salary raises reduced to dollars and cents gave much trouble to those who administered CPFF contracts, appraising the "reasonableness" of such fringe benefit features of salary as retirement pay and group insurance was even more difficult. Worse still were all those questions raised as to the reimbursement of bonus pay-

---

[30] See for example, Memo, OUSW for CofAC *et al.*, 23 Oct 41, and reply, Asst to Chief, Mat Div, to USW, 1 Nov 41, AFCF 161 CPFF.
[31] Interv with Mr. Schwinn, 25 Jul 55, WF.
[32] CPFF Administration, Lecture by Demuth.
[33] For an instance illustrating the desire of a manufacturer to switch his contract from the air arm to the Navy "because the Navy was more lenient with respect to maximum salaries," see Col Rae to IG, 30 Mar 42, AFCF 161 CPFF.

[34] CPFF Administration, Lecture by Demuth.

ments. Although the practice was to allow this kind of costs if they were general in application and clearly a part of the manufacturer's morale and incentive scheme, contracting officers knew well that as a rule bonus payments were almost certain to raise doubts and difficulties with GAO.[35]

Taxes were yet another field where the problems of allowable costs could be knotty for those who administered CPFF contracts. Once again a few illustrations may suffice to indicate something of the complexity faced.

Consider, for example, the matter of unemployment insurance payments by individual manufacturers. Under the statutes prevailing in most states the size of the payments made by manufacturers into the unemployment insurance fund depended upon their experience rating. Manufacturers with a highly stable employment record were rewarded with a lower rate of payment than that imposed on firms with a record of frequent lay-offs. Aircraft manufacturers entering fixed-fee contracts kept one eye on the inevitable decimation of employees expected at the end of the war. Prudently, they demanded protection against postwar increases in their tax rate brought on by circumstances entirely beyond their control. Air arm negotiators responded with an appropriate contract clause by which the government obligated itself to save the manufacturer harmless—as the lawyers put it—by agreeing to assume the burden of any such tax increase.

At least on the surface a "save harmless" clause applied to the unemployment insurance tax seemed valid enough, but it raised problems far beyond the immediate sphere of aircraft procurement. Would such unlimited promise to pay future increases in "experience rating" taxes pass scrutiny at GAO? In so binding the government were not procurement officers undertaking obligations for which no known appropriation was earmarked? Then too there was the question of equity. Would not the manufacturers who held conventional lump-sum contracts also suffer increased unemployment insurance tax rates as a result of war end lay-offs? Why then should they not receive the same protection granted to fixed-fee contractors? The subsequent evolution—one cannot say solution in matters of this sort—of the unemployment tax problem lies far beyond the province of this study. Here it should be sufficient to suggest the character of the tax problems confronting contracting officers who struggled to determine just which costs were allowable and which were not under fixed-fee contracts.

Excise taxes offer yet another case in point. In the prewar years it had been the settled policy of the government to refuse payment of all excise taxes on finished products. Excise taxes on components buried in the finished product were, however, paid without protest. Then in January 1942, in the very midst of the rush of war orders, the Treasury Department promulgated a new decision, TD–5114, which altered this practice profoundly. Henceforth, it was announced, the government would pay no excise taxes at all, including those on component parts buried in the end item.

---

[35] CPFF Contracts, Lecture by Sommers.

The new tax policy appeared at a most inopportune time. Manufacturers were already over their heads in a mass of intricate contractual details—they already had more paper work to do than their staffs could handle, they were under intense pressure to get results, and they were criticized at every turn for their slowness in signing contracts. Yet the Treasury, in the peak month of war order placement, handed down a decision that made manufacturers take one of two courses, both of them costly. The manufacturer could shrug his shoulders, sign the contract before him, and absorb the tax burden in his fixed fee, or he could insist on conducting a careful study to analyze each taxable element of material in every one of the hundreds and hundreds of purchase orders and subcontracts comprising his prime contract, thus delaying for days or even weeks the signing of the contract.

Manufacturers who chose to absorb the excise taxes in their own fees and those who inadvertently failed to identify the tax element in component prices as such lived to rue the day. Cumulatively the many seemingly trivial federal imposts ran into very large sums of money.

Much the same thing could be said of a whole series of state and local taxes applied to sales, use, and gross receipts on transactions between fixed-fee contractors and the federal government. A 3-percent California use tax, for example, applied to a Vega fixed-fee contract involving about $4,750,000 in taxable items, ran up a tax of $141,600, which could make a very big dent in the firm's so-called profit if subtracted from the fixed fee.[36] And this, it should be observed, was only one of a number of similar state and local taxes to which the contractor was subject.

State and local taxes threatened to become so burdensome indeed that War Department procurement officials began to cast about for means to avoid them. One solution, issued as a directive from the Under Secretary's Office, was to order all procurement officers to purchase directly, as agents of the United States, all materials needed by fixed-fee contractors that would be subject to burdensome state taxes. Along the same line, contracting officers were ordered to make direct payments from federal funds covering each fixed-fee contractor's entire payroll wherever states attempted to impose gross receipts taxes on such disbursements.[37] In short, the plan was to let the manufacturers hide from state taxation behind federal immunity. Superficially these techniques of tax avoidance may appear to have been ingenious, but as is so often the case, the proposed administrative cure threatened to do more harm than the tax disease itself.

Because full compliance with the order from the Under Secretary threatened virtually to wreck the rearmament effort, procurement officers at Wright Field felt they could not follow the directive received; at the same time they did not wish to disobey. Instead, they tactfully reported that they had "delayed compliance" to avoid plunging the procurement program into disastrous turmoil. The heart of the trouble was this: to

---

[36] Vega Airplane Co. to Asst Chief, Mat Div, 6 Sep 41, AFCF 161 CPFF.
[37] Memo, OUSW for CofAC et al., 7 May 41; OCAC TI–742, 12 May 41. Both in AFCF 161 CPFF.

execute the order would be to transfer a large portion of a manufacturer's responsibility for the timely execution of his contract to the shoulders of the government's agents. How could the government hold a manufacturer accountable for the delivery of aircraft by a given date when he was denied control over the purchase of the materials he required? Finding enough qualified air arm personnel to take over the manufacturer's purchasing role would in itself be difficult. Worse yet, responsible officers at Wright Field felt that air arm procurement methods with all their built-in statutory safeguards were "too slow and cumbersome." Such a course would inject "confusion, indecision and slowness" at a time when speed was more than ever essential.[38] This indictment of governmental procurement procedures was not entirely unconscious, for it was more or less a matter of settled policy at Wright Field to make the fullest possible use of the "freedom of initiative and resourcefulness" enjoyed by private businessmen, who were unhampered by so much of the statutory red tape that beset governmental procurement operations.

In the view of air arm procurement officials, there were only two appropriate alternatives insofar as state and local taxes (or for that matter even federal excises) were concerned. One was to pay the tax and settle the matter in the courts later if need be; the other, decidedly preferable, was to invite Congress to provide a statutory solution. A problem so complex as taxation obviously can never be entirely resolved, but it is of interest to observe that the course eventually taken in handling at least one of the many tax questions raised here followed along both alternatives. Beginning in March 1943, the Air Force policy was to include all federal excise taxes on component parts in the cost of the end product, thus presumably risking GAO refusals to reimburse. At the same time representations were made to Congress seeking relief. Eventually, in the revenue act of June 1944, Congress complied by authorizing manufacturers to include excise taxes as a cost of doing business, and a great many government agents got off the administrative merry-go-round of tax claims, certificates of exemption, and disallowances that took money out of one governmental pocket to put it into another at considerable expense in paper work.[39]

In the matter of state taxes, the federal government could, if it wished, hide behind a long line of precedents, from Justice Marshall on down, establishing its immunity to state imposts. Nevertheless, a number of sociological considerations indicated that a doctrinaire insistence upon the rule of other times and circumstances could lead to grave local hardships. For example, a California franchise tax on fixed-fee contractors might be found nonreimbursable, at least the Army JAG so opined, although the Navy JAG found otherwise, but the ruling only avoided the social realities. The erection of immense new aircraft plants hiring tens of thousands of peo-

---

[38] IOM, Actg Asst Chief, Mat Div, for Chief, Mat Div, 22 May 41, AFCF 161 CPFF.

[39] Lecture, Taxes and Their Effect on Procurement, by Maj Julian deB. Kops, AAF Contracting Officers School, WF, Winter 1944–45, WFHO. See also, Flexible Pricing in Fixed Price Contracts, Lecture by Dinkelspeil, pp. 16–17.

ple sometimes brought waves of suburban growth in one nearby community after another. Each such wave of expansion imposed costly burdens of fire and police protection, sewage disposal, street paving, school construction, and the like. Somehow these social costs had to be absorbed. Should the federal government as the exclusive buyer in some plants refuse to shoulder the cost? If so, was it reasonable to work toward further reductions in the manufacturer's fixed fee if this fee had to absorb all such tax costs as the one described above?[40]

In groping for answers to these and similar tax questions, state officials and legislators, hard-pressed manufacturers, federal judges, and War Department lawyers were engaging in a constitutional controversy of considerable significance. Individual contracting officers could and did play important roles in this process as they ruled on allowable costs in particular contracts, but it was easy to lose sight of these broader implications when confronted with seemingly impossible questions and when under relentless pressure to hasten on the pace of production.

Overhead costs, salary increases, and taxes—these were only a few of the troubles that plagued contracting officers trying to administer CPFF contracts. A host of similar matters ranging from constitutional law to the most technical questions of production made the determination of allowable costs an endless challenge. Gradually, as they accumulated experience and found certain repetitious patterns in the cases coming before them, they were able to generalize some of their experience for the benefit of the service as a whole. It may be one of the real tragedies of the procurement process that more lessons were not learned from the record of individual contracts. Unlike the records of common law courts, those of procurement do not enter a body of formal reports or case histories, readily accessible, where they can be studied in depth and with continuing perspective. Some lessons were indeed learned from the general procurement experience, but too many were lost.[41]

Although the lessons learned by contracting officers and negotiators were never collected during the war into a single grand synthesis, nor summarized in any comprehensive set of manuals or casebooks on allowable costs, procurement officers did manage to skim off a number of individual points for general application. Some appeared as command directives to contract writers and administrators. Others took the form of stock clauses for insertion in Article III of

---

[40] Congress explicitly recognized a responsibility for such local costs by the federal government by authorizing cash relief payments to communities abnormally burdened by war industries; see Public War Housing (Lanham) Act of October 14, 1940 (54 Stat 1125).

[41] Although procurement officers during World War II took great pains to see that the record of experience with CPFF contracts was preserved for the future, the record has shown an unusual propensity for vanishing. Even where determined efforts were made to distill wartime experience for postwar instruction, the results have not always lived up to expectations. Take, for example, the multivolume study of CPFF administration in the AAF prepared by Colonel Scarff at Wright Field during the war. Although dozens of persons devoted a great deal of time over many weeks searching for this study after the war, both in Washington and at Wright Field, no copy could be found in the official record repositories.

fixed-fee contracts, spelling out in detail just which costs would be allowed and which disallowed. Still others, those of broadest application, appeared as official cost interpretations for the guidance of buyers throughout the War Department. Thus it turned out that the air arm, which had begun the war relying upon a few general principles in TD–5000 and the discretion of its contracting officers, ended up, very much like the Navy and the Ordnance Department, with the cost stipulations of Article III in fixed-fee contracts running to as many as forty subclauses encrusted with legal jargon.[42]

In a characteristic pattern of government, the simple became complex. And as experience gradually revealed the infinite variety of facets in fixed-fee contracts, even a most casual observer could see that the essence of successful supervision lay in adequate procedures for accounting. Which is to say, no appraisal of fixed-fee administration is possible without an understanding of the methods and organizations for auditing and accounting that served the air arm.

Auditing and Accounting

Unfortunately for the cause of effective procurement, the prewar Air Corps had developed neither the organization nor the procedures for accounting needed to cope with the challenge imposed by the use of fixed-fee contracts. To be sure, a small staff had been established to conduct the audits of manufacturers' books that were authorized by the Air Corps Act of October 1926, but for over ten years the work of this group went along more or less mechanically with little or no influence on the procurement process. The auditors employed may have been competent enough, but their conception of the task assigned to them was sharply limited. Indeed that of the officers who directed their work was no wider since they regarded the auditors as watchmen to prevent fraud and collusion. At no time did the auditors try to summarize the results of their work or put it in a form useful to those engaged in the formulation of procurement policy. Until the rearmament crisis arrived, the air arm auditors were never regarded as an integral part of the procurement team.[43]

Not only was the audit staff on the eve of the war small and narrow in outlook, it was also inadequate in the matter of procedures. It lacked experience in precisely those problems of accounting that were to prove most troublesome during the war. The Vinson-Trammell Act, which Congress passed in 1934 to limit profits on munitions contracts, gave the Treasury Department sole power to administer its terms.[44] This proviso deprived the War and Navy Departments of an excellent opportunity, for had they been required to administer the act they would have been forced to perfect their organizations and procedures for accounting and auditing along lines that would have been advantageous when the war arrived.

---

[42] ASF Purchases Div, Purchasing Policies and Practices, pp. 269–70; CPFF Administration, Lecture by Demuth.

[43] IOM, Asst Chief, Mat Div, for Gen Brett, OCAC, 9 Nov 40, AFCF, 321.9–D. For evidence of the lag in exploiting the audit powers of the Air Corps Act, see SW to CofAC, 24 Oct 36, and Mat Div, GO 6, 9 Dec 36. Both in AHO Plans Div 145.91–391.

[44] ASW to W. W. Parrish, editor of *American Aviation*, 23 Jul 40, AFCF 132.2 Audits.

THE COST-PLUS-FIXED-FEE CONTRACT

The steps by which the small prewar audit staff finally did grow into an army of clerks and accountants need not be related here. Suffice it to say that the air arm audit staff, along with those of the other procurement services, gradually fanned out in an elaborate network of district, regional, and in-plant or resident auditors. Soon, as one Air Corps officer observed, a vast array of "Government lice" were swarming over contractors' plants reviewing every last voucher. In some instances not one but several sets of auditors fell upon a manufacturer at one time as Air Corps, Ordnance, and Navy agents worked over his books and got in each other's way. It takes little imagination to visualize how seriously this kind of duplication could impede a manufacturer's administrative operations.[45]

Some sort of high level co-ordination of effort was patently needed. As a matter of fact, as early as 1939 representatives of the War and Navy Departments had made some effort to avoid duplications, but this only led to the decision that both Departments would work on a manufacturer's books at one time so as to avoid handling the same set of records twice. Not until well into the war, in the spring of 1943, did the two services finally agree to accept each other's audits, leaving the whole job in any one plant to the service with the larger dollar volume in orders.[46] Why, one may ask, was this obvious expedient put off so long? There were a number of reasons why it proved so difficult to simplify and co-ordinate the accounting and auditing done on munitions contracts. In the first place, nearly every manufacturer had a different system of accounting. To achieve really uniform audits would require prior agreement on some standard system of accounting imposed from above. But against any gain in uniformity would have to be placed the confusion and lost motion involved in an attempt to tamper with the manufacturer's system of accounting in the midst of the hectic rush to rearm. Then too, even if a high degree of standardization could be achieved in the contractor's books, organizational differences in the services and in the various governmental agencies themselves made uniformity of procedure almost impossible to attain. Air arm procurement districts were not even coterminous with the districts of the Ordnance Department, let alone those of the Navy, and at the beginning of the emergency GAO maintained no field organization, insisting instead that all its auditing be centralized in Washington. Finally, the novel character of so many of the accounting problems encountered in each successive fixed-fee contract made co-ordination and simplification an elusive task. Auditors and contracting officers often made verbal statements on particular cost problems raised by manufacturers, so that even on individual contracts the governing rulings were not

---

[45] A brief published account of military audit organizations may be found in Co-ordination of Procurement Between the War and Navy Departments (Draper-Strauss Rpt), February 1945, by Col. William H. Draper, Jr., and Capt. Lewis L. Strauss, USNR. See vol. II, pp. 183ff. See also, CPFF Administration, Lecture by Demuth; Office of Fiscal Dir (Army), Hist of Fiscal Services, p. 834.

[46] Office of Fiscal Dir (Army), Hist of Fiscal Services, pp. 478–80.

always readily available in writing for careful study. Virtually the same thing could be said for the hundreds of unpublished memos that lay scattered through the contract files of the various procuring services.[47] As a consequence, improved procedures and interservice agreements on accounting were perfected very slowly and then only after the expenditure of an immense amount of time and effort on the part of officials whose abilities were already spread far too thin by the exigencies of the procurement program.

Although continued use of the CPFF contracts throughout the war years raised a never-ending series of problems in accounting and auditing, the first CPFF contract written for air matériel proved to be one of the most intricate ever entered. As such, it affords an excellent illustration of the bookkeeping problems confronting air arm officials. The contract was the three-party agreement of the British Government (or its agent, the British Purchasing Commission), the War Department, and the Packard Motor Car Company calling for some 9,000 Rolls Royce aircraft engines. A three-way allocation of costs was confusing enough in itself, but it became even more involved when Packard started work on the job in the same plant with the company's regular automobile production line.[48]

On one point the record of accounting experience handed down from World War I was clear: retroactive audits had but limited validity and were virtually impossible to conduct.[49] Nevertheless, despite this inherited lesson, there were a number of instances in World War II where major aircraft manufacturers worked for several months before an audit of their contract was initiated. However, there were extenuating circumstances. Many of the unaudited contracts were started under letters of intent long before the opening of negotiations over terms. Since conventional or lump-sum contracts were not currently audited, the prevailing policy was to refrain from assigning an audit force until it was definitely decided whether a fixed-price or a fixed-fee instrument would be used. In those cases where a letter of intent matured months later into a fixed-fee contract, the auditors arrived to find themselves faced with just the sort of situation inveighed against by the veterans of World War I air arm procurement.[50]

---

[47] For illustrative examples on this point, see Lockheed to Mat Div, 21 Jun 41, and Memo, Dir Fiscal Services, SOS, for Dir, Purchases Div, 3 Sep 42. Both in AFCF 161 CPFF. That the problem was still unresolved at the end of the war is evident from comments in MB Industrial Advisory Com on Military Contract Relationships, Rpt to MB, *Review of Major Problems in Military Procurement and Recommendations,* Aug 51, pp. 14–15. Copy in OCMH.

[48] SW to Compt Gen, 6 Dec 40, SW files, Airplanes, item 1898. See also, Memo, Chief, Finance Div, for Gen Brett, 7 Nov 40, AFCF 161 CPFF.

One cannot help wondering if the intricate accounting problems growing out of this situation may not have influenced the much criticized decision to build entirely new facilities in preference to the use of intermingled production lines in a number of plants.

[49] For an explicit recognition of this contention, see C. E. Orton to Chief, Finance Div, OCAC, 16 Jan 40, AFCF 004.4. See also, Air Service, History of the Bureau of Aircraft Production, 1919, microfilm copy in ICAF Library.

[50] Memo, Orton, Exec Accountant and Auditor, Hq AAF, for Gen Echols, 24 Jun 42, AFCF 333.5 Investigation of Contracts.

THE COST-PLUS-FIXED-FEE CONTRACT

The muddle resulting from retroactive auditing is typified by the situation that developed in the Douglas complex of plants. With over half a billion dollars in orders on seven fixed-fee and eight fixed-price contracts in three different plants, Douglas pushed production along for eight months before the accounting staff learned it would be necessary to conduct a retroactive audit on all CPFF work even though it would involve locating more than half a million supporting documents. Insofar as the record was available, it was possible to do this kind of *post facto* search although it proved expensive and consumed the energies of a score of clerks. But some types of audits simply could not be conducted after the fact. The normal procedure in current operations was to send a team out once a week, unannounced, to make an on-the-spot check of the payroll of a single department against the time cards punched at the clock. These in turn could be checked against the workers actually present. Since Douglas employed at the time about 20,000 people in a new and hastily expanded organization, it was obviously imperative that the paper record be verified against the facts.[51] Months later no such audit would be possible.

There is, of course, a great difference between recognizing a problem and doing something about it. If they had sensed the need for audits on all work done under letters of intent, air arm officials probably could have done little to secure them, for trained accountants were hard to find. Civil service recruiting procedures were painfully slow, and high-grade accountants were seldom on the registers in any event. Occasionally, by shuffling manpower within the federal agencies, it was possible to locate a few experienced men. Just before Pearl Harbor, for example, Wright Field officials were delighted when the Unjust Enrichment Division of PWA disbanded and released a considerable number of auditors for duty with the military procurement services. But the supply continually ran behind the demand. Most serious of all was the shortage of really imaginative men, outstanding minds capable of formulating the broad outlines of policy within which others could carry on the routine chores.[52] It may well be that many of the difficulties encountered with the CPFF contract were not, as so many critics have charged, inherent in the fixed-fee instrument itself but a direct outgrowth of faulty accounting, particularly in the early stages of the war.

Under the circumstances it is not surprising that GAO began to pile up a huge backlog of exceptions or stopped vouchers. Until air arm officials could perfect a really smoothly working system of auditing and accounting for fixed-fee contracts, discrepancies were bound to occur. By the fall of 1942 the Comp-

---

[51] Maj L. S. Friedman, IGD, to IG, 24 Oct 41, AFCF 333.1 Contract Inspection.

[52] 2d Wrapper Ind, Western Dist Supervisor to Asst Chief, Mat Div, 24 Dec 41, and Basic IG Rpt, 24 Oct 41, Maj Friedman to IG, 24 Oct 41, both in AFCF 333.1 Contract Inspection; IOM, Asst Tech Exec, WF, for Chief, Mat Div, OCAC, 3 Oct 41, AFCF 161 CPFF. See also, for comments on the quality of auditing personnel available, Rpt of Board, Western Proc Dist, 16 Mar 43, AFCF 004 Bulky. Some revealing insights can be found in the papers relating to the informer's suit of G. C. Wilbert, Plaintiff, vs. Douglas . . . *et al.*, filed 14 May 43, AFCF 004 Douglas Long Beach, Bulky.

troller General had accumulated more than 20,000 challenged vouchers representing millions of dollars in unpaid claims. The contractors involved grew increasingly disturbed. Would they have to enter the courts to recover their outlay? It was small comfort to recall that claims of this sort left over from World War I still remained in litigation during World War II. Beset with such fears, some prudent managers questioned whether or not to undertake any further government contracts—this at a time when procurement officials were straining every resource to exploit the nation's productive capacity to the utmost.[53] In short, the situation was rapidly moving to the absurdity in which the mighty Arsenal of Democracy was about to be defeated by a platoon of bookkeepers.

Soon after Pearl Harbor procurement officers recognized that drastic action would be needed to win the war on the paper work front. Two bookkeeping bottlenecks in particular offered likely areas for attack: air arm auditing techniques on the one hand, and the procedures of GAO on the other. Despite the tremendous increase in volume, air arm accountants were still conducting 100-percent audits, verifying and approving every voucher presented for payment. Perhaps it would be more accurate to say they were trying to audit every voucher; actually, they were falling dangerously behind. During the summer of 1942 the War Department as a whole finally resorted to the system of selective auditing or spot checking normally employed by commercial accountants. The manpower released by this simple expedient made it possible to stretch the limited staff over more contracts, but this was not the most significant advantage. Where the 100-percent audits of peacetime practice forced military accountants to devote as much time on minute items of cost as they did on giant expenditures, they could now concentrate their efforts in the most troublesome areas or on those most commonly vulnerable to abuse.[54]

The General Accounting Office constituted a bottleneck largely because the Comptroller General had insisted upon concentrating his operations in Washington. This committed contractors to the expensive necessity of sending supporting documents to the central office to substantiate their claims for reimbursement. Photostatic copies would not do; only the original documents themselves were acceptable, which could mean, for example, sending a bulky payroll for 20,000 employees across the continent twice. Sometimes, where the records of subcontractors were included, the supporting evidence backtracked along an absurd itinerary—in one instance from Santa Monica, California, to Detroit, then back to Burbank, California, to Wright Field, and, finally, to GAO in Washingington.[55] Little wonder that the Comptroller's staff accumulated a two-year backlog of unaudited vouchers that hung menacingly above every contractor's head, a continual threat of after-the-fact disallowances with the possibility of crippling financial loss. Even if the facts of

---

[53] Office of Fiscal Dir (Army), Hist of Fiscal Services, pp. 485, 829.

[54] Memo, Dir, Fiscal Div, SOS, for CGMC, 27 May 42, AFCF 132.2 Audits.

[55] Orton to Chief, Fiscal Div, OCAC, 17 Jan 42, AFCF 132.2 Audits.

a given case clearly favored payment of a contractor's claim, months (and sometimes years) later it was not easy to muster the requisite evidence. Turnover in personnel and imperfections in the written record tended to obscure the most valid vouchers. Then, too, even where there was no question of time lag, the sheer difficulty of written communication resulted in frequent disallowances because of simple misunderstandings.

When confronted with the overwhelming evidence of just how unworkable the system of centralized audits had become, the Comptroller General agreed to a change. After a preliminary trial in Detroit during the spring and summer of 1942, GAO set up a series of decentralized or field audit offices in the leading centers of production, ultimately some 287 in all, throughout the nation. Almost immediately the backlog of contested vouchers began to melt away. By the end of fiscal year 1943 the number had been cut from the 1942 high of 20,000 to less than 6,000. By the end of fiscal 1945 there were only 805 still outstanding. This represented approximately one-twentieth of 1 percent of the funds processed for military purposes in World War II, a figure in sharp contrast to the vouchers still outstanding four years after the 1918 armistice when about 12 percent of the Army's expenditures in World War I were still in contest.[56]

Decentralized auditing proved highly effective but did not work the entire cure. The presence of field audit teams did make it possible in some instances to secure final GAO approval on vouchers twenty-four hours after presentation, but also significant was the procedural change introduced in 1943 by which GAO agreed to a system of "informal exceptions." By this system the GAO auditor served notice that he intended to disallow a given voucher unless it could be justified by further evidence. If the contractor failed to provide such evidence within sixty days, the temporary disallowance would automatically become a formal suspension, which could only be cleared by the Comptroller General. Since 98 percent of all the exceptions raised by GAO were the result of *pro forma* failures of a minor character—the absence of a necessary signature or a supporting certificate of one sort or another—much of the work of clearing up suspensions was purely mechanical or clerical and readily done when the voucher stemmed from current operations for which all the pertinent records were immediately at hand.[57]

In short, what had begun as a bookkeeper's nightmare threatening to impair the nation's defense effort ended as a rather well-oiled administrative machine. Without question the whole business of auditing was annoying and costly. Inevitably there were shrill cries from contractors protesting the red tape involved.[58] Yet on balance the effort was undoubtedly worth the various difficulties encountered.

---

[56] Office of Fiscal Dir (Army), Hist of Fiscal Services, p. 485; Memo, Dir, Fiscal Div, SOS, for CGMC et al., 11 May 42, as well as Fiscal Officer, Hq, AAF, to CGMC, 1 Aug 42, both in AFCF 161 CPFF. See also, CPFF Administration, Lecture by Demuth.

[57] Office of Fiscal Dir (Army), Hist of Fiscal Services, p. 832; CPFF Administration, Lecture by Demuth. See also, CPFF Contracts, Lecture by Sommers.

[58] See, for example, Curtiss-Wright Airplane Div to CofAC, 14 Jul 41, AFCF 161 CPFF.

There simply is no way to determine just how valuable the data derived from audits were to those who subsequently made use of them when negotiating, re-negotiating, and terminating contracts. Surely it was not inconsiderable. But was auditing worth the dollar cost involved? Here, too, no final answer is possible. A staff study in 1943 revealed that auditing costs ranged from a low of $110 for every $100,000 of contract value to a high of $12,000 in costs on the same face value.[59] These figures, needless to say, prove nothing. An audit undoubtedly dissuades fraud to some extent by its mere presence. On the other hand, the vast bulk of the evidence available in air arm files suggests that fraud was far less significant than faulty administration as a source of loss. Thus, it would appear that if the cost of auditing is to be justified, it must be largely in terms of the wealth of information that audits can make available to the whole procurement team and only secondarily in terms of the deterrent effect that audits produce.

In appraising the work of the auditors in connection with fixed-fee contracts, whether dealing with agents of the air arm or GAO, it is well to remember that a policeman's lot is not a happy one. The GAO auditors sometimes seemed to be going out of their way to look for trouble. Air arm officers repeatedly protested that the Comptroller General's men were weighing not only the legality of payments but also their appropriateness. The GAO auditors, right or wrong, wielded effective power:

they could bring both contractors and contracting officers to grief. Procurement officials learned that it was far wiser to maintain harmonious relations with the Comptroller's staff and thereby effect easy accommodations and adjustments on contested vouchers whenever possible than it was to engage in bitter controversy on questions of jurisdiction, which all but defied definition. Contests generally led to antagonisms that poisoned all working relations and only served to hasten contractors who sought reimbursements into the labyrinth of the courts.[60]

If the police role was an uncongenial one, GAO officials at least enjoyed real power. Their rulings generally held water. When they spoke both the contractor and the contracting officer had to bow. By contrast, the position of the auditors on the air arm staff was far from enviable. Their role was entirely passive. Even when they uncovered abuses or errors, their sole function was advisory; they informed the responsible contracting officer, who could take action or not as he saw fit. As a consequence, the job of the air arm auditor tended to be frustrating or, at best, unrewarding. No doubt this circumstance contributed significantly to the high turnover that characterized the auditing force at work on fixed-fee contracts for the air arm.[61]

---

[59] Maj D. B. Lobree, IGD, to Dist Supervisor, Central Proc Dist, 7 May 43, AFCF 004 Contract Audit Sec (Bulky).

[60] Tangible evidence of War Department recognition of the need for harmony in dealing with GAO appeared in the publication of TM 14-1004, *Relations With the General Accounting Office*, 1 Aug 46. See also, CPFF Administration, Lecture by Demuth.

[61] Maj Lobree, to Dist Supervisor, Central Proc Dist, 7 May 43, AFCF 004 Contract Audit Sec (Bulky).

THE COST-PLUS-FIXED-FEE CONTRACT

In retrospect it seems clear that the failure of the auditors and accountants in the prewar Air Corps was, in a sense, the sum of their virtues. The auditors minded their own business; they devoted themselves so exclusively—and so narrowly—to the mechanics of their job that they and their supervisors lost sight of the larger problems of policy arising from their work. If auditing often proved frustrating and unrewarding to the many rank and file accountants and clerks recruited to carry the big wartime burden of fixed-fee contracts, it was equally true with respect to those in command of procurement operations. The accounting organization of the air arm was weak because it failed to attract the interest of able officers; it failed to attract able officers in the prewar years because operations in this functional area had never been one of the conventional or popular routes to high command. During the war the procurement organization desperately needed a substantial number of accountants with a philosophical turn of mind, men of broad general experience and high technical skill. Such men are hard to recruit at any time, but they proved particularly hard to secure in the wartime crisis because, with few exceptions, promotion-minded officers avoided the field. Men capable of bold and imaginative leadership generally turned elsewhere, to the great detriment of effective administration in fixed-fee contracts. Unfortunately, the auditing of dollars was only one of the accounting problems plaguing those who tried to administer fixed-fee contracts.

The Problem of Property Accountability

In many ways the problem of property accounting on fixed-fee contracts paralleled that of dollar accounting. Here, too, as soon as Congress authorized the use of the CPFF instrument, foresighted staff officers in the Office of the Assistant Secretary of War directed the procurement services to draw up appropriate procedural directives. A good deal of constructive thinking was required to do this, for the fixed-fee contract created a number of situations that simply did not exist in the conventional procurement operations of lump-sum or fixed-price contracts. Since the government paid the bill, did every pound of raw material purchased by the contractor with a fixed-fee arrangement become accountable government property? Were small hand tools bought for use on the production line to be so treated? And what of the elaborate jigs and fixtures so prominent in the fabrication and assembly of airframes? Were these and similar items to be picked up as "accountable property" on the record books of an office duly ordered to assume this responsibility in the public interest? Such questions as these had to be asked and answered. Since fixed-fee contractors would have in their possession many millions of dollars' worth of raw materials, component parts, and special tooling paid for by the government, the public's interest in the property had somehow to be safeguarded. The directive from OASW ordering the procurement services to face this burden was eminently sensible, but that did not make the order easy to obey.

The complexities of property accounting no less than those of dollar accounting proved difficult to anticipate. A staff officer behind his desk at headquarters could scarcely be expected to foresee the many intricacies subsequent events would gradually reveal. Little wonder that five months slipped by before any procedural directives appeared. And, as might have been expected, the OASW directive was expressed in the most general terms suggesting only in broadest outline the objectives sought and the administrative steps to be taken in attaining the objectives.[62] At best it was a skeleton. To flesh out the bones would require experience—actual operations in a multitude of plants with all the varying conditions they would afford—and administrators perceptive enough to see the significance of local conditions and aggressive enough to feed them back to the staff at headquarters, which then could generalize on the flow of information and arrive at sound decisions on policy.

The air arm directive on property accountability had scarcely reached the resident representatives in the field when experience began to show up its inadequacies. Under the original order, all items purchased by a fixed-fee contractor and classified as capital assets were to be considered accountable property by the responsible officer. It soon developed, however, that the definition of capital assets differed widely among contractors. One manufacturer classified all standard tools bought from a catalogue as expense items or charges to be borne by the government on a given contract just as though they were raw materials and, as such, consumed in use and therefore nonaccountable. In this group would be found small hand tools such as pneumatic drills. The same manufacturer designated as special tools all items requiring a special blueprint or drawing in their fabrication. This group, including dies, patterns, jigs, and fixtures, were considered nonexpendable items to be carried on the property account. On the other hand, another manufacturer used dollar valuations as a means of classification. All tools, of whatever the use, costing over $100 were regarded as durable items, capital assets to be carried as accountable property, while all items costing less than $100 were treated as expendable and accordingly dropped from the property records. Such differences obviously required a clarification of policy.[63]

Similarly, operational experience soon revealed that the salvage of scrap presented a great many headaches for property accounting. Where a manufacturer held both fixed-fee and fixed-price contracts in the same shop, the responsible officers had been instructed to see that the scrap from fixed-fee jobs was segregated from all other scrap in order to protect the government's salvage interest. In practice this proved just about impossible. Scrap on adjacent production lines had a way of getting intermixed despite vigorous preventative efforts. The greatest difficulty was not simple carelessness; under the pressure

---

[62] Mat Div GO No. 11, 13 Dec 40 (WF), AFCF 161 CPFF. See also the preliminary version drafted in Washington, Chief, Mat Div, to Asst Chief, Mat Div, 25 Nov 40, TI-425, AFCF 333.1 Contract Inspection.

[63] Draft copy of proposed Mat Div Office Memo, 26 Feb 41, AFCF 161 CPFF.

of wartime urgency manufacturers undertook to rework scrap whenever possible in order to salvage components desperately needed to keep the whole assembly line from stopping. As a consequence, "borrowing" salvageable parts between contracts was as common as "borrowing" standard GFE components. In either event, in factories employing thousands of workers who handled tens of thousands of parts, property officers were driven to distraction by the sheer impossibility of keeping their accounts accurate in the face of so many expedient and thoroughly understandable but administratively irregular transactions.

Annoying as the matter of scrap was to property officers, it ranked well below tooling as a source of trouble. Frequent modifications and model changes involved a corresponding flux among the various jigs and fixtures or special tools concerned. Sometimes they had to be replaced entirely; sometimes a previously scrapped tool could be reworked for use in an entirely different context. Such transfers and metamorphoses as these made endless trouble for property officers. The task of maintaining strict accountability on the vast array of tooling necessary for airframe production was thus quite difficult enough when confined to the prime contractor's plant, yet how much more confusing was the game when manufacturers began to expand their output by sending portions of their production to subcontractors, providing them not only with drawings but often with the requisite tools and tooling as well.[64]

Something of the chaos confronting a property officer may be inferred from the situation in the Boeing complex. Boeing held all of the following types of contracts at one time: fixed-fee and fixed-price contracts with the air arm, a fixed-price contract for the Navy, a fixed-fee contract under Defense Aid or Lend Lease, and subcontract work on aircraft assemblies for Douglas. In addition, Boeing held experimental contracts on the XB–29 Superfortress and production contracts with Pan American and the Canadian Government for flying clippers. The greater part of the effort involved the B–17 in production at several plants.[65]

Inevitably, there was interplant borrowing of tools, parts, and materials that doubtlessly facilitated output enormously but at the same time laid almost insurmountable burdens on the property officers concerned. When a prime contractor shipped several freight cars full of tooling to a branch plant or a subcontractor several hundred miles away, the property officer's records might reflect the consignment, but what happened thereafter? How was he to keep informed of each subsequent modification in use? A tool or item of tooling might be worn out or tossed out as obsolete by a subcontractor and then subsequently reworked for use in quite another capacity. Before they insisted upon ineradicable markings, property officers had no way of knowing whether a manufacturer was charging the government for a new tool when he was merely refurbishing an old one. But even ineradicable markings

---

[64] See, for example, Maj J. G. Allen, IGD, to IG, 5 Nov 42, and related correspondence, AFCF 333.1 (a) Douglas.

[65] Memo, Asst to Chief, Mat Div, for SW, 8 Sep 41, AFCF 161 CPFF.

were of little use when the property had been transferred to a remote subcontractor.

Property officers soon found they had to build up elaborate record systems to keep track of the elusive property assigned to their care. Since there were frequently more than a hundred thousand separate items to follow, it began to look as though every property officer would need a vast corps of clerks to sustain him unless something were done promptly to simplify the whole procedure. The nub of the difficulty was conceptual. When they first set up the system of accountability on fixed-fee contracts, the staff officers concerned used the administrative tools they found ready at hand—notably the procedures for military property accounting prescribed in Army Regulations. Since the regulations had stood the test of time, the decision to use them seemed natural. Unfortunately, the Army system rested upon a number of assumptions that simply did not hold true in an industrial context. A procedure geared to Army depots, which maintained stock record cards on every item, was not necessarily adequate for the production lines at Willow Run, where dozens of widely separated stockrooms had a turnover so rapid as to defy simultaneous inventory returns. Disturbed by the numerous reports on the failure of ever larger clerical staffs to keep their property accounts up to date and accurate, headquarters staff officers reconsidered the whole question.[66]

Why keep property accounts at all? In an Army depot such records were necessary in the absence of any others. But was this true in a fixed-fee contractor's plant? Since the terms of the contract required the manufacturer to maintain his own property accounts, why should the resident representative or one of his deputies build up a clerical empire at government expense to compile records almost exactly duplicating those kept by the contractor—also at government expense? The logical solution finally adopted was to leave the task of property accounting entirely to the manufacturer himself, confining the government's property officer to the task of auditing these records, spot checking them from time to time to ensure compliance. Once assured that the manufacturer's procedures were sound, the responsible officer could concentrate his energies on those areas most subject to abuse.[67]

In property accounting, as in dollar accounting, staff officers learned how difficult if not impossible it is to foresee all the eventualities that operations might turn up. Only experience revealed the problems. It follows, then, that a staff is most effective when it is most active in garnering meaningful experience from the operational front and distilling that experience into directives. The wise commander will see to it that his staff strives unceasingly to perfect its techniques for gathering significant lessons of the operating echelons and for-

---

[66] IOM, Asst Chief, Mat Div, for Chief, Mat Div, 2 Sep 41; Knudsen to Gen Brett, 31 Jul 41; Memo, Asst to Chief, Mat Div, for SW, 8 Sep 41. All in AFCF 161 CPFF.

[67] Relationship of the Contracting Officer to the Accountable Property Officer, Lecture, by Maj R. H. Demuth, AAF Contracting Officers School, WF, 16 Dec 44, WFHO. Evidence of the new concept of property accounting may be found in TM-14-910, 16 Feb 43.

THE COST-PLUS-FIXED-FEE CONTRACT

mulates from these lessons useful generalizations on policy. But the problem is not merely one of efficiently channeled information. A staff that could reflect at once broadly and sensitively the infinite variety of experience encountered along the operating front might still promulgate unsound policy if it lacked appropriate perspectives, if it failed to see the problem at hand in its proper conceptual framework. This kind of shortcoming appears to have been the cause for much of the difficulty that plagued property officers on fixed-fee contracts. So long as they continued to handle their accountable items as though they were Army property in a depot, they floundered further and further into deep water. But once they visualized the problem in an entirely new frame of reference, then, armed with a good many lessons from experience, they rapidly discovered practical solutions for their difficulties.

All of which is to say, perhaps somewhat paradoxically, that the effective military staff is one which can get the necessary information and then get above it. Exploration of yet another aspect of CPFF administration—the relationship of prime contractors to their subcontractors—should confirm this contention.

The Relation of Primes to Subs

Among the many problems of administration raised in the wake of the fixed-fee contract, certainly none proved more challenging than the matter of purchasing by prime contractors. What did it matter if the government's contract negotiators bargained skillfully and kept down the total of estimated costs and thus awarded correspondingly low fees if the contractors had been permitted to go out and buy freely from subcontractors with little or no regard for cost? To ignore the prices paid to suppliers and subcontractors on fixed-fee contracts was tantamount to exercising meticulous care in locking the gate while failing to build a fence along the far side of the pasture.

The very first CPFF contract entered by the air arm, the one with Packard, brought the whole question of purchasing by prime contractors into sharp focus.[68] What, asked the Packard management, are the rights and obligations of primes and subs in their relations with one another? Though with so much at stake—no less than the success or failure of fixed-fee contracting in principle—one might assume that procurement officials would prescribe regulations on this point in minute detail, the chief of the Contract Section at Wright Field resolutely refused to rule on the matter. The primes and subs, he believed, should decide for themselves just what the character of their association ought to be, since this was "largely a matter of good faith and sound business judgment." While this declaration may appear to have been a fatal abdication of responsibility, it actually represented a most realistic appraisal of the situation. Procurement officials in Washington and at Wright Field could not possibly know the infinite variety of circumstances, the special conditions, the trade or regional practices that necessarily made virtually every subcontract and every purchase

---

[68] Chief, Contract Sec, to Packard Motor Car Co., 16 Oct 40, AFCF 333.1 Contract Inspection; IOM, Chief, Contract Sec, for CGMC, 27 Jul 42, AFCF 161 CPFF.

from suppliers or vendors a particular case. To meddle would be to inject the hand of government where it was least competent at a time when the procurement staff at Wright Field was most swamped with work.[69]

In short, when the air arm officials entered a contract, they expected to buy not only the end products on order but also the managerial skills of the contractors concerned. This was a fundamental tenet in the procurement philosophy of the air arm. Procurement officials insisted upon but one caveat: subcontracts had to include a clause reserving the right of audit to the government. This would appear to have been a minimal protection of the public interest, yet in practice even this scant safeguard met opposition.

The old-line firms of the aircraft industry raised no objection to government audits of their books. They had become accustomed to the practice, which had been authorized ever since the Air Corps Act of 1926. But subcontractors were quite another matter. They took a very dim view of any contractual obligation that permitted government auditors to prowl through their books even if their work for a fixed-fee contractor constituted only a small fraction of their total volume of business. Their reluctance to open their books to investigators was not entirely without reason.[70]

Few indeed would protest the government's right to detect fraud, but the contractual clause imposing the right of audit upon subcontractors implied a wider activity. It required that access be granted to "any person designated by the head of any executive department."[71] This could mean agents of the Department of Justice on a fishing expedition for evidence with which to prosecute antitrust cases. To some extreme anti-New Deal businessmen the mandatory audit clause seemed like an open invitation to prolabor administrators to hunt evidence for use in the next round of union negotiations. Whether or not the fears were justified is beside the point; insofar as they were believed, they operated to keep some firms from signing as subcontractors under fixed-fee manufacturers.

At a time when numerous governmental agencies were making a tremendous drive to enlist every bit of available productive capacity in the war effort, the reluctance of the subcontractors to accept audit clauses was used as an argument to persuade air arm officials to drop the troublesome requirements entirely. This they could not do. If on the one hand they insisted on freeing both prime and sub from minute and detailed supervision in order to take the fullest advantage of the managerial skills inherent in business, they certainly could not then relinquish their right to be assured that this freedom was exercised with integrity.[72]

---

[69] For an effective statement of the air arm position, see Col Volandt to Contract Distribution Div, OUSW, 12 Jan 42, AFCF 165 Classes of Contract.

[70] See, Roycraft Walsh, United Aircraft, to Chief, Mat Div, 28 Mar 41, AFCF 161 Contract Requirements.

[71] See standard contract form, Article 23. Copy filed with correspondence in AFCF 161 Contract Requirements.

[72] Asst to Chief, Mat Div, to United Aircraft, 1 Apr 41, and 4 Apr 41, AFCF 161 Contract Requirements. For an interesting instance of subcontractor resistance to audit clauses, see W. N. Maguire (legal representative for the bearing manufacturers) to IPS, WF, 24 Oct 41, WF Contract files 360.01.

THE COST-PLUS-FIXED-FEE CONTRACT

For more than a year after the instrument came into use, fixed-fee contractors were left free, save for an after-the-fact audit, to carry out their purchasing programs as their best judgment dictated. But just before Pearl Harbor, the practice came under severe fire from the General Accounting Office. In a series of communications reflecting nothing less than official horror, GAO auditors reported that they had recently begun to receive a large number of vouchers on which payments had been improperly made. The vouchers, representing purchases by prime contractors, had not, the GAO officials protested, been signed and approved by the contracting officer before going out.[73] The Under Secretary's office picked up the GAO charges and repeated them: why indeed had air arm procurement officials permitted this situation to arise? With no little irritation and a sense of injured innocence, the contract chief at Wright Field set out to defend his policies.

In the first place, he pointed out, contracting officers were not required by the terms of their contracts to give prior approval to the purchases made by primes. It might save a good deal of time, he declared, if the GAO auditors would first read the contracts "they so frequently seek to criticize." But the complaints raised by GAO were not merely a case of carelessness or misapprehension. They represented a totally different philosophy of procurement from that held by the air arm. This the contract chief recognized. Implicit in the criticisms made by GAO was the view that the government should exercise a close supervision and even a decisive veto over every act of the contractor. Such a policy was diametrically opposed to the philosophy and practice of the air arm. If the GAO view were to prevail, it would prove to be, so the contract chief asserted, "a most efficient method" for ensuring "a total disruption" of the current procurement program.[74]

There were many reasons why air arm officials were convinced that fixed-fee manufacturers should never be required to get prior approval from contracting officers on all their purchases. To begin with, in giving such approval a contracting officer would inject himself as a party to the transaction and thus make it difficult if not impossible for the government to find fault subsequently with manner of its execution. Some shrewd manufacturers recognized this opening and actually urged the introduction of some scheme calling for the prior official approval of all contractor decisions.[75] A second and probably the most important consideration moving against any plan to provide for prior approval of all purchases was none other than the circumstance that led to the adoption of the policy in the first place—the air arm simply did not have men qualified to do the job.

Consider the veritable morass of detail in which a contracting officer would flounder if he attempted to grant approval on all orders placed by primes. If he were to grant more than a perfunc-

---

[73] Chief, Natl Defense Sec, GAO, to CofAC, n.d. but received 6 Dec 41; IOM, Chief, Contract Sec, to Chief, Mat Div, 21 Jan 42. Both in AFCF 161 CPFF.

[74] IOM, Chief, Contract Sec, for Chief, Mat Div, 12 Dec 41 and 21 Jan 42, AFCF 161 CPFF.

[75] IOM, Chief, Contract Sec, for CGMC, 27 Jul 42. AFCF 161 CPFF.

tory, *pro forma* approval, if he were to protect the public's interest in fact, the contracting officer would have to weigh the merits of each order. Is the price fair and reasonable? Is it the lowest available? Can the subcontractor or vendor deliver on time? Questions such as these would have to be asked and answered for each outgoing order.

Just how numerous the orders could be is suggested by the roster of suppliers for a single Curtiss-Wright contract. There were 29 CPFF subcontractors in all, 25 of them doing jobs involving more than $100,000 each. There were 7 fixed-price subs. Some 25 orders were of a type in which both purveyor and purchaser contributed to the design of the item in question. There were approximately 1,300 orders issued to firms fabricating small items to specifications supplied by the prime contractor. And, finally, there were about 2,000 purchase orders sent out for standard hardware items generally available in the open market. In all, the typical airframe manufacturer placed anywhere from 2,500 to 3,500 suborders on a single contract.

Obviously, individual contracting officers did not have the information with which to approve or disapprove prime contractor purchases. To assemble such a mass of data would require the services of a staff of skilled purchasing agents, who were not available. And even if they were to be found, the delays imposed while they did their work, duplicating that of the manufacturer, might well retard the whole procurement program by weeks or months.[76]

[76] AFMC-4A to USW, 8 Aug 42, AFCF 333.1 Contract Inspection.

To put the matter bluntly, neither the GAO auditors nor the officers in the Under Secretary's office, who echoed the GAO criticisms, fully grasped the nature of the problem in hand. But did they merit the strictures hurled at them by the contract chief at Wright Field? The character of his criticisms can be understood if not entirely condoned when it is recalled that his remarks were made under dreadful stress in the weeks immediately following Pearl Harbor when the procurement staff seemed to be fighting against utter collapse from fatigue, and production seemed far more important than penny pinching. From the vantage point of Wright Field, the GAO staff did no doubt seem to consist of pettifogging auditors, and headquarters officers in Washington could at times be most annoyingly ignorant of the situations they sought to control, but this was no justification for excoriation. If the auditors and headquarters staff officers were unfamiliar with the facts, as inevitably they must be by the nature of the administrative process, the task of subordinate echelons was not to complain but to educate. And education is a continuing process, not an isolated act.

Instead of protesting at the blindness or wrongheadedness of officialdom in Washington, procurement officers at Wright Field served far better when they set out to explain—and explain again and again when necessary—just why the proposed scheme to require prior approval of all purchases made by fixed-fee contractors was "administratively impossible." Headquarters officers were not, at least for the most part, willfully blind; they were usually quite willing to be educated. When, for example, it was

THE COST-PLUS-FIXED-FEE CONTRACT

explained to them that subcontract prices could seldom be verified at face value but had to be pursued down through tier on tier of sub-subcontracts, they could readily grasp the administrative difficulties involved.[77]

Without question, the procurement doctrine maintained at Wright Field had much to commend it. The purchasing organization could not exercise minute supervision over a large segment of the national economy even if it wished to do so, since a staff adequate to the task could never be mustered soon enough. The alternative, it seemed, was to place responsibility on the contractor, making it a matter of contractual obligation, subject to subsequent audit, for him to exercise sound business judgment in all his purchasing operations. Clearly this practice assumed that each prime contractor would be fully staffed with skilled and experienced purchasing agents who were, as a matter of course, capable of exercising sound business judgment. In the rapid expansion that characterized the wartime aircraft industry, however, virtually every old-line firm had to spread its cadre of trained men woefully thin. Even where they recognized the difficulty, it was not easy for manufacturers to do much about it. The main problem of purchasing by primes was not one of honesty but of talent; along with the military services, manufacturers found it extremely difficult to procure and train competent purchasing agents.

After conceding that the air arm could never hope to assemble a staff to verify or countercheck all purchases before they were made by fixed-fee contractors, it did not necessarily follow that no such checks should be undertaken. As a matter of fact, the very first instructions issued by the air arm for the administration of CPFF contracts had given this point careful consideration. While prior approval of the contracting officer for all purchases was undesirable and indeed impossible, it was nonetheless anticipated that the officers administering a fixed-fee contract would exercise a general supervisory function, spot checking from time to time to be sure that the contractor was living up to his contractual obligation.[78]

Occasional spot checking was something very different from requiring prior approval on all purchases. The latter course would impose an extra step in the sequence of operations, a step leading outside of the manufacturer's own chain of command, thus causing a substantial delay in the processing of orders; spot checking could be accomplished by leaning over the contractor's shoulder, so to speak, inspecting his records in process without introducing delay by requiring the records to be regularly routed through the contracting officer's hands. In this respect at least, the original instructions issued by the air arm for the administration of CPFF contracts were intelligently drafted. Unfortunately, they were not always explicitly obeyed.

If fixed-fee manufacturers found it difficult to live up to their contractual obligations for want of experienced staff,

---

[77] IOM, Chief, Contract Sec, to Chief, Mat Div, 3 Feb 42, and 2d Ind, Chief, Mat Div, to USW, 5 Mar 42, AFCF 165 Classes of Contract.

[78] Mat Div GO No. 11, 13 Dec 40 (WF), AFCF 161 CPFF. See also the preliminary version drafted in Washington, Chief, Mat Div, to Asst Chief, Mat Div, 25 Nov 40, TI-425, AFCF 333.1 Contract Inspection.

almost the same thing could be said of those air arm officials concerned with contract administration. It was all very well to draw up orders prescribing a pattern of supervision for prime contractor purchasing, but getting new, inexperienced, and badly harassed resident representatives to comply was quite another matter. As might have been expected, a number of abuses cropped up in the absence of adequate safeguards. Occasionally the auditors uncovered apparent frauds, cases of duplicate billings, for example, which might have been detected had contracting officers exercised a closer supervision.[79] But the mistakes in purchasing made by prime contractors were, in the main, the consequence of haste, ignorance, and inexperience. Sometimes primes blundered into writing subcontracts embodying cost-plus-a-percentage-of-cost (CPPC) features explicitly forbidden by law as a consequence of the abuses under this type of instrument in World War I.[80] More often, auditors found purchase orders that had gone out before any effort at competitive bidding or comparison of prices had been made. Sometimes purchasing agents invited bids or price quotations from several suppliers on a first order and thereafter bought from the same supplier without bothering to invite further quotations on repeat orders. A common practice was for manufacturers to send out purchase orders saying "Advise price," leaving it to the supplier to fill in the amount.[81] Seldom did the records show that the air arm resident representative had spot checked a prime's purchases as contemplated in the command's administrative instructions to be certain that the manufacturer's purchasing agents were actually employing sound procedures.[82]

Surely some sort of middle ground could be found between those who favored a 100-percent prior approval by the contracting officer on every purchase by primes and those who argued that such a course was not only administratively impossible but worked to the government's disadvantage. Under Secretary Patterson himself took an interest in the question and offered a common sense suggestion: while fixed-fee contractors did place thousands of individual orders on each contract, by far the greater dollar volume was attributable to a very small number of major subcontractors. If 100-percent prior approval was not possible and perhaps not even desirable, there was nothing to prevent contracting officers from insisting upon prior approval of all major subcontracts entered by fixed-fee manufacturers.[83]

---

[79] See, for example, MC Intelligence Rpt on possible conspiracy to defraud U.S. Govt, 23 Dec 43, AFCF 004 American Design . . . (Bulky).

[80] TI–1055, 31 Mar 42, AFCF 165 Classes of Contract.

[81] CPFF Administration, Lecture by Demuth. Typical examples of the slack that can creep into unsupervised purchasing by primes: material received over or short the quantity invoiced or the quantity ordered; sales tax not deducted; invoice price not the same as purchase order price; invoice cash discount not same shown on purchase order, etc. Maj Friedman, IGD, to IG, 4 Nov 41, AFCF 333.1.

[82] Col S. H. Ellison, IGD, to IG, 6 Nov 42, AFCF 333.1 Boeing. For extensive discussion of this problem, see Rpt, Inspection of Procurement Operations at Wright Field, Lt Col Friedman, IGD, to IG, 11 Nov 43, with 2d Ind, Hq AAF to IG, 12 Jan 44, AFCF 333.1 Inspection (Bulky).

[83] Memo, USW for Gen Echols, 7 Apr 42, AFCF 165 Classes of Contract; Memo, CGMC, for Brig Gen A. W. Vanaman, 29 Jun 42, AFCF 333.5 Investigation of Contracts.

THE COST-PLUS-FIXED-FEE CONTRACT 407

The Under Secretary's proposal set the pattern the Materiel Command ultimately adopted. Since 100-percent prior approval was impossible and spot checking by the resident military administrators was not working out in practice, the more or less obvious solution was to improve the machinery for spot checking. The original instructions for the administration of CPFF contracts were amended to establish special price analysis groups in each procurement district headquarters to be sent into the various manufacturing facilities of the district. Here they could survey the contractor's purchasing procedures for general suitability and spot check them in operation for satisfactory compliance.[84]

Although a thoroughgoing price analysis of even a few purchases made by a single fixed-fee contractor could absorb the energies of the district price analysis team for weeks on end, there were a number of relatively simple checks that could quickly be made in a large number of cases. Even a cursory survey of purchase orders would show whether or not the manufacturer's agents were actually taking advantage of every available discount for ordering in quantity, discount for paying cash, or allowance for salvage. Sometimes a quick phone call would reveal whether or not a vendor was supplying the same item to another user at a lower figure. Similarly, it was relatively easy to check the quantities of a given item placed on order by a manufacturer with the quantities he specified in the bill of materials submitted with his original estimate. Discrepancies here could mean that a manufacturer was surreptitiously buying materials on his fixed-fee contract to use on his regular fixed-price jobs.

Because of the acute shortage of men with accounting or production experience, it was several months before each of the procurement districts could round up staffs of ten to twenty competent individuals.[85] Once the teams began to function, they saved the government far more than they cost. While no grand totals are available to demonstrate this point, it may be indicative of the vast potential savings possible to cite a few of the cases handled. One team of price analysts saved the government $72,000 by spotting a single hitherto neglected discount on a high volume purchase. Another team scrutinized a selected group of orders intensively for several months and found savings amounting to about $210,000 on a face value of $750,000. Occasionally the price analysts caught up with a 100-percent middleman, one who signed a subcontract with no intention of performing the work and then subsubcontracted the entire job to someone else, rendering no legitimate service whatsoever.[86] To eliminate practices of this

---

[84] MC FO Memo 34 (subsequently reissued as 40), 10 Jul 42, AFCF 333.5 Investigation of Contracts.

[85] Since primes in each procurement district bought from subs in virtually every other district across the nation, administration of price analysis raised some difficult problems. See Capt I. D. Harris, Dist Contracting Officer, to CGMC, 31 Jul 42, AFCF 333.1 Contract Inspection. Different districts approached the problems of organizing price analysis teams in different ways with striking variations in effectiveness. For discussion, see TWX, Vanaman to Echols, TEX–T–577, 1 Aug 42, AFCF 161 CPFF, and IOM, CofS, Mat Center, to CGMC, 1 Oct 42, AFCF 161 Renegotiation.

[86] IOM, Chief, Proc Div, for CGMC, 12 Mar 43, AFCF 333.1 Misc.

sort was, of course, pure gain for the government.

All in all the district price analysis scheme worked out admirably. The use of analysts did not free the fixed-fee contractor from his legal obligation to exercise sound business judgment in making purchases, nor did it slow down the manufacturer's operations by injecting extra steps in the sequence of his purchasing operations. On the other hand, by specializing in price analysis work, the teams employed soon acquired a competence that made their efforts far more effective than the part-time efforts of a resident contracting officer could ever hope to be.

Perhaps the most enduring contribution of the price analysts lay in the field of procedure. For example, one group drew up a bid summary form requiring the buyer to list for each purchase the bids invited, the replies received, and the basis on which the award was made to a particular firm. An appropriate space on the form induced the manufacturer to indicate just when he had last surveyed the supplier's plant to be sure that adequate capacity was available and that the supplier was capable of maintaining the desired standard of workmanship.[87] Simple administrative tools of this sort did not solve all the problems of purchasing by fixed-fee contractors, but they simplified the job substantially by showing up the trouble spots.

Other analysts devised equally useful administrative tools. For example, by making manufacturers cite the page, date, and title of a supplier's catalogue when they substantiated a purchase order with the caption "catalogue price," analysts found they gave company buyers a decided check against carelessness and at the same time simplified the task of verification for themselves. Similarly, by requiring all subcontractors to certify officially that they did not sell the same item to any other user at a lower price, analysts discovered an easy way to spot hitherto unsuspected price differentials.[88]

Although the problem of checking purchases by fixed-fee manufacturers was but one of many significant facets in the administration of CPFF contracts, it nevertheless offers an unusual opportunity to investigate some of the fundamental difficulties of command on the matériel front. In retrospect it seems clear that the various officials who sought to work out effective procedures for dealing with fixed-fee contracts fell into two groups expressing rather divergent philosophies of administration. For convenience, these rival schools of thought may be identified as those favoring a contractual approach to administration and those who preferred a supervisory approach. Both deserve careful attention.

The advocates of the contractual ap-

---

[87] Prime contractors preoccupied with their own problems often failed to make adequate surveys to ascertain whether or not their subs and suppliers were bona fide concerns qualified to fill the orders placed with them. In February 1944 a leading airframe builder who had been lax in this respect finally uncovered one audacious character who had signed a subcontract with the firm and then contrived to get himself hired as a production worker so that he could carry semifinished parts into the plant, machine them on company time, then carry them home to be delivered back to the firm in his capacity as subcontractor. Rpt of Study on Curtiss-Buffalo, 8 Jul 44, AFCF 004 Bulky.

[88] Lecture, Administration of Letter Contracts, by Maj L. S. Robinson, AAF Contracting Officers School, WF, 18 Dec 44, WFHO. See also, CPFF Administration, Lecture by Demuth.

proach to procurement administration—a view most often expressed by procurement officials at Wright Field—took the position that the most effective means of procurement was to sign a contract and then leave the manufacturer more or less free to get results. This was a legal or instrumental approach. It was founded upon the old military axiom that without authority over means one should not be held responsible for results. To require military approval of a contractor's purchases or to impose restraints on his selection of subcontractors, some procurement officers argued, would not only force the government to duplicate many of the contractor's administrative functions but would also deny the businessman the free exercise of his managerial authority. In effect, this would amount to holding manufacturers responsible for results while curtailing their executive freedom. The best way to protect the public's interest, these officers contended, was to write appropriate clauses into a manufacturer's contract and then leave him free within these written stipulations.

The advantages in the contractual approach to contract administration should be evident, but its disadvantages must not be overlooked. While it did free the contracting officer from the awkward task of matching his business acumen against that of the manufacturer on every purchase made and every subcontract entered, the contractual approach to administration was entirely too inflexible. When using it, one had to assume that a contracting officer could anticipate every significant eventuality and write appropriate clauses in the contract to deal with each. Of course no such assumption could be made. Even the most prescient negotiators could not possibly foresee the infinite variety of problems that experience would reveal.

On the other hand, the advocates of the supervisory approach to contract administration favored a tight rein. They wanted a close and personal supervision of every move made by the contractor with the government's money. Procurement officers at Wright Field, under constant pressure for results in the form of airplanes rolling off the production line, were inclined to regard the supervisory approach as characteristically bureaucratic, something one might expect of officials remote from the practical problems encountered at the level of operations. And indeed it was the penny-counting auditors of the Comptroller General who most insistently called for closer supervision of fixed-fee manufacturers' purchasing operations. Nonetheless, there was considerable merit to the contentions of the supervisory school of thought.

To extract the maximum in initiative and aggressiveness from private enterprise, the manufacturer must be left as free as possible from detailed supervision. Yet it is equally clear that the contractual instrument is in itself an inadequate safeguard of the public interest, even when provided with backstops in the form of audits. On-the-spot military supervision is essential in fixed-fee contracts. To be sure, supervision that attempts to duplicate the manufacturer's decision-making role is patently harmful, yet it is evident that *ad hoc*, spot-checking supervision by a contracting officer genuinely capable of exercising discretion is imperative if the government's interests are to be preserved in fixed-fee contracts.

In wartime, neither the procurement officials at Wright Field nor the staff officers in Washington were much inclined to theorize on procurement doctrine or to promulgate philosophies of administration. Of necessity they were concerned with immediate results. The pressure of events seldom afforded them opportunities to stand back from their work to take in the grand panorama. In retrospect it becomes clear that both the contractual approach and the supervisory approach had merit. Effective administration of fixed-fee contracts requires a skillful combination of the two, exploiting the best potentialities of each. But what is the proper admixture? Here lies the challenge of command; the balance must be decided anew not only to suit the requirements of the ever-changing economy in which contracts are written, but also to accommodate the endless variety of special circumstances that make virtually every contract a unique undertaking. There may be cold comfort in the observation, but it is nonetheless interesting to note that in Britain the Ministry of Aircraft Production faced this very same question. And there, too, the solution was found, as in this country, by trial and error, pragmatic groping, as experience revealed the full complexity of the problem in practice—at best an expensive undertaking.[89]

Expensive experience may well be the necessary route to understanding, but if the lessons of experience are fully absorbed, even heavy dollar costs may be justified. Sometimes, however, experience bought at the most prodigious expense refuses to yield any really clear lesson for the instruction of the future. This seems to have been the case with CPFF contracting in principle. Was the fixed-fee instrument necessary? Was it economical? Was it really less economical than the fixed-price contract? Procurement officials under the critical scrutiny of congressional watchdogs would like clear-cut and emphatic answers to questions such as these. Just why they have never been entirely gratified is explained by the War Department effort to rewrite all fixed-fee instruments in conventional fixed-price form.

The Conversion of Fixed-Fee Contracts

From the moment Congress first approved the use of CPFF contracts in the summer of 1940, the officially stated position of the War Department held that CPFF contracts would be applied only where absolutely necessary—only as a last resort where a multitude of unknowns made the drawing of a conventional fixed-price contract unfeasible. While admitting that the instrument was highly desirable and even essential for emergency use, military spokesmen were usually careful to accompany this contention with a catalogue of reasons why its general application would be objectionable. It offered no strong incentive to economy and efficiency; the least efficient contractor could be paid the same percentage in fee as the most efficient. Since contractors were in keen competition with one another for la-

---

[89] W. Ashworth, *Contracts and Finance* (London, 1953), pp. 98–101.

THE COST-PLUS-FIXED-FEE CONTRACT

bor, materials, and tools, they could be entirely irresponsible in paying higher prices and higher wages and then pass the increased costs along to the government. With the government footing all material bills, a contractor could pile up excessively large inventories as a hedge against future shortages yet never suffer from tied up working capital, the normal restraint operating against this kind of abuse. Finally, as procurement officers repeatedly pointed out, fixed-fee contracts were both difficult and costly to administer.[90]

As is so often the case, however, stated policy and actual practice were two entirely different things. While the various procurement officials who reiterated official strictures against CPFF contracts were undoubtedly sincere, the fact remains that, during the first year the fixed-fee form was in use, it accounted for nearly half the money obligated by the War Department. Approximately the same thing could be said for all air arm supply contracts written before Pearl Harbor.[91] Since Congress had authorized the use of fixed-fee contracts in the first place only with the greatest reluctance, to many legislators this disparity between professions of policy and actual performance called for corrective action.[92]

The harassing fire of criticism to which the fixed-fee instrument had been subjected all along became violent rather abruptly in the summer of 1942 when the House Committee on Military Affairs issued a highly critical report. The time had come, the committee declared, when the military contractors' "honeymoon at the expense of the taxpayers" must end. The Army Air Forces was especially singled out for censure. The committee claimed to have found evidence of "reckless expenditure" in connection with fixed-fee contracts for air matériel.[93] Statements of this sort made excellent headlines for the tabloids but left air arm procurement officials in a difficult position.

While generous in condemnation, the report was rather scanty in documentation. In denouncing CPFF procurement the report made no distinction between construction and supply contracts. Actually, different instruments were used for the two purposes, building camps and bases on the one hand and procuring munitions on the other. No one would deny that some abuses were sure to exist under every kind of contractual instrument, but for all its denunciations the committee report did not cite a single instance of waste or excessive cost in the administration of Air Forces fixed-fee supply contracts. This placed procurement officials in a most uncomfortable spot, since vague and general charges made refutation impossible and gave no leads for corrective action.[94]

---

[90] Flexible Pricing in Fixed Price Contracts, Lecture by Dinkelspiel. See also, ASF Purchases Div, Purchasing Policies and Practices, pp. 235-36.

[91] Annual report of the Under Secretary of War, 30 Jun 41, p. 29; and ASF Purchases Div, Purchasing Policies and Practices, p. 265.

[92] Smith, *The Army and Economic Mobilization*, pp. 302-10. This account contains a valuable survey of the War Department response to the conversion problem.

[93] R&R, Brig Gen T. H. Hanley to AFAMC, 24 Jul 42, AFCF 161 CPFF.

[94] Memo by MC Contract Sec on H.R. 2272 (July 24, 1942), 11 Aug 42, AFCF 333.5 Investigation of Contracts.

The net impression left by the committee report was most unfortunate. The errors of the few branded the many. Worse yet, a useful and even necessary contractual instrument was discredited without reference to its particular merits; its "fixed-fee" character received less emphasis than its "cost-plus" features, which evoked so many memories of the notorious cost-plus-a-percentage-of-cost contracts of World War I. A bad press was serious enough if it induced congressmen beyond the confines of the Military Affairs Committee to condemn the CPFF instrument out of hand, but it was no less harmful if it misled the public at large. Air arm officers learned to their chagrin not long afterward just how far such damage could extend in an encounter with an official working on Air Forces cases for the War Labor Board: he did not realize that there was any difference at all between the CPFF form and the outlawed CPPC contract.[95]

As a consequence of the unfavorable publicity, the War Department was under heavy pressure to curtail future use of the fixed-fee form of procurement regardless of its merits or its capacity for improvement. This pressure was passed on to the AAF in a directive ordering conversion of existing fixed-fee contracts wherever possible and prohibiting use of the instrument in any future contract with very few exceptions. Dutifully the Contract Section at Wright Field wrote all its fixed-fee contractors urging them to begin planning for conversion. A month slipped by, but none of the contractors showed much if any inclination to move. Somewhat petulantly the contract chief scolded the manufacturers for showing more interest in how to get the maximum allowable fee than in ways and means of effecting rapid conversions to lump-sum contracts.[96] It began to be clear that the switch from a fixed-fee to a fixed-price basis was a lot easier to propose than to execute.

As a matter of general policy when writing CPFF contracts, air arm procurement officers tried to induce manufacturers to accept a clause calling for conversion to a fixed-price footing at some predetermined point, usually after 40 percent of the items on order had been delivered. But even where a manufacturer had consented to the inclusion of such a clause in his original contract, it did not force him to accept any particular lump sum as a fixed-price contract, nor for that matter did it obligate him to reach any agreement at all. The conversion clause only required a manufacturer to bargain in good faith; it had no teeth. There could be none, for there was no way of knowing at the time of signing the contract what the unit costs would prove to be when 40 percent of the deliveries were completed. If such costs could be determined prospectively, there would be no occasion for entering a CPFF contract in the first place since this was precisely the kind of information that would have made possible the use of conventional fixed-price contracts. About all a conversion clause could do was to exert a moral pressure on a man-

---

[95] Gen Arnold to Wilson, WPB, 4 Nov 43, AFCF 452.01–D.

[96] Memo, OUSW (AF Liaison Officer) for CGMC, 17 Sep 42, AFCF 161 CPFF; Chief, Contract Sec, WF, to manufacturers holding fixed-fee contracts, 14 Nov 42, AFCF 161 Contract Regulations.

ufacturer to try to reach an agreement on a lump-sum contract at the designated time on the basis of the information on costs accumulated by that time.[97]

The manufacturers' resistance to conversion was certainly not captious nor was it merely selfish. They had many valid objections to the War Department effort to convert existing fixed-fee contracts to fixed-price contracts. Of greatest significance were the many unknowns still plaguing many fixed-fee contractors long after they had reached the designated switch-over point.

Probably the most elusive factor inhibiting an orderly estimate of costs was the matter of design change. The demands of war made the introduction of modifications in design an unavoidable necessity. These modifications were totally unpredictable; in any single contract literally thousands of them might prove necessary. For the most part, modifications involved only slight changes readily introduced in the production line without serious dislocation. Some, however, required a redesign of major components. On occasion this could lead to the scrapping of millions of dollars' worth of previously completed assemblies and the complete revision of large numbers of jigs, fixtures, and tools, not only in the prime contractor's plant but also in a multitude of subcontractors' factories. Obviously, modifications of this sort were costly. Under a conventional fixed-price contract the introduction of a modification of any considerable size required the negotiation of a supplemental contract with all its occasions for wrangling, delay, misunderstanding, and disagreement. On the other hand, with a CPFF contract, modifications could be absorbed in almost unlimited number without special negotiation.

Another unknown that continued to militate against a firm projection of costs was the element of labor. As manufacturers in the aircraft industry were forced to recruit increasing numbers of inexperienced workers, they found their wage bills correspondingly harder to anticipate. Training costs were difficult to estimate, labor productivity proved erratic, and a high rate of turnover further complicated calculations.[98]

The advantages of the CPFF contract as a substitute for working capital constituted yet another reason why manufacturers continued to favor this instrument over the more conventional type. Every one of the nation's major aircraft manufacturers had been induced to undertake a volume of war business in marked disproportion to his capital structure. As a consequence each had reason to fear lest a small error in estimating costs wipe out the firm's entire capital. With monthly payrolls in some instances approaching original capitalization, manufacturers were hard put to meet current obligations. Advance or partial payments and V-loans (government-guaranteed loans) minimized this objection, but the arrangements were less expeditious and therefore less attractive to manufacturers than the rou-

---

[97] Flexible Pricing in Fixed Price Contracts, Lecture by Dinkelspiel.

[98] For an elaborate explanation of the factors militating against conversions, see Gen Arnold to Wilson, WPB, 4 Nov 43, AFCF 452.01–D.

tine payment of cost vouchers under a CPFF contract.[99]

Not least among the objections raised by manufacturers protesting the conversion of fixed-fee contracts were those stemming from fears regarding the attitude of the General Accounting Office. The Comptroller General repeatedly refused to regard conversion agreements signed by the Air Forces as final. Consequently with good reason contractors feared there would be retroactive disallowances that would upset the arrangements so laboriously made and produce destructive losses.[100]

The fixed-fee contractors were not the only ones to see objections to the conversion program. From the AAF point of view, the very same factors that led to the reluctant use of the CPFF form in the first place continued to operate against any uniform policy of conversion across the board to fixed-price arrangements. To write a really watertight fixed-price contract, government negotiators had to be in a position to arrive at a price high enough to provide the manufacturer with a fair profit yet low enough to force him to be efficient in all his operations. Since there continued to be a great number of unknowns that persisted well along in the life of many fixed-fee contracts, it often proved impossible to compute a close price when undertaking to effect a conversion. With the immense volume of war orders stretching production schedules on single contracts over as much as twenty-four months, manufacturers invited to enter fixed-price contracts had no alternative but to include heavy contingency allowances to cover possible future increases in labor and material costs.[101]

The fear of catastrophic losses stemming from abrupt termination of contracts gave manufacturers another incentive for insisting upon further allowances when negotiations were afoot to set the price in a fixed-price contract. Until Congress passed appropriate termination legislation and administrative procedures were worked out to ensure its functioning, contractors contemplating conversions were inclined to demand generous provision in the fixed price to cover such contingencies as inventory losses and the costs of delays in the settlement of claims arising from termination. Doubtlessly the memory of the chaotic terminations following World War I did much to condition attitudes on this point.

In short, AAF officials realized that there was no use in converting fixed-fee contracts into fixed-price contracts if the manufacturers concerned insisted on umbrella pricing. If the lump sum agreed upon were inflated with sums inserted as protection against every possible contingency, then the whole purpose of conversion would be defeated.[102]

The net result of the many considerations weighing against conversion was that very few were made. The annual report of the Procurement Division for 1944 hopefully noted that there were

---

[99] TWX, Contract Sec, WF, to Chief, Mat Div, 22 Mar 41, AFCF TWX file, Cong-T-471; North American Aviation, Brief History, 1945, WFHO, Research Materials.

[100] Smith, *The Army and Economic Mobilization*, p. 305.

[101] One possible exception to this generalization was the escalator clause. See below, pp. 422-28.

[102] Gen Arnold to Wilson, WPB, 4 Nov 43, AFCF 452.01-D.

THE COST-PLUS-FIXED-FEE CONTRACT

"only 67" firms still holding fixed-fee contracts with the Air Forces. This was disingenuous, to say the least, since among them the 67 concerns held 218 fixed-fee contracts involving a face value of some $21,500,000,000, or approximately 70 percent of all airframe contracts and 50 percent of all engine contracts.[103] Nonetheless, the unimpressive record of accomplishment reflected no lack of co-operation on the part of AAF officials looking to the widespread conversion of air arm contracts from a fixed-fee to a fixed-price basis; the simple fact was that such an operation presented formidable obstacles.

Broadly speaking, there were three different ways of approaching the job of conversion, each subject to serious administrative difficulties. The first alternative was to compromise, letting existing fixed-fee contracts run to completion without change while writing all follow-on contracts for added quantities of end items only on a fixed-price basis. Such a course avoided the normal headaches of conversion but introduced troubles of another sort. The simultaneous operation of two production lines in the same plant under different contracts raised a host of problems on allowable costs.[104] Moreover, the exigencies of production were such that employees borrowed parts from one contract for another with cavalier disregard for accountability. As a consequence, the obligation to maintain separate inventories for each type of contract imposed heavy clerical costs. By way of illustration, when the North American plant at Dallas put both its contracts there on a fixed-price basis, the company was able to lay off as many as 1,800 employees who had been engaged in property accounting and inventory work.[105]

A second technique of conversion from fixed-fee to a fixed-price footing was to take a physical inventory and start off on the new contract with a clean slate. Unfortunately, it was found that such an inventory was all but impossible to conduct while a plant continued to operate. The only feasible course was to shut down production. When Curtiss-Wright pursued this course to convert to fixed-price contracts at the request of the Air Forces in several plants, an eleven-day shutdown resulted—clearly an intolerable interruption in the midst of a war. If for no other reason, an inventory shutdown was not feasible because of the protests it engendered from the representatives of various labor groups.

The third technique of conversion, the one most frequently used by the Air Forces, was to go back to the beginning of the contract and assume that it had been a fixed-price arrangement all along with each paid voucher treated as an advance payment. After cutting off the fee to cover only work already completed, the negotiators then tried to establish a fixed price to cover the undelivered portion of the contract. Naturally all subcontractors on a CPFF basis had to be converted before the prime contractor could be considered. It takes little im-

---

[103] Annual Rpt, Proc Div, ATSC, WF, 1944, WFHO Research Materials; Negotiation and Administration of Contracts, Lecture by Scarff; Proc Statistics, Lecture by Tyson.
[104] See above, pp. 379ff.

[105] Negotiation and Administration of Contracts, Lecture by Scarff.

agination to visualize the staggering accounting problems involved in such a conversion. When the Fisher B-29 contract was changed to a fixed-price one, it took 200 girls two weeks just to type up the record of the transaction. The end result was a stack of papers fourteen feet high. Only manufacturers with large and highly trained accounting staffs could handle tasks of such dimensions. And during most of the war aircraft manufacturers simply did not have accounting organizations capable of this effort.

All the evidence in the record makes it clear that inadequate cost accounting lay at the root of most of the conversion difficulties. Few if any of the airframe manufacturers entered the war with cost-accounting staffs that could meet the demands imposed by CPFF contracting. "When we entered our contract," lamented one aircraft manufacturer, "we had no idea of the tremendous amount of accounting involved." Nor, he added, did anyone else.[106] This was substantially true for the responsible officials in the air arm as well as for most manufacturers.[107]

Even after they came to recognize the vital importance of adequate accounting, both industry and the AAF were hard put to obtain a sufficient number of trained accountants to compile the cost studies absolutely necessary in any attempt to convert fixed-fee contracts. Draft boards found it almost impossible to understand that accountants might be as important to the efficient conduct of the war as skilled mechanics.[108] The subject of accounting manpower and its proper utilization requires further study before any final conclusions can be drawn, but it may just be that the tendency to ignore the importance of "mere bookkeepers" constituted an Achilles heel in the over-all procurement effort.

Not until December 1943 did the Air Forces manage to effect a single major conversion, and this one, the North American B-24 contract at Dallas, was accomplished with the full and willing co-operation of the manufacturer. During 1944 a substantial number of conversions were completed, but relatively few were large dollar-volume contracts, and each required what the negotiators described as Herculean efforts. Experience revealed that even the smaller contracts required the unremitting effort of as many as half a dozen skilled negotiators for a matter of weeks to complete a conversion. Not the least of the reasons for the poor showing of the Air Forces in effecting conversions was the scarcity of negotiators. With the regular staff entirely absorbed in writing new contracts to meet the continuing demands of the war, it is hardly surprising that existing fixed-fee contracts were allowed to drift along without revision.[109]

From time to time critics in and out of Congress were inclined to ask why the Air Forces did not try to combine the advantages of the fixed-fee and fixed-price contracts in a single form. Whether

---

[106] J. R. Kauffmann to Col Volandt, 30 Sep 42, AFCF 161 CPFF.
[107] For a revealing indication of this, see Executive Accountant, AC, to Chief, Fiscal Div, 9 Dec 41, AFCF 132.2 Audits.
[108] Gen Arnold to Wilson, WPB, 4 Nov 43, AFCF 452.01-D.
[109] Negotiation and Administration of Contracts, Lecture by Scarff. ASF Purchases Div, Purchasing Policies and Practices, p. 233.

THE COST-PLUS-FIXED-FEE CONTRACT

described as incentive contracts, target-price contracts, or bonus contracts, all the proposals amounted to much the same thing. If the contractor could hold his actual costs under the estimated cost (determined after a trial run), he could share in the savings in the form of an addition to his fee; if he ran over the estimated cost, he would be penalized by a reduction in fee. Although the Procurement Regulations contained a boiler plate form to be used in drafting such a contract, air arm procurement officers made no use of it during the war. Attractive as the scheme may appear in theory, it suffered from a fatal defect—it required an even more elaborate system of cost accounting than did the unmodified form of fixed-fee contract actually employed during the war.

The heart of the problem was in fixing the initial estimated cost. An inaccurate estimate would reward or penalize a manufacturer on an utterly fictitious basis. Moreover, even if the parties could agree on a cost estimate, the introduction of modifications would still lead to endless difficulties. In addition, contractors would be under a greater than ever pressure to dispute the allocation of overhead and the contracting officer's decisions on allowable costs.[110]

At least until better accounting practices could be applied, incentive or target-price contracts were clearly less desirable than the existing fixed-fee contract form used by the Air Forces. Nevertheless, the record of British experience suggests that, with appropriate accounting, the bonus scheme could be used with good effect to stimulate the economical use of resources by fixed-fee manufacturers.[111]

As the complexity of converting CPFF contracts became more apparent with each passing month, Air Forces procurement officials began to experience grave doubts about the fixed-price contract itself as a panacea.[112] In one of the very first conversions accomplished, the unit cost under the final fixed-price agreement turned out to be somewhat higher than it had been in the original fixed-fee contract. Admittedly, this particular instance reflected a rather special set of circumstances, but it was nevertheless disturbing to those who had hitherto assumed without question the inherent superiority of the fixed-fee form of procurement.[113] The record of CPFF conversions undertaken in World War I, had it been available, might have shed a great many insights on this problem and could have provided forewarning on the dangers involved. However, for all practical purposes that valuable body of experience was not readily accessible. Once again the officials confronted with the issue had to blunder painfully while trying to amass enough information on the comparative merits of fixed-fee and

---

[110] ASF Purchases Div, Purchasing Policies and Practices, pp. 278–79. See also, 8 Federal Register 5210, April 21, 1943.

[111] The British Ministry of Supply found it effective to equate fees to production rather than to estimated cost to secure maximum incentives. See Rpt of Secy, Army, *Foreign Logistical Organizations and Methods*, 1947, p. 163. See also, Bonus Schemes and Target Price Mechanisms Employed in British Armament Procurement Contracts by W. S. Lacey, NDAC, 4 Dec 40, AFCF 161 Contract Regulations.

[112] ASF Purchases Div, Purchasing Policies and Practices, p. 246.

[113] Chief, Contract Sec, WF, to Chief, Mat Div, 28 Jan 42, AFCF 161 CPFF.

fixed-price contracts to derive sound policy.[114]

An argument often raised against the CPFF form of contract was that it lacked incentives. The manufacturer collected his fee or profit no matter how inefficient he may have been. This conception of the instrument is incorrect. The fixed fee was not a guaranteed profit; it was a predetermined maximum up to which a manufacturer could push his earnings. Fees were not paid out in lump sums but in increments geared to the contractor's rate of production. The faster he delivered the end items on order, the sooner he collected his total fee. The faster a manufacturer completed a contract and collected his fee, the sooner he could take on another contract and begin earning another fee.

Patently, then, the fixed-fee form was not devoid of the profit incentives of the conventional contracts. But to talk only of profit incentives was to miss the central point. Although in Congress and in the press the subject of profits captured by far the larger share of headlines, in terms of the total dollar cost of air power, profits ranked well down in the roster of expenses. Of infinitely greater concern should have been the incentives to the economical use of resources—manpower, materials, facilities, and so on. Why be so concerned with 6 percent of profits while virtually ignoring the other 94 percent of price?

Without question, a tightly negotiated fixed-price contract tended to exert a greater pressure on a manufacturer to make the most efficient use of his resources than did a fixed-fee contract in which he could pass most of his costs along to the government. But to determine a close price on a conventional contract, the government's negotiators had to have a great many detailed figures on costs at their disposal. If such figures were available, there would be no need to resort to the fixed-fee form at all. Thus it is idle to compare the respective merits of an efficiently drawn and closely priced conventional or lump-sum contract and a fixed-fee contract, which by its very nature is only for use where the facts necessary for close pricing are not available. A more appropriate comparison is to pit the fixed-fee contract with its admitted shortcomings against a fixed-price contract drawn in the dark, without detailed information —without facts—and therefore almost of necessity padded with heavy contingency allowances insisted upon by contractors understandably anxious to save themselves from loss.

When procurement officers at Wright Field looked back over the record of wartime contracting they found a confusing pattern. Some fixed-price contractors showed a better record of efficiency and lower unit costs than their competitors working under fixed-fee contracts. On the other hand, there were instances where exactly the reverse was true. For example, Studebaker, with a CPFF contract, turned in a lower unit cost than did Wright Aeronautical under a fixed-price contract, when both firms were producing the same engine. But, in fairness to the firms involved, it should be pointed out that there were far too many variables present to permit any direct comparisons.[115] Differ-

---

[114] Interv with Mr. Schwinn, 25 Jul 55.

[115] Flexible Pricing in Fixed Price Contracts, Lecture by Dinkelspiel.

THE COST-PLUS-FIXED-FEE CONTRACT

ences in tooling, availability of skilled labor, the timing of design changes and the like, all conspired to defy easy generalizations. Perhaps the only generalization that could be safely made was that the evidence did not weigh definitively for or against either type of contract. Each contract had its advantages and disadvantages contingent upon the circumstances to which it was applied.

The absence of a clear decision as to whether the fixed-fee or fixed-price form was superior did not mean that the experience of the war years produced no conclusions whatsoever on the topic. Those procurement officials who studied the subject most intensively concluded that CPFF contracts were probably essential, especially in the early phases of an emergency, and their use should continue to be authorized. By imposing a rigorous system of accounting from the very beginning of every CPFF contract entered, the whole problem of subsequent conversion to a fixed-price basis could be simplified if not actually made mandatory at a predetermined point.[116] In short, when properly administered, the fixed-fee contract, which permits a more detailed supervision by the government, was certainly to be preferred to umbrella pricing or a fixed-price contract written without sufficient information at hand to prevent the inclusion of unjustified contingency allowances.

That air arm procurement officials favored the continued use of CPFF contracts should occasion no surprise. Even before the instrument had been strengthened by closer administration and improved accounting procedures, they had urged its use as a necessity of war. Far more significant, it would seem, was the appearance of some shift in opinions on Capitol Hill. Congress had authorized the fixed-fee contract only with the greatest reluctance, and all through the war individual congressmen repeatedly sought to terminate its use. Some even offered bills looking specifically to that end. Nonetheless, by the end of 1944, after careful study a Senate subcommittee reported:

> The form of the contract is not the decisive factor in determining the efficiency or inefficiency with which manpower, materials, and machinery are put to use in war production. In fact, we found many situations where highly effective operations were being conducted under Cost Plus Fixed Fee contracts and where any other form of contract would have contributed to inefficiency.[117]

A single subcommittee does not speak for the Senate and certainly not for the Congress as a whole, but the omen was favorable. It showed what experience had so often revealed before: when a group of conscientious congressmen are shown the facts in full perspective, they will legislate soundly on highly technical questions. But the lesson should be clear: the congressmen must be informed. If procurement officials wish to operate within workable statutes, they must see to it that the facts in the record of experience are not only available but readily accessible. While this was particularly true with respect to the rival

---

[116] See especially, ASF Purchases Div, Purchasing Policies and Practices, p. 286.

[117] Year-End Rpt of the War Contracts Subcom to the Com on Military Affairs pursuant to S Res 8, 18 Dec 44, p. 1, quoted in Smith, *The Army and Economic Mobilization*, p. 306.

claims of the fixed-fee and fixed-price forms of contract, it was no less essential in all the other facets of contracting subject to statutory regulation. Certainly of equal importance in this regard was the whole subject of the redetermination of price, a veritable revolution in the canons of contract law.

CHAPTER XVII

Price Adjustment

Although most of the discussion thus far has concerned only two forms of procurement contracts—the fixed price and the cost plus fixed fee—there was a large middle ground between the two that embodied neither the rigidly fixed price of the conventional contract nor the risk-absorbing cost-plus character of the form authorized for use during the emergency. The in-between type of contract cannot be identified by any particular label or neat package of terminology. This middle ground was occupied by contracts based on an initial fixed price but containing price-adjustment features —contradictory as the description may seem.

In many ways the fixed-price contract with price adjustment features was merely the other side of the coin represented by the fixed-fee contract with bonus or incentive clauses added. The former provided incentives in principle and then added devices to minimize risks; the latter minimized risks in principle and then sought to add incentives for efficiency. Each approached the same goal, but from a different direction. Both foundered over the same two shortcomings: inadequate accounting and inability to predict the future.

The evolution of price adjustment features in air arm contracts accurately reflects the ebb and flow of social and political pressures besetting the nation during the years of crisis. In the period before Pearl Harbor, as long as air arm officials continued to think and act along the rigid lines of peacetime buying, aircraft manufacturers continually agitated for the inclusion of escalator clauses in their production contracts. They had good reason to do so. The threat of war and then war in Europe had a most unsettling effect upon the economy of the nation; wages and material prices showed a disconcerting tendency to move upward erratically and unexpectedly. When air arm buyers insisted on writing fixed-price contracts, the manufacturers felt they had to get whatever protection they could by means of escalator clauses drafted to cover fluctuations in the heaviest elements of their costs. Here price adjustment was primarily designed for the relief of the contractor.

After Pearl Harbor the problem of price adjustment assumed an entirely different character. Speed of production had a higher priority than economy. More and more frequently procurement officers resorted to CPFF contracts or sought to hasten the signing of fixed-price contracts by granting umbrella prices sufficiently high to allay fears manufacturers might entertain about hidden costs and possible losses. By 1942 the inevitable harvest of this policy became a subject of public concern. One manufacturer after another realized abnormally high profits as the contingencies allowed for in the contract prices failed to materialize. In such cases, price adjustment, which is to say adjustment downward, was required in the public interest.

Escalator Clauses

During 1939 so many aircraft manufacturers began to express an interest in including escalator clauses in their production contracts that they presented an industry-wide proposal through their trade organization, the Aircraft Chamber of Commerce. The formula they suggested to make adjustments in material and labor costs according to changes in the published indices of the Departments of Labor and Commerce looked, on first glance, like an exercise in higher mathematics:

$$\left[100 + \frac{I-i}{I}\right]\% \, M + \left[100 + \frac{I'-i'}{I}\right]\%$$
$$L + 80\% \, [L'] + P = X$$

Actually the formula is readily understood: M equals materials; L, labor; P, profit; and X, the adjusted or corrected price. I stands for the published material index at the time of repricing, i for the index at the time the contract was signed. I' and i' stands for the corresponding indices for labor. The 80 percent figure was an arbitrary weighting assigned to overhead or indirect labor. Applied every 60 days, the formula promised relief from unforeseen contingencies and fluctuations in prices that were fretting a number of aircraft contractors.[1]

Apparently the Chief of the Air Corps Materiel Division was not losing any sleep over threatened price increases. He found it "extremely improbable" that labor and material costs, as fixed at the time of contracting, would "fluctuate materially" before the completion of deliveries. Evidently he was thinking exclusively in terms of the tiny job lot orders for aircraft that had characterized so much of Air Corps procurement in the between-war years. The tendency to look only backward seemed to extend to foreign affairs as well as domestic, for the division chief went on to say that "in the absence of a drastic economic upheaval, such fluctuations would be negligible." Many newspaper readers at the time might have been inclined to suggest that the course of events gave every sign of a drastic economic upheaval in the very near future.[2]

The acting Chief of the Air Corps mirrored the myopia of the Materiel Division when in May 1939 he wrote to the Assistant Secretary of War urging rejection of the escalator proposal. In addition, he contributed an objection of his own: the administration of aircraft procurement contracts was already "sufficiently complex" without introducing

---

[1] ACC to ASW, 20 Apr 39, with Incls, AFCF 161 Contract Regulations.

[2] 1st Ind, Mat Div to CofAC, 24 May 39, AFCF 161 Contract Regulations. Even the facts were wrong in the Materiel Division staff paper reporting that the Navy was not using escalators in aircraft contracts. Actually, the Bureau of Aeronautics had begun to write escalator clauses three months earlier. See Memo, Adm Towers for Gen Arnold, 13 Sep 39, AFCF 161 Contract Regulations.

PRICE ADJUSTMENT

additional clauses unless they were decidedly in the government's interest.[3]

Contract negotiators in the Navy's Bureau of Aeronautics took an entirely different tack. They used escalator clauses for a brief trial period with positive results. On the basis of this evidence they included similar clauses in all subsequent production contracts.[4]

The Navy's decision in favor of escalator clauses forced the War Department to follow suit. To have done otherwise would have put Air Corps negotiators at a decided disadvantage when bargaining with manufacturers at a time when the competition between the services for facilities was becoming increasingly acute. As a consequence, the Chief of the Air Corps was forced to reverse his position and accept escalator clauses as a necessity.

While there were advantages to be gained from using escalator clauses there were also disadvantages. Closer pricing was the most obvious benefit anticipated. Manufacturers with contracts including options for large numbers of aircraft would no longer feel under such heavy compulsion to include contingency allowances against the unknown cost increases of the future. Then, too, Air Corps officers recognized that in begging for the inclusion of escalator clauses, the aircraft manufacturers were of necessity condemning themselves to an extremely burdensome chore of detailed cost accounting. The accurate cost figures essential to the computation of the escalators would also be of very real value to air arm procurement officers in future contract negotiations. Had the procurement officers tried to make the preparation of such data a requirement in every production contract, the manufacturers would have resisted, but of their own volition the manufacturers were accepting responsibility in a most involved area of accounting. When the accounting system subsequently proved both costly and difficult, the manufacturers were hardly in a position to protest.

On the negative side, escalator clauses suffered from a number of administrative defects. Existing law prohibited contracts incurring obligations beyond the sums available in current appropriations. Since an escalator constituted an open-end or uncertain obligation, the only legal way to apply it was to write in a maximum or cut-off figure beyond which the escalator would not ride. This involved tying up large sums of appropriated monies on the off chance that the escalator would ride up to its maximum allowable amount. Another objection raised was that manufacturers would no longer buy all their materials in bulk directly after signing a contract, thus losing the customary economies of quantity procurement. Still more important was the expressed fear that it might prove difficult in practice to get useful index figures for labor and material costs. As events were to prove, the last foreboding was entirely justified.[5]

When the Air Corps' negotiators ac-

---

[3] Memo, Actg CofAC for ASW, 27 May 39, AFCF 161 Contract Regulations.
[4] Memo, Adm Towers for Gen Arnold, 13 Sep 39, AFCF 161 Contract Regulations.

[5] Memo, CofAC for ASW, 5 Oct 39, AFCF 161 Contract Regulations.

tually sat down with the manufacturers' representatives during the trying months of crisis in 1940 and tried to write contracts containing escalator clauses, the dreadful turn of events in Europe placed them in a poor position to bargain effectively. Their backs were to the wall; they had to have aircraft. They could not wait, and a number of manufacturers were quite prepared to take full advantage of this opportunity. If only those in command had shown a little more initiative in directing their staffs to hammer out the escalator clause as a workable instrument before the emergency had arrived, they would have been in a stronger position in their hour of desperation. As it turned out, they had to flounder about by trial and error, attempting to evolve an intricate contractual clause under pressure, since they were subject to criticism at the time if they failed to place orders for airplanes with the utmost speed and were equally open to criticism later if they failed to drive close bargains in their negotiations.

Finding suitable indices on which to base escalator clauses proved to be the crux of the problem. The material price index presented no serious difficulty, but hourly wage rates were another matter. Air Corps officials wished to use a broad-based index that would accurately reflect any general movement in the wage structure of the national economy and thus protect aircraft manufacturers from increases in cost entirely beyond their control. On the other hand, the manufacturers preferred a local index. They were in the midst of a drive by labor unions to organize their plants and wanted to be protected against any wage increases they might have to grant, so they asked for an index based on the wage levels prevailing in their own communities. Needless to say, the negotiators resisted this move since it would encourage irresponsible wage increases by manufacturers in hot competition for a limited pool of skilled aircraft workers. When a number of leading aircraft manufacturers proved adamant on the point, air arm procurement officials had to relent and accept a compromise. They agreed to a labor escalator clause in aircraft production contracts based on the wage index published by the Bureau of Labor Statistics (BLS) for the aircraft industry.[6]

The compromise was not a happy one. The wage index published by BLS for the aircraft industry was actually a very narrow base on which to adjust escalators. Since some 18 or 20 major firms more or less constituted the aircraft industry, wage concessions by one or two leaders in the group were enough to tip the index. This was obviously unsound; the escalator became rather too directly responsive to wage decisions made by individual manufacturers.

Worse yet, use of the aircraft industry index placed the Air Corps out of step with the Navy. Negotiators for the Bureau of Aeronautics had built their escalators upon the BLS index of average hourly earnings in the durable goods manufacturing industries of the United States, a broadly based index patently not directly subject to the pressure of

---

[6] TWX, Cont–T–518, Contract Sec, WF, to Contract Sec, OCAC, 7 Mar 41; Memo, Asst to Chief, Mat Div, for ASW, undated, with 1st Ind, OASW to CofAC, 13 Mar 41. Both in AFCF 161 Contract Regulations.

any individual concern.⁷ Despite frequent protestations by the two services that they maintained a high degree of co-ordination in procurement matters, here was compelling evidence to the contrary. The Air Corps had accepted the use of escalator clauses in the first place only to keep pace with the Navy but had failed to maintain a united front with the Navy in its dealings with industry.

When it began to appear that air arm negotiators had been badly outmaneuvered at the bargaining table, the Under Secretary of War ordered corrective action. In the future, he directed, they were to tie all escalator clauses to the durable goods index used by the Navy. Further, he wished all existing escalator clauses to be rewritten to reflect the new policy.⁸

Climbing out of the hole into which they had dug themselves proved embarrassing to the officers involved. To be sure, about half the manufacturers concerned recognized the merits of the durable goods index and readily accepted the change-over. The remaining firms refused to do so. As one of them pointed out, between mid-February and mid-May the durable goods hourly wage index had gone up only two-thirds of one percent. In the same period, the aircraft industry index rose 4.6 percent. The manufacturer's own wage rates had increased 6.1 percent. Since a change to the durable goods index would leave him in a less desirable position than before, he was not inclined to regard his unwillingness to change indices as unpatriotic conduct.⁹

When confronted with resistance on the part of nearly a dozen major manufacturers, the chief of the Contract Section, on whom the task of changing the indices fell, discovered that a successful resolution of the matter was virtually impossible. To make the best of a bad job, he recommended amending the contracts of all those manufacturers who were willing to accept the durable goods index; the contracts of the others he would let run as written, even if they were of an inflationary character.¹⁰ This course may have been the only practicable one, but it was nonetheless blatantly inequitable. In essence it amounted to penalizing those who cooperated willingly while rewarding the holdouts. At best such a policy could only have harmful long-run effects, Manufacturers would be led to infer that it was better to be hard-boiled than to be fair minded when negotiating with the Air Corps.

The fiasco encountered in the first trial of escalator clauses by the Air Corps precipitated a decision by the Assistant Secretary of War to work out a really viable clause for general use in War Department contracts. In circulating drafts for discussion and comments, OASW staff officers uncovered many objections to the whole mechanism that might far better have been learned during the peacetime years had the escalator clause been tried then on a small scale in order to search out some of its

---

⁷ J. D. Biggers, Chairman, OPA Tax and Finance Com, to ASW, 20 Feb 41, AFCF 161 Contract Regulations.

⁸ Memo, OUSW for CofAC, 6 Mar 41, AFCF 161 Contract Regulations.

⁹ IOM, Chief, Contract Sec, for Chief, Mat Div, OCAC, 15 May 41, with Incls, AFCF 161 Contract Regulations.

¹⁰ *Ibid.*

inherent difficulties. For example, operation of the escalator clause presupposed the existence of an accurate inventory by the participating contractor. Few if any aircraft builders could begin to present such a record, and certainly none would be willing to shut down a production line for a week or more to take an inventory, nor would such a course have been to the advantage of the Air Corps.

Another objection to the escalator clause was that it would tend to negate an important incentive feature built into fixed-price aircraft production contracts by air arm negotiators. This was the practice of plotting costs along an assumed learner curve projected across the life of a contract. The negotiators allowed relatively high costs in the early periods of the curve and progressively lower payments thereafter. Thus contractors were given a powerful incentive to speed production in order to increase the number of units delivered during the period when a higher rate of return was authorized. The escalator clause proposed by OASW was conceived in such a way that the increase it granted would cancel out the decreases indicated on the learner curve assumed by the negotiators.

The most serious objection raised over the proposed escalator clause, however, was that it appeared to impose excessive administrative burdens. Even the President of the Aeronautical Chamber of Commerce, speaking for the industry as a whole, had come to recognize this, admitting that it was based upon archaic accounting theory. In view of the earlier comments of air arm officers on the problems of accounting, this was something of the pot calling the kettle black. It was not the fault of the military buyers that escalators might require a great deal of accounting—it was inherent in the contractual device itself.

Even so, the escalator clause, as contrived, seemed to ignore a whole series of vital considerations. It purported to cover increases in the cost of materials, but what are materials? The clause defined materials subject to escalation as anything going into the end item. But what about jigs and fixtures or tooling? Modifications late in the life of a contract could require many thousands of dollars of expenditure for costly tool steels and the like. Were these not to be protected by escalators too?

The treatment of labor in the proposed escalator was similarly deceptive. The clause as drafted would authorize escalation only for direct labor costs, yet most manufacturers knew from experience that the line between direct and indirect labor on an aircraft was extremely difficult to draw. Furthermore, insofar as indirect labor (guards, clerks, production expediters, and so on) was subject to collective bargaining, the manufacturer had as much need for escalation here as in the case of direct labor.[11]

A further cataloguing of the obstacles encountered in drafting a truly workable escalator clause would serve little purpose. Suffice it to say, to many both in industry and in the procurement services, the difficulties to be encountered in

---

[11] Memo, OUSW for CofAC et al., 14 Mar 41, and reply, IOM, Asst Chief, Mat Div, WF, for Chief, Mat Div, OCAC, 22 Mar 41, AFCF 161 Contract Regulations.

administering escalators seemed to outweigh the advantages. Since this was true with respect to prime contractors, it was even more so when applied to subcontractors, who protested outspokenly against the prohibitive accounting costs necessarily entailed. Air arm officers had never been enthusiastic about the use of escalator clauses, but by the time of Pearl Harbor they had come to feel that their use might actually prove more harmful than helpful. If manufacturers disagreed with the choice of index or feared that hidden administrative costs might arise when applying them, they would find means in one way or another to inflate their initial cost estimates to cover themselves. In so doing they would more than offset the gains anticipated by the government in the form of close pricing or realistic initial estimates of costs.[12]

The air arm continued to use escalator clauses to a limited extent in 1942 and thereafter, but following Pearl Harbor the question became largely academic. Increased payments adjusted according to the escalator formula were generally made only at the completion of a contract. With the spare parts portion of some airframe contracts running on for as much as two years, final settlements were often unreasonably delayed. Moreover, the whole process became absurd when both the manufacturer and the government tied up valuable negotiators in computing payments under escalator clauses while most of the manufacturers were at the very same time making refunds to the government from excess profits. In their final mutation, the escalator clauses used by the Air Forces dropped the formula or index approach in favor of *ad hoc* redetermination of price. Which is to say, escalation gave place to repricing by negotiation.[13]

Despite many failures, the foray into escalation was not in vain. Even where the clauses used had been badly drawn, if their application helped allay the manufacturers' fears of catastrophic loss, especially during the summer of 1940, and thereby hastened the nation's defense, escalation was worth the trouble involved. In retrospect, many of the manufacturers' fears proved groundless, but this does not mean that the anguish of the manufacturers at the moment of signing was any less real. Perhaps no one who has not himself sat down to sign a multimillion dollar fixed-price contract in a period of economic upheaval can ever really appreciate the psychological advantage of escalator clauses to those who expected so much from their use.

One final observation remains to be made. Taken all together, the many administrative difficulties that plagued every effort to apply escalator clauses effectively spell out a major reason why the air arm felt compelled to resort to the cost-plus-fixed-fee form of procurement for such a large portion of its total dollar outlay. When seen against the perspective of the ill-fated escalator

---

[12] Memo, OUSW for CofAC *et al.*, 17 Sep 41; R&R, Fiscal Div to Mat Div, 14 Oct 41; Jouett to USW, 27 Nov 41; Memo, C. J. Little, Glenn L. Martin, for Exec Officer, Legal Branch, Purchases Div, SOS, 8 Sep 42. All in AFCF ,61 Contract Regulations.

[13] IOM, Chief, Proc Div to Chief, Price Adjustment Office, WF, 2 Nov 43, AFCF 161 Renegotiation; Flexible Pricing in Fixed Price Contracts, Lecture by Dinkelspiel.

clauses, the heavy reliance of the air arm on fixed-fee contracts during the war is more easily understood.

Excess Profits and Voluntary Refunds

With the use of escalators demonstrated to be administratively cumbersome and the use of cost-plus-fixed-fee contracts still officially frowned upon, the air arm necessarily turned to the conventional lump-sum or fixed-price form of contract for the vast majority of contracts entered. Unfortunately, for want of adequate information with which to achieve close prices, air arm buyers frequently had to approve contracts they suspected but could not prove to be inflated with abnormally high contingency allowances—"fib factors" as some jocular negotiators called them. The inevitable consequence of this kind of buying was soon apparent. In the weeks immediately before Pearl Harbor, one manufacturer after another realized excess profits of surprising magnitude.

Not all excess profits were the result of faulty initial pricing. Even where the negotiators had done an excellent job on the basis of the facts available at the time, lower costs resulting from the substitution of nonstrategic materials, refinements in production techniques, improved labor efficiency, and the economies generally stemming from larger orders or longer production runs all combined to yield lower unit costs and unanticipated profits. But whatever may have been the ultimate reason for the unusual earnings in any particular case, the mere existence of abnormal profit levels in public contracts called for corrective action.

One means of recovering excess profits was to rely on voluntary refunds. In some instances patriotic manufacturers actually took the initiative in suggesting refunds. One airframe builder, for example, late in 1941 volunteered a reduction of $14,000,000 across the board on the firm's outstanding business.[14] More often than not, however, the voluntary refunds were made at the suggestion of air arm officials, whose studies showed where heavy profits were piling up. Although those manufacturers who responded to the prodding deserve credit for their co-operation, the record makes it quite evident that at least some of those who complied did so in the hope that they would receive correspondingly favorable treatment in subsequent negotiations.[15] Whether or not any scheme of voluntary refunds would have proved successful on a large scale as a technique of profit control is now impossible to say, because, before the voluntary refund program was fairly under way, Congress stepped in with a major piece of legislation authorizing compulsory renegotiation of contracts where excess profits were evident.

Statutory Renegotiation

The decision of Congress to legislate against excess profits came as a direct consequence of the unsavory details

---

[14] North American Aviation, Brief History, p. 123, copy in WFHO files.
[15] IOM, Chief, Contract Sec, WF, for CGMC, 26 Sep 42, and related correspondence, AFCF 400.19; Negotiation and Administration of Contracts, Lecture by Scarff.

found by a House committee investigating war contracts. Undoubtedly the most notorious case of profiteering disclosed by the congressmen was that of Jack and Heintz, Inc., a Cleveland firm newly organized to manufacture aircraft engine starters and other accessories. By charging $750 for starters actually costing about $292 to produce and resisting every suggestion of price reduction, the firm in short order piled up spectacular profits. By the time this company's record of fantastic profits and fabulous employee bonus payments—$40,000 to the owner's private secretary, for example—had been aired, Congress was in a mood to crack down on profiteering with punitive legislation.[16]

The Renegotiation Act, as the congressional profit curb came to be called, actually appeared in the form of an amendment tacked on to an appropriation measure.[17] In essence, it empowered the heads of departments to compel contractors to renegotiate contract prices wherever unconscionable profits appeared to exist. The law carried teeth too. If a contractor refused to agree on a revised price by renegotiation, the appropriate department head could make a unilateral decision binding on the contractor concerned. Future contracts in excess of $100,000 with both sub and prime contractors were required to include a renegotiation clause, but the act permitted renegotiation in contracts of any size when excessive profits appeared to be present.

The Organization for Renegotiation

To carry out the stipulations of the 1942 Renegotiation Act, the Secretary of War created a Price Adjustment Board within the War Department. This agency not only laid down policy and formulated procedures but served as a kind of referee, reviewing determinations made by officers in the several services within the Army to whom the detailed work had been delegated. On occasion, when the size, complexity, or novelty of a contract seemed to warrant such action, the board itself conducted the renegotiation proceedings, though the bulk of the task fell to the service staffs established for that purpose.

In the Air Forces a Price Adjustment Section located at Wright Field carried out the work of renegotiation. In short order this group encountered some trying problems of co-ordination.[18] The Contract Section at Wright Field, it will be recalled, already had a Cost Analysis Branch as one of its component units. Since price adjustment and cost analysis groups each conducted cost studies of selected contracts, it might appear that the newly added unit was a needless duplication. Both groups did deal in contractor costs, but they approached the subject from different angles. The primary objective of the Contract Section and its subordinate Cost Analysis Branch

---

[16] Vinson, Chairman, Naval Affairs Investigating Com, to SW, 25 Mar 42, AFCF 333.5 Investigation of Contracts. For a fuller account of this episode, see Smith, *The Army and Economic Mobilization*, pp. 351ff.

[17] Sixth Supplemental National Defense Act, April 28, 1942, Public 528, 77th Cong, 2d sess, sec. 403, title IV.

[18] MC TI-1258 with addendum 1, 16 Sep 42, AFCF 161 Renegotiation; McMurtrie, Hist of AAF MC: 1942, pp. 101–03.

was to negotiate contracts and thus get production as soon as possible. The implicit objective of the Price Adjustment Section was to prevent the accumulation of excess profits. The two groups therefore pulled in more or less opposite directions, and the decision to set them up as separate entities followed organizational doctrine in aligning form to function. To have done otherwise would almost inevitably have compromised one or another of the objectives sought.

Separate organizations for contracting and renegotiation at Wright Field were doubtlessly necessary to ensure an appropriate singleness of purpose in the pursuit of these different ends. But this very separation made the task of co-ordination doubly difficult. To avoid needless reworking of a contractor's books, the Price Adjustment staff had to take pains to exploit the findings of the Cost Analysis Branch to the utmost. The same was true of the data compiled by the Contract Audit Section of the Fiscal Division as well as the Legal Branch of the Contract Section. So long as renegotiation operations were conducted at Wright Field, this kind of co-ordination could be maintained at a high level of effectiveness. When the several procurement districts established price adjustment sections, however, and began to handle the renegotiations delegated to them, co-ordination proved rather more difficult to achieve.[19]

Decentralization of renegotiation to the districts threw the whole problem of co-ordination into focus. District price adjustment staffs would plunge into the record of an individual contract only to discover that a balanced view of the profit picture found there would require an appraisal of the firm's total business volume. Where this included contracts with the Navy or other governmental agencies, the renegotiators were blocked, since the organization established under the 1942 act envisioned the Price Adjustment Board of each department as a separate entity. During 1944 Congress rectified this weakness by creating a single War Contracts Price Adjustment Board with jurisdiction over the departmental boards to handle just such cases.

The creation of a single, centralized War Contracts Price Adjustment Board may have solved some problems, but it generated new ones. Where manufacturers held contracts with two or more services, the board proposed to assign the work of renegotiation to the service with the dominant dollar interest. This appeared logical enough, but such an obvious course had its drawback. An Air Forces price adjustment officer pointed out that in many instances the air arm renegotiation team members had worked long and hard not only to acquire an intimate knowledge of a manufacturer's special problems and the idiosyncrasies of his accounting methods but also to establish a close and friendly rapport with the company personnel. In assigning renegotiations to one or another of the services by formula on the basis of dollar volume, the board would ignore and perhaps lose the advantage of the delicate and useful relationship already established. The board subsequently did de-

---

[19] Deputy Chief, Price Adjustment Sec, to WDPAB, 10 Dec 43, AFCF 161 Renegotiation; Lecture, Statutory Renegotiation, by Maj S. L. M. McCorskey, AAF Contracting Officers School, WF, Winter 1944–45, WFHO.

velop an elaborate procedure of assignment.[20]

The lesson for administrators was obvious: a standing operating procedure may be easy to use and may by its very nature imply an equity that places the responsible official beyond reproach, but it is no substitute for the exercise of discretion based on common sense and a careful appraisal of the evidence in hand for a particular case.

The Administration of Renegotiation

From the outset the directives issued by the War Department of the subject of price adjustment reflected a deliberate intention to rely heavily upon common sense. Since detailed audits and cost studies on thousands of individual contracts would be virtually impossible administratively, renegotiators were instructed to consider each contractor's total business for a whole year then leave him a "reasonable" return, offsetting whatever losses may have been incurred against profits taken. The main objective was to get "uninterrupted, efficient, and maximum production at a minimum cost" rather than to try to squeeze out the "last increment of possible excess profit." To this end the individual officers concerned were admonished to take a "practical and realistic view" of their work. They were to maintain a "firm but friendly" attitude, and to try to make each final determination a matter of mutual agreement.

Although Congress passed the Renegotiation Act of 1942 in a punitive spirit and provided coercions for use in recalcitrant cases, the War Department took the position that the overwhelming majority of contractors had no wish to retain excessive profits. Moreover, the existence of such profits, the departmental directive was careful to observe, did not constitute prima-facie evidence of wrong doing since manufacturers working on novel items or in unusually large quantities could in all innocence miscalculate costs by a wide margin. The directive was emphatic in ordering renegotiators at all echelons to make every effort to sell the price adjustment program as a constructive step in the best interests of the industry. The return of abnormal profits would help contractors maintain good public relations by avoiding the nasty charge of profiteering. Renegotiation that worked toward closer pricing would provide an incentive to efficiency, which would leave contractors in better condition to meet the rigors of postwar competition. And by the same token, every official step that held down the cost of the war would redound to the advantage of industry by retarding inflation and lowering taxes.[21]

The mere promulgation of a directive at headquarters did not ensure compliance at the fringe of operations. However farsighted and well thought out the departmental directive may have been, it would remain a dead letter until it could be sold effectively—sold to the officers who could be expected to apply it to the contractors affected. The officers assigned

---

[20] Chief, Price Adjustment Br, Control Office, MM&D, to Price Adjustment Office, MC, 13 Jan 44, AFCF 161 Renegotiation. See also, Smith, *The Army and Economic Mobilization*, p. 363.

[21] Memo, Col Browning for Maurice Karker, Chairman, WDPAB, 8 Aug 42; WDPAB: Principles, Policy and Procedure To Be Followed in Renegotiation, mimeographed instructions, 10 Aug 42, revised 20 Nov 42. Both in AFCF 161 Renegotiation.

to this task showed a good deal of imagination and no little insight in contriving methods to be sure that the official policies actually did pass on down the line.

The problem in hand was essentially one of how best to communicate the spirit in which the law was to be administered. It was easy enough to draw up a directive telling who was to do what and when, but official directives have a way of falling short when it comes to expressing the mood or the attitude intended by those in authority. One clever remedy dreamed up by an Air Forces officer to meet this difficulty was to make use of the testimony on the profits question given by the Under Secretary before a congressional committee.[22] Reprints of this testimony could be sent not only to interested officers but to the president of each company about to be subjected to renegotiation. Inasmuch as the Under Secretary's remarks explored the full range of the topic and expressed at length the philosophy behind the department's stand, they served as an ideal supplement to the official renegotiation directive. The suggestion had particular merit because copies were immediately available from the Government Printing Office without the delays that would have been unavoidable in any attempt to prepare an explanatory pamphlet from scratch.

The need for communicating top level policy on renegotiation downward was a continuing one. The law itself was repeatedly amended, and as the renegotiation process embraced more and more contractors, the need for passing the word grew correspondingly. To this end Air Forces officers resorted to a number of ingenious expedients. They circulated the script of a radio debate on renegotiation and compiled rosters of officers whose experience with the subject qualified them to speak before industry groups whenever an appropriate occasion presented itself. In time a great many articles on renegotiation began to appear in various media. Taken all together, the literature presented a highly instructive cross section of ideas and experience on the price adjustment process, but inasmuch as some of the best articles appeared in trade journals and other similar publications not readily available to a wide public, AAF officers undertook to compile and circulate reproduced copies of these articles to interested persons.[23] A general bibliography of articles on renegotiation was yet another useful administrative tool employed.

The importance of communicating the spirit as well as the letter of the Renegotiation Act would be hard to understate. The very concept of compulsory renegotiation marked a radical departure from conventional business and legal practice. In its way, the 1942 act threatened to be no less significant than the original federal income tax legislation of 1913, for it opened administrative vistas down which even the most farsighted businessman could not see with certainty. While fair-minded men might agree that excessive profits should be recaptured by the government, they might honestly disagree on the definition of what was "excessive" and question the methods used to deter-

---

[22] Lt Col C. H. Dyson, AFAMC, to Price Adjustment Sec, MC, 20 Oct 42, AFCF 161 Renegotiation.

[23] Actg Chief, Price Adjustment Office, to ACofAS MM&D, 20 Jun 43; Chief, Price Adjustment Br, MM&D, to CGMC, 20 Sep 43; AFMM&D to CGMC, 1 Jan 44. All in AFCF 161 Renegotiation.

mine precisely what constituted a profit. Thus, even the most patriotic contractors who approved profit curbs in principle might be inclined to regard the approach of the renegotiators with concern, if not with suspicion. It was highly important for the price adjustment staffs to make sure that these fears were minimized by a full exposition of the departmental policy on renegotiation. They succeeded only imperfectly, for the response of the contractors ran the whole gamut from downright refusal to gratifyingly friendly co-operation.

Only a very few firms really resisted renegotiation. Some raised objections to the text of the renegotiation clause, suggested alternatives, and then finally capitulated. In one procurement district, many refusals to co-operate stemmed from the activities of a single law firm, which seems to have specialized in drumming up renegotiation cases. Adamant resistance to renegotiation, however, was rare.[24]

At the other extreme were manufacturers who proved almost too willing to renegotiate. In one case, a firm was refused the privilege of renegotiating despite its request to do so. In this instance the Department of Justice had a criminal action pending against the company in question and felt that a refund of excessive profits might prove fatal to the government's case by prejudicing the jury. An equally bizarre exception was the corporation that reported a return of 14.1 percent profit on sales only to be told by the renegotiators working on its books that because of an accounting error the margin was only 4.5 percent—scarcely an excessive profit.[25]

Excessive profits did not necessarily connote a greedy or dishonest management. Conveying a realization of this idea to industry was of the utmost importance, for once the point was made, contractors could co-operate freely without feeling they were on the defensive. By way of illustration, consider the case of an Air Forces contractor fabricating a tiny item of standard hardware much favored by the leading airframe builders. The outbreak of war literally swamped the small firm with orders. After a number of months of production, procurement officials discovered signs of abnormal profits; on some orders the manufacturer seemed to be making over 50 percent on sales. On the surface this looked like ruthless gouging, but investigation proved otherwise.

The contractor willingly agreed to lower his prices and even to do so retroactively. He was willing in spirit but weak in facts. The truth was, he simply did not have an adequate cost accounting system to tell him where he stood. This was typical of any number of small suppliers where the war brought rapid expansion, spreading management thin and posing difficult problems of production that absorbed attention from cost accounting. In the particular case at hand the excessive profits were readily explained. Even though the contractor had increased his output many times over and enjoyed all the economies of high volume production, his clerks had continued to bill each purchase order received at rates

---

[24] MM&D to Western Proc Dist, 19 Apr 44, and related correspondence, AFCF 161 Renegotiation.

[25] Chief, Price Adjustment Branch, Central Office, MM&D, to Mid-Central Proc Dist, 3 Aug 43, and to CGMC, 24 Jun 43, AFCF 161 Renegotiation.

scaled to the size of the individual order. Since the airframe manufacturers found it necessary to control the flow of materials into their plants with a series of purchase orders reflecting the need of the moment rather than total requirements, they ended up paying what might be called retail rates.[26]

In all probability it would be accurate to say that the typical AAF contractor accepted renegotiation as a necessary evil. However little he relished the prospect, he did agree to renegotiate. But persuading manufacturers to renegotiate in good faith was only the first hurdle to be cleared. Getting them to agree on a revised price or a refund was quite another matter.

What constituted an excessive profit? Finding an answer to this question was to be a source of friction. The Renegotiation Act itself gave little help. It held excessive "any amount of a contract or subcontract price which is found as a result of renegotiation to represent excessive profits." In the tradition of Gertrude Stein this was tantamount to saying that an excessive profit was an excessive profit. Bewildered AAF officers who wanted something less cryptic and elusive with which to work were told the following story:

A lady shopper one day asked a sales clerk how she could tell male goldfish from the females. "That's easy," replied the clerk, "the male goldfish eat male angleworms and the female goldfish eat female angleworms." "But," asked the lady, "how do I tell the male worms from the females?" "Sorry," replied the clerk, "that I can't tell you; we don't sell angleworms." [27]

In short, Congress recognized that there was no simple formula by which profits could be uniformly measured for all industries across the nation. Those who administered the law were left to work out an equitable solution as best they could in accord with the general spirit of the statute. Unavoidably this meant that there would have to be a period of fumbling and groping while the officers charged with the task of renegotiation acquired enough experience to formulate sound policy.

Since they had to start somewhere, the renegotiators decided as a general rule to aim at leaving contractors approximately 10 percent on sales before taxes. This was the basic profit margin used by procurement officers at Wright Field when they negotiated new contracts. The figure was not inflexible; it could be moved up or down as circumstances seemed to warrant. For example, where an individual concern or a group of concerns in a particular industry could show consistently higher earnings during the prewar years, renegotiators were inclined to permit them to retain a comparably high percentage of return on all wartime business up to their normal volume while applying the lower basic percentage figure for all volume above normal.[28]

In general, the renegotiators tried to determine profits in such a way as to take into account all those special considerations that happened to be present in any particular instance. In a typical case the following considerations led renegotiators to permit a contractor to retain a

---

[26] Chief, Procurement Div, to Western Proc Dist, 12 Jan 44, AFCF 161 Renegotiation.

[27] Statutory Renegotiation, Lecture by McCorskey.

[28] Negotiation and Administration of Contracts, Lecture by Scarff; Col Dyson to Central Proc Dist, 8 Dec 42, AFCF 161 Renegotiation.

PRICE ADJUSTMENT

profit of 15 percent on his sales: the end item he turned out was a high-quality precision product requiring a good deal of engineering skill to fabricate; the manufacturer was virtually a sole source for the item in question and therefore carried a heavy responsibility for maintaining production at the level required by the airframe builders who relied upon him; finally, because he produced only this one item, he might expect to suffer more seriously from postwar dislocation than would many other manufacturers.[29]

Manufacturers who had shown a general willingness to co-operate all along the line were also rewarded with higher profits in proportion to their contribution. The evidence presented to justify the generous margin allowed to one firm in the Western Procurement District will illustrate what the renegotiators regarded as unusual co-operation and contribution. The contractor, the Doehler Die Casting Company, had demonstrated unusual initiative in anticipating and breaking through production bottlenecks. In 1940, at its own expense, the firm expanded to meet the upsurge of war orders and was ready when the deluge came without having to resort to government financing. Doehler had been liberal in making the results of its research and development program available to the government. In general, Doehler's prices were the lowest in its branch of the industry. What is more, Doehler followed a policy of consistently cutting prices whenever the circumstances warranted. Finally, its deliveries were always on schedule or ahead of schedule. Obviously, contractors of this stamp deserved every incentive that could be extended to them.[30]

On the other hand, just because a contractor was co-operative, it did not necessarily follow that he deserved to keep a high profit margin. Once they learned that the renegotiators were not practicing confiscation, contractors would not infrequently turn up in great good humor, claiming to be fine fellows who had been anxious to do the right thing all along: produce at full blast, make deliveries on time, help win the war, and renegotiate willingly. This attitude was gratifying, but the officers involved found they still had to stick to the facts. Not only did they try to verify all such claims to virtue by cross-checking with the procurement record, but in addition tried to ferret out every other relevant consideration: Did the contractor use his own or government-financed facilities? Did he subcontract extensively? To what extent had he actually assumed risks?[31]

As might have been expected, the problem of allowable costs again and again plagued renegotiation teams. Whenever possible the teams turned to the rulings worked out by the Bureau of Internal Revenue for income tax purposes. If there were no such rulings, they had to exercise their own discretion and this they had to do over an extremely wide range of problems. Most often in contest were questions of executive salaries, reserves set aside for postwar use, bad debts, abnormal depreciation, and the allocation of overhead between government contracts and those for private interests.

---

[29] Col Dyson to Western Proc Dist, 28 Jan 43, AFCF 161 Renegotiation.

[30] Chief, Price Adjustment Br, MM&D, to CGMD, 30 Aug 43, AFCF 161 Renegotiation.

[31] Statutory Renegotiation, Lecture by McCorskey. See also, Deputy Chief, Price Adjustment Br, MM&D, to CGMC, 20 Oct 43, AFCF 161 Renegotiation.

Typical of the overhead problem was the matter of salaries paid to partners in an unincorporated business. As owners, partners could pay themselves extravagant salaries and thus have the company books show only a modest year-end profit. To forestall this, renegotiators disallowed all salaries to partners although it could properly be argued that the compensation of working partners might be as legitimate an element of cost as the salary of any corporation manager.[32] Here, obviously, was an area where discretion came into play.

Along the same line was the case of the corporate officials who paid themselves generous fees as patent holders for the company in which they held a major interest. If such payments, however excessive, were regarded as royalties, they became necessary costs of doing business. On the other hand, some officers regarded such payments as in the nature of dividends to stockholders and therefore not deductible as a business expense.[33] Here, too, discretion and not the letter of the law would have to guide the final decision.

In time, men of good will on both sides of the renegotiation table might be expected to hammer out wise policies serving the best interests of the contractors no less than those of the government. Unfortunately, time was running out. The Renegotiation Statute of 1942 contained a limiting clause. Unless proceedings were begun within one year after a manufacturer filed a report of his costs, no further action could be taken. As a consequence, the price adjustment teams at every echelon had to operate at forced draft, hastening into individual renegotiations even before they were sure what their general policies should be.[34]

Of one thing the negotiators were certain—they needed facts before they could work effectively. After an initial period of confusion, the Price Adjustment Board began to compile statistics on sales and earnings by industry and by product groups for use as guides in making individual determinations. Renegotiators working in the field were encouraged to send to Wright Field whatever data they could accumulate along this line, but at best it was slow work. Contractors who were willing to open their books in private were often reluctant to let their cost figures be published and circulated for fear their competitors might use the information to their detriment.[35] Not until late in 1943 did the War Department finally start a systematic and periodic publication of price levels and indices useful to renegotiators.[36]

While some facts were extremely hard to obtain, others piled up almost too fast. To be sure that contractors received full credit for whatever price reductions they

---

[32] For an illustrative case, see Col Dyson, to Atlantic Mfg. Co., Philadelphia, 14 Dec 42, AFCF 161 Renegotiation. Refusal to allow the partners' salaries in this instance was particularly ironic since the decision to disallow coincided with the award of an Army-Navy "E" to the firm for excellent performance as a subcontractor to Glenn L. Martin.

[33] Col Dyson to WDPAB, 19 Mar 43, AFCF 161 Renegotiation.

[34] C. Lynde, Asst to Air Inspector, Hq AAF, to Air Inspector, 22 Dec 42, AFCF 161 Renegotiation; Col Friedman, IGD, to IG, 11 Nov 43, AFCF 333.1 Inspection (Bulky).

[35] Budget Officer, AFAMC, to CGMC, 28 Jan 43; Price Adjustment Br, AFAMC, to WDPAB, 26 Jun 43. Both in AFCF 161 Renegotiation.

[36] Deputy Chief, Price Adjustment Br, MM&D, to Pricing Methods Br, Purchases Div, ASF, 18 Dec 43, AFCF 400.19; MM&D to CGMC, 31 Jan 44, AFCF 161 Renegotiation.

made during the life of a contract, they were instructed to report each price change as it occurred. This was sound enough in principle and no great burden so long as it was confined to airframe manufacturers or others turning out relatively few categories of end items, but a firm such as General Electric, for example, posed an entirely different problem. With literally thousands of different types of items on contract at any given time, many of them subject to rather frequent price changes, the reports of even a single firm such as General Electric could grow to a staggering volume. In short order the Price Adjustment staff begged for a change in procedure to keep from being buried under a mountain of paper.[37] Too much information could be as fatal to good administration as too little information; to have a crucial bit of data "lost in the files" when needed was hardly better than not to have it at all.

From bitter experience, renegotiators learned they had to give heed to the qualitative as well as the quantitative aspects of the information amassed for their use. They discovered that the most obvious parallels could turn out to be deceptive. Before making comparisons—using the profit ratios of one manufacturer to establish criteria for dealing with another—price adjustment officers had to be sure they were comparing the same things. If one manufacturer computed his profit on a sales volume including the cost of government-furnished equipment while another excluded all such costs, the two returns would bear little if any relation to one another.[38] The same was true in comparing seemingly identical end items. A case in point concerned aircraft engine starters. When one contractor quoted unit prices nearly $100 below another to the apparent detriment of the latter, a careful investigation revealed that the items in question were only remotely comparable since the more expensive one was fully equipped with all the necessary accessories while the less expensive one was not.[39]

Even where two manufacturers produced the same item according to a common specification, price adjusters found that it was dangerous to attempt comparisons. Production runs of different length, among other considerations, could bring surprisingly wide variations in price. A Jack and Heintz autopilot at $2,230 might appear to reflect a closer price than a Sperry autopilot at $3,215, but it was highly pertinent to know that Sperry had had only one-twentieth of the volume enjoyed by Jack and Heintz. Moreover, the size of the successive order increments awarded to Jack and Heintz, viz., 1,000, then 4,000, and finally 19,500, was considerably more favorable to production planning and tooling than the successive orders placed with Sperry—an initial order of 204, then an order for 921, and finally an order for 166 units.[40]

---

[37] Col Dyson, to CGMC, 5 Apr 43, AFCF 161 Renegotiation. For an insight on the difficulties of record keeping in renegotiation, see also 1st Ind, Chief, Price Adjustment Br, MM&D, to CGMC, 3 Nov 43, AFCF 161 Renegotiation.

[38] Col Dyson to CGMC, 6 Mar 43, AFCF 161 Contract Regulations.

[39] Memo, Dir, Purchases Div, ASF, for AFMM&D, 29 Apr 43; Chief, Procurement Br, MM&D, to Purchases Div, ASF, 26 May 43 with Incls. Both in AFCF 400.19.

[40] *Ibid.* See also, the warnings against unqualified comparisons in Chief, Price Adjustment Br, MM&D, to CGMC, 19 Jan 44, AFCF 400.19.

Thus, renegotiation was not a job for bookkeepers in the narrow sense of the term. The financial record alone was not sufficient. Since the determination of reasonable profit levels was left to discretion rather than to a formula, and since discretion involved such a wide variety of considerations, it followed that the officers who undertook the work of renegotiation had to understand the whole range of procurement problems—technical, financial, and legal. And what is more, they had to exercise the greatest care to be certain that all the pertinent factors were considered before they drew comparisons among producers and drafted settlements accordingly.

The conduct of price adjustment operations would have been complicated even had Congress seen fit to pass no legislation on the subject beyond the original Renegotiation Act of 1942. Of course, no such legislative stability was to be expected. A statute affecting so many individuals and often compelling a return of profits to the government was certain to provoke well-nigh endless complaint to Congress. The departmental renegotiators themselves would have welcomed a number of useful amendments. Operational experience had pointed out a number of places where administration of the act could be substantially improved by legislative action.[41]

The initiation of major amendments to the 1942 statute was not a step to be undertaken lightly. Once opened, there was no telling where the measure might end. Under pressure from outspoken and disgruntled constituents, Congress might finally turn out a watered down law even less satisfactory than the original act. When it appeared, however, that some form of amendment was probably inevitable, the War Department Price Adjustment Board decided to seize the initiative by proposing those changes that appeared administratively most desirable.

The full story of the War Department role in relation to the Renegotiation Act of 1943 lies beyond the compass of this study.[42] Nonetheless, consideration of one or two aspects of this episode may afford some insights on the interrelationships of military administration and the legislative process. Congress, in passing the original act of 1942, had moved against profiteering, and the act in many ways reflected a punitive spirit. This was all very well so long as the measure remained a matter only of discussion, but it became quite another matter when ordinary businessmen, who certainly did not regard themselves as unpatriotic profiteers, suddenly found that they too were expected to renegotiate.

Less than a year after they had been calling with righteous indignation for scalps, a number of congressmen qualified their anger by urging more care in the selection of scalps, especially those of small business.

The upshot of this congressional sensitivity to the cries of small business was a proposal to increase the volume of business automatically exempt from renego-

---

[41] Smith, *The Army and Economic Mobilization*, pp. 354-57.

[42] The renegotiation statute debated during 1943 was actually enacted as a section of the 1943 Revenue Act, passed February 25, 1944, as Public 235, 78th Congress. It applied to all war contracts in fiscal years ending after 30 June 1943. There were numerous minor amendments not mentioned here, enacted between 28 April 1942 and 25 February 1944.

PRICE ADJUSTMENT

tiation. Where the original act freed a firm from renegotiation if its government contracts totaled less than $100,000, the proposed amendment would raise the exemption to $500,000. Although this change implied at least the dubious assumption that small business was intrinsically less prone to profiteering than big business, the War Department actively supported the move. As the docket of renegotiation cases mounted steadily and price adjustment teams fell further and further behind, they welcomed any change that would cut the backlog to manageable proportions. Fully one-third of the cases in Air Forces files could be dropped if Congress accepted the higher exemption level.[43]

Had Congress moved promptly when the proposed amendment first came up, the task of administration undoubtedly would have been simplified. But Congress did not act promptly; it could not. By its very nature the legislative process is ponderous. There were hearings and debates; the issues involved were argued for months. Meanwhile, the officers engaged in price administration had to perform their duties against a background of continual uncertainty.

As soon as word of the impending increase in the exemption limit began to circulate, many contractors whose volume fell below the proposed $500,000 level began to drag their feet when invited to negotiate on new contracts. If they could stall off renegotiation until Congress acted, they reasoned, they might avoid having to make refunds. Reports of this kind of trouble began to appear at Wright Field in early 1943 and continued to plague the price administrators until Congress finally passed an amended Renegotiation Act in February 1944.[44]

While it was easy to blame the legislators, criticism of Congress was bootless. Administrators had to learn to live within the hazards inherent in self-government. In this case self-criticism would have been wiser, for the very policy the War Department had approved and even sponsored turned out to be most harmful. Manufacturers whose volume mounted toward the $500,000 limit sometimes showed a reluctance to accept additional orders, which would push them over the line and make renegotiation unavoidable. As a consequence, procurement officers actually reported instances where they found it difficult to place certain orders. Furthermore, by the time Congress raised the exemption level, the original justification presented by the War Department for such a move no longer existed. The discouraging backlog of cases in 1943 melted before an aggressive and determined assault carried out by price adjustment teams at Wright Field as well as in the districts. To make matters worse, a postwar appraisal revealed that some of the most outrageous and excessive profits were made by manufacturers whose limited volume automatically exempted them from renegotiation.[45]

To single out one unfortunate aspect of the 1944 amendment of the Renegotiation Act for analysis while ignoring all the other facets of that elaborate piece

---

[43] Actg Control Officer, MM&D, to WDPAB, 18 Dec 43, AFCF 161 Renegotiation.

[44] Col Dyson to WDPAB, 17 Mar 43, AFCF 161 Renegotiation.

[45] Smith, *The Army and Economic Mobilization*, ch. XVI, especially pp. 375–78.

of legislation would be grossly unfair. There were a number of constructive features. Not least among these was the stipulation requiring all contractors whose business brought them under the act to file regular statements on their finances and general operations for use by price adjustment personnel. This simplified the task of administration immensely, since it automatically placed most of the data necessary for a preliminary screening directly into the hands of those who needed it.

In a sense, a large part of the 1944 amendment only confirmed by statute what was already being done administratively. Although the revised measure refrained, as did the original law, from attempting the impossible—a uniform definition of excessive profits—it did list the factors to be taken into account in determining such profits. Actually the list was little more than a recital of the criteria already used by the negotiators, yet this was by no means wasted effort.[46] By making it compulsory for manufacturers to send in the factual data necessary and by formalizing the criteria to be used in determining profits, Congress took a long step forward. Thereafter the conduct of renegotiations became increasingly routine. Price adjustments could not be wrought by formula, but as experience was codified in standardized forms and simplified administrative procedures were hammered out, more and more cases could be handled by less skillful and less imaginative renegotiators. This freed the abler and more experienced staff members to deal with the many really novel problems of policy posed by the amended Renegotiation Act.[47] Among the most important of these was the task of accommodating the rather subtle transition in philosophy that characterized the new legislation, a transition from profit curbing to price setting.

Renegotiation and Repricing

Congress enacted the Renegotiation Act of 1942 to recover excess profits and to prevent profiteering. Nevertheless, the organization established within the War Department to carry out the terms of the act was called the Price Adjustment Board rather than the Profits Control Board. The terminology is significant; it shows that from the very beginning the Department's policy was to stress constructive pricing—close pricing in the interest of efficient operations—rather than the punishment of profiteers.[48] Yet for all these intentions, renegotiation during 1942 was largely a matter of profits recovery. This was probably inevitable. Umbrella pricing had characterized many of the fixed-price contracts written during the early period of rearmament, and during 1942 the renegotiation teams had had to devote most of their time to rendering the fat that experience had shown to be present in so many contracts.

By 1943, however, the situation was

---
[46] Statutory Renegotiation, Lecture by McCorskey. The criteria included, among other things: efficiency; similarity of wartime output to peacetime product; private or public financing; risks involved; and contribution, complexity, and extent of subcontracting.

[47] For a survey of the problems anticipated in 1944, see AFMM&D to WDPAB, 12 Jan 44, AFCF 161 Renegotiation.
[48] AFMM&D, to Mr. Emmons Bryant, jr., 12 Jan 44, AFCF 161 Renegotiation.

PRICE ADJUSTMENT

quite different. Profit recovery declined in importance as the emphasis shifted toward improved pricing, prospective as well as retrospective. In short, the work of the renegotiators began to converge with that of the procurement officers who negotiated new contracts. While functionally understandable, this convergence threatened to bring jurisdictional conflicts as the work of the negotiators and that of the renegotiators came to be in many respects identical. Moreover, there was an added difficulty.[49] Whatever may have been their avowed philosophy and sincere intention, during their first year of action the renegotiators had become identified in the business world with the refunding of profits. From the contractor's point of view this was often a most unhappy experience. As the renegotiators turned more and more of their attention to repricing, they did so under the stigma of their past activities as profit seizers.

Although the term *repricing* was often used in a loose sense to describe the work of the renegotiators, it actually had a rather narrow technical definition that should be differentiated from the several other operations generally comprehended under the word. To reprice a contract was to reopen the question of price for the contract as a whole. This meant renegotiating the price retroactively for the completed portion of a contract while at the same time setting a price on the portion yet undelivered. Forward or future pricing, as it was sometimes called, was somewhat different. This kind of pricing applied only to the undelivered portion of an existing contract.[50]

There were both advantages and disadvantages in these pricing techniques. Future pricing could be initiated at any point in the life of a contract and was therefore administratively convenient. But a contract could be so priced only once. This meant that the price for the undelivered portion of a contract would be set after a trial run, but once set, that price would remain fixed and any savings the contractor could effect thereafter would accrue to him. Repricing, on the other hand, applied to the whole contract and thus to the recovery of excess profits on the completed portions as well as closer pricing on the remaining deliveries. But repricing had to be accomplished at some predetermined point in the life of the contract, usually after completion of 40 percent of the deliveries or after a fair trial period for cost determination. To delay repricing further or to any point near the end of deliveries would have the effect of converting the procurement into a cost-plus-percentage-of-cost contract prohibited by law, since this would amount to negotiating a profit after the costs were known.

Still another variety of price adjustment was periodic repricing. Here the government and the contractor agreed in advance to reprice the undelivered portion of a contract either at periodic intervals set beforehand or at the option of either party. Periodic repricing was gen-

---

[49] AFMM&D to CGMC, 11 Jan 44; Chief, Price Adjustment Br, to CGMC, 19 Jan 44. Both in AFCF 161 Renegotiation.

[50] Flexible Pricing in Fixed Price Contracts, Lecture by Dinkelspiel. Forward pricing was first used by the Air Forces in December 1943. See Davis, History of AAF Materiel Command: 1943, WFHO, Jul 44, ch. II.

erally popular with air arm contractors. Among other features, it offered an alternative to the cumbersome and all but unworkable escalator clauses, which had proved to be so difficult to apply during the early phases of the rearmament program.[51]

The culminating development in the field of price adjustment during the war was the introduction of a practice called company pricing. Early in 1944 it became clear that neither the procurement officers who negotiated contracts nor the renegotiators who tried to reprice them were really getting the kind of close pricing that would compel manufacturers to be efficient and economical. Their most determined efforts frequently proved unsuccessful. Manufacturers continued to be fearful of losses, and even where they subsequently made refunds most willingly, they continued to seek umbrella prices with generous contingency allowances. And so long as this practice persisted, no matter how co-operative contractors were in returning excess profits, they were not under the continual pressure to seek efficiency that an initially close price would have exerted. Obviously, some means for arriving at closer initial pricing were urgently required. Company pricing appeared to provide an answer.

Company pricing was nothing more than a matter of getting an over-all perspective on the total volume handled by a single manufacturer.[52] A great many firms held contracts with two or more services, and co-ordination of procurement between the services was notoriously poor.[53] Thus, by arranging a pricing session at which representatives of all the procurement agencies concerned sat down with the contractor at one time, it was possible to arrive at closer prices. Duplicate charges for overhead, for example, could be eliminated as the renegotiators considered the entire picture of a manufacturer's operations.

The technique of company pricing can be illustrated by a single example. Procurement officers at Wright Field worked for weeks trying to reach agreement with Beech Aircraft on a fair price in a production contract for the UC–45, a light utility airplane. The combined efforts of the price analysis staff, auditors, and renegotiators at Wright Field indicated that $33,000 would constitute a fair unit price. Beech held out for $40,000. This spread was much too great to compromise, but Beech remained adamant. Then the negotiators tried the company pricing approach. In all, some twenty persons attended the conference called: fifteen representatives from the Army and Navy and five company men. After a good deal of parley, the root of the trouble became clear. The estimated $33,000 figure, the manufacturer admitted, was probably not far off, but the company executives were decidedly fearful of the losses they might have to absorb if this and the firm's other contracts were to be terminated abruptly. Here was the joker. Termination costs were an entirely uncertain factor; they could not be estimated

---

[51] Flexible Pricing in Fixed Price Contracts, Lecture by Dinkelspiel.

[52] Negotiation and Administration of Contracts. Lecture by Scarff.

[53] Draper and Strauss, Coordination of Procurement Between the War and Navy Departments, vol. II, p. 38ff.

PRICE ADJUSTMENT

in advance, so the manufacturer had tried to protect himself in the only way he knew how—by adding in a "fib factor" that no amount of price analysis could justify on a rational basis.

Once he was reassured that his total workload would be repriced if terminations set in, the manufacturer agreed to a unit price of $35,000 for the UC-45. When the contract was finally completed, an audit revealed that the manufacturer's unit costs actually turned out to be less than $35,000 and Beech made a substantial profit even after refunding a large sum. To be sure, renegotiation at the end of the contract could have recaptured any excess profits there may have been under a $40,000 unit price, but meanwhile the manufacturer would have been under virtually no pressure to be efficient and economical in his operations.[54]

After a trial period during the first half of 1944, company pricing became a regular AAF policy. Needless to say, since the Air Forces did business with several thousand contractors, the tremendous burden of cost accounting essential to a successful foray into company pricing made it imperative to establish some rational system of selection. One screening device used was to pick out all firms reporting a profit of 20 percent or more on sales. This gave a list of about a hundred firms, an entirely manageable number. Of course, a high profit did not always indicate the need for repricing. For example, one manufacturer of screw machine products in the Central Procurement District consistently reported profits well above 20 percent on sales, but with equal consistency his prices ran well below those of his competitors.[55] The services of the renegotiators would be far better used elsewhere.

Company pricing gave air arm procurement officials a weapon they had long needed. It opened the manufacturer's subcontract prices to possible revision. Hitherto, under a fixed-price contract, no matter how hard the negotiators worked to get a close price, they could not reach the subcontractors who operated through tier after tier below the prime. Inasmuch as roughly half of every dollar spent for air matériel went to suppliers below the prime contractor, a major portion of most fixed-price contracts was beyond reach. The Renegotiation Act of 1942 did make it possible to take away excess profits from subs as well as primes. But this was after-the-fact recovery. So long as the subs remained free to quote high prices to primes in the first instance, they executed their contracts under the protection of a price umbrella and without the pressure of a close price to force them to be economical in the use of materials, labor, and so on. Under the company pricing program, the renegotiators could study subcontract prices at first hand. Where the facts seemed to warrant, individual subs could be asked to lower their prices to the prime.

By the time company pricing got under way in 1944, the procurement services had acquired an additional weapon of coercion from Congress. As early as 1940 Congress wrote into the Selective Service Act a special grant of power to compel manufacturers to accept military contracts or submit to the seizure of their

---

[54] Company Pricing Program, lecture, AAF Contracting Officers School, WF, 15 Dec 44, WFHO.

[55] *Ibid.*

plants. This authority was of no use whatsoever in dealing with a subcontractor who was only too willing to take on war work—at a high price. In the Revenue Act of 1943, Congress tried to rectify this weakness. Title VIII of the act empowered the government to issue compulsory orders or unilateral determinations of contract price where manufacturers refused to quote prices regarded as reasonable by the government's negotiators.[56]

Just how effective the compulsory order could be is suggested by the following example. A well-known supplier quoted $136,000 for an order of special hand tools. Investigation revealed that the firm was actually subcontracting the job to another firm for $128,000. This second company in turn sub-subcontracted to a third at $86,000, but a cost study showed that this company had actually completed the order for $74,000. Since the original jobber held the design rights to the tool in question, a procurement could not be made directly from the company that had actually done the work. The alternative, when the original jobber refused to consider price adjustment, was a mandatory order. This was issued, and a fair price was worked out.[57]

With but one exception, as soon as a mandate was issued, the manufacturers involved fell into line. The mere threat of force was usually sufficient to get results. Perhaps "usually" is too strong a word. The Air Forces resorted to compulsory pricing in no more than seven cases during the war. There is, however, no record of the many cases where the threat of compulsion proved sufficient to win co-operation.[58]

A number of safeguards were written into Title VIII to prevent abuse of the mandating power. Before a compulsory order could be issued, it had to be shown that the company in question could make the item desired and that the item could not be procured elsewhere in comparable quantity and quality in the time allowed. The best guarantee that compulsion would not be overused was the simple circumstance that the whole process was very cumbersome to apply where a manufacturer wished to resist tooth and nail. Compulsory determination of price touched only a small portion of the total problem of negotiation. This still left such matters as license rights and other contract terms open to debate, so the resort to a mandate most assuredly did not guarantee the government an easy way out in difficult cases.

Renegotiation in Review

All together, the Air Forces renegotiators completed 13,344 individual price adjustment cases—17.6 percent of the total handled by the War Department. During the first year of operations, from April 1942 to April 1943, this brought in recoveries of excess profits amounting to just less than a billion dollars. By the end of 1943 the total recovered had grown to somewhat more than two bil-

---

[56] Section 801, title VIII, Revenue Act of 1943, February 25, 1944 (58 Stat 92).

[57] Mandatory Orders, Lecture by Robinson; Negotiation and Administration of Contracts, Lecture by Scarff.

[58] *Ibid.* See also, ASF Purchases Div, Purchasing Policies and Practices, pt. III, sec. II H, Compulsory Procedures, pp. 35off.

lions. The year 1944 saw another billion and a half added.[59]

Although big round billion-dollar figures make a splendid impression, they probably should not be taken too seriously. The billions refunded were important, but the exact totals reported do not begin to tell the whole story. Voluntary refunds can be added to the profits recaptured by statutory renegotiation. It is impossible, however, to compute the savings made in the form of lower prices agreed to during renegotiation that applied to future contracts or to the undelivered portions of existing contracts.

Lower prices undoubtedly contributed a greater proportion of "savings" than profit recoveries. While dollar recoveries from contractors look impressive, it should never be forgotten that these dollars were really cheap dollars since the excess profits taxes would have recovered about 75 percent of the total anyhow.[60] In short, profits do not tell the important story of savings. The really great contribution of renegotiation lay in the pressure it exerted on costs. Although no figures are readily at hand, the record implicit in the price adjustment operations conducted during the war years makes this clear. Renegotiation led to closer pricing, which in turn forced manufacturers to be more efficient in their operations if they were to make profits. Since the general ratio of costs to profits during the war was approximately nine to one, it is clear that costs offered a far more fruitful field for savings than did profits.

Although statutory renegotiation was one of the truly significant administrative innovations of the war years, the drawbacks inherent in the use of the tool should never be overlooked. There was grave danger that the use of renegotiation would tend to discourage incentive: "Why work hard? They will take it all away from you anyhow." To provide maximum incentives in order to encourage efficient management, price adjustment teams had to award high profits to those who earned them. But high profit percentages make bad headlines. They encouraged the cry of profiteering, for it was hard to make the public realize that low costs—not low profits—were the vital consideration. Renegotiation, to be an effective instrument for military procurement, required a continuing campaign of public education. At the very least the contractors had to be persuaded that efficiency would be rewarded in proportion to achievement and not according to some percentage yardstick popularly regarded as "reasonable."

---

[59] Smith, *The Army and Economic Mobilization*, p. 390, Table 41; AFBFO to CGASF, 12 May 43 and 15 Dec 43, AFCF 161 Renegotiation. See also, Proc Div Annual Rpt, WF, 1944, WFHO.

[60] Statutory Renegotiation; Lecture by McCorskey, North American Aviation, Brief History, p. 125.

CHAPTER XVIII

Contract Termination

The Background of Termination

On occasion military contracts had to be terminated or canceled before the completion of deliveries. Changing requirements during the period of hostilities as well as the unpredictable date of the enemy's surrender made large numbers of terminations inevitable. Just as inevitably, abrupt cancellations gave rise to an almost endless series of problems: what was to be done with partially completed work, with untouched inventory of raw materials, and with materials on order from suppliers and vendors? What compensation could the contractor expect for expenses already incurred and what were his obligations to the government? If the interests of buyer and seller alike were to be preserved equitably, these and many other problems had to be anticipated contractually.

The War Department had ample forewarning on the importance of carefully drafted termination clauses in military contracts. For want of such preparation, the sudden terminations made at the end of World War I brought chaos. Contractors went bankrupt and thousands of cases went into litigation in the Court of Claims. One of the largest of these was still unsettled when the Japanese struck Pearl Harbor. In all, the nation paid a high price for the contracts faultily drafted during World War I.

Many officers who lived through the termination fiasco after the armistice in 1918 were anxious to see that it was not repeated. But the best of plans easily went astray. Terminations had played virtually no part in peacetime buying, and, with many other more immediate problems pressing for attention, procurement officers gave little thought to the intricate task of polishing termination clauses. Some mobilization planners considered the question of termination clauses during the between-war years, but beyond recognizing the importance of the problem they did little.

Thus it came about, when war again broke out in Europe, that all six of the approved or standard contract forms used by the War Department contained standard or boiler plate termination provisions. Each form represented a stockpile of clauses that the procurement officers of the several services were free to use or not as the peculiar circumstances suggested. Even where they were used, the approved termination clauses left much to be desired. They were, to put it mildly, rather primitive beginnings. Indeed, the thinking of procurement officers on the whole complex question of terminations was almost totally undeveloped.[1]

---

[1] The foregoing paragraphs are based largely on Smith, *The Army and Economic Mobilization*, ch. XXVII.

One small but rather significant bit of evidence in the files at Wright Field gives a fair appraisal of the neglect characterizing the matter of contract termination during the first two years of the emergency. In these early months of rearmament, all papers relating to contract cancellation were placed in decimal file 164, the conventional file location for cases of nonperformance. Doubtless this was merely a continuation of the peacetime routine when just about the only terminations encountered were those arising from defaulting contractors. But cancellations for the convenience of the government—the justification for most wartime or war-end terminations—were something very different from defaults, which implied a failure of the contractor to perform.

By the eve of Pearl Harbor air arm officers had come to realize the inadequacy of their thinking on the over-all implications of termination. From all over the country complaints rolled in from subcontractors protesting what they regarded as the unjust cancellation clauses prime contractors were forcing them to accept.[2] The government's termination clauses with the primes were generous enough; they made the government liable for all obligations incurred. The primes, on the other hand, failed to extend the same generosity to their subcontractors. Should the primes be compelled to do so by contractual mandate? The air arm procurement staff decided against such action. Fixed-price contractors should solve their own problems. If the air arm tried to dictate the terms of relationship for tier after tier of subs, the procurement staff would be hopelessly swamped with work.[3]

Although much could be said for the wisdom of the air arm position, it did not answer the questions raised by the subcontractors. Fearful of the future, they pressed for further clarification of termination policy. In this they were perfectly correct; termination in its broadest implications should be explored and policies worked out accordingly. Unfortunately, when the matter came to a head the moment was scarcely propitious; it was the week after Pearl Harbor when every procurement officer in the air arm had his sights on the immediate goal—production. Termination seemed as far away as the end of the war. "There is," said the contract chief, "no time for such legal discussions."[4] Officers burdened with current operations could scarcely be expected to find leisure for speculative or philosophical reflection on long-range problems.

The Character of the Termination Problem

While the end of hostilities would most certainly produce an enormous wave of contract cancellations, the termination problem was by no means so far off. Procurement officers found occasion to cancel individual contracts even before the

---

[2] Memo, F. W. Ayers, OPM, for M. C. Meigs, 29 Oct 41, AFCF 161 CPFF; Maguire to IPS, WF, undated (Oct 41), WF Contract files, 360.01 and related correspondence.

[3] Memo, Asst to Chief, Mat Div, for Aircraft Br, Mfg Sec, OPM, 6 Nov 41, AFCF 161 CPFF; Col Volandt to Chief, Contract Sec, 3 Dec 41, 165 Classes of Contract. See also, Chief, Contract Sec, to Packard Motor Car Co., 16 Oct 40, AFCF 333.1 Contract Inspection.

[4] Chief, Contract Sec, to Chief, Mat Div, 18 Dec 41, WF Contract files, 360.01.

nation's forces had fairly engaged the enemy. For example, a design change sometimes forced a contractor to cancel a subcontractor. Where two different firms supplied the same item to a prime and one made faster deliveries at a lower cost than another, it could be wise to terminate the contract of the least efficient producer. Even airframe builders whose production became obsolete were occasionally terminated.[5]

In short, termination was a current problem. If the termination procedures were slow and cumbersome, the manufacturers concerned might be delayed for weeks and months. Litigation could drain off managerial energies better spent in breaking production records. Inventory disputes could tie up tons of material desperately needed for the war effort. From whatever angle one approached it, termination was an integral part of current procurement.

On the other hand, while the termination problem was very real, it was not entirely tangible. In a sense, the very core of the termination problem was psychological. It was more a question of what the contractors feared might happen than what actually was happening. The boiler plate cancellation clause included in all air arm contracts did guarantee to repay all primes and, by extension, their subs too, for all expenditures made. Nevertheless, as one major engine manufacturer put it, the contractors lived in "mortal terror" lest a hasty termination catch them in an overextended position and drive them into bankruptcy.[6]

The contractors' fears were not entirely groundless. Besides some old-line firms who could remember the disasters that followed World War I, there were others with long experience in government contracting who knew that after-the-fact disallowances by the General Accounting Office could turn a generous cancellation settlement into a serious loss. Finally, as every company comptroller knew, even full compensation for every penny of expenditure if long delayed in payment could wreck an otherwise prosperous concern.

At the root of the contractors' fears was the knowledge that virtually every leading manufacturer in the aviation field was overextended financially. By 1943, for example, the six largest airframe builders had outstanding commitments amounting to ten times their working capital. Unless promptly reimbursed by the government, these obligations could absorb the contractors' working capital in three weeks.[7] One manufacturer stated: "The payroll is so big and the job of paying off is so complex, . . . the outgo would break us before we could finish the task."[8]

As most manufacturers saw the problem, delays rather than disputes over amounts due offered the greatest threat. On the other hand, some were loath to be bound by the decisions of a contracting officer who might not allow many of the costs the manufacturer believed to be reasonable. Disagreements of this sort could be carried to the Court of Claims, but few if any contractors had illusions about this remedy. Common law reme-

---

[5] Relation of Procurement Activities to Readjustment . . . , Lecture, by Maj R. H. Demuth, AAF Contracting Officers School, WF, 28 Apr 45, WFHO.
[6] See, for example, Wilson, *Slipstream*, p. 256.
[7] Callery, "Review of American Aircraft Finance," *Air Affairs* (Summer 1947), p. 489.
[8] Wilson, *Slipstream*, pp. 261–62.

CONTRACT TERMINATION

dies were almost certain to be slow and costly, so much so as to make administrative solutions preferable.[9]

In the final analysis, a successful resolution of the termination problem would hinge upon the attitudes of the contractors. And this in turn would depend not so much upon the letter of the law—upon the wording of individual termination clauses—as upon the attitude of those who administered them. What was Air Forces policy on termination? How was it to be administered, and who would meet this special responsibility? Merely to ask such questions was to recognize how unprepared the procurement staff was in this important respect.

The termination problem came up again and again during the early months of the rearmament rush and was as often brushed aside. Other difficulties seemed more urgent. Then, during the fall of 1942, air arm procurement officers met a termination controversy too big to ignore. The company concerned was the Bendix Aviation Corporation, a major producer of aircraft accessories holding literally dozens of separate contracts. The problem at hand was to devise a termination article that would provide realistic protection for the company as well as the government.

The staff officers who sat down to work out solutions for the many issues raised by the Bendix case realized full well that whatever they did would be of more than immediate significance. The Bendix termination article would establish not only an administrative pattern but also set important precedents for policy.[10] Accordingly, they moved with caution. For weeks they conferred with Bendix representatives to hammer out successive drafts of a termination agreement describing both the procedures to be followed and the terms of settlement. They were careful to circulate each revision to the several echelons concerned. It was especially important to keep the Under Secretary informed. His approval would be necessary on the policies reflected in the final product, and the safest way to win his assent was to educate him, sharing with him the successive stages in the evolution of a paper. Then, they hoped, when the final draft came up for signature, he would be predisposed to sign it.

By the same token the headquarters staff officers in Washington who actually worked out the details with Bendix found it expedient to circulate the several drafts of their agreement to the working echelon at Wright Field. Procurement officers at Wright Field, with their wide experience, ought to be able to criticize the drafts with constructive discernment; moreover, they would be the individuals who would actually apply the termination policies finally agreed upon. Getting their criticisms in advance might save endless complaints later. As the sage old colonel said in November 1918, when asked if he had learned anything from the war: "Find out how your subordinates expect to tackle the job you assign, then write their orders accordingly."

A glance at a few of the questions raised by the Bendix settlement will sug-

---

[9] See, for example, Michigan Tool Co., to Chief, Proc Br, MM&D, 26 Apr 43, and to OCofOrd, 25 Jun 43, AFCF 164 Non Performance.

[10] Maj G. B. Brophy to Col Volandt, 21 Sep 42, AFCF 164 Non Performance; Volandt to Chief Contract Sec, WF, 19 Oct 42, AFCF 161 Renegotiation.

gest why the termination clauses used when war came marked only the beginning of the matter. Should the manufacturer be awarded a profit on partially finished work or work in process at the time of cancellation? If the final settlement were long delayed, should the government pay interest on the sums awarded; if so, what should be the rate? If the contractor accepted an agreement and Congress subsequently extended more generous terms, should the contractor benefit accordingly? These and dozens of similar questions convinced everybody concerned that contract termination was an extremely complex subject not to be brushed off as a remote postwar worry.[11]

Without prompt agreement on terminations, the Bendix representatives contended, the company would be forced to curtail its production program. The trouble stemmed largely from the dual position Bendix occupied as both prime and subcontractor. As a manufacturer of various accessory items and instruments purchased directly by the AAF as government-furnished equipment, Bendix was a prime contractor. But as the manufacturer of a variety of accessories in general use by airframe and engine builders, Bendix was a supplier and subcontractor to scores of firms throughout the industry. Taken all together, the hundreds of contracts Bendix had entered, both as prime and as sub, extended the corporation's obligations far beyond the point justified by its capital structure. Fearful lest the existing contract clauses prove entirely inadequate to prevent bankruptcy in the wake of large-scale terminations, the company managers were reluctant to enter any new contracts until their position was reinforced.[12]

The Bendix threat—for it amounted to that whether delivered as an ultimatum or not—put AAF policy makers in a difficult position. Bendix products were absolutely vital to the war effort. Any interruption in the placement of contracts could be disastrous. The only alternative was to produce a sound termination agreement. The months of preliminary discussion that had already taken place made it relatively easy to narrow the areas of disagreement. Bendix' role as a prime contractor raised no insurmountable difficulties since the cancellation terms offered to primes by the government were generally favorable. But Bendix the subcontractor was an entirely different matter. Here the company representatives claimed that they were inadequately protected and that a sudden wave of cancellations would leave them with crippling inventory losses.

With the remaining issue thus narrowly focused, the air arm staff cast about for specific solutions. They first considered a plan whereby the government would agree to acquire all Bendix' inventory of subcontract items and to assume all its obligations as a supplier. In addition, the proposal included a 2-percent margin on all work in progress. The 2 percent would serve more as a contingency allowance or cushion against overhead costs than as a profit. These terms looked generous, but they suffered from certain drawbacks. The 2-percent return was less than Bendix would receive un-

---

[11] Col Volandt to CGMC, 29 Oct 42, AFCF 161 Renegotiation.

[12] Memo, CGMC for USW, 4 Feb 43, 164 Non Performance.

der many of its existing contracts as a supplier. Moreover, in taking over the entire Bendix inventory, the government would acquire a host of problems for which it was ill prepared. As an alternative, the procurement staff suggested letting Bendix, in an eighteen-month period, try to dispose of the inventory through conventional channels, then applying the 2-percent rate to the remainder. Bendix preferred the alternative offer. Nonetheless, when the agreement went to the Under Secretary's office, it was returned without approval.[13] The negotiators had taken the precaution of keeping the upper echelons informed of every step along the way, but to no avail.

The trouble was that six months had elapsed between the time the Bendix case first came up and the day the settlement emerged. During the six months the whole complex picture of termination had come into focus. By the time the AAF negotiators were ready with their one prototype case, it had become clear that termination, like renegotiation, should be handled across the board, encompassing a manufacturer's entire workload in precisely the same fashion as company pricing.[14]

In sum, leadership in the field of termination was not for the individual procurement services within the Army nor even for the War Department alone, but for every department engaged in the war effort. The determination of broad outlines of policy passed more and more into the hands of a special joint organization established for the sole purpose of coping with the termination problem. The full story of how this organization evolved is a study in itself and quite beyond the scope of the present volume. Here it will be sufficient to indicate in briefest outline the structures erected and the policies worked out for general application.

The Organization for Termination

During November 1943 the six major contracting agencies of the war period—the Army, the Navy, the Maritime Commission, the Treasury, the Reconstruction Finance Corporation, and the Foreign Economic Administration—established a Joint Contract Termination Board to lay down over-all principles and procedures governing all war contracts. Although not fully appreciated as such at the time, the establishment of the board marked a major advance in the direction of co-ordination.

The first job before the board was to draft a uniform contract termination clause to simplify administration and bring equity in dealing with industry. This was only the beginning, since the procurement services had already learned that applying the law in particular instances posed the really difficult problems. The board had to work out standards of allowable costs, procedures for dealing with subcontractors, and techniques for company-wide terminations. Two matters of the utmost importance to contractors were plant clearance and interim financing. If manufacturers were to get back into useful production promptly, the board would have to de-

---

[13] Memo, CGMC for USW, 15 Mar 43; Col Volandt to CGMC, 25 Mar 43. Both in AFCF 164 Non Performance.

[14] For an excellent review and appreciation of this situation, see Agenda for Meeting With General Echols, 23 Feb 44, unsigned study in the reading file of Chief, Resources Div, MM&D, filed in AAG (AGAW-J) Rcd Group 506 (A-50-21).

vise means of removing and disposing of the government property—materials, special tooling, work in progress, and the like—that cluttered contractors' plants at the end of every job. Moreover, if the national economy were to avoid serious dislocation when the mass of war-end terminations arrived, some means of ensuring adequate financing for contractors in the throes of reconversion would also have to be found. Finally, the board would have to take steps to see that appropriate administrative procedures were worked out by the several services to ensure compliance all down the line.[15]

During the first half of 1944 the work of the board was vigorously debated in the press and on the Hill. Since a very large percentage of the nation's industries was concerned with military contracts, the debate attracted widespread public interest. Finally in July 1944 Congress passed a Contract Settlement Act, which not only gave legislative sanction to much of the work already done by the board but strengthened the existing establishment.[16] In general the act had one major objective—it sought to minimize dislocations of the national economy when mass terminations began. Speed in conducting termination proceedings was imperative. To this end the act specifically authorized negotiated settlements. Termination teams could sit down with industry representatives and write termination agreements just as though they were writing amendments or change orders to existing contracts in the normal course of business. Settlements reached in this way would be final, subject to review by the General Accounting Office only for the presence of fraud and for conformity with the terms of the settlement agreed upon.

Finality of settlement was crucially important to industry. Had they been subjected to the continuing threat of disallowances and reversals by the Comptroller General, few contractors could have moved boldly into the future. Instead of putting capital to work and increasing employment, they would have been induced to hold assets in reserve against contingencies.[17]

The Contract Settlement Act had other provisions for speeding the pace of termination. By authorizing negotiated settlements, the act minimized the enormous job of auditing that would have been necessary under the settlements by formula provided for in the boiler plate termination clause. But this still left the problem of physical assets. Here the act ensured speed by requiring the government to remove all property from a contractor's plant within sixty days after the contractor filed an inventory statement.[18]

Taken together, the Contract Settlement Act of 1944 and the administrative context in which it appeared—the work of the board as well as the regulations

---

[15] Memo, Chief, Contract Termination Br, for Chief, Resources Div, MM&D, 24 Dec 43, gives a rather full summary of the evolving termination organization. Resources Div reading file. See also, Smith, *The Army and Economic Mobilization*, ch. XXVII, especially pp. 628ff.

[16] Public 395, 78th Cong, 2d sess, July 1, 1944 (58 Stat 651).

[17] The contribution of Air Forces termination officials in defining the department's stand against the Comptroller General is clearly indicated in Memo, Charlton MacVeagh, Chairman, AAF Settlement Review Com, for Chief, Mat Div, MM&D, 5 Oct 43, AFCF 164 Non Performance.

[18] Memo, Chief, Contract Termination Br, for Chief, Resources Div, MM&D, 13 Dec 43, Resources Div reading file.

CONTRACT TERMINATION

and procedures it perfected—stand as a stimulating example of the high degree of co-operation that could be achieved among widely differing services when men of energy and imagination put their hearts into the effort. What was possible in unwinding contracts might equally well be possible when making them in the first place. But whatever influence the termination experience was to wield over those who looked toward improved co-ordination in the initial procurement process, lay in the future. This account deals only with the experience of the war years. Moreover, although an unusual degree of centralization was achieved in matters of policy formulation, the actual conduct of termination operations remained largely decentralized.

Within the War Department, the flow of policy downward from the interdepartmental apparatus of the Contract Settlement Act requires little explanation. The Under Secretary assigned primary responsibility for termination matters to a newly established Readjustment Division in the Army Service Forces. Since ASF and the Army Air Forces were separate but parallel commands, this created something of an anomaly by making the commanding general of the Air Forces look to a subordinate agency within ASF for policy in termination matters. An Air Forces representative was therefore made deputy director of the Readjustment Division, ASF, to ensure continual liaison.[19]

At Headquarters, AAF, a Settlement Review Committee officially handled all termination matters but actually delegated its operating functions to a Settlement Review Board at Wright Field. The organizations subsequently changed names from time to time, but the pattern of their operations remained substantially the same.

Implementing the joint termination operation proved to be anything but a routine task of administration. In view of the air arm struggles to build up a suitable staff of contract negotiators and renegotiators, the staggering problems encountered in lining up the necessary personnel for handling terminations can be appreciated. The negotiated contract authorized under the Settlement Act would prove a timesaver only if a skilled staff could be found to negotiate. When the war ended, virtually the entire force of negotiators and renegotiators could turn to termination work, but to wait until then would defeat the objectives of the Contract Settlement Act. Unless contracts were terminated promptly as the occasion demanded during the war, the backlog of unsettled cases would doubly compound the postwar rush. The only alternative was to recruit an entirely new staff of specialists to deal with terminations, though during 1944 the procurement organization was itself still recruiting personnel.[20] Here was the ultimate contradiction—the mobilizers and the demobilizers were in open competition in the midst of the war.

By the summer 1944, when the full implications of the task at hand became apparent, the Materiel Command was

---

[19] See ch. XIX, below, for further treatment of the Readjustment Division.

[20] Memo, Chief, Contract Termination Br, for Chief, Resources Div, MM&D, 4 Feb 44, Resources Div reading file; Study, prepared by Lt Col R. B. Murray, jr., Exec, Special Projects, Hq AAF, AFCF 164 Non Performance.

already building a large organization to specialize in this work. Termination activities were removed from the Procurement Division and entrusted to a newly formed Readjustment Division of equal status. Instead of the 300 terminators originally sought, the target was raised to 3,000. The new Readjustment Division hastily organized courses in a number of schools and began to teach contract termination. In all, 1,836 officers, 438 enlisted men, and 196 civilians took the training before fanning out into the procurement districts to form termination teams working with individual contractors.

Equally important was the need to make industry aware of the termination problem. To do this, the Readjustment Division helped conduct mass meetings attended by a total of more than 27,000 people representing contractors and subcontractors. Contractors in particular were urged to set up their own termination teams to meet the government's men halfway. By the end of 1944, 1,513 prime contractors had complied. Since the AAF at that time had only 1,562 prime contractors doing jobs in excess of $10,000, these crews more or less blanketed the field.

As usual, getting the proper information to the right people posed many problems. An information bulletin distributed to 2,500 Air Forces personnel and 14,000 manufacturers helped in some measure, and because a large portion of the termination burden lay in the tiers of subcontractors below the primes, the Readjustment Division made a special effort to persuade the primes to set up independent training programs for subs. Training kits were sent to primes willing to conduct classes of this sort. Wherever possible, the emphasis with primes and subs alike was on "pretermination"—lining up claims before the day of final termination arrived.[21] Spreading the word was important, but in the last analysis, the main job was to find the right people—and to find them without interfering with current procurement operations.

In a sense, the conflict of interests seen in the competition between the negotiators and the terminators reflected one of the basic dilemmas of the whole procurement problem. Those who made contracts and those who "unmade" them both served in the public interest. But they were to discover that the phrase "in the public interest" was a deceptively simple generalization. It tended to conceal the underlying reality. The public interest is not a single end; it is an enormously complex bundle of interests, often conflicting. Measures sincerely aimed at one portion of this interest may prove harmful to another. From hard experience officers learned that the real art of administration lies in the successful reconciliation of these conflicting pulls.

Some Illustrative Aspects of Administration

The business of war, it has been said, is much too important to be left to the generals. In a sense this might be said more pointedly of air arm procurement. War contracts have far too much impact on the national economy to be left exclusively to contracting officers. In theory, of course, these buyers were sup-

---

[21] Readjustment Div, ATSC, Annual Rpt, 1944, WFHO files.

posed to take the broad view. As written, the procurement regulations gave weight to a great many social and economic considerations well beyond the minimum of bare military necessity. For example, the procurement regulations specifically directed contracting officers whenever possible to negotiate detailed termination provisions when entering new agreements. In practice the air arm buyer did no such thing. In haste to get production under way, both parties to the contract usually agreed to include the simple boiler plate termination clause and let the matter drop without further ado.[22]

In short, regardless of what the book said, the men who wrote contracts at Wright Field looked for immediate results. With considerable justice, they might argue that there would have been no weapons bought had they stopped to tie up all the loose ends in tidy contractual language. This attitude was entirely justified in the early days of the rush to rearm; far better an imperfect contract than defeat in the field for want of arms. But, once rooted, the idea persisted. Contract negotiators continued, more or less unconsciously perhaps, to ignore or minimize the social and economic implications of any given purchase. The whole termination apparatus, as one able procurement officer at Wright Field put it, was regarded by AAF buyers as something drawn up by the "termination brain trust in Washington" rather than as an integral part of the procurement process conceived by contracting officers in the field.[23]

The problem, then, confronting the high command of the air arm was the reconciliation of the conflicting interests present. To lessen the impact of cancellations on the economy, the terminators tried to favor areas of low labor utilization. Given two manufacturers of the same item, they would urge cancellation of the one in the area with the least unemployment even if that contractor were the more efficient of the two. Similarly, the terminators favored small business over large business. The Air Forces buyers, on the other hand, favored the most efficient contractors. Other things being equal, they preferred to terminate cost-plus-fixed-fee contracts before fixed-price contracts. And with one eye on long-range strategic considerations, they wished also to consider such factors as geographic dispersal and transportation.[24]

The task of accommodating the conflicting objectives of the negotiators and the terminators was by no means impossible. Once again, as the experience of the renegotiators had suggested earlier, the secret of sound and effective administration lay in having all the relevant considerations at hand before reaching a decision. Given the almost endless ramifications of any large contract, this might seem a counsel of perfection. At the very least, it suggests that the job required men of broad experience and wide-ranging imagination.

A typical wartime termination will illustrate something of the problem involved. During the fall of 1944 the output of B-22 turbosuperchargers ran ahead of requirements; a cutback was necessary. Three firms manufactured the

---

[22] Negotiation and Administration of Contracts, Lecture by Scarff.
[23] Ibid.

[24] Termination Activities of the Procurement Division, Lecture, by Maj J. Beattie, AAF Contracting Officers School, WF, Winter 1944-45, WFHO.

item: General Electric, with a capacity of 6,500 a month; Ford with a capacity of 3,500, and Allis-Chalmers with a capacity of 4,500. When demand dropped to approximatey 11,000 units a month, what action was to be taken? All three firms were efficient producers with comparable prices. A cut across the board would be equitable but would release a substantial number of skilled workers. Both General Electric and Allis-Chalmers were expected to begin production on a new model turbo in the near future, but until then they could not absorb the surplus labor. Rather than permit the trained force to drift into other jobs between contracts, it seemed wise to continue production of the B-22 turbo in these two plants at the normal rate.

The situation with Ford was quite different. The labor made available by a cutback on the B-22 turbo could be absorbed on existing contracts elsewhere in the plant. In addition, the labor shortage was currently more acute in the Detroit area than in the vicinity of the other two plants. Finally, since Ford was about to take on a subcontract from General Electric to work on jet engine parts, even more employees would be needed. But labor was not the only consideration involved. Where Ford had only two engineers working exclusively on turbo designs, both General Electric and Allis-Chalmers maintained large staffs for this purpose alone. Inasmuch as further modifications in the B-22 turbo were planned before the line was terminated entirely, it seemed wiser to make the whole cutback at Ford, leaving the firms with the larger engineering staffs to handle the modifications.[25]

[25] *Ibid.*

The foregoing illustration should make it clear that there was nothing arcane about the technique of reconciling procurement with termination. The job simply called for first-rate staff work. No formula could possibly be devised to encompass the many variables present; this kind of problem called for zealous application and imagination, not more elaborate regulations.

The entire termination operation conducted by the Air Forces offers fertile fields for those seeking lessons in administration. Of these, one of the most difficult was the peculiar problem of inventory disposal or plant clearance. In Army circles during the war, it was customary to write off the claim of "problems peculiar to the Air Force" as special pleading for separatism. These gibes were probably often merited; nonetheless, property disposal really did pose abnormal difficulties throughout the aircraft industry, and the administrative problems growing out of this situation merit close attention because they illustrate once again how hard it is to accommodate all the conflicting elements of the public interest with general statutes.

Long before the termination question began to take the center of the stage, prudent staff officers at Air Forces headquarters recognized that accumulated inventory in the hands of contractors would become a major termination stumbling block. Tighter inventory control imposed contractually would minimize the difficulty. Seen in the abstract, this was a perfectly logical course to follow, but at Wright Field the solution was rejected out of hand. Production control officers were doing everything they could to encourage manufacturers to order materials

CONTRACT TERMINATION

in advance, and the proposed action would only increase the contractors' fears of termination disallowances for inventories "unreasonably incurred."[26]

Here was the classic pattern of conflict. On the one hand were the dollar savers, on the other the production men who saw the main goal as speed of output. Both worked in the public interest. Sound administration lay somewhere between the two, but the complexity of the inventory problem made sound administration extremely difficult if not impossible to achieve.

There were a number of reasons why the inventory problem was abnormally complex in the aircraft industry,[27] but the root of the problem was that the demands of war forced the industry to expand more explosively than the industries on which the other arms and services were dependent. Output jumped from a total of approximately 6,000 aircraft in 1939 to nearly 100,000 in 1944. A carriage trade, job-shop industry leaped forward overnight, as it were, into an advanced stage of conveyer-belt mass production. The implications of such rapid growth become clear when one recalls that even a single-engine fighter may require as many as 10,000 different types of parts, each subject to all the ramifications implicit in the design changes so frequently introduced to meet the fierce competition of an aggressive and resourceful enemy. One major airframe manufacturer reported a total of 300,000 separate purchase orders outstanding at all times during the war. The stock clerks of the typical airframe firm posted an average of 5,000 entries a day; 20,000 postings a day were not unknown. Newly trained and inexperienced clerks, all knowing their jobs were only temporary, introduced further headaches, while absenteeism and a high turnover scarcely improved the accuracy with which the inventory records were kept.

In short, the aircraft manufacturers had neither time nor personnel during the war to take inventory. Even if they had done so, their findings would have been obsolete before they were reported, so rapid was the pace of production. For the most part they were so busy trying to catch up with themselves, so busy trying to perfect their records to the minimum required for efficient mass production, that inventory taking was out of the question.

The inventory control problem inherent in the expanded scale of wartime production was bad enough; worse yet were the difficulties growing out of critical shortages. Sometimes as many as 1,500 shortage reports would reach the Air Scheduling Unit at Wright Field in a single day. To keep production rolling, it was common practice to arrange exchanges of parts and materials between separate manufacturers or the different plants of a single firm. In five years 50,000 transfers of this type took place. In similar fashion, the widespread use of inexperienced subcontractors led to abnormally high wastage factors impossible to anticipate with accuracy.[28]

---

[26] Acting Chief, Procurement Div, to ACofAS MM&D, 20 Oct 43, AFCF 164 Non Performance.

[27] Monthly Progress Report, Readjustment Div, ATSC, 1944 (Annual Review for 1944), WFHO files; Agenda for Meeting With General Echols, 23 Feb 44, cited in unsigned study in the reading file of Chief, Resources Div, MM&D, AAG (AGAW-J) Rcd Group 506 (A50-21).

[28] J. K. Boyle, ACC, to Charlton MacVeagh, 29 Sep 44, AAG, AF Rcds, Rcds Group 506 (A51-66).

Under such circumstances, exact inventory control over each part and piece in every single contract was out of the question. Thousands of stock clerks and accountants might conceivably have allocated every item of expense to its appropriate contract, but to do so would have consumed much time, delayed reconversion, and proved prohibitively costly to boot. The only feasible alternative was to authorize termination teams to make company-wide settlements, sweeping all inventories into a single pot, so to speak, without waiting for an item-by-item allocation.[29] This was the Air Forces answer to the Under Secretary of War when he called for a "courageous" exercise of authority in disposing of excess property.[30]

That real courage was required to negotiate inventory settlements across the board is no exaggeration. The policy was entirely in accord with the spirit that had characterized so much of the work done by the aircraft industry during the war. It stressed speed and expediency rather than contractual exactitude. Speedy and expedient settlements were possible, however, only where negotiators were willing to exercise discretion boldly, and every termination negotiated in the latter part of the war took place in the shadow of the Detroit tool scandal, which could scarcely serve as an inducement to action unhampered by petty regulations that so often ensured precision of detail while defeating the larger objectives sought.

---

[29] For a concise account of the whole termination operation and property disposal techniques, see Training Section, Readjustment Division, Materiel Command, Readjustment Training Course Manual, 1945, especially Part IV, copy in ICAF Library.

[30] Memo, USW for CGs, AAF and ASF, n.d. (6 Jan 44), AFCF 164 Non Performance.

The essential facts of the Detroit tool case can be stated briefly. During 1941 air arm procurement officers decided to switch Studebaker from work on the R-2600 engine to the more urgently needed R-1820 engine. Large numbers of tools purchased for the first job but unsuited to the second remained on the contractor's hands. Although a number of firms working on similar projects were invited to pick them over and buy what they could use, a majority of the excess tools—valued at $1,750,000—were shipped to a government warehouse. Of this total, only about $250,000 worth represented standard tools, items such as bits and broaches or milling cutters that could be ordered directly from suppliers' catalogues. Officials at the Central Procurement District tool shortage warehouse in Detroit began a campaign to dispose of the items wherever possible. The tools were advertised in various media, offered to several Air Forces agencies, and one official even undertook to solicit orders by telephone from manufacturers in the Detroit area who might be interested. None of these efforts proved successful. There remained several thousand items ranging from small tools to heavy jigs and fixtures. Lacking trained tool men, the warehouse staff made slow progress in identifying and segregating the mass of material. The job became no easier when the warehouse staff sent their only set of blueprints to the War Production Board in Washington to get advice on disposal of the items.

The War Production Board suggested selling the special tooling as scrap. The Material Command then ordered disposal as salvage. Apparently there was a misunderstanding somewhere in the course

CONTRACT TERMINATION

of the telephone calls between Wright Field and Detroit. Somewhere along the line the recommendation of WPB relating only to the special tools was assumed to apply to all the items.

Down at the end of the long chain of command a second lieutenant began to dispose of the tools in the Detroit warehouse. Although the disposition was advertised as a sale at cost, the lieutenant in charge seems to have sold most of the tools as scrap. Unsorted lots of unidentified tools were trundled into trucks, weighed on the scales of a nearby coal dealer and sold at $18 a ton.[31]

A Detroit manufacturer who had come to the sale in search of standard tools, horrified by what he saw, reported the whole affair to WPB. Soon a local newspaper was howling for scalps, and the story went out to the nation at large. A local editorial writer raged at "maladministration, muddleheadedness, and apparent venality" and called for "appropriate punishment" of those responsible. The facts reported did indeed look bad; the newspapers indicated that the great bulk of the ninety tons of tools sold as scrap were actually general-purpose tools that could be absorbed by industry.[32]

The Air Forces reaction to this violent attack was just about what might have been expected. Several of the officers concerned were punished after an investigation. A lieutenant colonel was permitted to resign, one lieutenant was reclassified and another was dismissed from the Army only to be drafted into service again as an enlisted man. But the investigation also showed that the charges were not entirely warranted by the facts. That there had been mistakes was undeniable; nonetheless, it was also true that only about 10 or 12 percent of the material sold as scrap could be identified as general-purpose tools useful to manufacturers at large. Furthermore, it could not be said that the Air Forces had not made a determined effort to return the tools to use directly through commercial channels before selling them as junk.

At this distance, of course, censure and defense are relatively meaningless. The real significance of the Detroit tool case lies in the influence it had thereafter on Air Forces administration. Property disposal thereafter became a highly unpopular assignment among AAF officers. Boldness in the exercise of discretion might be the philosophy of the Under Secretary, but the officers who read the headlines, "Procurement Chief To Be Replaced," would think twice before they pursued a common-sense course if it involved any relaxation of the conventional regulations.[33] It was far safer to keep the record clear, even if it cost the taxpayers more.

The "play-it-safe" reaction of the Air Forces took the form of a Cutting Tools Warehouse centrally located in Chicago. To protect themselves from criticism, the officers in charge of this enterprise invited a panel of four well-known toolmen from industry to suggest procedures for dealing with the disposal of general-purpose tools. Subpanels of specialists on all the various categories of tools—drills, ream-

---

[31] Rpt of investigation of disposition of government-owned tools and equipment at GFE Warehouse No. 1 in Detroit, Mich., 27 Nov 43, AFCF 412.4 Bulky.

[32] The case was reported in the press generally, but see especially *Detroit Free Press*, October 30, 1943.

[33] *Detroit Free Press*, November 1, 1943.

ers, milling cutters, broaches, taps, dies, were called in to deal with whatever technical problems seemed to lie beyond the competence of the warehouse staff. In sum, the Cutting Tools Warehouse would absorb excess tools from all over the country and use skilled labor to inspect them, segregate them according to class, and catalogue them appropriately in an effort to feed as many tools as possible back into industrial channels.

The Cutting Tools Warehouse plan was certainly a safe one. There would be no more inexperienced second lieutenants selling off tools as scrap. But to play safe is expensive. The central warehouse cost the government $30,000 a year in rent and $74,000 to equip with bins to hold the tools stored. The cost of the military staff running the warehouse cannot be readily computed, but the civilians employed there cost the government $89,000 in a period of 15 months, and this figure does not include the fees paid to consultants.

There were still other expenses involved in running the warehouse. Cutting tools had to be wrapped carefully when shipped any great distance. The government had to absorb this expense. When experience showed that the single warehouse in Chicago was too remote, operations were started at new centers in Fresno, California, and Elyria, Ohio.

A final computation of the cost of playing safe with the Chicago Cutting Tools Warehouse makes disheartening reading. Industrial buyers could be induced to purchase only a minute percentage of the tools sent to the warehouse. The industrialists were hardly to be blamed for showing so little enthusiasm. All purchases had to be accompanied by a certified check. Purchases from regular tool sources, on the other hand, could be made by phone, and in addition they carried the guarantee of the seller's reputation. As a consequence, the total return from tools sold amounted to less than $75,000, or a mere 2.65 percent of the total value of the tools sent to the Chicago warehouse for disposal. Set against the administrative cost of the warehouse, computed at $222,000, it cost three dollars in overhead expense for every dollar realized in sales. Even at that, the administrative cost included neither office equipment and supplies nor the charges incurred in clearing and packing the tools for shipment to the central warehouse.[34]

The point scarcely needs belaboring. The taxpayers can have every contract supervised down to the last penny, if they wish to pay the price. But how many taxpayers want to pay three dollars for every dollar they save? Perhaps one of the real heroes of the Materiel Command was that lieutenant, possibly apocryphal, who shortly after V–J Day deliberately drove a tractor over a B–17 wing section to convert it into scrap rather than force the taxpayers to spend more than the item cost in crating and shipping it to a disposal depot.

An Afterword

If one accepts as evidence the absence of postwar litigation and the failure of a postwar depression to materialize, it can

---

[34] Capt E. O. Porter, History of the Cutting Tools Warehouse, Monograph prepared by historical officer in the Central Proc Dist, n.d. (Jun 45), WFHO. See also, Lt Col R. E. Cook to CGMC, 19 Aug 43, AFCF 412.4 Bulky.

be argued that the termination operations conducted by the War Department during and immediately following World War II were signally successful. Few would deny that the job done in 1944 and 1945 was superior to that of 1918 and 1919. In some respects it might be argued that the task of terminating contracts was more effectively accomplished than the writing of contracts in the beginning. If at first glance this seems paradoxical, it is worth recalling that termination policy was developed almost from scratch during the war. Nearly the whole debate took place over a period in which thousands upon thousands of business firms were vitally interested in the subject since they already held contracts with the military services. As a consequence, a vast literature grew up around the topic of terminations—indeed, far more has been written about the termination than about the negotiation of military contracts. Much, if not most of the technique of negotiating military contracts evolved during the prewar years of peace when relatively few businessmen gave any serious attention to military procurement or during the early days of the war when there was little or no time for public discussion over the means and methods employed. Thus, in retrospect, the whole termination operation conducted by the War Department appears far more effective, not only in principle but in detail, than were the original negotiations resulting in the contracts subsequently terminated.

CHAPTER XIX

Organization for Procurement

Many and perhaps most of the changes that seemed to be the continual lot of military agencies during the war reflected nothing more than an effort of those in command to accommodate organizations to the individuals available to man them. To record the successive mutations in structure stemming from this cause is a waste of time. On the other hand, some of the changes represented fundamental shifts in policy of crucial importance to the procurement process.

Although the various problems selected for discussion here represent rather distinct aspects of the over-all question of organization, all share one trait in common—they have suffered from a dangerous tendency to oversimplification. Military leaders no less than journalists and political figures have sometimes been inclined to see cures in catch phrases. During the war there was always someone ready to urge the merits of *centralized* or *unified* command while ignoring the costs of attaining that end. The same can be said of the continual cry for the "elimination of duplication." So, too, "centralized procurement" had its perpetual advocates. Would-be reformers have sometimes exploited the deep-rooted national adherence to the principle of civilian control by advocating and justifying centralized procurement of military supplies by some sort of civilian agency as a cure for the "red tape" of military procurement. Finally, *decentralized operations* has been a perennial catch phrase too often used in disregard of its broader implications and ultimate consequences.

What follows should shed some light, admittedly at the risk of repetition, on the nature of the problems of organization and some insight into the solutions wrought to cope with them.

Co-ordination, Control, and Command

Expanding the Procurement Organization for War

During most of the years between the formation of the Air Corps in 1926 and the coming of war in 1939, the Materiel Division operated as a subordinate bureau of the Washington headquarters—the Office of the Chief of Air Corps—and was physically located at Wright Field, Ohio.[1] There, six major agencies carried on the functions of the division. The Experimental Engineering Section monitored the research and development program, which explored the hither edge of aeronautical science. The Contract Section invited bids, wrote contracts, and administered them. The Production Engineering Section rode herd on the manufacturers who secured contracts for air-

---
[1] See above, pp. 93–101.

craft in quantity. The Inspection Section ensured compliance with the standards laid down in the procurement specifications. The Field Service Section supervised the supply and maintenance operations carried out at depots widely dispersed about the country and in the outlying possessions. The Industrial Planning Section prepared mobilization plans.[2]

The arrangements by which six such varied and complex staff functions were carried out so far from the rest of the Washington headquarters were not entirely satisfactory. For many years it had seemed expedient to locate the chief of the Materiel Division at Wright Field, where he could supervise his operational force personally, but there were decided disadvantages in this. So long as the chief of the Materiel Division remained outside of Washington, he had to make his decisions without the benefit of the easy co-ordination with the other divisions of OCAC that residence at headquarters would have afforded. By the same token, the Chief of the Air Corps did not have the ready and frequent access to his principal advisor on matériel matters that he enjoyed with his other division heads. The problem was the subject of staff studies for many months, and the coming of war in 1939 led the Chief of the Air Corps to move the chief of the Materiel Division to Washington, leaving the operating echelon at Wright Field in charge of an assistant chief.

Such a fundamental organizational shift brought all sorts of difficulties in its wake. In Washington the chief of the Materiel Division found himself bereft of the advisors upon whom he had relied when making decisions at Wright Field. Without their continuing support, he became progressively less useful as a well-informed source of technical information upon whom the Chief of the Air Corps could rely—the very reason for his transfer from Wright Field in the first place. His escape from this dilemma was to build up a personal staff patterned on the several operating activities at Wright Field. Although it had originally been contemplated that a very small staff would suffice, an elaborate organization gradually grew up around the chief of the Materiel Division in Washington as he drew one trusted subordinate after another from Wright Field to the OCAC headquarters.[3]

The Materiel Division at Wright Field could ill afford to lose the officers being drawn to Washington. Even before the migration to headquarters began, an investigating board in 1939 had found "an appalling lack of qualified personnel . . . particularly in the key positions" at Wright Field. At the same time, another study of the "pitifully inadequate" technical staff effectively underlined the point by observing that a single project officer with one civilian assistant was currently expected to perform the "manifestly impossible" job of co-ordinating three or four different production contracts for bombardment aircraft under construction in plants several thousand miles apart.[4] If the Materiel Division

---

[2] See the organization chart for the Materiel Division as of 18 August 1939, McMurtrie and Davis, Hist of AAF MC: 1926–41, app. A–7.

[3] AAF Hist Study 10, pp. 34–37.

[4] Rpt of com to study revision of Mat Div organization, 10 Jan 39, and civilian personnel study by Capt C. S. Irvine, 26 Jan 39, AC Project Rcds (Lyon Papers), bks. 18 and 19.

was to procure the immense quantities of equipment essential to a wartime air force, it would have to launch an aggressive program to recruit a vastly larger technical staff. During the two years before Pearl Harbor, this is what did happen.[5]

Explosive growth under any circumstances leads to organizational difficulties. With so slight a cadre to build upon, sound organization and effective administration proved hard to obtain in the rapidly growing Materiel Division. More than ever, the quality of the leadership available would determine whether or not the sprawling and hastily enlarged establishment would get results in the form of finished aircraft ready for the tactical units facing the enemy or become totally embroiled in its own housekeeping problems. The unimpressive record of production achieved by the procurement organization in World War I suggested, to some at least, that the latter outcome was not entirely beyond the realm of possibility.[6]

Despite the acute shortage of technical staff, the Materiel Division was fortunate in having at least a handful of officers whose peacetime service had given them a wide range of experience in the various activities of the division. In one sense the very paucity of staff was an advantage; for want of personnel, the few officers available had never been allowed to develop into specialists. Instead, they had been forced to take a turn at virtually every job in the division, and as a consequence many of them had acquired just the sort of general training necessary to equip general officers for the leadership expected of their rank.

One of the handful of officers at Wright Field who had acquired a broad knowledge of matériel problems was Lt. Col. Oliver P. Echols. In addition to a variety of lesser assignments, his apprenticeship had included duty as the technical executive at Wright Field and the post of assistant chief, Materiel Division, which he assumed shortly after war broke out in Europe. A year later, promoted to brigadier general, he was called to Washington to take over as the division chief. He remained at headquarters as the top-ranking officer in charge of matériel matters throughout the war, although his title and the organization he managed passed through a succession of mutations.[7]

If the transfer of the matériel chief to Washington was disturbing to the procurement organization, no less so was the War Department reorganization of March 1942. This epoch-making change swept away much of the military structure devised following World War I and established in its place a tripartite organization in which three separate commands —ground, air, and service—reported directly to the Chief of Staff. The impact of this departmental reorganization extended far down into the internal structure of the air arm.

Under the commanding general of the Army Air Forces, General H. H. Arnold, there were three distinct echelons of activity. Reporting directly to him was the Air Staff charged with policy formulation.

---

[5] McMurtrie and Davis, Hist of AAF MC: 1926–41, app. E, and p. 6a of the text.

[6] See, for example, David Lloyd George, *War Memoirs* (6 vols.; Boston: Little, Brown and Co., 1933–37), V, 451.

[7] McMurtrie and Davis, Hist of AAF MC: 1926–41, pp. 103ff.

ORGANIZATION FOR PROCUREMENT

Next came the directorates or so-called operating staff. This group, including directors of personnel, requirements, management control, and technical services, was intended to serve as a co-ordinating staff that grouped problems along functional lines. At the next echelon came the operating commands, embracing not only such activities as technical training, flying training, ferrying, matériel, and the like but also the numbered Air Forces or tactical units in the field.

However impressive the new title of Materiel Command may appear, the "command" was really little more than the old Materiel Division staff within OCAC. In fact, during the first few days of its existence the infant command was in danger of being eclipsed altogether as the newly formed directorates in the echelon above began to build up a staff of technical specialists—in armament, power plants, communications, and so on —paralleling those already established in the Materiel Command headquarters staff. Although an agreement was finally worked out that left responsibility for technical advice to the Materiel Command and thus avoided an unseemly scramble for scarce specialists, the episode clearly indicated the prevailing confusion as to the precise division of functions among the Air Staff, the directorates, and the operating commands.[8]

When a full year of trial failed to clear up the confusion among the various staffs, the whole scheme of directorates had to be eliminated. Thus in March 1943 the policy-making air staff and the operating directorates were combined into a single echelon of six sections: personnel; intelligence; training; operations commitments and requirements; plans; and matériel, maintenance, and distribution. Each of these was headed by an assistant chief of Air Staff who played a dual role. In their relations with the Commanding General, AAF, these officers acted individually as his personal advisors and collectively as his air staff. When facing in the other direction, each of the men presided over his specialized operating staff as its chief executive and in this capacity kept himself intimately informed of the details he needed in his role as advisor to the commanding general.[9]

As chief of the Materiel Division at the time of the March 1942 reorganization of the War Department, General Echols became commanding general of the Materiel Command then established. The position of assistant chief of the Materiel Division, Wright Field, was redesignated, Commanding General, Materiel Center, and Brig. Gen. A. W. Vanaman received the assignment. He remained there until the reorganization of March 1943, when General Echols became assistant chief of Air Staff for Materiel, Maintenance, and Distribution. At that time the title of Commanding General, Materiel Command, moved out to Wright Field where it was assumed by Brig. Gen. Charles E. Branshaw. This officer came to Wright Field from the Western Procurement District, where he had been serving as district supervisor, a circumstance that was to have a considerable influence on the line of policy he subsequently pursued. The transfer of the title, Commanding

---

[8] AAF Hist Study 10, pp. 53–55; McMurtrie, Hist of AAF MC: 1942, pp. 2–3.

[9] For a discussion of the shortcomings in the directorates, see AAF Hist Study 10, pp. 46–51, 92–107.

GENERAL BRANSHAW

General, Materiel Command, to Wright Field did not mean that any large migration of command personnel from Washington took place. The headquarters organization of the old Materiel Command simply combined with the former policy and operating staff and stayed in the capital.[10]

During all the months of 1942 and 1943 when the Air Forces headquarters staffs were being shuffled and reshuffled in an effort to find a workable and efficient arrangement, the organization at Wright Field was equally subject to change. The successive permutations of structure introduced to keep the ever-growing organization manageable would be far too tedious to recount here, but by the fall of 1942 the major activities of the Materiel Command had been concentrated in three main divisions reporting to the commanding general. For the most part these divisions—engineering, production, and procurement—were composed of sections and units already in operation but now regrouped to provide more effective functional control.

While the matériel organization at Wright Field grew rapidly during the defense period, doubling and redoubling in the two years before Pearl Harbor, thereafter it grew at a rate that career officers thinking in terms of the scanty peacetime budget regarded as nothing less than phenomenal. During 1942 officer strength at Wright Field increased from 627 to 1,684. This growth was almost entirely made up of reservists, since the number of Regular Army officers on duty remained virtually constant at 90-odd men throughout the year. Civilian personnel strength increased from 7,828 in January 1942 to 11,226 at the end of the year. And this figure excludes those civilians working in the procurement districts. Counting these, the command employed 28,673 civilians in December 1942. By the end of 1943 the combined total reached 34,270 civilians along with 3,742 officers and 5,658 enlisted men. Although still more manpower was added to the command in the following year, by then the rate of growth was much slower.[11] This was certainly fortunate, since staggering growth had long since begun to compound the normal difficulties of coordination and control experienced by

---

[10] McMurtrie, Hist of AAF MC: 1942, p. 172; and Russel, Hist of AAF ATSC: 1944, p. 48, n. 8.

[11] McMurtrie, Hist of AAF MC: 1942, app. 7; Davis, Hist of AAF MC: 1943, app. 3; Russel, History of AAF ATSC: 1944, app. 3.

those who tried to direct the multifarious activities of the Matériel Command.

Problems of Co-ordination and Control

Although the statistics of personnel increases in the Materiel Command after Pearl Harbor may look impressive in retrospect, it would be a mistake to assume that these thousands upon thousands of inexperienced and untrained employees were all promptly absorbed and put to work efficiently. To begin with, they soon outstripped the available floor space despite additions from an extensive building program. The post garage and a number of other buildings including some storage sheds were hurriedly converted into offices. Even these expedients failed to meet the need, and finally some units had to set up their offices in the corridors of existing structures. With anywhere from 600 to 800 visitors coming to Wright Field on business every day during 1942, little imagination is required to understand how hard it was to perfect a smoothly functioning procurement organization under such circumstances.[12] Nevertheless, the difficulties, while aggravating, were no more than those to be expected by any rapidly growing force, and in time many of them were eliminated. More fundamental were the difficulties actually inherent in the structure or form of the organizations erected to encompass the added thousands of employees at Wright Field.

As the functions performed by the several divisions increased not only in volume but also in complexity, extensive subdivision of operating sections was not only desirable but necessary. Inexperienced staff members could often be trained to handle a narrow range of jobs effectively in a relatively short time, and each further subdivision made it possible to deal expeditiously with the continually mounting mass of details. Thus, for example, what had started out in October 1942 as the Production Division with four internal sections (production engineering, production control, industrial planning, and special projects) had been subdivided three months later into five sections, which included some twenty-five branches. These in turn were broken down into smaller units and subunits.

By way of illustration, consider a single section within the Production Division. By July 1943 it had parceled its functions out to 4 branches that contained in all sixteen units and sixty-three subunits. This meant that even within this section alone an officer in one of the subunits who sought to co-ordinate some matter of significance was confronted with an array of 70-odd organizations and more than a hundred officers to whom he might address an inquiry—all within his own immediate operational area. If his problem extended beyond his own section, he might have to approach any one of more than 400 officers in the Production Division as a whole. If it involved co-ordination with one of the other divisions his difficulties mounted still further, for there were over 800 officers in the Engineering Division and over 100 in the Procurement Division.[13]

Inevitably there was a good deal of

---

[12] McMurtrie, Hist of AAF MC: 1942, p. 168ff.

[13] Hist of Materiel Command: 1943, app. 3.

overlapping activity and lost motion in this hurriedly assembled multitude. Sometimes section and branch chiefs set up units and subunits to do jobs that, unbeknown to them, were already being attacked somewhere else in the sprawling matériel organization.

While the multiplication of branches, units, and subunits was indeed an important factor in causing confusion and in complicating the task of co-ordination within the operating divisions, it was by no means the only source of difficulty. In a large measure the trouble stemmed from the character of the task at hand. In peacetime the engineering staff supervised the development of aircraft and the procurement staff bought them, but even before the outbreak of war those in command recognized the need for a substantial measure of separation between production engineering on the one hand and experimental or developmental engineering on the other, lest the endless strivings after perfection of the experimental engineers delay production.[14] Some went so far as to believe—erroneously as it turned out—that experimental and production engineering could be entirely separated. General Arnold, for instance, as Chief of the Air Corps, had urged his matériel staff to build a "Chinese wall" between the two.[15] What he wanted was a staff of production engineers who would make quick decisions on changes in design or specifications proposed by contractors trying to step up output or eliminate critical materials in short supply.

Out of this beginning grew the organization that in time became the Production Division.

The very existence of a Production Division raised formidable problems of co-ordination. In the first place, the division would have to maintain the very closest kind of relationship with the Engineering Division if the airplanes turned out in quantity were to incorporate the latest improvements perfected under the supervision of experimental engineers. Inevitably there were misunderstandings between the two groups. The research staff complained that the production men did not consult it often enough and frequently ignored the advice it gave. The production men replied that the experimental engineers were too slow and too concerned with minor refinements. At this, the research men pointed out that the production men too often went ahead and made decisions on inadequate technical knowledge and then came running to the Engineering Division for help when changes did not work out.[16] Obviously only a highly efficient system of co-ordination and co-operative effort would avoid such conflicts.

In addition to co-operating with the Engineering Division, the production men had to work in the utmost harmony with the officers of the Procurement Division, since their work dovetailed at a great many points. In practice such relationships proved hard to achieve.

A number of circumstances contributed to the want of accord between the two divisions. Maj. K. B. Wolfe, the offi-

---

[14] Russel, Hist of AAF ATSC: 1944, p. 7.

[15] The conflicts of continuing development versus mass production are treated in Chapter XX, below. For General Arnold's view, see Memo, CofAC for Gen Brett, 17 Feb 39, WFCF 400.12.

[16] This paragraph is taken almost verbatim from the brief but excellent summary of the problem presented in Russel, Hist of AAF ATSC: 1944, pages 31–37.

ORGANIZATION FOR PROCUREMENT

cer who built up the Production Division and ultimately rose to the rank of major general for his efforts, was an unusually aggressive leader and a masterful personality. He saw clearly that no matter what other considerations were involved, in the final analysis the Production Division would be judged on the speed with which it sent large numbers of aircraft to the tactical units in combat. Surrounding himself with a strong staff of able production engineers and business executives, he imbued them with one goal: production. Following his contagious leadership, these men repeatedly seized the initiative in taking on new functions and creating new organizations to cope with them as opportunity presented.

The Procurement Division, on the other hand, was far less aggressive. Perhaps this was because so many of its officers were lawyers and less inclined to boldness than the production men recruited from industry. In any event, the Production Division gradually absorbed all sorts of activities that might logically have fallen to others. This was particularly true with respect to the contractual adjustments stemming from the deviations authorized by production engineers.[17]

Undoubtedly General Wolfe and his hard-working staff deserve well of the nation. They provided much of the power behind the drive that ultimately sent aircraft output to the spectacular levels achieved during the war. But the bulldozing methods that brought these results left a lot of casualties along the way. Contractors in particular found it difficult to know just where to turn for deci-

GENERAL WOLFE. *(Picture taken in 1947.)*

sions or assistance at Wright Field. Sometimes they made changes in delivery schedules or design details on the verbal assurance of project engineers in the Production Division only to discover subsequently that the changes had been cleared neither by Procurement Division nor by Engineering Division personnel. Sometimes contractors were able to exploit this lack of co-ordination to play one division

---

[17] *Ibid.*, pp. 8–10.

off against another. More often it led only to confusion, overlapping activity, and hot-tempered disputes.[18]

Typical of the overlapping effort that characterized the hastily erected matériel organization was the multiplication of agencies performing more or less identical contract follow-up functions. A control section in the Procurement Division pursued this line as did a similar section in the Production Division. And to complicate matters still further, so did a section in the Air Service Command (ASC), the supply and maintenance organization that had been formed as a separate command from the old prewar Field Service Section of the Materiel Division. As the supply service of the Air Forces, ASC was responsible for initiating all spare parts purchases. Inasmuch as the tactical units required spares as soon as they received their aircraft, ASC put heavy pressure on the Procurement Division to order spares at the same time as the aircraft needing them. It frequently happened, however, that in trying to turn out spares concurrently, manufacturers had to cut down on their output of finished aircraft or other end items. This brought ASC into conflict with the Production Division.[19]

A few other instances of the contrary interests that led to misunderstandings among the divisions of the Materiel Command and between the Materiel and Air Service Commands may be worth considering. In addition to aircraft, the Engineering Division was forever perfecting many new and different items of personal equipment such as flying suits, oxygen outfits, and escape kits. Naturally the engineers doing this work wanted the latest and most improved items procured for issue to the units in combat. The supply and maintenance people in ASC, however, were faced with some rather different objectives. They had to satisfy the tactical units with an immediate flow of items in quantity. Furthermore, they had to resist the introduction of too many models if they hoped to simplify maintenance and training as well as provide up-to-date technical orders and instruction manuals for the equipment they sent out. To attain these ends, ASC sometimes refused to order a newly developed item or asked for it only in small quantities. This vexed not only the engineers but the production men as well. Understandably enough, the latter found it easier to plan for the production of large quantities all at once than to deal with a succession of lesser purchases. Caught in this web of conflicting interests, officers in the Procurement Division found it hard to please anyone.[20]

Where so many entirely different agencies did business with individual contractors, conflicts were almost impossible to avoid. When, for example, ASC officers learned from their supply organization that a certain spare part was no longer required, they wired the manufacturer to discontinue production. Because this action was not properly cleared with the Procurement and Production Divisions in the Matériel Command, a whole train of misfortunes followed. Unaware of the cancellation, a contract com-

---

[18] McMurtrie, Hist of AAF MC: 1942, p. 28.
[19] *Ibid.*, pp. 59–79. See also, MC Letter of Instruction, 9 Mar 42, AFCF 400.12 Methods and Program of Proc.

[20] Russel, Admin Hist of AAF ATSC: 1944, pp. 78–80.

ORGANIZATION FOR PROCUREMENT

pliance unit continued to follow up the initial order, and a production expediter continued to urge the baffled manufacturer on to greater effort. Here was the epitome of un-co-ordinated action. The bad impression such a situation made on contractors only served to emphasize what those in command already knew: co-ordination within the matériel organization was faltering at a great many points.[21]

Eventually, late in 1944, the top Air Forces command undertook a major overhaul of the matériel system in an effort to eliminate some of its more serious weaknesses. The Materiel Command and the Air Service Command were combined into a single Air Technical Service Command (ATSC), and within this new command the procurement and production functions were combined into a single division. The intent of this rearrangement was to concentrate, insofar as possible, the points of contact between the manufacturers and the matériel staff along a narrow front and thus eliminate conflicting decisions.

There were many advantages to be derived from gathering all the matériel functions within a single command, but perceptive officers realized that putting a number of activities under a single head by no means guaranteed that conflicting decisions would thereafter disappear. Even where two activities were merged within a single division, officers were still confronted with the same formidable problems of co-ordination that had plagued matériel operations throughout the war.[22]

In a large measure the proliferation of overlapping subunits and the repeated instances of faulty co-ordination were a direct product of the isolation of command from day-to-day operations. Successive commanders at Wright Field during the war struggled hard to maintain contact with their burgeoning divisions. General Branshaw in particular kept his door open to all comers, making a valiant effort, ultimately at the cost of his health, not to lose the personal touch in exercising his command.

In the peacetime years the chief of the old Materiel Division at Wright Field was able to keep in touch more or less effectively with all the important operations going on under his supervision. All papers going up or down the chain of command flowed through his office, and by conscientious effort he could keep himself rather well informed. His office and those of his section chiefs were conveniently adjacent. Effective co-ordination could be achieved by the most informal of contacts.

In wartime the comfortable ways of peace were no longer possible. As sections and branches grew more numerous, and each in succession spawned units and subunits, the officer in top command at Wright Field soon found himself four, five, or even six echelons above the level where many operations were being per-

---

[21] McMurtrie, Hist of AAF MC: 1942, pp. 78–79. For elaboration of the problems raised here, see IOM, MC Comptroller to CofS MC, 12 May 44, in Analysis of AAF Proc and Shipment Rcds, 12 May 44, by MC Comptroller, WFHO files.

[22] Russel, Hist of AAF ATSC: 1944, p. 89ff. For an illustration of the difficulties encountered in achieving internal co-ordination even after merging the commands in ATSC, see the B-29 tools controversy described in Study of Proc of Special Tools, Supply Div, ATSC, 5 Dec 44, WFHO Research file, Tools and Equipment.

formed. To have insisted on routing all correspondence through his office would have swamped him with details and set up a fearful bottleneck. Much the same thing applied to the division and section chiefs. To avoid the delays encountered in passing communications up and down the chain—the practice of "layering" as Donald Nelson described it—subordinate units were authorized to communicate directly with their opposite numbers in other organizations. This proved expeditious, but the saving in time was paid for with a loss of personal contact that the commanding general and his division heads found progressively more detrimental as the months wore on.

To save themselves from complete loss of contact with the teeming organizations below them, those in command positions gradually came to realize that they had to create elaborate administrative instruments to control and co-ordinate the operations that had grown too vast for personal supervision. These new tools of command took many forms, of course, but it was not uncommon to find officers in policy-making positions served by three different kinds of staff agencies. Almost always there was an administrative unit to handle housekeeping details such as running a typing pool and a system of files. There was usually an executive staff to distribute the workload carried on by the organization and ensure internal co-ordination as well as to provide for liaison with other services or commands. And, finally, especially in larger organizations, there was likely to be a control unit serving the officer in command. The control unit imposed standards of record keeping on the subordinate units, established follow-up procedures, studied workloads, backlogs, staff loading, and personnel requirements, collected statistics and recurring reports, and compiled summaries for the use of command.

Without a doubt the expansion of the upper echelon administrative staff was necessary if officers in command positions were to keep positive control over the operations going on within their purview. Nonetheless, as time wore on, some critics were inclined to feel that these special staffs had become top-heavy monsters out of proportion to actual need, even outweighing the operating activities they were designed to serve. Whether such charges were valid could only be determined by a close study of individual cases. Nonetheless, it was certainly true that by the end of 1943 these administrative staffs had flowered luxuriantly within the Matériel Command.

Just how large the special administrative staffs could become may be suggested by a brief résumé of the establishment maintained for this purpose by the Procurement Division in March 1944. The division chief had four clerks in his immediate office. His two technical assistants were served by a total of 18 people. The administrative staff for housekeeping employed 80 persons. Some 60 of these performed the highly important work of keeping the central file of all contracts written and all correspondence relating to the contracts. In addition, there was a Procurement Control Section with 108 people working to keep a current situation report on the status of all contracts. Altogether, this made a total of over 200 people in the upper echelon of the division performing housekeeping

ORGANIZATION FOR PROCUREMENT

and supervisory jobs. And below this top layer at the level of operations, the purchasing, contracting, and terminating sections all had similar staffs under a variety of guises such as administrative units, record units, or control units. Taken all together, upward of one-third of the total strength of the Procurement Division was absorbed in the function of providing tools for the use of command.[23]

Even as the explosive and often ill-digested organizational growth of 1942 had led those in command to appreciate the need for improved tools in the form of special staffs for co-ordination and control, by 1944 they had come to realize that the cures might have been carried too far. Admittedly, some of the specialists in organizational planning seemed to believe the heavy top staffs were justified. They pointed out that whereas in January 1943 it took 6.79 persons in the Materiel Command for every aircraft turned out by Air Force contractors, in November 1943 only 4.87 persons were required.[24] But, like so many seemingly impressive statistics, these figures may have been utterly meaningless since such an infinite variety of factors quite apart from the organization at Wright Field entered into the acceleration of aircraft production. The doubts of those who actually shouldered the burdens of command were mirrored in the annual report of the Procurement Division in 1944:

> The necessary early policy of getting the job done by "expedient" methods has been supplanted by accomplishing the job properly through planning and control. The impact of the change on responsible operating personnel accustomed to considerable independence of decision was quite noticeable. With the advent of new (and) exacting administrative controls—forms controls, reports controls, project controls, classified data controls, and correspondence controls—considerably more manpower hours were required away from primary functions. While undoubtedly these mechanisms will result in getting the administrative job done better, they do conflict with the technical jobs—those of getting material produced as fast as possible for combat. Overemphasis should not be placed on burdensome control mechanisms which do not result in improvement in efficiency.[25]

Whether or not the Materiel Command overemphasized and overbuilt control mechanism is now beside the point. Nevertheless, to recognize the lessons implicit in the experience of the war years is very much to the point. Clearly, the manual techniques of record keeping and the informal methods of administration (especially in the matter of co-ordination) that worked well enough with the low-volume characteristic of peacetime were no longer feasible when the rush of war work prohibited personal surveillance. Special staffs for co-ordination, control, and administration could be and were erected to keep command from being swamped in a mass of details, but these staffs themselves got out of hand. The continuing task of command, then, was to keep the administrative mechanisms, the overhead staff for co-ordination and control, sensitively adjusted to the volume of business handled and to the size or complexity of the organization controlled.

---

[23] Russel, Hist of AAF ATSC: 1944, p. 73ff.
[24] Office of Organizational Planning, Materiel Command Operational Problems; Appraisal as of 1 Dec 43, WFHO Research file.

[25] Quoted in Russel, Hist of AAF ATSC: 1944. p. 74.

While the problems of co-ordination and control within the air matériel organization were indeed highly involved, they were hardly unique. Almost exactly the same pattern of difficulties beset the officials of the War Department who tried to exercise their supervisory responsibility over the procurement effected for the Army's air arm.

The Army and the Air Arm

The epochal Defense Act of 1920 placed two major responsibilities on the Assistant Secretary of War. He was to plan for the mobilization of the national economy in the event of hostilities and supervise current Army procurement. The actual mechanics of buying, of course, were left to the technical services —Ordnance, Quartermaster, Air Corps, and the others—but the Assistant Secretary was expected to police their operations and hold them to an acceptable standard of performance. Above all, he was supposed to prevent the unseemly scramble that had marred the procurement record in World War I when contracting officers within the Army actually bid against one another for the services of industry. To prevent this, the Assistant Secretary laid down standard contract forms, drew up uniform procurement regulations, and then set out to maintain a comprehensive view of the far-flung procurement activities of the services to insure adequate co-ordination among them.[26]

In December 1940, Congress created a new position—the Under Secretary of War (USW)—which absorbed all the procurement functions formerly assigned to the Assistant Secretary. The incumbent Assistant Secretary, Robert P. Patterson, became the first Under Secretary. Soon thereafter the President appointed Robert A. Lovett to fill the post of Assistant Secretary of War for Air, which had remained vacant since the early thirties. Although this position carried no statutory power to direct procurement matters in the sense that the Under Secretary's did, Mr. Lovett took an active interest in air arm production problems.[27] While the precise character of Mr. Lovett's duties was never clearly defined by statute during the war, his very presence opened a direct and personal line of communication to the Secretary of War that could prove useful in the event of misunderstandings or disagreements between the Under Secretary and the air arm. Few such end runs around the Under Secretary proved necessary, largely because of the tactful leadership of Mr. Patterson and his principal subordinates throughout the war years. On the other hand, the Assistant Secretary's effectiveness was further enhanced by the personal access he enjoyed in the Office of the Chief of Staff by virtue of his intimate relationship with General Arnold. From October 1940 until the time of the War Department reorganization of 1942, General Arnold served as Deputy Chief of Staff for Air, and thus readily bridged the gap between Assistant Secretary Lovett and General Mar-

---

[26] Defense Act of June 4, 1920, sec. 5a, as amplified in 5 series Army Regulations and *Handbook for the War Department General Staff*, Oct 23, ch. 8. See also, Act of December 16, 1940 (54 Stat 1224).

[27] 44 Stat 784, sec. 9. See also, Craven and Cate, eds., *Plans and Early Operations*, p. 115.

ORGANIZATION FOR PROCUREMENT

shall, the Chief of Staff, when procurement matters required the latter's attention.

In actual practice there was a wide field open for disputes between the Office of the Under Secretary (OUSW) and the technical services. By the terms of the Defense Act of 1920 as amended, the technical services were left in the ambiguous position of serving two masters: the Chief of Staff on matters military and the Under Secretary on matters relating to procurement. Inasmuch as the distinction between "military" and "procurement" questions was frequently impossible to make, collisions of authority were increasingly frequent as the rearmament program gathered momentum. Of the various reorganizations considered to rectify this situation, one in particular found ready adherents. The scheme called for the establishment of a single military business manager over all the technical services, somewhat along the lines of the Purchase, Storage, and Traffic Division commanded by Maj. Gen. George Goethals in World War I.[28]

The agitation for a single military supervisor to co-ordinate procurement matters was considerably stimulated by the increasing frequency with which the technical services met obstacles and delays in their dealing with OUSW. Needless to say, the Under Secretary's staff was suffering from the usual pangs of wartime expansion.[29] In less than a year it grew from its peacetime strength of about 80 to nearly 500. The old familiar techniques of personal and informal co-ordination broke down just as they had at Wright Field when rapid organizational growth set in. But OUSW suffered from a still more grievous malady according to a firm of management consultants called in to study the office at work. No one, declared the consultants, really understood the purpose for which OUSW existed—neither the personnel of that organization itself nor those in the technical services subject to the Under Secretary's supervision.[30] Criticisms of this sort helped bring to a head the agitation that led to the major overhauling of the War Department in March 1942.

The reorganization of March 1942 divided the Army into three separate forces: air, ground, and service—Army Air Forces, Army Ground Forces, and Army Service Forces—each under a commanding general reporting to the Chief of Staff. To overcome the criticisms made by the technical services before the reorganization that they served two masters in reporting to the Under Secretary as well as the Chief of Staff, the details of the policy-making and co-ordinating functions hitherto carried out by OUSW in regard to procurement were moved downward and assigned to the service force under the command of Lt. Gen. Brehon B. Somervell. Originally designated as Services of Supply (SOS), General Somervell's command was subsequently and more popularly known as the Army Service Forces (ASF).

The plan of reorganization for 1942 spelled out in War Department Circular

---

[28] This whole problem is treated at length in John D. Millett, *The Organization and Role of the Army Service Forces*, UNITED STATES ARMY IN WORLD WAR II (Washington, 1954).

[29] Anderson, Hist of OUSW: 1914–41, ch. 6, especially sec. 3, The Organization and Working of the Office.

[30] Millet, *Organization and Role of ASF*, p. 27.

59 placed procurement responsibility for the Army on the Commanding General, ASF, with one significant exception. The mission of the ASF was to provide services and supplies to meet all requirements "except those peculiar to the Army Air Forces." This meant that while Ordnance, Quartermaster, Chemical Warfare, and the other technical services would report to Commanding General, ASF, the Materiel Command would remain a part of the AAF. Any other arrangement was scarcely possible. The thinking of responsible air arm officers in the upper echelons of command had been thoroughly conditioned by the struggle for autonomy. At the eleventh hour it was hardly to be expected that they would relinquish direct control over the procurement of the equipment vital to their mission. Nevertheless, the available evidence suggests that the decision to leave air arm procurement with the AAF was as much a matter of political compromise as it was deference to the desires of the air officers. The officials who planned the reorganization of 1942 apparently felt that the vociferous advocates of air arm autonomy on Capitol Hill would launch an immediate drive for a separate air force unless some such compromise were made. And in the chaotic months following Pearl Harbor the administrative delays inevitable in effecting complete autonomy might well have proved disastrous.[31]

While there were sound arguments for leaving air arm procurement entirely within the AAF, the arrangement would have raised a number of difficulties. When the Under Secretary relinquished to the Commanding General, ASF, the task of imposing uniform procurement procedures on all Army procurement, the responsibility then resided in an echelon parallel to the AAF. The three forces, AGF, ASF, and AAF were coequal; each reported independently to the Chief of Staff. How, then, could ASF impose uniform procurement policies on the Army as a whole? The difficulty plagued the staff planners for some time until finally they resolved the matter by leaving the job of supervising air arm procurement to the Under Secretary, as had been the case before the reorganization. This expedient they showed on their organizational charts as a dotted line running from the AAF Materiel Command directly to OUSW rather than through ASF.

When Under Secretary Patterson saw the scheme proposed by the planners, he immediately sensed its inherent weakness. It was, he said, "awkward and unsound." He could not exercise effective supervision over Air Force procurement without a staff; authority to control policy without an adequate staff organization to follow up the details gave only the form and not the substance of power. This was axiomatic. But the March 1942 reorganization stripped most of the Under Secretary's staff from him and placed it under the Commanding General, ASF. Moreover, unless both the AAF and the ASF pursued a uniform course in procurement matters, there was real danger of a return to the confusion and interbranch competition that had discredited Army contracting in World War I.

To escape from the dilemma confronting him, the Under Secretary finally hit

---
[31] *Ibid.*, pp. 30–34; Memo, G. H. Dorr, Notes on the Activities of an Informal Group in Connection With Supply Reorganization in the War Dept, Jan–May 1942, OCMH files.

ORGANIZATION FOR PROCUREMENT

upon an expedient solution. It was natural for him to work with the officers of his old staff who had moved into the ASF. He knew them as individuals and understood something of their activities. So he continued to use them, instructing them to impose uniformity in contract procedures on the AAF Materiel Command as well as the technical services within ASF. But when dealing with air arm matters they were to do so "for the Under Secretary personally" and not in their capacity as ASF officers. In practice, this bit of fiction actually involved one man, Col. A. J. Browning, an industrialist newly commissioned from private life. Colonel Browning as chief of the Purchase Division, ASF, was the officer to whom the Commanding General, ASF, had delegated most matters of procurement policy. Thus, when dealing with the AAF Materiel Command, Colonel Browning acted as the "Special Representative of the Under Secretary of War." In dealing with the other technical services he acted as the chief of the Purchases Division, ASF, down the normal chain of command, even when sending out directives identical to those issued to the AAF.[32]

While expedient, the Under Secretary's "Special Representative" formula for using the ASF to impose policy on the air arm was not without its shortcomings. Even among the men who drew up the reorganization in 1942 the subterfuge was regarded as "not particularly dignified,"[33] and from the point of view of procurement officers at Wright Field, still more serious objections could be

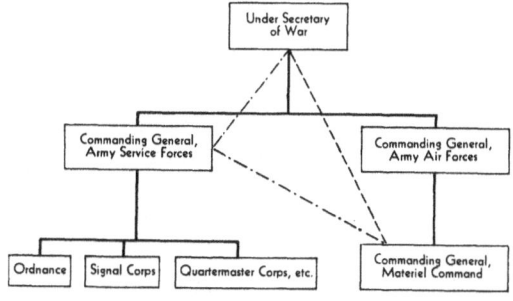

CO-ORDINATION BETWEEN USW AND MATERIEL COMMAND

Organizational chart showing the expedient arrangement by which the USW retained direct policy control over the Materiel Command, AAF, after the War Department reorganization of March 1942 placed responsibility for procurement procedures within the ASF.

— — — — — line of co-ordination in original reorganization plan.

— · — · — · — · line of co-ordination suggested by Under Secretary Patterson.

raised. No matter how much it was sugar coated with fictions, the arrangement still left the formulation of procurement policy in the hands of ground force officers. To minimize resistance on this score, the Under Secretary provided two built-in safeguards. He directed ASF to establish an Air Forces liaison office to clear all proposed directives with the AAF Materiel Command before issue. Where agreement could not be reached on a proposed procurement regulation or similar matter, air arm officers were empowered to carry appeals personally to the Under Secretary for a decision.[34]

The officers in charge of Air Forces matériel were quite willing to go along with the Under Secretary's polite fiction,

---

[32] Dorr Memo, cited n. 31; Millett, *Organization and Role of ASF*, p. 125.

[33] Dorr Memo, cited n. 31.

[34] USW to CGs, ASF and AAF, 9 Apr 42, AFCF 400.12 Method and Program of Proc; Function of Proc Function of the AAF, Lecture by Swatland.

GENERAL SOMERVELL

since they recognized the need for uniform procurement regulations. Three months later they were even willing to acquiesce silently when he delegated his job of approving certain classes of Air Forces contracts to Colonel Browning as his special representative. In effect this meant that contracts for air matériel involving the largest dollar volume could not be officially approved by a major general in the AAF but had to await the signature of a colonel in the ASF who was actually two echelons below the Under Secretary. Colonel Browning's promotion to brigadier general scarcely altered the incongruity. And when he in turn redelegated the authority for granting deviations in standard contract forms to Mr. W. C. Marbury, a Baltimore lawyer serving in the Purchases Division, ASF, Air Forces officers began to wonder if the fiction had been carried too far.[35]

The matter came to a head during the major reorganization of the AAF headquarters staff in March 1943.[36] The staff planners in the management control office who worked out the details of the reorganization discovered in studying their little boxes and black lines of authority that the arrangement contrived a year before in the reorganization of March 1942 was really quite impossible. The unique relationship of the air arm and the Under Secretary was symbolized on the organizational charts by a dotted line running from the Commanding General, Materiel Command to the Under Secretary. But the reshuffling of the AAF headquarters in March 1943 saw the title Commanding General, Materiel Command, move out to Wright Field. General Echols, who had held that position, became Assistant Chief of Air Staff, Materiel, Maintenance and Distribution, on the Air Staff.

To leave the relationship of the Under Secretary (or his special representative) and the Commanding General, Materiel Command, unchanged, would be to cut the whole Washington headquarters organization of the AAF from consideration of matériel questions. On further reflection the staff planners realized that for the whole year, or so long as the "dotted line" had run directly from the Commanding General, Materiel Command, to the Under Secretary on the official organizational charts, the Commanding General, AAF, himself, had been entirely left out of the procurement picture.[37]

By rephrasing a few directives, the lines of authority could be straightened

---

[35] Memo, Maj R. G. Storey for ACofAS Management Control, 1 Oct 42; Memo, Col G. R. Perera for Lt Col G. A. Brownell, 17 Oct 42. Both in AFCF 400.12 Method and Program of Proc.

[36] See above, p. 265.

[37] Memo, Chief, Management Control, for CofAS, 30 Apr 43, AFCF 161 Renegotiation.

GENERAL BROWNING   ROBERT P. PATTERSON   GENERAL ECHOLS

out, but the mere fact that the "impossible" pattern laid down in the reorganization of 1942 had worked for a whole year suggests how little it mattered what the organizational charts and directives said. The really important consideration was how the system actually worked. And it did work despite the absurdities and incongruities. The AAF got what its partisans wanted: its procurement operations were not swallowed up by ASF as some had feared would happen; and for all practical purposes, Air Forces officers retained substantial control over the procurement of air matériel even while the Under Secretary met his statutory obligation to maintain uniformity in the procurement practices of the Army.

In establishing the relationship of the air arm to the rest of the Army, it would seem that the precise form of the organizations employed was less important than the attitudes of the men who ran them. Fortunately, Under Secretary Patterson, General Browning, and General Echols were all men of good will who worked together in harmony. The special representative arrangement employed by the Under Secretary may have horrified the experts who drew up neat and symetrical organizational charts, but it worked so well it was subsequently taken over more or less intact and applied again at least twice in other situations.[38]

Seen in retrospect, the command requirement of co-ordination and control presents a surprisingly similar pattern at any echelon. Whether one views the problem within the matériel organization at Wright Field, within the larger framework of the AAF, or within the still larger structure of the Military Establishment as a whole, the necessity for ever larger staffs at the supervisory level is clear. As the size of every operating organization mounted, officers in respon-

---

[38] The special representative device was used to co-ordinate price adjustment and termination policies of both the Renegotiation Division and the Readjustment Division, ASF, with the AAF. Perhaps the best evidence of the broad latitude ASF left to the AAF is in the almost total neglect of AAF problems in the Purchases Division. ASF Purchases Div, Purchasing Policies and Practices, especially pp. 91–92.

sible positions found a comprehensive over-all view progressively more difficult to maintain. They had to resort to larger staffs, yet these staffs themselves generated problems that in turn had to be resolved. Nevertheless, the experience of the war years demonstrated beyond question that few of these difficulties defied solution if the officers concerned made a genuine effort to take a broad view, striving conscientiously to perceive the interests of every echelon concerned with a particular question. Admittedly, that broad view was often difficult to take. Few aspects of matériel procurement revealed more vexing features of control and co-ordination than did the efforts at cross procurement undertaken within the Military Establishment.

Cross Procurement

The terms of the 1942 reorganization of War Department placed responsibility for Army procurement on ASF, except for items "peculiar to Army Air Forces." This was clear enough so long as the planners thought in terms of aircraft and other such obvious end items. But what about the borderline cases that might or might not be regarded as "peculiar to the AAF"? Who was going to draw the line? Here was a test of precisely that kind of supervision and over-all leadership envisioned for the Assistant Secretary of War in the Defense Act of 1920. By March 1942 the Assistant Secretary's procurement duties had been absorbed by the newly established office of Under Secretary, but the principle remained the same. To prevent duplication of effort where two or more of the technical services used an item in common, the Under Secretary could assign procurement responsibility to a single service, which would then buy in quantity for all users, a procedure known as single service procurement or cross procurement.

Jurisdictional disputes between the services were almost inevitable in any program of cross procurement. The job of the Under Secretary was to resolve them, but could he do so to the satisfaction of all the parties concerned? To attempt an answer is to come firmly to grips with the knotty problem of procurement assignment.

Procurement Assignment

In 1942 procurement assignment was not new to the War Department—at least in theory. As far back as 1934 the Assistant Secretary had set up the Procurement Assignment Board to make assignments for cross procurement by a single service. In practice, the board virtually dried up for want of cases referred to it. There were indeed many instances of overlapping, but the technical services repeatedly found that cross procurement was slower than direct procurement and involved a good deal of tedious administrative effort to boot.[39]

The Procurement Assignment Board continued to exist, but the technical services often managed to circumvent cross procurement by the simple expedient of ignoring the board. Typical of this pattern was the case of the Graflex camera. In 1940 the Signal Corps and the Air Corps each signed a large contract for ex-

---

[39] See, for example, IOM, Asst Chief, Mat Div, for Chief, Mat Div, 11 Oct 40, AFCF 400.12.

actly the same model Graflex; the only difference in their orders was that the Air Corps specification called for a leather carrying case while the Signal Corps required one of plastic.[40] If ever there was an opportunity for cross procurement, this was it. Such bald evasions led some to feel that the main purpose of the Procurement Assignment Board was to stand as a monument that could be pointed to during congressional hearings as evidence that "duplication" had been eliminated from military buying.

One might well argue that the frequent evasion of procurement assignment in peacetime caused no great damage and might even have been beneficial. A great deal could be said for maintaining the closest possible ties between the using service and the manufacturer. Moreover, it could also be shown that in some cases the costs of duplication in contracting were no greater than the cost of administering the interservice transfers resulting from cross procurement. On the other hand, by avoiding cross procurement in peacetime the Army entered the war with only limited experience in its administration. Scarcity of materials and acute competition for production facilities in wartime made the elimination of minor differences in specifications and the consolidation of departmental requirements for common items nothing less than mandatory. To fail to use cross procurement was to invite justifiable criticism from industry and open the way for a civilian superagency to impose cross procurement forcefully from outside the Military Establishment.[41]

The flood of buying that followed Pearl Harbor produced so many instances of duplicate buying among the services that the Under Secretary resolved to take vigorous corrective action. But since a large part of his organization had been transferred to ASF, he had no staff of his own to handle this kind of problem and thus had to delegate the job to the ASF. There, at his behest, the Director of the Purchases Division set up a new Procurement Assignment Board and laid out a set of operating procedures for it to follow. The new regulations called for cross procurement whenever there was significant competition over a common item, the dollar value was of consequence, one service was the predominant user, or confusion existed within the Army as to just where procurement responsibility should be for any given item.[42]

Looking back at a later date, the chairman of the new board was inclined to believe that a number of substantial benefits had flowed from the board's operations. Among other gains, the board had eliminated "priority competition" among the services, simplified the planning of facility expansions, guaranteed a uniform price on common items, and cut costs by reducing administrative overhead.[43] In some measure these contentions were true, but to accept them at face value would be to succumb to the old refrain, "we have eliminated dupli-

---

[40] Col Volandt to Asst Chief, Mat Div, 18 Oct 42, AFCF 400.12.

[41] For illustration of appreciation for this point within the military organization, see OCAC, Letter of Instruction No. 79, 4 Oct 40, AFCF 400.12.

[42] Draper-Strauss Rpt, II, 61–62. For further information on joint Army-Navy procurement and the Draper-Strauss Rpt, see Millett, *Organization and Role of ASF*, ch. 18.

[43] *Ibid.*

Problems of Cross Procurement

Although the historian of the ASF has observed that the AAF was "favorably disposed" toward the work of the new Procurement Assignment Board, in doing so he rather generously overlooked the considerable opposition to the board initially offered by the air arm.[44] At first AAF resistance followed the traditional pattern of evasion that had helped sidetrack the earlier assignment board. When ASF requested a list of AAF items that might be regarded as suitable candidates for procurement assignment, the Air Forces blandly denied using any such items and declined to make recommendations for possible action by the board.[45]

There were a number of reasons why many Air Forces officers resisted cross procurement. To many the growth of ASF represented a real threat. They did not deny the importance of and need for centralized, Army-wide supervision over procurement and the elimination of the more egregious examples of overlapping effort. And so long as the Assistant Secretary or the Under Secretary had performed this supervisory role at the departmental level, they were inclined to be co-operative. But when the Under Secretary passed many of his functions down to ASF, Air Forces officers feared they would be left at the mercy of a board dominated by the ground arms.

Some AAF officers believed, moreover, that cross procurement was only a camel's nose under the tent. Would the Procurement Assignment Board stop with common items, or would it go on eventually to take over the whole range of air matériel procurement including even airplanes and engines? Whether justified or not, views such as these were expressed during 1942 when ASF, under General Somervell's aggressive leadership, was expanding rapidly in many directions.[46]

By no means all of the Air Forces resistance to cross procurement was attributable to the impetus toward autonomy or mere branch consciousness; there were very real disadvantages in any scheme that placed procurement of any AAF item in the hands of another service. To appreciate this, AAF officers had only to look at what happened when they themselves controlled procurement and another service looked to them for supplies. The North American AT-6 two-place trainer offered a case in point. Although the AAF was the sole military agent in contracting with the manufacturer for this aircraft in quantity, a portion of the order was on cross procurement for the Navy. When the Navy asked for some modifications on its portion of the order to make the aircraft suitable for naval use, the production staff at Wright Field resisted on the grounds that any tampering with production would reduce the

---

[44] Millett, *Organization and Role of ASF*, p. 126.
[45] Memo, Dir, Proc and Distribution Div, SOS, for CGMC, 3 Jun 42, and reply, 18 Jun 42, AFCF 400.12 Method and Program of Proc. Compare this evasion with the same practice a year earlier, Memo, Chairman, Proc Assignment Board, OUSW, for CofAC, 8 Aug 41, and 1st Ind, 26 Aug 41, in reply, AFCF 400.12.

[46] For illustrative examples of opposition within the AAF to cross procurement in principle, see R&R, Comment 5, AFASC to AFDAS thru AFAMC, 18 Dec 42, and Comment 6, AFAMC 4A to AFDAS, 31 Dec 42, AFCF, 161 Purchasing and Contracting Officers.

ORGANIZATION FOR PROCUREMENT

total number of units turned out.[47] If the AAF could do this to the Navy—or any of the services—the same practice might be expected in return.

Probably the most important single factor in generating resistance to the cross procurement idea was the fear that assignment to another service would result in loss of control over the design characteristics and production output of the equipment being purchased. By injecting a third party—often one with decided interests of his own—between the manufacturer and the user, the resort to cross procurement could stimulate conflicts. If Air Forces officers in 1942 were reluctant to move into an extensive program of cross procurement, it is well to recall that their attitudes were conditioned by a number of unhappy episodes arising from an essay in cross procurement the previous year.

The case of the Norden bombsight offers an excellent example of the difficulties attending any attempt at cross procurement involving highly technical apparatus. Although the AAF was the major user of the precision device, absorbing up to 90 percent of output at the time of Pearl Harbor, all procurement took place through the Navy. Norden had developed the sight for the Navy in the early thirties, and the Norden plant had been under Navy cognizance ever since. If the sight had been of static design, most of the trouble might have been avoided. But the design was far from static. Like the bombers in which it was employed, the Norden sight was subject to continuous modification that left a trail of related changes in its wake. Instruction manuals got out of date, but complaints could only be forwarded to the Navy. Parts lists and drawings of use in planning spares orders and training programs took more than a year to reach Army air arm users through Navy channels. The manufacturer was quite willing to communicate directly with air officers, but, to maintain effective control, the Navy prohibited this with only a few exceptions.[48]

Officers in the Navy Department were not deliberately sabotaging the interests of the Army air arm. The delays and inconveniences that marked the cross procurement of the Norden sight were simply those inherent in any procurement system that injected a third party between the maker and user. Because of the inadequacies in the existing arrangements, a number of officers holding important positions in AAF headquarters were persuaded that cross procurement was unsound in principle and especially undesirable when applied to equipment of any considerable complexity.[49] Nevertheless, after extensive consideration matériel officers on the air staff had to concede that single service procurement was imperative in many instances in order to prevent unseemly competition within

---

[47] TWX, Tech Exec (WF) to Tech Exec (OCAC), 16 Sep 40, WF Contract files, 360.01.

[48] Craven and Cate, eds., *Plans and Early Operations*, p. 598; R&R, Chief, Inspection Div, to Mat Div, 29 Apr 41, AFCF 452.1 Airplanes, Gen; ASW to USN, 11 Jul 41, AFCF 400.12 Proc; Asst Tech Exec (WF) to Chief, Mat Div, OCAC, 17 Dec 41, AFCF 319.1 Misc Rpts.

[49] For an illustration of AAF resistance to the assignment of procurement responsibility to other services, see Memo, Chief, Aircraft Sec, Hq, SOS, for CGMC, 1 May 42, and undated 1st Ind, Hq AAF, to CG, Armored Forces; Chief, Supply Div, ASC, to Chief, Field Services, ASC, 20 May 42. All in AFCF 400.12 Method and Program of Proc.

the Military Establishment.⁵⁰ Any attempt to put AAF interests ahead of all others was to take a position manifestly untenable. Cross procurement raised many grave difficulties in operation, but abandoning the principle would only bring about another set of problems. Obviously, the sensible course was to recognize the new Procurement Assignment Board and make its work effective by reconciling conflicts of interest with the utmost good will.

Cross Procurement in Action

Despite the initial resistance of the AAF to cross procurement, a great many classes of matériel were successfully subjected to single service assignment once it became AAF policy. In addition to such obvious items as food and clothing, the list included an incredible array ranging from insecticides, locomotives, and dry cells to flags, fuels, and fork lifts. Of course, cross procurement did not invariably mean that some other service purchased for the air arm; sometimes the reverse was true, most notably in the matter of aircraft. In 1942, for example, 34.7 percent of all airframes ordered by the Navy were procured through Air Forces channels.⁵¹

As procurement officers in the several services acquired experience in co-operating with one another, they modified and improved the techniques of cross procurement and introduced novel forms of collaboration. Typical of these was the Army-Navy Petroleum Board established in October 1943 as a joint agency to co-ordinate the procurement activities of all military users of petroleum products. Although the board left the actual mechanics of contracting with the several services, it consolidated requirements, set up common specifications, and agreed on maximum prices to be paid. Since some 62 percent of the nation's 200 major suppliers of petroleum products sold to both the Army and the Navy, including the various using services within each department, this form of collaboration was obviously of great advantage.⁵²

While the numerous experiments in co-operation undertaken by military buyers during the war gradually won adherents as successful practice led to mutual confidence, there were some areas of procurement that remained trouble spots throughout the war. Special tools offer a case in point. Even in October 1945, after the war was over, the Army and the Navy were still in open competition when purchasing aircraft tools despite the efforts of several boards and commissions to settle the matter.⁵³ Although the available evidence is inconclusive, it seems clear that the character of the problem rather than any want of good will lay behind this failure.

By their very nature, tools, especially small hand tools, were bound to pose difficulties for procurement officers. In the first place, infinite variety in design and use in widely different environments under rapidly changing conditions com-

---

⁵⁰ R&R, ACofAS-4 to AAG, 26 Feb 43, AFCF 161 Purchasing and Contracting Officers.

⁵¹ Millett, *Organization and Role of ASF*, p. 127; Draper-Strauss Rpt, III, 143. In 1943 the figure fell to 26.8 percent and in 1944 to 13.3 percent.

⁵² Draper-Strauss Rpt, III, 43.

⁵³ Supply of Tools, one of several miscellaneous unsigned reports complied 25 October 1945 in response to a directive from T-5 (Management Control and Plans), WFHO Research file, AMC, Experience in Wartime Expansion. See also, Draper-Strauss Rpt, III, 155-57.

ORGANIZATION FOR PROCUREMENT

bined to make seemingly simple tools as unsuited to cross procurement as the highly complex apparatus on which the tools were to be used. While a single service such as the Quartermaster Corps might successfully procure carpenter's hammers for all the Army technical services including the AAF, and the Navy too for that matter, this was hardly true of the tools used in maintaining aircraft and aeronautical accessories. Virtually every new aircraft engine, instrument, and accessory of any complexity required from one to a multitude of special tools for maintenance. In a sense, the tools were really a part of the equipment on which they were to be used. Under these circumstances, even though a certain amount of duplication resulted, direct procurement by the using service was probably justified. To have insisted on the "economies" of cross procurement in such a situation might well have turned out to be penny wise and pound foolish.

In any dispute over a proposed candidate for cross procurement, Air Forces officers always held one important trump card: if they believed emphatically that it would be in the best interest of the service to procure directly a certain item of equipment, they could declare it "peculiar to the AAF"—they could write up a specification that would put the item beyond the jurisdiction of the Procurement Assignment Board. Since direct procurement was generally quicker than cross procurement, air arm buyers were sometimes tempted to declare borderline cases "peculiar to the AAF" in the interests of speed. At Wright Field, so some humorists claimed, contracting officers in a hurry even went so far as to buy "technical broomsticks." Although this particular taunt was probably a canard, the method was nevertheless occasionally used to evade cross procurement.[54]

Evasion of cross procurement was not always possible, even when it may have seemed desirable in particular instances to air arm officials. Some items of equipment of absolutely vital significance to the air arm, especially in the communications and ordnance categories, clearly fell within the jurisdiction of other technical services. There was substantial justification for cross procurement in these cases. Both the Ordnance Department and the Signal Corps had built up large staffs of specialists as well as impressive laboratories and testing sites that would have had to be duplicated to some extent if the air arm had attempted direct procurement. On the other hand, cross procurement of equipment so obviously complex as the Ordnance and Signal items was bound to raise endless difficulties of coordination.

In a very real sense, both communications and ordnance items are intrinsic elements of military aircraft. Air arm doctrine tirelessly reiterated that the combat airplane was nothing more than a gun platform. To achieve maximum effectiveness the airplane had to be designed around the weapons it mounted—whether these be machine guns, cannon, rocket launchers, or bomb racks. And the same applied to communications equipment, a broad category that extended far beyond radio apparatus to embrace a whole series of radar devices for navigation, target identification, and electronic gun-laying. Although cross

---

[54] Pringle Papers, item 22, Tab: AAF.

procurement under such circumstances was an open door to conflicts, at least down to the beginning of guided missile development the Ordnance Department and the Air Forces were able to resolve their problems without serious delay.[55]

Relations between the Air Forces and the Signal Corps proved rather more turbulent. During each year of the war, the procurement of radio and radar items for the AAF led to administrative difficulties. Even before the outbreak of hostilities in 1939, air arm officers had studied the possibility of assuming responsibility for the procurement of such items but rejected the idea on its merits. They were anxious not to "precipitate a fight" with the Signal Corps on the eve of war, and they recognized that the technical specialists required to do the job might be hard to find.[56] As a compromise, the Signal Corps agreed to establish a procurement organization at Wright Field to handle all signal equipment relating to aviation.

Physical proximity of the Signal Corps procurement staff to the laboratories of the Engineering Division at Wright Field proved immensely helpful in simplifying the task of co-ordination. Nevertheless, the relationship remained an awkward one, especially as each successive year of the war witnessed great strides forward in the technology of electronics.[57] Radio-radar devices became more than ever an integral part of aircraft and a proportionately higher percentage of their total cost. After months of study General Marshall, as Chief of Staff, finally decided in July 1944 that the AAF was indeed entitled to direct control over procurement of aviation communications equipment. Although the official transfer of responsibility was set for April 1945, the procurement omelet proved hard to unscramble, and some details were still being worked out when the war ended.[58]

In looking back upon the experience of the war years it seems clear that the problem of overlapping or duplication of effort admitted of no simple or clearcut solutions. On the one hand it is evident that the purchase of common items could not be left entirely to the individual services, for un-co-ordinated buying leads to competitive chaos, costly to the taxpayers and harmful to the best interests of the military users. Nor, on the other hand, was procurement assignment a full and sufficient answer to every case of duplication and conflict. As the record of the war reveals, there were some types of equipment for which the administrative inconvenience and the loss of sensitive control over technical details attendant upon cross procurement were too high a price to pay for the elimination of duplication. Whenever possible the avoidance of overlapping effort was desirable, but there was grave danger in reducing this objective to a formula.

---

[55] Constance McL. Green, Harry C. Thomson, and Peter C. Roots, *The Ordnance Department: Planning Munitions for War*, UNITED STATES ARMY IN WORLD WAR II (Washington, 1955), p. 233.

[56] Rpt of com to study Mat Div organization, 10 Jan 39, AC Project Rcds (Lyon Papers), bk. 18.

[57] The dissatisfaction was not all one-sided. For evidence that the Signal Corps found the air arm a most difficult customer to satisfy, see Dulany Terrett, *The Signal Corps: The Emergency*, THE UNITED STATES ARMY IN WORLD WAR II (Washington, 1956) ch. X, *passim*.

[58] AAF Hist Study 10, pp. 100–101. See also, Millett, *Organization and Role of ASF*, p. 128, and Russel, History of AAF ATSC: 1944, pp. 132–35.

ORGANIZATION FOR PROCUREMENT

CHART 5—ARMY AIR FORCES ORGANIZATION: 9 MARCH 1942

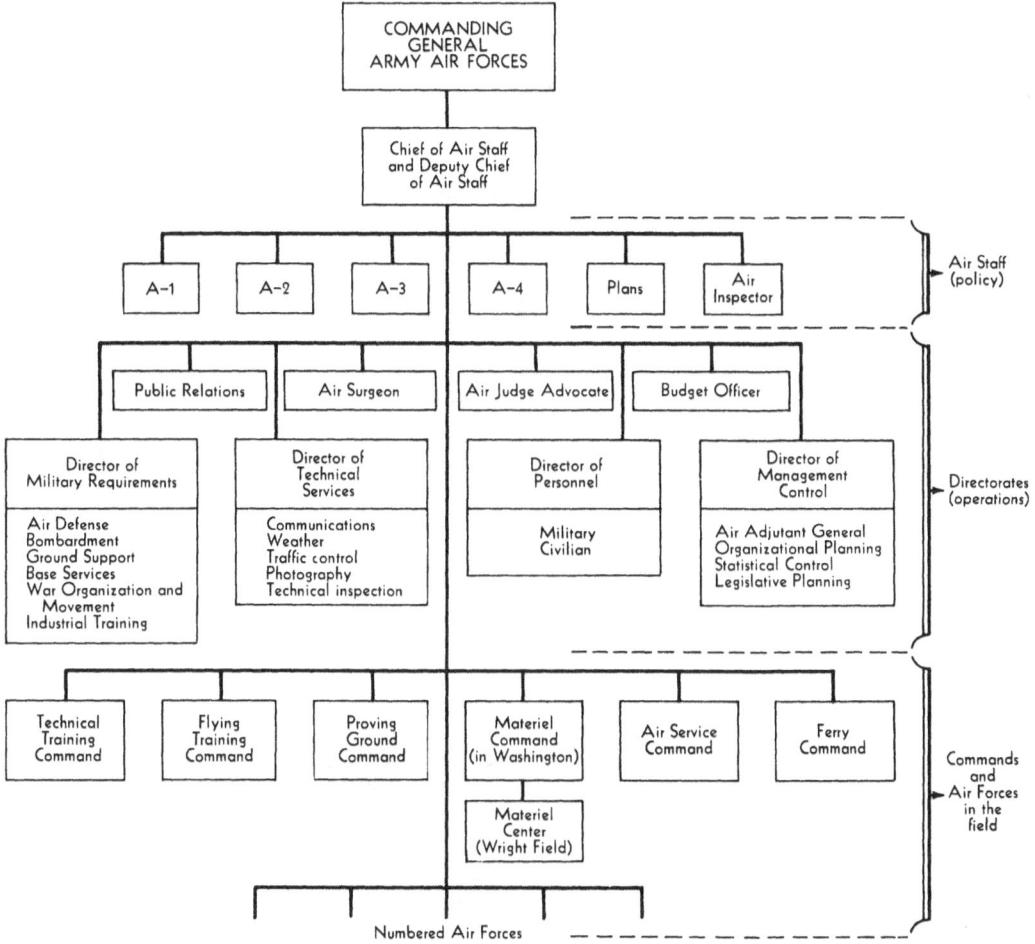

Source: Based on Chart 4, AAF Hist Study 10.

The selection of an appropriate pattern of procurement—single-service purchasing by assignment, collaborative buying through the establishment of some joint central agency, or out-and-out duplication of effort by several services—rested upon the circumstances prevailing in each particular case.

Centralization and Decentralization

Administrative organizations in the field of military procurement have two main purposes. On the one hand, they must provide those in authority with the information, the facts and figures, neces-

CHART 6—ORGANIZATION OF THE MATERIEL COMMAND: 19 OCTOBER 1942

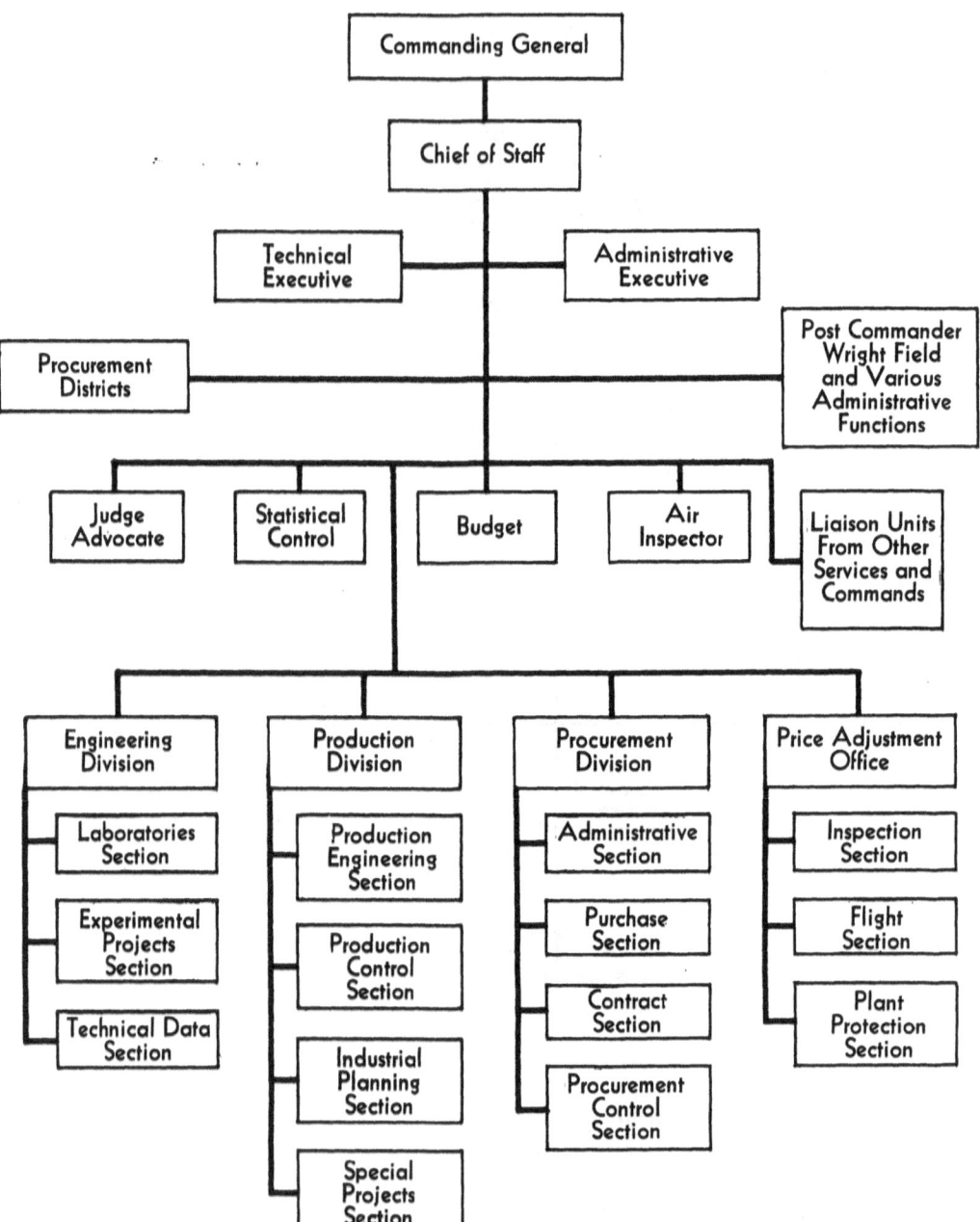

Source: Based on chart in Appendix 56, McMurtrie, History of Materiel Command: 1942.

ORGANIZATION FOR PROCUREMENT

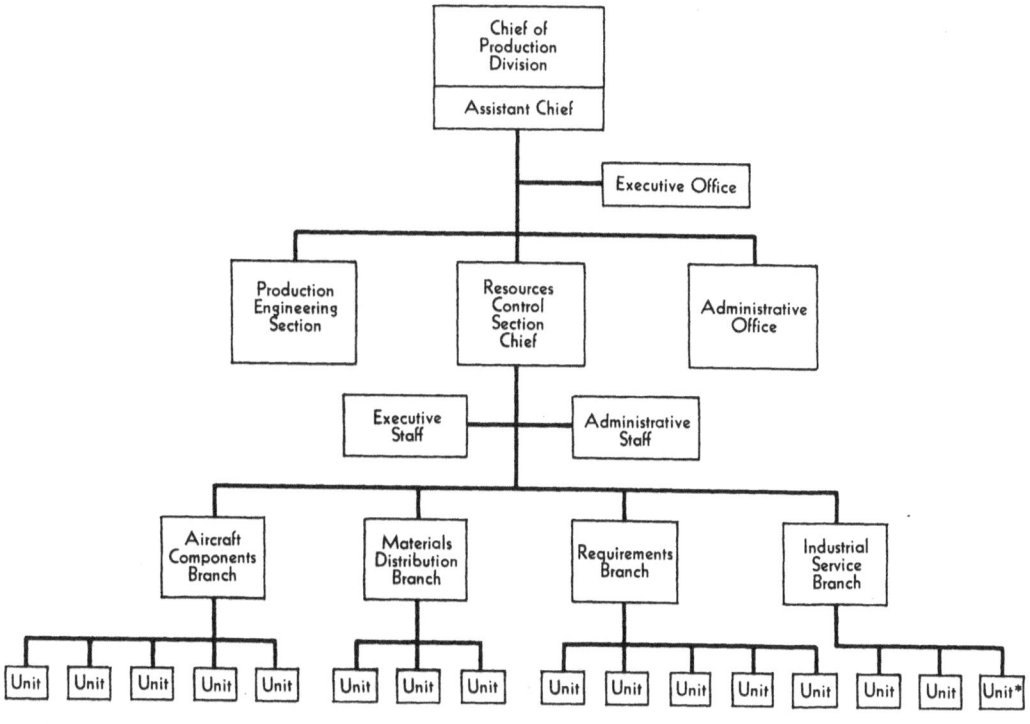

Chart 7—Organization of the Resources Control Section of the Production Division, Materiel Command: July 1943

*In some instances units were still further subdivided.
Source: Based on Appendixes 37 and 38, History of the Materiel Command: 1943.

sary to exercise the decision-making functions of command. And on the other hand, they must provide the nation's manufacturers, the thousands of contractors who produce the equipment purchased by the government, with all those services they require to do the jobs expected of them. By and large, the foregoing pages of this chapter have been concerned with the former of these two functions: they have dealt with the problems implicit in the successive steps by which the threads of control were concentrated in the upper echelons of command. No less essential was the need for organizations to provide an effective relationship with industry.

What kind of a procurement organization would best serve the needs of industry in wartime? Ever since the passage of the Air Corps Act in 1926, this question had been debated by air arm planners. In peace, of course, the relatively small volume of business transacted made it feasible to centralize all procurement at Wright Field, but from time to time proposals to decentralize the procurement function to outlying district offices in the

CHART 8—ARMY AIR FORCES ORGANIZATION: 29 MARCH 1943

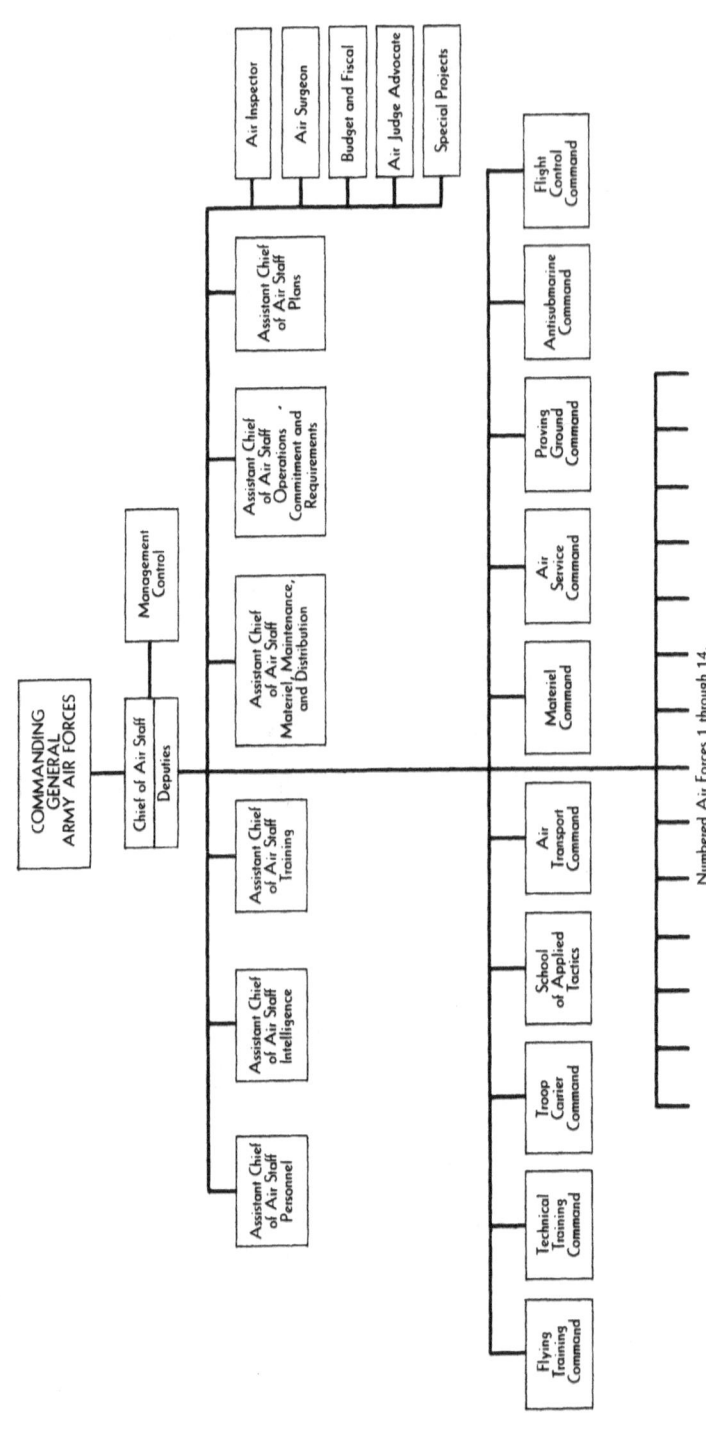

Source: Based on Chart 6, AAF Historical Study 10.

ORGANIZATION FOR PROCUREMENT

event of hostilities received consideration.[59]

The issue was still under discussion when war broke out in Europe and the rearmament program got under way at home. Since the nation was still technically at peace, it was natural for those in command to continue using the existing procurement organization. Thus, by the time the country actually began fighting after Pearl Harbor, the buying operation was already so far advanced at Wright Field that the decision between a centralized and a decentralized organization had already been decided by default in favor of the former.[60]

Centralized Procurement

When the rearmament program began, the procurement districts as such did not exist. From the establishment of the Air Corps in 1926 through 1939, the so-called districts were actually two entirely separate entities, one to provide local centers to inspect the supplies purchased and the other for industrial mobilization planning purposes. Not until the very end of 1939 were these functions combined to form three new procurement districts, the Eastern, the Central, and the Western, with offices in New York City, Detroit, and Santa Monica, California. Even then the caption *Procurement District* was something of a misnomer, since the functions of the districts were almost entirely limited to the administration of contracts written at Wright Field, and none of them built up elaborate staffs to negotiate large contracts.[61]

A number of other considerations made centralized procurement a logical course to pursue. In the first place, by far the largest dollar volume of air arm expenditures during the war went into aircraft contracts. This meant that most of the money would go to a limited number of firms, not more than seventy-five at the outside, including engine and propeller manufacturers as well as airframe builders.[62] Since only a handful of men were trained to undertake the enormously complex business of negotiating aircraft contracts for the government, it was of obvious advantage to have the few available do the whole job at Wright Field. The big manufacturers expected to negotiate there as they always had. Indeed, many of them maintained nearby offices especially for this purpose.[63] Moreover, since virtually every tactical aircraft ordered during the emergency was still in the process of development and subject to frequent changes in design, it was of the utmost importance for procurement

---

[59] See, for example, Exec, OCAC, to Chief, Mat Div, 6 Feb 28, and related Inds, WFCF 381 Mobilization, 1939.

[60] For a discussion of this problem, see Russel, Hist of AAF ATSC: 1944, p. 141ff.

[61] McMurtrie and Davis, Hist of AAF MC: 1926-41, ch. III.

[62] H. G. Silverman, Central Office, MM&D, to Col S. A. Rosenblatt, 11 Jun 43, AFCF 400 Small Plants. A Wright Field study showed the following distribution during the Korean War: only 5 percent of the contracts written exceeded a million dollars, but this 5 percent accounted for over 90 percent of the money obligated. See Decentralization Presentation for Area Commanders, AMC, 17 Apr 52, WFHO Research file.

[63] Some have been inclined to regard these offices as the "Dayton lobby" for use in subverting weak-willed contracting officers. While a few of them may have been so misused at times, some such local offices were certainly needed to handle the mass of detailed business a number of firms carried on at Wright Field.

officers to maintain the closest sort of co-ordination with the technical staff of the Engineering and Production Divisions. Finally, the myriad details arising in connection with facility expansions, the provision of machine tools, and other matters of this sort requiring co-ordination with the national superagencies, afforded still further justification, if any were needed, for concentrating aircraft procurement at Wright Field.

However justifiable it may have been in terms of efficiency and economy to negotiate contracts at a single center, in concentrating the entire purchasing operation there, air arm officials left themselves wide open for criticism. The officials of large aircraft or engine firms dickering for multimillion dollar orders might find it no great hardship to fly across the country for this purpose, but to thousands of small businessmen who wished to bid on lesser items this was hardly the case. And while the lion's share of the matériel dollar went into a few contracts calling for complete aircraft and other major end products, by far the larger number of contracts drawn at Wright Field went to relatively small firms supplying minor but important items of equipment. In this category were to be found most of those firms supplying small accessories and personal equipment such as flying suits, as well as the host of concerns providing all the servicing and maintenance equipment required by modern aircraft. With few exceptions, manufacturers in this group relied upon correspondence and mailed bids when seeking contracts from the air arm.

The difficulties of trying to initiate a contract by mail with a military procurement agency scarcely need elaboration. In the first place, thousands of small companies anxious to get government orders found it difficult to locate the right buyer. For example, a ceramics manufacturer specializing in porcelain eggs for homing pigeons who wrote vaguely to "the Aviation Department" had to be referred to the Signal Corps. Another would-be supplier who wrote to the "Air Corps, Maritime Commission, Treasury Procurement Division" all in one breath, as it were, had to be shown that this shotgun approach was quite unnecessary. In fact, whenever the President made a radio address mentioning the aircraft program, officials all over Washington had to devote untold hours for weeks thereafter referring misdirected letters into the proper channels. Out of this confusing welter of correspondence, those few who could supply items of interest to air arm buyers were put on the appropriate advertising registers at Wright Field to await subsequent invitations to bid.[64]

Unfortunately, as many hopeful manufacturers were to discover, listing on one of the Wright Field advertising registers did not in itself solve the problem of bringing buyer and seller together. When Contract Section officials sent out circular proposals to the manufacturers on the list, the need for equipment was so urgent that they could seldom allow more than two weeks before opening the bids. In this short time, even old-line suppliers, manufacturers who had been doing business at Wright Field for years, sometimes found it difficult to prepare and return bids. For manufacturers with no experience in military contracts or in

---

[64] AFCF 163 Bids, Alphabetical file, especially for 1940–41, *passim*.

ORGANIZATION FOR PROCUREMENT 493

working to government specifications, two weeks were often entirely inadequate.

Suppliers on the west coast in particular suffered a disadvantage in trying to get their bids in on time. As one manufacturer in California complained, it took anywhere from five to seven days for circular proposals to reach the coast from Wright Field. The invitations were not always mailed the day they were issued, and even then they traveled by regular post rather than by air, sometimes leaving the manufacturers a scant four days to prepare bids. Moreover, since it was obviously impractical to send out bulky specifications and blueprints to every firm listed on the advertising register, would-be bidders often had to visit the nearest procurement district office and vie with one another for an opportunity to study them there—provided the appropriate papers had arrived at the procurement district office, which was not always the case.[65]

In time, as administrative procedures were refined and the staff strengthened at Wright Field, many of the difficulties encountered by bidders on supply contracts were overcome. To be sure, the fundamental disadvantage of centralized procurement—the lack of direct personal contact between buyer and seller—remained. Nonetheless, while this did lead to a number of complaints from individual contractors, in general their remarks looked to improved administration rather than any basic change in the existing organization.[66]

The loudest criticism of the procurement system came not from those who found it difficult to do business with the government but from those who found they could get no business at all. During 1940 each successive month had seen the supply of critical raw materials grow scarcer as the rearmament program at home and exports to foreign nations absorbed an ever larger share of the national economy. As the system of priorities established by the civilian superagencies began to pinch tighter, one manufacturer after another found himself forced to make a choice: he must either secure a military contract and the priority rating on materials that went with it or go out of business.[67] Thus confronted, droves of manufacturers who had hitherto never dreamed of looking for government contracts descended upon the military services. Regrettably, most of those who found their way to Wright Field came away empty-handed, though some who could convert their plants to manufacture one or another of the items purchased directly by the air arm did get contracts.

The reasons for not securing contracts are not hard to perceive. Since by far the greater part of the sums spent at Wright Field went to the relatively small number of firms capable of producing major end items such as bombers, fighters, power plants, gun turrets, superchargers, and the like, all but the strongest firms

---

[65] A. T. Case Co., Los Angeles, to Chief, Contract Sec, WF, 10 Jul 41; Case to Senator Hiram Bingham, 10 Jul 41; SW to Senator Bingham, 4 Aug 41. All in AFCF 163 Bids.

[66] For a typical example of the kind of problems raised by disgruntled bidders, see SW to Compt Gen, 16 Jan 41, AFCF 016.

[67] For an illustration of this trend, see J. C. Paddock Co., Spartanburg, S.C., to Representative J. R. Bryson, 13 Nov 41, along with numerous similar letters, in AFCF 163 Bids. See also, *Business Week* (August 16, 1941), p. 7, "It's Shut Down or Show Down Now."

were virtually precluded from entering such contracts because of their cost and complexity. If small business concerns wished to share in the millions of dollars being spent on this category of air matériel, they would have to do so as subcontractors. This meant that they would have to look to the few manufacturers holding prime contracts for major end items rather than to the contracting officers at Wright Field if they were to find work.

From the point of view of the air arm buyers, this surrender of power to the primes appeared as useful as it was unavoidable. It was useful because passing responsibility for the selection of subcontractors to the prime contractors freed procurement officers at Wright Field of a tremendous burden they were ill equipped to handle; at no time throughout the war were there ever enough really skilled negotiators available in the Matériel Command even to do the work required.[68] It was unavoidable for another reason. If the manufacturers who signed prime contracts were to be held responsible for the timely delivery of large quantities of intricate equipment made to exacting specifications, then they had to be left free to select the means they would employ to attain the desired results, and the means included the subcontractor they chose to help them. While air arm officers might recommend a potential sub to a prime, they could not compel the prime to accept their suggestions.[69] At best they could stipulate in a prime contract that a certain percentage of the total cost was to be subcontracted. To intrude further would be to destroy the whole concept of contractual responsibility upon which the procurement program was erected.[70]

On the other hand, there were a number of desperate manufacturers who regarded the matter in an entirely different light. Because they were unable to see the problem in full perspective, they felt they were being squeezed into bankruptcy by the priorities pinch and found it difficult to understand why they were unable to get supply contracts. In the newspapers they read almost daily accounts of the acute shortage of productive capacity, yet when they offered their own at Wright Field their facilities were spurned. To some at least, this pattern of events seemed to be the rankest kind of inequity: if the contracting officers at Wright Field were not personally guilty of favoring big business, then surely the procurement system itself must be unsound. Protests of this sort reached Congress with increasing frequency and a political response followed.

---

[68] See above, pp. 343-48. Something of the staggering burden of detailed purchasing that air arm officers would have had to handle if all subcontracts were channeled through Wright Field may be suggested by the 965 suppliers located in 287 cities in 38 states required to serve the B-24 facility at Willow Run alone. ATSC Industrial Planning Project Case History: Ford Willow Run, 1946, WFHO.

[69] Memo, Asst Chief, Mat Div, for J. H. Amberg, OSW, 4 Sep 41, with Incl, Utilization of Small Manufacturers in the Aircraft Industry, AFCF 335.5 House and Senate Investigations.

[70] In 1940 airframe primes subcontracted an average of about 5 percent of the face value of their contracts; by 1944 they subcontracted about 37 percent. See ATSC Industrial Planning study, Analysis of the Aircraft Industry, undated (1945), WFHO research file. By April 1944 Air Force prime contractors were passing an estimated 50 percent of every contract dollar on to subcontractors and suppliers. Proc Function of the AAF, Lecture by Swatland.

ORGANIZATION FOR PROCUREMENT

Military Buying Under Fire

The political reaction stirred up by the protests of unhappy manufacturers lies somewhat beyond the scope of this volume. The air arm was only one of a number of procurement agencies within the military services, and criticism by the manufacturers was by no means confined to the activities centering at Wright Field. The problem was thus a general one and as such has been treated at length by the historian of Army procurement as a whole.[71] Nonetheless, the various steps taken by Congress and the civilian superagencies to reform military buying cannot be entirely ignored here, for they had a profound influence upon the subsequent structure of the air arm procurement organization.

In general, political criticism of military agencies tended to concentrate on the charge that the services favored big business over small business. The bulk of the air arm procurement dollar had to go to big business. This, the civilian mobilizers recognized, but continuing complaints from all over the country convinced them that even where the buyers at Wright Field and the other service centers could deal with small firms they continued to award contracts to the larger concerns with which they had long done business. To be sure, the Under Secretary of War repeatedly admonished the technical services about "spreading the load" and "broadening the production base," but the exhortations did not seem to produce practical reforms in procedure.[72] Contracting officers in the military services were judged by their ability to get results—delivery of essential war matériel—and not by the effect their work had on the national economy. Confronted with a choice of two manufacturers, one large, financially powerful, and of known reputation, the other an unknown small business concern, the buyer under pressure for immediate results made the obvious selection. The civilian mobilizers, first in the National Defense Advisory Commission and later in the Office of Production Management, were convinced that military buyers would persist in this pattern in the face of endless directives to the contrary. They decided, therefore, to take corrective action on their own account.

To rectify the alleged preference shown by military buyers for big business, the civilian mobilizers required all contracts over a given dollar value to be routed through their hands in Washington. Ostensibly, no contract would be approved, or granted clearance as the current jargon called it, until the agency officials had satisfied themselves that the military buyers had complied with all the necessary requirements with regard to priorities, use of small business, special consideration to distressed areas, and so on. Unfortunately, the clearance system proved awkward. In effect, it injected the civilian agency into the military chain of command. Moreover, it gave the agency a responsibility it was ill equipped to meet; to pass judgment on a contract the civilian officials had to have access to information not evident in the body of

---

[71] Smith, *The Army and Economic Mobilization*, pt. IV.

[72] Exec, OUSW, to Chiefs of Supply Arms and Services, 10 Sep 41, AFCF 400.12.

the contract itself. To assemble such information involved delays that jeopardized the military procurement program.[73]

After Pearl Harbor the whole scheme of contract clearance was thoroughly overhauled, but long before that happened the civilian mobilizers had come to realize that contract clearance, or after-the-fact supervision, was not ensuring small business an adequate share of the defense dollar. As they saw it, the problem was simply one of bridging the gap between the contracting officers of the military services and would-be contractors. And since they believed the military were not doing the job effectively, they proposed to provide a remedy themselves. To this end, in February 1941, the Office of Production Management established a Defense Contract Service of its own.[74]

In order to reach the small businessmen who had been ignored by the military buyers, the OPM Defense Contract Service opened suboffices in each of the Federal Reserve's twelve banks and twenty-four branch banks scattered about the country. By calling on the staff members of the Federal Reserve system with their wide knowledge of local conditions, regional OPM officials could size up the capabilities of potential suppliers with considerable accuracy. Informed appraisals of this sort, they felt, would go far to offset the objections raised by military buyers to placing important orders with untried firms. At the same time the regional OPM staff could help channel orders to small business by publicizing invitations to bid and other procurement information they could obtain from the military services and by helping inexperienced firms surmount the technicalities encountered when preparing bids on government business.[75]

The official histories of the civilian superagencies have charged that the War Department made only grudging use of the OPM Defense Contract Service.[76] At least insofar as the air arm is concerned, this contention does not appear justified. Officers at Wright Field actually welcomed the new service as a useful adjunct and frequently sought its help. But the best of intentions and endless well wishing could not in themselves make the OPM agency accomplish all that was expected by its proponents.[77]

As might have been expected, it was the intrinsic difficulty of bringing small business into the defense program rather than the attitude of the military buyers that thwarted the high hopes of OPM officials. In a sense, the OPM service was parallel to the regular air arm procure-

---

[73] An excellent discussion of the general administrative difficulties attending contract clearance by the civilian superagencies will be found in Smith, *The Army and Economic Mobilization*, ch. IX. See also, Anderson, Hist of OUSW: 1914–41, ch. VI, pp. 122–27. For evidence of the air arm reaction to contract clearance, see Memo, Exec, OCAC, for ASW, 11 Oct 40, AFCF 400.112.

[74] Memo, USW for Chiefs of Supply Arms and Services, 17 Feb 41, AFCF 165 Classes of Contract. For the background of this organization in NDAC, see, Civilian Production Administration, "Industrial Mobilization for War," vol. I, *History of the War Production Board and Predecessor Agencies: 1940–1945* (Washington, 1947), pp. 63, 145–46.

[75] Organization of Defense Contract Service, manual prepared by OPM, Feb 41, copy in AFCF 334.8 OPM. On 4 September the organization was renamed, somewhat more functionally, the Contract Distribution Division. See Executive Order 8891.

[76] CPA, *History of WPB*, pp. 145–46.

[77] R&R, Maj F. C. Langmead to Col Lyon, 4 Apr 41, AFCF 004.4, and other items in this file. See also, A. R. Griswold, OPM, to Chief, Mat Div, 18 Dec 41, and reply 24 Dec 41, AFCF 163 Bids; Chief, Contract Sec, to CGMC, 6 Oct 42, AFCF 004.

ORGANIZATION FOR PROCUREMENT

ment system and because of this it suffered from many of the same shortcomings. There was the same initial period of confusion as the new service built up its staff and gained recognition from the various organizations and individuals with whom it had to do business. But even after this shakedown period was substantially over, the Defense Contract Service's troubles were by no means past. The same old problem of time-lag that had plagued air arm relations with small business in the past continued even after OPM undertook to improve on the job being done by military buyers.

One need not go very far into the problem to understand why the elaborate administrative structure created by the Defense Contract Service did not entirely succeed in closing the gap between small business and the military contracting officers. The general practice was for the military services to forward to OPM, insofar as practical, copies of all invitations to bid and all plans for negotiated procurements. The OPM staff then disseminated this information through its regional outposts where the local officials would do what they could to bring contractual opportunities to the attention of appropriate manufacturers in the locality. Meanwhile, the buyers at Wright Field were circularizing the firms already on their mailing lists. Thus it turned out time and again that while the OPM staff did an excellent job in lining up potential bidders with suitable facilities, financing, and the like, they did so too late to win contracts. The time lost in getting the information on outstanding orders analyzed, reproduced, and distributed to the field offices was so great that the offering sometimes actually expired before the manufacturers located by OPM could even begin to prepare their bids.[78]

A single example, admittedly an extreme case, will be useful not only to illustrate the difficulties confronting the Defense Contract Service but also to suggest the political heat it brought down on the air arm procurement system. Just before Pearl Harbor, on 3 December 1941, an invitation went out from Wright Field calling for bids on a small piece of equipment. The official opening was to be on the 19th of the month. On 11 December a manufacturer in Texas learned of this opportunity from a notice that had been sent out by the OPM service on the 9th. He immediately wired Wright Field asking for particulars: blueprints, specifications, and the like. These were mailed on 15 December but did not reach his plant in Texas until the eighteenth, or the day before the invitation expired. After spending all day and most of the night preparing his bid, the manufacturer sent it off to Wright Field for evaluation. A week later it was back again marked "not considered." The Post Office cancellation mark showed an hour later than the prescribed deadline on bids. On investigation the manufacturer found that while his bid had actually gone in before the deadline, his local postmaster had set his cancelling machine for a time just before the train went out when he ran off all the accumulated mail at once.

---

[78] IOM, Chief, Contract Sec, for CGMC, 2 Oct 42, explaining policy in response to WPB, Production Service Dept, to Chief, Mat Div, AC, 25 Sep 42. Both in AFCF 161 Renegotiation. See also, CPA Special Study 25, Field Organization and Administration of the War Production Board and Predecessor Agencies: May 1940–May 1945, 1945, pp. 7–14.

The irate manufacturer, understandably furious, availed himself of the great American privilege and dashed off a red hot letter to his congressman. He poured out his pent-up frustrations, blaming all and sundry for this miscarriage. "Does the government really want small business to have military contracts?" he asked. "If they don't want us in and have set up the [OPM Contract Service] merely as a front to stall us along until we shall have discovered for ourselves the hollowness of it all, why then, in common decency, don't they have the guts to come out flatfootedly and tell us that the best thing for us to do is to close up for duration and seek employment where we might be able to buy it from some union." For the sake of hundreds of small businessmen, he urged, "somebody up the line better get going." [79]

Although one can only sympathize with the small manufacturer who saw himself being squeezed out of business, the evidence suggests that the situation was nowhere near as sinister as he pictured it. On his own showing of the facts, by any reasonable standard of judgment, the OPM Contract Service appears to have done a rather creditable job in passing the word on anticipated procurements down the line. In view of all the inevitable delays in reproducing and distributing such notices, the elapsed time between the date the original invitation was issued and the date it was received by the manufacturer in Texas seems surprisingly short, especially when one recalls that this particular invitation was only one of thousands issued at Wright Field every month. Under such circumstances, to get nationwide distribution of information on an offering within about a week, the OPM organization must have been remarkably effective.

A further investigation of the case in question dredged up facts clearly indicating that procurement officials at Wright Field were making a determined effort to include small business firms in the supply program. The invitation, which had seemed so unfair to the angry Texan, actually brought no less than 85 replies to Wright Field. Moreover, instead of awarding the entire contract to a single firm—which would have been less trouble—it was broken into increments and given to 3 of the 85 bidders.[80] Surely any system garnering 85 bids in 16 days could not have been as bad as its critics alleged.

The real trouble was that tens of thousands of small concerns simply did not know how to do business with the government. The irate Texan would have served himself far better had he spent more energy in learning the ropes and less in complaining to Congress. Once a manufacturer was listed on the appropriate advertising registers and had indicated his financial and technical reliability, he would find contracting officers far more inclined to negotiate. This educational process took time, and all too often, as in the case of the Texan, the disappointed manufacturer rushed off to tell his troubles to Congress. Without all the facts, he saw the matter entirely as heartless discrimination against small business.

There was no absolute solution to the problem of enlarging the volume of con-

---

[79] Letter to Representative M. H. West, 29 Dec 41, AFCF 004.4.

[80] AAF draft reply for SW to Representative M. H. West, 14 Jan 42, AFCF 004.4; SW to West, 26 Feb 42, SW files, Airplanes, item 2122.

tracts for air matériel going to small business. At the beginning of 1941 many civilian mobilizers and political leaders were convinced that the military buyers were doing a bad job upon which they could improve. Some of the critics felt certain that a civilian agency could do far better. Nevertheless, the experience of the OPM Defense Contract Service during the year showed that their attempt to build up a contract distribution system had not brought the results desired. Instead of improving the existing bridge between the military buyers and small business, OPM had merely built another bridge parallel to that maintained by the military, and in some respects the new structure was inferior to the existing one. Mr. Donald Nelson seems to have grasped this point when he took charge of the newly formed War Production Board soon after Pearl Harbor. He abandoned the old pattern of contract clearance and distribution by separate and parallel civilian agencies in favor of a scheme placing responsibility for these objectives on the military buyers themselves. Nelson transferred the civilian staff that had been engaged in this work to positions within the several military procurement organizations. Instead of dispersing its energies building up parallel and competitive schemes, the civilian agency could then concentrate on supervision, policing the policies and operations of the military buyers—not least with respect to placing contracts with small business.[81]

Before the new WPB policy of supervision from within could get in motion, the whole problem of contracts for small business suddenly grew to enormous proportions. Once the nation was actually engaged in a shooting war, procurement by negotiation rather than by invitation to bid became the order of the day, and negotiation worked to the advantage of those manufacturers already doing business at Wright Field. The desperate plight of the military forces falling back before the enemy in the Pacific gave contracting officers every incentive to place their orders with firms they knew they could trust to deliver the goods on time and without deviation in the quality required. In practice this meant all too often that the larger and stronger manufacturers got the orders. At the same time, the increased demand for all kinds of munitions absorbed more scarce raw materials and the resulting squeeze in priorities drove further hordes of manufacturers to seek government contracts as their only means of remaining in business. When this new wave of contract seekers encountered the usual difficulties in landing military orders, Congress echoed with their protests.

The congressional reaction to the cries of the manufacturers left out of the armament program was the Small Business Act of June 11, 1942.[82] To "mobilize aggressively the productive capacity of all small business concerns," the measure provided for action along several different fronts. For example, by exempting them from the antitrust laws, it encouraged small firms to form pools that could handle contracts too large for any of the

---

[81] Smith, *The Army and Economic Mobilization;* D. Nelson, *Arsenal of Democracy,* pp. 198ff.; and CPA, *History of WPB,* p. 216.

[82] Public 603, 77th Cong, 2d sess (56 Stat 351), sometimes called the Smaller War Plants Act. A small plant was defined as "an independently owned concern employing less than 500 wage earners." See WD PR 35, par. 225.

member firms acting individually. To offset the higher costs resulting from lower volume, the measure authorized contracting officers to place orders with small firms even when they quoted prices somewhat higher than those of large producers.

The Small Business Act was by no means limited to passive or permissive features, some of its provisions carried teeth. Specifically, the measure set up a novel governmental entity, the Smaller War Plants Corporation (SWPC) to act, among other things, as a prime contractor to the military services. In effect, the SWPC was to serve as a kind of official middleman. The corporation would contract to supply the services with items of military equipment that it could then procure from small business concerns. The coercion entered at this point; if the chairman of WPB so directed, the military services were required to place with SWPC any contract he specified.

From the military point of view, the discretionary power placed in the hands of the civilian mobilizers by the Small Business Act represented a serious threat. Used aggressively, the coercive powers might prove to be a fatal encroachment upon the authority traditionally exercised by military officials. The military buyers felt that if they were to be held responsible for the nation's defense, they had a right to retain immediate supervision over the means employed. Above all, they feared that the civilian officials of SWPC in their zeal to help small business would hand over vitally important contracts to unqualified firms. From sad experience all too frequently repeated, procurement officers knew what havoc resulted when a single supplier failed to come through with equipment manufactured to the desired specifications on schedule. For want of one essential component, a whole production line might be shut down.

For several months after Congress acted, the activities of SWPC gave military officials little reason to believe they could trust the new agency with important munitions contracts.[83] At Wright Field in particular the organization got off to a poor start. Because the authorities in Washington were slow to hammer out policies and procedures, few directives arrived to guide the SWPC staff assigned to open a branch office in the Materiel Command. In fact, almost everything the SWPC men knew about their own organization they learned through the courtesy of the Air Force liaison officers assigned to work with them. The civilian officials representing SWPC were conscientious men, but they lacked guidance; in their enthusiasm to get things started, they tended to duplicate each other's efforts and get in one another's way.[84] Given enough time, the SWPC staff might have eliminated most of these procedural kinks, but the new agency was not left to build soundly at its own pace. Congress, impatient for results and goaded by small business constituents, urged immediate action. The results were most unfortunate. In order to make a showing for political purposes the SWPC hurried into some ill-advised contracts that it compelled the Air Force

---

[83] The organizational confusion that marked the early months of the SWPC is described at length in CPA Special Study 25, ch. IX.

[84] These harsh judgments are not those of Air Force critics but of SWPC staff members themselves. See J. K. Weddell, SWPC History, 2 Apr 46, an account of the AAF Branch of SWPC filed in WFHO.

ORGANIZATION FOR PROCUREMENT

to accept. Then when the small firms working for SWPC failed to produce the desired equipment on time, the organization was discredited.[85]

In spite of the mistrust inspired by its early operations, the local branch of the SWPC eventually managed to co-operate harmoniously with the procurement staff at Wright Field. After working together for some months the two groups came to appreciate each other's problems somewhat better. Thus informed, they drew up a series of operating agreements that defined their relationship and laid down procedures for working together. For their part, Materiel Command officials made an honest effort to place more orders with small business, and wherever possible they gave administrative help to SWPC. For example, they had blueprints converted to isometric projections to simplify their use by inexperienced suppliers, and they brought pressure to bear on big patent holders to release their patents to SWPC, which could then cultivate new sources at will. On the other hand, the local SWPC staff at Wright Field made substantial concessions too. The staff virtually abandoned the coercive powers given to their organization. Moreover, they agreed never to seek contracts for certain items admittedly too complex and too technical to be entrusted to untried or unproved sources. Included on this so-called waiver list were such things as aircraft spares and accessories.

Freed from the fear that the aircraft procurement program might be wrecked by enthusiastic but inexperienced outsiders, procurement officers at Wright Field were far more inclined to co-operate with the SWPC in those areas where co-operation was feasible.[86]

Although the various representatives of SWPC and the Materiel Command learned to pull together in harness by the end of 1943, to dwell upon their ultimately harmonious relations would be to mask the profoundly disturbing impact the passage of the Small Business Act had upon the Air Force procurement organization during the first year or so after it was passed by Congress. As it subsequently came about, the SWPC did not build up an elaborate procurement system more or less parallel to the existing military structure. What is more, its representatives at Wright Field had the good sense to realize that they would only breed opposition by invoking their power to compel the Air Force to award contracts to them. But during the summer and fall of 1942, all this was not clear. Then the threat of a civilian agency seizing control over large segments of the military procurement program seemed very real indeed, and the leaders of the Materiel Command responded accordingly. Hastily they set about getting their house in order to meet the criticism that they were not giving small business its fair share of Air Force contracts.

How could the Air Forces give more contracts to small business, especially to firms not already working on war orders? Under the pressure of outside criticism,

---

[85] *Ibid.* An example of a contract placed at the insistence of SWPC with disastrous results is recited with full details in 2d Ind, MC (Chief, Proc Div), to CGAAF (ACofAS MM&D), 1 Oct 43, AGO files, Rcd Group 205.03, Purchase Div, ASF 334 SWPC. Others may be found in Maj B. H. White to Lt Col E. McD. Kintz, 20 May 43, AFCF 004 Small Plants.

[86] Weddell, SWPC Hist; Proc Function of the AAF, Lecture by Swatland.

responsible officials in the Materiel Command began to sense the true character of the difficulty. Most of the manufacturing jobs that small firms were able to perform fell in the area of subcontracts passed out by the major primes. For all practical purposes this put the problem virtually beyond reach for Materiel Command officials. They could cajole the prime contractors to place more work with small subs; they could encourage the primes in this by suggesting qualified subs uncovered for them by the production staff at Wright Field; and, finally, they could force the primes contractually to subcontract a certain percentage of the total cost. All these courses the air arm buyers did pursue.[87] At best, however, the steps constituted only an indirect approach to the problem. And no matter how beneficial these efforts may have been in getting work for small concerns, they did not provide a politically persuasive reply to the charge that the overwhelming dollar value in the prime contracts written by the Air Force went to big business.

If the air arm was to meet its critics, no matter how unfair or uninformed many of them were, somehow means had to be found to increase the number of prime contracts given to small business. Contracting officers at Wright Field were not congenitally prejudiced against small business. In fact, many suppliers who received important contracts for air matériel could be classed as very small business by any yardstick. Contracting officers were not guilty of malevolent discrimination; rather they were victims of an inability to deal with the unknown. There were thousands of small firms scattered across the country of whose very existence air arm buyers were unaware. But even where one of the small manufacturers succeeded in bringing his facilities to the contracting officers' attention, they could not safely deal with him until they knew a great deal about his capabilities.

Before contracting officials dared entrust a contract to some newly discovered supplier, they had to inform themselves on a number of points: could a given firm undertake an intricate technical job to close tolerances with every assurance of success? Was the firm's management capable and reliable? Could it be trusted with confidential specifications? Did the firm have adequate capital to carry a job to completion? If not, did it have a credit rating that would permit it to borrow freely? These and many similar questions were thoroughly justified by military necessity and prudent business practice, yet so long as air arm procurement remained centralized at Wright Field, it operated to the disadvantage of small business.

If they were to increase the flow of prime contracts to small business, Materiel Command leaders realized that they must somehow make good the lack of information that kept contracting officers at Wright Field from dealing with unknown or inexperienced concerns. The heart of the difficulty was the remoteness

---

[87] For evidence of the Materiel Command role in finding subs and urging them on primes and in encouraging primes to give more work to subs, see FO Memo 50, Mat Center, 5 Oct 42; Chief, Contract Sec, WF, to CGMC, 6 Oct 42; Small Industrial Concerns, Brought Into the AAF Procurement Program, list prepared by Industrial Planning Sec, Prod Div, Mat Center, 10 Nov 42; and Deputy ACofAS MM&D to Senator J. E. Murray, Chairman, Special Com to study problems of small business, 5 Apr 43. All in AFCF 004 Small Plants.

ORGANIZATION FOR PROCUREMENT

of the buyers centralized at Wright Field from the many small potential suppliers scattered across the nation. The OPM Defense Contract Service had tried to overcome this difficulty by building up an organization that would, in effect, bring the small business man to the contracting officers of the Materiel Command. Although better than nothing, this approach failed to solve the problem. The mechanics of liaison between the military and the hastily erected civilian agency proved unwieldy. An obvious alternative was to carry the buyers to small business by decentralizing contracting operations to the procurement districts.[88]

Decentralized Procurement

The directive on decentralized procurement, which appeared in December 1942, clearly reflected the considerations that had motivated adoption of the new policy.[89] The chief of the Contract Section at Wright Field was to review all authorizations for purchases sent from the headquarters in Washington to determine which could be sent out to the procurement districts and negotiated by contracting officers located there. At first, only relatively uncomplicated items were to be considered for decentralized procurement. And in making assignments, the contract chief was specifically instructed to stress the utilization of small business and hitherto untapped sources of supply. To ensure compliance with the spirit of the directive, periodic reports were required showing the number and value of all contracts placed with firms employing fewer than 100 persons, 500 persons, and so on.

Despite the emphatic directive from command, the districts were slow to begin writing contracts. Never was the spread between giving an order and getting it carried out more evident. But the districts were not to blame. They could not negotiate contracts until they received specific assignments from Wright Field, and few could be sent until the districts built up staffs fully competent to carry on this difficult work. The procurement chief at Wright Field was ordered to send out cadres for the purpose, but he was slow to move. Few officers wished to be uprooted from Wright Field. Civilian employees who were ordered to go could resign and accept well-paid positions with industry. What is more, individual branch, section, and unit chiefs were little inclined to be enthusiastic about reducing their own importance by releasing the members of their staff to other organizations. Under the circumstances, it is hardly surprising that the people they did send out not infrequently were the least experienced, the culls and the misfits.[90]

Even after the districts had built up elaborate contracting organizations, they received only a trickle of purchasing assignments from the Materiel Command. Quite apart from any considerations of rivalry or ambition, contracting officers at Wright Field were genuinely reluctant to place any great number of negotiations in district hands. In the first place, they believed the district staffs were still unready to assume major responsibilities;

---

[88] McMurtrie, Hist of AAF MC: 1942, ch. VIII, passim.

[89] FO Memo 61, Mat Center, 24 Dec 42, app. 20; McMurtrie, Hist of AAF MC: 1942.

[90] Russel, Hist of AAF ATSC: 1944, pp. 145–46.

the difficulties of co-ordination raised as objections against decentralized procurement when the war began were no less valid a year later. As a consequence, during the first three months of 1943, of the 10,000-odd purchase directives received at Wright Field, fewer than 500 were passed on to the districts—less than 2 percent of the funds obligated in that quarter.[91]

The negotiation of contracts in the districts seemed destined to continue at a limping pace until April 1943 when General Branshaw became the commanding general of the Materiel Command. If the leaders of the Air Force really wished to exploit a policy of decentralization, General Branshaw was an excellent choice. Coming to his new position from a tour of duty as supervisor of the Western Procurement District, he had great faith in the district organizations and believed them quite capable of shouldering large responsibilities. As if to prove this, soon after taking over at Wright Field he launched an aggressive program of decentralization.

General Branshaw made "decentralized operations with centralized control" the cornerstone of his command.[92] He identified himself with the policy personally. In so doing he may have hoped to inspire ready compliance, but at the same time he assumed certain liabilities; if the policy failed, he would be inextricably linked to it. Although he intended to apply his policy generally to all the functions of the Materiel Command, General Branshaw was particularly concerned about placing the mechanics of contracting out in the districts wherever possible. He aimed to have them negotiate 50 percent of all contracts if at all feasible, and because 50 percent by dollar value would be impossible so long as all major end items were purchased at Wright Field, he even undertook to send aircraft contracts out for the districts to negotiate.[93]

General Branshaw's vigorous program to decentralize procurement was as forthright as it was aggressive. The critics who had protested the military neglect of small business could not question the sincerity with which his campaign was launched. Unfortunately, sincerity was no guarantee of success. The best of intentions on the part of command could not escape the formidable array of problems raised by the effort.

The Difficulties of Decentralization

Perhaps the biggest challenge confronting the officers who were assigned to work out the details of the decentralization was to overcome the objection that district procurement would lead to a seri-

---

[91] J. P. Walsh, History of the Eastern Procurement District, Materiel Command, Army Air Forces: 1943, (hereinafter cited as Walsh, Hist of Eastern Proc Dist: 1943), 1945, pp. 321–27, filed at Air University. See also, Office for Organizational Planning, MC, Report on Decentralization of Procurement Division, 11 Sep 43, Exhibit F, WFHO Research file. For the arguments against decentralization presented following Pearl Harbor, see Chief, Mat Div, to USW, 20 Dec 41, and 2d Ind, Asst Chief, Mat Div, to USW, 7 Jan 42, AFCF 400.12 Method and Program of Proc.

[92] CO 40, MC, 5 Aug 43, cited in Davis Hist of AAF MC: 1943, p. 3, n. 6.

[93] Office for Organizational Planning, MC, Rpt on Decentralization of Proc Div. As it ultimately turned out, the districts negotiated not a single aircraft contract to the point of approval during the war. Negotiation and Administration of Contracts. Lecture by Scarff.

ous loss of co-ordination. Their answer to this was to prescribe a rigid parallelism between the organization at Wright Field and the organizations in the district offices. The districts were ordered to establish what amounted to a mirror image of the Wright Field counterpart. Thus where the central organization divided a procurement branch into seven offices, each of which was subdivided into units, the districts were expected to do likewise. The rationale behind this parallelism was that it would facilitate the flow of papers between the field and the central staff and thus eliminate confusion.[94] There was a certain advantage in this arrangement, but it carried with it many contingent liabilities.

The trouble with trying to sustain an organizational parallelism between Wright Field and the districts was that every time the former changed, the latter had to change too. This kept the district offices in continual chaos, a result all the more absurd because the organizational changes at Wright Field often reflected nothing more than an effort to accommodate the personalities occupying positions of command there. Thus, to impose an organization that mirrored Wright Field, the districts had to ignore the personal traits and talents of their own officers. When a district supervisor protested this elevation of mere organization charts over human considerations, General Branshaw vigorously defended the principle of parallelism. If "rank or personalities" made the charts unworkable, he said, arrange to transfer the individuals concerned so the charts would work.[95]

In the long run, the attempt to maintain an organizational parallelism between Wright Field and the districts turned out to be more harmful than helpful in co-ordinating procurement activities. The endless effort to juggle the people available in the districts to fit the master organizational charts kept the district staff from concentrating on the work in hand. As one officer complained, "the District has been organized to death." As a consequence, the scheme designed to simplify the channels of communication turned them into mazes instead.[96]

The task of getting the district procurement organizations in working order was complicated immeasurably by the continuing shortage of experienced personnel. After Pearl Harbor, when patriotic motivations operated rather more forcefully, a number of really able businessmen were induced to accept commissions and work in the procurement field. But for every experienced executive thus acquired, two or three new positions were created and had to be filled. The demand for talent seemed insatiable. By way of illustration, one district contract section in January 1943 had a staff of thirteen. By September there were seventy-four people at work in the section and over sixty more were needed to fill the available job openings.[97]

The importance of the procurement role played by reservists—businessmen in

---

[94] Office for Organizational Planning, MC. Progress Rpt on Decentralization of Proc Div, 30 Sep 43, WFHO Research file, Proc Div; Proc Div Office Memo, 43–99, 1 Jun 43, Organization and Functions of Dist Proc, app. 20, Davis Hist of AAF MC: 1943. See also, Russel, Hist of AAF ATSC: 1944, p. 141ff.

[95] Walsh, Hist of Eastern Proc Dist: 1943, pp. 59–66.

[96] *Ibid.*, pp. 58, 116.

[97] Office for Organizational Planning, MC, Progress Rpt on Decentralization of Proc Div.

uniform—would be hard to overstate. In the Eastern Procurement District office in New York, to take but one example, during 1943 the civilian staff of more than 6,000 employees was led by approximately 400 officers, of whom only about a half dozen were Regular Army. Most branches and sections of the decentralized procurement organizations were built around the abilities of key reservists, many of whom were recruited in the large cities where the district offices were located. Unfortunately, many of these men had hardly begun to pull their weight when the General Staff ruled that reservists must be assigned to stations away from their homes.[98] There was nothing to do but uproot them and start over again to build up a new staff.

The shortage of competent officer and civilian personnel to carry on decentralized procurement was further aggravated when the districts themselves were subdivided and the district staffs were called upon to provide cadres for the new organizations. It will be recalled that there were originally three procurement districts, East, Central, and West. The theory of these district offices was that they would overcome the evil effects of centralized procurement at Wright Field by providing local and personal contact with small business men. However, so long as there were only three districts for the entire United States, the theory was hardly tenable. The Eastern Procurement District stretched from Maine to Florida. Its office in New York City was hardly "local" to a manufacturer in North Carolina.

The solution to the problem of making the districts truly local was to break them down into smaller geographical units. This was done in a succession of steps until eventually there were six districts in all including the Midwestern (Wichita), the Midcentral (Chicago), and the Southeastern (Atlanta) carved out of the original three. Even these subdivisions covered immense geographical areas embracing many states in each instance, and each district had to be still further broken into areas, each with a local office. For example, the Eastern District, before the Southeastern District was established, maintained area offices at Binghamton, Rochester, Philadelphia, Newark, New Haven, Worcester, Boston, Baltimore, and Atlanta, each manned with a staff of three, six, or sometimes more officers. And every time the existing districts were required to drain off staff to set up new district or area offices their own organizations were left reeling from the shock.[99]

Questions of organization and personnel seriously interfered with the decentralization of procurement, but even without these complications the job was fundamentally difficult. The role of district officers in the procurement process was such that they had to work almost continually in two areas of uncertainty: they were seldom fully informed as to precisely what was wanted or whom they could find to supply it.

Just why the districts found it hard to learn what the procurement staff at Wright Field wanted them to buy needs a word of explanation. On the surface the procedure appeared routine enough.

---

[98] Walsh, Hist of Eastern Proc Dist: 1943, pp. 3, 67, 86–88.

[99] Mimeograph pamphlet, Procurement Field Organization: 1920–1948, WFHO Research file; Walsh, Hist of Eastern Proc Dist: 1943, pp. 72, 78.

ORGANIZATION FOR PROCUREMENT

When Procurement Division officers at Wright Field decided that a given item could be conveniently purchased in a district, they wrote out an Authority for District Purchase (ADP) and sent it out to one or more of the districts. The ADP indicated the required number of items, the specifications, the time and place of delivery, packaging, and so on. In theory, all the district officers had to do was locate one or more suppliers with whom to negotiate. In practice the game was never so simple.

By way of illustration, consider the example of an ADP calling for an electrically operated hand tool, a power drill, or some such implement. When approached by district officers with an order, one manufacturer offered to supply the item promptly at a very favorable price, provided a deviation in the specification could be arranged to permit him to use a model he already had in production for commercial sales. Could the district officers grant such a deviation? If they stopped to find out by writing to Wright Field, the procurement would be delayed. In this instance, to play safe, they did seek approval first. Protracted correspondence finally revealed that a commercial item definitely would not do; the order, although placed through the Air Force, was for a foreign aid account and the ultimate user operated on a 240-volt, 50-cycle system rather than the domestic 110-volt, 60-cycle system for which the tools were wired.[100]

In trying to function in the field without all the relevant facts, district procurement officers suffered a serious disadvantage. Even though they were free to negotiate individual contracts, almost unavoidably they were tied to the central organization where their orders initiated. And this dependence, so obvious to the manufacturers with whom the district officers had to deal, brought district procurement into contempt. The original Wright Field directive authorizing decentralized procurement had specifically stated that the district contracting officers were to enjoy plenary authority to negotiate, but the facts of the situation ruled otherwise. Power without information to guide its use was ineffectual.

Even when district contracting officers knew precisely what was required on an ADP, they still had to find a suitable source of supply. The whole *raison d'être* of decentralized procurement was to increase the flow of contracts to small business and hitherto untapped facilities. This meant that insofar as possible district contracting officers had to avoid suppliers already familiar to them and go out of their way to cultivate new sources. The district officers deliberately had to take the hard way.

The task of uncovering new suppliers among the smaller firms in any of the districts was by no means simple. Prewar surveys by industrial planning officers gave only limited help. The war extended the variety as well as the number of items purchased far beyond the scope anticipated by the mobilization planners. At peak, the districts purchased up to 200,000 different kinds of items for the Air Force. Obviously, to compile and maintain an up-to-date list of sources capable of turning out all these items was in itself an immense administrative undertaking.

---

[100] Walsh, Hist of Eastern Proc Dist: 1943, pp. 329-31.

Various devices were employed to find new sources. A vigorous campaign of advertising and the missionary work of individual officers sent into the major industrial centers uncovered a number of leads. Even more effective was a continuing study of the subcontractors listed in the contract status report submitted periodically by all Air Forces prime contractors. Although some of these secondary sources were already swamped with orders from the primes, others welcomed the opportunity to take on contracts let by the procurement districts. Just how necessary this proselytizing was is suggested by the results of a survey conducted by one of the districts during the summer of 1943. When interviewed, no less than 8,400 of the firms working in the district as subcontractors to major AAF suppliers admitted that they had never even heard of the district organization and did not realize they could seek contracts from the procurement officers there.[101]

The lists of subcontractors abstracted from the reports prepared by the Materiel Command Statistical Control Office, while exceedingly helpful, did not provide a thoroughgoing survey of every manufacturer in the districts. In the first place, the lists covered only Air Forces contracts and thus ignored the suppliers and their subs holding contracts from the other services. Secondly, each prime contractor reported only those subs with whom he dealt directly. This meant that all the sub-subcontractors, tier on tier of them, remained yet unidentified.

Some of the many obstacles besetting the district officers who tried to locate and serve sub-subcontractors and suppliers may be seen from the case of a manufacturer of precision gears with a plant located in New York state. The concern was turning out parts for a Detroit manufacturer of aircraft gun turrets purchased by the Air Forces as government-furnished equipment. When the New York manufacturer failed to keep up to schedule, a Wright Field official wrote a letter lacerating the district staff for failing to follow up on this critical procurement with sufficient attention. The bewildered district officer had never even heard of the gear maker. Since the firm in question supplied a manufacturer in a different district, the Eastern District had no record of him as a subcontractor. What is more, subsequent inquiry revealed that the manufacturer himself did not realize that his gears were to be used in an item of Air Forces equipment. He made his products to the specifications provided with no questions asked, so he had no way of knowing that he could turn to the district office not only for help in getting needed priorities on tools and materials, but also for possible contracts. Under such circumstances district officers were understandably annoyed when Wright Field officials criticized them for not knowing what was going on under their very noses.[102]

At best, the effort to decentralize procurement never achieved the goals anticipated. Even at a time when the commanding general of the Materiel Command was exerting the utmost pressure to this end, the results achieved were not impressive. In August 1943, for example, only 27.4 percent of all Air Forces

---

[101] *Ibid.*, pp. 171–73.

[102] *Ibid.*, pp. 169–70.

ORGANIZATION FOR PROCUREMENT

purchases were negotiated by the districts. This represented not more than 14 percent of the total dollar value involved.[103]

By the summer of 1944 the Materiel Command program of decentralized procurement had run into so many snags that a reappraisal of policy seemed called for. After a year and a half of trial, the disadvantages of district procurement seemed to outweigh the advantages. Nevertheless, since the commanding general had identified himself so emphatically and so personally with the policy of decentralization, any proposal to return all procurement to Wright Field threatened to be a rather delicate matter. There is evidence extant that at least some officers, fully aware of the commanding general's predilections, were inclined to be wary in writing on the question.[104] General Branshaw's relief for reasons of health in July 1944 after a long illness simplified the task considerably, for then the decision could be made with no loss of face by the new commander, Brig. Gen. K. B. Wolfe.

To procurement officials at Wright Field it seemed clear that the attempt to decentralize had been unwise. There were, of course, many functions that would always be performed most advantageously in the districts. As a general rule these included all the myriad details of contract administration—inspection, production expediting, on-the-spot studies of costs, and so on—wherever a close and continuing personal contact was required at the local level between buyer and seller. On the other hand, experience showed that the negotiation of contracts in the districts had led to serious delays in the production and delivery of vital military equipment. And in wartime, from the military point of view, this was reason enough to abandon the attempt and return Air Forces buying to Wright Field.[105]

For students of military command the whole episode merits careful attention for several reasons. To begin with, almost without exception time and trial validated the objections raised to decentralized procurement by Wright Field officers long before the policy was attempted. Their fears that district procurement would lead to difficulties in co-ordinating complex engineering details were entirely justified, as were their forebodings on the difficulties of maintaining uniform and equitable procedures when buying through a number of centers. Moreover, although decentralized procurement was initially undertaken to increase the share of Air Forces contracts going to small business and otherwise untapped facilities, these objectives were scarcely mentioned when the decision was made to return procurement to Wright Field.[106] All of which suggests that the original decision to decentralize procurement to the districts

---

[103] Russel, Hist of AAF ATSC: 1944, p. 158.

[104] Walsh, Hist of Eastern Proc Dist: 1943, p. 116, especially the following comment: "The tendency of some to remove from the files what was derogatory or, what was more common, the tendency to prevent what was derogatory from becoming a matter of record, leaves only the favorable or mildly critical for evaluation. Rumors, off-the-record comments of persons engaged in the work of decentralization, modify any conclusions . . . which a . . . scrutiny of district directives and letters indicates."

[105] *Ibid.*, p. 82; see also Russel, Hist of AAF ATSC: 1944, pp. 151–58.

[106] Negotiation and Administration of Contracts, Lecture by Scarff.

was not so much the result of careful planning as it was a hasty change of front made under considerable political pressure.

In retrospect, procurement officials at Wright Field ruefully admitted that they had been forced to learn the hard way the important distinction between control and operation.[107] There was a certain irony in the circumstance that even while reiterating axioms about "centralized control and decentralized operations" the command directives had proceeded to order just the opposite. Instead of confining district procurement staff officers to the role of honest brokers, finders, or middlemen without commission, dedicated to the task of bringing in more small business firms to share in Air Forces orders, the command directives ordering decentralized procurement turned them into contracting officers with all the ultimate responsibilities that function entailed. As a consequence, control at the level of command was seriously weakened, and the main objective, aid to small business, was lost in the welter of administrative difficulties that district buying entailed. A better example of the grave dangers awaiting those who resort to glib formulas would be hard to find. Axiomatic simplicity all too often merely conceals complex realities.

---

[107] Proc Div Annual Rpt, 1944, WFHO Research file.

CHAPTER XX

Production

The Problem Defined

The term *production* is an omnibus word; it conveys a host of meanings. To use it is to conjure visions of long assembly lines crowded with workers, machine tools turning out precision parts, heavy presses forming intricate shapes, hundreds of draftsmen bending over drawing boards, and thousands of clerks posting entries in endless records of parts and materials to keep them flowing in uninterrupted succession to the point of need. Production also describes the sum of the parts, the end product turned out in large quantities.

To tell the complete story of aircraft production in World War II would require a history of industrial America as a whole during the war years, for the aircraft industry in its complexity embraced a very large portion of the national economy. True, a handful of major airframe builders received most of the publicity, but behind them lay the subcontractors and the suppliers or vendors, tier after tier, spreading out into every state in the union. Each firm, from the giant industrial complex to the tiny three-man backyard job-shop turning out bits and pieces, played a significant role in the collective enterprise called aircraft production.

Large or small, every manufacturer participating in the aircraft program was confronted with new and baffling problems imposed by the demands of war. Until these were resolved and output was accelerated, air arm leaders knew that air power would remain a concept rather than a reality.

Though Air Forces officers were of necessity interested in every aspect of aircraft production, the full range of this far-flung story cannot be recited in a study such as this.[1] Within its prescribed limits, this chapter can only analyze some of the factors of peculiar importance to military officers—those concerned with day-to-day administration as well as those in command—who work for large-scale mass production when haste is all essential. The point of view taken is that of the officer, not that of the businessman. Another consideration has influenced the selection of the topics discussed. Almost

---

[1] Because the term *production* covers planning and control functions as well as manufacturing, a bibliography of the subject tends to spread out, like spokes from a hub, along specialized lines. Much of the best material in each of these lines is to be found in periodicals of the time. In addition to the general periodicals of the aviation industry as a whole, there are the trade journals of all the contributory industries. Typical of the monographic literature in this area is T. Lilly *et al.*, *Problems of Accelerating Aircraft Production During World War II* (Boston: Harvard University Graduate School of Business Administration, 30 January 1946). For a general study of wartime labor that touches upon the special problems of the aircraft industry, see Byron Fairchild and Jonathan Grossman, *The Army and Industrial Manpower*, UNITED STATES ARMY IN WORLD WAR II (Washington, 1959).

without exception they represent problems that recurred again and again, not only in World War II but in World War I as well, since the record of aircraft production in World War I reflects a striking similarity to the pattern of problems encountered in World War II.[2]

The Dilemma of Mass Production

More Airplanes or Better?

The military force that can put more and better weapons into the field holds a long leg on victory. Quantity combined with quality, larger numbers, and superior performance, to say the very least, give a decided advantage. But this is an ideal combination hard to obtain.

Continuing superiority requires continual change. Every innovation introduced by the enemy must be outmatched. Superior performance in aircraft is the sum total of many components—range, speed, climb, maneuverability, fire power, and the like—each conditioned by thousands of features of design: here a change in engine cowling to improve cooling and increase horsepower, there a better gun mount to enlarge the field of fire, and so on in an endless procession suggested by experience in the field and innovations on the drawing board. When one is pitted against an aggressive and determined foe, to maintain superiority is to accept the absolute necessity of frequent change, modification of existing designs to incorporate improvements whenever possible and, ultimately, replacement of old models with new ones. Fluidity of design is a requisite for superior weapons. Mass production, on the other hand, lies at the opposite extreme.

Mass production and design stabilization are complementary concepts. To freeze design is to facilitate production. Mass production involves a good deal more than just an enlarged scale of operation. The economies that stem from bulk purchase, long production runs without retooling, and the wider use of jigs and fixtures that permit more extensive employment of semiskilled labor, all require stability of design as well as sheer quantitative increase. When design is repeatedly subject to alteration, bulk purchasing of materials can be hazardous, production planning more complicated, and retooling continual. What is more, in such circumstances every significant shift in design may necessitate a program for retraining labor. In short, only by minimizing design change is it possible to obtain maximum production.

Possibly no other single problem posed air arm officials such hard choices on so many occasions as the eternal equation of quantity and quality. Repeatedly, officers concerned with the production of weapons faced the question: to freeze or not to freeze? Which was more important at any given moment: a higher volume of output or changes in design that would sharpen the cutting edge? In the staff school exercise it may be possible to resolve this equation neatly, but to those actually in command, especially in wartime, the imponderables were hard to count.

---

[2] See, for example, Report on Aircraft Supply of Great Britain, extract from a study by the British War Cabinet, 1917, in Smithsonian Misc Collection, vol. 69, No. 7, Jun 18. See also, Maj H. H. Arnold, Analysis of Aircraft Production in World War I, Jan 22, WFHO. This study perfectly illustrates how superficial was the study given the production experience of World War I.

PRODUCTION

In retrospect, the quantity-quality equation is clear: aircraft output must reflect a skillful compromise between maximum output and maximum performance made possible by continual innovations in design. To the officers who faced this problem in the months leading into the war, this commonplace was never so clear. They were certainly aware of the tug-of-war between quantity and quality, but they saw the issue in different terms.

In place of continuing compromise, they tended to think in terms of successive phases. For them, aircraft procurement followed orderly programs: first a design and development phase, then a production phase. In October 1939, for example, when the 5,500 program loomed as the biggest rush project of the year, the General Staff ordered the Chief of the Air Corps to be sure that the experimental and service test phases were completed before production orders went out for the equipment to be used by tactical units.[3]

The General Staff directive cannot be dismissed as a failure of ground officers to appreciate the peculiar problems of the air arm; Air Corps officers themselves had been thinking in terms of freezing designs before going into mass production. In working out their mobilization plans, they expected to separate engineering from procurement. This would entail turning over complete control to the procurement organization once the decision to freeze a given aircraft design had been made.[4] The staff planners feared that the engineering officers would never relinquish an aircraft for production unless they did this. Project engineers always had "one more really vital improvement" just over the horizon.

The conception of a production freeze was not confined to military circles. Aircraft manufacturers were equally prone to talk about freezing designs to get maximum production.[5] But always the freeze was to take place at some point in the future, presumably on some distant M-day, when all-out production became mandatory. Meanwhile, the engineers at Wright Field went on working with the airframe firms all over the country, continually injecting design changes in production model airplanes.

During the summer of 1940 the realization gradually dawned that there would be no M-day in the accepted sense of the term. The nation was already in the midst of a creeping M-day in many respects. And in the light of this circumstance, many air arm officers became increasingly disturbed at the faltering pace of aircraft output. They believed that designs should be frozen immediately without waiting for a declaration of war.

One headquarters staff officer returned from a tour of the industrial front convinced that "drastic action" was necessary if the pace of output was ever to increase significantly. He urged the Chief of the

---

[3] TAG to CofAC, 30 Oct 39, AFCF 452.1 Aircraft Requirements Program. The General Staff directive was in line with the prevailing concept of "standardizing" before entering production. On the whole subject of standardization, see USAF Hist Study 67, Standardization of Air Materiel, 1939–1944: Controls, Policies and Procedures, by Dr. M. P. Claussen, Air University Hist Div, Nov 51.

[4] Notes on Detailed Plans for Execution of Emergency Program, 1 Dec 38, staff paper, AC Project Rcds (A. J. Lyon Papers).

[5] See, for example, Donald Douglas, "Speeding Aircraft Production," *Aviation* (August 1940), p. 44ff.

Air Corps to set up a board of officers who thoroughly appreciated the importance of "production rather than perfection." He wanted "full authority" for the board to determine the changes to be permitted in aircraft already on the production line. The plan for a board as such was rejected, but the spirit of the scheme received approval as a matter of general Air Corps policy.[6]

A few days later the Assistant Secretary of War circulated a letter reinforcing the policy laid down for the Air Corps. Quoting from the dispatch of a military attaché in London, he wrote:

It has been reported that one of the factors contributing to the present desperate position of the British is the failure to freeze designs. The technical services are never satisfied with anything less than a perfection which is always unobtainable. The best is the enemy of the good. If we are to avoid the catastrophe of "too little and too late," there must be a decision as to production types. Germany has demonstrated that thousands of imperfect tanks on the battlefield are better than scores of perfect tanks on the testing ground.

"Failure to freeze designs," admonished the Assistant Secretary, "must be constantly guarded against." For maximum impact, this message was reproduced and distributed down through every echelon at Wright Field, so that the officers and civilian engineers who worked on design changes could reflect on its significance.[7]

At no time, of course, could it be said that the Air Corps actually prohibited change in production airplanes. No freeze could be absolute. Modifications found necessary to safe and effective operation and those that could be introduced with little or no trouble continued to be made. But this circumstance in no way negated the significance of the decision to freeze. Modifications that were desirable but difficult to accomplish would not be undertaken, and, perhaps of even greater moment, the manufacturers were instructed to give all experimental work a priority lower than that assigned to the problems of production.[8]

So long as output lagged, there was undoubtedly a good deal to be said for giving top priority to production, but the policy had its dangers. Would it be wise for the Air Corps to order Douglas to drop all work on the four-engine C-54 transport in order to press production on the twin-engine C-47? Such a step was seriously considered.[9] The C-47 did turn out to be the indispensable work horse of the war, but it could never make the long-range ocean hops that war in the Pacific would subsequently make so necessary. If to freeze designs was to perpetuate the production of yesterday's weapons, the decision to freeze might prove fatal.

When the Chief of the Air Corps decided to freeze the designs of production model airplanes during the summer of 1940, he presumably believed that such a freeze was possible. A year later he must have been less certain. There was

---

[6] R&R, Inspection Div, OCAC, to CofAC, 14 Aug 40; Mat Div to CofAC, 6 Sep 40. Both in AHO Plans Div 145.91-246. See also, R&R, CofAC to Chief, Mat Div, 30 Aug 40, AFCF 452.1 Airplanes, Gen.

[7] Memo, ASW for CofAC, 26 Aug 40; OCAC, CTI-96, 7 Sep 40. Both in AFCF 452.1 Airplanes, Gen. See also, Military Attaché, London, Rpt 41,443, 31 Jul 40, CADO WF, Doc 70/146.

[8] Mat Div Memo Rpt, Exp-M-50-476, 17 Oct 40, AFCF 452.1 (Bulky) Means of Accelerating Aircraft Production.

[9] Memo, Maj Langmead for Chief, Mat Div, 8 Jul 40, AFCF 452.1 Airplanes, Gen.

PRODUCTION

still a tremendous public and political pressure on the Air Corps for large numbers of aircraft.[10] Qualitative superiority involved considerations far too subtle for easy comprehension by the general public; numbers, on the other hand, made obvious headlines and even the uninformed could count. Nevertheless, in the fall of 1941 the nation was not yet at war, and counteracting the pressure for more airplanes was the natural desire of all Air Corps officers to get the very best airplanes they could. Thus, despite the freeze order of August 1940, all sorts of changes continued to be made on production aircraft.

The turn of events in Europe during 1941 was one of the factors helping to melt the freeze order of the previous summer. The Battle of Britain had been fought and won. The few "to whom so many owed so much" had demonstrated that a marked superiority in performance was a consideration not to be ignored. Fifty-two fighter squadrons and a chain of radar sets had helped to hold the Luftwaffe at bay. Air Corps observers stationed in England sensed the change that had taken place in the year following the disaster at Dunkerque. At the time of Dunkerque all-out production had been the cry; now the emphasis was shifting back to superior performance. One of the observers made a special point of warning those in command in the United States to avoid "political production" or sheer numbers for the record. "This war," another observer added, "cannot be won by producing great numbers of airplanes that are not up to combat standards." [11]

The pendulum was swinging back from quantity to quality. Then came Pearl Harbor. The shift in emphasis noted by the observers in Britain was accurately reported, but it was, after all, a British policy; it reflected the needs of a particular situation. After Pearl Harbor numbers again loomed in importance and all-out production took first priority.[12]

To trace each pulse beat of the war, each surge in priority from more aircraft to better aircraft and back again to more aircraft would serve no purpose. On the other hand, a single illustration may epitomize the problem. By the middle of 1943 the military forces of the United States were engaged on a truly world-wide front. In the Pacific the amphibious campaigns were soon to be in full swing. The troops in North Africa had moved across the Mediterranean and invaded Sicily, while in Britain the build-up for a cross-Channel attack had begun. Moreover, by this time the Air Forces was deeply committed to the strategic assault on Germany with heavy bombers. Month after month, each of these operations called for ever larger numbers of airplanes. Manufacturers in the United States were breaking all records with their output, but still there were not enough. Demand exceeded supply. As always, the continual temptation to get

---

[10] The continuing political pressure for increased output is reflected in Memo, USW for CofAC, 10 Sep 41, AFCF 161 Contract Regulations.

[11] Gen Brett to "Dear Hap" (Maj Gen H. H. Arnold), 10 Nov 41; Lt Col E. M. Powers to Chief, Mat Div, 4 Nov 41. Both in AFCF 452.1 Sales Abroad.

[12] For a revealing appreciation of this situation, see Memo, CGMC (WF) for ACofAS MM&D, 4 Jun 43, AFCF 452.01–B Production.

better aircraft had led to design changes that slowed production.

In desperation, the Chief of the Air Staff finally decided that only drastic action would keep the engineers from retarding output by their eternal quest for improvements. In September 1943 he ordered all production aircraft to be frozen on an "as is" basis. Even modifications deemed absolutely essential for safe operation were not to be undertaken without express approval from the Office of the Chief of Air Staff.[18] As might have been expected, the order raised a quick cry of protest.

Matériel officers on the air staff were quite willing to admit that there had been a tendency to permit an excessive number of changes on the production lines. They realized that in seeking "nothing but the best" they had sometimes incorporated relatively minor improvements that slowed production far beyond the point where the qualitative gain justified the quantitative loss. On the other hand, it would be dangerous to ignore the urgent requests for design changes sent from tactical units confronting the enemy in the field. For example, where a theater commander reported that gunners found the field of vision from a certain turret inadequate, immediate modification was the only acceptable course, even if it involved extensive structural changes. The alternative was to lose bombers for want of effective defensive fire.

At long last the concept of freezing production lines was changing. Few responsible officers still thought it would ever be literally possible to freeze production. The Chief of the Air Staff recognized this implicitly when he ordered all exceptions to clear through his office. The question, then, was no longer to freeze or not to freeze at all; it had now become a matter of degree. This in turn resolved itself into a question of procedure. What was the best way to handle decisions as to which changes were to be allowed and which rejected?

There were serious drawbacks to the directive that put the final decision on all production line modifications into the hands of the Chief of Air Staff. In the first place, the time element militated against such a scheme. Delays were inevitable in the headquarters paper mill, and even vital changes could be delayed for weeks awaiting *pro forma* approval. Then, too, with over a dozen different aircraft in production status, each one involving thousands of intricate technical considerations, the Chief of Air Staff and his immediate entourage were scarcely in a position to make sound decisions on such matters of detail. As the matériel staff pointed out, air staff would soon be swamped with hundreds of requests awaiting decision. And just how, for example, would the Chief of the Air Staff know whether or not a request for closer riveting to strengthen the engine cowling of a particular aircraft was really justified?

As a counterproposal, the matériel staff suggested that it would be wiser to let the engineers at Wright Field decide on all minor points, sending suggested major changes—armament, structural design, and the like—to Washington for approval. Since the matériel specialists at Air Forces headquarters were obviously more famil-

---

[18] R&R, DCofAS to ACofAS MM&D, 22 Sep 43, AFCF 452.01–C Production. The only exception to the freeze order was the B-29, which was then being pushed into production under a special program.

PRODUCTION 517

iar than the Chief of the Air Staff with the technical details of production, they preferred to keep all decisions on changes in their own hands. But the staff chief was adamant. He insisted that every design change on all important production contracts had to clear through his office. He was absolutely determined to speed up production, and he knew that every earlier freeze order had been vitiated by just such concessions to the engineers.

Still persuaded that their position was the wiser one, the matériel staff returned with a compromise that the Chief of the Air Staff finally accepted. A true freeze was unrealistic. Perhaps the most convincing argument was the obvious one: freezing production designs would accomplish little indeed if it subsequently turned out that the proposed changes were essential after all and had to be tacked on to the airplanes out in the field at great inconvenience and expense.

Here was the gist of the problem. There was to be no more talk of freezing design; it was a matter of improving procedures to minimize changes. In short, the compromise plan aimed at an appropriate balance between more aircraft and better aircraft. The engineers at Wright Field were empowered to approve any change made necessary by faulty operation or the dictates of safety as well as any that might actually speed up the pace of production. All other suggested changes were to be sent to Washington for study by the matériel specialists. They in turn could present each major modification to the Chief of Air Staff for a decision.

Most significantly, the new procedure required the engineers at Wright Field to buttress each request with facts: Who asked for the change and why? When could the proposed change be injected into the production line, and what would be the estimated impact of the proposal upon deliveries? Facts plus a carefully planned system for dealing with them would help make it possible to balance the quantity-quality equation.[14] There need be no more unrealistic swings of the pendulum, no more impossible freeze orders—provided the system could be made to work.

Making the system work was by no means easy. The new directive had been in force hardly more than a month when the matériel staff at the headquarters in Washington found occasion to chide the engineers at Wright Field for continuing to permit changes that did not lie "within the spirit" of the directive. In this short period, it seems, the Materiel Command had authorized 75 changes on the P–38 alone. In addition, there had been 43 on the A–20 and 94 on the P–63. Theater commanders were beginning to complain that the multiude of design changes injected on the production line were flooding the tactical units with a heterogeneous collection of equipment. With every few aircraft in a given production sequence different in numerous particulars, supply and maintenance became unduly complicated.

There was a certain grim irony in this turn of events. In the case of the P–40, for example, unit commanders sent back frantic messages demanding modifications in production models to make them tactically suitable. The threat of enemy

---

[14] R&R Comment 2, ACofAS MM&D, to CofAS, 23 Sep 43, and successive replies, 30 Sep, 2 Oct, and 16 Oct, AFCF 452.01–B Production. See also, Memo, Actg ACofAS MM&D for CofAS, 29 Oct 43, same file.

superiority made such changes imperative. But after the improvements had been incorporated at the cost of a considerable slowdown in total output, the unit commanders in the theater complained that the logistical difficulties imposed by these changes nullified the gains anticipated.[15] Since the distribution of revised technical orders and instruction manuals lagged well behind the pace of modification, the complications of supply and maintenance under such circumstances defied imagination.

In short, the quantity-quality equation was paralleled by another one that balanced qualitative improvement against the resulting complexity of supply and maintenance. Neither permitted all-or-nothing solutions. Both required compromises. And to be truly effective, the compromises had to derive from a careful consideration of the relevant facts in each instance. Mustering these facts required staff work of a high order. And good staff work was possible only when it rested upon a foundation of sound administration. For the keenest of officers was helpless in the face of an administrative system that failed to provide him with a timely and adequate flow of information on which to premise decisions.

Better staff work brought results. On that point the record is clear. Nonetheless, while the details of administration were gradually being perfected, the need for ever larger output continued. The decision makers remained under heavy pressure for results. Under the circumstances, those in command were repeatedly tempted to take short cuts that promised to pay big dividends in the form of increased production. Sometimes, of course, the short cuts contained pitfalls that negated the gains they seemed to promise. In this respect the whole experiment in maximum tooling for mass production at Willow Run is peculiarly well worth investigation.

Willow Run: A Tooling Triumph?

June 1940 was probably the most disastrous month of the war. Almost in desperation, Air Corps officers cast about for alternatives and expedients to speed the pace of production. Among other things, they looked to Detroit, the very symbol of mass production in the United States if not the world.

A conference with the top management at the Ford Motor Company brought results. After the Ford staff expert had studied a P-40 flown to Detroit for the purpose, Henry and Edsel Ford and C. E. Sorensen declared that they saw "no difficulty" in adapting such an aircraft to mass production. They suggested further that production at the rate of one an hour was not an unreasonable anticipation, provided the aircraft design were frozen before they began. On this point they were emphatic. Changes "would have to be tabooed" to get the promised output.[16]

The Ford offer was indeed tempting. Airplanes at the rate of one an hour after a tooling-up period of eight months, while not exactly fantastic, certainly exceeded anything planned by the regular aircraft industry. And the enormous prestige of the Ford empire gave credence to

---

[15] Chief, Mat Div, MM&D, to CGMC, 13 Dec 43, AFCF 452.01-D Production.

[16] TWX, EES to Chief, Mat Div, 13 Jun 40, AC Project Rcds (Lyon Papers), vol. 33.

the predicted achievement. Nonetheless, on reflection, the matériel staff concluded that the Ford scheme could not be executed.

The Ford proposition was not feasible if only because none of the military aircraft needed in large numbers could really be frozen. Almost without exception the designs chosen had been earmarked for production while still in the experimental stage. In an effort to get the newest and the best equipment as soon as possible, the customary service tests had been telescoped so that production planning in many instances coincided with the development of the original experimental model. In a few instances, the manufacturers had started production planning even before the designs had come off the drawing board. Under such circumstances, a true design freeze was patently impossible. But the dream of mass-produced airplanes was difficult to kill.

The idea of military aircraft rolling off the end of a Ford assembly line stirred up a good deal of public enthusiasm. Soon queries from political leaders on the Hill began to reach the War Department. Why not turn out fighters and bombers in Detroit? The answers sent back reflected the stand that had been official policy ever since 1938.[17] "Military aircraft of combat type are not adaptable to mass production techniques." So wrote the Assistant Secretary of War, who went on to explain that where automobiles might be standardized for a full year at a time, aircraft had to be modified at entirely "unpredictable intervals." Mass production on a Detroit scale would only result in large numbers of obsolete aircraft unsuited for combat—a "poor bargain" at best, the Assistant Secretary declared.[18]

The demise of the Ford proposal to mass-produce airplanes did not, of course, mean that the capacity of the automobile industry would not be used. Negotiations proceeded, albeit haltingly, for aircraft engines, and the vast potential of Detroit held considerable promise as a source of parts and subassemblies for the old-line aircraft industry. To this end negotiators continued through the latter part of 1940 and into early 1941. Finally, in May 1941, Ford agreed to sign as a major subcontractor supplying sets of knocked-down parts or components for the four-engine B–24 heavy bomber to be assembled by Consolidated and Douglas. But Ford had little interest in remaining a secondary producer of parts for others.

Once captivated by the dream of mass-produced aircraft, the Ford management could never rest content with making parts. Intentions are hard to document, but every shred of evidence in the War Department files makes it clear that from the very beginning of the negotiations leading to the B–24 parts contract, the Ford management hoped to turn out bombers on its own account as soon as possible. Not the least significant evidence of this intention is the Willow Run plant itself.[19]

Ostensibly erected as a parts plant, the

---

[17] See ch. XV, above.

[18] Actg SW (Louis Johnson) to Senator Sheppard, 26 Jun 40, SW files, Air Corps Gen Questions, item 1019.

[19] Except where otherwise indicated, the description of the Willow Run operation is based on ATSC Industrial Planning Project Case Hist: Ford Willow Run.

Willow Run facility had all the earmarks of an assembly plant. The main structure—there were ultimately 16 in all counting hangars, offices, warehouses, and so forth—covered some 67 acres, one of the largest single industrial buildings in the world. The main production areas under this roof embraced two major bays 150 feet wide, 30 feet high, and 2,000 feet long. Overhead cranes with capacities running to 19 tons served this expanse. Taken all together, the building, its dimensions, and its equipment clearly signified that Ford intended to do far more than turn out a couple of hundred sets of knocked-down parts per month.

Even before it signed as a subcontractor for parts, the Ford Company had succeeded in getting a contract for one B-24 as an "educational order." And around this single airplane the Ford team began planning for mass production on their own account. They virtually ignored the original schedules for parts deliveries laid down by the military planners and from the very beginning set their eyes on a target of one bomber per hour. All their production plans were premised upon this ultimate goal.

Such planning was costly; since it went far beyond what the contract authorized, the company had to use its own funds to carry on. The gamble paid off. While other manufacturers dutifully accepted the official schedules and planned to meet them, only to complain at the dislocations inevitable when the schedules were subsequently enlarged repeatedly, Ford planned initially far in excess of schedule and took each successive increase in stride.

In October 1941, the Ford management got a contract authorizing the production of complete bombers at Willow Run.[20] The contract regularized the Ford position. By absorbing all the advance outlays made by the company from its own funds, it rewarded Ford's initial boldness. But of greater moment, it gave official sanction to the Ford dream of mass-produced military aircraft.

The Ford empire possessed in depth the resources required for large-scale production. An old and experienced purchasing organization understood the art of close pricing when dealing with vendors and suppliers. A large staff of production men, tool designers, engineers, expediters, and machinists was already at hand. So too were the hundreds of machine tools in the Ford pool, ready and waiting to supplement the new equipment installed at Willow Run by the Defense Plant Corporation. These were important aspects of the Ford plan, but the key to the one-an-hour pace of mass production can be summed up in a single word: tooling.

The very essence of Ford's dream for Willow Run was production tooling. Here was a technique the automobile industry had carried further than any other industry in the world, a technique that the aircraft industry was only beginning to comprehend. The disparity between the levels of tooling employed by the two industries is readily demonstrated. For example, in a single prewar year when a leading automobile manufacturer spent $10,000,000 in tooling up for a year's output, one of the most production-minded aircraft builders spent only $150,000. Airplanes were still built mostly by hand. Rivets, generally speaking, were ham-

---

[20] Although the contract was not signed until October 1941, negotiations had been under way since the previous June.

mered in one at a time—and there were more than 250,000 rivets in a bomber. At this rate it was easy to understand why aircraft production costs were estimated to range from $5.00 to $8.00 a pound against the 15 or 20 cents average experienced by the automobile industry.[21] Admittedly, even then airplanes were far more intricate than automobiles, but these figures suggest how slight was the tooling used by the old-line aircraft firms.

Production tools are of two kinds: those designed to simplify and speed the pace of production and thereby cut costs and those designed to ensure accuracy and interchangeability. Typical of the first group is a fixture permitting the use of a gang drill where one employee controlling a single spindle runs a whole bank of drills performing identical operations. Tooling for accuracy and interchangeability includes a wide variety of jigs and fixtures for holding work and ensuring perfect matings when separately fabricated parts are brought together for final assembly. Increased use of tooling can speed production along a geometric curve. As more tooling is added, the level of skills required falls and trained labor becomes less important as a limiting factor. A steel die in a press turning out intricately shaped cowlings or fuselage fillets can obviously outstrip the most skillful workman making the same items by hand on a drop hammer—once the die is completed.

The over-all Ford production program called for maximum use of both kinds of tooling. In fact, the Ford plan was premised upon mechanization at every feasible point. The B-24 was to be broken into 70 major component sections. These were to be completely prefabricated in their own special areas and then moved on conveyors to the final point of integration on the main assembly line. Like the whole Ford undertaking, this scheme of production was bold in conception and exciting in promise. It was to prove immensely difficult in execution.

The Willow Run story began even before Ford signed the original contract as a parts supplier. Two months earlier, during March and April of 1941, a team of Ford representatives, ultimately numbering 200, spent weeks at the main Consolidated plant in San Diego making careful studies. They photographed every one of the 30,000 detailed drawings of every different part and assembly going into the bomber. They struck off copies of all blueprints, bills of materials, and engineering releases and made reproductions of the loft boards used by Consolidated. When they returned to Detroit, it took two freight cars to transport the records and materials they had accumulated. They believed they had enough information to get bomber production under way, but they were soon to be disillusioned. No sooner had the engineers returned to Detroit than their real troubles began.

A large part of the difficulty lay in the B-24 itself. The bomber simply was not ready for mass production. Conceived in 1938, the XB-24 was built and flown in 1939. Although Consolidated had turned out 139 of the craft on a British contract, a "production order" by prewar standards, the B-24 was still a "shop engineered" aircraft. It had not been designed

---

[21] J. H. Kindelberger, President, North American Aviation, The Aircraft Industry, Lecture, 19 Nov 37, AIC. See also, C. T. Gilliam to SW, 8 Nov 40, ASF Planning Br files 452.11 Aircraft, AGO Rcds 205.04.

initially with an eye to mass production, at least not in the sense that Detroit used that phrase.

Then too, the transfer of drawings from Consolidated to Ford turned out to be more difficult than anticipated. The automobile manufacturers and the airframe builders found they spoke different languages, and translation injected its inevitable obscurities. Where Consolidated used fractional dimensions—the survival of a cruder age of aircraft construction—Ford used decimal notations entirely. Moreover, the Consolidated draftsmen all presumed that their drawings would be interpreted by experienced foremen. They made use of all sorts of signs and symbols without amplification. Worse yet, the Ford engineers found numerous discrepancies between the duplicate loft boards and the detailed drawings of parts they had brought from San Diego. The Consolidated engineers knew of these errors in many cases, but under tremendous pressure, they customarily left it to the skill of their production men to reconcile them on the line.

For the engineers in Detroit who were trying to prepare precision tools for mass production, the discrepancies in the Consolidated drawings were devastating. They decided they would have to re-do the drawings—30,000 in all. Before they were through, what with the many design changes introduced along the way, they had to turn out twice that number, work enough to occupy a whole regiment of draftsmen for several years.

Sometimes the engineers working on a particular part could discover no drawing for it among the reams of paper brought from San Diego to Detroit. On one occasion, when a Ford draftsman was unable to locate an adequate drawing for the B-24 toilet paper container, he wired to the west coast requesting further details. To his surprise the reply came back that there were no drawings. Consolidated had found it cheaper to buy the item in a local dime store.

The difficulties initially encountered in transferring the Consolidated designs to Ford tended to compound as they ramified through the whole operation in Detroit.[22] During the year after the Consolidated drawings were first brought back, a tool design group with upward of a thousand men worked continually to prepare the jigs, fixtures, and dies—the tooling—with which they hoped to achieve wonders of production. The Ford management knew there were risks in planning tools while the aircraft itself was still being engineered for production. Subsequent design changes would force them to scrap production tools already made up, but the risks seemed worth taking in the interest of speed. Consequently, by April 1942 one whole set of production tools was ready for use.

As it turned out, the decision to tool up without waiting for the B-24 to be thoroughly engineered for production was a wise one even though it cost a good deal of lost motion at first. Some 15 percent of the tools originally made had to be scrapped or reworked because of design changes. Nonetheless, it was only because Ford had fabricated a large number of tools well before the assembly line was scheduled to start that the production men had time to discover in their tools some of the serious shortcomings that had

---

[22] Not until the spring of 1942 did the production staff move out to the new plant under construction at Willow Run.

to be worked out before production could begin. Above all, this forehandedness gave them time to learn how faulty their basic assumption had been. Ford's whole program rested on the premise that the production techniques of the automobile industry could be applied directly to aircraft. Experience showed this was not quite true.

The Ford engineers had planned to use dies far more extensively than was customary among the old-line aircraft firms. By using dies for blanking, piercing, forming, and drawing, the production men hoped to reach hitherto undreamed of levels of output. Once set up, tested, gauged, and put into action, high-speed presses manned by relatively unskilled employees could turn out extremely accurate parts in large quantities in very little time. Dies were expensive and hard to make. They required the services of highly skilled die-sinkers and the use of special machine tools. But in these resources the Ford empire was rich. The Ford toolmakers were world famous and the Ford tool room no less so. For example, in the main toolroom the B-24 engineers had, in addition to the usual array of standard machine tools, a battery of 23 hard-to-get Kellett profilers, each worth $80,000, ready to cut the dies needed for the bomber program. Here were resources far beyond those possessed by any of the aircraft manufacturers.

The Ford plan to make maximum use of dies proved disappointing. To begin with, the production men had to learn from bitter experience that aluminum is not the same thing as steel. When they began using their forming dies on aluminum sheets, they discovered that the dies scratched and defaced the surface of the stock, which was considerably softer than steel. Scarred surfaces cannot be tolerated on aircraft exteriors for aerodynamic reasons, so it was absolutely essential to correct this difficulty. A trial of chrome plated dies proved abortive. After considerable experimentation, it turned out that highly polished steel dies would work acceptably. But all this took time, the very item the production engineers had hoped to save by the use of dies.

Still more troublesome was the matter of spring-back. The Ford engineers discovered that unlike steel, aluminum would not retain the exact shape given it by a forming die. To correct this they had to design a sequence of two or more dies to perform deep draws in successive steps where a single pass would have sufficed with steel. As a consequence of these discoveries, the Ford engineers ended up by making 29,000 dies although not more than 15,000 were actually used. Moreover, about 2,400 of these had to be reworked, some of them repeatedly, before they were satisfactory.

The use of dies proved disappointing in other respects. The automobile men had originally expected to effect economies by the widespread use of presswork. Where the airframe builders laboriously drilled holes, one at a time, or sometimes faster with gang drills, the automotive men planned to punch out the holes for an entire skin section with one pass of a press. The idea was alluring but it did not always work. Aluminum skin sheets showed a distressing propensity for stretching irregularly and thereby failing to mate properly when they reached the point of assembly.

Finally, the inevitable problem of design change militated against the use of dies. One of the major economies anticipated was the long production run with semiskilled labor. A single tool setting, the engineers hoped, would suffice for the full number of items on any given contract. But the high frequency of design change destroyed this economy entirely. The planners found it was unwise to stamp out more than a 60-day supply of any part since beyond that point the introduction of a design change could make scrap losses extremely serious. Furthermore, it often turned out that shortages of critical materials made even a limited 60-day run impossible. Here, too, the expected economies failed to materialize.

Although the Ford engineers made extensive use of tooling to speed up the fabrication of individual parts, it was in jigging up for final assembly that they carried their ideas on tooling to the ultimate. They built fixtures for every single assembly operation. Often these were sturdy frames or benches of welded steel to ensure stability and rigidity while the work of assembly was in process.

One of the most important—and impressive—assembly jigs was the massive device used in assembling the B-24 center wing section, the wing root on either side, and the heavy structure where these roots joined the fuselage. A predrilled and precut aluminum sheet to make the top wing was placed in Fixture No. 1, where rivets were inserted in the holes. Fixture No. 2 then closed down on this skin to hold it in place. Fixture No. 3 held splicer bars in position while they were riveted to the skin. The next two fixtures passed up stringers and locked them into place while they too were riveted to the skin, and a sixth fixture held both stringers and splicers while they were riveted to each other. Finally, an overhead conveyor moved in, lifted out the finished component, and carried it off to the assembly line.

When production finally reached its peak at Willow Run, there were seven banks of wing assembly fixtures, each bank holding five separate wings. Thus thirty-five individual wing center sections were under construction simultaneously. Each fixture was sixty feet long and fifteen feet high, a mass of cast iron and steel. They were costly and required months to build, but once in operation, they needed only one-sixth the labor required by conventional methods of aircraft construction.

If the center section jig was impressive, even more so was the huge milling apparatus installed to machine the finished subassembly. This special machine tool, conceived by Ford engineers, was constructed by the Ingersoll Milling Machine Company at a cost of $168,000. Using it, a seven-man crew did some forty-two machining operations in three and one half man-hours. With conventional tools the same job would have required 500 man-hours. But the major advantage of this heavy tool was less the saving in labor than the gain in accuracy that it permitted. With the device, all four-engine mounting pads could be milled and drilled simultaneously in perfect alignment. So too were the landing-gear bearing holes. Thus, at one stroke, the Ford engineers contrived to master the immensely taxing problem of alignment.

The other tooling along the Willow Run production line need not be described. Suffice it to say that the main center section passed on down through a long succession of stations where fuel

Assembly Jig, B-24 Center Wing Section, Willow Run

tanks, electrical gear, nose section, fuselage, and so on were added until the completed bomber rolled off the end of the line on its own wheels. The whole process represented a remarkable example of production engineering. It was bold in conception and dramatic, even breathtaking, to watch in operation. Nevertheless, it too suffered from the fundamental error of premise that underlay so much of the Ford experiment.

The whole Ford production plan rested upon two major assumptions. One was that the B-24 design would be reasonably stable; the other was that there would be a continuous flow of parts and semifinished components to the assembly line. In the event, both of these assumptions proved to be unfounded. Frequent, almost continual changes in design characterized the whole production life of the B-24. Many if not most of the changes required revisions in the elaborate tooling devised to speed production at each step along the way. And every time a major change in tooling proved unavoidable, the whole production line had to stop. Continuous fabrication on the final

B-24 ASSEMBLY LINE AT WILLOW RUN

assembly line involved a careful interlocking of every adjacent item. Since there were 152,000 separate parts in the B-24, 30,000 of them entirely different, the implications of the continual flux in design are not hard to imagine. All together, the Ford production men built 21,000 jigs and fixtures, but only about 11,000 were finally put to use. Little wonder then that the total cost of tooling Willow Run—dies, jigs, and all—ranged between $75,000,000 and $100,000,000.

The realization that the B-24 design could never be frozen came hard to the Ford engineers. Only gradually did they begin to understand that design change was a perfectly normal attribute of military aircraft even at a time when production had been accelerated to the scheduled level. It is no exaggeration to say that the last B-24 turned off the Willow Run production line was an entirely different aircraft from the initial item. The original Ford educational order called for one B-24E. The last production model, 18 contracts later, was designated the B-24L. In between, 130 major changes and thousands of minor ones had been introduced. And the original aircraft design had burgeoned from a gross weight of 41,000 pounds to 60,000 pounds as operations in combat showed the need for adding turbosuperchargers, self-sealing fuel tanks, full-feathering constant-speed propellers, three heavily armored power-operated gun turrets, and camouflage paint—a not inconsiderable weight—to mention but a few of the many changes made during the life of the airplane.[23]

Was the Willow Run attempt at mass production really a success? Did the whole undertaking vindicate the automobile engineers' conception of production tooling? Or did it only prove that the automobile makers' approach was unsuited to military aircraft in general? Clear-cut answers to questions such as these are hard to find.

In some respects the Willow Run project was a success. If success is measured in terms of more airframe pounds produced with the least cost in dollars and man-hours, there is much to be said for the Ford B–24. At its best, toward the end of 1944, the Willow Run plant turned out one airframe pound with 0.30 man-hours of labor. This was a decided margin of superiority over the industry average of 0.47 man-hours. Economy in the matter of dollar costs is somewhat harder to compute. Assuming a total of approximately 9,000 items, including completed airplanes and equivalent sets of knocked-down parts, and dividing this number into the outlay (not forgetting the cost of tooling) of approximately a billion and a half dollars, the unit cost averages approximately $167,000. This too compares very favorably with the industry as a whole. Of course, such comparisons are not necessarily definitive. Far too many variables impinge upon the picture to permit mathematically exact and scientifically objective evaluations.

No accurate evaluation of the Willow Run operation will ever be possible since the Ford plant was never really run at maximum capacity. In part this stemmed from the labor shortage that plagued the undertaking from beginning to end. At peak, 42,500 people were employed. About 10,000 of these were transferred from other Ford units, but the rest had to be drawn from outside the Ford orbit. When the labor shortage was most acute, Ford recruiters went as far afield as Tennessee and Texas to find workers. Those they found may have been willing, but they were certainly untrained. Thus inexperienced labor and the chronic shortage of labor both operated to retard production at Willow Run entirely without reference to the feasibility of the tooling provided there.

Willow Run was not operated at maximum capacity for yet another reason. By the time the plant hit its stride, the Air Forces no longer needed B–24 bombers in unlimited quantities. By March 1944 the monthly output amounted to 309 units plus parts equivalent to 112 units or a computed total of 421 bombers. Thereafter increases in output up to 600 a month would have been technically possible, but the tactical units in the field were unable to absorb anything like that quantity. As it was, the long rows of completed but unused bombers that began to accumulate became a matter of acute embarrassment to the Air Forces. Had Ford

---

[23] For an itemized description of each master change in the B–24, see ATSC, Model Designations: Army Aircraft, 11th ed., Jan 46.

been permitted to operate at maximum capacity to the end of the war, the ratio of airframe pounds to man-hours and the ratio of units to dollar costs would undoubtedly have been improved markedly in the company's favor. But these ratios are not definitive either.

If the real test of success in military aircraft is the production of tactically suitable weapons at the time required, then the Willow Run record may not appear in such a favorable light. Compared with some of the old-line aircraft manufacturers, Ford's rate of acceleration was only fair. From the start of the project, three years elapsed before the assembly line reached peak production. From the day the project began to the day the first production item was accepted in July 1942, seventeen months elapsed. This was somewhat better than average for airframe builders as a group, but Ford's production acceleration thereafter was decidedly below average for at least six months. Here, too, external variables such as Ford's unavoidable subservience to Consolidated in matters of aeronautical design make final judgments impossible.

At the end of the war a group of officers was assigned the task of appraising the Willow Run operation as a whole for future reference. In their report they recognized how seriously the delay in getting adequate design data had retarded the acceleration of output. But they went on to observe that the Ford system was "not flexible enough" to use on a product that had not been "completely engineered and ready for mass production." Was there ever such an aircraft in wartime? The high rate of flux characterizing the B–24 was far from exceptional; indeed, it might be said that the aircraft design that remained relatively stable during the war was the real exception. The following figures showing total direct engineering hours expended in the war years on another typical production bomber, the North American B–25, should suggest how normal continual change in design actually was: [24]

Year	Hours
1940	329,415
1941	419,060
1942	695,488
1943	461,213
1944	200,321

Surely, then, it is useless to talk of the levels of mass production attainable with a completely engineered aircraft ready for production. Such an aircraft will probably never exist.

To debate the "success" or "failure" of the Willow Run program is hardly useful. The Ford management may have been in error in assuming that a design freeze was possible. Certainly the air arm officers who let them go ahead on that assumption were then equally in error. Yet, in a sense, both these errors, if they were such, combined to produce an exceedingly worthwhile experiment. If the automobile makers came to the realization that military aircraft could not be slapped out like so many passenger vehicles, so too the old-line airframe builders were given some substantial lessons in techniques of mass production hitherto unknown to them.

Above all, the Willow Run experiment demonstrated the necessity of compromise in the quantity-quality equation. The automobile makers tended to em-

---

[24] North American Aviation, Brief History, p. 62.

PRODUCTION 529

phasize quantity. The engineering staffs of the old-line aircraft builders were primarily concerned with quality; at heart they were designers rather than producers. Their tendency was to work toward aircraft of high performance, even to the neglect of such vital considerations as armament. But the dreadful urgency of war demonstrated once and for all that both quantity and quality were necessary. Both the production-minded automobile makers and the performance-minded aircraft designers came to realize that the real test of success lay in the ability of the industry to incorporate design changes on the production line with the least reduction in output.

Resolving the Dilemma

The dilemma of mass production is implicit in the quantity-quality equation. Clearly, these conflicting objectives can never be entirely reconciled, but during World War II the Air Forces did contrive a working compromise between the two. The compromise was called modification.

Modification: A Working Compromise

Like so many other aspects of wartime procurement, the techniques of modification did not spring into operation full born; they evolved slowly, in part from accidents of circumstance and in part as an outgrowth of hard experience. Although the necessity of finding an accommodation between more and better airplanes was to become grimly urgent in the fight for survival after Pearl Harbor, the practice of modification actually began nearly two years earlier when the joint Anglo-French purchasing missions began buying equipment in the United States.[25]

American-built aircraft such as the B-17 and the B-24 bombers when sold abroad required a good many changes to make them acceptable to foreign users. Communications equipment, armament, oxygen systems, and other such accessory items had to be altered to French and British specifications. To make these changes on the assembly lines in the United States would delay production. And this, of course, was out of the question; export sales of aircraft built to U.S. specifications were already in serious competition with deliveries to the Air Corps.[26] The solution was to establish modification centers abroad, where production aircraft from the United States could be refitted as the occasion required. Such a scheme had proved workable in World War I and could be used again.

After Pearl Harbor the situation was almost exactly reversed. Hundreds of military aircraft ordered by foreign customers, from Sweden to Siam, were taken over in haste by the air arm. Many of the items had to be reworked before they could be used with standard Air Corps accessories,[27] but the aircraft manufacturers concerned showed no interest in undertaking the job. They were under heavy pressure to turn out still more air-

---

[25] USAF Hist Study 62, The Modification of Army Aircraft in the United States: 1939-1945, by V. G. Toole and R. W. Ackerman, Aug 47, p. 11. Except where otherwise documented, the following section is based on this study.

[26] See above, ch. IX.

[27] Sometimes the aircraft diverted from foreign buyers were pressed into service without change. The author recalls the somewhat disconcerting experience of flying during 1942 in an airplane with Swedish instrument markings and instruction plates.

planes at top speed. And, needless to add, they were already swamped with problems inevitable in the rapid expansion of an entire industry. Here again the modification center idea seemed to offer a workable solution to the problem.

Another consideration leading to the decision to open modification centers in the United States was the need to free the airframe manufacturers of the large numbers of aircraft that began to pile up at the end of their production lines. In the rush after the outbreak of war it frequently happened that vital components or accessories were not available in sufficient numbers to keep pace with the flow of production. Rather than slow down or stop the assembly lines, nearly completed aircraft were hauled outside to await the arrival of the missing parts. Soon dozens and even hundreds of units cluttered the open areas around most major airframe plants. These seemingly completed aircraft had a depressing effect upon the employees, who were constantly being exhorted to redouble their efforts to increase output.[28] Sending the airplanes to separate modification centers, the morale problem would be solved and the missing parts could be installed without delaying production.

The formal decision to open modification centers in the United States not unlike those set up earlier in Britain came in January 1942. Although the manufacturers themselves at that hectic moment were far too busy to take on any additional problems, the repair and maintenance shops of the nation's major airlines seemed to offer a convenient alternative. They had hangars, airfields, machinery, and a nucleus of skilled mechanics who could be employed immediately. Within a week plans were afoot to make use of the American Airlines base at El Paso, the United Airlines base at Cheyenne, and the TWA shops at Kansas City and Los Angeles, as well as numerous others. By May 1942, some ten airline maintenance bases were in full swing doing modification work for the Air Forces.

As 1942 wore on, the broader implications of the modification problem gradually became apparent. Modification was far more than a matter of reconditioning aircraft originally ordered for foreign purchasers or adding parts left off on the assembly line because of a momentary shortage. Operations by tactical units in the field began to show up all sorts of deficiencies and malfunctionings in the aircraft currently being turned out. But the need for more airplanes was desperate, and maximum production was then possible only by stabilizing designs. To undertake corrective action by introducing changes on the production line itself would be to buy qualitative improvement at too great a cost in terms of the total number of units produced. Modification offered the only feasible middle course. The production lines could continue their output unabated, yet the tactical units at the front need not be denied those modifications they regarded essential.

About twenty permanent modification centers were opened during the war although not all were in operation at any one time. Some were so near the production lines they served that aircraft could be towed to them. Others required a

---

[28] AAF Hist Study 40, p. 158. See also, Maj Friedman, IGD, to IG, 24 Oct 41, AFCF 333.1 Contract Inspection.

ferry flight of hundreds of miles from the assembly plant to the modification area. The Birmingham, Alabama, center, for example, was primarily engaged in modifying B-24 bombers coming from the Willow Run plant in Michigan. Weather considerations weighed heavily in the selection of the center sites. The more southerly locations not only offered more flying days per year, but permitted a great deal of work to be done out of doors.

In a sense, good weather was one of the nation's secret weapons. A warm sunny climate made it possible to enlarge floor space and productive area at no greater expense than the cost of constructing hardstands. With nightlighting and portable canvas "nose hangars," the outdoor capacity was enhanced still further. The importance of this supplementary space is evident: against 5,000,000 square feet of covered floor space in the modification centers as a whole, outside working areas totaled approximately 12,000,000 square feet.

Modification centers may have been a necessary wartime compromise, but to say the very least that compromise was purchased dearly. The $75,000,000 spent on facilities at the various centers was only a small part of the total outlay. Inevitably, operating costs were abnormally large. By its very nature modification was makeshift and expedient work. Improvisation was the order of the day. Drawings and detailed instructions were seldom available. Installations frequently had to be made with "tin snips and stove bolts." Speed rather than polish was the prevailing criterion; so long as a modification was safe and functional, it was generally acceptable. In the jargon of the time, this kind of job had to be "quick and dirty." [29]

Modifications were normally made with hand tools rather than production jigs, and labor costs soared accordingly. Several centers ran up charges for more than a million man-hours a month doing by hand what might better have been done by machines. Installing an extra fuel tank in the leading edge of a P-38 wing, to cite but one example, absorbed 300 man-hours at a modification center; the same installation on the production line could have been done in a matter of minutes. During the initial rush of 1942, makeshift arrangements of this sort were entirely understandable, but as time wore on they showed no sign of diminishing. On the contrary, in 1943 the modification load grew larger.[30]

By the middle of 1943 it was sometimes difficult to tell where the production line left off and modification began. One center reported an expenditure of 8,000 man-hours to complete a miscellaneous lot of modifications on an aircraft that had required only 9,000 man-hours to build in the first place.[31] As long as this expenditure was directed toward making last-minute changes found necessary by the tactical units in the field, no one could justly complain. But some officers were inclined to believe that too often the manufacturers were using the centers to accomplish work that should have been

---

[29] For a contemporary account, see Paul Gallico, "Quick and Dirty," *Saturday Evening Post* (October 10, 1943), p. 9ff.

[30] B. Kinsey and J. V. C. Gregory, Modification Centers and Tactical Availability, Lecture, AFSC Project Officers School, WF, 18 Sep 45, copy in ICAF file.

[31] Materiel Command, Proc Div, Decentralization Progress Rpt, 30 Sep 43, WFHO.

done on the production line. The airplanes some of the prime contractors turned out, as one officer protested, were hardly recognizable as such. "They send them over to the modification center," he complained, "and build themselves an airplane at Government expense." [32]

This charge was not quite fair. It was true that anywhere from 25 to 50 percent of the total labor spent in turning out military aircraft was actually performed at the centers. But in theory at least the original prime contractors were charged for all work required to make good deficiencies stemming from shortages along the production line. In practice, of course, it was extremely difficult to keep such accounts straight. The line between deficiencies in assembly on the one hand and modification directed by demands from the field on the other was not always easy to define. Moreover, the paper record was difficult to keep in phase with the facts. A heterogeneous array of items in job-lot quantities flown in from all over the map in great haste posed acute difficulties of property accounting. The lack of adequate storage bins caused trouble, and the outdoor operations characterizing so many centers only aggravated the problem. In one way or another, unless the closest sort of supervision could be exercised, the government would end up paying nearly twice over for many of the aircraft it received.[33]

At Wright Field, where a Modification Section had been set up in the Production Division to ride herd on the various centers, the officer in charge put his finger on the heart of the trouble. The existing system gave no real incentive to the airframe manufacturers to absorb the work of the centers by incorporating as many modifications as possible on the production line. Aircraft coming out of the factories were inspected, then "accepted" or officially credited for payment, and then ferried to a center for modification. After being reworked there, they were again "accepted" from the center contractor, who was duly credited for payment also. So long as the prime contractor and the modifier were separate firms, the prime had no economic incentive to incorporate modifications on the production line since he was paid for the number of units he produced whether they were modified or not.

If the existing pattern of "double acceptance" operated to delay the incorporation of changes on the assembly line, the production officers at Wright Field believed that the way out was to make each prime contractor responsible for the modification center where his aircraft were reworked. No aircraft would then be "accepted" or credited for payment until it had been completely modified and was ready to ferry off to a tactical unit. Single acceptance would encourage both fixed-price and cost-plus-fixed-fee contractors to absorb changes on the line whenever possible inasmuch as their respective lump sum payments and proportionate fees were paid on the basis of deliveries.

By the middle of 1944, most of the centers had been put under the management of the prime contractors whose airplanes were being reworked. The arrangement was not without its drawbacks. When each center was identified with a particular production line, it proved to be rather

---
[32] Walsh, Hist of Eastern Proc Dist: 1943, p. 298.
[33] Ibid., pp. 272–73.

more difficult than formerly to distribute the load. By its very nature modification was feast or famine work. Hurry calls from the strategic planners in Washington frequently demanded deliveries beyond the capabilities of the center assigned to the particular aircraft in question. To spill the load over into another center assigned to another contractor at work on a different model would only lead to the confusion that had prevailed before the centers had been specialized and placed under the control of the prime contractors. Nevertheless, the problem of rush orders and peak loads had to be faced.

The solution finally worked out was to earmark two big centers, the United Airlines shop at Cheyenne and the Bechtel-McCone-Parsons base at Birmingham, as overflow facilities to handle rush orders beyond the capabilities of the specialized centers. When these resources proved inadequate, it was always possible to call upon the repair and maintenance depots operated by the Air Service Command. In fact, by 1944 approximately 25 percent of the total modification load was actually being done in the air depots along with the normal maintenance and repair work regularly performed there. In the main, the depots concentrated on the job of adding modifications to aircraft already accepted and put into service by the Air Forces.

Not every modification could have been made in the factory. Even where the contractor was entirely willing and co-operative, there were some changes that did not lend themselves to mass production. Although the term *modification* is often used loosely to describe all the changes made in a "completed" aircraft, there were actually several rather different categories of work encompassed by the word.

Some modifications were minor alterations of the "tin snip and stove bolt" variety. If an escape hatch showed a tendency to fly open in flight, it was a relatively easy matter to rivet on an extra latch at a center. Or when operations in North Africa indicated the need to relocate the P–38 rear vision mirror to widen the field of vision, this too could be accomplished at a center. In time, of course, such trivial additions or adjustments could easily be performed on the production line with little trouble. But there were other more basic changes that gave greater difficulty.

Basic modifications were those requiring a great deal of careful engineering.[34] These involved major structural changes in the airframe or the design and installation of an entirely new assembly or component. When fighter pilots complained of high stick forces in flying the P–38, it proved necessary to install hydraulic boosters on the ailerons.[35] Similarly, when Luftwaffe attacks on Air Forces bombers making deep penetrations over Germany became too costly to bear, there came a hurry call for escort fighters with greater fuel capacity for longer ranges. Difficult modifications such as these could be performed at the centers, but it would have been less costly and far more desirable, from an engineering standpoint, to make the modifications on the production line as soon as feasible.

[34] See ATSC Regulation 152-3, 24 Feb 45, for definitions of the various classes of modifications.

[35] For a typical cross section of modifications suggested by tactical units in the field, see Actg Chief, PES, to CGAAF, 11 Sep 43, AFCF 452.01–D Production.

On the other hand, there were still other modifications, both major and minor, that would always be done at the centers. Included in this category were all those modifications undertaken to equip aircraft for special missions or to make them suitable for operations in a particular theater. Typical of the former was the conversion of a standard fighter into a weather reconnaissance aircraft. Theater modifications included "desert proofing" aircraft for operation in North Africa and "winterizing" aircraft destined for the Soviet Union via the Alaska-Siberia route. These were highly specialized conversions required on a relatively small portion of the total number of aircraft produced and thus entirely unsuited for introduction on the contractors' assembly lines.

Even where it was highly desirable to make a modification or group of modifications in the factory, it was not easily accomplished. Most prime contractors resisted the efforts of Air Forces officers in this direction. Until the single acceptance scheme was inaugurated, they actually had an economic incentive to delay since the introduction of substantial modifications on the line almost invariably cut down on the number of finished aircraft being turned out and thus affected their rate of compensation.[36] But this was not the only reason the manufacturers were slow to incorporate modifications on their assembly lines. The truth of the matter was that they simply could not do so without serious loss of output until they had brought the whole production process into complete control with every part and process so perfectly scheduled that the cost in dollars and in the rate of output for any proposed change could be predicted with reasonable accuracy.

The following figures showing some of the time and dollar costs encountered when making seventy-three modifications in a group of 1,000 P-38's should give at least a general impression of why it was that airframe contractors had such a hard time mastering their production lines:[37]

Aircraft Designation	Engineering Hours	Tooling Hours	Tooling Materials Cost
P-38F — 5	10,450	6,200	$ 4,650
P-38G — 1	23,250	23,760	18,000
P-38G — 3 to 5	5,000	4,000	3,000
P-38G — 10	19,200	18,400	13,800

Only an extremely proficient and well-organized production staff could hope to co-ordinate the multiplicity of details evident in changes such as these to the point where they could be incorporated on the line without disrupting the whole assembly process.

In some ways it was actually harmful for a manufacturer to insert modifications in the assembly line before his production organization was sufficiently skilled to handle them properly. The Martin B-26 facility in Omaha offers a case in point. This government-built assembly plant was a war baby; its management had been built around a cadre drawn from the already badly overextended Martin home plant near Baltimore. Under pressure from Air Forces officers, the managerial staff at the Omaha plant did try to move

---

[36] For an unusually clear statement by a manufacturer of the impact modifications had on output, see G. F. Smith of Lockheed to AAF Resident Representative (Lockheed), 22 Oct 43, AFCF 452.01-D Production.

[37] Ibid.

PRODUCTION 535

a number of modifications from the centers to the production line, but the attempt misfired. No distinction was made between minor changes and "must" items —between the desirable and the necessary. What is more, there was no master plan controlling the point in the production line at which any given modification was made. The changes were tacked on haphazardly whenever it seemed convenient rather than at fixed stations planned in advance. As a consequence, once an airplane left the factory no one knew just what equipment it did or did not have. Under such circumstances repair and maintenance in the field was certain to become a nightmare. Nor was this an isolated example.[38] Other airframe manufacturers experienced a similar confusion.

The effective answer to the problem of incorporating modifications on the assembly line itself lay in improved production control. During the spring of 1944 the Production Division at Wright Field finally established a more or less standard procedure by which all modifications were actually scheduled down to the last rivet on the production line. The heart of this scheme was the so-called block system, which had been evolved earlier by some of the more proficient airframe builders.

The block system was nothing more than an arbitrary pattern of model identification. Thus a B–24J, after being equipped with a different type of life raft and improved sights on the waist guns, might be designated the B–24J–15 to distinguish it from the B–24J–10, the last previous block without these additions. The series letter "J" would be changed only when there were modifications affecting major alterations in structure or the primary armament of the aircraft. Thus the B–17F became the B–17G after the chin turret was added. The B–17, which was finally to be the most modified aircraft in the Air Forces during the war, went through eight different series from the B–17A to the B–17G, and each of these series had many different blocks. For example, the B–17F had 56 blocks and the B–17G had 48.[39]

By lumping many small modifications into a single change and by running a pilot model to spot potential production bugs, it was possible to eliminate some of the confusion.[40] But not until the production staff in any given facility could obtain accurate information on inventory, machine loading, labor availability, and the like, was it possible to maintain a truly positive control over the incorporation of modifications into the production line. As machine records replaced manual techniques of accounting and inventory control, manufacturers found they could effect modifications with a minimum of dislocation.[41]

What this meant in terms of aircraft output may be suggested by the hypothetical learner curve in Chart 9. Modifications introduced along the assembly

---

[38] Chief, Prod Div to CGMD, 26 Jan 43, AFCF 452.01–A Production.

[39] USAF Hist Study 62, p. 3. See also, ATSC, Model Designations: Army Aircraft, 11th ed., Jan 46.

[40] See Memo, ACofAS MM&D for CGMC, 4 Jun 43, AFCF 452.01–B Production; and North American Aviation, Annual Report, 1942, p. 33, AFCF 452.01 (Bulky).

[41] See for example, descriptions in North American Aviation, Brief History, pp. 64–65, and ATSC Industrial Planning Project Case History: Ford Willow Run, pp. 67–68.

CHART 9—HYPOTHETICAL LEARNER CURVE

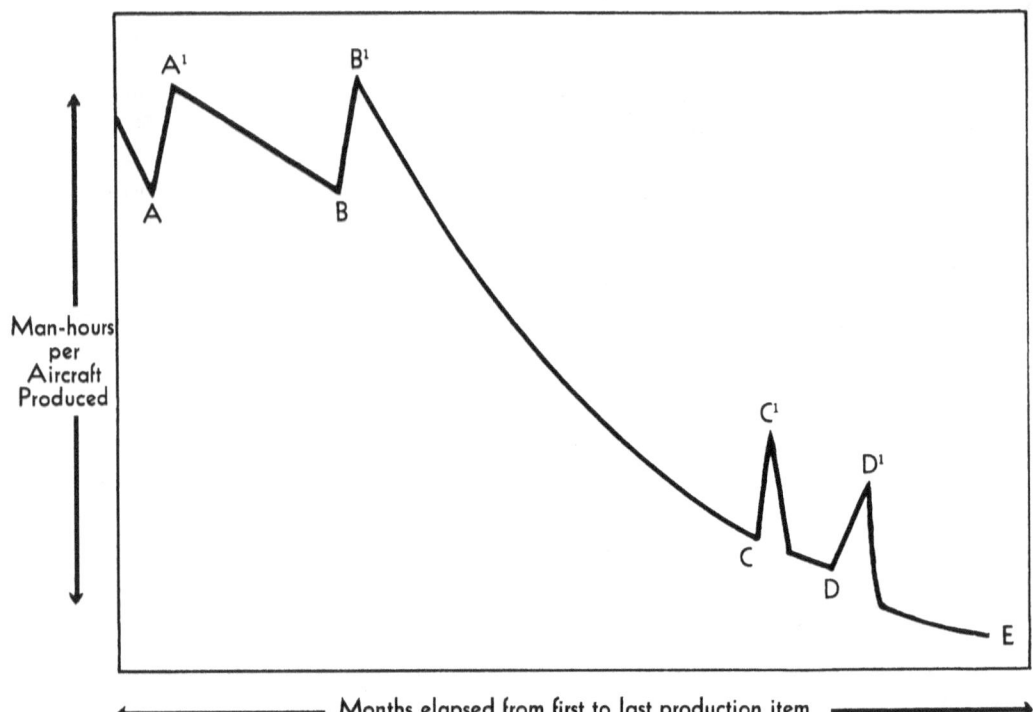

line (at A, B, etc.) before the manufacturer had close control over all the factors of production resulted in rather abrupt and substantial increases in the number of man-hours required to complete each aircraft (A–A^1, B–B^1 etc.). Moreover, the recovery rate was slow (A^1 to B etc.). But modifications introduced after the manufacturer's production engineers had established adequate systems of control (as at C and D), imposed only relatively small increases in man-hours (C–C^1, D–D^1, etc.) and the recovery rate was rapid (as in C^1–D, etc.). Consequently, only a slight loss in the rate of production resulted.

Table 7 gives a panoramic view of the modifications spread across the block system of the B–24 bombers produced at Willow Run up to March 1944, the point of peak production. Although all the early blocks show a large number of changes, it was not until the beginning of the H series that the most difficult modifications were introduced. At this point more than 50 master changes were made. These included the installation of a nose turret, a retractable lower ball turret, a crew passage through the bomb bay, a central fuel transfer system and numerous others. Despite the complexity of these modifications, it will be observed from a comparison of the number of aircraft delivered, the dates of delivery and the

PRODUCTION

TABLE 7—B-24 MODIFICATIONS AT WILLOW RUN

Block Number	Quantity in Block	Delivery Date First Item in Block	Number of Master Changes Involved	Sequence of Aircraft in Block
B-24E- 1	29	1 September 1942	129	1–29
- 5	60	16 January 1943	82	30–89
-10	57	15 March 1943	95	90–146
-15	49	27 March 1943	27	147–195
-20	58	21 April 1943	23	196–253
-25	235	7 May 1943	68	254–488
B-24H- 1	253	30 June 1943	51	489–741
- 5	89	18 September 1943	42	742–830
-10	189	6 October 1943	37	831–1019
-15	540	11 November 1943	75	1020–1559
-20	228	4 February 1944	38	1560–1787
-25	266	24 February 1944	18	1788–2053
-30	215	17 March 1944	12	2054–2268

Source: ATSC Industrial Planning Project Case History: Ford Willow Run, 1946, p. 58.

number of changes involved that improved production control made it possible to introduce a relatively large number of modifications while still maintaining a high level of output.

At Wright Field, the Chief of the Production Division regarded the whole program for incorporating modifications in the factories on a regularly scheduled basis as one of the outstanding achievements of 1944. It virtually put an end to the buck passing that had previously marked the relations of the primes and the center contractors. This kind of scheduling not only saved man-hours of labor but also cut down materially on the flow time between the beginning of fabrication and delivery of a completed and tactically suitable aircraft to the combat theater.[42] All in all, the whole modification center scheme was an important mechanism for bridging the gap between the stability of design essential for mass production and the flexibility of design essential to tactical suitability. During the course of the war the twenty centers and the twelve air depots (which devoted anywhere from 30 to 45 percent of their "repair" time to modifications) reworked a total of 58,741 aircraft as follows: 1942, 4,038; 1943, 22,007; 1944, 25,048; 1945, 7,218. Experience showed that nearly all of the bombers and cargo aircraft produced had to be sent off to modification centers before entering service; only 30 to 50 percent of the fighter output had to be modified before use.

To be sure, the centers were staggeringly expensive to operate. To retain a sufficient degree of flexibility they had to be run on "open end" cost-plus-fixed-fee contracts so loosely drawn as to permit the contractors in charge to cope with whatever rush program chanced to come along.

---

[42] Production Div, ATSC, WF, Annual Rpt, 1944, WFHO files, pp. 11–12. For evidence on flow time through centers, see Kinsey and Gregory, Modification Centers and Tactical Availability.

Such an arrangement was scarcely conducive to economy, but what was the alternative? Fixed-price contractors could not undertake to incorporate substantial modifications on the production line without entering supplementary contracts, and such contracts took time to negotiate. Aircraft manufacturers with CPFF contracts could introduce modifications with fewer financial difficulties, but in either case the manufacturers concerned could not begin to incorporate modification on the line as a matter of smoothly operating routine until the aircraft industry had begun to master the arts of production control.

In short, the modification centers of World War II were a necessary evil. They served as an expedient stopgap until the managerial skills of the prewar job-shop airframe builders caught up with the industrial giant that the war had made of the airplane business.[43] If they did no more than win time for the aircraft manufacturers to grow up to their responsibilities, the modification centers of the war years were probably worth their cost.

Modification centers were indeed important in reconciling the quantity-quality equation during World War II. However, as the foregoing account has suggested, the experience of the war years clearly demonstrated that improved production control contained the ultimate solution to the problem. For this reason, the role of the military—of staff and command—in the perfection of production control devices throughout the aircraft industry takes on particular significance.

It is patently impossible to describe here all the many mechanisms by which a high degree of control was finally achieved over the enormous manufacturing enterprise sponsored by the Air Forces in the course of the war. Many of the most successful were those contrived by the production engineers and managerial staffs of the manufacturers themselves. Others were the work of the civilian agencies such as OPM and WPB and their subordinate branches working in close collaboration with officers in the procurement services of the Army and Navy. Needless to say, any and every refinement in production control techniques, by whomever evolved, was of interest to air arm officers. But in one area in particular their interest and participation contributed substantially to one of the more important administrative innovations of the war: the co-ordinating committees for joint production programs.

Co-ordinating Committees:
An Effective Solution

If the introduction of effective systems of production control within a single factory posed staggering tasks for management, how much more difficult were the problems raised by the need to co-ordinate the construction of identical aircraft in a number of factories at a great distance from one another and run by different companies. But difficult or not, during World War II such a course proved necessary. The techniques evolved to co-ordinate these enormously complex joint manufacturing undertakings deserve close study. To begin with,

---

[43] How well the aircraft builders profited from this respite may be indicated by the remarkable speed with which they incorporated production line changes when the Korean emergency came along. Republic, for example, averaged 315 modifications a week in the P-84.

however, it may be useful to understand just how the problem came about.

Before the war, the Air Corps officers engaged in mobilization planning found themselves in a difficult position. They knew that the aircraft manufacturers were bitterly opposed to any policy that would permit the government to take their proprietary designs, the fruits of their research and development, and hand them over to a rival firm to put into mass production. Ever since the 1920's the aircraft manufacturers had vigorously fought against any scheme along this line. The decision of 1938 not to use the automobile manufacturers to mass-produce aircraft in wartime was a typical reflection of their opposition.[44] On the other hand, the Air Corps planners knew full well that in wartime it would be foolish to mass-produce any aircraft other than the best. To keep four or five different airframe firms at work, each building bombers of its own design after experience had demonstrated that one or two of the designs were markedly superior might satisfy the manufacturers but would scarcely turn out the best aircraft in the largest numbers.

Down to the very eve of World War II, the mobilization planners had been unable to resolve this conflict of interests.[45] Little wonder then that they entered the emergency with no detailed plans for coordinating the production of identical items in remotely situated factories under different managements. The interplant production control systems perfected during the war had to be evolved from the beginning.

The character of the difficulties encountered when the air arm finally did decide to produce identical airplanes of the best available design in several different factories has already been foreshadowed in the account of the Willow Run operation. And what was true there was true elsewhere. In fact, there is a certain irony in the complaints the management at the North American plant in Dallas leveled against Ford in the course of their mutual effort to mass-produce the Consolidated B-24. The North American engineers made almost the same criticisms of Ford that Ford was making of Consolidated: production in Dallas was hindered by faulty liaison. The drawings provided by Ford arrived in unsatisfactory condition. As experienced airframe builders, the North American engineers fully expected changes in design, but they were disturbed by the laggard pace at which the 180,000-odd change notifications had cleared through Ford during the first few months of production. And just as the Ford staff before them had reworked all the drawings received from Consolidated, the North American engineers finally decided to redraw all the prints sent them from Willow Run.[46]

The difficulties besetting the joint production effort on the B-24 recurred again and again elsewhere. In fact, every company attempting to step up production by subcontracting the fabrication of major components encountered many similar troubles. For the problems of co-ordinat-

---

[44] See chs. V, VI, VII, and XIV, above.
[45] See, for example, Chief, Mat Div, to CofAC, 14 Dec 38, on Boeing's reluctance to have Consolidated build the B-17, AC Project Rcds (Lyon Papers), bk. 1.

[46] North American Aviation, Annual Rpt, 1942, AFCF 452.01 Bulky.

ing a prime with a number of key subs were much the same as those encountered in a joint production effort. The Martin B-26 program offers a case in point.

The B-26 twin-engine Marauder was developed and originally produced at the Martin Baltimore plant. When the Martin Omaha plant was completed, a parallel production line opened there. The new facility was to be supplied with major components from the automotive industry. Chrysler, Goodyear, and J. L. Case were to fabricate wings; Hudson would turn out other structural items. Soon the inevitable complaints began to roll into Wright Field from the major subcontractors. Martin in Baltimore was slow sending out engineering change notifications. Drawings for modifications scheduled on the line for October were not even received until December. Production expeditors at Wright Field began to doubt whether the wings and other assemblies turned out by the several different major subcontractors would actually be interchangeable when they arrived in Omaha.[47]

Some sort of system to co-ordinate those diffuse activities had to be concocted before the whole aircraft production program bogged down in a hopeless chaos of delays, misunderstandings, and mutual recriminations. Fortunately, a practical solution was already at hand—the co-ordinating committee system that had been devised to speed production of the Boeing B-17 long before the disaster at Pearl Harbor. The origin, organization, and operation of this committee merit careful attention, for the committee idea as such was to have a profound influence on aircraft output in the United States during the war.

Early in 1941 President Roosevelt ordered the Air Corps to initiate a program looking to the production of 500 heavy bombers a month. Air arm officials hurriedly cast about for ways and means to meet such a tremendous schedule. After numerous conferences with the leading aircraft and accessory firms, they decided that a joint production project would be absolutely necessary if they were to meet the goal demanded by the President. No individual manufacturer could hope to achieve this level of output singlehandedly. Since the Boeing B-17 and the Consolidated B-24 seemed to be the most promising heavy bombers available at the time, the two were selected for mass production by half a dozen firms. The combination of contractors who agreed to work on the B-24 has already been described. For the B-17, Douglas and Lockheed were persuaded to enter the joint endeavor with Boeing.[48]

The B-17 co-ordinating committee established in May 1941 to unify the activities of the three contractors working on the Flying Fortress seems to have developed more by accident than as a result of planning. A group of Douglas engineers and production men were just leaving Washington after a conference when an air arm officer suggested that it might be

---

[47] IOM, Col Mulligan for Chief, Prod Div, 30 Dec 42, AFCF 452.01-A Production.

[48] This paragraph and a substantial portion of the factual basis for the account that follows are based upon Maj P. H. Breuckner, Joint Airplane Production Programs, Lecture, ATSC Project Officers Training School, WF, 1945. A somewhat superficial but readable account of the joint production programs will be found in S. A. Zimmerman, Procurement in the United States Air Forces: 1938-1948, WFHO, Aug 50, vol. II, ch. VI.

Boeing B-17 Assembly Line *under joint production program at Douglas Long Beach plant.*

well if they returned to California by way of Seattle to discuss their common problems in person with the staff at Boeing. They followed the suggestion and soon afterward the three interested contractors formed a joint production organization that came to be known as the BDV Committee—for Boeing, Douglas, and Vega, the latter being the subsidiary of Lockheed that was actually going to work on the B-17 program.

What brought on this new-found harmony after so many years of opposition to any and every proposal to hand over the aircraft designs of one company for mass production by another? Undoubt-edly the military and diplomatic disasters of the previous months played some part. But it may also be true that the air arm decision to bring Detroit into the aircraft program was not without its effect. Were the old-line aircraft firms suddenly converted to the desirability of close co-operation only when confronted with an alternative such as Willow Run, even then well on its way to realization?

Broadly speaking, the function of the BDV Committee was to co-ordinate all the production activities of the member contractors, their related subcontractors, and the various air arm organizations with which they had dealings. This involved a wide variety of specialized activities. The committee undertook to review all material purchases, to regulate the selection and assignment of subcontractors, to prepare master production schedules (on which nearly every other decision hinged), to control the release and distribution of engineering drawings and other technical information, and to establish uniform inspection criteria. In general, the committee was to serve as a clearinghouse for information and a check point or control station on all decisions affecting the joint production program.

In time, the BDV Committee came to be a rather elaborate organization. The committee proper was a small group with one representative from each of the prime contractors concerned and one air arm spokesman, but below this top level group were a number of working subcommittees established to execute the details of co-ordination. At the peak of its activity, the committee, its subcommittees, and their associated clerical helpers numbered approximately two hundred people. The whole group was located in a downtown office building in Seattle not far from the Boeing home plant.

The secret of the BDV Committee's effectiveness seems to have been in its authority to act decisively. Each member of the main committee came to it with the power to act for the organization appointing him. The contractors' representatives were responsible corporate officials; the air arm representative was the chief of the Production Division at Wright Field or his alternate. This arrangement in itself afforded the committee a considerable measure of power, but its position was still further enhanced by a special charter giving official sanction to the committee as such. The charter, agreed to by the participants and approved by the Chief of the Air Corps, was officially authorized by the Assistant Secretary of War for Air.

Since the Assistant Secretary enjoyed broad, if somewhat nebulous, statutory powers for mobilizing the national economy for war, his authorization gave legal sanction to what might otherwise have proved a most elusive relationship. Certainly the contracts drawn with the several member firms never provided the necessary machinery of co-ordination in legally binding terms. In the final analysis, however, legal sanctions probably played a far less significant role than did good will. If the contractors concerned had not entered into the scheme with a spirit of co-operative enthusiasm, the whole idea of a joint committee to co-ordinate production would undoubtedly have come to nought.

The imperative necessity of willing co-operation was implicit in virtually every action of the BDV Committee. Even so, it would be a mistake to assume that the committee functioned on any simple principle of majority rule. To be sure, the committee members did try to find common ground for agreement, but in a showdown the air arm representative held, as the chief of the Production Division expressed it, "one more vote than the combined contractors." [49] Nevertheless, coercion was foreign to the whole spirit of the committee and could only be exercized with the utmost restraint if the committee system were to thrive.

---

[49] *Ibid.*, p. 9.

PRODUCTION

To understand the organization and functioning of the BDV Committee, one must first be aware of the unique contractual relationship that lay behind it. Although Boeing had designed and developed the B-17 and was required by contract to provide the other two participating firms with all the necessary drawings, engineering data, lofts, templates, and so on, these companies did not assume the role of subcontractors to Boeing. Instead, both Lockheed and Douglas held prime contracts from the government calling for the B-17 in production quantities. To avoid confusion, Boeing was designated the design prime contractor while the other two firms were called participating prime contractors.

The existence of three primes on one project created a somewhat anomalous situation. In the normal course of events when a design firm sought assistance in production, it did so by calling in subcontractors, who undertook to manufacture components to specifications provided by the design firm. The relationship of the sub to the prime was a contractual one: the prime provided engineering services and designs while the sub returned finished components. Since the prime's output hinged upon the performance of his subs, he was under pressure to see to it that his subs performed effectively. On the other hand, under a joint production arrangement, while the participating primes looked to the design prime for engineering information (and in some instances actually negotiated a contract for these services), they delivered their final output to the government and not to the prime.

The drawback in the novel joint production arrangement was that the design prime was under no great pressure to see to it that the participating primes were informed with the utmost speed of every design change and alteration of tooling made on the B-17. The design prime's output and his level of profit were not connected with the performance of the participating primes. For this reason, the creation of a co-ordinating group such as the BDV Committee assumed especial importance. In effect, it was an effort to provide administratively what would ordinarily have been supplied contractually.

Just how the BDV Committee functioned should be clear from a brief description of its operating procedures. During its first four months of life, the committee met daily. For the rest of 1941 it met weekly and thereafter only on call. The minutes of the committee's deliberations were recorded and published for circulation to serve as guides for subcommittees, contractors, and various governmental agencies concerned. A few subjects chosen from the bulletins issued by the committee early in its life give a fair picture of the nature and scope of its operations. Bulletin No. 1 covered the organization and functions of the committee itself. No. 2 dealt with channels of communications. Numbers 3 to 5 dealt with policy in regard to tooling, purchasing, and subcontractor facilities. No. 9 set up a procedure for instituting committee action on a problem. No. 10, appearing in August 1941 after three months of experience, laid down a series of standard definitions. Subsequent issues spelled out a wide variety of procedures for the most part concerned with engineering changes—No. 20, changes in specifications; No. 22, drawing release schedules; No. 24, tooling data release schedules; No. 26, schedules for master gages.[50]

Although the formal BDV Committee itself exercised the final power of decision, it was in the working subcommittees that the practical details were first hammered out. Probably the most important of these was the engineering subcommittee. The very heart of the joint production program was the engineering and design data provided by the design prime contractor. But the transmission of such information, even between the engineers of two old-line aircraft firms, inevitably raised problems of interpretation as well as problems of timing with respect to design changes and the distribution of drawings.

In the matter of interpretation especially, the engineering subcommittee more than proved its worth. No two aircraft firms turned out precisely the same kind of drawings or used the same format in issuing engineering releases.[51] Some were more complete than others, depending upon the level of skills known to exist in the shop. Moreover, the character of the drawings issued reflected in large measure the particular kinds of supplementary media employed to convey information. Practices differed according to the extent they relied upon parts lists, dimensional layouts, templates, and plaster patterns of contoured surfaces.

Every transfer of information from one contractor to another provided an opportunity for misunderstanding or confusion. The job of the engineering subcommittee was to ensure uniformity of interpretation. Sometimes supplementary information of one sort or another had to be issued to bring positive results; at others, the subcommittee anticipated difficulties and saw to it that the data initially released by the design prime was sufficiently detailed to permit of no confusion.

Another function of the engineering subcommittee was to serve as a clearinghouse on deviations in design. The drawings turned out by the design prime contractor often reflected the production practices commonly employed in his plant. The mere fact that certain types of machine tools happened to be available there often determined the form given to a particular part on the drawing board whereas another manufacturer with a somewhat different array of tools might turn out the same part much more readily if permitted to alter the design in some measure. Such requests were readily processed by the subcommittee, which could weigh manufacturing feasibility against the need for design uniformity or standardization and interchangeability to the best interests of all parties. In this respect the work of the subcommittee was considerably enhanced by the presence of Boeing engineers. Since they had laid out the aircraft originally, they were able to give firsthand interpretations of whatever design features came into question.

The engineering subcommittee helped keep the bomber design from becoming needlessly rigid in other ways as well. The normal flow of information was from

---

[50] BDV Committee Bulletins, WFHO files. See also, ATSC Industrial Planning Project Case History: Ford Willow Run, p. ix.

[51] For interesting evidence on this point, see Chief, EES, to General Lofting Corp., Van Nuys, Calif., 7 Nov 40, AFCF 452.1 Production; Chief EES, to Lockheed, 11 Dec 40, and TWX, PES to Production Engr Br, OCAS, 30 Jun 41, both in WFCF 412.5 (1941).

the design prime to the participating primes. But it did not invariably follow that the designer's way of constructing any given part or component was necessarily the only way or even the best way of doing the job. Sometimes the participating primes or one of their subcontractors came up with a revised design that simplified production, cut down on the use of critical materials, or resulted in superior performance. Where the idea warranted such action, the engineering subcommittee might recommend the revised design as standard for all concerned including the design prime. In this way the subcommittee helped good ideas flow up as well as down.

One of the more important continuing functions of the engineering subcommittee was the determination of the effective point at which modifications would be introduced on the assembly line of the various primes. In fact, it was the pioneering work of the BDV engineering subcommittee in this subject that led to the development of the master change record system, which subsequently became more or less standard practice on all Air Forces contracts. Where shortages of engineering talent threatened to delay the introduction of modifications at the appropriate time by one or another of the primes, the subcommittee even went so far as to arrange for loans of engineers between plants or for transfer of design tasks to subcontractors.

The operation of all the other subcommittees need not be described in detail. Suffice it to say that other working groups dealt with problems of tooling to insure uniformity and interchangeability, with procurement scheduling to synchronize purchases from vendors and suppliers for all the primes, and so on. In bringing face to face representatives of the various primes (and sometimes their subs as well), these subcommittees evolved a large number of effective devices for improved co-ordination and used the experience of one contractor to save the others from grief. The tooling subcommittee, for instance, found that it was often wise to have a single subcontractor manufacture all the tooling required for an assembly operation performed by each of the primes. Again, the procurement subcommittee discovered that it was often possible to solve temporary shortages of critical raw materials or machine tools by transfers within the participating contractor and subcontractor group without recourse to the formal channels through governmental agencies such as the Air Scheduling Unit, the Aircraft Resources Control Office, or the War Production Board.[52] This was creative imagination at work exploring the outer limits of industrial co-operation.

The work of the BDV Committee and its several subcommittees in time became so effective that Air Forces officers began to urge the committee system on other manufacturers engaged in joint production programs. All in all, six other committees were set up after the BDV precedent. Not until nearly a year after the BDV Committee began to function was a similar one established for the B-24 program. And that was precisely the period in which the services of such a co-ordinating committee were most desperately needed as the account of the Willow Run operation revealed. The other joint production programs subsequently utilizing

---

[52] See above, ch. XII.

the committee system involved the B–26, the PT–13 and PT–23, the C–46, the AT–21, and the B–29.

The committee system did not always prove successful. With the B–26 in particular, the committee system failed to bring immediate results. A production expediter at Wright Field was inclined to blame the design prime contractor for failing to provide adequate leadership, but he overlooked one vital consideration. When Hudson and Chrysler dealt with Martin, it was in their capacity of subcontractors. They felt constrained by their legal or contractual obligation to the design prime. No such restriction affected Lockheed or Douglas in their dealings with Boeing on the BDV Committee. A more important consideration may have been the fact that they spoke on aircraft problems with the assurance of old-line design firms. On the other hand, as automobile builders, Hudson and Chrysler felt themselves on uncertain ground when discussing aircraft problems with an experienced design firm such as Martin. Moreover, while Chrysler and Hudson were obliged to deliver components acceptable to Martin's inspection, Douglas and Lockheed did not have to get Boeing approval on the bombers they delivered to the government. The two situations were hardly comparable. Genuine co-operation thrives better in the company of equals than it does in a master and servant relationship.

The Production Division expediter at Wright Field put his finger on another weakness in the B–26 committee. The experience of every other joint production program seemed to indicate that successful operations were possible only where working subcommittees actively engaged the problems of production as they appeared. After four months of life, the Wright Field critic complained, the B–26 committee had only one subcommittee—the one on engineering. This group had met only once, he said, and then had "consumed itself in parliamentary debate on questions of membership and jurisdiction." What is more, the minutes showed that no discussion of engineering problems had taken place.[53]

Even the best of the co-ordinating committees had their weaknesses. The BDV Committee, for example, early recognized that it would have been helpful if somewhat more control had been exercised in the organization of subcommittees and the evolution of their operating procedures. Sometimes the subcommittees were rather too "loosely woven" and this made it difficult to harmonize their operations with one another as well as with the committee proper. By creating an executive organization to ride herd on the working subcommittees, the later joint production programs took advantage of the lessons learned from experience acquired by the pioneer BDV group.

One consideration loomed above all others in determining the success or failure of the committee system. It would not work unless the committee and its subcommittees were staffed with men of the highest caliber. They had to be men with a considerable grasp of technical skills and wide production experience, but even more, they had to be men who could speak with authority for the organizations they represented. The experience of the war years demonstrated the

---

[53] IOM, Col Mulligan for Chief, Prod Div, 30 Dec 42, AFCF 452.01–A Production.

PRODUCTION 547

importance of this point repeatedly. In those instances where the member contractors replaced their top caliber men with underlings after the most challenging initial period of getting production under way had passed, the committee system was less effective. The heart of the system was the speed with which authoritative decisions could be reached and accommodations arranged to the mutual convenience and advantage of the participating firms. Whenever top corporate officials withdrew in favor of less decisive subordinates, the committee system began to suffer a stifling paralysis.[54]

The committee system met its severest test in the Boeing B–29 program. The B–29 Superfortress, a four-engine bomber twice as heavy as the earlier B–17, was originally to have been manufactured entirely by Boeing. But soon after Pearl Harbor, when the strategic planners assigned it a vastly larger role, the matériel staff decided that only by a joint production program would it be possible to turn out the required number of bombers in time. In addition to Boeing, the Fisher Body Division of General Motors, Bell Aircraft, and North American Aviation were drawn in as participating contractors. By the summer of 1942 North American had to leave the program in order to concentrate on other commitments and the Boeing-Renton facility took up this slack. A year later Martin of Omaha replaced Fisher Body as a participating prime, although Fisher continued on as a parts supplier. There were, in addition to these assembly plants, five participating primes—Chrysler, Hudson, Goodyear, McDonnell, and Republic—supplying major components and assemblies to the others.[55]

The B–29 program was the most complex joint production undertaking of the war. This in itself made effective co-ordination a requisite of the utmost importance. The many changes in contractors along the way only served to emphasize the need for the closest kind of production control. So too did the highly experimental character of the bomber itself, which meant that design changes were numerous in every stage of the program. There were, for example, 1,174 engineering changes introduced even before the first item was officially accepted by the Air Forces. Some 900 of these had to be rushed through at the last minute as a result of findings made during flight tests.

Before the end of the war the various participating contractors turned out 3,898 B–29 Superforts for the sustained aerial assault on Japan,[56] one of them carrying "the" bomb that finally precipitated victory. All this was possible only because tens of thousands of diverse details in factories all over the country were successfully harmonized into a single effective program.

---

[54] ATSC Industrial Planning Project Case History: Boeing-Seattle: B–17, 1946, p. xi, WFHO. See also, comments of Chief, Prod Div, on committee system, in Gen Wolfe to Fairchild *et al.*, 23 Dec 42, AT–21 case history, Doc 26, WFHO.

[55] ATSC Industrial Planning Project Case History: Boeing B–29, WFHO, 1946, p. xii.
[56] Smith, *The Army and Economic Mobilization,* Table 11.

CHAPTER XXI

The Procurement Record

A Statistical Summation

The forces of the United Nations assaulting Hitler's troops across the beaches of Normandy in 1944 were magnificently equipped. The Arsenal of Democracy had come a long way since the awful summer of 1940. Under Secretary of War Robert P. Patterson made this point dramatically when he rephrased Churchill's famous words to say "never were so many provided with so much." [1] Certainly this statement was true with regard to air power. During the years 1939 through 1945 the nation's manufacturers turned out a total of 324,750 aircraft: [2]

Year	U.S. Military Services	Others
1939	921	4,935
1940	6,019	6,785
1941	19,433	6,844
1942	47,836	None
1943	85,898	None
1944	96,318	None
1945	47,714	2,047

Of the 304,139 aircraft procured by the military services over the years 1939–45, the lion's share or more than 231,000

[1] OASW annual report, 30 Jun 44, p. 6.
[2] CAA, *Statistical Handbook, 1948*, p. 43. The U.S. military aircraft include those built in Canada but financed in the United States. Deliveries under "Others" for 1939 include both civil and military aircraft built for export. Thereafter during the war all aircraft sales, including civilian transports, were made through the military services.

were actually purchased under AAF auspices. While impressive, this total somewhat obscures the true character of the production triumph it represents by making no distinction between massive bombers and tiny puddle jumpers or between single-place fighters and four-engine transports. The same statistics expressed in terms of airframe pounds procured by the AAF provide a far more accurate summary of the ascending curve of output: [3]

Year	Pounds
1940	20,279,000
1941	68,064,000
1942	239,858,000
1943	542,397,000
1944	797,120,000
1945	421,718,000
Total	2,089,436,000

No less impressive was the record of engine production. Table 8 shows Air Forces and Navy purchases. Because so many engines were bought on cross procurement, AAF acceptances alone would not begin to reflect the scale of the industrial effort actually required to build power plants for aircraft. The table excludes aircraft engines manufactured for use in tanks.

[3] Abstracted from R. H. Crawford and L. F. Cook, Statistics: Procurement, OCMH, Table PR–16, pp. 78–79.

THE PROCUREMENT RECORD

TABLE 8—ENGINE PRODUCTION BY TYPE: 1940–45

Year	Total	Procuring Agency		Type		
		AAF	Navy	Air-Cooled (Radial)	Liquid-Cooled (In-Line)	Jets
Total	812,615	660,950	151,665	685,964	125,321	1,330
1940	22,667	15,346	7,321	21,524	1,143	0
1941	58,181	39,502	18,679	51,684	6,497	0
1942	138,089	103,809	34,280	115,933	22,156	0
1943	227,116	188,803	38,313	193,728	33,388	0
1944	256,911	223,861	33,050	213,495	43,294	122
1945	109,651	89,629	20,022	89,600	18,843	1,208

Source: Abstracted from Table PR-18, Crawford and Cook, *Statistics: Procurement*, p. 80. The source table gives the figures by quarters as well as annually.

TABLE 9—ENGINE PRODUCTION BY HORSEPOWER: 1940–45

Year	Under 300 hp.	300–999 hp.	1000–1599 hp.	1600 hp. and up
1940	9,138	4,422	7,149	1,958
1941	18,652	12,841	17,526	9,162
1942	23,724	23,098	61,265	30,002
1943	29,741	23,871	127,011	46,493
1944	11,101	13,267	146,585	85,836
1945	3,366	857	46,169	58,050

Source: CAA, *Statistical Handbook 1948*, p. 47.

TABLE 10—PROPELLER PRODUCTION: 1940–45

Year	Units Accepted
Total	713,717
1940	14,290
1941	39,123
1942	106,136
1943	213,937
1944	243,741
1945	96,490

Source: Abstracted from Table PR-17, Crawford and Cook, *Statistics: Procurement*, p. 79. The figures are for controllable-pitch types only.

Just as aircraft acceptance statistics must be read against the record of airframe pounds produced to be truly meaningful, the figures for engine output presented in Table 8 should be qualified by a breakdown into horsepower groups. In Table 9 all jet engines are excluded. Nevertheless, across the war years the trend is clearly discernible from the lower powered engines used in trainers to the higher powered engines at the hither edge of development used in the most advanced tactical aircraft.

Propellers were no less essential to air power than engines. Table 10 reflects

TABLE 11—NUMBER OF AIRPLANES PROCURED BY ARMY AIR FORCES, BY TYPE AND BY YEAR OF ACCEPTANCE: JANUARY 1940–DECEMBER 1945[a]

Type and model	Total	1940	1941	1942	1943	1944	1945
All types	231,099	5,054	15,860	41,092	68,600	69,956	30,537
Very heavy bombers—total	3,899	0	1	3	92	1,161	2,642
B–19	1	0	1	0	0	0	0
B–29, Superfortress	3,898	0	0	3	92	1,161	2,642
Heavy bombers—total	31,000	60	313	2,576	9,393	14,887	3,771
B–17, Flying Fortress	12,692	53	144	1,412	4,179	5,352	1,552
B–24, Liberator	18,190	7	169	1,164	5,214	9,519	2,117
B–32, Dominator	118	0	0	0	0	16	102
Medium bombers—total	16,070	62	459	3,271	5,413	5,228	1,637
B–25, Mitchell	9,816	0	171	1,554	2,954	3,677	1,460
B–26, Marauder	5,157	0	263	803	2,364	1,551	176
B–42	1	0	0	0	0	0	1
Other models	1,096	62	25	914	95	0	0
Light bombers—total	18,113	891	2,396	4,055	5,175	3,861	1,735
A–20, Havoc	7,385	297	1,011	1,785	1,975	2,317	0
A–24, Dauntless	615	0	0	0	615	0	0
A–25, Helldiver	900	0	0	1	585	314	0
A–26, Invader	2,450	0	0	0	9	711	1,730
A–28, A–29, Hudson	2,189	170	1,100	836	83	0	0
A–30, Baltimore	1,575	0	146	505	675	249	0
A–31, A–35, Vengeance	1,931	0	0	786	875	270	0
A–36 (P–51 type), Mustang	500	0	0	142	358	0	0
Other models	568	424	139	0	0	0	5
Fighters—total	68,712	1,422	3,784	9,102	17,628	24,174	12,602
P–38, Lightning	9,536	1	205	1,265	2,213	4,186	1,666
P–39, Airacobra	9,588	13	926	1,973	4,947	1,729	0
P–40, Warhawk	13,738	778	2,246	4,454	4,258	2,002	0
P–47, Thunderbolt	15,683	0	1	532	4,428	7,065	3,657
P–51, Mustang	14,686	0	138	634	1,710	6,908	5,296
P–59, Airacomet (jet propelled)	66	0	0	0	1	36	29
P–61, Black Widow	702	0	0	0	34	449	219
P–63, Kingcobra	3,292	0	0	0	31	1,786	1,475
P–70, night fighter type of A–20	60	0	0	60	0	0	0
P–80, Shooting Star (jet propelled)	243	0	0	0	0	5	238
Other models	1,118	630	268	184	6	8	22
Reconnaissance—total	1,117	65	203	223	284	95	247
F–2 (version of C–45)	55	13	0	0	0	20	22
F–4, F–5 (version of P–38)	500	0	2	214	284	0	0
F–6 (version of P–51)	299	0	0	0	0	74	225
Other models	263	52	201	9	0	1	0

TABLE 11—NUMBER OF AIRPLANES PROCURED BY ARMY AIR FORCES:
JANUARY 1940–DECEMBER 1945[a]—*Continued*

Type and model	Total	1940	1941	1942	1943	1944	1945
Transports—total	22,885	233	398	1,738	6,817	9,276	4,423
C-43, Traveller	352	7	0	27	157	161	0
C-45, Expeditor	1,771	19	41	0	60	1,060	591
C-46, Commando	3,180	0	1	46	353	1,321	1,459
C-47, Skytrain	10,368	115	165	1,057	2,595	4,900	1,536
C-54, Skymaster	1,162	0	0	26	72	356	708
C-60, Lodestar	620	45	98	180	297	0	0
C-61, Forwarder	1,009	11	51	147	400	400	0
C-64, Norseman	756	0	6	1	209	454	86
C-69, Constellation	15	0	0	0	1	3	11
C-78 (AT-17 type), Bobcat	3,206	0	0	187	2,548	471	0
C-87, Liberator Express	291	0	0	41	110	140	0
C-117 (DC-3 type)	17	0	0	0	0	0	17
Other models	138	36	36	26	15	10	15
Trainers—total	55,712	2,320	8,036	16,978	19,491	7,578	1,309
AT-6, Texan	15,094	595	2,235	3,705	4,024	3,298	1,237
AT-7, AT-10, AT-11, Navigator (AT-7)	5,775	0	191	1,853	2,661	1,070	0
AT-8, AT-17, Bobcat	2,153	6	618	1,248	281	0	0
BT-13, BT-15, Valiant	11,537	232	1,841	4,132	4,049	1,283	0
PT-13, PT-17, PT-27, Kaydet	7,539	376	1,523	2,217	2,643	708	72
PT-19, PT-23, PT-26, Cornell	7,802	253	913	1,758	4,141	737	0
Other models	5,812	858	715	2,065	1,692	482	0
Communications—total	13,591	1	270	3,146	4,307	3,696	2,171
L-1, Vigilant	324	1	171	152	0	0	0
L-2, Grasshopper type	1,940	0	24	529	1,161	226	0
L-3, Grasshopper type	1,439	0	24	813	522	80	0
L-4, L-14, Grasshopper type	5,611	0	44	1,595	1,249	1,904	819
L-5, Sentinel	3,590	0	0	10	1,116	1,361	1,103
R-4, R-5 (helicopter)	161	0	0	1	14	116	30
R-6 (helicopter)	224	0	0	0	0	8	216
Other models	302	0	7	46	245	1	3

[a] Compiled from Army Air Forces Statistical Digest, 1946, p. 100, published Jun 47 by Director, Statistical Services, Comptroller, Hq, U.S. Air Force. Procurement data represent factory acceptances or receipt of legal title by resident factory representative of procuring agency. Includes all airplanes procured by the AAF regardless of subsequent distribution to Army, Navy, recipients of lend-lease, or others. Also includes United States-financed Canadian and experimental models.

Source: Table PR-14, Crawford and Cook, Statistics: Procurement, pp. 76–77.

only the production of the highly complex and difficult-to-manufacture controllable pitch propellers. All others, from the simple wooden blades used on puddle jumpers or liaison aircraft to the rather more expensive steel or dural fixed-pitch blades fitted to some trainers, are excluded. Here, as with engines, the widespread use of cross procurement makes it imperative to show AAF and Navy acceptances combined.

The foregoing statistics may accurately chronicle the pace at which the vital ingredients of air power were assembled, but they do not in themselves bespeak that power. However valuable airframe pounds or delivered horsepower may be as indices of productivity, they are no substitute for the end product itself. The soldier who wields the sword would rather see the blade than be told of its metallurgy to five decimal places of accuracy. Table 11 presents in one grand panorama the story of how the cutting edge of the Air Forces grew larger and stronger. Here, with their popular names, are shown the airplanes familiar to millions as they became available in increasing numbers through the successive years of the war.

Although some have charged that the production triumphs of the aircraft industry were achieved only by padding the record with large numbers of small inexpensive liaison aircraft to inflate the total, a careful perusal of Table 11 will show that this was not the case. Moreover, the figures in the table do not reflect the productive effort that went into the construction of gliders. Many different types of gliders were turned out during the war: bomb, power, training, and the like, to a total of 15,697 units. Of these, the overwhelming majority, 14,583, were troop-carrying gliders, almost all of them of the CG–4 design, a model capable of carrying 15 fully equipped men or a 75-mm. pack howitzer and 5 men in addition to a glider crew of 2. The total number of gliders accepted was as follows: [4]

Year	Number
1940	0
1941	4
1942	1,601
1943	6,243
1944	4,410
1945	3,439

The Measure of Success

The grand totals of aircraft, engine, and glider production spread out in the several tables above make an impressive showing, especially when they are interpreted against the miniscule levels of procurement that characterized the military buying of prewar years. But sheer quantities are never enough. In war, timely delivery is also crucial. Therefore, any summary of air power to be meaningful must consider the pace at which those quantities became available. How soon did the air arm buyers manage to provide the weapons required in the volume desired? A study of Table 12 should go far to answer this question. Shown here is the record of deliveries to the AAF from July 1940 through December 1945.

Readily apparent in the figures of Table 12 will be the gradual shift of emphasis of types from training through de-

---

[4] Abstracted from Table PR–15, Crawford and Cook, Statistics: Procurement, p. 77.

THE PROCUREMENT RECORD

fense to offense. During 1940 and 1941 deliveries of training aircraft far outnumbered the other categories. Even in 1942, after the nation had entered the war, trainers constituted almost half of the total produced. Not until after the disaster at Pearl Harbor did the United States even begin to receive heavy bombers in quantity. Indeed, the figures make it quite clear that the whole idea of strategic air power was little more than a paper doctrine, insofar as the AAF was concerned, until late 1942 or early 1943. Moreover, with the immensely long ranges required to reach Japan from most island bases in the Pacific, land-based strategic air power in that theater had to await the appearance of very heavy bombers, the Boeing B-29's, and deliveries of that aircraft had hardly begun by the first quarter of 1944, more than twenty-four months after the nation had begun to fight.

The time consumed in accelerating production to the levels required for application of strategic air power is expressed somewhat more simply and in rather more generalized terms in Table 13. The figures indicate once again that accelerating bomber output involves not a few months but years. Despite the prolonged period of limited emergency or cold war before Pearl Harbor, twenty-six months from the outbreak of war in Europe and nearly eighteen months from the fall of France, it will be noted that the major increase in the number of bombers produced still did not come until after the nation began fighting. March, 1944, was the month of maximum output for the war period. In that one month the AAF alone accepted 6,800 aircraft of all categories. Navy acceptance for the same thirty-day period brought the national total to 9,113 aircraft.[5]

Perhaps the most significant yardstick by which the air arm procurement effort can be measured is to be found by comparing the nation's strength in air power with that of its allies and enemies. (*Table 14*) This, however, is more easily suggested than done. Production figures, whether labeled acceptances or actual deliveries, are highly deceptive. Acceptance, as this study has had occasion to reveal, does not always mean that a given aircraft is available for delivery. Even delivery by flight does not invariably indicate that an aircraft is ready for use.[6] From the point of view of the strategic planner, tactical availability is the only statistic that really counts. But tactical availability depends upon many considerations that not only lie well beyond the scope of this study but also defy objective statistical presentation. For this reason, even while recognizing the limited validity of bare production figures in making international evaluations, Table 15 compares total military aircraft production by four of the five major powers. No reliable figures are available for Russian output.

From 1941 onward aircraft production in the United States exceeded the combined output of both its major enemies by a generous margin. The implications of this disparity become more pointed when one probes behind the bare figures. Over the years shown, both Germany and Japan turned out progressively fewer heavy bombers as they were driven step

---

[5] Table PR-13, Crawford and Cook, *Statistics: Procurement*, p. 75, and CAA, *Statistical Handbook, 1948*, p. 45.

[6] See above, ch. XI, p. 245.

TABLE 12—AIRCRAFT DELIVERIES TO THE AAF: JULY 1940–DECEMBER 1945[a]

Period	Total	Very Heavy Bombers	Heavy Bombers	Medium Bombers	Light Bombers	Fighters	Recon-naissance	Trans-ports	Trainers	Com-munications
Total	160,070	3,899	27,874	11,836	7,785	47,775	1,216	15,947	34,469	9,269
1940 (last half)	1,209	0	19	24	16	187	10	5	948	0
Third quarter	695	0	9	23	10	138	10	5	500	0
Fourth quarter	514	0	10	1	6	49	0	0	448	0
1941	8,723	0	181	326	373	1,727	165	133	5,585	233
First quarter	1,105	0	21	24	73	170	1	12	795	9
Second quarter	1,818	0	29	62	58	226	17	13	1,377	36
Third quarter	2,383	0	7	80	88	567	84	46	1,445	66
Fourth quarter	3,417	0	124	160	154	764	63	62	1,968	122
1942	26,448	4	2,241	2,429	1,153	5,213	195	1,264	11,004	2,945
First quarter	5,537	1	322	177	322	1,007	37	79	2,988	604
Second quarter	6,168	0	406	483	102	941	65	245	2,905	1,021
Third quarter	6,901	0	665	859	337	1,777	52	429	2,021	761
Fourth quarter	7,842	3	848	910	392	1,488	41	511	3,090	559
1943	45,889	91	8,695	3,989	2,247	11,766	320	5,072	11,246	2,463
First quarter	9,693	0	1,224	1,031	579	1,992	120	939	3,517	291
Second quarter	11,073	0	1,895	1,302	295	2,681	0	1,351	3,086	463
Third quarter	11,776	19	2,455	838	540	3,118	88	1,454	2,360	904
Fourth quarter	13,347	72	3,121	818	833	3,975	112	1,328	2,283	805
1944	51,547	1,147	13,057	3,636	2,276	18,291	241	6,430	4,861	1,608
First quarter	14,822	160	3,749	1,132	550	4,707	0	1,751	1,994	779
Second quarter	13,782	233	3,959	1,049	591	4,591	0	1,887	1,201	271
Third quarter	12,504	281	3,146	804	734	4,598	113	1,528	1,029	271
Fourth quarter	10,439	473	2,203	651	401	4,395	128	1,264	637	287
1945	26,254	2,657	3,681	1,432	1,720	10,591	285	3,043	825	2,020
First quarter	11,587	784	2,137	837	611	4,468	130	1,278	622	720
Second quarter	9,776	1,032	1,443	411	865	4,001	115	998	96	815
Third quarter	4,210	825	94	183	241	1,626	40	668	107	426
Fourth quarter	681	16	7	1	3	496	0	99	0	59

[a] Compiled from United States Air Force Statistical Digest, 1947, p. 120, and errata sheets for same, published by Director of Statistical Services, Comptroller, Hq, U.S. Air Force, Aug 48. Data represent transfer of possession of airplanes from resident factory representative of procuring agency to representative of the Air Transport Command or other transporting agency for delivery to Army Air Forces. Includes all military airplanes designated for delivery to the Army Air Forces regardless of their procurement by Army Air Forces or U.S. Navy. Data are not adjusted deliveries to compensate for any subsequent reallocations to other recipients such as the U.S. Navy, other Government agencies, or recipients of lend-lease or others. Data also include United States-financed Canadian production and experimental airplanes.

Source: Table PR-19, Crawford and Cook, Statistics: Procurement, p. 81.

THE PROCUREMENT RECORD

TABLE 13—HEAVY BOMBERS ACCEPTED BY THE AAF

Year	Number	Percent of Five-Year Total	Percent Increase Over Preceding Year
1940	61	.2	—
1941	313	1.1	413
1942	2,576	9.0	723
1943	9,485	33.3	268
1944	16,045	56.3	69

Source: Abstracted from table in Craven and Cate, eds., *Men and Planes*, p. 359.

TABLE 14—TOTAL MILITARY AIRCRAFT PRODUCTION OF FOUR MAJOR POWERS: 1939-44

Year	Japan	Germany	United Kingdom	United States
Total	68,057	111,787	117,479	257,645
1939	4,467	8,295	7,940	2,141
1940	4,768	10,826	15,049	6,019
1941	5,088	11,776	20,094	19,433
1942	8,861	15,556	23,672	47,836
1943	16,693	25,527	26,263	85,898
1944	28,180	39,807	24,461	96,318

Source: Craven and Cate, eds., *Men and Planes*, p. 350. The figures credited to the United States for 1939 do not agree with the totals shown in the first table of this chapter, because the compiler included military aircraft for export. The discrepancy of sixty-seven items in the total for 1940 in the source cited above has been adjusted to agree with the totals given in the CAA, *Statistical Handbook, 1948*, page 43, and Civilian Production Administration special release of 1 May 1947, *Official Munitions Production of the United States*, pages 1 and 54.

by step to take the defensive. By 1944 more than 50 percent of the production reported for Japan and 75 percent of that for Germany consisted of fighter aircraft.[7] In the United States, on the other hand, the trend was in the opposite direction with increasing emphasis on the construction of heavy bombers. These big aircraft required up to four times as many engines and propellers as fighters and absorbed far larger allocations of all other types of resources—labor and facilities as well as materials. As a consequence, the spread between the output of the United States and its combined enemies was really substantially greater than the production totals alone may at first appear to indicate.

In yet another sense, the production figures presented in the foregoing tables require qualification. Even within a single category of aircraft such as bombers, the total output shown for any one year cannot be compared accurately with the

---

[7] United States Strategic Bombing Survey, Overall Economics Division, *The Japanese Aircraft Industry* (Washington, May 1947), pp. 166-67, and USSBS, Aircraft Division, *The Effects of Strategic Bombing on the German War Economy* (October 1945), pp. 149, 158, and 277.

output of another year. Designs changed with such rapidity during the war period that bombers in 1945 were very different from the bombers of 1940. The rising curve of airframe gross weights makes this point clear. Where bombers in the United States averaged 7,709 pounds in 1940, by 1945 they had increased to more than 20,000 pounds.[8] In short, the figures for total production in the later years of the war represent more airplane in every sense of the word than they did in the earlier years.

One final word of warning. In at least some of the statistics provided by British sources during the war, the figures purporting to reflect the total number of aircraft produced actually included a large number of items returned damaged from operations to the manufacturers for major rebuilding.[9] Unless one is fully informed of considerations such as this, it would be easy to draw grossly misleading conclusions from seemingly objective data. If this is true of production figures, it is certainly no less true when applied to the dollar costs of the wartime aircraft program.

Counting the Cost

Between July 1940 and August 1945, when the war ended, the AAF received just over 43.5 billion dollars worth of air matériel. Aircraft accounted for 82.5 percent of this sum, which represented 37 percent of the total value of all matériel bought by the War Department.

The value of the air matériel procured by the Army and Navy together amounted to just under 25 percent of the nation's 185 billion-dollar outlay for munitions of all sorts in this period.[10] Sums of these magnitudes may be awe inspiring, but they are so large as to lose meaning for most readers. Unless they can be broken down and presented in terms that can be equated with rather more commonplace statistics, they serve little purpose.

Congressional appropriations offer at least one familiar point of departure for students of military procurement. Table 15 shows direct cash appropriations for air matériel and expenditures from these appropriations. The figures are given for the full decade 1935–45 in order to place the war years against an ample peacetime perspective. The disparity between the two columns in Table 15 requires explanation. Funds appropriated in one year may be spent in that year, in subsequent years, or not at all. Sums obligated, that is, written into contracts, may be paid out across a period of deliveries stretching over many months; they may be recovered by means of renegotiation or not paid out at all as a consequence of cutbacks or terminations. For this reason, in wartime, the status of funds obligated may often provide a far more meaningful indicator of the current production pattern than either the size of the annual appropriation or the actual rate of expenditure in any one year.

Thus, for example, as of 30 June 1945, the end of fiscal year 1945, the cumula-

---

[8] Airframes only. CAA, *Statistical Handbook, 1948*, p. 45.
[9] Memo, CofS MC for USW, 22 Jan 43, AFCF 452.01–A Production.

[10] Crawford and Cook, Statistics: Procurement, p. 10, and CPA, *Official Munitions Production*, p. 363.

THE PROCUREMENT RECORD

TABLE 15—AAF CASH APPROPRIATIONS AND EXPENDITURES: 1935–45

Fiscal Year	Direct Cash Appropriations	Expenditures From Appropriations
1935	27,918,000	20,338,000
1936	45,600,000	32,027,000
1937	59,620,000	41,055,000
1938	58,851,000	50,875,000
1939	71,099,000	83,164,000
1940	186,563,000	108,170,000
1941	2,173,609,000	605,409,000
1942	23,049,935,000	2,554,863,000
1943	11,317,417,000	9,391,855,000
1944	23,655,998,000	13,087,280,000
1945	1,610,717,000	11,357,390,000

Source: Abstracted from Office of Statistical Control, AAF, *Army Air Forces Statistical Digest: World War II*, 1945, p. 297. (The 1945 edition should not be mistaken for the 1946 edition labeled "first [*sic*] annual edition.") The last three digits have been rounded off in each figure given. Appropriations here listed are for air materiel only, aircraft, gasoline, etc. Supplies contributed by other technical services such as QM are not included.

tive obligations or contracts entered by the AAF but not paid off amounted to 15.33 billions. Yet by November, after the war had ended, terminations rather than deliveries played a major role in whittling this backlog down to about five billions. Obviously any statistical compilation that looked only to actual expenditures would neglect a vast area of effort simply because it did not mature into payments. Moreover, expenditures from direct appropriations take no account of foreign aid funds. Since in 1942 alone obligations from this source ran to nearly 2.5 billion dollars, it must be clear that statistics on appropriations give at best a partial view of AAF procurement.[11]

If one bears in mind the significant difference between funds obligated and funds actually spent, Table 16, showing expenditures by major categories, may be helpful in giving some idea of how the AAF appropriation dollar was used from July 1942 through August 1945, the period during which the heaviest payments were made.

Although the tabulations in Table 16 do help to express procurement expenditures in terms more comprehensible than the big totals recorded earlier, it would be a serious mistake to assume that they represent anything like the true cost of the air matériel bought during the war. Certainly some consideration must be given to expenditures for research and development, the heavy outlays made for new facilities, and various other overhead expenses. New facilities, including the cost of tools as well as floor space financed directly by the government, absorbed more than three billion dollars of federal funds. Another half billion must be added to this if one includes the indirect costs to the government from tax amor-

---

[11] I. R. Friend, History of the Air Technical Service Command: 1945, AMC Hist Office, Aug 50, p. 43; and McMurtrie, Hist of AAF MC: 1942, app. 3.

TABLE 16—AAF EXPENDITURES BY MAJOR CATEGORIES: 1942–45

Items Procured	(In thousands of dollars)			
	1942[a]	1943	1944	1945[b]
Standard aircraft	2,174,752	9,367,194	8,569,578	4,850,330
Guided missiles				15,071
Balloons and accessories		40,773	6,583	
Gliders and accessories	34,346	165,648	81,831	74,048
Materials for maintenance	113,255	452,567	562,202	248,677
Aircraft fuel and oil	42,050	332,820	398,265	464,538
Personal and organizational equipment	52,020	630,275	426,751	205,347
Photo equipment and supplies	8,273	23,158	23,408	15,346
Maps and mapping	2,605	6,604	9,032	3,911
Service test items	15,730	11,827	21,063	6,374

[a] Last six months.
[b] First eight months.
Source: Abstracted from *AAF Statistical Digest*, 1945, pp. 298–99.

tizations authorized to manufacturers by the AAF.[12]

Expenditures for research and development on AAF projects are somewhat harder to compute. A substantial proportion of the spectacular advances in design that marked the war years was underwritten, directly or indirectly, in the sums obligated on production contracts. Then too, the funds allocated for modifications in accepted aircraft contributed appreciably to the pace of development. As Table 17 indicates, the total charges attributable to modification were actually greater than the direct expenditures earmarked for research and development.

Yet another element of overhead that cannot be ignored in appraising the cost of air matériel is the payroll of the large number of employees in the Materiel Command. At peak strength in mid-1943, there were more than 10,000 civil-

TABLE 17—EXPENDITURES FOR MODIFICATIONS AND RESEARCH AND DEVELOPMENT: 1942–45

Year	Modifications	Research and Development
Total	$350,771,000	$294,296,000
1942[a]	23,920,000	22,232,000
1943	51,372,000	92,368,000
1944	177,433,000	106,914,000
1945[b]	98,046,000	72,782,000

[a] Last six months.
[b] First eight months.
Source: Abstracted from *AAF Statistical Digest*, 1945, pp. 298–99.

ians employed at Wright Field. Wage and salaries for these people obligated nearly 48.5 million dollars a year. At the same time more than twice as many civilians were on the federal payroll in the various procurement district offices, which continued to build up to a peak strength of 27,000 a year later. In addition, during the same period the payroll

---
[12] AAF Hist Study 40, p. 232.

TABLE 18—COMPARISON OF CIVILIAN PAYROLL TO NEW AIRCRAFT AND RESEARCH AND DEVELOPMENT: 1938-41

	FY 1938	FY 1939	FY 1940	FY 1941
Funds Obligated in Dollars				
New aircraft	36,146,428	35,012,034	175,704,034	2,675,709,593
Research and development	4,348,995	3,525,252	9,882,116	97,103,641
Wright Field civilian payroll	2,595,096	3,169,464	4,599,864	8,352,552
District civilian payroll	52,440	52,800	98,760	3,148,420
Number of Personnel				
Civilian personnel at Wright Field	1,335	1,690	2,478	4,915
Civilian personnel in districts	215	219	418	1,381
Military personnel at Wright Field	95	245	169	323
Aircraft contracted for	610	865	3,122	36,661

Source: McMurtrie and Davis, Hist AAF MC: 1926-41, app. E-2. Personnel figures excluded troops attached from Signal Corps, Ordnance, and so forth, and all maintenance employees of the Field Service Section who later transferred to the Air Service Command.

for nearly 10,000 military personnel at Wright Field and in the districts must be taken into account.[13]

From the various facts and figures recorded here it should be apparent that no accurate total can ever be compiled to represent the true "cost" of the air matériel purchased during the war. Nevertheless, the data presented may open up a number of thought-provoking vistas for those who would understand the problem of procurement costs in their broadest context, including the record of prewar experience. Table 18 should go far to provide this necessary perspective.

Whatever the observations made upon these figures, one conclusion seems inescapable. In light of the billions spent in wartime on air matériel, it would appear that even the most modest increases in payroll during the prewar years might well have led to disproportionately large dividends in terms of better preparedness—faster procurement at lower cost and a less disturbing impact on the national economy. For example, is it entirely idle to speculate on what savings might have been expected if a few more really able contract negotiators could have been hired before the war? Was it a real economy to keep the procurement staff continually shorthanded and so modestly paid? Clearly it is not without significance that the average salary paid to civilian employees at Wright Field in the period from 1938 through 1941 was never higher than $1,944 per annum.[14] What is more, the same sort of questions could be raised with regard to research and development expenditures. If air matériel cost too much during the war, surely one of the principal reasons for this was that it cost too little before the war.

---

[13] Davis, Hist of AAF MC: 1943, app. 2 and 3; Russel, Hist of AAF ATSC: 1944, app. 3.

[14] McMurtrie and Davis, Hist of AAF MC: 1926-41, app. E-2.

TABLE 19—AVERAGE UNIT COSTS OF SELECTED AIRCRAFT: 1939–45

Aircraft and Manufacturer	1939–41	1942	1943	1944	1945
Boeing B-17	$301,221	$258,949	. . . .	$204,370	$187,742
Consolidated B-24	379,162	304,391	. . . .	215,516	. . . .
North American B-25	180,031	153,396	151,894	142,194	116,752
Martin B-26	261,062	239,655	212,952	192,427	. . . .
Douglas A-20	136,813	124,253	110,324	100,800	. . . .
Lockheed P-38	134,280	120,407	105,567	97,147	. . . .
Bell P-39	77,159	69,534	. . . .	50,666	. . . .
Curtiss P-40	60,562	59,444	49,449	44,892	. . . .
Republic P-47	113,246	105,594	104,258	85,578	83,001
Beach C-45	67,743	. . . .	66,189	52,507	48,830
Curtiss C-46	341,831	314,700	259,268	233,377	221,550
Douglas C-47	128,761	109,696	92,417	88,574	85,035
Douglas C-54	516,552	370,492	400,831	285,113	259,816
North American AT-6	29,423	25,672	. . . .	22,952	. . . .

Source: Abstracted from *AAF Statistical Digest*, 1945. Figures given show average cost per unit computed to reflect the several costs resulting from different contracts, renegotiated prices on uncompleted portions of contracts, and so forth. Cash refunds from renegotiations are not taken into account. Costs as shown cover complete flyaway aircraft with engines, propellers, and factory installed signal and ordnance equipment but exclude value of spares and equipment installed at modification centers.

Although the increased number and growing skill of Wright Field procurement staff during the war years did lead to closer pricing and lower costs, probably the most important factor in securing this result was the introduction of mass production techniques by the industry. The decline in unit costs occurring during the war is indicated in Table 19. The economies resulting from mass production suggested by these figures become considerably more impressive when it is recalled that all of these aircraft were modified into heavier and more complex types in each successive year of the war. The reductions in unit costs, while remarkable, offer only one indication of the prodigious accomplishments of the aircraft industry as a whole during the war years. For a fuller index of the industry's wartime achievement, a number of different yardsticks are clearly necessary.

The Contribution of Industry

The contribution of the aircraft industry to the war effort cannot be measured solely in terms of deliveries to the AAF. As the following table clearly reveals, the Air Forces received just over half the total number of aircraft turned out in the United States between July 1940 and August 1945: [15]

Recipient	Number of Aircraft
U.S. AAF	158,880
U.S. Navy	73,711
U.S. other	3,714
British Commonwealth	38,811
USSR	14,717
China	1,225
Other foreign	4,901
Total	295,959

[15] Abstracted from *AAF Statistical Digest*, 1945, p. 127.

THE PROCUREMENT RECORD

Of this grand total, 230,287 aircraft were actually procured under AAF cognizance regardless of the ultimate recipient.[16] The aircraft builders who helped to achieve the total production record are listed in Appendix B, along with the number and types of aircraft they built. On the basis of the production figures cited in Appendix B, the top fifteen manufacturers of aircraft under AAF cognizance were:

Manufacturer	Aircraft Accepted AAF	Navy
North American	41,839	0
Consolidated	27,634	3,296
Douglas	25,569	5,411
Curtiss	19,703	6,934
Boeing	17,231	291
Lockheed	17,148	1,929
Republic	15,663	0
Bell	12,941	1
Martin	7,711	1,272
Beech	7,430	0
Ford	6,792	0
Fairchild	6,080	300
Cessna	5,359	0
Piper	5,611	330
Taylor	1,940	0

When the aircraft under Navy cognizance are added in, the order is changed substantially, especially when the four firms, Grumman, Eastern, Chance-Vought, and Goodyear, which produced nothing for the AAF, are added into the sequence with 17,448, 13,449, 7,896, and 3,940 aircraft, respectively.

If airframe pounds rather than individual aircraft accepted by the AAF and the Navy are used as a yardstick, the order of importance is changed somewhat further, the makers of heavy bombers and transports in the leading position. On this basis the top producers in the order of their output were:[17]

Manufacturer	Percent of Total
Douglas	15.3
Consolidated	14.6
Boeing	11.3
North American	10.5
Lockheed	9.0
Curtiss	6.9
Martin	6.3
Ford	6.2
Republic	3.9
Grumman	3.7
Bell	2.7
Eastern	2.4
Chance Vought	1.4
Goodyear	0.7
All others	5.1
	100.0

The foregoing makes it clear that AAF procurement policy placed major reliance upon the old-line aircraft firms. With the exception of Ford, every one of the principal manufacturers for the AAF could be classed as an old-line firm with a continuous history of prewar operations in the aircraft field. This pattern of policy by no means held true with the wartime production of aircraft engines. While the two old-line firms, Pratt and Whitney and Wright Aero, continued to lead the field, a substantial share of the total engine output came from firms licensed by them. *(Appendix C)* The licensees did include some of the smaller old-line aircraft engine builders, but the total output achieved by them was small in comparison with the records made by firms of the automobile industry without recent experience in air-

---

[16] *AAF Statistical Digest*, 1945, p. 118.

[17] From table in Craven and Cate, eds., *Men and Planes*, p. 355.

TABLE 20—PRODUCTION OF TURBOJET ENGINES: JULY 1940–AUGUST 1945

Manufacturer	Plant Location	Turbojet Engines	Description
General Electric	West Lynn, Mass.	40	J–33 used in P–80
		337	J–31 used in P–59
	Syracuse, N.Y.	211	J–33
		588	
Allison	Indianapolis, Ind.	297	J–33
		16	J–31
		313	

Source: CPA, *Official Munitions Production*, pp. 65, 68, 70.

craft engine work. Appendix C lists the major aircraft engine producers with their licensees in the order of their importance according to the number of units produced. A listing in terms of total horsepower capacity produced would not significantly alter the sequence. To the record of production in conventional, reciprocating engines must be added the first trickle of output in turbojet engines which appeared toward the end of the war. *(Table 20)*

The pattern of production in the propeller industry was similar to that prevailing in the engine industry. The old-line firms led the field insofar as design was concerned, but manufacturers outside the aviation industry supplied much of the wartime capacity. The two leading old-line firms were Curtiss Electric, a subsidiary of Curtiss-Wright, with an automatic controllable pitch propeller system operated by electric devices, and Hamilton Standard, a subsidiary of United Aircraft, using a hydraulic control. Both firms followed the corporate policy they had laid down when expanding engine production. Curtiss increased output by additions to plant and increased subcontracting; United took these steps too but also resorted to licensing on a large scale. The third major source of military propellers was Aeroproducts, a division of General Motors established in 1940 when the corporation acquired a small Dayton, Ohio, concern that had developed an adjustable pitch propeller with a hydraulic control system.

Table 21 gives production figures for automatic controllable pitch propellers only. Although the Curtiss scheme of concentrating production under an experienced management enjoyed certain advantages from the point of view of design co-ordination and quality control, production could not be expanded indefinitely in this fashion since management resources would be spread dangerously thin. On the other hand, although the policy of licensing pursued by United involved difficulties of technical supervision, it did enlist substantial additions of managerial talent. The production record for engines as well as propellers seems

TABLE 21—PRODUCTION OF AUTOMATIC CONTROLLABLE PITCH PROPELLERS: JULY 1940–AUGUST 1945

Manufacturer	Output
Curtiss Electric	144,863
Hamilton Standard	233,021
Nash-Kelvinator	158,134
Frigidaire	76,626
Remington Rand	62,354
Canadian Propellers Ltd.	12,497
Aeroproducts Division of General Motors	20,773

Source: CPA, *Official Munitions Production*, pp. 73–80.

to suggest that the latter course had much to commend it.[18]

While no array of statistics can convey an adequate impression of the full contribution to air power made by industry during the war years, the following figures may add substantially to the tabulations already presented. Where the foregoing statistics spelled out the achievements of individual manufacturers in turning out airframes, engines, and propellers, the following data gives some idea of the size of the industry as a whole and the enormous complexity of the task undertaken.

At peak production in early 1944, some fifty different firms held prime contracts for military airframes. Taken all together, these concerns had over 100 million square feet of floor space representing an investment of more than a billion dollars. On this production base they managed to achieve a monthly output of more than 9,000 aircraft or better than 100 million airframe pounds excluding spares. This feat required a labor force of over 750,000 people working in assembly plants and a third of that number working for subcontractors. These figures for peak production are best understood when seen against the airframe industry in June 1940, when the major wartime growth began. Then, some 85,000 employees in 8 million square feet of floor space turned out only a little more than 2 million airframe pounds a month, excluding spares and experimental aircraft.[19]

Although airframe manufacturers ranged in size from one small firm with only 100,000 square feet of space to the largest with 7 million square feet, over 95 percent of the airframe weight produced came from those manufacturers with more than 2 million square feet of available space. Approximately half the total number of airframe contractors fell in this category. The necessity for such

---

[18] See especially, Lilley *et al.*, *Problems of Accelerating Aircraft Production During World War II*, sec. V.

[19] Undated monograph prepared in 1945 in conjunction with the postwar industrial mobilization planning project, Technical and Statistical Analysis of the U.S. Aircraft Industry, WFHO, Research file: Aircraft Industry, Analysis (hereafter cited as Statistical Analysis: 1945). See also, CAA, *Statistical Handbook, 1948*, pp. 46 and 56.

large production areas is implicit in the vital statistics of the typical tactical airplanes turned out during the war. Fighters weighed up to 31,000 pounds and had wing spans up to 70 feet. Heavy bombers ranged from 35,000 to 130,000 pounds and had spans from 100 to 130 feet. The *empennage* assemblies for some heavy bombers built during the war were almost as large as the whole of a typical fighter of a few years earlier. Rudders on the big bombers stood anywhere from 18 to 47 feet in the air.

If the sheer size of military aircraft explains why the bulk of wartime airframe output fell to a relatively small number of large assembly plants, even the briefest catalogue of the component parts in the various types of tactical aircraft will suggest the magnitude of the production problems faced by these concerns. A typical fighter might embody 10,000 or more different kinds of parts, 10,000 feet of wiring, 3,000 feet of hydraulic tubing, and 36,000 rivets. A bomber might contain 16,000 parts, 24,000 feet of wiring, and over 200,000 rivets. The B-29, to cite but one example, required 23,652 pounds of sheet aluminum, 1,418 forgings, 618 castings, and 11,308 separate extrusions for every airplane turned out. Obviously only those manufacturers who mastered the techniques of production control could hope to keep one jump ahead of chaos in such a welter of parts.

Yet another factor of significance in appraising the contribution of industry to the wartime expansion of air power is the pace at which airframe manufacturers had to recruit, train, and absorb additional employees. From a total of 59,000 employees in January 1940, the labor force in the airframe industry rose to a peak of 936,000 in November 1943. Individual manufacturers had payrolls of anywhere from 700 to 80,000 people. Table 22 shows the distribution of employment in the airframe industry as of April 1945.

That the aircraft manufacturers finally did achieve an impressive mastery over both men and materials is attested by the following production ratios: where airframe builders in January 1943 required an average of 2.3 man-hours of direct labor per pound of airframe accepted, by July 1944 they had reduced this ratio to the point where it required an average of just under one man-hour for every airframe pound accepted. As Table 23 suggests, under certain circumstances where the volume was high and the number of design changes was closely controlled, some manufacturers achieved records far superior to this average. In conjunction with Table 23, it may be useful to note that the manufacturers of heavy bombers averaged between 1.5 and 2 airframe pounds of output per square foot of floor space. For fighter aircraft the ratio was 1 to 1.5 airframe pounds per foot.

As a group, the aircraft engine manufacturers can be measured in much the same fashion as the airframe builders.[20] The 18 firms holding prime contracts for military engines at peak production employed over 339,000 people and occupied 75 million square feet of floor area. In addition, another 120,000 persons were engaged by subcontractors to the engine manufacturers. The engine firms together turned out more than 24,000 engines or 42 million horsepower in the

---

[20] The rest of this chapter is based on Statistical Analysis: 1945, unless otherwise indicated.

TABLE 22—DISTRIBUTION OF EMPLOYMENT IN AIRFRAME INDUSTRY: APRIL 1945

Range of Payroll	Plants in Range	Total Employees
Under 10,000	33	110,000
10–20,000	14	273,000
20–30,000	8	183,000
Over 30,000	3	188,000

Source: Statistical Analysis: 1945; CAA, *Statistical Handbook, 1948*, p. 56.

TABLE 23—DIRECT MAN-HOURS PER AIRFRAME POUND ACCEPTED

Month	Ford Willow Run B–24	Consolidated San Diego B–24	Boeing Wichita B–29	Republic Farmingdale P–47
January 1943	5.03	1.11		3.82
February 1943	2.52	1.10		2.78
March 1943	1.72	1.04		2.49
May 1943	1.03	.92		1.90
July 1943	1.13	.87		1.70
September 1943	.81	.70	5.60	1.62
November 1943	.70	.67	3.25	1.62
January 1944	.56	.63	2.60	1.42
March 1944	.52	.52	2.36	1.38
May 1944	.56	.50	1.55	1.12
July 1944	.38	.50	1.39	0.99
September 1944	.32	.64	1.13	1.02
December 1944	.36	.60	0.86	1.61

Source: AFF Hist Study 40, pp. 178–79. No direct comparisons can be made from the figures shown. Even in the case of the B–24, where two firms produced the same items, differences in expenditures on tooling and previous production experience preclude valid comparisons as to relative efficiency of production.

peak month of August 1944. By the way of contrast, the engine industry in January 1940 shipped 856 military engines producing a total of 646,000 horsepower. At that time only about 16,000 persons were employed in this work.[21]

Throughout the war the aircraft engine manufacturers not only turned out more and better products but also made continual strides toward higher productivity. Over the five-year war period, the number of man-hours per horsepower output in air-cooled engines dropped from 5.82 to .86. For liquid-cooled engines the drop was from 3.14 to .80 man-hours per horsepower output. And all this, it should be observed, was accomplished at a time when the turnover in labor was climbing rapidly. Whereas in 1941 the annual turnover rate was 27 in 100, by 1943 the rate was 30 in 100. In the airframe industry, by way of compar-

---
[21] CAA, *Statistical Handbook, 1948*, pp. 48, 56–57.

ison, the turnover rate increased from 30 in 100 in 1940 to 50 in 100 by 1943.

In addition to the three major propeller firms and their licensees already mentioned, there were eight other concerns making propellers for training aircraft, and ten firms turning out the light wooden blades used on liaison aircraft. In all, these lesser facilities and those of the major producers of propellers represented about 10 million square feet of floor space with perhaps 10 million more in subcontractors' plants. At peak, in January 1944, the propeller manufacturers employed over 57,000 people, a 23-fold increase over the level of employment in January 1940. In this period, production of military propellers increased from 648 a month to more than 22,000 a month.[22]

Although airframes, engines, and propellers constituted vital ingredients of air power in World War II, they were only the most important in a long list of components. Beyond the essentials lay dozens of accessories and items of subordinate or corollary equipment that cannot be neglected when surveying the role of the aircraft industry as a whole. The list of firms manufacturing these items is entirely too long to identify individual concerns by name and too diverse to lend itself readily to statistical treatment. Nonetheless, a few facts and figures may give at least some impression of the magnitude of this collateral facet of the aircraft industry.

The fabrication of landing-gear assemblies provides an excellent illustration of the sizable complexes organized to produce the many vital accessories so often neglected in the emphasis generally placed on airframes, engines, and propellers. By 1944 there were over 100 firms engaged in this effort. Included on the roster were 15 companies turning out oleo struts, 3 making wheel and brake components, 6 making tires, and 80-odd contributing parts for retracting gear mechanisms. At peak these manufacturers produced 35,300 units a month.

Without question, the oleo strut, or compressible hydraulic shock absorber, was the most difficult item to manufacture in the whole assembly. Ranging in size from 1 to 15 inches in diameter, from 6 inches to 8 feet in length, and from 75 to 700 pounds in gross weight, the struts required the most exacting precision work to produce. Approximately 85 percent of the man-hours spent on them were machine time—turning, boring, and honing. But emphasis on the close tolerances required in strut construction should not obscure the achievements of the many other manufacturers contributing to the fabrication of landing-gear assemblies. For example, many of the development problems and production headaches encountered in manufacturing aircraft tires ranging from 6 inches to 9 feet in diameter and weighing anywhere from 6 to 600 pounds should be more or less implicit in these bare statistics.

One large but nebulous group of suppliers and contractors serving the aircraft industry is vaguely referred to as the electrical equipment manufacturers. In 1939 three major concerns with upward of 50 subs met the needs of the airframe builders. All together, the principal primes then had about 1,000 people on the payroll. By 1945 at least 50 firms

---
[22] CAA, *Statistical Handbook, 1945*, p. 49; Statistical Analysis: 1945.

held major prime contracts in this field and relied upon more than 1,000 subcontractors in addition. Over a million persons were employed in 1945 by these electrical equipment manufacturers who turned out such items as generators, motors, starters, solenoids, switches, ignition coils, and the like.

Some indication of the problems posed by the requirements for electrical equipment can be seen in the production of aircraft generators. Before the war two manufacturers turned out all the generators needed by the Air Corps, a total of about 500 units a year. By the end of 1944 seven different manufacturers were shipping a total of more than 38,000 units a month—a rate of over 450,000 per year. Since the firms supplying the auto industry had mass-produced as many as 10,000 generators a day before the war, the achievement of the manufacturers who entered the aircraft field during the war may not seem remarkable at first glance. But aircraft quality called for far more exacting standards than those prevailing in the automobile industry at that time, and aircraft generators were by no means the same as those used in cars. Where the latter operated at 600 revolutions per minute, aircraft generators ran at a minimum of 24,000 revolutions per minute. Moreover, there was a considerable span between the 300-watt capacity of an automobile generator and the 9,000-watt model used in a B-29.

The war years marked an almost revolutionary shift in the use of electric motors in aircraft. And although no special industry grew up to serve the airframe builders on this account, the regular electrical manufacturers gave increasing attention to the problem of light, fractional horsepower motors. Before the war such units were virtually unknown in fighter aircraft. By 1945 one fighter model mounted 11 and the B-29 used more than 140 of them.

The aircraft instrument makers no less than the electrical equipment manufacturers supplied a diversity of items but constituted a rather more cohesive and identifiable group. A wide variety of skills was required to produce the more than 60 instruments found on the panel of a heavy bomber. These included both navigational instruments such as altimeters and turn and bank indicators and engine instruments such as tachometers, manifold pressure gages, and temperature gages for cylinders, bearings, and so on. In 1940 15 firms turned out these instruments. They subcontracted about 50 percent of their work to some 1,200 other concerns. This unusually high percentage of subcontracting laid a base of experience that made it possible to avoid extensive expansions by the major primes during the war. Instead, the 15 old-line concerns recruited up to 4,000 subs, mostly from the watch and musical instrument manufacturers, to meet their production requirements.

Perhaps no single accessory epitomizes the contributions of industry more effectively than the turbosupercharger, an exhaust-driven compressor designed to offset the effect of altitude on engine performance. Before 1940 only one manufacturer in the United States was engaged in producing the item; it had a staff of 38 employees and 68,000 feet of floor space. By the end of 1944, five manufacturers had 2,750,000 square feet of space and over 12,000 employees devoted to supercharger work. At peak these concerns turned out 13,800 units a month. Although the finished product was small, weighing from 140 to 260 pounds, the various stages of fabrication required a large number of specialized skills and expensive pieces of equipment such as heat treating ovens, X-ray inspection devices, and metallurgical laboratories in addition to such production tools as the heavy drop hammers required to forge turbine blades. This complexity was an important consideration in minimizing subcontracting. At the most, only about 10 percent of the total work involved was passed out to subs who numbered no more than 200 in all.

Manufacturers of the accessory items ranged from tiny one-room shops turning out such products as the almost microscopic machine screws used by instrument makers to giant industrial corporations with numerous branch plants and thousands of employees making such elaborate mechanisms as power-operated gun turrets weighing hundreds of pounds and embracing thousands of parts. Similarly, no generalizations are possible regarding the role of subcontracting since practices and policies varied widely among the various manufacturers concerned. Nor can these firms be neatly and exactly identified as elements of the aircraft industry. Unlike the makers of airframes, engines, and propellers, with few exceptions the manufacturers of accessories and other related items did not confine their activities to the aircraft field. As a consequence, meaningful generalized conclusions on this segment of the industry are difficult if not impossible to draw.

The mass of facts and figures presented in this chapter and those preceding it do make one conclusion patent: the procurement record achieved during World War II resulted from the combined contributions of the military organization and the manufacturers of the nation. In a study such as this the preoccupation with problems of military administration, while inevitable, may tend to give a false emphasis, stressing the contribution of the air arm rather than that of industry. No such distortion is intended. Governmental agencies guided the course and controlled the process, but industry built the airplanes. In the final analysis, perhaps the best measure of industry's contribution is to be seen in the weapons used against the enemy. The nation that desperately and ineffectually sought to defend itself against Japanese attacks in December 1941 by sending a few ancient P-26 and obsolete P-35 fighters into the air was striking in 1945 with tens of thousands of aircraft, many of them models that had not even been test flown when the war broke out. Surely this is the true measure of the industry's achievement.

CHAPTER XXII

Some Concluding Observations on Military Procurement

The more the author has reflected upon the complex mass of evidence presented in this book, the less he is inclined to dogmatic certainties regarding the existence of a right or a wrong course in military buying. He is persuaded that there are no simple formulas, no neatly packaged principles to be memorized in axiomatic form. Yet for all of this, some observations of more than fleeting significance may be abstracted from the book. If these be conclusions, they are no more than tentative conclusions, offered rather as suggestions for discussion than as essential lessons distilled beyond all shadow of doubt.

What Is Air Arm Procurement?

Buying Aircraft presents one thesis above all others: the procurement process itself is a weapon of war no less significant than the guns, the airplanes, and the rockets turned out by the arsenals of democracy. Just as these more conventional weapons must be continually changed to keep pace with those of the nation's enemies, so too the procurement process must be continually modified and improved to meet the emerging demands of the future. But improvement requires understanding, and the enormous complexity of military procurement makes even the most rudimentary understanding a difficult goal to achieve.

Air arm procurement embraces a panorama of considerations far beyond the range of the regulations and procedures hammered out by military officials. Inescapably, in any appreciation of military procurement, one encounters a host of others factors: the prevailing federal statutes, court decisions, the rulings and opinions of various regulatory agencies, the attitudes of Congress, the economic health and character of the aircraft industry, the state of research and development, and so on. Indeed, even the term *aircraft industry* is an all-too-easy generalization that requires elaboration and explanation, for it encompasses not merely the ten to twenty leading airframe manufacturers but a whole congeries of related industries as well—suppliers, vendors, and subcontractors—in seemingly endless array. To understand the procurement process is to appreciate the full gamut of problems raised by this bewildering hierarchy of firms no less than the internal administrative procedures of the military buyers.

Procurement and Politics

In an era of total war, supplying the voracious demands of armed forces becomes a major function of the national economy. The requirements for matériel send out shock waves of increasing severity until scarcely an individual in the nation remains unaware of their impact. Inexorably, air arm procurement becomes a question of widespread popular and therefore political interest. To ignore or even to minimize the frankly political aspects of military buying is to be less than candid and, at the very least, unrealistic.

The sum total of the record, in two world wars and the years of peace between them clearly reveals the necessity for a high level of experience as minimal equipment for staff officers dealing with Congress. Hill tactics are profoundly important. Officers inexperienced in this specialized function, no matter how high ranking or meritorious in every other respect, operate at a serious disadvantage and to the detriment of the service they represent. Staff officers who would provide continuity of support for procurement programs must develop political sagacity of the first order; they must learn to anticipate the shifting tides of congressional opinion that reflect the fevers of the body politic, changes in administration, fluctuations in the national economy, and shifts in foreign policy.

Above all, officers who serve on the Hill, operating as they do in a political milieu, must develop a sensitivity to "political" realities. They must learn that congressmen are not always free to pursue a straight-line course toward a clearly defined goal but must heed the sometimes irrational and usually contradictory dictates of their constituents or they will no longer represent them. In short, the interests of the military may best be served if the officers who deal with Congress recognize the character of political necessity and learn to accommodate it as best they can, standing ever ready, with imagination and flexibility, to concoct alternatives when their proposed measures or programs prove politically unacceptable. Politicians are under continual pressure to come up with easy solutions, quick expedients, and flashy panaceas that promise national security without presenting the voters a higher tax bill. As they come to understand this, military officers can expect to operate with increasing effectiveness on the Hill.

Although a number of staff officers may become highly competent specialists in Hill tactics, it is hardly to be expected that more than a very few congressmen will ever acquire more than a general grasp of military procurement. The evidence of air arm relations with the Hill over the years clearly reveals that the demands of elective office militate against the development of any such expert knowledge even when an enlightened and dedicated legislator makes a determined effort to understand the technicalities of the procurement process. For this reason, the impressions formed by Congress on the subject of military procurement are highly significant. Procurement officials would do well to recognize that in any given problem they present to Congress, whether it be a budget proposal or the draft of a new law, the symbolic significance of the measure is often just as important as the particular details in question. Which is to say, procurement officials must recognize that the impact of any proposal in shaping congressional opinion may in the long run be fully as important as or even more important than the objectives sought for the immediate future.

The relationship of military officers to the executive branch of government is also of crucial significance. The record of air arm procurement before and during World War II revealed repeatedly that military leadership is neither exclusively the task of professional soldiers nor of the politicians in the executive branch. Together they must find adjustments between the demands of the soldiers, stated as minimum requirements, and programs that the politicians believe to be politically feasible. If this equilibrium is to be attained, both the soldiers and the politicians must have a clear conception of their differing roles. If the soldiers begin by trimming down their stated requirements to a level that they regard as politically acceptable, they deprive the President of their best technical and professional advice on the needs of national defense. If the President fails to keep soldiers aware of the nature of the nation's changing diplomatic and political commitments, responsible military leaders can scarcely be expected to give him adequate professional advice on military matters.

Procurement Leadership in Wartime

Procurement leadership is not, however, confined to the precincts of Capitol Hill and dealings with government officials. Those who set out to mobilize the nation's air power for World War II discovered anew that their decisions had a symbolic significance within the military organization and throughout the ranks of industry and labor no less than among the politicians. Those officers who wielded effective command learned that the programs they launched were most successful when they were somehow endowed with a leader's personality. Any number of minor functionaries could have spelled out the right answers for this or that procurement program, but even the right answers when spoken by the wrong people have a way of failing to gain acceptance. The soundest of policies often need the prestige of a famous name before they succeed. Sometimes the magic of a name alone is not enough; then it is necessary to simplify the issues at hand and reduce a statement of policy to well-nigh axiomatic form. Clever indeed is the leader, be he politician or general, who can lay down policy in an epigram; one bon mot by a leader—or his ghost writer—is sometimes worth a host of bone-dry staff studies, detailed, accurate, and unimpeachable, when those studies are written by unknowns. Sound staff work is always essential, but successful leaders give to it an added dimension.

Procurement leadership also calls for courage. The experience of air arm officers in the era of World War II underlined this requirement endlessly. Whatever may have been the temptation to stay within convention, to "play it safe" and follow the usual routines, on occasion an able executive had to make daring use of his discretionary powers. Where necessary, he had to assume political risks and display a bold willingness to make decisions stretching the powers of his office to the limit. A significant difference between the able executive and the mere administrator is to be found at precisely this point: the former clearly apprehends those situations that call for innovation and acts accordingly; the latter continues in faithful execution of a routine long after it has ceased to be important.

During the war years, however, air arm officers found that bold leadership also involved knowing when *not* to act. They learned how important it was not to assume that innovation meant inevitable improvement. The truly effective leader is the one with enough imagination to see the need for innovation and enough sense to know when and whether it should or should not be introduced.

Sometimes effective leadership calls for quite another kind of courage, the courage to delegate power. By sharing discretionary powers with trusted subordinates, by granting them authority to make final decisions, a bold officer can substantially enlarge his effectiveness. To share power calls for character: the timid man is afraid to delegate, the selfish man refuses to.

Air Power and Organization

In one respect at least, the coming of war vastly simplified the task of procurement leadership. In the nation's hour of danger, Congress authorized sweeping grants of power to those charged with the nation's defense as concern for cost to the taxpayers gave place abruptly to a consuming interest in the immediate delivery of essential weapons. But power, no matter how all embracing, does not of itself ensure success. To exercise power is to make decisions, and, as leaders at every echelon soon learned, sound decisions require a continuing flow of appropriate information.

One of the significant tasks of procurement leaders, then, is to contrive organizations that will ensure an adequate flow of information into the decision-making centers of command. Experience, sometimes of the most frustrating kind, gradually revealed that organizations—whether they were of the decision-making or the information-gathering variety—worked best when they were kept flexible, almost as living entities, sensitively atuned to the changing needs of the moment. While it is usually obvious when an organization needs to expand, an able leader must recognize when an organization should be reduced or abolished.

One fundamental dilemma inescapably confronts the air arm, and for that matter, every tactical arm of the defense establishment. Somehow, military men must reconcile the conflicting objectives of more weapons and better weapons—quantity and quality. The technical necessities of mass production put a premium upon stability of design, but the exigencies of battle, the need for weapons that will outperform the enemy in action, require continual changes in design to ensure superiority. During World War II air arm officers learned that these conflicting and seemingly contradictory ends could be effectively reconciled. The solution, they found, lay not in abnormal and extraordinary powers conferred on command, but in organization. Once the major functions to be carried out were clearly understood, it became only a matter of diligent effort before an organization of suitable form was contrived to ensure mastery over the immense array of details involved.

Just as the experience of the air arm in World War II proved that the horizontal equation of quantity and quality could be resolved, so too the war years revealed that the vertical equation of command

SOME CONCLUDING OBSERVATIONS

and operations could be accommodated by imaginative innovations and organization. Military doctrine has traditionally held that command should be centralized and operations decentralized, but to centralize command and decentralize operations may spell isolation for both. Centralized command separates the decision-makers from day-to-day operations, the roots that nourish them with information; at the same time decentralization of operations tends to remove the operators from the seats of power, away from the commanders who alone can pass down the authoritative decisions required for efficient operations. Those in authority had to discover suitable means for bridging this gap. After several false starts during the war years, air arm leaders evolved an organization that did just this. Each assistant chief of staff was assigned a dual role. In his first capacity he served as the chief of a functional staff division, coping with issues of current interest and thus acquiring personal and intimate knowledge of the problems in his specialized area. In his second capacity he sat on the top policy-making staff as an expert advisor to the commanding general. By this arrangement, with its analogy and precedent in the Presidential Cabinet, the officers of the policy staff remained in close touch with the problems of the operating echelons and were thus in a position to feed realistic and informed advice to the top command while transmitting necessary decisions promptly down the chain.

In sum, effective procurement for national defense calls for a high order of leadership. Those who buy the nation's armament must develop sound political insight, a keen understanding of the arts of organization, and, no less than the officers who lead troops in the field, must display unusual courage. But they would do well to remember that there is no simple set of rules governing military procurement. To pretend to have found any such certainty is to court disaster. Continuing and unremitting study is the only alternative. In the struggle for superior weapons, the administration of procurement is of crucial importance, a vital aspect of the whole process. Yet, in a nation that has piled up a significant portion of its federal debt in buying weapons, no aspect has been studied less.

Appendix A

MEMBERSHIP IN THE AERONAUTICAL CHAMBER OF COMMERCE: 1938

Manufacturers producing civil aircraft only:

Aeronautical Corp. of America, Cincinnati, Ohio
Culver Aircraft Corp., Columbus, Ohio
Fairchild Aircraft Corp., Hagerstown, Md.
Fleetwings, Inc., Bristol, Pa.
Luscombe Airplane Corp., West Trenton, N.J.
Monocoupe Corp., Robertson, Mo.
Piper Aircraft Corp., Lockhaven, Pa.
Porterfield Aircraft Corp., Kansas City, Mo.
St. Louis Aircraft Corp., St. Louis, Mo.
Spartan Aircraft Co., Tulsa, Okla.
Stearman-Hammond Aircraft Corp., San Francisco, Calif.
Stinson Aircraft Division of Aviation Mfg. Corp., Wayne, Mich.
Taylorcraft Aviation Corp. (Taylor-Young Airplane Co.), Alliance, Ohio
Waco Aircraft Co., Troy, Ohio
White Aircraft Co., Leroy, N.Y.

Manufacturers producing both civil and military types:

Beech Aircraft Corp., Wichita, Kans.
Bellanca Aircraft Corp., Newcastle, Del.
Boeing Aircraft Corp., Seattle, Wash.
Consolidated Aircraft Corp., San Diego, Calif.
Douglas Aircraft Co., Santa Monica, Calif.
Grumman Aircraft Engineering Corp., Bethpage, Long Island, N.Y.
Kellett Autogiro Corp., Philadelphia, Pa.
Lockheed Aircraft Corp., Burbank, Calif.
North American Aviation Corp., Inglewood, Calif.
Saint Louis Airplane Division of Curtiss-Wright Corp., Robertson, Mo.
Solar Aircraft Co., San Diego, Calif.
Stearman Aircraft Division of Boeing Aircraft Corp., Wichita, Kans.
Vought-Sikorsky Aircraft Division of United Aircraft Corp., Stratford, Conn.
Vultee Aircraft Division of Aviation Mfg. Corp., Downey, Calif.

Manufacturers producing military types only:

Bell Aircraft Corp., Buffalo, N.Y.
Brewster Aeronautical Corp., Long Island City, N.Y.
Curtiss Aeroplane Division, Curtiss-Wright Corp., Buffalo, N.Y.
Seversky Aviation Corp., Farmingdale, Long Island, N.Y.

Source: Hearings, House Subcommittee of Committee on Appropriations, Supplemental Military Establishment Bill for 1940, pp. 319–20.

Appendix B

WARTIME PRODUCERS OF AIRCRAFT*

Manufacturer	Plant Location	AAF Acceptances	Character of Major Items Produced
Aeronca Aircraft Corp.	Middleton, Ohio	2,439	PT-19, PT-23 (995), L-3, (1,439)
Beech Aircraft Corp.	Wichita, Kans.	7,430	C-45 (1,771), AT-7, AT-10, AT-11 (5,175), including 47 items bought for Navy in 1941 and 1942
Bell Aircraft Corp.	Atlanta, Ga.	652	B-29
	Buffalo, N.Y.	12,941	P-39 (9,588), P-63 (3,273), and 1 Navy fighter
Bellanca Aircraft	New Castle, Del.	42	C-50 (3), AT-21 (39)
Boeing Aircraft Corp.	Renton, Wash.	1,000	B-29 (998), C-97 (2)
	Seattle, Wash.	7,339	B-29 (3), B-17 (6,942), A-20 (380), and 1 Navy patrol bomber
	Vancouver, Canada	0	290 Navy patrol bombers
	Wichita, Kans.	9,890	B-29 (1,595), PT-13, PT-17 (7,839), including 600 trainers bought for Navy in 1940 and 1941
Brewster Aircraft Corp.	Johnsville, Pa.	0	1,997 Navy light bombers and fighters
	Long Island City, N.Y.	2	A-32
Budd Mfg. Co.	Philadelphia, Pa.	0	17 Navy transports
Canadian Car Co.	Fort Wilham, Canada	0	832 Navy light bombers
Cessna Aircraft Co.	Wichita, Kans.	5,359	C-78 (3,206), AT-8 (673), AT-17 (1,480)
Cessna Aircraft Division of United Aircraft	Stratford, Conn.	0	7,897 Navy light bombers, reconnaissance aircraft, fighters, and transports
Columbia Aircraft	Valley Stream, N.Y.	0	319 Navy transports
Consolidated-Vultee, Aircraft Corp. (2)	Allentown, Pa.	0	174 Navy light bombers
	Downey, Calif.	11,687	BT-13, BT-15, (11,537), A-31 (2)
	Fort Worth, Tex.	3,148	B-24, (2,743), B-32 (114), C-87 (291)
	Nashville, Tenn.	1,966	A-31, A-35 (1,529), B-38 (113), L-1
	New Orleans, La.	0	221 Navy patrol bombers
	San Diego, Calif.	6,729	B-24 (6,725), B-32 (4)
	Wayne, Mich.	4,104	AT-19 (500), L-5 (3,590)
Culver Aircraft Corp.	Wichita, Kans.	19	Liaison types

APPENDIX B

Wartime Producers of Aircraft*—Continued

Manufacturer	Plant Location	AAF Acceptances	Character of Major Items Produced
Curtiss-Wright Corp.	Buffalo, N.Y.	17,489	P-40 (17,738), P-47 (354), C-46 (2,674), and 86 new light bombers and fighters
	Columbus, Ohio	0	6,343 Navy light bombers, reconnaissance aircraft
	Louisville, Ky.	458	C-46 (438)
	St. Louis, Mo.	2,261	A-25 (900), C-46 (29), AT-9 (791), and 505 Navy trainers
DeHaviland Aircraft of Canada	Toronto, Canada	200	PT-24
Douglas Aircraft Co., Inc.	Chicago, Illinois	629	C-54
	El Segundo, Calif.	3	A-26 and 5,411 Navy light bombers and transports
	Long Beach, Calif.	9,439	B-17 (3,000), A-26 (1,155), A-20 (999), C-47 (4,285)
	Oklahoma City, Okla.	5,319	C-47, C-117
	Santa Monica, Calif.	7,309	A-20 (6,006), P-70 (60), C-54 (460)
	Tulsa, Okla.	2,870	B-24 (964), A-26 (1,291), A-24 (615)
Eastern Aircraft Division of General Motors	Linden, N.J.	0	5,927 Navy fighters
	Trenton, N.J.	0	7,522 Navy light bombers
Engineering and Research Corp.	Riverside, Md.	1	C-55
Fairchild Aircraft Division	Burlington, N.C.	105	AT-21
	Hagerstown, Md.	5,975	C-82 (2), C-61 (1,012, including 3 for Navy)
	Montreal, Canada	0	PT-19, PT-23, PT-26 (4,958), 300 Navy light bombers
Fisher Body Division of General Motors	Cleveland, Ohio	14	P-75
Fleet Aircraft Corp.	Fort Erie, Canada	1,150	PT-23, PT-26
Fleetwings, Inc.	Bristol, Pa.	25	BY-12
Ford Motor Co.	Willow Run, Mich.	6,792	B-24
G & A Aircraft Corp.	Willow Grove, Pa.	7	Rotary wing aircraft
Globe Aircraft Corp.	Fort Worth, Tex.	600	AT-10
Goodyear Aircraft Corp.	Akron, Ohio	0	3,940 Navy fighters
Grumman Aircraft Corp.	Bethpage, Long Island, N.Y.	0	17,478 fighters, light bombers, and transports for Navy
Higgins Aircraft, Inc.	New Orleans, La.	2	C-46

Wartime Producers of Aircraft*—Continued

Manufacturer	Plant Location	AAF Acceptances	Character of Major Items Produced
Howard Aircraft Corp.	Chicago, Ill.	349	PT-23 and 483 transports and trainers for Navy
Interstate Aircraft and Engineering Corp.	El Segundo, Calif.	259	L-6 (251), L-8 (8)
Kellett Autogiro Corp.	Philadelphia, Pa.	7	O-60 autogiro
Lockheed Aircraft Corp.	Burbank, Calif. Plant A	3,764	B-17 (2,750) B-24 (1,014), and 1,929 Navy patrol bombers
	Plant B	13,384	A-28, A-29 (2,189), P-38 (9,423), P-80 (115), F-4, F-5 (500), C-69 (14), including 1 Navy transport in 1941
Glenn L. Martin Co.	Baltimore, Md.	5,611	B-26 (3,572), A-30 (1,575), and 1,275 Navy patrol bombers
	Omaha, Neb.	2,100	B-29 (515), B-26 (1,585)
McDonnell Aircraft Corp.	Memphis, Tenn.	30	AT-21
	St. Louis, Mo.	1	P-67
Nash-Kelvinator Corp.	Detroit, Mich.	201	R-6 helicopter
Naval Aircraft Factory	Philadelphia, Pa.	0	1,302 Navy patrol bombers, reconnaissance aircraft, light bombers, and trainers
Noorduyn Aviation Co., Ltd.	Montreal, Canada	2,252	C-64 (752), AT-16 (1,500)
North American Aviation, Inc.	Dallas, Tex.	18,784	B-24 (966), P-51 (4,552), E-6 (299), AT-6 (12,967)
	Inglewood, Calif.	16,447	B-25 (3,208), A-36 (500), P-51 (9,949), AT-6 (2,163), including 36 trainers for Navy in 1940
	Kansas City, Kans.	6,608	B-25
Northrup Aircraft, Inc.	Hawthorne, Calif.	1,083	A-31 (400), P-62 (682), and 24 Navy light bombers
Piper Aircraft Corp.	Lockhaven, Pa.	5,611	L-4, L-14, and 330 Navy trainers and liaison
Platt-LePage Aircraft Co.	Eddystone, Pa.	2	R-1 helicopter
Rearwin Aircraft	Kansas City, Kans.	25	Liaison
Republic Aviation Corp.	Evansville, Ind.	6,225	P-47
	Farmingdale, N.Y.	9,438	P-43 (272), P-47 (9,006), etc.
Ryan Aeronautical Corp.	San Diego, Calif.	1,443	PT-20, PT-21, PT-25 (392), P-22 (1,048), and 42 Navy fighters
St. Louis Aircraft Corp.	St. Louis, Mo.	363	PT-19, PT-23 (350)
Sikorsky Aircraft Division of United Aircraft	Stratford, Conn.	151	R-4 (130), R-5 (16), R-6 (5) helicopters

APPENDIX B

Wartime Producers of Aircraft*—Continued

Manufacturer	Plant Location	AAF Acceptances	Character of Major Items Produced
Spartan Aircraft Corp.	Tulsa, Okla.	0	201 Navy trainers
Taylorcraft Aviation Corp.	Alliance, Ohio	1,940	L-2
Timm Aircraft Corp.	Van Nuys, Calif.	0	262 Navy trainers
Universal Aircraft	Bristol, Va.	19	L-7
Vickers Canadian, Ltd.	Montreal, Canada	0	230 Navy patrol bombers
Waco Aircraft Co.	Troy, Ohio	6	PT-14 (2)

*In those instances where a firm produced only for Navy cognizance or for the Navy as well as the AAF, the number of units so produced is indicated in the column on the right along with the description of the principal items turned out.

Note: Figures in parenthesis show the total production for each aircraft or group of similar aircraft.

Source: *AAF Statistical Digest*, pp. 113–17. (Dec 45)

Appendix C

Major Producers of Aircraft Engines: July 1940–August 1945*

Manufacturer	Plant Location	Conventional Reciprocating Engines Produced	Description, Approximate Horsepower, and Use (Major Items Only)	
Pratt & Whitney	East Hartford, Conn.	122,302	R-2800	
			R-1830	
			R-1340	R-2800: Double Wasp 18 cylinder twin row, 2000 hp. used on B-26, C-54, etc.
			R-985	
	Kansas City, Mo.	7,815	R-2800	
Licensees of Pratt & Whitney				R-1830: Twin Wasp 14 cylinder twin row, 1200 hp. used on B-24, C-47, etc.
Ford	Dearborn, Mich.	57,178	R-2800	
Buick	Melrose Park, Ill.	74,198	R-2800 (Flint)	
			R-1830	
Chevrolet	Tonowanda, N.Y.	60,766	R-2800	R-1340: Wasp 9 cylinder 650 hp.
			R-1830	
Nash-Kelvinator	Kenosha, Wis.	17,012	R-2800	R-985: Wasp Junior 9 cylinder 450 hp.
Jacobs	Pottstown, Pa.	11,614	R-1340	
			R-985	
Continental	Muskegon, Mich.	5,100	R-1340	
		355,985		
Wright Aeronautical	Patterson, N.J.	77,554	R-3350	
			R-2600	
			R-1820	R-3350: Cyclone 18, 18 cylinder twin row, 2200 hp. used on B-29
			R-975	
			R-760	
	Lockland, Ohio	61,940	R-3350	R-2600: Cyclone 14, 14 cylinder twin row, 1600 hp. used on A-20, B-25, etc.
			R-2600	
Licensees of Wright Aero				R-1820: Cyclone 9, 9 cylinder 1200 hp. used on B-17, etc.
Dodge (Division of Chrysler)	Chicago, Ill.	18,349	R-3350	
Studebaker	South Bend, Ind.	63,789	R-1820	R-975: Whirlwind 9 cylinder 450 hp.
Continental	Muskegon, Mich.	19	R-975	
Naval Aircraft Factory	Philadelphia, Pa.	1,385	R-975	R-760: Whirlwind 7 cylinder 225 hp.
			R-760	
		223,036		

APPENDIX C

Major Producers of Aircraft Engines: July 1940–August 1945*—Continued

Manufacturer	Plant Location	Conventional Reciprocating Engines Produced	Description, Approximate Horsepower, and Use (Major Items Only)	
Allison	Indianapolis, Ind.	69,305	V-1710:	12 cylinder 1500 hp., liquid cooled; P-38, P-39, P-40
			V-3420:	24 cylinder 2000 hp., liquid cooled
Rolls Royce license to:				
Packard	Detroit, Mich.	54,714	V-1650:	Merlin, 12 cylinder, 1800 hp., liquid cooled; P-51
Continental	Muskegon, Mich.	797		
		55,511		
Continental	Muskegon, Mich.	23	I-1430:	12 cylinder 1350 hp., inverted V, liquid cooled
		11,828	R-670:	7 cylinder 220 hp.; PT-13, etc., PT-19, etc.
		16,977	O-170:	4 cylinder 80 hp.; opposed; L-4, etc.
		28,828		
Lycoming	Williamsport, Pa.	12,476	R-680:	9 cylinder 295 hp.; AT-8, AT-10, etc.
			O-435	
			O-290	4-6 cylinder 50–210 hp.; L-5, etc.
			O-235	
		12,395	O-145	
		24,871		
Jacobs	Pottstown, Pa.	5,759	R-915:	7 cylinder 330 hp.
		14,746	R-755:	7 cylinder 225 hp.; AT-17, etc.
		20,505		
Ranger	Farmingdale, N.Y.	2,748	V-770:	12 cylinder 520 hp., air cooled; AT-21, etc.
		11,518	L-440:	6 cylinder 200 hp., in line, air cooled; PT-19, etc.
		14,266		
Air Cooled Motors	Syracuse, N.Y.	178	O-805:	12 cylinder 500 hp.
		6,044	O-405; O-300; O-200; O-175:	4-6 cylinder 80 to 200 hp.; L-6, etc.
		6,222		
Kinner Motors	Glendale, Calif.	2,356	R-540:	5 cylinder 165 hp.; PT-22, PT-25
		802	R-440:	5 cylinder 135 hp.; PT-20, PT-24
		3,158		

Major Producers of Aircraft Engines: July 1940–August 1945*—Continued

Manufacturer	Plant Location	Conventional Reciprocating Engines Produced	Description, Approximate Horsepower, and Use (Major Items Only)	
Warner	Detroit, Mich.	184	R–550:	7 cylinder 200 hp.; R–4 helicopter
		1,704	R–500:	7 cylinder 175 hp.
		127	R–420:	7 cylinder 110 hp.
		2,015		
Menasco	Burbank, Calif.	525	L–365:	4 cylinder 125 hp., inverted in line, air cooled

*Because cross procurement played such an important role in engine production, total rather than AAF acceptances are shown.

  Source: Official Munitions Production, p. 61 ff.; Lilley, *Problems of Accelerating Aircraft Production During World War II,* ch. V and apps. B and C.

Bibliographical Note

During the more than fifteen years that have past since the author started work on this volume, he has consulted the contents of over a thousand published volumes and over 5,000 tightly packed file drawers containing the working papers of the major agencies and organizations concerned with the procurement of air matériel. Expressed another way, in the course of his research the author worked through sheaves of papers that, piled one upon another, would stand well over two miles high. Thus physical stamina and good eyesight were prerequisites to research in this subject every bit as important as scholarly objectivity. These depressing observations are here recorded not to frighten off the student interested in procurement, but rather to impress him with the necessity for some sort of guide to the many scattered repositories housing the enormous mass of official records pertaining to procurement. The paragraphs that follow are to be regarded as a road map designed to simplify the task of leading the researcher to the information he needs rather than as an exhaustive bibliography covering all the many sources consulted.

Broadly speaking, the volume rests upon three types of sources: first, and most significantly, the actual working papers generated by various procurement agencies at the several echelons from the President on down; second, the unpublished historical monographs and other secondary studies produced during and after World War II by a number of the agencies interested in the procurement process; and, third, published materials, both primary and secondary, issuing from sources ranging from organizations for which procurement was a central mission to those having only a remote or indirect interest in the subject. As a matter of convenience, the following description of these sources is presented by organization or by repository rather than by the type of source involved.

As a point of departure, one should consult the National Archives volumes, *Federal Records of World War II:* Volume I, *Civilian Agencies* (1950), and Volume II, *Military Agencies* (1951). Much of the bibliographical information that would otherwise have to be spelled out in great detail is already available in these two volumes. Not only do they describe most of the major collections of materials used by the author, they also provide a great deal of indispensable collateral information such as a description of the War Department decimal filing system. The comments that follow should be regarded for the most part as supplementary to *Federal Records of World War II*.

The most significant body of records in the Washington area used for this book was the official headquarters files of the Air Service, Air Corps, and Army Air Forces, and their subordinate staff sections, covering the period from World War I to the end of World War II. For a description of these records, see *Federal Records of World War II*, Volume II, items 255ff. (Hereafter, unless otherwise noted, all references to item numbers refer to descriptive items in Volume II.) Throughout the span of years covered in this study, the successive headquarters maintained a central file, the Air Force Central File (AFCF). (Items 256a and 256b) Although materials relevant to procurement were found scattered through virtually the whole range of decimal or subject headings, the following file numbers generally were most rewarding in both the classified and the unclassified portions of the central file:

000.71	Interviews
004.4	Firms and Factories; Manufacturers
030	Misc. President and Congress
031	The President
032	Congress
111.3	Estimates
112.4	Apportionment of Funds
161	Contract Regulations
161	Contracts
230.433	Labor
319.1	Reports
321.9	Organization
334.7	Boards, Misc.
337.1	Conferences
360.01	War Dept. Policy on Aviation, Programs, etc.
360.02	Foreign Aviation
381	War Plans
381.3	Lend Lease
400.12	Procurement
400.174	Priority
452.1	Procurement of Aircraft
452.1	Production
452.1	Requirements
452.1	Bomber Program
452.1	Sales Abroad
452.1	Airplanes, General
452.1–191	Price of Aircraft

The shortcomings of the War Department decimal system as applied to the Air Force Central File during the war years is clearly indicated by the concentration of subjects under a single heading such as 452.1.

Although all subordinate staff sections were supposed to use the facilities of the central file, almost all of them also built up file systems of their own. While these accumulations duplicate the materials in the central files in many respects, they do contain large quantities of unique materials and should be consulted. Especially valuable for the purposes of this volume were the papers generated by the subordinate sections of the headquarters matériel and requirements staffs in their successive organizational guises (items 281, 287, 287a and b, 289, 290, 291, and 292). Also useful were the planning staff files (items 296–98).

For the crucial period of expansion before 1941, one of the most helpful collections of materials on procurement is known as the Air Corps Project Records, assembled by Col. A. J. Lyon while serving as executive for the incumbent chief of the Materiel Division, Brig. Gen. G. H. Brett. An index and a summary provide a guide to the 124 binders that comprise the collection (item 289). A microfilm copy of this whole series is available in the Historical Office at Wright Air Force Base, Dayton, Ohio.

In addition to the air arm records described above, the author used many other file collections within the War Department. These include those of the Secretary of War (items 133–34); the Under Secretary (item 137a–c); the Assistant Secretary (item 139); and the Assistant Secretary of War for Air (item 142). Necessary for certain aspects of procurement were the files of the Office of the Chief of Staff (items 165ff.), particularly the War Plans Division (Operations Division) papers (items 197ff.). Also helpful were certain records from the Legislative and Liaison Division, War Department Special Staff (items 205, 213).

An extremely valuable body of materials relating to procurement law and its interpretation is to be found in the files maintained by The Judge Advocate General's Office (item 765). Of particular interest are Contract Division files (item 773) and Patents Division files (item 775). These include formal opinions, related correspondence, and working papers concerned with proposed legislation, all preserved in a well-organized collection employing the standard War Department decimal system of filing. For the period after the formation of the AAF, consult the files of the Air Judge Advocate (item 304).

Although the working papers of the various military organizations dealing with procurement described above provided the real core of this book, an almost equally useful body of materials can be found in the repositories maintained by such organizations as the Air Historical Office (item 258); the Office, Chief of Military History (items 130b, 182, and 253); the National War College Library (item 253); the Pentagon Library (item 141); the Library of Industrial College of the Armed Forces (item 138); and the Documentary Reference and Research Branch (Administrative Reference Branch, Director of Administrative Services, USAF).

The files of the Air Historical Office (item 330) contain a large quantity of material on procurement. In addition to the elaborate series of historical monographs and studies prepared by this organization during and after the war, the office files contain several collections of working papers of operating agencies that were taken over bodily at the end of the war. Most useful among these were the files of the Plans Division, Office of the Chief of Air Corps, and the records of the prewar Air Corps Board.

The Library of the Industrial College of the Armed Forces maintains, in addition to its unequalled collection of published materials dealing with economic mobilization, a system of files containing a large number of fugitive items obtainable nowhere else. Without the resources of this collection it would have proved difficult, if not impossible, to complete this book.

The Documentary Reference and Research Branch, USAF, collection was built upon the nucleus of files accumulated before the war by the Information Division, Office, Chief of Air Corps. A number of scattered files in this collection were especially useful for the prewar period. Materials in this collection are filed under a Library of Congress cataloguing system.

In addition to the several collections mentioned above, the author made extensive use of two other large bodies of materials in the Washington area. At the National Archives, the records of the President's postwar Air Policy Commission, 1947–48 (Record Group 220), was most useful. Also valuable were the files and reference collection of the Aircraft Industries Association (Aeronautical Chamber of Commerce).

The author did not make direct use of the working files of the War Production Board and all its related civilian agencies concerned with mobilizing the national economy in wartime. (See *Federal Records of World War II, Volume I.*) For data regarding the activities of these agencies, he was dependent upon the large number of monographs and other studies, published and unpublished, turned out by the Civilian Production Administration and its predecessors. In the same way, the author had to rely upon the manuscript monographs prepared by the Naval History Division (item 799) when he was unable to consult the working files of the Bureau of Aeronautics.

Outside of Washington, the principal air arm procurement records are those located at Wright Field (Wright-Patterson Air Force Base), Dayton, Ohio, where four separate collections of working papers and files contributed significantly to the preparation of this volume (items 321 and 321a–e). These included the Materiel Division (Materiel Command, Air Technical Service Command) Central Files, the Procurement and Contract Files, the Judge Advocate General's files, and the collections designated as the Central Air Documents Office (CADO). The first of these, cited in this study as Wright Field Central File (WFCF) for simplicity and convenience, is the local equivalent of the headquarters central file in Washington. It, too, employs the War Department decimal filing system for the major part of its accessions, and, like its Washington counterpart, is divided into two parallel collections, one classified, the other unclassified.

The procurement organization at Wright Field in all of its successive mutations of name and structure has maintained a major record repository, independent of the central file, comprising the record copy of all air arm contracts, as amended, along with the correspondence pertaining to them, the regulations governing procurement, and the various administrative tools, periodic reports, and so forth employed by the procurement organization. Although the latter are filed under a War Department decimal system, all contracts are filed by contract number.

The files of the Judge Advocate at Wright Field proved to be extremely rich in materials supplementing the official central file on problems raised by contests with the Comptroller General and in staff papers reflecting the efforts of air arm officers to hammer out effective interpretations of the successive statutes governing the procurement of air matériel.

The Central Air Documents Office at Wright Field, established to administer enemy records and other air intelligence materials, assumed custody of the technical data library files accumulated before World War II. This archive was especially valuable for its extensive holdings on foreign procurement methods, industrial planning, Air Corps and Navy procurement procedures before 1939, and military attaché reports.

The records in the Wright Field Historical Office (WFHO), though relatively small in bulk, constitute one of the most important sources of information employed in the preparation of the volume.

In addition to writing annual organizational histories, monographs, and documented case histories on special topics, the staff of this office has been particularly active in saving and filing a wide variety of items otherwise unobtainable. These include lecture transcripts, manuscript histories of contractors' operations, and personal copies of various reports, staff papers, procedural manuals, and the like secured from interested participants across the whole range of air arm procurement operations.

The records of the procurement district offices subordinate to the authorities at Wright Field contain a number of blocks of files of considerable use in the preparation of the volume (item 322). Although the wartime working papers of the several districts have been retired to a central repository, copies of the histories prepared by district historians during the war are on file in the archive of the Air University Library, Maxwell Air Force Base, Alabama.

Although any one seriously interested in the problems of air arm procurement would find it essential to consult virtually all of the several repositories listed above, there is a vast quantity of pertinent source material readily available in any major Federal depository library. In addition to the immense array of factual data to be found in the hearings and reports published by congressional committees, there are the published reports and records of various special committees and commissions appointed by the President, the published opinions of the Attorney General, decisions of the Treasury Department, reports of the Civil Aeronautics Board, and such other agencies.

Glossary

AAF	Army Air Forces
AAG	Air Adjutant General
ACAD	Automotive Committee for Air Defense
ACC	Aeronautical Chamber of Commerce
ACofAC	Assistant Chief of Air Corps
ACTS	Air Corps Tactical School
Actg	Acting
Admin	Administrative; administrator
ADP	Authority for District Purchase
AFAMC	Air Forces Air Materiel Command
AFMM&D	Air Forces Materiel, Maintenance, and Distribution
AG	Adjutant General
AHO	Air Historical Office
AGF	Army Ground Forces
AIA	Aircraft Industries Association
AIC	Army Industrial College
AMA	Automobile Manufacturers Association
AMC	Air Materiel Command
ANB	Army-Navy-British
ANMB	Army and Navy Munitions Board
ARCO	Aircraft Resources Control Office
ASC	Air Service Command
ASF	Army Service Forces
ASU	Air Scheduling Unit
ASW	Assistant Secretary of War
ATSC	Air Technical Service Command
AWPD	Air War Plans Division
BLS	Bureau of Labor Statistics
BPC	British Purchasing Commission
Br	Branch
Bull	Bulletin
CAA	Civil Aeronautics Administration
CAB	Civil Aeronautics Board
CAS	Chief of Air Staff; Chief of Air Service
CADO	Central Air Documents Office

GLOSSARY

CGMC	Commanding General, Materiel Command
CofAC	Chief of Air Corps
Com	Committee
Comm	Commission
CofS	Chief of Staff
Compt Gen	Comptroller General
Cong	Congress
CPA	Civilian Production Administration
CPFF	Cost plus fixed fee
CPPC	Cost plus percentage of cost
DCofS	Deputy Chief of Staff
Dir	Director
Dist	District
Doc	Document; documentary
DPC	Defense Plant Corporation
EES	Experimental Engineering Staff
Engr	Engineer; engineering
EPF	Emergency plant facility
Exec	Executive
FDR	Franklin Delano Roosevelt
FO	Field Order
G–1	Personnel section of divisional or higher staff
G–2	Intelligence section of divisional or higher staff
G–3	Operations and training section of divisional or higher staff
G–4	Supply section of divisional or higher staff
GAO	General Accounting Office
GFE	Government-furnished equipment
GHQAF	General Headquarters Air Force
GOCO	Government-owned, contractor-operated
H Doc	House document
H.R.	House bill
ICAF	Industrial College of the Armed Forces
IG	Inspector General
IOM	Interoffice memorandum
Interv	Interview
IPS	Industrial Planning Section

JAC	Joint Aircraft Committee	
JAG	Judge Advocate General	
JAGD	Judge Advocate General's Department	
JAGO	Judge Advocate General's Office	
Jt	Joint	

LI	Letter of intent

Mat	Matériel
MB	Munitions Board
MC	Materiel Command
MID	Military Intelligence Division
MM&D	Materiel, Maintenance, and Distribution

NACA	National Advisory Committee for Aeronautics
NDAC	Advisory Commission to the Council of National Defense

OASW	Office of the Assistant Secretary of War
OCAC	Office, Chief of Air Corps
OCofOrd	Office, Chief of Ordnance
OCofS	Office, Chief of Staff
OEM	Office for Emergency Management
OPA	Office of Price Administration
OPM	Office of Production Management

P&A	Priorities and Allocations
PES	Production Engineering Section
PMP	Protective Mobilization Plan
Proc	Procurement
PR	Procurement Regulation
PWA	Public Works Administration

RAF	Royal Air Force
Rcd	Record
R&D	Research and Development
Res	Resolution
RFC	Reconstruction Finance Corporation
Rpt	Report
R&R	Routing and record; reference and research

S	Senate
SAE	Society of Automotive Engineers
Sess	Session

GLOSSARY

SGS	Secretary, General Staff
SN	Secretary of the Navy
SOS	Services of Supply
SSUSA	Special Staff, U.S. Army
Stat	Statutes; statistical
SW	Secretary of War
SWPC	Smaller War Plants Corporation
TAG	The Adjutant General
Telg	Telegram
T&O	Training and Operations
TWX	Teletypewriter exchange
UAW	United Auto Workers
USCA	United States Code Annotated
USW	Under Secretary of War
WD	War Department
WDPAB	War Department Price Adjustment Board
WF	Wright Field
WPB	War Production Board
WFCF	Wright Field Central File
WFHO	Wright Field Historical Office
WPD	War Plans Division
WRA	War Resources Administration
WRB	War Resources Board

UNITED STATES ARMY IN WORLD WAR II

The following volumes have been published or are in press:

The War Department
    Chief of Staff: Prewar Plans and Preparations
    Washington Command Post: The Operations Division
    Strategic Planning for Coalition Warfare: 1941–1942
    Strategic Planning for Coalition Warfare: 1943–1944
    Global Logistics and Strategy: 1940–1943
    Global Logistics and Strategy: 1943–1945
    The Army and Economic Mobilization
    The Army and Industrial Manpower
The Army Ground Forces
    The Organization of Ground Combat Troops
    The Procurement and Training of Ground Combat Troops
The Army Service Forces
    The Organization and Role of the Army Service Forces
The Western Hemisphere
    The Framework of Hemisphere Defense
    Guarding the United States and Its Outposts
The War in the Pacific
    The Fall of the Philippines
    Guadalcanal: The First Offensive
    Victory in Papua
    CARTWHEEL: The Reduction of Rabaul
    Seizure of the Gilberts and Marshalls
    Campaign in the Marianas
    The Approach to the Philippines
    Leyte: The Return to the Philippines
    Triumph in the Philippines
    Okinawa: The Last Battle
    Strategy and Command: The First Two Years
The Mediterranean Theater of Operations
    Northwest Africa: Seizing the Initiative in the West
    Sicily and the Surrender of Italy
    Salerno to Cassino
    Cassino to the Alps
The European Theater of Operations
    Cross-Channel Attack
    Breakout and Pursuit
    The Lorraine Campaign
    The Siegfried Line Campaign
    The Ardennes: Battle of the Bulge
    The Last Offensive

    The Supreme Command
    Logistical Support of the Armies, Volume I
    Logistical Support of the Armies, Volume II
The Middle East Theater
    The Persian Corridor and Aid to Russia
The China-Burma-India Theater
    Stilwell's Mission to China
    Stilwell's Command Problems
    Time Runs Out in CBI
The Technical Services
    The Chemical Warfare Service: Organizing for War
    The Chemical Warfare Service: From Laboratory to Field
    The Chemical Warfare Service: Chemicals in Combat
    The Corps of Engineers: Troops and Equipment
    The Corps of Engineers: The War Against Japan
    The Corps of Engineers: The War Against Germany
    The Corps of Engineers: Military Construction in the United States
    The Medical Department: Hospitalization and Evacuation; Zone of Interior
    The Medical Department: Medical Service in the Mediterranean and Minor Theaters
    The Ordnance Department: Planning Munitions for War
    The Ordnance Department: Procurement and Supply
    The Ordnance Department: On Beachhead and Battlefront
    The Quartermaster Corps: Organization, Supply, and Services, Volume I
    The Quartermaster Corps: Organization, Supply, and Services, Volume II
    The Quartermaster Corps: Operations in the War Against Japan
    The Quartermaster Corps: Operations in the War Against Germany
    The Signal Corps: The Emergency
    The Signal Corps: The Test
    The Signal Corps: The Outcome
    The Transportation Corps: Responsibilities, Organization, and Operations
    The Transportation Corps: Movements, Training, and Supply
    The Transportation Corps: Operations Overseas
Special Studies
    Chronology: 1941–1945
    Military Relations Between the United States and Canada: 1939–1945
    Rearming the French
    Three Battles: Arnaville, Altuzzo, and Schmidt
    The Women's Army Corps
    Civil Affairs: Soldiers Become Governors
    Buying Aircraft: Materiel Procurement for the Army Air Forces
    The Employment of Negro Troops
    Manhattan: The U.S. Army and the Atomic Bomb
Pictorial Record
    The War Against Germany and Italy: Mediterranean and Adjacent Areas
    The War Against Germany: Europe and Adjacent Areas
    The War Against Japan

Index

A-20's, 517, 550, 560, 576–77, 580
A-24's, 550, 577
A-25's, 550, 577
A-26's, 241, 243, 550, 576
A-28's, 550, 578
A-29's, 550, 578
A-30's, 550, 578
A-31's, 242, 550, 576, 578
A-32's, 576
A-35's, 550, 576
A-36's, 550, 578
Absenteeism, 457
ACAD, 305
ACC. *See* Aeronautical Chamber of Commerce.
Accelerated depreciation. *See* Depreciation; Facility financing, by accelerated depreciation.
Acceptances of aircraft, 243n, 244–45, 370, 532, 534, 553, 560, 564. *See also* Aircraft production; Deliveries; Delivery schedules.
"Accepted schedules," 152–55
Accessories, 6, 8, 198, 210, 273. *See also* Components.
  Bendix role, 450
  contract negotiation, 354
  educational orders for, 160, 183
  experimental development, 97, 99
  exports influence, 197
  facility expansion, 294, 310, 320–21, 324, 328
  manufacturers' profits, 36
  production, 530, 566ff.
  production capacity, 180
  proposed nationalization of supply, 124–25
  shortages, 183
  small business role, 492, 501
  special tools problem, 485
  standardization, 267
Accident ratios, 50. *See also* Attrition rate.
Accidental loss. *See* Aircraft accidents; Attrition rate.
Accountable property, 397. *See also* Property accounting.
Accountability. *See* Property accounting.
Accountants, 354, 360, 393, 407, 416
Accounting, 34–35, 125, 282, 300, 419, 535
  in CPFF contracts, 380–81, 392, 415
  escalation problem, 423, 427
  impact on finances, 36, 38
  inadequacies, 391, 394, 397, 416, 421, 433
  in modification centers, 532
  organization and procedures, 390
  savings, 367
Accounting office. *See* General Accounting Office.

Accuracy. *See* Standardization; Tolerances.
Act of 24 June 1936, 171–72. *See also* 2,320 aircraft program.
Administration. *See* Administrative procedures.
Administration Branch, Materiel Division, 98
Administrative controls, 473. *See also* Management control; Organizational planning; Statistical Control Office.
Administrative discretion. *See* Discretionary powers.
Administrative history, 271
Administrative organization, 329
Administrative overhead. *See* Overhead.
Administrative personnel, 403. *See also* Civil Service; Civilian personnel; Enlisted men; Officers.
Administrative procedures
  analysis of, 106, 109–11, 128, 272, 338, 352, 408–09
  for CPFF contracts, 408
  delay procurement, 274, 307, 331–32, 350, 353
  in facility expansions, 296–98
  standardized forms, 473
  for termination, 452
  weaknesses, 105, 261, 380
  Wright Field, 99, 104, 493
Administrators, qualities required, 147. *See also* Discretionary powers; Leadership; Officers; Personnel.
ADP. *See* Authority for District Purchase; Data processing.
Advance payments, 284–85, 413, 415. *See also* Partial payments.
Advanced trainers, 482, 546, 551, 560, 576–78, 581
Advertising, promotional, 382
Advertising for bids, 80, 89–90, 128, 275, 508. *See also* Bids; Circular proposals; Competitive bidding; Competitive procurement.
Advertising registers, 492, 497–98
Advisory Commission to the Council of National Defense. *See* National Defense Advisory Commission.
Aerial navigation, 13
Aeronautical Board, 211, 213
Aeronautical Chamber of Commerce, 8–9, 187
  Army-Navy agreements, 89
  capacity studies, 178, 188, 193n
  criticizes procurement methods, 145, 277, 422, 426
  relations with Air Corps, 87–88, 145, 188, 426
  site selection check list, 307
Aeronautical Corporation of America, 575
Aeronautical engineers. *See* Aircraft designers; Design engineers; Design staffs.

Aeronautical journals, 275
Aeronautical research. *See* Research and development.
Aeronautical Section, NDAC, 256–57
Aeronca Aircraft Corp., 321, 576. *See also* PT-19's; PT-23's.
Aero Supply Corp., 7–8, 8n
Aeroproducts Division of GMC, 562–63
AGF, 241, 475
Agreements, interservice, 392. *See also* Aeronautical Chamber of Commerce; Army-Navy; Interbranch competition; Interservice rivalry; Joint Army and Navy Board.
Aid for Britain, 199
Air arm. *See* Air Corps; Army Air Forces; Bureau of Aeronautics; Royal Air Force, *etc.*
Air arm versus ground forces, 173. *See also* Interbranch competition.
Air arsenals, 176–79, 185, 277, 291. *See also* Facilities, nationalization; Nationalization of industry.
Air Associates, Inc., 7–8, 8n
Air bases, 77–78, 216–17, 411. *See also* Depots.
Air Board, 220
Air Commerce Act of 1926, 13–14, 17
Air-cooled engines. *See* Engine manufacturers; Engine production; Radial engines.
Air Cooled Motors, Inc., 6n, 581
Air Corps
  administrative procedures, 75, 78, 127, 260–61, 261n, 380
  airmail, 15, 121
  auditing, 35, 390
  authorized strength, 43, 48–51, 50n, 59–61, 63–75, 171–75, 206
  balanced program, 77–78
  as combat arm, 48
  co-operation with Navy, 212–13
  defers to export orders, 202–03
  educational orders, 160, 183
  expansion program, 170, 178–79, 283
  expenditures for aircraft, 1926–34, 117
  50,000 program, 228n
  finances, 67, 70, 172–73. *See also* Appropriations; Expenditures for air matériel.
  inadequately armed, 43, 208, 244–45
  JAC members, 266
  manufacturers, 21
  mission, 48, 53, 63, 101, 124, 169–70, 210. *See also* Doctrine.
  mobilization planning, 159, 161–62, 168, 178–79, 206, 225, 249, 291
  obsoletion policy, 50
  oleo strut procurement, 318
  OPM relations, 270
  personnel, 64
  prewar procurement, 3, 20, 66, 332, 346
  procurement procedures, 130, 143. *See also* Procurement procedures.

Air Corps—Continued
  profits on contracts, 126
  relation to Congress, 48, 55–57, 76–77, 92, 119, 144–45, 277, 280, 283
  relations with NDAC, 192, 256, 262
  relief funds, 67–68
  research policy, 23–25
  rivalry with British, 263
  studies requirements, 51–52, 63
  spares policy, 74, 215
  Standards Book, 132
Air Corps Act of 1926, 47, 49, 59, 64, 89
  Air Corps policy on, 116, 124
  alleged violations of, 118, 123
  amendment considered, 52, 116, 116n, 127–28, 276
  auditing provisions, 390, 402
  creates ASW (Air), 53, 94
  data for negotiation, 344
  expenditures, 1926–34, 117
  interpretations, 51, 92–93, 100, 114–16, 126–28, 171–72
  operating experience, 50–51, 61, 106, 137, 148
  procurement procedures, 92–93, 106ff., 113ff., 130
  used in emergency, 275, 278
Air Corps Board, 94–95, 106, 217
Air Corps officers. *See* Officers.
Air Corps Technical Committee, 94, 97, 97n, 104, 106–07
Air defense plans, 52, 95. *See also* War planning.
Air depots, 98, 244–45, 533, 537. *See also* Depots; Field Service Section, Materiel Division; Maintenance; Supply.
Air force, concept of, 45
Air forces. *See* Army Air Forces; German Air Force; Royal Air Force.
Air Mail Act of 1925, 12, 14, 17
Air Mail Act of 1934, 15, 56
Air Ministry, 165, 266. *See also* British Purchasing Commission; Joint Aircraft Committee; Royal Air Force; United Kingdom.
Air power. *See also* Doctrine.
  Army advocates silenced, 212
  Army views on, 174
  Baker Board views, 56
  British, 224
  character of, 5
  doctrines discussed, 52, 63, 101, 156, 169, 233
  factors influencing, 41, 52, 171–74, 210–11, 237, 553
  German, 169
  GHQ Air Force role, 102
  Johnson's views, 181
  Lassiter Board views, 45
  newspaper comment on, 195
  procurement law role, 278
  requirements for, 210
  Rogers Committee views, 123–24
  Roosevelt's strategy on, 172–73
  War Department views, 48, 157, 172, 210–11

INDEX

Air Scheduling Unit, JAC, 269–73, 457
Air Service
 aircraft expenditures in 1920–24, 85
 engineering center, 112
 policy on composition, 45, 47
 procurement officer, 144
 procurement program, 44–46
 strength in 1926, 48
"Air service," concept of, 45
Air Service Command, 470–71, 487, 533
Air Staff, AAF, 241, 465, 478, 487. *See also individual elements of staff, e.g.*, Materiel, Maintenance, and Distribution, Air Staff.
Air Technical Service Command, 471
Air trust, 123
Air War Plans Divisions, 237–38
Airacobra. *See* P–39's.
Airacomet. *See* P–59's.
Aircraft. *See also* Engines; Manufacturers.
 A–20's, 517, 550, 560, 576–77, 580
 A–24's, 550, 577
 A–25's, 550, 577
 A–26's, 241, 243, 550, 576
 A–28's, 550, 578
 A–29's, 550, 578
 A–30's, 550, 578
 A–31's, 242, 550, 576, 578
 A–32's, 576
 A–35's, 550, 576
 A–36's, 550, 578
 Advanced trainers, 482, 546, 551, 560, 576–78, 581
 AT–6's, 482, 551, 560, 578
 AT–7's, 551, 576
 AT–8's, 551, 576
 AT–9's, 577
 AT–10's, 576–77
 AT–11's, 576
 AT–16's, 578
 AT–17's, 576, 581
 AT–19's, 576
 AT–21's, 546, 576–78, 581
 attack, 64
 attack bomber, 72, 275
 autogiros, 275, 278
 B–10's, 117, 142, 163–64
 B–15's. *See* Aircraft, XB–15's.
 B–17's, 20, 76, 77n, 142, 148, 214, 245, 246, 250, 257, 282, 302–03, 306, 309, 362, 460, 529, 540, 550, 560, 576–78, 580
 B–18's, 76–77, 77n, 142, 245
 B–19's, 550
 B–23's, 246
 B–24's, 306, 309, 310, 326–27, 416, 494n, 519–21, 524, 526–27, 529, 531, 535–36, 539, 540, 545, 550, 560, 576–78, 580
 B–25's, 241, 306, 308, 528, 550, 560, 578, 580
 B–26's, 241, 243, 302, 306, 308, 366, 534, 540, 545–46, 550, 560, 578, 580

Aircraft—Continued
 B–29's, 156, 303, 308, 325, 399, 415, 546–47, 550, 553, 564, 567, 576, 578, 580
 B–32's, 308, 550, 576
 B–38's, 576
 B–42's, 550
 bomber (general), 45, 52, 64, 72, 72n, 75, 77–78, 77n, 117, 142, 156, 204n, 210, 537, 553–56, 576–77
 BT–12's, 577
 BT–13's, 551, 576
 BT–15's, 576
 C–32's, 136
 C–43's, 551
 C–45's, 551, 560, 576
 C–46's, 546, 551, 577
 C–47's, 136, 551, 560, 577, 580
 C–50's, 576
 C–54's, 514, 551, 560, 577, 580
 C–55's, 577
 C–60's, 551
 C–61's, 551, 577
 C–64's, 551, 578
 C–69's, 551, 578
 C–78's, 551, 576
 C–82's, 577
 C–87's, 551, 576
 C–97's, 576
 C–117's, 551
 cargo, 514, 537
 civilian, 8–9, 11, 20, 126, 575
 CS–2's, 85–86
 DC–2's, 136
 DC–3's. *See* Aircraft, C–47's.
 E–6's, 578
 F–2's, 550. *See also* Aircraft, C–45's.
 F–4's, 550, 578. *See also* Aircraft, P–38's.
 F–5's, 550, 578. *See also* Aircraft, P–38's.
 F–6's, 550. *See also* Aircraft, P–51's.
 fighter, 45, 110, 112, 156, 228, 233, 237, 239, 244–45, 269, 278, 310, 457, 533, 537, 564, 567, 576–79
 four-engine bomber, 302–03, 319
 glider, 373, 552, 558, 577
 heavy bomber, 233, 237, 244, 253, 564, 567
 L–1's, 551
 L–2's, 551, 579
 L–3's, 551, 576
 L–4's, 551, 578, 580
 L–5's, 551, 576, 580
 L–6's, 578, 580
 L–7's, 579
 L–8's, 578
 L–14's, 578. *See also* Aircraft, L–4's.
 liaison, 11, 552, 566, 576–79
 light bomber, 244
 medium bomber, 244, 302, 308
 observation, 45, 64, 156–57
 P–26's, 568
 P–35's, 568

Aircraft—Continued
  P-38's, 517, 531, 533-34, 550, 560, 578, 581
  P-39's, 245, 302, 550, 560, 576, 581
  P-40's, 228, 517-18, 550, 560, 577, 581
  P-43's, 578
  P-47's, 550, 560, 577-78
  P-51's, 550, 578, 581
  P-59's, 550, 562
  P-61's, 550
  P-62's, 578
  P-63's, 517, 550, 576
  P-67's, 578
  P-70's, 550, 577
  P-75's, 269, 577
  P-80's, 550, 562, 578
  P-84's, 538n
  PT-13's, 546, 551, 576, 581
  PT-14's, 579
  PT-17's, 551, 576
  PT-19's, 551, 576-78, 581
  PT-20's, 578, 581
  PT-21's, 578
  PT-22's, 578, 581
  PT-23's, 546, 551, 576-78
  PT-24's, 577, 581
  PT-25's, 578, 581
  PT-26's, 551, 577
  PT-27's, 551
  R-1's, 578
  R-4's, 551, 578, 582
  R-5's, 551, 578
  R-6's, 551, 578
  reconnaissance, 576-79
  rotary wing, 577-79
  strategic bomber, 212
  tactical, 170, 225, 225n, 241, 244
  transport, 12, 16, 110, 134ff., 183, 551, 576-79
  UC-45's, 442-43
  utility, 442-43
  XB-15's, 149
  XFM-1's, 199
  YB-10's, 117
Aircraft acceptances. *See* Acceptances of aircraft.
Aircraft accidents, 121. *See also* Accident ratios; Loss rates.
Aircraft armament. *See* Armament, aircraft.
Aircraft Board, 82, 82n
Aircraft Branch, Materiel Division, 97-99
Aircraft Branch, WPB, 273
Aircraft characteristics, evaluation of, 111. *See also* Aircraft performance; Military characteristics; Performance characteristics; Specifications.
Aircraft, civilian. *See* Civilian aircraft.
Aircraft design. *See also* Design *et seq.*
  data flow studied, 308, 541
  evaluation of, 89-90, 109-110, 113, 131
  freeze of, 187
  impact on profits, 36

Aircraft design—Continued
  influences mobilization, 157
  interpretation problems, 469, 522, 544
  Martin B-10, 117
  Reuther misconception of, 311
Aircraft designers. *See also* Design engineers; Design staffs; Engineers.
  automotive industry lacks, 290
  danger of loss by, 114-15, 302
  fees allowed, 377
  indispensable to government, 177, 182
  spare parts problem, 342
  specify engines desired, 127
Aircraft Designers Handbook, 131
Aircraft engineers. *See* Aircraft designers; Engineers.
Aircraft engines. *See* Engine manufacturers; Engines.
Aircraft expenditures, 117, 556-59
Aircraft grounded for repairs, 50. *See also* Depots; Maintenance; Spare parts.
Aircraft on hand. *See also* Authorized strength.
  average number, 50
  factors influencing, 44, 56-59, 70-71, 171
  lack equipment, 246
  1941 GHQ Air Force, 244
  1929-40 period, 55, 61, 66, 129, 230
  reported not actual, 50
Aircraft hardware, 8, 404, 433. *See also* Accessories.
Aircraft Industries Association, 188n. *See also* Aeronautical Chamber of Commerce.
Aircraft industry
  accepts audits, 402
  accounting practices, 34-35
  Air Corps Act impact, 93
  Air Corps representatives with, 99. *See also* Resident representatives.
  alleged banker control, 123
  alleged frauds, 122
  capacity estimates, 161, 186. *See also* Production capacity.
  character of, 6-10, 27
  contract negotiating practices, 286, 355-56
  contributions, 568
  co-operation needed, 182
  cost-cutting requirements, 297
  criticizes procurement procedures, 86-87
  dollar value output, 27
  economic status, 26-27, 46, 93, 127, 130, 141, 143, 147, 159-61, 178, 325, 569
  educational orders, 159-60
  facilities expansion, 41, 70, 175-78, 193, 291, 302, 307
  fear of nationalization, 38, 124-25, 277. *See also* Air arsenals; Nationalization of industry.
  financing, 17, 19, 21, 33-41, 70, 184, 451. *See also* Advance payments; Capital investment; Facility financing; Loans; Partial payments; Stock market; V-loans.
  floor space, 29, 294-95, 310

INDEX

599

Aircraft industry—Continued
  foreign order impact, 200. *See also* Exports.
  impact of secrecy, 18. *See also* Release policy; Security classification.
  inventory problem, 457
  job-shop views, 164
  lacks adequate staff, 405. *See also* Aircraft designers; Employment; Engineers.
  lobby, 145. *See also* Aeronautical Chamber of Commerce.
  managerial experience, 304
  market, 11ff., 17, 21–22, 41, 179. *See also* Exports; Foreign orders.
  mobilization planning, 152–55, 181ff., 207
  NRA code, 8
  operating ratios, 40–41
  order backlog, 179–80, 202, 234
  output per worker, 26–27
  political influence on, 38
  prewar production experience, 26ff.
  research bid policy, 24–25
  resists strategic dispersal, 307. *See also* Geographic dispersal.
  shortages, 180, 258
  statutory aids for, 281
  technical changes in, 148, 246. *See also* Research and development.
  training engineers, 23
  wage indices, 424–25
Aircraft innovations, 107. *See also* Design; Experimental aircraft; Experimental contracts; Research and development.
Aircraft instruments. *See* Instruments, aircraft.
Aircraft losses. *See* Aircraft accidents; Attrition rate; Loss rates.
Aircraft Maintenance Branch, Materiel Division, 98
Aircraft manufacturers. *See* Airframe manufacturers; Manufacturers.
Aircraft "on order," 49, 66, 67n. *See also* Aircraft industry, order backlog.
Aircraft performance, 3–4, 110–14, 116, 127, 130. *See also* Military characteristics; Performance characteristics; Specifications.
Aircraft Planning Committee, ANMB, 252
Aircraft Procurement Branch, Wright Field, 348
Aircraft production, 511, 511n
  acceleration, 189, 315, 324, 518, 520, 528, 553
  cost curves, 344
  design change role, 26, 32, 468, 516. *See also* Design freeze; Quantity versus quality.
  Detroit conversion for, 314
  directly from design, 251
  efficiency yardstick, 326–27
  factors delaying, 27, 246, 274, 306, 468
  first large-scale, 16
  by foreign powers, 169n, 553ff.
  goals change, 257, 304
  impact of nationalization, 201

Aircraft production—Continued
  lags behind automobile, 27
  legal obstacle, 274
  neutrality impact, 201
  1939–45 total U.S., 241n, 548, 555
  1922–35 total U.S., 10, 21n, 26–28
  one-an-hour rate, 518
  organization for, 273
  peak monthly, 553, 563
  prewar resources, 7–9, 26ff.
  rate determines fee, 418
  relation to training, 225
  scheduling and co-ordination, 263–64, 266–67, 270, 273. *See also* Airframe manufacturers, scheduling.
  steps leading to, 106ff.
  stressed over experimentation, 257n, 514
  wartime expansion, 457
  Willow Run efficiency, 527
  World War I, 84n
Aircraft Production Board, WPB, 273
Aircraft Production Board of 1917, 82n
Aircraft program. *See* Procurement program; *individual programs by name.*
Aircraft Resources Control Office, 273
Aircraft seats, 267n
Aircraft Section, OPM, 266, 270
Aircraft strength. *See* Air Corps, authorized strength; Aircraft on hand.
Aircraft tools, 484
Aircraft unit costs. *See* Unit costs.
Aircraft weight. *See* Airframe pounds; Airframes, average gross weights.
Airframe manufacturers, 6–9, 293n, 563, 575–79
  accounting, 416, 423
  aluminum, 180, 250–51, 257
  attitudes and practices, 119, 185, 251, 318, 333, 356, 356n
  audits, 344, 392
  automotive industry relations, 306, 522, 541
  capacity studies, 111, 185–87, 191, 290, 292. *See also* Production capacity.
  competition, 127, 141
  conference in 1938, 166
  contract negotiations, 277, 336, 355
  costs per pound, 521
  criticize procurement procedures, 87n, 114–15, 129, 142, 145, 370
  design role, 8, 32, 132, 513, 529
  dollar volume, 491
  educational orders, 160, 183
  employees, 564–66
  exports impact, 200, 202, 294–95
  facility expansions, 29, 162, 165, 177–78, 184–85, 290, 299, 301–02, 321, 324–25
  fear automotive competition, 290–91, 304
  fear government facilities, 124–25, 178. *See also* Air arsenals; Nationalization of industry.

Airframe manufacturers—Continued
  fear of loss, 286, 297, 332–33, 345, 383, 421, 424, 427
  financial condition, 35–36, 40, 126, 130, 141–43, 289, 448
  floor space, 29
  inventory value, 40–41
  lobbying, 68. *See also* Aeronautical Chamber of Commerce.
  mass production, 324, 348, 520, 528, 538. *See also* Production contracts.
  modifications, 303, 531–32, 535, 538
  neutrality problem, 196, 201, 201n. *See also* Exports; Foreign orders; Release policy.
  oleo strut shortage, 318
  order backlog, 29, 376
  priorities problems, 259–60
  productivity rank, 561
  purchase orders, 457
  scheduling, 263–64, 267, 269–70, 274, 277
  subcontracting, 182, 184, 282
  suborders, 404, 457
  suppliers, 251
  views on Reuther, 312
Airframe pounds, 190, 548, 551, 556, 563–64. *See also* Airframes, average gross weights.
Airframe spares. *See* Spare parts.
Airframes, average gross weights, 72, 243, 527, 556. *See also* Airframe pounds.
Airframes, security classification, 198. *See also* Release policy; Security classification.
Airlines. *See also* Modification centers; *individual airlines by name.*
  alleged profiteering, 119
  aircraft market, 11–12, 17, 20, 143
  airmail contracts, 12–13, 121
  description, 11ff.
  engines borrowed, 250
  finances, 15–17, 123
  modifications role, 530
  passenger traffic, 14–16
  pilots' experience aids planners, 222
  priorities problem, 259, 262
  production scheduling, 265–66
Airmail, 14–15, 55, 119, 121, 279
Airplane Division, NDAC, 293
Airstrips, 77–78. *See also* Air bases.
Akron, Ohio, 9
Alaska, 242, 534
Albert Kahn, Inc., 28n
Alcoa, 250–51
Alignment, 524
All-metal aircraft, 16
Allis-Chalmers, 455–56
Allison Division of GMC, 6n, 269, 293n, 309, 562, 581. *See also* V–1710 engine; V–3420 engine.
Allocation of contracts, 88. *See also* Approved lists.
Allocation of costs, 362, 392. *See also* Accounting.

Allocation of industrial capacity, 152, 247, 269. *See also* Facilities, requirements; Facilities Division, OASW; Mobilization planning; Office of Assistant Secretary of War.
Allowable costs
  in CPFF contracts, 379–82
  French policy, 378
  in renegotiation, 435
  in terminations, 451
Altimeters, 567
Aluminum
  airframe weights, 180
  mobilization planning for, 158
  production problems, 523
  requirements, 257, 564
  shortages, 250–51, 271n
Aluminum industry, 180. *See also* Alcoa.
AMA, 305
Amendment of contracts, 366–67. *See also* Change orders; Escalator clauses; Price adjustment; Renegotiation.
American Airlines, 530
Amortization of costs, 85. *See also* Deferred development charges.
Amortization specialists, 354. *See also* Facility financing, by accelerated depreciation.
ANMB. *See* Army and Navy Munitions Board.
Annual reports, War Department, 3
Antikickback acts, 281
Antitrust statutes, 499
APB, 273
Appeals, 370, 477. *See also* Board of Contract Appeals; Federal courts.
Applied research, 22–25. *See also* Experimental aircraft; Experimental contracts; Research and development; Service tests.
Appropriations. *See also* Estimates.
  administration of, 43, 73–74, 78, 104–05, 144, 154, 298, 300, 423
  buy less than intended, 76
  congressional responsibility, 70
  for Defense Aid, 267
  discretionary fund sought, 78
  distinguished from authorization, 43
  for 50,000 program, 229
  funds maldistributed, 78
  impounded by President, 67, 128
  inadequate between wars, 63
  Lampert Committee recommendations, 46
  Morrow Board recommendations, 47
  in 1940 crisis, 179–80, 230
  for 1935–45 fiscal years, 556–57
  no substitute for procurement skills, 79
Appropriations Committee. *See* House Committee on Appropriations.
Approved lists, 88, 120
Aqua system, 209
ARCADIA Conference, 238

INDEX
601

ARCO, 273
Area offices, 506
Area representatives, 361. *See also* Resident representatives.
Argentina, 3
Armament, aircraft, 203, 267, 529. *See also* Ordnance Department.
Armament Branch, Materiel Division, 98
Armament dealers, 196. *See also* Neutrality legislation.
Armor, 203, 245, 269
Arms and Services, 93–94, 104, 152–53. *See also* Technical Services; *individual arms and services by name*.
Army
  air power views, 106, 174, 211, 213. *See also* Air Corps; Air power; Army Air Forces; General Staff, War Department, doctrine.
  bids versus Navy, 150. *See also* Army-Navy; Interservice rivalry.
Army Air Corps. *See* Air Corps.
Army Air Forces
  criticized, 411
  1942 procurement, 346
  organization, 475, 487, 490
  relation to ASF, 453, 477
  relation to Signal Corps, 486
  relation to SWPC, 500
  relation to USW, 478
  resist procurement assignment, 482
  retains procurement control, 479
Army cognizance, 293
Army co-operation aircraft, 54. *See also* Close-support role; Liaison aircraft.
Army depots, 400
Army Ground Forces, 241, 475
Army Industrial College, 151, 247
Army-Navy
  ANMB resolves conflicts, 258
  cognizance agreement, 293n
  contract procedures criticized, 317
  co-ordination problems, 230, 424, 442
  discussion silenced, 212
  DPC mediation role, 300
  "E" awards, 436n
  facility expansion roles, 293
  priorities problem, 260
  procurement statutes, 285
  requirements, 250, 252
  roles and missions, 212. *See also* Doctrine.
  terminations, 451
  total wartime expenditures, 556
Army-Navy-British Purchasing Commission Joint Committee, 263–67, 270–71. *See also* Air Scheduling Unit, JAC.
Army and Navy Munitions Board. *See also* Office of Assistant Secretary of War.
  mobilization role, 152, 155, 247, 252

Army and Navy Munitions Board—Continued
  organization, 151, 213, 253, 261
  priorities problems, 261–62, 258–59
Army-Navy Petroleum Board, 484
Army–Navy procurement. *See* Joint procurement.
Army Regulations
  on procurement, 94, 116–17
  on property accounting, 400
  sole source defined, 129
  on technical committees, 104
Army Service Forces, 453, 475–76, 482
Arnold, General Henry H., 112, 234, 244–45, 465. *See also* Chief of Air Corps; Commanding General, AAF.
  on aircraft ceiling, 171–73
  aircraft program, 170, 170n
  on aircraft reserve, 204n
  approves CPFF, 335
  disciplines President's critics, 205
  on expansion difficulties, 177
  50,000 program comment, 243
  JAC role, 266
  legislative tactics, 204
  mistrusts mobilization plans, 205
  and obsolescence problem, 203n
  orders conversion survey, 322
  preparedness views, 181–82
  production goals, 242
  rejects supply ministry, 272–73
  release policy, 197n, 205, 207
  seeks capacity yardstick, 185, 188, 190
  seeks negotiation authorization, 278
  separates production and engineering, 468
Arsenal of Democracy, 304
Artillery shells, 296
Artillery spotting, 45. *See also* Army co-operation aircraft; Liaison aircraft.
Aruba, 282
ASC. *See* Air Service Command.
Assembly lines
  ASU curbs stoppages, 271
  for B-24, 309, 521
  conversion of, 315
  impact of standardization, 264
  incorporating changes, 516, 530, 532, 534–35, 537. *See also* Modifications.
Assignment of claims, 288. *See also* Loans.
Assistant Chief of Air Staff, AAF, 465, 478, 573
Assistant Secretary of Navy, 88–89, 247
Assistant Secretary of War, 3–4, 118, 279, 352. *See also* Davis, D. F.; Johnson, Louis B.; Office of Assistant Secretary of War; Patterson, Robert P.; Woodring, H. H.
  ANMB role, 247
  backs sample aircraft, 133
  and bottlenecks, 248
  considers design freeze, 514
  CPFF role, 334

Assistant Secretary of War—Continued
  development role, 107
  favors proprietary rights, 88
  limits educational orders, 183
  mass production views, 519
  mobilization planning, 151, 153, 154n
  procurement assignment, 480
  Procurement Regulations role, 339
  procurement role, 93–94, 100, 128–30, 336, 474
  reaction to negotiated contracts, 129
  studies escalation, 425
Assistant Secretary of War for Air, 53, 94, 101, 241, 378, 474, 542
ASU. *See* Air Scheduling Unit, JAC.
ASW. *See* Assistant Secretary of War.
ASW (Air). *See* Assistant Secretary of War for Air.
AT–6's, 482, 551, 560, 578
AT–7's, 551, 576
AT–8's, 551, 576
AT–9's, 577
AT–10's, 576–77
AT–11's, 576
AT–16's, 578
AT–17's, 576, 581
AT–19's, 576
AT–21's, 546, 576–78, 581
Atlanta, Ga., 303, 506
Atom bomb, 547
ATSC, 471
Attachés. *See* Military attaché reports.
Attack aircraft, 64. *See also* A–20's *et seq.*
Attack bombers, 72, 275
Attorney General
  defines executive discretion, 81
  opinions on Air Corps Act, 51, 128
  procurement role, 80, 137, 147, 275, 339
  seeks statutory loopholes, 281
Attrition rate, 70, 214, 217–18, 225. *See also* Loss rates; Obsoletion, problem of; Operational losses.
Auditing
  administration of, 35n, 364, 390, 393
  contractor complaints of, 396
  data for negotiators, 344, 358
  minimizes fraud, 357, 406, 409
  Navy contracts, 126
  overhead role, 382
  for renegotiation, 431
  retroactive, 392
  subcontractors resist, 402
  terminations, 452
Auditors, 391, 396, 406, 442
Austin automobile, 165
Australia, 200
Authority for District Purchase, 507
Authority for purchase, 503
Authorization, distinguished from appropriation, 43, 61, 65

Authorized strength, 43, 48–51, 50n, 59–61, 63–75, 171–75, 206
Autogiros, 575, 578. *See also* Rotary wing aircraft.
Automatic data processing. *See* Data processing.
Automobile industry
  aircraft manufacturers influenced by, 304, 541
  aircraft production problems, 162–63, 162n, 522, 528
  aircraft role considered, 162, 290, 304–05, 314
  capacity estimates faulty, 164
  establish aircraft committee, 305
  components role, 540, 567
  conversion considered, 290, 314–15, 322
  costs per pound, 521
  CPFF salary increases, 384
  designers, 290, 306
  facilities expansion, 306, 309
  fees allowed, 377
  labor allegations, 313–14, 316
  mass-production views, 164, 529
  mobilization role, 163, 166, 539
  1937 wages, 26
  output per worker, 26–27
  Reuther Plan views, 311
  survey, 27
  tooling expenditures, 520
  World War I engines, 6. *See also* Liberty engines.
Automobile Manufacturers Association, 305
Automobile model change, 311–16
Automobile production, 26, 310, 314–15
Automotive Committee for Air Defense, 305
Autonomy for air arm, 476, 482
Autopilots, 183, 437
Aviation Engineering Center, proposed, 277
Aviation gasoline. *See* Fuel.
Aviation magazine, 184
Aviation Manufacturing Corp., 6n. *See also* Lycoming, Stinson, and Vultee Divisions *of the corporation.*
Aviation periodicals, 89–90. *See also* Magazines.
Aviation Procurement Committee, 124n
Aviation shares, 119. *See also* Aircraft industry, economic status; Aircraft industry, operating ratios; Airframe manufacturers, fear of loss; Capital investment; Stock market.
Award of contracts, 81, 115, 134–38, 279, 317, 498–500. *See also* Procurement procedures.
AWPD, 237–38
Axis air power, 195

B–10's, 117, 142, 163–64
B–15's. *See* XB–15's.
B–17's, 148, 282, 362
  costs, 20, 142, 560
  engines, 250, 580
  facilities, 302–03, 306, 309
  joint production program, 540
  modification, 529

INDEX

603

B-17's—Continued
  parts, 214, 245, 460
  performance compared, 77n, 246
  production, 550, 576–78
  production opposed, 76, 257
B-18's, 76–77, 77n, 142, 245
B-19's, 550
B-23's, 246
B-24's, 306, 309, 326–27, 416
  engines, 310, 580
  joint production program, 540
  modification, 529, 531, 535–36
  production, 550, 576–78
  unit costs, 560
  Willow Run, 494n, 519–21, 524, 526–27, 539, 545
B-25's
  engine, 580
  engineering, 528
  production, 241, 306, 308, 550, 578
  unit costs, 560
B-26's
  engine, 580
  facility expansion, 302
  modification, 534
  production, 550, 578
  production co-ordination problems, 540, 545–46
  production discussed, 241, 306, 308
  supply problems, 243
  termination problems, 366
  unit costs, 560
B-29's, 399, 415, 546–47, 553
  component parts, 156, 564, 567
  engine, 580
  facilities, 303, 308, 325
  production record, 547, 550, 576, 578
B-32's, 308, 550, 576
B-38's, 576
B-42's, 550
Backlog, 472
Bad debts, 435
Bad faith, 383
Baker Board, 56, 58–59, 159n
Baker, Newton D., 55–56
Balance sheets, bidders', 357, 363. *See also* Financial statements.
Balanced force, 174
Balanced program, 77–78
Baldwin-Southwark, 31
Ball turrets. *See* Gun turrets.
Balloons, 558
Baltimore (light bomber). *See* A-30's.
Baltimore, Md., 9, 37, 506, 540
Baltimore & Ohio R.R., 307
Bank loans. *See* Loans.
Bankers, 123, 284, 298–99
Bankruptcy
  industry fears of, 130, 150, 178, 333
  from sample aircraft, 142

Bankruptcy—Continued
  small business, 494
  from terminations, 448
Bankruptcy Act, 37
Banks. *See* Facility financing; Federal Reserve System; Loans.
Barracks, 77–78
Basic training aircraft, 551, 576–77
Battle of Britain, 232–33
BDV Committee, 541–45
Bearings, antifriction, 271n
Beaverbrook, Lord, 209, 228
Bechtel-McCone-Parsons base, 533
Beech Aircraft Corp., 293n, 302, 321, 442. *See also* AT-7's; AT-10's; AT-11's; C-45's; UC-45's.
  production, 561, 575–76
Belgium 200, 207–08, 224
Bell Aircraft Corp., 38–39, 259, 293n, 303–04, 376. *See also* B-29's; P-39's; P-63's; XFM-1's.
  B-29 role, 547
  facility expansion, 302ff., 321
  production, 245, 561, 575–76
Bell, L. L., 190
Bellanca Aircraft, 321, 576. *See also* AT-21's; C-50's.
Bendix Aviation Corp., 7–8, 8n, 449–50
Bibliography on renegotiation, 432
Bid bonds, 288
Bid summary form, 408
Bidders, 92–93, 131, 133, 197. *See also* Air Corps Act of 1926.
  inadequate number of, 142–43, 145–46, 358
Bidders lists, 492, 497–98
Bids
  contractor tactics, 108–09, 114, 138, 350
  evaluation of, 131, 133, 136–37
  preparation problems, 275–76, 492–93, 496–98
  wartime limitations, 358
Big business
  AAF dollar volume, 502
  alleged favoritism, 317, 493–95
  negotiating contracts with, 356–57, 499
  political implications, 125, 312
  renegotiation, 439
Bill of materials, 153–54, 270, 407, 521
Billing, 406
Binghamton, N.Y., 506
Birmingham, Ala., 531, 533
Birmingham (England), 165
Black, Hugo, 55n, 119, 121
Black Widow. *See* P-61's.
Blitzkrieg, 194, 211, 222–24
Block system modifications, 535, 537
BLS, 424
Blueprints, 99, 251, 305, 493, 501
  interpretation problems, 86, 361, 483, 521–22, 539, 544
Board of Contract Appeals, 371, 379

Boards of Officers, 59, 110–11. *See also* Air Corps Board; Investigations; Procurement Planning Board, Materiel Division.
Bobcat. *See* AT–8's; AT–17's; C–78's.
Boeing Aircraft Corp., 9, 293n, 575. *See also* A–20's; B–17's; B–29's; C–97's.
  contract administration, 349, 399, 540ff.
  facility expansion, 29, 299, 302, 325
  financing, 34, 38n, 40n
  production, 7, 21n, 373, 376, 547, 561, 565, 576
Boeing-Douglas-Vega Committee, 541–45
Bogey contracts, 82–83. *See also* Bonus contracts; Incentive contracts; Incentives.
"Boiler plate," 340–41, 448, 455. *See also* Contract forms.
Bomber aircraft, 117, 204n. *See also* B–10's *et seq.*; Four-engine bombers; Heavy bombers.
  armament, 156
  doctrine and use, 45, 52, 72n, 156, 210
  gross weight, 556
  modification, 537
  Navy, 576–79
  number of parts, 72, 564
  production, 553–55
  program, 64, 75, 77–78, 77n
  unit costs, 142
Bomber competition, 145
Bomber plant program, 305–08
Bombsights, 246, 483
Bonds, 36–37, 288
Bonus, 379, 385, 429. *See also* Incentives.
Bonus contracts, 417. *See also* Bogey contracts; Incentive contracts; Incentives.
Book of standards, 107
Bookkeeping, 282, 300. *See also* Accounting.
Boring mills, 259
Borrowing, 298. *See also* Emergency plant facility contracts; Loans.
Borrowing of parts, 399, 415
Bottlenecks, 160, 183, 257, 271, 292, 294. *See also* Shortages.
BPC. *See* British Purchasing Commission.
Brakes, 566
Branch plant, 399. *See also* Facility expansion.
Brand names, 314
Branshaw, Brig. Gen. C. E., 465, 471, 504–05, 509
Breakage, 342
Breaker points, 250
Breeze Manufacturing Co., 7–8, 8n
Brett, Maj. Gen. George H., 266
Brewster Aeronautical Corp., 7–8, 8n, 293n, 575–76
British Army, 208
British Commonwealth, 560
British Purchasing Commission, 200, 262, 266, 392
British Supply Council, 263, 266
British War Relief, 382
Brokers. *See* Capital investment; Middlemen.
Browning, Brig. Gen. A. J., 477–79

BT–12's, 577
BT–13's, 551, 576
BT–15's, 576
BuAer. *See* Bureau of Aeronautics.
Budd Manufacturing Co., 576
Budget
  estimates, 62, 64, 70–72, 74–75, 173, 204
  impact on requirements, 219, 221, 232ff.
  procedures, 60–61, 79, 125, 143–44, 171–74, 192
Budget and Accounting Act, 43, 173–74
Budget Director, 68–69
Budget Officer, Materiel Division, 98, 107
Buffalo, N.Y., 29, 153, 302
Buick Motor Division of General Motors, 310, 580
Bulk purchase, 512
Bullitt, William C., 169, 226
Bureau of Aeronautics, 9, 21, 59
  fears Air Corps Act amendment, 116n
  escalator clauses, 422n, 423–24
  JAC members, 266
  NDAC tie, 256
  priorities problem, 262
  sample aircraft difficulties, 142
  scout bomber contract, 85–86
Bureau of Air Commerce, 13
Bureau of Air Production, 102
Bureau of the Budget. *See also* Appropriations; Budget estimates.
  procedures, 60–61
  relations with Air Corps, 43, 60, 63–64, 69–71, 195, 215, 232, 232n
Bureau of Internal Revenue, 336, 435. *See also* Tax amortization *et seq*.
Bureau of Labor Statistics, 424
Bureau of Ordnance, 362
Burns, Maj. Gen. James H., 224–25, 231, 231n
Business machines. *See* Data processing.
Business Week, 316n
Businessmen. *See also* Big business; Small business.
  attitudes of, 271, 316n, 340, 438
  employed by AAF, 468, 505
  influence policy, 129, 169
  mobilization role, 247
Buy American Act, 90, 280, 282–83, 286
Buyers. *See* Contract negotiators; Purchasing agents.

C–32's, 136
C–43's, 551
C–45's, 551, 560, 576
C–46's, 546, 551, 577
C–47's (Douglas DC–3), 136, 551, 560, 577, 580
C–50's, 576
C–54's, 514, 551, 560, 577, 580
C–55's, 577
C–60's, 551
C–61's, 551, 577
C–64's, 551, 578
C–69's, 551, 578

INDEX 605

C-78's, 551, 576
C-82's, 577
C-87's, 551, 576
C-97's, 576
C-117's, 551
CAA, 13
CAB, 13-14
California, 299, 299n, 387-88
California Institute of Technology, 256
Canada, 199-200, 201n, 213, 229, 399
Canadian Car Co., 576
Canadian Propellers, Ltd., 563
Cancellations. *See* Termination.
Cannibalization, 240
Capacity. *See* Production capacity.
Capital. *See* Capital investment; Defense Plant Corporation; Facility financing; Financing; Working capital.
Capital assets, 398
Capital investment. *See also* Bonds; Stock market.
   in aircraft industry, 36-40
   Bendix, 450
   CPFF problem, 411, 413
   evaluation of, 22, 111, 141-42, 333, 373, 448. *See also* Airframe manufacturers, fear of loss; Bankruptcy; Losses by contractors; Risk taking.
   in facilities, 29, 70, 292, 322, 563. *See also* Facility financing.
   foreign order impact, 200-201
   influences subcontracting, 182
   per worker, 26
   in production tools, 31-33. *See also* Production tooling.
   for research and development, 21
   return, 34, 376. *See also* Aircraft industry, economic status; Airframe manufacturers, financial condition; Profits.
   small business problem, 502
   sources of, 33, 125, 179, 184
   World War I profits on, 83
Capital reserves, 435. *See also* Cash reserves.
Carburetors, 183, 294
Career officers, 212. *See also* Regular Army officers.
Cargo aircraft, 514, 537. *See also* C-32's *et seq.*; Transport aircraft.
Case, J. L., 540
Case histories, 389
Case law, 374
Cash and carry neutrality law, 196, 201n
Cash reserves, 299. *See also* Capital reserves.
Castings, 180, 250, 264
Catalogues, 408, 458. *See also* Mail-order catalogue parts supplier.
Cave, W. S., Col., 270n
Ceiling on aircraft strength. *See* Authorized strength.
Censorship, 382. *See also* Witnesses.
Central Procurement District, 443, 458, 491

Centralization. *See also* Decentralization.
   of procurement, 462, 489, 493
   of production control, 273
   of renegotiation, 430
   of termination policy, 453
Certificates of exemption, 388
Certificates of necessity, 336
Certification of facility costs, 297-98, 300
Certified public accountants, 360
Cessna Aircraft Division of United Aircraft, 293n, 561, 576. *See also* AT-8's; AT-17's; C-78's.
Chaco war, 196n
Chance-Vought Division of United Aircraft Corp., 22, 561
Change notifications. *See* Engineering change notifications.
Change orders, 99, 146, 366. *See also* Amendment of contracts.
   potential abuse, 108-09, 303
   rectify errors, 140
   termination agreements, 452
Chemical Warfare Service, 476
Chemidlin, Capt. Paul, 199
Chevrolet Division of GMC, 26, 580
Cheyenne, Wyo., 530, 533
Chicago, Ill., 153, 310, 459, 506
Chief of Air Corps. *See also* Arnold, General Henry H.; Foulois, Maj. Gen. Benjamin D.; Westover, Maj. Gen. Oscar.
   air arm strength role, 52, 55, 62, 70, 74, 78-79, 120, 124, 171, 173-74, 173n, 245
   alleged misconduct, 127
   criticizes relief funds, 67
   fears loss of discretion, 116
   GHQ Air Force role, 102
   Materiel Division relations, 463
   minimizes design changes, 514
   mobilization planning, 153, 162, 166, 177, 179, 181ff., 259
   political problems, 57-58, 68-69
   procurement role, 94, 97, 100, 107, 138-39, 542
   resists escalator clauses, 422-23
   responsibilities of, 182, 210
   statistical tools, 192n
   urges procurement changes, 51-52, 142
   uses negotiated production contracts, 129
   views transport case, 136
Chief of Air Service, 44
Chief of Air Staff, 516
Chief of Contract Section, Materiel Command, 345, 401, 403-04, 412, 425, 447, 503
Chief of Materiel Command, 242
Chief of Materiel Division, 100-03, 239, 303, 422, 463, 471
Chief of Procurement Division, Materiel Command, 352
Chief of Production Division, Materiel Command, 537, 542

Chief of Purchases Division, ASF, 477
Chief of Staff. *See also* Craig, General Malin; MacArthur, General Douglas; Marshall, General George C.
  air power views, 3, 62n, 66, 171, 176, 211
  controls GHQ Air Force, 102
  on political maneuvering, 57–58
  procurement role, 93, 146
  relations with Arnold, 474
  relations with ASW (Air), 53, 53n, 101
  relations with USW, 475
  requirements role, 93, 217, 220
Chief of Supply Division, OCAC, 103
Chiefs of Arms and Services, procurement operations, 93
China, 19, 196, 217, 560
Chokepoints. *See* Bottlenecks; Shortages.
Christmas Island, 213
Chrome plating, 523
Chrysler Corp., 312, 377
  B-26 role, 308, 540, 546
  B-29 role, 547
  Dodge engine facility, 321, 580
Churchill, Winston S., 223–24, 233, 238
Cincinnati, Ohio, 9, 320
CIO, 310. *See also* Unions.
Circular proposals. *See also* Advertising for bids; Bidders; Bids; Defense Contract Service; Invitations to bid.
  difficulties in drafting, 140
  distribution problems, 492
  few responses to, 141–42, 145
  manufacturers' tactics on, 108–09
  procedures, 80, 89–90, 99, 113, 130–31
  wartime use, 358
Civil Aeronautics Authority, 13
Civil Aeronautics Board, 13–14
Civil Service, 104, 125, 285n, 345–46, 393, 558. *See also* Civilian personnel.
Civilian aircraft, 8–9, 11, 20, 126, 575. *See also* Airlines; Cargo aircraft.
Civilian control, 247, 462. *See also* Civilian superagency.
Civilian personnel, 106, 147, 158, 261n, 354. *See also* Civil Service.
  in district offices, 503, 506
  fraud, 355
  in Materiel Command, 270, 345, 350, 360, 466, 559
  shortages, 505
  wages and salaries, 558–59
Civilian requirements, 152, 317
Civilian superagency, 155, 322, 481, 495–96. *See also* National Defense Advisory Commission; Office of Production Management; War Production Board; War Resources Administration.
  abortive organization, 247–49
  liaison problems, 192
  need for, 251–55, 262, 265

Claimant agencies, 247
Claims, 124, 393
Clark, Bennett Champ, 199
Classified data, 473. *See also* Secrecy; Security classification.
Clearance Committee, ANMB, 252
Cleveland, Ohio, 153
Cleveland Pneumatic Tool Co., 7–8, 8n, 318–319
Climate. *See* Weather, influence of.
Close Pricing
  by escalation, 423
  illustrated, 363
  methods, 358–59
  objectives, 431, 440
  problems, 343, 414, 418, 428
  by repricing, 441
Close-support role, 45, 52, 157. *See also* "Air service", concept of; Army co-operation aircraft.
Clothing, 250, 470, 484
Coastal defense, 211, 213
Code law, 374
Coercion. *See also* Compulsory directives; Mandatory orders; Plant seizure.
  for administrative convenience, 338n
  emergency legislation for, 287
  in renegotiation, 431–32
  by SWPC, 500–501
Coffin, Howard, 87–88
Cognizance agreement, 293, 293n, 561. *See also* Acceptances of aircraft; Allocation of industrial capacity; Army-Navy; Cross procurement.
Cold war, 281, 283
Collector rings, 7, 183
Collusion, 110–11, 390. *See also* Fraud.
Color plans, 53, 95. *See also* RAINBOW plan.
Columbia Aircraft, 576
Combined versus joint, 266n
Collective bargaining, 426. *See also* Unions.
Command. *See also* Discretionary powers.
  analysis of, 272, 424, 480, 518, 571
  centralization and decentralization, 509–10, 509n, 573
  organizational problems, 243, 268, 471. *See also* Organization.
  personal factors, 352
  political restraints on, 316
  procurement problems, 397, 408, 410, 455, 512, 538
  relation to doctrine, 212
  tools for, 450, 472–73, 572
Command post exercises, 167
Commandeering. *See* Plant seizure.
Commander in Chief, 213. *See also* President of the United States; *Presidents by name*.
Commanding General, AAF, 453, 465
Commanding General, ASF, 477
Commanding General, Materiel Command, 352, 465, 471, 478
Commando. *See* C-46's.

INDEX

607

Commercial carriers. *See* Airlines.
Commercial items, procurement of, 358, 381, 392, 507. *See also* Open market procurement.
Commissioner of Internal Revenue, 285
Committee on Appropriations. *See* House Committee on Appropriations; Senate Committee on Appropriations.
Committee on Military Affairs. *See* House Committee on Military Affairs; Senate Committee on Military Affairs.
Commodities Division, OASW, 247
Common items, 481
Communications. *See* Signal Corps.
Communications aircraft, 551. *See also* L series and R series of aircraft; Liaison aircraft; Rotary wing aircraft.
Communications equipment, 72, 267, 529
Company pricing, 442–43
Company-wide termination, 458
Comparative prices, 359
Compensation. *See* Excess profits; Fees; Fixed fees; Profits; Salaries; Wages.
Competitive bidding
  below cost, 114–15
  contractor purchasing without, 406
  incompatible with relief, 67–68
  influenced by accounting, 35
  lack of bidders, 145. *See also* Circular proposals.
  opposed, 88–89
  permitted, 358
  uncertainty on requirement, 92–93
Competitive economy, 316
Competitive procurement
  abandoned, 123, 343
  administrative alternatives, 374
  adverse effects of, 85, 142–43
  in aircraft industry, 185
  circumvention of, 285
  compensating losers, 143–46
  cross procurement role, 483
  difficulties of administering, 130, 138, 140, 274
  equity in, 140
  evaluation problem, 111, 141
  favored, 80–81, 84, 124, 127–28, 148, 277–78
  from foreign orders, 202–03
  impact of renegotiation, 431
  indirectly achieved, 127
  inhibits cost disclosures, 436
  interservice, 272. *See also* Army-Navy; Interservice rivalry.
  merits of, 146–47
  in 1940 emergency, 280
  reconciling price and performance, 130–31, 135
  sometimes impractical, 81, 84–85, 91, 116, 274
  in wartime, 358–59
Competitors, provision for appeals, 90
Complaints, 94, 281, 380, 493. *See also* Appeals; Criticism.

Components. *See also* Accessories.
  in B-24's, 521
  delay production, 530
  educational orders for, 160
  Ford supplier role, 519
  manufacture of, 6–7, 9
  number per aircraft, 564
  scheduling problems, 257, 259, 264, 266–67, 270, 271n. *See also* Materials; Parts; Raw materials; Spare parts.
Comptroller General. *See also* General Accounting Office.
  capacity for delay, 138
  centralized operations, 394–95
  corporate seal ruling, 332
  CPFF conversion views, 414
  criticizes procurement procedures, 118, 128, 134–37
  curbed in terminations, 452
  defines executive discretion, 81. *See also* Discretionary powers.
  disallowances, 329, 383, 393. *See also* Allowable costs; Disallowances.
  Eight-Hour ruling, 281
  favors supervised contracts, 409
  influences procurement regulations, 339
  independence, 383
  mutual mistake role, 366
  procurement role, 147
  on proprietary rights, 89n
  rules on fees, 376
Compulsory directives, 271, 444. *See also* Mandatory orders.
Concurrent delivery, 342
Concurrent procurement, 294, 470
Conferences, 181ff., 238. *See also* White House conference.
Confiscation, 435. *See also* Plant seizure.
Congress
  air arm strength role, 43, 45, 51, 78, 172
  Air Corps Act views, 92, 116, 127–28
  Air Corps liaison, 105, 119, 144
  Air Mail Act, 15
  appropriations impounded, 128
  authorizes plant seizure, 443
  authorizes priorities, 258
  authorizes wide discretion, 289
  CPFF views, 284, 412, 419
  delays defense, 64, 71, 75, 79, 175, 179, 235, 301
  defense responsibilities, 3, 5, 43, 62, 130
  economy minded, 52, 66, 73–74, 195, 202, 204
  educational order role, 159–60, 183
  establishes CAA and CAB, 13
  establishes NACA, 23
  expansion programs, 179–80, 194, 243
  facility financing, 297, 301, 304
  favors aircraft over facilities, 50, 77–78
  favors quantity versus quality, 64–65
  fraud problem, 121, 355, 357

Congress—Continued
  impact on procurement, 88–89, 118, 120–21, 133, 136, 495, 570
  manufacturing by government, 125
  neutrality legislation, 196, 201, 201n
  opposes negotiated contracts, 277
  procurement views change, 148, 283
  proposes aviation center, 277
  relation to Executive, 68, 74, 78, 91, 131, 137, 169–71, 276
  renegotiation problem, 430–31, 438
  secrecy legislation, 197. *See also* Release policy; Secrecy; Security classification.
  small business problem, 498, 500
  social legislation, 72, 281, 389n
  sources of information, 55, 57–59, 62–63. *See also* Congressional investigations; Investigations.
  spare engine policy, 215
  split awards views, 280
  termination legislation, 452
  views on emergency, 229–30, 280
  views on profits, 418, 429
Congressional appropriations. *See* Appropriations.
Congressional authorization, 43, 61, 65. *See also* Authorized strength.
Congressional investigations, 107–08, 111, 118–24. *See also* Investigations; Lampert Committee; Rogers Committee; Truman Committee.
Congressional Record, 122
Connally, Tom, 287
Consolidated Aircraft Corp. (Consolidated-Vultee), 293n, 575. *See also* A–31's; A–35's; AT–19's; B–24's; B–32's; B–38's; BT–13's; BT–15's; C–87's; L–5's.
  criticized, 539
  facilities, 10, 29, 309, 326
  finances, 38n, 40n
  Ford collaboration, 521–22
  joint production program, 540
  production record, 21n, 561, 565, 576
  Reuben H. Fleet's role, 144
Constellation. *See* C–69's.
Constitutional law, 389
Construction contracts, 411
Continental Motors Corp., 6n, 293n, 580–81
Continental U.S., 52–53, 213. *See also* Hemisphere defense.
Contingency allowances
  impair CPFF conversion, 414
  pad fixed-price contracts, 418, 422. *See also* Umbrella pricing.
  policy liberalized, 323
  sought by manufacturers, 428, 442
  in termination, 450
Continuity of orders, 67, 87
Contraband, 199
Contract administration, 364; 368ff., 491, 509

Contract Administration Branch, Materiel Division, 98
Contract amendments. *See* Change orders.
Contract Audit Section, 430
Contract audits. *See* Auditing.
Contract authorization, 73
Contract awards. *See* Award of contracts; Procurement procedures.
Contract cancellation. *See* Termination.
Contract carriers. *See* Airlines.
Contract changes. *See* Change orders.
Contract clearance, 495–96, 499
Contract Compliance Unit, 470
Contract distribution, 499
Contract Distribution Division, 496n. *See also* Allocation of contracts; Defense Contract Service.
Contract files, Procurement Division, Materiel Command, 472
Contract follow-up, 470
Contract forms. *See also* Form 32.
  boiler plate clauses, 340
  British experience, 165
  for CPFF, 334–36, 389
  data purchase clause, 186
  deviations, 340, 478
  disputes clause, 370
  formulation of, 330, 409, 419, 474
  selection of, 344
  simplify negotiation, 339
  standard, 365
  termination clauses, 446
  World War I, 150
Contract negotiation
  abandoned by districts, 509
  alleged laxity in, 126
  audit data used, 390, 395
  business fears, 340
  co-ordination with renegotiation, 430
  delays, 71, 73, 109, 350
  described, 112n, 339, 343, 350, 355
  with letter of intent, 338
  literature lacking, 461
  procedures, 107, 347, 353–55, 358, 509. *See also* Procurement procedures.
  spare parts problem, 342
  specialists for, 104, 353–54. *See also* Contract negotiators; Contracting officers.
  wartime volume, 346
  Wright Field advantages, 491
Contract negotiators. *See also* Contracting officers.
  allowable costs problem, 379
  anticipate problems, 409
  bargaining position, 423–24
  conflict with termination, 453
  educate businessmen, 363
  effectiveness, 357, 442
  escalation, 423, 427

INDEX

Contract negotiators—Continued
fee views, 376
incentive payments, 426
minimize nonmilitary ends, 455
morale, 355
need for data, 345, 348, 357, 418
prewar experience, 345
profits allowed, 375
shortage, 337, 344, 416, 494, 559
specialization introduced, 347–48
statistical tools, 192
training of, 344, 346
verification methods, 362
Contract placement, 482. *See also* Allocation of contracts; Cross procurement.
Contract Section, Wright Field
circular proposal problems, 492
cost analysis role, 429
CPFF conversion, 412
fee problem, 378
operations, 462
organization, 345–47, 349, 473
Contract Settlement Act, termination statute, 452
Contract status report, 508
Contract termination. *See* Termination.
Contracting officers. *See also* Contract negotiators; Procurement officers.
alleged violations of, 123
approves costs, 379
basis of evaluation, 495
bid bond waivers, 288
Buy American problems, 283
criticized, 87, 491n, 494
delayed by industry, 301
difficulties, 354–55, 367, 369–70, 382, 409
encounter shortages, 250
favor negotiated contract, 117–18
fear political criticism, 81, 115, 332
monitor contractor purchasing, 403–05
need for information, 507
on negotiating team, 354
overhead problem, 382
reconciling price and performance, 130
relations with GAO, 396
require production options, 127
reversal of rulings, 383
scope of discretion, 80–81, 88–89, 289, 352, 385, 499–500. *See also* Discretionary powers.
seek loopholes, 275
skills required, 409
small business views, 502
status and role, 353, 364–65, 368, 389
use Naval Aircraft Factory costs, 125
verbal rulings, 391
Contracting procedures. *See* Procurement procedures.
Contracting regulations. *See* Procurement Regulations.

Contractors. *See also* Participating prime contractors; Prime contractors; Subcontractors.
accountability threatened, 388
adjustment of compensation, 108–09. *See also* Renegotiation.
auditing, 391
bidding tactics, 108–09, 317, 469
criticize procurement procedures, 492–93
decision-making role, 409
disallowance of costs, 383
disclosures required, 357
excise tax problem, 387
facilities role, 297–98, 328
fear inventory problems, 457
financial statements, 440
inadequate business methods, 363, 406, 416
joint production program, 540, 547
losses on contracts, 114
need for education, 377
negotiations scheduled, 337
priority conflicts, 258
procurement procedures monitored, 360, 403–05, 407
profits allowed, 122, 375, 385n
relations with subcontractors, 447
renegotiation views, 435, 439
reports required, 282, 349
respect for law, 332
responsibilities, 402, 405, 408
schedules unreliable, 187
statutory limitations on, 281
terminations, 448, 452, 454
Contracts. *See also* Amendment of contracts; *by type of contract*.
administrative alternatives to, 543
advance preparation of, 175
allocation of costs, 362
amendment of, 366–67
by big business, 493–94
civilian agency evaluation, 495
commingling of, 398
co-ordination of, 350ff.
correspondence files, 99, 472
delays, 297, 301, 315, 332, 353
delegation of approval, 478
distribution by size, 491n
for district negotiation, 504
drawn by Procurement Section, 99
EPF, 298–99
experience not extracted, 389
final settlement delayed, 427
for 50,000 program, 243
Ford B–24 series, 526
impact of, 246
inadequate provisions, 207
independent GAO review, 383
interpretation of, 331
maldistribution of, 277

Contracts—Continued
  modification authorized, 284. *See also* Change orders.
  monthly average negotiation, 346
  negotiations summarized, 337
  philosophy of, 408–09
  processing speeded, 331–32
  rate of revision, 367–68
  renegotiation clause, 429
  small business volume, 492
  split awards, 498
  status record, 472
  by SWPC, 500
  Treasury co-ordination of, 253
  in World War I, 446
Contributions, 383
"Contributory items," 156
Control, distinguished from operations, 510. *See also* Command.
Control units, administrative, 472
Conventions, political, 253
Conversion of CPFF contracts, 412, 414–15
Conversion of facilities. *See also* Facility expansion; Mobilization, facility policy; Mobilization planning.
  Air Corps policy, 319
  by automobile industry, 309
  conversion versus construction, 326, 328
  costs appraised, 327
  delays, 321, 325–26
  difficulties, 319, 322
  enforced by WPB, 323
  inadequate planning for, 163–66, 321
  inadequately emphasized, 317, 320
  machine tool, impact on, 328
  in mobilization, 161
  obstacles to, 315
  policy revised, 290, 323
  priorities control of, 322
  secures military orders, 493
  by small business, 316
Conveyors, 521
Coolidge, Calvin, 46
Co-operation by contractors, 538ff., 542, 546. *See also* Interplant borrowing.
Co-ordinating agency, abortive, 124n
Co-ordinating committees, production control role, 538ff.
Co-ordination. *See also* Army and Navy Munitions Board; Joint Army and Navy Board; Liaison.
  AAF directorate role, 465
  Air Corps emphasis on, 107–08
  aircraft exports, 252–53
  Army-Navy failure, 424
  of audits, 391
  Curtiss policy, 562
  by informal methods, 471, 473
  inhibited by decentralization, 491–92, 504–05, 509

Co-ordination—Continued
  in mobilization, 254, 262–63
  of modifications, 534
  organization for, 265, 472
  in procurement, 101, 109, 350ff., 467ff., 480, 484. *See also* Cross procurement.
  Signal Corps–AAF, 486
  users and suppliers, 102
Cornell. *See* PT-19's; PT-23's; PT-26's.
Corporate Profit Unit, 348
Corporate seal, 332
Corps of Engineers, 296
Correspondence, 471, 473, 492
Corruption. *See* Fraud.
Cost accounting, 416–17. *See also* Accounting.
Cost in relation to performance, 130
Cost analysis
  District field studies, 509
  faulty, 433
  illustrated, 363–64
  by Navy, 86
  problems involved, 298, 344–45
  for renegotiation, 429–31
  required by negotiators, 357–60
Cost Analysis Branch, 348, 429
Cost estimates, 114, 360–64
Cost-plus-fixed-fee (CPFF) contracts
  accounting, 393
  administrative instructions, 409
  authorized, 285, 334
  conversion to fixed price, 412, 414–15
  criticized, 335–36, 372, 411
  drawbacks, 373, 410
  evaluation, 373, 410, 418–19
  fee reduced, 288
  first written, 335
  forms, 334, 339
  history lost, 389
  influenced by escalation, 427
  for modifications, 532, 537
  problems raised, 336
  savings effected, 364
  termination policy, 455
  use limited, 334, 418
Cost-plus-percentage of-cost (CPPC) contracts
  accidentally employed, 406, 441
  confused with CPFF, 412
  defined, 82
  discredited, 83–84
  prohibited, 284, 372
Cost-plus principle, 82, 372
Costs. *See also* Allowable costs; Cost accounting; Cost analysis; Unit costs.
  bids below, 114
  bombers, 141–42
  civilian aircraft, 20
  in CPPC contracts, 82
  estimating, 343–44, 413, 427, 431

INDEX

611

Costs—Continued
  of facility expansions, 298
  foreign order impact, 204–05
  of GFE, 132
  gliders, 373
  impact of inflation, 303
  increased by subsidies, 146
  increases cut procurement, 128
  influence capacity yardstick, 189–90
  influence President, 170–71
  mass production economies, 560
  of modification, 532, 534
  per airframe pound, 521, 527
  as procurement objective, 330
  relation to profits, 364n, 418, 445
  statistical tools for, 192
  yardsticks, 125, 277
Council of National Defense, 82n, 254. *See also* National Defense Advisory Commission.
Courier service, 331
Court of Claims, 446, 448. *See also* Federal courts.
Court rulings. *See* Judicial decisions.
CPFF. *See* Cost-plus-fixed-fee contracts.
CPPC. *See* Cost-plus-percentage-of-cost contracts.
Craig, General Malin, 3, 57, 171–73, 199
Cranes, 520, 524
Crankcases, 250
Crashes, 121
Credit, 18. *See also* Loans.
Credit rating, 502
Crew exhaustion, 218
Criminal action, 433. *See also* Department of Justice.
Critical raw materials, 319. *See also* Materials; Priorities; Raw materials; Shortages.
Criticism. *See also* Complaints.
  of auto manufacturers, 178
  of centralized procurement, 492
  Materiel Command reaction to, 501
  of military procurement, 495, 502
  procurement leaders risk, 352
Cross procurement, 480–85, 552. *See also* Joint procurement; Joint production programs.
CS-2's (Curtiss scout-bombers), 85–86
Culver Aircraft Corp., 575–76
Current ratio in aircraft industry, 39–41
Curtiss Aeroplane and Motor Co., 85
Curtiss Electric Division of Curtiss-Wright, 562–63
Curtiss-Wright Corp., 7–8, 8n, 190, 256, 293n, 575. *See also* A-25's; AT-9's; C-46's; CS-2's; P-40's; P-47's.
  Condor transport, 15
  CPFF conversion, 415
  delayed by shortages, 180–81
  engine profits, 33
  facility expansion, 29, 302, 320–21
  finances, 37–39
  neutrality violations, 196n
  policy evaluated, 562

Curtiss-Wright Corp.—Continued
  production record, 7, 21n, 561, 577
  subcontractors and suppliers, 404
  transport bid, 134
Cutting Tools Warehouse, 459–60
Cyclone engine, 580. *See also* Wright Aeronautical Corp.
Dallas, Texas, 302, 539. *See also* North American Aviation Corp.
Data contracts, 186–87
Data processing, 32, 261, 271, 473, 535. *See also* Information processing.
Dauntless. *See* A-24's.
Davis, D. F., 46, 88
Dayton, Ohio, 177, 562. *See also* Wright Field, Dayton, Ohio.
"Dayton lobby," 491n
Dayton-Wright Airplane Co., 83
DC-2's, 136
DC-3's. *See* C-47's.
Dealers, automobile, 314
Decentralization
  of operations, 273, 395
  of procurement, 462, 489, 491, 503–05, 507–08, 509n, 573
  of renegoiation, 430
  of termination, 453
Decision making. *See also* Contract negotiation; Contracting officers; Delegation of authority; Discretionary powers; Leadership; Procurement procedures.
  organizations for, 265, 268, 272–73, 573
  in procurement, 352, 571
  in production engineering, 468, 516, 544, 547
  requires information, 572, 518
Decisions. *See* Judicial decisions.
Defaulting contractors, 365, 365n, 447. *See also* Bankruptcy; Losses by contractors.
Defense Act of 1916. *See* National Defense Act of 1916.
Defense Act of 1920. *See* National Defense Act of 1920.
Defense Aid contract, 267, 399
Defense Contract Service, 496–98, 503
Defense contracts, 285, 317
Defense Plant Corporation, 284, 299–301, 303, 315, 323, 520
Defense policy. *See* Doctrine.
Deferred delivery, 207
Deferred development charges, 34–36
DeHaviland Aircraft of Canada, 577. *See also* PT-24's.
Delaney, John J., 121
Delaney Committee, 122–23
Delays, 71, 150, 240, 313, 365, 509, 516
Delegation of authority, 272, 351–52, 572
Deliveries, 71, 240, 330, 361, 426, 494
  advantage in deferring, 201–03

Deliveries—Continued
  of aluminum forgings, 251
  influence contract negotiation, 317, 435, 499
  influence facility policy, 301, 320
  mobilization role, 157, 251, 269
  modifications impact, 532, 537
  1940–45 aircraft, 552–54. *See also* Acceptances of aircraft.
  procurement yardstick, 495
Delivery schedules, 244, 362, 365, 469, 520
Delivery scheduling, 240, 251, 266, 270. *See also* Air Scheduling Unit, JAC.
Denver, Colo., 177
Department of Air, proposed, 59
Department of Commerce, 13, 222, 422
Department of Defense, proposed, 124–25
Department of Justice, 84, 402, 433
Department of Labor, 94, 422
Department of State, 196
Depots, 50, 77–78, 215
Depot repair, 322
Depreciation, 125, 285, 289, 296, 435
Depression
  imposes economies, 10, 65–66, 384
  influences attitudes, 41, 129, 178, 184, 291
Deputy Chief of Air Staff, 241
Deputy Chief of Staff for Air, 474
Dern, George H., 56–57, 59–60, 210
"Desert proofing," 534
Design. *See also* Aircraft design.
  financing, 85–86
  NDAC influence, 257n
  specification problem, 86, 132, 138, 140
  standardization, 264, 266
  time lag, 108
Design changes, 16ff. *See also* Design freeze.
  affect market, 10, 17
  affect obsoletion policy, 51
  complicate contract administration, 25–26, 319, 365, 413, 448
  complicate cross procurement, 483
  excessive numbers of, 240, 516–17
  favor centralized procurement, 491–92
  foreign impact, 203
  impact on costs, 20, 36, 40–41, 72, 75–76
  impact on labor, 362
  mobilization impact, 156, 207
  prevent contract comparison, 419
  production problems, 32, 251, 468, 512, 522–23, 547
  require organization, 572
  spare parts problem, 342
Design competitions
  administration of, 104, 106, 108
  advocated, 91–92, 124
  Navy, 85–86
  procedures outlined, 89–90
  tried and abandoned, 113–14, 139–40
  used in emergency, 275–76

Design data, 145–46. *See also* Data contracts.
Design engineers, 163. *See also* Design staffs.
Design freeze
  illustrated, 242, 516, 518–19, 525
  problem discussed, 137, 166–67, 187, 512–14, 513n
Design prime contractors, 543–46
Design rights, 85, 87, 166, 444. *See also* Proprietary designs.
Design stabilization. *See* Design freeze.
Design staffs, 88, 139. *See also* Design engineers.
Designers. *See* Aircraft designers; Engineers.
Detroit, Mich., 9, 290, 323, 519
  aircraft role, 304ff., 519
  Procurement District, 153, 491
Detroit tool case, 458ff.
Development. *See* Research and development.
Development project, 106
Developmental engineering, 468
Deviations, 478, 544
Die forming, 30–31, 521
Die-sinkers, 251, 523
Die steel, 250
Dies, 251, 398, 523
Direct labor. *See* Labor.
Director of Military Requirements, 241–42
Directorates, 465, 487
Directory of Allocated and Reserved Facilities, 152
Disallowances. *See also* Allowable costs.
  in terminations, 448, 452
  Treasury guide, 380
  under CPFF, 380, 388, 394–95, 414
Discounts, 360, 406n, 407
Discretionary fund, 78
Discretionary powers. *See also* Command; Comptroller General; Decision making; Executive discretion; Leadership.
  Congress grants, 111, 113, 285–86, 289
  fiscal limitations, 78
  proposed enlargement, 276–87
  require skill and courage, 84, 115, 286, 571
Discrimination, 317
Dishonesty. *See* Fraud.
Dispersal, 328, 455. *See also* Site selection; Strategic dispersal.
Disputes
  between divisions, 469
  in contract administration, 370, 379, 383, 448
  JAC role, 266
Distribution pipeline, 216–17, 222
District representatives. *See* Procurement Planning District representatives; Resident representatives.
District Supervisor, 465
Dive bombers, 142, 239
Dividends, 34, 436. *See also* Profits.
Division of Military Aeronautics, 102
Dockweiler, John F., 59n

INDEX

Doctrine
  advanced by Douhet, 45
  air arm, 4–5, 52–54, 101–02, 157, 237. See also Procurement doctrine.
  Air Corps Board role, 95
  on centralized command, 573
  difficulties in formulating, 210–12, 233
  influences requirements, 106, 156, 210, 217, 232–33
  on mobilization, 265
Dodge Division, Chrysler Corp., 321, 580
Doehler Die Casting Co., 435
Dollar volume yardstick, 189–90. See also Yardstick, for productive capacity.
Dominator. See B-32's.
Donations, 383
Douglas Aircraft Corp., 199, 201, 241, 293n, 575. See also A-20's; A-24's; A-26's; B-17's; B-24's; C-47's; C-54's; P-70's.
  B-18 costs, 142
  contract administration, 378n, 393, 393n
  facility expansion, 9, 299n, 309, 321
  finances, 38n, 40n
  production, 21n, 540, 561, 577
  production problems, 264, 315, 362, 519
  relation to Boeing, 540–41, 543, 546
  transports, 15–17, 134, 136–37, 514
Douglas *Airview*, 382
Douhet, Giulio, 45
DPC. See Defense Plant Corporation.
Draft boards, 416
Draftees, 384
Draftsmen, 522
Drawings. See Blueprints.
Drop hammers, 521, 568
Drum, Maj. Gen. Hugh A., 53, 56
Drum Board, 53–56, 58, 119
Dunkerque, 208
Duplication of effort, 86, 103–04, 468, 471, 480–81, 485. See also Army-Navy; Cross procurement.
Durable goods index, 424–25. See also Bureau of Labor Statistics.

E-6's, 578
Earnings. See Profits.
Eastern Aircraft Division of GMC, 561, 577
Eastern Procurement District, 491, 506, 508
Echols, Maj. Gen. Oliver P., 167n, 464–65, 478–79
Economic controls. See Army and Navy Munitions Board; National Defense Advisory Commission; Office of Production Management; War Production Board.
Economic czar, 247
Economic dislocation, 315, 435, 452
Economic feasibility, 232
Economic mobilization, 313, 316. See also Mobilization planning.
Economic planning, 150ff.
Economy Board, 213

Economy drives, 65–67, 73, 124–25, 128, 175
Economy-mindedness, 181n
Edison, Charles, 224
Educational orders
  data contracts, 291
  exports replace, 195
  faulty application, 159–60, 183
  Ford B-24, 520, 526
  need for, 152–53, 183
Efficiency. See also Labor, productivity; Productivity.
  of centralized procurement, 492
  contractor negotiation role, 364, 418, 421, 443, 445
  in labor utilization, 362
  production ratios, 564
Eight-Hour Law, 280–81
1,800 aircraft program, 49, 51, 53, 66, 71, 128. See also Air Corps Act of 1926; Five Year Program.
El Paso, Texas, 530
Elections, 194, 203n, 265
Electric power, 150, 247–48, 308
Electrical equipment, 156, 271. See also Fractional horsepower motors.
Electrical equipment manufacturers, 566–67
Electronics, 486. See also Communications equipment; Radios; Signal Corps.
Elyria, Ohio, 460
Embargo. See Neutrality legislation.
Emergency facilities. See Facility expansions.
Emergency plant facility contracts, 298–99, 302
"Emergency" procurement, 275
Emerson Electric, 378
Empennage, 564
Employees, 281, 467. See also Civil Service; Labor.
Employment. See also Labor.
  aircraft and automobile industry, 27
  factors influencing, 7, 200–201
  insurance rating, 386
  as procurement objective, 330
  reports on, 181, 187, 282
Engine accessories, 271
Engine change, 110
Engine instruments, 567
Engine manufacturers, 6–8, 123, 186–87, 281, 293n, 312. See also Engine production.
  contract negotiations, 336, 355, 561
  educational orders, 183
  export sales, 19, 200, 205
  facility expansions, 184, 201, 302, 309, 320–21, 324
  floor space, 294–95
  productivity, 564–65
  profits, 35–36, 36n, 120, 126
Engine overhaul, 215–16. See also Engine change; Maintenance.
Engine production, 292, 381, 392, 580. See also Engines, acceptances.
  factors influencing, 16, 27–28
  1929–37, 7, 20
  peak monthly output, 565

Engine production—Continued
  World War I, 6
Engine production scheduling, 267. *See also* Air Scheduling Unit, JAC.
Engineering change notifications, 99, 366, 539–40, 543. *See also* Change orders.
Engineering Division, 358, 361, 466–67, 486
Engineering drawing releases, 521, 541
Engineering drawings, 554. *See also* Blueprints.
Engineering information, 543
Engineering and Research Corp., 577
Engineering Section, Materiel Division, 97–98, 106ff.
Engineering versus production, 513
Engineers, 186, 188, 361, 456, 545. *See also* Aircraft designers; Corps of Engineers; Design staffs.
Engines, 309–10, 458. *See also individual engines by number and manufacturers by name.*
  acceptances, 548–59. *See also* Deliveries.
  aluminum needs studied, 257
  costs, 20, 83, 142
  critical shortages, 250
  Cyclone, 580
  four-engine bombers, 302–03, 519
  horsepower, 16, 20, 580–82
  in-line, 309, 565
  indirect competition, 127
  jets, 456, 562
  Liberty's, 64, 83
  liquid cooled, 309, 565
  Merlin, 309, 580
  mounting methods, 524
  Packard-Rolls Royce, 301
  production data, 580–82
  spare, 74, 215–16
  spare parts, 215
  special tools, 485
  World War I, 64
England. *See* United Kingdom.
Englewood, Calif., 302
Enlisted men, 466
EPF. *See* Emergency plant facility contracts.
Equipment Branch, Materiel Division, 98
Equity
  in contract procedures, 335, 377, 385, 509
  in escalation, 425
  for small business, 494
  in terminations, 451
Equity capital. *See* Capital investment.
Escalator clauses
  repricing as alternative, 442
  sought by contractors, 332, 421
  use of, 423–25, 427
Escape kits, 470
Espionage Act, 197
Estimates, 361. *See also* Appropriations, administration of; Budget, estimates.
Estimators, 360–61

Ethiopia, 196
Europe, 18. *See also* Exports.
Evaluation procedures, 90, 108–12, 110n, 114, 131, 133–38, 140, 146
Exceptions to contracting requirements, 80–81. *See also* Disallowances.
Excess profits. *See also* Profits, statutory curbs.
  attitudes on, 83, 277
  causes, 428
  contract negotiation problem, 330, 348, 380, 384, 422
  induce voluntary refunds, 428
  problem of definition, 431–32, 434
  offset escalation, 427
  recapture, 431, 441, 443–44
Excess profits tax, 289, 298, 301
Excise taxes, 386, 388
Executive branch, 79, 137. *See also* President of the U.S.; *Presidents by name.*
Executive budget. *See* Appropriations, administration of; Budget, estimates.
Executive discretion, 68, 78, 81, 84, 92. *See also* Discretionary powers.
Executive Office, 213
Executive order, 124n, 367
Executive session. *See* Secrecy; Security classification.
Exemptions, 80–81
Exhaust manifolds, 7, 183
Expansion program
  planning, 176–78
  problems met, 181–83, 191, 193–94, 200, 202–05, 216, 281, 294
  shifting conception of, 304
Expansion versus conversion, 325
Expediters, 520. *See also* Aircraft production, acceleration; Co-ordination; Liaison.
Expeditor. *See* C–45's.
Expendable property, 398
Expenditures for air matériel, 117, 556–59
Experience factors, 215–16
Experience rating, 386
Experimental aircraft, 246, 514, 519. *See also* Experimental contracts.
Experimental contracts, 90, 117, 278, 399
  competitive procurement, 132
  with design competitions, 124, 139–40, 143, 145
  expenditures, 117, 143–44
  losses on, 88–89, 115, 126
  negotiated contracts, 84–86, 114
  relation to production contracts, 113–14, 127
  in sample competition, 140–41
Experimental development procedures, 97, 106–08
Experimental engineering, 104, 468
Experimental Engineering Section, Materiel Division, 462
Export-Import Bank, 196, 198
Export licensing, 18

INDEX

Exports. *See also* Foreign orders.
  complicate U.S. procurement, 252, 260, 263–65, 493, 529
  Draft Act curbs, 288
  influence financing, 204–05, 223n, 286
  mobilization role, 195–96, 201, 203, 205, 253
  neutrality limitations on, 196
  1940–45, 560
  peacetime market, 10, 17–19
  secrecy release problem, 18, 197–98, 200
Extrusions, 180

F–2's, 550. *See also* C–45's.
F–4's, 550, 578. *See also* P–38's.
F–5's, 550, 578. *See also* P–38's.
F–6's, 550. *See also* P–51's.
Facilities. *See also* Capital investment; Floor space; Production capacity; *individual firms by name.*
  Air Corps representatives in, 99. *See also* Contract administration; Resident representatives.
  Army-Navy cognizance, 273
  in contract negotiations, 340–41, 357
  design of, 28n, 298
  expenditures for, 557
  foreign investment in, 201
  nationalization, 201. *See also* Facility expansion; Nationalization of industry.
  obsolescence, 29
  requirements, 17, 290. *See also* Allocation of industrial capacity; Facilities Division, OASW; Mobilization planning; Office of Assistant Secretary of War.
  security restrictions, 18
  seizure authorized, 286n, 288
  shortage of, 250, 330
Facilities Division, OASW, 247
Facility allocation. *See* Allocation of industrial capacity.
Facility conversion. *See* Conversion of facilities; Mobilization, facility policy.
Facility costs. *See* Facility financing.
Facility expansion
  by accessory firms, 310
  administrative problems, 274, 297, 392, 435, 267
  air arsenal plan, 176–79
  British experience, 165. *See also* Shadow factories.
  conversions. *See* Conversion of facilities.
  50,000 program, 293–94
  financing. *See* Capital investment; Facility financing.
  foreign order impact, 200
  foreign subsidies taxed, 296
  industry views on, 41, 175, 184–85, 201
  by instrument firms, 567
  labor requirements, 564
  policies, 203–04, 317, 319–20
  President's views, 291
  private sites, 285

Facility expansion—Continued
  requirements planning, 70, 161–62, 177, 182–83, 190, 192–93, 264, 292, 304, 307, 481
  reviewed, 301ff., 310, 321, 323–26
  for spares, 294
  by small business, 316
  World War I, 87
Facility financing
  by accelerated depreciation, 285, 289, 296–98, 301. 324. *See also* Depreciation.
  by DPC, 284, 299ff. *See also* Defense Plant Corporation.
  by EPF, 298ff.
  funds for, 296, 324
  by private funds, 181, 184, 292, 294–95, 309, 557
  reconversion costs excluded, 315. *See also* Reconversion of facilities.
  relation to investment, 40
  reviewed, 293–95, 327–28
  tactics, 187
Facility surveys, 153–55, 186, 189ff., 322, 408. *See also* Industrial Planning Section; Mobilization planning; Office of Assistant Secretary of War; Yardstick Board.
Factory plans, 152–55, 163, 186, 290
Failure. *See* Bankruptcy; Defaulting contractors; Loss of bids; Losses by contractors.
Fairchild Aircraft Corp., 38–39, 134, 293, 561, 575, 577. *See also* AT–21's; C–61's; C–82's; PT–19's; PT–23's; PT–26's.
  facility expansion, 302, 321
Fairey Aircraft Ltd., 165
Fairey, C. R., 266
Farmingdale, N.Y., 565
Farrel-Birmingham press, 30
Favoritism
  allegations of, 317, 357–58
  dangers of, 88–89
  procedures to avoid, 90–91, 93, 111, 139–40, 145
Federal Aviation Commission, 55–59
Federal courts, 92, 150, 333n, 389. *See also* Appeals.
Federal Reserve System, 496. *See also* Defense Contract Service.
Fees
  in CPFF contracts, 364, 372, 410. *See also* Fixed fees.
  incentive contracts, 417
  not entirely profit, 418
  related to modifications, 532, 534
  tied to production, 417n
Ferry Command, 487
Ferry pilots, 243n
Ferrying, 465, 530–31
Field audit offices, 395
Field Service Section, Materiel Division, 98–99, 463, 470. *See also* Air Service Command; Air Technical Service Command.
Field servicing equipment, 209

5,500 aircraft program, 174–75, 202–03, 230, 513
50,000 aircraft program
  aluminum requirements, 257
  implementation of, 229, 232–33, 235–37, 243, 249–50
  influences legislation, 283
  origins, 209ff., 221, 226, 228, 228n
  productive capacity required, 253, 293
Fighter aircraft. *See also* P-38's *et seq.*
  Bell P-39 production delays, 245
  doctrine, 45, 156, 233
  evaluation of, 110, 233, 237, 239, 278
  Fisher P-75, 269
  modifications required, 533, 537
  Navy, 576–79
  1941 strength on hand, 244
  parts problems, 457, 564, 567
  production ratios, 564
  Reuther Plan for, 310
  weight, 564
Figure of merit on competition, 90
Filing, 437
Final settlement, 427. *See also* Termination.
Financial statements, 440. *See also* Balance sheets, bidders; Contract negotiation; Cost analysis.
Financing. *See* Advance payments; Aircraft industry, financing; Capital investment; Defense Plant Corporation; Facility financing; Government financing; Interim financing; Loans; Partial payments; V-loans.
Fire control, 45
Fire protection, 389
First Aviation Objective, 235–36
First Aviation Strength, 236
First War Powers Act, 289
Fiscal decisions. *See* Procurement Planning Board, Materiel Division.
Fiscal Division, 430
Fiscal obsoletion, 219
Fiscal program. *See* Budget.
Fisher Body Division of GMC, 269, 309, 321, 382, 415, 547, 577. *See also* P-75's.
Five Year Program, 46–47, 49. *See also* Air Corps Act of 1926.
  delayed by Congress, 64–66, 69–70, 78–79
  proves unworkable, 51
Fixed fees, 372. *See also* Fees.
  absorb disallowed costs, 379, 383–84, 389
  determination of, 375–76, 378, 385
Fixed-price contracts
  administration of, 303, 365–66, 370, 386
  auditing, 390, 392
  defined, 82
  Form 32, 339
  modification problems, 413, 532, 537–38
  negotiation problems, 335, 339, 414, 428
  relation to CPFF, 285, 410, 412
  subcontractors, 443
  terminations, 447, 455

Fixed-price contracts—Continued
  wartime performance record, 418
Fixtures. *See* Jigs and fixtures.
Fleet Aircraft Corp., 577. *See also* PT-23's; PT-26's.
Fleet, Reuben H., 144
Fleet-in-being, 158
Fleetwings, Inc., 575, 577. *See also* BT-12's.
Flight testing, 110, 131
Floor space. *See also* Aircraft industry, floor space; Airframe manufacturers, floor space.
  for airframe industry, 294–95, 303, 310, 563
  costs, 327
  data sought, 181, 187
  in engine industry, 321, 564
  factory plan for, 163–64
  50,000 program needs, 293
  financing, 298, 557. *See also* Facility financing.
  open air, 531
  production ratios, 564
  in propeller industry, 566
  Reuther Plan for, 310
  in supercharger industry, 567
  at Wright Field, 467
Flow charts, 270
Flow time, 537
Flying Clippers, 399
Flying Fortress. *See* B-17's.
Flying suits, 250, 470
Flying training, 465
Flying Training Command, 487
Follow-on contracts, 415
Follow-on orders, 367
Food, 484
Ford, Edsel, 305, 518
Ford, Henry, 518
Ford Motor Co. *See also* B-24's.
  B-24 role, 309, 519–23
  criticized, 311, 314n, 539
  facility problems, 299, 299n, 326–27, 520
  managerial skills, 312
  P-40 plan, 518
  Pratt & Whitney licensee, 309, 580
  production record, 528, 561, 565, 577
  protests fee, 372
  supercharger contract, 455–56
  suppliers, 494n
  trimotor transport, 15
Foreign aid, 214, 222, 399, 451, 507, 557
Foreign Economic Administration, 451
Foreign orders. *See also* Exports.
  compete with Air Corps, 202, 252, 260, 262, 285
  complicate scheduling, 265–66
  impact on industry, 200
  mobilization role, 195–96, 202–03, 205, 207, 294–95
  neutrality act curbs, 196
  relation to appropriations, 204
  require modifications, 529
  1940–45 total, 560

INDEX

Foreign orders—Continued
  secrecy release problem, 200
Foreign policy. *See also* Rearmament.
  aircraft export impact, 202, 204, 208
  shapes requirements, 213, 570
Foreign procurement authorized, 90. *See also* Buy American Act.
Foreign sales. *See* Foreign orders.
Foremen, 322, 522
Forging dies, 251
Forgings, 156, 180, 250–51, 564, 568. *See also* Aluminum.
Form 32, 339–41. *See also* Contract forms; Standard contract form.
Forming dies. *See* Dies.
Forms, 473. *See also* Administrative procedures; Contract forms.
Formula for evaluating bids, 138
Fort Wayne, Ind., 310
Fort Worth, Texas, 308–09
Forward pricing, 441
Forwarder. *See* C–61's.
Foulois, Maj. Gen. Benjamin D., 120–21, 127, 136, 138–39, 279
Four-engine bombers, 302–03, 519. *See also* Bomber aircraft; Heavy bombers.
Fractional horsepower motors, 156, 567
France, 208–09
  accelerated depreciation, 297
  fee policy, 378
  mobilization experience, 159
  nationalization of production, 201
  procurement in U.S., 185, 195–96, 198–99, 201, 296
Franklin, 6n, 581
Fraud
  allegations of, 120–21, 123, 125
  audit role, 390, 396, 402
  in CPFF purchasing, 406
  prevention of, 137, 284, 351, 383
  in procurement contracts, 355–56, 355n
  by subcontractors, 408n
  in terminations, 452
Freedom of expression, 57–58
French Purchasing Mission, 200
Fresno, Calif., 460
Frigidaire Division of GMC, 563
Fringe benefits, 378, 385
Fuel, 282, 484, 558
Fuel cells (tanks), 203, 245, 250, 267n, 527, 531, 533
Fuel transfer system, 536
Fundamental research, 22–26. *See also* Research and development.
Funded debt. *See* Bonds.
Funds expended, 556ff. *See also* Appropriations; Budget, estimates; Expenditures for air materiel.
Fungibles, 282
Furniture manufacturers, 373
Future pricing, 441

G–2, WDGS, 105, 223
G–4, WDGS, 217, 221
G & A Aircraft Corp., 577. *See also* Rotary wing aircraft.
Gallup poll, 313
Gang drill, 521, 523
GAO. *See* General Accounting Office.
Gasoline. *See* Fuel.
Gauges, 160, 523, 543
General Accounting Office, 128, 138, 147, 300. *See also* Comptroller General.
  on CPFF contracts, 379–82, 385, 387, 391, 393–96, 403–404, 414
  on terminations, 448, 452
General Electric, 437, 455–56, 562
General Motors Corp. (GMC), 6n, 26, 255, 269, 293n, 309, 310, 312, 321, 382, 415, 561, 562–63, 577, 580, 581
General Staff, War Department, 44–45, 52, 63, 104, 106
  doctrine, 56n, 57, 101, 157, 210, 212, 212n
  5,500 program views, 513
  mobilization policy, 157, 206
  requirements role, 48, 62–63, 93, 155–57, 222–23, 238
  Reserve officer ruling, 506
Generators, 567
Geneva, 210
Geographic dispersal, 455. *See also* Dispersal; Site selection; Strategic dispersal.
German Air Force
  procurement experience, 112, 190, 214, 514
  strength, 169, 194
Germany, 194–95, 205, 207–08, 283
  aircraft production, 169n, 201, 553–55
  influences U.S., 169, 224, 250
GFE. *See* Government-furnished equipment.
GHQ Air Force, 54, 77, 102, 244
Gibbs and Cox, 188n
Gifts, 295
Glenn L. Martin. *See* Martin, Glenn L.
Glider manufacturers, 324
Gliders, 373, 552, 558, 577
Globe Aircraft Corp., 577
GOCO, 295–96
Goethals, G. W., 475
Goodyear Aircraft Corp., 308, 540, 547, 561, 577
Gorrell, E. N., 56n
Government aircraft factory, 87, 124–25
Government contracts, 129, 362
Government factories. *See* Government-operated facilities; Government-owned, contractor-operated; Government-owned facilities; Naval Aircraft Factory; Unfair competition.
Government financing, 291, 328, 375, 435. *See also* Defense Plant Corporation; Emergency plant facility contracts; Facility financing.
Government-furnished equipment, 166, 187, 340, 342, 450, 508

Government-furnished equipment—Continued
  aids standardization, 132
  costs per aircraft, 142
  organization, 348, 369
  prewar volume, 345
  property accounting, 399
  renegotiation problem, 437
Government-furnished facilities, 306, 308–09. *See also* Defense Plant Corporation; Emergency plant facility contracts; Facility expansion, air arsenal plan; Facility financing; Shadow factories.
Government-operated facilities, 166
Government-owned, contractor-operated, 295–96
Government-owned facilities
  feasibility considered, 166, 175–177, 182, 184
  industry fear of, 185, 277. *See also* Nationalization of industry.
  influence profit allowed, 375
  site selection, 306ff.
Government ownership. *See* Nationalization of industry.
Government procurement, aircraft as special case, 130
Government warehouse, 458
Graflex camera, 480–81
Graham, William J., 84n
Graham-Paige, 163
Grand Rapids, Mich., 373
Grasshopper. *See* L–2's; L–3's; L–4's; L–14's.
Gray, C. G., 4
Great Britain. *See* United Kingdom.
Green, William, 254
Grievances. *See* Complaints.
Gross weight. *See* Airframes, average gross weights.
Ground crews, 209
Ground forces, 173. *See also* Army Ground Forces; Army Service Forces; Close-support role; Interbranch competition; Jurisdictional disputes.
Grumman Aircraft Engineering Corp., 21n, 293n, 561, 575, 577
Guarantees, 130. *See also* Bid bonds; Liquidated damages.
Guggenheim Fund, 22
Guided missiles, 485–86, 558
Gun-synchronizers, 180
Gun turrets, 245–46, 310, 378, 508, 516, 527, 536
"Guns and butter," 314, 316
Gyro-pilots. *See* Autopilots.

Hagerstown, Md., 321
Hamilton-Standard Division of United Aircraft Corp., 7–8, 8n, 562–63
Hammond Aircraft. *See* Stearman-Hammond Aircraft Corp.
Hand tools, 397, 444, 484
Handbook for Aircraft Designers, 132
Hardstands, 531
Hardware. *See* Aircraft hardware.

Harrisburg, Pa., 177
Hartford, Conn., 6, 9, 28
Havoc. *See* A–20's.
Hawaiian Islands, 52–53, 212–13
Hawthorne, Calif., 321
Hearings. *See* Congressional investigations; Investigations.
Heat treating, 568
Heavy bomber program, 205, 239, 540
Heavy bombers, 233, 237, 244, 253, 564, 567. *See also* Bomber aircraft; Four-engine bombers.
  1940–44 acceptances, 555
Helicopters. *See* Rotary wing aircraft.
Helldiver. *See* A–25's.
Hemisphere defense, 213, 222, 246
Hides, 250
Higgins Aircraft, Inc., 577. *See also* C–46's.
High speed, evaluation of, 110
Hillman, Sidney, 254–55, 265, 313, 316
Hitler, Adolf, 112, 169, 200
Holding company, 299
Holland, 207–08
Honesty. *See* Integrity.
Hopkins, Harry, 170, 238–39, 241
Horsepower, 549, 564
Hourly earnings. *See* Wages.
Hours of employment, 260–61, 261n
House Committee on Appropriations
  aircraft funds, 43, 51, 64–65, 195, 204. *See also* Air Corps, relation to Congress; Air Corps, expenditures for aircraft, 1926–34; Appropriations.
  condemns relief funds, 68
  opposes B–17, 76
  overtaken by price rises, 71
  procedure, 171
  pursues Baker report, 58–59
  reduces engine reserve, 71
House Committee on Military Affairs
  air arm hearings, 43, 48, 119. *See also* Investigations.
  aircraft program, 59, 61, 174. *See also* Authorized strength.
  criticizes CPFF contracts, 411
  freedom of witnesses, 58n
  influence on War Department, 139n
  military advisors, 48
  procurement problems, 123, 139, 145, 277, 279, 283–84
  suspects General Staff, 55
House Committee on Naval Affairs, 121–22, 284
Housekeeping, administrative, 472. *See also* Administrative procedures.
Housing, 77–78, 308, 326, 389n
Houston, Texas, 318
Howard Aircraft Corp., 578. *See also* PT–23's.
Howell, Clark, 56
Howell Commission, 55–59
Howitzers, 552
Hudson. *See* A–28's; A–29's.

INDEX

619

Hudson Motor Car Corp., 163, 308, 546–47
Hughes, C. E., 37
Hughes Tool Co., 318
Hull, Cordell, 209, 228
Humping, 66, 70
Hydraulic pumps, 180–81
Hydraulic tubing, 564

I–1430 engine, 581
Ickes, Harold, 68
Ignition coils, 567
Improprieties, 110. *See also* Fraud.
Improvisation, 301
Incentive contracts, 416–17, 421. *See also* Bogey contracts.
Incentives, 83, 85, 182, 333, 335, 358, 426. *See also* Liquidated damages.
  in CPFF contracts, 373, 384, 386, 410, 418
  in CPPC contracts, 82
  negated by escalation, 426
  influence modification, 532, 534
  impact of renegotiation, 445
  role in pricing, 343
  statutory provisions, 284, 287–89
  substitutes for, 374
Income tax, 299, 385, 432, 435
Indianapolis, Ind., 309, 562
Indices. *See* Durable goods index.
Indirect labor. *See* Labor; Wages.
Industrial Cost Unit, 348
Industrial mobilization, 217, 292. *See also* Mobilization.
Industrial Mobilization Plan, 151
Industrial planning. *See* Mobilization planning.
Industrial Planning Section, 98–99, 153–68, 463, 467
  data inadequate, 186, 188–89, 191
  transferred to Washington, 206
Industrial potential. *See* Production capacity.
Industrial wages. *See* Wages.
Inexperienced officers, 354–55
Inflation, 303, 344, 350, 425, 431
Influence
  attempts to cultivate, 69
  improper, 110, 356n
Informal contracts. *See* Purchase orders.
Informal exceptions, 395
Information contracts. *See* Data contracts.
Information processing, 186–87, 349, 572. *See also* Data processing.
Information Division, OCAC, 105
Informers, 357, 393n
Ingersoll Milling Machine Co., 524
Initiative, by contractors, 388, 435
In-line engines, 309, 565. *See also* Allison Division of GMC.
Innovations, 107, 140
Insecticides, 484

Inspection, 99
  BDV Committee role, 541
  contract stipulations, 340–41, 364
  in procurement districts, 491, 509
  by X-ray, 568
Inspection Branch, Materiel Division, 98
Inspection Section, Materiel Division, 463
Inspector General, 376
Instruction manuals, 470, 483, 518
Instrument manufacturers, 321, 567
Instruments, aircraft, 12, 72, 271n, 294, 485
Insurance, 354, 386
Integrity, 353, 355–56
Intelligence, 194, 465. *See also* G–2, WDGS; Military Intelligence Division, WDGS.
Interbranch competition, 476, 484. *See also* Jurisdictional disputes.
Interchangeability, 501, 540, 544. *See also* Standardization.
Interdepartmental Committee for Coordinating Foreign and Domestic Military Purchases, 252–53, 263
Interest charges, 299, 303, 450. *See also* Loans.
Interim financing, 451
Interplant borrowing, 399, 415
Interservice rivalry, 272. *See also* Army-Navy; Jurisdictional disputes.
Interservice transfers, 481
Interstate Aircraft and Engineering Corp., 578. *See also* L–6's; L–8's.
Invader. *See* A–26's.
Invention, stimulation of, 93
Inventory, 32, 72. *See also* Aircraft industry, inventory problem; Airframe manufacturers, inventory value; Stock control.
  control problems, 216, 251, 426, 457, 535
  CPFF problem, 411, 414–15
  termination problem, 446, 448, 451–52, 456
Investigations, 59, 119, 107–08, 357. *See also* Congressional investigations.
  Air Corps, 55
  aircraft industry, 37
  Detroit tool, 459
  of excess profits, 429
  Lampert, 46
  Morrow, 47
  War Department policy, 57
  World War I, 84n
Investment brokers, 141–42
Investments. *See* Capital investment.
Invitations to bid, 80, 89–90, 358. *See also* Advertising for bids; Circular proposals.
  distribution delays, 493, 497–98
  OPM role, 496–97
IPS. *See* Industrial Planning Section.
Iraq, 200
Iridium, 250
Irving Airchute, 7–8, 8n

Isolationists, 175, 197, 199
Isometric projections, 501. *See also* Blueprints.
Italy, 196
IV-1430 engine, 581

J-31 jet engine, 562
J-33 jet engine, 562
JAC. *See* Joint Aircraft Committee.
Jacobs Aircraft Engine Co., 6n, 293n, 580
Jack and Heintz, Inc., 429, 437
James, W. F., 58n, 124n
Janeway, Eliot, 257n
Japan, 196, 553-55
Jet engines, 456, 562
Jet fighter, 112
Jigs and fixtures. *See also* Production tooling.
  contract negotiation, 341-42
  costs, 363, 413, 426
  disposal problem, 458
  educational orders, 159-60
  production use, 512, 521, 524, 526
  property accounting, 397
Job-shop, 190, 511
Jobbers, 444
Johnson, Louis A.
  leadership, 4, 175-76, 225n
  on military requirements, 223, 225, 232n
  on mobilization plan, 248n
  preparedness views, 181
  on production capacity, 186, 193, 224
  urges statutory revision, 283
Johnston, S. Paul, 256
Joint Aircraft Committee, 264n, 266-68, 271-73
Joint Army and Navy Board, 213
Joint Contract Termination Board, 451
Joint procurement, 124. *See also* Cross procurement.
Joint production programs, 538-41, 543, 547
Joint versus combined, 266n
Jones, Col. A. E., 354n
Judge Advocate, Wright Field, 99, 349
Judge Advocate General (Army)
  defines executive discretion, 81
  interprets 1926 Act, 51, 115, 128
  officers in OCAC, 105-06
  on procurement, 139, 147, 276, 388
Judge Advocate General (Navy), 388
Judicial decisions, 353, 569
Judicial review. *See* Federal courts.
Jurisdictional disputes, 480, 485. *See also* Army-Navy; Duplication of effort; Interbranch competition; Interservice rivalry.
Justice. *See* Department of Justice.

Kahn, Albert, 28n
Kansas City, Kans., 9, 308, 530
Kaydet. *See* PT-13's; PT-17's; PT-27's.
Keller, K. T., 305
Kellett Autogiro Corp., 575, 578

Kellett profilers, 523
Kelly Act, 12, 14, 17
Kelvinator. *See* Nash-Kelvinator Corp.
Kennedy, Joseph P., 226
Kettering, Charles, 257
Kindelberger, James H., 169n, 190
Kingcobra. *See* P-63's.
Kingston, Ontario, 213
Kinner Airplane and Motor Co., 6n, 580
Knockdown airframes, 309, 519
Knudsen, William S.
  approves CPFF, 335
  on bomber program, 305
  NDAC role, 255-56, 263
  OPM role, 265, 270, 313, 316
  recruits automobile industry, 304, 308
  on requirements, 292-93
  on Roosevelt, 232n
  urges facility conversion, 322
Korean emergency, 538n
Kraus, Capt. S. M., 256

L-1's, 551
L-2's, 551, 579
L-3's, 551, 576
L-4's (L-14's), 551, 578, 580
L-5's, 551, 576, 580
L-6's, 578, 580
L-7's, 579
L-8's, 578
L-14's, 578
L-365 engine, 582
L-440 engine, 581
Labor, 340, 357, 393, 419, 429, 521. *See also* Employment; Semiskilled labor; Skilled labor; Unions; Unskilled labor; Wages.
  attitudes, 322, 415, 530, 565-66
  availability, 241, 250, 323, 535
  costs, 141, 348, 360, 362, 422, 426, 531
  influences site selection, 9, 177, 303, 308, 328
  influences termination, 455-56
  productivity, 191, 413, 564
  reports on, 282
  requirements, 192, 293, 361-63
  statutory protection, 281
  training of, 319
  waste of, 242-43
  at Willow Run, 326, 524, 527
Labor Department, 94, 422
Labor force, 310
  in airframe industry, 563-65
  in electrical industry, 567
  in engine industry, 564-65
  in supercharger industry, 567
Labor leaders, 254, 311, 313-14. *See also* Green, William; Hillman, Sidney; Lewis, John L.; Reuther, Walter; Unions.
Labor-management co-operation, 311

INDEX

Labor unions. *See* Unions.
Laboratories, Wright Field, 99
Lampert, Florian, 46
Lampert Committee, 46, 57n, 87, 89, 122, 124, 130
Landing field. *See* Air bases; Airstrips.
Landing gear, 271, 310, 566
Langley Field, Va., 23
Lassiter, Maj. Gen. William, 44
Lassiter Board, 44–46, 48
Latin America, 18, 196
Laws. *See* Procurement statutes; Revised Statutes; Social welfare legislation.
Lawyers, 105–06, 353, 433, 469. *See also* Judge Advocate, Wright Field; Judge Advocate General; Legal advisors.
Lay-offs, 386
"Layering," 471
Lead time, 275
Leadership, 272, 397, 401
  Air Corps lack of, 261n
  in business, 364n
  character of, 181, 353, 404, 449, 459, 471–72. *See also* Command; Decision making; Discretionary powers.
  examples of, 172–73, 182, 468, 474
  in mobilization, 207, 243, 249, 254
  in procurement, 335–36, 346, 351, 464, 480, 571
  in renegotiation, 431
  in termination, 458
Leakproof fuel cells, 245
Learner curve, 344, 361–62, 426, 535–36
Leather, 250
Leavenworth, 303
Lectures, 432
Legal Branch, Contract Section, 349, 430
Legal advisors, 147, 228. *See also* Judge Advocate, Wright Field; Judge Advocate General; Lawyers.
Legal problems, 99, 105–06, 296. *See also* Judge Advocate General.
Legislation. *See also* Congress.
  by appropriation, 43, 62n
  innovations feared, 116, 116n, 353
  organization for, 92, 95, 104–06
  proposals for, 119, 176–77, 276–78, 297
  regulations and procedures for, 57, 133, 286
Legislative draftsmanship, 61
Lend-Lease contracts, 399
Lenses, 183
Lessons learned, technique for, 400
Letter contracts, 338
Letter of intent
  drawbacks, 337–38, 392
  origin and use, 257, 302, 318, 336
Lewis, John L., 254
Liaison, 58, 165, 192, 472. *See also* Co-ordination; Production control.
  with ASF, 477

Liaison—Continued
  with manufacturers, 539
  with SWPC, 500
Liaison aircraft, 11, 552, 566, 576–79. *See also* Aeronca Aircraft Corp.; Consolidated Aircraft Corp.; Interstate Aircraft and Engineering Corp.; L–1's *et seq.*; Piper Aircraft Corp.; Rearwin Aircraft & Engines, Inc.; Universal Aircraft.
Liaison Committee. *See* President's Liaison Committee.
Liberator. *See* B–24's.
Liberator Express. *See* C–87's.
Liberty engines, 64, 83
Library, OCAC, 105. *See also* Technical Data Library, Wright Field.
Licensing, 444, 561–62, 566, 580
Light bombers, 244
Lightning. *See* P–38's.
Limited emergency, 194
Limited profit contracts, 333. *See also* Cost-plus-fixed-fee (CPFF) contracts.
Line and staff, 381
Linen, 250
Lippmann, Walter, 316
Liquid-cooled engines, 309, 565
Liquidated damages, 203, 207, 332
Litigation, 333n, 446, 460. *See also* Federal courts.
Load-carrying capacity, 110
Lobby, 491n. *See also* Aeronautical Chamber of Commerce.
Loans, 36, 196, 284, 298. *See also* Advance payments; Assignment of claims; Partial payments.
Local taxes, 387
Lockheed Aircraft Corp., 30, 200, 293n, 376, 541, 575, 578. *See also* A–28's; A–29's; B–17's; B–24's; C–69's; F–4's; F–5's; P–38's; P–80's.
  B–17 production role, 540, 543, 546
  financing, 38, 38n, 40n
  wartime production, 561
Lockland, Ohio, 309
Locomotives, 484
Lodestar. *See* C–60's.
Lodge, Henry Cabot, Jr., 203n
Loening, Grover C., 88
Lofting, 521–22, 543
Logistics. *See* Maintenance; Supply.
Lombard, A. E., Jr., 256
Long Beach, Calif., 299
Los Angeles, Calif., 9, 153, 530
Loss of bids, procedures for appeals, 90, 147. *See also* Appeals.
Loss rates, 50, 217. *See also* Attrition rate.
Losses by contractors, 34, 115, 299n, 333, 348
  on experimental contracts, 115n, 126
  in renegotiation, 431
Lovett, Robert A., 241, 474. *See also* Assistant Secretary of War for Air.

Low bid, basis of award, 80–81, 92–93, 108–09, 113, 359, 366. See also Advertising for bids; Competitive procurement.
Lubricants. See Fuel.
Luftwaffe, 43, 175, 194, 232, 533
Lump-sum contracts. See Fixed-price contracts.
Luscombe Airplane Corp., 578
Luxembourg, 224
Lycoming Division of Aviation Manufacturing Corp., 6–8, 8n, 156n, 259, 293, 309, 581. See also R–680 engine.

M-day, 249. See also Mobilization; Mobilization planning.
  plans, 153, 155, 161, 207, 513
  requirements, 52–54, 216
MacArthur, General Douglas, 3, 53n, 62n, 66, 211
McCarl, John R., 118
Machine guns, 246. See also Armament, aircraft; Ordnance Department.
Machine loading, 32, 535
Machine records tabulation. See Data processing.
Machine tools in automotive industry, 311, 313, 323, 520, 523–24
  in contract administration, 267, 341–42, 411, 508, 545
  expenditures, 77–78, 323, 557
  influence design, 544
  influence facility policy, 326–27
  mobilization planning for, 158, 163–64, 187
  shortages, 150, 250–51, 258–59
McCook Field, Dayton, Ohio, 112
McDonnell Aircraft Corp., 547, 578. See also AT-21's; P–67's.
McNary-Watres Act of 1930, 14
McSwain, John J., 44, 55, 59–60, 145
  Air Corps Act role, 90–93
  investigates procurement procedures, 113, 123
  proposes procurement bill, 133, 139, 139n
Magazines, 275
Maginot Line, 195
Magnaflux, 30
Magnesium casting, 320
Magnetos, 183, 294, 321
Mailing lists, 497. See also Advertising registers; Bidders lists.
Mail-order catalogue parts supplier, 8
Maintenance, 110, 243, 246, 517. See also Malfunctioning; Unsatisfactory Report.
  organizations, 99, 470. See also Air Service Command; Air Technical Service Command; Depots; Field Service Section, Materiel Division; Materiel Division.
  equipment, 209, 492
  materials, 558
  shops, 530
Malfunctioning, 530. See also Engine overhaul; Maintenance; Modifications; Unsatisfactory Report.

Man-hours, 361–62, 531, 534, 537, 564. See also Efficiency; Employment; Labor; Manpower; Productivity.
Management consultants, 475
Management control, 478. See also Administrative procedures; Organizational planning; Statistical Control Office.
Managerial skills. See also Businessmen; Leadership.
  corporate policy on, 562
  dilution of, 309, 380, 405, 433
  improvement in, 304, 538
  influence site selection, 303
  needed by government, 177, 261
  remuneration, 382, 384
  small business problem, 502
  utilization of, 311–12, 322, 402, 409, 448, 534
Mandatory orders, 378n, 444. See also Compulsory directives.
Maneuverability, 110
Manifold pressure gauges, 567
Manpower
  in air arm, 45, 77–78. See also Civil Service; Civilian personnel; Enlisted men; Officers; Personnel.
  in airframe industry, 191. See also Employment; Labor.
  auditing, 394
  lack of skilled, 261
  in mobilization planning, 44, 154, 157, 224, 330
  at Wright Field, 466
Manuals, 221, 389. See also Contracting officers; Technical orders.
Manufacturers. See also Airframe manufacturers; Engine manufacturers.
  of accessories and subassemblies, 6
  Aeronautical Corporation of America, 575
  Aeronca Aircraft Corp., 321, 576
  Aeroproducts Division of GMC, 562–63.
  Air Associates, Inc., 7–8, 8n
  Air Cooled Motors, Inc., 6n, 581
  Albert Kahn, Inc., 28n
  Allis-Chalmers, 455–56
  Allison Division of GMC, 6n, 269, 293n, 309, 562, 581
  alphabetical file of, 358
  Aviation Manufacturing Corp., 6n. See also individual divisions.
  Baldwin-Southwark, 31
  Beech Aircraft Corp., 293n, 302, 321, 442, 561, 575–76
  Bell Aircraft Corp., 38–39, 245, 293n, 302ff., 376, 547, 561, 575–76
  Bellanca Aircraft, 321, 576
  Bendix Aviation Corp., 7–8, 8n, 449–50
  Boeing Aircraft Corp., 7, 9, 21n, 29, 34, 38n, 40n, 293n, 299, 302, 325, 349, 373, 376, 399, 540, 547, 561, 565, 575, 576
  Breeze Manufacturing Co., 7–8, 8n
  Brewster Aeronautical Corp., 7–8, 8n, 293n, 575–76

INDEX

Manufacturers—Continued
  Budd Manufacturing Co., 576
  Buick Division of GMC, 310, 580
  business practices, 354, 360, 363, 403, 409
  Canadian Car Co., 576
  Canadian Propellers, Ltd., 563
  Case, J. L., 540
  Cessna Aircraft Division of United Aircraft, 293n, 561, 576
  Chance-Vought Division of United Aircraft Corp., 22, 561
  Chevrolet Division of GMC, 26, 580
  Chrysler Corp., 312, 377
  Cleveland Pneumatic Tool Co., 7-8, 8n, 318-19
  Columbia Aircraft, 576
  Consolidated Aircraft Corp. (Consolidated-Vultee), 10, 21n, 29, 38n, 40n, 144, 293n, 309, 326, 521-22, 539, 540, 561, 565, 575, 576
  Continental Motors Corp., 6n, 293n, 580-81
  criticisms by, 281-82, 495. *See also* Aeronautical Chamber of Commerce; Lampert Committee; Morrow Board.
  Culver Aircraft Corp., 575-76
  Curtiss Aeroplane and Motor Co., 85
  Curtiss Electric Division of Curtiss-Wright Corp., 562-63
  Curtiss-Wright Corp., 7-8, 8n, 15, 21n, 29, 33, 37-39, 134, 180-81, 190, 196n, 256, 293n, 302, 320-21, 404, 415, 561, 562, 575, 577
  Dayton-Wright Airplane Co., 83
  DeHaviland Aircraft of Canada, 577
  delayed by Congress, 301, 439
  Dodge Division of Chrysler Corp., 321, 580
  Doehler Die Casting Co., 435
  Douglas Aircraft Corp., 9, 15-17, 21n, 38n, 40n, 134, 136-37, 142, 199, 201, 241, 264, 293n, 299n, 309, 315, 321, 362, 378n, 393, 393n, 514, 519, 540-41, 543, 546, 561, 575, 577
  Eastern Aircraft Division of GMC, 561, 577
  Emerson Electric, 378
  excise tax problem, 387
  Fairchild Aircraft Corp., 38-39, 134, 293, 561, 575, 577
  Fairey Aircraft Ltd., 165
  fears of, 357, 373, 376, 379, 413, 442
  Fisher Body Division of GMC, 269, 309, 321, 382, 415, 547, 577
  Fleet Aircraft Corp., 577
  Fleetwings, Inc., 575, 577
  Ford Motor Co., 15, 299, 299n, 309, 311, 312, 314n, 326-27, 377, 455-56, 494n, 518, 519-23, 528, 539, 561, 565, 577, 580
  Frigidaire Division of GMC, 563
  G & A Aircraft Corp., 577
  General Electric, 437, 455-56, 562
  General Motors Corp., 255, 312, 321. *See also individual divisions.*
  Globe Aircraft Corp., 577

Manufacturers—Continued
  Goodyear Aircraft Corp., 308, 540, 547, 561, 577
  Graham-Paige, 163
  Grumman Aircraft Engineering Corp., 21n, 293n, 561, 575, 577
  Hamilton-Standard Division of United Aircraft Corp., 7-8, 8n, 562-63
  Higgins Aircraft, Inc., 577
  Howard Aircraft Corp., 578
  Hudson Motor Car Corp., 163, 308, 546-47
  Hughes Tool Co., 318
  Ingersoll Milling Machine Co., 524
  Interstate Aircraft and Engineering Corp., 578
  Irving Airchute, 7-8, 8n
  Jacobs Aircraft Engine Co., 6n, 293n, 580
  Jack and Heintz, Inc., 429, 437
  Kellett Autogiro Corp., 575, 578
  Kinner Airplane and Motor Co., 6n, 580
  Lockheed Aircraft Corp., 30, 200, 293n, 376, 541, 575, 578
  Luscombe Airplane Corp., 578
  Lycoming Division of Aviation Manufacturing Corp., 6-8, 8n, 156n, 259, 293, 309, 581
  McDonnell Aircraft Corp., 547, 578
  Martin, Glenn L., 9, 21n, 26, 37, 38n, 40n, 85ff., 88, 117, 142, 163, 169n, 184-85, 241, 293n, 299, 302, 308, 319, 436n, 534, 561, 578
  Menasco Manufacturing Co., 6n, 293n, 580
  Monocoupe Corp., 575
  Murray Corporation of America, 315
  Nash-Kelvinator Corp., 563, 578, 580
  Naval Aircraft Factory, 125-26, 578, 580
  Noorduyn Aviation Co., Ltd., 578
  North American Aviation Corp., 21n, 30-31, 38n, 40n, 200, 241, 293n, 302, 308, 321, 414-15, 482, 539, 547, 561, 575, 578
  Northrop Aircraft, Inc., 38-39, 321, 578
  Packard Motor Car Co., 83, 163, 301, 309, 367, 392, 401, 580
  Piper Aircraft Corp., 561, 575, 578
  Platt-LePage Aircraft Co., 578
  Porterfield Aircraft Corp., 575
  Pratt & Whitney Aircraft Division of United Aircraft Corp., 6, 7, 28, 200-201, 293n, 309, 561, 580
  Rearwin Aircraft & Engines, Inc., 9, 578
  relations with procurement officers, 140, 364-65, 369. *See also* Contract administration; Contract negotiation; Procurement procedures.
  Remington Rand, 563
  Republic Aviation Corp., 38-39, 293n, 302, 321, 376, 538n, 547, 561, 565, 578
  Rolls-Royce, 301, 309, 367, 392, 580
  Ryan Aeronautical Corp., 293, 302, 578
  St. Louis Aircraft Corp., 575, 578
  St. Louis Airplane Division of Curtiss-Wright Corp., 575
  Seversky Aviation Corp., 575

Manufacturers—Continued
 Sikorsky Aircraft Division of United Aircraft Corp., 578
 Solar Aircraft Corp., 575
 Spartan Aircraft Co., 293n, 575, 579
 Sperry Corp., 7–8, 8n, 437
 Stearman Aircraft Division of Boeing Aircraft Corp., 293n, 575
 Stearman-Hammond Aircraft Corp., 575
 Stinson Aircraft Division of Aviation Manufacturing Corp., 293n, 575
 Studebaker Corp., 310, 377, 418, 458, 480
 Taylor Aircraft Corp., 32n
 Timm Aircraft Corp., 579
 United Aircraft Corp., 6, 33, 38–39, 184, 187n, 256, 297, 562. *See also individual divisions.*
 United States Steel, 255
 Universal Aircraft, 579
 Vega Airplane Co., 387, 541
 Vickers Canadian, Ltd., 579
 Vought-Sikorsky Aircraft Division of United Aircraft Corp., 273n, 575
 Vultee Aircraft Division of Aviation Manufacturing Corp., 242, 293n, 302, 575
 Waco Aircraft Co., 373, 575–76
 Warner Aircraft Corp., 582
 Warner-Swasey, 259
 White Aircraft Co., 575
 Wright Aeronautical Corp., 6, 200–201, 293n, 309, 418
Manufacturing methods, 153–54, 522
Manufacturing plants. *See* Facilities.
Mapping, 558
Marauder. *See* B-26's.
Marbury, W. C., 478
Maritime Commission, 188n, 451
Markets for aircraft. *See* Airlines; Civilian aircraft; Exports; Foreign orders.
Markets for aircraft parts, 7–8
Market economy, 373
Market prices, 344, 360. *See also* Open market procurement.
Marshall, General George C. *See also* Chief of Staff.
 on aircraft program, 202–04, 202n, 203n, 204n, 207, 231
 on aluminum shortage, 251
 appoints Air Board, 220
 aviation communications policy, 486
 relations with Arnold, 474
Martin, Glenn L., 88, 169n, 293n. *See also* A-30's; B-26's; B-29's.
 B-10 bomber, 117, 142, 163–64
 early development role, 85ff.
 facility expansions, 9, 184–85, 299, 302, 308
 factory plan, 163
 finances, 26, 37, 38n, 40n
 production record, 9, 21n, 561, 578
 wartime contract problems, 241, 319, 436n, 534

Mass production, 512
 costs, 327, 560
 data required for, 185–87
 designing for, 110–11, 187, 264. *See also* Standardization.
 examples of, 180, 320, 518ff., 540
 exports impact, 200
 influences spares policy, 215
 labor role, 348
 proprietary rights inhibit, 539
 Reuther Plan for, 310
 time lag before, 108
Master changes in modifications, 536–37, 545. *See also* Change orders; Modifications.
Materials
 cost analysis, 348, 359, 422, 424
 definition problems, 426. *See also* Critical raw materials; Raw materials.
 escalation influences purchase, 423.
 requirements studies, 252
 shortages, 263–64, 317, 330, 468
Materials Branch, Materiel Division, 98
Materiel Center, 465, 487. *See also* Wright Field.
Materiel Command
 decentralization policy, 503–10
 organization, 270, 245–46, 465, 471–72, 476–77, 487. *See also* Materiel Division; Wright Field.
 procurement role, 242–43, 318, 337, 341. *See also* Contracting officers; Negotiation of contracts; Procurement doctrine; Procurement officers; Procurement procedures.
 small business problems, 502
 staff, 273, 350, 558. *See also* Civil Service; Civilian personnel; Enlisted men; Officers; Reserve officers.
 SWPC role, 501
 termination organization, 453–54
Materiel Division
 co-ordination problems, 463
 mobilization role, 153, 179, 188–89, 193, 258. *See also* Industrial Planning Section; Mobilization; Mobilization planning.
 OCAC, 97–106
 organization, 462, 465
 relations with OPM, 270
 staff, 463–64
 statistical tools, 192
Materiel Liaison Section, OCAC, 95, 102–03
Materiel, Maintenance, and Distribution, Air Staff, 465, 478
May, Andrew J., 285
Mead, George J., 256
Medium bombers, 244, 302, 308. *See also* Bomber aircraft.
Meigs, Merrill C., 266
Melrose Park, Ill., 310
Memorandum Report, 110–11
Menasco Manufacturing Co., 6n, 293n, 580

INDEX 625

Merchants of Death, 119–20, 125, 129, 155, 196
Merlin engine, 309, 580. *See also* Packard Motor Car Co.
Metallurgical laboratories, 568
Methods of manufacture. *See* Manufacturing methods.
Midcentral Procurement District, 506
Middle River, Md., 37
Middlemen, 407, 444, 500, 510
Middletown, Ohio, 321
Midway Island, 213
Midwestern Procurement District, 506
Militarism, 67
Military Affairs Committees. *See* House Committee on Military Affairs; Senate Committee on Military Affairs.
Military attaché reports, 165, 169n, 514. *See also* G-2, WDGS.
Military characteristics, 110, 214, 257n, 316
   defined, 106, 210n. *See also* Aircraft characteristics; Aircraft performance; Performance characteristics; Quality; Specifications.
Military Intelligence Division, WDGS, 105
Military justice, 349. *See also* Judge Advocate General.
Military mission. *See* Mission.
Military personnel. *See* Enlisted men; Materiel Command, staff; Officers; Reserve officers.
Military priority. *See* Priorities.
Military services. *See* Arms and Services; Army; Navy Department; *individual services by name.*
Minimum wage, 281. *See also* Walsh-Healey Act.
Ministry of Aircraft Production, 410
Ministry of Supply, concept of, 272
Ministry of Supply (British), 341, 417n
Miscellaneous Maintenance and Supply Branch, Materiel Division, 98
Mission, 210–13, 217–18, 220, 222. *See also* Air Board; Air Corps, mission; Air Corps Board; Air power; Army-Navy; Doctrine; Joint Army and Navy Board; Requirements.
Mitchell. *See* B-25's.
Mitchell, Brig. Gen. William, 45–46, 112
Mobilization
   Buy American Act delays, 283
   Detroit role, 316
   facility policy, 290, 292, 315–19, 322, 325, 329
   foreign order role, 195–96
   labor seeks voice in, 313
   legislation for, 286–87
   makeshift character, 235, 252
   organization, 246–48, 255, 262, 265
   status in 1940, 254
Mobilization and War Planning Branch, Materiel Division, 98
Mobilization plan, 225, 225n, 252. *See also* Protective Mobilization Plan.

Mobilization planning, 54, 150–68, 177–78, 181, 205–08. *See also* Factory plans; Industrial Planning Section; Office of Assistant Secretary of War.
   appraisals of, 152, 155, 160–61, 166–67, 178, 181, 205–07, 253, 258, 265, 268, 301–02, 304, 507
   conceptions, 155, 157ff., 249, 273, 291n, 307, 513
   of contract negotiation, 347
   data lacking, 186
   educational order use, 183
   by procurement districts, 491
   proprietary design problems, 539
   of termination clauses, 446
   tools for, 191–92, 267
Mock-up, 140, 140n
Model changes, 470, 526, 535, 537. *See also* Change orders; Modifications.
Modification centers, 324, 529–33, 537
Modification Section, Production Division, 532
Modifications
   attempted freeze, 514–17
   BDV Committee role, 545
   of bombers, 117, 526
   contract administration problems, 366–67, 399, 413, 417, 426, 482–83
   expenditures, for, 557–58
   exports pay costs, 203
   need for, 242, 245, 512, 529ff.
   procedures for, 108–09, 167, 530–34, 540
Moffett, Rear Adm. W. A., 116n
Monocoque construction, 16, 20, 51
Monocoupe Corp., 575
Monopoly, 127. *See also* Negotiated contracts; Sole source.
Moody's *Industrials,* 33
Morale, 355, 361, 382, 386, 530
"Morgan interests," 249
Morgenthau, Henry, Jr., 224, 224n, 252–53, 252n, 263
Morrow, Dwight W., 46
Morrow Board, 46–47, 50, 57, 87, 89, 122, 130
Motor vehicles, military, 315
Motors, electric. *See* Fractional horsepower motors.
Multiple awards, 280
Multiple-shift operations, 182, 187, 191, 287. *See also* Employment; Labor.
Munitions Control Board, 196. *See also* Exports; Neutrality legislation.
Munitions manufacturers, 120, 125
Munitions program, 231, 235–36, 238, 331. *See also* 50,000 aircraft program.
Murray Corporation of America, 315
Musical instrument manufacturers, 567
Mussolini, Benito, 208
Mustang. *See* A-36's; P-51's.
Mutual mistakes, rectification, 366
Myers, B. E., 240n

NACA. *See* National Advisory Committee for Aeronautics.
Nash-Kelvinator Corp., 563, 578, 580. *See also* R–6's.
National Advisory Committee for Aeronautics, 22–23, 256
National defense
 Air Corps conceptions of, 41, 53, 124, 182, 213, 234
 exports impact on, 196n, 200, 205
 politics of, 3, 66, 79, 175
 requirements for, 44, 52–53, 169–70, 172–73
National Defense Act of 1916, 82n
National Defense Act of 1920, 44–45, 93, 151, 159, 339
 ambiguities, 475
 ASW role, 474, 480
 authorizes negotiated procurement, 275, 339, 474–75, 480
 exceptions authorized, 84n
National Defense Advisory Commission
 capacity studies, 192, 293–94
 facility expansion, 302, 304
 organization, 254–58, 261–65, 313, 318, 322
 views of military, 495
National Defense Expediting Act, 284
National economy, 454, 493, 511
National Guard, 48
National Recovery Administration, 8
National security. *See* National defense; Rearmament.
Nationalization of industry
 in France, 201
 industry fear of, 38, 185, 277, 291
 proposed, 124–25, 177–79
Naval Aircraft Factory, 125–26, 578, 580
Navigation instruments, 567
Navigator. *See* AT–7's; AT–10's; AT–11's.
Navy Department, 74–75, 89n, 161. *See also* Bureau of Aeronautics; Bureau of Ordnance; Joint Army and Navy Board; Naval Aircraft Factory.
 air power views, 211–13
 contract administration, 362, 379, 388, 390–91, 422n, 422–24, 430, 442
 cross procurement, 482–83
 mobilization role, 151, 196, 241, 247, 262
 organizational relationships, 256, 266, 270, 306
 procurement procedures, 120, 138n, 142, 150, 284
 procurement program, 230, 234
 procurement record, 548, 552–53, 560–61, 576–79
 profits on contracts, 120, 122, 126
 requirements, 44, 53–54
 termination role, 451
NDAC. *See* National Defense Advisory Commission.
Negotiated contracts
 amendment sought, 276–80, 287
 authorization for, 82, 91–92, 113, 117, 275–76, 284–85, 289, 234, 258
 Congress views on, 118–20, 127, 148, 276
 for experimental aircraft, 86, 90–91, 114, 131
 for production orders, 129, 144

Negotiated contracts—Continued
 sometimes unavoidable, 84, 122, 130
 use before 1926, 91
 use discussed, 117, 127, 127n, 139, 141, 143, 146–47, 286, 338, 343, 373, 497, 499
Negotiated settlements, 452
Negotiation of contracts. *See* Contract negotiation.
Newspapers, 122, 124, 170, 199. *See also* Magazines; Public opinion; Public relations; Publicity.
 political use of, 173n, 173–74, 195
 publicize irregularities, 119–20, 122, 459
 Reuther Plan coverage, 311–14, 313n
Nelson, Donald, 228n, 239n, 272–73, 322, 471, 499
Netherlands, 224
Neutrality legislation, 18–19, 196–97, 200–201, 201n, 228, 249
New Castle, Del., 321
New Deal, 248–49, 316n, 402
New Haven, Conn., 506
New York, N.Y., 153, 491
New York Stock Exchange, 119
New York *Times,* 122, 223
Newark, N.J., 506
Noncompetitive procurement. *See* Negotiated contracts; Purchase orders; Sole source.
Nonferrous metal, 271n
Nonperformance, 447. *See also* Terminations.
Noorduyn Aviation Co., Ltd., 578. *See also* AT–16's; C–64's.
Norden bombsight, 198, 483
Norseman. *See* C–64's.
North Africa, 534
North American Aviation Corp., 30–31, 200, 241, 293n, 539, 547, 575. *See also* A–36's; AT–6's; B–24's; B–25's; B–29's; P–51's.
 CPFF contract, 415–16
 cross procurement, 482
 facility expansion, 302, 308, 321
 financing, 38n, 40n
 production, 21n, 561, 578
Northrop Aircraft, Inc., 38–39, 321, 578. *See also* A–31's; P–62's.
Norway, 200, 224
Nose turrets. *See* Gun turrets.
NRA. *See* National Recovery Administration.
Numbered air forces, 487
Numbers racket, 239ff.
Nye, Gerald Prentice, 55n, 199
Nylon, 250

O–60's, 578
O series engines, 581
OASW. *See* Office of Assistant Secretary of War.
Obligation of funds, 71–73, 76, 556–57. *See also* Authorization, distinguished from appropriation.
Observation aircraft, 45, 64, 156–57
Observation balloons, 206

INDEX 627

Observers, reports of, 218, 515. *See also* Military attaché reports.
Obsolescent aircraft
  influence current production, 203, 234, 267
  influence mobilization planning, 158–59
  retention of, 64, 242, 245
  spare parts impact, 342
Obsoletion, problem of, 49–51, 49n, 66–70, 197, 204, 219
OCAC. *See* Office, Chief of Air Corps.
OEM. *See* Office for Emergency Management.
Office, Chief of Air Corps. *See also* Chief of Air Corps.
  introduces machine records, 261n
  organization, 94ff., 268, 462
  priorities role, 258–62
  procurement role, 100, 102–05
  relations with NDAC, 256
  seeks procurement law, 276
Office of Assistant Secretary of War. *See also* Assistant Secretary of War.
  policies and procedures, 160, 183–84, 231, 276, 374, 397
  procurement role, 94, 100, 151, 247
Office for Emergency Management, 254
Office of Production Management, 192, 257n, 495
  co-ordinating role, 265–66, 270, 313, 538
  Defense Contract Service, 352, 496–97
  facility policies, 303, 321
  Wright Field unit, 270
  inadequacies, 272, 322
Office of the Secretary of War, 62. *See also* Secretary of War.
Office space, at Wright Field, 349–50
Office, Under Secretary of War. *See also* Under Secretary of War.
  anticipates conversion dislocations, 315, 403–04, 475
  co-ordination problems, 475
  disputes with services, 475
Officers. *See also* Contracting officers; Personnel; Regular Army; Reserve officers; Staff officers; Trained personnel.
  attitudes, 115, 240, 304, 509
  delay production decisions, 306
  in District offices, 503, 506
  frauds, 355
  industrial training, 162n
  at Wright Field, 466–67, 559
Offices, at Wright Field, 467
Official history, 482, 496
Ogden, Utah, 177
Oleo struts, 7, 160, 183, 318, 373, 566
Omaha, Neb., 308, 534, 540, 547
Open end contracts, 537
Open market procurement, 122, 248, 250, 343, 365
Operating expenses, fixed-fee role, 384
Operating ratios, aircraft industry, 40–41

Operating statements, financial, 357, 363
Operational experience, 381, 400
Operational losses, 217. *See also* Attrition.
Operations
  distinguished from control, 510
  influence organization, 93
Operations Commitments and Requirements, Air Staff, 465
Operations Division, OCAC, 97
OPM. *See* Office of Production Management.
Options, 127, 278, 332, 423
Order backlog, 234
Order maldistribution, 88, 274
Ordnance Department, 258
  CPFF practices, 379, 390–91
  cross procurement, 485
  GOCO contracts, 296
  relation to AAF, 486
  relation to ASF, 476
Organization, 93, 261, 271–272, 573. *See also* Doctrine; Organizational planning; Procurement procedures.
  charts, 476, 479, 505
Organizational planning, 347, 473, 476–78. *See also* Organization.
Organized labor. *See* CIO; Green, William; Hillman, Sidney; Reuther, Walter; Unions; United Auto Workers.
Organized Reserve, 48
Orwell, George, 218
OSW. *See* Office of the Secretary of War.
Overhaul, 50, 54–55, 74. *See also* Depots.
Overhead, 125, 282, 360, 362–63, 381, 383, 435
Overhead cranes, 524
Overlapping organizations, 103–04. *See also* Army-Navy; Cross procurement; Duplication of effort; Interbranch competition; Interservice rivalry.
Overseas procurement, 90. *See also* Buy American Act.
Overtime, 261n, 281
Oxygen systems, 267, 470, 529

P–26's, 568
P–35's, 568
P–36's, 198, 245
P–38's, 517, 531, 533–34, 550, 560, 578, 581
P–39's, 245, 302, 550, 560, 576, 581
P–40's, 228, 517–18, 550, 560, 577, 581
P–43's, 578
P–47's, 550, 560, 577–78
P–51's, 550, 578, 581
P–59's, 550, 562
P–61's, 550
P–62's, 578
P–63's, 517, 550, 576
P–67's, 578
P–70's, 550, 577
P–75's, 269, 577

P-80's, 550, 562, 578
P-84's, 538n
Pacifists, 73
Packard Motor Car Co.
    factory plan, 163
    purchasing problems, 401
    Rolls-Royce contract, 301, 309, 367, 392, 580
    World War I profits, 83
Packing, 341
Pan American Airlines, 399
Panama Canal Zone, 52–53, 282
Panel instruments. See Instruments, aircraft.
"Paper aircraft," 246
Parachute harness, 250
Partial payments, 73, 284, 368, 413. See also Advance payments; Progress payments.
Participating prime contractors, 543–45, 547
Partnerships, 436
Parts. See also Accessories; Components; Spare parts.
    fighter aircraft, 457
    number per aircraft, 564
    production of 306, 308–09, 381
Parts lists, 483, 544
Parts manufacturers, 182, 324
Parts supplier, mail order, 8
Patent lawyers, 105–06
Patent Liaison Section, 98–99
Patent licensing, 308
Patents, 46, 80–81, 319, 341, 436, 501
Patriotism, 271, 323, 364n, 384, 428, 505
Patrol bombers, 211, 576–79
Patterns, 398
Patterson, N.J., 6
Patterson, Robert P. See also Assistant Secretary of War; Office of Assistant Secretary of War; Under Secretary of War.
    appointed USW, 474ff.
    criticizes Air Corps, 261n
    criticizes legal organization, 349
    quoted, 548
    personal relationships, 479
    procurement role, 335, 351–52, 406
Paving, 389
Pay of officers, 212
Pay-as-you-go research. See Research and development.
Payroll, 393, 448. See also Wages.
Peacetime attitudes, 307
Peacetime strength. See Aircraft on hand; Authorized strength.
Pearl Harbor, 238–39, 249, 289, 316, 320
Pecora, Ferdinand, 119
Peculation. See Fraud.
Penalties, 357, 365
Penalty clauses. See Liquidated damages.
Performance characteristics. See also Aircraft performance; Military characteristics.

Performance characteristics—Continued
    design change role, 512
    evaluated in procurement, 93, 140. See also Evaluation procedures.
    impact of increased range, 52
    maximum sought, 130
    relation to price, 131, 134–38
Periodic repricing, 441
Periodicals. See Aviation periodicals; Magazines.
Personal equipment, 470, 492
Personal and organizational equipment, 558
Personalities, influence on procurement, 272n, 353, 355, 505
Personnel. See also Civilian personnel; Labor; Manpower; Officers; Skilled labor; Trained personnel.
    AAF directorate role, 465
    inexperienced, 110–11, 354–55, 369
    recruitment problem, 349, 360, 453
    requirements studies, 472
    shortages, 99, 104–05, 109
    Wright Field statistics, 466
Petroleum products, 484. See also Fuel.
Philadelphia, Pa., 125, 506
Philippine Islands, 52–53
Photography, 558
Piano manufacturers, 373
Pilot training, 225
Pilots, 11, 78, 121
Pipeline. See Distribution pipeline.
Piper, W. T., 32n
Piper Aircraft Corp., 561, 575, 578. See also L-4's.
Pirating of labor, 181
Planning, 44, 294. See also Mobilization planning; Policy formulation; Procurement planning.
Planning Branch, Materiel Division, 98
Planning Branch, OASW, 151ff., 165
Planning districts. See Procurement Planning Districts.
Plans Division, OCAC, 94–95, 105–106, 176–77
Plant clearance, 451–52, 456
Plant seizure, 322. See also Coercion; Confiscation; Seizure of facilities.
Plant Site Board, 307
Plant site selection. See Site selection.
Plant surveys. See Facility surveys.
Plants. See Facilities.
Plaster patterns, 544. See also Lofting; Templates.
Platt-LePage Aircraft Co., 578
PMP. See Protective Mobilization Plan.
Point system in aircraft evaluation, 111
Poland, 195, 205, 211
Police protection, 389
Policy formulation, 381, 401. See also Chief of Air Corps; Chief of Staff; Congress, defense responsibilities; Decision making; General Staff, War

INDEX 629

Policy formulation—Continued
  Department; House Committee on Military Affairs; Leadership; Senate Committee on Military Affairs.
Political parties, 253
Political slogans, 237
Political symbols, 229, 571
Politics. *See also* Congress; Decision making; Leadership; Procurement statutes; Public opinion.
  business allegations on, 316n
  influence aircraft industry, 37–38
  influence aircraft program, 172, 232n, 233, 515, 519, 569–71
  influence decentralization policy, 509–10
  influence design decisions, 515
  influence procurement leadership, 115, 188, 272n, 352–53
  in mobilization, 208, 248, 253–54, 265, 320
  plant seizure problem, 322
  in priorities problem, 494–95
  in procurement process, 55–58, 68–69, 106, 421
  in relief funds, 68–69
  in Reuther Plan, 312
  Roosevelt's tactics, 170–74
  separate air arm, 476
  in site selection, 308
  small business pressure, 497, 500, 502
Pools, formed by businessmen, 499
Porterfield Aircraft Corp., 575
Post Office Department, 12–13, 15, 497
Postmaster General, 14
Postwar economy, influence, 295–98, 431, 438
Power Plant Branch, Materiel Division, 98
Power plants. *See* Engine manufacturers; Engines; Jet engines; Liberty engines.
PR. *See* Procurement Regulations.
Pratt & Whitney Aircraft Division of United Aircraft Corp., 6, 28, 293n. *See also* R–985, R–1340, R–1830, *and* R–2800 engines.
  engine production, 7, 561, 580
  license Ford production, 309
  1939 foreign orders, 200–201
Precision work. *See* Tolerances.
Preparedness, 158, 164–65, 178, 225–26, 312. *See also* Mobilization planning; National defense.
President of the United States. *See also* Coolidge, Calvin; Roosevelt, Franklin D.
  Air Corps relations with, 69
  discretionary powers, 285, 289
  influence on procurement, 148
  mobilization role, 247
  requirements role, 63, 571
Presidential Budget. *See* Budget.
President's Liaison Committee, 252–53, 263, 265
Press. *See* Magazines; Newspapers; Public relations; Publicity.
Press, heavy forming, 30–31

Pretermination, 454
Price
  as factor in award, 93, 115, 138, 330, 343
  market policing of, 343
  procedure for evaluating, 134
  profit as factor in, 418
  relation to performance, 130–31, 134ff., 138. *See also* Performance characteristics.
  statute to minimize, 127
Price adjustment, 369, 421, 479n. *See also* Amendment of contracts; Renegotiation.
Price Adjustment Board, 429–30, 436–37, 440
Price Adjustment Section, 429
Price analysis, 407–08, 407n, 442
Price comparison, 358
Price competition, 130. *See also* Price.
Price increases, 108
Price indices, 358, 422–24, 436
Price quotations, 357
Price trends, 359
Prices
  accelerated depreciation lowers, 297
  contracting officer monitoring, 403–04
  excessive, 123
  foreign order impact, 204–05
  historical records, 359
  impact of renegotiation, 445
  Naval Aircraft Factory leverage on, 125
  reporting changes, 437
  verification, 360
Pricing, 87, 192, 357, 428
Primary training aircraft. *See* PT–13's *et seq.*
Prime contractors. *See also* Contractors.
  for airframes, 563
  favor facility expansions, 319
  favored over subs, 8, 317
  1942 volume, 346
  profits allowed, 375
  property accounting, 399
  purchasing problems, 401
  renegotiation clause, 429
  responsibilities, 494
  subcontractor relations, 319, 406, 447, 454, 494, 500, 543
  utilize small business, 323, 502
  views on modification, 531–32
Priorities
  district role, 508
  Draft Act provisions, 288
  for facility expansion, 321
  military compliance, 495
  OASW mobilization assignment, 247–48
  pinch small business, 262, 316–20, 493–94, 499
  procedures, 258–60, 262
  rivalry for, 259–60
Priorities and Allocations Section, OCAC, 259
Priority competition, 481

Private aircraft. *See* Civilian aircraft.
Private enterprise, 125, 388, 409
Procurement
 annual, 67, 87
 total expenditures, 556
Procurement, Army-Navy. *See* Joint procurement.
Procurement assignment, 480–81. *See also* Co-ordination, in procurement; Cross procurement.
Procurement Assignment Board, 480–85
Procurement Control Section, 472
Procurement cycle, 331–32. *See also* Procurement procedures.
Procurement district representatives, 167
Procurement districts
 complicate audits, 391
 contracting officers, 368–69
 data for negotiators, 358
 organization, 491, 506–08. *See also* Procurement Planning Districts.
 personnel problems, 466, 503, 505, 558–59
 price analysis groups, 407
 procurement role, 489, 493, 503–04, 504n, 508–10
 renegotiation role, 430, 433
 termination teams, 454
Procurement Division, Materiel Command
 cadres for districts, 503
 co-ordination with production, 468–69
 CPFF conversions, 414
 description, 466, 469–70, 472–73
 officer strength, 467
 sheds termination role, 454
Procurement Division, Treasury Department, 124n
Procurement doctrine
 on allowable profits, 434
 ASW role, 93
 auditing role, 390
 on contractor role, 388, 401–05
 favors established firms, 561
 formulated by ASF, 477
 GAO encroachment, 383
 impact of termination on, 453
 interpretations of, 80, 84, 209, 381, 408, 410, 573. *See also* Procurement policy; Procurement procedures.
 on organization, 430
 on renegotiation, 440
 on subcontracts, 494, 502
 supervision costs problem, 460
 on termination, 447
Procurement Engineering Branch, Materiel Division, 98
Procurement hump, problem of, 49
Procurement legislation. *See also* Procurement statutes.
 organization needed, 104–05
 revisions considered, 88
 specialists needed, 106, 349
 turning point, 283–84

Procurement officers. *See also* Contracting officers.
 attitudes of, 107–08, 401–02
 authority, 289, 500
 circumvent procurement curbs, 275
 close pricing failures, 442
 contractor pressure on, 317
 co-operate with SWPC, 501
 criticism of, 84
 criticism of ASF, 477
 defend contractor purchasing, 403, 409
 designer contracts restricted, 140
 educational role, 404, 419
 experience recorded, 389
 facility views, 319–20, 328
 fee views, 376
 inadequate staffs, 328
 neglect termination, 446, 449, 455
 oleo strut problem, 318
 problems confronting, 330ff.
 profit goals, 434
 qualities required, 147, 317, 343, 377
 question CPFF conversion, 419
 relations with GAO, 281, 396
 resist tax directive, 387
 shed subcontractor problem, 494
 swamped with data, 349
 use OPM services, 496
 value co-ordination, 351
 volume of negotiation, 346
Procurement organization. *See also* Materiel Command; Materiel Division; Procurement districts; Procurement Division, Materiel Command.
 congressional impact, 495
 criticism of, 345–46, 381
 district parallelism prescribed, 505
 functional subdivision, 346–48
 functions analyzed, 487
 housekeeping, 467
 lacks estimators, 361
 morale, 355
 personnel strength, 350
 reaction to criticism, 404
Procurement planning. *See also* Industrial Planning Section; Mobilization planning; Office of Assistant Secretary of War.
 design freeze planned, 513
 by OASW, 93, 151
 practical difficulties, 166n, 235–36
 requirements computation, 223
Procurement Planning Board, Materiel Division, 94, 97
Procurement Planning District representatives, 98, 153–54
Procurement Planning Districts, 153, 181n
Procurement policy, 82, 132, 141. *See also* Procurement doctrine; Procurement procedures; Procurement Regulations.
"Procurement priority," 262

INDEX
631

Procurement procedures. *See also* Contract negotiation; Contracting officers; Procurement doctrine; Procurement Regulations; Procurement statutes.
 AAF retains control, 479
 administering samples difficult, 133, 140
 ASW (Air) role, 94
 avoid favoritism, 140
 business instruction needed, 498
 change orders, 108–09, 303
 Chief of Air Corps role, 94
 complexity of objectives, 6, 104, 107, 112, 146–47, 209, 330, 569, 573
 congressional interest, 48, 121, 124
 contractor purchasing supervised, 360, 403
 co-ordination problems, 100–101
 criticism of, 75, 84–86, 113, 139, 350–51, 388
 described, 79, 81, 89, 99, 106–08, 113, 128, 148, 388, 513
 detailed specifications undesirable, 137–38
 evaluation methods, 110–11, 133
 Field Service Section role, 99
 General Foulois' views, 120
 German, 112
 impact of organization, 93
 impact of termination, 453
 innovations feared, 353
 internal record keeping, 358
 investigation of, 123
 irregularities alleged, 121–22, 127
 legal aspects, 105–06
 Navy's approved, 122
 negotiated contracts, 88, 129
 political aspects of, 106
 precedents for, 109–10
 price analysis, 408
 reconciling price and performance, 130
 revision urged, 86–89, 109, 124, 128, 131, 142, 145, 331ff.
 rival conceptions, 408
 simplified by Johnson, 175
 small business complaints, 493
 standardization required, 132
 subcontractor stipulations, 494
 USW role, 476
 upset by war, 146
Procurement program. *See also* Air Corps, balanced program; Air Corps, expansion program; Air Corps Act of 1926; Authorized strength; 1,800, 2,320, 5,500, and 50,000 aircraft programs; Mobilization; Rearmament program.
 Air Service, 46
 complexity of, 229
 civilian agency interference, 495–96
 delays, 71, 334
 implications discussed, 236
 influenced by doctrine, 5–6, 211, 233
 lack of, 44
 Morrow Board, 46–47

Procurement program—Continued
 need for continuing, 47
 revision in, 239
Procurement Regulations
 ASF role, 477
 authorize discretion, 81
 condition negotiations, 356
 on contracting officers, 353, 369
 define fair price, 357
 described, 339
 drafted by ASW, 474
 evasions, 367
 incentive contract, 417
 literal compliance, 459
 nonmilitary objectives, 455
 problem of formulation, 478
 procurement assignment, 481
Procurement Section, Materiel Division, 99, 106ff., 116. *See also* Procurement Division.
Procurement statutes. *See also* Legislation; Procurement legislation; Revised Statutes; Social welfare legislation.
 ACC role, 87–88
 administration of, 80ff., 94, 104–05, 125, 147, 419
 complexity, 147
 danger of tampering, 116, 128, 131, 276, 353
 discourage designers, 86–87
 discretionary powers ignored, 115
 evasion of, 275–367
 impact of, 569
 inadequacies, 100, 274–75, 280, 283
 interpretation of, 81, 114–15, 172
 limit fees, 375
 penalties for fraud, 357
 permit wartime deviations, 359
 renegotiation provisions, 429, 432, 438–39
 revisions sought, 89, 126, 276, 279–80
 strict compliance harmful, 85
 termination, 452
Procurement without competition, 89, 113–17, 123, 127. *See also* Air Corps Act of 1926; Allocation of contracts; Negotiated contracts; Sole source.
Production, 511, 511n. *See also* Aircraft industry, prewar production experience; Aircraft production.
Production analysis, 163–64. *See also* Factory plans.
Production capacity. *See also* Aircraft industry, capacity estimates; Mobilization, facility policy; Mobilization planning.
 for accessories, 180, 294
 allocation of, 152, 155–56, 247
 in aluminum, 180
 in automobile industry, 304
 in conception of mobilization, 159, 178, 234, 329
 expansion of, 143, 176–77, 182, 232, 304, 320, 324–25. *See also* Facility expansion.
 foreign order impact, 18, 195, 197, 200–203
 impact of nationalization, 201

Production capacity—Continued
  measurement of, 175, 181, 181n, 185–92, 291, 294, 305, 321, 408
  misuse of, 242
  needed for spares, 294
  of oleo struts, 318
  out of doors, 531
  problem of maintaining, 178–79, 234
  reports on, 186
  requirements, 168n, 169, 186, 224–25, 252, 290, 292, 507
  shortage of, 150, 181, 250
  in small business, 317, 494
  subcontracting inadequate for, 184
  turbosuperchargers, 455–56
Production contracts
  to amortize research, 25, 85, 88, 114
  Beech UC–45 discussed, 442
  budgetary problems, 72, 128, 143–44
  competition required, 84–85, 115, 124, 131
  co-ordination problems, 463
  delayed by development, 75–76, 108
  by design competition, 90–91, 276
  evaluation of, 131
  facility financing, 295
  indirect competition on, 127
  JAG rulings on, 115
  political influence on, 115
  procedures for, 107, 274
  profits on, 126
  sample required, 140–42
  specifications, 86
  without competition, 88, 91, 116–17, 127n, 144, 146
Production control. *See also* BDV Committee; Co-ordination; Joint production programs; Production Division, Materiel Command; Production planning.
  industry failures in, 32
  for modifications, 516–17, 535, 538
  need for, 564
  termination problem, 456
Production Control Section, 467
Production data contracts, 291
Production Division, Materiel Command
  aids negotiators, 358, 361
  co-ordination problems, 468–69
  officer strength, 467
  organization, 466, 469
  schedules modifications, 532, 535
Production Division, NDAC, 256, 262
Production engineering, 32, 468
Production Engineering Section, Materiel Command, 270, 462, 467, 482, 502, 517
Production engineers, 186, 188, 306, 361, 468, 538
Production expediting, 364, 471, 509. *See also* Aircraft production, acceleration.
Production failures, 240
Production lines. *See* Assembly lines.

Production methods, 156. *See also* Aircraft production; Manufacturing methods.
Production models, 331
Production options, 127
Production orders, procedure for, 113
Production versus performance, 75
Production planning. *See also* Production control.
  BDV Committee role, 541
  during design phase, 519
  faulty premises, 294
  Ford initiative, 520
  influences renegotiation, 437
  for modifications, 534
  statistical tools, 192
Production processes. *See* Aircraft production; Manufacturing methods.
Production programs. *See also* procurement programs and individual programs by name.
  Air Staff "ultimate," 237
  airframe weight factor, 243
  criticized, 4, 239
  design changes influence, 156
  Ford Willow Run, 521
  goals change, 304
  President's, 238, 240, 571
  require symbolic leadership, 571
Production ratios, 564. *See also* Aircraft industry, output per worker; Airframe manufacturers, cost per pound; Production time.
Production scheduling. *See also* Production control; Production planning; Scheduling.
  by JAC, 266–69
  NDAC initiates, 263
  periodic revision of, 264
  unreliable, 187
Production statistics. *See* Aircraft production.
Production targets, feasibility questioned, 240
Production time, airframes, 141. *See also* Time lapse, production.
Production tooling. *See also* Jigs and fixtures.
  accelerated depreciation for, 297
  Air Corps failure, 190n
  in aircraft industry, 17, 28, 30–31
  BDV Committee on, 543, 545
  complicates contract authorization, 73
  in contract negotiation, 341–42
  cost analysis of, 348, 360, 363
  costs, 31, 141, 413, 526
  delays encountered, 325–26
  disposal, 458–59
  duplicate charges for, 399
  economies, 26–27, 33, 327, 367, 512
  educational order, 159–60
  escalation for, 426
  evaluation of, 111
  exports impact, 200
  influences facility policy, 327
  influences renegotiation, 437

INDEX

Production tooling—Continued
  in modification costs, 534
  paucity of literature, 32
  prevents contract comparison, 419
  property accounting, 397, 399
  spare parts impact, 342
  upsets capacity yardstick, 189-90
  at Willow Run, 518-27
Productivity
  in engine industry, 565
  of labor, 191, 361
  ratios, 564
Products, alphabetical file of, 358
Profit limitations
  impact on industry, 35-36
  impact on priorities, 259-60
  legislation, 280, 288, 297, 301. *See also* Vinson-Trammell Act.
  in negotiated contracts, 279
  regulations, 380
Profiteering
  adverse publicity, 445
  alleged in aircraft industry, 59, 126, 384
  alleged in airlines, 119, 121
  alleged in Navy contracts, 120, 122
  alleged in World War I, 46, 83, 119. *See also* Nye, Gerald Prentice.
  compared with treason, 84
  Congress curbs, 429. *See also* Price adjustment; Renegotiation; Vinson-Trammell Act.
  infrequent on military contracts, 126
  procedural changes against, 124
  Renegotiation Act role, 431, 438
Profits. *See also* Excess profits.
  allowable margins, 375, 434
  Army-Navy contracts, 126
  automobile industry views, 314
  Congress studies curbs on, 119-20, 123-26
  on cost-plus contract, 82, 372
  faulty industry index, 40
  in fee setting, 378
  foreign order impact, 197, 201, 203-04, 260
  inadequate capital source, 36
  misunderstood by public, 445
  Naval Aircraft Factory control of, 125
  Navy contracts, 120, 122
  on negotiated contracts, 121
  1926-38 aircraft industry, 33, 35-36, 39, 126
  preferred to preparedness, 178
  recapture. *See* Profit limitations; Renegotiation; Repricing; Vinson-Trammell Act.
  reduce fraud temptation, 357
  reduction, 364
  relation to costs, 360, 364n, 418, 445
  in renegotiation, 431, 440, 443. *See also* Renegotiation.
  role in pricing, 343-44, 348

Profits—Continued
  statutory curbs on, 284-85. *See also* Profit limitations; Renegotiation; Repricing; Vinson-Trammell Act.
  tax impact on, 299n
  termination allowance, 450
  on unfinished work, 450
  in World War I, 83, 150
Programs. *See* Procurement planning; Procurement program; Production programs; *individual programs by name*.
Progress payments, 73, 284. *See also* Partial payment.
Progress reports, 368
Project engineers, 269, 366, 513. *See also* Project officers.
Project officers, 97, 99, 358, 361, 463
Promotion, 212, 354, 384
Propeller manufacturers, 7-8, 8n, 183, 294-95, 566
Propellers, 562-63. *See also* Hamilton-Standard Division of United Aircraft Corp.; Nash-Kelvinator Corp.
  aluminum needs studied, 257
  concurrent spares production, 294
  for Ford B-24, 527
  mobilization plans for, 156
  P-39 production delays, 245
  production, 549, 563
  production acceleration, 566
  production scheduling, 267
  types procured, 552
  variable pitch, 72, 156
Property accounting, 397-98, 400, 415, 532
Property disposal, 456, 458-60
Property officers, 399-400
Proposal form, 357
Proposals. *See* Circular proposals.
Proprietary designs, 87-89, 160, 319, 539. *See also* Licensing; Patents; Sole source.
Protective Mobilization Plan, 151, 166, 206, 221, 225, 225n
Proving Ground Command, 487
Psychological targets, 228-29, 234, 236-40, 242-43
PT-13's, 546, 551, 576, 581
PT-14's, 579
PT-17's, 551, 576
PT-19's, 551, 576-78, 581
PT-20's, 578, 581
PT-21's, 578
PT-22's, 578, 581
PT-23's, 546, 551, 576-78
PT-24's, 577, 581
PT-25's, 578, 581
PT-26's, 551, 577
PT-27's, 551
Public advertising. *See* Advertising for bids.
Public exigency, 80

Public opinion. *See also* Congress; Magazines; Newspapers; Politics; Public relations; Publicity.
  dilemmas for command, 243
  manipulation of, 172–73
  misled by minority report, 122
  on production goals, 241, 310, 316
  on profits problem, 445
  relation to air power, 3–5
Public relations, 105, 378, 431
Public War Housing Act, 389n
Public works, statutory requirements for, 281, 376
Public Works Administration, 67, 128–29, 393
Publications, 382
Publicity, 124, 312, 412, 454, 459, 496. *See also* Advertising for bids; Magazines; Newspapers; Public relations.
Puddle jumpers. *See* Liaison aircraft.
Pumps, 271n
Purchase Branch, Materiel Division, 98, 347–48
Purchase of land, 327
Purchase orders. *See also* Purchasing; Suborders.
  business volume, 346, 457
  excise tax problem, 387
  forms, 339
  monitoring, 404, 407–08
  noncompetitive, 406
  retail pricing, 434
Purchase Section, Materiel Command, 348, 473
Purchase, Storage, and Traffic Division, 475
Purchases Division, ASF, 481
Purchasing. *See also* Contract administration; Contractors, procurement procedures monitored.
  abuses, 406
  Buy American requirement, 280
  by contractors, 403
  co-ordinating committee role, 541, 543, 545
  improved procedure, 408
  requires specialized skills, 405
Purchasing agents, 404–06
Purchasing missions, 195–96. *See also* British Purchasing Commission; French Purchasing Mission.
Purchasing organizations, automotive, 312
Pursuit aircraft. *See* Fighter aircraft; P–26's *et seq.*
PWA. *See* Public Works Administration.
Pyrotechnic equipment, 267n

Quality. *See also* Aircraft performance; Performance characteristics; Specifications; Tolerances.
  problem of achieving, 112, 116
  control, 562
  versus price, 330
Quantity procurement, 132, 134, 140–41. *See also* Production data contracts.
Quantity versus quality, 64–65, 75–77, 144, 241–43
  compromises required, 512–18, 528
  modification role, 530, 538

Quantity versus quality—Continued
  NDAC interest, 257n
  organization required, 572
Quartermaster Corps, 258, 476

R–1's, 578
R–4's, 551, 578, 582
R–5's, 551, 578
R–6's, 551, 578
R–420 engine, 582
R–440 engine, 581
R–500 engine, 582
R–540 engine, 581
R–550 engine, 582
R–670 engine, 581
R–680 engine, 309, 581
R–755 engine, 581
R–760 engine, 580
R–915 engine, 581
R–975 engine, 580
R–985 engine, 580
R–1340 engine, 580
R–1820 engine, 458, 580
R–1830 engine, 309–10, 580
R–2100 engine, 309
R–2600 engine, 310, 438, 580
R–2800 engine, 309, 580
R–3350 engine, 580
R&D. *See* Research and development.
Radar, 485. *See also* Communications equipment; Radios; Signal Corps.
Radial engines, 309, 565
Radiator caps, 32
Radio Corporation of America, 7–8, 8n
Radio programs, 432
Radios, 246, 271, 486
RAF. *See* Royal Air Force.
RAINBOW plan, 211n
Railroads, 327
Ramsey, Capt. D. C., 266
Range, impact of increased, 52. *See also* Aircraft performance.
Ranger Engineering Co., 6, 28n, 273n, 580
Raw materials. *See also* Critical raw materials; Materials.
  Buy American Act role, 282
  costs, 303, 360. *See also* Market prices; Price quotations; Price trends.
  CPFF problems, 411
  interplant transfers, 545
  mobilization problems, 158, 259, 267, 269–70. *See also* Air Scheduling Unit, JAC; Priorities; Scheduling; Shortages.
  shortages, 241, 250, 271n, 317, 493
  waste of, 242
RCA, 7–8, 8n
Readjustment Division, ASF, 453
Readjustment Division, Materiel Command, 454

INDEX

635

Rearmament. *See also* National defense.
 foreign order role, 195–96
 stimulus to, 175, 179–80, 194
 U.S. policy on, 169
Rearmament program, 210, 274, 281–83, 300, 314, 493. *See also* 5,500 aircraft program.
Rearwin Aircraft & Engines, Inc., 9, 578
Rebates, 281
Reconnaissance aircraft, 576–79
Reconstruction Finance Corporation, 284, 299, 451
Reconversion of facilities, 315, 323, 377, 452, 457
Record-breaking flights, 3
Record keeping, 473. *See also* Data processing.
Recovery rate, 536
Recruiting, 355
Red Cross, 382
Red tape, 388, 395. *See also* Procurement procedures.
Reform, 123–25. *See also* Investigations.
Reformation of contracts, 366n
Refunds, 434. *See also* Renegotiation; Voluntary refunds.
Regular Army officers, 212, 506. *See also* Officers; Reserve officers.
Regulations. *See* Army Regulations; Procurement Regulations.
Rehabilitation. *See* Reconversion of facilities.
Reimbursement, 380–81. *See also* Contract administration; General Accounting Office.
Release policy, 197–200, 207. *See also* Neutrality legislation; Secrecy; Security classification.
Relief appropriations for aircraft, 67–69, 128
Relief payments, 389n
Remington Rand, 563
Renegotiation, 289, 355, 358, 377, 396, 429–30
 administration of, 433–43, 453
 criteria, 440n
 objectives, 431
 summarized, 444–45
Renegotiation Act
 amended, 438–39
 lacks profit definition, 434
 passed, 429
 spirit and philosophy, 431–32, 436, 443
Renton, Wash., 547. *See also* Boeing Aircraft Corp.
Reorganization of Army, 475, 480
Repair shops, 530. *See also* Depots.
Repairs. *See* Maintenance.
Replacement aircraft, 49, 66, 70, 74–75, 217–19, 225
Replacements. *See* Spare engines; Spare parts.
Reports, 349, 473. *See also* Contract administration; Management control; Statistical Control Office.
Repricing, 355, 377, 422, 427, 441
Republic Aviation Corp., 38–39, 293n, 538n, 547. *See also* B-29's; P-47's; P-43's; Seversky Aviation Corp.
 facility expansion, 302, 321
 production record, 376, 561, 565, 578

Requirements
 for aluminum, 158
 for aluminum forgings, 250
 changing character, 241, 291, 304, 446
 conflicting objectives in, 130, 172
 design factors in, 130, 140, 156
 estimates, 61–62, 70, 153, 224–25, 225n
 factors influencing, 48, 172, 216, 218ff., 238, 321
 industry capacity for, 161, 178. *See also* Allocation of facilities; Facility expansion; Mobilization planning.
 interbranch consolidation, 481
 Johnson views on, 181
 organizations involved, 52, 63, 65–66, 93–95, 99, 231, 241, 252, 257, 271, 465
 for petroleum products, 484
 Roosevelt role in, 169–73, 214, 225–26, 237–40, 292
Requirements Branch, Materiel Division, 98
Requirements computation
 in Air Service, 44–45
 defects in, 220–22
 doctrinal basis, 211, 231–33
 Drum Board studies, 53
 methods of, 52–53, 155–58, 209–14, 222–23, 223n, 231, 525, 571. *See also* Troop basis.
 political factors behind, 213
Research and development, 10. *See also* Aircraft innovations; Experimental aircraft; Experimental contracts; Scientific advances; Service tests.
 design firms favored, 22, 88
 facilities, 23, 99
 financing, 21, 36, 70, 85, 144, 557–59
 impact of procurement, 569
 industry losses on, 24–25
 influences renegotiation, 435
 procedures for encouraging, 25, 90
 procurement statute role, 85, 92, 141. *See also* Aeronautical Chamber of Commerce; Air Corps Act of 1926; Procurement statutes.
 university role, 23
Reserve aircraft, 54, 74, 157, 204. *See also* Spare engines; Spare parts.
Reserve Branch, Materiel Division, 98
Reserve officers, 158, 466, 505–06. *See also* Officers; Regular Army officers.
Resident representatives, 98–99, 358, 361, 369–70, 391, 406, 406n. *See also* Contract administration; Procurement districts.
Resources, 247–48. *See also* Raw materials.
Resources Control Section, Materiel Command, 489
Retirement pay, 385
Retraction gear, 180–81, 566
Retrenchment. *See* Economy drives.
Reuther, Walter, 310–15, 314n
Reuther Plan, 310–14
Revenue Act of 1943, 444
Revenue Act of 1944, 388

Revised Statutes, 80, 275. *See also* Procurement statutes.
RFC. *See* Reconstruction Finance Corporation.
Risk taking, 82, 200–201, 421
River Rouge (Detroit) facility, 309
Rivets, 564
Rochester, N.Y., 506
Rogers, W. N., 123, 136
Rogers Committee, 55n, 123–24, 124n, 127
Rolls-Royce, 301, 309, 367, 392, 580. *See also* Packard Motor Car Co.
Roosevelt, Franklin D.
  airmail role, 15
  ARCADIA Conference, 238
  Arsenal of Democracy, 304
  and ASW (Air), 53, 102
  Aviation Procurement Committee, 124n
  budget minded, 60, 67, 71, 128, 195, 231, 232n
  criticized, 234, 236, 239–43, 277, 291, 313
  decision to rearm, 169–71, 174
  declares emergency, 193–95
  export policy, 202, 205, 207, 210, 252
  50,000 aircraft program, 209, 224, 226, 230, 240, 250, 283, 332
  initiates bomber program, 540
  military leadership, 213, 228, 240, 274–75, 279, 302, 385, 492
  on nationalization of facilities, 125, 177–79. *See also* Air arsenals; Government-owned facilities; Nationalization of industry.
  NDAC role, 253–55
  neutrality policy, 19, 196, 198–99
  OPM role, 265, 270
  orders aviation investigation, 56
  political skill, 170–75, 173n, 249
  on Reuther Plan, 313n
  role in requirements, 169–73, 214, 225–26, 237–40, 292
  WPB role, 322
  WRB role, 248–49
Roosevelt, James, 68–69
Roosevelt, Theodore, Jr., 88–89
Rosenman, Samuel, 228n
Rotary wing aircraft, 551, 577–79, 582
Rotation in office, 109
Roush, F. E., 354n
Royal Air Force, 51, 218. *See also* British Purchasing Commission; United Kingdom.
Royalties, 357, 436
Rubber, 322
Rudders, 564
Rulings. *See* Judicial decisions. *See also* Comptroller General; General Accounting Office.
Rumors, 170
Russia, 200, 242, 246, 534, 553, 560
Rutherford, Col. H. K., 184
Ryan Aeronautical Corp., 293, 302, 578. *See also* PT–20's; PT–21's; PT–22's; PT–25's.

Safety belts, 267n
St. Louis, Mo., 9, 378, 575, 578
St. Louis Aircraft Corp., 575, 578. *See also* PT–19's; PT–23's.
St. Louis Airplane Division of Curtiss-Wright Corp., 575
Salaries, 154, 382, 384–85, 435, 558–59. *See also* Wages.
Sales abroad. *See* Foreign orders; Exports.
Sales taxes, 387, 406n
Salvage, 398, 407, 458. *See also* Plant clearance; Property disposal; Scrap; Surplus aircraft.
Salvageable parts, 399
Sample aircraft competition, 114, 131–36, 139–49, 274, 331
San Diego, Calif., 9, 29, 565, 575
Santa Monica, Calif., 9, 491
"Save harmless" clause, 386
Scamping, 181
Scandal, 15, 55, 118, 123, 458ff.
Scarcities. *See* Shortages.
Scarff, Col. J. G., 389
Scheduled carriers. *See* Airlines.
Scheduling, 251, 267, 270, 537, 541. *See also* Delivery scheduling; Production scheduling.
School construction, 389
Schools for contract termination, 454
Schwinn, J. W., 354n
Scientific advances, 97. *See also* Aircraft innovations; Research and development.
Scrap, 398, 458, 522, 524. *See also* Salvage.
Screw machine, 443
Sealed bids, 343. *See also* Advertising for bids; Bidders; Bids; Circular proposals; Competitive procurement.
Seattle, Wash., 9, 299, 542
Second Aviation Objective, 236
Second Aviation Strength, 236
Second Revenue Act of 1940, 288–89
Second-shift operations. *See* Multiple-shift operations.
Secretary of the Air Force, 378
Secretary of the General Staff, 211
Secretary of Labor, 282
Secretary of Navy
  discretionary powers, 88–91, 115, 284
  emergency powers, 286
  establishes Munitions Board, 151
  urges air study, 46
  urges discretionary funds, 224
Secretary of State, 209
Secretary of Treasury, 224, 252–53, 256, 265, 282
Secretary of War. *See also* Davis, D. F.; Baker, Newton D.; Dern, George H.; Stimson, Henry L.; Woodring, H. H.
  anticipates private financing, 292–93
  approves Bell EPF, 302
  backs sample aircraft, 133, 143, 148
  Buy American suspension, 283

INDEX

637

Secretary of War—Continued
  conflict with Comptroller, 137
  curtails negotiated contracts, 334
  on design change, 156
  design competition role, 89–90
  discretionary powers, 88–89, 111, 113, 115–16, 136–38, 276
  emergency powers, 82, 286
  establishes Munitions Board, 151
  50,000 program contracts, 243
  investigates air arm, 4, 44, 46, 48, 55–57
  negotiated procurement authorized, 275
  plant seizures authorized, 288
  Price Adjustment Board, 429
  procurement role, 91, 100, 107
  rejects conversion study, 163
  relations with ASW (Air), 53
  resists McSwain, 59–60, 139n
  studies facility financing, 294
  transport case views, 137
  urged to spread contracts, 129
Secrecy, 124, 185, 197, 207. *See also* Release policy; Security classification.
Secret procurement, 279n
Secret weapon, 112
Section 10, Air Corps Act, 89–93, 278, 344
Securities, sale of. *See* Capital investment; Stock market.
Security classification, 18, 188, 198, 502. *See also* Classified data; Release policy; Secrecy.
Self, Sir Henry, 266
Seizure of facilities, 286n. *See also* Coercion; Confiscation; Plant seizure.
Selective auditing, 394
Selective Service, 157
Selective Service Act, 288, 338n, 378n, 443. *See also* Draft boards; Draftees.
Seller's market, 287
Semiskilled labor, 348, 512, 524
Senate Committee on Appropriations, 43
Senate Committee on Military Affairs, 43, 61, 284
Senate Committee on Naval Affairs, 284
Seniority, 322
Sentinel. *See* L-5's.
Separate air force, 476
Service pay, 212
Service testing, expenditures, 558
Service test contract, 278
Service test squadron, 107
Service tests, 24, 107–08, 113, 117, 203, 509
Serviceable aircraft, defined, 51
Services of Supply, 475
Settlement. *See* Termination.
Settlement Review Board, 453
Settlement Review Committee, 453
Seversky Aviation Corp., 575. *See also* Republic Aviation Corp.
Sewage disposal, 389

Shadow factories, 164–66, 184, 290n
Shaw, Col. F. P., 354n
Sherwood, Robert, 239n
Shock absorbers. *See* Oleo struts.
Shooting Star. *See* P-80's.
Shop practices, 86. *See also* Manufacturing methods.
Shortages. *See also* Bottlenecks; Critical raw materials; Priorities.
  in aircraft industry, 180–81, 250, 258
  ASU alleviation role, 271, 271n
  BDV Committee solutions, 545
  complicate inventory control, 457
  cut production economies, 524
  foster procurement assignment, 481
  50,000 program reveals, 250
  ground aircraft, 50
  hurt small business, 318
  industry warnings of, 180
  influence bidders, 493
  influence modification policy, 530
  influence procurement objectives, 330
  influence on subcontracting, 182
  Materiel Division personnel, 99, 104–05
  spare parts, 55
  in World War I, 150
Shutdown, 415
Siam, 529
Signal Corps, 109–10, 480–81, 486
Sikorsky Aircraft Division of United Aircraft, 578. *See also* R-1's; R-4's; R-5's; R-6's; Vought-Sikorsky Aircraft Division of United Aircraft Corp.
Site selection, 177, 307–08. *See also* Facility expansion.
"Sitzkrieg," 195
60,000 aircraft program, 238–39
Skilled labor. *See also* Labor; Skilled personnel; Trained personnel.
  in aircraft industry, 348, 522
  airlines as source, 530
  dispersal feared, 179
  Eight-Hour law impact, 281
  lost during conversions, 322
  mobilization planning for, 158, 163, 187
  shortages, 181
  termination problem, 456
Skilled personnel, 104
Skymaster. *See* C-54's.
Skytrain. *See* C-47's.
Slogans, 54, 229
Small business. *See also* Smaller War Plants Corporation.
  congressional concern for, 121, 288, 438, 498
  conversion for defense, 319–20, 323
  defined, 316
  favored by competition, 127
  favors decentralization, 492, 510
  influences termination, 455

Small business—Continued
    integrity, 346
    military procurement from, 317, 495–96, 498
    profiteering, 439
    resents disclosures, 357
    seeks defense contracts, 317, 493
    subcontract role, 494
    volume of contracts, 492
Small Business Act, 499, 501
Small claims, 349
Smaller War Plants Corporation, 500–501
Social costs, 389
Social security, 386
Social Security Building, 273
Social welfare legislation, 72, 141, 280–81, 285n
Socialism, 277. See also Nationalization of industry.
Socialists, 297
Society of British Aircraft Constructors, 188
Solar Aircraft Corp., 575
Sole source, 80, 108, 116–18, 127, 129, 435. See also Licensing; Patents; Proprietary designs; Purchase orders.
Solenoids, 567
Somervell, Lt. Gen. Brehon B., 475, 482
Sorties, 217
SOS, 475
South Bend, Ind., 310
Southeastern Procurement District, 506
Spain, 217
Spare engines, 74, 215–16
Spare parts
    ASC purchasing, 470
    concurrent production, 294
    contract stipulations, 342
    cross procurement problem, 483
    delay contract settlement, 427
    Field Service Section role, 99
    impact on procurement, 80–81
    importance, 210
    influence production decisions, 243
    influence release policy, 198
    lacking for B–17, 245
    production cut, 240
    requirements computation, 214–16, 342
    shortages ground aircraft, 50, 55
    standardized, 267n
    SWPC policy, 501
Spark plugs, 214, 250
Spartan Aircraft Co., 293n, 575, 579
Special-purpose tools, 342, 484
Special tooling, 452. See also Production tooling.
Specialization, 347–50, 354
Specifications. See also Standardization.
    advantages in delaying, 145
    compliance problems, 492–93
    Comptroller misunderstands character of, 137
    in contract negotiations, 130, 140, 340–41, 366, 497
    co-ordination of, 543

Specifications—Continued
    curb cross procurement, 485
    for data contracts, 186
    decisions on changes, 468
    deviation problems, 108, 507
    by Engineering Section, 97
    for first airplane, 110n
    foreign policy influences, 214
    indexed, 132
    influence mobilization plans, 155
    interbranch differences, 480–81
    needed for priorities, 259
    never complete, 86
    petroleum products, 484
    restrict scope of competition, 130
    small business problem, 502
    subcontractor role, 404
    for suppliers, 251
    time in formulation, 108
    Wright Field files, 99
Speculators, 39
Sperry Corp., 7–8, 8n, 437
Spitfire, 228
Split awards, 280, 283, 498
Spot checking, 394. See also Auditing.
Staff-loading studies, 472
Staff manuals. See Manuals.
Staff officers. See also Officers.
    education, 404
    lack of, 381, 476, 479
    modification role, 518
    need political skill, 570
    termination role, 456
Staff paper. See Memorandum Report.
Staffing problems. See Personnel.
Standard designs, 107. See also Standardization.
Standard contract form, 365. See also Contract forms.
Standard hardware. See Accessories; Aircraft hardware.
Standard Oil of N.J., 282
Standard Proposal Form, 357, 359, 363
Standard tools, 459. See also Hand tools.
Standardization
    Air Corps Technical Committee role, 107
    in aircraft, 519
    of aircraft accessories, 131, 267
    of audit procedures, 391
    co-ordination of, 544
    Engineering Section role, 97
    guidebooks, 131–32
    inhibits design change, 26
    JAC role, 266, 268–269
    need for, 264, 293
    organization needed, 264
    prewar conception, 513n
    procedures for, 107, 132
    proprietary design problem, 539

INDEX 639

Standardized forms, 440. *See also* Contract forms; Form 32.
Standardized parts, 8, 160
Standards book, 132
Stand-by facility. *See* Government-owned facility; Shadow factories.
Stand-by reserve, 195
Standing operating procedures, 147. *See also* Administrative procedures; Procurement procedures.
Starters, aircraft, 183, 294, 429, 437, 567
State taxes, 299–300, 387–88
Statistical Control Office, 508
Statistics, 191–93, 216, 261, 472. *See also* Data processing.
Status of Equipment Book, 99
Statutes. *See* Legislation; Procurement statutes; Revised statutes; Social welfare legislation.
Stearman Aircraft Division of Boeing Aircraft Corp., 293n, 575
Stearman-Hammond Aircraft Corp., 575
Steel, electric furnace, 250
Steel, weight in airframes, 180
Steer hides, 250
Stettinius, Edward R., Jr., 255
Stein, Gertrude, 434
Stimson, Henry L., 335
Stinson Aircraft Division of Aviation Manufacturing Corp., 293n, 575
Stock control, 32, 400, 457
Stock market, 119, 121, 141–42. *See also* Capital investment.
Stock record cards, 400
Stockholders, 436. *See also* Stock market.
Stoppages, 271
Strategic bombers, 212. *See also* Four-engine bombers; Heavy bombers.
Strategic dispersal, 9, 177, 307. *See also* Dispersal.
Strategic mission, 54. *See also* Air power.
Strategic requirements, 55, 172
Strategic vulnerability. *See* Strategic dispersal.
Strategy, influence of, 225, 307
Strength in aircraft. *See* Aircraft on hand.
Strength ceiling, 170–72. *See also* Authorized strength.
Strength report. *See* Aircraft on hand.
Stopped vouchers. *See* Disallowances.
Stretching devices, hydraulic, 31
Stretch-out, 280
Structural defects, 245
Structural steel, 267, 321
Studebaker Corp., 310, 377, 418, 458, 480. *See also* Wright Aeronautical Corp.
Subassemblies, 6–7, 290, 303, 305–06, 309, 324. *See also* Components.
Subcontracting
  in airframe industry, 191
  co-ordination problems, 539
  by Curtiss Electric, 562
  discussed, 7–8, 182–84, 317, 502, 568

Subcontracting—Continued
  dollar volume, 494n
  in engine industry, 564
  excise tax problem, 387
  in 50,000 program, 293
  influences bidding, 359
  influences renegotiation, 435
  by instrument firms, 567
  in propeller industry, 566
  small business seeks, 317
  in supercharger industry, 568
Subcontractors
  escalation accounting, 427
  in automobile industry, 290, 309
  Bendix role, 450
  close pricing, 361
  contract stipulations, 342
  contracting officer monitoring, 368, 404, 408n
  CPFF conversion problem, 415
  distribution of, 511
  facility conversion, 315
  facility expansion, 320
  feared as competitors, 319
  Ford role, 494n, 519
  inventory problem, 450
  labor force, 282, 563
  listings inadequate, 508
  mobilization planning for, 153–54
  obligations, 401
  prewar description, 7
  price certifications, 408
  priorities problems, 258
  profit curbs, 285, 289
  property accounting, 399
  relation to primes, 543, 546
  renegotiation, 429
  repricing, 443
  right of audit, 402
  small business role, 494
  studied as sources, 508
  termination, 447, 451, 454
  1942 volume, 346
Suborders. *See* Purchase orders.
Subsidies, 119, 143–44, 146
Sub-subcontractors, 405, 407
Superagency. *See* Civilian superagency.
Superchargers. *See* Turbosuperchargers.
Superfortress. *See* B–29's; Boeing Aircraft Corp.
Supervision
  in CPFF contracts, 408–09. *See also* Contract administration; Contracting officers, monitor contractor purchasing; Suppliers, contracting officer monitoring.
  difficulties of, 403, 472–73, 479. *See also* Command; leadership.
Supplementary agreement. *See* Supplementary contracts.

Supplementary contracts, 366–67, 413. *See also* Change orders.
Suppliers. *See also* Vendors.
   in automobile complex, 305, 309
   Bendix role, 450
   and Buy American Act, 282
   catalogues, 408, 458
   close pricing, 360
   contracting officer monitoring, 404, 408n
   co-ordination, 545
   distribution of, 511
   DPC role, 300
   of electrical equipment, 566–67
   facility conversion, 315
   facility expansion, 320
   faulty cost accounting, 433
   Federal Reserve survey, 496
   50,000 program orders, 250
   Ford Willow Run, 494n
   impact of failures, 500
   materials production, 180
   need design data, 251
   petroleum products, 484
   scheduling helps, 264
   share of funds, 443
   SWPC aids inexperienced, 501
   west coast disadvantages, 493
Supply, 99, 470, 517. *See also* Air Service Command; Field Service Section, Materiel Division; Supply Division, OCAC.
Supply contracts defined, 411
Supply Division, OCAC, 95, 102–04
Supreme Court, 8. *See also* Federal courts; Judicial decisions.
Surplus, capital, 126
Surplus aircraft, 234
Surveys, 257, 270, 294, 507–08. *See also* Aircraft industry, capacity estimates; Production capacity, measurement of.
Swatland, Brig. Gen. D. C., 360n
Sweden, 200, 529
Switches, electric, 567
SWPC. *See* Smaller War Plants Corporation.
Symbolism, 571. *See also* Command; Leadership; Slogans.
Symington, W. S., 378
Syracuse, N.Y., 562

Tables of Organization, 206
Tachometers, 567
Tactical aircraft, 170, 225, 225n, 241, 244
Tactical availability, 245–46, 553
Tactical life. *See* Obsoletion, problem of
Tactical mission, 246
Tactical performance, 110
Tactical suitability, 107
Tactical units, 64, 107, 110, 245–46, 470
Tank trucks, 209

Tankers, 282
Tanks, 514
Target-price contract, 417. *See also* Incentive contracts.
Targets, combat, 246
Tax accountants, 354
Tax amortization, 296–97, 324, 557–58. *See also* Depreciation; Tax concessions.
Tax avoidance, 387
Tax claims, 388
Tax concessions, 296, 313. *See also* Depreciation.
Tax exemption certificates, 368
Taxation, 195, 202, 285, 296, 299–300, 357, 386–87, 431. *See also* Depreciation; Excess profits tax; Excise taxes; Income tax; Sales taxes.
Taxpayers, 72–73, 329
Taylor Aircraft Corp., 32n
Taylor-Young Airplane Co. *See* Taylorcraft Aviation Corp.
Taylorcraft Aviation Corp., 561, 575, 579. *See also* L–2's.
TD–5000, Treasury directive, 380
Technical Committee. *See* Air Corps Technical Committee.
Technical Data Library, Wright Field, 165
Technical executive, Materiel Division, 464
Technical innovations. *See* Design changes.
Technical orders, 470, 518
Technical revolution, 148. *See also* Design.
Technical Services, 475–77, 480. *See also* arms and services and individual services by name.
Technical training, 465
Technical Training Command, 487
Technological advance, 97. *See also* Research and development.
Telephone calls, 307, 331, 337
10,000 aircraft program, 275
Tennessee, 527
Temperature gauges, 567
Templates, 543–44. *See also* Lofting.
Termination, 367, 369, 396, 414, 442, 470–71, 479n, 556
   problems, 446–55
   success, 461
Termination clauses, 449, 451–52, 455
Termination Section, 473
Terminators, 453–55
Testimony, 57
Texan. *See* AT–6's.
Texas, 527
Theater commanders, 517
Theaters of operations, 246
Three-party contract, 367
Thunderbolt. *See* P–47's.
Time cards, 393
Time lapse, production, 108–09. *See also* Production time, airframes.

INDEX

641

Time magazine, 195
Time studies, 361
Timm Aircraft Corp., 579
Tires, 566
Tolerances, 7, 164, 312, 319, 435, 502, 523, 566
Tool and die industry, 305, 311
Tool design, 520, 522
Tooling. *See* Production tooling.
Toolmakers, 523
Tools. *See* Hand tools.
Tools warehouse, 459
Towers, Rear Adm. J. H., 266
Trade associations, 188, 382. *See also* Aeronautical Chamber of Commerce.
Trade journals, 432
Trained personnel, 66, 77–78
Training, 225, 243, 355, 454, 467, 521
Training aircraft. *See also* AT–6's *et seq.*; BT–12's *et seq.*; PT–13's *et seq.*
  cross procurement, 482
  educational order, 183
  engines and propellers, 309, 549, 566
  Navy, 576–79
  production, 551, 553
  program, 239, 241, 244
  requirements, 64, 66, 170, 246
Training program, 66, 204, 483
Training schools, 64. *See also* Schools for contract termination.
Transportation, 247–48, 308, 330, 360, 455
Transport aircraft, 12, 16, 110, 134ff., 183, 551, 576–79. *See also* Cargo aircraft; C–32's *et seq.*
Traveller. *See* C–43's.
Treasury Department, 94, 124n, 262–63
  allowable costs role, 380, 390
  excise tax rule, 386
  facility financing, 294, 301
  Form 32, 341
  termination role, 451
Trial balloons, 172–73, 253
Troop basis, 44–45, 48, 52, 157, 225, 231
Truman Committee, 317, 320
Trusts, 127
Tulsa, Okla., 308–09.
Turbosuperchargers, 294, 321, 455–56, 527, 567
Turn and bank indicators, 567
Turnover in labor, 413
Turret lathe, 259
Turrets. *See* Gun turrets.
TWA, 530
2,320 aircraft program, 55–56, 58, 60–62

UC–45's, 442–43
Umbrella pricing, 414, 419, 421, 440, 442
Under Secretary of War. *See also* Patterson, Robert P.
  contract role, 343, 351–52, 425, 495
  CPFF role, 387, 406
  cross procurement, 480–81

Under Secretary of War—Continued
  organizational status, 474–78
  renegotiation role, 432
  termination role, 449, 451, 453, 458
Unemployment, 315, 322–23, 455
Unemployment insurance, 386
Unfair competition, 87
Unification, 471, 475
Unified command, 462
Uniformity. *See* Standardization; Tolerances.
Unilateral determinations, 444
Unincorporated business, 436
Unions, 129, 249, 310–14, 402, 424. *See also* Green, William; Hillman, Sidney; Lewis, John L.; Reuther, Walter.
Unit costs
  for aircraft, 20, 86, 233, 442, 560
  to amortize facilities, 295
  in CPFF contracts, 417–18
  estimating, 192, 344, 412
  factors influencing, 11, 16–17, 20, 26–27, 32–33, 72, 141, 197, 264, 297, 367, 428
  higher than bids, 114
  impact on procurement, 10, 70–71, 74, 76
  records on, 32, 189–90
  World War I engines, 83
United Aircraft Corp., 6, 33, 38–39, 184, 187n, 256, 297, 562. *See also* Cessna Aircraft Division; Chance-Vought Division; Hamilton-Standard Division; Pratt & Whitney Aircraft Division; Vought-Sikorsky Aircraft Division.
United Airlines, 530, 533
United Auto Workers, 310
United Kingdom
  aircraft orders, 18n, 195–96, 199, 201, 234. *See also* British Purchasing Commission.
  aircraft procurement, 521, 555, 560
  aircraft production qualified, 556
  chief of production, 209
  contract forms, 341, 417
  engine requirements, 310
  experience influences U.S., 242, 290n, 315, 514
  impact of aircraft orders from, 237, 246, 263, 296
  Ministry of Aircraft Production, 410
  Packard contract, 301, 309, 392
  representation in U.S., 195–96, 266, 270
  shadow factories, 164–65
United States Army. *See* Army.
United States Steel, 255
Universal Aircraft, 579. *See also* L–7's.
Unjust Enrichment Division, PWA, 393
Unpreparedness, 150
Unsatisfactory Report, 97, 99, 530
Unskilled labor, 200, 523, 527
UR. *See* Unsatisfactory Report.
Use taxes, 387
Users versus suppliers, 102
USSR. *See* Russia.

USW. *See* Under Secretary of War.
Utility aircraft, 442-43

V-770 engine, 581
V-1650 engine, 309, 581
V-1710 engine, 581
V-3420 engine, 269, 581
V-loans, 413
Valiant. *See* BT-13's; BT-15's.
Valves, 271n
Vanaman, A. W., 465
Vaughan, G. W., 29
Vega Airplane Co., 387, 541
Vendors, 7-8, 8n, 205, 250, 264, 300
  in auto industry, 304
  monitoring of, 404, 407
Vengeance. *See* A-31's; A-35's.
Venezuela, 282
Verbal rulings, 391
Vickers Canadian, Ltd., 579
Victory Program, 238
Vigilant. *See* L-1's.
Vinson, Carl, 121-22, 284
Vinson, F. M., 91
Vinson Act, 284-85
Vinson-Trammell Act, 35-36, 279, 297, 380, 390
Voluntary refunds, 428, 445
Voters, 352
Vouchers, 379, 383, 403
Vought-Sikorsky Aircraft Division of United Aircraft Corp., 273n, 575. *See also* R-1's; R-4's; R-5's; R-6's.
Vultee Aircraft Division of Aviation Manufacturing Corp., 242, 293n, 302, 575

Waco Aircraft Co., 373, 575-76. *See also* PT-14's.
Wages. *See also* Payroll; Salaries.
  in aircraft industry, 26
  in capacity yardstick, 189
  in contract administration, 344, 360, 411, 413
  in Materiel Command, 558
  reports and indices, 282, 359, 424. *See also* Labor.
Wagner Act, 311
Waiver list, 501
Walsh-Healey Act, 280, 282, 340. *See also* Employment; Labor.
War Contracts Price Adjustment Board, 430
War Department
  air power views, 211, 213
  Air Service policies, 43-48
  aircraft release problem, 199, 202
  annual report, 3
  auditing policy, 391
  contracting officer powers, 383
  Drum Board survey, 53-57
  educational orders, 159
  emergency procurement legislation, 278-79, 281
  establishes GHQ Air Force, 102

War Department—Continued
  facilities expansion, 290, 298-99, 301, 315
  initial air mobilization role, 159, 170, 173n, 174, 181
  legislative liaison, 57-58, 92
  March 1942 reorganization, 464, 475, 489
  perfects procurement policies, 81, 86, 89n, 116, 118, 129, 144-45
  price index, 358
  rearmament program, 202, 204, 210, 246-47
  requirements role, 62-64
  responsibility for delays, 79
  seeks relief funds, 67
  studies Buy American, 282
  World War 1 procurement, 150
War Department Circular, 475-76
War Department General Staff. *See* General Staff, War Department.
War Department Price Adjustment Board, 438
War games, 167
War Labor Board, 412
War planning. *See* Industrial Planning Section, Materiel Division; Mobilization planning; Office of Assistant Secretary of War; Plans Division, OCAC; War Plans Division, WDGS.
War Plans Division, WDGS, 52, 57, 211, 217, 220
War Policies Commission, 119
War Powers Act of 1941, 367
War prevention, 125. *See also* Nye, Gerald Prentice; War Policies Commission.
War Production Board. *See also* Civilian superagency; National Defense Advisory Commission; Office of Production Management; War Resources Administration.
  organization, 272-73, 322
  production control, 358, 499, 538
  statistical tools, 192
  SWPC role, 500
War Production Board, tool disposal, 458
War profiteering. *See* Profiteering.
War reserve. *See* Reserve aircraft.
War Resources Administration, 247, 249, 265
War Resources Board, criticized, 248-49
Warhawk. *See* P-40's.
Warner Aircraft Corp., 582
Warner-Swasey, 259
Washington Post, 118
Washouts. *See* Accident ratios; Attrition rate.
Wasp aircraft engine, 256, 580
Wastage. *See* Attrition rate.
Waste, 83, 411, 457
Watch manufacturers, 567
Watson, Brig. Gen. E. M., 68, 223
WDGS. *See* General Staff, War Department.
Weapons design, 257n. *See also* Aircraft design; Design; Design changes.
Weather, influence of, 218, 308, 531
Weather reconnaissance aircraft, 534

INDEX

643

Weatherizing. *See* Winterization.
Wehrmacht, 283
Wedell-Williams Air Service Corp., 139
Weight. *See* Airframes, average gross weights.
Welfare legislation. *See* Social welfare legislation.
West coast, 493
West Lynn, Mass., 562
Western Hemisphere defense. *See* Hemisphere defense.
Western Procurement District, 435, 465, 491, 504
Westover, Maj. Gen. Oscar, 68, 166, 199
West Wall, 195
Whirlwind engine, 580
White Aircraft Co., 575
White House conference, 169–70, 175, 210, 213, 274
Wichita, Kans., 9, 302, 321, 506, 565
Wilbert, G. C., 393n
Williamsport, Pa., 6
Willow Run, Mich. *See also* Ford Motor Co.
  criticism of, 314n, 321, 326
  described, 518ff.
  facility planned, 309
  modifications, 531, 536
  production control problems, 539
  production ratios, 565
  project evaluated, 527–28
  property accounting, 400
  suppliers, 494n
Wilson, C. E., 273, 305
Wilson, E. E., 186n
Wilson, H. R., 169, 169n
Wind tunnels, 23
Windshields, 269
Wing spans, 164, 564
Winterization, 242, 534. *See also* Modifications.
Witnesses, 57. *See also* Congressional investigations; Investigations; War Department, legislative liaison.
Wolfe, Brig. Gen. K. B., 354n, 468–69, 509
Woodring, H. H., 4, 66, 128–31, 138, 170n, 253, 253n
Worcester, Mass., 506
Work week, 260–61, 261n
Working capital, 39–40, 284, 288, 373, 377, 448. *See also* Advance payments; Assignment of claims; Capital investment; Loans; Partial payments.
Workload, 294, 472
World War I
  accounting experience, 392, 395
  contract litigation, 333n, 393
  contract terminations, 414, 446, 448
  cost-plus contracts, 372, 412, 417

World War I—Continued
  foreign order impact, 195–96
  incentive contracts, 83
  interbranch competition, 474, 476
  lessons learned and ignored, 84, 207, 209, 222, 272, 355n
  mobilization experience, 161, 166–67, 247
  modification centers, 529
  Navy aircraft, 125
  procurement organization, 102
  procurement procedures, 81, 112
  production record, 84n, 150, 189, 464, 511–12
  profits, 82, 84n, 119
  Purchase, Storage, and Traffic Division, 475
  secrecy, 197
WPB. *See* War Production Board.
WPD. *See* War Plans Division, WDGS.
WRA. *See* War Resources Administration.
Wright Aeronautical Corp., 6, 200–201, 293n, 309, 418, 561, 580. *See also* R–760, R–975, R–1820, R–2600, and R–3350 engines.
Wright Field, Dayton, Ohio
  Industrial Planning Section, 153
  matériel role, 95, 99, 128, 131, 492
  OPM unit, 270
  organization and personnel, 141, 345–46, 349–50, 466–67, 558–59. *See also* Materiel Center; Materiel Command; Materiel Division.
  relation to district offices, 505. *See also* Procurement districts.
  relation to Washington headquarters, 102, 106, 331, 463
  termination file, 447
Wright, Theodore P.
  capacity yardstick, 190–92, 304
  devises learner curve, 344
  JAC role, 266, 267n
  NDAC role, 256
  reports on Germany, 169n

X-ray inspection, 568
XB–15's, 149
XFM–1's, 199

YB–10's, 117
Yardstick, for productive capacity, 125, 185, 188–90, 277, 294. *See also* Learner curve.
Yardstick Board, 191–93, 291

Zinc dies, 31

www.ingramcontent.com/pod-product-compliance
Lightning Source LLC
Chambersburg PA
CBHW022004300426
44117CB00005B/31